ATOMIC AUDIT

Atomic Audit

The Costs and Consequences of U.S. Nuclear Weapons since 1940

Stephen I. Schwartz, editor

Bruce G. Blair, Thomas S. Blanton, William Burr, Steven M. Kosiak, Arjun Makhijani, Robert S. Norris, Kevin O'Neill, John E. Pike, and William J. Weida, contributing authors

Brookings Institution Press
Washington, D.C.

ABOUT BROOKINGS

The Brookings Institution is a private nonprofit organization devoted to research, education, and publication on important issues of domestic and foreign policy. Its principal purpose is to bring knowledge to bear on current and emerging policy problems. The Institution maintains a position of neutrality on issues of public policy. Interpretations or conclusions in publications of the Brookings Institution Press should be understood to be solely those of the authors.

1775 Massachusetts Ave., N.W. Washington, D.C. 20036

Library of Congress Cataloging-in-Publication Data
Atomic audit: the costs and consequences of U.S. nuclear weapons since 1940 / Stephen I. Schwartz, editor.
p. cm.
Includes bibliographical references (p.) and index.
ISBN 0-8157-7774-4 (cloth)
ISBN 0-8157-7773-6 (pbk.)
1. Nuclear weapons—United States—Costs. 2. Nuclear weapons—United States—History. I. Schwartz, Stephen I.
U264.3 .A874 1998
355.8'25119'0973—ddc21 98-19746
CIP

9 8 7 6 5 4 3 2 1

The paper used in this publication meets the minimum requirements of the American National Standard for Information Sciences—Permanence of Paper for Printed Library Materials: ANSI Z39.48-1984.

Typeset in New Baskerville with Officina display

Composition by Harlowe Typography, Inc.
Cottage City, Maryland

Printed by R. R. Donnelley & Sons Co.
Harrisonburg, Virginia

Contents

Appendixes

Foreword

This book assembles for the first time anywhere the actual and estimated costs of the U.S. nuclear weapons program since its inception in 1940. Countless books and articles have examined the role of nuclear weapons as implements of deterrence, instruments of coercion, and, not least, weapons of war, but the details concerning the numbers of weapons, their characteristics, and their deployment remained largely classified information during the cold war and were seldom assessed. Moreover, all the books, articles, and congressional debates concerning what was arguably the principal focus of U.S. national security for the latter half of the twentieth century said little about the not inconsequential costs of basing national security on the deployment of large numbers of nuclear weapons, of embracing the notion that such weapons provided a "bigger bang for a buck."

This book rectifies that omission. The authors, led by Stephen I. Schwartz, provide a unique perspective on nuclear policy and nuclear weapons, tracing their development from the Manhattan Project of World War II to the present day and focusing on each aspect of the program, including research, development, and testing; deployment; command and control; and defenses. They also look at the costs of dismantling nuclear weapons, problems of managing large quantities of radioactive and toxic wastes arising from their production, compensation for persons harmed by their production and testing, nuclear secrecy, and the economic implications of nuclear deterrence.

A central finding of the book is that government officials made little effort to ensure that limited economic resources were used as efficiently as possible so that nuclear deterrence could be achieved at the least cost to taxpayers. While the costs of individual programs were debated from time to time, the near total absence of data documenting either annual or cumulative costs of the overall effort made effective democratic debate and oversight all but impossible, contributing to the justification of many nuclear weapons programs on grounds that often had little to do with clearly defined military requirements or objectives. The authors carefully examine this lack of accountability and its implications for historical and present-day programs and policies. They recommend further areas of study and ways of strengthening fiscal accountability in the government's management of nuclear weapons programs. One essential step in this direction, they argue, would be for the government to compile an annual report documenting all current and projected costs of nuclear weapons and weapons-related programs.

Earlier drafts of this book were reviewed in whole or in part by Steven Aftergood, Lynn Eden, Richard L. Garwin, Emilia Govan, Peter Gray, Richard N. Haass, Daniel Hirsch, Peter A. Johnson, Seymour Melman, Janne E. Nolan, Henry S. Rowen, Roger A. Schwartz, Herbert F. York, and James D. Werner. The authors thank these reviewers for their thoughtful criticism and suggestions, all of which improved the final product. Any errors or omissions are, of course, the sole responsibility of the authors.

The success of any endeavor as lengthy and complex as the one that resulted in this book is necessarily due to the contributions of many people. The authors wish to thank the following persons for providing critical documents and data and for invaluable advice and assistance: Cheri E. Abdelnour, Ricardo Aguilera, Robert Alvarez, Barbara Arnold, Lori Azim, Tom Bell, Magaly Carter Bernazsky, Chuck Broscious, Lois Chalmers, William E. Davis, Terry Freese, Michele S. Gerber, Skip Gosling, Chuck Hansen, Roger Heusser, Ronald L. Kathren, Peter Kuran, John C. Lonnquest, Jeffrey Mason, Joseph McDermott, Melba Meador, Jonathan Medalia, Daniel Reicher, Karen Rosenthal, Ted Saunders, Kenneth Schafer, Kathryn Schultz, A. Bryan Siebert, Jim Thomas, Lisa K. Wagner, Jonathan Weisgall, Andrew Weston-Dawkes, and Thomas Wheeler.

The authors are especially grateful to officials at the Department of Defense who agreed to review and declassify substantial portions of the hitherto classified Future Years Defense Program historical database, greatly facilitating the in-depth budgetary analysis found in chapters 2 through 4.

They are indebted to a number of people at Brookings Institution: John Steinbruner and Richard Haass, for agreeing to host the project and for their guidance and advice through the various stages of its development; Melanie Allen, Bridget Butkevich, Julien Hartley, Christina Larson, and Andrew Solomon for verifying the manuscript; Megan deLong for helping to edit early drafts of chapters 3, 4, and 8; Sarah Chilton, Mary Fry, and the rest of the library staff for their help in locating critical research materials; and Winnie Alvarado, Dave Barnette, John Grimes, Carol McHale, Anhtuan Phan, and Tibor Purger for essential computer support. Vicky Macintyre edited the manuscript, Larry Converse and Susan Woollen prepared it for publication, Linda Humphrey designed the book, Sally Martin proofread it, and Julia Petrakis provided the index.

Funding for this project was provided by the W. Alton Jones Foundation, whose generous support is gratefully acknowledged. Special thanks are owed to George Perkovich, director of the foundation's Secure World Program, whose interest in this project was instrumental in its success.

The views expressed here are those of the authors alone and should not be ascribed to any of the aforementioned individuals or institutions or to the trustees, officers, or other staff members of the Brookings Institution.

Michael H. Armacost
President

May 1998
Washington, D.C.

Abbreviations and Acronyms

ABCC	Atomic Bomb Casualty Commission
ABM	antiballistic missile
ACDA	Arms Control and Disarmament Agency
ACM	advanced cruise missile
ADCOM	Air Force Air Defense Command
ADM	atomic demolition munition
AEC	Atomic Energy Commission
AEDS	Atomic Energy Detection System
AFOAT-1	Air Force Deputy Chief of Staff for Operations, Atomic Energy Office, Section One
AFSWP	Armed Forces Special Weapons Project
AFTAC	Air Force Technical Applications Center
ALCM	Air-Launched Cruise Missile
ALMV	air-launched miniature vehicle
AMARC	Aerospace Maintenance and Regeneration Center
ANMCC	Alternate National Military Command Center
ANP	aircraft nuclear propulsion
ARAACOM	Army Antiaircraft Command
ARADCOM	Army Air Defense Command
ARPA	Advanced Research Projects Agency
ASA	Army Security Agency
ASAT	antisatellite
ASROC	antisubmarine rocket
ASTOR	antisubmarine torpedo

ASW	antisubmarine warfare
ATB	advanced technology bomber
ATSDR	Agency for Toxic Substances and Disease Registry
AVLIS	atomic vapor laser isotope separation
AWACS	airborne warning and control system
BAMBI	ballistic missile boost intercept
BMD	ballistic missile defense
BMDO	Ballistic Missile Defense Organization
BMEWS	Ballistic Missile Early Warning System
BOB	Bureau of the Budget
BRAC	Base Realignment and Closure
CBO	Congressional Budget Office
CDC	Centers for Disease Control and Prevention
CEBMCO	Army Corps of Engineers Ballistic Missile Construction Office
CIA	Central Intelligence Agency
CNO	chief of naval operations
CNWDI	critical nuclear weapons design information
CoG	continuity of government
CRP	crisis relocation planning
CRS	Congressional Research Service
C^3I	command, control, communications, and intelligence
CTBT	Comprehensive Test Ban Treaty
CTR	cooperative threat reduction
DASA	Defense Atomic Support Agency
DERA	Defense Environmental Restoration Account
DERP	Defense Environmental Restoration Program
DEW	distant early warning
DGZ	designated ground zero
DIA	Defense Intelligence Agency
DISA	Defense Information Systems Agency
DLA	dispersed landing area
DMA	Defense Mapping Agency
DNA	Defense Nuclear Agency
DNFSB	Defense Nuclear Facilities Safety Board
DNSI	defense nuclear surety inspections
DOB	dispersed operating base
DOD	Department of Defense
DOE	Department of Energy
DMSP	Defense Meteorological Satellite Program
DPA	dispersed parking area

DSP	Defense Support Program
DSWA	Defense Special Weapons Agency
DU	depleted uranium
DWPF	Defense Waste Processing Facility
EAM	emergency action message
ELF	extremely low frequency
EMP	electromagnetic pulse
EPA	Environmental Protection Agency
ERDA	Energy Research and Development Administration
ERWM	environmental restoration and waste management
ESD	environmental sensing device
ES&H	environment, safety, and health
FAA	Federal Aviation Administration
FBI	Federal Bureau of Investigation
FBM	fleet ballistic missile
FCC	Federal Communications Commission
FCDA	Federal Civil Defense Administration
FEMA	Federal Emergency Management Agency
FFCA	Federal Facilities Compliance Act
FOIA	Freedom of Information Act
FPU	first production unit
FRD	formerly restricted data
FUSRAP	Formerly Utilized Site Remedial Action Program
FYDP	Future Years Defense Program
GAC	General Advisory Committee
GAO	General Accounting Office
GDP	gaseous diffusion plant
GDP	gross domestic product
GLCM	Ground-Launched Cruise Missile
GNP	gross national product
GPS	global positioning system
GWEN	Ground-Wave Emergency Network
HE	high explosive
HEU	highly enriched uranium
HLW	high-level waste
IAEA	International Atomic Energy Agency
ICBM	intercontinental ballistic missile
ICF	inertial confinement fusion
ICPP	Idaho Chemical Processing Plant

IEER	Institute for Energy and Environmental Research
IHE	insensitive high explosives
INEEL	Idaho National Engineering and Environmental Laboratory
INF	Intermediate-Range Nuclear Forces Treaty
INFOSEC	information security
IRBM	intermediate-range ballistic missile
IOC	initial operational capability
IRS	Internal Revenue Service
JCAE	Joint Committee on Atomic Energy
JCS	Joint Chiefs of Staff
JEN	Junta de Engeria Nuclear
JMIP	Joint Military Intelligence Program
JSTPS	Joint Strategic Target Planning Staff
KAPL	Knolls Atomic Power Laboratory
LANL	Los Alamos National Laboratory
LCC	launch-control capsule
LEU	low-enriched uranium
LLNL	Lawrence Livermore National Laboratory
LLW	low-level waste
LoADS	Low-Altitude Defense System
MADM	medium atomic demolition munition
MED	Manhattan Engineer District
MEECN	Minimum Essential Emergency Communications Network
MFD	military first destination
MFP	major force program
MHV	miniature homing vehicle
MIDAS	Missile Defense Alarm System
MILSTAR	Military Strategic and Tactical Relay
MIRV	multiple independently targeted reentry vehicle
MLC	Military Liaison Committee
MOL	manned orbiting laboratory
MOX	mixed oxide (fuel)
MRV	multiple reentry vehicle
NAE	National Academy of Engineering
NAOC	National Airborne Operations Center
NARA	National Archives and Records Administration
NAS	National Academy of Sciences

NASA	National Aeronautics and Space Administration
NATO	North Atlantic Treaty Organization
NAVSEA	Naval Sea Systems Command
NAVSTAR/GPS	navigation satellite tracking and ranging/global positioning system
NCMC	NORAD Cheyenne Mountain Complex
NDEW	nuclear-directed energy weapon
NDRC	National Defense Research Committee
NEACP	National Emergency Airborne Command Post
NECPA	National Emergency Command Post Afloat
NEPA	Nuclear Energy for the Propulsion of Aircraft
NEST	Nuclear Emergency Search Team
NFIP	National Foreign Intelligence Program
NIE	national intelligence estimate
NIF	National Ignition Facility
NIMA	National Imagery and Mapping Agency
NMCC	National Military Command Center
NOAA	National Oceanic and Atmospheric Administration
NORAD	North American Air Defense Command
NOSS	naval ocean surveillance system
NPR	New Production Reactor
NRC	Nuclear Regulatory Commission
NRF	Naval Reactors Facility
NRO	National Reconnaissance Office
NRTS	National Reactor Testing Station
NSA	National Security Agency
NSC	National Security Council
NSI	national security information
NSTDB	National Strategic Target Database
NSTL	National Strategic Target List
NTPR	Nuclear Test Personnel Review
NTS	Nevada Test Site
NUDET	nuclear detonation
NWTRB	Nuclear Waste Technical Review Board
OCDM	Office of Civil and Defense Mobilization
OECD	Organization for Economic Cooperation and Development
O&M	operations and maintenance
OMB	Office of Management and Budget
OPM	Office of Personnel Management
O&S	operation and support
OSIA	On-Site Inspection Agency
OSRD	Office of Scientific Research and Development
OTA	Office of Technology Assessment

OTH-B	over-the-horizon backscatter
PACCS	Post-Attack Command and Control System
PAL	permissive action link
PAR	perimeter acquisition radar
PAVE PAWS	PAVE (air force code word) phased-array warning system
PHS	Public Health Service
PNAF	Prime Nuclear Airlift Force
PNET	Peaceful Nuclear Explosions Treaty
PPG	Pacific Proving Ground
PRP	Personnel Reliability Program
PSNS	Puget Sound Naval Shipyard
PTBT	Partial Test Ban Treaty
rad	radiation absorbed dose
RCRA	Resource Conservation Recovery Act
RD	restricted data
R&D	research and development
RDT&E	research, development, testing, and evaluation
REAC	Radiation Emergency Assistance Center
REACT	Rapid Execution and Combat Targeting
rem	roentgen equivalent man
RERF	Radiation Effects Research Foundation
SAC	Strategic Air Command
SACEUR	Supreme Allied Commander Europe
SADM	special atomic demolition munition
SAGE	Semiautomatic Ground Environment
SALT	Strategic Arms Limitation Talks
SAM	surface-to-air missile
SAMOS	Satellite and Missile Observation System
SAR	synthetic aperture radar
SCATANA	security control of air traffic and navigation aids
SCI	sensitive compartmentalized information
SDI	Strategic Defense Initiative
SDIO	Strategic Defense Initiative Organization
SGT	safeguards transporter
SIGINT	signals intelligence
SIOP	Single Integrated Operational Plan
SIP	Stockpile Improvement Program
SIS	special isotope separation plant
SLBM	Submarine-Launched Ballistic Missile
SLCM	Sea-Launched Cruise Missile
SNM	special nuclear materials

SOSUS	Sound Surveillance System
SRAM	Short-Range Attack Missile
SRS	Savannah River Site
SSBN	nuclear-powered ballistic missile submarine
SSM	surface-to-surface missile
SSN	nuclear-powered attack submarine
SST	safe secure transporter
STS	space transportation system
START	Strategic Arms Reduction Treaty
STRATCOM	Strategic Command
SUBROC	submarine rocket
TACAMO	"take charge and move out"
TIARA	Tactical Intelligence and Related Activities
TRU	transuranic (waste)
TTBT	Threshold Test Ban Treaty
TTR	Tonopah Test Range
UCNI	unclassified controlled nuclear information
UMTRA	Uranium Mill Tailings Remedial Action Program
USAFE	United States Air Forces Europe
USEC	United States Enrichment Corporation
USGS	United States Geological Survey
USPS	United States Postal Service
USTUR	United States Transuranium and Uranium Registries
VLF	very low frequency
WATPL	wartime air traffic priority list
WDD	Western Development Division
WIPP	Waste Isolation Pilot Plant
WSMR	White Sands Missile Range
WTR	Western Test Range
WWMCCS	Worldwide Military Command and Control System

A Methodological Note

Except where indicated, all figures in this book have been adjusted for inflation and are expressed in constant fiscal 1996 dollars. "Then-year dollars" represent the prices of goods or services current at the time they were sold. "Constant dollars" have been adjusted for the effects of inflation. Dollar costs for past expenditures are adjusted by adding inflation. This permits a comparison of expenditures over time that, although still imperfect, is less distorted than if current dollar expenditures were used, and it allows the reader to view costs in terms of the dollar's approximate purchasing power at the present time. Except where noted, these adjustments have been made using standard Department of Defense (DOD) deflators. More specific methodological considerations are taken up in each chapter, as necessary.

Except as noted, all years referred to in this volume are fiscal years. Before 1976 the government's fiscal year ran from July 1 to June 30. In 1976 the beginning of the fiscal year was moved back to October 1, so that year has a transition quarter (76T) from July 1 to September 30.

This volume makes extensive use of the DOD's Future Years Defense Program (FYDP) historical database, a computerized budgeting system inaugurated by Secretary of Defense Robert S. McNamara in 1961 to track all major defense programs via unique "program element" numbers. This database is classified and access to it is strictly controlled. Requests under the Freedom of Information Act by private researchers for its declassification were routinely denied. In response to a December 1994 request by the authors, however, most of the historical data on funding for the more than seven hundred program elements relating to nuclear weapons were declassified and made available in March 1996. These data enabled us to analyze and compare annual direct program costs for most major DOD nuclear weapons programs over fiscal 1962–95. In conjunction with the publication of this book, portions of the FYDP data are being made available on the World Wide Web (http://www.brook.edu/fp/projects nucwcost/weapons.htm), affording scholars, journalists, and others unprecedented access to this information in a useful, interactive format.

The budgetary data in this book come from several major sources. Whenever possible, we have used original and not derivative data and turned to secondary sources such as books, scholarly journals, and newspaper accounts only as necessary. For data on Department of Energy (DOE) nuclear weapons programs, we relied principally on the official semiannual and annual reports of the Atomic Energy Commission (AEC), 1946–75, official AEC histories, the *Budget of the United States Government*, and hearings before various congressional committees. We also consulted reports of the General Accounting Office (GAO), the files of the Joint Committee on Atomic Energy (JCAE) at the National Archives, and declassified government documents available at the nongovernmental National Security Archive at George Washington University in Washington, D.C.

For DOD programs, data for fiscal 1946–61 come principally from semiannual and annual reports of the Secretary of Defense, official histories of various programs, other DOD publications, and the *U.S. Historical Military Aircraft and Missile Data Book*.[1] For data after fiscal 1961, we relied on the FYDP historical database, along with a variety of other publications. Additional data come from GAO reports, congressional hearings, papers at the National Archives, and declassified government documents available at the nongovernmental National Security Archive.

This study assesses only those nuclear weapons costs borne by the federal government, although state and local governments also shoulder some of the burden. This includes support for law enforcement (such as assisting facility security forces and accident response training), environmental monitoring programs, road maintenance, and sewage treatment. We have not attempted to count such costs in this study, but they should be considered when measuring the overall costs of nuclear weapons.

1. Ted Nicholas and Rita Rossi, *U.S. Historical Military Aircraft and Missile Data Book* (Fountain Valley, Calif.: Data Search Associates, 1991).

The full power which resides within the American people will be evoked only through the traditional democratic process: This process requires, firstly, that sufficient information regarding the basic political, economic and military elements of the present situation be made publicly available so that an intelligent popular opinion may be formed. Having achieved a comprehension of the issues now confronting this Republic, it will then be possible for the American people and the American Government to arrive at a consensus. Out of this common view will develop a determination of the national will and a solid resolute expression of that will. The initiative in this process lies with the Government. . . . A large measure of sacrifice and discipline will be demanded of the American people. They will be asked to give up some of the benefits which they have come to associate with their freedoms. Nothing could be more important than that they fully understand the reasons for this.

—United States Objectives and Programs for National Security (NSC 68), April 14, 1950

FIGURE 1. Estimated Minimum Incurred Costs of U.S. Nuclear Weapons Programs, 1940–96[a]

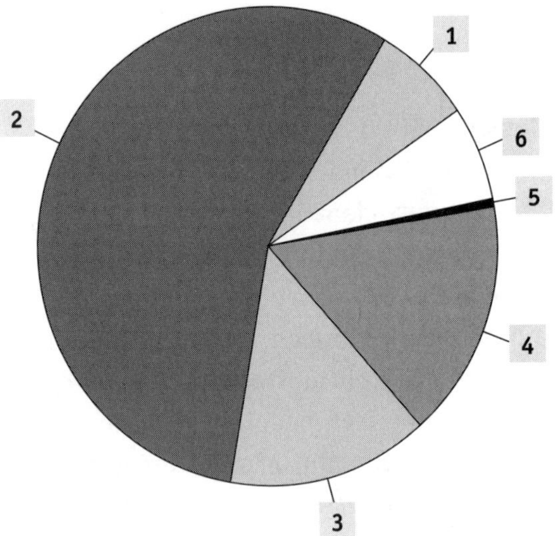

Total: $5,821.0 billion

1 Building the bomb
$409.4 billion / 7.0%

2 Deploying the bomb
$3,241.0 billion / 55.7%

3 Targeting and controlling the bomb
$831.1 billion / 14.3%

4 Defending against the bomb
$937.2 billion / 16.1%

5 Dismantling the bomb
$31.1 billion / 0.5%

6 Nuclear waste management and environmental remediation
$365.1 billion / 6.3%

Not Shown

Victims of U.S. nuclear weapons
$2.1 billion / 0.04%

Nuclear secrecy
$3.1 billion / 0.05%

Congressional oversight of nuclear weapons programs
$0.9 billion / 0.02%

a. In constant 1996 dollars. Includes average projected future-year costs for nuclear weapons dismantlement and fissile materials disposition and environmental remediation and waste management. Total actual and estimated expenditures through 1996 were $5,481.1 billion.

Introduction

Stephen I. Schwartz

Why conduct an atomic audit? The cold war is over, the Soviet Union is but a fading memory, and both the United States and Russia are dismantling large parts of their nuclear arsenals. Why assess either the costs or the consequences of the U.S. nuclear weapons program? Are not these costs already well known and, in any event, largely irrelevant given the successful and peaceful outcome of the cold war? Such questions reflect today's conventional wisdom about the cold war, nuclear weapons, and the federal government's budgetary accounting practices. They are, however, short-sighted and in several critical respects completely wrong.

We will document that the United States spent vast amounts on nuclear weapons without the kind of careful and sustained debate or oversight that are essential both to democratic practice and to sound public policy. In most cases, even rudimentary standards of government policymaking and accountability were lacking. Today, with an estimated $35 billion expended annually on nuclear weapons and weapons-related programs (in 1998 dollars), government officials remain by and large unaware of both the overall size of and rationale for such costs. Notwithstanding frequent debates about arms control treaties, the nature of deterrence, the size and mix of nuclear forces, or the threat these forces were intended to counter, the decisionmaking process did not allow for a rigorous examination of the costs associated with U.S. nuclear policy. This rendered it politically and fiscally unaccountable.

Although U.S. and Russian nuclear stockpiles are significantly smaller than at their peak levels, they remain quite formidable, with approximately 10,000 warheads apiece.[1] Despite renewed calls from some quarters for the eventual worldwide elimination of nuclear weapons, neither the U.S. nor Russian governments have indicated an intention to pursue such a goal. The significant costs of maintaining these arsenals will thus continue for the foreseeable future. *As large as they are, the U.S. government has no clear idea of these overall costs, past or present, because it has never attempted to track them over time.*

Many people attribute the containment and ultimate defeat of the Soviet Union and the peaceful conclusion of the cold war in large measure to the fact that the United States deployed and maintained a substantial nuclear arsenal.[2] This view is open to question, however, and plausible arguments can be made for and against this proposition. What does seem clear is that the United States, in managing to end the cold war on its own terms, has created a very dangerous and costly post–cold war situation. The "losing side" has roughly equivalent amounts of nuclear materials and weapons as the "winning side." Meanwhile, the dangers posed by the loss of control of nuclear weapons and by nuclear black markets are greater today than ever before; the risk of accidental nuclear war continues to be a significant problem. Under the circumstances, it has become all the more urgent to have full knowledge of the costs and consequences of U.S. nuclear weapons in order to accurately assess their apparent benefits, and to ascertain whether "a bigger bang for a buck" actually was realized.[3]

Atomic Audit is the first comprehensive effort to tally the total costs of the U.S. nuclear weapons program, from developing and deploying nuclear weapons to managing and ultimately disposing of the wastes created in the process. Along the way, we examine how and why key decisions were made, what factors influenced those decisions, and whether alternatives were considered. Cost is a prism through which

1. Robert S. Norris and Thomas B. Cochran, *US-USSR/Russian Strategic Offensive Nuclear Forces, 1945–1996,* NWD-97-1 (Natural Resources Defense Council, January 1997), tables 9, 10; author's telephone conversation with Robert S. Norris, January 13, 1998.

2. Proponents of the belief that nuclear weapons kept the cold war cold frequently ignore or discount the impact of much larger U.S. expenditures on conventional forces (see figure 2) and the fact that these forces, in contrast to nuclear weapons, were used in actual combat (for example, in Korea and Vietnam).

3. Although it can be argued that the benefits ascribed to nuclear deterrence remain constant regardless of their costs, the objective in any endeavor—including the maintenance of national security—is for the benefits to outweigh the costs. If the benefits of deterrence remain constant (as they must, given that deterrence is an either/or proposition) and costs increase (as they did throughout much of the cold war), then one would be forced to conclude that higher costs cannot be justified because the benefits can be obtained at a lower cost. In fact, the impetus to manufacture and deploy large numbers of nuclear weapons gathered strength *because* nuclear weapons were considered *less* expensive than conventional ones. Even after this assumption was disproved, the buildup continued, despite rising costs. Had these costs been more transparent and widely known, there almost certainly would have been a debate about the wisdom of this approach. That there was not is the subject of this book.

we are able to separate and analyze the various aspects of the overall endeavor. Our purpose is neither to praise all nuclear weapons programs undertaken during the decades of uncertainty nor to criticize all nuclear weapons expenditures as dangerous and wasteful. Rather, we seek to explain the process by which an arsenal consisting of but two primitive weapons in 1945 was eventually expanded to more than 32,000, what this process cost, and how the costs and consequences of the program were viewed by policymakers at the time.

What Have U.S. Nuclear Weapons Cost?

Since 1940, the United States has spent almost $5.5 trillion (in constant 1996 dollars) on nuclear weapons and weapons-related programs (see table 1). This figure—which is based on an unprecedented four-year analysis of historical budget data and, where necessary, conservative estimates of costs that either remain classified or are not clearly apportioned to the nuclear program—does not include $320 billion in estimated future-year costs for storing and disposing of more than five decades' worth of accumulated toxic and radioactive wastes and $20 billion for dismantling nuclear weapons systems and disposing of surplus nuclear materials. When these amounts (at least one of which is likely to exceed current official estimates) are factored in, the total incurred costs of the U.S. nuclear weapons program exceed $5.8 trillion (see figure 1).

The amount spent through 1996—$5.5 trillion—is 29 percent of all military spending from 1940 through 1996 ($18.7 trillion).[4] This figure is significantly larger than any previous official or unofficial estimate of nuclear weapons expenditures, exceeding *all* other categories of government spending (see figure 2) except nonnuclear national defense ($13.2 trillion) and social security ($7.9 trillion). This amounts to almost 11 percent of all government expenditures from 1940 through 1996 ($51.6 trillion). During this period, the United States spent on average nearly $98 billion a year developing and maintaining its nuclear arsenal (see box 1).

A Short History of Nuclear Weapons Cost Analysis

Given the significant sums expended on nuclear weapons and their central role in the cold war, it is striking that so few have expressed an

4. This figure is for what the government terms "national defense." Additional defense-related costs are categorized separately under "veterans benefits and services" ($1.8 trillion). Neither of these items includes the $1.2 trillion spent on "international affairs," which incites foreign aid and encompasses the broader aspects of U.S. foreign policy.

TABLE 1. Breakdown of Total Actual and Estimated U.S. Expenditures for Nuclear Weapons, 1940–96

Billions of 1996 dollars

Activity	*Cost*
Building the bomb (chapter 1)	409.4
Deploying the bomb (chapter 2)	3,241.0
Targeting and controlling the bomb (chapter 3)	831.1
Defending against the bomb (chapter 4)	937.2
Dismantling the bomb (chapter 5)	11.1
Nuclear waste management and environmental remediation (chapter 6)	45.2
Victims of the bomb (chapter 7)	2.1
Costs and consequences of nuclear secrecy (chapter 8)	3.1
Congressional oversight of the bomb (chapter 9)	0.9
Total	5,481.1

interest in either the cumulative or the annual costs. Ironically, the first effort to review the costs was undertaken in response to congressional complaints that *too little* was being spent on nuclear weapons. On September 18, 1951, Senator Brien McMahon (Democrat of Connecticut), chairman of the Joint Committee on Atomic Energy (JCAE), introduced Senate Concurrent Resolution 46, which claimed in its preamble: "The cost of military fire power based upon atomic bombs is hundreds of time cheaper, dollar for dollar, than conventional explosives. . . . [S]ince 1945, only 3 cents out of each American dollar paid for military defense has been spent on atomic weapons. . . . [P]resent expansion plans still assign 3 cents in the military dollar to these weapons."[5]

5. S. Conc. Res. 46, 82 Cong. 1 sess., introduced September 18, 1951, and referred to the Joint Committee on Atomic Energy.

FIGURE 2. U.S. Government Historical Obligations by Function, 1940–96[a]

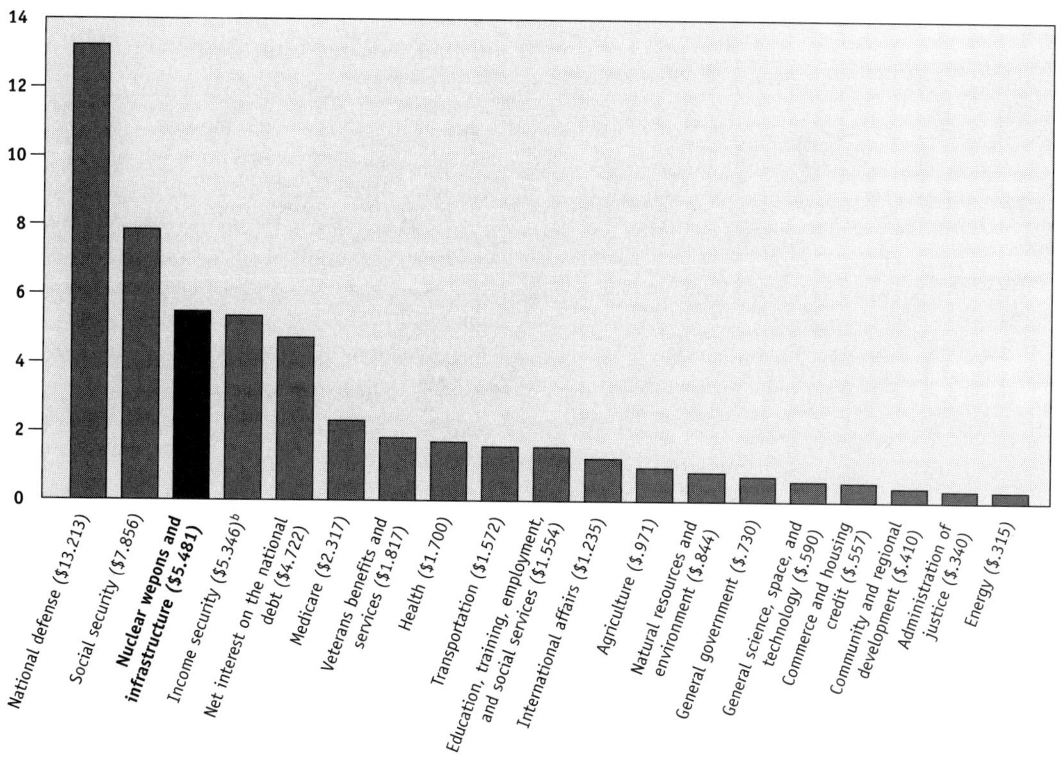

Note: National defense category has been adjusted to exclude nuclear weapons and infrastructure costs. Nuclear weapons costs are a combination of actual and estimated expenditures. Program totals do not match overall total because of rounding and the addition of undistributed offsetting receipts (not shown).

a. (Total = $51,557,983,000,000).

b. Income security as defined by the Office of Management and Budget includes programs such as federal employee retirement and disability, unemployment compensation, housing assistance, and other "welfare" programs.

Sources: Office of Management and Budget, *Budget of the United States Government, Fiscal Year 1998* (GPO, 1997), pp. 42–49; U.S. Nuclear Weapons Cost Study Project.

These findings were actually the result of a questionable accounting exercise undertaken by the JCAE staff the previous year; the "3 cents in the military dollar" referred only to a portion of the Atomic Energy Commission's (AEC) budget and completely excluded any research undertaken by the Department of Defense (DOD) as well as the costs of building and operating strategic bombers, the principal nuclear delivery vehicle at that time (see chapter 9). However, McMahon used them to argue that current nuclear expenditures were "unreasonably and

Box 1

Visualizing the Cost of Nuclear Weapons

Distributed evenly to everyone living in the United States at the start of 1998, the total estimated cost of nuclear weapons equals $21,646 per person. Represented as bricks of new $1 bills (such as one can obtain at a bank, bound at $200 to the inch) stacked on top of one another, $5,821,027,000,000 would stretch 459,361 miles (739,117 kilometers), to the Moon and nearly back. If $1 was counted off every second, it would take almost 12 days to reach $1 million, nearly 32 years to reach $1 billion, 31,709 years to reach $1 trillion, and about 184,579 years to tally the actual and anticipated costs of nuclear weapons. Laid end to end, bricks of $1 bills equivalent to the sum actually expended on U.S. nuclear weapons since 1940 ($5,481,083,000,000) would encircle the Earth at the Equator almost 105 times, making a wall more than 8.7 feet (2.7 meters) high.

imprudently small" and that the United States "must go all-out" to equip each military service with large numbers of nuclear weapons.[6]

Although this resolution was never brought to a vote (its sentiments were nevertheless realized in subsequent AEC budgets; see chapter 1), it prompted immediate concern within the military. As an official air force history of the period records, "The McMahon Resolution focused attention on the fact that *there existed no itemized record of the military expenditures, either direct or indirect, for the atomic energy program.*" Some maintained that the resolution was not necessarily aimed at the air force, which therefore needed to make no response. Others were disturbed by it. In late November 1951 Wilfred J. McNeil, the assistant secretary of defense (controller), issued a request for estimates of the support of the atomic program in the army, navy, and air force. The air force, through its Directorate of the Budget, began compiling the information, including costs, for fiscal 1947–51: "*At once it became apparent that it was difficult to draw sharp lines between those activities which pertained to the atomic energy program and those which were outside its limits. This lack of clarity was one of several factors which made it impossible to arrive at exact sums either spent or to be spent for atomic energy*" (emphasis added).[7]

Following the exercise prompted by McMahon's resolution, the secretary of defense directed the air force to prepare its fiscal 1954 budget with the costs for nuclear weapons broken out and itemized. An accurate accounting was still deemed "inherently impossible because of the overlap with other programs resulting from the broad scope of

6. S. Conc. Res. 46, 82 Cong. 1 sess., September 18, 1951.

7. Lee Bowen, Robert D. Little, and others *A History of the Air Force Atomic Energy Program, 1943–1953,* vol. 3: *Building an Atomic Air Force, 1949–1953* (Washington, D.C.: U.S. Air Force Historical Division, 1959), pp. 471–72 (formerly top secret; declassified in 1980).

the atomic effort, and for the same reason the atomic program was not made a separate division of the budget."[8]

The 1954 budget was the last time the air force attempted to estimate the direct and indirect costs of its nuclear weapons programs. Although Major General Howard G. Bunker, the air force's assistant for atomic energy, believed that a revamped method of data collection would provide a more valid measure of direct and indirect costs, the deputy chief of staff for the comptroller found the estimates sufficient "to demonstrate to the [JCAE], and other reviewing authority, that the Military Services are pursuing actively their use of modern atomic weapons and that the cost attributable thereto includes a great deal more than the production costs for atomic bombs and warheads." A detailed reporting system, he said, would be inapplicable, and the compromise reached "was apparently to discontinue the effort entirely."[9]

The success of the overall effort may be judged from the opening chapter of the air force history, published as a top secret document nine years after McMahon introduced his resolution:

> This chapter was originally intended to be a detailed account of the cost and funding of the Air Force atomic energy program, 1943–1953. However, it was found to be impracticable to treat the subject in that manner. *From 1943 through 1951, there was no current, systematic account of Air Force atomic costs, since with some few exceptions no effort was made to distinguish these from other budget categories of which they formed a part.* Consequently, this chapter, except for consideration of certain episodes and procedures, unavoidably became a study of the estimated costs of the Air Force atomic program.[10] (Emphasis added)

As unreliable as they are, by the air force's own admission, these costs are in all likelihood the only data currently available that document what the both the air force and DOD spent on the nuclear weapons program during its early years (see table 2).

Several things are interesting about these data. First, although the air force maintained a monopoly on the delivery of nuclear weapons until the early 1950s, it did not begin to spend sizable amounts of money on its nuclear mission until 1949 (two years after achieving independence from the army). The other services, especially the navy, were clearly laying out more than the air force (the army continued to manage the Manhattan Engineer District until January 1, 1947, and the army and navy together also helped to support the AEC's costly testing program in the Pacific; see chapter 1). Second, the enormous increase in nuclear budgets in 1951 reflects efforts to respond to the

8. Bowen, Little, and others, *Building an Atomic Air Force*, p. 488.

9. Bowen, Little, and others, *Building an Atomic Air Force*, p. 495.

10. Bowen, Little, and others, *Building an Atomic Air Force*, p. 460.

TABLE 2. Estimated Air Force and Overall DOD Expenditures for Nuclear Weapons, 1944–54

Billions of 1996 dollars

Year	*Total DOD nuclear*	*Nuclear as percentage of total DOD*	*Total AF nuclear*	*AF as percentage of DOD nuclear*	*AF nuclear as percentage of total AF*
1944	—	—	0.038	—	00.02
1945	—	—	0.040	—	00.02
1946	—	—	0.159	—	00.25
1947	34.842	27	5.038	14.50	37.30
1948	26.376	27	5.762	21.85	46.20
1949	45.487	32	20.365	44.77	67.30
1950	39.221	34	16.966	43.26	42.00
1951	102.173	30	76.721	75.09	53.70
1952	115.061	27	74.043	64.35	53.60
1953	—	—	83.320	—	48.00
1954	—	—	69.785	—	51.50
Total	363.161		352.237		

Source: Little, *Building an Atomic Air Force,* pp. 487–89, 496. Column 4 was not in the original document but was derived from data therein. This report carefully qualified these figures, noting that it was impossible "within our present framework of operation to develop ground rules and assumptions on which to base irrefutable estimates of the portion of Air Force funds which contribute to the 'Atomic Effort. . . .' For this reason, the use of these estimates should be qualified in every instance as only broad order of magnitude estimates" (p. 494).

first Soviet atomic test in August 1949, the coming to power of the Communist party in China later that year, and the start of the Korean War in June 1950, events that proved particularly unsettling to civilian policymakers and the military. Third, the air force's—principally the Strategic Air Command's (SAC's)—growing control of DOD nuclear-related funding from 1947 through 1952 is clearly evident. This fiscal dominance, due both to SAC's attempts to control the nuclear weapons budget and the support of Congress in this endeavor, pushed the army and navy to create requirements for nuclear weapons, not only to protect their traditional missions from usurpation by the air force but to gain control of some of the budgetary largesse created by the decision to base national security on nuclear deterrence. This interservice rivalry was a major reason for the wide variety and sizable number of nuclear weapons ultimately deployed (see chapter 2). Fourth, it is apparent, from the rate of expenditures after 1950, that the United States spent its first $1 trillion on nuclear weapons within fifteen years of the end of World War II.

This early air force assessment stands out not just because it is the only known official attempt to calculate annual nuclear weapons costs. It shows that, as a percentage of total U.S. military spending for a few years during the most intense period of the cold war, expenditures on nuclear weapons were about the same as the average we have calculated for the *entire* cold war. Strong pressures, it would appear, have tended to maintain nuclear weapons spending at an approximately constant fraction of overall military spending. Moreover, the air force estimates omit AEC nuclear testing and weapons production costs. With the addition of these costs, the air force estimate is slightly greater than ours in terms of the percentage of overall military spending: about 33 percent on average between 1948 and 1952.

While most in Congress were relatively complacent about the high costs of nuclear weapons (not least because those costs were never fully presented to or understood by them), some occasionally voiced concern and frustration. On May 24, 1957, Representative Errett P. Scrivner (Republican of Kansas), a leading member of the House Appropriations Committee, called for some explanation—either by the Defense Department or "perhaps some outsiders"—of the current and long-term costs of nuclear weapons:

> One plane today can carry more potential death and destruction by 1 drop in 1 bomb than all of the planes carried in all of the sorties during all of World War II in both the Pacific and the Atlantic. . . . Somebody ought to tell us how much it is going to cost to deliver a megaton bomb, whether it is an atom bomb or a hydrogen bomb, by missile, by bomber, by carrier, by submarine. Somewhere, some place, there ought to be an answer as to which is the best and the most economical method. You know and I know that all of our services cannot be kept perpetually at peak effort to fight an atomic war all the time, one which may never come. . . . When you see some of these figures for a 10-year program I would expect your hair to sizzle.[11]

The situation had changed little by February 1960, when recently retired army chief of staff, General Maxwell D. Taylor, testified before a Senate subcommittee that the DOD made little effort to assess its overall needs and that both its planning and budgeting were haphazard:

> *We never look at our forces; we never build our forces in a budget sense in terms of military functions such as atomic retaliation, limited war capability, antisubmarine warfare, continental air defense.* We don't case our books in that form. So as a result, *I never know, and I doubt personally that anyone knows, exactly what we are buying with our budget.* . . . The Joint Chiefs of Staff were never in the budgetmaking business in this sense.[12] (Emphasis added)

11. *Congressional Record,* 85 Cong. 1 sess., vol. 103, pt. 6 (May 24, 1957), pp. H7619–20.

12. *Missiles, Space, and Other Major Defense Matters,* Hearings before the Preparedness Investigating Subcommittee of the Senate Committee on Armed Services in Conjunction with the Committee on Aeronautical and Space Sciences, 86 Cong. 2 sess., (Government Printing Office, 1960), p. 199. The AEC, meanwhile, had its own problems. In presenting the commission's first budget to Congress in 1947, Chairman David Lilienthal had no obvious means of justifying his request because "we didn't have a set of books showing costs, since the Army's Manhattan District didn't have or keep any" (see chapter 1 in this volume). This situation had not significantly improved by 1950, when Representative Francis Case (Republican of South Dakota) admonished the AEC: "No other agency of the Government has been able to get by the

At the start of the Kennedy administration in 1961, Secretary of Defense Robert S. McNamara moved to rectify this predicament. McNamara created the Five-Year (later "Future Years") Defense Program (FYDP) and assigned unique program element numbers to every major program in the department's budget.[13] Supplementing the organizational system in place since World War II (if not before), which grouped programs by service, McNamara created eleven major force programs (MFPs) to organize everything by function. These included strategic forces, general purpose forces, intelligence and communications, airlift and sealift, research and development, central supply, and maintenance. For the first time, officials were able to make accurate, long-range forecasts of budgetary requirements and, no less important, to assess historical expenditures.

Although the FYDP was a watershed development in DOD accounting, it did little to resolve the dilemma created a decade earlier by McMahon's resolution: it made no provision to track spending for nuclear weapons in general. Except in the case of strategic forces, the most visible part of the nuclear arsenal, the costs of tactical nuclear weapons, most weapons-related research and development, command, control and communications, nuclear-related intelligence, training, and other vital costs were intermingled among the MFPs. This situation made extraction and quantification difficult and posed continuing problems for policymakers.

On May 2, 1962, President John F. Kennedy called on the Bureau of the Budget, in cooperation with the Secretary of Defense, to develop a procedure for compiling "a statement of the costs of nuclear weapons provided for the national defense, including both the cost of delivery systems provided in the Defense budget and costs of weapons funded in the budget of the Atomic Energy Commission." Kennedy issued this directive in the context of the overall defense program he had initiated, which was increasing substantially the size of the nuclear stockpile (see chapter 2). Kennedy "stressed the extreme importance of holding down expenditures and requests for additional appropriations," a task obviously complicated by the lack of the aforementioned

Appropriations Committee with the lax presentation of detailed estimates that the [AEC] has. No other agency of the Government, so far as I know, has been able to come up and cloak itself with the aura of a scientific subject and get by with such general justifications." Quoted in Harold P. Green and Alan Rosenthal, *Government of the Atom: The Integration of Powers* (New York: Atherton Press, 1963), p. 225. In 1952 Commissioner T. Keith Glennan sent his colleagues a memorandum warning that the agency was then spending more than $100 million each month ($715 million in 1996 dollars), yet, "I am continuously at sea as to the status of our budgets, of our expenditures and particularly of any real basis for judging the quality of the financial performance of our various offices." Memorandum, T. Keith Glennan to Chairman Gordon Dean and others, May 9, 1952, Record Group 324, Records of the Atomic Energy Commission, Office of Secretary, General Correspondence, box 73, File: Organization and Management 8, Progress Reports by Division, vol. 1, National Archives.

13. The FYDP was renamed the Future Years Defense Program in 1988 when a six-year planning horizon was instituted.

data.[14] Despite the president's pressing interest in the issue, no "procedure" was devised for ascertaining the full costs of nuclear weapons on an annual basis; certainly none exists today.[15]

In the 1970s the Brookings Institution undertook an annual analysis of the defense budget as part of its *Setting National Priorities* series of books. Although the Brookings analysts did create a methodology for assessing nearly all nuclear weapons costs (excluding those for antisubmarine warfare and the costs borne by the AEC for warheads), they focused entirely on present and future year costs. Their figures were therefore of limited utility in gauging historical trends.[16] In 1973 Brookings published *Strategic Forces: Issues for the Mid-Seventies.* Building on the methodologies used in *Setting National Priorities,* authors Alton H. Quanbeck and Barry M. Blechman offered a careful assessment of the strategic nuclear triad (bombers, intercontinental ballistic missiles, and submarine-launched ballistic missiles, or SLBMs) and the costs of alternative force structures. This important contribution to understanding the potential future costs associated with the strategic nuclear arsenal did not delve into past expenditures, however.[17]

In the early 1980s interest in the cost of nuclear weapons arose anew, following the announcement of the Reagan administration's ambitious strategic modernization program. Among the more detailed

14. Memorandum, Charles E. Johnson for the record, "President's Decisions at the Meeting on Nuclear Weapons Requirements on May 3, 1962" (draft), May 4, 1962 (formerly top secret/restricted data), National Security Archive, p. 1. Officials present at this meeting included national security adviser McGeorge Bundy, military representative General Maxwell D. Taylor, Deputy Secretary of Defense Roswell L. Gilpatric, and AEC chairman Glenn T. Seaborg.

15. In September 1994 the DOD released the results of a year-long "Nuclear Posture Review" (NPR). Included in the briefing materials was a chart purporting to show the "Annual Budget—All Nuclear" for the years 1964, 1989, 1994, and 2003. Yet Secretary of Defense William J. Perry, referring to these data, asserted: "During the peak of our spending [1964 on the chart] we were spending about $50 billion a year on our *strategic* nuclear programs" (emphasis added). In subsequent congressional testimony on the NPR, Deputy Secretary John M. Deutch stated: "We are spending 70 percent less dollars on our nuclear programs than in 1988 and have 70 percent fewer individuals involved in these programs." DOD officials were asked by the author to supply the underlying data used to prepare this chart, and to describe what weapons systems and programs were included along with the methodology used to arrive at a total figure. An official eventually responded eight months later that the DOD was unable to comply with this request because neither the data nor the methodology were available. In its 1995, 1996, and 1997 *Annual Reports,* the DOD produced charts showing historical and anticipated future-year costs (in then-year dollars) for just strategic offensive nuclear forces, but many have misinterpreted these data to mean that they represent *total* nuclear weapons expenditures (see chapter 11 in this volume). See Department of Defense, "Press Conference with Secretary of Defense William J. Perry, General Shalikashvili, Chairman, JCS, Deputy Secretary of Defense John M. Deutch, Mr. Kenneth Bacon, ATSD-PA," News Release 546-95, September 22, 1994; *U.S. Nuclear Policy,* Hearing before the House Committee on Foreign Affairs, 103 Cong. 2 sess. (GPO, 1994), pp. 3, 51; author's telephone conversation with Laura Holgate, special assistant to the assistant secretary of defense for international security policy, June 20, 1995; Department of Defense, *Report of the Secretary of Defense to the President and the Congress* (GPO, February 1995), pp. 166–68; Department of Defense, *Report of the Secretary of Defense to the President and the Congress* (GPO, February 1996), pp. 215–17; Department of Defense, *Report of the Secretary of Defense to the President and the Congress* (GPO, April 1997), pp. 209–11.

16. Charles L. Schultze with Edward K. Hamilton and Allen Schick, *Setting National Priorities: The 1971 Budget* (Brookings, 1970), pp. 17–23; Charles L. Schultze and others, *Setting National Priorities: The 1972 Budget* (Brookings, 1971), pp. 39–50, 94–102, 107–17; Charles L. Schultze and others, *Setting National Priorities: The 1973 Budget* (Brookings, 1972), pp. 46–57, 93–109; Edward R. Fried and others, *Setting National Priorities: The 1974 Budget* (Brookings, 1973), pp. 307–15.

17. Alton H. Quanbeck and Barry M. Blechman, *Strategic Forces: Issues for the Mid-Seventies* (Brookings, 1973).

efforts to quantify the probable costs of this program were two studies by the nongovernmental Center for Defense Information. Like the Brookings analyses of a decade earlier, these reports focused on future year costs, but went somewhat further and included, for instance, warhead production costs borne by the Department of Defense.[18]

Attention soon turned to the "problems" of trying to estimate funding for strategic nuclear weapons. Without an accurate "funding aggregation," remarked a Congressional Research Service paper in 1984, "DOD estimates of strategic forces funding are often subject to misinterpretation."[19]

But it was not until October 1994 that the nongovernmental Defense Budget Project (now the Center for Strategic and Budgetary Assessments) produced the first estimate of the historical costs incurred by the U.S. nuclear weapons program. According to its assessment (which was linked to this analysis but not intended to provide a comprehensive review of each aspect of the nuclear weapons program), the total costs incurred were $4.1 trillion, while actual expenditures through 1994 were $3.7 trillion (in constant 1995 dollars). The methodology developed for this assessment greatly informed the present study.[20]

Key Factors Affecting the Pace and Scale of the U.S. Nuclear Weapons Program

Needless to say, the United States did not develop its nuclear arsenal in a vacuum. A variety of international and domestic factors profoundly influenced the scale and pace of the nuclear buildup. Among the most compelling of these, as discussed in chapter 1, was the fear of many scientists, especially those recently emigrated from Europe, that Adolf Hitler would try to acquire an atomic bomb. Though atomic research had been proceeding in earnest for many years, a major war in Europe spearheaded by a ruthless dictator was a powerful incentive to develop a bomb sooner rather than later.

---

18. Center for Defense Information, "Preparing for Nuclear War: President Reagan's Program," *Defense Monitor*, vol. 10, no. 8 (1982); Center for Defense Information, "More Bang, More Bucks: $450 Billion for Nuclear War," *Defense Monitor*, vol. 12, no. 7 (1983). In 1990 the center revisited the issue in Center for Defense Information, "Preparations for Nuclear War: Still More than $1 Billion a Week," *Defense Monitor*, vol. 19, no. 7 (1990). More recent of the center's analyses of nuclear weapon costs are in Center for Defense Information, "Nuclear Weapons after the Cold War: Too Many, Too Costly, Too Dangerous," *Defense Monitor*, vol. 22, no. 1 (1993); and Center for Defense Information, "The Nuclear Nineties: Broken Promises, Misplaced Priorities," *Defense Monitor*, vol. 24, no. 8 (1995).

19. Alice C. Maroni, "Estimating Funding for Strategic Forces: A Review of the Problems," Congressional Research Service Report 84-652F, May 31, 1984, p. 2.

20. Steven Kosiak, "The Lifecycle Costs of Nuclear Forces: A Preliminary Assessment," Defense Budget Project, Washington, D.C., October 1994. This report also estimated probable future-year costs for the U.S. nuclear arsenal under the START I and START II treaties.

Once the Allied victory in World War II had been secured, in part through the use of two atomic bombs against Japan, the nuclear weapons program began to grow. Unease about developments abroad—the Soviet Union's swift consolidation of control over Eastern Europe and the first Soviet atomic test on August 29, 1949—also spurred the pace of nuclear developments in the United States. Other worrisome international developments followed: the victory of China's Communist party in October 1949, the Soviet-Chinese alliance the following February, the start of the Korean War on June 25, 1950, and China's entry into the war that October.[21] When Senator Joseph McCarthy began charging that there were communist spies at home and Klaus Fuchs and Julius and Ethel Rosenberg were brought to trial for atomic-related espionage activities, vigilance toward the threat increased, as did the role of nuclear weapons in the defense of U.S. interests.

Spurred on by the small (eighteen-member) but singularly powerful congressional Joint Committee on Atomic Energy and the Atomic Energy Commission, the United States responded to these various events by developing the more powerful hydrogen bomb, as well as smaller "tactical" nuclear weapons for battlefield combat. It also increased nuclear testing, opened a nuclear test site on the mainland (to permit more frequent and less costly tests), and created an extensive series of new production facilities. These developments were driven by the advice of scientists working on the nuclear program.[22]

Another domestic factor contributing to increased spending on nuclear weapons was, ironically, President Harry S Truman's determination to control postwar government spending and inflation. His May 1948 decision to impose a $14.4 billion (then-year dollars) ceiling on military spending led to increased reliance on nuclear weapons, which were widely regarded as less costly than conventional weapons.[23] With

21. Before the Korean War, U.S. policymakers had become concerned that it might be only a matter of time before the Soviet Union believed it was strong enough to attack the United States. Military conquest in order to impose communism around the world was presumed to be the Soviet Union's prime objective. U.S. military planning was pegged to a year of "maximum danger," when the balance of forces would be most unfavorable to the United States. To head off this threat, plans were put forward to rearm the nation. The North Korean attack appeared to confirm the predictions about Soviet aspirations and many analysts considered the possibility that it was but the opening phase of a general war, with further aggression possible in Europe, the Middle East, or elsewhere.

22. Despite their expertise, there has been for decades a serious but largely unacknowledged conflict of interest in permitting scientists—whose personal and professional livelihood depends on the continued production of nuclear weapons—to appear before congressional committees or other government entities as supposedly dispassionate experts to make recommendations on which weapons or policies to pursue.

23. This is equivalent to $142.6 billion in 1996 dollars. "During the next eight months, despite military protests, [Truman] refused to raise the limit he had imposed. The [Joint Chiefs of Staff] estimated that a budget of $21–23 billion [$213 billion to $233 billion in 1996 dollars], or even a compromise of $16.9 billion [$171.4 billion], would allow the United States to maintain adequate conventional forces to retain some foothold in Europe as well as to carry out naval operations in all or part of the Mediterranean in the event of war. They feared that the $14.4 billion budget would result in the total loss of Western Europe; conventional forces would have to be cut back so far, the JCS argued, that the only offensive operation the United States could undertake to meet an emergency would be an atomic air offensive from the British Isles and the Cairo-Suez area." David Alan Rosenberg, "American Atomic Strategy and the Hydrogen Bomb Decision,"

the creation of the North Atlantic Treaty Organization (NATO) in April 1949 and the explicit commitment of the United States to defend its members against a Soviet attack, the argument that a defense against conventional attack should now be based on nuclear weapons became even more compelling, especially as it was believed that Soviet conventional forces in Europe were overwhelmingly superior to those of the United States.[24] As historian David Alan Rosenberg notes, this decision "launched the United States on a one-sided strategic arms race *before* the Soviet atomic test of August 1949."[25]

The decision was made even more attractive by the fact that the AEC budget was considered separately from the defense budget and thus did not fall under Truman's spending ceiling. In addition, because the military services incurred few costs for the development of nuclear weapons, there was no financial disincentive not to seek their development in large numbers.[26] Truman's policy was continued and broadened under President Dwight D. Eisenhower's "New Look," which led to the production and deployment of thousands of nuclear weapons. Although, as explained shortly, the belief that nuclear weapons delivered "a bigger bang for a buck" came into serious question immediately, it continued to hold sway in government circles.

The unsettling international events of 1949 and 1950 prompted Truman to order a comprehensive statement of national security policy. That statement, known as NSC 68 and delivered to Truman in April 1950, argued the Soviet Union was economically and technologically competitive with the United States and sought to dominate the world.[27] Absent changes in U.S. or Soviet policies, the report con-

---

Journal of American History, vol. 66, no. 1 (June 1979), p. 69. In fact, Truman had a plan—known as universal military training—to provide sufficient manpower for a robust conventional military. But the Republican-controlled Congress defeated this proposal, siding with the air force (which had pointedly broken ranks with the other services to promote its own interests) in favoring the development of a seventy-group air force (capable of dropping atomic bombs on the Soviet Union) over increasing personnel strength and easing reliance on nuclear firepower. See Lynn Eden, "Capitalist Conflict and the State: The Making of United States Military Policy in 1948," in Charles Bright and Susan Harding, eds., *Statemaking and Social Movements: Essays in History and Theory* (University of Michigan Press, 1984), pp. 233–61.

24. This belief, which only became widely accepted following the start of the Korean War, was subsequently shown to be, if not false, at least greatly exaggerated. See Alain C. Enthoven and K. Wayne Smith, *How Much Is Enough?: Shaping the Defense Program, 1961–1969* (New York: Harper & Row, 1971), p. 136; John Lewis Gaddis and Paul Nitze, "NSC 68 and the Soviet Threat Reconsidered," *International Security*, vol. 4, no. 4 (1980), pp. 170–76; Matthew A. Evangelista, "Stalin's Postwar Army Reappraised," *International Security*, vol. 7, no. 3 (1982/83), p. 121. For a fuller treatment of the perceptions and realities of the Soviet military threat in general, see Andrew Cockburn, *The Threat: Inside the Soviet Military Machine* (New York: Vintage Books, 1984).

25. Rosenberg, "American Atomic Strategy," p. 86. Emphasis added.

26. The services were responsible, however, for the cost of all nuclear delivery vehicles (such as aircraft, missiles, and submarines) except for gravity bombs. According to comments made in July 1965 by "a former high government official who had had full access to relevant classified information. . . . '[T]here would have been many fewer weapons designed and many fewer weapons produced if the money had come out of the relatively fixed ceiling on DOD funds. The result is, there is no incentive for DOD to be sparing on its nuclear weapons demands. . . . [T]he greatest beneficial restraint on the proliferation of nuclear weapons would come from making the Department of Defense budget for these weapons.'" Quoted in Harold Orlans, *Contracting for Atoms: A Study of Public Policy Issues Posed by the Atomic Energy Commission's Contracting for Research, Development, and Managerial Services* (Brookings, 1967), p. 179.

27. In assessing the Soviet Union's economic capabilities,

cluded, the Soviet Union stood a good chance of winning. To thwart Soviet intentions, NSC 68 suggested significant increases in defense spending. This idea was strongly resisted by Secretary of Defense Louis A. Johnson, a fiscal conservative, but it nevertheless set the stage for an arms race with the Soviet Union.[28]

Another important reason that the U.S. nuclear program proceeded as it did was the government's refusal, through the mid-1950s, to engage the Soviet Union in discussions on arms control or nuclear disarmament.[29] For the next decade after Soviet authorities rejected the 1946 Baruch plan calling for all other countries to forgo developing nuclear weapons as a precondition for eventual U.S. disarmament, the U.S. government dismissed all Soviet arms control proposals as mere propaganda. In July 1949 Truman told his senior policy advisers: "I am of the opinion we'll never obtain international control. Since we can't obtain international control we must be strongest in atomic weapons."[30] When in May 1955 the Soviet Union presented a plan for verifying arms reductions—a plan that matched Western proposals—the United States, after initially praising the offer, withdrew from the Geneva disarmament conference and nearly two years later explicitly renounced the goal of disarmament altogether.[31]

---

the report concluded that "as the Soviet attainment of an atomic capability has demonstrated, the totalitarian state, at least in time of peace, can focus its efforts on any given project far more readily than the democratic state." Yet the Soviet atomic bomb effort had actually taken *longer* than the Manhattan Project. Even discounting that Soviet atomic research was initiated before World War II (as was also the case in the United States)—a fact not then known by U.S. officials—the Manhattan Project required just thirty-five months *during wartime* (August 13, 1942, to July 16, 1945) to design, manufacture, and test an atomic bomb, as well as construct all the facilities necessary to produce the materials needed for the program. By comparison, the Soviet Union, after the war and with the crucial knowledge unavailable to the United States that such weapons could indeed be manufactured, needed more than forty-eight months (August 20, 1945, to August 29, 1949) to accomplish the same task, even though it had essentially copied the Trinity device and had access to important details of the U.S. program both from its spies and from open U.S. publications about the Manhattan Project (see chapter 8). August 20, 1945, is the date the State Defense Committee "adopted a decree setting up a special committee to direct 'all work on the utilization of the intra-atomic energy of uranium.'" The creation of this committee prompted the immediate acceleration of work on an atomic bomb. See David Holloway, *Stalin and the Bomb: The Soviet Union and Atomic Energy, 1939—1956* (Yale University Press, 1994), p. 129.

28. The full text of NSC 68 (United States Objectives and Programs for National Security) can be found in Thomas H. Etzold and John Lewis Gaddis, *Containment: Documents on American Policy and Strategy, 1945–1950* (Columbia University Press, 1978), pp. 385–442.

29. Significantly, NSC 68 argued that because a growing Soviet atomic stockpile would threaten U.S. military installations and because a jockeying for nuclear superiority (coupled with fears of inferiority) when both countries had attained large stockpiles "might well act, therefore, not as a deterrent, but as an incitement to war . . . it appears it would be to the long-term advantage of the United States if atomic weapons were to be effectively eliminated from national peacetime armaments." Quoted in Etzold and Gaddis, *Containment,* pp. 416–17.

30. Quoted in David Alan Rosenberg, "The Origins of Overkill: Nuclear Weapons and American Strategy, 1945–1960," in Steven E. Miller, ed., *Strategy and Nuclear Deterrence* (Princeton University Press, 1984), pp. 131–32. Roger M. Anders, editor of AEC chairman Gordon Dean's office diary, writes: "Like the president and Senator McMahon, Dean judged the immediate Soviet threat a greater danger than the potential long-range costs of a nuclear arms race. He found a transitory military superiority more congenial than attempts to negotiate long-range security. *Dean never seems to have considered whether an unrestrained arms race posed far more danger to America than negotiating with Stalin*" (emphasis added). Roger M. Anders, ed., *Forging the Atomic Shield: Excerpts from the Office Diary of Gordon E. Dean* (University of North Carolina Press, 1987), p. 19.

31. In the words of Harold Stassen, Eisenhower's special assistant on disarmament: "It is our view that if an effort is made to reduce armaments, armed forces, and military expenditures to a level that is too low . . . it would not be con-

In October 1957 the Soviet Union stunned Americans by launching a missile carrying the earth's first artificial satellite. If Soviet scientists could launch a Sputnik, U.S. analysts reasoned, they would soon be able to loft nuclear warheads to the United States.[32] The implications were profound: warning times decreased from hours to minutes and, more important, there was no known means of defending against a ballistic missile attack. Congressional Democrats blamed the Eisenhower administration for the "missile gap," and Senator John F. Kennedy used the issue to help defeat Vice President Richard Nixon in November 1960. Though Kennedy discovered, upon assuming office, that the missile gap was not only illusory but favored the United States by a margin of nearly 6 to 1 for ICBMs (or 2 to 1 when SLBMs were included), he was unwilling to rescind his charges for political reasons and thus authorized a sizable increase in U.S. strategic nuclear forces. In so doing the administration failed "to recognize that the large American deployment under way, and specifically endorsed by [a top secret interdepartmental review of a recent national intelligence estimate] as being necessary, would contribute to decisions by the Soviet Union to increase its own capabilities: in the near run by the Cuban deployment, in the longer run by pushing ahead with the SS-9 and SS-11 ICBMs and Y-class submarine program. This was perhaps the most important error of all."[33]

Spending on U.S. nuclear weapons was also greatly affected by two factors that arose somewhat later. In December 1979 the Soviet Union invaded Afghanistan, only weeks after the seizure of the U.S. embassy in Tehran by Iranian militants. At that point, U.S.–Soviet relations took an abrupt turn for the worse, as many in the United States became concerned about their nation's apparent military weakness and resurgent Soviet hegemonic aspirations. In response, President Jimmy Carter requested a considerable increase in defense spending and signed Presidential Directive 59, calling on the United States to develop and maintain the capability to wage a protracted nuclear war.

After defeating Carter in the 1980 presidential election, Ronald Reagan entered office determined to undertake an unprecedented

---

ducive to stability in the world. . . . It is our view that if armaments. . . are brought down to too low a level, then . . . the danger of war is increased." Quoted in David Goldfischer, *The Best Defense: Policy Alternatives for U.S. Nuclear Security from the 1950s to the 1990s* (Cornell University Press, 1993), p. 109. For more on this issue, see pp. 107–16.

32. Deputy Secretary of Defense Donald Quarles tried to put the threat in perspective on November 18, 1957, by pointing out that "it takes us years to produce a new weapon system like the B-52 bomber. The ballistic missile problem is even more difficult and takes even longer because of the many tough technical problems that have to be solved. The very size of the equipment and test facilities adds to the difficulty. In our experience, there is a long time period between the first test firings and the final operational weapons. We have no reason to believe it is significantly different with them." Quoted in Charles H. Donnelly, *The United States Guided Missile Program*, prepared for the Preparedness Investigating Subcommittee of the Senate Committee on Armed Services, 86 Cong. 1 sess. (GPO, 1959), p. 17.

33. Norris and Cochran, *US-USSR/Russian Strategic Offensive Nuclear Forces*, tables 1 and 2. Raymond L. Garthoff, *Intelligence Assessment and Policymaking: A Decision Point in the Kennedy Administration* (Brookings, 1984), p. 13.

peacetime military buildup as a means to increase economic pressure on the Soviet Union and force an end to the cold war.[34] Though the Soviet Union did indeed collapse in 1991—the cause, said Reagan supporters, was the president's actions, whereas opponents credited the reforms of Russian leader Mikhail Gorbachev—there is no evidence, as discussed in chapter 4, that the Soviet Union increased its military spending to match the Reagan administration's program. This is not to say that the military burden on the Soviet economy was not substantial; it was. However, if the Soviet Union's expenditures—as estimated by the Central Intelligence Agency (CIA)—were substantially unaltered during this period and the state collapsed anyway, then it was the United States that ended up racing against itself.[35] In fiscal terms, this modernization program contributed to the $2 trillion added to the U.S. national debt during Reagan's two terms.[36] Moreover, a June 1993 report from the General Accounting Office following a three-year analysis of the administration's strategic modernization program (the first governmental analysis of strategic nuclear forces in more than thirty years) indicated that the DOD had misled Congress about the necessity, cost, and effectiveness of many of the weapons, as well as the vulnerability of bombers and ICBMs to Soviet attack.[37]

---

34. For more on this policy, see Lou Cannon, "Arms Boost Seen as Strain on Soviets," *Washington Post,* June 19, 1980, p. A3; Richard Halloran, Leslie H. Gelb, and Howell Raines, "Weinberger Said to Offer Reagan Plan to Regain Atomic Superiority," *New York Times,* August 14, 1981, p. A1; Richard Halloran, "Pentagon Draws Up First Strategy for Fighting a Long Nuclear War," *New York Times,* May 30, 1982, p. 12.

35. In fact, some argue that the U.S. buildup may have postponed the reforms—including reductions in military spending—that Gorbachev sought to implement, thereby prolonging the cold war and the costs to the United States. From 1985 to 1994 disinformation supplied by known or suspected Soviet double agents (emplaced with the assistance of confessed spy Aldrich Ames) was provided by the CIA to Presidents Reagan, Bush, and Clinton and other top officials. The result, according to an unnamed former top intelligence official, was that "the U.S. released publicly wrong information and may have wasted millions of dollars retooling military equipment to meet fabricated changes in Soviet capabilities." An internal review of the affair by CIA director John M. Deutch determined that although not much money was expended on the basis of the tainted data, it "had a substantial role in framing the debate" on U.S. military strategy and "in some cases our military posture was altered slightly." Deutch added that the disinformation effort was designed "to affect R&D and procurement decisions of the Department of Defense" by misleading officials into believing "that the Soviets remained a superpower and that their military R&D program was robust." Consequently, "we overestimated their capability." Walter Pincus, "CIA Passed Bogus News to Presidents; Ames Aided KGB Effort to Deceive, Reports Show," *Washington Post,* October 31, 1995, p. A1; Tim Weiner, "C.I.A. Tells Panels It Failed to Sift Tainted Spy Data," *New York Times,* November 1, 1995, p. A1; Walter Pincus, "Tainted Moscow Data Swayed U.S., CIA Says; Information Concealed Soviet Decline, Hill Told," *Washington Post,* December 9, 1995, p. A1.

36. "The Numbers Behind the Budget: Federal Debt," *Washington Post,* August 30, 1990, p. A21. By way of comparison, it took from 1776 to 1981—205 years—to amass the first $1 trillion of the national debt.

37. The capabilities of many existing weapons were downplayed and their vulnerabilities exaggerated in order to make the weapons proposed under the modernization program appear both necessary and cost-effective. In the words of Eleanor Chelimsky, assistant comptroller general for program evaluation and methodology in the General Accounting Office (GAO): "A general conclusion from our study is that there exist systematic disparities between what the data showed and DOD's claims and estimates for (1) the Soviet threat, (2) the performance of mature systems, and (3) the expected performance and costs of proposed upgrades. I say *systematic* disparities, because they seem to follow a particular pattern, tending to overstate threats to our weapon systems, to understate the performance of mature systems, to overstate the expected performance of upgrades, and to understate the expected costs of those upgrades." See *Evaluation of the U.S. Strategic Nuclear Triad,* Hearing before the Senate Committee on Governmental Affairs, 103 Cong. 1 sess., S. Hrg. 103-457 (GPO, 1994), p. 8. See also Tim Weiner, "Military Accused of Lies over Arms," *New York Times,* June 28,

Equally important, the strength of the U.S. economy made it relatively easy and less controversial to maintain and expand the nuclear weapons program throughout the cold war. Propagating such a large and diverse program over so many years would have been more problematic had the economy been smaller or less robust. In addition, plentiful supplies of natural uranium precluded any significant resource constraints on the ultimate size of the program.

A "Bigger Bang for a Buck"?

As just mentioned, both Truman's and Eisenhower's defense policies were predicated on the assumption that nuclear weapons were a cost-effective means of addressing the Soviet military threat. The genesis and validity of this belief merit a closer examination. The general notion that nuclear weapons are less expensive than conventional ones can be traced to the fact that a given amount of fissile material (plutonium or highly enriched uranium, HEU), when fissioned in a nuclear bomb, can produce more explosive power than an equivalent amount of conventional high explosives. Therefore, the reasoning went, while 10 pounds of high explosives might kill or injure 100 people, 10 pounds of plutonium could kill or injure 100,000 people.[38]

The phrase used to promote this idea was "a bigger bang for a buck," which may well have been coined long before the advent of the atomic bomb. The press seems to have first used it in a 1954 *Newsweek* profile on Secretary of Defense Charles E. Wilson. The article criticized the administration's "leading spokesmen" for describing the defense program with "catchy, all embracing phrases like 'the new

1993, p. A10. During this period the Soviet Union became increasingly dependent on the policy of launch on warning to ensure that its forces would not be destroyed by a surprise U.S. attack. Yet government intelligence analysts wrongly suggested that the Soviet Union was actually planning for a first strike and the entire U.S. strategic modernization program instituted by the Reagan administration was justified and implemented on this basis. "Unfortunately, during the professional and public debate over the programs, the intelligence community did not weigh in with its abundant evidence that the Soviet nuclear planning system was almost totally preoccupied with scenarios in which the West strikes first. The intelligence community in effect repressed a competing view of Soviet strategic motivations and activities, and as a result of this bias, the United States pursued what could be considered a dangerously misguided nuclear policy." Bruce G. Blair, *Global Zero Alert for Nuclear Forces* (Brookings, 1995), pp. 44–45.

38. As early as 1949, Vannevar Bush, head of the National Defense Research Committee during World War II, warned against making such comparisons: "The cost of trinitrotoluol, the TNT that is the most common high explosive, is less than a dollar a pound when it is manufactured in quantity. Built into bombs, delivered on a target hundreds of miles distant by an intricate aircraft manned by a highly trained crew subject to the attrition of war, its cost may well mount to hundreds of dollars a pound. Behind this ratio lies the opportunity for gross fallacies in reasoning. . . . Moreover, it is not to ignore the important element that the cost of atomic bombs is largely a peacetime cost, for they cannot be manufactured in a hurry during war, as can high explosive. Costs, that is, effort in terms of labor and materials, are necessarily spread over a long interval to produce atomic bombs, and this fact greatly affects our reasoning concerning them." Bush, *Modern Arms and Free Men: A Discussion of the Role of Science in Preserving Democracy* (New York: Simon & Schuster, 1949), pp. 94, 106.

look.' They have talked of getting more for less, of 'a bigger bang for a buck.'"[39]

Although the exact origins of the phrase are uncertain, the thinking leading to it is readily apparent in a speech delivered by Senator McMahon on September 18, 1951. In it, McMahon made the case for his concurrent resolution calling for an "all-out" nuclear weapons program. After remarking on the steadily climbing defense budgets, he asked, with rhetorical flourish: "Can we forever scale these giddy heights without crashing downward? May not history some day come upon the bones of a broken economy and a bankrupt people?"[40] The answer, for the time being at least, was that it was "better to scrape the bottom of the tax barrel than to scrape atomic rubble from the streets of New York, London and Moscow. Better to balance the armed power of the Kremlin than to balance the national budget"; but such a policy, if continued for very much longer, could have only two "ultimate destinations: military safety at the price of economic disaster or economic safety at the price of military disaster."[41]

This outcome, McMahon proposed, might be prevented by increasing reliance on the atomic bomb. Although a "hideous weapon," it could, if deployed by the thousands, deter Stalin until "his enslaved millions break their chains and join hands with us in peace and brotherhood."[42] The "startling fact," he continued, was that atomic deterring power was "actually hundreds of times cheaper than TNT."

> Money spent upon the atomic bomb could pulverize a dozen enemy war plants at no more expense than destroying a single plant with TNT, to say nothing of the fact that one plane can deliver one A-bomb as against the huge armadas needed to deliver an equivalent cargo of block-busters. . . . If we mass-produce this weapon, as we can, I solemnly say to the Senate that the cost of a single atomic bomb will become less than the cost of a single tank.[43]

By making nuclear weapons the "real backbone" of its peace power, the United States would be able to hit the enemy anywhere and everywhere so that "if he dares attack he will have no place to hide."[44] This would save the country from economic ruin because

39. "Defense and Politics . . . Battle of the Potomac," *Newsweek*, March 22, 1954, p. 28. Interestingly, this article goes on to report that "atomic weapons do come into the new look, but in a totally different way—to build up the fire power of the Army, not to provide the same fire power with fewer men. The U.S. can do that because it's now producing atomic weapons in quantity" (p. 30).

40. *Congressional Record*, 82 Cong. 1 sess., vol. 97, pt. 9 (September 18, 1961), p. S11496.

41. *Congressional Record*, vol. 97, pt. 9 (September 18, 1951), pp. S11496–97.

42. *Congressional Record*, vol. 97, pt. 9 (September 18, 1951), p. S11497.

43. *Congressional Record*, vol. 97, pt. 9 (September 18, 1951), p. S11497. This did not, in fact, occur, because the economies of scale associated with conventional weapons were largely absent in the nuclear realm, as evidenced by the large size and resulting high cost of the weapons production complex necessary to produce even a small number of weapons.

44. *Congressional Record*, vol. 97, pt. 9 (September 18, 1951), p. S11498.

> in all logic and common sense, an atomic army and an atomic navy and an atomic air force ought to mean fewer men under arms. They ought to mean a major reduction in the tens of billions of dollars we would otherwise spend upon stacks and stacks of conventional armaments. They ought to mean a sloughing off of outmoded operations and outdated expenses.[45]

Others, too, believed that more energy could be released for a dollar expended. At a January 16, 1952, meeting of the National Security Council (NSC) (attended by President Truman) to discuss the pending decision to proceed with work on the hydrogen bomb and the multibillion-dollar expansion program linked to this effort, Secretary of Defense Robert A. Lovett took the argument a step further. He pointed out how expensive high explosive was compared with fissionable material "from the standpoint of energy release for dollar expended . . . something on the order of twenty to one in favor of nuclear detonations. . . . Even if this material is not exploded, it can be useful for our peacetime economy." To this, Gordon Dean, AEC chairman, responded:

> While none of the material processed into plutonium or U-235 is wasted, in the sense that you could use it eventually in one form or another for power reactors, one would not spend any money on additional gaseous diffusion plants or production reactors themselves if our goal was commercial power. . . . [W]e must not kid ourselves into thinking that this program could be justified as a purely peacetime measure. . . . [T]he gaseous diffusion plants and production piles themselves would be wasted if we did not have a tense international situation.[46]

But what of the belief that nuclear weapons would save money by replacing conventional forces? Army chief of staff General J. Lawton Collins noted at a press conference on September 6, 1952, that nonstrategic nuclear weapons would not reduce "the number of divisions required initially for the defense of Europe," but they would "result ultimately in the ability to do the job with a smaller number of divisions."[47] After studying the issue in two-sided war games during the winter of

45. *Congressional Record,* vol. 97, pt. 9 (September 18, 1951), pp. S11496–509. McMahon also told his colleagues that once this goal had been attained, the fissile materials in these many weapons could be put to peacetime uses: "That selfsame material will not be barren and wasted; it will not become obsolete and useless; and money spent creating it will not be lost" (p. S11498). For the reality of how these materials are treated today, see chapter 6 in this volume. Two days after this speech, J. Robert Oppenheimer called AEC chairman Dean and, among other things, stated that "he thought the Senator's suggestions . . . will not save that much money." Quoted in Anders, *Forging the Atomic Shield,* p. 164. The following month, Representative Henry M. Jackson (Democrat of Washington), McMahon's colleague on the JCAE, delivered an even more forceful speech and called for an even larger expansion program than McMahon's. See *Congressional Record,* 82 Cong. 1 sess., vol. 97, pt. 10 (October 9, 1951), pp. H12866–73.

46. Anders, *Forging the Atomic Shield,* p. 193.

47. Quoted in Robert Endicott Osgood, *NATO: The Entangling Alliance* (University of Chicago Press, 1962), p. 105.

1952–53, Lieutenant General James M. Gavin, commander of the Seventh Army Corps, observed: "More rather than less manpower would be required to fight a nuclear war successfully." These findings were confirmed in subsequent war games in 1955 and 1958.[48] In 1953, General Mathew P. Ridgway, the supreme Allied commander Europe (SACEUR), "held that the new tactical nuclear weapons would not only demand more manpower but would also increase the cost of defense to the taxpayer." His successor, General Alfred B. Gruenther, cautioned that "new weapons frequently have the effect of adding new problems and new tasks without eliminating those that previously confronted us."[49]

Notwithstanding such warnings, Secretary of State John Foster Dulles, in a widely noted speech before the Council on Foreign Relations on January 12, 1954 (in which he explained the Eisenhower administration's new policy, which would become known as "massive retaliation"), insisted that the administration's plan "to depend primarily upon a great capacity to retaliate, instantly, by means and at places of our choosing" meant that "it is now possible to get, and share, more basic security at less cost."[50] However, as late as June 1973, in discussing the cost of the current generation of atomic artillery, then SACEUR General Andrew J. Goodpaster told a subcommittee of the JCAE that the "'more bang for a buck' type of analysis . . . is open to serious question."[51]

48. James M. Gavin, *War and Peace in the Space Age* (New York: Harper & Brothers, 1958), p. 139; Osgood, *NATO,* pp. 118–19. Interestingly, this conclusion did nothing to shake Gavin's faith in nuclear weapons. In 1956 and 1957 he told the JCAE that the army required 151,000 nuclear weapons for battlefield use (see chapter 2 in this volume). In his 1958 book, he continued to maintain that cost savings were just around the corner: "Nuclear weapons will become conventional for several reasons, among them cost, effectiveness against enemy weapons, and ease of handling. By 1965 the cost of nuclear weapons will be far less than present high-explosive weapons of equivalent yield and effectiveness. Many millions of dollars spent in the manufacture, shipping, storage and handling of high-explosive projectiles and bombs will be saved through the use of nuclear weapons moved by air to combat areas" (p. 265).

49. Quoted in Osgood, *NATO,* p. 107. This was true not least because the weapons deployed to Europe were quite complicated and required a large number of highly trained technicians to operate and maintain them. In addition, the greater explosive power of nuclear weapons would yield a larger number of casualties. To compensate for these anticipated losses and minimize their impact on the outcome of the battle, larger numbers of reserve troops would be required, as well as an expanded medical corps to treat the wounded.

50. Quoted in David N. Schwartz, *NATO's Nuclear Dilemmas* (Brookings, 1983), pp. 24–25. Conversely, some army officers believed that by 1958 the high cost of nonstrategic nuclear weapons and the corresponding cuts in conventional military capability had "dangerously restricted the development and production of conventional weapons without producing sufficient nuclear weapons" (Osgood, *NATO,* p. 119). Army Chief of Staff Maxwell D. Taylor testified before a Senate subcommittee in January 1958 (in the wake of Sputnik): "We have found our missile programs have lived up to their technological expectations, but unfortunately they have come very high in dollar costs. So within the comparatively limited budgets we have had to work with, to a large extent we have had to pay for the missile program out of what you might call conventional equipment. I am always disturbed by that, and each year we try to strike a reasonable balance so we can be sure of replacing our equipment, which is not in the missile category, at a reasonable rate." Astonishingly, the subcommittee's special counsel, Edwin L. Weisl, who was conducting the questioning of Taylor, did not pursue this critical issue, turning instead to the issue of deploying mobile versions of the Jupiter and Redstone missiles. *Inquiry into Satellite and Missile Programs,* Hearings before the Preparedness Investigating Subcommittee of the Senate Committee on U.S. Armed Services, 85 Cong., 1 and 2 sess. (GPO, 1958), pt. 1, p. 477. Concerns such as these encouraged the development of the policy of flexible response during the Kennedy administration and led to increased funding for conventional military capabilities.

51. *Military Applications of Nuclear Technology,* Hearing before the Subcommittee on Military Applications of the

The Indeterminate Nature of Deterrence

The final and most significant factor affecting the scale and pace of the U.S. nuclear buildup is perhaps the least understood by those not intimately familiar with the arcana of nuclear policy. There is clear historical evidence, going back to the Manhattan Project and as recently as the 1994 U.S.–North Korean–South Korean nonproliferation agreement and the ongoing India–Pakistan nuclear standoff, that even the possession of nuclear weapons usable materials and actual or presumed nuclear expertise can, in some circumstances, serve as a deterrent. Similarly, there is also evidence that a state with a relatively small proven arsenal, such as China or France, can deter nuclear attacks by states with far larger arsenals. Furthermore, there is no evidence that a huge nuclear arsenal is more effective than a small one in deterring a conventional attack, although military and civilian strategists tended to think along these lines, reasoning that if a few nuclear weapons were good for deterrence, more would be better.

The unconstrained U.S.-Soviet nuclear arms race that actually occurred (until the advent of the Strategic Arms Limitation Talks, SALT, in November 1969), with its escalating targeting requirements and tit-for-tat responses to qualitative and quantitative changes on both sides, did not derive from any analysis of the size of an arsenal needed for deterrence. Instead, a variety of other factors drove the process, including a lack of reliable information on the strength and disposition of an opponent's forces, interservice rivalry and pork-barrel pressures for military spending. In fact, there has never been a consensus on the number of weapons needed for deterrence, although the estimates of many senior policymakers tended to be significantly lower than the number of weapons actually deployed at any given time (see figure 3).

Official statements about deterrence during the nuclear era tended to reflect this action-reaction view of deterrence, rather than a view that derived from any historical analysis of what had deterred various states. General Thomas S. Power, commander in chief of SAC, stated in February 1960: "The closest to one man who would know what the minimum deterrent is would be Mr. Khrushchev, and frankly I don't think he knows from one week to another. He might be willing to absorb more punishment next week than he wants to absorb today. Therefore, deterrence is not a concrete or finite amount."[52] This gets to the crux of the problem, namely that deterrence is predicated on ascertaining as accurately as possible what will prevent an opponent

Joint Committee on Atomic Energy, 93 Cong. 1 sess. (GPO, 1973), pt. 2, p. 101.

52. *Missiles, Space, and Other Major Defense Matters,* Hearings, p. 15.

FIGURE 3. How Much Was Enough?
Official Estimates of Nuclear Weapons Requirements, 1957–95[a]

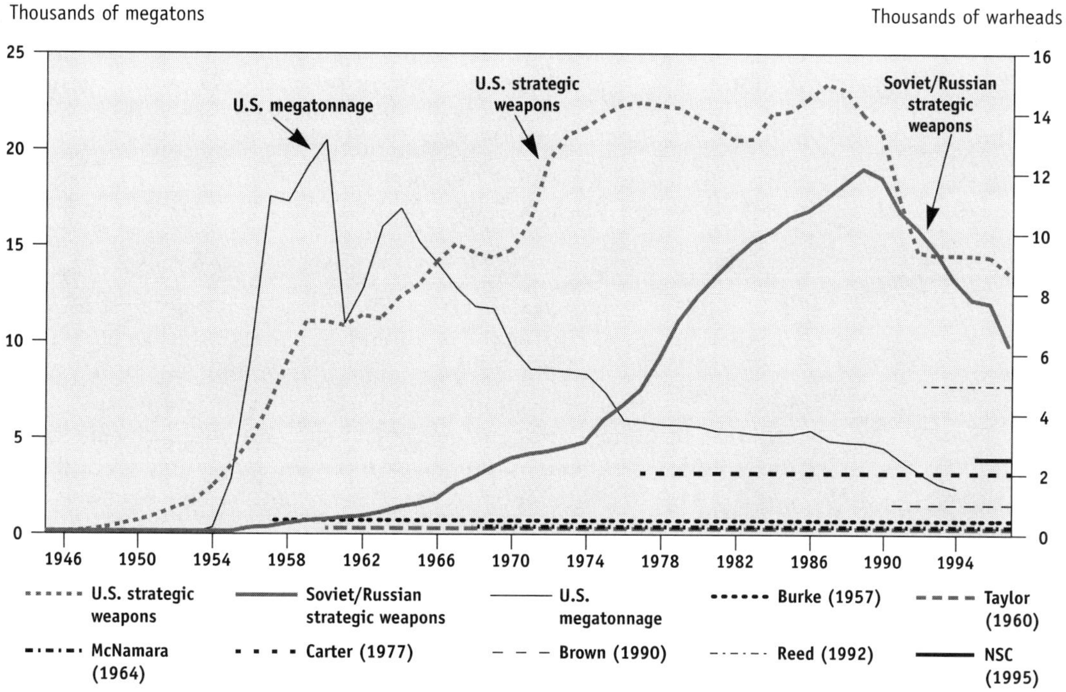

a. U.S. and Soviet/Russian warhead totals exclude an estimated 39,958 and 35,000 nonstrategic weapons, respectively. U.S. megatonnage figures are actual totals released by the Department of Energy and do not distinguished between strategic and nonstrategic weapons (data after 1994 remain classified). Burke is Admiral Arleigh Burke, former chief of naval operations, who stated in 1957 that a fleet of forty-five Polaris submarines (with twenty-nine always deployed) was enough to ensure deterrence and destroy the Soviet Union. Although Burke believed that only 232 warheads were required to destroy the Soviet Union (these could be carried on fewer than fifteen Polaris submarines [16 missiles per submarine/1 warhead per missile]), a larger fleet was deemed necessary to ensure the required number would survive a Soviet attack. Taylor is General Maxwell Taylor, who in 1960 asserted that "a few hundred" missiles were sufficient to deter the Soviet Union (for this calculation, "a few hundred" is assumed to take into account 300 warheads). McNamara is former Secretary of Defense Robert McNamara's 1964 calculation that 400 "equivalent megatons" (megatons weighted to take into account varying blast effects from weapons of different yields) were enough to achieve Mutual Assured Destruction and thus deterrence (one EMT is roughly equivalent to a one-megaton warhead). Carter is President Jimmy Carter's 1977 query to the Defense Department about reducing U.S. and Soviet strategic nuclear delivery vehicles between 200 and 250 each, which is equal to a maximum of 2,000 warheads for the United States. Brown is former Secretary of Defense Harold Brown, who argued in 1990 that a U.S. arsenal of 1,000 warheads would constitute "a very stable deterrent." Reed is Thomas C. Reed, a former secretary of the air force (1976–77) and NSC staffer who coauthored a report for the Strategic Command, "The Role of Nuclear Weapons in the New World Order," which, among other things, called for a reduction in the U.S. strategic arsenal to about 5,000 weapons (plus or minus 20 percent). NSC refers to a 1995 proposal by the National Security Council (subsequently rejected by the Joint Chiefs of Staff) to reduce the strategic stockpile to 2,500 weapons.

from initiating a conflict or otherwise threatening one's security. As the Scowcroft Commission put it in 1983:

> Deterrence is not an abstract notion amenable to simple quantification. Still less it is a mirror image of what would deter ourselves. *Deterrence is the set of beliefs in the minds of the Soviet leaders, given their own values and attitudes,*

> *about our capabilities and our will.* It requires us to determine, as best we can, what would deter them from considering aggression, even in a crisis—*not to determine what would deter us.*[53] (Emphasis added)

Such definitions, when coupled with the prevalent view that the Soviet Union was an expansionist power bent on ruling the world, naturally led military leaders to base their plans on worst-case scenarios. The belief that Soviet leaders did not value human life as much as Americans also led to increased "requirements," just in case a threat that would stop any Western leader cold was insufficiently destructive to deter a communist.[54]

Shortly after World War II, when production capabilities were limited and the means of delivery of nuclear weapons was restricted to bombers (owing to the large size of early weapons), the vagueness and uncertainty of deterrence did not appear to present much of a problem. But as the production of fissile material increased and more efficient and smaller designs were introduced into the stockpile, there was no effective check on the ability to field larger numbers of different types of weapons, which were, in any event, treated largely as free goods by the military. Indeed, the air force, navy, and army each assessed their nuclear requirements largely in isolation, without considering the forces of their sister services. This led to duplicative targeting, which threatened both the safety and effectiveness of U.S. attacking forces. It also raised the problem of overkill (see chapter 3).

For instance, by the summer of 1959 the navy, under the direction of Chief of Naval Operations (CNO) Admiral Arleigh Burke, proposed a finite deterrent force of submarine-based missiles aboard forty-five relatively invulnerable Polaris submarines with twenty-nine deployed at all times. This force could destroy 232 targets in the Soviet Union and hence was considered "sufficient to destroy all of Russia." The cost for this program was projected to be $7 to $8 billion (in then-year dollars), with annual operating costs of $350 million. When this plan was presented to the Bureau of the Budget (BOB), Budget Director Maurice

53. *Report of the President's Commission on Strategic Forces,* April 6, 1983, in *S. Con. Res. 26, A Resolution to Approve Funding for the MX Missile,* Hearings before the Senate Committee on Appropriations, 98 Cong. 1 sess. (GPO, 1983), p. 67.

54. For example, during a May 24, 1956, meeting between Army Chief of Staff General Taylor and President Eisenhower, Taylor argued against current administration policy (which envisioned the use of nuclear weapons across a spectrum of conflict scenarios) on the grounds that within a few years each side would have enough thermonuclear weapons so that both would be deterred from hostile action. If hostilities did occur on even a small scale, however, the administration's plan was designed to lead to full-scale war. For these reasons, Taylor also argued against the use of tactical nuclear weapons in local conflicts. Eisenhower was unmoved, convinced that tactical weapons were as likely to trigger a larger conflict as much as conventional "twenty-ton blockbusters." His overriding interest was in eliminating the possibility of another war such as Korea. Eisenhower told Taylor that his (Taylor's) approach rested "on an assumption that we are opposed by people who would think as we do with regard to the value of human life." The Soviet Union would not hesitate to use nuclear weapons "in full force" in a "life and death struggle" with the United States. Massive retaliation, insisted the president, was the only acceptable alternative in the face of such a threat; indeed, it was the "key to survival." Quoted in Rosenberg, "The Origins of Overkill," p. 152.

Stans inquired why the United States needed "other IRBMs [intermediate-range ballistic missiles], or ICBMs, SAC aircraft, and overseas bases." Navy officials, who had for years chafed at SAC's dominance of the nuclear arsenal, appreciated Stans's perspective but demurred, saying the issue "was somebody else's problem."[55]

An even larger problem surfaced when the Soviet Union began deploying its own offensive nuclear weapons. Destroying these weapons to blunt any damage to the United States—whether in a preemptive or a retaliatory attack—became one of SAC's principal missions. But the fragmentary intelligence data available before the start of U-2 flights and, later, satellite reconnaissance, led to large overestimates of Soviet forces, which in turn boosted U.S. requirements for nuclear weapons, creating a spiraling cycle of weapons requirements to attack an essentially infinite target base.

From time to time, members of Congress became aware of the economic ramifications of the forces driving the creation of excessive numbers of weapons. For example, in February 1960, in the midst of the sizable increase in IRBMs and ICBMs prompted by Sputnik (see Chapter 2), Senator John Stennis (Democrat of Mississippi) engaged in a discussion with recently retired army chief of staff General Taylor over the size and cost of the still developing ballistic missile program:

> SENATOR STENNIS: I notice that the cost of the [Jupiter] missile alone—and we expect to have quite a few of them operational—is astronomical, even for only 1 year.
>
> GENERAL TAYLOR: That is why it is so important to know now how much is enough. What is our goal? Why do we need 10 or 100, or 150, or whatever the number happens to be?
>
> SENATOR STENNIS: Yes. Well, I can visualize one group of missiles for one type—ICBMs—costing anywhere from 4 to 8 billion dollars per year just to keep the supply line going and keep up the numbers. That is just for one single type of missile. Something must be done now. . . . Otherwise, this

55. Quoted in Rosenberg, "The Original Overkill," p. 167. SAC, and in particular General Curtis LeMay, viewed Polaris as a serious threat to its control of the strategic nuclear arsenal and alternatively tried to eliminate it or bring it under SAC control. Around this time, LeMay was reported to have "adorned his office with a model of the sub painted with SAC's insignia just to irk Navy visitors." See Michael R. Beschloss, *Mayday: Eisenhower, Khrushchev and the U-2 Affair* (New York: Harper & Row, 1986), p. 106. Ironically, Burke's exercise was essentially repeated more than two decades later, when early in the Reagan administration Chief of Naval Operations Admiral James D. Watkins attempted to ascertain, on the basis of strict targeting criteria, how many Trident submarines the navy should purchase. However, "he quickly realized that this was impossible without knowing how many B-2 bombers and MX missiles would be operating at the same time. But the air force calculated its 'needs' separately. Watkins started to agitate on behalf of joint criteria for strategic requirements but became discouraged when it grew apparent that this would serve only to fulfill the air force's long-standing hegemonic ambitions. Given the disproportionate influence of air force officers in SAC planning, a joint process would essentially give them control of the navy's strategic assets. The effort was quickly abandoned." Janne Nolan, *Guardians of the Arsenal: The Politics of Nuclear Strategy* (New York: Basic Books, 1989), p. 273.

> cost is going to mushroom and become so astronomical that it could well undermine the soundness of the free enterprise system.
>
> GENERAL TAYLOR: The only encouraging factor from a fiscal point of view, I would say, is the fact that we really don't need many of these, if they are *really* good, if they are accurate, and we are sure of getting them on target. . . .
>
> SENATOR STENNIS: Well, I think that is certainly a good comment. But, if we continue building all these different types and kinds of ICBMs and IRBMs as well as battlefield and tactical, air-to-ground, ground-to-air, air-to-air, and other missiles, it is going to run into the many, many billions of dollars a year. Just to supply the missiles alone, without the launching pads or the operation and maintenance costs, could soon run from 5 to 8 or 9 billion dollars for 1 year, alone. Do you know what we should do now to try to impress someone with the idea of making plans to reduce the number of different type missiles and thereby reduce the cost?
>
> GENERAL TAYLOR: I am afraid I can only repeat myself, Senator, and say my only solution is to make the military come up with an engineering kind of estimate of how much we need. We are building the structure of our defense without knowing what the factors of safety are. If you were running an engineering company, you would go bankrupt on that basis.[56]

In fact, some critical decisions on weapons force size were arrived at through less than rigorous means (see chapter 2). In determining how many Minuteman ICBMs to build, for example, Secretary of Defense McNamara was presented with requests from the air force for as many as 10,000 missiles as well as studies by the BOB indicating that anything above 450 would contribute essentially nothing to U.S. military effectiveness. Faced with competing and powerful bureaucratic interests, McNamara delayed making a final decision. Then, at a December 22, 1964, meeting at President Lyndon Johnson's ranch in Texas, McNamara and General Curtis LeMay began debating whether 1,000 or 1,200 Minuteman missiles should be procured: "President Johnson asked BOB Director Kermit Gordon to enter the argument, knowing from an earlier meeting with Gordon in early November that he favored only 900. Gordon's entry . . . had the desired effect—he was 'jumped on' by both McNamara and LeMay, and Johnson was able to get 1,000 accepted as a compromise."[57]

Deputy Secretary of Defense Roswell Gilpatric later admitted that "1,000 was really just a horse trade."[58] But why did McNamara choose the figure 1,000?

> According to [General Taylor] 1,000 was simply the result of a 'visceral feeling' on the part of McNamara and his aides that that figure was a satisfac-

56. *Missiles, Space, and Other Major Defense Matters,* Hearings, pp. 222–23.

57. Desmond Ball, *Politics and Force Levels: The Strategic Missile Program of the Kennedy Administration* (University of California Press, 1980), p. 251.

58. Ball, *Politics and Force Levels,* p. 252.

tory and viable compromise. And the choice of exactly 1,000 (rather than, say 983 or 1,039, or any other prime number) can be explained in terms of the simple *salience* of that figure, rather than in terms of precise calculation.[59]

Such instinctual analysis remains in use today. In late March 1997, C. Paul Robinson, director of Sandia National Laboratories, told reporters: "My gut feeling [with regard to the future size of the arsenal] is we wouldn't want to go below 2,000."[60]

For all these reasons and more, the United States came to associate deterrence with tens of thousands of nuclear weapons. Logic and fiscal accountability were subordinated to uncertainty, fear, interservice rivalries, pork-barrel politics, and an ultimately futile attempt to maintain the upper hand in the face of unimaginable destruction.[61]

Nuclear Insurance: A Sound Policy?

Over the years, a number of observers have compared nuclear weapons and nuclear deterrence to an insurance policy, one that you

59. Ball, *Politics and Force Levels,* p. 275.

60. "Military Can Meet Threat with 2,000 Nukes, But Not Less, Official Says," *Inside the Air Force,* March 28, 1997, p. 12; Paul Richter, "U.S. Nuclear Cuts Could Increase Risk to Civilians, Expert Warns," *Los Angeles Times* (Washington edition), March 28, 1997, p. A9. These sorts of decisions and justifications are not unique to the United States. When senior British military officers first recommended developing nuclear weapons, they wrote to Prime Minister Clement Attlee on January 1, 1946: "It is not possible to assess the precise number which we might require but we are convinced we should aim to have as soon as possible a stock in the order of hundreds rather than scores." A subsequent report in July 1947 by the Defense Research Policy Committee (DRPC) contended that 1,000 bombs were required. This figure "was based on conclusions of the Home Defense Committee, which had reported that 25 atomic bombs would be sufficient to knock Britain out of a war. The DRPC concluded that because the Soviet Union was roughly forty times the size of the United Kingdom a deterrent force could be worked out on the basis of 25 bombs times 40, making a figure of 1,000! As historian Margaret Gowing has concluded, however, this 'methodology was so ridiculous' that its conclusions were worthless." In 1961, a paper by the British Nuclear Deterrent Study Group called for a review of assumptions behind the level of damage necessary to deter the Soviet Union. Discussions focused on a choice of forty cities (the current planning level), ten cities, and five cities. "In the end, the compromise figure of fifteen cities was agreed by the Defense Committee as the basis for strategic planning." Apart from being arbitrary, this figure was also criticized because it did not take into account NATO or U.S. forces. As one official noted, the group "was operating on the completely false assumption that government policy was based on the need for 'a strategic nuclear force sufficient to deter Russia *on its own*' . . . [when] the key question was what size of force would make the United States believe that Britain was making a major contribution to the western deterrent." John Baylis, *Ambiguity and Deterrence: British Nuclear Strategy, 1945–1964* (Oxford University Press, 1995), pp. 50, 52, 368–69.

61. For example, during a September 12, 1963, meeting of the NSC to consider a study on the projected results of a general war between 1963 and 1968, Secretary McNamara stated: "Defense Department studies showed that even if we spend $80 billion [$470 billion in 1996 dollars] more than we are now spending, we would still have 30 million fatalities in the U.S. in the 1968 time period, *even if we made the first strike against the USSR*" (emphasis added). Nevertheless, General Leon W. Johnson, head of the Net Evaluation Subcommittee, argued that the number of casualties could be diminished "by undertaking additional weapons programs" to destroy Soviet weapons. (A memorandum prepared in advance of this meeting declared that the study found that U.S. "offensive and defensive weapons currently programmed will not reduce damage from a full nuclear exchange to an acceptable level. Consequently, there is a need for development of new offensive and defensive weapons.") When President Kennedy inquired "if this doesn't get us into the overkill business," Johnson said "no," and reiterated that deploying more and more accurate U.S. missiles would reduce damage to the United States. Secretary of State Dean Rusk characterized the "present nuclear situation" as one of "deep schizophrenia." See "Summary Record of the 517th Meeting of the National Security Council," in David W. Mabon, ed., *Foreign Relations of the United States, 1961–1963,* vol. 8: *National Security Policy* (GPO, 1996), pp. 499–507.

purchase but hope you will never need. For example, when SAC established its airborne alert program with B-52 bombers in the early 1960s, several members of Congress remarked that it was a very inexpensive insurance policy against a surprise Soviet attack, even though it was estimated to cost some $6 billion a year (see chapter 2). In 1974 columnist Joseph Alsop argued:

> If you are able to pay for an adequate insurance policy, what kind of chance of national destruction is it proper to take? . . . The real chance that your house or my house will burn to the ground is far, far less than the chance that everyone in the CIA will be dead wrong about any given matter. Yet I spend a lot on fire insurance, and so do you if you are prudent. The same rules that apply to fire insurance for our houses ought to apply to insurance against the destruction of the United States.[62]

In 1988 former undersecretary of the navy R. James Woolsey wrote: "In strategic modernization, we are dealing, in a sense, with a major insurance policy against an admittedly unlikely eventuality. But it is insurance against the most catastrophic of imaginable losses, and it is a curious kind of policy—one where paying the premiums can make the catastrophe less likely."[63] In 1994 chairman of the Joint Chiefs of Staff (JCS) General John M. Shalikashvili told officers at the United States Strategic Command (STRATCOM, the successor to SAC): "It is the ultimate insurance policy for the United States, what SAC did and now what Strategic Command is doing. It will always remain our ultimate insurance policy."[64]

This is clearly a popular characterization, one that resonates with nuclear policymakers. Yet it is also flawed in two critical respects. First, as has already been demonstrated, the actual fiscal costs of this "policy" have never been apparent, either to military and government officials or to the general public. Insurance policies can indeed be a prudent investment, but few would purchase one without knowing the premiums up front. Second, to view nuclear weapons as insurance and then conclude that the absence of nuclear war means that the policy worked is to ignore the consequences had the policy failed. After all, nuclear weapons were not designed merely to sit in silos, submarines, or depots; they were and are routinely tested and operated and maintained to be used. As the Scowcroft Commission explained in 1983:

62. Joseph Alsop, letter responding to article by Albert Wohlstetter, *Foreign Policy*, no. 16 (Fall 1974), pp. 87–88.

63. Quoted in Nolan, *Guardians of the Arsenal*, p. 272.

64. Master Sergeant Dave Bryan, "Chairman Characterizes STRATCOM as Nation's 'Ultimate Insurance Policy,'" *STRATUS*, vol. 2, no. 8 (1994), p. 1. In January 1997 Vice Admiral Dennis A. Jones, STRATCOM's deputy commander, told the *New York Times*: "We think of ourselves as an insurance policy." That comment was echoed two months later by Major General Donald G. Cook, commander of F. E. Warren Air Force Base, who said of the Minuteman ICBMs he oversees: "It's a mighty cheap insurance policy." See James Brooke, "Former Cold Warrior Has a New Mission: Nuclear Cuts," *New York Times*, January 8, 1997, p. A12; James Brooke, "Counting the Missiles, Dreaming of Disarmament," *New York Times*, March 19, 1997, p. A16.

"Deterrence is not, and cannot be, a bluff. In order for deterrence to be effective we must not merely have weapons, we must be perceived to be able, and prepared, if necessary, to use them effectively against the key elements of Soviet power."[65] Paradoxically, nuclear insurance *heightened* the risks of war even as it sought to reduce them. While nuclear war did not occur, this cannot be ascribed to the large arsenals that were built, given that deterrence of nuclear attack has historically been achieved with a variety of arsenal sizes. But amassing huge arsenals did exacerbate the potential for inadvertent or accidental nuclear war as well as accidents associated with keeping nuclear forces on high levels of alert.

U.S. nuclear weapons did not exist in a vacuum. They interacted in complex ways with Soviet forces (and still do). Accidents were routine (between 1950 and 1968, eleven nuclear weapons fell out of or crashed with U.S. aircraft and were never recovered).[66] False alarms were not uncommon. As detailed in chapter 3, the vulnerable command, control, and communications networks and the hair-trigger launch policies adopted by both the Soviet Union and the United States interacted and presented an extreme and unnecessary risk of accidental or unintentional nuclear war.[67] That is the downside of the nuclear insurance policy. Woolsey's observation that "paying the premiums can make the catastrophe less likely" misses the point that both the premiums and the policy itself are expressly designed to unleash the catastrophe they are also supposed to deter. Here again the insurance analogy fails, for who would purchase a life insurance policy that may actually increase one's risk of death? What homeowners, to follow Alsop's analogy, would buy fire insurance knowing that by doing so they increased—even slightly—the possibility of not only burning down their home but ensuring that the fire would be uncontainable?

In his insightful history of the early years of the Soviet nuclear weapons program, David Holloway concludes that little evidence is available to suggest that through at least 1953 U.S. nuclear weapons forced the Soviet Union "to do things it did not want to do." Even the case for the deterrent effect of the atomic bomb, especially during the Berlin crisis, is inconclusive: "The United States did not have enough atomic bombs in the early postwar years to be able to prevent the Soviet Union from occupying Western Europe; and the Soviet leaders were aware of this. There is no evidence to show that Stalin intended to

---

65. *Report of the President's Commission on Strategic Forces*, April 6, 1983, p. 67.

66. "U.S. Nuclear Weapons Accidents: Danger in Our Midst," *Defense Monitor*, vol. 10, no. 5 (1981); Chuck Hansen, *The Swords of Armageddon* (Sunnyvale, Calif.: Chuckelea Publications, 1995), vol. 8, pp. 98–146; "Lost Bombs," Atwood Keeney Productions, Inc., 1997).

67. For a particularly disturbing manifestation of this danger, see Robert M. Gates, *From the Shadows: The Ultimate Insider's Story of Five Presidents and How They Won the Cold War* (New York: Simon & Schuster, 1996), pp. 113–15.

invade Western Europe, except in the event of a major war; and his overall policy suggests that he was anxious to avoid such a war, and not merely because the United States possessed the atomic bomb. . . . Stalin had concluded after Hiroshima that atomic diplomacy rather than war was the immediate danger, and this assumption underpinned his policy until 1949. . . . Stalin did not want war with the West; he did not believe that the Soviet Union was ready for war. . . . [T]he bomb had a dual effect. It probably made the Soviet Union more restrained in its use of force, for fear of precipitating war. It also made the Soviet Union less cooperative and less willing to compromise, for fear of seeming weak."[68]

Implications for The Future

Today the U.S. nuclear weapons program faces an uncertain future. Although the production of nuclear explosives, fissile materials, and nuclear weapons testing have all ceased, an ambitious and expensive "stockpile stewardship" program, directed by the Department of Energy, is gearing up to allow for the support and limited production of weapons components into the indefinite future, at a higher annual cost—$4.5 billion (in 1998 dollars)—than the costs incurred, on average, for similar activities between 1948 and 1991—$3.6 billion—when large-scale production and testing were under way. No new nuclear delivery systems are in production at present, and the debate over the next phase of arms reductions has shifted dramatically since late 1996, with future stockpiles of only hundreds of weapons being discussed as potentially viable options.[69] Although many of the production-related aspects of the nuclear arsenal are moribund, at an operational level forces still remain on high levels of alert equaling those of the cold war era.[70] Here, too, serious discussions are under way to consider "de-

68. Holloway, *Stalin and the Bomb,* pp. 271–72. However, there is ample evidence that U.S. nuclear policy in the period after Stalin's death, especially the provocative deployment of Jupiter missiles in Turkey, drove Nikita Khrushchev to adopt high-risk policies in relation to the United States and led directly to the Cuban Missile Crisis. A document discovered in the archives of the former Soviet Union following the publication of Holloway's book reveals that although Stalin did not seek a war with the United States, he was willing to risk one by urging the Chinese to intervene in the Korean War. In an October 1950 letter to North Korean leader Kim Il Sung, Stalin recounts a letter he sent to Mao Tse Tung explaining why he believed the United States was not ready for a "big war" and therefore why such an intervention would be beneficial to both China and the Soviet Union. Even if Chinese intervention in the Korean War led to a wider conflict involving the United States, wrote Stalin, China and the Soviet Union "together will be stronger than the USA and England, while the other European capitalist states (with the exception of Germany which is unable to provide any assistance to the United States now) do not present serious military forces. If a war is inevitable, then let it be waged now, and not in a few years when Japanese militarism will be restored as an ally of the USA and when the USA and Japan will have a ready-made bridgehead on the continent in the form of the entire Korea run by Syngman Rhee." See "Letter, Fyn Si [Stalin] to Kim Il Sung (via Shtykov) 8 [7] October 1950," Document 13, translated in *Cold War International History Project Bulletin,* Issues 6-7 (Winter 1995/1996), pp. 116–17.

69. See, for example, Committee on International Security and Arms Control, *The Future of U.S. Nuclear Weapons Policy* (Washington, D.C.: National Academy Press, 1997).

70. For an example of the current risks posed by such alert postures, see David Hoffman, "Cold-War Doctrines Refuse to Die," *Washington Post,* March 15, 1998, p. A1.

alerting" large numbers of U.S. and Russian nuclear weapons and to consider removing warheads from ballistic missiles to substantially reduce the risk of accidental or unauthorized launch while retaining, for now, the warheads themselves and their associated delivery vehicles.

U.S. nuclear weapons currently consume some $35 billion a year, with about $25 billion going toward operating and maintaining the arsenal and the remainder allocated to environmental remediation and waste management, arms reduction measures, and the storage and disposition of excess fissile material (these figures are in 1998 dollars). This equals 14 percent of all defense spending. Although these overall costs are substantially lower than cold war levels, they are likely to remain in this range barring substantial changes in either the operational posture or the total number of deployed weapons. It is therefore important to understand how and why the arsenal of today was developed, not least because of the numerous factors beyond genuine security requirements that shaped it. Once policymakers understand the actual costs of nuclear weapons and the often bureaucratic and arbitrary forces influencing the size and composition of U.S. nuclear forces, they may plan for the future in realistic fashion, free of cold war biases and myths.

The preceding analysis has demonstrated that for all the reasons behind the buildup of U.S. nuclear forces, military and civilian policymakers paid too little attention to the short- and long-term costs of the policies they sought to enact. While the domestic and international pressures of the Cold War made the financial aspects of the arms race of secondary importance to ensuring U.S. security, there is no justification today for continued inattention. Indeed, tighter federal budgets and the shrinking size of the arsenal make it imperative to understand the future costs and consequences of the program and ensure an adequate level of accountability. The discussion now turns to the costs and consequences of the U.S. nuclear weapons program, beginning with the production of the weapons themselves.

FIGURE 1-1. The Costs of Building the Bomb[a]

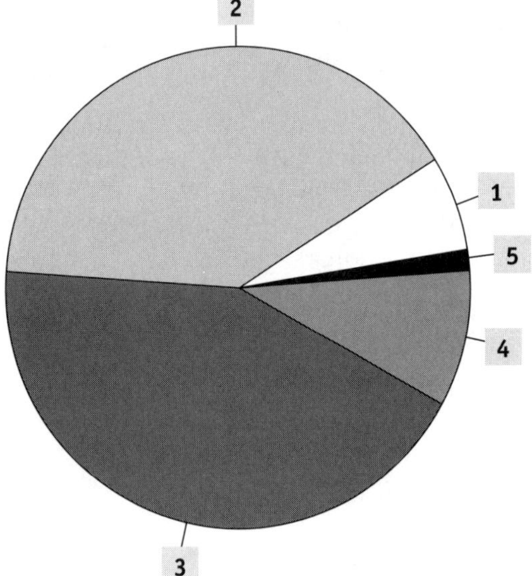

TOTAL: $409.4 BILLION

1 Manhattan Engineer District
$25.6 billion[b] / 6.3%

2 Fissile materials production
$165.5 billion / 40.4%

3 Research, development, testing, and weapons production
$174.6 billion[c] / 42.6%

4 Department of Defense development and testing
$37.4 billion / 9.1%

5 Other

Atomic Energy Commision (January–June 1947)
$1.6 billion / 0.4%

Materials safeguards and security
$1.6 billion / 0.4%

Project Plowshare
$0.8 billion / 0.2%

Community support (Los Alamos, Oak Ridge, and Hanford)
$2.3 billion / 0.6%

a. In constant 1996 dollars.

b. Includes spending by the National Defense Research Committee and the Office of Scientific Research and Development.

c. Excludes an estimated $3.0 billion spent on nuclear weapons retirement and dismantlement activities at the Pantex and Y-12 plants from 1991 to 1996 (counted in chapter 5 but not disaggregated from the total in table A-2) and an estimated $2.2 billion spent from 1984 to 1991 on research related to the Strategic Defense Initiative (counted in chapter 4). Thus the actual total for this category is $179.8 billion.

1

Building the Bomb

Kevin O'Neill

Between 1945 and 1990 the United States produced more than 70,000 nuclear weapons. The cost—for the acquisition and production of fissionable materials and for weapons research, development, testing, and manufacturing—was approximately $409 billion and was divided among several agencies (see figure 1-1). Before World War II and up to the end of fiscal 1947, expenditures totaled $27.3 billion, of which nearly $26 billion went to the Manhattan Project and other, smaller government efforts during the war. After World War II, the Department of Defense invested more than $37 billion in nuclear weapons effects and related research. But by far the largest amount was spent by civilian agencies. Together, the Atomic Energy Commission (1947–75), the Energy Research and Development Administration (ERDA, 1975–77), and the Department of Energy (DOE, 1977 to the present) have spent $345 billion since 1947 to produce nuclear materials, to conduct research, and to develop, test, and manufacture nuclear weapons. This chapter covers the costs incurred during World War II, the Manhattan Project, and the cold war. Other costs, such as the historical and future costs of weapons dismantlement, environmental remediation, and waste management, are taken up in chapters 5 and 6.

Methodology and Sources

The inherent secrecy of the U.S. nuclear weapons program, the almost total lack of detailed budgetary data from the 1940s through at least the early 1960s, and the multipurpose nature of many weapons facilities make it virtually impossible to audit the U.S. nuclear weapons development program on a site-by-site basis. In addition, a calculation of actual year-by-year expenses by program is complicated by standard budgeting practices, which generally record budget authority and obligations.

Still, budget authority and obligations make it possible to estimate expenditures over time. Budget authority is the right granted to an agency by Congress to allocate a given amount of money for certain specified purposes, while obligations represent an agency's commitment to allocate this amount as specified. These obligations may be discharged within a single fiscal year or over a period of several years, as in the case of construction projects and capital equipment purchases. Therefore, budget authority and obligations provide an accurate record of historical expenditures, but not of actual spending in a given year.

Most of the data presented in this chapter can be found in government documents presented to the Congress and to the public. Beginning in the early 1960s, annual AEC, ERDA, and DOE budget requests were presented to Congress and printed as part of the official records of hearings of the Joint Committee of Atomic Energy. After this committee was abolished in 1977, separate House and Senate appropriations subcommittees continued the practice. Before the early 1960s, these records did not typically present budget data in a useful fashion, although the Bureau of the Budget (later, the Office of Management and Budget, or OMB) annually published such data in the *Budget of the United States Government.* Some of the data have only recently been released to the public or made available by the DOD and DOE at the request of this project's participants.[1]

Several deflators have been used. OMB total defense outlays were used as a deflator for Manhattan Project expenditures, which are expressed as actual expenditures by the sources used.[2] Otherwise, DOD deflators are used for total obligational authority and for budget authority, where applicable.[3]

1. In January 1997 the DOE provided a chart delineating research, development, testing, and evaluation costs since 1951 to a *New York Times* reporter. In several instances, these data differ significantly from the figures assembled here. According to the official with DOE's Defense Programs office who generated the data for the *Times,* the costs he provided were from material collected beginning in the 1950s and had not been historically evaluated so it is not fully known "exactly what these costs are for." In his view, the data assembled in this book are "better documented than the DOE data." Memorandum, Kevin O'Neill to Stephen I. Schwartz, March 21, 1997.

2. Office of Management and Budget, *Budget of the United States Government for Fiscal Year 1996,* table 10.1, p. 143.

3. Department of Defense, *National Defense Budget Estimates for Fiscal Year 1996,* tables 6.1, 6.8, and 6.11 for fiscal 1948–49, and tables 5.4 and 5.9 for fiscal 1950–96.

The Nuclear Weapons Production Complex

Historically, the United States has expanded or reduced its weapons production complex whenever policy decisions, perceived military requirements, and costs deemed it necessary. At present, the complex consists of thirteen major facilities around the country (three of which are inactive). These facilities occupy nearly 3,300 square miles (8,547 square kilometers), a land area greater than that of Delaware, Rhode Island, and the District of Columbia combined (see figure 1-2 and appendix C for a complete list of active and inactive facilities).

Producing the Nuclear Materials

The most difficult step in manufacturing nuclear weapons lies in producing highly enriched uranium (HEU) and plutonium, the fissionable materials used in nuclear weapons. Only certain isotopes of uranium and plutonium are suitable for making weapons. Isotopes are forms of an element that have nearly identical chemical properties but whose nuclei contain different numbers of neutrons. Naturally occurring uranium is composed of almost 99.3 percent uranium-238, which is not suitable for nuclear explosives, and only 0.7 percent uranium-235, the fissionable isotope used in weapons. The level of uranium-235 must be increased or enriched before it can be used in nuclear weapons or even in most common nuclear power reactors. Plutonium is also problematic: it occurs naturally only in minute quantities and must be produced in a nuclear reactor.[4]

Uranium Enrichment. Most nuclear power reactors use uranium fuel enriched to 2–5 percent, but the U.S. nuclear program used "highly enriched uranium," defined as greater than 20 percent uranium-235, to manufacture warhead pits and secondaries for thermonuclear weapons, for naval reactor fuel, and as fuel for some production reactors at its Savannah River Site (SRS).

The Manhattan Project—officially known as the Manhattan Engineer District (MED)—used a combination of three enrichment methods to produce HEU. The first method, called electromagnetic isotopic separation, achieved enrichment with the aid of large electromagnets in a device called a calutron.[5] The second method relied on

4. About two billion years ago, a high concentration of uranium ore in what is now Gabon, West Africa, formed a "natural" underground reactor and produced some plutonium, long since transformed into other elements through the process of radioactive decay. A very small proportion of spontaneous fissions that occur in natural uranium today produces neutrons, which in turn create minute quantities of plutonium. See Merill Eisenbud and Thomas Gessel, *Environmental Radioactivity* (San Diego, Calif.: Academic Press, 1997), pp. 198, 200.

5. Calutrons enrich uranium by accelerating uranium ions through a magnetic field. Because uranium-238 and uranium-235 have slightly different weights, they take slightly different paths through the field.

FIGURE 1-2. U.S. Nuclear Weapons Research, Testing, and Production Facilities[a]

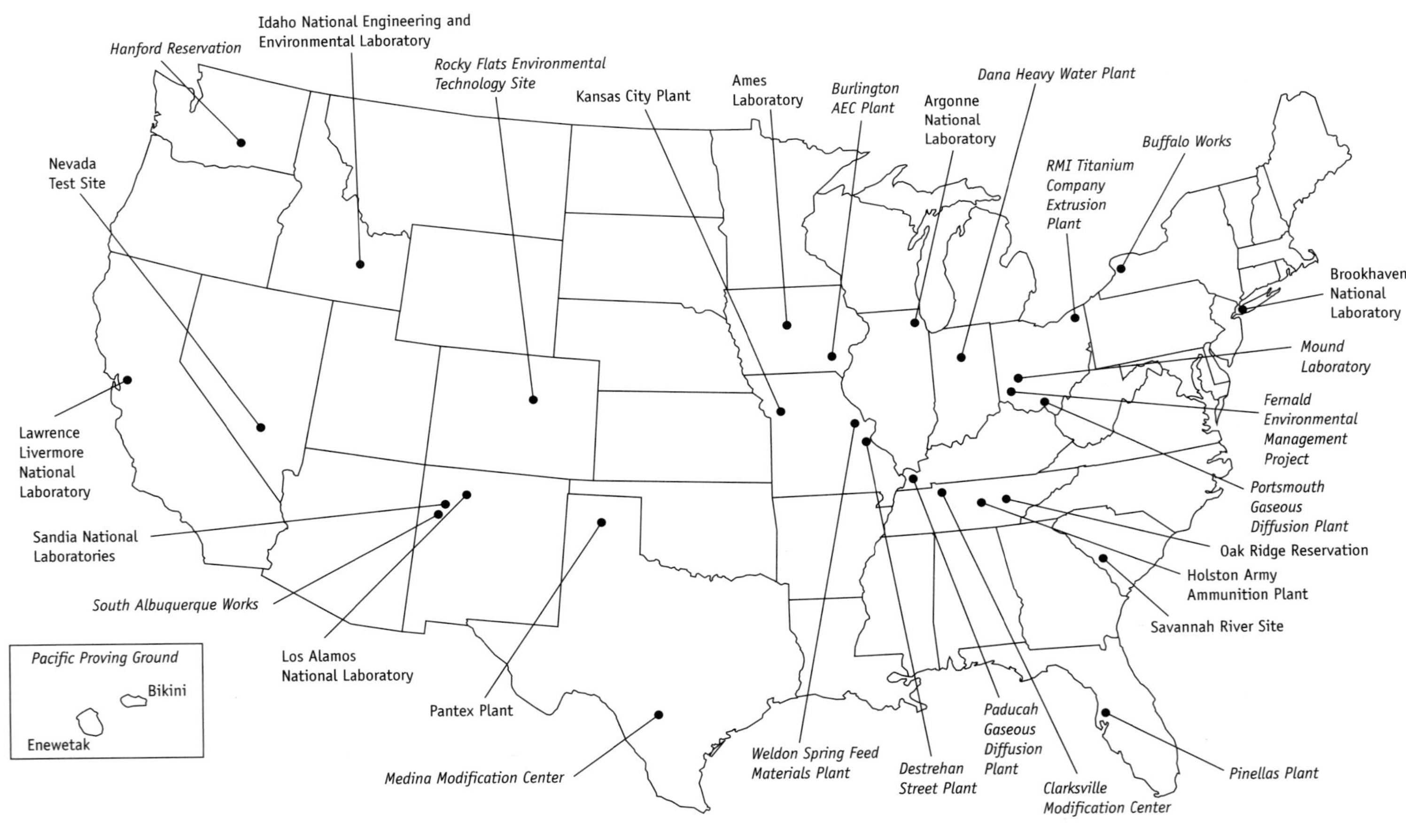

Source: U.S. Department of Energy.

a. Sites no longer involved in research, development, testing, or production activities are shown in italics.

gaseous diffusion. Gaseous diffusion enrichment operates on the principle that heavier gaseous molecules move more slowly than lighter gaseous molecules. In this method of enrichment, gaseous uranium tetrachloride molecules are circulated into a series of cylindrical containers, each divided into two sections by a porous barrier. The molecules containing the lighter uranium-235 hit the barrier more frequently than the heavier molecules and therefore collect on one side of the barrier. This was the primary method used by the United States to enrich uranium during the cold war. Large plants housing the calutrons (Y-12) and gaseous diffusion "cascades" (K-25) were built at what is now the Oak Ridge Reservation in Tennessee. A third method, thermal diffusion, was initially considered and then abandoned after electromagnetic and gaseous diffusion were deemed more promising for large-scale production. However, the S-50 Thermal Diffusion Plant at Oak Ridge—built for an estimated $179 million—was used to provide enriched feed material to the Y-12 and K-25 plants.

After World War II, in response to the first Soviet detonation of an atomic bomb and the outbreak of the Korean War, the AEC expanded the Oak Ridge gaseous diffusion plant and built large new facilities in Portsmouth, Ohio, and Paducah, Kentucky. These facilities have also produced low enriched uranium for commercial nuclear power plants. In April 1964 the United States unilaterally ceased production of HEU for weapons, although two of the plants continued to produce HEU for naval nuclear reactors, plutonium production reactors, and civilian research reactors. As a result of this decision, HEU production declined 40 percent (at the same time, plutonium production fell 20 percent).

Plutonium and Tritium Production. Unlike uranium-235, which can be isolated from other naturally occurring uranium isotopes, all of the plutonium used by the United States to build nuclear weapons has been produced in nuclear reactors. Plutonium is created when uranium-238 absorbs neutrons during a chain reaction. The uranium-238 forms the isotope uranium-239, which through a process called "beta decay" quickly transforms into another element, neptunium-239. A second beta decay then results in plutonium-239, the principal isotope used in weapons.[6]

Once the plutonium is produced, it is chemically separated from the spent reactor fuel in a procedure known as "reprocessing." Because

6. Some of the plutonium-239 produced in a reactor will continue to absorb neutrons, forming plutonium-240, plutonium-241, and plutonium-242. All plutonium isotopes can be used to make nuclear weapons, although the even-numbered isotopes make it more difficult (because the "excess" neutrons they produce can trigger a premature chain reaction). "Weapon-grade plutonium" contains less than 7 percent of these other isotopes, while "fuel-grade plutonium" contains between 7 and 18 percent plutonium-240 and "reactor-grade plutonium" contains 18 percent plutonium-240 or more.

spent reactor fuel is highly radioactive, reprocessing must be conducted in remotely operated or automated facilities. Plutonium and uranium can be separated from the highly radioactive waste by dissolving the spent fuel in acid. Subsequently, the plutonium and uranium are separated from each other using nitric acid in a process known as solvent extraction. The plutonium is then used to manufacture weapons, and the uranium is recycled back into the fuel production pipeline of the weapons complex (see figure 1-3).

During the cold war, the United States produced plutonium at two sites: Hanford Reservation, near Richland, Washington; and the Savannah River Site, near Aiken, South Carolina (known as the Savannah River Plant until April 1, 1989). Hanford produced the plutonium for the Manhattan Project. Of the nine reactors built at Hanford, eight were in operation by the mid-1950s but were all shut down by 1971. A ninth reactor was constructed in the early 1960s and produced both weapon-grade and fuel-grade plutonium until 1987. The irradiated fuel containing the plutonium was stored on site, and the plutonium was extracted in as many as five reprocessing plants at Hanford, nicknamed "Queen Marys" by plant workers because of their great size (which significantly exceeded that of their maritime namesake).

Between 1951 and 1955, five reactors were constructed at the SRS. Unlike the light-water, graphite-moderated reactors at Hanford, the Savannah River reactors were moderated and cooled by heavy water and used HEU fuel. HEU and plutonium were recovered from spent fuel at the Savannah Site's H and F chemical separation plants.

The United States also used the Savannah River reactors to produce the materials needed to build boosted and thermonuclear weapons. These weapons employ tritium and deuterium to increase the explosive yield or decrease the amount of fissile materials required to achieve the same yield. In boosted weapons, a mix of tritium and deuterium gas is released into the hollow, fissioning mass of plutonium, or HEU, called a "pit" or "core," shortly before detonation.[7] Energy generated by the fission explosion causes tritium atoms to join, or "fuse," with deuterium and release neutrons. The release of neutrons by the tritium causes more of the plutonium or HEU to fission and thereby increases, or "boosts," the yield.

In thermonuclear weapons, tritium is formed in situ from lithium deuteride components and fuses with deuterium in the thermonuclear "secondary." The energy released through fusion in thermonuclear weapons is sufficient to increase the yield of an atomic weapon from tons or kilotons to the megaton range. If a uranium tamper (composed of uranium-238) is placed around the secondary, high-energy neutrons

7. By 1983, 85 percent of weapons in the stockpile (about 19,800 weapons) required tritium to ensure proper operation.

Figure 1-3. The Nuclear Weapons Complex, Mid-1950s to Mid-1960s

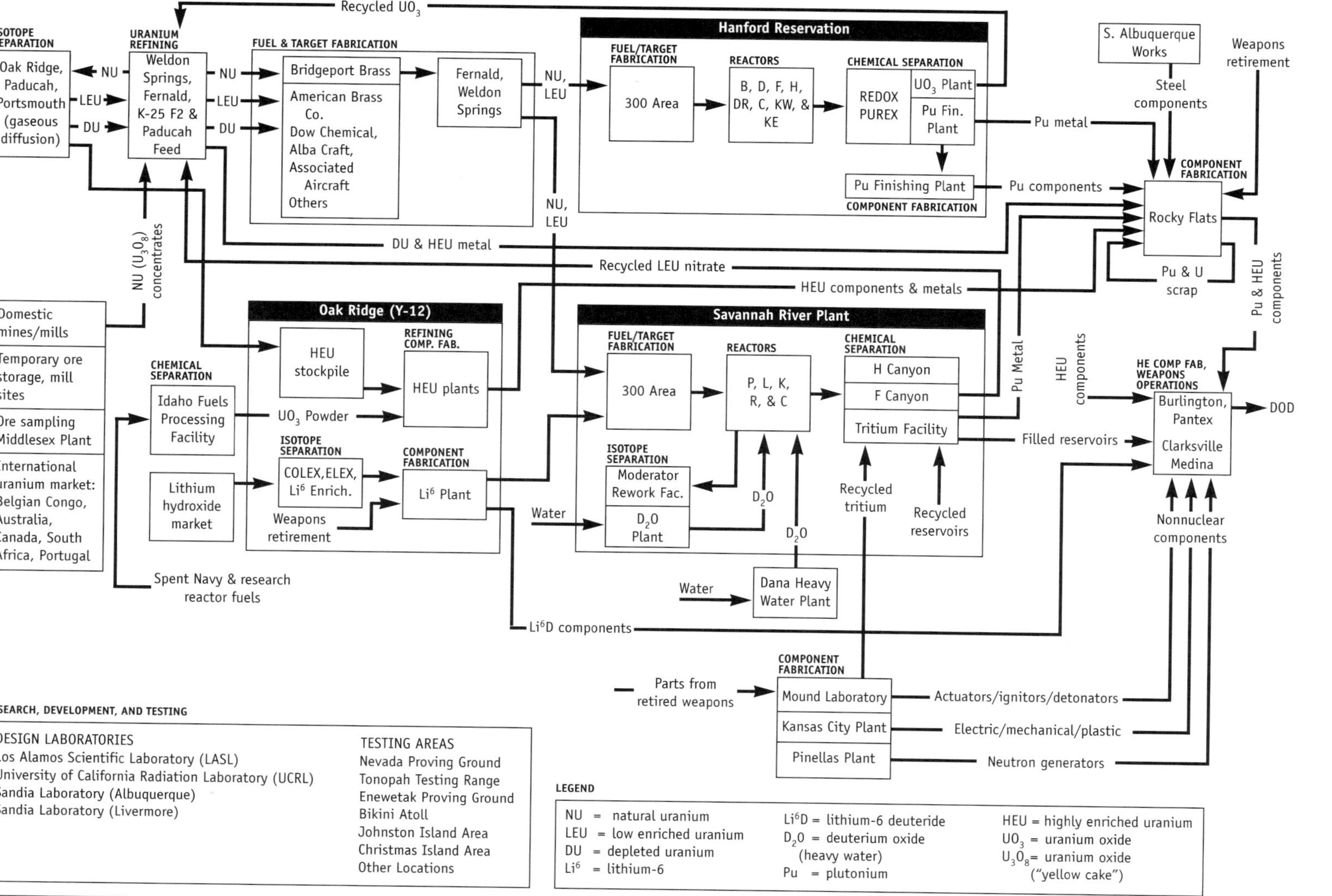

Source: U.S. Department of Energy.

released by the fusion reaction will fission the tamper and increase the yield even more.

The United States needed to isolate sufficient deuterium from heavy water and produce tritium to manufacture boosted and thermonuclear weapons. Heavy water occurs in nature in a concentration of about 0.015 percent and may be separated from raw water through a combination of distillation and chemical exchange between hydrogen sulfide and water or through electrolysis. To isolate heavy water, the Manhattan Project and the AEC constructed several plants, including one at Savannah River that operated from 1952 to 1982.[8] Tritium was produced in the heavy water–moderated reactors by bombarding lithium-6 targets with neutrons. At the Tritium Recovery Facility at SRS, engineers then recovered the tritium from the irradiated targets in a fashion analogous to reprocessing spent uranium fuel.

The United States relied on various sources to obtain the natural uranium needed to produce HEU and plutonium and to fuel the production reactors. Much of the Manhattan Project uranium—4,810 tons in all—came from the Belgian Congo in colonial Africa (today the Democratic Republic of Congo). Belgium sent this uranium to the United States at the beginning of the war to prevent it from falling into the hands of Nazi Germany.[9] In the spring of 1943 the Manhattan Project initiated a highly secretive effort, known as the Murray Hill Area Project (named after a neighborhood in Manhattan that was the location of MED headquarters), to purchase the rights to as many of the high-grade uranium ore deposits as possible around the world, in a deliberate effort to monopolize existing supplies and prevent other nations from acquiring the raw materials necessary to build atomic weapons. To keep the program secret and avoid having to obtain Congressional approval, the government transferred funds directly from the MED into the personal bank account of Brigadier General Leslie Groves, head of the MED. Initial funding in 1943 was in excess of $37 million (more than $400 million in 1996 dollars).[10]

8. A plant similar to the one at Savannah River operated in Dana, Indiana, from 1952 to 1957. The Dana Plant and three others (in Trail, British Columbia; Morgantown, West Virginia; and Montgomery, Alabama) were constructed during the Manhattan Project at a cost of approximately $306 million. Had the graphite-moderated reactors at Hanford proven unworkable, the heavy water was to have been used to moderate a different plutonium production reactor.

9. In late 1995 John Lansdale, Jr., a former army lieutenant colonel involved with intelligence and security matters during the Manhattan Project, disclosed in an interview that 1,232 pounds (560 kilograms) of uranium oxide (containing an estimated 7.7 pounds [3.5 kilograms] of uranium-235) carried aboard a German U-boat captured in May 1945 while en route for Tokyo and taken to a submarine base at Portsmouth, New Hampshire, eventually found its way into the MED's uranium supply line. This uranium may have been included in the "Little Boy" bomb dropped on Hiroshima less than three months later, although there is as yet no documentary evidence for this. See William J. Broad, "Captured Cargo, Captivating Mystery," *New York Times*, December 31, 1995, p. A22.

10. Murray Hill was thus the seminal U.S. effort to stem the proliferation of nuclear weapons. See Charles A. Ziegler, and David Jacobson, *Spying without Spies: Origins of America's Secret Nuclear Surveillance System* (Westport, Conn.: Praeger, 1995), pp. 21–22. This effort proved quite successful. On December 3, 1945, Groves informed Secretary of War Robert Patterson that the Combined Development Trust—

After the war, the AEC purchased uranium from a variety of foreign sources, including Canada, Portugal, Australia, and South Africa. By the end of 1955 some 925 uranium mines were in operation in the United States. That figure held relatively steady through the early 1960s (as total production per mine increased) and then declined until mining operations for the weapons program ceased in 1970.[11] Accounting records do not allow for an estimate of uranium purchase costs in the immediate postwar years, but by 1954 the AEC was spending $1 billion or more annually on uranium (see appendix table A-1).

Other Materials. Other important materials besides HEU, plutonium, tritium, and deuterium are needed to make nuclear weapons. Very pure fluorine gas is required to make uranium-hexafluoride (UF-6), the corrosive gas used in the enrichment process. The United States needed high-quality graphite to moderate Chicago Piles 1 and 2 (CP-1 and CP-2, the first experimental reactors at the University of Chicago), the X-10 reactor at Oak Ridge (the first plutonium production reactor and the model for the Hanford reactors), and weapons reactors at Hanford. Beryllium, a strong but lightweight metal, was used to fabricate shields around the core to reflect and amplify neutrons back into the critical mass (early weapon designs also incorporated beryllium in neutron initiators). Lithium-6 was needed to produce tritium, and mercury was needed to produce lithium-6. Significant quantities of precious metals, including gold, silver, and platinum, were also used in the manufacture of nuclear weapons (see chapter 5). Many of these materials—most notably plutonium, beryllium, and mercury—are highly toxic; environmental contamination by these and other materials continues to pose a significant concern at weapons complex sites (see chapter 6).[12]

From Materials to Warheads and Bombs

More than two dozen facilities in the United States have conducted nuclear weapons research and helped to design, test, and manufacture

comprising the United States, Great Britain, Belgium, Brazil, and the Netherlands—controlled 97 percent of the world's uranium production and 65 percent of the world supply of thorium (which through the process of neutron absorption and radioactive decay becomes uranium-233, which is fissionable). See David Holloway, *Stalin and the Bomb: The Soviet Union and Atomic Energy, 1939–1956* (Yale University Press, 1994), p. 174.

11. U.S. Atomic Energy Commission, *Nineteenth Semiannual Report of the Atomic Energy Commission* (GPO, January 1956), p. 31. Beginning with the Manhattan Project, the AEC relied on the U.S. Geological Survey (USGS) and the Bureau of Mines for assistance in locating and exploiting uranium and other critical mineral deposits and conducting basic geological research applicable to the AEC's mission. From 1949 to 1960, the USGS received funds from the AEC for this work, with annual funding fluctuating between $20 million and $50 million annually. Details on expenditures by the Bureau of Mines are unavailable, but presumably the AEC funded its operations as well. Telephone conversation with Ted Saunders, Office of the Director, U.S. Geological Survey, April 18, 1995.

12. To produce lithium-6, from 1950 to 1962 the Lithium Enrichment Facility at the Y-12 Plant at the Oak Ridge Reservation used 24 million pounds of mercury, equal to two years

nuclear warheads and bombs. The process can be illustrated by examining the primary functions of several of these facilities.

Weapons Research, Design, and Testing. The primary mission of nuclear weapons research and development has been to create new nuclear explosive devices. The scope of the research and the direction and growth of the nuclear arsenal have often been dictated by laboratory breakthroughs rather than military requirements, especially during the early years of the cold war. From the beginning, the services were not greatly concerned about specialization: "As long as their specific requirements could be met, they felt that interchangeability of nuclear materials among several systems was a good thing. . . . As soon as the nuclear designers learned and pointed out that higher efficiencies would be obtained if weapons were tailored to specific systems, the Services accepted the idea gladly."[13] Even as late as 1973, a senior DOD official told Congress, "the laboratories have often led. They have bright people. They know the military problems. In many cases, they travel, they interact and quite often, they come up with solutions to military problems before the military people know that a solution is possible."[14]

As weapons technology evolved, however, the services began requesting not only more and different kinds of bombs and warheads, but also extra features or capabilities that significantly increased the per unit cost. Because the military services have never had to pay for their own nuclear bombs and warheads—all of the costs were borne by the AEC, ERDA, and the DOE—there was never any fiscal incentive *not* to "require" large quantities of the most sophisticated kinds that could be produced.

Between 1945 and 1991, the DOE and its predecessors designed and built 65 types of bombs and warheads for 116 kinds of delivery systems, ranging from battlefield, or "tactical," nuclear weapons to the strategic bombs and warheads based in the United States or on board ballistic missile submarines (see box 1-1). Land mines, antisubmarine depth charges, artillery shells, gravity bombs, and cruise missiles are among the various weapons systems that have employed nuclear warheads (a complete chronological list of U.S. nuclear bombs and warheads appears in table 1-3).

of the entire world supply of mercury in 1993 and enough to fill 11 billion thermometers. Poor production practices and lax environmental controls contributed to the "loss" of at least 750,000 pounds of mercury to the environment, principally the east fork of Poplar Creek, which runs near the Y-12 Plant. See U.S. Department of Energy, "Openness Press Conference Fact Sheets," December 7, 1993, pp. 47–52.

13. Herbert B. Loper, assistant to the secretary of defense (atomic energy), address delivered before the Air War College, Montgomery, Alabama, November 19, 1956, pp. 12–13 (formerly classified Secret, at the National Security Archive, Washington, D.C.).

14. *Military Applications of Nuclear Technology,* Hearings before the Subcommittee on Military Applications of the Joint Committee on Atomic Energy, 93 Cong. 1 sess. (GPO, 1973), pt. 2, p. 28.

Three dedicated nuclear laboratories—at Los Alamos, New Mexico; Livermore, California; and Albuquerque, New Mexico—have designed, tested, and sometimes manufactured nuclear weapons. The AEC inherited the Manhattan Project's main research laboratory at Los Alamos in 1947. Scientists there continued to pursue new weapons concepts and to manufacture atomic bombs. As the weapons complex grew, manufacturing activities were performed elsewhere, while the Los Alamos National Laboratory (LANL), as it is known today, continued to be a primary focus of nuclear research and weapons development. Over time, its numerous assets have grown to include facilities for processing plutonium, handling other radioactive materials, manufacturing test devices, and testing new design concepts short of a full-scale test.

The Lawrence Livermore National Laboratory (LLNL), in Livermore, California, was established in 1952, primarily to expand research into thermonuclear weapons. In the late 1940s, some scientists, AEC commissioners, and influential members of Congress began to argue that insufficient resources at Los Alamos were being dedicated to thermonuclear work and that a new laboratory was needed.[15] Manhattan Project physicists Edward Teller and Ernest O. Lawrence were particularly insistent that a new laboratory be established (Teller even resigned from Los Alamos to lobby the administration on this point). Pressure also came from Senator Brien McMahon (Democrat of Connecticut), chairman of the Joint Committee on Atomic Energy and an ardent advocate of increased production of nuclear weapons, who tried to interest the Department of Defense in establishing a second laboratory. Teller personally lobbied air force officials on this point, forcing AEC chairman Gordon Dean to choose between creating a laboratory at Livermore or ceding the hydrogen bomb program to the DOD. Under this pressure, the AEC established the Livermore Radiation Laboratory in 1952.[16] Ironically, the first thermonuclear device tested by the United States in the November 1952 "Ivy-Mike" test and most of the more advanced weapons detonated during the "Castle" test series in 1954 were designed at Los Alamos.[17] However, the AEC argued that two research laboratories were needed to create competition, fostered by "independent peer review" among weapons designers, which would lead to faster and cheaper breakthroughs. In turn, this

15. For more on the early development of thermonuclear weapons, see Richard Rhodes, *Dark Sun: The Making of the Hydrogen Bomb* (New York: Simon & Schuster, 1995).

16. Roger M. Anders, *Forging the Atomic Shield: Excerpts from the Diary of Gordon E. Dean* (University of North Carolina Press, 1987), pp. 201–02; Richard G. Hewlett and Francis Duncan, *Atomic Shield: A History of the United States Atomic Energy Commission,* vol. 2: *1947/1952* (Oak Ridge, Tenn.: U.S. AEC Technical Information Center, 1972), pp. 581–84; Harold Orlans, *Contracting for Atoms* (Brookings, 1967), p. 176.

17. However, following "Ivy-Mike," the first test of an experimental thermonuclear device in which the fusion of hydrogen isotopes generated a large percentage of the energy released, the news media incorrectly credited Livermore with designing the weapon. Under the secrecy rules in place at that time, the laboratory could not correct the misstatement, which was deeply resented by scientists at Los Alamos. See Herbert York, "The Origins of the Lawrence Livermore Laboratory," *Bulletin of the Atomic Scientists,* vol. 31 (September 1975), p. 13.

BOX 1-1

Growth and Evolution of the U.S. Nuclear Stockpile

Sixty-five warhead types have been produced and deployed, configured for approximately 116 weapons systems. The air force has used 42 types of nuclear weapons, the navy and Marine Corps 34 types, and the army 21 types. Another 25 warhead types were canceled before production, because another warhead type was chosen, or in some cases, because the delivery system itself was canceled. Some warhead types have had wide applicability, used in one configuration as a bomb, and in another as a warhead for one or perhaps several kinds of missiles.[1]

The last completely new warhead was a W88 assembled at the Pantex Plant on July 31, 1990, for the Trident II missile.[2] Although production has not resumed, Pantex recently converted approximately fifty existing B61-7 bombs into B61-11 bombs, to allow them to penetrate 10 to 20 feet (3 to 6 meters) into the earth's surface and destroy hardened underground targets. The principal modification is the emplacement of the existing "physics package" into a new needle-nosed, hardened, depleted uranium casing. This has increased the bomb's weight by 449 pounds (204 kilograms) and its length by just over 3 inches (8 centimeters). In addition, the drogue parachute has been removed, to permit the bomb to fall freely upon release and thus achieve maximum velocity before impact. While this program does not appear to contravene U.S. government pledges to foreswear development and deployment of entirely new nuclear weapons, it has raised serious questions about when a modified bomb becomes a new weapon. The B61-11 was first deployed with the B-2A bomber at Whiteman AFB in Missouri in April 1997. Scientists at Sandia National Laboratories are already designing a new nuclear glide bomb (based on the B61-11 but utilizing a new guidance system) to be dropped from the B-2A bomber, even though the air force has no requirement for such a weapon.[3]

Other warhead modifications are under way: the W76 warhead for the Trident I missile is being revalidated (to ensure its continued conformity with military requirements in the absence of nuclear testing) and the pit for the W88 is being rebuilt (to address safety concerns pertaining to accidental detonation and plutonium scattering accidents first raised in 1990). In addition, the navy and the weapons laboratories are engaged in a joint SLBM

---

1. For more information, see David Alan Rosenberg, "U.S. Nuclear Stockpile, 1945 to 1950," *Bulletin of the Atomic Scientists,* vol. 38 (May 1982), pp. 25–30; Robert S. Norris, Thomas B. Cochran, and William M. Arkin, "History of the Nuclear Stockpile," *Bulletin of the Atomic Scientists,* vol. 47 (August 1985), pp. 106–09; William Arkin, "The Buildup That Wasn't," *Bulletin of the Atomic Scientists,* vol. 45 (January/February 1989), pp. 6–10.

2. Letter from Gloria E. Inlow, Deputy Director, Office of Intergovernmental and External Affairs, Albuquerque Operations Office, U.S. Department of Energy, to Stephen I. Schwartz, July 19, 1991; R. Jeffrey Smith, "U.S. to Halt H-Bomb Production," *Washington Post,* January 25, 1992, p. A1.

3 Greg Mello, "New Bomb, No Mission," *Bulletin of the Atomic Scientists,* vol. 53 (May/June 1997), pp. 28–32; Matthew L. Wald, "U.S. Refits a Nuclear Bomb to Destroy Enemy Bunkers," *New York Times* (Washington edition), May 31, 1997, p. A1; William B. Scott, "Test Drops of B61-11 Penetrator Weapon Continue," *Aviation Week & Space Technology,* June 9, 1997, pp. 75–76; Jonathan S. Landay, "U.S. Quietly Adds A Bunker-Buster to Nuclear Arsenal," *Christian Science Monitor,* April 8, 1997, p. 1; Jonathan Landay, "Why U.S. Lab Is Designing Bomb No One Asked For," *Christian Science Monitor,* July 24, 1997, p. 1; Jeff Erlich, "Bunker-Busting Bomb Prompts U.S. Discord," *Defense News,* February 24–March 2, 1997, p. 1; William M. Arkin, "New, and Stupid," *Bulletin of the Atomic Scientists,* vol. 52, no. 1 (1996), p. 64; Jonathan Weisman, "Old Nuclear Warheads Get New Life," *Tri-Valley Herald* (Livermore, California), September 21, 1995, p. A1; John Fleck, "Sandia Redesigns N-Bomb," *Albuquerque Journal,* September 22, 1995, p. A1; Jonathan Weisman, "Burrowing Nuclear Warhead Will Take Out the Atomic Trash," *Oakland Tribune,* September 22, 1995, p. A1; Art Pine, "A-Bomb against Libya Target Suggested," *Los Angeles Times* (Washington Edition), April 24, 1996, p. A4.

Box 1-1
(continued)

warhead protection program, the goal of which is to design and fabricate (but not actually produce) a new warhead for either the current or the next generation of SLBMs by 2004.[4]

The historic high for the stockpile was reached in 1966 when about 32,200 nuclear warheads were simultaneously active. As can be seen in figure 1-4, the U.S. buildup started in the late 1950s and consisted almost entirely of tactical nuclear weapons, made possible by the rapid AEC production expansions in the early 1950s and the Eisenhower administration's "New Look" military program, which emphasized nuclear weapons over conventional forces. Annual production of nuclear weapons exceeded 7,000 a year in 1959–60, and more than 5,000 in 1961: this amounted to almost 19,500 new warheads in three years, or a rate of about 25 per workday.

In 1954 hydrogen bombs—hundreds of times more powerful than their fission predecessors—began to enter the stockpile in great numbers, and the megatonnage increased sixtyfold in five years. It peaked in 1960 when it equaled almost 20.5 billion tons of TNT—equivalent to nearly 1.4 million Hiroshima-sized bombs—largely because the Strategic Air Command dominated the nuclear force of the day with a fleet of some 1,600 bombers, armed with thousands of high-yield bombs (the explosive power of the arsenal today equals some 120,000–130,000 Hiroshima-sized bombs).

With the sudden retirement of about 940 warheads in 1961, the megatonnage was cut almost in half. The reason was that the retired bomb, the B36, had a yield of 10 megatons. Until recently, the largest warhead in the arsenal was the 9-megaton B53 bomb, though only about fifty remained and were replaced following the introduction of the B61-11 into the active stockpile in April 1997.[5] As ballistic missiles were introduced and accuracy improved, high-yield weapons were further reduced. The rule of thumb is that making a weapon twice as accurate allows an eightfold reduction in yield to achieve the same level of destruction. Lower yields also permitted the use of substantially less plutonium and highly enriched uranium in warheads, lowering the cost of many weapons and contributing to the eventual surplus of fissile materials.

—Robert S. Norris and Stephen I. Schwartz

---

4. Zerriffi, and Makhijani, *The Nuclear Safety Smokescreen*, p. 39; Elaine M. Grossman, "Navy, Energy Department Seek Back-Up Warhead Design for Trident Missiles," *Inside the Pentagon*, May 9, 1996, p. 1; Elaine M. Grossman, "STRATCOM Has No Requirement for Alternative Trident Missile Warhead," *Inside the Pentagon*, August 29, 1996, p. 6; John Fleck, "Labs Craft Warhead Backup," *Albuquerque Journal*, July 23, 1997, p. A1; U.S. Department of Energy, *FY 1998 Congressional Budget Request*, vol. 1, DOE/CR-0041 (GPO, 1997), pp. 57, 78; Office of the Secretary of Defense, *Nuclear Weapon Systems Sustainment Programs* (GPO, May 1997); Christopher E. Paine and Matthew G. McKinzie, *End Run: The U.S. Government's Plan for Designing Nuclear Weapons and Simulating Nuclear Explosions under the Comprehensive Test Ban Treaty*, Natural Resources Defense Council Nuclear Program (August 1997). The W76 recertification is necessary because when warhead production stopped in 1990, only about four hundred W88 warheads for the Trident II had been built. The W76 (which was not originally intended to be deployed on the Trident II) is thus being loaded on these missiles to offset the shortfall, and the program is to ensure that it will operate as designed.

5. Susanne M. Schafer, "B-2 Bombers Ready for Missions," Associated Press, March 31, 1997.

FIGURE 1-4. Global Nuclear Stockpiles, 1945–97[a]

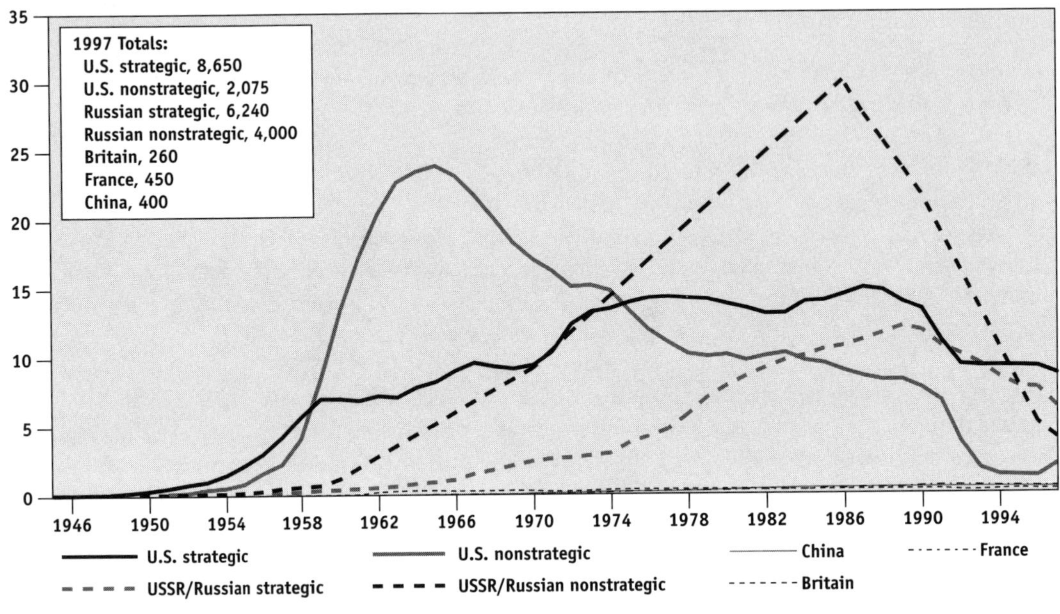

Sources: Robert S. Norris and Thomas B. Cochran, "U.S.-U.S.S.R./Russian Strategic Offensive Nuclear Forces, 1945–1996," Nuclear Weapons Databook Working Paper 97-1 (Washington, D.C.: Natural Resources Defense Council, January 1997); Robert S. Norris, "Nuclear Arsenals of the United States, Russia, Great Britain, France and China: A Status Report," presented at the Fifth ISODARCO Beijing Seminar on Arms Control, November 12–15, 1996; Robert S. Norris, Andrew S. Burrows, and Richard W. Fieldhouse, *Nuclear Weapons Databook,* vol. 5: *British, French, and Chinese Nuclear Weapons* (Boulder, Colo.: Westview Press, 1994).

a. These figures are for active nuclear weapons, including spares. They do not include inactive but intact weapons awaiting dismantlement. For the United States, these warheads are estimated as follows: 241 (1988), 642 (1989), 752 (1990), 2,330 (1991), 5,261 (1992), 5,789 (1993), 4,916 (1994), 3,635 (1995), 2,542 (1996), and 1,350 (1997). For the USSR/Russia, these are estimated as follows: 4,277 (1986), 4,141 (1987), 3,670 (1988). 3,183 (1989), 3,485 (1990), 5,394 (1991), 6,744 (1992), 8,215 (1993), 9,933 (1994), 11,385 (1995), 12,278 (1996), and 12,200 (1997). There is a great deal of uncertainty as to the exact number of U.S.S.R./Russian nonstrategic nuclear weapons. Israel (not shown) is assumed to have 100–150 nuclear weapons.

competition contributed to the development of new weapons designs that exceeded military expectations and, by some accounts, spurred nuclear weapons developments as much as the competition with the Soviet Union.[18]

Both the Los Alamos and Lawrence Livermore laboratories concentrated on developing sophisticated "physics packages" for nuclear weapons. A laboratory for nonnuclear research, known as the Sandia

18. At the February 1992 Fourth International Workshop on Nuclear Weapon Elimination and Nonproliferation held in Washington, D.C., Evgeni N. Avrorin, the head of Chelyabinsk-70 (the Soviet counterpart to Livermore), recalled a recent visit to Los Alamos and marveled that two long-time opponents in the design of nuclear weapons could meet in such a friendly atmosphere and discussing cooperation on joint ventures. At this point Avrorin said, Sigfried (Sig) Hecker, Los Alamos's director, interjected, "Ah, but you were not our enemy. Livermore was." Avrorin then told his

National Laboratories (SNL), was established at Albuquerque, New Mexico, in 1945 and also Livermore, California (in 1956).[19] Sandia worked on other important bomb components, such as electronics equipment; safing, fuzing, and firing devices; and drogue parachutes. Consequently, while LANL and LLNL scientists independently produced new warhead designs, Sandia engineers contributed to the efforts of both laboratories.

Once new nuclear explosives were designed, the AEC and DOD collaborated to test them.[20] The United States conducted "Operation Crossroads," its first post–World War II nuclear tests, at Bikini Atoll (part of the Marshall Islands) in the Pacific in July 1946, before the Manhattan Project was disbanded (the operation is discussed later in the chapter). In 1948, the United States began testing its nuclear weapons on Enewetak Atoll,[21] also in the Marshalls and the site of the first thermonuclear test (Ivy-Mike) on November 1, 1952.[22] Together, these atolls became the prime facilities of the AEC's Pacific Proving Ground (PPG), which was the site of sixty-six atmospheric and underwater tests until 1958.[23]

However, only a limited number of tests could be conducted at this site, owing to the complex logistics of maintaining such a facility so far

audience, "And now I can tell you that just as the real competition was between Livermore and Los Alamos, so in our country the competition was between Arzamas 16 and Chelyabinsk 70." Personal communication, George Perkovich, Director, Secure World Program, W. Alton Jones Foundation, April 11, 1997. Such attitudes are supported by cultural anthropologist Hugh Gusterson's recent survey of scientists at Livermore: "From the start, then, Livermore, which has always represented itself as the more energetic and innovative of the two weapons laboratories, has consistently defined itself against the Los Alamos establishment." Gusterson adds in a footnote, "Los Alamos scientists felt the same way about Livermore. . . . One told me that the levels of classification were 'confidential,' 'secret,' 'top secret,' and the strictest of all, 'hide from Livermore.'" Hugh Gusterson, *Nuclear Rites: A Weapons Laboratory at the End of the Cold War* (University of California Press, 1996), pp. 24, 256, n. 13.

19. Sandia also maintains the Barking Sands Pacific Missile Range in Kauai, Hawaii, and operates the Tonopah Test Range, 140 miles (225.3 kilometers) northwest of Las Vegas, Nevada (see chapter 2).

20. To generate meteorological data before and after nuclear tests, the AEC enlisted the help of the U.S. Weather Bureau (now the National Weather Service). As late as 1994, the Weather Service maintained a staff of thirty-eight with a $1 million annual budget at the Nevada Test Site. An official with the Weather Service has confirmed that the AEC/ERDA/DOE provided all the funds for this effort. In July 1994 these functions were transferred to the Oceanic and Atmospheric Research division of the National Oceanic and Atmospheric Administration (NOAA). Telephone conversation, Stephen I. Schwartz with John Potts, Management and Budget Office, National Weather Service, May 2, 1995.

21. During the years of testing in the Pacific, the name of the atoll was spelled Eniwetok. In 1974 the U.S. government, spurred by increasing concern for Marshallese sensibilities, altered the spelling of all Marshallese names to conform more closely to actual pronunciation by native speakers. This convention is adhered to throughout this book.

22. This massive 10.4-megaton test (equivalent to 10.4 million tons of TNT), the largest on earth at that time, generated a fireball that grew to a diameter of 3½ miles (5.6 kilometers), completely vaporizing Elugelab Island and leaving in its place a crater 164 feet (50 meters) deep and 6,240 feet (1,902 meters) in diameter. See Chuck Hansen, *U.S. Nuclear Weapons: The Secret History* (Arlington, Tex.: Aerofax, 1988), pp. 58–60, 95 (note 190). To illustrate the scale of this event, the AEC later produced a photograph on which the outlines of fourteen Pentagon buildings were superimposed over the crater. See Anders, *Forging the Atomic Shield*, p. 150.

23. In addition, on April 28, 1958, the United States conducted the Yucca test 85 nautical miles (157.4 kilometers) northeast of Enewetak, detonating a W25 warhead (with a yield of 1.7 kilotons) attached to a helium balloon more than 16 miles (25.7 kilometers) in the air. See Robert S. Norris and Thomas B. Cochran, *United States Nuclear Tests: July 1945 to 31 December 1992,* NWD-94-1 (Natural Resources Defense Council, February 1, 1994), pp. 29, 58–59. It appears that government officials occasionally referred to the PPG as the "picnic grounds." See Anders, *Forging the Atomic Shield,* p. 257.

from U.S. shores and adverse weather conditions in the fall and winter.[24] Defending the atolls against Soviet spies and possible outright attack was also difficult.[25] Following the outbreak of the Korean War in June 1950, the army and navy—eager to break the air force's monopoly on atomic weapons and develop devices small enough to be used on the battlefield—requested small, low-yield weapons deliverable by carrier aircraft and artillery pieces.[26] After studying several locations, the AEC in December 1950 designated the areas in and around the Las Vegas Bombing and Gunnery Range as the dedicated continental nuclear test site (on the selection of the test site, see box 1-2). The first test occurred a month later. This would be the primary test site for the remainder of the cold war. Although the United States continued to test high-yield thermonuclear weapons in the Pacific until the signing of the Partial Test Ban Treaty in 1963, 904 (88 percent) of the total 1,030 tests it conducted occurred at the Nevada Test Site (NTS) (see figure 1-5).[27]

Weapons Assembly, Production, and Storage. The manufacture and storage of nuclear weapons is a complicated process. Nuclear and nonnuclear components must be manufactured to stringent specifications. Assembly, production, and storage facilities must impose the strictest of security, health, and safety regulations to ensure that dangerous materials are not stolen and to minimize the health risk to workers and the offsite population.[28] For example, metallic plutonium, which is susceptible to spontaneous combustion, must be handled in an enclosed and controlled environment. To shield workers from exposure and to reduce the risk of fire through accidental releases to the environment, this material is handled remotely in airtight "glove boxes."

24. For example, Operation Greenhouse—a series of four tests (including the first two thermonuclear experiments) conducted at Enewetak between April 7 and May 24, 1951—involved more than 9,000 AEC and military personnel and 15,000 mice, pigs, and dogs (to test the effects of blast, thermal pulse, and radiation). More than 275,000 tons of equipment was moved by sea and air transports an average of 8,000 miles (12,822 kilometers) from points across the United States to Enewetak (requiring fourteen days by sea and three days by air). The total cost for this one series of tests was nearly $1 billion ($114 million in then-year dollars)—with about $700 million consumed by operating costs. These figures prompted AEC chairman Gordon Dean, who traveled to Enewetak to witness the third test, to remark in his diary on the "amazing complexity in cost of the total operation." See Anders, *Forging the Atomic Shield,* pp. 5, 145; Department of Defense, *Costs: Operation Greenhouse, Joint Task Force Three* (circa 1951), n.p.

25. Top secret documents declassified in 1995 revealed that in January 1951, before early tests of hydrogen bomb concepts, the DOD drew up a plan, code-named "Operation Lazybones," to defend Enewetak Atoll from a Soviet assault long enough to allow the evacuation of weapons scientists and bomb materials. See Associated Press, "U.S. Anticipated Soviet Attack on H-bomb Test Site," *Washington Times,* August 23, 1995, p. A3.

26. Bernard J. O'Keefe, *Nuclear Hostages* (Boston: Houghton Mifflin, 1983), p. 148.

27. See U.S. Department of Energy, Openness Press Conference Fact Sheets, December 7, 1993, p. 1, and June 27, 1994, p. 140; Norris and Cochran, "United States Nuclear Tests."

28. Nevertheless, health and safety measures were frequently bypassed or ignored in the interest of containing costs and not impeding production requirements (see chapters 6 and 7).

Beginning in the early 1950s, components made of plutonium and HEU metal were assembled at the Rocky Flats Plant near Denver, Colorado, and the Y-12 Plant at Oak Ridge, Tennessee. Specially equipped machine shops at Rocky Flats produced pits and other nuclear weapons components from plutonium, HEU, depleted uranium, beryllium, and other materials. Scrap plutonium from the assembly line, plutonium metal not deemed waste, and plutonium metal from retired warheads was purified and recycled into new components at the site. Originally, HEU pit components were manufactured and shaped at Oak Ridge's Y-12 Plant before shipment to Rocky Flats, but Y-12 ultimately assumed responsibility for the full assembly of these components while Rocky Flats consolidated its work on plutonium. Thermonuclear secondary components were also assembled at Y-12.

Of the many facilities that contributed nonnuclear components, only the Kansas City Plant, near Kansas City, Missouri, remains in operation. It supplies various electrical, electronic, and plastic components, including arming, fuzing, and firing systems, radars, and coded safety locks known as permissive action links (PALs).[29]

Since 1945 nuclear and nonnuclear components have been assembled into completed nuclear explosive devices at seven locations: Los Alamos; Sandia National Laboratories in Albuquerque, New Mexico; Buffalo Works in Buffalo, New York; the Burlington AEC Plant in Burlington, Iowa; the Clarksville Modification Center in Clarksville, Tennessee; the Medina Modification Center near San Antonio, Texas; and the Pantex Plant, outside Amarillo, Texas. Only Pantex performs these functions today (see appendix C).[30] The most sensitive and dangerous procedure takes place in containment cells known as "Gravel Gerties,"[31] where high-explosive chemicals are layered around the spherical nuclear explosive pits. Each Gravel Gertie (there are thirteen in all at Pantex) holds some 17 feet (5.2 meters) of gravel on its roof and is designed to collapse should the chemical explosive detonate

29. PALs were introduced in the 1960s after the JCAE expressed concern about the security of warheads and bombs, particularly at overseas installations (see box 9-2). Early versions were simple mechanical combination locks with a single code. The most recent versions are electronic switches utilizing a twelve-digit code that not only allows the release of individual warheads but also designates the warhead's yield (for devices with variable yields). See Thomas B. Cochran, William M. Arkin, and Milton M. Hoenig, *Nuclear Weapons Databook,* vol. 1: *U.S. Nuclear Forces and Capabilities* (Cambridge, Mass.: Ballinger, 1984), p. 30.

30. In mid-1993 construction was completed on the $109 million Device Assembly Facility, a 100,000-square-foot (9,300-square-meter) building within a highly secured 22-acre portion of the Nevada Test Site. The facility includes five Gravel Gerties, three weapon assembly bays, two radiographic areas, a component testing laboratory, storage bunkers, two decontamination facilities, three small vaults, and extensive security measures. Designed in the mid-1980s to assemble forty to fifty weapons a year in what was expected to be a significantly increased test program (the last time more than forty weapons were tested in one year was 1969), the facility sits unused, at a cost of $8 million a year. See Robert Macy, "Nearly Completed Nuclear Test Site in Need of Mission," *Philadelphia Inquirer,* April 6, 1997, p. A2; U.S. Department of Energy, *FY 1993 Congressional Budget Request: Atomic Energy Defense Activities—Project Data Sheets,* vol. 1, DOE/CR-0008 (January 1992), pp. 173–77.

31. Named after a character in the "Dick Tracy" comic strip.

Box 1-2
Selecting a Continental Test Site

By 1948 the Joint Chiefs of Staff had initiated plans for a continental test site.[1] But they had to contend with public concerns about the radiological hazards of such a move. To encourage the public to take a more "realistic" attitude and to reduce public relations and political difficulties, an aide to the army chief of staff thought it prudent to "reeducate" the public, in order to allay its "unhealthy, dangerous and unjustified fear of atomic detonations" and to lay to rest "the ghost of an all pervading lethal radioactive cloud which can only be evaded by people on ships, airplanes and sandpits in the Marshall Islands."[2]

Officials in charge of selecting a continental site understood that nearly the only parts of the country that would escape fallout were on the East Coast. As a U.S. Air Force meteorologist reported in 1948, that region was "predominantly under the influence of westerly winds" and might provide a suitable site.

By 1950 the government had ruled out anything north of Cape Hatteras (because ocean currents could bring fallout on shore and because fallout could also affect important fishing grounds) and concentrated on five locations, three of which were owned by the Department of Defense, in order to avoid the costly and time-consuming process of acquiring the land (a site south of Cape Hatteras, which the aforementioned meteorologist indicated would be ideal for avoiding "all fallout," was rejected for this reason): Alamogordo-White Sands Guided Missile Range, New Mexico (where the Trinity test took place); Dugway Proving Ground-Wendover Bombing Range, Utah; Las Vegas-Tonopah Bombing and Gunnery Range, Nevada; an area in Nevada, about 50 miles wide, extending from Fallon to Eureka; and the Pamlico Sound–Camp Lejeune area of North Carolina. The last two sites were not under government control, and, faced with possible delays in their acquisition, they were removed from further consideration. In the end, convenience carried the day, despite the warnings of Colonel Stafford Warren (the chief of radiological safety at the Trinity test who later headed the AEC's Division of Biology and Medicine). After monitoring the fallout from Trinity, he urged that tests not be conducted within a 150-mile radius of human habitation. Gordon Dean, then chairman of the AEC, stated in 1950: "A geographical location as close as possible to the Los Alamos Laboratory, to enable accelerating the pace of the weapons development program, is obviously a characteristic of such desirability that it could outweigh partial deficiencies in other respects."

1. This box draws on International Physicians for the Prevention of Nuclear War and the Institute for Energy and Environmental Research, *Radioactive Heaven and Earth: The Health and Environmental Effects of Nuclear Weapons Testing in, on, and above the Earth* (New York: Apex Press, 1991), pp. 50–56.

2. Memorandum, Lieutenant General J. E. Hull, U.S. Army, to the Chief of Staff, United States Army, "Location of Proving Ground for Atomic Weapons," formerly Top Secret (n.d., circa May 1948), pp. 2–3; Memorandum, Rear Admiral W. S. Parsons to Commander, Joint Task Force Seven, "Location of Proving Ground for Atomic Weapons," for-

during the assembly process, thus containing the explosion and any radioactive debris it produces.[32]

At first, high explosives for the Manhattan Engineer District were manufactured at the Salt Wells Pilot Plant in Inyokern, California (at

32. They would not, of course, contain a nuclear explosion. For more on Pantex and other warhead assembly facilities, see Robert S. Norris and William M. Arkin, "Nuclear Notebook (Pantex Lays Nukes to Rest)," *Bulletin of the Atomic Scientists*, vol. 48 (October 1992), pp. 48–49; Ann Arnold Lemert, *First You Take a Pick and Shovel: The Story of the Mason Companies* (Lexington, Ken.:

BOX 1-2
(continued)

On January 8, 1951, three days before the selection of the test site was officially announced, Dean was informed by Dr. Charles Dunham, chief of the medical branch of the AEC's Division of Biology and Medicine, that while no evaluation had actually been done, there were no serious problems with potential fallout in Nevada and that monitoring would be done mainly for "record purposes." Dunham said: "The only ones we are concerned with are the people who live in the first valley—a town called Alamo. It is not the first valley from the test site; it is about fifty miles as the crow flies."[3] Dean continued to ask what would happen to the people in the surrounding areas. "If there was a pretty good sized burst," replied Dunham, "there might be trouble in the valley, if it poured right after, that is a remote possibility." But the people would not be affected "if they get out and . . . they would have several hours to evacuate—it would not have to be done in a matter of a few minutes," and even if rain fell within two hours of a test, the worst thing that could possibly happen would be "minor skin burns." The sheep, on the other hand, "cannot be controlled."[4]

In reality, large amounts of fallout routinely drifted far from the test site, depositing highly radioactive debris across the United States, but especially in eastern Nevada, southern Utah, Idaho, and Montana (see figure 7-3). Radiation levels were monitored, but even when they became quite high no evacuations were ordered. Instead, reassuring press releases were issued and people were told to stay indoors and, if caught outdoors, to simply remove and wash their clothes and themselves to eliminate any marginal hazards (see chapters 7 and 9).[5] Even before the very first test, the AEC clearly intended to announce that testing posed no risk whatsoever.

—Stephen I. Schwartz

merly Top Secret, May 12, 1948 (attached to previous item), p. 7.

3. Anders, *Forging the Atomic Shield*, p. 94.

4. Anders, *Forging the Atomic Shield*, p. 97. In a conversation with a reporter on January 12, Dean was asked what assurances the AEC had given to Nevada officials about hazards from testing. Dean responded that "we assured them that every precaution was being taken; that there was less danger in it than taking an automobile from here [Washington, D.C.] to Richmond" (p. 103).

5. During the Upshot-Knothole series of tests from March 17 to June 4, 1953, shot Simon (43 kilotons) on April 25 deposited fallout across local highways, forcing the AEC to stop traffic and hose down contaminated vehicles. Shot Harry (32 kilotons), on May 19, sent fallout over St. George, Utah, leading the AEC to caution people to remain indoors that morning. Significant fallout from Upshot-Knothole tests was also detected in Troy, New York, and there was increasing concern that it had also led to an unusual number of sheep deaths in Utah. Consequently, a proposal by scientists at Los Alamos to add an eleventh high-yield test (to avoid the expense of conducting it as originally planned at Enewetak) generated a heated controversy within the AEC, with Chairman Dean making the final decision in favor of doing so. See Anders, *Forging the Atomic Shield*, pp. 238–39, 256–58. For more on the sheep deaths, see Stewart L. Udall, *The Myths of August: A Personal Exploration of Our Tragic Cold War Affair with the Atom* (New York: Pantheon Books, 1994), pp. 203–16.

what is now China Lake Naval Air Warfare Center), under the code name Project Camel. In 1955 the bulk of production moved to the Holston Army Ammunition Plant at Kingsport, Tennessee (which has been the sole supplier since 1961).[33] Newly manufactured warheads (or

John Bradford Press, 1979), pp. 160–89; George T. West, "United States Warhead Assembly Facilities (1945–1990)," Mason & Hanger—Silas Mason, Pantex Plant, March 1991; "Pantex Historical Perspective," available on the World Wide Web at http://www.pantex.com/ds/pxgenal.htm).

33. Robert S. Norris and William M. Arkin, "Nuclear

FIGURE 1-5. Global Nuclear Weapons Tests, 1945–96[a]

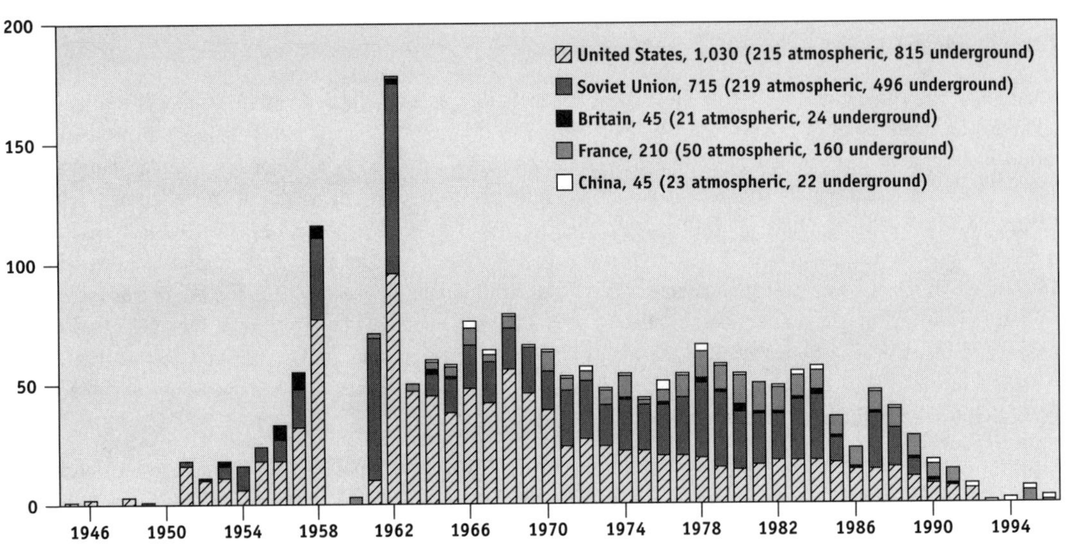

Sources: U.S. Department of Energy; Natural Resources Defense Council, Nuclear Weapons Databook Project.

a. India conducted an underground nuclear test on May 18, 1974. The U.S. total does not include the two atomic bombs dropped on Hiroshima and Nagasaki in August 1945. The United States and the Soviet Union conducted 27 and 116 "peaceful nuclear explosions," respectively, which are included in the above totals.

those returned to Pantex for routine surveillance or modification) are stored at Pantex and remain in DOE custody until the military takes control of them at an operational base or military storage depot.

Pantex also served as one of four plants that routinely disassembled retired warheads, a function it still performs (see chapter 5). After disassembly, nuclear components are transferred from Pantex back to their point of origin—either Rocky Flats or Y-12—for recycling and reuse. Since the cessation of production activities at the Rocky Flats Plant in 1989, Pantex has stored all plutonium components on site, although HEU secondaries are returned to the Y-12 Plant at Oak Ridge. Nonnuclear components were returned to the Pinellas Plant near Clearwater, Florida; the Mound Laboratory in Miamisburg, Ohio;

Notebook (Tennessee Fireworks)," *Bulletin of the Atomic Scientists,* vol. 47 (July/August 1991), p. 47; Richard G. Hewlett and Oscar E. Anderson, Jr., *The New World: A History of the United States Atomic Energy Commission,* vol. 1: *1939/1946* (Oak Ridge, Tenn.: U.S. AEC Technical Information Center, 1972), p. 626; "China Lake Weapons Digest," *The Rocketeer,* November 4, 1993 (available on the World Wide Web at http://www.nawcwpns.navy.mil/clmf.weapdig.html). Before 1961 this powder was apparently also manufactured at a second facility, the Cornhusker Army Ammunition Plant in Grand Island, Nebraska. High-explosive lenses fabricated at the Salt Wells used ingredients obtained from Holston and possibly Cornhusker. Previous production and assembly of high explosives took place at the Los Alamos Scientific Laboratory, Kirtland Air Force Base (assembly only), and the Iowa Army Ordinance Plant. Telephone and facsimile communication with Michael S. Binder, Military Site Reclamation and Conversion, August 14, 1996.

and the Kansas City Plant. Since 1995, most work on nonnuclear components has been consolidated at the Kansas City Plant.

Assessing the Costs

Of course, many laboratories besides Los Alamos, Livermore, and Sandia conducted research and developed processes for handling nuclear materials, and dozens of facilities produced nonnuclear components and handled radioactive materials (see appendix C and chapters 5 and 6). The very size of the nuclear weapons complex, not to mention the secrecy surrounding many of its activities, the lack of rigorous accounting procedures, and poor historical records, make it extremely difficult to determine the costs incurred at each facility. It is much easier to assess costs by program among the lead agencies that contributed to the development of the U.S. nuclear stockpile. The ones considered here are the Manhattan Project; the AEC, ERDA, the DOE, and DOD.

The Manhattan Project

The U.S. nuclear weapons program began shortly before the country entered into World War II. At first it was a modest program of basic research conducted under the supervision of President Franklin Delano Roosevelt and his closest advisers. Under wartime conditions it quickly expanded into a $25 billion project. Three offices—the National Defense Research Committee (NDRC), the Office of Scientific Research and Development (OSRD), and the Manhattan Engineer District—guided this work under what is more commonly known as the Manhattan Project.

National Defense Research Committee. The NDRC was created in June 1940, when atomic physics was still in its infancy. Indeed, that uranium was fissionable had only been demonstrated two years earlier, and it was not yet known if building an atomic bomb was practical. In the fall of 1939, in response to a letter from Albert Einstein, President Roosevelt established the Uranium Committee of the National Research Council under the leadership of Lyman J. Briggs, Director of the National Bureau of Standards.[34] The committee coordinated research into the properties of uranium, but very little money was spent on this effort.[35] Less than a year later, information that Germany had begun

34. The text of Einstein's letter is reprinted in Robert C. Williams and Philip L. Cantelon, eds., *The American Atom: A Documentary History of Nuclear Policies from the Discovery of Fission to the Present, 1939–1984* (Philadelphia: University of Pennsylvania Press, 1984), pp. 12–14.

35. The first known disbursement of government funds

its own research into uranium spurred Roosevelt to expand U.S. activities, and in June 1940 the Uranium Committee was reconstituted under the newly created NDRC.

Led by Vannevar Bush, a former vice president of the Massachusetts Institute of Technology, the NDRC investigated the fissile properties of uranium-235 and uranium-238 and began to evaluate methods for separating isotopes of uranium. The NDRC also coordinated research into the fissile properties and potential weapons applications of the newly discovered transuranic element number 94, later to be called plutonium.[36]

Work coordinated by the NDRC was absorbed by the OSRD beginning in the summer of 1941. According to historical financial reports released by the AEC, the NDRC had spent $468,000, or $6.4 million in 1996 dollars, up to this time.

Office of Scientific Research and Development. Although the creation of the NDRC had demonstrated the importance of atomic research, organizational problems led the government to change its support in the following year. As a scientific and research organization, the NDRC was not equipped to "fill the gap between research and procurement orders that engineers called 'development.'"[37] Furthermore, it had to compete for resources with the laboratories operated by the army and navy and thus found access to funding restricted. To remedy these shortcomings, Bush persuaded President Roosevelt to elevate the priority assigned to the military application of atomic energy.

At Bush's recommendation, Roosevelt created the Office of Scientific Research and Development (OSRD) in June 1941. The OSRD was located within the Office of Emergency Management in the Executive Office of the President and was placed under Bush's direction. James Bryant Conant, the president of Harvard University, replaced Bush at the NDRC, which continued to exist under the OSRD. Under this arrangement, the NDRC made recommendations for further research, while the OSRD guaranteed access to the president and the promise of

for atomic research occurred in February 1940, after navy and army officials agreed to provide $6,000 ($90,361 in 1996 dollars) for work proposed by Briggs. This money was provided to the National Bureau of Standards, which in turn allotted it to Columbia University. There, physicist Enrico Fermi and his colleagues used it to purchase large quantities of pure graphite, measure graphite's ability to absorb neutrons (and thus moderate a chain reaction), and begin designing what would become the world's first nuclear reactor. See Hewlett and Anderson, *New World,* pp. 19–21; Vincent C. Jones, *Manhattan: The Army and the Atomic Bomb* (Washington, D.C.: Center for Military History, U.S. Army, 1985), pp. 22–23.

36. Plutonium was discovered in February 1941 by a team at the University of California at Berkeley led by Glenn T. Seaborg (building upon critical early investigations by Edwin M. Mcmillan and Philip M. Abelson) and including Emilio Segrè, Joseph W. Kennedy, and Arthur C. Wahl. It was named the following year for Pluto, the Greek god of the underworld (a god of the Earth's fertility and also the god of the dead), and after the ninth planet from the Sun following Martin Klaproth's inspiration in 1789 to link the discovery of Uranus to his discovery of a new element, uranium. See Richard Rhodes, *The Making of the Atomic Bomb* (New York: Simon & Schuster, 1986), pp. 353–55.

37. Hewlett and Anderson, *New World,* p. 41.

more resources. Research directed by Bush and Conant continued to explore different isotope separation methods, such as electromagnetic separation in calutrons and centrifuges and by means of gaseous diffusion. Work also continued on producing plutonium in a uranium-graphite "pile," although real breakthroughs were about a year away.

The OSRD was succeeded by the Manhattan Engineer District in 1942. It remained in existence until 1947, however, and its budget was intimately tied to the hidden accounts of the MED as well as other military research efforts. Official AEC sources report that the OSRD's independent contribution to the bomb program was $14.6 million, or $170.8 million in 1996 dollars.

Manhattan Engineer District. By far the largest and best-known World War II organization involved in the building of the bomb was the Army Corps of Engineers' Manhattan Engineer District.[38] Although the OSRD had made progress in all its endeavors to separate uranium isotopes and produce plutonium, the design and construction of production-scale plants were beyond the scope of the office's expertise and mandate. It had long been recognized that the help of the army would be needed to construct facilities large enough for full-scale atomic bomb production, and the military became involved while the program was still under the direction of the OSRD. By September 1942 the project was in the hands of the MED.

Under the leadership of Brigadier General Leslie Groves, who had recently supervised construction of the Pentagon, the MED built the nucleus of the U.S. nuclear weapons production complex. Far from pilot facilities, however, these full-scale plants were designed from the start to generate enough materials for a sizable stockpile of atomic bombs.[39]

In September 1942 Groves selected Oak Ridge, a site near Clinton, Tennessee, for the production of enriched uranium. Over the next two years the MED constructed several facilities there, including the Y-12 Plant, which housed the calutrons; the K-25 Plant for gaseous diffusion; and the S-50 Plant, where uranium was enriched through thermal diffusion. In the process, about one thousand families were displaced.[40]

38. So named because the principal Corps of Engineers office supervising the project was based in Manhattan. General Groves and his staff considered several code names before deciding on this one as being the least likely to draw the unwanted attention of either domestic or foreign interests.

39. In May 1942, for example, the OSRD estimated optimistically that it would cost approximately $148 million (in then-year dollars, about $1.7 billion in 1996 dollars) to construct and operate the facilities needed to build "a few atomic bombs by July 1, 1944, and about twice as many each year thereafter." See Hewlett and Anderson, *New World,* p. 71. A May 7, 1945, report from Oppenheimer to Groves stated: "It seems to us [at Los Alamos] that our first obligation, as long as hostilities continue, and possibly for some little time beyond that, will be uninterrupted production of the gadget models so far developed [the Little Boy and Fat Man devices]." Quoted in Barton J. Bernstein, "Eclipsed by Hiroshima and Nagasaki," *International Security,* vol. 15, no. 4 (1991), p. 153.

40. Hewlett and Anderson, *New World,* p. 116.

The Oak Ridge calutrons and gaseous diffusion separators were developed by physicists and engineers at several university laboratories, primarily the University of California, the University of Chicago, and Columbia University, while the MED contracted out construction, labor, and management tasks to firms such as the Tennessee Eastman Corporation (a subsidiary of Eastman Kodak), Union Carbide, and Stone and Webster, establishing a pattern that survives to the present.[41] Shortages of essential materials caused by the war sometimes led to innovative substitutions in the design and production of these technologies.

A notable and expensive example of such *ersatz* craftsmanship involved the use of silver, rather than copper, to manufacture the electromagnetic coils for the calutrons. Because copper was scarce, silver—a good electrical conductor and not a critical war material—became a substitute. On August 29, 1942, Secretary of War Henry L. Stimson requested the transfer of 175 million fine troy ounces (about 6,000 tons) of silver to the War Department for a "highly secret" project. By 1944 the amount had increased to 14,700 tons, worth nearly $3.3 billion in 1996 dollars.[42]

On December 2, 1942, Enrico Fermi achieved the first chain reaction in natural uranium in CP-1, a graphite-moderated "pile" under the University of Chicago's Stagg Field.[43] Surveying for the proper location for full-scale plutonium production reactors took place during the last two weeks of 1942 even before Fermi's experiment was complete. General Groves, in consultation with scientists in Chicago and Du Pont engineers, drew up a list of eight criteria for the site, encompassing available water and power supplies, land area, distance

41. The selection of these principal operating contractors and others into the 1950s "were determined more by the rapid judgment of a few men [especially Gen. Groves, from 1942 to 1946] in key places than by a protracted, methodical process of examining and evaluating possible alternatives . . . essentially 'closed circle' decisions of a few key individuals up to and including the President." During the war, the system was also remarkably informal, with Groves personally handling correspondence and operating "almost entirely on personal oral discussions, either face to face or by telephone." The primary consideration was speed. As the official history of the period paraphrases his remarks during an October 1942 meeting, "A wrong decision that brought quick results was better than no decision at all. If there were a choice between two methods, one of which was good and the other promising, build both. Time was more important than money." See Orlans, *Contracting for Atoms,* pp. 32–33, 116–18; Hewlett and Anderson, *New World,* p. 181.

42. In August 1942, when Lieutenant Colonel Kenneth Nichols of the Army Corps of Engineers initially approached Undersecretary of the Treasury Daniel W. Bell to inquire about the availability of silver, he did not provide specific details of the project requiring the silver. Bell was nonetheless receptive, asking how much silver Nichols had in mind. "About 15,000 tons," replied Nichols. An astonished Bell exclaimed, "Young man . . . I would have you know that when we talk of silver we speak in terms of ounces." Although an agreement between the Treasury and War departments stipulated the return of all the silver within five years, the AEC did not relinquish the last of it until May 1970. See Jones, *Manhattan,* pp. 66–67.

43. Several safety measures were put in place in case the reaction threatened to run out of control, among them a control rod named "Zip," suspended over the "pile" and designed to be dropped into it either automatically or at the push of a switch. This red button "was labeled, almost as a joke, 'scram.' That word, of course, became part of the language, both as a verb and a noun, in the nuclear world; at the time, it reflected the evacuation plan of those less confident than Fermi." See Rodney P. Carlisle with Joan M. Zenzen, *Supplying the Nuclear Arsenal: American Production Reactors, 1942–1992* (Baltimore, Md.: Johns Hopkins University Press, 1996), pp. 21–22.

to existing communities, highways and railroads, and a suitable climate. From a list of twenty potential sites, Groves indicated that he preferred the ones in the Pacific Northwest. A three-man team—two engineers with E. I. Du Pont de Nemours and a lieutenant colonel from the Manhattan Engineer District—inspected the five most promising: Coulee and Hanford in Washington State; and Pit River, Needles, and Blythe in California. Their report, completed by January 2, 1943, recommended Hanford, finding that the other sites were deficient in one or more of the requirements (Needles, for example, was in an earthquake zone and would necessitate relocating a highway, and Blythe, which was 50 miles (80.5 kilometers) from the Mexican border, was excluded on security grounds). Hanford's only disadvantage was a lack of natural camouflage, owing to the flat, desertlike land. Formal acquisition of the land around Hanford began on February 9, 1943.[44] Meanwhile, the MED would construct the X-10 "pile" at Oak Ridge, to validate Fermi's research on controlled chain reactions.[45]

In all, three reactors and three separation facilities were constructed at the Hanford Reservation during World War II. In September 1944, less than two years after the start of the unprecedented project, the first reactor went "critical," and soon separated plutonium was available for research and weapons use.

As at Oak Ridge, the MED relied on inexpensive construction labor and contracted out with private corporations to carry out most of the design and operations. E. I. Du Pont de Nemours and Company was selected to produce the uranium slugs and construct the reactors at the site. With the influx of tens of thousands of workers and technicians, new communities sprouted up and disrupted the lives of about five hundred residents in the nearby farming communities of Richland, Hanford, and White Bluffs, along with a handful of Wanaapum Indians who fished and foraged along the Columbia River. The purchase of the land itself involved complicated negotiations with the two thousand owners of the more than three thousand tracts that were required. Not only the living were inconvenienced; the area's cemeteries were all closed and the graves exhumed and relocated.[46]

---

44. See Carlisle and Zenzen, *Supplying the Nuclear Arsenal,* pp. 23–25.

45. X-10 was originally to be built in Argonne Forest, 20 miles (32.2 kilometers) from downtown Chicago. A safety review in early 1943 concluded that an accident there would deposit lethal radiation within a 5-mile (8-kilometer) radius, so instead it was built at Oak Ridge (site X) in 1943–44 (where the site's geography would provide somewhat more isolation from the surrounding community) and subsequently operated to confirm the validity of the graphite reactor design. It was shut down in 1947 and is now a national historical site.

46. Hewlett and Anderson, *New World,* p. 213; Kim Murphy, "Nature's Nuclear Surprise," *Los Angeles Times* (Washington edition), June 27, 1996, p. A1. Shortly after selecting Hanford, Groves decided against formally taking the land immediately in order to be "fair and give the owners plenty of time to settle their affairs and get relocated." His decision "cost the government a considerable amount of money, for reasons I did not foresee. Growing conditions that spring and early summer proved to be astoundingly good, so that the crops were better than they had been at almost any time since farming began in that area, and were extremely profitable to the growers. When it came time for the courts to settle the

Weapons design and production took place at Los Alamos, run by the University of California under contract with the MED. The property was acquired in part from a boys' school at the site, although possession was disputed by Pueblo Indian and Hispano farmers, ranchers, and sheepherders living in the area.[47] Until Los Alamos was founded in 1942, scientists had conducted weapons research at many different facilities across the country. By putting them all in one place, General Groves hoped to minimize security risks and foster collaboration. Isolated atop a high mesa in New Mexico, Los Alamos was ideal for both purposes.

What Did the Manhattan Project Cost? On July 16, 1945, an experimental plutonium-fueled device, nicknamed the "Gadget," was detonated from a tower 100 feet (30.5 meters) above the New Mexico desert near Alamogordo. The test was code-named "Trinity." Less than three weeks later, on August 6, a uranium-fueled atomic bomb, nicknamed "Little Boy," was detonated over Hiroshima (this "gun-type" device was considered so reliable that it was never tested). On August 9 a third bomb, named "Fat Man" and a virtual copy of the Trinity device, was dropped on Nagasaki.[48] Two days later, Japan surrendered and World War II ended.[49]

The cost of building the facilities to produce these bombs far exceeded the government's expectations (see footnote 39). According to the AEC, actual Manhattan Project (NDRC, OSRD, and MED) expenditures through the end of 1945 totaled $1.9 billion in then-year dollars ($21.6 billion in 1996 dollars).[50] Of that amount, uranium enrichment accounted for $1.2 billion (about $13.6 billion in 1996 dollars); plutonium production for $390.1 million (about $4.5 billion in

land values, the juries decided on much higher values than had been anticipated, or, in our opinion, were fair." See Leslie R. Groves, *Now It Can Be Told: The Story of the Manhattan Project* (New York: Harper & Brothers, 1962), pp. 76–77. A new historical account of the creation of the Hanford Reservation does not square with Groves's recollection that landowners had "plenty of time" to settle their affairs and that the monetary settlement reached was equitable. Peter Bacon Hales, *Atomic Spaces: Living on the Manhattan Project* (University of Illinois Press, 1997), pp. 60–69.

47. Hales, *Atomic Spaces*, pp. 16, 57–60. Other groups displaced by the bomb program include the Bikini Islanders in 1946 and Western Shoshone Indians living on and around what would become the Nevada Test Site, in 1951. Similar problems arose elsewhere. The Soviet Union's test site in Kazakhstan imparted a terrible toll on the surrounding Kazakh population. Britain's early atmospheric nuclear weapons tests took place on aboriginal lands in South Australia, on the Monte Belle Islands off Australia's northwest coast, and at Christmas Island, south of Java. France maintained a test site in Algeria until political unrest forced a relocation to Moruroa, near Tahiti in the South Pacific. China's test site at Lop Nur in northwestern China lies to the west of Mongolia.

48. The yields of the "Gadget," "Little Boy," and "Fat Man" were 23 kilotons (±3 kilotons), 15 kilotons, and 21 kilotons, respectively. Norris and Cochran, *United States Nuclear Tests*, p. 22.

49. One or two additional "Fat Man"–type bombs were in various stages of preparation but were not available for use before Japan surrendered. See Thomas B. Cochran and others, *Nuclear Weapons Databook*, vol. 2: *U.S. Nuclear Warhead Production* (Cambridge, Mass.: Ballinger, 1987, p. 14, fn. 1.

50. This excludes $76 million spent by the Army Air Forces on Project SILVERPLATE from September 1943 through September 1945. This project covered the modification of 46 B-29 bombers in support of the Manhattan Project, trained the personnel of the 509th composite bombing group, and provided logistical support for units based at Tinian Island, launching point for the attacks on Japan.

1996 dollars); and weapons research, design, testing, and production (including work at Los Alamos) for $143.7 million (about $1.6 billion).[51] In addition, $103.4 million ($1.2 billion) was spent on raw materials, primarily uranium, including ore from Canada and Belgium, along with extremely pure graphite, fluorine, and other materials needed to produce separated plutonium, enriched uranium, and nuclear weapons.[52] The costs of individual programs encompassed by the Manhattan Project are presented in table 1-1.

Only a handful of people knew the enormous sums of money involved. General Groves and other officials secured what was essentially a blank check for the MED from the congressional leadership. To facilitate the appropriations process without revealing too many details, senior War Department and military officials (not including Groves) briefed House leaders in February 1944 (seventeen months after the project got under way) about finances, construction, procurement, and schedules, as well as the project's overall connection to the war. "The Congressmen indicated their approval without reservation" and said further explanations "would not be necessary." The Senate leadership concurred. Thus most members of Congress remained "completely in the dark" about the MED's work.[53]

Atomic Energy Commission

After World War II ended in August 1945, the MED, under the direction of General Groves, continued to manage the weapons complex. At least one more bomb was in the pipeline in August 1945, and Oak Ridge and Hanford remained operational under their wartime contracts. Gradually, the production of uranium-235 at Oak Ridge and plutonium at Hanford declined.[54] Work at Los Alamos also wound down,

51. This included $142 million spent to build a 214-ton steel container—nicknamed "Jumbo"—that was 25 feet (7.6 meters) long and 12 feet (3.7 meters) wide and had walls 14 inches (36 centimeters) thick. At one time, scientists wanted to place the first test device in it, on the theory that if it "fizzled" the container would keep the valuable plutonium from scattering across the New Mexico desert. As the Hanford reactors began to produce greater quantities of plutonium and calculations reduced the chance of a fizzle, Jumbo was abandoned (it was exposed to the Trinity test and came through unscathed). At the time, Jumbo was the heaviest item ever shipped by rail; several of the trestles between the plant in Ohio where it was manufactured and the Trinity site were damaged by its great weight and had to be rebuilt. See Hewlett and Anderson, *New World,* p. 319; Robert W. Seidel, "Trinity—Completion of the Wartime Mission," December 17, 1993 (available on the World Wide Web at http://bang.lanl.gov/video/history/lanl50th/12-17-93.html).

52. Hewlett and Anderson, *New World,* p. 723.

53. Groves, *Now It Can be Told,* pp. 361–63. Groves said that in 1943 the MED had had "a bad moment" when Congressman Albert J. Engel (Republican of Michigan) inquired about construction at Oak Ridge and stated his intention to visit the site in the near future, but he was persuaded to "forget his contemplated visit." Other members of Congress made similar inquiries from time to time, and were again discouraged but accepted the War Department's explanations, "with some reservation, no doubt," and observed its request for secrecy. Before being selected as Roosevelt's running mate in 1944, Senator Harry Truman (Democrat of Missouri) had chaired the Senate's Committee to Investigate the National Defense Program, which attempted to examine the purpose behind the very large expenditures for the MED. But Truman called off the investigation after being told by Secretary of War Stimson not to pursue his inquiry. See Rhodes, *Making of the Atomic Bomb,* p. 617.

54. Hewlett and Anderson, *New World,* pp. 624–33; Hewlett and Duncan. *Atomic Shield,* pp. 39–40.

TABLE 1-1. Auditing the Manhattan Project: Where Did the Money Go?

Cumulative costs in millions of dollars as of December 31, 1945

Site/program	*Then-year dollars*[a]	*Constant 1996 dollars*
Oak Ridge (total)	1,188.35	13,565.66
K-25 Gaseous Diffusion Plant	512.17	5,846.64
Y-12 Electromagnetic Plant	477.63	5,452.41
Clinton Engineer Works—HQ and central utilities	155.95	1,780.26
Clinton Laboratories	26.93	307.44
S-50 Thermal Diffusion Plant	15.67	178.90
Hanford engineer works	390.12	4,453.47
Special operating materials	103.37	1,180.01
Los Alamos Project	74.06	845.38
Research and development	69.68	795.45
Government overhead	37.26	425.29
Heavy-water plants[b]	26.77	305.57
Total	1,889.61	21,570.83

Source: Original data from Hewlett and Anderson, *1939/1946,* p. 11.

a. Includes capital and operations costs from 1942 through 1945. Costs adjusted using a base year of 1944. Actual costs per facility per year are apparently unknown.

b. Designed and constructed by E. B. Badger and Sons and the Consolidated Mining and Smelting Company of Canada in Trail, British Columbia, and by E. I. Du Pont de Nemours and Company in Morgantown, West Virginia; Montgomery, Alabama; and Dana, Indiana.

but preparations for "Operation Crossroads" kept about one-eighth of the scientists busy.[55] There was no question, however, that the program would continue after the war. At a meeting of the Interim Committee on May 31, 1945 (formed by Secretary of War Stimson to consider post-war policy options for the atomic bomb and including Stimson, Groves, Army Chief of Staff George C. Marshall, Oppenheimer, Lawrence, Bush, MIT president Karl T. Compton, Undersecretary of the Navy Ralph A. Bard, Assistant Secretary of State William L. Clayton, and Secretary of State-designate James F. Byrnes), Lawrence spoke forcefully in favor of continued production, recommending "that a program of plant expansion be vigorously pursued and at the same time a sizable stock pile of bombs and material should be built up" to ensure that the nation would "stay out in front." Later in the meeting, Byrnes "expressed the view, *which was generally agreed to by all present,* that the most desirable program would be to push ahead as fast as possible in

55. Jonathan Weisgall, *Operation Crossroads: The Atomic Tests at Bikini Atoll* (Annapolis, Md.: Naval Institute Press, 1994), p. 137.

production and research to make certain that we stay ahead and at the same time make every effort to better our political relations with Russia."[56]

The only issue was under whose authority it would do so. Because the entire endeavor was conducted in strict secrecy, there was never any public or congressional discussion as to the profound military, economic, political, or environmental implications of this decision.[57]

Meanwhile, Congress decided to replace the Manhattan Project with a civilian peacetime agency. In 1946, through the Atomic Energy Act (sponsored by freshman senator Brien McMahon), it established the Atomic Energy Commission, with broad powers to conduct, control, and regulate nuclear research. All materials, facilities, equipment, items, and property related to atomic energy research, and all property in the custody or control of the Manhattan Engineer District—including nine completed "Fat Man"-type bombs—were to be turned over to the AEC by January 1, 1947.[58] The military aspects of the MED were incorporated in the new Armed Forces Special Weapons Project (which in turn became the Defense Atomic Support Agency, DASA, on May 6, 1959; the Defense Nuclear Agency, DNA, on July 1, 1971; and the Defense Special Weapons Agency on June 26, 1996).[59]

Before this transfer was complete, the MED spent an additional $3.1 billion, most notably on the manufacture of nine new bombs, the development of more advanced plutonium weapons, continued research into thermonuclear weapons, and support for the Army-Navy

56. See Rhodes, *Making of the Atomic Bomb,* pp. 628–29, 643–46.

57. In announcing the bombing of Hiroshima on August 6, 1945, President Truman called on Congress "to consider promptly the establishment of an appropriate commission to control the production and use of atomic power within the United States." (Quoted in Williams and Cantelon, *American Atom,* p. 70). Groves initially believed that a civilian commission would take control within just a few months after the end of the war. He therefore proceeded to complete construction projects already in progress and improve the efficiency of various production processes pending a turnover. By late 1945, as hopes for a quick resolution faded, Groves switched tactics and made unilateral decisions (with the approval of the secretary of war) to retain key contractors, continue production, stockpile materials, and assemble weapons. At Hanford, new contractor General Electric's orders were to keep the reactors operating in order to maintain the presumptive lead over the Soviet Union. Interestingly, in an April 1947 meeting with the AEC and its Military Liaison Committee, Groves dismissed calls to build new reactors immediately, questioning whether the sizable number of weapons they would fuel were truly necessary. See Hewlett and Anderson, *New World,* pp. 624–33; Carlisle and Zenzen, *Supplying the Nuclear Arsenal,* pp. 55, 57, 65.

58. This included the communities of Los Alamos, Oak Ridge, and Hanford. According to itemized obligations in *The Budget of the United States Government* (for fiscal 1952–75, inclusive), the AEC spent nearly $2.3 billion operating and maintaining these cities from 1950 to 1973. These costs are considered part of the AEC's overall support of the nuclear weapons program and are included in figure 1-1 (nonweapon programs constituted a small portion of the work at these three sites, but their creation and continued existence were inextricably linked to nuclear weapons).

59. DNA was renamed to "more accurately reflect the Agency's mission under its 1995 charter." This charter broadened DNA's mission to include chemical and biological weapons. See U.S. Department of Defense, "Defense Nuclear Agency Changes Name," Press Release 378-96, June 26, 1996. On November 10, 1997, Secretary of Defense William S. Cohen announced that as part of an agency-wide reform plan, the DSWA, the On-Site Inspection Agency, and the Defense Technology Security Administration would be consolidated into a new Threat Reduction and Treaty Compliance Agency. Department of Defense, "Secretary Cohen Reshapes Defense for the 21st Century," Press Release 605-97, November 10, 1997.

Joint Task Force in conducting Operation Crossroads.[60] Except for Crossroads, specific costs for these activities are unknown. On January 1, 1947, the AEC formally assumed control of the Manhattan Project. The transfer list included thirty-seven installations in nineteen states and Canada; and authority over 254 military officers, 1,688 enlisted men, and about 38,000 contractor employees.[61]

As table 1-2 indicates, the AEC spent $1.6 billion during the last six months of fiscal 1947. The accuracy and completeness of this figure is uncertain. When the newly formed AEC went to Capitol Hill in 1947 to present its budget request for fiscal 1948, its chairman, David E. Lilienthal, wrote:

> The committee itself refused to look at the secret tables we had prepared, but I insisted on it; then we withdrew them. But the secret tables contained large lump sum amounts—140 million for this, 200 for that. The committee members were baffled, and we admitted frankly we didn't know how to present a budget when (a) we didn't have a set of books showing costs, since the Army's Manhattan District didn't have or keep any; and (b) to disclose details would be to breach security.[62]

As the AEC's controller subsequently explained: "The weapon—not the expense—was properly the primary consideration during the war. For this reason, financial controls as a tool of management were largely lacking. . . . In the main, Manhattan District financial management was aimed merely at justifying the reimbursement of expenditures made by cost-type contractors, in conformity with law and Government regulations." As a result, the commission had "an exceptionally poor basic program on which to work."[63]

AEC, ERDA, and DOE Weapons-Related Activities

Between 1947 and 1996, the AEC and its successor agencies—ERDA and DOE—spent about $345 billion on nuclear weapons, roughly divided between materials production, on one hand, and weapons

---

60. Military expenditures for Operation Crossroads in addition to MED expenditures are tabulated in the section on military contributions to nuclear weapons research, development, and testing later in this chapter.

61. Hewlett and Anderson, *New World,* p. 2.

62. David E. Lilienthal, *The Journals of David E. Lilienthal,* vol. 2: *The Atomic Energy Years, 1945–1950* (New York: Harper & Row, 1964), p. 181. In testimony before the Joint Committee on Atomic Energy almost exactly two years later, Lilienthal remarked: "When the Atomic Energy Commission assumed its responsibility 2½ years ago, the atomic weapons position of this country was nothing less than tragic. Continuity of production of fissionable materials was threatened. The morale of scientific forces was at a very low ebb. No real inventory of fissionable materials or of secret documents existed. The state of physical security was defective. The crucial supply of raw materials was tenuous." These conditions were elaborated upon in a series of papers provided to the committee. *Investigation into the United States Atomic Energy Project,* Hearing before the Joint Committee on Atomic Energy, 81 Cong. 1 sess. (GPO, 1949), pt. 23, p. 1114.

63. *Investigation into the United States Atomic Energy Project Hearings,* pp. 1085–86.

TABLE 1-2. Manhattan Project and AEC Expenses, July 1, 1940, to June 30, 1947

Millions of dollars

Program/fiscal year	*Then-year dollars*	*Constant 1996 dollars*
NDRC	0.468	6.4
OSRD	14.6	170.8
MED		
1943	77.1	838.0
1944	730.0	8,333.3
1945	856.9	10,189.1
1946	356.1	4,208.0
1947[a]	171.4	1,881.4
Total, Manhattan Project	2,206.6	25,449.8
AEC		
1947[b]	146.1	1,645.3
Total, FY 1941–47	2,352.7	27,272.3

Sources: For NDRC, OSRD, and AEC, see *Annual Financial Report of the Atomic Energy Commission for FY 1953,* p. 73; for the MED, see Hewlett and Anderson, *1939/1946,* p. 724.

a. From July 1, 1946, through December 31, 1946.

b. From January 1, 1947, through June 30, 1947.

research, development, testing, and manufacturing, on the other. Construction at the weapons complex during this period cost an estimated $79 billion, and operations an estimated $227 billion.

Nuclear Materials Production Costs.

Official budget information suggests that the AEC, ERDA, and DOE have spent more than $165 billion to produce fissile and special materials for nuclear weapons, including an estimated 725 metric tons of HEU (estimated average enrichment of 93 percent), 103.5 metric tons of fuel and weapon-grade plutonium, and an estimated 225 kilograms of tritium since fiscal 1948.[64] Of this amount, $76.7 billion was spent on operating costs, $35.1 billion on source materials procurement, and $51.1 billion on construction and capital equipment purchases (see appendix table A-1). An additional $1.6 billion was spent between 1968 and 1995 to safeguard these materials against theft or diversion while

64. An estimated additional 100 metric tons of HEU (estimated average enrichment of 97 percent) was produced for the naval nuclear propulsion program from 1964 to 1992. See David Albright, William Walker, and Frans Berkhout, *Plutonium and Highly Enriched Uranium 1996: World Inventories, Capabilities, and Policies* (New York: Oxford University Press, 1997), p. 87.

in DOE custody and (to a lesser extent) to implement production-related safety measures. (This amount is for program direction only; each facility has its own safeguards and security budget, which historically was not disaggregated from other spending.) Data on the unit cost of fissile and special nuclear materials, though tracked by the DOE, are classified. Whatever data exist on the total costs of producing each material (or even the total costs at each facility) also appear to be classified. It is therefore not possible to ascertain with any degree of specificity how much was expended just to produce, say, plutonium, highly enriched uranium or tritium (see figure 1-6).

When examined against the background of the ebb and flow of the AEC's materials production activities, the available time-consistent budget data fall into four distinct periods: 1948 to 1964, which was when fissile materials stockpiles rapidly increased; 1964 to 1980, a period of retrenchment in which the United States ceased producing HEU for weapons and sharply curtailed plutonium production activities; 1981 to 1988, which saw a rapid resurgence in materials production under the Reagan administration's military buildup; and 1989 to the present, which has witnessed the collapse of the materials production complex because of age and neglect and the reorientation of DOE's nuclear weapons missions.

Expansion: 1948–64. Not long after it was established, the AEC aggressively expanded U.S. capacity to produce fissile materials in response to the breakup of the wartime "Grand Alliance" and the deterioration, between 1946 and 1948, of U.S.-Soviet relations. Three important factors behind these developments were the domestic discord over the agreement negotiated at Yalta in February 1945 by President Roosevelt, British Prime Minister Winston Churchill, and Soviet leader Josef Stalin, which granted control of postwar Eastern Europe to the Soviet Union (in part to maintain the military alliance and end WWII); the resulting "German question"; and the Marshall Plan. Although the United States had a massive industrial mobilization base and a booming economy (both thanks to the war), not to mention the atomic bomb, the perceived superiority of the Red Army and the thought of it occupying Eastern Europe raised alarms in Washington about Soviet intentions and Western disadvantages should conflict break out.

To prevent war and maintain global influence, the Truman administration and its successors decided, among other things, to further embrace nuclear weapons, especially thermonuclear weapons. The first Soviet detonation of an atomic bomb in 1949 (which came as a shock to many observers),[65] the fall of China to the Communists that

65. Although a number of Manhattan Project scientists confidently (and accurately) predicted that acquisition of the atomic bomb by the Soviet Union would take about four to five years, civilian policymakers and U.S. intelligence agen-

FIGURE 1-6. Expenditures for U.S. Nuclear Weapons Materials Production, 1942–96[a]

Billions of 1996 dollars

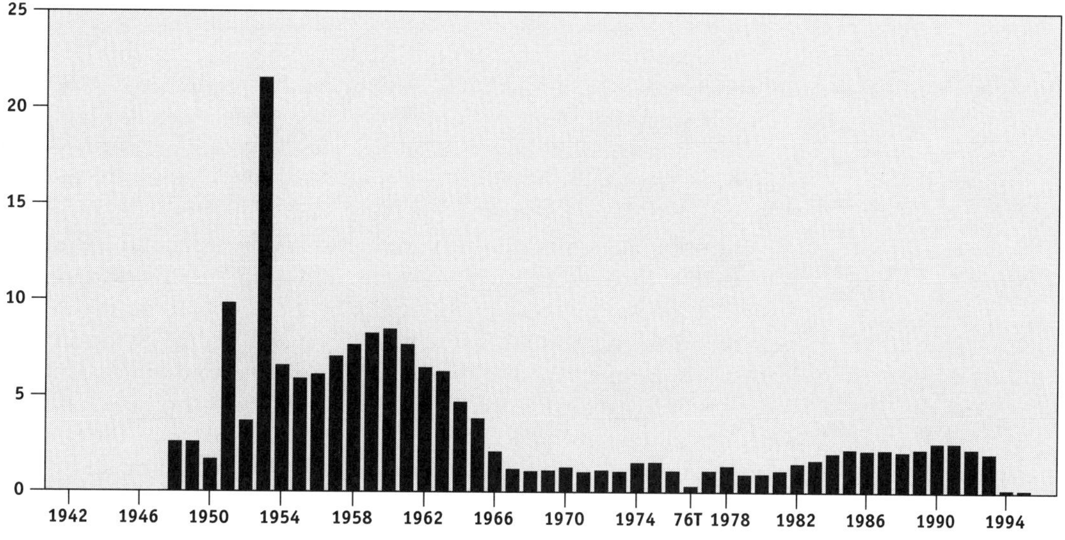

a. The fissile materials production budget was not disaggregated from the AEC's overall weapons budget until 1948.

same year, and the outbreak of the Korean War on June 25, 1950, seemed to confirm policymakers' worst fears about Soviet expansionism (embodied most strongly in NSC 68, issued in April 1950) and spurred the United States to accelerate its nuclear weapons program. Apprehension about possible Soviet thermonuclear weapons also played a significant role in the expansion of the U.S. effort.

One day after North Korean forces attacked South Korea, Senator Brien McMahon (Democrat of Connecticut), now chairman of the

cies had differing views. General Groves, believing that the Soviet Union had no access to uranium ore, asserted that it could not produce nuclear weapons for at least twenty years. In June 1945 Secretary of State–designate James F. Byrnes concluded "that any other government would need from seven to ten years, at least, to produce a bomb." The estimates of those with actual experience with the Manhattan Project also varied greatly, ranging from three years to never. On September 20, 1949—twenty-two days *after* the Soviet test—the CIA issued Intelligence Memorandum 225, "Estimate of Status of Atomic Warfare in the USSR," which concluded: "The earliest possible date by which the USSR might be expected to produce an atomic bomb is mid-1950 and the most probable date is mid-1953." The CIA's reasoning reflected the tendency of many analysts to accept the initial prediction of about four years. However, this period of time was never fixed to a starting point, so that each year the Soviet Union did not demonstrate the capability, the time estimate was advanced into the future, inspiring the false hope that the U.S. monopoly on nuclear weapons might be maintained indefinitely and contributing to the shock at the actual event. Truman subsequently confided to a senator that he could not believe "those asiatics" were capable of constructing a weapon as complex as the atomic bomb. See Hewlett and Anderson, *New World,* p. 354; Rhodes, *Making of the Atomic Bomb,* pp. 649–50; Michael Warner, ed., *CIA Cold War Records: The CIA under Harry Truman* (Washington, D.C.: Central Intelligence Agency, 1994), p. 319; Lawrence Freedman, *U.S. Intelligence and the Soviet Strategic Threat,* 2d ed. (Princeton University Press, 1986), p. 64; Rhodes, *Dark Sun,* p. 373; Charles Ziegler, "Intelligence Assessments of Soviet Atomic Capability, 1945–1949: Myths, Monopolies and *Maskirovka,*" *Intelligence and National Security,* vol. 12 (October 1997), pp. 1–24.

Joint Committee on Atomic Energy (JCAE), asked AEC commissioner Sumner Pike to estimate the cost of increasing planned nuclear weapon production rates by 50 percent over the next few years.[66] Before the AEC could respond, Truman submitted to Congress on July 7 a supplemental appropriation of $260 million ($1.8 billion in 1996 dollars) for the AEC. McMahon supported the request and took the relatively small figure (3 percent of the overall 1951 defense budget) to mean that thermonuclear weapons were not very expensive and therefore were well within the reach of the Soviet Union. McMahon then asked William L. Borden, the JCAE's executive director, to assess the requirements for further expanding weapons production. Borden prepared a three-page memorandum outlining his belief that the Soviet Union was not only pursuing the hydrogen bomb but was likely well ahead of the United States.[67] To keep the United States in the lead, Borden called for the establishment of a second Hanford, with three to five reactors of the existing graphite and the newer heavy-water design (according to intelligence reports at this time, the United States had only a one-pile advantage over the Soviet Union, and superiority in gaseous diffusion technology was also threatened; such dire analyses anticipated the bomber and missile "gaps" that were to materialize—and just as quickly fade away—later in the decade). "If we act to increase our supply of atomic weapons and they turn out to be unnecessary, we may lose a few hundred million dollars," Borden explained. "If we fail to produce these weapons and they do turn out to be necessary, we may lose our country."[68]

Convinced of Soviet capabilities, the need for nuclear weapons in the U.S. defense posture, and the importance of research on these weapons, the Truman administration expanded the weapons complex during 1949–52. All the while the pressure for more nuclear weapons, especially large numbers of tactical weapons, and hence for fissionable materials, was building: it came from the JCAE, primarily Senators McMahon and Henry M. Jackson (Democrat of Washington); Robert

66. By this time, improvements such as new fuel slug designs and efficiencies had boosted output, cut material requirements significantly, and reduced costs. General Electric, for example, operating the Hanford Reservation, found itself producing "40 percent more plutonium per dollar of operating cost in 1949 than in 1947." Carlisle and Zenzen, *Supplying the Nuclear Arsenal,* p. 65.

67. In fact, though the United States was the first to test successfully an experimental thermonuclear device (weighing 82 tons) on November 1, 1952, the Soviet Union was the first to test a fully deliverable thermonuclear weapon (weighing substantially less), on August 12, 1953.

68. Hewlett and Duncan, *Atomic Shield,* pp. 522–23; Carlisle and Zenzen, *Supplying the Nuclear Arsenal,* pp. 93–94. When Chinese forces attacked U.S. forces in late November 1950, catching them unprepared and forcing a retreat, Truman announced that the United States would do what was necessary to meet the threat, which meant using "every weapon we have." On December 1 Truman asked Congress for an additional $16.8 billion ($117 billion in 1996 dollars) for military spending, including just over $1 billion (more than $7 billion in 1996 dollars) to expand the production of uranium and plutonium. Some of these additional funds went to General Electric for the construction of a sixth production reactor at Hanford, even though the commissioners stated that such a reactor was not "absolutely required" to meet production requirements. See, Hewlett and Duncan, *Atomic Shield,* pp. 532–33; Carlisle and Zenzen, *Supplying the Nuclear Arsenal,* p. 95.

LeBaron, assistant to the secretary of defense for atomic energy and chairman of the Military Liaison Committee (MLC), the DOD's link to the AEC: and the Joint Chiefs of Staff (largely following LeBaron's recommendations). The AEC, which preferred to base its production goals on a clear number of weapons rather than an arbitrary percentage increase in production, was troubled both by the huge costs associated with the increases and by the DOD's position that the AEC had no role in setting nuclear weapons policy but rather served essentially as a contractor to DOD, providing nuclear weapons and materials as required. (However, the AEC, as authorized by the Atomic Energy Act, retained custody of the nuclear stockpile, releasing weapons to the military only upon the authorization of the president. The JCS chafed at this arrangement, eventually gaining control of the arsenal from the AEC in stages from 1951 to 1967).

At a meeting with the MLC on October 5, 1951, Commissioner Henry Smyth, speaking for the AEC, stated that the military was moving far too quickly in deciding to increase production so dramatically. Given the cost of the proposals and their impact on the economy, Smyth argued, the decision to proceed lay not with the JCS or the AEC but with the president, the National Security Council, and Congress. The AEC, the MLC, and others were fully aware that the sizable outlays for the expansion program proposed in 1951 (and approved by Truman on January 16, 1952) would not have any meaningful impact on the size of the nuclear stockpile until 1956 and thus were of no use in addressing the threats raised by the Korean War (and could potentially divert resources necessary to prosecute the war). Indeed, Charles E. Wilson, with the Office of Defense Mobilization (and secretary of defense from 1953 to 1957), had written a memorandum criticizing the JCS for failing to justify the expansion program in light of these facts and during a meeting with Truman at the White House on January 16, 1952, argued that he saw no alternative, given the stated need for large numbers of weapons, although "the estimated requirements for critical materials and equipment had appalled him."[69]

Between 1951 and 1955, the AEC obligated nearly $35 billion for construction at fissile material production sites, primarily to build new reactors and to expand the capacity of the gaseous diffusion plants. Carleton Shugg, the AEC's acting general manager, assessing the expansion proposed in 1950 (as a direct result of the outbreak of the Korean War) for 1951, considered the proposed expenditure of $883 million ($6.2 billion in 1996 dollars) in that one year to be a "fantastic sum," exceeding the peak annual expenditures of the Manhattan Project just seven years earlier. Completing the program, he realized,

69. See Hewlett and Duncan, *Atomic Shield,* pp. 547–49, 556–61, 567–68, 576–77.

would clearly exceed the costs incurred during World War II.[70] In 1953, at the beginning of the so-called 50-150 expansion program, the AEC obligated more than $19 billion for construction activities at materials production sites, or slightly less than the amount spent on the entire Manhattan Project during *all* of World War II.[71]

As a result of these expenditures, both uranium enrichment and plutonium production capabilities were greatly increased. By 1954 the AEC had added four new buildings to the Oak Ridge gaseous diffusion plant and constructed a new five-building gaseous diffusion plant near Paducah, Kentucky. Two years later, a three-building plant was finished at Portsmouth, Ohio. Five new reactors—H, DR, C, KW, and KE—were constructed at Hanford and were producing plutonium by 1955. In addition, five new heavy-water reactors—R, L, P, K and C—were built at the new Savannah River Plant especially for producing plutonium, tritium, and other materials needed to build thermonuclear weapons. Large new reprocessing plants were built at both Hanford and Savannah River as well.[72]

Operating costs also increased, although not as steeply as those for construction. Between 1950 and 1954, operating expenses increased threefold, from $710 million to more than $2.1 billion. By 1957, with all thirteen reactors and all three gaseous diffusion plants operating, the AEC had obligated more than $3.8 billion to produce fissile materials. These operations would make possible the rapid increases in the weapons stockpile to come (see box 1-1).

Obligations for procuring source materials, especially uranium, increased with the AEC's uranium enrichment and plutonium production capacities. Initially, the availability of uranium ore severely constrained Defense Department planning for nuclear weapons and AEC capabilities to produce uranium and plutonium. According to AEC documents, "the shortage of raw materials dictated the magni-

70. Hewlett and Duncan, *Atomic Shield,* pp. 526–27.

71. Refers to the plan approved by President Truman on January 16, 1952. Its goal was to increase plutonium production by 50 percent and HEU production by 150 percent. See Memorandum to the President, "Atomic Energy: Expansion of the Atomic Energy Program," President's Secretary's Files, National Security Council (Atomic), Box 202, Harry S Truman Library (declassified), January 17, 1952. See also Anders, *Forging the Atomic Shield,* pp. 152, 189–95; Hewlett and Duncan, *Atomic Shield,* pp. 576–78. The expansion efforts of the early 1950s were so immense that "the concrete required by the Savannah River plant at Aiken [was] sufficient to lay a sidewalk five feet wide and 6 inches thick from coast to coast, and the excavation work will turn up enough earth to form a wall ten feet high and six feet wide from Los Angeles to Boston. . . .The materials required to build the Savannah River plant would fill a string of railway cars stretching all the way from New York to St. Louis." About 5 percent of the "total construction force of the nation" participated in this expansion. Gordon Dean, *Report on the Atom: What You Should Know about Atomic Energy* (London: Eyre & Spottiswoode, 1954), pp. 66–67.

72. As with the facilities built during World War II, construction of the Savannah River Plant forced existing communities to relocate. Du Pont recommended acquiring 240,000 acres, including land encompassing the rural towns of Ellenton, Jackson, and Snelling, home to 1,500 families. Two AEC commissioners responded that the site boundaries could be shifted slightly to bypass Ellenton, but in the end the AEC approved Du Pont's request, relocating the towns and 150 cemeteries. See Hewlett and Duncan, *Atomic Shield,* p. 531; Andre Carothers, "The Death of Ellenton," *Greenpeace,* vol. 13 (May/June 1988), pp. 13–19.

tude of military requirements. Not only were existing sources small in comparison with needs [in 1947] . . . no known uranium source could supply the projected military requirements, and the extractive metallurgy of these sources had only begun to be studied."[73]

During the closing days of World War II, the United States and Great Britain jointly sought rights to the high-grade uranium ore deposits in the Belgian Congo and moved to purchase lesser ores from gold mine tailings in South Africa and other foreign sources. When it was discovered that even lower grade ores could be processed to extract uranium concentrates, these foreign efforts were largely abandoned and significant resources were devoted to domestic production.

In 1948 the AEC stimulated domestic production by guaranteeing minimum prices for ten years for high-grade uranium concentrates and offered a $10,000 (then-year dollars, about $99,000 in 1996 dollars) bonus for the discovery of new high-grade deposits.[74] Over the next twelve years, domestic raw materials production increased rapidly, as did procurement costs. Hence spending on raw materials increased throughout the 1950s. Eventually, actual uranium purchases by the AEC surpassed planned or even optimal processing requirements. Whereas the 1953 expansion assumed an optimal receiving rate of 9,150 tons of ore a year through the end of the decade, by 1958 domestic sources alone were producing nearly 18,000 tons of concentrate, while significant quantities of foreign uranium were also being purchased. Domestic production was then curtailed, but receipts from all sources did not peak until 1960, when the AEC purchased 34,600 tons.[75]

By 1955 obligations for source materials were more than $1.5 billion, up from $334 million in 1950. By 1959 spending was in excess of $4.3 billion, and twenty-three ore-processing plants were operating in the United States.[76]

Curtailment: Mid-1960s through 1980. The rapid growth of plutonium and HEU production in the 1950s led the United States to consider curtailing its production activities in the early 1960s. Satisfied that fresh material stocks, together with materials recycled from retired weapons, were sufficient to accommodate planned weapons produc-

73. Atomic Energy Commission, *History of Expansion of AEC Production Facilities,* AEC 1140 (August 16, 1963), DOE Archives, declassified, p. 55. In fact, the JCS based its "requirement" for nuclear weapons on the AEC's production capacity, a practice criticized by the JCAE because it set what were viewed as arbitrary limits on an effort that it believed required greater numbers of weapons and, hence, a larger stockpile of nuclear materials. This was a key reason behind the JCAE's support of large increases in the AEC's production capacity.

74. Atomic Energy Commission, *History of Expansion of AEC Production Facilities,* p. 56.

75. Atomic Energy Commission, *History of Expansion of AEC Production Facilities,* p. 56.

76. The number of plants peaked at twenty-six in 1961. U.S. Atomic Energy Commission, *Major Activities in the Atomic Energy Programs, January–December 1959* (GPO, January 1960), pp. 57–59; U.S. Atomic Energy Commission, *Major Activities in the Atomic Energy Programs, January–December 1961* (GPO, January 1962), p. 167.

tion, the Johnson administration determined that the need to produce additional fresh plutonium and HEU had dramatically decreased.[77]

These considerations led the United States to propose a fissile material production cutoff to the Soviet Union in 1963. The United States hoped to capitalize on the momentum generated by the recent signing of the Partial Test Ban Treaty (PTBT) and the Washington-Moscow Hotline Agreement, and it sought to further reduce tensions between the superpowers while retaining a clear nuclear advantage.

Citing the substantial U.S. advantage, the Soviet Union refused to curtail fissile material production. In fact, some aspects of the Soviet program, in particular the gas centrifuge program to produce enriched uranium, were only then reaching maturity and full-scale operations.[78] Had the Soviet Union cut production, it would have been left with far less fissile material than the United States, and more than a decade's worth of research and development would have been wasted.

Despite the Soviet refusal, the Johnson administration took several steps to reduce fissile material production. First, it unilaterally stopped producing HEU for weapons in 1964. While the AEC would continue to produce enriched material, primarily low-enriched uranium (LEU) for commercial nuclear power plants and HEU for naval propulsion reactors, the gaseous diffusion plants ceased to play a central role in materials production for nuclear weapons.

Plutonium production also was scaled back dramatically in the mid-1960s. Between 1964 and 1971 the administration closed the original eight Hanford reactors and converted the N reactor, in operation between 1964 and 1966, to maximize electricity production (it would

77. AEC chairman Gordon Dean raised an important question in June 1952: Noting that Air Force Chief of Staff Hoyt Vandenberg had indicated on January 16, 1952 (during the meeting with Truman where the 50–150 program was approved) that a very large number of weapons would be required for all-out war (Dean omitted the figure from his draft, but other contemporary documents quote Vandenberg as saying that *at a minimum* "perhaps five or six thousand Soviet targets . . . would have to be destroyed in the event of war") Dean calculated that this figure would be reached by 1960 (owing to the speed and efficiency of AEC operations, it was actually attained between 1957 and 1958) and that twice that amount would be reached by 1964 or 1965 (it was accomplished between 1958 and 1959). This led Dean to ask, "What should be the course that the U.S. atomic energy program should follow when it has produced the number which the military state to be necessary for a total conflagration . . . [or] when it has reached twice the amount which the military state to be necessary for the defense of the United States? Is there any point in producing bombs beyond this point?" Recognizing the military's propensity for devising ever-expanding target lists, Dean asserted, "When this point has been reached, regardless of all the claims that can be made for an infinite number of 'targets of opportunity,' it simply means by any method of reasoning that we have more than enough." The country, he concluded, should "close down the entire operation at Paducah [and nearly all of the remaining enrichment facilities] . . . in 1965." It was thus possible for Dean to dismiss calls for even larger expansion programs, such as the 100 percent increase in plutonium and 300 percent increase in highly enriched uranium advocated by Senator Henry Jackson in October 1951 (see chapter 9). President Lyndon Johnson curtailed all HEU production for weapons and most plutonium production beginning in 1964. Production of new weapons, however, did not cease until 1990. See Anders, *Forging the Atomic Shield,* pp. 265–70; David Alan Rosenberg, "The Origins of Overkill: Nuclear Weapons and American Strategy, 1945–1960," in Steven E. Miller, ed., *Strategy and Nuclear Deterrence* (Princeton University Press, 1984), pp. 132–33.

78. For a history of Soviet uranium enrichment capabilities, in particular the Soviet centrifuge program, see Albright and others, *Plutonium and Highly Enriched Uranium 1996,* pp. 94–116.

be reconfigured to produce weapon-grade material in the early 1980s). At the Savannah River Plant, two reactors were shut down between 1964 and 1968, while the remaining three continued to produce plutonium and tritium until mid-1988.

Reprocessing was also scaled back. At Hanford, operations ceased in 1972 (although they resumed in the early 1980s). Spent fuel from the N reactor was stored in large concrete pools on site beginning in 1972. The fuel-grade plutonium in the spent fuel was to be recovered in the future for use in the never-realized U.S. breeder reactor program.[79] However, the F and H canyons at Savannah River continued to operate.

Production budgets soon felt the impact of these trends. In 1964 annual obligations for operating expenses were more than $2.5 billion, not including the additional billions dedicated to procuring uranium and other materials. Ten years later, spending on source materials had virtually disappeared, and annual operating expenses were nearly one quarter of what they had been. By 1979, total budget authority for materials production, including both operating expenses and capital equipment and construction purchases, had fallen below $1 billion for the first time ever.

Resurgence: 1981–88. With the start of the Reagan administration, trends in materials production spending again reversed direction. Several Soviet policies—including continued adventurism in Central America, Africa, and Asia; the decision to deploy mobile SS-20 intermediate-range ballistic missiles capable of targeting bases and cities in Western Europe; and the 1979 invasion of Afghanistan—soured U.S. decisionmakers on détente. The Reagan administration responded in part by expanding significantly fissile materials production to fuel a planned nuclear weapons modernization program calling for as many as 14,000 to 17,000 new warheads, according to some unofficial calculations.[80] Between 1981 and 1988 the DOE obligated or was authorized to spend $14 billion, including more than $10 billion for operating expenses and $3.5 billion for construction and capital equipment (appendix table A-1).

79. Breeder reactors are designed to create or "breed" at least as much fuel as they consume and therefore in theory offer an endless source of plutonium-239. Concerns that the proposed breeder reactor at Clinch River, Tennessee, would undermine U.S. nonproliferation policy and the increasing cost of the program led to its cancellation in December 1983, after the expenditure of more than $1.6 billion (in then-year dollars) and a vote by Congress to terminate construction funding.

80. In fact, from 1980 to 1988 the total size of the nuclear stockpile actually declined by 3 percent as these plans were scaled back and the aging production complex proved unable to meet the demand. For an analysis of why the administration's plans to increase the size of the arsenal were never realized, see William Arkin, "The Buildup That Wasn't," *Bulletin of the Atomic Scientists,* vol. 45 (January/February 1989), pp. 6–10; David C. Morrison, "The Nuclear Buildup That Wasn't," *National Journal,* November 26, 1988, p. 2994.

Several programs were initiated or resumed under the Reagan administration to increase the U.S. fissile materials stockpile. The Hanford N reactor was reconfigured to produce weapon-grade plutonium beginning in 1982, Hanford was reprocessing again in 1983, and the Savannah River L reactor was restarted in 1985. These programs incurred significant costs: $112 million was spent in 1983–84 on restarting Hanford reprocessing and an initial $41.3 million on restarting the L reactor.[81]

With the demise of the breeder reactor program in late 1983, the DOE also sought to increase weapon-grade plutonium stocks by recovering the fuel-grade material produced in the N reactor since 1966. This effort took two main tracks. First, in 1985, the DOE configured the Savannah P, K, and C reactors to produce "supergrade plutonium." This material was then blended with some of the N-reactor material to produce weapon-grade plutonium.

Second, scientists explored new methods of isotope separation. After the fuel-grade plutonium was recovered, the DOE proposed that the material should be enriched by using lasers at a new facility called the Special Isotope Separation (SIS) Plant, to be located at the Idaho National Engineering Laboratory (INEL; now known as the Idaho National Engineering and Environmental Laboratory, or INEEL). The SIS would outlast the second Reagan administration, with work continuing under President George Bush. Estimated research and development obligations for the SIS Plant, including a pilot-scale facility built at Lawrence Livermore National Laboratory, totaled $774 million before the program was canceled in 1990 owing to a lack of need and serious proliferation concerns.[82]

Collapse: 1988–93. During the mid-1980s, citizens' groups living near Hanford, Savannah River, the Fernald Plant in southwestern Ohio, and other such sites became increasingly concerned that the restarted facilities posed unacceptable risks to the environment and to the health and safety of both workers and the surrounding populations. Early in the decade, a few groups managed to keep facilities closed or to postpone their reopening. The Natural Resources Defense Council, for one, challenged DOE efforts to restart the L reactor and succeeded in delaying restart by two years.[83] However, it was not until the Chernobyl

---

81. Energy and Water Development Appropriations Subcommittee, House Appropriations Committee, *Atomic Energy Defense Activities for FY 1985* (GPO, 1984), pt. 6, p. 854.

82. On February 22, 1988, Energy Secretary John Herrington told the House Appropriations Energy and Water Development Subcommittee: "We're awash in plutonium. We have more plutonium than we need." See Eric Pryne, "DOE Chief: 'We're Awash in Plutonium,'" *Seattle Times,* February 23, 1988, p. B2. On May 1, 1995, the Atomic Vapor Laser Isotope Separation (AVLIS) program at LLNL was transferred to the United States Enrichment Corporation (USEC), which hopes to utilize it to enrich uranium for commercial nuclear power programs after 2004. Although AVLIS components remain at LLNL and the technology continues to have important weapons-related applications, all work is now funded by the USEC.

83. Carlisle and Zenzen, *Supplying the Nuclear Arsenal,* pp. 180–81.

accident in April 1986 that these grass roots groups began to achieve real success. Like Chernobyl, the Hanford N reactor was graphite-moderated. Unlike Chernobyl, it did not even have a system for monitoring or controlling hydrogen. It also lacked a containment vessel.[84] Indeed, only the five reactors at the Savannah River Site had containment vessels and none of the fourteen military production reactors built and operated in the United States had the pressurized steel and reinforced concrete containment building required by law for all civilian power reactors.

Under mounting public and congressional pressure, the DOE eventually acknowledged that environmental, safety, and health protection measures at production reactor sites and at other materials complex facilities were inadequate or nonexistent. Secretary of Energy John Herrington tried to persuade Congress to obligate billions of dollars to rebuild the complex and continue weapons production, but severe environmental and safety problems eclipsed stockpile concerns and the strategy backfired (see chapter 9). Ultimately, the DOE's failure to comply with environmental standards or adequately invest in maintaining its increasingly brittle infrastructure—despite reports of serious deficiencies as early as 1981—brought production and reprocessing activities to an abrupt halt in 1988.[85]

Spending at materials production sites did end, however. Under George Bush and Bill Clinton, the DOE committed almost $12 billion to the materials production facilities—nearly as much as President Reagan spent during his two terms in office—even though the United States has not produced any new plutonium or tritium since mid-1988. Much of the DOE's investment since 1988 has gone toward upgrading facilities to satisfy environmental, health, and safety concerns. Between 1988 and 1993, the DOE spent more than $2 billion to restore the Savannah River K, L, and P reactors alone, although efforts to restart them were ultimately abandoned, and they never resumed operation.[86]

In addition, both the Bush and Clinton administrations sought to resume the production of tritium, which had stopped when the K reactor shut down on April 10, 1988. Although plutonium stocks eventually were deemed more than sufficient to permit the reactor shutdowns, some officials within the Reagan and Bush administrations argued that because tritium had only a 12.3-year half-life such shutdowns would render the U.S. nuclear arsenal impotent, and its weapons would have

84. Carlisle and Zenzen, *Supplying the Nuclear Arsenal,* p. 189; Ben A. Franklin, "Key U.S. Reactor to Shut 6 Months for Safety Moves," *New York Times,* December 13, 1986, p. 1; Matthew L. Wald, "Hanford Reactor Is Troubled Link in Aging Production Chain," *New York Times,* December 13, 1986, p. 10.

85. Keith Schneider, "Defects in Nuclear Arms Industry Minimized in Early Reagan Years," *New York Times,* November 7, 1988, p. A1.

86. U.S. House of Representatives, Energy and Water Development Appropriations Subcommittee, House Appropriations Committee, *Atomic Energy Defense Activities for FY 1993* (GPO, 1992), pt. 6, p. 1780.

to be dismantled and cannibalized.[87] The Bush administration initially proposed building a New Production Reactor (NPR) at SRS to produce tritium but deferred construction in September 1992, citing a lack of immediate need for new tritium. The Clinton administration terminated the reactor program in 1995, after $2.2 billion in expenditures, but has not given up efforts to produce tritium entirely. It spent $182 million on basic research on nonreactor options such as particle accelerators in 1993, $75 million in 1996, and $150 million in 1997.[88]

Weapons Production Costs. Between 1948 and 1996 the DOE and its predecessors spent an estimated $178 billion on weapons research, development, testing, and production. This estimate, based on data in appendix table A-2, includes $150 billion in operating costs and $28 billion in construction and capital purchases (see figure 1-7). From 1948 through 1956 these costs kept pace with the steady increase in weapons production as new facilities were built and new weapons designs were introduced. They reached their first peak in 1964, the period of the most rapid buildup in the stockpile. Since 1965 they have had a mixed pattern.

Steady Growth: 1948–56. The AEC inherited many wartime facilities, notably the Manhattan Project's Los Alamos laboratory. As in the case of materials production, weapons production expenditures increased as the tension between the United States and the Soviet Union mounted. Advances in the Soviet nuclear arsenal and breakthroughs by weapons designers in the United States also helped push up expenditures.

The only constraint on the growth of the weapons production complex in the 1950s was the supply of nuclear materials. Scientists at Los Alamos were already designing new atomic weapons at the end of World War II, trying to optimize the yield of the weapons without increasing the amount of fissile materials and thus maximize the ratio of yield to weight. Such concepts as levitated cores, composite pits, and "boosted" weapons were considered during the Manhattan Project but not acted upon until the war had ended.

The AEC also spent increasingly large sums of money on thermonuclear research after World War II. Even before President Truman

87. Keith Schneider with Michael R. Gordon, "Reactor Shutdown Could Impede Nuclear Deterrent, Officials Say," *New York Times,* October 9, 1988, p. 1. Other officials were more sanguine. See Robert Gillette, "Tritium Supply Called Enough for Defense Needs," *Los Angeles Times,* October 18, 1988, p. 16; Fred Kaplan, "Tritium Shortage Isn't Critical Yet, Pentagon Says," *Boston Globe,* January 22, 1989, p. 3.

88. The DOE is also weighing the use of one or more commercial power reactors to generate small amounts of tritium, an approach that has been criticized for breaching the long-standing separation of civilian and military uses of nuclear power. A reactor at Hanford is also under consideration. See Matthew L. Wald, "U.S. to Put a Civilian Reactor to Military Use," *New York Times,* August 11, 1997, p. A10; Jim Simon, "U.S. Eyes New Task for Reactor at Hanford," *Seattle Times,* January 18, 1998, p. A1.

FIGURE 1-7. Expenditures for U.S. Nuclear Weapons Research, Development, Testing, and Production, 1942–96

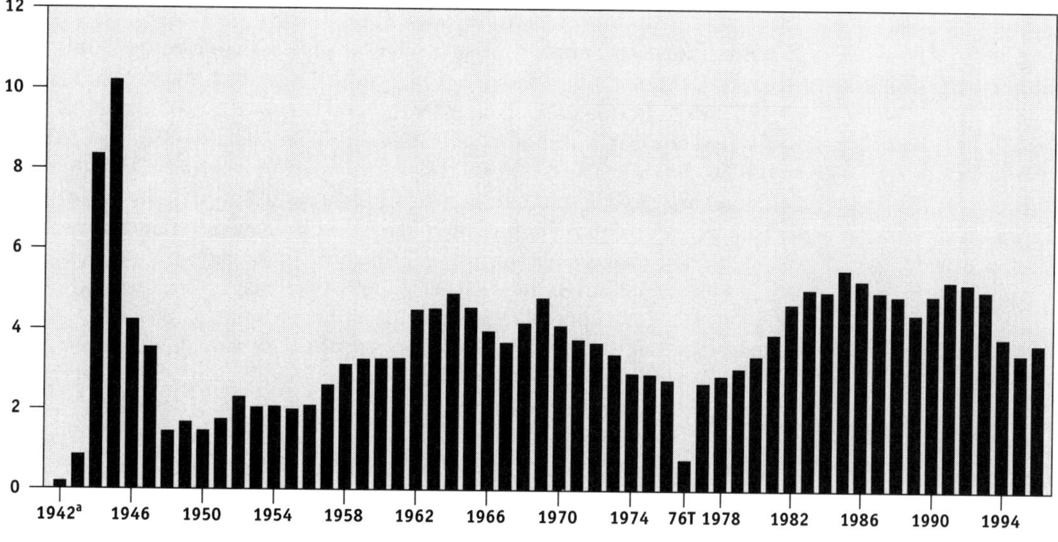

a. Figure for 1942 includes funds expended from 1940 to 1942 by the National Defense Research Committee and the Office of Scientific Research and Development. Data from 1942–47 include materials production costs.

ordered the crash development of the "so-called hydrogen or super-bomb" on January 31, 1950, the AEC had investigated the question of building thermonuclear weapons.[89] Significantly, with the exception of certain air force planners and members of the AEC's MLC, the military—particularly the Joint Chiefs of Staff—was not active in the early debates. In fact, the JCS concluded in January 1948 that "the majority of targets do not require a more powerful bomb because of area limitations [that is, hydrogen bombs were deemed too big for all but a limited number of targets]."[90]

89. Statement by the President on the Hydrogen Bomb, January 31, 1950, reprinted in Williams and Cantelon, *American Atom,* p. 131.

90. David Alan Rosenberg, "American Atomic Strategy and the Hydrogen Bomb Decision," *Journal of American History,* vol. 66 (June 1979), pp. 80–81. The MLC, "the only military planning group with direct access to the AEC's most secret atomic energy information," was instrumental in formulating JCS policy on the hydrogen bomb. In the main, developing the new weapon was considered psychologically important, because the Soviet Union should not be allowed to acquire it first. Once developed, the reasoning went, it would take the place of larger numbers of atomic bombs, providing greater destructive power while utilizing smaller amounts of critical (and expensive) fissile materials. When the JCS eventually endorsed the program in January 1950, it stressed that a "crash" program was not required. Because the AEC's budget was exempt from cuts that Truman was making in all other military programs, the support by the JCS of the hydrogen bomb had no immediate fiscal implications for the military. Had this not been the case, and had other programs been subject to reductions to allow it to get under way, Rosenberg concludes, the JCS "probably would have been reluctant to recommend it" (pp. 82–83). The JCS estimated the additional cost of the hydrogen bomb would be between $100 million and $200 million ($875 million to

In October 1949, shortly after the Soviet Union tested its first atomic bomb, the AEC's General Advisory Committee, chaired by J. Robert Oppenheimer, was asked to make recommendations on pursuing a highly accelerated program to build the Super (as the thermonuclear program was then known). In its October 30, 1949, report, the six-member GAC unanimously opposed such a program, arguing

> that the extreme dangers to mankind inherent in the proposal wholly outweigh any military advantage that could come from this development. Let it be clearly realized that this is a super weapon; it is in a totally different category from an atomic bomb. . . . We are alarmed as to the possible global effects of the radioactivity generated by the explosion of a few super bombs of conceivable magnitude. If super bombs will work at all, there is no inherent limit in the destructive power that may be attained with them. Therefore, a super bomb might become a weapon of genocide. . . . In determining not to proceed to develop the superbomb, we see a unique opportunity of providing by example some limitations on the totality of war and thus of limiting the fear and arousing the hopes of mankind.[91]

The AEC split on the recommendation of the GAC, with the majority agreeing not to proceed with a crash program. But physicists Edward Teller, Ernest O. Lawrence, and Luis Alvarez challenged the AEC's decision and aggressively promoted the idea that scientists had a fundamental duty to pursue new knowledge, whatever the costs. AEC chairman Lilienthal, in a meeting with Truman on November 9, 1949, expressed deep-seated reservations about the hydrogen bomb, arguing that it would "intensify in a new way" the arms race and signal that the United States had "abandoned our program for peace and are resigned to war." Staking national security on the Super, he asserted, would result in a "costly cycle of misconception and illusion."[92]

The JCS responded to the GAC's recommendation in a January 13, 1950, memorandum to Secretary of Defense Louis A. Johnson siding with Teller and his colleagues: "Such a weapon would improve our defense in its broadest sense, as a potential offensive weapon, a possible deterrent to war, a potential retaliatory weapon, as well as a defensive weapon against enemy forces. . . . [T]he United States would be in an intolerable position if a possible enemy possessed the bomb and the United States did not."[93] Through the end of fiscal 1952, just before

$1.75 billion in constant 1996 dollars), finding these sums "within the capability of the United States without materially interfering with improvement of existing weapons and other means of defense." See "Memorandum by the Joint Chiefs of Staff to the Secretary of Defense," January 13, 1950 (Top Secret), in S. Everett Gleason and Fredrick Aandahl, eds., *Foreign Relations of the United States 1950,* vol. 1: *National Security Affairs; Foreign Economic Policy* (GPO, 1977), pp. 503–11.

91. U.S. AEC General Advisory Committee Report on the "Super," October 30, 1949, reprinted in Williams and Cantelon, *American Atom,* pp. 120–27.

92. Quoted in Carlisle and Zenzen, *Supplying the Nuclear Arsenal,* p. 69

93. "Memorandum by the Joint Chiefs of Staff to the Secretary of Defense," January 13, 1950 (Top Secret), in Gleason and Aandahl, *Foreign Relations of the United States 1950,* pp. 505, 508.

the Ivy-Mike test, total Manhattan Project and AEC operating costs on thermonuclear weapons research exceeded $586 million (in then-year dollars).[94]

As the capacity to produce fissile materials increased, weapons production costs also increased. Until 1957 obligations for operating expenses remained below $2 billion a year (appendix table A-2). The growth of the stockpile and low annual production rates through 1957 suggest that the total obligations for operating expenses from 1948 to 1957 ($11 billion), were principally for research, development, and testing.

In comparison with the large obligations for building additional nuclear reactors, reprocessing plants, and gaseous diffusion plants, the cost of adding to or building new weapons production facilities was small. At this point, there was less need to build new facilities. Many weapons production complex sites were left over from the Manhattan Project, while industrial plants that would contribute nonnuclear components only needed to be converted from other defense contracting work. Of the new facilities, most were built or converted in the late 1940s and early 1950s. Construction at the Mound Laboratory began in 1947, and at the Kansas City Plant in 1949. Operations at NTS and Rocky Flats began in 1951 and 1952, respectively. The Pantex Plant (originally used to load TNT into conventional shells during WWII) was renovated in 1950 and began assembling nuclear weapons in 1952. The Lawrence Radiation Laboratory was founded in 1952. In 1956, a branch of Sandia Laboratories opened at Livermore.[95]

Peak of Buildup: 1957–65. By 1960 the output of AEC's plutonium production and uranium enrichment plants was sufficient to produce nuclear weapons at an unprecedented rate: more than 7,000 warheads annually, compared with only about 140 in 1950–51. Between 1959 and 1961, the United States produced 14,884 warheads, bringing its total stockpile to 24,173 warheads and bombs, or three times the total number in 1957.[96]

The growth in R&D and production obligations at the end of the decade is consistent with the development and manufacturing of large quantities of new and more sophisticated weapons. Research costs between 1957 and 1961 increased by $202 million, while production obligations nearly doubled, from $1 billion in 1957 to $1.9 billion dur-

94. Letter from AEC Chairman Lewis Strauss to JCAE Chairman Sterling Cole, November 20, 1953, AEC 493/26, Secretariat Collection, Box 4930, Folder MR+A Thermonuclear Weapon, vol. 2, DOE Archives.

95. The details of how these and other weapons production facilities were sited can be found in History Associates Incorporated, *History of the Production Complex: The Methods of Site Selection*, prepared for U.S. Department of Energy, Assistant Secretary for Defense Programs, Office of Nuclear Materials (September 1987).

96. Robert S. Norris and Thomas B. Cochran, *US-USSR/Russian Strategic Offensive Nuclear Forces, 1945–1996*, NWD-97-1 (Natural Resources Defense Council, January 1997), table 9.

ing the same period. Obligations for both R&D and production would remain above $1 billion a year for the rest of the decade.

By contrast, obligations for nuclear testing at the end of the 1950s steadily declined. This reflected the Eisenhower administration's decision, effective October 31, 1958, to observe a one-year nuclear testing moratorium (joined by the Soviet Union and the United Kingdom and subsequently extended through the end of 1959) and to attempt to negotiate a comprehensive test ban with the Soviet Union. During the course of these negotiations, in 1960 and 1961, both countries refrained from testing despite the expiration of the joint moratorium. When General Secretary Nikita Khrushchev announced on August 30, 1961, that the Soviet Union intended to resume testing—and then proceeded, between September 1 and November 4, to detonate fifty-nine nuclear devices, including a massive 50-megaton blast (a reduced yield version of a 100-megaton bomb)—U.S. officials were taken by surprise, and the AEC scrambled to resume testing. (Within two weeks the first U.S. test was conducted underground at NTS; eight more would follow by the end of the year. It was not until the following spring that the United States resumed atmospheric testing, reflecting the difficulty and expense of testing at the Pacific Proving Ground.) The test ban negotiations eventually resumed during the spring of 1962. Following the Cuban Missile Crisis in October 1962, which sobered both Khrushchev and President John F. Kennedy on the potential for nuclear war, the two sides continued to talk. Concerns about verification and the opposition of the JCS to a total ban (see footnote 112) eventually led to the Partial Test Ban Treaty, which prohibited all nuclear testing in the atmosphere, underwater, and in outer space.

As a result of the moratorium, testing expenditures declined from $473 million in 1958 to $124 million in 1961.[97] Testing aboveground resumed briefly in 1961, before the PTBT forced all nuclear testing underground.[98] The decision to conduct underground tests freed the

97. Expenditures did not decline to zero because the United States retained the capability to resume testing on short notice and because forty-six very low yield tests were conducted at Los Alamos and the Nevada Test Site between 1958 and 1961 in order to study the unforeseen risk of an accidental explosion caused by a serious defect in a warhead (probably the W47, which was rushed into production just before the moratorium and deployed with the Polaris SLBM). One analyst noted that in developing this warhead, scientists at Livermore "paid much more attention to achieving workable designs than to avoiding vulnerabilities." See R. E. Kidder, *Maintaining the U.S. Stockpile of Nuclear Weapons during a Low-Threshold or Comprehensive Test Ban*, UCRL-53820 (Livermore, Calif.: Lawrence Livermore National Laboratory, October 1987), pp. 16–17; letter from K. J. Germeshausen, President, Edgerton, Germeshausen & Grier, Inc., to V. W. Luckett, Contract Administrator, Albuquerque Operations Office, U.S. Atomic Energy Commission, October 13, 1961, DOE Archives. (This letter states in part, "As you are aware, during the moratorium we maintained a capability and were able to recently place in the field experienced personnel on very short notice.") See also Robert N. Thorn and Donald R. Westervelt, "Hydronuclear Experiments," Los Alamos National Laboratory, February 1987 (available in Virginia Foran, ed., *Nuclear Nonproliferation, 1945–1990* [Alexandria, Va.: Chadwick-Healey, 1992]); "U.S. N-testing Violations in 1958–61 Found," *San Jose Mercury News*, February 27, 1987, p. 8F.

98. Between September 15, 1961, and November 4, 1962, the United States conducted 114 nuclear tests, 94 of which took place in 1962 alone. Forty-three of these tests were in the atmosphere. Totals do not include five Plowshare tests.

U.S. testing program from the constraints imposed by seasonal weather changes and also limited (but did not eliminate) the incidence of nuclear fallout and its impact on the environment, an issue that had made aboveground testing controversial from the beginning. Now that the AEC was able to conduct more tests per year, costs again rose.[99] In addition, the cost per test increased because preparing for an underground test necessitated the drilling of test and monitoring shafts. These factors pushed annual testing obligations beyond $1 billion in 1964, where they stayed for the next several years.

With the resumption of nuclear testing, the AEC ran into serious public relations problems. Attempting to cast nuclear weapons as a constructive rather than destructive force, it proposed Project Plowshare, which would demonstrate the use of atomic explosions to dig harbors, cut through mountain passes, and perhaps even dig a new Panama Canal. One group, which included Edward Teller, proposed detonating nuclear weapons in natural gas fields to stimulate the production of that resource. Studies of that concept began in 1958, with twenty-seven nuclear tests conducted in Nevada, Colorado, and New Mexico from 1961 to 1973.[100] Although the AEC claimed that fallout from such projects would be minimal, experience proved otherwise. The PTBT also severely hampered the ability to test the basic principles of the program. That, coupled with fierce public opposition and a decrease in available funds due to the escalating costs of the war in Vietnam, led to Plowshare's ultimate demise in 1977 (by which time the program was known as Peaceful Nuclear Explosions). Costs for the program were more than $770 million.[101]

99. In 1956 and 1957 the United States conducted 18 and 32 tests, respectively. In 1964 and 1965, the number of tests rose to 45 and 38, respectively. See NRDC Nuclear Notebook, "Known Nuclear Tests Worldwide, 1945–1995," *Bulletin of the Atomic Scientists,* vol. 52 (May/June 1996), pp. 61–63.

100. The Soviet Union had an even more ambitious program: between January 1965 and September 1988 it exploded 116 nuclear devices for civil engineering projects and geological exploration. In 1996 China expressed interest in using a nuclear blast to divert water from the Brahmaputra River to irrigate its northwest territory (however, some considered this a last-minute effort to create an exception to the Comprehensive Test Ban Treaty). Health and safety were not always paramount concerns for the Soviet Union. On September 16, 1979, a low-yield (0.3-kiloton) nuclear device was secretly detonated in a coal mine in Ukraine, near the town of Yunokommunarovsk in an attempt to disperse explosive methane gas. One day later, thousands of miners were told to return to work, with no warnings or inclination of any dangers. Until 1992 Russian authorities continued to tell the 8,000 townspeople that high local radiation levels were the result of the 1986 accident at Chernobyl, despite the fact that this event occurred at the other end of the region. See Kathy Lally, "Soviet Building Projects Used 116 Nuclear Blasts," *Baltimore Sun,* November 2, 1994, p. 1; Thomas B. Cochran, Robert S. Norris, and Oleg A. Bukharin, *Making the Russian Bomb: From Stalin to Yeltsin* (Boulder, Colo.: Westview Press, 1995), pp. 45–46; John Horgan, "'Peaceful' Nuclear Explosions," *Scientific American,* June 1996, pp. 14–15; John-Thor Dahalburg, "Soviet Nuclear Bomb Drive Took a Vast Human Toll," *Los Angeles Times* (Washington edition), September 3, 1992, p. A1; Ministry of the Russian Federation for Atomic Energy and the Ministry of Defense of the Russian Federation, *USSR Nuclear Weapons Tests and Peaceful Nuclear Explosions: 1949 through 1990* (Sarov, Russia: RFNC-VNIIEF, 1996), p. 36.

101. For the fascinating history of Project Chariot, Edward Teller's pet project to blast a harbor near Point Hope, Alaska, with nuclear weapons, see Dan O'Neill, *The Firecracker Boys* (New York: St. Martin's Press, 1994). Although Project Chariot never proceeded to the blasting phase, nearly $27 million was spent on a massive and unprecedented environmental survey of the area around Point Hope before the effort was canceled. For a detailed history of the Plowshare program, see Trevor Findlay, *Nuclear Dynamite: The Peaceful Nuclear Explosions Fiasco* (Sydney: Brassey's Australia, 1990).

Mixed Pattern: 1965 to the Present. Between 1965 and 1975 the total budget authority, including operating expenses and capital purchases, at first rose (to $4.8 billion in 1969) and then dropped below $3 billion by the mid-1970s. Then, during the late 1970s and continuing into the early 1990s, annual spending increased to levels well above the peak production years of the late 1950s.

Research and Development. Between 1966 and 1996 research and development budget authority totaled an estimated $34 billion, or approximately 27 percent of the overall weapons program operating expenses. As appendix table A-2 shows, R&D expenditures divided among the three nuclear weapons laboratories and other DOE laboratories surpassed $1 billion a year for the better part of the 1960s before declining during the next decade. Indeed, estimated annual operating costs for R&D in 1979 were $278.3 million lower than they had been in 1966.

These trends reversed course toward the end of the Carter administration with the commencement of the Stockpile Improvement Program (SIP). In 1979 the DOD and DOE initiated the SIP to identify both strategic and tactical warheads and weapon systems that needed to be "modernized, retired, or replaced."[102] Embracing this effort, the Reagan administration rapidly increased nuclear weapons R&D to well over $1 billion a year by the middle of the decade.

Today research and development spending often is committed to ongoing, "big-ticket" programs, such as lasers, particle accelerators, or other sophisticated test and research facilities that are designed to simulate the conditions of a nuclear explosion in the absence of actual full-scale tests. The inertial confinement fusion (ICF) program is such an attempt, with research efforts divided between the three weapons labs. In the ICF program, high-powered lasers are focused on a small target of tritium and deuterium, causing the target materials to fuse. Since 1974 this program has cost approximately $4 billion, which includes operating and capital expenses. The DOE is currently building a new, multibillion ICF facility called the National Ignition Facility (NIF) at Livermore. NIF has a projected $4.5 billion price tag (not factoring in inflation), which includes annual operating costs for its expected thirty-year life span.[103] Proponents of NIF say it will help maintain confidence in the nuclear stockpile in the absence of nuclear

102. *Energy and Water Development Appropriations for Fiscal Year 1989,* Hearings before the Energy and Water Development Appropriations Subcommittee of the House Appropriations Committee, 100 Cong. 2 sess. (GPO, 1988), pt. 6, p. 966.

103. U.S. Department of Energy, *FY 1996 Congressional Budget Request: Project Data Sheets,* vol. 1, DOE/CR-0031 (February 1996), pp. 327–33. Between February 1996 and February 1997, NIF's total project construction cost increased by $125.3 million to $1.2 billion owing to changes in its design and a one-year delay in initial operations (to mid-2003). See U.S. Department of Energy, *FY 1998 Congressional Budget Request: Atomic Energy Defense Activities,* vol. 1, DOE/CR-0041, (February 1997), pp. 129–30.

testing and keep weapons scientists from leaving the weapons laboratories by allowing them to conduct cutting-edge physics experiments. Critics counter that crucial precursor experiments to demonstrate NIF's validity will not be completed until well after construction has begun and that the program is actually a payoff to the laboratories in exchange for their support for the CTBT.[104]

A second major program to receive significant R&D funding during the 1980s and early 1990s was the effort to develop a space-based X-ray laser to shoot down Soviet ballistic missiles. Developed in conjunction with President Reagan's Strategic Defense Initiative (SDI), this program proposed using the detonation of a nuclear device to generate and direct beams of focused X-ray energy at Soviet ballistic missiles, destroying them in their first few minutes of flight.[105]

Press accounts in October 1987 revealed that two years earlier Roy D. Woodruff, a former associate director for defense systems at Livermore, had charged that Edward Teller and others at the laboratory had provided many senior policymakers, including President Reagan's science adviser George Keyworth and CIA director William Casey, with "overly optimistic, technically incorrect" information about the program (they suggested, for example, that the laser could be made as small as a desk and could fire up to 100,000 separate laser beams to destroy ballistic missiles as they were boosted into orbit). According to Woodruff, laboratory director Roger E. Batzel was "fully aware" of the misleading information but refused to correct it and forbade Woodruff to do so. Unable to reign in the erroneous statements and unwilling to make the classified matter public, Woodruff resigned as associate director on October 29, 1985 (his charges were later leaked to the press). A

104. See William J. Broad, "Vast Laser Would Advance Fusion and Retain Bomb Experts," *New York Times,* June 21, 1994, p. C1; William J. Broad, "U.S. Will Build Laser to Create Nuclear Fusion," *New York Times,* October 21, 1994, p. A1; Hugh Gusterson, "NIF-ty Exercise Machine," *Bulletin of the Atomic Scientists,* vol. 51 (September/October 1995), pp. 22–26; Jacqueline Cabasso and John Burroughs, "End Run around the NPT," *Bulletin of the Atomic Scientists,* vol. 51 (September/October, 1995), pp. 27–29; Loren Stein, "New Superlaser to Test Nuclear Arms," *Christian Science Monitor,* December 18, 1995, p. 4; Tom Zamora Collina, "The National Ignition Facility: Buyer Beware," *Technology Review,* vol. 100 (February/March 1997), pp. 35–40; Andrew Lawler, "NIF Ignites Changes at Livermore," *Science,* vol. 275 (February 28, 1997), pp. 1252–54; letter from Thomas B. Cochran, Christopher E. Paine, and Barbara A. Finamore, Natural Resources Defense Council, to Professor Henry W. Kendall, Massachusetts Institute of Technology, April 17, 1997.

105. Reagan first proposed SDI during a nationally televised speech on March 23, 1983. He did not mention that the nuclear-pumped X-ray laser would be used to destroy other nuclear weapons. An administration official later claimed the president was unaware of the laser's power source at the time of the speech, despite being briefed on the system by Edward Teller. The day after Reagan's speech, Secretary of Defense Caspar W. Weinberger reportedly asked Richard DeLauer, his undersecretary for research and engineering, whether it was in fact a bomb. DeLauer suggested that in upcoming testimony before the Senate Weinberger characterize it as "a nuclear event." Weinberger, said one DOD official, "close[d] his eyes to reality" and instead said it was "like an X-ray generating device." Weinberger and Reagan surprised SDI officials in February 1985 when they stated that the program's goal was a nonnuclear defense, seemingly ruling out the X-ray laser, which at that time was crucial to the program. Deployment of the X-ray laser would have violated the Outer Space Treaty of 1967 and the ABM Treaty of 1972. See Janne E. Nolan, *Guardians of the Arsenal: The Politics of Nuclear Strategy* (New York: Basic Books, 1989), pp. 165–67; Gregg Herken, "The Earthly Origins of Star Wars," *Bulletin of the Atomic Scientists,* vol. 43 (October 1987), pp. 20–28.

1988 GAO report and a subsequent congressional investigation confirmed Woodruff's accusations.[106]

This misinformation altered, perhaps profoundly, the course of and expenditures for SDI, as well as strategic arms control negotiations with the Soviet Union. At the October 1986 summit in Reykjavik, Iceland, President Reagan adamantly refused to limit SDI research and testing to the laboratory (thus dashing any hope that *all* nuclear weapons would be eliminated within ten years, as agreed in earlier talks at the summit between Reagan and Soviet President Mikhail Gorbachev), at least in part because he believed that the X-ray laser—then the centerpiece of SDI—was a viable weapon system.[107] Yet, had SDI been limited and this sweeping and historic agreement enacted, the threat SDI was designed to address might by now have disappeared. Between 1984 and 1992 (when the X-ray laser was effectively canceled), the DOE labs obligated an estimated $2.2 billion of R&D funds to this and other weapons concepts making up the directed-energy weapons program.[108] This cost is covered in chapter 4 and does not count toward the overall total in this chapter.

After leveling off during the Bush administration, expenditures once again began to rise under President Clinton. Much of this funding has been directed to basic research. In recent years, the DOE has assigned high priority to "the fundamental scientific, engineering and facility capabilities" that underlie specific nuclear weapons research, even though there are currently no plans to develop new weapons.[109] Proponents of technology-based research argue that even under a comprehensive test ban weapons labs need to maintain a certain level of expertise in order to ensure that the nuclear stockpile remains safe and reliable in the absence of nuclear tests. Much of the funding under the Bush and Clinton administrations has gone to such activities. In fiscal

106. Dan Morain and Richard E. Meyer, "Teller Gave Flawed Data on X-Ray Laser, Scientist Says," *Los Angeles Times*, October 21, 1987, p. A1; William J. Broad, "Dispute on X-Ray Laser Erupts at Weapons Lab," *New York Times*, October 22, 1987, p. 11; U.S. General Accounting Office, *Strategic Defense Initiative Program: Accuracy of Statements Concerning DoE's X-Ray Laser Research Program*, NSIAD-88-181BR (June 1988); Robert Scheer, "The Man Who Blew the Whistle on 'Star Wars'," *Los Angeles Times Magazine*, July 17, 1988, pp. 7–14, 29–32; William J. Broad, "Scientist's Optimism on Powerful Lasers Fostered 'Star Wars,'" *New York Times*, August 1, 1988, p. A13.

107. A cogent account of the Reykjavik summit can be found in Raymond L. Garthoff, *The Great Transition: American-Soviet Relations and the End of the Cold War* (Brookings, 1994), pp. 285–99.

108. Ten known tests of the X-ray laser were conducted between 1978 and 1988. The third test was conducted just three days after Reagan's speech. Three of the tests were failures. At least one additional test—said to cost some $110 million—was in preparation when the Bush administration, in an effort to head off congressional calls for a test ban, restricted nuclear testing in mid-1992 to safety and reliability purposes. Of the many proposed NDEW concepts, only the X-ray laser proceeded to the development phase. See Norris and Cochran, "United States Nuclear Tests: June 1945 to 31 December 1992," pp. 47–52; Michael R. Gordon, "'Star Wars' X-Ray Laser Weapon Dies As Its Final Test Is Canceled," *New York Times*, July 21, 1992, p. A1.

109. U.S. Congress, Energy and Water Development Appropriations Subcommittee, House Appropriations Committee, "Atomic Energy Defense Activities," FY 1995, vol. 20 (GPO, 1994), pt. 4, p. 82; Eric Rosenberg, "A Debate Brews over Whether to Build a New Nuclear Warhead," *Defense Week*, August 16, 1994, p. 1; Eric Rosenberg, "Military Is Undecided over Building New Nuclear Warhead," *Defense Week*, August 22, 1994, p. 2; Elaine M. Grossman, "DoD Says It Needs No New Nuclear Designs, But Leaves Door Open," *Inside the Pentagon*, October 9, 1997, pp. 5, 6.

1996, the DOE moved in this direction under the stockpile stewardship and management program. Projected average annual costs over the next decade for stockpile stewardship (formerly R&D, testing, and weapons production)—$4.5 billion (in 1998 dollars)—are now higher than the average annual costs during the cold war ($3.6 billion).[110]

Nuclear Testing. The United States formally discontinued nuclear tests aboveground, underwater, and in outer space following the enactment of the Partial Test Ban Treaty on October 10, 1963.[111] However, 825 underground tests were conducted at NTS beginning in 1957, the last in September 1992. Although the PTBT outlawed all but underground tests, a little-noticed provision, known as Safeguard C, allowed the United States to maintain the capability to resume atmospheric testing promptly, should national security imperatives require it to do so. This safeguard was secured by the Joint Chiefs of Staff in exchange for the military's support for the treaty's ratification.[112] For thirty years, the DOE (and its predecessor agencies), working with the Defense Nuclear Agency and its predecessors, maintained Safeguard C facilities in Nevada, Hawaii, and Johnston Island (the site of a command post shielded against the effects of nuclear blasts), about 800 miles (1,287 kilometers) southwest of Honolulu, Hawaii. If a president decided to resume testing, scientists and engineers at the post would remove Thor ballistic missiles and nuclear warheads from storage and would mate and launch them. The program was equipped with ships, aircraft, laboratories, launch pads, and a dedicated staff to keep everything ready for use on short notice.[113] Up to 1993—when Congress became aware of the program and canceled it—the DOD and the DOE and its predecessors had spent at least $1.6 billion, and perhaps as much as $3 billion, on Safeguard C.[114]

110. Ralph Vartabedian, "Cost of Keeping Nuclear Arms Rises, U.S. Says," *Los Angeles Times*, September 27, 1997, p. A15; Pete V. Domenici, "New Nuclear Policy," Letter to the Editor, *New York Times*, December 7, 1997, sec. 4, p. 16.

111. The last atmospheric test actually occurred on November 4, 1962, 13 miles (20.9 kilometers) above Johnston Island in the Pacific.

112. The members of the JCS at the time the treaty was being negotiated consisted of General Maxwell D. Taylor (chairman), General Earle G. Wheeler (army), General Curtis E. LeMay (air force), Admiral George W. Anderson (navy), and General David M. Shoup (Marine Corps). Safeguard C was one of four requirements agreed to by President Kennedy in order to secure passage and ratification of the PTBT. The other three were a commitment by the president "to conduct a comprehensive and continuing underground test program, to maintain the vitality of the weapons laboratories, and to improve verification capabilities." See Committee on International Security and Arms Control, *Nuclear Arms Control: Background and Issues* (Washington, D.C.: National Academy Press, 1985), p. 195; *Public Papers of the Presidents of the United States, John F. Kennedy, 1963* (GPO, 1964), pp. 669–71.

113. Tim Weiner, "If a Call Comes: Bomb Team Set for More Tests," *New York Times*, June 9, 1993, p. A1.

114. The joint administration of this program by DOD and AEC/ERDA/DOE, the secrecy surrounding it, the fact that the program was never audited in its thirty-year existence, and fragmentary budget data prevent a more accurate accounting of all the associated costs. In 1992 the DOE estimated that it would spend "approximately $113,000 ($120,700 in 1996 dollars) in 1993 to support Safeguard C activities. See letter from Richard A. Claytor, Assistant Secretary for Defense Programs, Department of Energy, to the

Testing costs between 1966 and 1996 were approximately $20 billion, or about 20 percent of the total weapons budget since 1966. Annual costs are listed in appendix table A-2. The expenditures on nuclear testing, like those for R&D, rose steadily through the 1960s, declined during the 1970s, and increased rapidly in the 1980s. After peaking in 1969 at nearly $1.4 billion, spending began to decline. By 1974, as superpower relations warmed under détente, spending on nuclear testing dropped to $515 million in new budget authority. New test ban initiatives, such as the Threshold Test Ban Treaty (TTBT) in 1974 and the Peaceful Nuclear Explosions Treaty (PNET) in 1976 were initialed by the United States and the Soviet Union, and in 1977 new talks on a comprehensive test ban were begun. Testing expenditures during the 1970s were regularly one-half of expenditures during the previous decade.

Under Presidents Reagan and Bush, this trend was reversed with estimated annual operating expenses for nuclear testing reaching as high as $700 million or more in the mid-1980s. Between 1981 and 1992, when the United States conducted its most recent nuclear test, the DOE spent some $7.2 billion on testing.[115]

Production and Surveillance. Producing new warheads and maintaining the operational readiness of existing warheads is by far the most expensive aspect of the nuclear weapons program. Between 1966 and 1996 the DOE and its predecessor agencies spent $53 billion on weapons production activities, or 49 percent of the total operating budget (appendix table A-2). In every year of this period except 1976 and 1977, new budget authority for weapons production and surveillance was in excess of $1 billion. Production spending fell during 1966–69, rose to more than $1.4 billion per year in 1971–72, fell again (to $953 million) in 1977, then resumed its climb. Annual spending exceeded $2 billion in 1983—the first time in nearly twenty years—and remained in excess of $2 billion a year for the next ten years.

Honorable Michael J. Kopetski, U.S. House of Representatives, April 15, 1992, p. 3.

115. Although no full-scale nuclear tests have been conducted since September 21, 1992, the DOE plans to conduct six subcritical or "zero-yield" experiments underneath the NTS in 1997 and 1998 as part of its stockpile stewardship program; the first three were carried out on July 2 and September 18, 1997, and March 25, 1998. The experiments reportedly cost $15 million each, but by July 1997, just preparing for them had consumed between $77 million and $100 million (in then-year dollars). These are not nuclear tests in the classical sense and will not result in a self-sustaining chain reaction or a nuclear explosion (events banned under the CTBT). See U.S. Department of Energy, "Statement of the Secretary of Energy Federico Peña on the Schedule for Subcritical Experiments," April 4, 1997; Keith Rogers, "Nuclear Material Tests Planned," *Las Vegas Review-Journal,* April 5, 1997, p. 1A; Ralph Vartabedian, "Plan to Build Nuclear Weapons Facilities Is Illegal, Suit Says," *Los Angeles Times* (Washington edition), May 1, 1997, p. B5; Matthew L. Wald, "Lab's Task: Assuring Bomb's Quality without Pulling Nuclear Trigger," *New York Times* (Washington edition), June 3, 1997, p. A15; Peter Weiss, "Costs Spiral on Underground Nuclear Testing," *Valley Times,* July 1, 1997, p. A1.

Paradoxically, spending increased while the number of stockpiled weapons declined. According to reliable, unclassified estimates, the stockpile peaked at about 32,200 warheads in 1966 and declined to approximately 10,400 in 1996.[116] In fact, this overall decline was irregular. After initially declining in the late 1960s, the stockpile increased to about 28,500 warheads in 1973. Much of this increase was due to the production of multiple independently targeted reentry vehicle (MIRV) warhead systems on intercontinental and submarine-launched missiles. The strategic component of the U.S. stockpile increased by 5,300 bombs and warheads between 1966 and 1974, even as the total stockpile declined from 32,200 warheads to 28,300 warheads over the same period.

The next period of significant budgetary increase—during the Reagan administration—also corresponds to increases in the strategic arsenal. Calling for substantial modernization, the administration forged ahead with new bombs and warheads for several new weapons systems. Many systems, notably the W87 (MX), W88 (Trident II/D-5), the W-80 (Air-Launched Cruise Missile), and the B-83 gravity bomb, replaced existing weapons, while others, such as the W79 artillery shell, W84 (Ground-Launched Cruise Missile), and W85 (Pershing II Missile) were deployed along with existing forces (see table 1-3).

Stockpile maintenance also pushed up costs even as the arsenal dwindled in size. The AEC, ERDA, and DOE periodically disassembled and inspected stockpiled warheads to certify that they would explode as designed. Since the AEC began its Stockpile Evaluation Program (SEP) in 1958, more than 13,800 weapons of forty-five types have been disassembled, inspected, and tested, and only 400 findings have been deemed "actionable," requiring a modification to either the warhead or the production process that created it or a lowering of the warhead's presumed yield or reliability. Most of these findings occurred within the first few years of a warhead's entry into the stockpile; as weapons age, fewer fixes have been required. What age-related problems have occurred are almost entirely within the realm of nonnuclear components and thus can be fully assessed and corrected without resorting to nuclear tests. Between 1980 and 1992, 1,414 weapons were disassembled, inspected, and ultimately disposed of while another 2,449 were disassembled, inspected, and then reassembled using original or replacement parts. The weapons in this latter category were then redeployed.[117] This work continues today (see chapter 5). Warheads were

116. Norris and Cochran, *US-USSR/Russian Strategic Offensive Nuclear Forces*, table 9.

117. Letter and enclosures, Elva Ann Barfield, Freedom of Information Officer, Albuquerque Operations Office, Department of Energy, to Hisham Zerriffi, Staff Scientist, Institute for Energy and Environmental Research, January 5, 1996. This document is extensively analyzed in Hisham Zerriffi and Arjun Makhijani, *The Nuclear Safety Smokescreen: Warhead Safety and Reliability and the Science Based Stockpile Stewardship Program* (Takoma Park, Md.: Institute for Energy and

TABLE 1-3. U.S. Nuclear Warheads, 1945–97

Warhead[a]	*Yield (Kt)*	*Delivery system*	*Service*[b]	*Entered military service*[c]	*Retirement*	*Laboratory*[d]	*Number*[e]
Little Boy[f]	15	Bomb (B-29)	AF	August 1945	1950	LANL	5
Fat Man	21	Bomb (B-29)	AF	August 1945	1949	LANL	8
Mk-III (B3)	18–49	Bomb (B-29, B-50)	AF	1947	1950	LANL	150
Mk-IV (B4)	1–31	Bomb (B-29, B-50, B-36, A-2)	AF	1949	1953	LANL	550
Mk-5 (B5)	11–47	Bomb (B-29, B-50, B-45, B-47, B-66, A-2, A-3)	AF,N	1952	1962	LANL	140
Mk-5 (W5)	11–47	Regulus I	N	1955	1962	LANL	200
		Matador	AF	1955	1961	LANL	65
		Rascal GAM-63[g]	AF	Canceled March 1956		LANL	0
		Rigel SSM[g]	N	Canceled August 1953		LANL	0
		Hermes SSM[g]	A	Canceled August 1953		LANL	0
Mk-6 (B6)	8–160	Bomb (B-29, B-50, B-36, B-47, B-66, A-2, A-3)	AF,N	1951	1960	LANL	1,100
Mk-7 (B7)	8–61	Bomb (B-45, B-57, F-84, F-100, F-101, A-1, A-2, A-4, F-1, F-2, F-9)	AF,N	1952	1967	LANL	470
B7 (Betty)	8–61	Depth Bomb (P-2, S-2, SH-34)	N	1955	1960	LANL	225
Mk-7 (W7)	2–40	BOAR (A-1)	N	1953	1966	LANL	225
	0.09–47	Corporal	A	1954	1964	LANL	300
	2 and 30	Honest John	A	1954	1958	LANL	300
		Project A ADM	A	1954	?	LANL	25
Mk-8 (B8)[f]	25–30	Bomb (Elsie) (A-1, A-2, A-3, A-4, F-2, F-3, B-45)	N, AF	1952	1957	LANL	40
Mk-8 (W8)	25–30	Regulus I	N	Canceled May 1955		LANL	0
Mk-9[f]	15	280-mm howitzer	A	1952	1957	LANL	80
TX-10 (B10)[f]	12–15	Bomb	AF,N	Canceled May 1952 (B12)		LANL	0
Mk-11 (B11)[f]	?	Bomb (A-1, A-4, F-3)	N	1953	1960	LANL	40
Mk-12 (B12)	12 and 14	Bomb (F-86, A-2, A-3, A-4, F-1, F-3, F-9)	AF,N	1955	1962	LANL	250
Mk-12 (W12)	?	Talos/TADM	N,A	Canceled November 1955 (W30)		LANL	0
TX-13 (B13)	32	Bomb	AF	Canceled August 1954 (B18)		LANL	0
TX-13 (W13)	32	Snark/Navajo SSM[g]	AF	Canceled September 1954		LANL	0
EC-14[h]	5,000–7,000	TN Bomb	AF	February 1954	10/54	LANL	5
Mk-15 (B15)[h]	1,690 and 3,400	TN Bomb (B-36, B-47, B-52, A-3)	AF,N	1955	1965	LANL	1,200
Mk-15 (W15)[h]	1,690 and 3,400	Snark/Redstone	AF,A	Canceled January 1956 (W39)		LANL	0

EC-16[h]	?	TN Bomb	AF	March 1954	4/54	LANL	5
EC-17[h]	?	TN Bomb	AF	May 1954	11/54	LANL	5
Mk-17 (B17)[h]	10,000–15,000	TN Bomb (B-36)	AF	1954	1957	LANL	200
Mk-18 (B18)	500	Bomb (B-36, B-47)	AF	1953	1956	LANL	90
S19[f]	15	280-mm howitzer	A	1956	1962	LANL	80
B20	?	TN Bomb	AF	Canceled August 1954 (B15)		LANL	0
B21	4,000–5,000	TN Bomb (B-36, B-52)	AF	1956	1957	LANL	50
B22	1,000	TN Bomb	AF	Canceled April 1954 (B21)		LANL	0
S23[f]	15–20	16-inch gun	N	1956	1962	LANL	50
EC24	?	TN Bomb	AF	April 1954	11/54	LANL	10
B24	10,000–15,000	TN Bomb (B-36)	AF	1954	1956	LANL	105
EC25	1–2	Genie	AF	November 1956	7/57	LANL	20
W25	1–2	Genie (F-89, F-101, F-106)	AF	1957	1984	LANL	5,000
		Honest John Jr.	A	Canceled February 1956		LANL	0
B26	?	TN Bomb	AF	Canceled in favor of B21		LANL	0
B27	2,000	TN Bomb (A-2, A-3, A-5)	N	1959	1964	LLNL	700
W27	1,900	Regulus I, II	N	1959	1965	LLNL	25
		Triton SSM[g]	N	Canceled December 1955		LLNL	0
		Matador	AF	Canceled November 1956 (W28)		LLNL	0
B28	70, 350, 1,100, 1,450	TN Bomb (B-47, B-52, B-66, F-100, F-101, F-104, F-105, F-4, F-111, FB-111, A-3, A-4, A-5, A-6, A-7)	AF,N	1958	1991	LANL	5,000
W28	11–1,100	Hound Dog (B-52)	AF	1960	1975	LANL	600
		Mace A/B	AF	1959	1969	LANL	100
B29	?	TN Bomb	AF	Canceled August 1955 (B15/39)		LANL	0
W30	2	Talos	N	1959	1978	LANL	300
		TADM	A,MC	1961	1966	LANL	300
		Bomarc	AF	Canceled early 1959 (W40)		LANL	0
W31	2 and 30	Honest John	A	1958	1984	LANL	1,750
	2, 20, and 30	Nike Hercules	A	1958	1988	LANL	3,000
	1–40	ADM	A,MC	1960	1965	LANL	300
		Crossbow ASM[g]	AF	Canceled January 1957		LANL	0
S32	?	240-mm howitzer	A	Canceled May 1955 (W48)		LANL	0
W33[f]	5–10	8-inch howitzer	A,MC	1957	1991	LANL	1,200

TABLE 1-3. U.S. Nuclear Warheads, 1945–97 (*Continued*)

Warhead[a]	*Yield (Kt)*	*Delivery system*	*Service*[b]	*Entered military service*[c]	*Retirement*	*Laboratory*[d]	*Number*[e]
W34	11	Lulu (Mk-101) (P-2, S-2, SH-3, SH-34, A-1)	N	1958	1971	LANL	1,000
		Hotpoint (Mk-105) (A-1, A-3, A-4, F-1)	N	1958	1965	LANL	600
		ASTOR torpedo	N	1960	1977	LANL	600
W35	1,750	Atlas	AF	Canceled December 1957 (W49)		LANL	0
		Titan	AF	Canceled (W38)		LANL	0
		Thor	AF	Canceled December 1957 (W49)		LANL	0
		Jupiter	AF	Canceled December 1957 (W49)		LANL	0
B36	10,000	TN Bomb (B-36, B-47, B-52)	AF,N	1956	1961	LANL	940
W37	?	Nike Hercules	A	Canceled October 1956 (W31)		LANL	0
W38	4,500	Atlas E/F	AF	1961	1965	LLNL	110
	4,500	Titan I	AF	1962	1965	LLNL	65
B39	3,000–4,000	TN Bomb (B-36, B-47, B-52, B-58)	AF	1957	1966	LLNL	700
W39	3,000–4,000	Snark	AF	1960	1961	LLNL	30
	425 and 3,800	Redstone	A	1958	1964	LLNL	60
		Navaho SSM[g]	AF	Canceled July 1957		LLNL	0
W40	10	Bomarc	AF	1959	1972	LANL	400
	1.7 and 10	Lacrosse	A/MC	1959	1964	LANL	1,000
		Corvus ASM[g]	N	Canceled August 1960		LANL	0
B41	5,000	TN Bomb (B-47, B-52)	AF	1960	1976	LLNL	500
W41		Unnamed ICBM	AF	Canceled July 1957		LLNL	0
W42		Hawk SAM[g]	A	Canceled December 1960		LLNL	0
		Falcon	AF	Canceled June 1961 (W54)		LLNL	0
		Sparrow AAM[g]	N	Canceled January 1958		LLNL	0
		Eagle AAM[g]	N	Canceled circa March 1961		LLNL	0
B43	70, 500 and 1,000	TN Bomb (B-47, B-52, B-57, B-58, F-100, F-101, F-104, F-105, F-4, F-111, FB-111, A-1, A-3, A-4, A-5, A-6, A-7, F-1)	AF,N,MC	1961	1991	LANL	3,000
W44	10	ASROC	N	1961	1989	LANL	600
W45	<1–15	MADM	A,MC	1965	1986	LLNL	350
	1.7 and 10	Little John	A	1962	1965	LLNL	500
	1.7	Terrier	N	1962	1987	LLNL	300

	<1–15	Bullpup B (F-100)	AF	1962	1976	LLNL	100
B46	Megaton range	TN Bomb	AF	Canceled October 1956 (B53)		LANL	0
W46	Megaton range	Titan II	AF	Canceled October 1956 (W53)		LANL	0
		Redstone	A	Canceled April 1958		LANL	0
EC47	600 and 1,200	Polaris A1	N	April 1960	6/60	LLNL	300
W47	1,200–1,500	Polaris A1/A2	N	1960	1974	LLNL	350
W48	0.02–0.04	155-mm howitzer	A,MC	1963	1991	LLNL	1,000
W49	1,450	Thor	AF	1959	1963	LANL	70
	1,450	Jupiter	AF	1961	1963	LANL	35
	1,450	Atlas D	AF	1959	1964	LANL	35
W50	40 and 440	Pershing I	A	1963	1990	LANL	280
	60, 200, 400	Nike Zeus ASAT	A	1964	1967	LANL	6
		Hopi ASM[g]	N	Canceled December 1958		LANL	0
		Minuteman	AF	Canceled December 1958 (W59)		LANL	0
W51	0.022	Davy Crockett	A	Canceled January 1959 (W54)		LLNL	0
		Falcon	AF	Canceled January 1959 (W54)		LLNL	0
W52	40 and 150	Sergeant	A	1962	1977	LANL	300
B53	9,000–10,000	TN Bomb (B-52, B-58)	AF	1962	1997	LANL	340
W53	9,000–10,000	Titan II	AF	1963	1987	LANL	65
W54	0.25	Falcon (F-102)	AF	1961	1972	LANL	1,900
	0.01, 0.02–1	Davy Crockett	A	1961	1971	LANL	2,000
B54	0.01, 0.02–1	Special ADM	A,MC,N	1964	1988	LANL	250
W55	25	SUBROC	N	1964	1988	LLNL	300
W56	1,200	Minuteman I/II	AF	1963	1991	LLNL	950
B57	5–20	Bomb/ASW,Strike (B-52, F-100, F-104, F-105, F-4, F-111, FB-111, A-3, A-4, A-5, A-6, A-7, F/A-18, P-3, S-2, S-3, SH-3)	N,MC,AF	1963	1993	LANL	3,100
W58	200	Polaris A3	N	1964	1981	LLNL	1,450
W59	800 and 1,200	Minuteman I	AF	1962	1969	LANL	175
		Skybolt ASM[g]	AF	Canceled December 1962		LANL	0
W60	?	Typhoon SAM[g]	N	Canceled March 1964		LLNL	0
B61-0,-1,-7	10–300	TN Bomb (B-52, B-1B, B-2A)	AF	1968	Active	LANL	900
B61-2	10–150	TN Bomb	AF,N	1975	1993	LANL	265
B61-3	0.3, 1.5, 60, 170	TN Bomb	AF	1979	Active	LANL	520

Table 1-3. U.S. Nuclear Warheads, 1945–97 (*Continued*)

Warhead[a]	*Yield (Kt)*	*Delivery system*	*Service*[b]	*Entered military service*[c]	*Retirement*	*Laboratory*[d]	*Number*[e]
B61-4	0.3, 1.5, 10, 45	TN Bomb	AF	1979	Active	LANL	680
B61-5	10–150	TN Bomb	AF,N	1977	1993	LANL	435
B61-10, Mods 2-5,10	0.3, 5, 10, 80	TN Bomb (F-100, F-104, F-105, F-4, F-15, F-16, F-111, FB-111, F-117, A-4, A-6, A-7, F/A-18)	AF	1990	Active	LANL	200
B61-11	1.7–300	TN Bomb (F-16, B-1B, B-2A)	AF	1997	Active	LANL	~50
W62	170	Minuteman III	AF	1970	Active	LLNL	1,800
W63 (ER)		Lance	A	Canceled November 1966 (W70)		LLNL	0
W64 (ER)		Lance	A	Canceled September 1964 (W63)		LANL	0
W65 (ER)		Sprint	A	Canceled January 1968 (W66)		LLNL	0
W66 (ER)		Sprint	A	1974	1976	LANL	70
W67		Minuteman III	AF	Canceled December 1967 (W62)		LANL	0
		Poseidon	N	Canceled December 1967 (W68)		LANL	0
W68	40–50	Poseidon	N	1971	1991	LLNL	5,250
W69	170–200	SRAM (B-52, FB-111)	AF	1972	1991	LANL	1,250
W70-0-1-2	1–100	Lance	A	1973	1991	LLNL	900
W70-3 (ER)	1–100	Lance	A	1981	1991	LLNL	380
W71	5,000	Spartan	A	1974	1976	LLNL	45
W72	0.06	Walleye	N	1970	1979	LANL	300
W73		Condor ASM[g]	AF	Canceled September 1970		LANL	0
W74		155-mm howitzer	A,MC	Canceled June 1973		LANL	0
W75		8-inch howitzer	A,MC	Canceled June 1973		LLNL	0
W76	100	Trident I	N	1979	Active	LANL	3,275
B77	Up to 1,000	TN Bomb	AF	Canceled December 1977		LLNL	0
W78	335	Minuteman III	AF	1979	Active	LANL	1,000
W79 (ER)	?	8-inch howitzer	A,MC	1981	1991	LLNL	550
W80-0	< 1–5, 150	SLCM	N	1984	Active	LANL	350
W80-1	< 1–5, 150	ALCM/ACM (B-52)	AF	1981	Active	LANL	1,850
W81	2	Standard-2	N	Canceled June 1986		LANL	0
W82 (ER)	2	155-mm howitzer	A,MC	Canceled October 1983		LLNL	0
W82		155-mm howitzer	A,MC	Canceled May 1992		LLNL	0
B83	1,000	TN Bomb (B-52, B-1B, B-2A)	AF	1983	Active	LLNL	650

W84	0.02–150	GLCM	AF	1983	Inactive	LLNL	400
W85	0.3–80	Pershing II	A	1983	1991	LANL	200
W86		Pershing II EP	A	Canceled September 1980		LANL	0
W87	300	MX	AF	1986	Active	LLNL	560
W87		Small ICBM	AF	Canceled 1992		LLNL	0
W88	475	Trident II	N	1990	Active	LANL	400
W89	200	SRAM II	AF	Canceled September 1991		LLNL	0
B90		Depth/Strike Bomb	N	Canceled 1992		LANL	0
W91	10, 100	SRAM-T	AF	Canceled September 1991		LANL	0
Total Warhead Production 1945–90							70,299

Sources: Department of Energy, table B, "Cumulative History of Weapons Programs Key Dates and Time Spans," December 31, 1984; table C, "Cumulative History of LANL/DOD and EC Programs and Weapons Programs Suspended or Cancelled," December 31, 1983; Department of Energy, Office of Military Application, *A History of the Nuclear Weapons Stockpile FY 1945–FY 1985* (TID-26990-7), December 1986, declassified with deletions; Atomic Energy Commission, Division of Military Application, "Weapon Program Background for Study Relative Effects of a Limitation in Test Operations," February 14, 1956, declassified with deletions, August 12, 1987; Colonel Virgil D. Kempton, DOE Office of Military Application, letter to Robert S. Norris, February 21, 1986; National Atomic Museum, Albuquerque, N.M.; Thomas B. Cochran, William M. Arkin, and Milton Hoenig, *Nuclear Weapons Databook*, vol. 2: *U.S. Nuclear Warhead Production* (Cambridge, Mass.: Ballinger, 1987), pp. 10–11; Robert S. Norris and William M. Arkin, "NRDC Nuclear Notebook," *Bulletin of the Atomic Scientists*, May 1987 to date.

a. All current nuclear bombs are designated either "B" or "W" followed by a number. Gravity bombs are designated with a "B." In the 1940s and 1950s nuclear warheads were assigned "Mark" ("Mk") numbers, which were used interchangeably with the designations B and W. Other designations include "TN" (thermonuclear), "TX" (experimental but canceled warheads), "EC" for emergency capability, "S" for some atomic artillery shells, "ER" for enhanced radiation (that is, the "neutron bomb"), and "EP" for earth penetrator.

b. AF = air force; N = navy; A = army; MC = Marine Corps.

c. The dates are estimates for when a weapon system achieved initial operational capability (IOC) with a military command and when it was removed from operational service. The dates for the warhead phases for when it was produced and dismantled can be found in Cochran and others, *U.S. Nuclear Warhead Production*, pp. 10–11.

d. LANL = Los Alamos National Laboratory; LLNL = Lawrence Livermore National Laboratory. Both laboratories have undergone slight name changes over the years (see appendix C). Though the term "National Laboratory" dates from the 1970s, we have standardized the abbreviations back to their beginnings.

e. Estimate of weapons produced from 1945 to 1990 developed by Robert S. Norris.

f. Gun-assembly weapon.

g. Indicates a delivery system that either was never deployed or never deployed with a nuclear warhead.

h. First thermonuclear designs.

first disassembled at Pantex (or one of the other assembly/disassembly plants) before the component parts were returned to their points of origin. Rocky Flats (and later, Los Alamos) inspected plutonium pits, while the HEU secondaries were sent to the Y-12 Plant at Oak Ridge. The Savannah River Site examined tritium reservoirs, and other non-nuclear components were evaluated at the Kansas City Plant, Mound Laboratory, and the Pinellas Plant.

The cost of warhead inspections and dismantlements is not disaggregated from other production-related costs (estimated costs since fiscal 1991 are included in chapter 5). As the United States retired large numbers of warheads in the 1970s, they were dismantled at the Burlington AEC Plant and at Pantex, and their components and materials were recycled into new warheads or discarded as waste. In the late 1980s and early 1990s, as the United States greatly reduced its active stockpile of tactical nuclear bombs and warheads deployed in Europe and elsewhere, retirement and dismantlement activities increased, keeping so-called production costs high. All warhead production ceased in 1990, but the DOE is at present upgrading a facility at Los Alamos National Laboratory known as TA-55 to give it the capability to produce up to twenty pits a year. This capability was demonstrated in March 1998, and full production is planned to be available by 2007, although problems encountered in modifying the necessary facilities and the resulting cost overruns threaten to delay this.[118]

In 1994 the nuclear weapons laboratories formed the Nuclear Weapons Information Group (NWIG) to document and archive their nuclear weapons engineering knowledge to allow the stockpile to be maintained into the future and—if so desired—provide the data necessary to resume production. This multiyear effort was spurred by the Defense Nuclear Facilities Safety Board, which in December 1993 urged the DOE to develop a means of retaining the collective knowledge of fifty years of nuclear weapons production so that it is not lost as facilities shut down and personnel retire.[119] John D. Immele, direc-

Environmental Research, 1996). See also Kent Johnson and others, "Stockpile Surveillance: Past and Future," Lawrence Livermore National Laboratory, Los Alamos National Laboratory, Sandia National Laboratories, September 1995; Norris and Cochran, *United States Nuclear Tests,* p. 16.

118. U.S. Department of Energy, "Record of Decision: Programmatic Environmental Impact Statement for Stockpile Stewardship and Management," 6450-01-P, December 19, 1996; Keith Earthouse, "LANL Slowing Upgrades for Plutonium Pits," *Santa Fe New Mexican,* December 12, 1997, p. A1.

119. Defense Nuclear Facilities Safety Board, "Recommendation 93-6 to the Secretary of Energy," December 10, 1993 (available on the World Wide Web at http://www.dnfsb.gov/recommend/93-6.asc). However, a great deal of information related to the design and production of nuclear weapons is tacit knowledge, which cannot be communicated entirely via words and equations: motor skills, intuition, "common sense," and judgment based on experience. It is often said that nuclear weapons can never be disinvented. While the fundamental physical principles underlying nuclear weapons can never be completely unlearned or forgotten, the same cannot be said for the tacit knowledge essential to the engineering of nuclear weapons and the facilities that produce them. See Donald MacKenzie with Graham Spinardi, "Tacit Knowledge and the Uninvention of Nuclear Weapons," in Donald MacKenzie, ed., *Knowing Machines: Essays on Technical Change* (Cambridge, Mass.: MIT Press, 1996), pp. 215–60; Donald

tor of nuclear weapons technology at Los Alamos, told the *Los Angeles Times* in 1995: "You have to have the intellectual capability to respond to future developments. This lets our adversaries know that we still know what to do."[120] With an annual budget of about $14 million, researchers are scouring old safes and file cabinets for useful materials, which are then recorded on optical disks, magnetic tapes, and printouts. For the time being, each lab is archiving its own materials, but future plans call for a secure computer network that will allow the labs and other nuclear weapons facilities to share information. By August 1995 researchers at Los Alamos had collected about 800,000 drawings, 1 million photographs, 2,000 videotapes, and 7 million pages of documentation. As part of the project, current and former weapons designers are being interviewed and videotaped to preserve knowledge that would otherwise be lost. New technology has been developed to permit indexed keyword searches of these materials to allow users to locate information about specific warheads or production processes. At Los Alamos, this effort is called the Nuclear Weapons Archiving Project; at Sandia, the Knowledge Preservation Project; and at Livermore, the Nuclear Weapons Information Project.[121]

What Do Nuclear Bombs Cost?

The government has never disclosed the cost of individual nuclear warheads and bombs.[122] However, over the past half century the occasional lapses of government censors have revealed selected warhead cost data for a handful of systems. An otherwise heavily censored transcript from a 1973 congressional hearing on nuclear weapons and technology, for example, contains this question: "Whereas the conventional shell for the 155-millimeter weapon [the W74] costs $191 each, the nuclear shell in production costs $452,000 each; and, whereas the 8-inch shell [the W75] in production will eventually cost $56 apiece, the nuclear shell in production cost over $400,000 apiece?"[123] Within

---

MacKenzie, "Moving Toward Disinvention," *Bulletin of the Atomic Scientists,* vol. 52 (September/October 1996), p. 4.

120. Ralph Vartabedian, "U.S. Launches Race to Save Nuclear Arms Know-How," *Los Angeles Times,* August 28, 1995, p. A1. On March 13, 1996, C. Paul Robinson, director of Sandia National Laboratories, testified before a Senate Armed Services subcommittee about the weapons laboratories' long-term plans for replacing many of the weapons currently in the arsenal, indicating that the laboratories expect to be active for at least the next quarter- to half-century. He stressed the need for qualified people to handle this work: "They need to work on real systems. We cannot expect them to acquire critical design skills merely by performing piecemeal component replacement work and development simulations. They have to design whole systems with real deliverables to fully develop their capabilities. Ideally, we would like to train our junior weapon design engineers alongside experienced engineers, but this will not be possible during a decades-long hiatus of no weapon development." Prepared statement of C. Paul Robinson to the Strategic Forces Subcommittee of the Senate Armed Services Committee, March 13, 1996, quoted in Zerriffi and Makhijani, *Nuclear Safety Smokescreen,* p. 37.

121. Nancy Garcia, "Minding Sandia's Business Is the Mission of Weapons-Project 'Oral Historians,'" *Sandia Lab-News,* May 10, 1996; "Preserving Nuclear Weapons Information," *Science and Technology Review,* May 1997, pp. 18–19.

122. This section is by Stephen I. Schwartz.

123. *Military Applications of Nuclear Technology,* Hearings before the Subcommittee on Military Applications of the Joint Committee on Atomic Energy, 93 Cong. 1 sess. (GPO, 1973), pt. 2, p. 101.

a month of this hearing, these weapons were canceled by the JCAE and never produced because they were considered to be "more of the same." The committee stated it was important to develop weapons that "can utilize the latest glide bomb technology, radar guidance and other remote controlled delivery means."[124] In constant 1996 dollars, the unit cost of these weapons would have been $1.5 million and more than $1.3 million each, respectively. However, the army and the nuclear weapons laboratories continued to pursue the nuclear artillery shell and later in the decade proposed building the W79 8-inch shell and the W82 155-millimeter shell, both of which were to be "enhanced radiation warheads," commonly known as neutron bombs (the W79 was produced beginning in 1981, but the W82 was canceled in 1983; a non-ER version was later canceled in 1992). The W82 would have been even more expensive, estimated at more than $4 million a copy.[125]

Congressional testimony in 1981 revealed that the W84 warhead for the Ground-Launched Cruise Missile was expected to cost $630 million for 530 warheads, or $1.1 million apiece ($1.9 million in 1996 dollars).[126] The actual cost may have even been higher, owing to a shortened production run (400 were built but were retired in the late 1980s under the Intermediate Nuclear Forces [INF] Treaty) and production problems.

In August 1990 the GAO inadvertently revealed the W80-1 warhead costs for the Advanced Cruise Missile (ACM) to be about $720,000 apiece ($845,000 in 1996 dollars), on the basis of the eventual procurement of 1,461 ACMs. In the face of rising costs and operational deficiencies, only 460 were built and only 400 warheads were produced for these; as with the W84, these changes almost certainly pushed up the cost.[127] The W80-1 is also used in the Air-Launched Cruise Missile (ALCM) and a variant, the W80-0, is in the Sea-Launched Cruise Missile (SLCM), so costs for these systems are likely similar (see footnote 130).

The preceding is all that has ever been released (albeit in error) from official sources on the cost of nuclear warheads since 1945.[128] Since many of these weapons no longer exist and all production, not

124. *Report of the Executive Secretariat of the President's Blue Ribbon Task Group on Nuclear Weapons Program Management,* vol. 5 (Case Studies): *Part 1, Artillery-Fired Atomic Projectiles (AFAPS)* (March 1985), p. 2 (formerly Secret/Restricted Data, Sigma 3).

125. Cochran and others, *U.S. Nuclear Forces and Capabilities,* p. 15.

126. Cochran and others, *U.S. Nuclear Forces and Capabilities,* p. 15.

127. U.S. General Accounting Office, *Strategic Weapons: Long-Term Costs Are Not Reported to the Congress,* NSIAD-90-226 (August 1990), pp. 47–48.

128. Following the midair collision of a B-52 bomber and a KC-135 refueling tanker over Spain in 1966 (see box 7-3), the DOD informed the Joint Committee on Atomic Energy that the "salvage value" of the B28 bomb lost off the coast was $164,000 (about $830,000 in 1996 dollars). As damage to this weapon was limited to dents in its casing, missing parts of its tail section, and (presumably) water damage to various internal components, we can assume that this figure covers much of the original cost of the weapon. See Memorandum, Edward J. Bauser, Deputy Director, Joint Committee on Atomic Energy, to the files, February 15, 1968, JCAE General Correspondence Files, Record Group 128, Box 453, National Archives.

to mention the cold war, has ceased, we hoped that the DOE might be willing to release historical data on unit costs. To make matters easy, we requested a declassified copy of a 1985 presidential study conducted at the behest of Congress (which at the time was greatly concerned about the escalating cost of nuclear warheads).[129] This study contains tables and other data on the costs of nuclear weapons going back to 1960 and thus includes most of the information we needed to conduct our analysis. Although large portions of the report and its supporting documentation were ultimately released to us after nearly two years, all of the data pertaining to warhead costs (with a single partial exception) were deleted.[130] Despite repeated efforts to obtain any additional data from this report, the DOE (in conjunction with the DOD, which under the Atomic Energy Act must concur in any release of formerly restricted data) has steadfastly refused our requests.

Why such secrecy, even today? The information, it seems, remains classified because "it is counter to U.S. nonproliferation goals to tell proliferants precisely how much special nuclear material is used in a weapon, or to provide details on the mix of fuel materials the United States has found optimal for its weapons."[131] Such reasoning makes good sense, which is why we scrupulously avoided asking for the cost of the nuclear materials themselves, requesting data on the *total* cost of the weapon, on a unit basis, and, where possible, broken down by its components (with the cost of the nuclear materials lumped together under the "physics package" category).[132] We had no desire to thwart U.S. nonproliferation objectives; on the contrary, the release of such

129. *Report of the President's Blue Ribbon Task Group on Nuclear Weapons Program Management* (July 1985). The members of the task group were William P. Clark (chairman and former national security adviser to President Ronald Reagan), James R. Schlesinger (former secretary of defense and secretary of energy), Harold M. Agnew (former director of Los Alamos National Laboratory), Jeane J. Kirkpatrick (former ambassador to the United Nations), Frederick J. Koresen (former commander in chief, U.S. Army, Europe), and William J. Perry (former undersecretary of defense for research and engineering).

130. This exception—a table comparing warhead costs and listing components for the W80-0 (SLCM), W80-1 (ALCM/ACM), and W84 (GLCM)—is quite revealing. The costs of the physics system (the heart of the warhead, containing its fissile materials) a subtotal category, and the total warhead costs were deleted, along with an unknown item (possibly the tritium reservoir and its contents or the lithium-deuteride secondary components). The total cost of each warhead (minus the physics system and the unknown item) is $105,000 for the W80-0 and W80-1 and $239,500 for the W84. When these figures are subtracted from the already known *total estimated cost* of these three warheads, the physics system and unknown item/tritium reservoir account for perhaps $740,000 of the cost of the W80 and W80-1 and $1.67 million of the W84. This difference appears generally consistent with the weights of the warheads (292 pounds for the W80/W80-1 versus 375 pounds for the W84), their selectable yield features (5–150 kilotons for the W80/W80-1 and 0.2-150 kilotons for the W84), and the fact that the W84 is known to have experienced significant cost increases (16 percent above original estimates) attributable to design and production difficulties. These figures reveal no information that would allow anyone to determine with any degree of certainty how much plutonium, HEU, or tritium is contained in each warhead or in what combination. The only thing these data reveal is that the fissile and special nuclear materials comprise the bulk of the cost of a warhead, something that is already both obvious and very well known. See *Report of the President's Blue Ribbon Task Group on Nuclear Weapons Program Management,*, appx. 3, pp. 4, C-2, and vol. 5 (Case Studies): *Part 5, Cruise Missile Warheads,* pp. 3, 31.

131. Letter from A. Bryan Siebert, Director, Office of Declassification, Office of Security Affairs, U.S. Department of Energy, to Stephen I. Schwartz, May 12, 1997.

132. Letter from Stephen I. Schwartz to the Honorable Hazel R. O'Leary, July 16, 1995.

data could bolster those objectives by revealing the high cost of such weapons. Fundamentally, we wanted to report to taxpayers what they had received for their multibillion dollar investment in nuclear deterrence. To argue that decades-old data on the total unadjusted cost of a particular type of weapon would somehow reveal the precise quantities of materials contained within it is farfetched, akin to being given the price of an automobile and from that and that alone ascertaining the exact types and quantities of materials used to assemble it and how all those parts function together.[133]

In fact the GAO reported in 1972 that for at least the first twenty-five years of its existence the AEC had no means of calculating accurately discrete warhead costs, and in any case its accounting system "was not designed to accumulate production costs by weapon system."[134] Thus production costs for each weapon system delivered during the year, as computed by the AEC, represented the standard costs of the system adjusted for a share of the variance between total standard costs and total production costs incurred during the year for all weapon systems.[135] The AEC assigned a share of the total variance to each weapon system on the basis of a uniform percentage, *regardless* of the variance experienced in producing each system. This system created significant distortions. For example, the unit costs incurred by one contractor during fiscal 1970 for its part of a warhead were more than the total unit costs that the AEC attributed to the production of the entire warhead for the year.[136] According to the GAO, when the AEC provided estimates of the total costs of producing individual weapon systems, its manner of assigning cost variance to individual weapon systems was not a satisfactory basis for identifying cost growth that may have occurred on such systems. To complicate matters, contractors were permitted to develop production data from their own cost accounting systems (subject to AEC approval).

133. Privately, several DOE officials agreed with this line of reasoning and stated that DOD officials were responsible for continuing to withhold the data.

134. U.S. General Accounting Office, *Improved Production Cost Data for Individual Nuclear Weapon Systems to Be Provided to the Congress by the Atomic Energy Commission,* B-165546 (February 29, 1972). "In September 1967, AEC prepared an initial estimate of the total costs to develop and produce the warheads for the SENTINEL (now SAFEGUARD) antiballistic missile system. Prior to initiation of planning for the antiballistic missile system, the AEC generally did not prepare total cost estimates for developing and producing its part of nuclear weapon systems. In September 1969, the AEC prepared cost estimates for all major systems in the development engineering or production phases" (p. 7).

135. Standard costs, developed by each contractor for each warhead component, consist of direct labor costs, direct material costs, and indirect costs. The standard cost of a completed weapon is the sum of all the standard costs ascribed to manufacturing and assembling the weapon's various components. The total cost variance is the difference between the total production costs actually incurred in a given year and the total standard costs of all weapons components actually produced.

136. "One contractor's unit cost report for fiscal 1970 showed a cost variance of about $182,000 above standard costs [$763,743 in 1996 dollars]. Because the total cost variance for the weapons production complex is allocated to the various weapon systems on the basis of the same percentage of standard costs, the cost variance assigned by AEC to the complete warhead was about $72,000 [$302,140 in 1996 dollars] above standard costs. The distribution of the $72,000 cost variance to the warhead resulted in a total unit cost which was about 8 percent lower than the costs reported by the contractor for its part of the warhead alone, even though the contractor's standard cost accounted for a relatively small percentage of the total standard cost of the completed warhead." General Accounting Office, *Improved Production Cost Data.*

In 1977, a new cost-estimating procedure was formally adopted under Phase 2A (Design Definition and Cost Study), and the Weapon Design and Cost Report (WDCR) was established.[137] The 1985 presidential study—requested by members of Congress frustrated with the DOE's explanation of weapons costs—found that the DOE's reporting of costs to Congress was inadequate and that the department failed to use the production costs of individual weapons "as a basis for program management," and declared: "DOE's apparent reluctance to adopt customary, and thus more understandable, concepts of cost measurement and presentation requires serious attention."[138]

AEC and DOE data on weapons costs appear to have consisted largely of estimates, and the way those estimates were derived, especially before 1977, makes it highly questionable that they accurately represent the total cost of each type of nuclear warhead. Of the sixty-five types of weapons actually produced since 1945, evidently only two—the W87 (MK/Peacekeeper) and W88 (Trident II/D-5)—were ever subjected to the improved and more rigorous accounting method (comprising a scant 3 percent of all warhead types ever manufactured). Therefore, any attempt to use these data to obtain any insight into the inner workings of any particular type of weapon would be fraught with tremendous methodological difficulties.

Because the DOE released figures in June 1994 documenting the total number of weapons built, dismantled, and in the stockpile from 1945 through 1961 (release of complete data after 1961 was overruled by DOD, on the grounds that it would reveal information about weapons currently in the stockpile), a gross calculation can be made from the data in appendix tables A-1 and A-2 of the average annual cost of warheads produced from 1948 through 1961. While this method is far from satisfactory, not least because larger weapons utilizing more nuclear materials would tend to be more expensive than smaller ones, it is unfortunately the only method available that provides any degree of accuracy for any given year. Another drawback of this approach is that the AEC and DOE historically entered the cost of a particular warhead on the books only at the time the first production units were delivered, even though significant costs may have been incurred in earlier years (another practice that tends to distort actual costs).

This method of calculation reveals that when the cost of weapons research, development, testing, production, and materials production are combined and divided by the total number of warheads produced in a given year, the average per unit cost of nuclear weapons declined from $92.5 million each in 1948 to $2.1 million each by 1961. When

137. This was five years after the AEC told the GAO it planned to improve its cost accounting systems.

138. *Report of the President's Blue Ribbon Task Group ib Nuclear Weapons Program Management,* appx. 3, p. 3.

materials production costs are excluded—which might be considered reasonable given that in any one year the total spent on materials was applicable to more than one year, especially in light of the tremendous sums expended on the expansion programs in the early 1950s—the figures are $33.2 million and $633,000, respectively. However, these latter figures ignore *all* nuclear materials costs and thus dramatically understate the true cost of the weapons in any given year.

Another approach is to add the cost of RD&T and production ($151.4 billion), and materials production ($158.4 billion) from 1948 (the first available data, aside from the Manhattan Engineer District) through 1990 (the last year of actual production) and divide it by the estimated total number of warheads built (70,299, see table 1-3). The resulting figure is $4.4 million per warhead. Adding in the estimated and known costs attributable to DOD weapons research and testing ($37.4 billion) raises this figure to $4.8 million per warhead. As before, this is a less than satisfactory approach, masking as it does both those weapons that were very expensive along with those that were less so. Furthermore, not all of these costs are attributable to the actual production of new weapons; in 1985, for example, "nearly one-third of the [DOE production and surveillance] workload was in support of stockpile maintenance, stockpile reliability, process development, and other weapon programs."[139] Such an estimate also provides no sense of how costs have fluctuated over time and whether costs per unit had gone down over time, as production increased and the technology improved (as would be expected in other large-scale industrial processes).

The 1985 presidential task group report found that the average unit cost of production (in constant dollars) increased at an average rate of 7 to 8 percent a year from 1962 to 1985. This trend reflected the increasing emphasis on more complex and technically sophisticated weapons designed to provide greater flexibility of employment, enhanced safety and control, and improved yield efficiency.[140]

The W79 and W82 AFAPs and the W84 for the GLCM all "experienced design and production difficulties which have increased costs above early estimates." In addition, "the costs of weapons which rely to a greater extent on well-understood technology and processes, or existing components appear to be estimated with considerably greater accu-

139. *Report of the President's Blue Ribbon Task Group on Nuclear Weapons Program Management,* appx. 3, p. A-7.

140. *Report of the President's Blue Ribbon Task Group on Nuclear Weapons Program Management,* appx. 3, pp. 2–3. These increases are attributed not only to the addition of new features—such as PALs, selectable yields, increased miniaturization, improved electrical systems, and insensitive high explosives—but also to the decline in the number of weapons produced, hence the "abnormally high average unit costs" in the late 1960s and late 1970s (pp. A-8, A-9). Gravity bombs and tactical warheads have experienced the greatest annual cost growth (6 to 8 percent) in contrast to strategic missile warheads (which have experienced about 4 percent). This difference is attributed to "the features that have been added to these types of weapons" (pp. A-11, A-12).

racy than more challenging designs."[141] Absent actual data, however, and forced to approximate costs via gross annual averages, these important trends remain invisible.

Military Expenditures

With the exception of the Manhattan Project, this chapter has thus far concentrated on expenditures by civilian agencies. However, the DOD—through the Defense Special Weapons Agency (DSWA) and its predecessor agencies, the Defense Nuclear Agency (1971–96), the Defense Atomic Support Agency (1959–71), and the Armed Forces Special Weapons Project (1947–59)—has allocated billions of dollars to nuclear weapons research, development, and testing. The individual services also supported their own research efforts to develop new weapons. The DOD appears to have spent more than $37 billion to support nuclear weapons research, development, and testing (see figure 1-8). A more accurate estimate is not possible, given the lack of complete expenditure data before 1962 and possible classified expenditures not yet publicly available.

Most of these expenditures went to support studies of the effects of nuclear explosions on different pieces of equipment, communications systems, weapons systems, and materials and to devise techniques to make these more survivable. Some nuclear weapons tests, such as those including military maneuvers at Camp Desert Rock (the Nevada Test Site) in the early- to mid-1950s, studied blast effects on tens of thousands of troops, many of whom were exposed to dangerously high levels of radiation. The tests were designed to simulate a nuclear battlefield and provide both combat training and data on the psychological effects of nuclear attack on troops (see chapter 7). However, all troops involved in the exercise "were thoroughly briefed in advance on the nature and characteristics of the weapon and were told that they were safe."[142] Hence, as a secret 1952 Army study reported, "the results were highly indeterminate and unconvincing. . . . No well-controlled studies could be undertaken which could presume even superficial validity.... To attempt to probe into men's private fears and anxieties when all danger of death or injury . . . has been excluded by the exercise seemed superfluous." Despite the enormous expense and risk of these exercises, the Army still did not know "how—or if—troops would endure close-in nuclear fires, unannounced detonations or multiple bursts."[143]

Weapons Research and Testing 1946–95. The military's involvement in post–World War II nuclear testing began with Operation Crossroads at

141. *Report of the President's Blue Ribbon Task Group on Nuclear Weapons Program Management,* appx. 3, p. 4.

142. John J. Midgley, Jr., *Deadly Illusions: Army Policy for the Nuclear Battlefield* (Boulder, Colo.: Westview Press, 1986), p. 23.

143. Midgley, *Deadly Illusions,* p. 23.

FIGURE 1-8. DOD Expenditures for U.S. Nuclear Weapons Research, Development, and Testing, 1946–95[a]

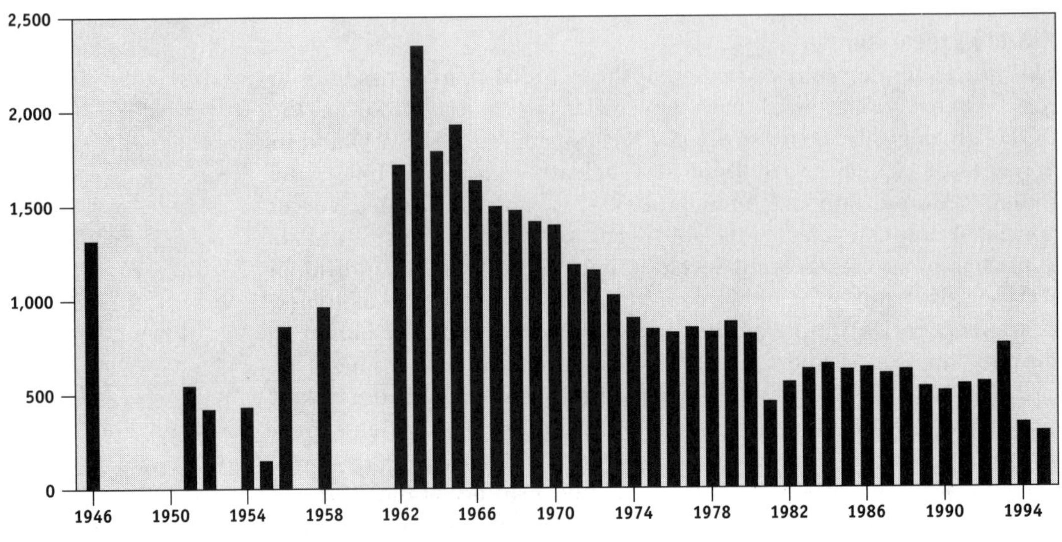

a. Research, development, and testing costs are only partial estimates for 1946–61.

Bikini Atoll in July 1946. Organized under the command of Admiral George Blandy, the stated objective was to determine the effects of atmospheric, shallow underwater, and deep underwater nuclear blasts on naval vessels. The entire exercise was also strongly motivated by a desire to counter claims by the U.S. Army Air Forces that atomic bombs had rendered naval vessels obsolete.[144] Two atomic implosion-type bombs, similar to the bomb dropped on Nagasaki, were detonated. The first bomb, code-named "Able," was dropped by a modified B-29 and missed its target by several hundred yards. The second shot, "Baker," was moored 90 feet (27 meters) beneath a landing craft in Bikini's lagoon. The Baker explosion produced a massive surge of radioactive water, spray, and other debris, which severely contaminated many of the ships in the lagoon to an extent not foreseen by the military. In part because of this contamination, the third deep underwater blast, code-named "Charlie," was canceled.

Operation Crossroads presaged the enormity of the DOD's eventual involvement in nuclear testing. To prepare the atoll for the tests, military authorities persuaded the native population to relocate from their homes

144. For a thorough account of the first post-war atomic tests see Weisgall, *Operation Crossroads.*

to other, less habitable islands in the Pacific, foreshadowing the forced removal of the people of Enewetak Atoll in the 1950s.[145] The operation was carried out by 42,000 military and civilian personnel. Ninety-five ships, including personnel landing ships, submarines, destroyers, aircraft carriers, and battleships, were moored in Bikini's lagoon. The total estimated cost of Operation Crossroads was an astonishing $1.3 billion, far more than any of the subsequent thermonuclear test series conducted during the 1950s, most of which tested many more thermonuclear devices than the two atomic bombs detonated at Crossroads.

During the 1950s, the DOD sponsored numerous additional weapons effects tests both in the Pacific and in Nevada. Because testing in the Pacific involved formidable logistical considerations, many of these tests were conducted in conjunction with AEC-sponsored weapons development tests. The AEC and the military maintained two test sites in the Pacific (Enewetak and Bikini) for similar reasons. The DOD also conducted weapons effects tests in Nevada; between 1975 and 1992 twenty-five such tests were conducted at a cost of nearly $1.3 billion.[146] Some of these were used to determine whether proposed civil defense measures (such as hardened structures) and military equipment could withstand the impact of atomic explosions. All of them were carefully documented by extensive still and motion-picture photography. A full cost accounting of this documentary effort is beyond the scope of this study (if complete records even exist), but an AEC report on Operation Castle (a four-test series in 1954 to verify the successful design of the hydrogen bomb) indicates that costs for "scientific photography" were more than $7.5 million. Data from official reports prepared by the 1352d motion picture squadron (known as Lookout Mountain Laboratory) for the air force historical office indicate that for fiscal 1958 and 1959 photographic costs for the testing program in Nevada and Enewetak were $10.3 million. During this period, 108 tests were conducted—70 in Nevada, 32 at Enewetak or Bikini, 3 in the South Atlantic, 2 over Johnston Island, and one 85 miles (137 kilometers) northwest of Enewetak. In 1997 the DOE began to declassify and release many of these films.[147]

145. For a contemporaneous account of the relocation, see Carl Markwith, "Farewell to Bikini," *National Geographic,* vol. 90 (July 1946), pp. 97–116. For an overview of Bikini today, see Nicholas D. Kristof, "An Atomic Age Eden (but Don't Eat the Coconuts)," *New York Times,* March 5, 1997, p. A4.

146. Norris and Cochran, *United States Nuclear Tests,* pp. 45–53. Many of these tests were detonated underneath Rainier Mesa at the NTS. Since the cessation of all underground testing in September 1992, fourteen of the sixteen test tunnels in the mesa have been closed. Author's communication with Derek Scammell, DOE Nevada Operations Office, December 10, 1997.

147. Air Photographic and Charting Service, Military Air Transport Service, U.S. Air Force, "History of the 1352nd Motion Picture Squadron (Lookout Mountain Air Force Station), 1 January 1958—30 June 1958," pp. 43–45; Air Photographic and Charting Service, Military Air Transport Service, U.S. Air Force, "History of the 1352nd Motion Picture Squadron (Lookout Mountain Air Force Station), 1 January 1959—30 June 1959," pp. 40–45; Bob Post, Blast from the Past," *Los Angeles Times* (Washington edition), October 22, 1997, p. B1. An excellent compilation of some of these films gathered from high-quality master copies in DOD archives can be seen in *Trinity and Beyond: The Atomic Bomb Movie,* produced by Peter Kuran, VCE Inc., 1995.

According to the best available evidence, the Defense Department spent at least $4.7 billion on nuclear weapons research and testing through the end of fiscal 1961 (table 1-4). This figure comes from a tabulation of known expenditures for test series conducted during the period together with partial expenditures from other test series (four major test series involving forty-eight detonations remain unaccounted for). Therefore, this estimate may undercount total costs by as much as several billion dollars.

From 1962 to 1995 the DOD spent in the neighborhood of $32.8 billion to support the development of nuclear weapons and to explore the effects of atomic and thermonuclear explosions. (appendix table A-3) This estimate includes research and testing programs ($27.5 billion), nuclear weapons development programs ($1.6 billion), and overhead costs ($3.7 billion).

Conclusion

Since 1940 the United States has spent at least $409 billion to produce fissile materials and to amass a nuclear weapons stockpile of more than 70,000 bombs and warheads (although these weapons were not all deployed at the same time). As large as this total figure seems, it is only 7 percent of total estimated U.S. spending on nuclear weapons. Producing a small, yet potent nuclear arsenal is relatively inexpensive; one recent estimate placed the costs at $130 million to $326 million.[148] Building delivery systems, creating the military infrastructure to deploy the arsenal, maintaining the weapons, and developing effective command and control systems entail far greater costs, as is discussed in the following chapters.

Despite our best efforts to compile a complete record of historical spending, poor record-keeping and continued classification of key documents ensure that there will always be more details to uncover. The Department of Defense has released substantial and unprecedented amounts of formerly classified budgetary data to the authors of this book, some of which is incorporated in this chapter. However, no complete records of spending in the 1950s have been kept by either the AEC or the DOD. According to one DOE official, any such records were stored in "shoebox-like" fashion. To what extent they can be retrieved or have even survived to the present day remains unknown.

148. Stephen M. Meyer, *The Dynamics of Nuclear Proliferation* (University of Chicago Press, 1984), pp. 194–203, cited in U.S. Congress Office of Technology Assessment, *Technologies Underlying Weapons of Mass Destruction,* Background Paper IS-115 (GPO, December 1993), pp. 155–58. This estimate is based on facilities sufficient to produce about one nuclear weapon's worth of plutonium (approximately 10 kilograms for a crude weapon) per year and assumes that the nation building the facilities does not provide them with heavy radiation shielding or try to keep them secret. Accordingly, it is unrealistically low. Iraq's nuclear weapons program, for example, is estimated to have cost several billion dollars.

TABLE 1-4. Estimated DOD Expenditures on Nuclear Testing, Research, and Development, 1946–61

Millions of 1996 dollars

Known test or test series	*Total known DOD expenditures*[a]
Crossroads, 2 shots (Bikini, 1946)	1,314.3[b]
Greenhouse, 4 shots (Enewetak, 1951)	543.7
Ivy, 2 shots (Enewetak, 1952)	240.9
Castle, 6 shots (Bikini/Enewetak, 1954)	398.7
Teapot, 14 shots (Nevada Test Site, 1955)	52.0
Wigwam, 1 shot (400 miles SW of San Diego, Calif., 1955)	95.0
Redwing, 17 shots (Bikini/Enewetak, 1956)	857.5
Hardtack I, 35 shots (Bikini/Enewetak/Johnston Island, 1958)	915.0
Subtotal	4,417.1
Other known tests	256.4[c]
Estimated total	4,673.5

a. Costs derived from official test manager reports and histories, except for Greenhouse and Ivy (Joint Task Force 3 Final Report and AEC Test Manager's Report); Castle (Moore and Bechanan and AEC report); Teapot (Joint Test Organization, Report of the Test Manager, "Operation Teapot," RG 374, Defense Nuclear Agency, Location WNRC; Access no. 61A1525 Box 3/6; Folder Report of the Test Manager, JTO, Operation Teapot, Exhibit A, p. 2); Redwing (Chuck Hansen, *U.S. Nuclear Weapons,* p. 75; AEC report); Hardtack (AEC Test Manager's Report); Wigwam ("Underwater Test in the Pacific Area," transcript of an executive session hearing before the Subcommittee on Military Applications of the Joint Committee on Atomic Energy, May 9, 1955, p. 23, Record Group 128, Series 1: Executive Session, Boxes 18–24, JCAE no. 4605, at the National Archives).

b. Includes $520 billion for operating costs and $780 billion for maintaining the target and support ships and personnel. On the former, see Joint Chiefs of Staff Evaluation Board for Operation Crossroads, "The Evaluation of the Atomic Bomb as a Military Weapon," Truman Library Archives, (declassified) June 30, 1947, p. 16; on the latter, see Weisgall, *Operation Crossroads,* p. 294 and fn. 9, p. 371.

c. Includes partial spending data (in 1996 dollars) for the following test series: Buster-Jangle (7 tests, 1952), $137.2 million; Tumbler-Snapper (8 tests, 1952), $41.5 million; Upshot-Knothole (11 tests, 1954), $31.8 million; and Plumbob (24 tests, 1958), $46 million. For Buster-Jangle and Tumbler-Snapper, see "First History of the Armed Forces Special Weapons Project 1947–54," vol. 5: "1952," document DNA1.941128.004, chap. 3. For Upshot-Knothole, see Armed Forces Special Weapons Command Semiannual Historical Report, *Activities for the Period 1 July 1953–31 December 1953* (declassified), in FCTXE, Building 220363, Field Command, DNA, Folder "Field Command," AFSWP History, July 1–December 31, 1953; p. 324. For Plumbob, see Armed Forces Special Weapons Project, *Justification of Estimates for Fiscal Year 1958: Appropriation– Research and Development, Army,* p. 52.

We encourage future researchers to build upon what we have presented here despite the enormity of the challenge.

Designing and building nuclear weapons was only the first step in creating a nuclear arsenal. For these weapons to be useful, they had to be delivered to their targets. Chapter 2 examines the development of these delivery systems, including strategic bombers, ballistic missiles, and submarines.

FIGURE 2-1. The Costs of Deploying the Bomb[a]

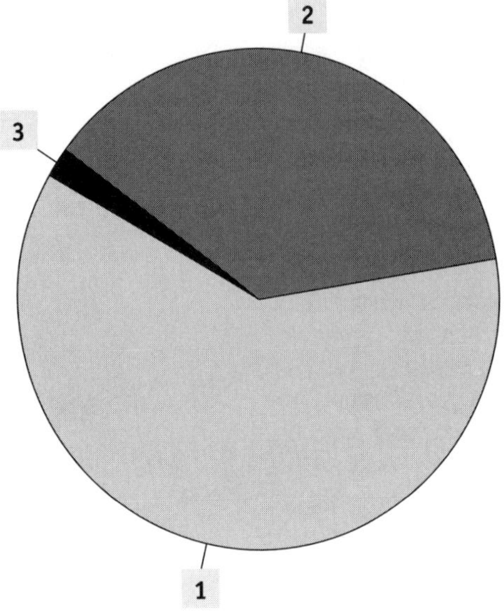

Total: $3,241 billion

1 Strategic offensive forces
$1,980 billion / 61.1%

2 Tactical offensive forces
$1,200 billion / 37.0%

3 Other

Aircraft nuclear propulsion
$7 billion / 0.2%

Naval nuclear propulsion
$51 billion / 1.6%

DOE warhead transportation
$3 billion / 0.1%

a. In constant 1996 dollars.

2

Deploying the Bomb

Robert S. Norris, Steven M. Kosiak, and Stephen I. Schwartz

Once nuclear weapons have been designed, tested, and built, a means must be found to deliver them to their intended target. Early nuclear bombs were extremely large, heavy devices that could only be carried in specially modified B-29 bombers. But as the technology was refined, nuclear weapons became small enough to fit into everything from ballistic missiles to backpacks. As this chapter explains, the United States tested and produced a great number and variety of nuclear weapons delivery systems.

Summary

—The estimated total cost of offensive U.S. nuclear delivery systems is $3.2 trillion (figure 2-1). This covers all known costs to deploy and support the nuclear arsenal, including $1.2 trillion as a conservative estimate of the amount of money used to produce, deploy, and support nuclear weapons integrated into U.S. general-purpose (that is, nonnuclear) forces.

—The United States manufactured some 6,135 strategic ballistic missiles at a cost of $266 billion. This figure does not include many expenses—considered separately in this chapter—such as constructing the silos, purchasing the submarines and naval reactors, buying the nuclear warheads, operating the missile force, or providing the routine maintenance that keeps the missiles in service.

—Since 1945 the United States has purchased and fielded twelve types of nuclear-capable bombers. Excluding air force B-29 bombers, most of which were built and used as conventional bombers in World War II, the United States procured 4,680 nuclear-capable bombers over this period, at a cost of about $227 billion (an additional $22 billion was spent on the B-70 and B-1A programs, neither of which resulted in operational aircraft). The most expensive of these aircraft is the B-2A Spirit, at nearly $2.6 billion per plane. These figures include only the cost of developing and producing the aircraft themselves. They do not include the cost of acquiring the nuclear weapons carried on these aircraft. Nor do they include the cost of acquiring a wide variety of associated equipment, including, for example, refueling tankers, ground support equipment and base facilities, or the annual cost of operating and maintaining these planes.

—The United States purchased 3,160 intercontinental ballistic missiles (ICBMs) at a cost of $169 billion. Per missile, the MX has been the most expensive, at $189 million each. Minuteman ICBMs were a relative bargain at $34 million to $37 million each. The early Atlas ICBMs cost $92 million each; the Titan Is, $131 million; and the Titan IIs, $100 million.

—The United States bought 2,975 submarine-launched ballistic missiles (SLBMs) at a cost of $97 billion. Per missile, the Trident II SLBM has been the most expensive, at $65 million a copy. Polaris missiles were $24 million each; Poseidon SLBMs, $22 million; and the Trident Is, $37 million (see figure 2-2).

Overall Cost of Delivering the Bomb

Between the end of 1945 and the end of 1996, the United States spent some $644 billion developing and procuring weapon systems primarily intended to deliver strategic nuclear weapons. This figure includes $266 billion to buy 3,160 ICBMs and 2,975 SLBMs, about $227 billion to acquire some 4,700 strategic bombers (plus $22 billion for the B-70 and B-1A programs and $7 billion for the nuclear-powered aircraft program), and $123 billion to procure and later retrofit 59 ballistic missile submarines. As enormous as these figures are, they represent only the tip of the nuclear expenditure iceberg. To measure the true cost of U.S. spending on offensive nuclear forces since 1945 (defensive forces are covered in chapter 4), it is necessary to include a far broader range of costs. Altogether, including both direct and indirect costs, the United States spent some $1.98 trillion equipping, manning, operating, and supporting U.S. offensive nuclear forces during this period.

FIGURE 2-2. Average Unit Acquisition Costs for Strategic Nuclear Delivery Vehicles[a]

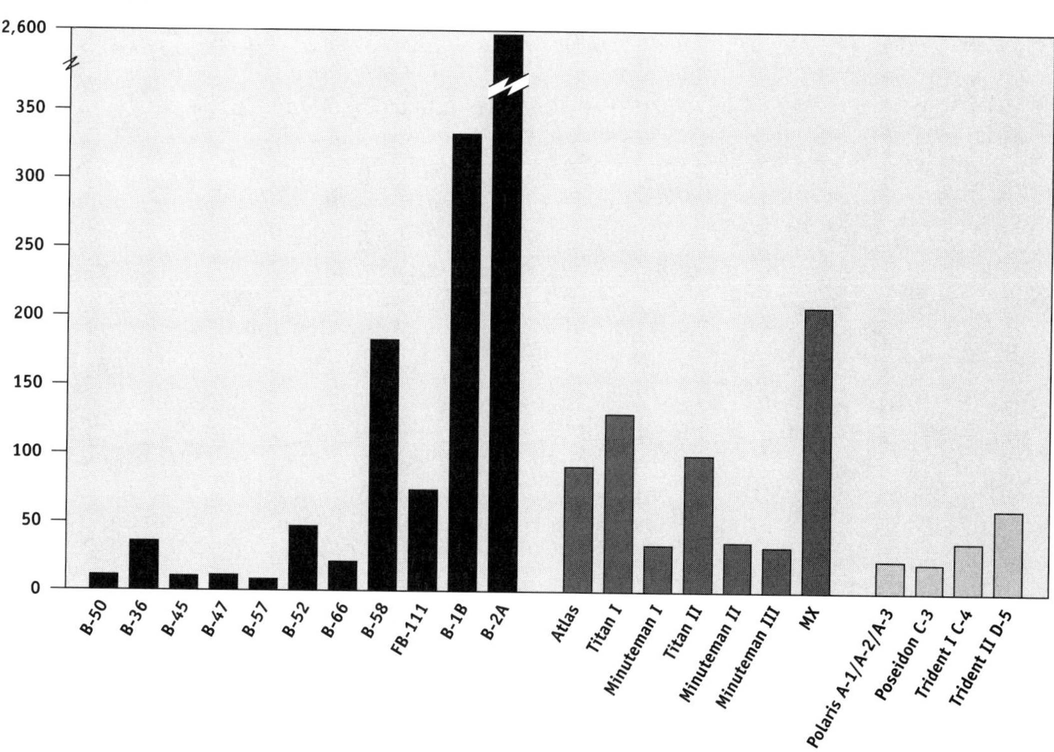

a. Acquisition costs include research, development, testing, and procurement costs. Bomber and ICBM costs exclude air base and launch pad/silo construction costs. SLBM costs do not include associated submarine costs. Also excluded are the B-70 ($4.6 billion each) and B-1A ($4.2 billion each) bombers, which were never operationally deployed.

Figures compiled by the Department of Defense itself suggest that the United States spent perhaps $1.26 trillion on offensive *strategic* forces during the cold war.[1] However, this estimate does not include a number of costs that should be attributed to the strategic offensive mission because the DOD has never assessed costs in this fashion. Most significantly, it does not include the R&D costs associated with developing new strategic weapon systems or a wide variety of indirect or "overhead" support costs. Moreover, by definition these expenditures do not include the sizable cost of general-purpose forces equipped with tactical and theater nuclear weapons.

The cost of developing and producing nuclear-capable missiles, aircraft, and other weapon systems is only the most obvious cost incurred

1. The derivation of this figure is explained later in this chapter.

by the DOD in its preparations for nuclear war. Like any other weapon, to be effective these systems require constant and costly maintenance once operational. Operations and support (O&S) costs are funded primarily out of two DOD budget accounts: the military personnel and operations and maintenance (O&M) accounts. The former pays the salaries of active and reserve military personnel, while the latter covers the salaries of DOD civilian personnel, as well as the costs of most supplies (including fuel and some spare parts), health care, training activities, and equipment maintenance and repair work. The military construction and family housing accounts also fund some important O&S functions, including, respectively, the construction and repair of base facilities (such as having environmentally controlled hangers for the B-2A bomber) and the provision of housing for military dependents. Finally, some O&S items (such as some spare parts) are funded through the services' procurement accounts.

The Congressional Budget Office (CBO) has estimated the annual O&S costs for a number of strategic weapon systems, including the Minuteman missile ($1.6 million per missile), the MX missile ($2.9 million per missile), the B-52 bomber ($11.4 million per aircraft), the B-1B bomber ($16.1 million per aircraft), and the Trident submarine ($49.5 million per boat).[2] At the request of this project, the DOD released some relatively detailed data on funding for strategic offensive forces during 1962–95. According to DOD data, the direct costs during this period of equipping and operating strategic bomber squadrons, for example, amounted to about $171 billion. This estimate includes $93.5 billion for B-52 squadrons, $40 billion for B-1B squadrons, and $16.8 billion for B-2A squadrons. The DOD estimates the direct costs of ICBM squadrons to have been some $142 billion, including $101.6 billion for Minuteman squadrons, $12.4 billion for MX squadrons, $18.5 billion for Titan squadrons, and $8.4 billion for Atlas squadrons. And DOD estimates of direct costs associated with the Trident I SLBM program total some $83 billion.

Among the less direct costs for offensive strategic forces, the DOD estimates that between 1962 and 1995 the air force spent approximately $53 billion on equipping and operating the KC-135 and KC-97

2. U.S. Congressional Budget Office, *The START Treaty and Beyond* (GPO, 1991), p. 140. For consistency, CBO's estimates have been converted here into 1996 dollars. It is noteworthy that annual O&S cost data produced by the air force and the navy is consistently much lower than that produced by the CBO, for example, $427,000 for the Minuteman III missile, $1.96 million for the MX missile, $3.3 million for the B-52 bomber, $5 million for the B-1B bomber, and $24 million for the Trident submarine (which excludes the cost of Trident missiles and other infrastructure costs). Furthermore, both these sets of figures differ from the FYDP data maintained by the DOD and provided to this project. This suggests there exists no definitive, objective measure of these costs. See facsimile communication, Captain Sam McNiel, SAF/PAM, U.S. Air Force, to Stephen I. Schwartz, April 12, 1996; letter from Captain W. A. Peters, Submarine Warfare Division, U.S. Navy, to Stephen I. Schwartz, March 11, 1996. For the curious way in which the navy calculated the price of its Trident I/C-4 and Trident II/D-5 SLBMs (at a time when it was seeking to upgrade its SLBM force), see Eric Rosenberg, "The Price of Navy Nuclear Missiles? Take Your Pick," *Defense Week*, August 8, 1994, p. 2.

tanker aircraft to provide aerial refueling for the strategic bomber force. In January 1958 more than 700 KC-97s were in operation.[3] Some 820 KC-135s (a militarized version of the Boeing 707 aircraft) were ultimately delivered (beginning in June 1957), and by early 1982 about 640 were still supporting the B-52 and FB-111 bomber forces.[4] In 1997 the air force's tanker fleet still included some 551 KC-135s used to support both strategic bombers and other aircraft.[5] Base operations and base communications added another $67 billion and $2.3 billion, respectively, to the cost of supporting U.S. strategic forces. In addition, the DOD estimates that it spent about $23.1 billion on minor construction and maintenance and repair at the base facilities used by U.S. offensive strategic forces.

For planning purposes, the DOD breaks down its budget into eleven "major force programs" (MFPs). Four of these programs can be considered primarily combat oriented: strategic forces, general-purpose forces, mobility forces, and special operations forces. The DOD estimates that over the 1946–95 period, strategic forces absorbed about $1.75 trillion.[6] Of this total, perhaps $1.26 trillion was allocated to strategic offensive forces, with the remaining funding split between strategic defense and strategic command, control, communications, and intelligence, known as C^3I (see chapter 3).[7] Beside these four combat-oriented MFPs, the DOD budget supports separate MFPs for intelligence and communications, R&D, and guard and reserve forces, and four MFPs related to overhead support functions. To accurately calculate total U.S. spending on offensive strategic forces, it is necessary to include a portion of the costs included in some of these other non-combat-oriented MFPs.

Research and Development

The strategic forces MFP covers only a fraction of the R&D costs associated with developing strategic weapon systems, namely that portion

3. *Inquiry into Satellite and Missile Programs,* Hearings before the Preparedness Investigating Subcommittee of the Senate Committee on Armed Services, 85 Cong. 1 and 2 sess.(GPO, 1958), pt. 2, p. 1999. During the late 1940s and 1950s the air force also used KB-29 tankers, 143 of which were in use in December 1953. See "Document One: Memorandum Op-36C/jm, 18 March 1954," reprinted in David Alan Rosenberg, "'A Smoking Radiating Ruin at the End of Two Hours:' Documents on American Plans for Nuclear War with the Soviet Union, 1954–1955," *International Security,* vol. 6, no. 3 (1981/82), pp. 19–20.

4. U.S. Congressional Budget Office, *Aerial Tanker Force Modernization* (GPO, March 1982), p. 1. These large fleets are the result of air force decisions in the late 1950s and early 1960s, supported by Congress, to attempt to provide a one-to-one ratio of tankers to bombers. SAC commander General Curtis LeMay told the Senate in January 1958 that this ratio was required to "get a really efficient intercontinental [bomber] force." See *Inquiry into Satellite and Missile Programs,* Hearings, p. 2000.

5. Susan H. H. Young, "USAF Almanac: Gallery of USAF Weapons," *Air Force Magazine,* May 1997, p. 182.

6. For the 1962–95 period, this estimate was derived from Department of Defense, *National Defense Budget Estimates for FY 1997* (GPO, April 1996), table 6-5, p. 71. For the 1946–61 period, this estimate was derived from Department of Defense, *National Defense Budget Estimates for FY 1985* (GPO, March 1984), table 6-2, p. 79.

7. DOD figures released in November 1988 indicate that about 72 percent of DOD strategic forces funding between 1962 and 1989 was allocated to strategic offensive forces (see *Armed Forces Journal International,* November 1988, p. 80). The $1.26 trillion estimate assumes that strategic offensive forces absorbed roughly this same share of strategic forces funding over the entire 1946–95 period.

related to modifications and upgrades of these systems once they have already been fielded (so-called operational systems development). Over the 1968–94 period the DOD claims to have allocated an average of about 20 percent of its total R&D funding to strategic programs. If this figure holds for the *entire* cold war, and if the development of offensive strategic forces accounted for about 72 percent of total strategic R&D funding,[8] then a reasonable estimate of the level of funding spent on offensive strategic forces between the end of 1945 and 1996 would be about $150 billion.[9]

Overhead Support Functions

Although most of the O&S costs that are directly related to maintaining U.S. offensive strategic forces are included within the strategic forces MFP, many indirect and overhead O&S costs are not. Rather, they are separated out by the DOD and allocated to the central supply and maintenance, training, medical and other general personnel activities, administration and associated activities, and support of other nations MFPs. If the costs of these four overhead MFPs were allocated proportionally to the strategic forces, general-purpose forces, mobility forces, guard and reserve forces, intelligence and communications, and special operations MFPs, the share for the strategic forces MFP would be about $780 billion.[10] This suggests that a reasonable estimate of the overhead and indirect O&S costs associated with offensive strategic forces would be some $570 billion since World War II. Altogether, the costs of equipping, operating, and supporting U.S. strategic offensive forces therefore probably amounted to at least $1.98 trillion between the end of 1945 and the end of 1996 ($1.26 trillion + $150 billion + $570 billion).[11]

As for the U.S. theater and tactical nuclear forces, there is no reliable way to document or estimate the costs associated with them. The biggest problem is that the vast majority of theater and tactical nuclear weapons built during the cold war—more than 25,000 warheads and

8. This would be consistent with the share of total funding in the strategic forces MFP absorbed by offensive strategic forces.

9. According to the DOD, R&D funding (MFP 6) totaled about $1.03 trillion over the 1946–96 period.

10. Strategic forces accounted for just 18.6 percent of all funding allocated to the six MFPs listed above during the 1946–96 period, while funding for the five overhead MFPs totaled about $4.23 trillion. The proportional share of overhead costs reasonably attributable to the strategic forces MFP is thus about $780 billion.

11. No part of the intelligence and communications MFP is included in this estimate, even though some portion of those costs are used, at least indirectly, to support U.S. offensive strategic forces. Instead, they are accounted for in chapter 3. Neither are any portion of the guard and reserve sources MFP included in this estimate. Some U.S. National Guard and reserve military personnel have in the past been used to support offensive strategic forces (in particular, Air National Guard and Air Force Reserve units have provided much of the tanker support for bombers) and defensive strategic forces (in particular, the large commitment to air defense in the 1950s and 1960s). However, the *overall* proportion of national guard and reserve personnel assigned such missions has been very small over the past half century. Thus these costs are not considered here. Some guard and reserve forces costs associated with strategic defensive missions are included in chapter 4.

bombs, 36.5 percent of all U.S. nuclear weapons—were designed to be delivered by "conventional" military systems, such as air force and navy tactical fighters, army ground-based and navy shipborne surface-to-air missiles (SAMs), navy antisubmarine warfare (ASW) systems, and army and Marine Corps artillery pieces. The DOD includes forces that operate such dual-capable weapon systems in the general-purpose forces MFP.

Some portion of these costs clearly should be allocated to the cost of preparing for nuclear war, but *what* proportion? If even 15 percent of the cost of equipping, operating, and supporting U.S. general-purpose forces over the past fifty years were allocated to the nuclear mission, the costs associated with the nuclear weapons activities outlined in this chapter would grow by another $1.2 trillion, to more than $3 trillion.[12] Moreover, given the extent to which nuclear weapons were integrated into the training and doctrine of U.S. general-purpose forces during much of the cold war, especially during the 1950s and 1960s, 15 percent might well be a serious underestimate of the extent to which U.S. general-purpose forces were involved in nuclear missions.[13] Nevertheless, to be conservative this analysis includes only the 15 percent figure in its estimate of the total cost of "deploying the bomb."[14]

U.S. Nuclear Bombers

For a decade and a half after World War II, the U.S. strategic bomber force served as the main means of delivering nuclear weapons.[15] Begin-

12. According to the DOD, the general forces MFP accounted for about $5.55 trillion of the DOD's budget between 1946 and 1996. Assuming a proportional share of the four overhead MFPs was also allocated to general-purpose forces, this would bring total DOD spending on general-purpose forces to about $8.0 trillion. Fifteen percent of $8.0 trillion is about $1.2 trillion. From this total, $161 billion is subtracted to avoid double counting the cost of general purpose forces with nuclear-related missions accounted for in chapter 4 (that is, forces used for strategic antisubmarine warfare).

13. For example, one analyst has argued that given the Eisenhower administration's deemphasis of conventional forces from 1953 to 1960 in favor of increasing tactical nuclear capabilities, "it seems reasonable to assume that more than half the budget for general purpose forces [during this period] was nuclear-related." See Jerome H. Kahan, *Security in the Nuclear Age: Developing U.S. Strategic Arms Policy* (Brookings, 1975), pp. 16–17.

14. Furthermore, the potential understatement of total costs arising from this calculation is offset to some extent by the fact that some small portion of the costs of U.S. offensive strategic forces should be allocated to conventional (rather than nuclear) missions. This is true in particular because U.S. strategic bombers were used to drop conventional bombs in all three of the major wars fought by the U.S. military over the past 50 years (the Korean, Vietnam and Gulf wars). The FYDP, however, provides no means for segregating these costs.

15. This section draws heavily on several excellent works, especially Ray Wagner, *American Combat Planes*, 3d ed. (Garden City, N.Y.: Doubleday, 1982); Marcelle Size Knaack, *Encyclopedia of U.S. Air Force Aircraft and Missile Systems*, vol. 2: *Post–World II Bombers, 1945–1973* (Washington, D.C.: Office of Air Force History, 1988); Lindsay Peacock, *Strategic Air Command* (London: Arms & Armour Press, 1988); Michael E. Brown, *Flying Blind: The Politics of the U.S. Strategic Bomber Program* (Ithaca, N.Y.: Cornell University Press, 1992); David S. Sorenson, *The Politics of Strategic Aircraft Modernization* (Westport, Conn.: Praeger, 1995); Norman Polmar, *Strategic Weapons: An Introduction* (New York: Crane, Russak & Company, 1975); Ted Nicholas and Rita Rossi, *U.S. Historical Military Aircraft and Missile Data Book* (Fountain Valley, Calif.: Data Search Associates, 1991); and Walton S. Moody, *Building a Strategic Air Force* (Washington, D.C.: Air Force History and Museums Program, 1996).

ning with a few specially modified B-29s in 1945, the inventory of the Strategic Air Command increased to more than 1,850 bombers by 1959. Over five decades SAC has developed fourteen kinds of strategic bombers, twelve of which were ultimately deployed (at a cost of $227 billion) and two of which never got beyond testing ($22 billion), plus three kinds of air-to-surface missiles, and two dozen varieties of gravity bombs with yields from 10 kilotons (equal to 10,000 tons of TNT) to 15 megatons (equal to 15 million tons of TNT).[16] Excluding the still operational B-52, B-1B, and B-2A bombers, the average service life of these aircraft was just nine years (see table 2-1).

B-29 Superfortress

The atomic bombs that devastated Hiroshima and Nagasaki in August 1945 were dropped from B-29 Superfortress bombers. With two large piston (propeller) engines on each wing and a gross weight of some 110,000 pounds (50,000 kilograms), the B-29 was by far the largest of the bombers used in World War II. Moreover, it was the only aircraft that could carry early atomic bombs (the two bombs dropped on Japan each weighed about 10,000 pounds, or 4,545 kilograms) to targets located more than 1,000 miles (1,609 kilometers) away (thanks largely to the use of supercharging, which allowed for more fuel-efficient, high-altitude flight). Boeing won a contract in September 1940, before the United States had entered the war, to build two XB-29 prototypes. In June 1941, with the prospect of war looming large, the U.S. Army Air Corps placed a production order for 1,644 B-29s before the first prototypes had even flown. Altogether, 3,960 B-29s were built, with the last aircraft delivered to the U.S. Army Air Forces in May 1946.[17]

At the close of World War II, the U.S. Army Air Forces operated a fleet of some 2,900 B-29 bombers. By 1947, as a result of postwar reductions, only about 300 B-29s remained in service with SAC. Furthermore, only one of the six bomb groups into which the B-29 force was then organized had aircraft configured to carry nuclear bombs (this was the 509th Bomb Group at Roswell Air Force Base in New Mexico). Thus, when the Berlin crisis began in June 1948, SAC had only thirty-two nuclear-capable B-29 bombers.[18] Because of the B-29's limited

16. By way of comparison, the bombs detonated over Hiroshima and Nagasaki in August 1945 had yields of 15 and 21 kilotons, respectively.

17. Because most, if not all, of the B-29s were ordered before the end of World War II, this study excludes the estimated $27 billion spent to procure them. However, between September 1943 and September 1945, the U.S. Army Air Forces, in an effort known as Project SILVERPLATE, spent $76 million to modify forty-six B-29 bombers to carry the first atomic bombs ($285,000 each) and to provide crew training and logistical arrangements in support of the Manhattan Project. Project SILVERPLATE continued after the war, providing support to Operation Crossroads at Bikini and modifying nineteen additional aircraft through May 1947. Its total costs over this period were $282.6 million. See Lee Bowen, Robert D. Little, and others, *A History of the Air Force Atomic Energy Program, 1943–1953*, vol . 3: *Building an Atomic Air Force, 1949–53* (Washington, D.C.: U.S. Air Force Historical Division, 1959), pp. 462–66 (formerly Top Secret, declassified in 1980).

18. David Alan Rosenberg, "American Atomic Strategy

TABLE 2-1. U.S. Strategic Bombers, 1945–97[a]

Designation	Name	In-service dates	Gross weight (pounds/kilograms)	Maximum speed (mph/kph)	Acquisition costs (millions of then-year dollars)	Acquisition costs (millions of 1996 dollars)	Notes
B-29	Superfortress	1943–54	110,000(50,000)	367(591)	2,530[b]	27,400[b]	3,960 built
B-50	Superfortress	1948–55	173,000(78,636)	380(611)	423[b]	4,200[b]	B-50D data; 370 built
B-36	Peacemaker	1948–58	358,000(168,200)	439(706)	1,425[b]	14,100[b]	B-36D data; 385 built
B-45	Tornado	1949–58	81,000(36,364)	571(919)	154[b]	1,600[b]	B-45A data; 142 built
B-47	Stratojet	1951–66	175,000(79,545)	630(1,014)	4,153	23,400	B-47E data; 2,041 built
B-57	Canberra	1955–59	54,000(24,545)	598(962)	559	4,300	B-57B data; 403 built
B-52	Stratofortress	1955–	448,000(203,636)	645(1,038)	6,250	31,900	B-52H data; 744 built
B-66	Destroyer	1956–65	83,000(37,727)	631(1,015)	891	6,400	B-66B data; 294 built
B-58	Hustler	1960–70	160,000(72,727)	1,385(2,228)	3,166	19,400	B-58A data; 104 built
B-70	Valkyrie	n.a.	500,000(227,273)	2,000(3,218)	1,468	9,200	2 built; never operational
FB-111	Aardvark	1971–91	110,000(50,080)	Supersonic	1,229	5,700	76 built
B-1A	n.a.	n.a.	395,000(179,545)	Supersonic	4,493	12,500	3 built; never operational
B-1B	Lancer	1986–	434,000(197,273)	Supersonic	27,700	33,700	100 built
B-2A	Spirit	1994–	376,000(170,909)	High subsonic	45,200	54,500	21 ordered; 10 deployed

Sources: Technical data are primarily from Norman Polmar, *Strategic Weapons: An Introduction* (New York: Crane, Russak, 1975), p. 147; Ray Wagner, *American Combat Planes,* 3d ed. (Garden City, N.Y.: Doubleday, 1982); Ted Nicholas and Rita Rossi, *U.S. Historical Military Aircraft and Missile Data Book* (Fountain Valley, Calif.: Data Search Associates, 1991). Then-year dollar cost estimates are taken from Nicholas and Rossi, except for the B-1B and the B-2, which were taken, respectively, from the DOD, "Selected Acquisition Report (SAR) Summary Tables," September 30, 1992, p. 11; and *National Defense Authorization Act for Fiscal Year 1993: Report of the Committee on Armed Services, House of Representatives,* 102 Cong. 2 sess. (GPO, 1992), p. 18.

a. The production and cost totals provided in this table include costs associated with bombers later used in conventional roles, as well as reconnaissance and some other combat support roles. Except where noted, acquisition cost estimates include research and development (R&D) and procurement costs. The 1996 dollar cost estimates for the B-29, B-50, B-36, B-45, B-57, B-66, B-58, and B-70 bombers represent very rough estimates. They were derived by dividing the then-year dollar cost estimate for each aircraft by the deflator for the year they first entered service. For the B-47 and the B-52, 1996 dollar cost estimates were derived by using data from William E. DePuy, Jr., and others, *U.S. Military Aircraft Cost Handbook* (Falls Church, Va.: Management Consulting & Research, 1983), to estimate the total flyaway procurement costs of the aircraft, and by assuming that the funding required to cover the remaining R&D and procurement costs associated with these aircraft were provided at the same rate and over the same years as the flyaway procurement funding. The 1996 dollar cost estimate for the FB-111 was derived by applying deflators to the annual funding totals provided in Nicholas and Rossi, *Military Aircraft and Missile Data Book,* tables 2-6, 2-7. For the B-1A, it was derived by applying deflators to the annual funding totals provided in the fiscal 1970–79 annual statements and reports of the secretary of defense. For the B-1B, it was derived by applying a deflator to the B-1B base year (fiscal 1981) dollar estimate provided in the SAR, p. 5. For the B-2A, the 1996 dollar cost estimate was derived by applying deflators to the estimates included in Dagnija Sterste-Perkins, "Long-Range Bomber Facts: Background Information," Congressional Research Service Report for Congress, March 10, 1995, p. 4, for fiscal 1989–95, and the Congressional Budget Office (CBO), "Selected Weapons Costs from the President's FY 1996 Program," June 1995, p. F1, for fiscal 1996–2000. The 1996 dollar cost estimate for fiscal 1988 and previous years (for which annual funding levels are classified) was derived on the simplifying assumption that all B-2 classified funding (about $17 billion) was provided in fiscal 1986.

b. Estimates include *only* total "flyaway" procurement costs (besides excluding R&D, flyaway procurement costs exclude some procurement costs directly associated with buying aircraft, such as spare parts and ground support equipment).

range, had the Berlin crisis escalated to war, the planes would have been flown to staging bases in the United Kingdom to be refueled before being sent on to strike their targets in the Soviet Union. The B-29 remained in active service until 1954.

B-50 Superfortress

In May 1945 the air force began to test a B-29 equipped with new, larger engines. This aircraft, designated the XB-44, became the prototype of the air force's next heavy bomber, the B-50. Essentially an upgraded version of the B-29, the B-50 Superfortress even kept its predecessor's name. The first B-50s entered service in February 1948. Altogether, Boeing built 370 B-50 bombers, including 44 reconnaissance versions, with the last B-50s delivered in February 1953. The B-50 remained in service until 1955.

B-36 Peacemaker

In April 1941 the U.S. Army Air Corps—concerned that Nazi Germany might gain control of all of Europe—held a competition for the design of a bomber with intercontinental range. The winner was the B-36 Peacemaker, entered by Consolidated Vultee Aircraft Corporation.[19] The B-36 was a huge aircraft, requiring a crew of sixteen. With a wing span of 230 feet (70 meters) and a gross weight of some 370,000 pounds (168,200 kilograms), it weighed three times more than the B-29 and more than twice as much as the B-50.

The B-36 was powered by six piston engines (three on each wing) located on the trailing edge of the wings, which were used to "push" the aircraft, later supplemented by four jet engines in wing pods. By the time the contract for the first hundred B-36s was signed in August 1944, the wartime need for an intercontinental bomber had all but vanished. By then U.S. forces had captured the Mariana Islands, from which B-29s were able to stage bombing missions against Japan. Nevertheless, the decision to procure the B-36 was reaffirmed after the Japanese surrender in August 1945. The cold war provided a new justification for an intercontinental bomber; its target simply shifted from Nazi Germany and Imperial Japan to the Soviet Union. The first B-36s entered service with the air force in June 1948.

A number of factors combined to make the B-36 program highly controversial. By contemporary standards it was enormously expensive. The first 95 production aircraft cost more than $6 million apiece (in then-year dollars), and the total program cost more than $14.1 billion

---

and the Hydrogen Bomb Decision," *Journal of American History*, vol. 66 (June 1979), p. 65.

19. The Consolidated Aircraft Corporation and Vultee Aircraft, Inc., merged on March 17, 1943. The new Consolidated Vultee Aircraft Corporation (Convair) became the Convair Division of the General Dynamics Corporation on April 29, 1954.

($1.4 billion in then-year dollars). Moreover, in May 1949 the Soviet Union displayed its new MiG-15 jet fighter, which raised serious concerns about the survivability of the B-36. The controversy peaked in 1949, when congressional hearings were held to examine charges that Secretary of Defense Louis A. Johnson (a former Convair director) had shown favoritism to his former company in selecting the B-36. In the end, the B-36 survived the hearings, and a total of 385 aircraft, including 143 reconnaissance aircraft, were built.[20] The last B-36 was delivered in August 1954, and the aircraft remained in service until 1959.

B-45 Tornado

The first American bomber to be equipped with jet engines was the experimental XB-43, ordered in March 1944. Just a month later, more than two years before the XB-43 made its first flight, the air force held a competition to develop a jet-powered medium bomber with a 1,000-mile (1,609-kilometer) range and a speed of 500 miles (805 kilometers) per hour. Five prototype designs emerged, all of which were first flown in 1947: the North American XB-45, the Consolidated XB-46, the Northrop YB-49, the Martin XB-48, and the Boeing XB-47.[21]

In January 1947, two months before the XB-45 was first flown, the air force decided to order 96 B-45 bombers from North American, making it the first jet bomber to go into production in the United States. With a gross weight of 81,000 pounds (36,364 kilograms), the B-45 Tornado was powered by two 5,200-pound (2,364-kilogram) thrust jet engines under each wing. The first B-45 was delivered in November 1948. The air force eventually purchased a total of 142 B-45s, including 33 for reconnaissance, at a cost of $1.6 billion. The last B-45 flew in 1958.

B-47 Stratojet

The real winner of the air force's competition was the Boeing XB-47. Its development had been delayed long enough for captured German research on swept-wing technology to be incorporated into its design. The XB-47 was first flown in December 1947, and in October 1948 the air force ordered production of the first 10 B-47s. The B-47 had a gross weight of about 175,000 pounds (79,545 kilograms) and was powered by three jet engines under each wing. The first B-47 Stratojet entered service with SAC in October 1951, ushering in what turned out to be a massive program. A total of about 2,041 B-47s were eventually built (at

20. Knaack, *Post–World II Bombers, 1945–1973,* p. 53. Some of the reconnaissance versions also carried nuclear weapons.

21. The Northrop YB-49 was dubbed the "flying wing" for its radical design. Although the YB-49 did not become part of the bomber fleet, Northrop resurrected the design in the 1970s for the B-2 bomber program.

a cost of $23.4 billion), making it the largest jet bomber program ever—with the possible exception of the Soviet Union's Tu-16 Badger bomber program.

Before actual full-scale testing of the hydrogen bomb, many officials expressed concern about the dangers of delivering this unprecedentedly powerful weapon via manned aircraft. Accordingly, from 1951 to 1953 the air force undertook Project BRASS RING, an effort to reconfigure the B-47 as an autonomous H-bomb delivery system. Following the Operation Ivy test series in the fall of 1952 (during which the hydrogen bomb design developed by Edward Teller and Stanislaw Ulam was confirmed), these concerns abated, and the air force abandoned the program, which was growing rather expensive. Its total cost was close to $72 million.[22]

The B-47 had a maximum speed of some 630 miles (1,014 kilometers) an hour, which made it faster than even many interceptor aircraft in service at the time. The air force compensated for the relatively short combat radius (about 1,600 miles, or 2,574 kilometers) by establishing SAC bases in the United Kingdom and Morocco[23] and periodically rotating bombers through other forward bases, and by purchasing large numbers of KC-97 tanker aircraft (more than 700 were operational by 1958) to provide the B-47 with inflight refueling. The B-47s were retired by 1966.

B-57 Canberra

When the Korean War began in June 1950, the air force had no jet-powered light bombers to support U.S. ground forces. In March 1951, in order to rapidly compensate for this deficiency, the air force took the highly unusual step of asking Martin to build a foreign-designed aircraft, the English Electric Canberra, a two-engined aircraft with a gross weight of about 54,000 pounds (24,545 kilograms). However, the first B-57s did not enter service with the air force until after the war. In addition to 316 bomber versions, 87 reconnaissance versions of the B-57 were eventually produced, at a cost of $4.3 billion. The B-57 left active service in 1959.

B-52 Stratofortress

In January 1946 the air force issued specifications for an intercontinental jet bomber and the following January awarded the design contract to Boeing. In July 1948 it ordered two XB-52 prototypes. The first

22. Delmer J. Trester, *History of Project Brass Ring,* vol. 1: *Text* (Dayton, Ohio: Wright Air Development Center, November 1953), formerly Top Secret/Restricted Data (declassified and available at the National Security Archive, Washington, D.C.).

23. U.S. Air Force, *SAC Operations in the United Kingdom, 1948–1956* (Washington, D.C.: Historical Division, 7th Air Division, n.d.); Colonel Gerald M. Adams, USAF (Ret.), *A History of U.S. Strategic Air Bases in Morocco, 1951–1963* (Omaha, Nebr.: Moroccan Reunion Association, 1992).

prototype flew in April 1952, the first production aircraft were ordered in December 1952, and in June 1955 the air force took delivery of the first intercontinental range jet-powered bomber, the B-52 Stratofortress.[24] The B-52 has a gross weight of 448,000 pounds (203,636 kilograms), making it roughly 20 percent heavier than the B-36 and three times heavier than the B-47. The B-52 has eight jet engines (four pairs of two) suspended under its 35-degree swept back wings. By October 1962, when the last B-52 was delivered to SAC, Boeing had built a total of 744 of the bombers, including 27 reconnaissance versions. The B-52 has proven remarkably durable, remaining in service longer than any other combat aircraft. The air force still had 94 B-52Hs at the end of 1996. According to the latest air force plans, some 71 B-52H bombers are to remain in service for the foreseeable future, for both nuclear and conventional bombing missions.[25] The total acquisition cost of the B-52 program was about $32 billion.

B-66 Destroyer

In February 1952 the air force decided to purchase a variant of the Navy's carrier-based Douglas A3D Skywarrior. Dubbed the B-66 Destroyer, this jet-powered "light" bomber had a gross weight of some 83,000 pounds (37,727 kilograms). The first B-66 was test flown in June 1954, with the first aircraft entering service with the air force in 1956. Altogether, the air force procured 294 B-66 aircraft, including 186 reconnaissance versions, at a cost of $6.4 billion. The B-66 was retired in 1965.

B-58 Hustler

The first supersonic bomber was the four-engine B-58 Hustler, which entered service with the air force in March 1960. Built by Convair, it

24. During a May 5, 1956, press conference at the height of the "bomber gap" controversy, President Eisenhower, under attack for not authorizing more B-52 bombers to stay ahead of Soviet bomber production, was asked if it was "vital that we try to stay ahead of Russia in production of the long-range bomber." Eisenhower responded: "No. I say it is vital that we get what we believe we need. That does not necessarily mean more than somebody else does. We have got to get what we need. Now, certainly, when you come and talk about the quality of the thing, I saw we mustn't be behind anybody. . . . [W]e need what our requirements demand." See *Study of Airpower,* Hearings before the Subcommittee on the Air Force of the Senate Committee on Armed Services, 84 Cong. 2 sess. (GPO, 1956), vol. 1, pp. 458–59. In 1958 Eisenhower—having been thwarted in his efforts to reorganize the DOD to prevent the individual services from pursuing their own parochial programs and responding to the "missile gap" in the wake of Sputnik—authorized an additional 100 B-52 bombers, though he observed caustically, "If 600 won't do the job, certainly 700 won't." Pressured by the air force to fund still more planes Eisenhower snapped, "I don't know how many times you can kill a man, but about three should be enough." Quoted in Nick Kotz, *Wild Blue Yonder: Money, Politics, and the B-1 Bomber* (New York: Pantheon Books, 1988), p. 33.

25. General Accounting Office, *Air Force Bombers: Options to Retire or Restructure the Force Would Reduce Planned Spending,* NSIAD-96-192 (September 1996), pp. 2, 31. The Clinton administration's 1994 "Nuclear Posture Review" actually determined that sixty-six B-52Hs should be retained, but this number was subsequently increased "to provide a larger attrition reserve force to hedge against potential future losses." The air force estimates that the remaining B-52H force will remain structurally sound "until about 2030," sixty-eight years after the last aircraft entered the force. For an overview of the results of the Nuclear Posture Review, see William J.

had a gross weight of about 160,000 pounds (72,727 kilograms) and a delta-wing design and was capable of speeds in excess of Mach 2. The air force selected Convair's design in October 1952 and ordered 13 test aircraft two years later. The first XB-58 prototype was flown in November 1956, and deliveries of production aircraft began in September 1959. Although the B-58's supersonic dash capability made it an impressive performer, ultimately only 104 bombers were purchased (at a cost of $19.4 billion), and the aircraft was retired from service by 1970. Built to optimize speed, the much smaller B-58 lacked the payload capacity and range of the B-52. More important, by the time the B-58 was deployed, advances in Soviet surface-to-air missile capabilities had rendered the high-speed, high-altitude mission for which the aircraft had been designed relatively dangerous.

B-70 Valkyrie

In December 1957 the air force awarded North American a contract for the XB-70 Valkyrie, a prototype of a bomber intended to replace the B-52 (which had entered service less than three years earlier) as SAC's premier intercontinental bomber. With a gross weight of about 500,000 pounds (227,273 kilograms), the six-engine, delta-wing XB-70 was even larger than the B-52. In contrast to the B-52, however, the XB-70 was designed to cruise over its targets at Mach 3 at an altitude of some 75,000 feet (22,860 meters). Unfortunately for the XB-70, the potential vulnerability of even high-speed aircraft flying at high altitude became apparent on May 1, 1960, when a Soviet SA-2 SAM missile apparently brought down an American U-2 spy plane over Sverdlovsk, at an officially reported altitude of 68,000 feet (20,726 meters; see chapter 3). At the same time, the growth of the ICBM force raised questions about the need for a new bomber.[26] Therefore despite intense congressional and air force pressure, in March 1961 President Kennedy decided to limit the program (then designated the RS-70) to a prototype effort. In the end, just two XB-70 prototypes were built and flight-tested.[27] The total program cost some $9.2 billion.

Perry, *Annual Report to the President and the Congress, February 1995* (GPO, 1995), pp. 83–92; and Perry, *Annual Report to the President and Congress, March 1996* (GPO, 1996), pp. 174–75.

26. During a February 1960 hearing, Senator Stuart Symington (Democrat of Missouri), a staunch supporter of the air force, touted the B-70's speed as its greatest asset while arguing against its cancellation. Questioning Admiral Arleigh Burke, the chief of naval operations, Symington complained, "We are eliminating all research and development on something that . . . might go Mach 10, and at the same time are putting billions of dollars of the taxpayers' money into something [the Polaris SSBN] that goes only a very small fraction of Mach 1." Burke replied that effectiveness depended on "a lot more" than speed: "What gives [Polaris] its power is that it is hidden. It can't be destroyed." See *Missiles, Space, and Other Major Defense Matters,* Hearings before the Preparedness Investigating Subcommittee of the Senate Committee on Armed Services in Conjunction with the Committee on Aeronautical and Space Sciences, 86 Cong. 2 sess. (GPO, 1960), pp. 296–97.

27. One of the test aircraft was destroyed on June 8, 1966, after touching wing tips with an F-104 fighter while flying in formation during a photo opportunity arranged for the General Electric Company by the air force (G.E. wanted to photograph the five air force planes powered by its engines). The other XB-70 prototype was put on display at the air force museum at Wright-Patterson Air Force Base outside Dayton, Ohio, where it remains today. See Kotz, *Wild Blue Yonder,* p. 86.

FB-111 Aardvark

In December 1965, almost five years after the cancellation of the B-70 program, Secretary of Defense Robert S. McNamara announced that SAC would buy a version of the General Dynamics F-111 Aardvark tactical fighter-bomber, begun as the Tactical Fighter Experimental (TFX) in 1960, configured for strategic bombing. The Defense Department originally planned to build some 1,700 of the variable-geometry ("swing-wing") F-111s. They were to have a wide variety of functions, including both carrier air defense and interdiction, and were to be used by the air force, navy, and Marine Corps. As a consequence of Soviet advances in high-altitude air defense capabilities, SAC decided to shift to low-level penetration, and the F-111, with its terrain-following radar, was optimized for this approach.

Deliveries of the strategic bomber version of this aircraft, the FB-111, began in October 1969. McNamara had originally ordered 263 FB-111s to be built, but in March 1969 the new secretary of defense, Melvin Laird, reduced the order to 76 aircraft. The decision to halt production of the FB-111 was due in large part to substantial cost growth.[28] Although the air force had initially estimated that 263 FB-111s could be purchased for $1.75 billion (in then-year dollars), the ultimate cost of buying just 76 of the aircraft came to more than $1.2 billion ($5.7 billion in 1996 dollars).

B-1A Bomber

Still searching for a new intercontinental bomber with a large payload to replace the B-52, the air force in June 1970 awarded North American Rockwell a contract to produce five B-1A test aircraft, later reduced to three. Like the FB-111, the B-1A had variable geometry wings. However, the B-1A was a much larger aircraft, with a gross weight of about 395,000 pounds (179,545 kilograms), compared with 110,000 pounds (50,000 kilograms) for the FB-111. The first B-1A prototype flew its first test flight in December 1974.

By this time, Rockwell had subcontracted the work for the plane to more than five thousand corporations in forty-eight states, creating a formidable lobbying coalition with clout in Congress. During annual consideration of the defense budget, Rockwell and air force lobbyists "armed themselves with meticulous lists of every B-1 subcontract location, cross-referenced by state, town, and congressional district." Surveys by Rockwell and the air force "showed how many dollars of B-1 money flowed into a congressional district each month . . . allow[ing] the lobbyists to show members of Congress, down to the last dollar,

28. Robert J. Art, *The TFX Decision: McNamara and the Military* (Boston: Little, Brown, 1968).

how their constituents benefited from the B-1."[29] By June 1976 the air force had two more B-1As and planned to purchase 244 by 1986.

In June 1977, however, President Jimmy Carter, who had campaigned against the B-1, decided to cancel production after completion of the last B-1A. Instead he focused on developing and procuring long-range (1,500-mile, 2,414-kilometer) cruise missiles that could be launched from B-52 bombers.[30] Since each B-52 was capable of carrying as many as twenty such missiles, there seemed to be no immediate need for a new penetrating bomber. Only in 1980 did the administration publicly acknowledge another reason for its decision to cancel the B-1A: the air force already had another bomber under development, the stealthy (radar-evading) Advanced Technology Bomber (ATB).[31] Total costs for the B-1A program were $12.5 billion.

B-1B Lancer

Four years after being canceled by Carter, however, the B-1 program was quickly revived by newly elected President Ronald Reagan.[32] In October 1981 the new administration announced that it would procure 100 B-1Bs, a derivative of the B-1A. Although closely resembling the B-1A in most respects, the B-1B was modified to optimize its capability to fly at low altitude at high subsonic speeds, and features designed to allow for a high-altitude supersonic dash capability were largely eliminated. The administration argued that the B-1B was needed as an interim penetrating bomber—to be used in conjunction with B-52s equipped with cruise missiles—until the stealthy ATB could be deployed. Despite substantial opposition, Congress eventually approved $27.7 billion ($33.7 billion in 1996 dollars) to buy the 100 B-1Bs proposed by the Reagan administration. The first B-1B was delivered to the air force in April 1985 and the last (on schedule) in April 1988.

The B-1B has been plagued by technical problems. Early in its service life, its terrain-following radar did not function properly, it experienced fuel leaks and in-flight stalling, and its offensive and defensive

29. See Kotz, *Wild Blue Yonder*, pp. 127–29.

30. This decision subsequently led to the cancellation of the high-yield (up to 1-megaton) B77 strategic gravity bomb, which had been developed in tandem with the B-1 for low-level delivery against "hard irregular targets." The rising cost of the B77 also contributed to this decision. See *Report of the President's Blue Ribbon Task Group on Nuclear Weapons Program Management*, vol. 5: *Case Studies, Part 2—B77/83 Strategic Gravity Bombs* (March 1985), pp. 7–9 (formerly Secret/Restricted Data, Sigma 3).

31. The developmental name given to what became the B-2 bomber.

32. Despite Carter's cancellation of the B-1A, the program was quietly provided more than $1 billion over the next several years through the efforts of four military and civilian officials in DOD (including Secretary of the Air Force Hans Mark and Seymour Zeiberg, deputy undersecretary of defense for research, engineering, and space) working together with select members of Congress and Rockwell International, the B-1's prime contractor. Funds were obtained by earmarking them for Rockwell under numerous smaller, nondescript programs that would not draw the attention of either Carter—who was known to scrutinize detailed budget documents—or the B-1s opponents on Capitol Hill. This funding was sufficient to keep the B-1 alive until after the 1980 election. See Kotz, *Wild Blue Yonder*, pp. 180–99.

avionics were found to be incompatible, which meant the plane might be vulnerable to attack or unable to carry out its assigned missions. Although some of these shortcomings have been addressed, others persisted long after the B-1 was first declared operational. The most serious deficiency concerned the aircraft's defensive avionics, which are intended to provide warning and jamming capabilities against enemy radars and radar-guided missiles.[33] Currently, the air force plans to retain the B-1B for the foreseeable future, but to equip the plane only for conventional bombing missions under a $3 billion conversion program. The B-1B will therefore not be counted as a nuclear weapon carrier under the START II Treaty. By the end of 1997, all ninety-five remaining operational B-1Bs were removed from the nuclear mission with a portion of the force assigned to the Air National Guard.

B-2A Spirit

The latest U.S. bomber is the B-2A, informally referred to as the Stealth bomber. The B-2A has a gross weight of 376,000 pounds (170,909 kilograms) and a "flying wing" shape incorporating advanced composite materials designed to make the aircraft very difficult to detect and track with radar. The fact that the air force was working to develop a stealthy bomber was first disclosed by the DOD on August 22, 1980. Originally, the air force had planned to buy a total of 132 B-2A bombers. However, because of declining defense budgets, the end of the cold war, and growing congressional opposition, in April 1990 it reduced this number to 75. Yielding to a further increase in budgetary pressures and congressional opposition, the Bush administration announced in January 1992 that only 20 B-2A bombers would be procured.

The Clinton administration, though originally committed to ending production of the B-2A bomber after the twentieth aircraft is completed, in 1996 authorized the conversion of an early test model to operational status, at a cost of nearly half a billion dollars.[34] As part of its 1994 Nuclear Posture Review, the Clinton administration decided to retain the twenty (now twenty-one) B-2s as dual-capable bombers for use in both conventional and nuclear roles. In then-year dollars, acquisition costs for the B-2A totaled about $45 billion ($54.5 billion in 1996

33. This problem and others kept the B-1B from participating in the Gulf War. Thirty-year-old B-52s were used instead. B-52s were also used to launch conventionally armed cruise missiles (air-launched cruise missiles, their nuclear warheads replaced by conventional warheads) in an attack on Iraq in September 1996. In November 1997 two B-1Bs were deployed to Bahrain to augment U.S. firepower during a crisis with Iraq. See Tony Capaccio, "A New Look at Why B-1B Bombers Sat Out the Gulf War," *Defense Week,* September 12, 1994, pp. 3, 14; Steven Komarow "Deployment of B-1s Marks New Strategy," *USA Today,* November 24, 1997, p. A1; Lisa Hoffman, "Revised B-1 Bombers Fill New Strategic Niche for U.S.," *Milwaukee Journal Sentinel,* December 7, 1997, p. 30.

34. Bradley Graham, "U.S. to Add One B-2 to 20-Plane Fleet," *Washington Post,* March 22, 1996, p. A20; John Pike, "Buying Votes with B-2s," *Bulletin of the Atomic Scientists,* vol. 52 (May/June 1996), p. 4.

dollars), including some $24 billion for R&D and $20 billion for procurement.[35] This makes the B- 2A the most expensive bomber program ever, in terms of its total development and procurement cost and its unit cost.[36]

The first three B-2As were delivered to the air force in 1994, and the twenty-first bomber is scheduled for delivery after 2000. The B-2A was integrated into the Single Integrated Operational Plan (SIOP), the nuclear war plan, and thus became fully operational on April 1, 1997. Eight B-2As based at Whiteman Air Force Base (AFB) in Missouri now carry the B61-11, a nuclear gravity-bomb capable of penetrating the earth at high speed to destroy underground facilities, such as Russian command posts (see box 1-2).[37]

Some members of Congress and others, including manufacturer Northrop Grumman, have advocated the production of additional B-2As, arguing that more aircraft are needed for conventional missions. The air force has estimated that twenty additional B-2 bombers would cost more than $20 billion. In May 1997, the CBO estimated that nineteen additional B-2s (bringing the size of the total fleet to forty aircraft) would cost $24 billion to $27 billion, noting that O&S costs for twenty years would add another $26 billion to $27 billion. Congressional B-2 supporters tried to add $331 million to the 1998 defense budget as a downpayment on nine additional aircraft, but only suc-

35. Final costs may be higher because flight testing and program modifications are being done concurrently with production. The above cost estimates assume these efforts would be completed on schedule and with no additional costs (however, the air force scaled back the testing program in order to conclude it by June 30, 1997, to avoid incurring extra expenses, and testing will continue until at least March 1998. See U.S. General Accounting Office, *B-2 Bomber: Status of Efforts to Acquire 21 Operational Aircraft*, NSIAD-97-11 (October 1996); William B. Scott, "Follow-on B-2 Flight Testing Planned," *Aviation Week & Space Technology*, June 30, 1997, p. 48.

36. As of January 30, 1998, each B-2A bomber was worth more than five times its weight in gold (based on gold selling for approximately $300 a troy ounce, or $3,600 a troy pound, with an empty B-2A weighting 134,146 troy pounds and thus equivalent to $482.9 million in gold). In 1996 the General Accounting Office disclosed that "the B-2 will be by far the most costly bomber to operate on a per aircraft basis [$31.9 million annually], costing over three times as much as the B-1B [$9.6 million annually] and over four times as much as the B-52H [$6.8 million annually]." A key reason for this is the extreme care required to maintain the aircraft's stealthy properties, especially its special low-observable coatings and skin. In September 1997, each hour of B-2 flight required 119 hours of maintenance; several months earlier the figure was 132 hours (comparable figures for the B-52 and B-1B are 53 and 60 hours, respectively). Air force officials say the figures, while high, are not unusual for a new aircraft and that they will decline over time. However, this has had an impact on the aircraft's readiness, at times reducing it far below acceptable air force rates and raising serious questions about the ability to deploy the B-2 overseas, where special climate-controlled hangars essential to maintaining the plane are as yet unavailable. Consequently, the air force has dropped its previous requirement to be able to base the B-2A overseas. The B-2A is designed to fly low altitude bombing missions, as low as 600 feet (183 meters). But such missions increase wear and tear on the aircraft far more than high altitude flight. See U.S. General Accounting Office, *Air Force: Options to Retire or Restructure the Force Would Reduce Planned Spending*, NSIAD-96-192 (September 1996), pp. 53, 56; Tony Capaccio, "The B-2's Stealthy Skins Need Tender, Lengthy Care," *Defense Week*, May 27, 1997, p. 1; David A. Fulghum, "B-2's Durability Faces Foreign Test" *Aviation Week & Space Technology*, September 22, 1997, pp. 82–84; U.S. General Accounting Office, *B-2 Bomber: Cost and Operational Issues*, NSIAD-97- 181 (August 1997); Mark Walsh, "DoD Testers: Stealth Unreliability Hampers B-2," *Defense News*, August 4–10, 1997, p. 1; Bradley Graham, "Maintenance Problems Postpone Overseas Basing of Air Force B-2 Bomber," *Washington Post*, August 22, 1997, p. A16; Tony Capaccio, "Top Pentagon Tester Gives B-2 Mixed Review," *Defense Week*, September 8, 1997, p. 1; Philip Shenon, "B-2 Bomber Gets a Bath to Prove That It Does Not Melt,'" *New York Times*, September 13, 1997, p. 9.

37. Susanne M. Schafer, "B-2 Bombers Ready for Missions," Associated Press, March 31, 1997.

ceeded in getting an additional $157 million in the budget (to be used at the Clinton administration's discretion to either upgrade existing planes or purchase new ones). Many military officials, including former chairman of the Joint Chiefs of Staff General John Shalikashvili and U.S. Air Force chief of staff General Mike Ryan are strongly opposed to the purchase of any additional B-2s, arguing that to do so would require unacceptable cuts in existing conventional and nuclear-capable aircraft to pay for the new planes.[38]

Nuclear-Powered Aircraft

Between 1946 and 1961, the air force and the AEC are estimated to have poured more than $7 billion into the Aircraft Nuclear Propulsion (ANP) program (nearly 50 percent of which went toward the development of a reactor power plant), largely at the behest of the Joint Committee on Atomic Energy, which strongly supported the concept.[39] The ANP program was originally called the Nuclear Energy for the Propulsion of Aircraft (NEPA) program and was briefly known as the continuously airborne missile launching and low-level penetrating weapons system (CAMAL). The air force had a twofold interest in the program: it hoped to develop a high-performance aircraft, capable of exceeding the speed of sound, and to field a bomber capable of flying over enemy territory for days or weeks without refueling, dropping atomic bombs, and performing aerial reconnaissance.[40]

As early as 1942 physicist Enrico Fermi envisioned the potential of using atomic power to propel aircraft.[41] Yet in February 1946, three months before the official start of the ANP program, *Scientific American*

38. On August 23, 1996, Speaker of the House Newt Gingrich (Republican of Georgia) said: "I absolutely believe the minimum number of B-2s we should have is 50. We need to make a commitment and let industry know our intentions." In March 1997 Northrop Grumman circulated a briefing arguing nine additional aircraft could be built for $9.3 billion, making the total number of B-2s produced sufficient to fill out three squadrons of eight planes each. "This is [the] absolute minimal operational need," the company declared. See "Gingrich Proposes Bigger B-2 Fleet," *Washington Times*, August 25, 1996, p. A2; "B-2 Backers Press for Nine More Bombers," *Inside the Pentagon*, March 27, 1997, p. 7; Holly Porteous, "Congress Eyes Prospects for More B-2 Bombers, Navy Warships," *Inside the Pentagon*, May 29, 1997, pp. 3–4; "Proceeding," *Defense Week*, April 21, 1997, p. 4; Tony Capaccio, "Nine More B-2s Carry $20 Billion Price Tag," *Defense Week*, June 16, 1997, p. 1. Bryan Bender and John Robinson, "Shali: More Stealth Bombers Means Less Combat Power," *Defense Daily*, August 5, 1997, p. 206; Douglas Berenson and Elaine M. Grossman, "Ryan Warns of 'Glaring Capability Gap' If Air Force Buys More B-2s," *Inside the Pentagon*, September 18, 1997, p. 1.

39. For an overview of the influential role of the JCAE, see Harold P. Green and Alan Rosenthal, *Government of the Atom: The Integration of Powers* (New York: Atherton Press, 1963), pp. 242–47.

40. The potential benefits were of particular interest to certain members of Congress as well. In February 1960 Senator Clinton Anderson (Democrat of New Mexico), chairman of the JCAE, asked General Bernard Schriever of the air force: "Would there not be some advantage to you to have something that is nuclear-propelled that could stay up in the sky for 2,000 hours [83 days] or 25,000 hours [1,042 days], if need be?" Schriever responded, "We have been extremely interested in the nuclear-propelled aircraft." See *Missiles, Space, and Other Major Defense Matters*, Hearings, pp. 110–11.

41. R. W. Bussard and R. D. DeLauer, *Fundamentals of Nuclear Flight* (New York: McGraw-Hill, 1965), p. 1.

called into question the entire array of portable nuclear power sources then being proposed in popular books and magazines. The weight of the minimum quantity of uranium and uranium oxide needed to sustain a chain reaction (plus the graphite necessary to control the reaction), it pointed out, would be close to 20 tons. The necessary cooling and shielding would only add further weight, making atomic-powered cars and planes completely impractical.[42]

Nevertheless, the air force and AEC scientists continued to work on the problem, enlisting the services of several contractors, including the Fairchild Engineer & Airframe Company, the Pratt & Whitney Company, the General Electric Company, and Oak Ridge National Laboratory. By 1951 the air force made the program its number-two priority, second only to development of ballistic missiles.[43] As predicted, there were significant difficulties, not only with designing a reactor to power a plane but with providing enough shielding to protect the crew from a fatal dose of radiation (cognizant of these dangers, the air force sought out test pilots who were beyond child-rearing age). Although no aircraft ever flew under nuclear power, between July 1955 and March 1957, the air force flew a three-megawatt air-cooled operational test reactor forty-seven times aboard a converted B-36 bomber to demonstrate the feasibility of the concept and study ways to shield the crew. The NB-36H, dubbed the Nuclear Test Aircraft, carried the reactor in its aft bomb bay and incorporated a new nose section, which housed a 12-ton lead and rubber-shielded crew compartment with leaded-glass windows 10 to 12 inches (25 to 30 centimeters) thick. Water pockets in the fuselage and behind the crew compartment also absorbed radiation (because of weight constraints, nothing was done to shield the considerable emissions from the top, bottom, or sides of the reactor).[44]

42. Leonard I. Katzin, "Industrial Uses of Atomic Energy," *Scientific American*, February 1946, pp. 74–78, cited in Paul Boyer, *By the Bomb's Early Light: American Thought and Culture at the Dawn of the Atomic Age* (New York: Pantheon Books, 1985), pp. 115–16.

43. Ralph E. Lapp, *Atoms and People* (New York: Harper & Brothers, 1956), p. 209. Given the resources allocated to this effort by the air force and the navy compared with those of the ballistic missile program ($617 million versus $166 million from 1946 through 1954), it is clear that the air force's determination to build a nuclear-powered aircraft was a critical factor in delaying the development of the ballistic missile, an outcome sharply criticized by Congress following the Soviet launch of Sputnik in 1957. Data derived from tables in *Aircraft Nuclear Propulsion Program,* Hearings before the Subcommittee on Research and Development of the Joint Committee on Atomic Energy, 86 Cong. 1st sess. (GPO, 1959), p. 118; and *Missiles, Space, and Other Major Defense Matters,* Hearings, p. 509.

44. Although the flight test program was conducted in absolute secrecy, the air force and the AEC remained concerned about the possibility of accidents. Accordingly, a B-50 aircraft accompanied the test plane on each run. Had the test aircraft crashed or been forced to jettison the reactor (a concept that was studied but never implemented), the B-50 would have flown low over the impact zone and dropped darts with warning markers to stay clear of the area. Then, specially trained paratroopers would have jumped from the plane to prevent unauthorized entry into the area and awaited the arrival of cleanup crews. The plane flew from a Convair plant at Carswell Air Force Base in Fort Worth—directly over Lake Worth, the principal water source for Fort Worth—to a base near Roswell, New Mexico. In New Mexico, the reactor was turned on and the plane sent aloft. When not in use, the reactor was stored in an underground bunker at Carswell AFB. See *Aircraft Nuclear Propulsion Program,* Hearings, p. 32; Knaack, *Post–World II Bombers, 1945–1973,* pp. 46–48; *American Portrait—ANP,* WFAA-TV (Dallas), 1993.

Two massive railway-mobile reactor engines weighing 250 and 270 tons were built and tested (twenty-one times between 1956 and 1961) at the National Reactor Testing Station (NRTS, now known as the Idaho National Engineering and Environmental Laboratory) in southeastern Idaho. Because the reactors were direct cycled and air cooled—air was sucked into the jet engine, compressed, passed directly over the fuel rods to extract heat energy, and then discharged through a jet nozzle—any accidental or deliberate releases of radiation would immediately reach the atmosphere.[45] In all, 4.6 million curies of radiation were released as a result of various ANP reactor tests at NRTS, with one test series in the spring of 1956 responsible for lofting more than 1.9 million curies of radiation.[46] To simulate and assess the consequences of a reactor accident, the air force burned portions of ANP reactor fuel at the Dugway Proving Ground in Utah (southwest of Salt Lake City) in high-temperature, open-air furnaces, tracking the radioactive cloud downwind as far as 20 miles (32 kilometers; although it traveled much further). Between August 5, 1959, and October 25, 1959, eight such tests were conducted at Dugway, releasing more than 215 curies of radiation (primarily from barium-140, cerium-141, strontium-89, and iodine-131), more than fourteen times the amount released by the accidental meltdown at Three Mile Island.[47]

Around 1952 a large shielded hanger with 8-foot-thick (2.4-meter) walls was constructed at NRTS (which was designated a flight-test base)[48] for the as-yet unbuilt plane, which would become highly radioactive after each flight. In 1953 the flying "testbed" program was terminated, rendering that investment a total loss (a planned 20,000-foot runway was never built). Despite a distinct lack of progress and efforts by an air force committee to scale back the program, the navy in November 1955 created a requirement for a subsonic nuclear-powered seaplane (this effort, named PRINCESS, eventually led the navy, in 1971, to award a contract to Lockheed to develop concepts to transform its giant C-5A into a nuclear-powered seaplane).

45. Scientists running the program were concerned enough about *their* exposure to radiation from the tests to locate the testing site in a remote area of the already remote NRTS. The site consisted of an underground control building and the reactors, which when operating were connected to a 150-foot-tall (45.7-meter) exhaust stack. During tests, the exhaust plume rose to over 1,200 feet (366 meters). See Chuck Broscious, *Citizens Guide to the Idaho National Engineering Laboratory* (Troy, Idaho: Environmental Defense Institute, February 1996), pp. 18–22.

46. For comparison, the accident at Three Mile Island in 1979 released 15 curies of Iodine-131. See Broscious, *Citizens Guide to the Idaho National Engineering Laboratory,* p. 18.

47. Lee Davidson, "How Dangerous Were Secret Dugway Tests?" *Deseret News* (Utah), October 9, 1994, p. B1. An earlier test on March 20, 1957, at NRTS consisted of placing part of a fuel rod in a section of fuselage and covering it with burning jet fuel. It was code-named Operation Wiener Roast because live animals were used to test radiation exposure. This and similar tests at NRTS released 502.7 curies of radiation. See Broscious, *Citizens Guide,* p. 18.

48. Six other sites were considered: Edwards and Hunter-Ligget Air Force bases in southern California; Mona Island, between the Dominican Republic and Puerto Rico; Cape Sable, Florida; and Mesquite Rincon on the Gulf Coast of Texas. NRTS was selected after the effects of potential crop damage, population density, and wind patterns were considered. See *American Portrait—ANP.*

The excessive cost of the ANP program, its lack of progress in resolving the fundamentals of nuclear-powered flight, and the development of long-range ballistic missiles and in-flight refueling for bombers eventually rendered the program obsolete, and it was terminated by President Kennedy on March 28, 1961.[49] The stubborn insistence of AEC scientists, air force officials and, most important, the unbridled advocacy of the Joint Committee on Atomic Energy—which called for a crash program in 1954 and an immediate flight test after Sputnik in 1957 (to boost prestige and create a "psychological victory")—kept the (largely secret) program alive far longer than warranted.[50] Some of the technology for the ANP reactor was subsequently incorporated into the TIMBERWIND program, a highly secretive effort in the 1980s and early 1990s to develop a nuclear-powered rocket for space defense applications (see chapter 4).

U.S. Missiles

By the late 1950s, the bomber was beginning to be supplanted by various kinds of missiles designed to deliver nuclear warheads.[51] Since World War II the United States has produced about fifty types of such missiles. They have come in every conceivable shape and size and with ranges from a few kilometers to distances that span continents. The number of ballistic missiles purchased—with short, medium, intermediate, and intercontinental ranges—comes to some 24,500, including

49. At the time of this decision, at least 3,500 AEC contractor employees were working on the program for General Electric and Pratt & Whitney, with as many as 10,000 involved overall. See Harold Orlans, *Contracting for Atoms* (Brookings, 1967), pp. 12–13; *American Portrait–ANP.*

50. *Aircraft Nuclear Propulsion Program,* Hearings; *Aircraft Nuclear Propulsion Program,* Report of the Joint Committee on Atomic Energy, 86 Cong. 1st sess. (GPO, 1959); H. Peter Metzger, *The Atomic Establishment* (New York: Simon & Schuster, 1972), pp. 203–08. The widely reported existence of a nuclear aircraft program in the Soviet Union also drove this effort, on the theory that the United States could not risk ceding the technological advantage, however dubious (see *Aircraft Nuclear Propulsion Program,* Hearings, pp. 201–415). One reported Soviet design, proposed in 1950, was a flying boat with a weight of 1,000 tons. With a wing span of almost 437 feet (133 meters), its four turbo-prop engines would exceed half a million horsepower. The design envisioned a load of 1,000 passengers and 100 tons of cargo and a speed of over 600 miles (965 kilometers) an hour. See Roman Grigorevich Perellman, *Soviet Nuclear Propulsion* (Yadernyye Dvigateli) (Washington, D.C.: Triumph, 1960), p. 31. In December 1958, however, President Eisenhower stated categorically: "There is absolutely no intelligence to back up a report [in *Aviation Week Intelligence*] that Russia is flight-testing an atomic-powered airplane" (Metzger, *Atomic Establishment,* p. 206). Noted aerospace intelligence analyst James Oberg, who met with Russian scientists and designers in the 1980s and 1990s, also determined that no Soviet nuclear aircraft program ever proceeded beyond the conceptual phase. See *American Portrait—ANP.*

51. Sources for information in this section include Strategic Air Command, *SAC Missile Chronology: 1939–1988,* 3d ed. (Offutt Air Force Base, Nebr.: Office of the Historian, Headquarters Strategic Air Command, 1990); Strategic Air Command, *From Snark to Peacekeeper: A Pictorial History of Strategic Air Command Missile* (Offutt Air Force Base, Nebr.: Office of the Historian, Headquarters Strategic Air Command, 1990); J. C. Hopkins and Sheldon A. Goldberg, *The Development of the Strategic Air Command, 1946–1986: The Fortieth Anniversary History* (Offutt Air Force Base, Nebr.: Office of the Historian, Headquarters Strategic Air Command, 1986); John C. Lonnquest and David F. Winkler, *To Defend and Deter: The Legacy of the United States Cold War Missile Program,* USACERL Special Report 97/01 (Rock Island Ill.: Defense Publishing Service, November 1996). For cruise missiles, see Kenneth P. Werrell, *The Evolution of the Cruise Missile* (Maxwell Air Force Base, Ala.: Air University Press, 1985).

3,160 ICBMs and 2,975 SLBMs. The acquisition cost for all nuclear-capable missiles—including ballistic, cruise, surface-to-air, and other missiles—amounts to more than $380 billion (including more than $35 billion for missiles with defensive missions, which are counted in chapter 4). This estimate does not include operations and maintenance, personnel, and other costs incurred to support these weapons systems after deployment (these costs are discussed later in this chapter). During the cold war, the DOD also produced more than 50,000 nuclear-capable nonballistic missiles, including air-to-air, air-to-ground, and surface-to-air missiles, as well as cruise missiles (although many of these were dual-capable weapon systems).

Strategic Land-Based Missiles

U.S. ballistic missile programs date back to World War II. In November 1943 Theodore von Kármán, director of the Guggenheim Aeronautical Laboratory, California Institute of Technology, submitted a proposal to U.S. Army Ordnance for the development of long-range, surface-to-surface missiles. This effort was inspired in part by knowledge of German advances in rocketry that had become known to American officials and scientists. Authorities in Washington were greatly concerned about what the Nazis might use as payload for these new rockets: it might be an atomic bomb—the Germans were suspected of developing such a weapon—poison gas, biological agents, or radioactive materials.[52] At a very early stage, well before the Trinity explosion of July 16, 1945, the connection was made between missiles and atomic bombs.

In the last year of the war the United States developed a group of missiles patterned after the German V-1 and powered by pulse jet engines, including the JB-1, JB-2, and JB-10. The JB-2, a somewhat improved version of the V-1, actually went into production but not into operation.[53] As early as 1945 some believed that a quick "marriage" between the atomic bomb and the guided missile could occur. A variety of air-to-air, air-to-surface, surface-to-air, and surface-to-surface missile programs with atomic potential were explored throughout the late 1940s and early 1950s, but technical problems and a strong bias in favor of aircraft on the part of the air force (which consistently received the largest share of the defense budget during this period and zealously guarded "its" strategic mission) prevented the production of practical and economical weapon systems.[54]

52. Thomas Powers, *Heisenberg's War: The Secret History of the German Bomb* (New York: Alfred A. Knopf, 1993), p. 353.

53. When production terminated in September 1945, U.S. industry had delivered about 1,385 JB-2s to the War Department. Werrell, *Evolution of the Cruise Missile*, p. 65.

54. Edmund Beard, *Developing the ICBM: A Study in Bureaucratic Politics* (New York: Columbia University Press, 1976), especially pp. 4–9, 86–92, 147–48, 154, 223–24.

By 1953 the situation was beginning to change. Breakthroughs in thermonuclear designs made lightweight, high-yield warheads practical.[55] Fission warheads as well were becoming smaller in diameter and significantly lighter than the first-generation atomic bombs. The steady advances in missile technology being pursued by the army, navy, and air force showed promise of increased range and greater accuracy. A fierce interservice and intraservice rivalry stimulated competition, which in turn spawned a myriad of programs.[56] Contributing to the process was the awareness of, and suspicions about, Soviet advances in the field.

Between 1950 and 1953, the army developed four surface-to-surface missiles with ranges from 12 to 600 miles (19 to 965 kilometers): the Corporal, Honest John, Hermes A-3, and Redstone. There were also surface-to-air missiles, including the Nike Ajax, Hawk, and Nike Hercules. Among the navy's developments were the Regulus, Rigel, Triton, Terrier, Talos, and Sparrow. The air force brought out the Matador, Snark, Navaho, Bomarc, Falcon, and Rascal in these early years.

Another category of missiles were decoys, designed to confuse, dilute, and degrade enemy air defenses by mimicking SAC bombers. The air force undertook several programs to simulate various bomber types, planning to put six Buck Ducks (XGAM-71) on each B-36 bomber before the program was canceled in January 1956. The Bull Goose (XSM-73) was an intercontinental-range, surface-launched, decoy missile intended to simulate a B-52. At one point the air force planned to buy 2,328 (plus 53 for R&D) of the 33-foot-long, 7,700-pound (10-meter, 3,500-kilogram) delta-winged Bull Goose decoy missiles for initial deployment in the first quarter of 1961. In early December 1958, how-

---

Despite studies demonstrating that ballistic missiles were more cost-effective than bombers, the air force essentially ignored the issue until Sputnik forced the matter into the public spotlight. Before that time, "no money was made available; so no research was done. No research was done; so no missiles were produced. No missiles were produced; so no demonstration of usefulness and capability was made. No demonstration of usefulness was made; so no money was made available" (p. 239). In August 1950, Undersecretary of the Air Force John A. McCone wrote to Secretary Thomas K. Finletter arguing that a Manhattan Project-type crash program (with a single manager responsible to the president) to develop the ballistic missile was required because interservice rivalries and insufficient funding had compromised "the urgent need" for such weapons. McCone called for minimum initial spending on "the order of $2 or $3 billion," equal to $14 to $21 billion in 1996 dollars. A missile "czar" was eventually appointed in October 1950, in the person of K. T. Keller, president of the Chrysler Corporation. But Keller ceded the budgetary and administrative authority necessary to carry out McCone's plan and he declined to implement a crash program, instead initiating a study of relevant issues and providing advice to the president (pp. 123–27).

55. Even before this, however, the air force had planned (since the three tests constituting Operation Sandstone in April–May 1948 demonstrated the effectiveness of newer, lighter warheads) to equip Snark and Navaho missiles with nuclear warheads, indicating that concern about warhead weight was not the principal limiting factor on the development of the ICBM. See, Beard, *Developing the ICBM,* p. 141.

56. Beard, *Developing the ICBM,* pp. 15–44. At this time great emphasis was being placed on the relatively primitive Atlas, which was nevertheless considered "so promising because of its invulnerability" (p. 146). This measure of invulnerability was taken against slower cruise missiles (such as Snark and Navaho) and bomber aircraft, both of which could be shot down by Soviet antiaircraft defenses. It thus refers *only* to invulnerability while en route to target. Few appear to have realized that once the Soviet Union had deployed ICBMs of its own, weapons like Atlas (not to mention the entire United States) would become quite vulnerable to attack *before* being launched.

ever, the air force canceled the missile because it did not appear to be a B-52 on the radar screen.[57] But by then the Bull Goose had amassed a total of 28½ test-flight hours and incurred costs totaling $460 million.

After these failures the air force finally did deploy a decoy missile, the Quail (GAM-72), which was carried on the B-52 and B-47 and became operational in early 1961. At peak deployment in 1963, there were 492 Quails with fourteen B-52 squadrons. By 1971 its credibility as a decoy was minimal and it was withdrawn. The total cost of this program is unknown.[58]

On October 31, 1953, the Strategic Missiles Evaluation ("Teapot") Committee was established to examine strategic missile programs. It was chaired by John von Neumann—a highly esteemed Hungarian-émigré mathematician who was part of the Manhattan Project—and was composed of prominent scientists and engineers. The committee's recommendations, submitted February 10, 1954, were that an ICBM could be quickly developed and deployed if enough resources were committed to the project, and that Convair's Project Atlas, the only ICBM then under development, should be reoriented and accelerated. The recommendations were approved by the air force and the DOD.

On July 1, 1954, the secret and innocuously named Western Development Division (WDD) was activated, under the command of Brigadier General Bernard A. Schriever, to develop the Atlas missile. Within a year the WDD was also charged with developing the Titan ICBM, a backup program should the Atlas fail. By the end of 1955, the WDD was developing yet another missile: the Thor intermediate-range ballistic missile (IRBM).

The launch of the Soviet satellite Sputnik by an ICBM on October 4, 1957, had an immediate impact on budgets for strategic programs, as did subsequent boasts by Nikita Khrushchev, first secretary of the Communist party, about Soviet missile prowess.[59] Neil H. McElroy, who

57. An equal if not greater problem was that the missile, once launched, could not be recalled. It was therefore deemed incompatible with the B-52, which might be sent aloft on ambiguous warnings. Launching an unrecallable missile intended to simulate a strategic bomber toward the Soviet Union posed an obvious safety risk and apparently contributed to the decision to cancel the program. See Edward A. Kolodziej, *The Uncommon Defense and Congress, 1945–1963* (Ohio State University Press, 1966), p. 340.

58. Werrell, *Evolution of the Cruise Missile*, pp. 123–28.

59. Walter A. McDougall, *The Heavens and the Earth: A Political History of the Space Age* (New York: Basic Books, 1985), pp. 141–56. Moscow radio reported on August 26, 1957, that a "super-long distance intercontinental multi-stage ballistic missile . . . flew at a very high, unprecedented altitude . . . [and] landed in the target area," but this received little public notice. See Beard, *Developing the ICBM*, p. 208. On October 9, 1957, Khrushchev told the *New York Times*, "I think I will not be revealing any military secret if I tell you that we now have all the rockets we need: long-range rockets, intermediate-range rockets and close-range rockets. Of course, these are not the limits of what can be achieved, for engineering is not marking time, but these means fully insure our defense." Approximately one month later, Khrushchev told a United Press correspondent: "Our designers have developed rockets that could, in the event of an attack on our country, strike any base in Europe, Asia, and Africa. On the very first try our missile fell exactly in the target area. . . . We have developed an intercontinental ballistic missile with a hydrogen warhead too." Quoted in Charles H. Donnelly, *The United States Guided Missile Program,* Prepared for the Preparedness Investigating Subcommittee of the Senate Committee on Armed Services, 86 Cong. 1st sess. (GPO, 1959), pp. 18–19.

became secretary of defense just five days after Sputnik, took a number of important steps in its aftermath. In November the number of planned ICBM squadrons was more than doubled, from eight to seventeen, and the deployment date was advanced. Funding increased dramatically, as more than 25 percent of the military budget was channeled to strategic programs alone: ballistic missile funding more than doubled, rising from $9.7 billion in 1957 to $20.8 billion in 1961.[60] In addition, on the eve of a November 27, 1957, appearance before a Senate investigating subcommittee chaired by Senator Lyndon Johnson (Democrat of Texas), McElroy resolved to settle the long-standing controversy between the Thor and Jupiter IRBMs by authorizing the production and deployment of both missiles.[61]

The domestic political atmosphere of the late 1950s became charged with emotion over the missile "gap" between the United States and the Soviet Union, as politicians tried to outdo each other in taking a strong stance on the issue. Missiles of every sort, along with other kinds of nuclear weaponry, became symbols of resolve in the global contest against communism.

Intercontinental Ballistic Missiles

The first U.S. intercontinental ballistic missile was placed on alert in October 1959, just five years after the approval of the Teapot Committee's recommendations and two years after Sputnik. The remarkable speed of this effort—managed by the air force—can in part be attributed to its scope: it was "the largest single military program ever undertaken by the United States" and had the support of "more than 30 major contractors, 200 major subcontractors, and 200,000 suppliers in industries across the Nation, whose joint resources include skills of thousands of scientists, engineers, and technicians." As of May 1960 the air force had obligated about $43 billion of its funds to this program and subsequently spent about $12 billion a year for research, development, testing, production, and operational deployment of the ballistic missiles. Hundreds of millions were also spent on new research, development, test, and production facilities for this program.[62]

60. *Missiles, Space, and Other Major Defense Matters,* Hearings, p. 509.

61. As Michael Armacost has written of this decision, "It hardly seems coincidental that [it] was reached only late in the evening prior to McElroy's appearance" before Johnson's subcommittee, which was investigating the impact of Sputnik I and II (launched on November 3, 1957) on national security, especially the alarming concerns that the United States had "slipped dangerously behind the Soviet Union in a number of very important fields." Johnson called the decision "good news" and hoped there would be "more reassessments, followed by more good news." See Michael H. Armacost, *The Politics of Weapons Innovation: The Thor-Jupiter Controversy* (Columbia University Press, 1969), p. 177; *Inquiry into Satellite and Missile Programs,* Hearings, pt. 1, pp. 1–3, 194–95. For a list of the fourteen important decisions made within the first two months after Sputnik, see *Inquiry Into Satellite and Missile Programs,* pp. 2080–82.

62. U.S. General Accounting Office, *Findings Resulting*

To date the United States has deployed four versions of ICBMs divided into nine types (Atlas D/E/F, Titan I/II, Minuteman I/II/III, and MX/Peacekeeper). These missiles have carried eight types of warheads with yields ranging from 170 kilotons to 10 megatons.

The first generation of ICBMs, Atlas D/E/F and Titan I, were large, liquid-fueled missiles launched from "soft" aboveground launchers (Atlas D), "semihard" coffin-type launchers (Atlas E), or "hard" silo-lift launchers (Atlas F, Titan I). Between October 31, 1959, and December 20, 1962, thirteen Atlas squadrons of 129 missiles and six Titan I squadrons with 108 missiles were operational. Because the liquid propellants used by these missiles, especially the Titan I, required cryogenic storage, however, the missiles could not be kept fueled except for a very brief period before launch without risking serious damage to the missiles themselves.[63] This situation necessarily limited their utility and prompted the search for less volatile, storable fuels.

Soon after these milestones were achieved, SAC began to replace the missiles with second-generation ICBMs: the Titan II and the solid-fueled Minuteman I. Three Titan II squadrons achieved operational status between June and December 1963. The first Minuteman I missiles went on alert on October 27, 1962, in the midst of the Cuban Missile Crisis. By year's end, two flights of 20 missiles (10 each) were operational. Eventually, 800 Minuteman I ICBMs were housed in unmanned, hardened, and widely dispersed (at 3- to 7-mile [4.8- to 11.3-kilometer] intervals) underground launch facilities (known as silos). A DOD directive issued on December 11, 1964, established the Minuteman force at 1,000 missiles, and this level was reached in April 1967 (for more on how this figure was derived, see the Introduction and pages 185–86). The first third-generation missile—the Minuteman III—with the new multiple independently targeted reentry vehicle began testing in 1968. Between 1970 and 1975, 550 Minuteman IIIs were deployed. By mid-July 1975, the Minuteman ICBM force consisted of 450 Minuteman IIs and 550 Minuteman IIIs.

While the number of land-based missiles remained relatively constant between 1967 and 1991, their military effectiveness was continuously improved. The original Mk-12/W62 reentry vehicle/warhead on 300 of the 550 Minuteman III missiles was replaced with a higher-yield Mk-12A/W78 between December 1979 and February 1983. The accuracy of Minuteman II and Minuteman III missiles has been constantly improved through the integration of new and more accurate guidance systems. To confuse, overwhelm, and jam the limited antiballistic missile system around Moscow, penetration aids (penaids) were deployed along with the missile reentry vehicles. Penaids reflect radar signals,

---

from Initial Review of the Ballistic Missile Programs of the Department of the Air Force, B-133042, December 27, 1960 (formerly Secret; declassified December 19, 1991), p. 8.

63. U.S. General Accounting Office, *Findings*, p. 22.

simulating or concealing actual reentry vehicles. The most common types are chaff (fine wires), aerosols (tiny beads that reflect infrared light), and active or passive decoys (which resemble or mimic a reentry vehicle). Targeting flexibility and remote retargeting options have been improved through the development of newer, faster, and more responsive systems. The latest such upgrade is a $632 million system called Rapid Execution and Combat Targeting, or REACT, though it is more commonly known among missileers as "Windows for Armageddon." REACT allows, for the first time, truly rapid and flexible retargeting for both individual missiles and the entire force.[64] The Nuclear Posture Review recommended retaining the Minuteman III (even as the much newer MX is retired) for the foreseeable future. As evidence of the missile's sturdy design and the air force's extensive and expensive maintenance and upgrade program, the U.S. Strategic Command (STRATCOM) expects the Minuteman force, with missiles now between twenty-two and twenty-seven years old, to remain viable until at least 2020.[65]

Construction of Missile Silos and Launch Pads

Between 1960 and 1967 contractors excavated and built a total of 1,180 underground silos for missiles, plus another 57 aboveground launch sites for the Atlas D and E and more than 100 Minuteman launch-control capsules (LCCs). The work was managed by the Army Corps of Engineers and the Army Corps of Engineers Ballistic Missile Construction Office (CEBMCO). The expenditures were credited to CEBMCO, which oversaw the effort, keeping it off air force budgets and helping to deflect concern about the already high cost of the ICBM program. The United States constructed ICBM launchers and support facilities for six types of missiles at sites on or near twenty-two air bases on land purchased or leased in seventeen states (see table 2-2).[66] The cost of this vast program was nearly $14 billion, which was about two-thirds of what it cost to develop the first atomic bombs during the Manhattan Project.[67]

64. William M. Arkin, "The Six-Hundred Million Dollar Mouse," *Bulletin of the Atomic Scientists*, vol. 52 (November/December 1996), p. 68.

65. By contrast, General Eugene Habiger, commander in chief of STRATCOM, has stated that Russian forces, most of which are newer than the Minuteman, will begin wearing out around 2005 because of aging and a general decline in Russian military readiness. Elaine M. Grossman, "Strategic Command Chief Sees Russian Nuclear Forces Degrading by 2005," *Inside the Pentagon*, August 29, 1996, pp. 5–6.

66. The decision to locate ICBM bases on or adjacent to existing air bases (which were presumably already targets) was questioned by Senator Henry M. Jackson during a 1960 hearing. Jackson wondered how this decision, taken for reasons of "economy and efficiency," in the words of Secretary of Defense Thomas Gates, contributed to the survivability of the ICBMs and, hence, their deterrent value. See *Missiles, Space, and Other Major Defense Matters,* Hearings, pp. 505–06.

67. The total cost per missile system was Atlas D/E, $1.5 billion; Titan I, $2.4 billion; Atlas F, $2.1 billion; Titan II, $2.1 billion; and Minuteman, $3.8 billion. An additional $1.9 billion went toward various tests and training facilities. U.S. Army Corps of Engineers Ballistic Missile Construction Office, "U.S. Air Force ICBM Construction Program," Corps

TABLE 2-2. Missile Silos and Launch Facilities Constructed in the United States, 1960–67

Type	Description	Construction: Started	Construction: Completed
Atlas D	30 soft launchers	June 13, 1957	June 15, 1960
Atlas E	27 semihard coffin	May 12, 1959	April 24, 1961
Atlas F	72 silo-lift	March 22, 1960	May 29, 1962
Titan I	54 silo-lift	May 1, 1959	March 16, 1962
Titan II	54 silo	December 7, 1960	March 4, 1963
Minuteman I/II	450 silo	March 15, 1961	1964
Minuteman III/MX	550 silo	1961	1967

State	Launch facilities, by state: Air force base	Near	Missiles
North Dakota	Minot	Minot	150 MMIII
	Grand Forks	Grand Forks	150 MMIII
Montana	Malmstrom	Great Falls	200 MMII/III
South Dakota	Ellsworth	Rapid City	150 MMII
	Ellsworth	Rapid City	9 Titan I
Missouri	Whiteman	Kansas City	150 MMII
Nebraska	F. E. Warren	Kimball	82 MMIII
	Lincoln	Lincoln	12 Atlas F
	Offutt	Omaha	6 Atlas D
	F. E. Warren	Kimball	1 Atlas E
Wyoming	F. E. Warren	Cheyenne	68 MMIII/MX
	F. E. Warren	Cheyenne	15 Atlas D
	F. E. Warren	Cheyenne	3 Atlas E
Colorado	F. E. Warren	Sterling	50 MM III
	F. E. Warren	Ft. Collins	5 Atlas E
	Lowry	Denver	18 Titan I
Kansas	Forbes	Topeka	9 Atlas E
	Schilling	Salina	12 Atlas F
	McConnell	Wichita	18 Titan II
Arizona	Davis-Monthan	Tucson	18 Titan II
Arkansas	Little Rock	Little Rock	18 Titan II
Washington	Fairchild	Spokane	8 Atlas E
	Larson	Moses Lake	9 Titan I
California	Beale	Sacramento	9 Titan I
	Vandenberg	Lompoc	6 Atlas D
Texas	Dyess	Abilene	12 Atlas F
	Altus	Fargo	1 Atlas F
New Mexico	Walker	Roswell	12 Atlas F
Oklahoma	Altus	Altus	11 Atlas F
New York	Plattsburgh	Plattsburgh	10 Atlas F
Idaho	Mountain Home	Mountain Home	9 Titan I
	Fairchild	Rockford	1 Atlas D
Iowa	Offutt	Missouri Valley	3 Atlas D
Vermont	Plattsburgh	Alburg/Swanton	2 Atlas F

Source: Lonnquest and Winkler, *To Defend and Deter.*

Various contractors bid for the right to work on the lucrative program, described in some quarters as "the largest and most extensive building program of its kind at that time."[68] At Whiteman AFB in Missouri, construction activities between 1962 and 1964 called for 168,000 yards (153,620 meters) of concrete, 25,355 tons of reinforcing steel, 15,120 tons of structural steel, and a vast underground intersite network of cable: "Enough of this cable was installed to run a line from Whiteman AFB to 100 miles [161 kilometers] beyond Los Angeles."[69]

Of the nineteen states that house missile bases, historically North Dakota has had the most silos (300) and Vermont the fewest (2, at Alburg and Swanton).

Atlas D

The Atlas D missile was stored horizontally aboveground on an unprotected launcher, then raised to a vertical position for fueling and firing. The typical configuration was in a group of three; in all, thirty were deployed. There were also aboveground launch buildings nearby. The average cost per launch facility was $26.3 million.[70]

Atlas E

The Atlas E was also stored horizontally, but in this case it was buried underground, in a concrete coffin 154 feet (46.9 meters) long. A heavily reinforced concrete roof covered the launcher and provided some protection against nuclear blast. Just before fueling and launch, the roof was retracted and the missile raised to a vertical position. Each of the twenty-seven missiles was deployed separately at an average cost of $26.3 million apiece and required a launch-control facility nearby.

Atlas F

The Atlas F was stored vertically on an elevator in an underground silo 180 feet (54.9 meters) deep. The doors would retract and the missile would be raised to the surface before firing. Each of the seventy-two silos had its own LCC and was built for an average cost of $29.2 million.[71]

---

of Engineers Historian's Office, Alexandria, Va., circa 1965, chart; C. D. Hargreaves, *Introduction to the Historical Report of the Corps of Engineers Ballistic Missile Construction Office and History of the Command Section, Pre-CEBMCO Thru December 1962* (Los Angeles, California: CEBMCO, circa 1963), esp. p. 8.

68. Jacob Neufeld, *Ballistic Missiles in the United States Air Force: 1945–1960* (Washington, D.C.: Office of Air Force History, 1990), p. 202.

69. "A Brief History of Whiteman AFB, Mo." (n.d., available on the World Wide Web at http://www.whiteman.af.mil/guide/wafbhist.html).

70. The Atlas D was quite vulnerable, both to attack from Soviet weapons and to snipers. During a February 1960 Senate hearing, JCS chairman General Nathan W. Twining was shown a photograph of an Atlas site from *Life* magazine and asked by Senator Stuart Symington if the missiles could be destroyed by a rifle or a single ICBM. Twining's answer was affirmative to both questions. See *Missiles, Space, and Other Major Defense Matters,* Hearings, p. 414.

71. For a history of the local impact of the Atlas F construction program at Walker AFB in New Mexico, see Terry Isaacs, "Silos and Shelters in the Pecos Valley: The Atlas

Titan I

The Titan I was deployed underground in a complex of three silos, connected to one powerhouse and other ancillary facilities, all interconnected by tunnels. Like the Atlas F, the Titan I would be raised to the surface before firing. One LCC was used to control three missiles. This practice reduced personnel and excavation costs, but it also cut down the number of targets necessary for an adversary to render the force useless. Eighteen of the three-missile complexes were deployed at five air force bases, at an average cost of $44.4 million per missile.

Titan II

The Titan II was deployed in silos 160 feet (48.8 meters) deep. Each of the fifty-four missiles had its own LCC. Eighteen were concentrated in a rectangle measuring 1,875 square miles (4,856 square kilometers) in an area north of Little Rock, Arkansas, and Little Rock AFB. Eighteen were scattered over 2,500 square miles (6,975 square kilometers) around Tucson, Arizona, and Davis Monthan AFB. Another eighteen were spread over 2,000 square miles (5,180 square kilometers) to the east and the west of Wichita, Kansas, and McConnell AFB. The average cost per missile was $38.9 million.

Minuteman

Minuteman I, II, and III missiles were placed in hardened dispersed silos in seven states: North Dakota, Montana, Missouri, South Dakota, Nebraska, Wyoming, and Colorado. One thousand silos and 100 underground LCCs were built, at an average cost per silo of $3.8 million. Each silo is buried 120 feet (36.6 meters) belowground, under a 110-ton concrete door (which would be blasted off before launch). Each LCC, located 60 to 120 feet (18.3 to 36.6 meters) underground and sealed off by an 8-ton metal door, is manned twenty-four hours a day by two air force launch-control officers (members rotate shifts—they are usually awake for eighteen hours and sleep for six—so that one person is always awake; each crew serves two to three shifts a week).

MX/Peacekeeper

In the mid-1980s fifty Minuteman III missiles were removed from their silos at F. E. Warren AFB in Wyoming and replaced with MX missiles. The Minuteman and MX silos and LCCs are widely dispersed over an area of 67,000 square miles (173,530 square kilometers), which is approximately the size of the state of Washington.

ICBM in Chaves County, New Mexico, 1960–1965," *New Mexico Historical Review*, vol. 68 (October 1993), pp. 347–70. Each of the twelve silos at this base utilized 7,500 yards (6,858 meters) of concrete and 350 tons of structural steel. Costs at this one base alone eventually totaled more than $230 million.

Submarines and Sea-Based Missiles

Like the Minuteman, the Polaris SLBM was a product of technological advances in solid propellants and lighter warheads.[72] The decision to proceed with a sea-based ballistic missile was made by Admiral Arleigh Burke, who had become chief of naval operations (CNO) in August 1955. An accelerated Polaris program was launched in January 1957, and in less than four years it proceeded from preliminary design to operational deployment: the first nuclear-powered ballistic missile submarine (SSBN), the USS *George Washington,* departed on its first patrol on November 15, 1960.

Initially, the navy worked with the army in developing plans for the liquid-fueled Jupiter IRBM as a shipboard or land-based system. Jupiter's length, weight, and diameter, as well as the difficulties and dangers of handling the cryogenic liquid fuel, led navy fleet ballistic missile (FBM) program managers in the CNO Special Projects Office to turn to a solid propulsion system. In March 1956 the navy received authorization to proceed with the study of such a system; by that summer the navy had assembled a proposal for a 30,000-pound (13,636-kilogram) solid-fuel missile (the Jupiter would have weighed 162,000 pounds, or 73,636 kilograms), made feasible by the expected development of relatively lightweight, high-yield nuclear warheads by the 1960s, as forecast by the AEC. At the end of 1956, the navy terminated its Jupiter program and initiated the Polaris program. In the following years, work proceeded with such intensity that the navy achieved its major goals ahead of schedule. Indeed, all three Polaris missiles, the A-1, A-2, and A-3, would be delivered much more quickly than the first generation of ballistic missiles while meeting all of their program and performance objectives.[73]

The next question to address was what kind of submarine would carry the missiles, and how many could it handle? The more missiles, the longer the submarine and the more difficult it would be to maneuver. Although more missiles per submarine might reduce costs, greater numbers might make the submarine a more tempting target. After weighing many factors, the authorities decided on sixteen missiles per submarine. Also crucial was the decision on how many submarines to build. Some early projections envisioned a fleet of up to 100. More disciplined planning reduced this to 45, and the final decision in September 1961 limited the Polaris program to 41 submarines (656 SLBMs).[74]

72. R. A. Fuhrman, "The Fleet Ballistic Missile System Polaris to Trident," American Institute of Aeronautics and Astronautics, February 1978.

73. Fuhrman, "The Fleet Ballistic Missile System," p. 5.

74. This figure was not based on any demonstrated need for a particular number of submarines or missiles. According to Alain Enthoven, the DOD official principally responsible for determining the final number, it was "simply a historical

Since 1960 the U.S. Navy has had three classes of SSBNs and four basic types of SLBMs. The initial Polaris A-1 SLBMs had a limited range and were soon replaced by the more capable A-2s and eventually by the multiple reentry vehicle (MRV) A-3.[75] A significant increase in capability began in 1971 with the introduction of MIRVed Poseidon SLBMs, which in the next five years increased the number of SSBN-based warheads from about 1,500 to 5,500. At the same time, numerous improvements had begun to take place in the communications, computing, and quieting systems of missiles and submarines, not to mention their electronics equipment.

Poseidon SLBMs were deployed on thirty-one converted Polaris submarines beginning in 1971. Between October 1979 and December 1982, twelve of these SSBNs were retrofitted to receive the Trident I SLBM. Trident I missiles also armed the first eight Ohio-class SSBNs deployed in the Pacific at Bangor Naval Submarine Base in Bangor, Washington. The Trident II SLBM is being deployed with the ten SSBNs of the Atlantic Fleet, based at Kings Bay Naval Submarine Base, Georgia. As a result of the Nuclear Posture Review, four of the Bangor-based submarines will be retrofitted to carry the Trident II. The future force, if all of the current plans are implemented and START II is enacted, will be a fleet of fourteen Ohio-class SSBNs armed with twenty-four Trident II SLBMs each, and each SLBM will carry up to five W88 warheads.[76]

Although the cold war has ended and nearly all Russian SSBNs have retreated to their home bases, data obtained from the navy reveals that U.S. SSBN operations were slow to adjust to these realities. From 1989 through at least 1993, U.S. SSBNs were at alert levels 11 to 18 percent higher than annual rates during the 1970s and 1980s and higher than at any time since 1969. Furthermore, more than 50 percent of the fleet was at sea on average in 1992 and 1993 (versus an average rate of 47 percent from 1970 to 1990, which dipped to as low as 37 percent in 1982). To support these high levels, the navy continues to maintain two separate "blue" and "gold" crews of about 160 personnel for each submarine (for a total of some 5,750 personnel for the eighteen-submarine fleet).[77] As a veteran Trident captain recently reported, "At our

accident. There was no precise calculation of the necessary number of missiles. The administration had inherited a program of 19 [submarines] then added 10, and then six and six, for 41." At this time, the number of proposed submarines ranged between 40 and 47. McNamara, by choosing 41, left open the possibility of a future increase (he testified in 1962 that this was not a "final decision") and thus increased his bargaining power with the navy in later years. Quoted in Desmond Ball, *Politics and Force Levels: The Strategic Missile Program of the Kennedy Administration* (University of California Press, 1980), pp. 242–44, 274–75.

75. Unlike the MIRV system (which came later), the A-3 MRV warheads were not capable of striking different targets.

76. In fact, all Trident SLBMs on "hard alert" (at sea within range of their targets), and thus presumably all other operational SLBMs, are already armed with five warheads apiece. Elaine M. Grossman, "Briefing Shows Navy Now Loads Trident Missiles with 5 Warheads, Not 8," *Inside the Pentagon,* February 5, 1998, pp. 5–6.

77. In 1996 there were eight Ohio-class SSBNs deployed at Kings Bay and a total of 2,607 personnel assigned to these submarines (for an average crew complement of 163 for each

end of the stick, things are pretty much the way they used to be." In January 1998, STRATCOM revealed that just four SSBNs were on alert patrols at any given time, rather than the six submarines (one-third of the fleet) assumed by independent observers."[78]

Deployment, it should be added, is not just a matter of loading a submarine with missiles. The submarine itself needs to be supplied, repaired, and overhauled. Crews need to be trained, rotated, rested, retrained, and paid. "Continuous readiness requires communication facilities, support bases, a logistics train, and realistic exercises. . . . The typical pattern in a weapon system with a life expectancy of an FBM submarine (20 years) is for the cumulative operating costs to almost equal the system's entire development and investment costs."[79]

Between 1956 and 1967 the Polaris program—with its 41 submarines and more than 5,000 Polaris missiles—cost an estimated $64 billion.[80] For the peak spending years, 1959 to 1964, the Polaris accounted for 8 to 14 percent of the total navy budget (this considerable expense, coupled with the Eisenhower administration's refusal to provide additional money for the program, led the navy to cut funding for all other projects by about 10 percent, engendering significant opposition to Polaris among those navy officials who favored surface warships). A dozen elements from DOD's future years defense program (FYDP) historical database for the period 1962–95 show that the price for SSBNs, including strategic submarine and weapons system support, support ships, Trident I, and Trident II came to $256 billion (acquiring 18 Ohio-class SSBNs between 1974 and 1991 cost $34.8 billion, or 14 percent of this total). An additional $572.7 million was spent between 1967 and 1986 on efforts to silence submarine platforms, "making them more compatible with installed sonars by reducing self and radiated noise . . . to define noise problems, develop corrective designs, materials, and procedures, and determine effectiveness of silencing measures."[81] These activities take place at Carr Inlet, Puget Sound. This accounting—$320.5 billion—

submarine). The total payroll for these crews was $68.9 million, for an average annual cost per submarine of $4.3 million and an average annual salary of $26,428 per crew member. In all, the base employed 9,212 personnel and had personnel and operating costs of $285.5 million. See Navy and Marine Corps Team of Northeast Florida and Camden County, Georgia, *Fiscal Year 1996 Regional Shareholders Report,* Office of Public Affairs, Naval Air Station Jacksonville, Fla., n.d. (circa Spring 1997).

78. William M. Arkin and Robert S. Norris, *Nuclear Alert after the Cold War,* NWD 93-4 (Natural Resources Defense Council, October 18, 1993); Ed Offley, "Trident Patrols Go On," *Seattle Post-Intelligencer,* May 12, 1997, p. B- 1; Grossman, "Briefing Shows Navy Now Loads Trident Missiles with 5 Warheads, Not 8," p. 5.

79. Harvey M. Sapolsky, *Creating the Fleet Ballistic Missile System: The Interaction of Technology and Organization in the Development of a Major Weapon System* (Cambridge, Mass.: MIT Press, October 1969), p. 220. According to the FYDP historical database, the annual operating and support costs for each Ohio-class SSBN are at least $59.5 million. For the fleet of eighteen submarines, this works out to more than $1 billion a year.

80. Sapolsky, *Creating the Fleet Ballistic Missile System,* p. 221.

81. Office of the Comptroller, Department of Defense, *FYDP Program Structure,* DOD7045.7-H (October 1993), pp. 2–97. Some, perhaps the majority, of these costs were for silencing nuclear-powered attack submarines (SSNs) but are included here because there is no obvious way of apportioning them between the two programs.

captures most, but probably not all, of the costs incurred by the SSBN program.

Naval Nuclear Propulsion

Naval vessels, particularly submarines, have used nuclear power for propulsion since the 1954 commissioning of the nuclear-powered attack submarine USS *Nautilus* (SSN-571).[82] In April 1994 the navy celebrated the nearly accident-free steaming of 100 million miles (161 million kilometers) with naval nuclear reactors.[83]

Research into naval nuclear propulsion began in 1946, under the aegis of the navy and the Manhattan Engineer District and the firm direction of Captain (later Admiral) Hyman G. Rickover, who in time earned the appellation, "father of the nuclear navy." In 1947 the Knolls Atomic Power Laboratory (KAPL) was established with sites in Schenectady, New York, and Windsor, Connecticut, to design, test, and build prototype naval reactors.[84] One year later, a second facility, the Bettis Atomic Power Laboratory, was opened in West Mifflin, Pennsylvania, to perform similar work.

Production of uranium-235 for the naval reactor program took place from 1952 to 1992 at the Oak Ridge, Paducah, and Portsmouth gaseous diffusion plants (GDP), though by the end of this period only

82. The *Nautilus* actually became operational on January 17, 1955. Richard G. Hewlett and Francis Duncan, *Nuclear Navy: 1946–1962* (University of Chicago Press, 1974); Joshua Handler and William M. Arkin, *Nuclear Warships and Naval Nuclear Weapons 1990: A Complete Inventory*, Neptune Papers no. 5 (Washington, D.C.: Greenpeace, September 1990); *Energy and Water Development Appropriations for 1996*, Hearings before the House of Representatives Subcommittee on Energy and Water Development of the Committee on Appropriations, 104 Cong. 1 sess. (GPO, 1995), pt. 6, pp. 385–92.

83. The navy maintains a high degree of secrecy around its nuclear operations. While the limited information supplied by the navy suggests that its safety record is quite good, it is not flawless. In addition to the sinking of the USS *Thresher* (SSN-593) and USS *Scorpion* (SSN-589) in 1963 and 1968, respectively, known accidents include a primary coolant leak aboard the USS *Guardfish* (SSN-612) on April 21, 1973, while running submerged 370 miles (595 kilometers) south-southwest of Puget Sound, Washington, and a propulsion casualty of unknown origin on November 24, 1985, aboard the USS *Swordfish* (SSN-579). The navy also acknowledges a primary coolant leak aboard the aircraft carrier USS *Nimitz* (CVN-68) on May 11, 1979. See William M. Arkin and Joshua Handler, *Naval Accidents 1945–1988*, Neptune Papers no. 3 (Washington, D.C.: Greenpeace, June 1989), pp. 5–7.

84. Knolls was initially established by General Leslie R. Groves, head of the Manhattan Engineer District, as an incentive to the General Electric Company to run the Hanford Reservation. When Du Pont, which had agreed to run Hanford during the war but always intended to quit at its conclusion, informed Groves in late 1945 that it planned to withdraw no later than October 31, 1946, Groves approached General Electric about assuming the contract. The company was initially reluctant, given the uncertainty surrounding the future of the atomic program and its own plans to reconvert its operations to nonmilitary functions, but later, after repeated entreaties from the War Department, G.E. accepted Groves's offer, agreeing to manage both Hanford and a new government-owned laboratory in Schenectady. The company also insisted on and received contract provisions guaranteeing full recovery for all costs associated with its operations at Hanford and Knolls and freeing it from all liability (see chapter 6). The AEC spent two months reviewing the details of this contract, which it did not like "at all," because, among other things, "the company could stop the operation of Hanford almost whenever it chose, and still have the laboratory." Nevertheless, General Electric managed Hanford from 1946 until 1964 and Knolls from 1947 until 1993. See Rodney P. Carlisle with Joan M. Zenzen, *Supplying the Nuclear Arsenal: American Production Reactors, 1942–1992* (Johns Hopkins University Press, 1996), pp. 54–55; David E. Lilienthal, *The Journals of David E. Lilienthal*, vol. 2: *The Atomic Energy Years, 1945–1950* (New York: Harper & Row, 1964), p. 113.

Portsmouth was still producing the fuel. Production was terminated in 1992 after the DOE and the navy determined that existing stockpiles and material available from the planned retirement of nuclear warheads would satisfy all its future requirements. Since 1949 the Naval Reactors Facility (NRF) at the Idaho National Engineering and Environmental Laboratory has been examining used naval reactor cores in its expended core facility and then reprocessing them (beginning in 1953) at the Idaho Chemical Processing Plant (ICPP) to extract uranium-235 and krypton-85. HEU was reused in the weapons program (as fuel for the Savannah River reactors, beginning in 1968) and krypton-85 was sold commercially (ICPP was one of only two sources of this gas; the other was the Soviet Union). Reprocessing was halted in 1992 after the DOE determined there was no need for additional quantities of HEU. Operating and capital equipment costs for ICPP from 1952 through 1995 totaled more than $8.7 billion.[85]

Several other facilities also contributed to the naval reactors program. From 1957 to 1978 a plant in Apollo, Pennsylvania, converted uranium hexafluoride (UF-6) into highly enriched reactor fuel.[86] Similar work took place at the United Nuclear Corporation Plant in Hermatite, Missouri, from 1961 to 1972. Since 1978, the navy's sole facility to convert UF-6 (from the Portsmouth Gaseous Diffusion Plant) into HEU fuel is Nuclear Fuel Services, Inc., in Erwin, Tennessee (see appendix C for more detailed descriptions of these facilities).

The naval nuclear propulsion program has historically operated nine land-based prototype reactors to train naval personnel and study new reactor designs; five of these are at KAPL and four at INEEL. One reactor at KAPL's site in Windsor, Connecticut, was shut down in March 1993 (see chapter 5). Six others were closed through 1996. The cost to build the reactors at KAPL (which were completed in 1959) was

85. During thirty-nine years of operation, the ICPP recovered more than $1 billion worth of HEU (in unadjusted dollars) from spent naval reactor fuel and spent fuel from some government and nongovernment research and test reactors (through 1984 ICPP had recovered 23 metric tons of HEU). This HEU was then blended at the Y-12 Plant at the Oak Ridge Reservation with HEU recovered at the Savannah River Site and converted to metal form for use as fuel elements in SRS reactors. See Thomas B. Cochran and others, *Nuclear Weapons Databook*, vol. 3: *U.S. Nuclear Warhead Facility Profiles* (Cambridge, Mass.: Ballinger, 1987), pp. 37–39; INEEL Fact Sheet, "Idaho Chemical Processing Plant," February 1997 (available on the World Wide Web at http://www.inel.gov/about/facts/icppfactsheet2.html); facsimile communication, Kelly Lemons, Budget Services Division, Idaho Operations Office, U.S. Department of Energy, to Stephen Schwartz, August 4, 1995.

86. The privately owned facility, run from 1957 to 1967 by the Nuclear Materials and Equipment Corporation (NUMEC), was suspected by the CIA of diverting some 200 pounds of HEU to Israel's nuclear weapons program in 1965. When decontamination efforts began in 1989 (eleven years after the plant had closed due to diminishing orders from the navy), however, officials from Babcock & Wilcox, who took over the facility in 1971, reported extremely heavy contamination, necessitating the removal of many sections of the concrete floor. By 1992 the Nuclear Regulatory Commission had documented the recovery of more than 100 kilograms of HEU, the amount allegedly diverted to Israel, with still more being recovered in subsequent years. The cleanup effort was funded, in part, with $34 million appropriated by Congress in October 1990. See Seymour M. Hersh, *The Samson Option* (New York: Random House, 1991), pp. 187–88, 242–57, 331.

approximately $140 million to $150 million, which was double the original estimate.[87]

At the end of 1997 there were 131 operational sea-going naval reactors (compared with 108 operating U.S. civilian power reactors). These reactors powered 113 vessels, including 80 SSNs, 20 SSBNs (two of which are used as shore-based training platforms), 8 aircraft carriers (CVNs), 4 cruisers (CGNs), and 1 deep submergence research vessel (NR-1) (for more on NR-1, see chapter 3).[88] The total number of nuclear-powered vessels built or still under construction comes to 191 submarines, 9 cruisers, 9 aircraft carriers, and the NR-1. In 1988 the number of operating reactors peaked at 169. Plans to expand the fleet were curtailed in the early 1990s with the cancellation of 37 new submarines.

Over its lifetime, the naval propulsion program has designed, built, and operated more than thirty distinct types of reactors and conducted more than 300 refuelings/defuelings.[89] Nuclear-powered vessels require unique handling, and this is accomplished at specially outfitted shipyards. Such ships are built at two shipyards: General Dynamics Electric Boat Division in Groton, Connecticut, and Newport News Shipbuilding in Newport News, Virginia. With the end of the cold war and the navy's decision to forgo many planned vessels, both yards now find themselves in fierce competition for the remaining work.[90] Refuelings/defuelings and maintenance activities take place at Charleston Naval Shipyard, South Carolina; Norfolk Naval Shipyard, Virginia;

87. Matthew L. Wald, "Citing Peace, Navy Will Shut Reactor Prototype," *New York Times*, December 7, 1991, p. 29; Daniel P. Jones, "Sub Reactor's Disposal Raises Questions in Windsor," *Hartford Courant*, August 7, 1996, p. 1.

88. Submarines use one reactor each, nuclear-powered cruisers two each. The nuclear-powered cruisers are gradually being retired as they reach the end of their service life. Seven Nimitz-class aircraft carriers are powered by two reactors each. The USS *Enterprise* (CVN-65), the first nuclear-powered carrier, is a one-of-a-kind ship utilizing eight reactors. Under design and construction from 1951 to 1961, its total cost during that time increased by more than $600 million, to an estimated $2.9 billion. As a result of this experience and the high cost of other nuclear-powered vessels, no nuclear carriers were funded from 1974 to 1980 (by contrast, four new carriers were funded from 1983 to 1988 as part of the Reagan administration's military buildup). See Hans M. Kristensen, William M. Arkin, and Joshua Handler, *Aircraft Carriers: The Limits of Power*, Neptune Papers no. 7 (Washington, D.C.: Greenpeace, June 1994), pp. 6–7.

89. Early naval reactors had a lifetime of about two years. The most modern reactor cores can now last fifteen years between refuelings, thereby reducing both waste generation and overhaul time and, therefore, overall costs. The navy is currently designing reactor cores to last fifty years for aircraft carriers, forty years for SSBNs, and thirty years for SSNs. These would eliminate the need for refuelings altogether, reduce costs and environmental hazards, and increase operational readiness. The navy has argued for decades that nuclear power offers aircraft carriers virtually unlimited range at maximum speed, the ability to remain on-station indefinitely without refueling, and greater storage capacity for essential materiel, such as jet fuel and ordnance. However, a 1994 analysis of navy data found that the claims are not matched by actual operational practice and that in most regards, nuclear-powered carriers are merely equal to or less effective than their conventionally powered counterparts, owing in large part to maintenance requirements. For example, over an expected operational life of fifty years, a nuclear carrier will spend more than sixteen years—nearly one-third of its life—in shipyards undergoing defueling/refueling, overhauls (each costing more than $2 billion) and other maintenance associated with its nuclear power plant. Extended life reactor cores have the potential to reduce these problems significantly. See Kristensen and others, *Aircraft Carriers*.

90. Associated Press, "Splitting Contracting of Sub to Raise Cost by $2 Billion, but Will Save Jobs," *Washington Post*, September 15, 1997, p. A4.

Portsmouth Naval Shipyard, Maine; and Puget Sound Naval Shipyard, Washington. Whenever the navy decides to retire a nuclear-powered vessel, several of these shipyards participate in dismantling the ship or submarine and removing its highly radioactive spent fuel and reactor compartment (these steps are described in detail in chapter 5).

Accounting for the costs of the naval nuclear propulsion program is problematic because its relationship to the nuclear weapons mission is not self-evident. Reactors for ballistic missile submarines should clearly be included in the total, but what about those for SSNs and surface ships? As discussed in chapter 4, not all SSNs have been dedicated to the strategic antisubmarine warfare mission, one wholly concerned with nuclear weapons. As for surface ships, as discussed later in this chapter, nuclear weapons were deployed extensively by the navy from the late 1950s until 1992, meaning that a sizable portion of the nuclear propulsion program for that period for these vessels is related to the nuclear weapons mission. Unfortunately, budgetary records of the AEC, ERDA, DOE, and DOD provide no ready means of segregating these costs by mission.

According to the available data, the joint DOD-DOE naval nuclear program has expended at least $30 billion since 1948. The cost of enriching HEU for naval reactors from 1952 to 1964 (see appendix table A-1) cannot be segregated from the overall enrichment total, although $9.6 billion was expended for such work from 1967 to 1993. Nor does this figure include the $8.7 billion expended at the ICPP from 1952 through 1995 (about 50 percent of which went toward reprocessing naval reactor fuel).[91] The reactor-related costs for the *Nautilus* and its land-based prototype (exclusive of the cost of building the submarine itself) totaled approximately $836 million. Six discrete program elements from the FYDP indicate that the navy on its own spent at least $3.5 billion on research for nuclear propulsion technology between 1962 and 1995, including $539 million for reactor development for Nimitz-class aircraft carriers and $327 million for reactors to power destroyers. Perhaps another $1.5 billion was expended before 1962.[92]

91. Historical AEC and DOE budgetary breakdowns for the program did not always include construction and capital equipment costs. Therefore this figure is only a minimum estimate. Testifying in February 1960, Admiral Rickover stated that the cumulative cost of the program to that date was "about $850 million" for "all of our laboratories . . . five land prototypes of atomic power plants . . . all of the research and development over this period . . . [and] the atomic power plants for the *Nautilus* and the *Seawolf*." In 1996 dollars, this is about $6 billion. See *Missiles, Space, and Other Major Defense Matters,* Hearings, p. 169. A vague reference in a June 9, 1953, diary entry by AEC chairman Gordon Dean appears to indicate that cumulative costs to that time for just six years of operations at Bettis Field (now Bettis Laboratory) totaled $4.2 billion, or about $30 billion in 1996 dollars. If this is correct, it would mean that official AEC and navy reports on the costs of the naval reactor propulsion program are gross understatements. See Roger M. Anders, ed., *Forging the Atomic Shield: Excerpts from the Office Diary of Gordon E. Dean* (University of North Carolina Press, 1987), p. 259. In 1992 the naval reactors program assumed budgetary responsibility for the DOE's efforts to shut down HEU production capabilities at the Portsmouth Gaseous Diffusion Plant. From 1992 to 1995, the cost for this activity was $323 million.

92. Hewlett and Duncan, *Nuclear Navy,* p. 403. Data provided by the navy indicate that among the costs it considers part of the overall naval nuclear propulsion program are shipbuilding expenses for new submarines and aircraft carri-

O&S costs for reactor maintenance, overhaul, and refuelings/defuelings are not identified separately and may be included in the overall program cost for particular classes of nuclear-powered submarines and surface ships. For 1991, however, records show that the Puget Sound Naval Shipyard expended $308 million for the following work on nuclear-powered vessels: to inactivate four submarines, recycle nine submarines, dispose of the reactor compartments of fourteen submarines, refuel overhauls of a cruiser and submarine, carry out nonrefueling overhauls on an carrier and submarine, perform maintenance on one aircraft carrier, and conduct classified work on two submarines and one cruiser.[93]

Because the joint DOD-DOE effort underlies the entire naval reactor effort, from research and development to training, we include its total costs on the grounds that if it did not exist the entire program would cease to function. To assess DOD expenditures, we considered that as of March 31, 1986, the navy operated 148 nuclear-powered ships and submarines, which represented about 40 percent of its submarine, aircraft carrier, and major surface combatant force. Of those 148 vessels, 135, or 91 percent, were submarines (38, or 25.5 percent, were SSBNs; and 97, or 65.5 percent, were SSNs).[94] This percentage decreased slightly—to 89 percent—by 1990 as the overall size of the navy declined. By 1997 SSBNs and SSNs accounted for 76 percent of all operating naval reactors (14 percent and 62 percent, respectively). Using these data and the conservative approach taken in chapter 4 of allocating just half the cost of SSNs to the antisubmarine warfare mission, we allocate just 50 percent of the overall costs from 1948 to 1996 in navy records and the FYDP (counting 100 percent of the SSBNs and approximately 50 percent of the SSNs over the duration of the program), or $2.5 billion. Thus a total accounting for naval nuclear propulsion research, development, testing, and production comes to at least $46 billion. Including the total O&S costs for naval reactors could add $10 billion to the total, with perhaps $5 billion of that attributable to nuclear weapons missions. That would bring the overall total to $51 billion.

Intermediate-Range Ballistic Missiles

At the same time that the first generation of ICBMs was being developed, work was under way on intermediate-range ballistic missiles. Also

ers and aircraft carrier inactivation. These costs are considered separately here.

93. U.S. General Accounting Office, *Nuclear-Powered Ships: Accounting for Shipyard Costs and Nuclear Waste Disposal Plans*, NSIAD- 92-256 (July 1992), p. 13.

94. Ronald O'Rourke, Congressional Research Service, Foreign Affairs and National Defense Division, *Nuclear-Powered and Nuclear-Weapon-Capable Ships in the U.S. Navy: An Aid to Identification*, Report 86-659F (Washington, D.C: Library of Congress, April 16, 1986), table 1, p. CRS-2.

liquid-fueled, their range was about 1,500 nautical miles (2,777 kilometers). Arguing that they could be produced and deployed before ICBMs, the 1955 Killian Report (the product of a committee established by the National Security Council to review strategic nuclear weapons programs) recommended their early development. Thus in December 1955 President Eisenhower assigned both the IRBM and ICBM highest national priority.[95] Their range necessitated deployment in countries in Europe and elsewhere around the Soviet periphery. Although some DOD officials saw unnecessary duplication in the Thor and Jupiter projects, Eisenhower supported a competitive approach to determine which missile worked better.[96] As a result, two powerful interest groups (comprised of the army and the air force, their respective industrial teams, and their congressional allies) emerged, prepared to do whatever was necessary to sustain their programs.[97] In the wake of the Soviet Union's success with Sputnik in 1957, the U.S. government supported immediate production and deployment of IRBMs in Western Europe to alleviate anxieties about Western vulnerability (see box 2-1).

By late 1957 the Thor and Jupiter programs were well along, both having been authorized for deployment. However, these decisions were made *before* consultations with America's allies, since it was assumed they would gladly accept the missiles in light of the ominous new threat emanating from the Soviet Union. When the allies, especially the United Kingdom, balked, U.S. policymakers were taken aback (Secretary of State John Foster Dulles quickly and publicly disavowed any intention of pressuring allies to accept the IRBMs.) Whereas U.S. officials considered their plans to be supportive of European security concerns, by demonstrating U.S. resolve to respond forcefully to any Soviet attack, some Europeans saw the planned deployments as bringing them a step closer

95. This "tended to confer a measure of immunity from deep budget cuts." In addition, neither the Bureau of the Budget (today the Office of Management and Budget) nor the Defense Department's comptroller "regularly employed systems analysis or cost-effectiveness tests to evaluate comparatively the weapons proposals advanced by the services. . . . Budgets were fashioned with an eye to inputs rather than outputs. The long-range cost implications of weapons decisions were not systematically examined." Armacost, *The Politics of Weapons Innovation*, p. 281.

96. Trevor Gardner, the assistant secretary of defense for research and development, favored focusing on development of ICBMs and testified as early as 1956: "We need to be more decisive and place our bets with more accuracy. Having a whole family of ballistic missile programs not only slows the programs down but it is wasteful of national funds." Quoted in Beard, *Developing the ICBM*, p. 198. Moreover, the decision to authorize two parallel IRBM programs—whether to hedge bets on technology or simply because a choice was politically impossible—"was not apparently informed by any clear conception as to how the technological yield of such competition could be maximized." Indeed, as Admiral Arthur Radford, chairman of the Joint Chiefs of Staff testified in 1958 (after he had stepped down as chairman at the end of his four-year term), "Well, the way it works out, I imagine for the most part we have tended to make a decision which gave each service a chance to do something. And that in some cases has cost us a lot of money." Armacost, *The Politics of Weapons Innovation*, pp. 76, 261.

97. An assistant secretary of defense stated in 1958 that "if the Defense Department suggested canceling the Air Force's Thor program, a Congressional delegation from California would be down our necks. And elimination of the Army's Jupiter program would have half the Alabama delegation plus a couple of representatives from the Detroit area fighting us." In fact, in a move anticipating the Rockwell Corporation's contracting scheme for the B-1 bomber, the two services dispersed Thor and Jupiter contracts across the country, ensuring the broadest possible support and political leverage for their programs. See Armacost, *The Politics of Weapons Innovation*, pp. 177, 254.

to becoming "cannon fodder."[98] In addition, the successful test of an Atlas ICBM on December 17, 1957, the day after heads of state of the North Atlantic Treaty Organization convened to discuss the proposed deployments, indicated that the IRBMs and their bases were likely to be only an interim system and thus not something requiring a political quid pro quo.[99] As journalist Marquis Childs opined, the entire affair was "the winter of our discontent following on the autumn of our disillusion."[100]

The original plan was to deploy eight Thor squadrons (120 missiles) at three bases in the United Kingdom. In a February 1, 1958, agreement between the United States and Great Britain, this was reduced to four squadrons (60 missiles); the first squadron became operational in June 1959. The launch pads stretched from East Anglia to the edge of the Yorkshire Moors.[101] Royal Air Force crews came to the United States and trained in Arizona. On August 1, 1962, the British minister of defense announced that the Thors would be phased out by the end of 1963 (after hearing from Secretary McNamara in May that the United States would soon end its logistical support for the program). During the Cuban Missile Crisis, 59 of the 60 Thors were put on a higher level of alert. By August 1963 they had been removed from operational duty and the phaseout was complete.

The Jupiter missile would have an equally short service life. On March 26, 1959, Italy and the United States signed an agreement to deploy thirty Jupiter missiles to Italy. The first Jupiter was placed in Italy in July 1960, and in Turkey in November 1961; by 1963 all forty-five had been deactivated (under a secret agreement between the United States and the Soviet Union negotiated during the Cuban Missile Crisis). The Thor program cost $9.4 billion and the Jupiter $5.2 billion.[102]

98. Henry Jackson, who favored the large-scale production of tactical nuclear weapons, believed that such weapons would eventually be used against "soldiers in uniform and against troops in the field" and that with them Americans would outflank Stalin's armies and halt the Red Army "in its tracks," thus increasing "Western Europe's will to resist." If anything, comments and plans such as this increased European resistance to U.S. efforts to create an atomic battlefield. *Congressional Record*, 82 Cong. 1 Sess., vol. 97, pt. 10 (October 9, 1951), p. 12867.

99. In fact, "it appears that the request for overseas bases for the Thor and Jupiter missiles was prompted at least as significantly by the political advantages of immediately capitalizing on available weaponry as by a sober and systematic evaluation of the strategic requirements of the situation. Even the political advantages subsequently proved illusory." Armacost, *The Politics of Weapons Innovation*, p. 210.

100. Quoted in Armacost, *The Politics of Weapons Innovation*, p. 199. Sites in Alaska, Okinawa, Guam, Formosa (Taiwan), the Philippines, the Azores, North Africa, and Thule, Greenland, were also considered as potential IRBM bases, but all were ultimately rejected. The difficulties in finding suitable bases, coupled with the discovery that the missile gap did not exist and the cost and vulnerable nature of the missiles, made "additional deployment unnecessary and uneconomical." The Thor and Jupiter production lines were accordingly shut down (pp. 212–13). See also *Missiles, Space, and Other Major Defense Matters, Hearing*, pp. 389–92.

101. These deployment plans indicate that while dispersion of forces would have made sense militarily, economic factors, chiefly the savings in logistics resulting from a smaller number of bases relatively near to each other, were foremost on the mind of SAC when it came to finalizing the deployments. Furthermore, the missiles were quite vulnerable to all sorts of attacks, including snipers. A more protective basing mode was deemed too expensive. Thus the Thors would only have been useful had they been launched in a first strike against the Soviet Union. Yet the deployment agreement gave Britain a political veto on their use, making a first strike an unlikely prospect at best. The British government paid an estimated $175 million to construct facilities for the Thor missiles and provide other necessary support.

102. Thor missiles were later reused in the U.S. antisatel-

Box 2-1

Europe and American Nuclear Strategy

Western Europe figured heavily in American nuclear strategy and nuclear deployments during the cold war, primarily because American leaders were convinced that West European security was a vital national interest; for them, what happened in Europe was laden with implications for the world balance of power and the future of American political and economic institutions. Beginning with World War II, if not earlier, American leaders worried that a Western Europe dominated by a hostile power could present a dangerous challenge. The concept of national security that crystallized during the 1940s started with the premise that the United States had to avoid at all costs a situation in which a potential foe had substantial control over the resources of Europe and Asia: "Even the specter of such a situation would force the United States to prepare for conflict, to reconfigure its economy, to limit its political freedoms, and to become a garrison state."[1]

From President Franklin Delano Roosevelt forward, American leaders entertained those fears because they believed that U.S. institutions could not flourish in a hostile world. If hostile powers, whether fascist or communist, dominated industrial Europe and world trade, the United States would have to start regimenting its foreign trade to compete effectively and to acquire necessary imported raw materials. Moreover, an unfriendly European hegemon would present a formidable military challenge that could require the United States to rearm on an immense scale, which would mean further economic regimentation.[2]

Concerns about European security persisted long after World War II, although during the cold war Washington was less anxious about a Soviet surprise attack on Western Europe than it was about the risk of miscalculation in a crisis and the political impact of the Soviet Union's military power. What especially troubled U.S. policymakers was that if West European allies perceived a shift in the balance of power that favored the Soviet Union, they might reconsider their alliance relations with Washington and drift toward neutralism, perhaps even making separate security arrangements with Moscow. American officials saw that as an intolerable prospect, which would quickly turn the United States into a "beleaguered island and a garrison state."[3]

Changes in the balance of power could easily be precipitated by an American failure during a foreign policy crisis, for example, "if we let down West Berlin and Turkey." To prevent such an outcome and to strengthen Western Europe's alignment with the United States, policymakers continually pondered the problem of European morale and political confidence and the actions needed to assure (or reassure) European leaders that American security guarantees were credible.[4]

As the Soviet Union became a nuclear power during the 1950s, American policymakers took it for granted that Western Europe's confidence depended upon U.S. military strength and pledges that Washington would use

1. Melvyn P. Leffler, *The Specter of Communism: The United States and the Origins of the Cold War, 1917–1953* (New York: Hill & Wang, 1994), p. 48.

2. Leffler, *The Specter of Communism*, pp. 30–31.

3. Memorandum, Walter W. Rostow to the Secretary of State, "Alliances and Their Inhibiting Effect on U.S. Action at a Time of Crisis," November 15, 1962, State Department Records, Policy Planning Staff Records for 1962, Box 229, Chron File, November–December 1962, National Archives.

4. Memorandum, Rostow to the Secretary of State, "Alliances and Their Inhibiting Effect."

Box 2-1
(continued)

nuclear weapons in a crisis. Thus in April 1950, NSC 68 declared that the Soviet Union's newly acquired atomic capabilities had caused "increasing nervousness in Western Europe" and an "increasing temptation" to "seek a position of neutrality." Washington could revive "confidence" only by greatly expanding its nonnuclear and nuclear capabilities. Although the Eisenhower administration would deemphasize the buildup of conventional forces, it too assumed that Washington needed to maintain the confidence of its European allies through nuclear protection.[5]

In the late 1950s, Soviet breakthroughs in launching satellites and testing ICBMs led U.S. policymakers to ponder whether U.S. strategy still enjoyed European confidence. Now the perennial question in European minds was, would Washington sacrifice New York for Hamburg or Paris in the event of a Soviet nuclear strike? American policymakers began to fret that if a "nuclear death neurosis" did not drive the Europeans toward neutralism, it might lead to the equally unpalatable option of greater nuclear proliferation.[6]

What did U.S. policymakers have to do to improve and maintain European confidence? During the decades of the cold war, confidence-building measures included dispersing thousands of tactical nuclear weapons across Europe, establishing NATO nuclear stockpiles, temporarily deploying Jupiter missiles in Italy and Turkey and Thor missiles in Great Britain, enduring deployments of Pershing missiles in Germany, forming nuclear planning committees, and embracing a nuclear first-use policy. Even if the Europeans were uncertain, secretaries of state such as John Foster Dulles and his successors would declare that the United States would "pay the price" of nuclear war. For Dulles, Washington would "come to the aid of its friends" not out of "love" for them but "out of the belief that if we did not . . . we would be faced with a worse alternative later."[7]

Washington never cured Western European fears of "nuclear death," and NATO's growing nuclearization plainly aggravated the problem. Whether State Department officials overestimated the possibility of neutralism or the levels of forces needed to ensure Western Europe's transatlantic orientation is open to question.[8] Nevertheless, preoccupations with Western Europe were central to the U.S. nuclear policy and posture during the cold war.

—William Burr

5. John P. Glennon and others, eds., *National Security Affairs: Foreign Economic Policy*, vol. 1 of S. Everett Gleason and Fredrick Anndahl, gen. eds., *Foreign Relations of the United States* GPO, (1950), pp. 277, 284.

6. See memoranda of conversations, April 7 and June 17, 1958, Department of State Records, Policy Planning Staff Records, 1957–61, National Archives.

7. Memorandum of conversation, June 17, 1958. The "worse" alternative was that "we would be crowded and crowded by the Soviet Union." See Dean Rusk's speech, classified "top secret" before NATO Council, December 14, 1961, indicating U.S. resolve to use nuclear weapons in the event of a Soviet attack. USRO/Paris Polto-A 718, December 15, 1961, Policy Planning Staff Records, Box 160, Europe. See also David Goldfischer, *The Best Defense: Policy Alternatives for U.S. Nuclear Security from the 1950s to the 1990s* (Cornell University Press, 1993), p. 216.

8. Anxiety that the wrong nuclear policies could generate neutralist tendencies and expand Soviet influence endured. See. for example, NSSM 84 Inter-Departmental Steering Committee, "U.S. Strategies and Forces for NATO" (National Security Study Memorandum 84 Report) (n.d., circa May 1970), copy at the National Security Archive.

Ballistic missiles were only one way to deliver nuclear warheads. Other kinds of missiles were also developed, tested, and deployed, among which cruise missiles were particularly popular. Land-based intercontinental cruise missiles, such as the Navaho and Snark, and the sea-based Regulus I and Regulus II cruise missiles were among the first types developed in the 1940s and 1950s (for costs and production numbers, see table 2-3).[103] But they proved cumbersome and unreliable and soon were supplanted by ICBMs and SLBMs.

Several shorter-range cruise missiles saw duty. The modern air-launched and sea-launched types deployed in the 1980s are among the most accurate, sophisticated, and versatile weapons in the U.S. arsenal and can be launched from several types of aircraft as well as surface ships and submarines. During the 1991 Gulf War, the United States fired 282 conventionally armed Sea-Launched Cruise Missiles (SLCMs) and 35 specially converted conventionally armed Air-Launched Cruise Missiles at Iraq. In June 1993 an additional 23 SLCMs were launched against Baghdad in retaliation for Iraq's role in the attempted assassination of President George Bush. To protest Iraqi attacks on the Kurds in northern Iraq, the United States in September 1996 fired another 31 SLCMs at missile sites, radar batteries, and command and control facilities in southern Iraq. Thirteen ALCMs were also fired from B-52 bombers flying from Guam. The nuclear-armed versions of the ALCM and SLCM cost $3.5 million and $3.9 million each, respectively (not including the warhead). Because of their high cost, fewer conventionally armed versions were deployed.[104]

---

lite program from 1964 to 1976 (see chapter 4), in the Safeguard C atmospheric test readiness program from 1963 until 1993 (see chapter 1), and for three high-altitude nuclear tests at Johnston Island in 1962. For a comprehensive analysis of the controversy surrounding the Thor and Jupiter programs, see Armacost, *The Politics of Weapons Innovation*; and Philip Nash, *The Other Missiles of October: Eisenhower, Kennedy, and the Jupiters, 1957–1963* (University of North Carolina Press, 1997).

103. By late January 1959, four submarines and four cruisers were equipped to fire the Regulus I. The Regulus II was canceled in December 1958 (after twenty-five were built) in favor of the Polaris SLBM. See *Missile and Space Activities,* Joint Hearings before the Preparedness Investigating Subcommittee of the Committee on Armed Services and the Committee on Aeronautical and Space Sciences, 86 Cong. 1 sess. (GPO, 1959) pp. 19, 86; James Norris Gibson, *The History of the U.S. Nuclear Arsenal* (Greenwich, Conn.: Brompton Books, 1989), pp. 153–54.

104. Department of Defense, *Conduct of the Persian Gulf War,* Final Report to Congress Pursuant to Title V of the Persian Gulf Conflict Supplemental Authorization and Personnel Benefits Act of 1991, Public Law 102-25 (April 1992), appx. T, pp. T-178–T-180, T-199–T-203; Gwen Ifill, "Raid on Baghdad; U.S. Fires Missiles at Baghdad, Citing April Plot to Kill Bush," *New York Times,* June 27, 1993, p. A1; Eric Schmitt, "Raid on Iraq: The Strategy; Targets Were Chosen to Punish and Weaken Hussein, U.S. Officials Say," *New York Times,* September 4, 1996, p. A9; John Cushman, Jr., "Raid on Iraq: The Weapon; Pentagon Defends Missiles' Accuracy," *New York Times,* September 5, 1996, p. A10; John Mintz, "U.S. Cruise Missiles Have Long Lineage; Improvements Solve Gulf War Problems," *Washington Post,* September 4, 1996, p. A23. During the Gulf War, 288 SLCMs were actually launched, 6 unsuccessfully. The ALCM was originally only a nuclear-capable weapon. Under a secret program begun in 1988, several hundred of the 1,787 originally purchased have been converted (at an additional cost of $260,000 per missile) to carry conventional warheads. Although SLCMs were produced in nuclear and conventional versions, during the Gulf War nuclear versions had to be offloaded from Navy ships in order to free up space for conventional ones. William M. Arkin, "Calculated Ambiguity: Nuclear Weapons and the Gulf War," *Washington Quarterly,* vol. 19, no. 4 (1996), p.10; Robert S. Norris and William M. Arkin, "Nuclear Notebook—U.S. Strategic Nuclear Forces, End of 1996," *Bulletin of the Atomic Scientists,* vol. 53 (January/February 1997), p. 71.

TABLE 2-3. U.S. Missiles, 1945–97[a]

Missile	Service	Start of development	Start of production	In service	Number produced	Warhead	Acquisition costs (millions of dollars)	
							Then-year	1996
Short-range ballistic missiles (up to 600 nm)								
Corporal MGM-5	Army	1944	1951	1954–67	1,101	W7	322	2,460
Honest John MGR-1	Army	1950	1951	1954–84	9,311	W7, W31	322	2,460
Lacrosse MGM-18	Army	1951	1955	1959–64	1,194	W40	320	2,010
Lance MGM-52C	Army	1967	1971	1972–91	2,314	W70	1,163	4,190
Little John MGR-3A	Army	1956	1958	1962–65	2,404	W45	85	520
Pershing 1/1a MGM-31A/B	Army	1958	1961	1964–90	750	W50	1,500	8,450
Sergeant MGM-29	Army	1955	1959	1962–77	475	W52	479	2,880
Medium-range ballistic missiles (600–1,500 nm)								
Jupiter PGM-19A	Air force	1956	1957	1961–63	98	W49	830	5,160
Pershing II	Army	1975	1981	1983–91	234	W85	2,567	3,100
Redstone PGM-11A	Army	1951	1952	1958–64	120	W39	512	3,400
Intermediate-Range Ballistic Missiles (1,500–3,000 nm)								
Thor PGM-17A	Air force	1955	1957	1959–63	224	W49	1,500	9,440
Intercontinental ballistic missiles (3,000–8,000 nm)								
Atlas D/E/F CGM-16D/E/F	Air force	1955	1957	1959–65	343	W49, W38	5,080	31,590
Minuteman I LGM-30A	Air force	1958	1962	1962–69	925	W59, W56	5,349	32,110
Minuteman II LGM-30F	Air force	1962	1964	1966–91	668	W56	4,855	24,550
Minuteman III LGM-30G	Air force	1966	1968	1970–	840	W62, W78	6,724	28,140
Titan I LGM-25A	Air force	1955	1962	1962–65	155	W38	3,330	20,320
Titan II LGM-25C	Air force	1960	1960	1963–87	127	W53	2,170	12,750
MX LGM-118A	Air force	1974	1983	1986–	102	W87	15,909	19,320
Submarine-launched ballistic missiles (3,000–8,000)								
Polaris A-1/UGM-27A	Navy	1956	1959	1960–64		W47	?	?
Polaris A-2/UGM-27B	Navy	1958	1961	1962–74		W47	?	?
Polaris A-3/UGM-27C	Navy	1962	1963	1964–81	1,278 (all)	W58	5,059 (all)	30,370
Poseidon C-3/UGM-73A	Navy	1965	1969	1971–91	640	W68	3,542	13,940
Trident I C-4/UGM-96A	Navy	1968	1976	1979–	595	W76	10,915	22,270
Trident II D-5/UGM-133A	Navy	1977	1987	1990–	462	W88	22,480	30,120

TABLE 2-3. U.S. Missiles, 1945–97[a] (*continued*)

Missile	*Service*	*Start of development*	*Start of production*	*In service*	*Number produced*	*Warhead*	*Acquisition costs (millions of dollars)*	
							Then-year	*1996*
Cruise missiles								
ALCM AGM-86B	Air force	1974	1978	1982–	1,787	W80	4,118	6,260
ACM AGM-129A	Air force	1983	1986	1991–	484	W80	4,802	5,530
GLCM BGM-109G	Air force	1977	1981	1983–91	443	W84	3,285	4,120
Matador MGM-1C	Air force	1946	?	1955–61	>1,000	W5	?	?
Mace MGM/CGM-13	Air force	1955	1958	1959–69	?	W28	?	?
Regulus I RGM-6-A	Navy	1946	1953	1954–64	514	W5, W27	370	2,860
SLCM BGM-109A/B	Navy	1972	1979	1984–	363	W80	990	1,420
Snark SM-62	Air force	1946	1956	1960–61	30	W39	677	4,180
Air-to-air missiles								
Falcon AIM-26A	Air force	1947	1961	1961–72	1,900?	W54	872	5,340
Genie AIR-2A	Air force	1954	1955	1957–84	10,171	W25	133	920
Air-to-ground missiles								
Bullpup B AGM-12D	Air force	1954	1958	1962–76	?	W45	?	?
Hound Dog AGM-28B	Air force	1957	1958	1960–75	722	W28	859	5,240
SRAM AGM-69A	Air force	1966	1971	1972–90	1,541	W69	1,149	4,140
Walleye AGM-62	N	?	?	1970–79	?	W72	?	?
Surface-to-air/antiballistic missiles								
Bomarc CIM-10A/B	Air force	1950	1957	1959-72	700	W40	2,303	14,320
Nike Hercules MIM-14	Army	1953	1955	1958–88	10,077	W31	?	?
Sprint	Army	1963	1968	1975–76	112	W66	842	2,350
Spartan LIM-49	Army	1965	1967	1975–76	72	W71	992	2,760
TALOS RIM-8	Navy	1944	1959	1959–79	2,404	W30	572	3,600
Terrier RIM-2D	Navy	1949	1950	1956–88	3,000	W45	186	1,350
Naval ASW missiles								
ASROC RUR-5A	Navy	1956	1959	1961–89	12,020	W44	326	1,990
SUBROC UUM-44	Navy	1958	1964	1965–90	611	W55	471	2,610
Other								
Davy Crockett M-28/29	Army	1956	1959	1961–71	2,100	W54	89	540

Sources: Ted Nicholas and Rita Rossi, *U.S. Missile Data Book, 1995*, 19th ed. (Fountain Valley, Calif.: Data Search Associates, November 1994); DOD Selected Acquisition Reports.

a. For most of these systems, constant fiscal 1996 dollar cost estimates were computed by using the beginning in-service date and dividing the then-year acquistion cost by the deflator for that year. The resulting figure was then rounded to the nearest $10 million. For a rigorous cost accounting, one would need a yearly breakdown for all acquisition costs from the beginning of research and development through the last year of procurement. Such records do not exist for many of these systems (especially for programs initiated before 1961) or are extremely hard to come by. It seems reasonable for the computation to take as the base year the first year the missile entered service. Fiscal 1996 dollar cost estimates for the MX, Trident II, ALCM, ACM, Pershing II, and GLCM were derived from DOD Selected Acquisition Report (SAR) data.

Missiles were also used for air-to-surface missions, fired from bombers and fighters. The United States deployed two kinds of air-to-air missiles, the Genie and the Falcon, to destroy enemy aircraft. Also participating in air defense were surface-to-air missiles with various ranges, notably the Bomarc and the Nike Hercules. The navy had the ASROC (antisubmarine rocket) and SUBROC (submarine-launched rocket) missiles as part of its arsenal for the antisubmarine warfare mission. The costs of these defensive systems are considered in chapter 4.

Tactical Nuclear and Dual-Capable Forces

Throughout the cold war, U.S. nuclear warfighting doctrine, planning, and capabilities were focused almost exclusively on the strategic mission, that is, on preparing for strikes against strategic targets in the Soviet Union. To that end, the United States expanded its strategic nuclear forces from a handful of bombers in the mid-1940s into an arsenal that came to include thousands of nuclear-armed medium- and long-range bombers and land- and submarine-based ballistic missiles. No less remarkable, nuclear weapons eventually spread into virtually every corner of the U.S. military's general-purpose forces.

In April 1951 the three services (led by the air force) pooled their resources to sponsor a study of the potential utility of atomic weapons for ground and air tactical warfare. The study, named Project Vista (after the hotel in which much of the sensitive work was done), had its headquarters at the California Institute of Technology (Caltech) and was conducted by some fifty scientists, including J. Robert Oppenheimer and former AEC commissioner Robert F. Bacher. Its budget—$5 million—was quite large, equal to Caltech's total income at the time. Although the study group initially had no particular geographic area in mind, official briefings in Washington, D.C., concentrated on Europe and led the group to turn its attention there (the obvious choice would have been Korea, but a truce in July of that year tended to strengthen the notion that Europe was of longer-term interest).

The group's report, completed in early 1952, emphasized that large-scale production of tactical weapons could be "the decisive factor in the defense of Europe," especially as the United States held the lead in atomic weapons and could exploit it for maximum gain. Significantly, nuclear weapons were not viewed as inexpensive nor a substitute for conventional forces. In defending Europe, the report argued, the nations of NATO would achieve success and support by focusing on defeating the Soviet Union not through large-scale strategic bombing (the air force approach and the prevailing view of the day) but through battlefield engagements using smaller weapons against troop concentrations, supply depots, command headquarters, and the like. Multimegaton weapons were considered useless for these missions. Also important, the report did *not* advocate close-in combat with nuclear weapons but rather the selective use of such weapons 20 to 25 miles (32 to 40 kilometers) behind enemy lines to destroy supplies, supply lines, and lines of communication and thus weaken the enemy to the point where conventional forces could be brought in to achieve victory. Used in this fashion, nuclear weapons would "deny the attacker his most important maneuver—concentration on or near the battlefield."

The air force, which at that time had virtually a monopoly on nuclear weapons (though this was about to change), and its supporters strongly objected to the report, viewing it as a direct challenge to the emphasis (up to that time) on strategic bombing and, hence, as a threat to the future funding and existence of SAC. That the report further recommended the creation of a tactical atomic air force, which would of course compete with SAC, was also troubling.

Upon its completion, the air force recalled all existing copies of the report and effectively suppressed it. Most proponents of a crash program to build the hydrogen bomb considered smaller tactical weapons to be a dangerous diversion of resources. This point in particular was used as evidence against Oppenheimer during his security trial in 1954, even though, as his colleague Robert Bacher testified, Vista's recommendations would in no way have slowed the H-bomb program. This judgment turned out to be correct, even though the project's report apparently had little if any influence over the eventual size or composition of the tactical arsenal, as can be seen from examining most of the types of weapons deployed and the strategies for their use, both of which were significantly different than what Vista had proposed.[105]

Through the early 1950s the sheer size of atomic bombs—typically on the order of 10,000 pounds (4,595 kilograms)—made SAC's medium and long-range bombers about the only effective means of delivering these weapons. In 1953, however, the United States deployed the 5,000-pound (2,273-kilogram) Mk-5 and the 2,700-pound (1,227-kilogram) Mk-7 atomic bombs. Among other things, the development of these smaller weapons led President Eisenhower to conclude later that same year—in a speech before the United Nations announcing his "Atoms for Peace" program—that "atomic weapons have virtually achieved conventional status within our armed services . . . the Army, the Navy, the Air Force, and the Marine Corps are all capable of putting this weapon to military use."[106] That state-

105. For more on Project Vista, see David C. Elliot, "Project Vista and Nuclear Weapons in Europe," *International Security*, vol. 11, no. 1 (1986), pp. 163–83.

106. Address by President Dwight D. Eisenhower before the General Assembly of the United Nations, December 8, 1953, reprinted in U.S. Senate, *Atoms for Peace Manual: A Compilation of Official Materials on International Cooperation for Peaceful Uses of Atomic Energy, December 1953–July 1955*, 84

ment may have been premature, but within a few years nuclear weapons had been introduced into a broad range of U.S. general-purpose forces and in little more than a decade it was difficult to find a major element of those forces into which nuclear weapons had not been extensively integrated.

Army

Army officials were quick to recognize the potential of tactical nuclear weapons, both as a means of redressing conventional force imbalances and as a way to prevent the air force from controlling ever larger shares of the defense budget. On January 21, 1946, then General Dwight Eisenhower presented the army's case to the Joint Chiefs of Staff: "excessive reliance" on nuclear weapons should be avoided (at the expense of shrinking conventional forces), he said, but through study, experiment, and training officials would be able to determine "the best kind of an Army to build around the all-powerful atomic weapons." He urged that "all possible methods of delivery of atomic weapons . . . be studied and developed." The JCS included Eisenhower's remarks verbatim in their report on the consequences of the atomic bomb on military organization and gave some thought to limiting the range of army guided missiles and artillery to less than 150 miles (241 kilometers; with the former appearing to be the most promising means of atomic delivery).[107] However, such a move promised to give the air force complete control of all long-range systems. The assistant chief of staff for development at Army Field Forces therefore recommended the immediate development of a 500-mile (805-kilometer) guided missile, solely to preempt the air force's attempt to dominate the nuclear delivery field. Lacking any definitive basis for such a development and any clear understanding of how such a weapon would be used, the army simply argued that control of such weapons by its forces would be inherently better than control by the air force.[108]

The army's budget for missile development jumped from $199.5 million in 1950 to $387.1 million in 1951.[109] In its first efforts to estab-

Cong. 1 sess. (GPO, 1955), p. 2. Nearly two years earlier, AEC chairman Gordon Dean created a stir (both within the government and the general public) when in the midst of the Korean War he stated, "I would like to be able to tell you how far into this new [atomic] era we have advanced, but I cannot, for to do so would be to give the Communists the kind of information they would dearly like to have as a basis for their evil calculations. . . . [W]ith each passing day, our design and production progress is steadily adding to the number of situations in which atomic weapons can be tactically employed against military targets." These remarks, along with testimony by Dean before Congress, led the press to speculate that atomic bombs might be used in Korea. President Truman—who on September 4, 1951, created his own controversy by telling Democratic party leaders at a meeting in San Francisco that some "fantastic weapons" were under construction—told Dean through his national security adviser that "he was not worked up" about it. See Anders, *Forging the Atomic Shield*, pp. 172–76, 276–85.

107. John J. Midgley, Jr., *Deadly Illusions: Army Policy for the Nuclear Battlefield* (Boulder, Colo.: Westview Press, 1986), pp. 7–8.

108. Midgley, *Deadly Illusions*, pp. 11–12.

109. Midgley, *Deadly Illusions*, p. 13.

lish a nuclear role, the army concentrated on the development of a 280-millimeter (11-inch) atomic cannon (initiated in November 1944 and intended for conventional use in the final months of the war in Europe) and the Corporal surface-to-surface missile (SSM).[110] Both of these systems were successfully tested in 1953.[111] But both represented interim solutions at best. Weighing 83 tons and having a range of only 17 miles (27 kilometers), the cannon was pronounced technologically obsolete as soon as it was fielded (only 160 nuclear shells were ever manufactured for it between 1952 and 1956, see table 1-3). With a range of 75 miles (121 kilometers), the Corporal represented an improvement, but it was still too long (46 feet, or 14 meters), used liquid fuel propulsion, and needed to be repositioned from its carrier before launch.

Even though nuclear weapons rendered massed conventional fighting units vulnerable, efforts to develop a cohesive doctrine governing the use of these weapons (and those that followed) lagged behind their actual deployment. In 1953 the army began to address this problem and by 1956 had developed and deployed the "pentomic" fighting unit. These smaller, more maneuverable units were equipped with nuclear and conventional weapons and were thought to be the answer to the army's vulnerability and the key to victory on the atomic battlefield. However, subsequent tests of the pentomic concept in war games—*after it was put into effect*—demonstrated that these units "could not effectively wage two-sided nuclear operations," and that they "had no significant advantages over the unmodified 1956 infantry division if nuclear weapons were used by both sides."[112] Assessing the results of these war games, officials with the Continental Army Command concluded that "the *Pentana* organization is not suitable for combat in a situation involving a high level of atomic war. . . . there is a need for an organization of drastically reduced vulnerability and with an improved atomic target acquisition and weapons delivery system." Most tellingly, the "high level of atomic war" responsible for the defeat was strikingly small: the units were rendered inoperable "after strikes by seven to 14 nuclear weapons with yields of 40 kilotons or less."[113]

The crux of the problem was the incompatibility of the conventional and nuclear missions: each required different weaponry, tactics, and support. The army wisely decided against fielding forces capable only of waging atomic war but, for political and budgetary reasons, combined both missions in one unit. Because the pentomic unit was

---

110. For an excellent discussion of the early history of U.S. Army nuclear weapons programs, see also A. J. Bacevich, *The Pentomic Era: The U.S. Army between Korea and Vietnam* (National Defense University Press, 1986).

111. On May 25, 1953, in a test named Grable, a 280-millimeter cannon at the Nevada Proving Ground fired a projectile that detonated with a force of 15 kilotons 524 feet (160 meters) above Frenchman Flat. This was the first and only operational test of this weapon.

112. Midgley, *Deadly Illusions,* pp. 31–79 (quotations on p. 73).

113. Midgley, *Deadly Illusions,* p. 74.

designed to justify the procurement of large numbers of new nuclear weapons rather than develop a workable concept for employing them in time of war, the approach proved a failure.[114] In the end, the army received and deployed thousands of offensive nuclear weapons without ever finding a way to use them effectively. Furthermore, many of these weapons were under the decentralized control of commanders in the field, and their deployment increased the risk of accidental or unintentional nuclear war.

Nevertheless, the army tested and deployed a variety of other nuclear-armed SSM designs during the 1950s. Some of these missiles had far greater ranges than the Corporal. The Redstone, tested in 1954, could travel 240 miles (386 kilometers) and the Jupiter IRBM, tested in 1957, 1,500 miles (2,414 kilometers). Others were smaller, more mobile, short-range systems. The first of these, fielded in 1954, was the Honest John SSM, which weighed three tons, used solid fuel, and had a range of 22 miles (35 kilometers; see table 2-3).

In 1954 the army further increased its nuclear capability by deploying the first atomic demolition munition (ADM). ADMs (and later, special atomic demolition munitions, or SADMs, and medium atomic demolition munitions, or MADMs) were low-yield weapons (sub-1 kiloton to 15 kilotons) designed to be emplaced by special forces and commando teams behind enemy lines to destroy bridges, tunnels, harbors, dams, airfields, command posts, transportation and communication hubs and fuel depots, or to create obstacles to disrupt the movement of enemy forces, so as to force them through choke points to create targets for other, larger nuclear weapons.[115]

The next major step was the development in 1956 of a nuclear artillery round for the army's 203-millimeter (8-inch) howitzer. This step was made possible by the dramatic progress made in the miniaturization of nuclear weapons: by the mid-1950s, the United States was able to produce warheads weighing several hundred, rather than several thousand, pounds. By 1963 the army had also deployed a nuclear round for use with its 155-millimeter (6-inch) artillery. Having thousands of 203-millimeter and 155-millimeter artillery pieces in its arsenal, the army found that the development of nuclear artillery rounds, perhaps more than anything else, opened the door to its thorough nuclearization in the late 1950s and early 1960s. This development did not by any means mark the end of the army's integration of nuclear

114. "In the search for rationales useful in acquiring new technology, well-defined military missions were relatively unimportant. . . . [B]y the mid-1960s, the nuclear battlefield was merely a facade, useful in justifying procurement but lacking any explicit military rationale." Midgley, *Deadly Illusions,* pp. 174, 177.

115. These and other ADMs were designed to be emplaced by specially trained teams and, for security reasons, early versions were detonated by a short cable connected to the device, which was to remain within sight of the team. Later models utilized a time-delay detonator. ADMs and SADMs were also deployed with navy and Marine Corps units. See Frank Greve, "Suicide Squads Reportedly Were Trained to Use Nuclear Backpacks," *Dallas Morning News,* July 27, 1994, p. 4.

weapons into its planning and forces. In 1958, for example, it deployed the nuclear-tipped Nike Hercules SAM, which eventually played a large strategic defense role across the United States and in Europe, among both U.S. and allied forces.

Perhaps the most bizarre nuclear system ever developed by the U.S. Army, and the one that most clearly illustrates the army's procurement-driven force policy and the lack of understanding of the exact mission of these weapons was the Davy Crockett, fielded in 1961. This weapon had a maximum range of 1.24 to 2.49 miles (2 to 4 kilometers) and could be launched from either a 120-millimeter or a 150-millimeter recoilless rifle that could be fitted onto a jeep and fired by a four-man crew. Authority to launch this widely dispersed weapon—which was designed to be used in large numbers against massed Soviet troops in close proximity to American or NATO divisions—rested with battalion commanders or lower-level officers in the field. In fact, army planners recognized that its utility depended upon such decentralized control (the same factor was viewed quite negatively by the Kennedy administration and, by the late 1960s, field commanders in Europe, but was nevertheless also used by the army to justify fielding large quanitities of 8-inch and 155-millimeter nuclear artillery shells). According to one student of the army's nuclear planning during this period:

> The technical characteristics of systems developed in the late 1950s and early 1960s—particularly the Davy Crockett—exerted relentless pressure toward a strategy which relied on widespread, decentralized nuclear operations. Viewed in isolation . . . the new nuclear weapons appeared to offer significant military capabilities. However, analysis was never extended to the question of how the weapons would be employed in actual campaigns . . . and did not consider the difficulties imposed by enemy use of similar weapons. . . . In the Army's designs for the 1960s, the nuclear battlefield remained an ill-defined and little understood environment, useful as a justification for equipment and weapon procurement but not considered as a basis for force design.[116]

The W54 warhead used in the Davy Crockett weighed just 51 pounds (23.2 kilograms) and had a variable yield of 0.01 to 1 kiloton (equal to 10 tons of TNT) and 0.02 to 1 kiloton. As such, it was the lightest and smallest fission weapon (implosion type) ever deployed by the United States, but practice firings showed it to be "too inaccurate to deliver even low-yield nuclear fires." Nevertheless, it remained in service until 1971 (although there are unconfirmed reports that President Kennedy ordered its removal in 1963).[117] In all, 2,100 were produced at a cost of $540 million (excluding the cost of the warheads).

116. Midgley, *Deadly Illusions,* p. 112.

117. Midgley, *Deadly Illusions,* p. 112. The lowest yield of the W54 was two to five times more powerful than the ammonium nitrate bomb which destroyed the Alfred P. Murrah

The extent to which the nuclear mission came to dominate army thinking and spending is apparent in its 1957 R&D budget. Some 43 percent of that funding was allocated to nuclear programs. By comparison, army vehicle, artillery and aircraft programs accounted for, respectively, only 4.5 percent, 4.3 percent, and 4 percent of army R&D funding.[118] Early 8-inch nuclear howitzer battalions deployed in Germany during the late 1950s reportedly spent one-third of their training time on nuclear delivery training and maintenance. So great was the emphasis on the nuclear mission that "all officers were required to be proficient in assembly of these 1st generation weapons," and "each battery was required to establish a nuclear detachment of six personnel (out of 127 authorized) whose sole duty was the security, safety, and assembly and delivery of the nuclear weapons maintained by the unit." The diversion of resources required to maintain nuclear-capable forces apparently did not subside for some time.[119]

Even when the Kennedy administration embraced the doctrine of "flexible response" and the United States entered the Vietnam War, the army continued to expand its nuclear-warfighting capabilities: in 1962 it fielded the Sergeant and Pershing IA SSMs, in 1972 it deployed the Lance SSM, and in 1983 it deployed its last new SSM, the 1,100-mile (1,770-kilometer) range Pershing II missile. Over these years the army also fielded a series of improved nuclear artillery rounds and ADMs—including, in 1964, a special 163-pound (74-kilogram) ADM (the warhead weighed just 58.6 pounds, or 26.6 kilograms) that could be carried in a backpack by a single soldier.[120] The army remained heavily nuclearized through the 1980s. In 1984 it possessed more than 5,000 nuclear warheads, in addition to 300 nuclear-capable SSMs of various ranges, 200 nuclear-capable SAMs, 610 ADMs, and more than 4,300

federal building in Oklahoma City on April 19, 1995. Stockpiled W54 warheads were test-fired at the Nevada Test Site on July 7 and 17, 1962, during the Little Feller II and Little Feller I shots. In Little Feller II on July 7, the warhead was suspended on cables about 3 feet (0.9 meters) above the ground (yield was 22 tons). In Little Feller I on July 17, a Davy Crockett was fired from a stationary 155-millimeter launcher (in tandem with troop maneuvers) and detonated about 20 feet (6.1 meters) above the ground at a distance of about 1.8 miles (2.7 kilometers) from the launch point (yield was 18 tons). This test, the last atmospheric detonation at the Nevada Test Site, was observed by Attorney General Robert F. Kennedy and presidential adviser General Maxwell D. Taylor. Thomas B. Cochran, William M. Arkin, and Milton M. Hoenig, *Nuclear Weapons Databook,* vol. 1: *U.S. Nuclear Forces and Capabilities* (Cambridge, Mass.: Ballinger, 1984), pp. 60, 311; Robert S. Norris and Thomas B. Cochran, *United States Nuclear Tests: July 1945 to 31 December 1992,* NWD-94-1 (Natural Resources Defense Council, February 1, 1994), p. 35; Chuck Hansen, *Nuclear Weapons: The Secret History* (Arlington, Tex.: Aerofax, 1988), pp. 197–98; "The U.S. Army Presents MF20 9811: Ivy Flats Film Report," July 1962 (declassified December 22, 1997, and available through the U.S. Department of Energy's Coordination and Information Center, Las Vegas, Nev., accession no. 0800032).

118. Bacevich, *Pentomic Era,* p. 100.

119. Letter from Honorable William F. Burns, Major General U.S. Army (retired), to Stephen I. Schwartz, May 7, 1996. Burns goes on to describe a mission in the late 1970s at a NATO nuclear storage site he commanded near Giessen in West Germany that required the "diversion of 85 soldiers on a daily basis (out of about 1500 available . . .) to the sole duty of guarding the site. It also required a reinforced armored infantry company from a nearby armored division (about 200 men) to be immediately available at all times as a reinforcement and backup."

120. Cochran and others, *United States Nuclear Forces and Capabilities,* p. 311.

nuclear-capable artillery pieces.[121] Acquisition costs for the Pershing IA, the Lance, and the Pershing II were, respectively, about $8.5 billion, $4.2 billion, and $3.1 billion.

Navy

In 1948 and 1949 the navy—struggling to show that it remained relevant and effective in the atomic age—conducted a series of tests demonstrating that strategic nuclear strikes could be conducted from aircraft carriers.[122] However, this capability was extremely limited, to say the least. The early atomic bombs were far too large and heavy for regular carrier-based aircraft, so the navy employed eleven specially modified P2V-3 Neptune maritime patrol planes for this mission. These large planes could take off from—but not land on—the aircraft carriers and had to be lifted onto the carrier decks by cranes. They would have had to fly one-way missions in wartime.

The navy's strategic strike capability improved considerably in 1950, with the deployment of the AJ-1 Savage, which, unlike the Neptune, was designed for carrier takeoff and landing. Nevertheless, the largest aircraft carrier was capable of handling at most a dozen Savages, and the navy's nuclear strike capability remained very limited compared with SAC's. As in the case of the army, the diffusion of nuclear weapons throughout the navy was closely connected with the appearance of relatively lightweight nuclear weapons in the early 1950s. Initially, 25 carrier-based F2H-2B Banshee fighter-bombers and 165 carrier-based AD-4Bs were equipped to carry the relatively lightweight Mk-7 and Mk-8 nuclear bombs. The first navy attack aircraft designed from the outset to deliver small nuclear weapons, the A-4 Skyhawk, became operational in 1956.

That same year, the Navy introduced two other types of nuclear weapons into its general-purpose forces: the shipborne Terrier SAM system and the S23, a nuclear round for the 16-inch guns of the navy's battleships (the S23, only fifty of which were actually produced, was quickly retired three years later). In 1958 a nuclear depth bomb was

121. William M. Arkin and Richard W. Fieldhouse, *Nuclear Battlefields: Global Links in the Arms Race* (Cambridge, Mass.: Ballinger, 1985), p. 57.

122. Jeffrey G. Barlow, *Revolt of the Admirals: The Fight for Naval Aviation, 1945–1950* (Washington, D.C.: Naval Historical Center, 1994), p. 127. Such tests were necessary because most observers believed that the atomic bomb had rendered surface vessels obsolete, owing in part to the results of the July 25, 1946, Baker test conducted at Bikini Atoll as part of Operation Crossroads (where all but nine of ninety-five target ships were heavily contaminated and the 26,000-ton battleship *Arkansas* sank in seconds, along with thirteen other vessels). The navy, however, still considered ships to be "tough" and "among the least vulnerable of all targets on the surface of the earth, and immeasurably more so than any fixed base," because of all the "protective devices that are inherent in going to sea." Nevertheless, of the ninety-five ships contaminated by Baker, all but six were eventually deliberately scuttled because of dangerously high levels of lingering radioactivity. See, *Study of Airpower,* Hearings, vol. 1, p. 912, and vol. 2, pp. 1374–75. For more on Operation Crossroads, see Jonathan M. Weisgall, *Operation Crossroads: The Atomic Tests at Bikini Atoll* (Annapolis, Md.: Naval Institute Press, 1994).

deployed with navy carrier- and land-based ASW patrol planes. A nuclear-armed antisubmarine torpedo (ASTOR) was also developed in 1958. In view of its short range, however, a submarine firing the torpedo might well be damaged or destroyed by its nuclear blast.[123] Therefore in 1961 and 1965, respectively, the navy began deploying the nuclear-armed ASROC depth charge aboard its surface combatants and the SUBROC depth charge aboard its fleet of attack submarines. And in 1984 the navy brought the 1,500-mile (2,414-kilometer) range nuclear-armed land-attack SLCM aboard a wide variety of both surface combatants and attack submarines. The costs of ASTOR, ASROC, SUBROC, and other defensive tactical weapons are considered in chapter 4.

Although the navy has a long-standing policy of neither confirming nor denying the presence or absence of nuclear weapons, from time to time officials have discussed its general nuclear capabilities. Even then, the information has often amounted to such statements as "We can carry [thermonuclear weapons] on board," "We have the capability" (1956),[124] or "We have a Regulus I capability in some submarines and cruisers, which will carry a nuclear warhead" (1959).[125] In 1974 retired Rear Admiral Gene R. La Rocque went so far as to disclose:

> My experience has been that any ship that is *capable* of carrying nuclear weapons, *carries* nuclear weapons. They do not off-load them when they go into foreign ports such as Japan or other countries. If they are capable of carrying them, they normally keep them aboard ship at all times except when the ship is in overhaul or in for major repair.[126]

---

123. ASTOR was guided to its target via a spool of wire in its tail assembly. The length of the wire necessarily limited its range and gave the weapon a reputation for "dual kill capability": the Soviet target and the American submarine that launched it. Despite this serious operational limitation, ASTOR was retained in the arsenal until 1977. See Gibson, *History of the US Nuclear Arsenal*, pp. 182–83.

124. *Study of Airpower*, Hearings, vol. 2, p. 1433.

125. *Missile and Space Activities*, Hearings, p. 86.

126. *Proliferation of Nuclear Weapons*, Hearings before the Subcommittee on Military Applications of the Joint Committee on Atomic Energy, 93 Cong. 2 sess. (GPO, 1974), pp. 17–18, 25, cited in O'Rourke, "Nuclear-Powered and Nuclear-Capable Ships in the U.S. Navy," pp. CRS-5–CRS-6. La Rocque's reference to nuclear weapons entering Japan—which has had a strict nonnuclear policy since World War II—triggered a period of severe agitation, later dubbed "La Rocque Shock." The governor of Kanagawa, home to the immense U.S. Navy complex at Yokosuka, informed the Foreign Ministry that "if the testimony is true, we will be forced to refuse entry of U.S. ships to Yokosuka." Cabinet Secretary Susumu Nikado carefully replied, "I have no doubt that the United States is keeping its promise," adding, "however, the government is not in a position of being able to check every ship." Shortly after this testimony, American newspapers reported that the United States and Japan had signed a secret 1960 agreement "permitting U.S. warships to carry nuclear weapons into Japan during port calls and American aircraft to bring them in during landings." To allow the Japanese government to maintain deniability, the agreement was reportedly concluded without a Japanese text. Both this story and La Rocque's testimony were confirmed in 1981 by Edwin Reischauer, U.S. ambassador to Japan from 1961 to 1966. Quoted in David C. Morrison, "Japanese Principles, U.S. Policies," *Bulletin of the Atomic Scientists*, vol. 41 (June/July 1985), pp. 22–24; Geoffrey Murray, "Japan Reels under Reischauer's Nuclear 'Bombshell,'" *Christian Science Monitor*, May 19, 1981, p. 5; Geoffrey Murray, "Nuclear 'Facts of Life' Intrude Into Japan Defense Furor," *Christian Science Monitor*, June 3, 1981, p. 9. See also a series of declassified documents obtained by the U.S.-Japan Project of the National Security Archive in 1997 that further clarify the important but hitherto secret role of U.S. nuclear weapons in U.S.-Japan relations. The documents are available online at http://www.seas.gwu.edu/nsarchive/japan/okinawa/okinawa.htm.

The U.S. Navy's general-purpose forces remained heavily nuclearized until the early 1990s. In 1984 the navy had a total of some 2,900 nuclear bombs and warheads. Delivery systems for these weapons included about 900 nuclear-capable aircraft aboard the navy's 13 large carriers, 5 types of helicopters and vertical/short take-off and landing (VSTOL) craft aboard amphibious assault ships, 2 battleships, all 112 cruisers and destroyers, 64 attack submarines, and 61 of 86 frigates.[127] That U.S. general-purpose naval forces were (and to a large extent remain) extensively integrated into nuclear warfighting plans is clear from the fact that the primary mission of the navy's fleet of nuclear-powered attack submarines during the cold war was to track and, in wartime, hunt down and destroy Soviet SSBNs (see chapter 4).

Air Force

The first U.S. Air Force tactical fighter to be equipped to carry nuclear weapons was the F-84G Thunderjet. The F-84G was delivered to the 20th Fighter-Bomber Group in November 1951. In August 1953 the group was forward-deployed to the United Kingdom.[128] Soon thereafter the air force began to deploy nuclear bombs throughout much of its tactical forces. Here again, the development of relatively small nuclear weapons beginning in the early 1950s aided in nuclearizing general-purpose forces.

By 1953 the Tactical Air Command had placed orders for the first jet fighter-bomber designed from the beginning to carry nuclear weapons, the F-105 Thunderchief. The F-105 had an internal bomb bay large enough to carry the 2,000-pound Mk-28 nuclear bomb. Ironically, notwithstanding its nuclear-oriented design, the F-105 eventually became the workhorse of the air force's bombing campaign against North Vietnam.

In 1957 the air force tested the first nuclear-armed air-to-air-missile, the unguided Genie. This was followed, in 1961, with a nuclear version of the Falcon air-to-air guided missile. The Genie and the Falcon were extensively deployed with U.S. strategic air defense aircraft: 10,171 and 1,900, respectively, were purchased. In 1983 the air force began deploying the 1,500-mile-range ground-launched cruise missile (GLCM). Plans called for eventually deploying 464 GLCMs in five European countries: Great Britain, Belgium, the Netherlands, Italy, and West Germany (in addition, 108 Army Pershing II launchers were to go to West Germany). But these deployments were cut short by the signing of the Intermediate-Range Nuclear Forces (INF) Treaty in 1987.[129] Nevertheless, the air force still spent $5.7 billion on the GLCM program.

127. Arkin and Fieldhouse, *Nuclear Battlefields*, pp. 57, 62.
128. Wagner, *American Combat Planes*, p. 448.
129. In all, 234 Pershing IIs and 443 GLCMs were produced. In accordance with the INF Treaty, the first arms con-

In 1984 the air force had some 2,900 tactical nuclear weapons in its stockpile, including about 2,800 nuclear bombs (and approximately 100 GLCM warheads). Moreover, most of its tactical combat aircraft at this time, some 2,000 in all, were nuclear-certified designs.[130] Under a unilateral measure implemented by President Bush on September 27, 1991, most of these weapons, as well as those fielded by the army and navy, have been retired and many dismantled.[131]

The profusion of requirements, missions, and weapon types sparked by the revolutionary potential nuclear weapons seemed to offer reached a peak in the mid-1960s. Try as they might, military officials often found it difficult to rationalize the elaborate war plans and extensive exercises for many of their weapons. Once they began questioning whether such weapons could actually be used to fight wars, their infatuation with "nuclearization" subsided. Shortly after Bush unveiled his initiative, Vice Admiral William Owens, commander of the Sixth Fleet, stated that the removal of all strategic naval nuclear weapons was "a revolutionary thing. . . . There is a great deal to be said about the additional freedom it gives us to operate our ships. The training of people to maintain the nuclear weapons on those ships has been a continual drain on our resources." Admiral Frank Kelso, chief of naval operations, asserted that many naval officers had long felt that "if we had conflict at sea, we were better off with conventional weapons," because U.S. conventional superiority would be negated in a nuclear war at sea (see box 2-2).[132]

---

trol agreement requiring the complete destruction of an entire class of missiles, the last Pershing II was destroyed on May 6, 1991, and the last GLCMs were destroyed on May 1, 1991. The warheads carried by these missiles were not subject to dismantlement under the treaty, and the W85 warheads carried by the Pershing II were reconfigured by the DOE into the B61 Mod 10 tactical gravity bomb and returned to Europe for deployment at air bases. The W84 GLCM warheads remain in inactive reserve status. See Robert S. Norris and William M. Arkin, "Beating Swords into Swords," *Bulletin of the Atomic Scientists*, vol. 46 (November 1990), pp. 14–16.

130. Arkin and Fieldhouse, *Nuclear Battlefields*, p. 57.

131. All ground-launched and naval nonstrategic nuclear weapons were withdrawn from active deployment by July 2, 1992. *Public Papers of the Presidents of the United States: George Bush, 1992–93*, vol. 1: *January 1 to July 31, 1992* (GPO, 1983), p. 1062. See also Ann Devroy and R. Jeffrey Smith, "President Orders Sweeping Reductions in Strategic and Tactical Nuclear Arms," *Washington Post*, September 28, 1991, p. A1; R. Jeffrey Smith, "Initiative Affects Least Useful Weapons," *Washington Post*, September 28, 1991, p. A1; Eric Schmitt, "Bush's Plan Would Sharply Cut Nuclear Arms for Battlefield Use," *New York Times*, September 28, 1991, p. A5.

132. R. Jeffrey Smith, "6th Fleet at Sea on A-Arm Loss," *Washington Post*, October 17, 1991, p. A40. One noteworthy statement comes from Lieutenant General A. S. Collins (U.S. Army, ret.), deputy commander in chief of U.S. Army forces in Europe from 1971–74: "I do not believe that a tactical nuclear war could be fought in areas like Western Europe for more than a few days, or even a few hours, without getting out of control." See, A. S. Collins, "Current NATO Strategy: A Recipe for Disaster," in Gwyn Prins, ed., *The Nuclear Crisis Reader* (New York: Vintage Books, 1984), p. 31. Of greater import is what active duty officers thought when they were making critical decisions about various nuclear weapons systems and policies. These opinions are more difficult to uncover, but concerns must have been expressed, as is evident from the fact that while in the 1950s and 1960s, there were nuclear weapons for almost every conceivable military mission, by the 1970s and 1980s many of these weapons had either been canceled, retired, or replaced by conventional versions. The professional military had a central role in those decisions and concluded—for one reason or another—that nuclear weapons were not essential to carrying out combat missions. As a retired army colonel wrote recently, "My experience as an instructor in nuclear strategy at the Army War College [from 1979 to 1985] was that it was almost impossible to get military officers to use nuclear weapons even in war games that were specifially designed to force them to do so. They had a moral revulsion

BOX 2-2

Weapons That Did Not Make the Cut

Twenty-five weapons programs utilizing sixteen warhead types were canceled before production, because another warhead type was chosen, or in some cases, because the delivery system itself was canceled (see table 2-4). Each canceled program makes an interesting story, capturing as it does the thinking of the day. Some warhead types have had wide applicability, used in one configuration as a bomb, and in another as a warhead for one or perhaps several kinds of missiles. These delivery systems include the Navaho cruise missile ($4.9 billion); the Skybolt, an air-launched ballistic missile ($2.6 billion); the Midgetman or Small ICBM ($5.6 billion); the MX Rail Garrison basing plan ($3.4 billion); the SRAM II ($1.1 billion); and the PLUTO, a nuclear-powered, nuclear-armed, low-altitude cruise missile (about $780 million).

Navaho. From the vantage point of the early 1950s, it appeared that the cruise missile, rather than the ballistic missile, would be the first to be deployed.[1] The Navaho was a supersonic cruise missile whose roots could be traced to the early postwar American efforts to modify and upgrade the German V-1. By September 1950 the air force had proposed a three-phase program consisting of the design and construction of a test vehicle (plus a series of test flights), the development of an interim missile with a range of 3,600 miles (5,792 kilometers), and, finally, the development of an operational missile with a range of 5,500 miles (8,850 kilometers).

The test vehicle, called the X-10, used two Westinghouse turbojets to power the 70-foot-long (21-meter) missile. Eleven vehicles flew twenty-seven flights beginning in October 1953. In one test, the X-10 reached a speed of Mach 2.05. But the interim missile, known as the XSM-64, had repeated launch failures during 1956–57. With competition from the more promising ballistic missile programs under concurrent development, the air force canceled the Navaho on July 12, 1957. A limited number of test flights continued after cancellation, five of which occurred between August 12, 1957, and February 25, 1958, with two final tests taking place on September 11, 1958, and November 18, 1958. For a total of one and a half hours of flight time, U.S. taxpayers spent $4.9 billion. The Navaho itself never flew, although some of the technology developed for it was used in subsequent missile and space programs. The proposed intercontinental XSM-64A was 87.3 feet (26.6 meters) long, with a wing span of 40.2 feet (12.3 meters), and weighed 120,000 pounds (54,545 kilograms) at launch. There was also a 91.5-foot-long (27.9-meter), 169,500-pound (77,045-kilogram) booster to which the Navaho would ride piggyback for 110 seconds.

The Navaho, like the Snark (another cruise missile, thirty of which were deployed for four months at Presque Isle, Maine, at a cost of $4.2 billion), failed for a number of reasons.[2] The technology of the day could never match the ambitious requirements set by the air force. Loose corporate management led to cost overruns and

1. Werrell, *Evolution of the Cruise Missile,* pp. 97–108; U.S. Air Force, Air Research and Development Command, *Development of the SM-64 Navaho Missile, 1954–1958* (Historical Branch: Wright Air Development Division, January 1961). For a technical history of the program, see James N. Gibson, *The Navaho Missile Project: The Story of the 'Know-How' Missile of American Rocketry* (Atglen, Pa.: Schiffer Publishing, 1996).

2. Of Snark, Herbert York (the former director of defense research and engineering) would later write: "We realized, several years before Snark became operational, that it would become obsolete by the time it was finally deployed, and repeated recommendations for dropping the project were made. However, in this case as in so many others, the momentum of the project and the politics which surrounded it made it impossible to do so." Herbert F. York, *Race to Oblivion: A Partici-*

Box 2-2
(continued)

Table 2-4. Canceled U.S. Nuclear-Capable Missile Programs, 1943–91

				Total program cost (millions of dollars)	
Missile	*Service*	*Warhead/canceled*	*Start–end*	*Then-year*	*Constant 1996*[a]
Rigel SSM (SSM-N-6)	Navy	W5/August 1953	1943–53	38	380
Hermes SSM (A-1)	Army	W5/August 1953	1944–54	96	970
Sparrow I AAM (AIM-7A)	Navy	W42/January 1958	1945–56	196	1,370
Rascal ASM (AGAM-63)	Air force	W5/March 1956	1946–58	448	3,240
Triton (SSM-N-2)	Navy	W27/December 1955	1948–57	19	140
Navaho SSM (SM-64)	Air force	W13/September 1954	1954–57	680	4,910
Corvus ASM-N-8	Navy	W40/August 1960	1954–60	80	550
Regulus II RGM-15A	Navy	W27/?	1952–58	147	1,120
Nike Zeus	Army	W50/?	1955–65	3,000	18,360
Honest John, Jr. SSM	Army	W25/February 1956	?	?	
Crossbow ASM (GAM-67)	Air force	W31/January 1957	1957–58	75	520
Hopi ASM	Navy	W50/December 1958	?	?	
Hawk SAM	Army	W42/December 1960	?	?	
Typhon SAM (RIM-55)	Navy	W60/March 1964	1958–64	225	1,370
Eagle AAM-N-10	Navy	W42/c. March 1961	1959–61	53	320
Pluto	Air force	?	1959–64	128	780
Mobile Minuteman	Air force	?	1959–62	108	660
Skybolt AGM-48A	Air force	W59/December 1962	1960–63	440	2,640
MMRBM	Air force	?	1962–64	65	380
Condor ASM	Air force	W73/September 1970	?	?	
Hound Dog II	Air force	?	1972–73	12	40
SRAM II AGM-BIA	Air force	W89/1990	1983–90	858	1,020
SRAM-T AGM-B1B	Air force	W91/September 1991	1983–90	81	110
SICBM MGM-134A	Air force	W87/1991	1984–91	3,675	5,600
MX/Rail Garrison	Air force	W87/1991	1986–91	2,088	2,400
Total				12,512	46,880

Sources: Thomas B. Cochran and others, *Nuclear Weapons Databook*, vol. 2: *U.S. Nuclear Warhead Production* (Cambridge, Mass.: Ballinger, 1987); Nicholas and Rossi, *U.S. Missile Data Book*, pp. 3-11–3-13; U.S. Army Missiles Handbook (Office of Director of Progress and Statistical Reporting, Office Comptroller of the Army, OCS, January 15, 1960); Donnelly, "The United States Guided Missile Program."

a. Except for Skybolt, MMRBM, SRAM II, SICBM, and MX Rail Garrison, for which verified annual data exist, constant 1996 dollar totals were computed by using the midpoint of development to select an appropriate deflator (for example, a system in development from 1950 to 1960 would be adjusted using a 1955 deflator). The resulting figure was then rounded to the nearest $10 million. This is obviously a very rough calculation, but barring the discovery of annualized budgetary data for most of these programs, it is the most reasonable means available.

Box 2-2
(continued)

schedule slippage. The ballistic missile, though unproven as well, was winning the competition (it was more accurate and reliable and had a shorter flight time), and money, resources, and attention turned to it.

Skybolt. Skybolt was an effort by the air force to use B-52 bombers as ballistic missile launchers.[3] As originally conceived, Skybolt was to have been a 39-foot (11.9-meter), 11,000-pound (5,000-kilogram), two-stage missile with a range of some 950 nautical miles (1,759 kilometers) when dropped from a B-52 at a height of 40,000 feet (12,192 meters). At maximum range, it would reach its target in approximately twelve minutes. Other launch heights and ranges were also considered. Its mission, developed in an effort to regain ground lost with the introduction of the navy's new Polaris missile and submarine, was "defense suppression": destroying air defense batteries to allow SAC bombers clear paths to Soviet targets (that the Polaris, then being deployed, could already accomplish this task did not deter the air force from proceeding). The air force originally sought to purchase 1,000 missiles to equip twenty-two bomber squadrons by mid-1967 for $15.3 billion, of which $3.7 billion was for the missile's planned 800-kiloton warhead.

At the urging of the air force, the DOD on February 1, 1960, authorized the Skybolt R&D program. That March, the British government, eager to bolster its independent nuclear force, expressed an interest in using the Skybolt in conjunction with its Vulcan bombers. It received assurances from President Eisenhower that such a program would be developed and formed a joint project office to work with the air force (in a secret quid pro quo deal agreed to during a meeting that month at Camp David, British Prime Minister Harold Macmillan offered Eisenhower the use of Holy Loch, Scotland, as a strategic submarine base).

The Skybolt testing program, which included building and dropping full-size dummy missiles from both U.S. and British aircraft, failed to achieve much success and, with costs mounting, President Kennedy canceled it in December 1962, disappointing the air force, which had, ironically, been offered the project almost two years earlier as "compensation" for Kennedy's cancellation of the troubled B-70 bomber,[4] and straining relations with the British. Kennedy was prepared to offer Britain the data and materials from the Skybolt program in exchange for a $100 million (then-year dollars; $588 million in 1996 dollars) cash payment to cover development costs.

---

pant's View of the Arms Race (New York: Simon & Schuster, 1970), p. 80. General Thomas Power, head of the Strategic Air Command, stated in 1959 that "it is a subsonic missile. Let's face it, it came late. We are buying only a very few of them. They have a very limited value to SAC." Quoted in Beard, *Developing the ICBM*, p. 212, n. 30. As Beard notes, "It is possible, of course, that one factor at play in this period was a hesitancy to cancel Snark and Navaho on grounds of vulnerability because such arguments might also reflect poorly on large segments of the manned fleet." Beard, *Developing the ICBM*, p. 212, n. 30. The first Snark at Presque Isle went on alert on March 18, 1960, and on February 28, 1961, SAC declared the base fully operational with thirty missiles. One month later, President Kennedy ordered the Snark to be phased out because it was "obsolete and of marginal military value." By June 25, 1961, all Snarks were withdrawn from service. Gibson, *History of the U.S. Nuclear Arsenal*, p. 148.

3. Ian Clark, *Nuclear Diplomacy and the Special Relationship: Britain's Deterrent and America, 1957–1962* (Oxford: Clarendon Press, 1994), pp. 338–73; Richard E. Neustadt, *Alliance Politics* (Columbia University Press, 1970), pp. 30–55; Robert Standish Norris, Andrew S. Burrows, and Richard W. Fieldhouse, *Nuclear Weapons Databook*, vol. 5: *British, French, and Chinese Nuclear Weapons* (Boulder, Colo.: Westview Press, 1994), pp. 98–99.

4. Kennedy and McNamara offered this "compensation" despite strong reservations about the viability of Skybolt. After making the decision to terminate the bomber, Kennedy is reported to have remarked that he "used Skybolt to shoot down the B-70." See York, *Race to Oblivion*, p. 155.

Box 2-2
(continued)

But with Skybolt deemed a failure, British Prime Minister Harold Macmillan and his defense minister, Peter Thorneycroft, set their sights higher and eventually persuaded Kennedy (against the advice of the State Department, which was deeply concerned about the example this would set) to offer cooperation on the Polaris SLBM program.[5] In all, Skybolt cost nearly $2.6 billion by the time it was terminated.

Project PLUTO. Project PLUTO sought to combine the power of nuclear weapons with the presumptive versatility of a flying nuclear reactor by creating the world's first atomic-powered buzz bomb. Using a nuclear-powered ramjet engine and carrying a nuclear warhead, the PLUTO missile would have flown at supersonic speeds around treetop level (to avoid radar detection) and delivered its lethal cargo without need of refueling or a crew to guide it. The air force, AEC, and JCAE were all strongly supportive of the concept, which went as far as ground-testing of its turbineless engine at the Nevada Test Site in 1961.

But even as the concept was proving itself feasible, military officials began to have doubts about it. One basic problem was that the ramjet—like the engine then in development for the nuclear-powered aircraft—was essentially an open-ended nuclear reactor, meaning that even routine operations would spew vast quantities of dangerous fission products in its wake, to say nothing of the potential for in-flight accidents or crashes. When combined with a nuclear warhead, the need to transit allied territory on the way to its targets in the Soviet Union, and the missile's vulnerability to being shot down, PLUTO became less and less attractive. Moreover, the radioactive fallout generated by the vaporization of PLUTO's reactor engine would have been many times greater than for just a warhead alone, creating long-term risks downwind of any explosion site. The program was canceled in 1964, following expenditures of about $780 million.[6]

Project Orion. One other project deserves mention for it demonstrates the lengths scientists and engineers went to in attempts to utilize the power of nuclear weapons. Project Orion was a proposal to power a spacecraft by detonating nuclear bombs behind it, allowing the force of the blast to hit a specially designed plate on the back of the craft and thus propel it forward. Despite the obvious problem of safely launching such a vehicle from Earth, scientists worked up a number of studies of the concept, one of which modeled the device to eject the bombs from the craft on the bottle-dispensing mechanism in Coca-Cola vending machines.[7]

---

5. McNamara was prepared to offer the British the Hound Dog cruise missile, but this provoked disappointment and offense. How, Neustadt notes (citing Henry Brandon), "could Englishmen base 'independence' upon something labeled Hound Dog?" Neustadt, *Alliance Politics,* pp. 47–48.

6. Metzger, *The Atomic Establishment,* pp. 201–03; Letter from Representative Chet Holifield, Chairman, Joint Committee on Atomic Energy, to McGeorge Bundy, Special Assistant to the President, December 22, 1962, Record Group 128, General Correspondence, Box 668 (Project Pluto), National Archives. In this letter, Holifield reports "expenditure[s] of $128 million" in then-year dollars for PLUTO. However, available official budget data record only $94.3 million (then-year) in obligations through fiscal 1963 (total recorded obligations through 1965 were $110.3 million). Because relatively small programs like PLUTO were not always itemized in annual budgets and assuming that Holifield, a strong proponent of the program and at the time chairman of the JCAE, had access to all pertinent data, we choose to use his figure here, adjusting it to constant 1996 dollars using a base year of 1961.

7. John McPhee, *The Curve of Binding Energy* (New York: Farrar, Straus & Giroux, 1974), p. 174.

Box 2-2
(continued)

From 1958 until early 1965 the studies consumed nearly $50 million. In 1960 the program was transferred from the Advanced Research Projects Agency (ARPA) to the air force, which, seeing little weapons potential in it, appeared to abandon it. However, a recently declassified memorandum to General Curtis LeMay, dated June 9, 1964, indicates that the concept was kept alive through at least that date by the air force, General Atomics (a defense contractor), and scientists at Livermore Laboratory, who had transformed it into Project Helios, proposing to use lower-yield nuclear explosives to propel a smaller, lighter spacecraft from orbit.[8] Scientists at Livermore suggested proving the new concept via underground nuclear tests, an approach the Air Force Scientific Advisory Board favored as long as NASA and the AEC would take a direct financial interest in the project. The outcome of this proposal is unclear, but Orion never took flight.

A separate but related effort, known as Project ROVER (and later Nuclear Engine for Rocket Vehicle Applications, or NERVA) sought to build nuclear reactor engines to power missiles and rockets for both military and space exploration applications. Initially considered a possible means of powering ICBMs, the program later concentrated on their use as the second-stage motor of a lunar mission and for manned missions to Mars. In all, twenty-one reactor tests took place at the Nuclear Rocket Development Station at the Nevada Test Site between 1959 and 1969. On January 21, 1965, a Kiwi-B type reactor was deliberately destroyed by allowing it to blow apart in order to assess analytical models of the reactor's behavior during a rapid power excursion (only 50 percent of the reactor core could be accounted for after this test; the remainder was presumed to either have burned or been converted into fine particles and carried downwind in a cloud). The program was terminated following a shift in national priorities, principally a move away from large numbers of manned spaceflights following the success of the Apollo program. From 1961 to 1973, NERVA consumed $3.9 billion.[9]

8. Memorandum, James Ferguson, Lieutenant General, U.S. Air Force, Military Director, USAF Scientific Advisory Board, to General Curtis E. LeMay, June 9, 1964, Curtis LeMay papers, Library of Congress.

9. W. H. Robins, Analytical Engineering Corp., and H. B. Finger, consultant, "An Historical Perspective of the NERVA Nuclear Rocket Engine Technology Program," paper presented at the AIAA/NASA/OAI Conference on Advanced SEI Technologies, September 4–6, 1991, Cleveland, Ohio, AIAA (American Institute of Aeronautics and Astronautics) 91-3451; Daniel R. Koenig, "Experience Gained from the Space Nuclear Rocket Program (Rover)," Los Alamos National Laboratory, LA-10062-H, May 1985; Gary L. Bennett and others, "Prelude to the Future: A Brief History of Nuclear Thermal Propulsion in the United States," Special Commemorative Paper, NASA Symposia on Space Nuclear Power Systems, Preprint Log 092 (n.d., circa 1992). Budget data for ROVER/NERVA were obtained from successive volumes of Bureau of the Budget/Office of Management and Budget, *Budget of the United States Government,* Fiscal Year 1958 through 1975, and converted to constant 1996 dollars.

General Maxwell D. Taylor, army chief of staff under Eisenhower (and later chairman of the JCS under Kennedy), for one, subscribed to the theory of finite deterrence, according to which nuclear weapons exist solely to deter rather than fight nuclear wars. Hence the threat to destroy a finite number of targets, usually cities, would be enough to prevent any aggression. An adequate force, Taylor wrote in 1960, might consist of "a few hundred reliable and accurate missiles," which were "mobile, concealed, and dispersed" and supplemented by a small number of bombers. Taylor used what he called "simple arithmetic" to calculate that only a few score targets ("at most two hundred") had to be destroyed to undermine the enemy's war-making capacity: "Even after adding a heavy factor of safety to cover imponderables, the size of the required atomic retaliatory forces will be found to be much smaller than the bombers and missiles of our present force."[133] Going further still, Admiral Noel Gayler, former deputy director of the Joint Strategic Target Planning Staff (JSTPS), former commander in chief of Pacific Command, and former director of the National Security Agency, wrote in 1984 that he could find "no sensible military use for nuclear weapons, whether 'strategic' weapons, 'tactical' weapons, 'theater' weapons, weapons at sea or weapons in space." Once, when scrutinizing the whole of the Pacific command, he could not identify "any area where it would conceivably have made sense to explode nuclear weapons in order to carry our military objectives."[134]

General Norman Schwarzkopf wrote in 1992 that after Saddam Hussein closed the borders of Iraq and Kuwait on August 9, 1990, "if the Iraqis started executing U.S. embassy employees, say, and the President wanted to retaliate, Central Command had little to offer short of a nuclear strike on Baghdad. I would never have recommended such a course of action, and even if I had, I am certain the President would never have approved it."[135] Indeed, Bush had privately ruled out the use of nuclear weapons prior to the start of the Gulf War.

In 1994, shortly before he retired as commander in chief of Space Command, General Charles Horner (who served as allied air force commander during the Gulf War) declared the nuclear weapon "obsolete" and challenged the United States to take "the high moral ground" by completely eliminating its nuclear arsenal.[136] And in his 1995 autobiog-

---

toward inficting mass civilian casualties, particularly when they could see no practical military gain in unilaterally breaching the nuclear threshold." Harry G. Summers, Jr., "Doomsday Clock Reset," *Washington Times,* December 18, 1997, p. A19.

133. Maxwell D. Taylor, *The Uncertain Trumpet* (New York: Harper, 1960), pp. 148, 158.

134. Noel Gayler, "A Commander-in-Chief's Perspective on Nuclear Weapons," in Prins, *The Nuclear Crisis Reader,* p. 16. Gayler communicated this view in writing to his superiors, the Joint Chiefs of Staff. He later heard rumors that this action was considered sufficient grounds for his removal and that he would have been fired but for the intervention of Secretary of Defense James Schlesinger

135. H. Norman Schwarzkopf, *It Doesn't Take a Hero: General H. Norman Schwazkopf, The Autobiography,* written with Peter Petre (New York: Bantam Books, 1992), p. 313. Notwithstanding his unequivocal stance regarding the actual use of nuclear weapons, Schwarzkopf testified before the Senate Veterans' Affairs Committee in January 1997 that he believed the threat to use nuclear weapons played a key role in keeping Iraq from launching an attack with chemical weapons. Schwarzkopf said that he told General Colin Powell, chairman of the Joint Chiefs of Staff, "'This guy's a thug. There's only certain things he understands,' and I said, 'Hey, tell Saddam Hussein that, you know, he throws chemicals on our troops, we're going to blow him away with nuclear weapons, period. He'll understand that.'" Quoted in United Press International, "U.S. Threatened Iraq with Nukes," January 29, 1997. U.S. officials did not explicitly threaten the use of nuclear weapons, but in public statements and private communications with Iraqi officials, they strongly implied that any use of weapons of mass destruction would be "unconscionable," requiring the "strongest possible response" by whatever means necessary.

136. John Diamond, "Air Force General Calls for End to Atomic Arms," *Boston Globe,* July 16, 1994, p. A3; Associated Press, "General Wants U.S. to Get Rid of Nuclear Arms, *Seattle Times,* July 16, 1994, p. A3.

raphy, General Colin Powell recalled how, during a war-gaming exercise in 1986—when one of his senior officers matter-of-factly suggested using nuclear-armed short-range missiles and artillery shells to keep Warsaw Pact forces from crossing the Haune and Fulda rivers in what was then West Germany and cutting NATO forces in half—he realized that "no matter how small these nuclear payloads were, we would be crossing a threshold. . . . From that day on I began rethinking the practicality of these small nuclear weapons." While planning strategy prior to the Gulf War, Powell told Secretary of Defense Dick Cheney, "Let's not even think about nukes. You know we're not going to let that genie loose." Replied Cheney, "Of course not. But take a look to be thorough." Powell did and discovered that to "do serious damage to just one armored division dispersed in the desert would require a considerable number of small tactical nuclear weapons. I showed this analysis to Cheney and then had it destroyed. If I had had any doubts before about the practicality of nukes on the field of battle, this report clinched them."[137] Just months later, Powell's new thinking reached fruition as, at President Bush's direction, he helped to develop and then implement far-reaching measures to alter the nuclear status quo, including eliminating all short-range nuclear weapons and grounding the Strategic Air Command's airborne command post.

With more and more in the military subscribing to such views, one nuclear mission after another was eliminated. This pattern has continued to the present day. In 1995, for example, the nuclear strike mission from aircraft carriers, a mission more than forty years old, was terminated.[138] And in a speech delivered in December 1996, General George Lee Butler, the former head of the U.S. Strategic Command, issued the most far-reaching proposal ever made by someone of his background and rank: he called on the nuclear powers to abandon the notion that nuclear weapons are inextricably linked to security and to work toward eventually eliminating them.[139] This speech met with an immediate response from sixty retired generals and admirals from around the world. They urged nations to gradually take their nuclear weapons off alert and henceforth to base their security policies on "the declared principle of continuous, complete and irrevocable elimination of nuclear weapons." Although many commentators saw these views as somewhat extreme or impractical, few took issue with the suggested deep reductions in the U.S. nuclear arsenal or with the proposal to take nuclear weapons off alert.[140]

137. Colin L. Powell with Joseph E. Perisco, *My American Journey* (New York: Random House, 1995), pp. 323–24, 485–86, 540–41.

138. Perry, *Report of the Secretary of Defense to the President and the Congress* (1995), pp. 88–89.

139. Remarks by General Lee Butler (U.S. Air Force, retired) at the National Press Club, December 4, 1996. See also R. Jeffrey Smith, "Retired Nuclear Warrior Sounds Alarm on Weapons," *Washington Post,* December 4, 1996, p. A1; R. Jeffrey Smith, "The Dissenter," *Washington Post Magazine,* December 7, 1997, pp. 18–21, 38–45.

140. Stephen S. Rosenfeld, "Nuclear Abolitionism,"

Missile Test Ranges

The enormous scale of the U.S. nuclear endeavor cannot be fully appreciated without some attention to its testing programs and basing efforts. Testing alone requires a network of sophisticated instruments to record a missile's performance through all the stages of its development, from R&D to operational service. Testing begins in unrealistic (for example, static) conditions and becomes more realistic as initial deployment approaches. Even after deployment, missiles need to undergo flight testing. The JCS establish general guidelines for the testing of weapon systems, and the results help to determine the number of missiles that will be bought.[141] The individual services may alter the guidelines by applying more strict or less strict criteria than those specified by the JCS.

White Sands Missile Range, New Mexico

The White Sands Proving Ground, the first U.S. test range on land, was established on July 9, 1945, in the Tularosa Basin of south-central New Mexico, and rocket firings began in September. Many types of rockets, such as Corporal, Nike, and Lance, were tested there.

Today it is called White Sands Missile Range (WSMR). With headquarters 20 miles (32.2 kilometers) east of Las Cruces and 45 miles (72 kilometers) north of El Paso, Texas, it covers 3,200 square miles (8,288 square kilometers; which is greater than the area of Delaware and Rhode Island combined) and is the largest military installation in the country. WSMR also was used as an impact area for missiles fired from other locations. The range is equipped with a network of optical and electronic instruments to collect and process data. The first atomic bomb was exploded at Trinity site near the north boundary of the range. According to the FYDP historical database, it cost $5.1 billion to operate WSMR from 1962 to 1995.

The United States maintains two coastal test ranges for ballistic missile flight tests over the ocean. These tests require high-performance

---

Washington Post, December 6, 1996, p. A31; "Questioning Nuclear Arms," transcript of a debate between General Charles Horner and James R. Schlesinger, "The NewsHour with Jim Lehrer," December 4, 1996 (available on the World Wide Web at http://www1.pbs.org/newshour/bb/military/nuclear_debate_12-4.htm); David M. North, "Destroying Nukes Will Save More than Lives," *Aviation Week & Space Technology*, December 9, 1996, p. 98; Richard N. Haass, "It's Dangerous to Disarm," *New York Times*, December 11, 1996, p. A27; William Pfaff, "It's Time to Give Up the Bomb," *Baltimore Sun*, December 23, 1996, p. A12; "Don't Ban the Bomb," *Economist*, January 4, 1997, pp. 15–16. General Butler commented on these and other responses to his speech in remarks before the Henry L. Stimson Center on January 8, 1997. Excerpts appear in George Lee Butler, "Time to End the Age of Nukes," *Bulletin of the Atomic Scientists*, vol. 53 (March 1997), pp. 33–36. See also Committee on International Security and Arms Control, *The Future of U.S. Nuclear Weapons Policy* (Washington, D.C.: National Academy Press, 1997); and a series of perspectives and debates on nuclear arms control in a special edition of *Washington Quarterly*, vol. 20, no. 1 (1997), pp. 77–210.

141. For example, although the MX/Peacekeeper missile program was limited in the mid-1980s to just 50 deployed missiles, 102 were ultimately purchased, with the majority of the "extra" missiles designated for the ongoing flight test program.

telemetry reception equipment, radars for trajectory measurements, meteorological equipment, optical systems for tracking, and photographic equipment, among other things. Whether on land or at sea, all of this equipment must be available to record the test. Some of the equipment measuring ocean ranges may be placed on islands but may need to be supplemented by the use of ships and aircraft.[142]

Vandenberg Air Force Base, California

The air force's first missile base was established in September 1956 on a peninsula 55 miles (88.5 kilometers) north of Santa Barbara, California. It was then an army base called Camp Cooke, which dated from World War II. It was renamed Cooke AFB in June 1957 and changed to Vandenberg AFB in October 1958 (after former Air Force Chief of Staff Hoyt S. Vandenberg). The base encompasses 98,400 acres and is the third largest air force base. It includes 35 miles (56 kilometers) of Pacific coastline, 520 miles (836.7 kilometers) of road, 17 miles (27 kilometers) of railroad track, and 16 missile silos and is home to more than seven thousand personnel. On December 16, 1958, Vandenberg successfully fired its first missile: a Thor IRBM. As of August 1995, it had launched 1,714 vehicles: 978 ICBMs, 626 space boosters, 87 surface-to-air interceptor missiles, 22 IRBMs, and 1 GLCM.[143]

For an operational test of a Minuteman or MX missile, an ICBM is withdrawn from its silo, its warheads are removed, and it is transported via unmarked boxcars to Vandenberg.[144] Explosive safety devices are installed in the boosters to provide a means of destroying them should they deviate from their programmed flight pattern. Special telemetry and instrumentation equipment is installed to record flight performance. It is then placed in a silo and launched unarmed down the Western Test Range (WTR).

The WTR is a vast test and evaluation complex that begins at the coastal boundaries of Vandenberg and extends westward across the Pacific to the middle of the Indian Ocean. It includes a network of

142. In addition to these facilities, the DOD maintains six other bases and test ranges that have played important roles in the development of nuclear weapons systems. These include the Barking Sands Pacific Missile Range Facility (Kauai, Hawaii), China Lake Naval Air Warfare Center (Ridgecrest, California), Edwards Air Force Base (Edwards, California), Hill Air Force Base/Utah Test and Training Range (Ogden, Utah), Pacific Missile Test Center (Oxnard, California), and the Redstone Arsenal (Huntsville, Alabama).

143. Thirtieth Space Wing History Office, *The Heritage of the 30th Space Wing and Vandenberg Air Force Base* (GPO 1995), p. 21.

144. In the 1960s, to allay concerns that operational missiles might not launch when needed, SAC initiated Project Long Life. On March 1, 1965, a Minuteman I missile was launched from its silo at Ellsworth AFB in South Dakota (the second and third stages were inert and the first stage was tethered to a long elastic cord). The flight lasted seven seconds and covered just 2 miles (3.2 kilometers). However, subsequent tests with the Minuteman II on October 19 and 28, 1966, and August 14, 1968 (the latter named Giant Boost), were unsuccessful, leading to a new effort in 1970 to launch eight fully operational Minutemen from a SAC base. This program never got under way because members of Congress over whose states and districts these missiles would fly declined to authorize it. See Strategic Air Command, *SAC Missile Chronology: 1939–1988*; Gibson, *History of the US Nuclear Arsenal*, p. 23.

Herb Lehr, a member of the Manhattan Project's Special Engineering Detachment, holding the assembled plutonium core for the world's first atomic bomb in a special shock-absorbing case about 6:00 p.m. on July 12, 1945. The core was about the size of an orange and weighed some 13.5 pounds (6.1 kilograms).

Credit: Los Alamos National Laboratory

Los Alamos National Laboratory, birthplace of the atomic bomb and one of the three major laboratories responsible for creating and maintaining the U.S. nuclear stockpile.

Credit: Department of Energy

A casing for the *Little Boy* atomic bomb, similar to the one dropped on Hiroshima, Japan, on August 6, 1945. The bomb, which contained 132 pounds (60 kilograms) of highly enriched uranium, was 10 feet (3 meters) long, 28 inches (71 centimeters) in diameter, weighed 8,900 pounds (4,045 kilograms), and had an explosive yield of 15 kilotons. The scientists who designed it were so certain it would work that unlike the *Fat Man* plutonium bomb it was never subjected to a full-scale test.

Credit: U.S. Air Force

A casing for the *Fat Man* bomb of the type dropped on Nagasaki, Japan, on August 9, 1945. This bomb contained about 13.5 pounds (6.1 kilograms) of plutonium, was 12 feet (3.7 meters) long, 60 inches (1.5 meters) in diameter (at its widest point), weighed 10,800 pounds (4,909 kilograms), and had an explosive yield of 21 kilotons.

Credit: National Atomic Museum

The Gaseous Diffusion Plant at the Oak Ridge Reservation in Tennessee produced 483 metric tons of highly enriched uranium for nuclear weapons from 1945 until 1964. The original K-25 Plant built during the Manhattan Project (the large U-shaped building at right) covers some 2.3 square miles (6 square kilometers).

Credit: Department of Energy

More than 36 metric tons of weapon-grade plutonium were produced by reactors such as this one—the L-reactor—at the Savannah River Site in South Carolina between 1953 and 1988 (an additional 54.5 metric tons of weapon-grade plutonium was produced in reactors at the Hanford Reservation in Washington state). There are five such reactors at the Savannah River Site, all shut down.

Credit: Robert Del Tredici

Workers at the Savannah River Site use "master-slave manipulators" to handle highly radioactive fuel elements from the site's production reactors. The materials they are manipulating are behind about 12 inches (30 centimeters) of leaded glass and concrete.

Credit: Department of Energy

The Rocky Flats Environmental Technology Site (formerly the Rocky Flats Plant), located in the foothills of the Rocky Mountains 21 miles (34 kilometers) northwest of Denver, Colorado, fabricated plutonium cores and other nuclear weapons components from 1952 until 1990. It covers an area of 10.2 square miles (26.4 square kilometers). Some buildings at this facility are so contaminated that people cannot safely enter them.

Credit: Rockwell International Corp.

A worker at the Rocky Flats Plant (circa 1975) examines a plutonium "button" inside a glove box. The button will later be broken down and cast into a "pit" or core for a nuclear weapon.

Credit: Department of Energy

An enormous radioactive spray plume more than 1 mile (1.6 kilometers) high and containing 2 million tons of water rises from Bikini Atoll about one second after the detonation of the 23-kiloton Baker test, part of Operation Crossroads, on July 25, 1946. The Baker device, similar to the *Fat Man* bomb dropped on Nagasaki, was exploded 90 feet (27 meters) underwater, in the midst of a target fleet of ninety-five German, Japanese, and U.S. ships (all but nine of which were heavily contaminated by the blast).

Credit: Army Navy Task Force One (courtesy Jonathan Weisgall)

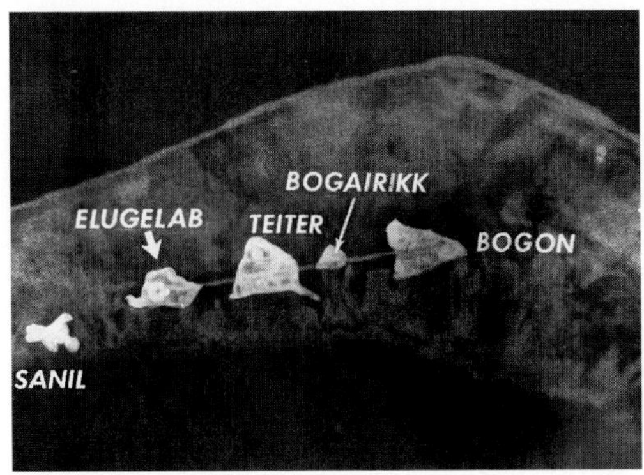

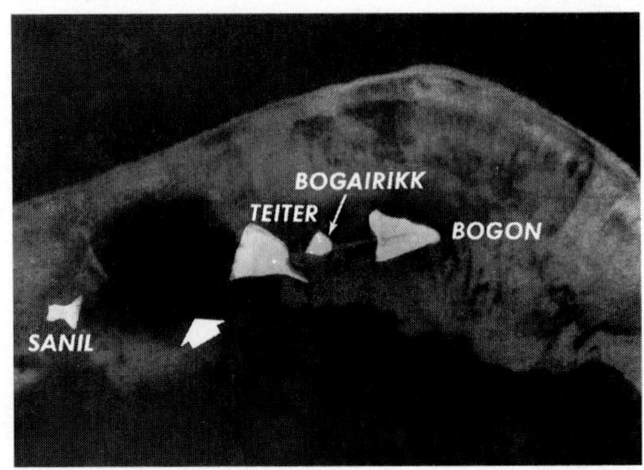

The photograph at left shows five of forty named islands comprising Enewetak Atoll before the "Mike" test of November 1, 1952 (the gray areas surrounding the islands are coral reefs). This test of an experimental thermonuclear device (weighing 164,000 pounds or 74,546 kilograms) had a yield of 10.4 megatons and completely vaporized the island of Elugelab as well as portions of Sanil and Teiter (right), leaving a crater 164 feet (50 meters) deep and 1.2 miles (1.9 kilometers) wide.

Credit: U.S. Air Force

This crater at the Nevada Test Site is 1,280 feet (390 meters) wide and 322 feet (98 meters) deep. It was created by the July 6, 1962, Sedan test, a 104-kiloton device buried 635 feet (194 meters) underground and used by the Plowshare Program to study potential excavation techniques using nuclear weapons. The blast ejected 12 million tons of rock and earth into the air, 8 million of which fell outside the crater. The vehicles near the lip of the crater at right show the scale.

Credit: Department of Energy (courtesy Natural Resources Defense Council)

In preparation for an underground nuclear test at the Nevada Test Site, miles of cables connect the nuclear device to diagnostic and monitoring instruments in trailers located a safe distance away from the test shaft. In the instant after the device detonates—destroying itself and everything in the test shaft—the cables relay critical measurements back to weapons scientists, allowing them to ascertain the device's yield, efficiency, and other characteristics. Note the subsidence craters from previous tests in the vicinity.

Credit: Lawrence Livermore National Laboratory (courtesy Natural Resources Defense Council)

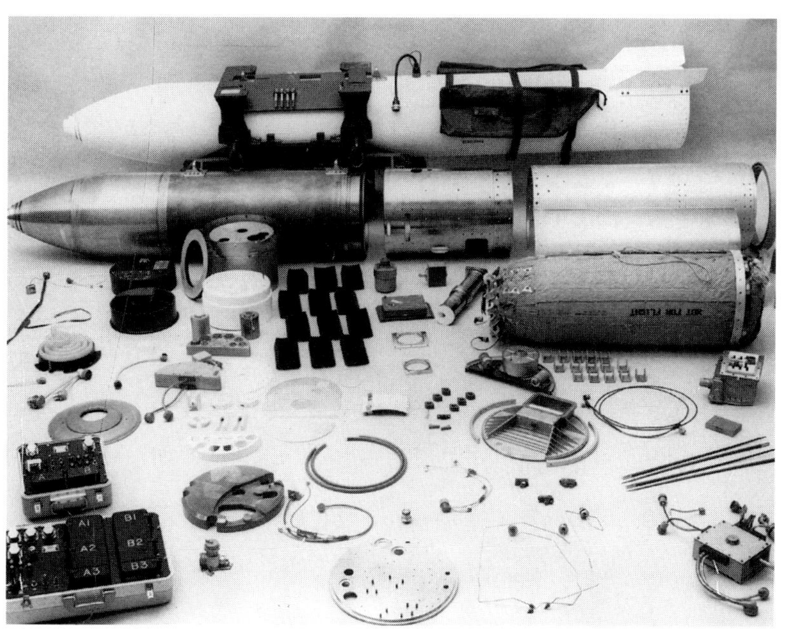

A B83 strategic gravity bomb shown fully assembled (background) and disassembled into its major components and subassemblies (its 1 megaton warhead is contained in the front section of the bomb). The B83 contains 6,619 parts and was first deployed in 1983. It can be carried by B-52 and B-2A bombers.

Credit: Department of Energy (courtesy Natural Resources Defense Council)

A fleet of giant B-36 Peacemaker bombers and their sixteen-person crews on display at Carswell Air Force Base, Texas in 1955. The B-36 had a wingspan of 230 feet (70 meters) and was operational from 1948-1958. In all, 385 aircraft were built.

Credit: National Archives

The crew of a B-58 bomber poses with their aircraft. Also on display are the plane's external fuel tank, warhead pod, and four B-43 nuclear gravity bombs. One hundred and four B-58s were built and deployed from 1960 to 1970.

Credit: General Dynamics (courtesy James Norris Gibson)

Air-launched cruise missiles being loaded aboard wing pylons on a B-52 bomber at Griffiss Air Force Base, New York, in December 1981. The open warhead compartment on one missile is clearly visible.

Credit: U.S. Air Force (courtesy Natural Resources Defense Council)

A KC-135 tanker refuels a B-2 bomber over Edwards Air Force Base, California, in November 1989.

Credit: Department of Defense

A B-52 bomber armed with two Hound Dog air-to-surface missiles. The Hound Dog, in service from 1960 to 1975, carried a warhead with a yield of up to 1.1 megatons. The first of 744 B-52s was deployed in 1955; 93 remain operational today.

Credit: U.S. Air Force

Three Mk-12A reentry vehicles atop a "bus" in the configuration used on the Minuteman III missile (the missile's nosecone is at right). Each reentry vehicle carries a single W78 warhead with a 335-kiloton yield and measures 5.9 feet (1.8 meters) tall and 1.8 feet (54.3 centimeters) in diameter at its base.

Credit: U.S. Air Force (courtesy Natural Resources Defense Council)

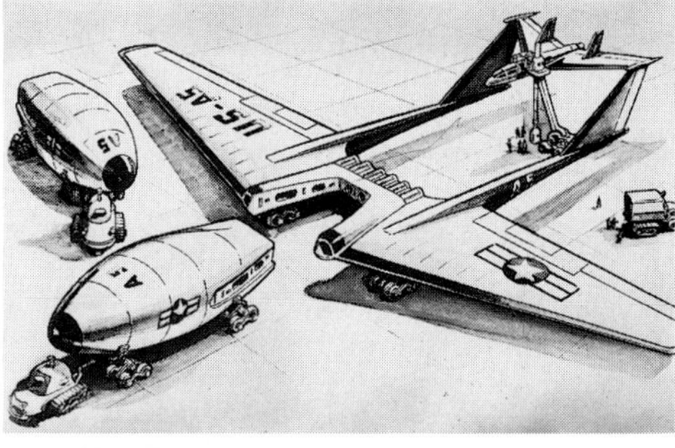

Between 1946 and 1961, the air force and the Atomic Energy Commission spent more than $7 billion trying to develop a nuclear-powered aircraft. One concept involved detachable reactor modules (bottom) that could be replaced as needed. In this artist's conception, the pilots were in the section forming part of the tail, which could be detached in case of emergency. The two prototype power plants (top, in a vertical and horizontal configuration) weighed 250 and 270 tons, respectively, and could only be moved by a shielded locomotive on a specially designed railway at the National Reactor Testing Station in Idaho.

Credits: Robert Del Tredici (top), U.S. Air Force (bottom)

A Titan I launch sequence is demonstrated at Vandenberg Air Force Base, California, in 1961. Fifty-four of these liquid-fueled missiles, each carrying a 4.5-megaton warhead, were deployed in groups of three at five air force bases between 1962 and 1965. Each missile was 98 feet (29.9 meters) tall. The elapsed time between the first and last frame is approximately 15 minutes. Note the persons in the first and last frames.

Credit: National Archives

A Minuteman II ICBM roars out of an aboveground test silo at the Kennedy Space Center in March 1970, on its way over the Eastern Test Range. Four hundred and fifty Minuteman IIs were on alert from 1966 to 1991.

Credit: U.S. Air Force

Unlike early aboveground ICBM facilities, all 1,000 Minuteman silos were designed to survive anything but a direct hit. Inserted into each silo shaft was a 62-foot (18.9 meter) reinforced steel liner that was then covered by poured concrete, forming the external silo wall. The missiles were inserted into the liner and the silos covered by a heavy steel and concrete door.

Credit: U.S. Army Corps of Engineers

The B17 (also known as the Mk-17) was the first deliverable thermonuclear weapon and the largest bomb ever deployed by the United States (only the B-36 bomber could carry it). The B17 was 24.8 feet (7.6 meters) long and 5.1 feet (1.6 meters) in diameter, weighed 21 tons, and had a yield of 10–15 megatons. Deployed for a little over three years, it was soon replaced with smaller, easier-to-handle weapons.

Credit: National Atomic Museum (courtesy Natural Resources Defense Council)

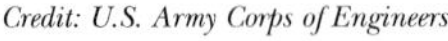

Construction of a Titan I missile site at Lowry Air Force Base, Colorado, November 1959. The missile control center is in the background and the powerhouse is in the foreground (the silo, propellant tanks, and associated buildings are not shown). Eighteen launch complexes (for fifty-four missiles) were built in California, Colorado, Idaho, South Dakota, and Washington state at an average cost of $44.4 million each. Titan I missiles were only on alert from 1962 to 1965.

Credit: U.S. Army Corps of Engineers

Soldiers with the 40th Artillery Group begin raising a large Redstone missile into firing position during training exercises at Eckweiler, Germany, in December 1958. This missile, which was deployed between 1958 and 1964, carried a warhead with a yield of either 425 kilotons or 3.8 megatons.

Credit: U.S. Army (courtesy Center for Defense Information)

The USS *George Washington,* the Navy's first ballistic missile submarine, is shown minutes after launching in Groton, Connecticut, on June 9, 1959. Powered by a single nuclear reactor, it carried sixteen Polaris A-1 missiles, each with a 1.2- to 1.5-megaton warhead.

Credit: U.S. Navy

Two views of the construction of Minuteman launch control capsules (LCCs) at Ellsworth Air Force Base, South Dakota, July 1962. At left, workers attach reinforcing steel to the capsule in preparation for covering it with concrete. The large hole in the capsule is the crew's escape hatch (to which a tube leading to the surface will later be attached). The large white tower is the elevator shaft to the capsule. The right view shows another site at a similar stage of construction. When completed, the capsules—59 feet (18 meters) long and 29 feet (8.8 meters) in diameter—were buried and a blockhouse constructed atop the site, housing crew quarters and support equipment. (Beginning in the late 1960s at Minuteman facilities in Missouri, North Dakota, and Wyoming, this vital equipment was moved underground into hardened capsules adjacent to the LCC.) Each capsule controls a flight of ten missiles.

Credit: U.S. Army Corps of Engineers

The petal-like shelter and supporter around a Jupiter missile being raised to enclose the missile during testing at Redstone Arsenal, Alabama, in May 1959. Forty-five intermediate-range Jupiter missiles carrying 1.45-megaton warheads were deployed briefly in Italy (30 missiles) and Turkey (15 missiles) but were withdrawn following the Cuban Missile Crisis in October 1963.

Credit: National Archives

On May 25, 1953, in its first and only live test (observed by senior army officials and members of Congress), a 280-millimeter atomic cannon at the Nevada Proving Ground fired a shell that detonated 524 feet (159.7 meters) above the ground with a yield of 15 kilotons. The mushroom cloud reached an altitude of 35,000 feet (10,668 meters). Only 160 nuclear shells were built for this system, which was considered by many to be technologically obsolete as soon as it was deployed.

Credit: National Archives

The Davy Crockett was the smallest and lightest nuclear weapon ever deployed by the U.S. military. The W54 warhead (inside the finned casing) weighed just 51 pounds (23.2 kilograms) and had a variable yield as small as .01 kiloton (equivalent to 10 tons of TNT). Launched from either a 120-millimeter or 150-millimeter recoilless rifle (the former is shown here at the Aberdeen Proving Ground in Maryland in March 1961), it was designed for use in Europe against Soviet troop formations.

Credit: National Archives

Scientists displaying the warhead (left) and packing container for the Medium Atomic Demolition Munition (MADM), a low-yield (1- to 15-kiloton) nuclear land mine designed to be deployed behind enemy lines and destroy tunnels, bridges, dams and disrupt enemy troop movements. The entire unit (including warhead) weighed less than 400 pounds and was deployed from 1965 to 1986.

Credit: Department of Defense (courtesy Natural Resources Defense Council)

A neat row of B83 strategic gravity bombs in a maintenance facility at Barksdale Air Force Base, Louisiana, in 1995. An estimated 650 B83s were built, each carrying a 1-megaton warhead. In the background at left are air-launched cruise missiles and an advanced cruise missile.

Credit: Paul Shambroom

The Department of Energy transports nuclear weapons and weapons components via custom-made trailers known as Safeguards Transporters. Drivers are specially trained, and all shipments are accompanied by highly armed escorts. The trucks are steel-lined and fire resistant and incorporate a number of active and passive features to thwart tampering or theft.

Credit: Department of Energy

launch, tracking, telemetry, and command and control systems that monitor a variety of developmental and operational ICBMs and space boosters launched from Vandenberg. Downrange instrumentation sites are in Hawaii and Kwajalein Atoll in the Marshall Islands, and uprange sites are located along the coast of California. Reentry for ICBMs takes place near Kwajalein. According to the DOD's FYDP historical database, WTR and the Pacific missile range operations cost $7.4 billion from 1962 to 1995. Communications and logistical support for the WTR cost an additional $1.2 billion, and facilities on Kwajalein Atoll $6.9 billion.

Eastern Space and Missile Center, Cape Canaveral, Florida

On October 1, 1949, the Pentagon activated a joint long-range missile proving ground on Cape Canaveral, later named Patrick Air Force Base.[145] In the early 1950s tracking and range stations were built at Grand Bahama Island, Eleuthera, San Salvador, Mayaguana, Gran Turk, the Dominican Republic, and Puerto Rico. To accommodate longer-range missiles such as the Snark and Navaho, additional stations were built at Antigua, St. Lucia, Fernando de Noronha, and Ascension. Telemetry ships filled in the gaps between Antigua and Ascension. Activities in all territories outside the United States were conducted under negotiated agreements with the host governments.

On July 24, 1950, the first missile, a Bumper, was fired at the Eastern Test Range. The first 5,000-mile (8,045-kilometer) mission, a Snark test flight, took place on October 31, 1957.[146] Throughout the 1950s Cape launches concentrated on aerodynamic or winged missiles, notably, the Matador, Snark, Bomarc, Navaho, and Mace. The Matador alone had more than 280 launches.[147]

By the 1960s, air force and navy ballistic missile tests came to dominate the range, along with the Mercury manned space program of the National Aeronautics and Space Administration (NASA). A wide variety of radars, tracking telescopes, and cameras were used and con-

145. Forty-fifth Space Wing History Office, *The 45th Space Wing: Its Heritage, History & Honors, 1950–1994* (GPO, 1995).

146. Of sixty-eight test launches of Snark between August 6, 1953, and September 19, 1958, only thirty-three were considered successful, which amounts to a failure rate of 49 percent. "The average miss distance was over 1,000 miles (1,609 kilometers). At least one [launched December 5, 1956] came down in the wrong hemisphere, in the interior of Brazil." This missile—whose radio command destruct system failed—was eventually discovered in January 1983 by a Brazilian farmer. See, Beard, *Developing the ICBM*, p. 224 (n. 15); Gibson, *History of the US Nuclear Arsenal*, pp. 146–48. In a similar incident in November 1960, "portions of a Thor missile that malfunctioned in flight during a satellite launch . . . impacted in Cuba, reportedly killing a cow and causing strong diplomatic protests from the Castro government." Parts of this missile's propulsion system "were sold by the Castro government to the government of the People's Republic of China, which used the pieces to design the second stage of its DF-5 (NATO designation CSS-4) ICBM." See Scott D. Sagan, *The Limits of Safety: Organizations, Accidents, and Nuclear Weapons* (Princeton University Press, 1993), p. 127.

147. Mark C. Cleary, *The 655th:Missile and Space Launches Through 1970* (45th Space Wing, Office of History, 1991), p. 27 (available on the World Wide Web at: http://www.pafb.af.mil/heritage/6555th/6555fram.htm).

stantly improved and replaced. Specially instrumented aircraft for communication and telemetry support were also needed.[148] Modified C-54s, C-130s, and C-135As were used from the 1950s to the 1990s. Between July 1950 and the end of 1994 there were 3,060 launches. According to the FYDP historical database, costs for the Eastern Test Range over the period 1962–92 came to $14.5 billion.

Tonopah Test Range, Nevada

The Tonopah Test Range (TTR) covers an area of 577 square miles (1,494 square kilometers) located 140 miles (225 kilometers) northwest of Las Vegas and is operated by Sandia National Laboratories. It was established in 1957 and was used on a limited basis after similar facilities at the Salton Sea Test Base and at Yucca Flat (on the Nevada Test Site) became inadequate. Testing activities at TTR

> have included air drops of simulated bombs, gun firings of artillery shells, ground launched rockets (for ballistics or materials properties measurements), rocket launches from aircraft, static rocket tests (e.g., for the Trident I), use of the range as an impact area for cruise missiles launched from ships and submarines at sea, and explosives tests on shipping and storage containers for nuclear weapons. Some of the latter tests have involved plutonium and kilogram quantities of depleted uranium and beryllium.[149]

Between February and June 1963, a series of tests code-named Roller Coaster were jointly conducted with Great Britain to study the spread of plutonium from the nonnuclear detonation of nuclear weapons configured in various transportation and storage modes. Four plutonium pits and forty-four mock-up pits were destroyed in nonnuclear explosions. In the process, a portion of the test site was contaminated. The results of the tests were used "as a basis of agreement . . . on mutual standards for the storage, transport and handling of plutonium-bearing weapons." The AEC and DOD costs for the exercise were $39 million.[150] Total costs for Tonopah are apparently included in Sandia's overall budget, which is counted in chapter 1. From 1993 to 1996, the only years for which Sandia officials said figures were available, the site cost $51.3 million to operate.[151]

---

148. Between 1981 and 1983, the navy spent $60.7 million to modify four P-3 Orion aircraft to "serve as mobile instrumentation platforms capable of acquiring ballistic missile reentry vehicle telemetry and performing missile impact scoring in broad ocean areas as required to support testing of Trident, MX and other strategic weapons systems." Department of Defense, *FYDP Program Structure*, p. 6N-121.

149. Cochran and others, *U.S. Nuclear Warhead Facility Profiles*, p. 125.

150. U.S. Atomic Energy Commission, Nevada Operations Office, *Project Manager's Report: Project Roller Coaster* (Nevada Operations Office: Reynolds Electrical and Engineering, and AEC, May 1964; formerly classified Confidential/Restricted Data, at the DOE's Coordination and Information Center in Las Vegas, Nevada), pp. 1, 44–45, 47.

151. Author's telephone and e-mail communication with Karen Rosenthal, Office of Consumer and Public Liaison, U.S. Department of Energy, August 6 and 14, 1997.

Aircraft Test Ranges

Aircraft, too, have training ranges to practice the performance of their missions. In the early years bomber crews dropped sand bags or dummy bombs on circles drawn on the ground.[152] Modern radar bomb scoring uses highly sophisticated electronic devices to assess the accuracy of simulated bomb drops. U.S. Strategic Command (formerly SAC) bombers use the Strategic Training Route Complex with ground radar sites near Powell, Wyoming; Forsyth, Conrad, and Havre, Montana; Dickinson, North Dakota; and Belle Fourche, South Dakota. Bombers fly most of the routes at altitudes of only 400 feet (122 meters).

To test the simulated effects of nuclear weapons, particularly the electromagnetic pulse (EMP), the DOD maintains a trestle-test facility at Kirtland Air Force Base, New Mexico. The trestle is the largest glue-laminated structure in the world, large enough to hold a B-52 bomber. Planes are brought to the trestle and subjected to 10 million volts of EMP energy to determine their resistance, or "hardness," to the pulse.

Bases and Basing

As in all military operations, the basing of nuclear forces, whether aircraft, missiles, or ships, was a paramount concern during the cold war. Airplanes need airfields to take off and, after the mission is accomplished, to land. Missiles, whether fired from mobile or fixed launchers, need to be placed in the most advantageous position to hit their targets.

Foreign Bases

One prominent feature of the cold war was the expansion of U.S. military forces abroad. The largest growth took place from the late-1940s to the early-1960s.[153] A major purpose of this extensive basing network, built through multilateral treaties such as NATO and numerous bilateral agreements, was to be better able to deliver nuclear weapons on

152. Training for the atomic bomb attacks on Japan occurred from September 1944 to July 1945 at Wendover, Utah, an isolated area of salt flats located on the Utah-Nevada border. B-29 bombers modified under Project SILVERPLATE, made test runs over the Mojave Desert and the Salton Sea in Southern California, as well as the Carribean (to gain experience navigating over water). Full-size mockups of the "Little Boy" and "Fat Man" bombs, some armed with high explosives, were used during practice drops. See Eric Malnic, "Remote Utah Town Became Launching Pad for A-Bomb," *Los Angeles Times*, August 6, 1995, p. A1.

153. Many bases were built during World War II. In the United States, a number of these were built in the South, to allow for year-round training. Following the war, the air force converted many of these bases into bomber bases, a decision that, while appearing cost effective, placed bombers hundreds of miles further away from their intended targets, increasing flying time and hence overall costs and reducing operational effectiveness. As General Curtis LeMay, commander in chief of SAC testified in 1956: "Our base system more or less grew instead of being properly planned from a tactical standpoint. . . . [W]e are there sort of by accident." This situation led General LeMay to request additional funding to build new bases in the northern part of the country (in addition to more planes and refueling tankers). See *Study of Airpower*, Hearings, vol. 1, pp. 157–58.

targets in the Soviet Union. By the mid-1960s the United States had established 375 foreign military bases and 3,000 lesser facilities in forty-three countries around the world, "virtually surrounding both the Soviet Union and Communist China in support of the policy of containment."[154]

In the event of an "emergency," all in the network would spring into action. Under the SAC emergency war plan, approved by the Joint Chiefs of Staff on October 22, 1951, the first strike would be made by heavy bombers flying from Maine, which would drop twenty bombs on the Moscow-Gorky area, then return to the United Kingdom.

> Simultaneously, medium bombers from Labrador would attack the Leningrad area with 12 weapons and re-assemble at British bases. Meanwhile, medium bombers based in the British Isles would approach the USSR along the edge of the Mediterranean Sea and deliver 52 bombs in the industrial regions of the Volga and Donets Basin: they would return through Libyan and Egyptian airfields. More medium bombers flying from the Azores would drop 15 weapons in the Caucasus area and then stage through Dhahran, Saudi Arabia. Concurrently, medium bombers from Guam would bring 15 bombs against Vladivostok and Irkutsk.[155]

Without overseas bases, SAC would have had to increase its strength "five or six times" in order to perform its missions.[156]

Since Europe was always considered the central area in which conflict was most likely, extensive bases were built there.[157] Those closest to the "Iron Curtain" were equipped with interceptors, fighters, and reconnaissance aircraft. NATO's nuclear strike aircraft were further back, in France and England. Tactical airlift forces were also in France, as well as Germany, while SAC's forward bomber bases were in central England.[158]

The drawback of forward basing, however, is that installations intended to facilitate reaching a target soon become targets themselves. Large concentrations of high-value military targets might even invite preemptive attack. These worrying implications of U.S.-provided security did not go unnoticed, either in the United States or in Europe. A study by Rand, the air force's think tank, commissioned by the air force in 1951 to help in the selection of overseas air bases pointed to this very problem.[159]

---

154. *Security Agreements and Commitments Abroad,* Report to Subcommittee on Security Agreements and Commitments Abroad of the Senate Foreign Relations Committee, 91 Cong. 2 sess. (GPO, December 21, 1970), p. 3.

155. Walter S. Poole, *The History of the Joint Chiefs of Staff,* vol. 4, *1950–1952* (Wilmington, Del.: Michael Glazer, 1980), pp. 169–70.

156. Poole, *1950–1952,* p. 170.

157. The air force experience is recounted in Lawrence R. Benson, *USAF Aircraft Basing in Europe, North Africa, and the Middle East, 1945–1980* (Ramstein Air Base, Germany: Office of History, Headquarters, United States Air Forces in Europe, April 23, 1981), released under the Freedom of Information Act.

158. Benson, *USAF Aircraft Basing in Europe,* p. 29.

159. The original report is, A. J. Wohlstetter, F. S. Hoff-

For year 1952, Congress had authorized $25.3 billion (some $3.5 billion in then-year dollars) for air base construction, about half of which was planned for overseas bases.[160] Selection was to be based not only on cost but also on the total number and kinds of bombers, combat radius and range, entry points and flight paths to target, air- and ground-refueling possibilities, potential losses, weather conditions—to name a few of the variables—all projected out five to ten years in the future. One conclusion of the Rand study was that the peacetime cost of operating bases overseas would by necessity be more than 50 percent higher than buying and maintaining a wing of bombers in the United States.[161] Extra costs would have to be incurred to better defend the foreign bases, either through passive means or active ones, such as surface-to-air missiles or interceptor aircraft, hardening, and/or dispersal. "When we are close," remarked one analyst, "not only is our power to attack the enemy very great, but so also is his power to attack us."[162]

The air force, fearing that the study's proposed changes would cost "millions," was at first unenthusiastic about its findings. After belatedly recognizing that perhaps the survival of the U.S. strategic force might be at stake, however, officials shifted their attention to reducing vulnerability.[163]

One possibility was a dispersal plan, an extensive network of dispersed operating bases (DOBs), dispersed landing areas (DLAs), and dispersed parking areas (DPAs), which would improve survivability. To hold down expenses, United States Air Forces Europe (USAFE) planned to use civilian airfields and even the German autobahn as landing fields. The study helped set in motion a host of costly "fixes" to protect SAC bombers and bases. But the goal proved elusive as efforts to protect against the powerful effects of nuclear weapons never succeeded.

SAC itself did not argue for extensive protective measures; confident that enough warning would always be available to allow all bombers to take off before any strike, and, more important, prepared to strike first if necessary, it had never considered itself vulnerable to a surprise attack. Rather, it pushed for more offensive bombers. Simple arithmetic dictated that if there were more bombers to begin with, more would survive an attack. This, it concluded, would be a wiser use of limited funds.[164]

man, R. J. Lutz, and H. S. Rowen, *Selection and Use of Strategic Air Bases,* Rand Corporation Report R-266 (April 1954). Commentary on the study can be found in E. S. Quade, "The Selection and Use of Strategic Air Bases: A Case History," in E. S. Quade, ed., *Analysis for Military Decisions* (Santa Monica, Calif.: Rand Corporation, 1964), pp. 24–63; and Fred Kaplan, *The Wizards of Armageddon* (New York: Simon & Schuster, 1983), pp. 88–110.

160. Quade, "A Case History," p. 26.

161. Quade, "A Case History," p. 41.

162. Quade, "A Case History," pp. 26, 41, 43.

163. Kaplan, *Wizards of Armageddon,* p. 103. By 1954, as USAFE's main operating bases grew in number, it was already acknowledged that "as few as 15 well-placed atomic weaons would constitute a fatal blow." Benson, *USAF Aircraft Basing in Europe,* p. 100.

164. Even four years later (September 1957), General LeMay told Robert C. Sprague, a member of President Eisen-

Eventually, as B-52 long-range bombers and ICBMs were deployed, the need for overseas basing diminished, although it did not end.[165] But the fear of vulnerability continued unabated, and it has been a constant in the calculations of targeters on both sides.[166] For SAC, it meant having to put B-52 bombers on airborne alert and, later, ground alert.[167] The army, eager to ease vulnerability concerns and carve out a strategic role for itself, proposed Project Iceworm in 1960, which would have deployed large numbers of a two-stage version of the Minuteman missile under the Greenland icecap. This idea was modified in 1962 to a suggested deployment of medium-range ballistic missiles accountable to NATO, but in the same fashion. While acknowledging that "the key to the enterprise" hinged on the Danish government's concurrence (Denmark controls Greenland and at the time maintained, and continues to maintain, a firm policy against the deployment of nuclear weapons on its territory in peacetime), the army noted numerous advantages to such a basing concept, including its relative invulnerability to all but a massive barrage attack with thermonuclear weapons, the ability of the base commander to launch limited attacks "without concern that an attack [by the Soviet Union on unlaunched missiles] . . . would expose his own homeland to blast and fallout," and the fact that prevailing winds would carry the fallout from any massive Soviet attack on the base "primarily over the USSR."[168]

---

hower's Gaither Committee (see chapter 4) that he was not worried about Soviet bombers catching his forces on the ground. "If I see that the Russians are amassing their planes for an attack, I'm going to knock the shit out of them before they take off the ground," said LeMay. A stunned Sprague responded, "But General LeMay, that's not national policy," LeMay replied, "I don't care. It's my policy. That's what I'm going to do." See Kaplan, *Wizards of Armageddon*, pp. 133–34.

165. In 1950 there were nineteen SAC bases in the continental United States and one overseas base in Puerto Rico. By 1957 there were thirty SAC bases overseas. The peak number of bases in the continental United States was forty-six in 1960 and 1961. Strategic Air Command, *The Development of the Strategic Air Command, 1946–1986* (Offutt Air Force Base, Nebr.: Office of the Historian, September 1, 1986).

166. Morton H. Halperin, *National Security Policy-Making: Analyses, Cases, and Proposals* (Lexington, Mass.: Lexington Books, 1975), p. 65 (n. 21).

167. Airborne alert was expensive to maintain. In February 1960, General Thomas White, air force chief of staff, testified that it would cost about $754 million ($4.6 billion in 1996 dollars) to achieve an airborne alert force in 1961 and about $1 billion ($6.1 billion) each year thereafter to maintain it. Lyndon Johnson, then Democratic senator of Texas, was "convinced" that "the number one order" of Congress was to provide sufficient funds to give the Strategic Air Command the money it needed "to get the planes in the air for an air alert as early as possible." General Lyman Lemnitzer, chief of staff of the army, Admiral Arleigh Burke, chief of naval operations, and General Nathan Twining, chairman of the Joint Chiefs of Staff and an air force officer, all favored developing the capability for an airborne alert posture but felt that actually implementing one was unnecessary. Twining testified that his preference would be to fund higher-priority programs, specifically the Polaris and Minuteman missiles. "I don't believe we need to put all our planes into the air now, so I say put this in an offensive weapons system. This way, when you end up the period you have something for your $3 or $4 or $5 billion. When you end up with the air alert, you have nothing but some worn out airplanes." *Missiles, Space, and Other Major Defense Matters*, Hearings, pp. 113, 152, 268, 297, 386–87, 464–65.

168. U.S. Department of Defense, "Deployment of NATO MRBM's in the Greenland Icecap (The U.S. Army's Iceworm Concept)," February 1, 1962, reprinted in Danish Institute of International Affairs, *Grønland under den Kolde Krig [Greenland During the Cold War]* (Copenhagen, 1997), vol. 2, pp. 314–54. Another advantage of Iceworm was its presumed ability to dissuade NATO members, particularly West Germany, from acquiring their own nuclear arsenals. The Army's concept envisioned deploying 600 Iceman missiles some 4 miles (6.4 kilometers) apart inside a series of tunnels 28 feet

As Soviet ICBMs grew in number and accuracy, some conservative policy analysts raised concerns about a potential "window of vulnerability" that was said to put U.S. ICBMs at risk.[169] This became a major political issue in the late 1970s, championed principally by the Committee on the Present Danger (many of whose members found positions in the Reagan administration, including Reagan himself). It eventually led officials to consider dozens of unusual and costly deployment schemes for the MX ICBM.[170]

ICBM basing costs in general are very difficult to ascertain, not least because much of the construction took place before the development of the FYDP database in 1961. Furthermore, it is necessary to know not only the costs of construction but also the costs of ongoing operations and support. Unfortunately, the FYDP does not allow these costs to be tracked by discrete bases; they are instead spread across a large number of program elements.[171]

The scope of base construction in the 1950s was impressive, especially for the air force. Its construction program encompassed base

---

(85 meters) below the icecap. The base would cover a 52,000-square-mile (134,680-square-kilometer) area—"approximately the size of Alabama"—would require 11,000 personnel to operate, maintain, and defend it (with nuclear-tipped Nike Hercules missiles), and would cost an estimated $14.5 billion to construct and $2.5 billion each year thereafter to operate. Electrical power would be provided by nuclear reactors. Despite the enormous size of the project and the complexity of construction in an Arctic environment, the Army optimistically predicted full operations could begin within three years provided that the missiles and the reactors to power the base could be built within that time. As for probable Soviet reactions, the army asserted that "in Soviet eyes, [Iceworm] would represent less of a threat and a danger than an MRBM force of comparable or greater strength deployed on the Continent, where reaction times would be shorter, where the chance of war by miscalculation would be greater, where the trend toward national and German capabilities would be inevitable, and where the commander could not, as with Iceworm, verify an initial strike before deciding to respond." (Significantly, this last point appears to tacitly acknowledge a policy of launch on warning regarding nuclear combat in Europe). While concluding that deployment of Iceworm "would doubtless in the short run accelerate the arms race," the army argued that the system could be used to bring the Soviet Union to the bargaining table and that, eventually, "Iceworm might at some stage serve as leverge to obtain Soviet concessions in the disarmament field." In many ways, Iceworm prophetically anticipated both the "window of vulnerability" and the furious debates over the MX "racetrack" system and "bargaining chips" nearly two decades later.

169. That weapons based aboard bombers and submarines were less vulnerable was routinely ignored in such calculations. So was the complex and highly coordinated series of events necessary to successfully carry out such an attack, as well as the fact that missiles launched over the North Pole would encounter largely unknown geomagnetic conditions that could induce enough error into guidance systems to render a first strike against ICBMs by either country highly problematic. This would have the effect of reducing significantly the confidence that such an attack could succeed and, hence, the likelihood that it would ever be attempted. For a concise overview of these issues, see James Fallows, *National Defense* (New York: Vintage Books, 1981), pp. 144–57; Matthew Bunn and Kosta Tsipis, "The Uncertainties of Preemptive Nuclear Attack," *Scientific American*, vol. 249 (November 1983), pp. 38–46; Andrew Cockburn and Alexander Cockburn, "The Myth of Missile Accuracy," *New York Review of Books*, November 20, 1980, pp. 40–44.

170. Among the options considered were orbital-based, shallow underwater missiles, scattered in the ocean (Hydra), anchored to the seabed (Orca), barges sailing coastal and inland waterways, launched from C-5 or 747-class aircraft or dirigibles, commercial rail cars, and off-road trucks. See Department of Defense, Office of the Deputy Undersecretary of Defense for Research and Engineering (Strategic and Space Systems), *ICBM Basing Options: A Summary of Major Studies to Define a Survivable Basing Concept for ICBMs* (December 1980); Office of Technology Assessment, *MX Missile Basing*, OTA- IS-140 (GPO, 1981); Cochran and others, *U.S. Nuclear Forces and Capabilities*, pp. 128–31.

171. At the local base and regional level there must exist some means of monitoring these costs; otherwise such bases and regional commands would not know how much money to request for operations in any given year. However, tracking down costs at this level, particularly historical expenditures, is beyond the means of this study.

facilities for 137 wings, the early warning system, and test and operational facilities for new weapons systems. The estimated cost, through year 1958, was in the neighborhood of $10 billion (approximately $74 billion in 1996 dollars). As a result, the total number of air force installations almost doubled (to 3,100), bringing the number to 204 active principal bases in the continental United States and 156 overseas. In addition, the air force program itself grew to be "more than twice as big as those of the other two services combined."[172]

Construction cost figures were sporadically provided in some early semiannual and annual reports of the secretary of defense and of the army and air force. They indicate that just from 1956 to 1957, the air force and army spent more than $16 billion on airfields and related projects around the world. As a conservative estimate, it appears that at least $50 billion was expended on building nuclear air, missile, and submarine bases and support facilities in the United States and overseas (not including the costs of ICBM bases).

Deploying Nuclear Weapons

Once a nuclear weapons system has been fully tested, it moves into production and deployment. If the weapon is a gravity bomb, it is produced by the DOE's nuclear weapons complex and delivered as a complete device (warhead plus casing) to the appropriate military service. If the weapon is a missile, the process consists of two steps, which may take place concurrently.

In step one, a defense contractor builds the delivery vehicle (for example, a cruise missile) and delivers it to the military. At the same time (step two), the DOE builds the warheads at the Pantex Plant. Once a number of warheads are finished, they are loaded aboard dedicated, unmarked, heavily armored, and fireproof tractor trailers known as safe secure transporters (SST)—each of which costs more than $1 million and can carry up to twenty-four warheads—and are driven to a military depot or staging area. There the warheads are offloaded, and custody is officially transferred to the military (see table 5-1 for a list of current DOD storage sites). SSTs travel mostly at night, in highly armed convoys, and along varied routes, never exceeding 55 miles (88 kilometers) per hour no matter what the posted speed limit.[173] Their locations are continuously monitored via satellite from the DOE's Albuquerque Operations Office, home of the Transportation Safeguards Division (created in 1975), with which the SSTs maintain constant radio contact. The steel-lined, fire-resistant trailers also incorporate various active and

172. *Study of Airpower,* Hearings, vol. 1, pp. 371–73.

173. Drivers and their escorts, who travel in Ford vans or Chevy Suburbans, carry .357 magnum pistols, shotguns, machine guns, and grenade launchers and are authorized to shoot to kill. Couriers currently earn between $28,000 and $48,000 a year.

passive measures to foil attempts at theft or tampering. The current number of SSTs and their annual cost is classified, but in 1984 there were reportedly 170 "couriers" or drivers, 70 support personnel, 45 tractors, 35 trailers, and 49 escort vehicles. A 1992 newspaper article reported a total of 51 trucks and 300 couriers.[174] In 1996 the DOE initiated a development program to replace the aging SSTs with a new safeguards transporter (SGT). Twelve units are currently in production, with the first to be delivered in December 1997.[175] Since 1975, SSTs have traveled some 80 million miles (129 million kilometers), yet have been involved in just four accidents, all relatively minor and none involving either fatalities or the release of radioactive materials.[176]

Nuclear weapons components (and, until at least the early 1980s, actual weapons) are also transported via aircraft. From 1948 until February 1970, this mission was performed for the AEC by Carco Air Service, Inc., of Las Vegas, Nevada. Since then, Ross Aviation, Inc., of Albuquerque, New Mexico, has handled all of the AEC's and DOE's air transport, including that of personnel. A typical air mission today might involve the transport of depleted tritium reservoirs from a military depot or base to the Savannah River Site for replenishment. Historical costs for the DOE's weapons transportation mission, while known, are apparently not readily available.[177] Those for 1990–94 are available, however, and they indicate that the DOE expended nearly $487 million over that period, which was when many weapons were being retired and returned to military depots for storage and to Pantex and Oak Ridge for dismantlement. (In 1996, for example, the DOE

174. William Hart, "Nuclear Arms Haulers Ready for Any Attack," *Dallas Morning News*, February 5, 1984, p. 1AA; Samuel H. Day, Jr., "H-bombs on Our Highways," *The Progressive*, November 1984, pp. 18–23; John Fleck, "Trucking Bombs Cross-Country," *Albuquerque Journal*, August 2, 1992, p. A6; letter from Richard W. Arkin, Deputy Director, Transportation and Safeguards Division, Deprtment of Energy, to Stephen I. Schwartz, August 19, 1995. The overall budget for the Transportation Safeguards Division in 1985 was $41.3 million. By 1994 it had increased to $97.1 million before dropping to $66.4 million in 1997.

175. Department of Energy, *FY 1998 Congressional Budget Request: Atomic Energy Defense Activities*, vol. 1 (GPO, 1997), p. 188. From 1957 until the early 1990s, the DOE also shipped some warheads and bombs via custom-built, unmarked railcars, commonly referred to as the "White Train" because of its distinctive appearance (necessary to help control temperatures inside the railcars). Sustained protests by antinuclear and peace groups in Washington State and elsewhere during the 1980s led the DOE to discontinue the trains.

176. The latest accident occurred on November 16, 1996, when an SST transferring two warheads from Ellsworth AFB in South Dakota to Pantex for apparently routine maintenance skidded on an icy two-lane highway (U.S. 83) 40 miles (64.4 kilometers) south of Valentine, Nebraska, and tipped over into a ditch. The truck was righted within hours of the accident, and the warheads were transferred to another SST and returned to Ellsworth. Mark Obmascik, "Denver's a Nuclear Interchange," December 15, 1996, p. 1A; James Brooke, "Road Mishap Puts a Focus on Shipments of A-Bombs," *New York Times*, December 19, 1996, p. A23; "Recovery of Upset Warhead Truck Was Operation Worthy of Praise," Editorial, *Omaha World-Herald*, February 22, 1997, p. 42.

177. An inquiry to the Transportation Safeguards Division requesting total budgets from 1988 to 1995 and a description of the level of activity supported by such budgets (that is, numbers of airplane flights and SST deliveries) was returned with a notice that the request would incur ninety-six hours of staff research at a cost of $2,160. This was actually a second, pared-down request, submitted after being told that retrieving older records would be even more difficult. See Memorandum, Richard W. Arkin, Deputy Director, Transportation Safeguards Division, Department of Energy, to Karen Rosenthal, Department of Energy, Office of Consumer and Public Liaison, June 22, 1995.

fleet transported 580 shipments of weapons and special nuclear materials more than 4.2 million miles [6.8 million kilometers]; this increased to 650 shipments and 5.1 million miles [8.2 million kilometers] in 1997.)[178] It therefore seems reasonable to assume that over the lifetime of the nuclear weapons program, the DOE and its predecessors have historically spent a total of at least $3 billion transporting nuclear weapons to and from military bases.

Once in military custody, weapons move according to the service to which they are attached. If naval weapons, they are loaded onto ships or submarines or placed in coastal depots. Before their retirement in the early 1990s, nuclear depth bombs were kept available for use on P-3 Orion antisubmarine warfare aircraft. If air force weapons, they might be either mated to a ballistic missile or taken to an air base and stored. From 1961 to 1968, fully armed B-52s operated on airborne alert. Two serious crashes over Palomares, Spain, on January 17, 1966, and Thule, Greenland, on January 21, 1968, helped bring that program to an end (part of the overall force was henceforth kept on constant runway alert).[179]

The army and Marine Corps are now nuclear-free, but until the early 1990s both had a wide variety of weapons at their disposal, including artillery shells, atomic demolition munitions, and, in the case of the army, ballistic missiles. Weapons for these systems were first transferred by the DOE to several depots—known as "military first destinations" or MFDs—within the United States, and from there a special unit of the air force flew the weapons to U.S. or overseas bases. The Prime Nuclear Airlift Force (PNAF) consists of specially trained C-130, C-141, and C-17 crews and support personnel. The PNAF moves weapons from or to the MFDs, depending on their destination.[180] Since 1978 transport needs on the West Coast were met by the 4th Airlift Squadron of the 62d Airlift Wing, stationed at McChord Air Force Base in Washington. With the creation of a new Air Mobility Command in 1992, the mission was transferred to the 60th Air Mobility Wing at Travis Air Force Base, near San Fran-

178. Letter from Richard W. Arkin, Deputy Director, Transportation and Safeguards Division, Department of Energy, to Stephen I. Schwartz, August 19, 1995; Department of Energy, *FY 1998 Congressional Budget Request*, p. 188.

179. The Palomares accident involved a fully loaded B-52, which collided with a KC-135 tanker during a refueling attempt. Both aircraft crashed near Palomares, killing seven of the eleven crewmen. The Thule accident involved a B-52, which crashed on the ice. Its four weapons were destroyed in the resulting fire and plutonium and debris were scattered over a wide area. See Center for Defense Information, "U.S. Nuclear Weapons Accidents: Danger in Our Midst," *Defense Monitor*, vol. 10, no. 5 (1981); Strategic Air Command, *Project Crested Ice: The Thule Nuclear Accident*, vol. 1: SAC Historical Study 113 (April 23, 1969), p. 39 (at the National Security Archive). See box 7-3, for further information on these accidents.

180. During the early 1970s (and perhaps before and after that time), the army used helicopters to move some of its weapons in the field. See *Military Applications of Nuclear Technology*, Hearings before the Subcommittee on Military Applications of the Joint Committee on Atomic Energy, 93 Cong. 1st sess. (GPO, 1973), pt. 2, pp. 26–27.

181. Robert S. Norris and William M. Arkin, "Nuclear Notebook (Ferrying Warheads)," *Bulletin of the Atomic Scientists*, vol. 48 (December 1992), p. 57.

cisco.[181] The costs of the PNAF are apparently aggregated with general airlift costs and are unknown. An analysis by the GAO in 1979 found that for a selected route, DOD transportation costs were nearly twice as much as those for the DOE (the actual costs were not disclosed).[182] If the historical expenditures of the DOE are any guide, it seems likely that at least several billion dollars have been spent on this mission.

Once nuclear weapons are deployed with the military, a series of extensive military security measures go into effect. Weapons not constantly mated to a delivery vehicle are stored in special containers inside special bunkers, surrounded by sensors, lights, and double fences with barbed wire. They are kept under constant surveillance by a special security force and are routinely inventoried (see box 2-3). Costs for these activities are not readily discernible from the FYDP, but three items do stand out. First, from 1962 to 1995 the DOD spent $4.4 billion on "Special Ammunition Control—Non–United States" for storing, securing, and managing nuclear warheads and bombs deployed in support of NATO, or an average of $132.3 million per year. Between 1964 and 1991 costs were well in excess of $100 million a year. In 1985 spending peaked at $254 million. With the withdrawal of most nuclear weapons from Europe over the period 1991–92, costs fell dramatically, with just $1.4 million expended in 1995.

Second, between 1984 and 1995, the air force expended $214 million procuring and installing the WS3 in Europe. The WS3 is "an underground nuclear weapon storage container to be installed in theater strike aircraft shelters to allow co-storage of nuclear weapons and strike aircraft. The system will increase weapons access denial time, increase survivability through dispersal of nuclear weapons, improve operational readiness, decrease weapons vulnerability and reduce ground convoy requirements."[183]

182. Letter from J. Dexter Peach, Director, Energy and Minerals Division, U.S. General Accounting Office, to the Honorable Harold Brown and the Honorable James R. Schlesinger, B-164105, August 1, 1979. This letter also notes that the Defense Department, "frequently picks up and ships nuclear weapons from the [Pantex] plant."

183. Department of Defense, *FYDP Program Structure*, p. 3-47. By relocating nuclear weapons away from highly visible storage bunkers to aircraft shelters, the WS3 also serves to reduce the overall visibility of such weapons at overseas bases. This has created confusion among some nongovernmental observers and in the news media about the current status and number of tactical weapons in Great Britain and other NATO countries. For example, in October 1996 the Campaign for Nuclear Disarmament jumped to the conclusion that all U.S. nuclear weapons had been removed from RAF Lakenheath after observing that storage igloos at the base were empty and unguarded. Only after this claim was widely reported did more careful analysts point out that the weapons, while reduced in number from years past, were still at the base, having been relocated to WS3 vaults. Adding to the confusion, British, NATO, and U.S. officials refused to formally confirm or deny any information about the weapons. See Christopher Bellamy, "Winds of Change as U.S. Removes Last Nuclear Bombs from Britain," *Independent* (London), October 28, 1996, p. 1; "U.S. Nuclear Era in Britain Ends with Removal of Last Bombs," *Baltimore Sun*, October 29, 1996, p. 7; Peter Almond, "NATO Nukes to Stay Put as Alliance Grows," *Washington Times*, October 31, 1996, p. A17; British American Security Information Council and Berlin Information-Center for Transatlantic Security, "U.S. Nuclear NATO Arsenals 1996," (draft), *Inside the Pentagon*, December 12, 1996, pp. 13–16.

Box 2-3

Keeping Track of the Bomb

Once built, every nuclear weapon is assigned a unique serial number.[1] This number is permanently emplaced by engraving or etching it onto the weapon. These numbers are used by the DOE and the DSWA (formerly the Defense Nuclear Agency) to track changes in custody, current weapon configurations, and changes in location. Since 1952, the DSWA and its predecessors have been charged by the secretary of defense and the chairman of the Joint Chiefs of Staff with inspecting and certifying all nuclear-capable units through a process known as a defense nuclear surety inspection (for the air force) or a navy technical proficiency inspection.[2] According to the DSWA, the inspection team currently consists of eleven personnel. No unit is permitted to exceed sixty months between inspections. Only a portion of the stockpile is examined each year (in the mid-1970s the sample size was 20–25 percent; today it is about 25 percent). In the 1970s the military units themselves were responsible for selecting the weapons to be inspected (DOD told GAO in 1977 that operational missions, training, and routine maintenance all took priority over inspections and that giving DNA the authority to select weapons to be inventoried was undesirable from the standpoint of military readiness). Today, DSWA inspection teams are responsible for selecting weapons for physical inspection. The military services also conduct their own inspections of certified nuclear units at least every eighteen months, with inspection teams ranging in size from 6 to 150 personnel, depending on the characteristics of the unit involved.

In addition to the weapons inventory, DSWA officials review management records, technical operations, security, and safety. In the mid-1970s (and presumably before), each nuclear-capable unit performed semiannual inspections to reconcile its lists with those maintained by the DSWA and reported its findings to the DSWA. However, many weapons on alert or emplaced in inaccessible containers were not physically inspected in this manner. Both the DOE and DSWA maintain secure computerized databases for this tracking information. A 1977 investigation by the General Accounting Office found the system immune to tampering and an accurate record of the current stockpile.

1. Drawn from U.S. General Accounting Office, *Accountability and Control of Warheads in the Custody of the Department of Defense and the Energy Research and Development Administration*, PSAD-77-115 (June 2, 1977); information provided via facsimile by Cheri E. Abdelnour, Public Affairs Office, Defense Special Weapons Agency, to Stephen I. Schwartz, February 1, 1998; and William M. Arkin, Robert S. Norris, and Joshua Handler, *Taking Stock: Worldwide Nuclear Deployments, 1998* (Washington, D.C.: Natural Resources Defense Council, March 1998), pp. 21–22.

2. A nuclear-capable unit is defined as one certified by one of the three services or, in the case of European units, the European command, as having the capability for assembly, maintenance, or storage of nuclear weapons, associated components, and ancillary equipment. There currently are about sixty-one nuclear-capable units in the U.S. military (thirty-four navy, twenty-six air force, and one army).

Third, from 1986 to 1995, the navy spent more than $196 million on personnel, support equipment, and facilities for "Sensitive Ordnance Security; Nuclear Security Ashore; Remote Sensors."[184] In addition, an October 1995 audit by the DOE inspector general found that

184. Department of Defense, *FYDP Program Structure*, p. 3-44.

between 1992 and 1994 the DOE spent $29 million to build or modify eighty-seven accident-resistant nuclear weapons transport containers for the air force, even though it knew the air force had no interest in using them. After the air force stated again that it had no need for the containers—and furthermore noted that they would not hold the weapons they were designed for (B57 and B61 bombs and W62 and W78 warheads) because of faulty specifications—the DOE spent an additional $35,000 after August 1992 to store the containers and related equipment at an army depot and continued to pay about $11,000 a year for this service.[185]

Since the 1960s the DOD has operated a personnel reliability program (PRP) to screen and monitor individuals with access to nuclear weapons in a maintenance or firing capacity; the DOE has a separate but related effort for its employees—the personnel assurance program.[186] If an individual is found to have one or more of several problems (such as alcohol or drug abuse, aberrant behavior, poor work performance), he or she is decertified. Between 1975 and 1984, 51,000 personnel, on average 4.5 percent a year, were decertified and removed from nuclear duties. In 1975 more than 119,000 personnel were part of the PRP. By 1990, as a result of changes in the size and composition of the nuclear stockpile, that figure had dropped to 66,510, and the annual decertification rate fell to 2.9 percent.

The expenses associated with the PRP are not fully known. However, testimony before the Senate Armed Services Committee in 1980 indicated that training personnel to perform nuclear weapons electronics and maintenance duties cost (over the first ten years) approximately $21,393 per person for the air force, $95,630 for the army, and $100,933 for the navy. Training for the subsequent ten-year period cost $41,324 for the navy and $49,186 for the army.[187] Much of this training occurs at the Defense Nuclear Weapons School, a field command of the Defense Special Weapons Agency based at Kirtland Air Force Base, New Mexico. Typical courses cover nuclear targeting, nuclear accident response and cleanup, nuclear weapons disposal, and the medical effects of ionizing radiation.[188]

185. U.S. Department of Energy, Office of the Inspector General, *Report on the Audit of the Department of Energy's Transportation Accident Resistant Container Program*, DOE/IG-0380 (October 1995). The containers, which weigh more than a ton apiece, are made from hardened steel and redwood. They were designed at Sandia National Laboratories and built at the DOE's Kansas City Plant.

186. For more information on the PRP, see Herbert L. Abrams, "Human Reliability and Safety in the Handling of Nuclear Weapons," *Science & Global Security*, vol. 2 (1991), pp. 1–26; Herbert L. Abrams, "Sources of Human Instability in the Handling of Nuclear Weapons," in *The Medical Implications of Nuclear War* (Washington, D.C.: National Academy Press, 1986), pp. 490–528; Lloyd J. Dumas, "Human Fallibility and Weapons," *Bulletin of the Atomic Scientists*, vol. 36 (November 1980), pp. 15–20.

187. Cochran and others, *U.S. Nuclear Forces and Capabilities*, p. 84.

188. A course catalog and other information is available on the World Wide Web at http://www.dswa.mil/dswainfo/dnws/index.htm.

Factors Influencing the Size and Composition of the Nuclear Arsenal

Many factors affected the size and composition of the nuclear stockpile, such as the phasing in of new production facilities, the provision of adequate delivery vehicles, the ultimate usages, and, of course, estimates of the other side's atomic weapon potential. Robert A. Lovett, secretary of defense from 1951 to 1953, did not believe that "the Joint Chiefs of Staff could or would state categorically . . . that a stockpile of 'X' number of atomic weapons would be sufficient conclusively to ensure the security of the U.S. . . . We must err . . . on the side of too much rather than too little."[189] Caspar Weinberger, who served as secretary of defense from 1981 to 1987 asserted in 1993: "You should always use a worst-case analysis in this business. You can't afford to be wrong. In the end, we won the cold war, and if we won by too much, if it was overkill, so be it."[190]

Whatever the size of the stockpile—large, medium, or small—much of the available evidence suggests that the production and deployment goals proposed and realized for nuclear weapons were essentially arbitrary. Although official reports and government testimony created the impression that military and political officials knew exactly what number of bombers or missiles would deter the Soviet Union (or conversely, what number would not), the reality is that the eventual size of a weapon program was arrived at through a number of interconnected factors and influences, including budget trade-offs, the perceived Soviet threat, interservice and intraservice rivalry, the promotion of jobs in states and districts by elected officials, corporate lobbying, cycles of technological obsolescence and novelty, and political charges and countercharges, to name but a few.

Herbert York, the first director of Lawrence Livermore National Laboratory and subsequently director of defense research and engineering at the DOD, made this abundantly clear some time ago. In retrospect, he said, the laboratory needed only three crash programs to develop long-range strategic missiles, in place of the six that were initiated: the Titan, the Minuteman, and the Polaris would have been "sufficient." He stated that "excessive technical conservatism" was probably responsible for the "overreaction," but that a valuable lesson can nevertheless be gleaned from the experience, "to be remembered the next time this sort of problem arises":

> From the point of view of military security such excesses were harmful because they caused us to stretch our resources thinner than was really nec-

189. Poole, *History of the Joint Chiefs of Staff*, p. 147.

190. Tim Weiner, "Military Accused of Lies over Arms," *New York Times*, June 28, 1993, p. A10.

> essary. . . . From the point of view of arms control and the arms race, these excesses in dollars and people also had serious consequences. The extra organizations and the extra people resulted in a larger constituency favoring weapons development . . . [which] in turn strengthened those forces in Congress 'which hear the farthest drum before the cry of a hungry child,' and consequently the whole arms race spiraled faster than before. Many of the leaders within this overexpanded missile industry correctly foresaw that they would be in trouble when all of these concurrent crash development programs finally resulted in some deployed hardware. They rightly anticipated that any follow-on developments would have a very hard time competing with the even larger funds needed for such deployments, and they provided some of the most strident voices among those proclaiming the 'missile gap' of the 1958–60 period.[191]

York also disclosed the arbitrary nature by which warhead yields (such as the 1-megaton version for the Atlas ICBM) were often determined: it was simply

> because one million is a particularly round number in our culture. . . . Human beings have two hands with five fingers each and therefore count by tens. . . . [I]f evolution had given us six fingers on each hand, our first ICBM warhead would have had to be three times as big, [and] the rockets to deliver them would have threatened the lives of up to three times as many human beings. . . . *It really was that arbitrary, and, what's more, that same arbitrariness has stayed with us.*[192] (Emphasis added)

Early in the Kennedy administration, a number of White House officials expressed opposition to the planned expansion of U.S. ICBM and SLBM forces. Several advisers, including Arthur Schlesinger and Theodore Sorensen, argued that the missile program was far in excess of what national security required. Jerome Wiesner, Kennedy's science adviser, noted that "some persons within the government" believed that 200–400 missiles, including Polaris, Titan II, and "a few" Minuteman missiles, would be sufficient. In 1960 Wiesner himself said that a force "in the range from 100 to 400 large nuclear weapons and accompanying delivery vehicles, either aircraft or missiles," would be adequate, expressing confidence in a force of 200 missiles. One year later, Weisner stated with more certainty that deterrence could be achieved with "two hundred relatively secure missiles . . . even in the absence of an agreement limiting force size."[193]

Officials with the Bureau of the Budget also supported minimal force levels, principally for economic reasons. They viewed a large

191. York, *Race to Oblivion*, pp. 102–04.
192. York, *Race to Oblivion*, pp. 89–90.
193. This and the following two paragraphs rely heavily on Desmond Ball, *Politics and Force Levels: The Strategic Missile Program of the Kennedy Administration* (University of California Press, 1980), pp. 81–87.

strategic buildup as an unnecessary diversion of limited resources. In December 1961 the formal White House position was presented to the president and the secretary of defense. Using DOD data, the officials assembled a graph that plotted McNamara's projected force numbers (950–1,050 Minuteman missiles) against "strategic effectiveness," demonstrating that the apex of the curve occurred at about 450 missiles. The additional 500–600 missiles contributed almost nothing to "effectiveness," regardless of the strategy pursued.

Following much discussion, Wiesner and an NSC staffer prepared a memorandum for the president, recommending a force of 600 Minuteman missiles, going beyond the "necessary" 450 missiles to provide both military and political insurance. Although McNamara apparently agreed with this assessment, he held to his planning figures, arguing that 950 was "the smallest number he could imagine asking Congress for and, in his words, 'not get murdered'" (see figure 2-3).[194]

To take a more recent example, during 1979 and 1980, a number of nuclear strategists argued that 200 MX missiles—to be shuttled around and hidden amid 4,600 shelters in a 40,000-square-mile (103,600-square-kilometer) area of the Great Basin in eastern Nevada and western Utah—were absolutely essential to the national security of the United States. Anything less would leave the country highly vulnerable to attack.[195] A GAO analysis of the air force's estimated life cycle costs of this option in 1981 found them to be nearly $76 billion, with the potential for significant increases owing to additional requirements. This included the cost to operate the system until 2000 but excluded the cost of the 2,000 warheads (10 per missile) required under the plan.[196] The mobility of the missiles was deemed necessary to reduce the perceived vulnerability of land-based ICBMs. But after a tortuous, very expensive, and ultimately unsuccessful effort to solve the problem of the "window of vulnerability," the strategic conundrum quietly disappeared, and 50 MX missiles were placed in fixed Minuteman silos, the very same silos that were called "vulnerable" a few short years

194. McNamara did eventually concede that the size of the missile force was excessive. In September 1967, after the programs he promoted had reached fruition, he stated that the United States' "current numerical superiority over the Soviet Union in reliable, accurate and effective warheads is both greater than we had originally planned and in fact more than we require." Robert S. McNamara, "The Dynamics of Nuclear Strategy," *Department of State Bulletin* 57 (October 9, 1967), p. 445.

195. This argument explicitly ignored the synergistic effects of the strategic triad, that is, the fact that no Soviet attack could possibly destroy *all* U.S. forces (although this synergism—and not the triad itself—was not in fact a deliberate creation but rather an outgrowth of the buildup initiated by the Eisenhower and Kennedy administrations, it has had important ramifications for the security of the strategic arsenal). An attack by bombers would provide enough time to launch bombers and ICBMs. An attack by ICBMs would allow some bombers to get off the ground and would not destroy all SLBMs, and an attack by SLBMs would also leave U.S. SLBM forces relatively unscathed. In short, whatever combination of forces the Soviets used, *some* U.S. forces would always survive, a sure incentive for any rational leader not to launch an attack in the first place. Irrational leaders, by definition, do not rely upon reason in making decisions and are therefore immune to the concept of deterrence.

196. U.S. General Accounting Office, *The MX Weapon System: Issues and Challenges*, MASAD 81-1 (February 17, 1981), pp. 4–7.

FIGURE 2-3. U.S. and USSR/Russian Strategic Offensive Nuclear Forces, 1945–97

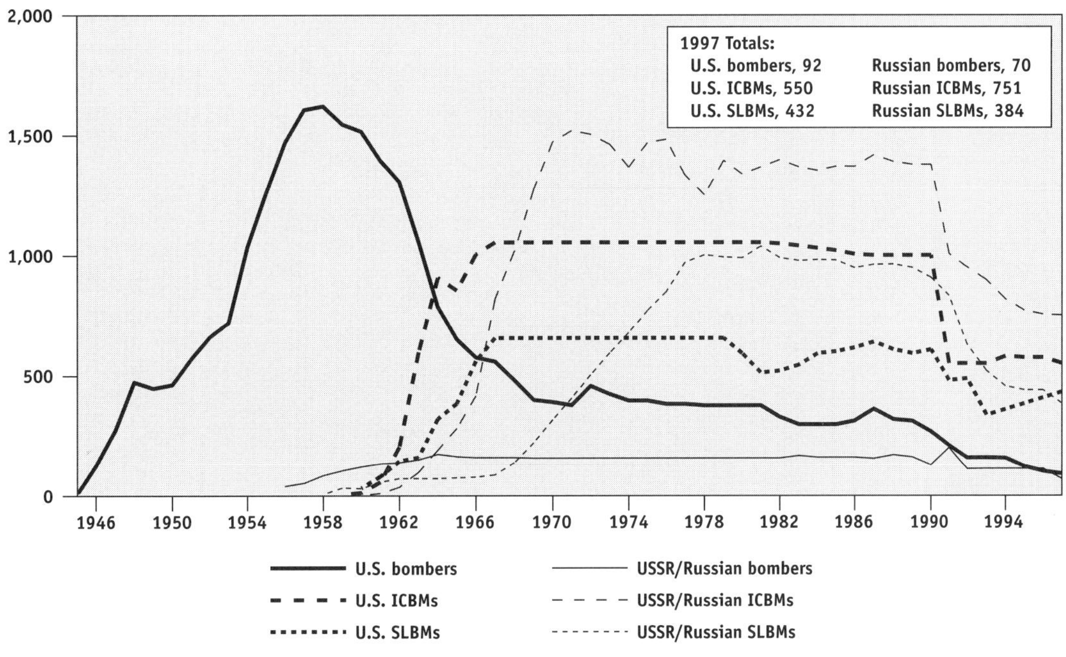

Source: Robert S. Norris and Thomas B. Cochran, "U.S.-U.S.S.R./Russian Strategic Offensive Forces, 1945–96," Nuclear Weapons Databook Working Paper 97-1 (Washington, D.S.: Natural Resources Defense Council, January 1997); Robert S. Norris and William M. Arkin, "NRDC Nuclear Notebook (U.S. Strategic Nuclear Forces, End of 1997)," *Bulletin of the Atomic Scientists,* vol. 54 (January/February 1998), pp. 70–72.

before. The effort and money that went into trying to come up with a survivable basing scheme are remarkable—between 1979 and 1984 the program consumed $14 billion—but not unique in the peregrinations that characterized the nuclear arms race. The 50 deployed MX missiles will be retired by 2003 if START II is fully implemented.[197]

Another arbitrary decision concerns the navy's plan to relocate its fleet of TACAMO ("take charge and move out") ballistic missile submarine communications aircraft. As discussed in chapter 3, TACAMO aircraft are designed to fly over the open ocean trailing a 5-mile-long (8-kilometer), very low frequency (VLF) antenna, which is used to relay orders to submerged submarines. The TACAMO planes act as a backup system in the event some or all of the nine land-based VLF transmitters are destroyed. In 1985 eighteen EC-130 aircraft in two

197. The 10 W87 warheads atop each missile are not subject to destruction under START II. One option under consideration is to download the 500 MX warheads onto the 500 remaining Minuteman III missiles, with one warhead per missile. The DOE is currently conducting studies to ensure the compatibility of the two systems.

squadrons based at Patuxent River Naval Air Station in Maryland and Barbers Point Naval Air Station, Hawaii, were assigned to communicate with SSBNs in the Atlantic and Pacific oceans, respectively. In January 1986 Secretary of the Navy John Lehman directed Chief of Naval Operations Admiral James D. Watkins to work with the air force and take immediate action to provide hanger and support facilities in the continental United States for the E-6A, an updated version of the existing TACAMOs based on the Boeing 707-320 airframe and the first aircraft to be designed specifically for the TACAMO mission.

From an initial list of twenty bases drawn up by the air force, the navy ultimately chose Tinker Air Force Base in Oklahoma, a location more than 1,000 miles (1,609 kilometers) in either direction from the Atlantic and Pacific, and further still from the operating areas of U.S. SSBNs. Although this move (completed in 1992) would reduce the vulnerability of the planes to surprise attack, it raised obvious questions about the ability of the TACAMO fleet to perform its mission. The navy claimed cost savings would result by consolidating the bases and moving them to Oklahoma (where similar aircraft based on the 707 airframe—the airborne warning and control system [AWACS]—were located), although a General Accounting Office audit was unable to verify this claim because the navy lacked the data to support its own estimates.[198] The GAO also warned that relocating the fleet to any site in the middle of the country might force the navy to purchase a sixteenth aircraft, at a cost of $60 million (in then-year dollars), to ensure the same degree of coverage as was available from two coastal bases (sixteen aircraft were ultimately purchased). Absent any compelling strategic rationale, it appeared that the navy's desire to move TACAMO to Oklahoma had less to do with cost savings than with politics.[199]

---

198. U.S. General Accounting Office, *Aircraft Basing: Decision to Base Navy TACAMO Aircraft at Tinker Air Force Base, Oklahoma,* NSIAD-87-106FS (April 1987).

199. Arkansas and Maryland lawmakers who argued, respectively, that Little Rock Air Force Base was better suited for the TACAMO mission and that the aircraft should remain at Patuxent, complained that the selection of Tinker (which was not on the air force's original list) was motivated by the Reagan administration's desire to reward Representative Mickey Edwards (Republican of Oklahoma). Edwards, the ranking minority member of the military construction subcommittee of the House Appropriations Committee, played an important role in securing passage of a military assistance package for the U.S.-backed Contras fighting the Nicaraguan government and announced the navy's intention to select Tinker shortly after that vote. Edwards denied any linkage between the two events, noting that he was a longtime supporter of the Contras and would have voted to assist them in any event. In July 1986, following Edwards' announcement of the selection of Tinker, Donald C. Latham, DOD assistant secretary of defense for command, control, communications and intelligence sent a memorandum to other officials stating, "Please note that Tinker is not in Mickey Edwards' district and he is somewhat puzzled by all this. Tinker is in [Democrat] Dave McCurdy's district. I still suggest we strongly reconsider Little Rock." See Randy Ellis, Navy Picks Tinker as Squadron Base," *Daily Oklahoman,* July 3, 1986, p. 1; Patti Case, "Lehman Wants E-6A Aircraft at Tinker, Say Navy Officials," *Journal Record* (Oklahoma City), July 11, 1986, n.p.; Eric Pianin and George C. Wilson, "Patuxent Aircraft to Be Phased Out; Navy Decision Will Cost Southern Md. Jobs, Economic Benefits," *Washington Post,* March 31, 1987, p. B1; Eric Pianin, "Plan to Shift Patuxent Planes 'Stopped Dead in Its Tracks'; Md. Lawmakers Push to Protect Jobs at Navy Base," *Washington Post,* April 3, 1987, p. C3; Maria Henson, "Political Battle Rages on Basing of Navy Squadron," *Arkansas Gazette,* June 12, 1988, p. 1C; Allan Cromley, "Funds Ok'd For E-6As at Tinker," *Daily Oklahoman,* June 16, 1988, p. 1.

Finally, it is important to remember that although the "triad" of nuclear bombers, land-based missiles, and sea-based missiles was and is often touted as a pragmatic and time-tested means both of ensuring that an adversary cannot, in a single blow, destroy the entire U.S. nuclear arsenal and insuring against the unforeseen catastrophic failure of any one leg, the triad itself developed not by design but in large measure because the air force and navy each wanted "a piece of the action," in the budgetary and mission-oriented sense. In fact, the triad was an "intellectual artifice developed in the 1960s to provide a framework for nuclear forces allocated among the three major services."[200] Even then, Secretary of Defense James Schlesinger admitted in testimony before the Senate Foreign Relations Committee in 1974 that "I think the rationale of the Triad was a rationalization."[201]

What Might Have Been

We now know—after more than fifty years of nuclear weapons production—that the United States manufactured more than 70,000 warheads, but we should recognize that along the way there were other expectations and possibilities. At one end of the scale, the army's Lieutenant General James M. Gavin, deputy chief of staff for research and development, under General Maxwell Taylor, told the JCAE in 1956 and 1957 that the total requirement for the army alone would be 151,000 nuclear weapons: 106,000 for tactical battlefield use, 25,000 for air defense, and 20,000 for support of our allies. Gavin estimated that a typical field army might use a total of 423 atomic warheads in one day of intense combat, not including surface-to-air weapons.[202]

Some navy officers in early 1958 spoke of a Polaris fleet of 100 SSBNs. This goal later dropped to between forty and fifty submarines. Forty-five became the accepted number, and eventually forty-one were bought between 1957 and 1964. Twenty additional Ohio-class SSBNs were once proposed, although only eighteen were actually purchased between 1974 and 1991.

The air force never proposed an exact goal for its ICBM force, but there were statements in the late 1950s envisioning several hundred to many thousands. At the high end was General Thomas S. Power, commander in chief of SAC from 1957 to 1964, who spoke of a requirement of 10,000 Minuteman ICBMs and is known to have personally suggested that figure to President Kennedy.[203] Actually, many air force

200. Janne E. Nolan, *Guardians of the Arsenal: The Politics of Nuclear Strategy* (New York: Basic Books, 1989), p. 275.

201. Graham T. Allison, "U.S. Strategic Forces in the 1960's," in *The Report of the Commission on the Organization of the Government for the Conduct of Foreign Policy*, appx. K, vol. 4, pt. 2 (GPO, 1975), p. 142.

202. *History of the Custody and Deployment of Nuclear Weapons, July 1945 through September 1977*, Prepared by the Office of the Assistant to the Secretary of Defense (Atomic Energy), February 1978, p. 50 (Formerly Top Secret, released under the Freedom of Information Act).

203. Former Secretary of Defense Robert McNamara

officers were not very enthusiastic about missiles, considering them a diversion and drain on resources for what really mattered: manned bombers. For nearly every bomber program, the air force's procurement goal exceeded the number of aircraft actually built as finite budgets and other factors led to a smaller program. This pattern was repeated with the two most recent bombers: the original program for the B-1 was 244 (100 were bought), and for the B-2 it was 132 (reduced to 75 and then again to 21).[204]

As proposed in 1958, the intermediate-range ballistic missile program, composed of Thors and Jupiters, was originally to have had sixteen squadrons (240 missiles; see table 2-5). This was adjusted downward in steps. At one point, in addition to four Thor squadrons in the United Kingdom, five other Thor squadrons were tentatively earmarked for Italy, Turkey, Okinawa, and Alaska. It was also envisioned that three squadrons of Jupiter missiles would become operational in France sometime between February 1959 and March 1960. The French, however, insisted on national control, which Washington refused to consider; sites in Germany and Greece were considered instead. Eventually two Jupiter squadrons (30 missiles) were deployed in Italy and one squadron (15 missiles) in Turkey, only to be withdrawn from service wtihin one to two years.

Conclusion

It is instructive to study the production of nuclear weapons in the context of the cold war. Owing to secrecy and the indeterminate nature of deterrence, strict military requirements were not the only, or even the major, factor responsible for the types and numbers of weapons built and deployed. Diplomatic and domestic political and economic influ-

related in a 1985 interview: "I remember being with President Kennedy in May of 1962, in California. We were visiting Vandenberg Air Force Base, and the Commander of the Strategic Air Command [General Power] met us when our plane landed. As we got into his car, he turned to the President and said, 'When we get the 10,000 Minutemen, Mr. President, I. . . .' At that moment, the President said, 'What did you say?' 'Well, I started to say that when we get the 10,000 Minutemen, we're going to do. . . .' The President said, 'I thought that's what you said.' And he turned to me and said, 'Bob, we're not going to get 10,000 Minutemen, are we?' I said, 'No, Mr. President, we're limiting it to 1,000.' . . . The Commander of the Strategic Air Command believed we should have 10,000. The Air Force had cut that back and, as I recall, had recommended to me that we procure 3,000. I had cut it back to 1,000. Now I think one could argue that 1,000 was too many. *And that's about as far as I thought I could go in the circumstances*" (emphasis added). Quoted in Michael Charlton, *From Deterrence to Defense: The Inside Story of Strategic Policy* (Harvard University Press, 1987), pp. 9–10.

204. A thorough investigation of the B-1 bomber program revealed, "from a military standpoint, the Air Force calculated [in 1980] that the United States could use a force of about 350 to 400 strategic bombers—far beyond any politically acceptable cost. The number of planes actually requested—100 B-1Bs and 132 Stealths—was calculated almost entirely on economic and political factors. The Air Force decided that both [Secretary of Defense Caspar] Weinberger's and Congress's choke point for the B-1B was $20 billion and Rockwell's [B-1B program manager] Buzz Hello claimed he could produce 100 B-1Bs for that cost. The Air Force requested more Stealths than B-1Bs to satisfy the Senate—where a coalition of zealous Stealth advocates and B-1B opponents might scuttle the B-1B." Kotz, *Wild Blue Yonder*, p. 205.

TABLE 2-5. U.S. Nuclear Delivery Systems, 1945–97

System	Warheads	Active[a]	Number[b]
AIRCRAFT[c]			
Air force bombers			
B-29 Superfortress (B)	B3, B4, B5, B6	1945–54	3,960
B-36B/D/F/H/J Peacemaker (C)	B4, B6, B15, B17, B18, B21, B24, B36, B39	1948–58	385
B-45A Tornado (NA)	B5, B7, B8	1949–58	142
B-47 Stratojet (B, D, L)	B4, B5, B6, B15, B18, B21, B28, B36, B39, B41, B43	1951–66	2,041
B-50A/D Superfortress (B)	B3, B4, B5, B6	1948–55	370
B-52B/C/D/E/F/G/H Stratofortress (B)	B28, B15/39, B36 B41, B43, B53, B57, B61, B83, Hound Dog (W28), SRAM-A (W69), ALCM (W80-1), ACM (W80-1)	1955–	744
B-57B Canberra (MT)	B7, B43	1955–59	403
B-58 Hustler (C)	B39, B43, B53	1960–70	104
B-66 Destroyer (D)	B5, B6, B15, B28	1956–65	294
B-1B Lancer (RW)	B61, B83	1986–	100
B-2A Spirit (N)	B61, B83	1994–	21
Air force fighters			
F-84G Thunderjet (R)	B7	1951–60	789
F-84F Thunderstreak (R)	B7	1954–64	1,496
F-86F/H Sabre (NA)	B12	1954–57	738
F-89J Scorpion (N)	Genie (W25)	1957–68	350
F-100A/C/D/F Super Sabre (NA)	B7, B28, B43, B57, B61, Bullpup (W45)	1955–72	2,247
F-101A/C/B Voodoo (M)	B7, B28, B43	1957–80	
F-101B/F Voodoo (M)	Genie (W25)	1957–80	
F-102A Delta Dagger (C)	Falcon (W42)	1956–78	875
F-104C/G/S Starfighter (L)	B28, B43, B57, B61	1958–	2,578
F-105B/D/F Thunderchief (R)	B28, B43, B57, B61	1958–73	828
F-106A/B Delta Dart (C)	Genie (W25)	1959–84	340
F-4C/D/E Phantom II (M)	B28, B43, B57, B61, Walleye (W72)	1964–91	857
F-15E Strike Eagle (M)	B61	1989–	132
F-16A/B/C/D Falcon (GD)	B43, B57, B61	1979–	780
F-111A/D/E/F (GD)	B28, B43, B57, B61	1968–92	454
FB-111A (GD)	B28, B43, B57, B61, SRAM-A (W69)	1971–91	76
F-117A Nighthawk (L)	B61	1983–	59
Navy and Marine Corps[d]			
A-1 (AD-4B) Skyraider (D)	B7, B8	1953–65	194
A-1H (AD-6) Skyraider (D)	Hotpoint (W34), BOAR (Mk-7), B43	1953–65	713
A-1J (AD-7) Skyraider (D)	Hotpoint (W34)	1953–65	72
A-2 (AJ-1/2) Savage (NA)	B4, B5, B6, B7, B8, B11, B12, B15, B27	1949–60	140
A-3A (A3D-1) Skywarrior (D)	B5, B6, B7, B8, B12, B15, B27, B28, B39, B43	1956–70	50

TABLE 2-5. U.S. Nuclear Delivery Systems, 1945–97 (*continued*)

System	*Warheads*	*Active*[a]	*Number*[b]
A-3B (A3D-2) Skywarrior (D)	B5, B27, B28, W34, B43, B57	1957–70	164
A-4B/C/E/J/M Skyhawk (D)	B7, B8, B12, B28, B43, B57, B61	1956–90	2,960
A-5A (A3J-1) Vigilante (NA)	B27, B28, B43, B57	1961–70	59
A-6E Intruder (G)	B28, B43, B57, B61	1972–91	205
A-7E Corsair II (LTV)	B28, B43, B57, B61	1964–91	1,567
F-1 (FJ-4B) Fury (NA)	B7, B12, Hotpoint (W34), B43	1957–62	219
F-2 (F2H-2B) Banshee (M)	B7, B8	1949–59	358
F-3C (F3H-2N) Demon (M)	B7, B8, B11, B12	1956–64	140
F-9J (F9F-8B) Cougar (G)	B7, B12	1954–59	601
F/A-18 Hornet (M)	B57, B61	1983–91	1,168
P-2 (P2V-3C) Neptune (L)	Betty (B7), Lulu (W34)	1949–63	11
P-2E/H (P2V-5F/7) Neptune (L)	Betty (B7), Lulu (W34), B57	1950–66	783
P-3A/B/C Orion (L)	B57	1962–91	396
S-2A/C/D/E Tracker (G)	Betty (B7), Lulu (W34), B57	1954–76	471
S-3A/B Viking (L)	B57	1974–91	187
SH-3D/H Sea King (S)	B57, Lulu (W34)	1961–91	140
SH-34J Seabat	Betty (B7), Lulu (W34)	1957–66	122
SUBMARINES			
Polaris (*George Washington* class)	Polaris A-1 [W47], A-2 [W47], A-3 [W58]	1960–82	41
Poseidon (*Lafayette, Madison,* and *Franklin* class)	Poseidon C-3 [W68], Trident I/C-4 [W76]	1971–93	31
Trident (*Ohio* class)	Trident I/C-4 [W76], Trident II/D-5 [W88]	1982–	18
ARTILLERY AND ATOMIC DEMOLITION MUNITIONS (ADM)			
280-mm atomic cannon	W9, S19	1952–57	160
Katie (16-inch naval gun)	S23	1956–62	50
M44, M53, M59, M114 (155-mm)	W48	1963–91	1,000
M55, M115 (203-mm)	W33 Y1, Y2	1957–91	1,200
M55, M115 (203-mm)	W79	1981–91	550
T4 ADM	B4	1950s	25
Mark 7 Project A ADM	B7	1950s	25
TADM	W30 Y1	1961–66	300
ADM	W31 Y1, Y2, Y3	1960–65	300
Medium ADM	W45	1965–86	350
Special ADM	B54	1964–89	250
NAVAL WEAPONS			
ASROC RUR-5A	W44	1961–89	12,020/600 warheads
ASTOR	W34	1960–77	600
Regulus I SSM-N-8	W5, W27 Y1	1955–64	228/200 warheads
Regulus II SSM-N-9	W27 Y1	1958–65	25
SLCM BGM-109A/B	W80-0	1984–	363/350 warheads
SUBROC UUM-44	W55	1965–90	611/300 warheads
Talos RIM-8	W30	1959-79	2,404/300 warheads

TABLE 2-5. U.S. Nuclear Delivery Systems, 1945–97 (*continued*)

System	*Warheads*	*Active*[a]	*Number*[b]
Terrier RIM-2D	W45 Y1	1956–88	3,000/300 warheads
TACTICAL MISSILES			
Bullpup B AGM-12D	W45 Y1	1962–76	100 warheads
Corporal MGM-5	W7	1954–67	1,101/300 warheads
Davy Crockett M-28/29	W54 Mod 2, Y1	1961–71	2,100/2,000 warheads
Falcon AIM-26A	W54 Mod 0, Y1	1961–72	1,900 warheads
Genie AIR-2A	W25	1957–84	10,171/5,000 warheads
GLCM BGM-109G	W84	1983–91	443/400 warheads
Honest John MGR-1	W7, W31	1954–84	9,311/1,750 warheads
Jupiter PGM-19A	W49 Y2	1961–63	98/30 warheads
Lacrosse MGM-18	W40 Y1, Y2	1959–64	1,194/1,000 warheads
Lance MGM-52C	W70-0,-1,-2,-3	1972–91	2,314/1,280 warheads
Little John MGR-3A	W45 Y2, Y3	1962–65	2,404/500 warheads
Mace A/B MGM-13/CGM-13B	W28 Y1, Y2, Y3	1959–69	100 warheads
Matador MGM-1C	W5	1955–61	65 warheads
Nike Hercules MIM-14	W31 Y1, Y2, Y4	1958–88	10,077/3,000 warheads
Nike Zeus LIM-49	W50 Y3	1963–67	6 warheads
Pershing 1/1a MGM-31A/B	W50 Y1, Y2, Y3	1964–90	750/280 warheads
Pershing II	W85	1983–91	234/200 warheads
Redstone PGM-11A	W39 Y2	1958–64	120/60 warheads
Sergeant MGM-29	W52 Y1, Y2	1962–77	475/300 warheads
Thor PGM-17A	W49 Y2	1959–63	224/60 warheads
Walleye AGM-62 (Mk 6, Mod 0)	W72	1970–79	300 warheads
STRATEGIC MISSILES			
Atlas D CGM-16D	W49 Y2	1959–64	30 warheads
Atlas E CGM-16E	W38 Y1	1961–65	27 warheads
Atlas F HGM-16F	W38 Y1	1962–65	72 warheads
ALCM AGM-86B	W80-1	1981–	1,787/1,715 warheads
ACM AGM-129A	W80-1	1991–	460/400 warheads
Bomarc A/B CIM-10A/B	W40 Y1	1959–72	700/400 warheads
Hound Dog AGM-28B	W28 Y1, Y2	1960–75	722/600 warheads
Minuteman I LGM-30A	W59 Y1, W56	1962–69	925/800 warheads
Minuteman II LGM-30F	W56 Y1, Y2, Y3, Y4	1966–91	668/500 warheads
Minuteman III LGM-30G	W62, W78	1970–	840/2,650 warheads
MX/Peacekeeper LGM-118A	W87	1986–	102/550 warheads
Polaris A-1 UGM-27A	W47 Y1	1960–64	163/100 warheads
Polaris A-2 UGM-27B	W47 Y1, Y2	1962–74	346/250 warheads
Polaris A-3 UGM-27C	W58	1964–81	644/1,450 warheads
Poseidon C-3 UGM-73A	W68	1971–91	640/5,250 warheads
Snark SM-62	W39 Y1	1960–61	30/30 warheads
Spartan LIM-49	W71	1975–76	72/45 warheads
Sprint	W66	1975–76	112/70 warheads
SRAM AGM-69A	W69	1972–90	1,541/1,250 warheads

TABLE 2-5. U.S. Nuclear Delivery Systems, 1945–97 (*continued*)

System	*Warheads*	*Active*[a]	*Number*[b]
Titan I LGM-25A	W38 Y1	1962–65	155/65 warheads
Titan II LGM-25C	W53 Y1	1963–87	131/65 warheads
Trident I C-4 UGM-96A	W76	1979–	595/3,250 warheads
Trident II D-5 UGM-133A	W76, W88	1990–	462/400 warheads

Sources: U.S. Air Force, *A History of Strategic Arms Competition 1945–1972,* vol. 2: *A Handbook of Selected U.S. Weapon Systems* (June 1976); Hopkins and Goldberg, *Development of Strategic Air Command; From Snark to Peacekeeper: A Pictorial History of Strategic Air Command Missiles* (Offutt Air Force Base, Nebr.: Office of the Historian, Headquarters Strategic Air Command, May 1, 1990); *SAC Missile Chronology, 1939–88,* 3d ed. (Offutt Air Force Base, Nebr.: Office of the Historian, Headquarters Strategic Air Command, May 1, 1990); Neufeld, *Development of Ballistic Missiles in the United States Air Force, 1945–1960;* Kenneth Schaffel, *The Emerging Shield: The Air Force and the Evolution of Continental Air Defense, 1945–1960,* Office of Air Force History (GPO, 1991); Werrell, *Evolution of the Cruise Missile;* Knaack, *Encyclopedia of U.S. Air Force Aircraft and Missile Systems,* vols. 1 and 2; *FBM Facts/Chronology: Polaris-Poseidon-Trident,* Navy Department (GPO, 1990); Thomas B. Cochran, William M. Arkin, and Milton M. Hoenig, *Nuclear Weapons Databook,* vol. 1: *U.S. Nuclear Forces and Capabilities* (Cambridge, Mass: Ballinger, 1984); Cochran and others, *Nuclear Weapons Databook,* vol. 2; Philip A. Karber and Michael D. Yaffe, *U.S. Strategic Nuclear Forces, 1946–1990,* vol. 1: *Land-Based Bombers,* vol. 2: *Land-Based Missiles,* and vol. 3: *Sea-Based Missiles* (Washington, D.C., Nuclear History Program, August 13, 1992); Peacock, *Strategic Air Command.*

a. The dates given are when the plane, missile, or weapon system was operational. Exactly when certain dual-capable systems were certified to carry nuclear weapons is less clear.

b. For air force bombers, peak number in inventory; for air force fighters, number accepted by air force; for navy fighters, number accepted; for artillery and ADMs, numbers are for warheads; for naval weapons, tactical missiles, and strategic missiles, the number of missiles purhased, followed by an estimate of the number of warheads built for that system.

c. Company in parentheses: B = Boeing; C= Convair; D = Douglas; G = Grumman; GD = General Dynamics; L = Lockheed; LTV = Vought; M = McDonnell; MT = Martin; N = Northrop; NA = North American; R = Republic; RW = Rockwell; S = Sikorsky.

d. Naval planes were redesignated in October 1962. Where two designations are listed, the first is the designation after October 1962, and that in parentheses before October 1962.

ences pushed and pulled the program in a number of directions, often contradictory.

The early years of the program set the parameters for everything that followed, and during these years the chief influence was the desire to acquire as many nuclear weapons as quickly as possible. What this would cost, how these weapons would increase U.S. security, and what would happen if they were ever used were questions that were seldom raised. Although the actions of the Soviet Union during this period were of great importance in rationalizing the program, giving it a focus and propelling it forward in several great leaps, in many ways the United States was racing against itself, as became evident when the bomber and missile "gaps," among others, turned out to be illusory, the product of limited intelligence data and a propensity to characterize the Soviet Union as the literal opposite of the United States. Future scholars would do well to study these factors and assess their importance on the programs of the other nuclear powers.

Notwithstanding the enormous U.S. investment in a plethora of delivery vehicles, the arsenal was ineffective without a network of command posts and communications systems to control their use, as well as a sophisticated intelligence-gathering system to collect information on Soviet (and Chinese) forces and plans, both to target those forces and devise strategies and weapons to counter them. The costs and consequences of these programs are taken up in chapter 3.

FIGURE 3-1. The Costs of Targeting and Controlling the Bomb[a]

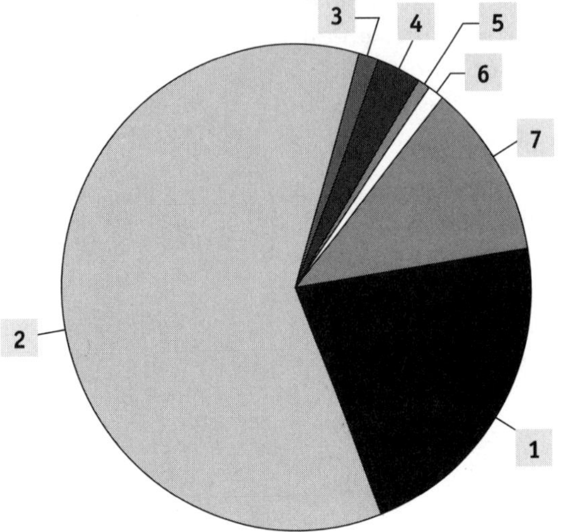

Total: $831.1 billion

1 Strategic command, control, and communications
$182.0 billion / 21.9%

2 Intelligence
$500.0 billion / 60.2%

3 Continuity of government/bunkers
$10.8 billion / 1.3%

4 Space Shuttle and space support
$26.0 billion / 3.1%

5 Other

Nuclear war planning
$2.4 billion / 0.3%

Defense Meteorological Satellite Program/weather support
$5.4 billion / 0.7%

6 Mapping, charting, geodesy, and oceanography
$9.5 billion / 1.1%

7 Overhead costs
$95.0 billion / 11.4%

a. In constant 1996 dollars.

3

Targeting and Controlling the Bomb

Bruce G. Blair, John E. Pike, and Stephen I. Schwartz

No decisions can be more fateful for Americans, and for the world, than decisions about nuclear weapons. Yet these decisions have largely escaped the control of the democratic process.

—*Robert Dahl, Controlling Nuclear Weapons*

Building the bombs and their delivery vehicles was only the beginning of the U.S. effort to create a nuclear fighting force. The decision to base national security on nuclear weapons opened a Pandora's box of complex and expensive operational burdens. To deter Soviet attack by credibly threatening to inflict apocalyptic destruction, the United States needed spy systems capable of gauging the strength of enemy nuclear forces, warning systems capable of detecting an imminent enemy attack, command systems capable of protecting the president and other key nuclear decisionmakers during wartime, and communications networks capable of transmitting the "go-code" to the dispersed nuclear forces. In short, the lethal offensive and defensive weapons at its disposal had to be placed under the tight operational control of a coherent war-fighting organization.

These requirements for fighting a nuclear war were coupled to another key goal: ensuring that a war would not start by accident, whether through inadvertent action, false alarms from early warning systems, or unauthorized acts. This task became increasingly difficult during the 1960s because of the vast numbers of U.S. and Soviet missiles on hair-trigger alert that could fly halfway around the globe in less than thirty minutes. Despite impressive efforts to make it safe, this posture of rapid reaction was inherently dangerous. Commanders were placed under great pressure to make fateful decisions in minutes, and to do so on the basis of incomplete intelligence and warning data.

Summary

—The United States spent an estimated $182 billion on strategic command, control, and communications systems.

—The United States spent approximately $1 trillion on intelligence-related activities, including $270 billion on spy satellites concentrated on the Soviet nuclear infrastructure, weapons, and operations in support of U.S. nuclear planning (offensive and defensive). A minimum of $100 billion of this amount can be attributed to nuclear weapons programs. A reasonable estimate of the cost of gathering intelligence on Soviet nuclear programs during the cold war is $500 billion, allowing that the costs were dominated by versatile satellite and other intelligence systems that gathered information on a wide range of topics and countries.

—Despite the enormous investment in these programs, the systems to control the use of nuclear weapons have always been vulnerable to attack, set on a hair trigger, susceptible to false alarms, and dependent on dubious measures of control such as predelegating nuclear launch authority to military officials other than the president. In addition, although surveillance and espionage enabled the United States to verify strategic arms control agreements, they failed to produce accurate and timely intelligence on many other important nuclear issues such as the size of the Soviet tactical nuclear arsenal and the increases in the alert level of Soviet strategic nuclear weapons during crises.

Nuclear War Planning and Targeting

Strategic war planning from 1960 to 1992 was carried out by the Joint Strategic Target Planning Staff, formed in 1960 at Strategic Air Command headquarters near Omaha, Nebraska. With the aid of satellite photographs, this staff drew up a long list of potential Soviet and Chinese targets—and plans to strike them—known as the Single Integrated Operational Plan.[1] Many tens of thousands of targets made the list during the height of the cold war. SAC staff assigned the most important targets to the U.S. strategic bomber, submarine, and land-based missile forces and scheduled the launch and delivery of U.S.

1. One of the few available military documents to discuss in detail the SIOP (in this case, the plan in effect as of April 15, 1961) can be found in Scott D. Sagan, "SIOP-62: The Nuclear Plan Briefing to President Kennedy," *International Security,* vol. 12, no. 1 (1987), pp. 22–51.

weapons to ensure maximum target destruction in wartime. On June 1, 1992, SAC became the U.S. Strategic Command and JSTPS was replaced by an organization called J-5. The change reflected both the end of the cold war and a decision to place all U.S. strategic forces under the control of a single commander. According to the historical database of the Future Years Defense Program, from 1984 to 1995, SAC/STRATCOM and JSTPS/J-5 spent $946 million on strategic war-planning activities. Spending before 1984 is not identified explicitly, but a reasonable estimate based on known data would be at least $1.5 billion from the 1950s until 1983, for a total of $2.4 billion.

Although the cold war has ended, the United States still aims its strategic forces at about two thousand targets in the former Soviet Union.[2] Several hundred additional targets in China are covered by U.S. strategic reserve forces, and a small but growing number of targets in Iran, Iraq, North Korea, Syria, and Libya are being added to the target list of U.S. strategic reserve forces and nonstrategic nuclear weapons.[3] Strategic reserve forces are the ICBMs, SLBMs, and long-range bombers that may be freed from their SIOP assignments (high-priority targets in the former Soviet Union) to cover other targets. Such forces could be rapidly prepared (hours or less) for launch against targets in the third world or elsewhere. The use of strategic forces in regional contingencies is provided by plans known as limited attack options and selected attack options. STRATCOM also draws up regional nuclear attack plans involving nonstrategic forces, mainly, Tomahawk nuclear-tipped sea-launched cruise missiles.

The SIOP

The main purpose of the SIOP has been to deter a Soviet nuclear attack against the United States and its allies, to deter an invasion of Western Europe by Soviet conventional forces, and to prevail in war should it break out.[4] The JSTPS at SAC headquarters assumed primary

2. As of May 30, 1994, under an agreement reached with Russia, U.S. ballistic missiles are now aimed largely at the Arctic Ocean. However, land- and sea-based missiles retain all their cold war targets in computer memory, preserving their ability to attack them as rapidly as ever. The time required to launch a first or second strike is the same because switching from ocean targets to military targets is roughly the equivalent of changing television channels by using a remote control. It takes only seconds to complete the retargeting procedure. See Bruce G. Blair, "Where Would All the Missiles Go?" *Washington Post,* October 15, 1996, p. A15; Douglas Berenson, "DOD Concedes Strategic Missile Detargeting Deal Is Easily Reversed," *Inside the Pentagon,* May 29, 1997, p. 1.

3. See Bruce G. Blair, *Global Zero Alert for Nuclear Forces* (Brookings, 1995), pp. 5–8; Hans Kristensen, "Targets of Opportunity," *Bulletin of the Atomic Scientists,* vol. 53 (September/October, 1997), pp. 22–28. In November 1996, in advance of a meeting between the presidents of the United States and China, the Clinton administration offered China a quid pro quo deal: it would not target U.S. missiles at China if China would not target its missiles at the United States. China rejected the deal and urged the United States to pledge it would not use nuclear weapons first. See George Wehrfritz, "Prepare to Ram," *Newsweek,* December 2, 1996, p. 42.

4. For more on the SIOP, see David Alan Rosenberg, "The Origins of Overkill: Nuclear Weapons and American Strategy, 1945–1960," in Steven E. Miller, ed. *Strategy and*

responsibility in 1960 for developing a plan that would ensure a coordinated strike by all three legs of the U.S. strategic triad—land-, sea-, and air-based weapons—against Soviet and Chinese nuclear and conventional forces, war-supporting industry, and political leadership.

Before the creation of the SIOP, war planning was carried out in less coordinated fashion by the Joint Chiefs of Staff and the military services. As a result, target plans frequently overlapped. In the Far East, in the mid-1950s, duplications of programmed weapons were found on 115 airfields and 40 complexes, and triplications on as many as 37 airfields and 7 complexes. In Europe duplications turned up on 121 airfields and 48 complexes, and triplications on 31 airfields.[5] Such multiple targeting was not only wasteful but could have impeded U.S. military objectives or killed or injured U.S. personnel had nuclear weapons been used. To add to the problems of the coordination system, individual commanders "were inclined to emphasize the needs of their own command over the objective of attack synchronization."[6] Although SAC had set a goal of eliminating all redundant targeting by 1954, by 1956 there had been a slight change of plan. In view of the increasingly larger number of weapons available (in part because of the duplication problem itself, which artificially boosted weapons requirements) and the growing number of targets identified by SAC, duplication could occur in the case of "highest-priority" targets. Such duplication, the reasoning went, would ensure the destruction of these targets in the event of a surprise attack.

Because SAC was semiautonomous, it prepared its own war plans, which it submitted to the JCS for review. But the JCS lacked the manpower and computing power to adequately review SAC's plans, especially the intelligence estimates behind them, which determined the targeting requirements and in turn drove the acquisition of nuclear weapons. In fact, from 1951 onward "General LeMay did not submit his annually updated Basic War Plans as required for JCS review, believing the details of operational planning should be closely guarded." In March 1954 a SAC briefing on current war plans revealed that "although SAC has been 'assigned' only a certain number of targets by the JCS, their planning has gone well beyond that number. A current plan . . . covers up to 1,700 DGZs [Designated Ground Zeros], which includes 409 airfields."[7] With lists unchecked and intelligence regu-

Nuclear Deterrence (Princeton University Press, 1984), pp. 113–81; Desmond Ball and Robert C. Toth, "Revising the SIOP: Taking War-Fighting to Dangerous Extremes," *International Security,* vol. 14, no. 4 (1990), pp. 65–92; Desmond Ball and Jeffrey Richelson, eds., *Strategic Nuclear Targeting* (Cornell University Press, 1986), esp. pp. 15–32, 35–83; and U.S. General Accounting Office, *Strategic Weapons: Nuclear Weapons Targeting Process,* NSIAD-91-319FS (September 1991).

5. *Study of Airpower,* Hearings before the Subcommittee on the Air Force of the Senate Committee on Armed Services, 84 Cong. 2 sess. (GPO, 1956), vol. 1, pp. 170–71.

6. Desmond Ball, "The Development of the SIOP, 1960–1983," in Ball and Richelson, *Strategic Nuclear Targeting,* p. 58.

7. "Document One: Memorandum Op-36C/jm, 18 March 1954," reprinted with David Alan Rosenberg, "'A Smoking Radiating Ruin at the End of Two Hours:' Documents on American Plans for Nuclear War with the Soviet Union, 1954–1955," *International Security,* vol. 6, no. 3 (1981/82), p. 18. The end result of this optimum strike plan,

larly suggesting possible new targets, the increase in estimates of weapons and force requirements is not surprising.[8]

During the first few years after World War II, military planners generally assumed that nuclear weapons would be used in any war with the Soviet Union, yet detailed plans were not drawn up until 1947. By 1959 the enormous growth in both weapons and delivery vehicles posed serious coordination problems. Of some 2,400 designated targets, about 300 were duplicated, with the result that "in each of the Joint Coordination Centers' exercises from 1958 to 1960, over 200 time-over-target conflicts were identified. Thus U.S. strategic delivery forces would likely destroy each other, and not only the targets attacked, in the event of nuclear war" (see box 3-1).[9] The JCS recognized the problem but could not agree on a solution. President Eisenhower, immensely frustrated with this state of affairs, authorized the creation of the JSTPS on August 11, 1960, whose task would be to prepare a National Strategic Target List (NSTL) and the SIOP. Because only SAC had the necessary computing power, the work was to take place at SAC headquarters in Omaha, to the distinct disadvantage of the army and navy. The first target staff was composed of 219 SAC personnel, 29 navy, 10 army, 3 Marine Corps, and 8 additional non-SAC air force officers. The first NSTL and SIOP were completed by November 1960.[10]

Rather than rectifying the problems with target planning, the creation of the SIOP in many ways exacerbated them. SAC's control over targeting doctrine, especially target selection and damage criteria, led to an increase in the number of targets and to multiple strikes on those targets to meet very stringent damage requirements. Out of a target database of 4,100 sites, JSTPS selected 2,600 installations for attack, which in turn became 1,050 DGZs in the NSTL.[11] Under the plan, the entire strategic force would be launched against the Soviet Union; nothing would be held back. Eisenhower was deeply troubled by this strategy, but with only a few more months left in office there was little he could do. The navy, especially chief of naval operations Admiral Arleigh Burke, complained that JSTPS "had failed to determine the *minimum* force necessary to achieve military objectives, and had failed to leave an adequate reserve for follow-up strikes." Furthermore, SAC's damage criteria only considered the immediate blast effects of a nuclear attack and ignored the secondary effects of fire and fallout (an omission that was only beginning to be reversed in 1996). The

as characterized by a navy officer at the briefing, "was that virtually all of Russia would be nothing but a smoking, radiating ruin at the end of two hours" (p. 25).

8. David Alan Rosenberg, "The Origins of Overkill," pp. 121, 147–48.

9. See "SIOP-62 Briefing: JCS 2056/281 Enclosure, September 13, 1961," *International Security*, vol. 12, no. 1 (1987), p. 42.

10. Rosenberg, "The Origins of Overkill," pp. 115–16.

11. One year later, some 80,000 potential targets were scrutinized, from which 3,729 installations "were determined to be essential for attack." This translated to 1,060 DGZs. See "SIOP-62 Briefing: JCS 2056/281 Enclosure, September 13, 1961," p. 44.

Box 3-1
Securing Control of the Skies

In the event of a confirmed warning of nuclear attack, NORAD, in conjunction with the Federal Aviation Administration (FAA) and the Federal Communications Commission (FCC), would order the immediate grounding of all commercial aircraft in U.S. airspace and off the U.S. coasts. Developed in the 1960s, this little-known plan—Security Control of Air Traffic and Navigation Aids (SCATANA)—authorizes NORAD, the FAA, and the FCC to impose these restrictions in order to clear the skies for bomber and missile operations.[1] Once SCATANA has been implemented, a wartime air traffic priority list (WATPL) is established to allow essential personnel and aircraft to use the airspace. Designated "priority one" on the WATPL are the president of the United States, the prime minister of Canada, their respective essential national security staffs, aircraft engaged in continental defense missions, retaliatory aircraft and their support aircraft (for example, refueling tankers), and airborne command posts.

While the military rationale for SCATANA is understandable, the feasibility of its implementation (particularly given the significant increase in air travel since the 1960s) is dubious. The program was (and presumably still is) tested regularly only via simulations.[2] According to the FAA, "Emergency security control of air traffic and/or the actual securing of navigational aids has never been accomplished." Therefore, "there are no recorded costs associated with the conduct of this program."[3] SCATANA has apparently been activated only once, by accident. During a false alert on November 9, 1979—triggered when a technician at NORAD inserted a computer tape used to simulate a nuclear attack into the on-line warning system—FAA controllers at some locations were directed to order commercial airliners to prepare to land immediately. When the indications of a full-scale Soviet attack were determined, after six agonizing minutes, to be false (on the basis of contrary data from early warning sensors), the order was rescinded.[4]

1. Under the Federal Aviation Act of 1958 (as amended), the Communication Act of 1934 (as amended), the National Security Act of 1947 (as amended), and Executive Order 11490. This need was recognized as early as 1956, when General Earl E. Partridge, commander in chief of the air defense and continental air defense commands, testified before Congress that with regard to identifying and destroying enemy aircraft in U.S. airspace, "in the event of an emergency . . . one of our first steps would be to eliminate all nonessential air traffic. The capability of our air defense system to identify aircraft tracks thereafter would be tremendously enhanced." See *Study of Airpower,*" Hearings, p. 311.

2. In April 1956 General Partridge also testified: "It is almost impossible for the Strategic Air Command to carry out a realistic test of [its ability to attack the Soviet Union]. . . . For example . . . the CAA [Civil Aviation Administration] must give [SAC] permission to operate without lights. This takes weeks, just in the making sure that everybody who is in the area on a particular night knows that there are going to be many aircraft in there at certain altitudes without lights." See *Study of Airpower,* Hearings, p. 294.

3. Letter, David J. Hurley, Director, Air Traffic System Management, Federal Aviation Administration, to Stephen I. Schwartz, August 9, 1994; and DOT/FAA/Federal Communications Commission (FCC) SCATANA Plan, 7610.4H, October 2, 1990, appx. 17.

4. Sagan, *Limits of Safety,* pp. 228–29.

"overkill" was particularly worrying: under SAC's criteria, "the damage caused by a 13 kiloton bomb on Hiroshima could only be assured by assigning 300 to 500 kilotons of weapons to a similar target."[12]

12. Rosenberg, "The Origins of Overkill," pp. 116–18 (emphasis added). This problem existed at least through the 1980s. A gas plant at Hiroshima, completely destroyed by secondary effects would, under the SIOP effective at that time,

Because the SIOP was shrouded in secrecy (all information pertaining to it has its own classification code, SIOP-ESI, "extremely sensitive information"), oversight of it was poor to nonexistent. When, in April 1974, Secretary of Defense James Schlesinger directed that SIOP forces "be able to destroy 70 percent of the Soviet industry that would be needed to achieve economic recovery in the event of a large-scale strategic nuclear exchange," this was taken to mean "70 percent of every factory or industrial installation rather than 70 percent of Soviet economic-industrial capacity as a whole" (an error only discovered years later, during a sweeping review of the SIOP process).[13] Even today, the overriding goal of the SIOP—ensuring the coverage and hence destruction of virtually all possible targets—drives the entire U.S. nuclear infrastructure, including targeting assignments, force deployments, warhead production and retirement, alert postures, and launch response times. A recent change of presidential guidance on the employment of nuclear weapons, issued as Presidential Decision Directive 60 in November 1997, will likely alter this requirement. The focus of targeting in future strategic war plans will be Russian strategic forces and nuclear command infrastructure. Russian war-supporting industry and conventional forces may have lower priority for targeting. The new guidance reportedly emphasizes potential targets in China and small proliferant states. Thus a partial shift away from Russia toward those countries appears to be under way in nuclear planning.[14] To understand the closeted world of the SIOP is to understand a good part of the history—and costs—of U.S. nuclear forces and policies since 1960.[15]

From Defense Secretary Robert S. McNamara onward, many civilian and some military officials responsible for nuclear planning have expressed varying degrees of concern about the way the SIOP has evolved (see box 3-2) and how U.S. nuclear forces would be used in an actual war. Admiral Noel Gayler, the former commander in chief of the Pacific and new deputy director of JSTPS in 1967, was particularly "bothered" by the "reverse" method of targeting weapons. Because of the enormous size of the arsenal—in 1966 the stockpile peaked at an

---

"be considered to absorb only 'moderate' damage . . . even though it could have several [thermonuclear] strategic warheads assigned to it" (each far larger than the single atomic bomb which destroyed Hiroshima). See Janne E. Nolan, *Guardians of the Arsenal: The Politics of Nuclear Strategy* (New York: Basic Books, 1989), p. 256. For more on SAC's decision to exclude secondary nuclear weapons effects—especially the intense thermal pulse capable of igniting firestorms—see Lynn Eden, *Constructing Destruction: Organizations, Knowledge, and U.S. Nuclear Weapons Effects* (Cornell University Press, forthcoming). For details of the U.S. Strategic Command's interest in a new nuclear strategy designed to maximize fallout and radiation in a nuclear attack on the former Soviet Union in order to do as much harm as possible to the civilian population, see William M. Arkin, "Bring on the Radiation," *Bulletin of the Atomic Scientists*, vol. 53 (January/February 1997), p. 72.

13. Ball, "Development of the SIOP, 1960–1983," p. 74; Ball and Toth, "Revising the SIOP," pp. 70–71.

14. R. Jeffrey Smith, "Clinton Directive Changes Strategy on Nuclear Arms," *Washington Post*, December 7, 1957, p. A1; Steven Lee Myers, "U.S. 'Updates' All-Out Atom War Guidelines," *New York Times*, December 7, 1997, p. A3.

15. For a discussion of the effects of targeting requirements on alert rates and launch-on-warning options, see Bruce G. Blair, *The Logic of Accidental Nuclear War* (Brookings, 1993), and *Global Zero Alert for Nuclear Forces*.

estimated 32,200 warheads and bombs—the idea was to find targets for excess weapons. When Gayler complained to his superior officer, he was told not to worry about it.[16]

One difficulty, of course, was that the copious intelligence data provided by satellites and other means, including espionage by the Central Intelligence Agency, could not divine intentions. Soviet strategic nuclear forces were systematically located and targeted, but detecting their preparation for attack was an entirely different matter. The massive effort devoted to collecting electronic and imagery intelligence on Soviet forces, initially with aircraft in the 1950s and subsequently with aircraft and spacecraft, was predicated on the assumption that detection of increased levels of alert would provide advanced warning of a possible Soviet attack, providing American commanders with the option of preemptively responding (see, for example, chapter 2, footnote 164). But on numerous occasions during the cold war when the Soviet Union raised the alert level of its strategic and theater nuclear forces, U.S. intelligence systems failed to notice every time.[17] Moreover, by the late 1960s Soviet strategic forces had reached a point where they required little or no advance preparation to mount a surprise nuclear strike on a massive scale.

This shortcoming in intelligence forced U.S. strategic planners to assume that a Soviet nuclear attack could come as a complete surprise. The standard "worst-case" scenario thus drove the United States to deploy missiles in hardened underground silos, stealthy submarines, and bombers on airborne (until 1968) and runway (until 1991) alert, to enable these forces to survive a massive attack launched without warning. But the harder task was to design command posts and communications networks that could ride out an attack, continue to function, and allow a coherent and coordinated U.S. response.

Vulnerability to Attack

Throughout the cold war, highly classified studies consistently showed that a surprise missile attack by a small fraction of the Soviet arsenal could decapitate the U.S. command system and destroy the communications links used to send the go-code (formally known as emergency

16. Two years later Gayler was "seduced" with an offer to head the National Security Agency, an offer he later came to believe "was to get me out of there." Admiral Noel Gayler (USN, retired), interview with Stephen I. Schwartz, April 11, 1996, Alexandria, Virginia. General Colin Powell criticized the same phenomenon more than twenty years later: "In the event of war, we were going to aim a warhead at a Soviet bridge *and* the city hall just blocks away. Under the current plan, nearly forty weapons were targeted for the Ukrainian capital of Kiev alone." See Colin L. Powell with Joseph E. Perisco, *My American Journey* (New York: Random House, 1995), pp. 540–41. See also Stansfield Turner, *Caging the Nuclear Genie: An American Challenge for Global Security* (Boulder, Colo.: Westview Press), pp. 7–8.

17. Blair, *The Logic of Accidental Nuclear War,* pp. 23–26, 178–83; Blair, *Global Zero Alert for Nuclear Forces,* p. 17–18.

Box 3-2

SIOP Milestones

Figure 3-2 shows the historical change in the number of targets in the SIOP.

—1960–61: First single integrated operational plan (SIOP-62) completed. It calls for a massive strike against all Soviet and Chinese targets. Strikes against all targets in Soviet and Chinese "satellites" could be withheld if sufficient notification were provided by civilian authorities in advance of the attack; otherwise the only flexibility in the plan was in whether to activate it as a preemptive or a retaliatory attack.[1] SIOP-62 took effect January 15, 1961.

—1962: First SIOP (SIOP-63) with "flexible options" introduced. It excludes some targets from an initial massive strike; the smallest option calls for a massive strike against Soviet nuclear forces and infrastructure. Options allow for individual countries such as China to be excluded, or for various targets sets within countries—such as the national leadership facilities in Moscow or Beijing—to be excluded.

—1976: First SIOP (SIOP-5) adopted allowing for selective strikes against "small" target sets (less than 100 targets). Twenty-five thousand targets in the National Strategic Target Database (NSTDB) in 1976; increased to 50,000 by mid-1980.

—1982: China dropped from the SIOP, but hundreds of Chinese targets retained in the strategic reserve force.

—1983: SIOP-6 takes effect on October 1, 1983. Revision and elimination of some SIOP missions and thorough review of NSTDB reduces the SIOP target base to 14,000 by 1987.

—1989: SIOP-6F takes effect on October 1, 1989. Emphasizes destruction of Soviet leadership, mobile targets (for example, SS-25 missiles), and development of "adaptive target planning."

—1990 to 1996: Dramatic reductions in Soviet and Russian SIOP targets as Soviet forces withdraw from Eastern Europe and former Soviet republics hand over nuclear forces to Russia;[2] strategic target planning focuses increasingly on third world countries that are developing weapons of mass destruction. Iran, North Korea, Syria, Libya, and Iraq are increasingly targeted by U.S. strategic weapons assigned to the strategic reserve force with a launch readiness measured in hours. The reserve force grows while the SIOP force aimed at the former Soviet Union and ready for immediate launch decreases. Although the United States and Russia agree in 1994 to stop targeting each other, all strategic forces on both sides retain their cold war targets in computer memory and preserve their ability to attack them as rapidly as ever.

—1997: President Clinton issues Presidential Decision Directive 60 delineating guidelines for the targeting of nuclear weapons, eliminating a 1981 directive by President Reagan to prepare to win protracted nuclear war and directing the military to focus instead on using nuclear weapons to deter the use of nuclear, chemical, or biological weapons by an adversary.

1. "SIOP-62 Briefing," pp. 49–50.

2. R. Jeffrey Smith, "U.S. Trims List of Targets in Soviet Union," *Washington Post*, July 21, 1991, p. A1.

FIGURE 3-2. The Evolving SIOP: Growth in Designated Targets for U.S. Strategic Nuclear Warheads, 1959–95

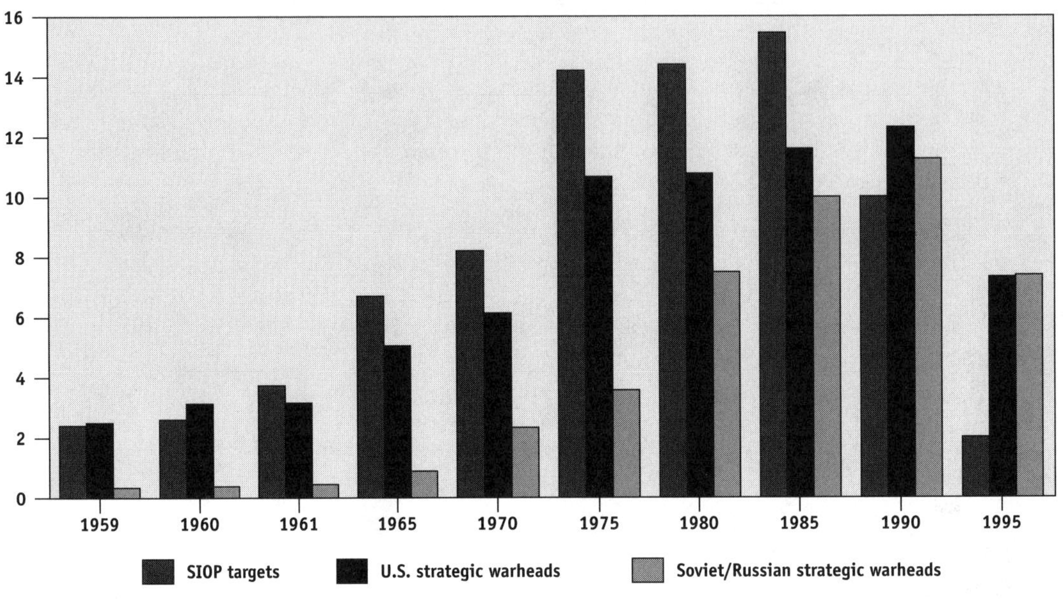

Sources: SIOP target figures for 1959–61 are from "SIOP-62 Briefing: JCS 2056/281, Enclosure, September 13, 1961." Subsequent figures are authors' estimates. Strategic warhead totals are for operational alert forces only and do not represent the entire strategic stockpile. These figures come from Robert S. Norris and Thomas B. Cochran, "U.S.-U.S.S.R./Russian Strategic Offensive Nuclear Forces, 1945–1996," Nuclear Weapons Databook Working Paper 97-1 (Washington, D.C.: Natural Resources Defense Council, January 1997), tables 1 and 2.

action messages, or EAMs) to retaliatory forces. An assessment presented to the National Security Council in February 1950 found that just sixteen properly targeted nuclear weapons could "most seriously disrupt" government operations.[18] The same conclusion emerged from authoritative detailed assessments conducted in the early 1960s, late 1960s, late 1970s, and mid-1980s.[19] The top political leaders, the senior military commanders, their fixed and mobile command posts,

18. Rosenberg, "Origins of Overkill," p. 141.

19. Leonard Wainstein and others, Institute for Defense Analyses, *The Evolution of U.S. Strategic Command and Control and Warning, 1945–1972,* Study S-467, June 1975 (formerly Top Secret, released under the Freedom of Information Act). See also Bruce G. Blair, *Strategic Command and Control: Redefining the Nuclear Threat* (Brookings, 1985). One pertinent study, written by Blair for the Office of Technology Assessment (OTA) between 1982 and 1985 and classified Top Secret, was retroactively classified SIOP-ESI by the Joint Chiefs of Staff. Most existing copies were rounded up and destroyed; the remainder were stamped and locked in a DOD safe. An outside reviewer of the study for the OTA recalled a colleague declaring, "This is the single most dangerous document I've ever seen." Members of Congress tried, without success, to obtain a copy of the report. See Tim Carrington, "The Ultimate Secret: A Pentagon Report Its Author Can't See," *Wall Street Journal,* February 18, 1986, p. 1.

and their communications links were all acutely vulnerable to sudden destruction by a few tens of Soviet weapons.

The historical and budgetary significance of this persistent finding is hard to overstate. It pressured the United States to emphasize heavily the ability to strike first or launch on warning: U.S. commanders needed to be able to authorize and implement the launch of U.S. forces *immediately* after detecting the imminent or actual launch of Soviet missiles. That is why launch authority was delegated to so-called pre-positioned national command authorities, namely, senior military commanders in the nuclear chain of command. Thus the hair trigger on the forces increased the risk of launching on false warning or of improperly exercising launch authority. This risk arguably exceeded the risk of deliberate, cold-blooded nuclear attack. That neither risk actually led to a nuclear war can be attributed to prudent leadership, effective safeguards, and sheer good luck during the numerous crisis situations and false alarms that brought the United States and the Soviet Union to the brink of war.[20]

Early in the Kennedy administration, the acute vulnerability of the U.S. nuclear command system came to the attention of Defense Secretary McNamara in a top secret report.[21] At the time, the main command posts for the president, Congress, other senior political leaders, the Joint Chiefs of Staff, and senior military commanders in the nuclear chain of command were surface and underground facilities that stood little chance of surviving a direct nuclear attack.[22] The main facilities in the Washington area reserved for the president and his top military advisers were not a secret: the National Military Command Center (NMCC) in the Pentagon, the Alternate National Military Command Center (ANMCC) in the Raven Rock/Site R underground complex (close to the president's retreat at Camp David, Maryland), and an austere protected post at Camp David.[23] Congress and execu-

20. See, for example, Blair, *The Logic of Accidental Nuclear War*; and Scott D. Sagan, *The Limits of Safety* (Princeton University Press, 1993).

21. Weapons Systems Evaluation Group Report 50, Enclosure C, September, 1960, quoted in Wainstein, *Evolution of U.S. Strategic Command and Control and Warning*, pp. 241–42. Among other findings, the study noted: "On the basis of tactical warning, the time the President may confidently think he has for the response decision, prior to bomb impact, is between *zero and about 15 minutes. In using the upper extreme of 15 minutes* he will be assuming that every procedural and physical element in the whole warning and strategic command and control structure *works perfectly* and that the enemy will not employ SLBMs or sabotage effectively against it. *A President could not be confident,* based on operating experience or exercises, *that the whole system would work perfectly.*"

22. Many of these facilities, particularly those reserved for the political leadership, were constructed using a highly classified fund established in 1957 by Congress and put under the direct control of the White House Military Office. The ITT Corporation built many of them, although when asked it could locate no records of the work, financial or otherwise. Letter from Brandon R. Belote III, Director, Public Relations, ITT, to Stephen I. Schwartz, May 22, 1995. By 1980 there were reportedly more than seventy-five sites around the country, all manned twenty-four hours a day by either ITT, the Federal Emergency Management Agency (FEMA), or the military. Total costs for the program under President Eisenhower (when most of the construction took place) are unknown, but spending under President Kennedy (1961–63) was $32.7 million. See Bill Gulley with Mary Ellen Reese, *Breaking Cover* (New York: Simon & Schuster, 1980), pp. 35–39, 182–83.

23. In 1959, in advance of a visit by Soviet president Nikita

tive branch officials were to evacuate to underground complexes at the Greenbrier resort in West Virginia and Mount Weather in rural Virginia, respectively (see box 3-3).

Although the existence and purpose of these other facilities was officially secret, it was probable that over time Soviet officials learned about and had targeted them, in which case they also stood little chance of survival. Similar vulnerabilities existed down the chain of command. The underground headquarters at the Strategic Air Command in Omaha, built in 1955–56 at a cost of $64.7 million, was another facility that would not have survived if it had been directly targeted. Even the North American Air Defense Command (NORAD) headquarters inside Cheyenne Mountain, Colorado (known as the NORAD Cheyenne Mountain Complex or NCMC), arguably the sturdiest of the bunkers, could not escape precisely directed high-yield thermonuclear weapons.

Recognizing the acute vulnerability of the ground-based facilities, Secretary McNamara secretly configured two Navy cruisers—the USS *Northampton* and the USS *Wright*—to serve as National Emergency Command Posts Afloat (NECPA). From 1962 through 1970, when the Navy terminated the program, more than $858 million was spent just on communications for NECPA. McNamara also formed an airborne command network out of a fleet of thirty-nine militarized Boeing 707 aircraft (known as EC-135s). The centerpiece of the aircraft network was the SAC airborne command post (nicknamed "Looking Glass") that rotating aircraft kept continuously aloft from February 3, 1961, until July 24, 1990 ("Looking Glass" is currently maintained on ground alert or occasional airborne alert). Other command aircraft were placed on fifteen-minute ground alert and put at the disposal of the president (whose doomsday plane was called the National Emergency Airborne Command Post, or NEACP, pronounced "Kneecap") and the various nuclear commanders in chief. Some aircraft in this so-called Post-Attack Command and Control System (PACCS) were equipped to fire nuclear-tipped Minuteman ICBMs by remote radio communications to the unmanned silos, should the launch-control centers on the ground be destroyed or cut off from communication with the missiles. They could also transmit an EAM to ten Minuteman emergency communications rockets deployed in 1967 at Whiteman Air Force Base in Missouri and launch the rockets that—for a limited period of time—would broadcast the EAM to bombers in flight, as well as to other

Khrushchev to Camp David (as part of a tour of the United States), laborers at Camp David "worked night and day to haul away truckloads of dirt and stone, making sure to hide every trace of their excavations before Khrushchev's arrival." A large flagstone deck was laid to cover the hole for the bunker, then under construction. "Little did Khrushchev know, as he stood smiling on the deck posing for photographers, the he was atop a presidential relocation site." Ted Gup, "How FEMA Learned to Stop Worrying about Civilians and Love the Bomb," *Mother Jones*, January/February 1994, p. 31.

strategic nuclear units. (This McNamara-initiated program, called the Emergency Rocket Communications System, or ERCS, was originally deployed in 1965 aboard unprotected Blue Scout rockets based on Wallops Island, just off the Virginia Coast, and was terminated in 1992. The Soviet Union developed and continues to operate a similar program—in conjunction with its "dead hand" system—using SS-17 and SS-25 missiles.)[24]

Until early 1991, other specially equipped EC-130 (later E-6A) TACAMO aircraft flown by the navy were on continuous patrol and could reel out a 5-mile-long (8-kilometer) very low frequency (VLF) antenna to radio the go-code to submerged ballistic missile submarines (the planes remain operational but, like "Looking Glass," are no longer on constant airborne alert). TACAMO costs, including twenty EC-130 and sixteen E-6A aircraft, are under "navy strategic communications" in the FYDP historical database and show $1.7 billion expended through 1995. Beginning in January 1998 and continuing through 2000, all EC-135 airborne command posts will be retired and replaced by the newest version of the TACAMO aircraft, the E-6B.

This airborne network, designed to ensure that U.S. strategic forces could be launched in the wake of a Soviet first strike, became the backbone of the wartime nuclear command system. But despite the substantial investment and periodic modernization of the elements (for instance, the president's doomsday plane was upgraded from a Boeing 707 to a 747 during the 1970s and a fleet of more than forty tractor trailers known as the Mobile Emergency Response Support fleet were deployed in the 1980s),[25] the potential for swift decapitation hardly diminished. Critical elements of the network, such as the president's doomsday plane on ground alert, became vulnerable to sudden attack by Soviet submarine missiles deployed off the east and west coasts of the United States during the late 1960s. For this and other reasons—

24. Blair, *Global Zero Alert for Nuclear Forces,* p. 52.

25. These 40-foot-long (12-meter) trailers, resembling moving vans but packed with state-of-the-art communications equipment, were mentioned publicly for the first and last time in Secretary of Defense Caspar Weinberger's 1983 annual report ("We will . . . develop and deploy terrestrial mobile command centers (MCCs) that could supplement or take over the key functions of airborne command posts if they could no longer operate effectively"). MCCs were financed by the Defense Communications Agency but actually purchased by the army under the code name "Island Sun." While their capabilities and even existence were considered highly classified by the DOD, Goodyear Aerospace, which manufactured them, freely distributed color brochures about its sophisticated product at trade shows. Speaking to a reporter, a Goodyear executive, while admitting that troops deployed with the vehicles would not likely survive a nuclear attack, asserted that reinforcements could be deployed to man the trucks. "Our equipment will last longer than theirs [the Soviets'], so in the long run we have an advantage," he said. Today, some of the trucks are under the control of FEMA and are deployed to assist communities recovering from natural disasters. The first two prototypes, completed in 1984, encountered serious problems. One was so packed with gear and special shielding that it sank into the road when first tested in rural Virginia. The other became stuck under a highway overpass, being taller than the available clearance. See *Report of the Secretary of Defense Caspar W. Weinberger to the Congress on the FY 1983 Budget, FY 1984 Authorization Request and FY 1983–1987 Defense Programs* (GPO, February 8, 1982), p. III-68; Fred Hiatt, "Building a Force for World War IV," *Washington Post,* July 27, 1986, p. A1; Steven Emerson, "America's Doomsday Project," *U.S. News & World Report,* August 7, 1989, pp. 26–31.

Box 3-3

Emergency Command Posts and the Continuity of Government

Several command posts have been established for use in the event of a nuclear emergency.

National Airborne Operations Center (NAOC)

A militarized Boeing E-4B (converted from a commercial 747-200) based at Offutt Air Force Base in Omaha, Nebraska, and ready for takeoff on fifteen minutes' notice, is available to the president and vice president for commanding nuclear forces from the air during a crisis.[1] At least one aircraft (there are four in all) is always on alert with a full battle staff. When the president travels around the country or overseas in *Air Force One* (the designation for one of several aircraft at the president's disposal in peacetime), a NAOC often flies to a nearby location.[2] While colloquially known as the "doomsday plane," the official code name for NAOC is "Night Watch." Classified assessments during the cold war questioned whether the president or his designated successor could actually reach the aircraft in the event of a nuclear attack, let alone get off the ground in time. Once airborne, the specially shielded and configured plane would allow the president to coordinate a nuclear war with senior military commanders (each of whom has his own airborne command post) and, if necessary, transmit EAMs to launch a nuclear attack.[3]

Although plans initiated under President Jimmy Carter and fortified during the Reagan administration envisioned a protracted nuclear war lasting days or weeks, NAOC, like all the other airborne command posts, can only remain aloft for seventy-two hours at most (assuming in-flight refueling from KC-135 tankers also kept on alert), at which point its engine oil will begin to break down and require replacement. A growing concern following the 1980 eruption of Mount St. Helens (whose ash drifted across much of the northern United States and forced the diversion of downwind commercial airline traffic) was that the large amounts of fallout generated by a Soviet attack on U.S. cities and military bases might clog the intakes of jet engines, further jeopardizing the survival of airborne command posts.[4]

Alternative Underground Command Posts

Alternative underground command posts were built in Pennsylvania, Colorado, Virginia (two), and West Virginia.

Site R/Alternate National Military Command Center (ANMCC): Raven Rock Mountain, Pennsylvania. Blasted out of Raven Rock Mountain, about 6 miles (9.67 kilometers) north of Camp David on the Pennsylvania-Maryland

---

1. Until 1983 this aircraft—then known as the National Emergency Airborne Command Post—was based at Andrews Air Force Base in Maryland, a short helicopter ride from the White House. That year, in response to long-standing concerns about the vulnerability of the aircraft to an attack by Soviet SLBMs, the DOD assistant secretary responsible for C^3I issues testified before Congress that NEACP would be moved inland to an undisclosed location where it could take off and rendezvous with the president, who would be evacuated from Washington by helicopter (maintained on alert at the Marine Air Corps Facility in Quantico, Virginia). The day after this testimony, Senator Dan Quayle (Republican of Indiana) surprised the DOD by issuing a press release announcing the stationing of NEACP at Grissom Air Force Base in Peru, Indiana (more than 50 miles [80.5 kilometers] north of Indianapolis). Quayle told reporters he had personally lobbied to have the aircraft transferred to Grissom to keep the base there open and to ensure that the surrounding community reaped the $4.6 million in extra spending generated by NEACP's presence. See Ford, *The Button,* pp. 136–37.

2. The first president to fly on NEACP was Jimmy Carter. The last was reportedly Ronald Reagan, who used it to travel from Texas to Washington, D.C., on November 15, 1981.

3. For a graphical depiction of NEACP and a general discussion of its capabilities, see Kenneth J. Stein, "America's Top-Secret Doomsday Plane," *Popular Mechanics,* May 1994, pp. 38–41.

4. Ford, *The Button,* p. 163.

Box 3-3
(continued)

border, this underground bunker was built in around-the-clock shifts between 1950 and 1953 as a backup Pentagon and communications center should Washington, D.C., be destroyed. Site R's "footprint" is 260,000 square feet (24,180 square meters); its total usable floor space is perhaps three times larger. Operated by nearby Fort Detrick, Site R's facilities are designed to handle 3,000 people and include sophisticated computer and communications equipment, a reservoir, medical and dental facilities, dining hall, barber shop, and chapel. Although twenty-four-hour staffing of the site ended in February 1992, by October 1997 more than 500 military and civilian personnel still worked at the facility.[5] Construction costs are unknown but likely match or exceed the $1 billion spent on Mount Weather. According to the FYDP, from fiscal 1962 to 1992 (the last year funds were recorded as being expended), maintaining and operating the ANMCC cost more than $1 billion.

NORAD Cheyenne Mountain Complex (NCMC): Cheyenne Mountain, Colorado Springs, Colorado. Planned in the mid to late 1950s and built by the U.S. Army Corps of Engineers between June 1961 and May 1964, the NCMC—dug out of Cheyenne Mountain—replaced NORAD's previous vulnerable aboveground facilities in a converted hospital at Ent Air Force Base, Colorado Springs, Colorado. The NCMC was designed to protect the headquarters of the North American early warning and control network (jointly operated by the United States and Canada) from nuclear attack. Its primary mission was to detect and assess a Soviet nuclear attack, notify senior military commanders, and coordinate the launching of retaliatory strikes before the first Soviet warheads detonated. Although shielded by 1,750 feet (533 meters) of granite, the NCMC became vulnerable to direct attack by Soviet missiles deployed in the late 1960s. Inside 4½ acres (196,020 square feet; 18,212 square meters) of the mountain, some 115,000 bolts shore up the walls (two noncommissioned officers continually check and tighten these bolts to keep the walls from weakening and collapsing). Fifteen buildings rest atop more than 1,300 large metal springs (3.95 to 4 feet [1.2 meters] long, 3 inches [7.6 centimeters] thick, and 20 inches [50.8 centimeters] in diameter), designed to cushion the shock of nearby detonations. The entire installation is sealed off by 30-ton blast doors, 3 feet (0.9 meter) thick, that can be hydraulically closed in less than a minute. The cost of the project by the end of 1965 totaled some $695 million.[6] At present, NORAD monitors data from early warning satellites and radars and tracks more than 8,000 objects in near-Earth orbit. Most of these objects (90 percent) are "space junk" consisting of paint chips, metal hardware, and other debris associated with past space missions. Using sophisticated radars and computers, NORAD monitors everything and reports potential hazards in order to avoid damage to orbiting satellites or the Space Shuttle.

Costs for the NCMC from 1962 through 1995 are listed in the FYDP under four program elements: 102310F "NCMC Tactical Warning and Attack Assessment" ($1.7 billion), 102311F NCMC "Space Defense Systems" ($3.0 billion),

5. From its creation until October 1, 1997, Site R was operated by Fort Ritchie, Maryland. The impending closure of Fort Ritchie under a base realignment initiative necessitated the shift to Fort Detrick. In 1992 Colonel Mark Scuerman, the site's commandant, proposed opening the facility for public tours, a plan rejected by DOD officials. See "Underground Pentagon Command to Be Shifted," *Baltimore Sun*, April 29, 1996, p. 2B; Associated Press, "Secret Ceremony Seals Hand-Over at Secret Site," *Washington Times*, October 13, 1997, p. A4.

6. David W. Shircliffe, *NORAD's Underground COC, Initial Requirement to Initial Operation: 1956–1966,* Historical Reference Paper 12, NORAD Public Affairs Office, January 1966 (classified, released with deletions under the Freedom of Information Act); U.S. Army Corps of Engineers (Omaha District), *The Federal Engineer—Damsites to Missile Sites: A History of the Omaha District, U.S. Army Corps of Engineers* (Omaha, Nebr., 1984), pp. 199- 213.

Box 3-3
(continued)

305906F "NCMC Tactical Warning and Attack Assessment" ($875 million), and 305907F "NCMC Space Defense Systems" ($49 million), for a total of $5.6 billion over thirty-three years.

High Point Special Facility (SF)/Mount Weather: Berryville, Virginia. The Mount Weather site is an unacknowledged continuity of government (CoG) facility operated by the Federal Emergency Management Agency. The 200,000-square-foot (18,600-square-meter) facility, with an estimated floor space of three times that amount, also houses FEMA's National Emergency Coordinating Center, which operates twenty-four hours a day, tracking worldwide disasters, both natural and manmade. Located on a 434-acre mountain site 48 miles (77 kilometers) (by air) from Washington, D.C., the surface complex includes about a dozen buildings staffed by more than 240 employees. The Bureau of Mines began constructing the facility's tunnels in 1954, which were completed by the Army Corps of Engineers under the code name "Operation High Point." Total construction costs, adjusted for inflation, are estimated to have exceeded $1 billion. Tunnel roofs are shored up with some 21,000 iron bolts driven 8 to 10 feet (2.4 to 3 meters) into the overhead rock. The entrance is protected by a guillotine gate and a 34-ton blast door that is 10 feet (3 meters) tall, 20 feet (6 meters) wide, and 5 feet (1.5 meters) thick and reportedly takes ten to fifteen minutes to open or close.

Completed in 1958, the underground bunker includes a hospital, crematorium, dining and recreation areas, sleeping quarters, reservoirs of drinking and cooling water, an emergency power plant, and a radio and television studio that is part of the Emergency Broadcasting System. From 1961 to 1970, the site was connected to the Bomb Alarm System, a network of sensors mounted on telephone poles adjacent to ninety-nine cities and military bases that would detect a nuclear detonation by its intense thermal flash and signal this event to Mount Weather and other military command posts, permitting both damage assessment and helping to confirm whether or not an attack had occurred. A large electronic map in a special room would indicate via tiny red lightbulbs where explosions had occurred (this system has since been replaced by more sophisticated space-based sensors).[7] A series of side tunnels accommodates a total of twenty office buildings, some of which are three stories tall. With an on-site sewage treatment plant that can process 90,000 gallons (340,650 liters) a day and two 250,000-gallon (946,250-liter) aboveground storage tanks, the facility can support a population of 200 for up to thirty days. Although it is designed to accommodate several thousand people (with sleeping cots for 2,000), only the president, the cabinet, and Supreme Court are provided private sleeping quarters.

For continuity of government, senior officials are divided into Alpha, Bravo, and Charlie teams: one would remain in Washington, another relocate to Mount Weather, and the third disperse to other relocation sites. Officials at Mount Weather track the location of everyone designated to succeed the president twenty-four hours a day. Designated evacuees carry special identification cards, and regular briefings and drills are conducted. Officials are

7. This system was entirely dependent on commercial telephone and telegraph lines and was thus susceptible to power outages and other phenomena that limited its reliability. Although it helped in at least one instance (during the Cuban Missile Crisis) to confirm a false warning of missile attack by failing to signal a nuclear detonation, during the Northeast power blackout on November 9, 1965, the system's console at Mount Weather correctly noted the power outage at twenty-two sensor sites but also reported that weapons had just exploded near Salt Lake City, Utah, and Charlotte, North Carolina. This condition triggered the full alert of the facility. It was only several days after the event that it was determined that the two detonation indications had been caused by faulty wiring in the console itself. Had such an error occurred during a time of international tension, the consequences could have been far more serious. See Sagan, *The Limits of Safety,* pp. 130, 171, 183.

Box 3-3
(continued)

not allowed to bring their families. The only full-scale activation of the facility came on November 9, 1965, during the great Northeastern power blackout.[8] The 1974 crash of a TWA plane into the mountain, killing ninety-two people, brought the site to widespread public attention. Until May 1991, the site's underground weather station issued daily reports on potential fallout patterns.

From the mid-1950s until 1970, the 2857th Test Squadron, a special group of helicopter pilots and rescue workers based at Olmstead Air Force Base in Pennsylvania, and known as the Outpost Mission, was trained to fly to the White House in the event of nuclear attack, retrieve the president and first family, and relocate them to Mount Weather or several other sites, including (from 1961 to 1970) the National Emergency Command Post Afloat. If the team should have difficulty reaching the White House before an attack, it carried specialized equipment to break into the bunker under the executive mansion; a backup unit with heavier equipment, including cranes, was also available if the damage proved more severe.[9]

Mount Pony: Culpeper, Virginia. For nearly three decades, the Federal Reserve Board operated a 139,800-square-foot (13,001 square-meter) radiation hardened facility inside Mount Pony, just east of Culpeper, Virginia. Dedicated on December 10, 1969, the 400-foot-long (122-meter) bunker is built of steel-reinforced concrete 1 foot (0.3 meter) thick. Lead-lined shutters can be dropped to shield the windows of the semirecessed facility, which is covered by 2 to 4 feet (0.6 to 1.2 meters) of dirt and surrounded by barbed-wire fences and a guard post. The seven computers at the facility, operated by the Federal Reserve Bank of Richmond, were the central node for the transfer of all American electronic funds.

Until July 1992 the bunker, about 70 miles (113 kilometers) southwest of Washington, D.C., also served as a facility for the continuity of government. With a peacetime staff of 100, the site was designed to support an emergency staff of 540 for thirty days, but only 200 beds were provided in the men's and women's dormitories, which would be shared on a "hot-bunk" basis by the staff, working around the clock. A pre-planned menu of freeze-dried foods for the first thirty days of occupation was stored on site; private wells would provide uncontaminated water following an attack. Other noteworthy features of the facility were a cold storage area for maintaining bodies that could not be promptly buried (owing to high radiation levels), an incinerator, indoor pistol range, and a helicopter landing pad. Until 1988 Mount Pony stored several billion dollars worth of currency, including a large number of $2 bills in its 23,500-square-foot (2,186-square-meter) vault, shrink-wrapped and stacked on pallets 9 feet (2.7 meters) high. This money was to be used "to replenish currency supplies east of the Mississippi."[10] In November 1997 Congress authorized the transfer of the facility from the Federal Reserve to the Library of Congress, which, using funds from a private foundation, will purchase and upgrade the site to house its extensive motion picture, television, and recorded sound collections.[11]

---

8. Ted Gup, "Doomsday Hideaway," *Time,* December 9, 1991, pp. 26–29.
9. Gup, "The Doomsday Blueprints," pp. 32–39.
10. Telephone conversation, Stephen I. Schwartz, with G. R. Schaar, vice president, Federal Reserve Bank of Richmond, December 31, 1997. After 1988, this money was dispersed to various Federal Reserve banks and passed into general circulation. Gold was also stored at the site for a time. Edward Zuckerman, *The Day after World War III* (New York: Viking Press, 1984), pp. 287–88; Gup, "The Doomsday Blueprints," p. 38; David C. Morrison, "And Not a Single Bang for Their Bucks," *National Journal,* August 13, 1994, pp. 1924–25.
11. Richard Tapscott, "In Virginia, a Fortress for a Film Collection," *Washington Post,* November 16, 1997, p. B3.

Box 3-3
(continued)

The Greenbrier (Casper): White Sulphur Springs, West Virginia. From 1962 until its decommissioning on July 31, 1995, this CoG facility, code-named Casper (later Greek Island), was to house the U.S. Congress. It is located on the grounds of the prestigious Greenbrier resort.[12] The 112,000-square-foot (10,416-meter) bunker is 64 feet (19.5 meters) beneath the West Virginia wing of the hotel and includes a complete medical clinic, a dining room (with wooden frames for false windows with country scenes painted on them), a television studio (to broadcast to the surviving citizenry), communications and cryptographic equipment, decontamination showers, and a "pathological waste incinerator" (otherwise known as a crematorium). Until 1992, the small staff maintaining the site—under the guise of a television repair company—quietly tracked all prescription medication for each member of Congress and kept fresh supplies on hand in the event the facility was called into action.[13]

Construction of the site—which required 50,000 tons of concrete—began in 1959 and took two and a half years to complete. The steel-reinforced concrete walls of the bunker, which is 20 feet (6.1 meters) below ground, are 2 feet (0.6 meter) thick. The facility includes separate chambers for the House of Representatives and the Senate, as well as a larger room for joint sessions. These are located in the "Exhibit Hall" of the West Virginia Wing, which includes vehicular and pedestrian entrances that can be quickly sealed by 20-ton blast doors. The site was designed to house about 1,000 people for two months, although plans called for commandeering the entire resort (capacity: 6,500 persons) in the event of an emergency. While the cost of maintaining the facility for more than thirty years is unknown, construction costs from 1959 to 1962 totaled some $86 million.[14]

12. Following the removal by the government of certain classified equipment, the Greenbrier's owner, the CSX Corporation, began offering tours of the bunker in April 1996.

13. Jim Stewart, report on the CBS Evening News, December 17, 1995.

14. Ted Gup, "The Ultimate Congressional Hideaway," *Washington Post Magazine,* May 31, 1992, pp. 10–15, 24–27; Tom Curley, "Inside Look at Cold War Secret," *USA Today,* November 7, 1995, p. 10A. (Construction costs of $14 million then-year dollars cited in this article were confirmed by Ted J. Kleisner, president and managing director of the Greenbrier, e-mail communication, July 31, 1997.)

not the least of which was the threat that a few nuclear weapons detonated at high altitude above the United States would generate an electromagnetic pulse (EMP) capable of burning out electronic circuits in command, control, and communications systems—top secret assessments concluded at the time that the United States might not be able to retaliate at all.

Strategic communications networks were also very vulnerable. A prominent example was (and is) the handful (nine) of very low frequency radio stations. These stations, at U.S. and overseas coastal locations, provided the primary link to ballistic missile submarines.[26] By

26. VLF transmitter/receiver sites are located in Northwest Cape, Australia; Yosami, Japan; Rugby and Anthorn, United Kingdom, Wahiawa, Hawaii; Annapolis, Maryland; Jim Creek, Washington; and Cutler, Maine. See William M.

their very nature, these facilities, with their extremely tall antenna complexes, were far more vulnerable than the nuclear forces they served. The navy sought to remedy this by building a survivable extremely low frequency (ELF) radio link, burying antennas in a grid encompassing 2,000 square miles (5,180 square kilometers) in particularly insulating parts of the earth's crust, to transmit retaliatory orders to submerged submarines.[27] But this program, designated Sanguine ELF, encountered strong opposition from citizens who feared that it would make the area a prime target of nuclear attack and that the radio emissions would pose health hazards. In any case, it proved too expensive and vulnerable to modern Soviet weapons and was eventually deployed in a scaled-down, aboveground version with 56 miles (90 kilometers) of cable suspended from telephone poles in an F-shaped pattern near K. I. Sawyer Air Force Base south of Marquette, Michigan, and 28 miles (45 kilometers) suspended at Clam Lake, Wisconsin. ELF became fully operational in October 1989. According to the FYDP historical database, its total cost through 1995 was $544 million.[28]

Spending on nuclear-related strategic command posts and systems totaled some $25 billion, of which more than $18 billion was spent from 1962 through 1995. Of the total amount, $858 million went to NECPA; $1 billion to the ANMCC at Raven Rock; $2.6 billion to the National Emergency Airborne Command Post; $6.7 billion to PACCS; $1.9 billion to Airborne Command Posts for the commanders-in-chief of the Pacific, Atlantic, and European Commands; $1.7 billion to the Minimum Essential Emergency Communications Network (MEECN) and the Ground Wave Emergency Network (which would be used to transmit SIOP messages to deployed nuclear forces); and $7.3 billion to the Worldwide Military Command and Control System (WWMCCS).[29]

Arkin and Richard W. Fieldhouse, *Nuclear Battlefields: Global Links in the Arms Race* (Cambridge, Mass.: Ballinger, 1985), p. 159 (n. 19).

27. Russia is believed to be working on a similar system in conjunction with its underground command post under construction in the Ural mountains. See Blair, *Global Zero Alert for Nuclear Forces,* p. 65.

28. Following construction of the ELF array, the navy—having survived years of determined local opposition to ELF—encountered another threat in the form of the pileated woodpecker, crow-size birds that peck "melon size" holes in some of the 1,492 wooden telephone poles supporting the antenna in Michigan. Michigan law prevents the navy from using repellant sprays or pesticides to deter the birds, so navy personnel routinely inspect and replace the poles as necessary. See Bruce Borchedt, "Woodpeckers Tapping U.S. Submarine Radio Network," *Chicago Tribune,* June 1, 1989, p. 4. According to one source, the two antennas together use $30,000 to $40,000 worth of electricity each month. See Doris Hajewski, "Submarine Technology Is No Fiction," *Milwaukee Journal,* March 12, 1995, p. B-3.

29. Because the WWMCCS supported both nuclear and conventional forces, only half of this figure—$3.6 billion—is included in the total above. In September 1996, DOD replaced the twenty-six-year-old WWMCCS with the Global Command and Control System (GCCS), a less expensive, more capable, easier-to-operate system. See Bryan Bender, "Military's New Global Command System Ready for Prime Time," *Defense Daily,* July 1, 1996, p. 6; George I. Seffers, "Pentagon: GCCS Saves $220 Million Since 1992," *Defense News,* June 16–22, 1997, p. 32. WWMCCS never operated as anticipated, in no small measure because the Honeywell computers purchased by the DOD in 1970 (apparently because they were thought to be the least expensive option) were never designed to handle large amounts of traffic in a real-time, interactive environment. Hence extensive and costly postinstallation modifications became necessary. Even then it never met command and control requirements yet was "very expensive to maintain, with no capacity for growth. . . . Some of the maintenance costs associated with [it] were frankly outrageous." See U.S. *Failures of the North American Aerospace Defense Command's (NORAD) Attack Warn-*

Launch on Warning

An enticing alternative to riding out a Soviet attack before retaliating was to launch the strategic forces after detecting the incoming Soviet missiles, but before those missiles arrived at their targets. Ballistic Missile Early Warning System (BMEWS) radars deployed in the early 1960s in Clear, Alaska, Thule, Greenland, and Fylingdales Moor, England, supported this option, though its feasibility was doubtful.[30] The three BMEWS radars covered all the attack corridors for Soviet ICBMs but provided only about fifteen minutes' advance warning before impact in America. In this brief period, a sequence of steps were required in order to launch on warning: the radars had to report the attack to NORAD in Cheyenne Mountain, Colorado; NORAD had to notify and brief the president and others; the national command authorities had to reach a decision; the Pentagon war room (or alternate war room) had to transmit the authorizing codes to the strategic forces; and the individual weapons commanders had to fire their weapons. Under the best of circumstances, these steps would have taken longer than fifteen minutes (unless retaliation was authorized by rote).

Over-the-horizon forward-scatter radars, with transmitter and receiver stations in Europe and Japan, were deployed in the 1960s to help remedy this shortcoming. In theory, these radars could detect the passage of ballistic missiles through the ionosphere above the Earth's atmosphere (the exhaust plumes of the missiles deplete the charged particles in the ionosphere, thereby hindering the passage of the forward-scatter radar beams). In practice the ionosphere, and the radars, proved too unpredictable and unreliable to render this scheme a dependable means of warning of missile attack. The Soviet Union experimented with similar schemes beginning in the late 1970s, and is not thought to have achieved more promising results.[31]

With the advent of early warning satellites, the United States gained an additional ten or fifteen minutes of warning against Soviet ICBM attack. Following the abortive development of the Missile Defense Alarm System (MIDAS) in the 1960s, Defense Support Program (DSP) satellites were launched beginning in 1971, carrying infrared sensors for detecting the hot exhaust plume of Soviet missiles during the early boost phase of flight. By the early 1970s the United States had "parked"

ing System, Hearings before a Subcommittee of the House Committee on Government Operations, 97 Cong. 1 sess. (GPO, 1981), esp. pp. 11–94; Peter Pringle and William Arkin, *SIOP* (London: Sphere Books, 1983), pp. 93–115; Daniel Ford, *The Button: The Pentagon's Strategic Command and Control System* (New York: Simon & Schuster, 1985), pp. 175–76, 188–90.

30. The November 1957 report by the Gaither Committee (see chapter 4) strongly endorsed a crash program of deploying such radars, "far in the north, possibly at Thule and Fairbanks."

31. V. Abramov, "Money for Defense: Four Monologues on the Secrets of 'Closed' Science," *Sovetskaya Rossiya* (August 5, 1990), p. 4, translated in Foreign Broadcast Information Service, *ABM Designer Sees 'Squandering' of Resources,* FBIS-SOV-90-151 (August 6, 1990), p. 1.

three of them in a geosynchronous orbit to continuously monitor missile fields in the Soviet Union, as well as potential SLBM launch areas.[32] Warning reports could be flashed quickly to the Pentagon and other nuclear command posts without stopping at NORAD headquarters.[33] This new warning capability significantly increased the feasibility of launch on warning, and the United States came to rely heavily on this option.

As of February 1997, eighteen DSP satellites had been launched, and the DSP constellation had been expanded to a total of five satellites (three primary operational units, along with two backups maintained on operational status).[34] On August 8, 1989, the Space Shuttle orbiter *Columbia,* on flight STS-28, deployed the first of a new generation of CIA measurement and signature intelligence sensors, which are carried aboard intelligence data relay satellites in geosynchronous and elliptical orbit under the HERITAGE program. As of early 1996, a total of two HERITAGE sensors were operating on satellites in elliptical orbit, and one in geosynchronous orbit. Although intended primarily for technical intelligence collection, these sophisticated "staring array" sensors also provide tactical warning of missile launches to a variety of military users.

Launch on warning was a dangerous option from the standpoint of safety, and its feasibility was questionable in the event of a Soviet attack spearheaded by submarines patrolling off the American coasts. Although DSP satellites (augmented in the 1980s by PAVE PAWS ground radars on each U.S. coast, which replaced the far less sophisticated FSS-7 radars that had performed this duty since the 1960s)[35] con-

32. DSP satellites are very sensitive. They have, for example, detected oil pipeline fires and the explosion of TWA Flight 800 on July 17, 1996. "DSP Satellites Provide No Clues to Explosion," *Space News,* March 17–23, 1997, p. 2; Benjamin Weisner, "In Graphic Simulation, F.B.I. Tries to Show Jet's Fiery End," *New York Times,* November 19, 1997, p. A1.

33. NORAD received the DSP (and BMEWS and PAVE PAWS radar) reports simultaneously, and the Pentagon, other command posts, and the president relied heavily on NORAD's assessment of the credibility of the reports. See Blair, *The Logic of Accidental Nuclear War,* pp. 185–91. During the Gulf War, the DOD gave Israel a real-time link to DSP data to allow that country to better prepare against missile attacks from Iraq. The link remains operational today. See Barton Gellman, "Israel Wants Warning of U.S. Attack on Iraq," *Washington Post,* February 2, 1998, p. A13.

34. Jeffrey T. Richelson, *The U.S. Intelligence Community,* 3d ed. (Boulder, Colo.: Westview Press, 1995), pp. 224–25; Jeffrey T. Richelson, "Scientists in Black," *Scientific American,* February 1998, p. 49.

35. PAVE PAWS is frequently expanded as precision acquisition of vehicle entry phased-array warning system. However, the PAVE prefix is a generic term used for Air Force Systems Command programs. It appears that this expansion was retroactively applied to the acronym, as none of the dozens of other PAVE programs have either expansions or even suffix acronyms that are related to the actual program content. PAVE PAWS are located at Beale Air Force Base, Marysville, California, and Cape Cod Air Station, Buzzards Bay, Massachusetts (in the mid-1980s, two additional radars were built near Goodfellow Air Force Base, San Antonio, Texas, and at Robins Air Force Base, Georgia. The radar at Robins was situated 2.5 miles (4 kilometers) from the end of a runway at the base. In 1989 the air force acknowledged that it had turned off the radar an average of fourteen times each month since November 1987, out of concern that the powerful radar emissions could trigger external electromagnetic explosives (used to jettison fuel tanks or fire air-to-air missiles) aboard aircraft landing at the base. This radar and the one near Goodfellow were shut down in September and June 1995, respectively). See Robert Lee Hotz, "Nunn Asks Air Force to Report on Radar System's Risks," *Atlanta Constitution,* January 6, 1989, p. 11; David Pace, "Moving $90 Million Radar from Robins Not 'Viable Option,'' A.F. Official Says," *Warner Robins Sunday Sun* (Georgia), February 12, 1989, p. 1.

tinuously monitored the ocean areas from which Soviet submarine missiles might have been fired, the flight time of these missiles was substantially shorter than ICBMs (thirteen to fourteen minutes compared with twenty-five to thirty for ICBMs). Launch on warning was thus no panacea for the problem of command vulnerability. Under the best of conditions, a president would have had only three to four minutes to get briefed and reach a retaliatory decision before Washington disintegrated. The danger of inadvertent war caused by false warning was as great as the risk that retaliation could not be authorized in time during an actual attack.

In all, upward of $35 billion has been spent on systems to warn of ballistic missile attack and to detect nuclear detonations. From 1962 through 1995 spending totaled $30 billion: more than $18 billion was spent on the DSP satellites, more than $6 billion on the BMEWS radar stations (with perhaps an additional $1 billion spent on BMEWS in prior years), and $1.6 billion on PAVE PAWS and other SLBM early warning radars.[36] Another $4 billion was spent on nuclear explosion detection, including $200 million for the Bomb Alarm System—an early network of autonomous ground-based sensors designed primarily to detect nuclear detonations by sensing their initial thermal flash and reporting that information to various command posts (see box 3-3)—and at least $760 million on the space-based nuclear detection (NUDET) system, which consists of multiple sensors placed aboard all twenty-four NAVSTAR (navigation satellite tracking and ranging) global positioning satellites (and other satellites, including DSP) capable of detecting the size and location of nuclear detonations anywhere in the world within several dozen meters and transmitting data in real-time to nuclear commanders in ground or airborne command posts.[37]

36. In the mid-to-late 1980s, the BMEWS radars in Greenland and England were upgraded, their aging mechanical radar dishes replaced with electronic phased-array platforms. This modernization program violated the Antiballistic Missile Treaty of 1972, which forbids the deployment of such radars outside U.S. (and Russian) territory. See Stephen I. Schwartz, *The ABM Treaty: Problems in Compliance* (University of California at Santa Cruz, Adlai E. Stevenson Program on Nuclear Policy, 1987); Gloria Duffy, *Compliance and the Future of Arms Control* (Palo Alto, Calif.: Stanford University, Center for International Security and Arms Control, 1988), pp. 93–98; Michael R. Gordon, "U.S. Presses Plans to Upgrade Radar Despite Concerns," *New York Times*, December 18, 1986 p. 1; David C. Morrison, "Radar Diplomacy," *National Journal*, vol. 19 (January 3, 1987), pp. 17–21; Peter Zimmerman, "The Thule, Fylingdales, and Krasnoyarsk Radars: Innocents Abroad?" *Arms Control Today*, vol. 17 (March 1987), pp. 9–11.

37. NAVSTAR was developed in the 1970s and deployed in the 1980s to provide U.S. and allied military forces with precise, continuous, all-weather, three-dimensional navigation and time reference data on land, sea, and in the air. NAVSTAR was particularly important for nuclear forces (especially submarines) because it allowed them to execute more precise attacks on Soviet nuclear forces and military installations, thus supporting the Reagan administration's plans for prolonged nuclear conflict. While the military encrypts the most accurate signals (said to be accurate within about 66 feet [20 meters]), civilian users can also receive NAVSTAR data with special receivers, pinpointing their location within about 328 feet (100 meters). On April 20, 1997, however, the normally encrypted military signals were openly broadcast for about nineteen hours, apparently to aid searchers looking for a missing A-10 aircraft that had crashed in mountainous terrain in Colorado (a shortage of equipment forces the military to use a number of the less accurate civilian receivers). During that period, civilian users found that NAVSTAR was providing data accurate to within 6.5 feet (2 meters). See Vincent Kiernan, "Is GPS Better than the Pentagon Lets On?" *New Scientist*, May 17, 1997, p. 5.

With these devices, the United States prepared to fight a protracted nuclear war through instant analysis of attacks on U.S. forces and the results of U.S. attacks on enemy forces.[38] These totals exclude spending for treaty verification purposes (for example, by the National Reconnaissance Office, NRO) and classified spending on space systems.

One important program thus excluded is Project VELA, created to help verify compliance with the Partial Test Ban Treaty of 1963 (and, subsequently, the Threshold Test Ban Treaty of 1974) by detecting nuclear explosions in the atmosphere and in space (such detection data would also have obvious military intelligence value).[39] VELA was developed by the Defense Advanced Projects Research Agency (DARPA) and consisted of three major programs. VELA Hotel used pairs of satellites to detect nuclear explosions in space or on the earth's surface, VELA Uniform used seismic and other equipment to detect underground and underwater explosions, and VELA Sierra used earth-based equipment to detect explosions in the atmosphere or in space.

VELA Hotel was managed by the Air Force Space Division of the Air Force Systems Command. A total of 12 satellites were placed in circular 60,000 mile (96,541 kilometer) orbits between October 1960 and April 1970. The program was phased out when the last satellite ceased operation on September 27, 1984 (this mission was handed off to the NUDET sensors). The Uniform and Sierra programs were overseen by the Air Force Technical Applications Center (AFTAC, discussed later in this chapter). Building on AFTAC's existing test detection network, VELA Uniform became operational in October 1960, with ten seismometers and 21 seismographs at the Wichita Mountain Seismological Observatory near Lawton, Oklahoma. Between October 1963 and July 1971, the Atomic Energy Commission conducted seven nuclear tests (four in Nevada, two in Mississippi, and one in Alaska) to assess and improve the system's detection capabilities.[40] Little has been published

38. In late 1996 General Eugene Habiger, commander in chief of STRATCOM, expressed concern that without $22 million in funding in fiscal 1998 the high accuracy NUDET mission will "virtually" disappear (the Air Force is funding work on sensors with a resolution of 0.6–6 miles [1–10 kilometers], but STRATCOM's requirements are more precise). Some officials believe that high-accuracy sensors can help with the threat of "loose nukes" in countries of the former Soviet Union and can provide critical data to keep crises from escalating. They would also be useful in verifying compliance with the Comprehensive Test Ban Treaty. STRATCOM officials apparently consider the maintenance of such precise sensor capabilities a prerequisite to further strategic nuclear force reductions. See Elaine M. Grossman, "USSTRACOM Sounds Alarm on Obsolete Nuclear Blast Detection Systems," *Inside the Pentagon,* February 20, 1997, p. 1; William B. Scott, Funding Fracas Imperils 'Nudet' Sensor," *Aviation Week & Space Technology,* January 5, 1998, pp. 29–30.

39. William E. Burrows, *Deep Black: Space Espionage and National Security* (New York: Random House, 1986), pp. 183–84; William M. Arkin, Joshua M. Handler, Julia A. Morrissey, and Jacquelyn M. Walsh, *Encyclopedia of the U.S. Military* (Philadelphia: Harper & Row, 1990), pp. 726–27.

40. Robert S. Norris and Thomas B. Cochran, *United States Nuclear Tests, July 1945 to 31 December 1992,* NWD-94-1 (Natural Resources Defense Council, February 1, 1994), pp. 36-43, 60. For more on AFTAC, see a series of articles by William B. Scott in *Aviation Week & Space Technology,* November 3, 1997: "USAF Nuclear Detectives Assume New Roles," (pp. 50–53); "Sampling Missions Unveiled Nuclear Weapon

about VELA Sierra. As an intelligence-related program subsumed in part under AFTAC, VELA's costs have not been publicly reported but they are included in this chapter's overall estimate of nuclear weapons-related intelligence expenditures. The cost of the AEC's VELA Uniform nuclear tests is counted in chapter 1.

An infusion of funds in the 1970s to buttress the nuclear command system had little effect, and the issue of command vulnerability resurfaced with a vengeance during the Carter administration. Another raft of top secret studies performed during the late 1970s validated the earlier grim assessments. The United States could not confidently ride out a sudden Soviet strike aimed at the command and communications network.[41] The president and his successors (stipulated by the Constitution and the Presidential Succession Act of 1947)[42] had not been afforded the level of protection necessary to ensure their survival, and key nodes in the network serving the subordinate nuclear commanders remained acutely vulnerable to a wide range of nuclear effects and to jamming. By this time, U.S. nuclear strategy depended heavily on prompt launch on warning, but even this operational shortcut, fraught with risk of nuclear inadvertence, did not guarantee retaliation.

The possibility that a sudden attack on the command system could neutralize the strategic retaliatory forces became even more salient as a result of safeguards instituted beginning in the late 1960s and continuing into the mid-1970s. Locking devices known as permissive action links had been installed on bomber and ICBM forces and physically prevented their use; the individual crews needed unlocking codes from a higher authority in order to launch. But the vulnerability of higher authorities cast doubt on the ability to disseminate the codes in wartime. Previously, it was doubted whether codes *authorizing* launch could be disseminated to the ICBM, bomber, and submarine crews; now the problem became compounded by a doubt that codes *enabling* launch could be distributed to the ICBM and bomber crews. (Similar locks on ballistic missile submarines were not installed until 1997 because of navy opposition and the fear that they would jeopardize the ability of submarine crews to carry out authorized launches.)[43] In

Secrets," (pp. 54–57); "Debris Collection Reverts to Ground Sites," (pp. 57–59).

41. Wainstein, *Evolution of U.S. Strategic Command and Control and Warning;* Blair, *The Logic of Accidental Nuclear War,* p. 186.

42. The act (now codified and amended at 3 U.S.C. § 19) stipulates that after the (1) vice president, the following officials, in sequence, are the designated successors to the president: (2) speaker of the House (3) president pro tempore of the Senate (4) secretary of state (5) secretary of the treasury (6) secretary of defense (7) attorney general (8) secretary of the interior (9) secretary of agriculture (10) secretary of commerce (11) secretary of labor (12) secretary of health and human services (13) secretary of housing and urban development (14) secretary of transportation (15) secretary of energy (16) secretary of education, and (17) secretary of veterans affairs.

43. PALs were originally produced for nuclear weapons allocated to NATO after members of the Joint Committee on Atomic Energy toured U.S. installations in Europe in late 1960 and came away very concerned about the legality of "custody" arrangements of short-range weapons deployed

response, the Carter administration further decentralized launch authority and widely distributed the enabling codes (see box 3-4).[44] Episodes like this illustrate a persistent dilemma facing nuclear planners: how to minimize the risk that a decapitating strike would neutralize the strategic retaliatory forces, while ensuring that the risk of unauthorized use was minimal. Efforts to reach a prudent balance between these competing priorities pervade the nuclear era.

Preparing to Fight a Nuclear War

Carter's efforts notwithstanding, the doubts persisted. The Reagan administration therefore gave nuclear command and control top priority in its early 1980s program of strategic modernization. While continuing the earlier practice of predelegating nuclear authority to guard against decapitation of the top civilian leadership, in 1982 it initiated a super-secret program called project 908, also known as the National Program Office or, more colloquially, as "continuity of government" (CoG). It was an amalgam of more than twenty highly classified programs designed to protect senior government officials and keep the government functioning during and after a nuclear war.[45] Strategic nuclear planners were directed to develop plans to fight a protracted nuclear war in which both strategic forces and their supporting command systems had to be able to endure for as long as six months. The war-fighting policy depended heavily on the endurance of ballistic missile submarines and a new command system built not around aircraft,

there. In particular, the handling of weapons on quick-reaction alert aircraft "raised grave questions," as U.S. nuclear weapons were mated to planes on runway alert, planes flown by non-U.S. pilots (for further details on the JCAE's role in promoting PALs, see box 9-2). On July 5, 1962, President Kennedy asked Congress for $23.3 million ($137 million in 1996 dollars) to allow the AEC to install PALs on U.S. nuclear weapons (initially just for weapons in Europe). Early PALs were simple mechanical locks. Later versions incorporate electronic switches requiring the entry of multiple digits before a weapon can be detonated. Repeated entry of an incorrect code renders the weapon unusable, whereupon it must be returned to an assembly facility for repairs. The most advanced PAL available in 1973 was reported to cost $110,000 apiece. A slightly less capable model (Category D) was priced at about $91,000 in the late 1970s to early 1980s. A Category F PAL (currently the most advanced) for the W84 warhead for the ground-launched cruise missile cost $106,000 a copy in 1985. See Jack Raymond, "U.S. to Install Locks on Atom Weapons as Extra Safeguard," *New York Times,* July 6, 1962, p. 1; *Military Applications of Nuclear Technology,* Hearings before the Subcommittee on Military Applications of the Joint Committee on Atomic Energy, 93 Cong. 1 sess. (GPO, 1973), pt. 1, pp. 47–48; Thomas B. Cochran, William M. Arkin, and Milton M. Hoenig, *Nuclear Weapons Databook,* vol. 1: *U.S. Nuclear Forces and Capabilities* (Cambridge, Mass.: Ballinger, 1984), p. 30; Ashton B. Carter, John B. Steinbruner, and Charles A. Zraket, eds., *Managing Nuclear Operations* (Brookings, 1987), pp. 46–51, 167–68; Chuck Hanson, *The Sword of Armageddon,* vol. 8 (Sunnyvale, Calif.: Chuckelea Publications, 1995), pp. 38–44.

44. In a 1983 book, Carter's secretary of defense, Harold Brown, wrote that "a decapitating attack should have the effect of making the response an all-out, unrestrained one." Quoted in Blair, *The Logic of Accidental Nuclear War,* pp. 49–50.

45. Emerson, "America's Doomsday Project." As an aide on the National Security Council, Lieutenant Colonel Oliver North helped establish CoG plans and programs, a fact he mentioned in his 1987 congressional testimony on the Iran-Contra scandal and his book *Under Fire: An American Story* (New York: HarperCollins, 1991). See David C. Morrison, "Nuking the Constitution," *National Journal,* December 7, 1991, p. 2993; "Doomsday Government," Cable News Network, November 17, 1991.

Box 3-4

The Football

The president's constant companion is a military aide carrying a briefcase nicknamed the "Football," which contains the *SIOP Decision Handbook.*[1] The *Handbook* explains—with the aid of cartoon-like drawings—the nuclear war plan and the available strike options. Typically, each president has received a short briefing on the briefcase and its contents, although Bill Gulley, former director of the White House Military Office and therefore custodian of the "Football" in the Johnson, Nixon, Ford, and Carter administrations, remarked in 1980 that no president has ever had a subsequent briefing even though the *Handbook* is regularly revised.[2]

Historically, this handbook, prepared by the JCS, has been provided to the president, vice president, secretary of defense, JCS, and the nuclear commanders in chief. This list thus excludes the vast majority of the president's legal successors (see footnote 42 in the text), while including military commanders who historically have been delegated the authority to launch the strategic forces in retaliation to an attack that decapitates the top political leadership.[3]

Contrary to popular belief, the "Football" does not contain the proverbial "go-code" or the unlock codes needed by the launch crews to fire their ground, sea, and airborne weapons. Those authorizing and enabling codes, created and maintained by the NSA, always remain in military custody at the national military command posts in the Pentagon and alternate sites around the country.

The president carries special codes to positively identify himself to the key nuclear commanders who might be ordered to launch a nuclear strike. But the military does not need these codes to launch the strike, although it may not accept an order from a president or successor who fails to "authenticate" correctly. Historically, few of the president's legal successors were provided the identification codes, and hence their nuclear authority might have been difficult to establish. Some presidents carried these codes in a pocket or wallet, and they have been misplaced on occasion, such as after the attempted assassination of President Ronald Reagan in 1981.[4] Although maintaining the "Football" obviously requires a great deal of communications, security, and cryptographic support, the White House Military Office denied a request for data on the overall costs of the effort citing, in part, an inability to segregate the emergency action duties of the president's military aides from their other duties and functions.[5]

1. The briefcase earned its nickname because the first SIOP was code-named "Dropkick."

2. Bill Gulley with Mary Ellen Reese, *Breaking Cover,* pp. 188–90.

3. Wainstein, *Evolution of U.S. Strategic Command and Control and Warning,* p. 358; Blair, *The Logic of Accidental Nuclear War,* pp. 46–52.

4. Douglas Waller, "Fumbling the Football: Now It Can Be Told," *Newsweek,* October 7, 1991, p. 26.

5. Letter, Stephen I. Schwartz to Alan Sullivan, Director, White House Military Office, April 4, 1996, and response from Alan P. Sullivan to Stephen I. Schwartz, April 11, 1996.

but around mobile trailer command posts, covertly established bunkers, and other novel means of command and communications.

A new satellite program called Military Strategic and Tactical Relay (MILSTAR)—its unclassified elements cost more than $15 billion from 1983 to 1996—became the centerpiece of the communications network planned for providing robust and enduring connectivity to support protracted nuclear operations. The proposed MILSTAR program envisioned twenty satellites costing $42 billion (in then-year dollars); this was later reduced by Congress to six satellites costing $17 billion (in then-year dollars). One of its many advanced features is an ability to operate autonomously for long periods (satellite station-keeping normally requires regular ground support).[46] MILSTAR satellites were also originally designed to evade attack by moving from a 23,300-mile (37,490-kilometer) orbit to one of 110,000 miles (176,991 kilometers).

In 1990 the Senate Armed Services Committee, troubled by the program's projected $35 billion to $40 billion price tag for an eight-satellite system, voted to terminate it. The committee stated unequivocally that the DOD had not "justified the extraordinary expense of this overdesigned system." General Colin Powell, then chairman of the JCS, defended MILSTAR as "absolutely critical," pointing out that with the winding down of the cold war just 30 percent of the system's communications capacity would be used by strategic nuclear forces. A House-Senate conference on the defense bill subsequently decided to keep the program but trimmed it to six satellites in orbit and ordered the removal of certain classified (and costly) capabilities no longer required in light of the system's reorientation. By 1994 the air force, saddled with most of the expense, sought to cancel MILSTAR, only to be opposed by the navy and army, which found the system's capabilities useful for its war-fighting operations. In the end, four of the six satellites were modified to enhance their capability to support army and navy tactical applications.[47]

The Reagan administration also started building the Ground-Wave Emergency Network (GWEN), linking nuclear command posts and forces by means of several hundred low-frequency radio towers scattered across the United States, for the most part away from densely populated areas (on the theory that the Soviet Union was unlikely to

46. The principal ground station for reconnaissance satellites, known as the "Blue Cube" for the distinctive color of its windowless control building, is located at Onizuka Air Station in Sunnyvale, California. For more than two decades, this facility (which used to maintain all air force satellites as well) had no backup, despite being located within 18 miles (29 kilometers) of three major earthquake faults and adjacent to an interstate highway. Air force communication, early warning, and weather satellites are now controlled from Falcon Air Force Base in Colorado Springs Colorado, which also provides some redundant capabilities to Onizuka.

47. Tim Weiner, "Questions Growing on New Satellites for the Pentagon," *New York Times*, January 17, 1994, p. A1; David C. Morrison, "Here's One Costly Relic," *National Journal*, January 29, 1994, pp. 247–49; John Mintz, "Space Battle: Is Milstar a Millstone?" *Washington Post*, July 23, 1994, p. F1.

expend nuclear weapons attacking single, isolated targets). GWEN was designed by the air force to be immune to EMP effects from high-altitude detonations and to disseminate EAMs following an initial nuclear attack and during and after a protracted nuclear war, automatically bypassing damaged or destroyed sites to deliver its messages.[48]

A glaring fault in the air force's logic was that even if some or all of the 299-foot-high (91-meter) GWEN towers survived the initial and subsequent attacks, few if any of the facilities with which they communicated (such as SAC missile and bomber bases and fixed and airborne command posts) would. Because of its high costs and strong local and congressional opposition (including a federal court suit), the program was gradually scaled back from 400–500 towers in 1984 to just 58 in January 1994, in a further blow to the administration's nuclear war fighting strategy.[49] The total cost for GWEN for research, development, training, and evaluation (RDT&E) and procurement was about $500 million. Current annual operating costs are likely to run in the range of several million dollars and are included under the MEECN program. Owing to operational problems, STRATCOM plans to phase out its reliance on GWEN, turning instead to portable MILSTAR terminals to transmit time-urgent messages under nuclear war conditions.

The Reagan administration wanted to be certain not only that strategic forces could be unleashed in the immediate wake of a Soviet surprise attack but also that they would receive coherent direction for months after an initial exchange. That expectation was unrealistic, from both an operational and economic point of view. Despite a sizable investment, this ambitious and expensive policy never got off the ground. The cold war ended first, and subsequent administrations reversed course. The Bush administration lowered the alert status of a large segment of the strategic forces (all bombers and 450 older Minuteman II missiles, as well as the bulk of the tactical nuclear arsenal) and parts of the nuclear command system, including NEACP and Looking Glass.

The Clinton administration went further, canceling or mothballing major pieces of the highly classified CoG program after it had reportedly cost some $8 billion (in then-year dollars).[50] It nonetheless reaf-

48. Gary K. Reynolds, Congressional Research Service, Foreign Affairs and National Defense Division, "The Ground Wave Emergency Network (GWEN)," March 27, 1989.

49. William M. Arkin, "Preparing for World War IV," *Bulletin of the Atomic Scientists,* vol. 41 (May 1985), pp. 6–7; Michael R. Gordon, "Value of Radio Towers for Nuclear Orders Debated," *New York Times,* February 17, 1986, p. A10; David C. Morrison, "Fuses Are Short over Tall Towers," *National Journal,* vol. 18 (May 31, 1986), pp. 1324–26; Nancy Foster, "Citizens Jam Nuclear Radio Network," *Bulletin of the Atomic Scientists,* vol. 44 (November 1988), pp. 21–26; Robert S. Norris and William M. Arkin, "GWEN Will I See You Again?" *Bulletin of the Atomic Scientists,* vol. 50 (March/April 1994), p. 62.

50. Tim Weiner, "Pentagon Book for Doomsday Is to Be Closed," *New York Times,* April 18, 1994, p. A1. Earlier published reports indicated that despite these expenditures, the program was unable to get its state-of-the-art communications system to function properly, that security had been breached at some secret bunkers and supply depots—which contained large amounts of food, drugs, and chemicals—and that contracting irregularities may have resulted in millions of dollars of unjustified costs. See Emerson, "America's

firmed the basic nuclear strategy of previous administrations and retained significant parts of the arsenal. A review of U.S. nuclear posture, completed in September 1994, staked out no major departures from past targeting principles or alert requirements, proposed no alteration of the rapid reaction postures of the past, and preserved some parts of the nuclear war-fighting mission.[51] However, one noteworthy improvement in safeguards was endorsed: in 1997 the Trident submarine fleet was equipped with special safes containing a vital launch key that cannot be opened unless and until a combination unlocking code is received from a higher authority.

More than $60 billion was expended on strategic offense communications, and command and control systems. From 1962 through 1995 spending totaled more than $50 billion, including the nearly $8 billion for fleet ballistic missile control system communications and more than $8 billion for SAC/STRATCOM headquarters activities. An estimated $8.8 billion was spent on nuclear-related mapping, charting, and geodesy, out of a total of $35 billion (25 percent of the total), including $30 billion from 1962 through 1995, primarily for the Defense Mapping Agency (DMA) and its predecessors.[52]

Other space-based programs included nuclear-related satellite communications, which cost $6.8 billion out of a total $27 billion (again, 25 percent). Some $1.9 billion was expended on nuclear-related navigation systems, primarily the NAVSTAR GPS, out of a total $7.5 billion from 1962 through 1995. To this should be added the $13 billion spent on nuclear-related space support activities, out of close to $50 billion all told, including $46 billion during the 1962–95 period for activities such as launch vehicles and the satellite ground support system.

Intelligence Support for Nuclear War

Only a few of the demanding goals established for command, control, communications, and intelligence (C^3I) were ever achieved. The notable successes included the development of spy satellites, which identified

Doomsday Project"; and Tim Weiner, "Army Whistle-blower Takes a Fall in 'Doomsday' Project," *Philadelphia Inquirer*, December 16, 1990, p. 1.

51. R. Jeffrey Smith, "Clinton Decides to Retain Bush Nuclear Arms Policy," *Washington Post*, September 22, 1994, p. A1.

52. This work includes, for example, preparing digital maps for the Terrain Contour Matching (TERCOM) guidance computer in cruise missiles. On October 1, 1996, the National Imagery and Mapping Agency (NIMA) came into being, consolidating the Defense Mapping Agency, the Central Imagery Office, and the Defense Dissemination Office in their entirety and incorporating the mission and functions of the CIA's National Photographic Interpretation Center. In addition, NIMA includes the "imagery exploitation, dissemination and processing elements" of the Defense Intelligence Agency (DIA), National Reconnaissance Office (NRO) and Defense Airborne Reconnaissance Office (DARO)." NIMA will also provide timely combat support data to military commanders. See U.S. Department of Defense, "National Imagery and Mapping Agency Established," Press Release 563-96, October 1, 1996; Pat Cooper, "New U.S. Spy Agency Melds Mapping, Imaging Services," *Defense News*, October 14–20, 1996, p. 68.

all Soviet missile launch pads, bomber bases, and submarine pens, along with most other major military installations.

From the comfortable remove of the late 1990s it is almost impossible to appreciate the full import of the astonishing revolution wrought by these technical collection systems. After long decades of use, decisionmakers and (indirectly) the public have become accustomed to, or at least developed a not-unreasonable expectation of, what passes for effective omniscience in matters concerning the number and disposition of such major strategic fixtures. Within a few years of the advent of imagery intelligence satellites, classified intelligence assessments provided excruciatingly detailed accounts of the status of Soviet special weapons facilities, noting with monotonous regularity the smallest movement of trucks and test articles at missile launch sites. Only by reading these recently declassified intelligence assessments and their supporting documents can one even begin to sense the enormity of this achievement in dispelling the fog that had hitherto engulfed the military arts.

The satellite intelligence revolution is all that stands between these comprehensive accounts and the finest distillations of the American intelligence community in the 1950s, which in retrospect seem little more than considered speculations leavened with a few rumors and scraps of information of World War II vintage captured from the Germans. Just how vast a fortune was expended on these efforts is difficult to ascertain, but there is little doubt that during the cold war it represented an investment of inestimable value.

It was soon recognized that the intelligence provided by space systems required vast and specialized organization. The National Reconnaissance Office, formed in August 1960, gradually evolved as a vehicle for coordinating the burgeoning technological opportunities and reconciling the competing requirements and interests of the CIA and the military services. The task of intercepting and deciphering military messages using satellites, aircraft, or other means was assigned to the National Security Agency (NSA), which along with the associated military service components accounted for a budget and personnel roster that at its peak rivaled that of the NRO and the CIA combined. The CIA, created in 1947, took the intelligence data provided by all sources and, in coordination with other agencies in the intelligence community, produced national intelligence estimates (NIE) that projected deployments and budgets of the Soviet nuclear force. These estimates proved highly accurate for current Soviet strategic deployments, inconsistently prescient for future deployments (including frequent underestimation and overestimation), and quite inconclusive for Soviet deployments of tactical and theater nuclear arsenals.

The problem here was that the estimates were often biased as a result of domestic political influences and the insular nature of the intelligence community. That community has its own "political structure." It is a hierarchical organization whose members share a particular adversary image that analysts, perhaps unconsciously, tend to adopt as their own, especially when the image is surrounded by a great deal of ambiguity. Estimators in a lowly position in such an organization "may come to feel that their lives will be easier and their careers will prosper if they close their minds to those heretical notions that contradict images held by their superiors."[53]

At the same time, many politicians expected assessments to conform to their view of the Soviet threat, and the military services naturally valued estimates that helped justify their programs and budgets.[54] Hence Soviet military strength was frequently overestimated and conclusions about Soviet doctrine and strategy were skewed.[55] One prevalent judgment during the 1970s and 1980s, for example, was that the Soviets believed that they could fight and win a nuclear war. Intelligence estimates also underwent a tortuous bureaucratic review that

53. Lawrence Freedman, *U.S. Intelligence and the Soviet Strategic Threat,* 2d ed. (Princeton University Press, 1986), pp. 184–85.

54. The bomber and missile "gaps" of the 1950s and early 1960s are two of the more well-known examples of this phenomenon (for more on the bomber gap see chapter 4). Working in an atmosphere of uncertainty and alarmist projections, air force analysts seemed so thoroughly convinced that "no government with any sense would be doing anything other than building a large ICBM force that this had become an article of faith." Freedman, *U.S. Intelligence and the Soviet Strategic Threat,* pp. 68, 79. In 1976 a group of outside hardline nuclear analysts was invited by CIA director George Bush (over the objections of his top analysts) to review the data used to develop the national intelligence estimate and issue its own findings. The Team B report concluded that the CIA had seriously underestimated the Soviet threat and was used by conservatives throughout the 1970s and 1980s to support large increases in defense spending. See *Intelligence Community Experiment in Competitive Analysis: Soviet Strategic Objectives—An Alternative View,* Report of Team "B," December 1976 (formerly Top Secret, declassified [with deletions], Record Group 263, at the National Archives); Anne Hessing Cahn and John Prados, "Team B: The Trillion Dollar Experiment," *Bulletin of the Atomic Scientists,* vol. 49 (April 1993), pp. 22–31. More recently, a CIA finding that no country will be able to threaten the United States with ballistic missiles for at least fifteen years was criticized by advocates of ballistic missile defenses as deliberately downplaying the threat. As in 1976, the CIA invited a team of nongovernmental analysts—headed by former CIA director R. James Woolsey—to scrutinize its data and issue its own conclusions. Ultimately, a special independent panel headed by former Director of Central Intelligence Robert Gates (himself accused by a former CIA official of politicizing NIEs during the Reagan administration) concluded that, if anything, the original CIA assessment had failed to include the full range of material that would substantiate its conclusions, and that whatever politicization had taken place was the result of congressional pressures to bolster the case for missile defense deployments. See Independent Panel's Report on NIE 95-19 DCI National Intelligence Estimate: "Emerging Missile Threats to North America during the Next 15 Years, November 1995" (available on the World Wide Web at http://www.fas.org/spp/starwars/offdocs/nie 9519/html); Rowan Scarborough and Bill Gertz, "Missile-Threat Report 'Politicized,' GOP Says," *Washington Times,* January 30, 1996, p. A1; Bill Gertz, "Report on Missile Threat to U.S. Too Optimistic, Woolsey Charges," *Washington Times,* March 15, 1996, p. A10; Bill Gertz, "CIA Will Let Private Analysts Examine Missile Readiness," *Washington Times,* March 26, 1996, p. A4; Bill Gertz, "Intelligence Report Warns of Missile Launches against U.S." *Washington Times,* May 14, 1996, p. A3; "Do We Need a Missile Defense System?" (reprint of a November 1995 President's Summary of the National Intelligence Estimate) *Washington Times,* May 14, 1996, p. A15; Associated Press, "Woolsey Disputes Clinton Missile-Threat Assessment," *Washington Times,* May 31, 1996, p. A3; Melvin A. Goodman, "Ending the CIA's Cold War Legacy," *Foreign Policy,* no. 106 (Spring 1997), pp. 128–43.

55. A distinct but related problem was noted by AEC chairman David E. Lilienthal, who wrote in his diary on June 30, 1948: "The thing that rather chills one's blood is to observe what is nothing less than a lack of integrity in the way the intelligence agencies deal with the meager stuff they have. It is chiefly a matter of reasoning from our own American experience, guessing from that how much longer it will take Russia using our methods and based upon our own problems of achieving weapons. But when this is put in a report, the reader, e.g., Congressional committee, is given the impression, and deliberately, that behind the estimates lies specific knowledge, knowledge so important and delicate that its nature and sources cannot be disclosed or hinted at." See David E. Lilienthal, *The Journals of David E. Lilienthal,* vol. 2: *The Atomic Energy Years, 1945–1950* (Harper and Row, 1964), p. 376.

often stifled internal dissent, encouraged a consensus based on the lowest common denominator, and produced analysis of little practical value. Too often, even the most carefully crafted intelligence estimates did not meet the needs of policymakers and were ignored.

Aerial Reconnaissance

Military appreciation of the potential application of aeronautics to survey the field of battle dates back to the Civil War, when both the Union and the Confederacy used balloons for this purpose to good effect. By the opening days of the World War I airplanes were typically attached to Signal Corps units to serve as reconnaissance platforms. Eventually a means of aerial combat developed to deny this advantage to adversaries. The true potential of aerial reconnaissance was fully unveiled in World War II, when all aspects of military operations, from strategic bombardment to amphibious assault, were predicated on comprehensive imagery intelligence from high-flying aircraft outfitted with cameras. Then specially designed reconnaissance aircraft emerged, with supercharged engines and vast wingspans that enabled them to fly above the enemy's air defenses.

In view of these prenuclear successes, it was only natural that aerial reconnaissance should be the first resort in intelligence collection during the atomic age. Taking a page from history, Americans first sought to pierce the Iron Curtain with balloons.[56] In 1946 the U.S. Army Air Forces inaugurated Project MOGUL, a top secret effort to detect Soviet nuclear test explosions by monitoring sound changes in the tropopause, the zone between the troposphere and the stratosphere. The project used "trains" of high-altitude balloons more than 600 feet (183 meters) long, radar reflectors (to assist in tracking), and acoustic sensors to detect distant blasts. Numerous tests of the apparatus were conducted in New Mexico in 1946 and 1947. When one of the models crashed outside of Roswell, New Mexico, in June 1947 (and was discovered by a rancher a month later), the unusual materials and markings and the air force's curious cover story led some to believe that an alien craft had crashed.[57]

---

56. Curtis Peebles, *The Moby Dick Project* (Washington, D.C.: Smithsonian Institution Press, 1991); and Merton Davis and William Harris, "RAND's Role in the Evolution of Balloon and Satellite Observation Systems and Related U.S. Space Technology" (Santa Monica, Calif.: Rand, 1988).

57. A press release issued by local U.S. Army Air Forces officials stated that the debris was from a "flying disc" (at the time, this term did not connote a spaceship but merely an unidentified object, possibly of Soviet origin, and therefore of concern to the Army Air Forces. Because Project MOGUL was a highly compartmentalized endeavor—even its name was top secret—it was not unusual for anyone not part of the project to have no knowledge of it). Only hours later, higher authorities insisted this was in error and that the debris was merely components from a weather balloon, including a metallic radar reflector used to track it from the ground. Nevertheless, the "admission" was splashed across the front pages of the July 8 and July 9 editions of the *Roswell Daily Record* and received national and international attention. See U.S. Air Force, *The Roswell Report: Fact vs. Fiction in the New Mexico*

Growing speculation by local citizens and others (beginning in earnest in 1978 with an article in the tabloid *National Enquirer*), coupled with the air force's refusal (until 1994) to disclose anything substantive about the objects recovered can be credited with helping to spawn and perpetuate the belief that alien visitors had landed near Roswell and that the air force withheld this information for fifty years. It also serves as a valuable lesson in the unintended effects of pervasive, long-term government secrecy.[58] Although Project MOGUL was tested at Enewetak, during Operation Sandstone in April and May 1948 as part of the air force's overall test-detection program named Operation FITZWILLIAM, the program was canceled in 1950, owing to difficulties in operating the system (the balloons would frequently drift beyond the range of radio communication and were extremely difficult to hide from public view) and the availability of more reliable acoustic and radiological monitoring methods (the latter of which actually detected the first Soviet atomic test in August 1949).[59] No bud-

Desert (GPO, 1995); U.S. Air Force, *The Roswell Report: Case Closed* (GPO, 1997); Dave Thomas, "The Roswell Incident and Project Mogul," *Skeptical Inquirer*, vol. 19 (July/August 1995), pp. 15–18 (also available on the World Wide Web at http://www.csicop.org/si/9507/roswell.html); Kal K. Korff, "What *Really* Happened at Roswell," *Skeptical Inquirer*, vol. 21 (July/August 1997), pp. 24–31 (also available on the World Wide Web at http://www.csicop.org/si/9707/roswell.html); Leon Jaroff, "Did Aliens Really Land?" *Time*, June 23, 1997, pp. 68–71; Amy Harmon, "Flying Saucer Buffs to Mark Half Century of Hazy History," *New York Times* (Washington edition), June 14, 1997, p. A1.

58. Nor was Project MOGUL the only nuclear weapons–related program to be linked to UFOs. With the start of high-altitude test flights of the U-2 in 1955, "commercial pilots and air traffic controllers began reporting a large increase in UFO sightings." U-2s flew more than 40,000 feet (12,192 meters) higher than commercial aircraft at that time and were therefore quite unusual. With their silver surface (later painted black), they often looked like "fiery objects to observers below." Although air force investigators found many UFO sightings related to U-2 flights (at least half, by one estimate), this information was not released to the public in order to keep secret the U-2 program. Gerald K. Haines, "CIA's Role in the Study of UFOs, 1947–90," *Studies in Intelligence*, vol. 1, no. 1 (1997), pp. 67–84 (available on the World Wide Web at http://www.odci.gov/csi/studies/97unclas/ufo.html); William J. Broad, "C.I.A. Admits Government Lied about U.F.O. Sightings," *New York Times*, August 3, 1997, p. 12; Dana Priest, "Cold War UFO Coverup Shielded Spy Planes," *Washington Post*, August 5, 1997, p. A4.

59. These efforts commenced in April 1947, after Lewis Strauss, newly appointed to the AEC, discovered that no program existed to detect a Soviet atomic test, despite the obvious importance of such an event for U.S. military and foreign policy (an oversight explained in part by the belief of many senior military and civilian officials that the Soviet Union was years away from being able to develop an atomic bomb [see chapter 1, fn. 65]; in fact, in June 1949 the Joint Committee on Atomic Energy tried to terminate the still seminal program, arguing that the proposed $20 million expenditure [$175 million in 1996 dollars] "might be spent more wisely in other fields of research and development"). Accordingly, the air force was directed to lead the effort and began focusing on sonic, seismic, and radiological detection (flying specially equipped B-29 bombers through mushroom clouds to collect debris via paper filters for later analysis). The Naval Research Laboratory concentrated on radiological detection via fallout contained in rainwater. All three methods were tested during Operation Sandstone, but only the radiological approach worked well. Subsequently the air force requested $32 million ($280 million in 1996 dollars) to equip more bombers with filter paper scoops. Anomalous readings were then analyzed by Tracerlab, Inc., a private radiological company based in Boston and with a laboratory in Berkeley, California, at a cost of $643,000 a year ($5.6 million in 1996 dollars). The navy's program—dubbed Project Rainbarrel—requested only $80,000 ($700,000 in 1996 dollars) to establish a network of monitoring stations in Alaska, Hawaii, the Philippines, and Washington, D.C. Both programs apparently continued through the 1950s. For more information, see Charles Ziegler, "Waiting for Joe-1: Decisions Leading to the Detection of Russia's First Atomic Bomb Test," *Social Studies of Science*, vol. 18, no. 2 (1988), pp. 197–229; Herbert Friedman, Luther B. Lockhart, and Irving H. Blifford, "Detecting the Soviet Bomb: Joe-1 in a Rain Barrel," *Physics Today*, vol. 49, no. 11 (1996), pp. 38–41; William B. Scott, "USAF Nuclear Detectives Assume New Roles," *Aviation Week & Space Technology*, November 3, 1997, p. 52; Lester Machta, "Finding the Site of the First Soviet Nuclear Test in 1949," *Bulletin of the American Meteorological Society*, vol. 73 (November 1992), pp. 1797–1806.

get data are apparently available for Project MOGUL, but the air force officer who managed it told the *New York Times* in 1994 that, "Money was no object. We seemed to have an unlimited budget."[60]

By 1947 research under Project SKYHOOK had produced novel materials and techniques that enabled free-flying balloons to reach unprecedented altitudes in excess of 90,000 feet (27,432 meters). In 1950 the air force initiated Project GOPHER, which sought a practical military application for the SKYHOOK breakthrough. Recalling Japanese attempts to use drifting balloons to start fires in the United States during the last years of World War II (see chapter 4, footnote 1), the air force hoped that the balloons would drift over interesting parts of the Soviet Union, with their cameras and film being recovered when the balloons drifted back into friendly airspace. A parallel project using similar balloons, MOBY DICK, was intended to provide useful meteorological data on the high-altitude winds that would guide (or misguide) GOPHER, as well as a cover for the imagery and signals intelligence collected by GOPHER. Some 640 MOBY DICK balloons were launched between February 1953 and June 1954, and testing of the GOPHER balloons began late in 1954. Renamed GENETRIX, at least 516 high-altitude camera-carrying balloons were unleashed over the Soviet Union from Western Europe and Turkey starting in January 1956. Nearly 2,000 additional balloons remained when the program was suspended one month later (and officially terminated by the air force in March) owing to generally poor performance, which one CIA official characterized as a "disaster": only forty-four cameras were recovered, with most providing views of clouds and empty stretches of countryside. A significant contributing factor to the program's termination was the Soviet Union's strong and immediate diplomatic protests.[61]

While these results were disappointing, they were not entirely surprising, and efforts to develop an effective piloted reconnaissance aircraft came to fruition not long after the futility of unmanned versions became apparent. During the late 1940s and early 1950s the United States flew dozens of unarmed reconnaissance missions against the

60. See William J. Broad, "Wreckage in the Desert was Odd but Not Alien," *New York Times,* September 18, 1994, p. 1.

61. A full accounting of the fruits of Genetrix remains unavailable. Despite a discouraging recovery rate of less than 10 percent of the balloons launched, the program did succeed in providing imagery covering 1.1 million square miles (2.9 million square kilometers), equivalent to some 8 percent of the Soviet Union. Analysis was complicated, however, by the fact that the location of the balloons when the photographs were taken was known only within broad parameters. With the impending arrival of the U-2, the CIA's institutional interests in deprecating the Genetrix product are not difficult to discern. However, the Genetrix product was not entirely useless. For instance, it provided critical evidence in evaluating the Urals electrical power grid that supported the Soviet nuclear weapons production complex. See Peebles, *The Moby Dick Project,* pp. 118, 125, 185; Jeffrey T. Richelson, *American Espionage and the Soviet Target* (New York: William Morrow, 1987), pp. 132–39; R. Gargill Hall, "The Truth about Overflights," *MHQ: Quarterly Journal of Military History,* vol. 9 (Spring 1997), pp. 24–39; Henry S. Lowenhaupt, "The Description of a Picture," *Studies in Intelligence,* vol. 11 (Summer 1967), pp. 41–53, National Archives.

Soviet Union, sometimes intruding up to 200 miles (322 kilometers) into Soviet airspace. Several craft were shot down and more than 100 personnel were presumed killed or captured. President Eisenhower, deeming the intelligence value of these missions of critical importance, later ordered fighters to accompany them, which triggered several tense dogfights with Soviet interceptors over the Sea of Japan.[62]

The U-2 high-altitude reconnaissance aircraft was developed in response to air force requirements issued in the fall of 1952 for a high-flying aircraft that would confound radar tracking.[63] Lockheed was selected to develop the aircraft for the CIA in November 1954, the first aircraft was completed on July 15, 1955, and the first prototype flew in August 1955 from a newly constructed base at Groom Lake (adjacent to the Nevada Proving Ground and thus away from prying eyes) built by Lockheed (with covert CIA funding) especially for the U-2.[64] On the basis of its operational altitude of over 75,000 feet (22,860 meters) and low radar visibility, the U-2 was initially expected to have an effective operational lifetime of two years, during which it would go undetected by Soviet air defenses. When this period was up (around 1958), flights would be halted. In fact, the U-2 was detected immediately, but the flights continued for years thereafter. While the U-2 was far and away the highest-flying aircraft in existence, reducing its visibility to the unexpectedly proficient Soviet radars proved difficult. Subsequent efforts to further reduce the plane's radar signature came at the price of greater weight and a lower operating ceiling.

Equipped with a variety of receivers to monitor Soviet radar emissions, the primary sensor on the U-2 was a camera system that could take up to 4,000 paired images (for stereoscopic viewing) each covering roughly 100 square kilometers. The first operational overflight of the Soviet Union was conducted on July 4, 1956. Although there was no Soviet reaction to this first flight, the second mission shortly thereafter produced a strong (though secret) protest from Moscow. Missions in August and September provided the first images of the ICBM and Sputnik launch facilities at Baikonur, the Semipalatinsk nuclear

62. Richelson, *American Espionage and the Soviet Target,* pp. 100–52; Ben R. Rich and Leo Janos, *Skunk Works: A Personal Memoir of My Years at Lockheed* (New York: Little, Brown, 1994), pp. 123–24; Hall, "The Truth about Overflights"; Paul Lashmar, *Spy Flights of the Cold War* (Annapolis, Md.: Naval Institute Press, 1996); Fern Shen, "A Memorial for 'Those Who Served in Silence,'" *Washington Post,* September 3, 1997, p. B3. See also footnote 73. Given the bellicose rhetoric of the day, one wonders how the United States would have reacted to similar incursions by the Soviet Union.

63. Jay Miller, *Lockheed U-2* (Austin, Texas: Aerofax, 1983); Chris Pocock, *Dragon Lady, The History of the U-2 Spyplane* (Shrewsbury, Great Britain: Airlife, 1989); and Bodø. Regional University, Cold War Forum, "U-2 Flights and the Cold War in the High North," available on-line at http://www.hibo.no/asf/Cold_War/.

64. Construction crews were provided by the AEC. In just a few months, working in 130-degree-Fahrenheit (54-degree-Celsius) summer heat, they built an airstrip, two hangars, wells, and a mess hall, all in the middle of the desert. The total cost was $800,000 ($6.1 million in 1996 dollars), said to be "one of the best deals the government will ever get," according to Kelly Johnson, head of Lockheed's "Skunk Works," developer of the U-2. Groom Lake remains in use today as a test base for highly classified aircraft. See Rich and Janos, *Skunk Works,* pp. 132–33; Michael R. Beschloss, *May-day: Eisenhower, Khrushchev and the U-2 Affair* (New York: Harper & Row, 1986), p. 93.

weapons test site in Kazakhstan, and naval facilities at Severomorsk and Murmansk.

Mindful of Soviet reactions, and apprehensive of greater than anticipated Soviet air defense capabilities, President Eisenhower halted direct flights over Soviet territory until July 1959, when he authorized new missions to help resolve the increasingly sensitive matter of the status of Soviet ICBM developments, which were the subject of a raging public (and private) debate over the extent of the "missile gap." Thus a half-dozen U-2 missions were conducted over the southern Soviet Union in the later part of 1959, covering the Kapustin Yar, Baikonur, Sary Shagan, and Semipalatinsk test sites, and the Sverdlovsk military industrial area. Although these missions revealed much of interest, they failed to detect operational ICBM launch sites.[65]

To lay the missile gap controversy to rest, the first of a series of more ambitious flights was scheduled, transversing the Soviet Union rather than merely intruding and quickly withdrawing.[66] The mission would depart from Pakistan; cover industrial facilities at Chelyabinsk, Kyshtym, and Sverdlovsk; then proceed to survey potential or suspected ICBM bases near Perm, Yurya, and Plesetsk; and culminate with coverage of naval facilities at Severodvinsk and Murmansk. Then, if all went well, it would land at Bodø, Norway. All did not go well. The U-2 piloted by Francis Gary Powers was brought down over Sverdlovsk on May Day 1960.[67]

65. Richard Bissell, who oversaw the U-2 program at the CIA, later stated that by 1959, "90 percent of our hard intelligence information about the Soviet Union" was provided by the U-2. See Beschloss, *Mayday,* p. 5. Another source indicates that by this date more than 20,000 targets identified by U-2 overflights had been assessed by SAC's war planners, and this greatly contributed to the assignment of targets to the SIOP. See Rosenberg, "A Smoking Radiating Ruin," p. 16.

66. Even as the U-2 program was proving to President Eisenhower and a small circle of senior administration officials that no missile gap existed (or rather, that the gap overwhelmingly favored the United States), the very secrecy surrounding the effort—notwithstanding the fact that the Soviet Union was fully aware of the flights and their purpose—served to perpetuate the missile gap mythos and prevented Eisenhower from responding to increasingly strident Democratic charges that he was undermining national security by allowing the Soviet Union to outpace the United States in missile development.

67. While it is popularly believed that the U-2 was shot down by a Soviet surface-to-air missile, how this might have occurred has always been uncertain, given that the U-2's maximum altitude was beyond the known range of Soviet air defenses. Among the explanations offered over the years have been a near-miss by an SA-2 missile, an engine flameout (forcing Powers to dive to a lower altitude to restart it), a faulty autopilot (contributing to a flameout), sabotage, and pilot error. The State Department, in a secret June 1960 report, concluded that the unusually good condition of the debris from the crash and its reported disposition over a 9.3-mile (15-kilometer) area was inconsistent with the plane having fallen from 68,000 feet (the height at which Powers told Soviet interrogators he was flying to conceal the true ceiling of the U-2). Powers himself could not say for certain what happened, having seen only an orange flash and felt an explosion from behind. Under pressure from Soviet officials (no doubt eager to allow the Soviet Union to claim a victory for its air defenses and, more important, halt any further overflights), he maintained during his interrogation and subsequent public espionage trial in Moscow in August 1960 that he was flying at maximum altitude when he was struck down by "something. . . . I have no idea what it was. I didn't see it." After examining photographs of the wrecked plane and interviewing Powers (following his return to the United States in 1962 in exchange for Soviet spy Rudolf Abel), Lockheed officials argued at a secret board of inquiry set up by the CIA that shockwaves from an SA-2 exploding near the plane knocked off the U-2's right-hand stabilizer. A National Security Agency analyst, however, testified that communications intelligence intercepts tracked the U-2 slowly descending to 30,000 or 40,000 feet (9,144–12,192 meters) before crashing. In its public report, the CIA downplayed the NSA's data (without citing the source), calling it inconsistent with Powers's testimony and internally contradictory. Director of

While the cost of the U-2 program is still officially classified, Ben Rich (Kelly Johnson's successor at Lockheed) revealed in 1994 that "more than $54 million was allocated for the U-2 program." This equals approximately $350 million to $370 million in 1996 dollars, or about $14 million to $15 million per aircraft (twenty-five were ultimately built). However, about 15 percent of the total U-2 production cost was refunded to the CIA, and five extra airplanes were built from spare fuselages and parts that were not needed because "both the Skunk Works and the U-2 had functioned so beautifully. This was probably the only instance of a cost *underrun* in the history of the military-industrial complex."[68]

President Eisenhower subsequently remarked on the "critical importance" of the intelligence provided by the U-2: "Perhaps as important as the positive information—what the Soviets *did* have—was the negative information it produced—what the Soviets *did not* have. . . . Armed with U-2 knowledge, which supplemented the strength of our Armed Forces, we were better able to plan our own political-military course." Furthermore, the U-2 kept down the air force budget, saving "billions of dollars," according to science adviser James Killian.[69] Yet only twenty-four deep penetrations of Soviet territory were conducted in the forty-four months before May 1960. Although these revealed much of interest to an American intelligence community that remained largely dependent on German aerial imagery from the World War II, they raised as many questions as they answered.

Central Intelligence John McCone privately told members of Congress that the CIA had concluded a near miss with an SA-2 had brought down the U-2. This was promptly leaked to the news media and quickly became the "official" explanation, exonerating both Powers and the CIA of any wrongdoing. Little new information was offered until October 1996, when a former Soviet fighter pilot, Igor Mentyukov, told the Russian newspaper *Trud* he was sent over the Urals in an unarmed Sukhoi Su-9 fighter and ordered to ram Powers's U-2. At 65,000 feet (19,812 meters), the U-2 "got into the slipstream of my Su-9. . . . It started to flip him over, his wings broke off. . . . It all happened by chance." Moreover, owing to confusion over aircraft codes, a barrage of 14 SA-2 antiaircraft missiles fired at the U-2 were mistakenly aimed at his fighter and actually destroyed a MiG-19 that was hunting the Su-9. Mentyukov said Soviet generals covered up these facts to win favor with Nikita Khrushchev, who harbored great faith in Soviet antiaircraft missiles. Because no thorough, impartial investigation of this incident was ever undertaken, its exact cause will likely never be known. See Reuters, "What Really Happened in 1960 U2 Crash," *Seattle Times,* October 12, 1996, p. A1. Elements of Mentyukov's account conform with facts offered by Rich and Janos, *Skunk Works,* pp. 159–60; and Burrows, *Deep Black,* pp. 53–54. See also Beschloss, *Mayday,* esp. pp. 355–63. President Eisenhower learned of the downing of Powers's U-2 during a mock evacuation exercise with his cabinet at the secret underground command post at Mount Weather in Virginia (see box 3-3). Upon reading a teletype report of the news, he reportedly exclaimed, "I'll be a son of a bitch." See Ted Gup, "The Doomsday Blueprints," *Time,* August 10, 1992, p. 35.

68. Rich and Janos, *Skunk Works,* pp. 143–44. Between 1967 and 1989, additional U-2s were procured at unknown cost for both strategic and tactical reconnaissance. There are currently thirty-six in the air force's active inventory.

69. Dwight D. Eisenhower, *The White House Years: Waging Peace, 1956–1961* (Garden City, N.Y.: Doubleday, 1965), pp. 547, 558; Beschloss, *Mayday,* p. 366. Following the downing of Gary Powers's U-2, CIA director Allen W. Dulles testified in closed session before the Senate Foreign Relations Committee: "The U-2 program has helped to confirm that only a greatly reduced long-range bomber production program is continuing in the Soviet Union. . . . [It] has provided valuable information on the Soviet atomic energy program . . . includ[ing] the production of fissionable materials, weapons development and test activities, and the location, type, and size of many stockpile sites. . . . the Soviet nuclear testing ground has been photographed with extremely interesting results more than once." Quoted in Richelson, *American Espionage and the Soviet Target,* pp. 151–52.

The Soviet Union was not the only target of military and political interest. Both during and after the penetrations of Soviet airspace, U-2s based in Germany, Turkey, and Japan covered areas ranging from Israel to Indonesia. Indeed, throughout the 1960s CIA-supplied Nationalist Chinese U-2s and U.S. Air Force RB-57s roamed extensively over mainland China, with many pilots suffering fates worse than Powers. Other reconnaissance aircraft such as the SR-71 Blackbird performed related missions.[70] When the United States in the late 1970s wished to assess the characteristics of a newly built missile early warning radar at Pechora, an SR-71 flew directly toward the radar and prompted Soviet operators to turn it on, which in turn enabled a variety of signals intelligence collectors to record the vital data.[71]

Over the period covered by the FYDP historical database, DOD spending on the SR-71 was $14.9 billion. Additional costs, not recorded in the FYDP, were borne by the CIA, including at least $3.7 billion to develop its extraordinary fuel-gulping engine (which burned 8,000 gallons [30,280 liters] an hour) and nearly $1 billion to build the first ten aircraft (thirty-one additional two-seater planes were later built for the air force). When it was retired in 1990 (after the air force argued that reconnaissance satellites and a soon-to-be-deployed unmanned drone made the aircraft an expensive and redundant capability), annual operating costs were about $305 million. This decision was strongly contested by many in Congress, which provided for a limited SR-71 emergency capability in 1995. President Clinton, with the support of the air force, vetoed the continuation of this program in 1997, arguing there was no requirement for it.[72]

The planning of bomber flights depended heavily on other reconnaissance operations such as RB-47 (an electronic intelligence version of the B-47 bomber) and subsequently RC-135 missions (a militarized Boeing 707 aircraft) around the borders of the Soviet Union (one of which may have contributed to the misidentification and shooting

70. This aircraft was originally designated the RS-71, but President Lyndon Johnson transposed the letters when he revealed its existence in 1964. "Instead of putting out a brief correction, the air force decided not to call attention to a very minor mistake by the commander in chief and ordered us to change about twenty-nine thousand blueprints at a cost of thousands of dollars so that they would read 'SR-71' and not 'RS-71.'" The large quantities of titanium required to build this Mach 3 aircraft were purchased (through a circuitous route managed by the CIA) from the Soviet Union, the intended target of the plane's reconnaissance missions. Rich and Janos, *Skunk Works,* pp. 202–04, 327. The SR-71's high rate of fuel consumption—a ninety-minute flight at cruise speed would empty its fuel tanks—required extensive refueling resources. For example, supporting the nine active aircraft stationed for many years at Beale Air Force Base near Sacramento, California, were twenty-five KC-135 refueling tankers. In an effort to defray the costs of the program, Lockheed proposed alternative uses of the plane for the air force, including launching ICBMs and an "energy bomb"—a 2,000-pound (909-kilogram) piece of high-density steel that could be dropped from an SR-71 at 80,000 feet (24,384 meters), hitting the ground like a meteor and blasting a hole 130 feet (40 meters) deep. President Kennedy, when made aware of the SR-71's capabilities and eager to cancel the air force's B-70 bomber, expressed interest in converting the plane into a long-range bomber (pp. 226–28, 241, 258–59).

71. Personal communication from a source serving in the U.S. intelligence community at the time.

72. Rich and Janos, *Skunk Works,* pp. 207, 227, 237, 258–59.

down of Korean Air Lines Flight 007 on September 1, 1983).[73] The planes collected the signals of Soviet air defense radars in order to enable bombers to fly around or jam those radars during their wartime incursions into Soviet territory. They also gathered telemetry data by monitoring the reentry of Soviet warheads over the Kamchatka Peninsula.

Assisting in this effort were the COBRA DANE and COBRA JUDY radars. COBRA DANE, approximately 100 feet high, and 94 feet wide (30 meters by 29 meters), is a phased-array radar based at Shemya, Alaska, at the tip of the Aleutian Islands. With a range of 28,000 miles (45,052 kilometers), it has monitored Soviet ballistic missile tests since 1977, tracking warheads as they reenter the atmosphere over the Kamchatka Peninsula or over the Pacific Ocean north of Guam. One analyst describes it as being able to "spot a spaceborne basketball at 2,000 miles" (3,218 kilometers).[74] COBRA JUDY is a large (22.5-foot [6.9-meter]-diameter) shipboard phased-array radar on the USNS *Observation Island,* a 563-foot-long (171.6-meter) former freighter refitted in the 1960s as a missile range and instrumentation ship. The ship also houses two geodesic radomes 32 feet (9.8 meters) in diameter housing passive antennas maintained by the NSA. Based in Hawaii, COBRA JUDY works with COBRA DANE to track warheads as they splash down in the Soviet/Russian Pacific test range. According to one source, the ship is "operated by the Military Sealift Command with a civilian crew for the Air Force Eastern Test Range."[75] However, costs are not itemized in the FYDP, and the funding mechanism for COBRA JUDY is too byzantine to explain usefully.

The cost of RC-135 aircraft and operations is clouded by continued classification. Although the air force is the lead service for the RC-135 fleet, including sixteen RC-135V/W RIVET JOINT aircraft for electronic surveillance, the operations of several of other aircraft have been funded jointly by the air force and the Defense Intelligence Agency (three RC-135S COBRA BALL for missile tracking), the National Security Agency (two RC-135U COMBAT SENT for analysis of

73. Burrows, *Deep Black,* pp. 19, 172–73, writes that an RC-135 was in the area that night "to gather telemetry from a scheduled Soviet ballistic missile test." In a December 1996 interview with the *New York Times,* Gennadi Osipovich, who shot down KAL 007 with his Su-15 fighter, maintained that even though he recognized the airplane as a civilian model it was still engaged in espionage activities. Michael R. Gordon, "Ex-Soviet Pilot Still Insists KAL 007 Was Spying," *New York Times,* December 9, 1996, p. A12. On September 2, 1958, an RC-130 spy plane conducting an electronic eavesdropping mission against the Soviet Union with a crew of seventeen crossed into Armenia and was shot down. The Soviet Union returned six mutilated bodies to the United States and maintained the plane had simply crashed. Eisenhower, insistent on retrieving the eleven other crewmen and aware (from NSA monitoring in Turkey) that the Soviet Union had indeed fired on the unarmed plane, authorized the leaking of the intercepted transmissions to the *New York Times,* where they were published on the front page, revealing officially for the first time that the United States spied on the Soviet Union. The Soviet Union remained unmoved and the missing Americans were never returned. See Beschloss, *Mayday,* pp. 158–59; Richelson, *American Espionage and the Soviet Target,* pp. 124–26.

74. Tom Gervasi, *The Myth of Soviet Military Supremacy* (New York: Harper & Row, 1986), p. 249.

75. Gervasi, *Myth of Soviet Military Supremacy;* Richelson, *American Espionage and the Soviet Target,* pp. 166–67.

electronic and infrared equipment), and the army (one RC-135X COBRA EYE to monitor U.S. missile launches).[76] Air force funding for the BIG SAFARI program, which included RC-135 operations, was approximately $100 million a year (in then-year dollars) during the mid-1980s.[77] However, this did not include related support costs, such as aerial tanker refueling, which might drive the annual operating costs to more than $200 million (in 1996 dollars).[78] Thus over the more than three decades of operations, spending on RC-135 operations certainly exceeded $5 billion.

Perhaps the most intriguing and secretive aerial reconnaissance program was conceived in 1962 by Lockheed's Skunk Works factory. Code-named TAGBOARD (and also known as D-21 SENIOR BOWL), it consisted of sophisticated titanium drones shaped like manta rays and launched piggyback style off SR-71s. These craft were capable of flying at Mach 3 to spy on China's Lop Nur nuclear testing site, 2,000 miles (3,218 kilometers) inland near the Mongolian border. After taking numerous photographs, the drones were programmed to return to their launch point and eject their film capsules, which would be retrieved by a waiting naval vessel. The drone would then self-destruct. The program, designed to avoid a repetition of the downing of Powers's U-2, was jointly funded by the CIA and the air force.

Following a test accident in July 1966, in which a drone crashed into and destroyed an SR-71 and one of the pilots was killed, the slower (and less expensive) B-52 was chosen as the launch platform. During tests in 1968–69, a B-52 loaded with two drones scored five successes and two failures. On November 9, 1969, the first Tagboard operational mission against Lop Nur was launched. The drone completed its mission undetected but was lost before its film could be retrieved (apparently it malfunctioned, missed its rendezvous point, and crashed when it ran out of fuel; a portion of this drone was later recovered by a shepherd in Soviet Siberia and given by a KGB agent to a CIA operative as a Christmas gift seventeen years later). In the fall of 1970, a second flight was attempted and, despite an otherwise flawless mission, the

76. The RC-135X COBRA EYE aircraft has been withdrawn from service and is being converted to perform COBRA BALL missions. It will be redeployed in late 1998. Jeffrey Richelson, "Cold War Recon Planes Find New Missions," *Defense Week*, September 5, 1995, p. 6; Robert S. Hopkins III, "Cobra Ball and Cobra Eye: Alaskan Observers," *World Air Power Journal*, vol. 8 (Spring 1992), pp. 128–39; Richelson, *American Espionage and the Soviet Target*, pp. 215–18. For more on Cobra Ball, see a series of articles by David A. Fulghum, "Cobra Ball Revamped for Battlefield Missions," "Endurance, Standoff Range Remain Crucial Attribute," "Multi-Sensor COBRA BALL Tackles Missile Defense," *Aviation Week & Space Technology*, August 4, 1997, pp. 48–57.

77. Department of the Air Force, Justification of Estimates for Fiscal Year 1986, Operations and Maintenance, "Force Program VII Central Supply and Maintenance," Submitted to Congress February 1985, vol. 1, p. 389.

78. Between January 1, 1991, and June 30, 1992, the RC-135 fleet logged 1,479 operational missions that required some 2,094 tanker sorties. Total tanker support costs from 1992 through 2020 were estimated at more than $1.5 billion (in then-year dollars), suggesting an annual cost of some $50 million. See U.S. General Accounting Office, *New RC-135 Aircraft Engines Can Reduce Cost and Improve Performance*, NSIAD-92-305 (1992), pp. 4–5. This report noted that other operating costs over the same period would bring the total (including tankers) to nearly $6 billion, suggesting an annual operating cost of approximately $200 million.

film capsule's parachute failed and it plunged into the sea. A third flight in March 1971 went perfectly. Unfortunately, seas at the recovery site were choppy and the film capsule was again lost. A fourth and final flight shortly thereafter penetrated 1,900 miles (3,057 kilometers) into Chinese territory before disappearing for reasons unknown. The program was terminated in mid-1972.

Although Lockheed's estimated cost for fifty drones was a relatively inexpensive $151 million, "the complex logistics surrounding each flight, involving recovery ships and rendezvous aircraft, cost a bloody fortune to stage."[79] The total costs of the program, if known, remain classified.

Eyes and Ears in Space

With its arsenal of thousands of nuclear weapons, the Soviet Union remained the main adversary, but hard as it might try, the United States could gather only sparse intelligence information with its automated balloons or highly risky high-altitude piloted aircraft. Theoretical studies dating back to the early months of the nuclear era had predicted that automated spacecraft would surpass the capabilities of piloted aircraft, without the associated human and political costs. The intelligence satellites proved them correct.

Imaging intelligence satellites use film and electronic cameras, or radars, to produce high-resolution images of objects on the ground at ranges of up to 622 miles (1,000 kilometers). Orbiting at altitudes several hundred miles, such satellites can readily identify and distinguish differing types of vehicles and equipment with resolutions better than 4 inches (10 centimeters). Resolutions of several meters are useful in locating vehicles and characterizing installations, while resolutions on the order of 33 feet (10 meters) have some applications for locating major facilities, such as airfields and ports.

Replacing the U-2 spy planes, photo-reconnaissance satellites managed by the NRO provided timely decisive intelligence on the strength of enemy nuclear forces, debunking fears of a missile gap favoring Russia. The first successful CORONA mission, Discoverer 14, launched on August 18, 1960, returned imagery covering more than 1.6 million square miles (4 million square kilometers), ten times the area covered by a single U-2 mission, with no risk to a pilot's life (or a president's prestige).[80] Although initially the resolution provided by CORONA was

79. Rich and Janos, *Skunk Works,* pp. 262–70.

80. Kevin C. Ruffner, ed., *CORONA: America's First Satellite Program* (Washington, D.C.: Center for the Study of Intelligence, Central Intelligence Agency, 1995), p. 2. The secret CORONA program was deployed under cover of the public Discoverer program, which was represented as an effort to test space launch vehicles and explore the environment of outer space. CORONA satellites took photographs as they

quite inferior to that of the U-2 (which accounts for the continuation of aerial reconnaissance missions over less heavily defended targets such as China), satellite imagery quickly improved to the point of providing evidence of the absence of widespread Soviet ICBM deployments, and soon thereafter helped to clarify many of the numerous other mysteries that had long bedeviled American intelligence.

As the satellites became more sophisticated, with their new sensors (such as cloud-piercing radar) and new missions (such as eavesdropping on Soviet military communications), the United States acquired a powerful means of monitoring and targeting Soviet strategic deployments. Satellites also created new opportunities for strategic arms control. They enabled the United States to enter into and verify compliance with agreements meant to slow the strategic arms race and codify stable deterrence.

But from the outset, the air force envisioned more ambitious goals for space reconnaissance systems, which it hoped would provide nearly instantaneous intelligence on the location of Soviet strategic forces, including bombers and mobile ballistic missiles. While aircraft such as the U-2 and the early film-return satellites provided unprecedented peacetime coverage of large fixed targets, such as the massive facilities used to launch early Soviet ICBMs, they were entirely unsuited to such wartime roles as locating bombers dispersed at auxiliary airfields, or mobile ICBMs that had left their garrisons.

Thus in the late 1950s and early 1960s the CIA perfected the CORONA film-return reconnaissance satellites (95 of which were successfully orbited between 1960 and 1972, out of a total of 145 launches). The total cost of the program was reportedly $850 million (in then-year dollars), or roughly $4 billion in 1996 dollars.[81] But this figure does not include many costs associated with launching and operating these spacecraft and was dwarfed by subsequent satellite expenditures. Meanwhile, the air force focused on the Satellite and Missile Observation System (SAMOS) program, which planned to electronically relay imagery in real-time to ground stations. When initial tests of

orbited over the Earth. Once the limited film supply was exhausted, the satellite was directed to eject its film capsule, which was then slowed by parachute and plucked from the air by specially modified cargo planes (or retrieved from the sea should airborne capture fail). Because intelligence requirements dictated a near-polar orbit (necessitating a launch to the north or south) and to avoid prying eyes, Vandenberg Air Force Base (near Santa Barbara California) was selected as the launch site. The trouble was, Vandenberg had a heavily traveled railroad passing through it. "Throughout its existence, the CORONA program was plagued by having to time the launches to occur during one of the intervals between passing trains." See Kenneth E. Greer, "Corona," *Studies in Intelligence,* Supplement 17 (Spring 1973), pp. 9–10, reprinted in Ruffner, *CORONA: America's First Satellite Program,* pp. 3–39.

81. "CIA Holds Landmark Symposium on CORONA," *Secrecy and Government Bulletin,* no. 49, June 1995. The CIA carefully deleted all budgetary data from the CORONA documents it declassified, even though the program ended twenty-three years earlier (see, Ruffner, *CORONA: America's First Satellite Program*). The cost was disclosed by former CIA deputy director John McMahon, who apparently did not agree with his former employer's decision. Ironically, while the budget remains officially classified, since 1995 the CIA has declassified and made available thousands of CORONA photographs.

SAMOS proved unsatisfactory, the air force turned to various schemes for rapidly returning film from satellites to ground processing sites for exploitation. In a parallel effort, between 1964 and 1970 the air force expended nearly $7 billion on a manned orbiting laboratory (MOL), a proposed space station with powerful reconnaissance cameras and onboard facilities for astronauts to examine film in minutes so that enemy military operations could be kept under continuous surveillance.

In November 1957 the air force initiated Project Dynasoar (from "dynamic-soaring") to test an ambitious, experimental craft that would be boosted into space to "bounce" off the upper atmosphere and then glide back to Earth and land. Among the applications proposed for the program were strategic reconnaissance, satellite inspection, and interception, and intercontinental bombardment. Between 1957 and 1959 the Boeing and Martin aerospace companies spent a combined total of $10.6 million refining the initial concept, concluding that Dynasoar should be an orbiting hypersonic test vehicle, which, if successful, could conduct reconnaissance and bombardment missions.

In April 1960 the DOD approved a three-phase development plan with the goal of producing a fully operational craft by 1966. The program's costs soon engendered opposition from Secretary of Defense McNamara and his staff, who tried to keep the effort experimental in nature and sought to increase support for the early phases of the U.S. space program such as Gemini. The air force resisted, citing the orbital flexibility of the Dynasoar (now called the X-20) and its reentry and landing capabilities as justification for continued work. But McNamara canceled the program anyway on December 10, 1963. At the same time, impressed with the equipment developed for the Gemini program, he authorized the MOL to study the feasibility and usefulness of maintaining orbiting reconnaissance platforms. According to the FYDP historical database, partial costs for Dynasoar between fiscal 1962 and 1964 totaled $1.7 billion, but another source indicates that $400 million (in then-year dollars) had been spent by the time the program was canceled, which equals about $2.4 billion in 1996 dollars.[82]

During the late 1970s and early 1980s, photographic satellites followed a fairly standard pattern. Two KH-11s (nicknamed KENNAN), each with an operational life of about three years, circled the Earth at all times, transmitting pictures to ground stations during every orbit. As an old satellite exhausted its maneuvering fuel, it would reenter the atmosphere on command (where it would burn up and disintegrate) and be replaced by a new satellite launched a week or two later. A KH-9 (HEXAGON) film-return satellite would be launched in late spring

82. Paul Stares, *The Militarization of Space: U.S. Policy, 1945–1984* (Cornell University Press, 1985), p. 97.

each year, and operate until around the end of the year. A KH-8 (GAMBIT) film-return satellite would be launched in early spring and operate for a few months.[83] The last KH-8 was launched in 1984, and the last KH-9 in the spring of 1986 (becoming the sole failure of the KH-9 program, owing to a launch vehicle explosion). By the early 1990s the KH-11 had been superseded by a more advanced KEYHOLE, offering considerably improved optical sensor capabilities.[84]

The cancellation of MOL in 1969 did not extinguish air force interest in continuous targeting from space.[85] By the early 1980s, a project was under way to develop a cloud-piercing synthetic aperture radar imaging intelligence satellite. These efforts finally bore fruit with the 1988 launch of the first LACROSSE satellite. But the three-decade-long quest for a real-time targeting capability was ultimately realized only after the collapse of the Soviet Union in 1991, following the launch of the second LACROSSE. The DOD is currently considering increasing its use of commercially operated imaging satellites as a way to both broaden its coverage of the globe and reduce its costs.[86]

Signals intelligence (SIGINT) satellites are designed to detect transmissions from broadcast communications systems such as radios, radars, and other electronic systems. The interception of such transmissions can provide information on the type and location of even low-power transmitters, such as handheld radios. However, these satellites are not capable of intercepting communications carried over land lines, such as undersea fiber optic cables (nor can they detect non-electronic communications, such as the spoken word).

The United States has operated four succeeding generations of SIGINT satellites in geostationary, elliptical, and low Earth orbits. The

83. See also Burrows, *Deep Black,* pp. 227, 302–05; and Richelson, *The U.S. Intelligence Community,* pp. 151–57.

84. The public has been afforded occasional glimpses of the extraordinary capabilities of these satellites. In 1984 naval analyst Samuel Eliot Morison leaked three KH-11 photographs of the Soviet aircraft carrier *Kuznetzov* under construction at Nikolayev shipyard on the Black Sea to *Jane's Defense Weekly.* Defense Secretary Caspar Weinberger was quite irritated when he saw the photographs, both because they contradicted claims in the latest issue of *Soviet Military Power* that the carrier was close to completion and because he had hoped to use such photographs (as opposed to sketches) in *Soviet Military Power* to buttress his case but had been turned down by the intelligence community. Weinberger therefore ordered Morison be prosecuted for espionage, an unprecedented and controversial charge as he had not transmitted the photographs to a foreign government. Morison, who also was the U.S. representative of *Jane's Fighting Ships* (and apparently hoped to gain full-time employment with the company as a consequence of his actions), was arrested and sentenced to prison for two years. Remarkably, on January 1, 1997, the *Washington Times* published a KH-12 photograph of the *Kuznetzov's* sister ship, the *Varyag* (now being scrapped). Three months later, the *Times* again published a KH-12 photograph, this time of a Chinese bomber converted into a refueling tanker. See Jeffrey T. Richelson, *America's Secret Eyes in Space: The U.S. Keyhole Spy Satellite Program* (New York: Harper & Row, 1990), pp. 201–02; Bill Gertz, "Ukraine Won't Finish Russian Flattop," *Washington Times,* January 1, 1997, p. A3; Bill Gertz, "Beijing Creates Military Monster," *Washington Times,* April 10, 1997, p. A1 (photograph is on A10). The photographs from these articles may be found on the World Wide Web at http://www.fas.org/irp/imint/. The photo leaked by Morison is reprinted in Burrows, *Deep Black.*

85. Spending on the program continued through 1970, which probably covered orderly program termination and the transition of MOL technology to other programs.

86. Vago Muradian, "DoD May Increase Consumption of Commercial Satellite Imagery," *Defense Daily,* February 11, 1997, pp. 214–15. The first private photoreconnaissance satellite was launched on December 24, 1997. See William J. Broad, "First Civilian Spy Satellite Soars into Space, Launched in Russia by a U.S. Company," *New York Times* (Washington edition), January 25, 1997, p. A14.

first generation consisted of a variety of small satellites in low Earth orbit, which were operated from the early 1960s through the early 1980s. The geostationary SIGINT constellation has consisted of approximately half a dozen satellites. The first generation of these, including the air force CANYON and CIA RHYOLITE programs, were launched in the late 1960s and early 1970s and had a receiving antenna with a diameter of more than 10 meters. The next generation of air force satellites, known as CHALET (and subsequently VORTEX), were first orbited in the late 1970s, and had an antenna with a diameter of several tens of meters. Concurrently, the air force deployed the JUMPSEAT satellites into elliptical orbits optimized for coverage of the Soviet Union. And starting in the mid-1980s the CIA launched the MAGNUM series (later renamed ORION), which featured very large deployable antennae with a diameter of approximately 100 meters.

Fourth-generation satellites with even larger antennae debuted in the mid-1990s, replacing both the MAGNUM and VORTEX systems. TRUMPET, the long-delayed replacement for JUMPSEAT, was also brought into service in 1994. With antennae of larger diameter, these satellites are able to detect lower-power transmissions, as well as determine the location of a transmitter with increased precision.[87]

To deploy intelligence-gathering and communications satellites, the DOD has relied on both expendable launch vehicles (such as Atlas rockets, long-retired as ICBMs) and, since the early 1980s, on the Space Shuttle. The DOD was intimately involved in the design of the shuttle, ensuring that its payload bay could carry the largest satellites it planned to launch. Beginning in 1979, a massive $3 billion (then-year dollars) launch site—Shuttle Launch Complex 6 or SLC-6 ("Slick Six")—was built at Vandenberg Air Force Base just for classified military missions, yet it was never used because shortly after the January 1986 explosion of the *Challenger,* the DOD and NASA decided for safety reasons not to launch shuttles from Vandenberg.[88] In January 1987 the DOD canceled plans to complete a $500 million (then-year dollars) classified shuttle control center at the new Consolidated Space Operations Center in Colorado Springs, Colorado, solely for managing military shuttle missions.[89] Since fiscal 1963, the DOD (principally the air force) has spent $12.4 billion on Space Shuttle and shuttle-related RDT&E and construction. We estimate that roughly half of that total, or $6.2 billion, can be conservatively attributed to supporting the nuclear weapons intelligence mission.

87. Craig Covault, "NRO Radar, Sigint Launches Readied," *Aviation Week & Space Technology,* September 1, 1997, pp. 22–24.

88. SLC-6 was originally designed and built between 1966 and 1969 as the launch site for the MOL, only to be mothballed after that program was canceled.

89. David E. Sanger, "Control Center for Space Shuttle Is Dropped from Pentagon Budget," *New York Times,* January 26, 1987, p. A25.

Meteorological and Geographic Reconnaissance

The military—especially the navy and the air force—have for decades operated extensive programs to analyze oceanographic, atmospheric, and geographic phenomena, all with the intent of improving military performance. The CIA and NRO have also amassed hundreds of thousands of photographs of the Earth's surface over several decades. Much of the data collected via satellites, aircraft, ships, and submarines are only now becoming available to civilian researchers, who hope to use it to track environmental trends and develop new meteorological models.[90] The navy, for example, has an array of data on variations in gravity across the seabed, gathered to improve the accuracy of submarine-launched ballistic missiles; geomagnetics, used for navigation; the thickness and types of seafloor sediments, used to better understand underwater sound propagation and improve tracking of ships and submarines); Arctic ice shape and depth (the Arctic was a key cold war battleground for submarines); highly detailed marine maps; temperature and salinity, used to study underwater sound propagation and improve tracking of ships and submarines; underwater visibility and bioluminescence, used to study the potential of visual detection of underwater objects.[91] Out of $28.4 billion expended on such programs between 1962 and 1995, we estimate that about one-third, or $9.5 billion, supported nuclear weapons operations.

The military maintained its own weather satellites—the Defense Meteorological Satellite Program (DMSP)—to forecast cloud cover (crucial for targeting photographic reconnaissance satellites), predict the behavior of low-altitude weather systems (to aid bomber and cruise missile operations), collect wind data (to predict fallout patterns), and track fallout. Other satellites study solar flares and auroral activity, both of which can affect high- frequency and shortwave communications, satellite orbits, and radar operations.[92] In response to tightening federal budgets, the government announced in May 1994 that the Defense Meteorological Satellite Program and the National Oceanic and Atmospheric Administration (NOAA) civilian satellite program would merge, thereby providing a constellation of four polar orbiting satellites (two each) capable of monitoring the Earth's surface and atmosphere from an altitude of 490 miles (788 kilometers) twice a day.[93] According to the FYDP historical database, between 1962 and 1995 the DOD spent $5 billion on DMSP and an additional $16.5 billion on "Weather Service" activities. We conservatively estimate that

90. See Richelson, "Scientists in Black," pp. 48–55.

91. William J. Broad, "Navy Is Releasing Treasure of Secret Data on World's Oceans," *New York Times,* November 28, 1995, p. C1; Curt Suplee, "Getting to the Bottom of the top of the World," *Washington Post,* August 22, 1997, p. A21.

92. Arkin and Fieldhouse, *Nuclear Battlefields,* pp. 26–28.

93. Warren E. Leary, "2 Weather Satellite Systems Will Merge to Save Money," *New York Times,* May 11, 1994, p. A21.

25 percent of the cost of these efforts—$5.4 billion—supported nuclear weapons operations.

The Air Force Technical Applications Center, established in 1959, is the successor to an Air Force agency created in September 1947 to "detect atomic explosions anywhere in the world" (see chapter 8). With headquarters at Patrick Air Force Base near Cocoa Beach, Florida, AFTAC operates the Atomic Energy Detection System (AEDS), a network of some 100 sites in more than thirty-five countries capable of detecting nuclear detonations underground, underwater, in the atmosphere, and in space. Most AEDS sites are seismic stations located on or near U.S. overseas military bases. Others, such as those in Pakistan, Finland, and Hong Kong, are concealed in embassies or commercial buildings.[94] In addition to seismic monitoring, AFTAC employs space-based, hydroacoustic, and radiological sensors. AFTAC monitors its AEDS sites twenty-four hours a day to assess compliance with the Partial Test Ban Treaty, Nuclear Nonproliferation Treaty, Threshold Test Ban Treaty, and the Peaceful Nuclear Explosions Treaty. AFTAC also maintains an airborne sampling capability with one TC-135 aircraft (sampling was previously carried out with C-130, B-52, U-2, and other specially modified aircraft; in 1962, at the height of Soviet atmospheric testing, eighty-four sampling aircraft were in use). From the late 1940s until the early 1990s, these aircraft flew long daily "tracks" along the periphery of the Soviet Union and China and over the North Pole to collect debris from nuclear weapons tests and bring it back to AFTAC laboratories for analysis (one early mission in 1949 helped detect fallout from the first Soviet atomic bomb test).

Since its creation, AFTAC has operated in extreme secrecy (even its mission and name were classified until the 1970s). This began to change in 1997, one year after AFTAC was given the lead role in collecting and assessing data to monitor compliance with the Comprehensive Test Ban Treaty. Under the CTBT, AFTAC will operate the National Data Center, which will feed information to and collect information from the new International Monitoring System, a proposed global network of 321 different sensors (40 of which will be in the United States), including new infrasonic (airborne acoustic) sensors in the southern hemisphere and 80 automated radionuclide collection/assessment devices (some of the U.S. controlled sensors, such as NUDET, will only provide information to U.S. analysts). A number of these will be installed by AFTAC.[95] Demonstrating the utility of a world-

94. Robert S. Norris and William M. Arkin, "Nuclear Notebook (Secret Test Monitors)," *Bulletin of the Atomic Scientists*, vol. 43 (July/August 1987), p. 63.

95. Once the CTBT enters into force (following its ratification by forty-four countries with actual or potential nuclear weapons capabilities), the CTBT Organization (CTBTO), based in Vienna, will begin formal operations, including managing the International Monitoring System and staging inspections to verify compliance with the treaty. In November 1997, Congress appropriated $13 million to cover part of the

wide monitoring regime, on August 16, 1997, the AEDS and other sensors detected a seismic event in the vicinity of Russia's nuclear test site at Novaya Zemlya. AFTAC dispatched a sampling aircraft to the site but found no radiological debris. On August 18, the CIA, using AFTAC's data, sent a high-priority classified report to senior U.S. government officials warning of a probable nuclear test, but subsequent analysis by government and private experts determined that the event in question was natural in origin and occurred some 81 miles (130 kilometers) to the southeast of the test site under the Kara Sea.[96]

In 1997 AFTAC employed some 1,000 personnel, 882 of whom were active duty military officers and enlisted personnel.[97] Its budget has traditionally been classified, but costs for some of the programs it manages (for example, NUDET) are known and included in this chapter.

Deep Ocean Reconnaissance and Retrieval

Since 1965 the navy has operated a submarine-based deep ocean reconnaissance and retrieval program under the nondescript title Submarine Development Group 1. The effort involves at least three converted nuclear-powered attack submarines, the now-retired USS *Seawolf* and USS *Halibut* and, beginning in 1976, the USS *Parche* (SSN-683). Among the missions these submarines have accomplished are deep ocean reconnaissance, the retrieval of Soviet nuclear warheads, and tapping into Soviet underwater communications cables.

The USS *Halibut* was the first of these special class of submarines, converted in 1965 to carry large spools of cable and reconnaissance equipment and outfitted with special thrusters to keep it motionless while under the ocean's surface. On April 11, 1968, a diesel-powered Golf-2 submarine, later identified as no. PL-722, exploded and sank 750 miles (1,207 kilometers) northwest of Hawaii in waters more than 3 miles (4.8 kilometers) deep. The Soviet navy searched in May and June for the submarine but without success. However, the U.S. Navy's Sound Surveillance System (SOSUS) (see chapter 4), detected the explosion and narrowed the submarine's location to within an area of

CTBTO's estimated $68 million budget. See Eve Kouidri Kuhn, "Nuclear Watchdog Lacks OK to Keep Eye on Tests," *Christian Science Monitor*, October 21, 1997, p. 6; congressional appropriation information courtesy of the Coalition to Reduce Nuclear Dangers, Washington, D.C., November 17, 1997.

96. On the basis of the CIA's report, the Clinton administration sent a strongly worded diplomatic note to Russia inquiring about the event and requesting more information. Russia consistently denied it had conducted a nuclear test. Two and a half months later, the CIA retracted its allegation, citing the findings of an independent panel that it appointed to review the available data. See Bill Gertz, "Russia Suspected of Nuclear Testing," *Washington Times*, August 28, 1997, p. A1; Bill Gertz, "Suspicion Grows of Russian Nuke Test," *Washington Times*, August 29, 1997, p. A1; R. Jeffrey Smith, "U.S. Officials Acted Hastily in Nuclear Test Accusation," *Washington Post*, October 20, 1997, p. A1; William J. Broad, "Hints of a Nuclear Test in Russia Are Disputed," *New York Times*, October 21, 1997, p. A12; R. Jeffrey Smith, "U.S. Formally Drops Claim of Possible Nuclear Blast," *Washington Post*, November 4, 1997, p. A2.

97. USAF Almanac, *Air Force Magazine*, May 1997, p. 126.

10 square miles (25.9 square kilometers). That summer, the *Halibut* examined the submarine, which had broken apart on the bottom, took photographs, and possibly removed equipment.[98]

During the 1980s the *Parche* conducted nine highly classified missions, earning five Presidential Unit Citations and three Navy Unit Citations. Although the navy will not comment in detail on the submarine's missions, published reports link it to the IVY BELLS program, in which a joint Navy-NSA team sailed into the Sea of Okhotsk, between the east coast of Siberia and the Kamchatka Peninsula, and attached two 6-ton monitoring devices to a Soviet underwater cable. The devices monitored all communications traveling through the cable via induction (as opposed to direct physical contact with the wires) and recorded data on special tapes, which were later retrieved and returned to the NSA for analysis. The program began in the 1970s but was compromised in 1981 after NSA analyst Ronald Pelton turned over information on it to the Soviet Union (which subsequently located and removed the electronic tapping devices). The *Parche* may also have picked up a mock Soviet nuclear warhead and its telemetry recorder fired during a missile test in 1981.[99]

The navy also maintains the NR-1, a small (146-foot-long, 44.5-meter), nuclear-powered, deep-sea diving submarine, which since 1969 has performed a number of highly classified missions and is now occasionally used for civilian research missions such as examining wreckage in the Mediterranean from the 1916 sinking of the *Titanic*'s sister ship, the HMHS *Britannic*. The NR-1 carries an array of sonar sensors, cameras, and laser mapping devices. In 1976 it assisted in the salvage of a sunken F-14 fighter and its Phoenix air-to-air missile, and in 1986 it helped recover debris from the *Challenger* explosion.[100]

Since the later years of the Eisenhower administration, the navy has also used submarines for electronic and photographic intelligence gathering. The effort is known by a variety of code names, most commonly HOLYSTONE but most recently BARNACLE. Through 1991 HOLYSTONE focused primarily on the Soviet Union, although China

98. William J. Broad, "Navy Has Long Had Secret Subs for Deep-Sea Spying, Experts Say," *New York Times*, February 7, 1994, p. A1.

99. Lloyd Pritchett, "Will Top-Secret Sub Be Able to Slip into Area Quietly?" *Bremerton Sun* (Washington), August 8, 1994, p. 1; Ed Offley, "Secret Navy Sub Finds New Home at Bangor Base," *Seattle Post-Intelligencer*, November 23, 1994, p. 1; Bill Gertz, "U.S. Gained Vital Data from Soviet Warhead Found in 1981," *Washington Times*, January 12, 1989, p. 4; Bob Woodward, *Veil: The Secret Wars of the CIA 1981–1987* (New York: Simon & Schuster, 1987), pp. 448–52. Another submarine, the USS *Grayback*, was identified by Russian Rear Admiral Anatoliy Shtyrov in 1992 as being a prime suspect in the retrieval of two nuclear weapons from a Soviet strategic bomber that crashed into the Sea of Okhotsk in 1976. See Nikolay Burbyga, "U.S. Said to Have Retrieved Soviet Weapons" (reprints of an interview with Rear Admiral Anatoliy Shtyrov and an article in *Izvestiya*, May 13 and 15, 1992), *Submarine Review*, January 1993, pp. 60–65.

100. William J. Broad, "Secret Sub to Scan Sea Floor for Roman Wrecks," *New York Times*, February 7, 1995, p. C1; Robert A. Hamilton, "Navy Research Sub to Begin Mission in Mediterranean," *New London Day* (Connecticut), July 20, 1995, p. B1; John Nole Wilford, "Roman Ships Found Off Sicily; New Sites Broaden Study," *New York Times* (Washington edition), July 31, 1997, p A3.

and Vietnam have also been targeted. All missions are conducted using nuclear-powered attack submarines (SSNs), which, until the early 1990s, were also armed with nuclear weapons. During these missions, to avoid detection by Soviet antisubmarine warfare devices, the crews are forbidden to use any active electronic or sonar equipment. This practice, in part, was the cause of nine collisions with other vessels during HOLYSTONE missions between 1966 and 1976.[101] Missions through 1975 helped provide critical information on the Soviet submarine fleet, including its size and organization, noise patterns, and missile firing capabilities. One mission collected the audio signature of Soviet submarines, enabling navy analysts to develop techniques for identifying individual submarines, even at great distances. Other missions provided telemetry data for SLBM tests and photographs of the underside of a Soviet submarine.[102]

Perhaps the "most complex and expensive single intelligence mission ever undertaken" was the CIA's retrieval of a portion of the Golf-2 submarine examined by the *Halibut* in 1968.[103] In the early 1970s the CIA, working with industrialist Howard Hughes, created a covert program, code-named Project AZORIAN, to build the 36,000-ton, 618-foot-long (188-meter), 115.5-foot-wide (35.2-meter) *Hughes Glomar Explorer.* The project also funded construction of an enormous submersible barge, the *HMB-1* (*Hughes Marine Barge*), whose sole purpose was to transfer a 180-foot-long (55-meter), 2,150-ton metal claw into the *Hughes Glomar Explorer*'s 199-foot-long (60.7-meter), 74-foot-wide (22.6-meter), 65-foot-high (19.8-meter) "moon pool" from underneath the water and retrieve it at mission's end. This was necessary both to disguise the true purpose of the ship and because the claw was simply too large and heavy to lift into or out of the ship from above. The

101. "The CIA Report the President Doesn't Want You to Read," *The Village Voice,* February 16, 1976, p. 88. This is the unofficial January 19, 1976, report by the House Select Committee on Intelligence concerning the U.S. intelligence community, otherwise known as the Pike Committee report. It was never officially released.

102. Richelson, *The U.S. Intelligence Community,* pp. 194–95.

103. Jeffrey T. Richelson and Desmond Ball, *The Ties That Bind: Intelligence Cooperation between the UKUSA Countries—The United Kingdom, the United States of America, Canada, Australia and New Zealand* (Boston: Allen & Unwin, 1985), p. 225. An equally remarkable effort during the 1980s, code-named ABSORB, was disclosed in 1997. Under this program, which was compromised by convicted spy Aldrich Ames, the CIA constructed a sophisticated radiation detector to count the number of MIRVs atop Soviet ICBMs as they were shipped by rail over the Ural Mountains from their assembly facility in the western Soviet Union to operational bases (the United States, by contrast, ships missiles and warheads separately, joining them together only when the missile is emplaced in its silo). Collaborating with Japan, the CIA tested its concept by hiding a specially triggered camera inside a shipping container; the camera returned numerous photographs of rail spurs to secret military installations. The CIA (again working with Japan) then secreted the actual device in a shipping container traveling from Vladivostok to Eastern Europe. Along the way, as the device passed trains carrying warheads, it measured the radiation emitted, allowing analysts to deduce the number of warheads per missile and their approximate yield. When the project was disclosed by Ames, Japan reportedly bribed the KGB to avoid being implicated, leading the KGB to boast that it had made money off the CIA. ABSORB reportedly cost the CIA an estimated $170 million. See Pete Earley, *Confessions of a Spy: The Real Story of Aldrich Ames* (New York: G.P. Putnam's Sons, 1997), pp. 117–19; Pete Earley, "Treason?" (book excerpt), *U.S. News & World Report,* February 17, 1997, p. 31; interview with Pete Earley on National Public Radio's "All Things Considered," WETA-FM, February 19, 1997.

moon pool—normally closed to the sea by heavy metal doors—would open once the ship reached its destination, whereby hundreds of sections of heavy pipe would be attached to the claw, lowering it to the sea floor, where it would grab a section of the submarine. Then the process would be reversed and the submarine would be hauled into the ship, to be cut apart and analyzed.[104] To mislead shipping industry observers and the Soviet Union (which would almost certainly have spotted the ship with its reconnaissance satellites), Hughes and the CIA promoted a cover story suggesting that the *Hughes Glomar Explorer* was designed to mine the seabed for minerals.

In June 1974 (its mission now renamed Project JENNIFER), the *Hughes Glomar Explorer* sailed to the site of the explosion and—according to former CIA directors William Colby and Robert Gates—retrieved a section of the submarine that lay 16,000 feet (4,877 meters) beneath the surface, including a forward crew compartment.[105] There are conflicting accounts as to whether the ship intended to retrieve the entire submarine or merely portions of it. Certainly the submarine, at 320 feet (97.5 meters) long, could not fit intact in the moon pool, although cut in half it could. One book published in 1978 claims that the whole submarine was indeed to be brought up, only to be cut apart by navy divers and hauled piece by piece into the ship. Another, published a year earlier, says that given the violence of the initial explosion and the depth to which the submarine fell, it was most certainly not intact on the seabed (conforming with what the *Halibut* found during its inspection of the site in 1968 but not publicly revealed until 1994) and, in any event, the ship's lift capacity was insufficient to bring it up in one piece. Moreover, cutting it apart while attached to the claw would have posed considerable engineering difficulties.[106]

News reports in 1975 and 1976 (stimulated by leaks from the Los Angeles Police Department, which was investigating a burglary at an office owned by the Hughes corporation from which documents describing the mission were apparently stolen), stated that during the salvage operation, operator error damaged the claw, causing it to break

104. One report, citing intelligence analysts, speculates that the motives for this effort include "the mission's raw intelligence value, the C.I.A.'s eagerness to outdo the Pentagon, and the Nixon administration's willingness to use Federal contracts as a 1972 re-election aid. The *Glomar Explorer's* main contractors were Hughes, Lockheed and Global Marine, all in the electoral plum of California." Lieutenant General Daniel O. Graham, deputy director of the CIA from 1973 to 1974, was aware of the *Halibut's* earlier mission, but defended proceeding with the *Glomar Explorer* because the CIA sought to retrieve all the submarine's warheads. "It would have given us better data points on their nuclear technology. That was a worthwhile endeavor, as far as I was concerned." See Broad, "Navy Has Long Had Secret Subs for Deep-Sea Spying, Experts Say," p. A1.

105. Colby stated that two nuclear torpedoes and the body of a Soviet nuclear expert (and his diary) were recovered.

106. Roy Varner and Wayne Collier, *A Matter of Risk: The Incredible Inside Story of the CIA's Hughes Glomar Explorer Mission to Raise a Russian Submarine* (New York: Random House, 1978); Clyde W. Burleson, *The Jennifer Project* (Englewood Cliffs, N.J.: Prentice-Hall, 1977). Although contradictory and necessarily incomplete, these remain the best sources of information on Project AZORIAN/JENNIFER.

and release the submarine as it neared the surface. Two nuclear torpedo warheads were reportedly recovered, but four-fifths of the submarine and its three ballistic missiles fell back to the ocean floor. However, other sources suggest that the mission was much more successful and that the CIA created the broken claw incident as a cover story to conceal this and thus avoid antagonizing the Soviet Union. In 1993 a panel of Russian scientists confirmed in a report to Russian President Boris Yeltsin that two warheads were recovered. Six bodies of Russian sailors (out of a crew of eighty-six) were recovered and buried at sea by the salvage team, a fact revealed by the CIA only in 1992 (but reported in a 1978 book on the project).[107]

After the recovery and while the *Hughes Glomar Explorer* returned to port in August 1974, analysts pored over the remains of the submarine, determining among other things that it was crudely constructed when compared with U.S. submarines. Efforts to recover the remainder of the submarine under the follow-on Project MATADOR were apparently abandoned after the details of the operation were disclosed in the press in 1975.

As a CIA covert program, the official cost of Project AZORIAN/JENNIFER has never been officially revealed. Published accounts put the then-year cost at between $200 million and $550 million, which is equivalent to some $665 million to $1.8 billion. Although controlled and expended by the CIA, funds for the project reportedly came from the navy's antisubmarine warfare budget.[108] One analyst pegs the total cost of the effort at "over a hundred million dollars," while a reporter describes it as a "half-billion-dollar" and "more than half a billion dollars" venture, which equates to roughly $400 million to $2 billion in 1996 dollars.[109]

Deciphering the "Secret" Intelligence Budget

Providing an estimate of nuclear-related intelligence spending is rife with methodological problems, both in collecting and in interpreting the data. Spending levels for most intelligence agencies and individual reconnaissance programs remain highly classified information (see figure 3-3 for the present organization of the intelligence community). Since 1972 the intelligence budget has been divided between the National Foreign Intelligence Program (NFIP) and Tactical Intelli-

107. William J. Broad, "Russia Says U.S. Got Sub's Atom Arms," *New York Times,* June 20, 1993, p. 14; Varner and Collier, *A Matter of Risk,* pp. 181–82.

108. Varner and Collier, *A Matter of Risk,* pp. 29–30, 190–91, 213; Burleson, *The Jennifer Project,* pp. 7, 49, 171.

109. Richelson, *American Espionage and the Soviet Target,* pp. 270–74; Broad, "Russia Says U.S. Got Sub's Atom Arms," p. 14; Broad, "Navy Has Long Had Secret Subs for Deep-Sea Spying."

gence and Related Activities (TIARA), and in 1995 a third category, the Joint Military Intelligence Program (JMIP), was added. These categories have never been hard and fast, and their relationship to what was in the 1950s termed "positive strategic intelligence" remains less than transparent (this aggregation appears to roughly correspond to the NFIP).

Since the beginning of the nuclear era, spending on intelligence and related activities has been among the most closely guarded secrets of the American government. The significant increase in CIA spending on covert operations in the early 1950s raised questions about whether the CIA budget should continue to be hidden in the State Department's finances, and spending on the U-2 reconnaissance aircraft prompted similar concerns. Although budget figures for individual intelligence-related activities have been and are released either sporadically in congressional hearings or systematically through military budget documents, spending levels for individual agencies have never been officially released and, until recently, neither has the total annual intelligence budget. On October 15, 1997, CIA director George J. Tenet, in response to a lawsuit filed by the Federation of American Scientists, stated that the total fiscal 1997 intelligence budget was $26.6 billion. At the same time, Tenet asserted that release of future budget figures "will be considered only after determining whether such disclosures could cause harm to national security by showing trends over time." He also refused to disclose any other intelligence spending data, either for agencies or individual programs, because such an action "could harm national security."[110]

The question of releasing a single annual figure for overall intelligence spending has been the subject of political debate for nearly two decades. Most recently, the report of the Commission on the Roles and Capabilities of the United States Intelligence Community concluded that the president "should disclose to the public the overall figure for the intelligence budget" and that "this can be done in manner that does not raise a significant security concern." Though necessarily limited, the information "would let the American public know what is being spent on intelligence as a proportion of federal spending . . . and may, to some degree, help restore the confidence of the American people in the intelligence function."[111] The commission went on to

110. Tim Weiner, "For First Time, U.S. Discloses Spying Budget," *New York Times* (Washington edition), October 16, 1997, p. A27; R. Jeffrey Smith, "Espionage Budget Totaled $26.6 Billion," *Washington Post,* October 16, 1997, p. A9; "Statement of the Director of Central Intelligence Regarding the Disclosure of the Aggregate Intelligence Budget for Fiscal Year 1997" (available on the World Wide Web at http://www.fas.org/sgp/foia/victory.html). Five months later, Tenet disclosed that the fiscal 1998 intelligence budget was $26.7 billion. Tim Weiner, "Voluntarily, CIA Director Reveals Intelligence Budget," *New York Times* (Washington edition), March 21, 1998, p. All

111. In response, on April 23, 1996, President William J. Clinton authorized Congress to release the "bottom line" intelligence budget figure in 1997. The proposal was quickly endorsed by Senator Arlen Specter (Republican of Pennsyl-

FIGURE 3-3. Organization of the U.S. Intelligence Community

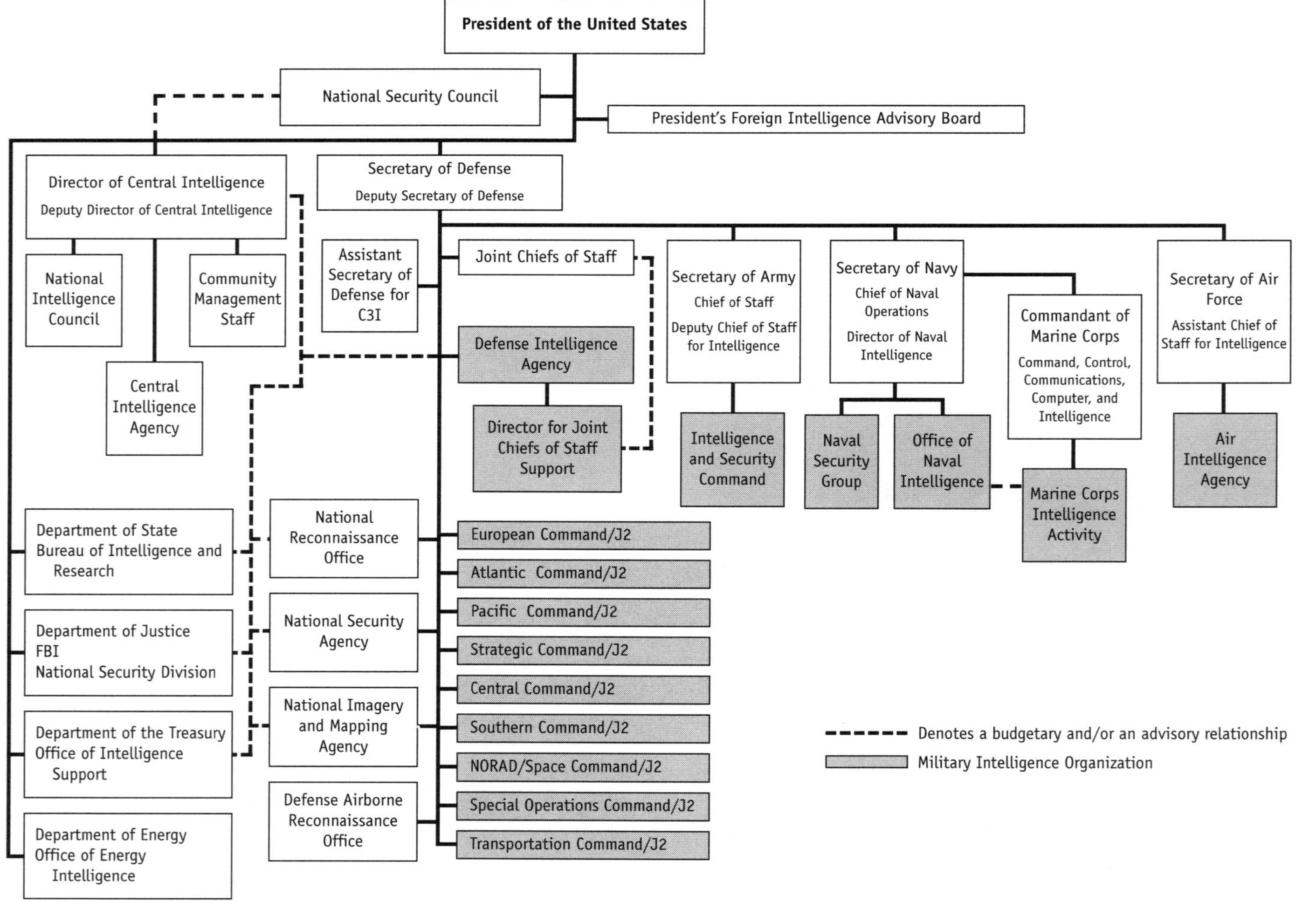

Source: Bernard C. Victory, ed., *Modernizing Intelligence: Structure and Change for the Twenty-first Century* (Fairfax, Va.: National Institute for Public Policy, September 1997).

recommend that "at the beginning of each congressional budget cycle, the President or a designee disclose the total amount of money appropriated for intelligence activities for the current fiscal year (to include NFIP, JMIP, and TIARA) and the total amount being requested for the next fiscal year. . . . No further disclosures should be authorized."[112]

At the same time, the commission's report provided a variety of charts that contained surprisingly detailed information concerning budget and personnel levels of individual agencies and programs.[113] As of this writing, the commission's recommendation, though embraced by the president, remains unimplemented in the face of congressional skepticism.

The classification problems extend not simply to public disclosure but also to congressional oversight. The primary congressional sources of information on the intelligence budget are briefings, the formal congressional budget justification books, and written questions for the record and answers thereto. But there are a variety of impediments to effective congressional oversight. For one thing, only a small number of people have full-time responsibility for important committee functions. In the case of the Senate Intelligence Committee, "six core staff and three designees have at least part-time responsibility for reviewing various NFIP programs and one core staff reviews the [TIARA] account for the Committee and develops the resulting set of annual recommendations this Committee makes to the Senate Armed Services Committee, which has jurisdiction over TIARA."[114]

This process is further constrained by the classified nature of the programs the committee reviews. That is to say, it lacks "alternative sources of information and points of view on intelligence budget requests, as there are few constituents with legitimate access to intelligence programs who wish to bring information forward to the Committees."[115]

The problems with NFIP budget submissions have been the focus of increasing congressional concern. Questions are being asked about

---

vania), chairman of the Intelligence Committee, and supported by the Senate. However, House members were opposed, and the 1997 Intelligence Authorization Act barred release of the total budget figure. In subsequent floor votes to amend the 1998 Intelligence Authorization Act to provide for release of the aggregate figure in that year and succeeding years, the Senate (56 to 43) and the House (237 to 192) both voted to oppose the release of any intelligence budget information. See Walter Pincus, "Clinton Approves Disclosure of Intelligence Budget Figure," *Washington Post,* April 24, 1996, p. A19; *Congressional Record,* June 19, 1997, pp. S5963–S5978; *Congressional Record,* July 9, 1997, pp. H4948–H4985 (these debates are available on the World Wide Web at http://www.fas.org/sgp/foia/victory.html).

112. Commission on the Roles and Capabilities of the United States Intelligence Community, *Preparing for the 21st Century: An Appraisal of U.S. Intelligence* (GPO, 1996), p. 142 (also available on the World Wide Web at http://www.access.gpo.gov/sv_docs/dpos/epubs/int/index.html).

113. Federation of American Scientists Intelligence Reform Project, "Intelligence Agency Budgets: Commission Recommends No Release but Releases Them Anyway," updated March 14, 1996 (available on the World Wide Web at http://www.fas.org/irp/commission/budget.htm).

114. Mary Sturtevant, "Congressional Oversight of Intelligence: One Perspective," *American Intelligence Journal,* vol. 13 (Summer 1992), p. 18.

115. Sturtevant, "Congressional Oversight of Intelligence," pp. 18–19.

not only the current method of depicting base expenditures but also the lack of details concerning base activities, which after all account for "the vast majority" of NFIP program costs. "This situation," says Congress, "is unacceptable."[116]

Given these limitations, it is not surprising that congressional supervision of the intelligence community has resulted in "oversight" in both meanings of that term. All of the various mechanisms with which the Congress attempts to regulate other components of the executive branch are atrophied or absent in the case of the intelligence community. Although Congress retains legal power over the community, legislative participation more frequently takes the form of political influence. Perception management, coalition building, and the formulation of policy are the products of public hearings, published reports, and press relations. Profound classification of information largely precludes these instruments of influence, the coin of the realm for the rest of the Congress, from being brought to bear on the intelligence community.

The irrelevance of the debate over releasing the aggregate total for intelligence spending becomes clear when it is understood that much more detailed budget data on America's most secret intelligence agencies is regularly revealed in the Pentagon budget. It is popularly believed that the intelligence budget is completely invisible. The astonishing fact is that it is thinly disguised, since it is hard to completely hide tens of billions of dollars.

To paraphrase Albert Einstein, the intelligence budget is subtle, but it is not perverse. Appreciation of this subtlety can provide surprising insight into the budgets of the NRO, the NSA, and the Defense Intelligence Agency (DIA). With a few clear exceptions, the annual budgets of NRO (more than $6 billion) and NSA (nearly $4 billion) are presented in the DOD's annual budget request and its unclassified supporting documents according to the same logic and rules as used by other less highly classified programs. Simple arithmetic readily reveals the budgets of these agencies, with a margin of error of perhaps 10 percent, to within a few hundred million dollars.

Central Intelligence Agency

It is popularly imagined that the CIA's budget is entirely obscured from public view. Some have implied that perhaps the agency is financed by

116. Adapted from House Permanent Select Committee on Intelligence, *Intelligence Authorization Act for Fiscal Year 1994—Classified Annex to the Joint Explanatory Statement of the Committee of the Conference (To Accompany H.R. 2330)* (1993), pp. 17–18, in *NRO Headquarters Project,* Hearings before the Senate Select Committee on Intelligence, 103 Cong. 2 sess. (GPO, 1995), pp. 108–10 (Top Secret, declassified and released in conjunction with the hearing).

a hidden accounting charge levied on a range of government agencies. Novelist Tom Clancy once even suggested that the agency's budget was to be found in the bowels of the Agriculture Department.[117] The reality is far more prosaic than the cult of secrecy would suggest.

The "Selected Activities" budget line item in "Other Procurement Air Force" includes the entire annual CIA budget of approximately $3 billion, as well as the CIA portion of the NRO satellite procurement budget. The CIA is clearly funded through this line item, for the outlay rates (the rate at which appropriated money is actually spent) for "Other Procurement Air Force" are much faster that for any other procurement budget category.[118] Personnel, operations, and RDT&E have much faster outlay rates (spending most of their budget in the first year or two) than do procurement accounts (whose outlays peak in the third year after the appropriation). Because "Selected Activities" accounts for roughly half of "Other Procurement Air Force" (and neither the army nor navy have such line items), it is apparent that this line item conceals the budget for an operational activity, rather than "other procurement." This operating activity is clearly not some other intelligence agency, since the budgets of other agencies, such as the NSA, are explicitly accounted for elsewhere in the budget (even if the details are slightly obscured).

What is unclear is the exact distribution within this line item between the CIA and the CIA's portion of NRO, given the uncertainties about the precise CIA budget. To complicate matters, at least some funding for satellite systems would be included in the budget for the CIA Science and Technology Directorate, which manages the development of CIA intelligence satellites. Because the accounting methodology used by the intelligence community to differentiate these two budget items is unavoidably obscure, there remains an uncertainty of several hundred million dollars as to how much money is allocated to the CIA and to the CIA's work that is funded through the NRO.

The Most Secret Agency

The NRO is America's most secretive intelligence organization. Although it was created on August 25, 1960, the public was unaware of its existence for more than a decade. The first major book on satellite

117. Tom Clancy, *Debt of Honor* (New York: G.P. Putnam's Sons, 1994), p. 22. Reflecting popular culture, Clancy suggests that portions of CIA's budget are variously concealed in authorizations for the Departments of Agriculture, Interior, or Health and Human Services. A moment's reflection would suggest, however, that shifting the CIA budget from agency to agency would expose CIA's finances to the inquiring minds of an extensive array of congressional and departmental staff, not all of whom might be predisposed to accommodate such maneuvers. It is also far easier to simply leave an unexplained sum in "Other Procurement Aircraft" than to have large inexplicable sums appearing and disappearing in the accounts of other agencies whose budgets are often subject to greater scrutiny than those of the Defense Department.

118. Department of Defense, Office of the Comptroller, *National Defense Budget Estimates for FY 1995* (March 1994), p. 47.

intelligence, published in 1971, gave no hint of such an entity.[119] More than a decade passed before the first (inadvertent) official mention of the NRO. Through an oversight during declassification of a 1973 Senate committee report, the NRO was included in a list of intelligence agencies whose budgets were recommended for public disclosure.[120] The NRO did not officially announce its existence until September 18, 1992; it was not until December 18, 1996, that the agency announced the launch of a reconnaissance satellite before the fact. According to an NRO spokeswoman, the move was a cost-saving measure: "We want to spend our resources protecting things that are worth protecting." In fact, one estimate puts the savings at hundreds of thousands of dollars per launch. All details of the satellites being launched, however, will continue to remain highly classified.[121]

Until its 1992 reorganization along functional lines (signals and imaging intelligence), the NRO was structured around its three executive agents: air force Program A, the CIA's Program B, and the navy's Program C. Thus one might expect the NRO budget to be divided along similar lines. Given the technical complexity and small numbers of intelligence satellites, however, the distinction between RDT&E funding and procurement funding is likely to be less clear (this is not unprecedented, as the first four MILSTAR communications satellites have all been procured from research and development funding).

Six line items in DOD's budget account for the NRO budget. Program Element 34111, "Special Activities," found in both the navy and air force RDT&E budgets, is displayed in the unclassified *RDT&E Programs R-1* budget document. The budget for these lines is usually deleted from unclassified budget documents, but it is easy to deduce the approximate value, since the *total* for Program 3 (intelligence) is given in the *R-1* budget document. To illustrate the inconsistency in the secrecy of the "secret" budget, the 1991 version of the *R-1* displayed budget figures for *all* the normally deleted line items, providing a check on calculations for other years.

It is clear that 34111 "Special Activities" funds the NRO, because unclassified *Program Element Descriptive Summaries* budget documents state that this budget item funds construction of support facilities for four classified spacecraft at Vandenberg Air Force Base, the primary NRO launch facility. Program Element 34111N "Special Activities Navy" funds all aspects of the navy's ocean surveillance signals intelli-

119. Philip J. Klass, *Secret Sentries in Space* (New York: Random House, 1971). Whether Klass's silence was engendered by ignorance or reticence on his own part is unclear, as there are several times at which he indicated possession of some point of information that he declined to publish in the national interest. This work remained the primary published source for over a decade, until the works of Burrows (*Deep Black*), and Richelson (*America's Secret Eyes in Space*).

120. Richelson, *The U.S. Intelligence Community,* pp. 29–32.

121. Associated Press, "U.S. Reveals Spy Satellite Launch Plan," *Washington Post,* December 19, 1996, p. A16; Reuters, "Pentagon Lifts Veil on Launch," *Washington Times,* December 19, 1996, p. A6.

gence program, variously referred to as White Cloud, Classic Wizard, and the Naval Ocean Surveillance System (NOSS). Program Element 34111F "Special Activities Air Force" funds the development of other new intelligence satellites.

The "Special Program" line item in "Missile Procurement Air Force," displayed in the *Procurement Programs P-1* unclassified budget document, funds production of intelligence satellites assigned by NRO to the air force. This is to be expected, because the missile procurement account funds acquisition of unclassified spacecraft as well. In another instance of the inconsistency of the NRO secrecy policy, unlike the "Special Activities" RDT&E line item, the funding for this procurement item is publicly reported each year in the unclassified *P-1* budget document, down to the nearest hundred thousand dollars. From all the available data, we conclude that the overall NRO budget nearly tripled during the 1980s, increasing from more than $3 billion in 1980 to more than $8 billion in the mid-1980s, with the 1996 Clinton administration request totaling more than $6 billion.[122]

The direct costing of spacecraft and launch vehicles provides another check on the validity of these estimates. Proceeding from the known payload capacities of launch vehicles used by the NRO, and assuming that these payloads cost somewhat more per pound than large NASA scientific satellites (such as the Gamma Ray Observatory or the Upper Atmosphere Research Satellite), the air force and CIA special program line items would support the procurement of one of each of the major types of intelligence satellites every year or two during the late 1980s. This is just the production rate to be expected on the basis of anticipated satellite lifetimes and required constellation sizes. These estimates are also consistent with the observation in 1987 by Representative George Brown (Democrat of California), then serving on the House Intelligence Committee, that the cost of a single KEYHOLE was $2 billion.[123]

No Such Agency

The National Security Agency is the nation's cryptologic organization, established in secret by President Truman on November 4, 1952, and tasked with making and breaking codes and ciphers. In addition, the NSA is a major center of foreign language analysis and research and

122. Another check on this total is possible given revelations by the NRO itself in 1996 that it unknowingly accumulated a surplus of nearly $4 billion in 1995, an occurrence likely to draw attention with anything less than a $7 billion annual budget. See Tony Capaccio, "Spy Agency's 1995 Surplus Tallied at Near $4 Billion," *Defense Week Special,* May 15, 1996, p. 1; Tim Weiner, "A Spy Agency Admits Accumulating $4 Billion in Secret Money," *New York Times,* May 16, 1996, p. A17.

123. *Congressional Record* (February 26, 1987), p. H850.

development within the government. The NSA is a high-technology organization, working on the frontiers of communications and data processing.[124] Compared with the CIA, the NSA has long been regarded as justly deserving the reputation of being so secretive that its initials really stand for "No Such Agency."

Whereas the CIA budget is regularly the subject of public reports, the NSA budget is seldom the subject of press speculation, and published reports vary widely, with some estimates running as high as $10 billion. A principal source of confusion is the distinction between the NSA proper and the associated military elements of the Central Security Service.[125] These service elements have historically been quite expensive, encompassing many thousands of personnel at overseas ground stations. In fact, the budget of the NSA itself turns out to be not much larger than that of CIA, and surprisingly, much more readily discernible from official public sources. For example, contracts with the NSA are routinely announced by the DOD, which coyly refers to the NSA as the "Maryland Procurement Office."

The annual *R-1* and *P-1* military budget documents provide total figures for RDT&E and procurement for all defense agencies, as well as funding for each individual agency, except for the NSA and DIA. The total for these two agencies is readily estimated, however, and since the NSA is much larger than the DIA, the bulk of this remainder must be for the NSA. Total RDT&E and procurement funding can thus be estimated at some $2 billion annually.

Unfortunately, there was until recently no "*O-1*" for the operations and maintenance account, but each year testimony is given to Congress that displays the operations and maintenance budget for defense agencies. As with the *R-1* and *P-1,* this display provides a total figure for all defense agencies, as well as funding for each agency, with a few exceptions. Another amusing example of the inconsistency with which the "secret" budget is publicly discussed is the presentation of the operations and maintenance budget, which provides an aggregate figure for intelligence *and* communications (about $2.8 billion). This

124. Adapted from U.S. Senate Select Committee on Governmental Operations with Respect to Intelligence Activities, *Foreign and Military Intelligence—Book I,* 94 Cong. 2 sess. (GPO, 1976), pp. 325–55.

125. This arrangement created obvious confusion in the mind of at least one senior senator during a May 1956 congressional hearing. Planning figures for defense-wide research and development expenditures in fiscal years 1956 and 1957 included (in 1996 dollars) $97.5 million and $96.9 million, respectively, for the NSA. When an army official explained that these costs (along with funds for the Armed Forces Special Weapons Project) had been part of the army's R&D budget since 1950 (accounting for about 10 percent of the total army R&D budget in fiscal 1957) but were not controlled by the army, Senator Stuart Symington, a former secretary of the air force, believing that the money came out of funds that would otherwise be available to the army, inquired why the army had to "carry" more of the budgetary load for these agencies than the other services. The funds were included, explained Army officials, merely as "an administrative device to put this into the budget."This response apparently assured him that critical R&D funds were not being diverted away from endeavors to stay ahead of the Soviet Union, and he proceeded to another line of inquiry, choosing not to ask the obvious question as to why the DOD was including a not insignificant portion of the NSA's budget in an army account. See *Study of Airpower,* Hearings, vol. 1, pp. 633–37, 754–55.

includes the NSA and DIA, as well as the Defense Information Systems Agency (DISA), which is lumped in the aggregate to avoid revealing the intelligence portion of this account (a reticence that does not extend to the RDT&E and procurement accounts). However, DISA has no reticence in revealing its annual operations and maintenance budget (nearly $400 million) in its annual report. Simple arithmetic reveals the total for the DIA and NSA, and the bulk of this remainder (about $2 billion) must be NSA.

The operations and maintenance account consists of spending for contractor services and civilian employees (uniformed service members are funded through the military personnel account). Reported NSA employment levels are consistent this $2 billion estimate, as seen by dividing the typical cost of an NSA government employee (about $60,000), to determine direct civil service employment, and the average pay scale of a Defense Department civilian worker (about $40,000) which can be used to estimate total employment, including service and support contractors personnel. On the basis of the precedent of other defense agencies, more than 20,000 government employees work at NSA, more than 90 percent of whom percent are civilians, along with an equal number of contractor support personnel.[126]

The Defense Intelligence Agency

The Defense Intelligence Agency was established in 1961 to increase the DOD's intelligence capability and to unify defense intelligence efforts. The DIA's mission is to meet the military intelligence requirements of both the civilian and military sectors of the Department of Defense. Through its director, the DIA serves as the primary intelligence adviser to the secretary of defense and other senior decisionmakers. The agency's director, who is also the intelligence staff officer on the Joint Chiefs of Staff, is responsible for providing intelligence support for military operational commands. Intelligence professionals at the DIA support DOD military and intelligence planners, executive and legislative decisionmakers, and operational armed forces overseas and in the United States.

With major elements located at Bolling Air Force Base and the Pentagon in Washington, D.C., and in Clarendon, Virginia, the DIA employs both military and civilian personnel. Approximately two-thirds of the DIA's work force are civilians, while among the military, approximately one-third are enlisted. The DIA's staff totaled about 4,500 in the early 1980s and has nearly doubled since then through the

126. For more on the NSA, see Scott Shane and Tom Bowman, "No Such Agency," reprint of a six-part series that appeared in the *Baltimore Sun* from December 3 to 15, 1995; and James Bamford, *The Puzzle Palace* (New York: Penguin Books, 1984).

addition of elements from other components of the military intelligence community.[127] Most of these personnel work in the agency's three principal organizational elements: the national military intelligence collection, production, and support centers.

The same analytical approach used in evaluating the NSA budget also reveals the budget of the DIA, which by the mid-1990s had reached about $800 million annually. These estimates are also consistent with authoritative reports based on classified documents.[128]

The Cost of Intelligence

Unlike many other nuclear-related activities, intelligence-related budget numbers—except for the overall 1997 and 1998 budgets—are not officially released by the government. As indicated by the preceding discussion, however, a combination of semiofficial leaks and a judicious reading of what little information has been officially released provides a fair outline of overall spending patterns. From the available evidence, it is clear that the National Foreign Intelligence Program—which includes the CIA, NRO, NSA, and related agencies and activities—has ranged from $10 billion to $20 billion annually since its creation in 1972, while Tactical Intelligence and Related Activities have ranged from approximately $10 billion to $15 billion a year over the same period.

Officially, the totals for both of these programs are classified, although unattributed informed sources are regularly cited in reporting on intelligence issues. The NFIP total for fiscal 1993 was reportedly $17 billion, with a $17.8 billion request anticipated that year for fiscal 1994.[129] This estimate provides a useful calibration for a graph depicting the NFIP in constant dollars from 1965 through 1994, reprinted in a 1993 Congressional report.[130] TIARA accounts for the remaining $10 billion for 1993, a substantial decline over prior years.

The total intelligence budget doubled from about $18 billion in 1980 to a peak of nearly $35 billion in 1987. Although both NFIP and TIARA grew at equal rates in the early 1980s, the subsequent 20 percent decline has been almost entirely from TIARA, reflecting general reductions in military spending. In contrast, the NFIP today remains at record cold war levels, twice as large as at the time of the 1979 Soviet invasion of Afghanistan.

127. Woodward, *Veil,* p. 98.

128. Tony Capaccio and Eric Rosenberg, "Deutch Approves $27 Billion for Pentagon Spy Budgets," *Defense Week,* August 29, 1994, p. 1.

129. Douglas Jehl, "Clinton Said to Seek Increase in Intelligence Funds," *New York Times,* April 15, 1993, p. A1.

130. U.S. House of Representatives, Committee on Appropriations, *Department of Defense Appropriations Bill, 1994,* 103 Cong. 1 sess., Report 103-254 (GPO, 1993), p. 14.

Given the somewhat arbitrary division of activity between NFIP and TIARA, it is not possible to completely reconstruct either of these programs from more fundamental agency or program line-item building blocks. However, it is clear that the bulk of NFIP is accounted for by three agencies: the CIA, NSA, and NRO (which has a budget roughly equivalent to the CIA and NSA combined).

Before the NFIP/TIARA budget schema, many but not all of the activities currently covered in the NFIP were termed "positive strategic intelligence," and annual spending on these programs during the mid-1950s ranged from $5 billion to $7 billion.[131] Although evidence for the antecedent and intervening years is lacking, it is not unreasonable to assume a fairly rapid buildup in the late 1940s, with programs currently counted under the NFIP reaching contemporary levels by the early 1960s, owing in large measure to the presence of the NRO.

Thus it may be said that over the past half century total spending on intelligence was approximately $1 trillion, more or less evenly divided between "national" and "tactical" intelligence. Total spending on intelligence satellite systems by the NRO may be estimated at $270 billion, and at least this much was spent on the exploitation and analysis of data derived from the NRO's and other technical systems.

Allocating Intelligence Costs to Nuclear Weapons

Although costs are thus relatively quantifiable, the question of interpretation is more complex. Estimating how much of this trillion dollars was devoted to matters pertaining to nuclear weapons is no easy matter, for the intelligence community itself does not construct its budget along such lines.[132] Indeed, it is precisely the absence of such budgetary constructions that even senior intelligence officials have acknowledged as one of the defects of the process.[133] Intelligence, particularly national intelligence, is provided to consumers as a "free good," with agency budgets focused on and structured around collec-

131. Note, Executive Secretary to the National Security Council, "Trends in National Security Programs and the Fiscal and Budgetary Outlook through FY 1959," NSC 5609, August 6, 1956. See also Department of State Records Relating to State Department Participation in the Operations Coordinating Board and the National Security Council, 1953–60, Record Group 59, Box 88, file NSC 5609, National Archives.

132. For example, on March 21, 1995, CIA acting director Admiral William O. Studeman in a letter to the *New York Times,* asserted: "By 1993 the Central Intelligence Agency allocated 13 percent of its resources to the former Soviet Union. That figure will decline to less than 10 percent by fiscal year 1996." ("It's Time to Drop the C.I.A. Caricature," March 25, 1995, p. A22). Yet when the authors of this study queried the CIA about obtaining similar breakdowns for prior years, an official responded that the calculations in Studeman's letter were unique, possible only because Studeman "requested it," that assembling the data would be extremely resource-intensive, and that "there is no one place we have all this information." Pearl Cohen, CIA Public Liaison Staff, Office of Public Affairs, personal communication with Stephen I. Schwartz, July 25, 1995; and Letter from Pearl Cohen to Stephen I. Schwartz, August 2, 1995.

133. Henry S. Rowen, "Reforming Intelligence: A Market Approach," *American Intelligence Journal,* vol. 14 (Autumn–Winter 93–94), pp. 49–54.

tion and exploitation inputs rather than policy outputs. The intelligence community generally bases its budgets on the costs of satellites and paid informants, rather than the costs of finished intelligence on Soviet nuclear weapons or Iraqi conventional forces.

Thus during the cold war the intelligence community, at least in this regard, came to resemble its main adversary, with the producers operating in a command economy environment largely free of market-pricing mechanisms. Although some reformers have advocated introducing precisely such market-pricing mechanisms to enable intelligence consumers to value various products, the task at hand is unavoidably one of divining retrospectively the "shadow prices" that would have prevailed had such pricing (that is to say, budgeting by analytical priorities and categories rather than collection disciplines) been established from the outset.

At one extreme, given the presumption that any conflict with a nuclear-armed adversary such as the Soviet Union or China would quickly escalate to a nuclear exchange, it is difficult to disengage entirely any significant portion of the intelligence budget from nuclear war planning, as virtually all intelligence-related activities could be characterized as either planning for or supporting the avoidance of nuclear war. This, however, is not a particularly elegant or useful conclusion.

Surely at least during the early years of its operation, the overwhelming bulk of the efforts of the NRO and the consumers of its product was devoted to nuclear threats, both strategic and tactical. Throughout this period, there must have been few targets that were worthy of coverage by technical collection systems that were not of interest to the nuclear planning community, even if the primary tasking requirement derived from other priorities. Simple extrapolation would suggest an estimate of roughly half a trillion dollars for nuclear-related intelligence.

Another approach to this problem might be to simply and naively assume that intelligence resources devoted to the Soviet Union pertained to nuclear weapons and related issues, while other intelligence collection targets did not. In this case, it is instructive to recall an observation made by Director of Central Intelligence Robert Gates in 1991: "Today, about half of the community's resources are focused on the Soviet Union."[134] It is not unreasonable to assume that, to the extent that such assessments can be made, a similar allocation of resources prevailed throughout this entire period: that is, the United States devoted roughly half a trillion dollars to intelligence coverage of the

134. Robert Gates, "The Future of American Intelligence," Address to the Intelligence Community, Washington, D.C., December 4, 1991, p. 6.

Soviet Union, with the remainder devoted to other targets, such as China. Again, this would suggest an estimate of roughly half a trillion dollars for nuclear-related intelligence.

A lower bound might be established by asserting that the NRO's early activities were devoted almost entirely to nuclear war planning, but that thereafter the products of technical intelligence found such a diversity of consumers that allocating the costs of these programs exclusively to nuclear weapons planning would fail to do justice to the broad contributions of technical collection during the cold war. By this standard, one might assert a lower bound of perhaps $100 billion. Thus one may conclude that during the past half century the United States spent at least $100 billion on intelligence related to nuclear weapons and probably as much as $500 billion on such intelligence.

Estimating the total costs of all C^3I programs poses a variety of methodological challenges. Before Defense Secretary McNamara inaugurated the budgeting system known as the Five-Year Defense Program (now Future Years Defense Program) in 1962, budget data were typically displayed at very high levels of aggregation and in categories that too frequently measured resource inputs rather than programmatic outputs. Even the somewhat confusing data that are available for the period 1945–61 are fragmentary, and in some cases lacking. Nevertheless, by any reasonable reckoning, it is clear that over the past half century the United States has spent hundreds of billions of dollars on nuclear command, control, communications, and related programs.

Conclusion

Despite the hundreds of billions of dollars spent on strategic C^3I, the United States never achieved a stable and safe posture for its nuclear forces. The classic notion of stable deterrence was that neither adversary would have any rational grounds for initiating a nuclear attack as long as both projected a credible threat of retaliation after riding out an attack by the other. Although many embraced this idea, its feasibility was another matter. The defense establishments charged with operating the deterrent forces concluded that it was not practical for various reasons, most notably the inherent vulnerability of command and control.[135] The United States underinvested in command protection

135. Blair, *Strategic Command and Control,* p. 285. In an interview in early 1985, President Reagan appeared to confirm that the United States relied on a policy of launch on warning: "The word comes that they're [the missiles] on their way. And you sit here knowing that there is no way, at present, of stopping them. So they're going to blow up how much of this country we can only guess at, and *your only response can be to push the button before they get here* so that even though you're all going to die, they're going to die too" (emphasis added). See Hugh Sidney, "'The Alternative Is So Terrible,'" *Time,* January 28, 1985, p. 29.

and compensated with low-cost operational shortcuts that geared the United States to launch on warning.

The tremendous destructiveness of nuclear weapons meant that even a small number threatened the coherence of vital command posts and communications networks. To protect these systems, the United States (and the Soviet Union) invested heavily in various schemes: combinations of active defenses, electronic hardening, mobility, and redundancy. The return on such investments proved unsatisfactory, however. The systems were intrinsically susceptible to severe disruption from the effects of nuclear weapons. Even massive investment, a luxury beyond the means of most nuclear states, could not have entirely eliminated the problem. Retaliation, strictly defined, was thus a particularly demanding task, not so much because an initial attack might have destroyed all the individual weapons required, but because an attack threatened the command and control system necessary to provide a coherent response. Nuclear forces were not unitary rational actors but large organizations whose internal procedures made it difficult to carry out the expectations on which the standard perspective depended. Standard assessments of the U.S.-Soviet strategic balance glossed over this vulnerability, calling into serious question their conclusions about the stability of deterrence during the cold war.[136]

The vulnerability of command and control systems to nuclear attack created strong pressures to buttress the credibility of the retaliatory threat by delegating alert and launch authority and shortening the reaction time of nuclear forces. The United States thus preauthorized nuclear launch authority to military commanders who were outside the chain of presidential succession, and it even more widely distributed the authorization and unlock codes used to unleash the strategic forces.[137] Such steps—along with the delay in introducing PALs for

136. This and the following three paragraphs are adapted with permission from Blair, *The Logic of Accidental Nuclear War,* pp. 6–8; and Blair, *Global Zero Alert for Nuclear Forces,* p. 3.

137. One army officer recalled recently that "at least during one crisis period over Berlin [in the late 1950s, nuclear howitzer] units were deployed with nuclear weapons and the capability (and perhaps authority) to use them . . . delegated to a rather low level" Letter from Honorable William E. Burns, Major General U.S. Army (retired), to Stephen I. Schwartz, May 7, 1996. "In April 1956, President Eisenhower apparently authorized the Air Defense Command to use . . . [Genie air-to-air and Nike Hercules surface-to-air nuclear-armed] missiles immediately in case of surprise attack when it would be infeasible to wait for orders. . . . To further reduce reaction time, on May 22, 1957, Eisenhower issued an 'authorization for the expenditure of nuclear weapons' still classified, which apparently went beyond the air defense authorization of the previous year, and gave permission for nuclear response under a variety of emergency conditions. The very complex instructions needed to implement this authorization required extensive consideration by the Departments of Defense and State, and were not approved until February 17, 1959. Other Emergency Action Documents, including possibly a secret executive order covering the transfer of nuclear weapons from the AEC to the military and their subsequent utilization, were also promulgated during this time. Finally, in 1960, a series of still classified directives regarding the use of nuclear weapons was issued to each of the unified and specified commanders." See Rosenberg, "The Origins of Overkill," pp. 153, 158–59. Sixteen documents recently released to the National Security Archive under the Freedom of Information Act (available on the World Wide Web at http://www.seas.gwu.edu/nsarchive/news/19980319.htm) confirm that in 1956 and 1957 Eisenhower authorized specific military commanders to use nuclear weapons under certain strictly defined circumstances. These highly sensitive arrangements continued at least through the late 1980s. See

bombers, ICBMs, and SLBMs; and the decision by the DOD, DOE, and the navy in 1983 to forgo the use of insensitive high explosives (IHE) and other safety features on the W88 warhead and to use an extremely volatile propellant in combination with a high-yield (475-kiloton) warhead in order to maximize the range and effectiveness of the Trident II missile—are further evidence that the perceived urgency of deterrence overrode safety considerations.[138]

The fact that deterrence was the primary commitment, and safety the secondary one, during the cold war is more obvious at the strategic planning level. If safety had been a governing influence on overall nuclear postures, strategic forces would not have been so numerous, so dispersed, or so geared to rapid use. Postures that worked at cross-purposes with safety in so many dimensions would not have been adopted in the first place. If policymakers indeed wanted to minimize the possibility of nuclear war, as Richard Betts points out, their policy declarations, military preparations, and diplomacy during crises would have been "consistent with the notion that nuclear weapons should be used for nothing but retaliation against nuclear attack. U.S. policy, however, has rested on the principle that there are interests for which the United States would make the first use of nuclear weapons rather than concede."[139]

Although not illegal, all of this occurred without informed public consent. Provocative and risky deterrent practices ranging from strategic targeting to launch on warning to predelegation were developed under minimal democratic oversight and influence. Civilian masters of the military establishment failed to exercise vigilant oversight of strategic planning and failed to deal decisively with deficiencies in the safety and performance of nuclear command, control, communications, and intelligence systems. All the while, the nuclear planners misrepresented U.S. strategic and command and control capabilities as sophisticated, flexible, and resilient.

The quick reaction posture adopted by the United States (and Soviet Union) relied heavily on early warning, imposing another huge

---

Walter Pincus, "Military Got Authority to Use Nuclear Arms in 1957," *Washington Post,* March 21, 1998, p. A1.

138. U.S. Navy, Chief of Naval Operations, "W88 Warhead for Trident II/D-5 Missile," Text of a briefing given to Dr. William J. Perry at Lawrence Livermore National Laboratory circa Spring 1985, reproduced in *Report of the President's Blue Ribbon Task Group on Nuclear Weapons Program Management,* vol. 5: *Case Studies,* pt. 4, pp. 36–90. This briefing describes the decision on whether to incorporate IHE in the Trident II's warheads as one of being willing to "accept significant operational penalties" and further notes that its use would afford higher levels of safety during manufacture and transportation. In addition, DOD policy at the time was to use IHE "absent overriding operational concerns." The "penalties" were defined as a "payload reduction of at least one warhead" and a decrease of "400 miles of range" (pp. 78–79). See also R. Jeffrey Smith, "Trident's Mix of Propellant with Warheads Raises Safety Questions," *Washington Post,* May 29, 1990, p. A6; U.S. House of Representatives, "Nuclear Weapons Safety," Report of the Panel on Nuclear Weapons Safety of the Committee on Armed Services, 101 Cong. 2 sess. (GPO, 1990), pp. 26–29; R. Jeffrey Smith, "Design Changes Urged for Nuclear Weapons Safety," *Washington Post,* December 19, 1990, p. A4; Robert Burns, "Navy Warhead," Associated Press, March 10, 1994.

139. Richard Betts, *Nuclear Blackmail and Nuclear Balance* (Brookings, 1987), p. 2.

burden on command and control systems. The two-sided deployment of forces with very short delivery times required each side to monitor the opponent's forces on a near real-time basis, to detect both preparations for attack and actual launches. Both countries thus acquired an extensive and costly reconnaissance infrastructure that also had to be linked to the command and control systems to permit timely decisions and rapid military responses. The result was a pair of command and control systems with a strong propensity to raise alert levels during a period of crisis as they interacted with each other. Both systems also became more prone to react quickly to the first signs of enemy launches, rendering them vulnerable to faulty warning indicators. Unmanageable crisis interactions, aggravated by erroneous early warning that in the extreme could trigger the release of launch codes, became more likely.[140]

The Soviet Union eventually gravitated to a quick-launch policy as well after investing hundreds of billions more than the United States in protecting its command and control network.[141] In the 1980s the USSR established and tested a backup system known as "dead hand," which would allow the quasi-automatic launch of thousands of nuclear warheads in the event senior nuclear commanders are killed or otherwise neutralized before they could issue the launch commands (the system is active today).[142] Russia remains heavily dependent on a posture of nuclear quick-draw while it pours scarce national treasure into excavating deep underground command posts.[143]

---

140. Evidence for this can be found in a series of widely publicized false alerts at NORAD in 1979 and 1980. Subsequent congressional investigations revealed inadequate management of the early warning system and severe deficiencies and significant cost overruns in the computer systems used by NORAD to both detect and track nuclear weapons launches and order responses. Some of the deficiencies remained unresolved as of 1997. See U.S. Senate, "Recent False Alerts From the Nation's Missile Attack Warning System," Report of Senator Gary Hart and Senator Barry Goldwater to the Committee on Armed Services, 96 Cong. 2 sess. (GPO, 1980); U.S. House of Representatives, "Failures of the North American Aerospace Defense Command's (NORAD) Attack Warning System," May 19–20, 1981; U.S. House of Representatives, "NORAD Computer Systems Are Dangerously Obsolete," Twenty-third Report by the Committee on Government Operations," H. Rept. 97-449, 97 Cong. 2 sess. (GPO, 1982); *Our Nation's Nuclear Warning System: Will It Work If We Need It?* Hearings before a Subcommittee of the House Committee on Government Operations, 99 Cong. 1 sess. (GPO, 1986); U.S. General Accounting Office, *Attack Warning: ADP Replacement for Warning and Assessment System Still Years Away,* IMTEC-86-15 (1986); U.S. General Accounting Office, *Attack Warning: NORAD's Communications System Segment Replacement Program Should Be Reassessed,* IMTEC-89-1 (1988); U.S. General Accounting Office, *Attack Warning: Costs to Modernize NORAD's Computer System Significantly Understated,* IMTEC-91-23 (1991); U.S. General Accounting Office, *Attack Warning: Status of the Cheyenne Mountain Upgrade Program,* AIMD-94-175 (GPO, 1994).

141. Blair, *The Logic of Accidental Nuclear War,* pp. 120–24, 131–45, 169–70.

142. Blair, *Global Zero Alert for Nuclear Forces,* pp. 51–56; Bruce G. Blair, "Russia's Doomsday Machine," *New York Times,* October 8, 1993, p. A35; William J. Broad, "Russia Has "Doomsday" Machine, U.S. Expert Says," *New York Times,* October 8, 1993, p. A6.

143. The existence of such shelters was first disclosed with great fanfare in Department of Defense, *Soviet Military Power: An Assessment of the Threat, 1988* (GPO, 1988), pp. 59–62. At that time, Defense Secretary Frank Carlucci argued: "These facilities contradict in steel and concrete Soviet protestations that they share President Reagan's view that nuclear war can never be won and must never be fought. These facilities reveal that they are preparing themselves for just the opposite." Left unsaid by Carlucci was that the United States maintained similar facilities on a smaller scale. See John M. Broder, "Underground Shelters Built for Soviet Leaders," *Los Angeles Times,* April 30, 1988, p. 6; The most recent examples of this appear to be large facilities

Such historical and ongoing rapid reaction postures imposed on the command and control systems a requirement for ironclad safeguards that reliably prevented the accidental or illicit firing of even a single nuclear weapon (negative control). Unlike the previous requirements, this one was relatively inexpensive, but it nonetheless represented a daunting challenge. Negative control was the dominant peacetime function, and elaborate safeguards were incorporated in the systems. But for all their sophistication and stringency, these technical and organizational measures were not tested and proved in every situation that the cold war might have presented. This is particularly true for crisis situations, which could have severely strained safeguards because of the competing demands of exercising positive control (dispatching forces on authoritative command) under severe time constraints. Negative control was counterpoised to the positive function associated with the central strategic purpose of nuclear forces: preparing to carry out enough destruction to deter the enemy. The challenge to the command systems was to preserve strict operational control while ensuring a convincing performance of the wartime mission.

These requirements clashed, especially in crisis circumstances. Measures that would facilitate the speedy deliberate use of nuclear weapons competed with measures that would minimize the risk of their aberrant use, and vice versa. The result was a system far more capable of initiating an inadvertent nuclear attack than has been generally understood. As analyst Scott Sagan has written: "It is important to recognize that the military commands controlling U.S. nuclear weapons have been asked to do the impossible. . . . In retrospect, it should be acknowledged that while [these] organizations . . . performed this task with less success than we knew, they performed with more success than we *should* have reasonably expected."[144]

To give but one example of the risks involved, on October 26, 1962—during the Cuban Missile Crisis—a U-2 aircraft flying a routine air-sampling mission (to detect radioactive debris from Soviet nuclear tests) from Eielson Air Force Base in Alaska took a new route over the North Pole, necessitating the use of celestial navigation and a primitive sextant to navigate (because the magnetic compass would not operate).[145] The pilot wandered off course when the aurora borealis inter-

under construction in Yamantau Mountain, reportedly covering more than 60 square miles (155 square kilometers), or roughly the size of Washington, D.C., and Kosvinsky Mountain, in the Urals. Russia also continues to build an underground subway network to allow military leaders to rapidly evacuate Moscow in the event of war. See Michael R. Gordon, "Despite Cold War's End, Russia Keeps Building a Secret Complex," *New York Times,* April 16, 1996, p. A1; "Mystery Solved?" *U.S. News & World Report,* April 29, 1996, p. 24; Bill Gertz, "Moscow Builds Bunkers against Nuclear Attack," *Washington Times,* April 1, 1997, p. A1; James Carney, "Moscow's Secret Plans," *Time,* August 10, 1992, p. 39; Mark Walsh, "U.S. Suspects Russia Is Building Super-Bunker," *Defense News,* July 28–August 3, 1997, p. 3.

144. Sagan, *The Limits of Safety,* pp. 278–79.

145. The following account comes from Sagan, *The Limits of Safety,* pp. 135–40.

fered with his attempts to get a celestial fix, and he flew deep into Soviet airspace over Chukotski Peninsula. Soviet MiG interceptors were ordered to intercept and attempt to shoot down the U-2 (recall that this occurred just two and a half years after the U-2 piloted by Francis Gary Powers was downed over the Soviet Union).

The U-2 pilot was able to contact a U.S. command center in Alaska and directed to turn due east and return to U.S. airspace. During this maneuver, the aircraft ran out of fuel over Siberia. The pilot radioed for help, unsure if he would make it back to base. Two F-102 interceptors were then scrambled from Galena Air Force Base to rescue the U-2 and keep the MiGs from entering U.S. airspace. Because of the crisis in Cuba, the Alaskan command was then at DEFCON (defense condition) 3 and the F-102s were carrying nuclear-armed Falcon air-to-air missiles under the direct control of the pilots (under normal conditions, conventional missiles would have been loaded). Over the Bering Straits, the U-2 sighted one of the interceptors and was escorted back to a remote airstrip. From there, the pilot was flown back to Eielson and then on to SAC headquarters to brief General Thomas Power and other SAC officials. (General Power issued no reprimand "and said only that he wished the U-2 had not been on a [sampling] mission, since if it had been equipped with photographic or electronic intelligence devices, SAC would have learned even more about Soviet military forces as their air defense system reacted to the overflight.")

Although U-2s on this mission had strayed into Soviet airspace before, no one considered the consequences of this during the crisis, and so the air sampling missions were flown as usual. As Scott Sagan also notes, "The possibility of an accidental, unauthorized, or mistaken use of a U.S. nuclear weapon during this incident was not remote." Furthermore, given the already tense international climate, the "risk of escalation after any initial use would not be negligible."

In researching this and other nuclear accidents and incidents, Sagan was troubled to discover that SAC was quite reluctant to acknowledge the danger posed by such events. In a number of cases, the organization's institutional memory was so spotty that very serious accidents were not recorded in official SAC histories. With such omissions there is a danger that the organization will fail to learn from its mistakes.[146]

146. This tendency is evident in a June 1984 interview with four senior SAC officers conducted by the air force historian's office. One of these officers, General David A. Burchinal, a former SAC wing commander and former chief of staff of the Eighth Air Force, recalled the Alaska incident and insisted that "the Russians knew what was going on anyway, because our controllers in Alaska contacted the aircraft on the radio, gave him his correct course, and got him back out of there. *There was no reaction on the Soviets' part, because they were stood down*. . . . They didn't make any move. They did not increase their alert; they did not increase any flights, or their air defense posture. They didn't do a thing; they froze in place. We were never further from nuclear war than at the time of Cuba, never further" (emphasis added). Richard H. Kohn and Joseph P. Harahan, "U.S. Strategic Air Power, 1948–1962," *International Security,* vol. 12, no. 4 (Spring

Against the backdrop of this generally negative view of command and control systems, the stunning achievements of the technical collection disciplines of the intelligence community must rank as one of the brightest spots in cold war history. The true magnitude of these achievements were long shrouded by impenetrable secrecy, which has only now begun to lighten. To read the various declassified intelligence estimates and reports is but to catch a glimpse of the extent of the enlightenment provided by satellite intelligence. From the outset, it dispelled the deep suspicions that had fueled the excesses of worst-case force planning. For example, Frank Madden, the chief engineer on the CORONA program, felt certain that "the CORONA pictures kept us from an even more accelerated arms race by giving us the power to make decisions based on facts rather than fear."[147] Soon thereafter satellite intelligence broke the deadlock on verification that had long frustrated the growing awareness that the nuclear genie had created common security interests between even ideological foes.

With future declassification of more detailed and more recent material pertaining to satellite intelligence, one may hope, however, for a more nuanced view. Although nothing can detract from the magnitude of the achievements of technical collection during the cold war, it must be admitted that these assets were unavoidably targeted against the most fearsome, and impressive, manifestations of Soviet state power: vast nuclear weapons facilities, missile silos scattered across millions of square kilometers, burgeoning antimissile test ranges, and the other trappings of nuclear power. All of these achievements of the Soviet state were intended to proclaim the might of the Soviet military, and as Soviet accomplishments matched Soviet pretense, they did so to an increasingly attentive audience in the skies.

One may wonder whether the American intelligence community, with technological systems focused on monitoring these technological accomplishments, was perhaps inadvertently complicit with Soviet efforts to "show the best and hide the rest." Entranced by the awful displays of nuclear might revealed by equally awesome intelligence collection systems, the American intelligence community was at least to

---

1988), p. 95. Burchinal appears oblivious to the fact that a stand-down is actually an alert step taken in preparation for war. As Blair has revealed, the Soviet Union did put its forces on alert during the crisis; the United States failed to notice. Equally troubling, a special chronology commemorating the air force's fiftieth anniversary, with entries designed to "tell a remarkable story of a powerful military institution's adaptation to 50 years of political, technological, and social change" and purporting to record "significant events and achievements from 18 September 1947 through 9 April 1997," fails to mention the 1962 U-2 incident, the nuclear weapons accidents over Palomares, Spain, and Thule, Greenland, in 1966 and 1968, respectively, or any other serious air force nuclear weapons accidents or incidents. See Frederick J. Shaw, Jr., and Timothy Warnock, *The Cold War and Beyond: Chronology of the United States Air Force, 1947–1997* (Maxwell Air Force Base, Ala.: Air University Press, 1997).

147. Seth Shulman, "Code Name: Corona," *Technology Review*, October 1996, pp. 22–31. While this assessment is accurate, it is nonetheless important to realize that the vastly improved photographic data provided by satellite reconnaissance also contributed to the increasing requirements for nuclear weapons by the military by identifying ever larger numbers of potential targets.

some extent thematically apperceptive of the state of the Soviet state.[148] And Soviet officials, of course, tried to "make the most of U.S. anxieties." There was, it seems, "a unique symbiosis between some purposive Soviet deception and some equally purposive U.S. gullibility."[149] Increasingly deluged by the products of our technological marvels, the intelligence community was disinclined to listen to those still small voices suggesting that the exertions of the cold war and the deformities and contradictions of the Soviet system were extracting a greater toll than perhaps anyone realized.[150] Building on the previous discussion, chapter 4 examines the elaborate systems developed since the 1950s to defend the United States as a whole, and in particular military equipment and installations, against nuclear attack.

148. Former chairman of the Joint Chiefs of Staff, General Maxwell Taylor, wrote that "the only perception of Soviet strength available to an observer with access to American sources is an image derived from interpretations of photographs and other technological data associated with the nuclear weapons which constitute the core of Soviet strategic strength—truly an image seen 'as through a glass, darkly.' A perverse skeptic might even wonder whether all this imagery might not be a clever Soviet contrivance with mirrors to lead Americans into error and thereby cause them to acquire an exaggerated impression of Soviet strength. After all, the Soviet Union has never seriously challenged the American estimates of their forces, whereas they challenge almost everything else. Their silence suggests that they are not dissatisfied with our figures." Maxwell D. Taylor, *Precarious Security* (New York: W. W. Norton, 1976), pp. 76–77.

149. Freedman, *U.S. Intelligence and the Soviet Strategic Threat,* p. 78.

150. A useful alternative perspective on this point may be found in Bruce D. Berkowitz and Jeffrey T. Richelson, "The CIA Vindicated: The Soviet Collapse *Was* Predicted," *National Interest,* no. 41 (Fall 1995), pp. 36–47; and Daniel Patrick Moynihan, Henry Rowen, Charles Wolf, Jr., and William T. Lee, "The CIA's Credibility" (letters in response), *National Interest,* no. 42 (Winter 1995/96), pp. 109–14.

4

Defending against the Bomb

John E. Pike, Bruce G. Blair, and Stephen I. Schwartz

After the events of August 1945, Americans, military and civilian alike, quickly recognized that the devastation visited upon Hiroshima and Nagasaki by one B-29 bomber carrying one atomic bomb could soon occur in the United States. Initial defensive efforts focused on the skies, as for more than a decade after World War II large aircraft were the only practical means of delivering a nuclear weapon over long distances. With the development of ballistic missiles in the late 1950s, efforts turned toward countering them. Around the same time, programs were initiated to attack and destroy satellites in orbit and to sink ships and submarines carrying nuclear weapons. While enormous sums of money were spent on all these efforts, none was able to significantly lessen the threat posed by the Soviet and later, Chinese, nuclear arsenals.

Summary

—Since the end of World War II, the United States has spent $937 billion on programs for strategic air and missile defense, antisatellite and antisubmarine warfare, and civil defense (figure 4-1).

—Despite this enormous investment, strategic defenses were generally unable to protect the U.S. population, the economy, or military

FIGURE 4-1. The Costs of Defending against the Bomb[a]

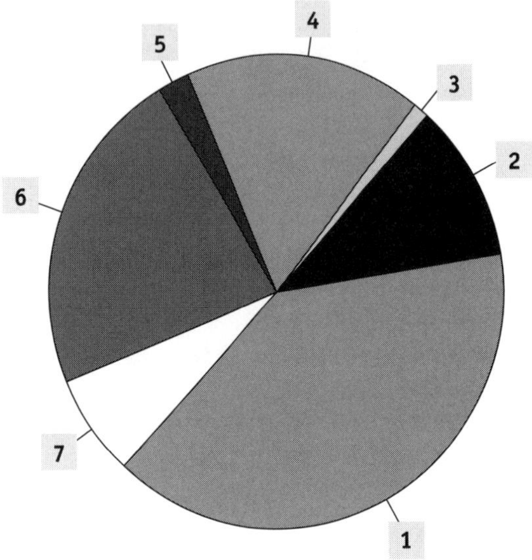

Total: $937.2 billion

1 Strategic air defenses
$371.0 billion / 39.6%

2 Ballistic missile defenses
$100.0 billion / 10.7%

3 Other

Antisatellite weapons/supporting programs
$7.2 billion / 0.8%

Nuclear Emergency Search Team
$0.5 billion / 0.1%

4 Strategic antisubmarine warfare
$161.0 billion / 17.2%

5 Civil defense/interstate highways
$19.5 billion / 2.1%

6 Overhead (Air/BMD/ASAT/CD)
$211.0 billion / 22.5%

7 Overhead (ASW)
$67.0 billion / 7.1%

a. In constant 1996 dollars.

forces—including strategic forces—from nuclear destruction by Soviet missiles and bombers. Despite periodic rejuvenation of strategic defense programs during the 1960s, 1980s, and 1990s, the rapid pace of the development of offensive countermeasures, coupled with extremely high projected costs and uncertain performance, left a trail of unfulfilled plans and fruitless expenditures on programs abandoned before completion. Whether past or future investment offer any realistic hope of strengthening American security at a reasonable cost against nuclear threats—from Russia, China, or the developing world—remains debatable, but history does not justify optimism.

The Desire for Defenses

The American political system has understandably never reconciled itself to its supreme vulnerability to nuclear destruction. For four centuries the United States has enjoyed isolation from Europe and Asia, behind oceanic barriers that have kept it largely free of the destructive invasions that were the normal course of history for most societies. In the event these oceanic barriers proved insufficient, from the early days of the Republic massive coastal defense artillery emplacements bristled around major harbors. These traditional means were augmented during World War II, when air defense wardens busied themselves with blackouts and other precautions against an aerial enemy that never materialized.[1]

The advent of the nuclear era abruptly exposed American society to the menace of sudden and utter destruction. This prospect, entirely without precedent in the American experience save perhaps for the devastation wrought by General William Tecumseh Sherman's march to the sea during the Civil War, was only slightly tempered by the knowledge that the terrors of nuclear war would be mutually inflicted on all participants. Throughout the nuclear era the national political scene was repeatedly convulsed with passing enthusiasms for applying updated equivalents of coastal defense artillery and air raid wardens to the hazards of atomic-age warfare.[2]

---

1. Although another attack on the scale of Pearl Harbor did not occur, Japan did mount three serious efforts to attack the mainland. On February 24, 1942, a Japanese submarine shelled an oil storage field near Santa Barbara with seventeen rounds of 5.5-inch ammunition, the first direct attack on the continental United States in 128 years. The submarine also sank two merchant ships. On March 4, 1942, a second attack on Pearl Harbor was launched using two large flying boats refueled by submarine. Overcast conditions prevented the bombers from locating their targets so the bombs were released "blindly." One fell into the sea, the second near Honolulu (this bomb was later blamed on U.S. aircraft). Additional flights were planned but later canceled. In August 1942, however, a specially outfitted reconnaissance aircraft was launched from the deck of a submarine in waters off Cape Blanco, Oregon. The floating plane flew 50 miles (80 kilometers) inland, released two incendiary bombs over a forest, and returned to the submarine. Later, a second such mission was flown. These were the first attacks by aircraft on the continental United States. By far the most elaborate air offensive mounted by Japan involved some 9,000 specially designed balloon bombs. These weapons were launched from the northeast coast of Honshu between November 1944 and April 1945 and lofted by the prevailing winds over the Pacific Ocean to the U.S. mainland. They carried incendiary and antipersonnel bombs and were designed to burn down American forests and cause widespread panic. Nearly 1,000 were estimated to have reached the United States (hundreds more landed in western Canada) and from November 4, 1944, and August 8, 1945, 285 "incidents" involving the balloon bombs were recorded. Once military officials recognized the threat, they sought to deny the Japanese government any propaganda or military gains by ordering the media not to report any balloon bomb incidents. Regrettably, this censorship precluded warning people about the danger from the balloons. On May 5, 1945, five children and a woman were killed near Bly, Oregon, when a bomb on a balloon they had found and were tugging on exploded. On May 22 the government rescinded its censorship order on the balloons and issued a warning describing them and warning persons to keep their distance. The only other recorded damage was two small brushfires and, ironically, a "scram" of the three Hanford "piles" on March 10, 1945, when a balloon bomb came in contact with off-site electrical lines and severed power for two minutes; it took three days to return the piles, then producing the plutonium fuel for the bomb that would be dropped on Nagasaki, to full power. Hanford thus became the only U.S. nuclear facility ever to come under enemy attack. See Dorr Carpenter and Norman Polmar, *Submarines of the Imperial Japanese Navy* (Annapolis, Md.: Conway Maritime Press, 1986), pp. 20–21; Nicholas D. Kristof, "Nobuo Fujita, 8J, Is Dead; Only Foe to Bomb America," *New York Times* (Washington edition), October 3, 1997, p. A14; Robert C. Mikesh, *Balloon Bomb Attacks on North America: Japan's World War II Assaults* (Fallbrook, Calif.: Aero, 1982), esp. pp. 1, 17, 25–27, 34–35, 38, 67–68; Rodney P. Carlisle with Joan M. Zenzen, *Supplying the Nuclear Arsenal: American Production Reactors, 1942–1992* (Johns Hopkins University Press, 1996), pp. 41–42.

2. Excellent synoptic sources on the history of the strategic defense debate include Samuel P. Huntington's *The Common Defense: Strategic Programs in National Politics* (Columbia University Press, 1961), which is the standard source on the period through the Eisenhower administration; and B. Bruce-Briggs's *The Shield of Faith: A Chronicle of Strategic Defense from Zeppelins to Star Wars* (New York: Simon & Schuster, 1988), which more or less takes up where Huntington leaves off and carries the story through the later years of the Reagan administration.

As with the preatomic continental defenses, nuclear strategic defenses never endured a trial by combat. Despite spending hundreds of billions of dollars, a modest down payment on the trillions that proponents advocated, the government carried few strategic air or missile defense programs through to completion, and none of them ever offered any reasonable prospect of protecting U.S. retaliatory forces or mitigating the tremendous social and economic destruction that would have attended a general nuclear exchange.[3]

Air Defenses

Although the U.S. Air Defense Command was formed in 1946 to protect U.S. territory from attack by enemy aircraft, a long history of freedom from direct threats to American territory relegated continental defense to a very low priority. But by early 1948 opinions were changing: the United States, said some, needed "the complicated defensive equipment of modern electronics and modern defensive fighter planes and ground defensive weapons," including a radar early warning system.

> But such a system, if designed to give complete and continuous coverage, would be extraordinarily expensive. Worse yet, it might divert us—as the Maginot Line diverted France—from the best defense against atomic attack, the counteroffensive striking force in being. . . . *No plans for defense should be made in derogation of the striking counter offensive air arm in being.*"[4] (Emphasis added)

Not surprisingly, then, the Project Charles Report would state in 1951 that "the air defense effort before 1949 was inadequate to the point of

3. The Soviet Union, too, invested heavily in air defenses, perhaps spending more than the United States. By 1948 Soviet air defenses employed 500,000 to 600,000 persons. Soviet offensive forces, by contrast, were paltry. Yet rather than accepting that the Soviet Union was adopting a defensive posture, ill-suited to massive surprise attack, the Truman administration and the Joint Chiefs of Staff believed just the opposite and supported a large buildup of offensive atomic-armed bombers. See David Goldfischer, *The Best Defense: Policy Alternatives for U.S. Nuclear Security from the 1950s to the 1990s* (Cornell University Press, 1993), pp. 103–06. Despite annual pronouncements from the DOD in the early-to-mid 1980s that these formidable Soviet defenses required the development of counterpoising forces such as the B-1 bomber and the air-launched cruise missile, they were unable to detect or halt the May 28, 1987, flight by nineteen-year-old West German pilot Mathias Rust in his single-engine Cessna aircraft from Helsinki to Moscow (which is also protected by an antiballistic missile system). Upon arriving in Moscow, Rust landed his plane in front of the Kremlin in Red Square before startled onlookers. Rust's flight took place, ironically, as the Soviet Union was celebrating Border Guards Day. See Felicity Barringer, "Lone West German Flies Unhindered to the Kremlin," *New York Times,* May 30, 1987, p. 1; "Pilot's Stunt in Red Square Shocks Soviets," *San Jose Mercury News,* May 30, 1987, p. A1.

4. Goldfischer, *The Best Defense,* p. 91, fn. 36. Yet even by 1957, after billions of dollars had been expended on air defense programs, the Gaither Committee (see the section on civil defense in this chapter) would report that "the system as it now exists, and as it is now planned to be, does not and will not provide this country with a significant level of protection. It has a number of 'Achilles' heels' which can be exploited by an intelligent enemy. It is ineffective in the face of electronic countermeasures, saturation tactics, and low-altitude attacks. . . . [W]hen we examine the history of air defense, we conclude that an effective air defense system is unlikely within the present organization framework." Security Resources Panel of the Science Advisory Committee, "Deterrence and Survival in the Nuclear Age," November 7, 1957, reproduced in Morton Halperin, *National Security Policy- Making: Analyses, Cases, and Proposals* (Lexington, Mass.: D.C. Heath, 1975), p. 103.

meaninglessness."[5] Fueling these defense concerns were the Berlin war scare in 1948, the September 1949 announcement of the first test of a Soviet atomic bomb, and the Korean War the following year. Here, suddenly, was the hitherto unprecedented prospect that the devastation of another world war might be visited upon the North American continent.

On January 1, 1951, the government reestablished the Air Force Air Defense Command (ADCOM) (it had been disbanded six months earlier), and by the end of the year its combat ready force had doubled, from 248 to 502 aircraft deployed at more than two dozen bases. By the close of 1952, the Army Antiaircraft Command (ARAACOM) had deployed more than 200 antiaircraft artillery batteries around nearly a dozen key locations, providing a point defense against low-yield fission bombs and bombers carrying conventional munitions.

Warning radar networks also blossomed. The air force, having failed in 1947 to obtain approval for the ambitious Supremacy network, which would have encompassed a nationwide system of 411 radar stations, contented itself with the modestly named Lash-Up radar network, intended to provide focused protection of major nuclear weapons production facilities.[6] Lash-Up grew from a mere seven sites in 1949 to fifty stations by the end of 1951, as it was gradually replaced by the so-called Permanent System, which numbered some seventy-four radars by June 1952.[7]

These radars were supplemented by the thirty-four stations of the Pinetree Line across Canada, providing the additional two hours of warning against piston-powered Tu-4 bombers needed to fully activate the remainder of the air defense system. The overall costs of these systems are, unfortunately, not recorded in any contemporaneous documents. Although the U.S. government provided approximately two-thirds of the construction costs of this network, U.S. participation was not revealed to the Canadian public until Pinetree was nearly complete in 1952.[8]

In August 1951 the Project Charles Report, the first product of the soon-to-be established Lincoln Laboratory at the Massachusetts Institute of Technology (MIT), outlined an ambitious program for future work, focused on improved radars and highly sophisticated (for the time) computers utilizing tens of thousands of vacuum tubes. When the air force learned of the study's probable recommendations in the summer of 1952, it took steps to censor and suppress them.[9] Air Force

5. President's Air Policy Commission, *Survival in the Air Age* (January 1, 1948), pp. 20, 25.

6. Air Defense Command, "The Air Defense of Atomic Energy Installations, March 1946–December 1952," ADCOM Special Historical Study, August 3, 1953.

7. Aerospace Defense Command, *Statistical Data Book—Radar,* vol. 2, April 1973, p. 122.

8. Joseph Thomas Jockel, "The United States and Canadian Efforts at Continental Air Defense, 1945–1957," Ph.D. dissertation, Johns Hopkins University, 1978, University Microfilms 7906466, p. 130.

9. At this time, the air force, especially the Strategic Air Command, opposed any proposals that would limit in any way SAC's offensive striking power, considered by the air

Secretary Thomas K. Finletter worried that the report might be too forceful in advocating defenses (in fact, it did identify the increasing vulnerability of the United States as a driving force behind the need to improve defenses).

The air force tried to prevent the circulation of the study, but was thwarted when President Harry S Truman learned of it from the director of the National Security Resources Board and ordered a National Security Council briefing on it. Ironically, this briefing was handled by an air force general, who delivered the study's data but hedged on implementing the report's recommendations.

Failing to gain support within the closed councils of the government and eager to influence the new administration, advocates of strategic air defense went public in early 1953 in an article provocatively titled "We Can Smash the Red A-Bombers." "If the Russians launched a transpolar A-bomb attack tomorrow," it stated, "we'd be lucky to stop one out of three of their planes. But there is a way for us to be sure of destroying 85%—even 95%—of the attacking force."[10] The comprehensive air defense network these advocates had in mind was expected to cost at least $20 billion, with some estimates ranging as high as $150 billion (roughly $147 billion to $1.1 trillion in 1996 dollars, anticipating the astronomical cost estimates of the Strategic Defense Initiative nearly three decades later).[11] Because the air force considered these costs a potentially serious drain on resources needed to field a modern strategic bomber force, it successfully opposed a major upgrade of the network. The central precept of strategic airpower—the belief that "the bomber will always get through"—provided doctrinal sanction for this offense-dominant posture. Having so recently achieved institutional independence on the wings of airpower doctrine, and having successfully portrayed the strategic bomber as the winning weapon of the World War II (despite evidence to the contrary in a major postwar survey), the air force was reluctant to sanction a force posture that challenged these fundamental assumptions.

Although the Project Charles report continued to receive serious consideration (by at least four groups in 1953), still no headway was made on defenses. In May 1953 *Fortune* weighed in with an anonymous air force–sponsored article characterizing the issue of defenses as a "life or death struggle," the stark choice being whether to discard, or at least greatly modify, the "retaliatory deterrence" principle embodied in the Strategic Air Command, or to go for a "defensive strategy" favor-

---

force to be the best and only means of defending the United States against Soviet aggression. Thus similar measures were instituted when the Project Vista report on the role tactical nuclear weapons could play in the defense of Europe was completed in early 1952 (see chapter 2).

10. Ralph E. Lapp and Stewart Alsop, "We Can Smash the Red A-Bombers," *Saturday Evening Post,* March 21, 1953, p. 19.

11. "The Truth about Our Air Defense," *Air Force* Magazine, May 1953, pp. 25–36.

ing "a renunciation of atomic-offensive power by both major adversaries." The latter suggestion was attributed to J. Robert Oppenheimer and three other scientists. The article falsely asserted that the Charles study purported to offer a "near leakproof defense," which, it countered, would force the United States "to throw away its strongest weapon merely because it is an offensive weapon. . . . The atomic advantage constitutes a 'shield' behind which the American people can work steadily for peace—until Mr. Eisenhower's proposals for world disarmament are universally accepted." In any case, it warned, foreshadowing the forthcoming Oppenheimer security hearings, "there was a serious question of the propriety of scientists trying to settle such grave national issues alone, inasmuch as they bear no responsibility for the successful execution of war plans."[12] What was a scientist to do, argued a frustrated Oppenheimer, when even "a high officer of the Air Defense Command" had stated that "it was not really our policy to protect this country, for that is so big a job it would interfere with our retaliatory capabilities." Commented Oppenheimer, "Such follies can occur only when even the men who know the facts can find no one to talk to about them, when the facts are too secret for discussion and thus for thought."[13]

The air force found further institutional support for its approach at the Atomic Energy Commission's weapons laboratories, where many scientists were more interested in developing the large hydrogen bombs carried by strategic bombers rather than the small nuclear weapons that might be needed for strategic air defense (choices that figured prominently in the increasing conflict between Edward Teller

12. "The Hidden Struggle for the H-Bomb," *Fortune,* May 1953, pp. 108–10, 210. Air defense proponents and journalists Joseph and Stewart Alsop ("We Accuse!" *Harper's* Magazine, October 1954, pp. 25–45) document the extent to which Oppenheimer's advocacy figured in the revocation of his security clearance. Kenneth Schaffel, *The Emerging Shield: The Air Force and the Evolution of Continental Air Defense, 1945–1960* (Washington, D.C.: Office of Air Force History, 1991), pp. 178–84, recounts this history in some detail, and dismisses some of the more sensational charges (even approaching treason) levied at the time. Oppenheimer and two other colleagues were said to have formed an informal committee to work for "world peace," and hence to have placed the air defense of the United States ahead of the development of "the thermonuclear weapon." As historian David Goldfischer notes, Oppenheimer and some of his colleagues—whose approach disdained the open-ended production of nuclear weapons favored by SAC—also "favored the 'no-first-test' H-bomb proposal, as well as supporting the Project Vista argument that Europe could be defended with tactical rather than strategic nuclear weapons. Whatever these proposals conveyed about the patriotism of their advocates, they clearly posed a basic challenge to Air Force doctrine and an immediate threat to the Air Force budget," especially SAC. Goldfischer, *The Best Defense,* p. 93. In deciding to revoke Oppenheimer's security clearance in 1954, the AEC's personnel security board cited as a key justification that the government must be certain that "underlying any advice [from outside specialists] is a genuine conviction that this country cannot in the interest of security have less than the strongest possible *offensive* capabilities in a time of national danger" (emphasis added). For further details, see Goldfischer, *The Best Defense,* pp. 90–96; U.S. Atomic Energy Commission, *In the Matter of J. Robert Oppenheimer: Text of Principal Documents and Letters of Personnel Security Board, General Manager, Commissioners,* Washington, D.C., April 12, 1954 through June 9, 1954 (GPO, 1954), p. 18. As Goldfischer remarks, it is striking how effectively, some would say ruthlessly, the air force discredited advocates of air defenses, not merely rejecting calls for defenses but denouncing those who issued such calls and questioning their loyalty for doing so. This is all the more noteworthy considering that the supporters (in and out of the government) of total disarmament and international control of nuclear weapons never encountered such outright hostility (*The Best Defense,* pp. 96, 117).

13. Quoted in Goldfischer, *The Best Defense,* pp. 93–94.

and Oppenheimer over the Super program).[14] As a result, the World War II–vintage air defense system performed poorly: it could detect and intercept only a small fraction of incoming enemy bombers.

The first Soviet thermonuclear explosion in August 1953 greatly increased the priority of air defense, even as the enormous power of the hydrogen bomb made the prospects for a successful defense much more difficult. The point defenses provided by antiaircraft artillery would be worthless in the face of the destructive potential of the hydrogen bomb.[15] The air force conceded in a 1952 study that it could hope to intercept only 23 to 37 percent of Soviet bombers by 1955, and that half of the attacking Soviet force would still penetrate to reach their targets by 1957.[16] Soon thereafter the NSC issued a report calling for dramatic improvements in continental air defense. The government quickly approved an array of ambitious programs including, notably, the Semiautomatic Ground Environment (SAGE) air defense control system and the Distant Early Warning (DEW) line, with the goal of providing from three to six hours of warning of aircraft attack.[17]

14. Testifying at Oppenheimer's security hearing in 1954, physicist Luis Alvarez recounted a conversation he had with Teller in 1952 about the Project Vista report, which Alvarez had signed. Asked why he had signed the report ("feeling the way you do about hydrogen bombs"), Alvarez replied that he did not see the pursuit of tactical weapons and the hydrogen bomb as mutually exclusive. Teller then said, according to Alvarez, "You go back and read that report and you will find that that essentially says that the hydrogen-bomb program is interfering with the small-weapons program, and it has caused me no end of trouble at Los Alamos. It is being used against our program. It is slowing it down and it could easily kill it." See U.S. Atomic Energy Commission, *In the Matter of J. Robert Oppenheimer,* pp. 788–89. However, one reviewer of an earlier draft of this book, a direct participant in nuclear weapons development during this period, contends: "The labs were equally interested across the board. We were just as interested in developing 'the smallest possible' (as in the Davy Crockett) as the biggest. For instance, [Livermore] designed a warhead small enough to fit the Nike Ajax (it was never produced), as well as one by [Los Alamos] for the larger Nike Hercules which was produced in large numbers." In the end, large numbers of tactical weapons *and* hydrogen bombs were developed and deployed, demonstrating that the conflict between the two programs was more apparent than actual. It is interesting to note the subsequent reversal in attitudes toward strategic defenses generally, as many of those who were early advocates, such as the *Bulletin of the Atomic Scientists,* became skeptics, and many of the early skeptics, such as Edward Teller, later became enthusiasts.

15. Headquarters ARADCOM, "The History of ARADCOM, Volume I: The Gun Era—1950–1955," Historical Project ARAD 5M-I, September 19, 1972, p. 99. The rings of air defense artillery extended to radii as great as 12 miles (19.3 kilometers), in the case of Washington, D.C. While this might have been adequate in the face of kiloton-yield fission (atomic) weapons with destructive radii of a mile (0.6 kilometer) or so, the blast effects of the new multimegaton fusion weapons were of the same scale as the entire area defended by artillery barrier defenses.

16. Jockel, "The United States and Canadian Efforts at Continental Air Defense, 1945–1957," p. 160. During a SAC test drill on July 11, 1953, SAC flew ninety-nine bomber sorties against U.S. cities, launching its coordinated "attack" using aircraft surreptitiously flown out of the country just before the commencement of the designated forty-eight-hour drill period and arriving within the first thirty minutes of the exercise. The Air Defense Command achieved only two "kills" of bombers before simulated bomb release and four "kills" after bomb release. See "Document One: Memorandum Op-36C/jm, 18 March 1954," reprinted in *International Security,* vol. 6, no. 3 (1981–82), p. 24.

17. Yet in January 1953 the Joint Chiefs of Staff remained convinced that offensive forces were still more important than defensive measures. Asked to approve DEW, they expressed outright hostility and even fear of the concept. "A statement of policy related to this one aspect of national security would focus undue attention on defensive measures as opposed to offensive measures. A chain reaction . . . might be set off which would result in so much effort being expended on home defense that the ultimate result would be the loss of any future war through failure to provide adequately for U.S. offensive capability." See Jockel, "The United States and Canadian Efforts at Continental Air Defense, 1945–1957," p. 185.

SAGE incorporated the latest radar and computer technology to support about fifty combat direction centers throughout the United States. Through these centers the Continental Air Defense Command would coordinate all weapons—mainly interceptor aircraft (such as the F-86D, F-89D, and F-94C interceptors) and antiaircraft missile batteries (including the air force Bomarc and the army's Nike Ajax and Nike Hercules) devoted to the air defense of the United States.

Although piloted interceptor aircraft were equipped initially with cannons and conventional missiles, investigation of the application of nuclear weapons to the air defense mission began in 1951, culminating in the HEAVENBOUND study, completed in June 1953.[18] This study concluded that the proposed concept of air-to-air bombing, in which a free-fall nuclear weapon would be dropped onto Soviet bomber formations, held little promise of providing an effective defense. It did recommend, however, the development of nuclear-tipped missiles that could be launched by air defense interceptor aircraft. Development of the MB-1 Genie air-to-air rocket culminated in the Operation Plumbob live fire test on July 19, 1957, with a Genie fired from an F-89J detonating 18,500 feet (5,639 meters) over the Nevada Proving Ground. The superior GAR-11 Falcon guided missile, carried on the F-102 Delta Dagger aircraft, was subsequently added to the inventory in 1961 (the Genie and Falcon were also carried on the F-101 Voodoo).[19]

The air force had been assigned responsibility for aerodynamic missiles on October 2, 1944, and studies of ram-jet powered ground-to-air missiles were initiated soon thereafter. Six years of studies culminated in 1950 with the initiation of the Bomarc (Boeing Michigan Air Research Center) long-range guided missile. This nuclear-tipped missile, with a planned range of more than 373 miles (600 kilometers), was initially intended to provide coverage of the entire continental United States. However, a seemingly unending series of test failures, low operational availability, and mounting costs plagued this program throughout its lifetime.[20]

Development of the army's Nike Ajax began in June 1945, with early test firings in 1950 demonstrating that initially challenging radar guidance problems had been resolved. Between July 1953 and May 1955 Nike Ajax replaced antiaircraft artillery at thirty-eight army battalions and by January 1959 sixty battalions were deployed around "the vital industrial, urban, and strategic areas of the United States." Six additional battalions were deployed in Europe.[21] Armed with a con-

18. Directorate of Historical Services, "Nuclear Weapons in the Air Defense System," Air Defense Command, Special Historical Study 2 (n.d.), p. 9.

19. Thomas W. Ray, "Nuclear Armament: Its Acquisition, Control and Application to Manned Interceptors, 1951–1963," Air Defense Command Historical Study 20 (n.d.).

20. Richard F. McMullen, "Interceptor Missiles in Air Defense," ADC Historical Study 30 (February 1965), for example, pp. 28, 107.

21. Charles H. Donnelly, *The United States Guided Missile Program*, prepared for the Preparedness Investigating Sub-

ventional high-explosive warhead, Nike Ajax was capable of engaging targets at ranges of up to 31 miles (50 kilometers) and altitudes of 12 miles (20 kilometers), but further improvements were imperative. The much larger nuclear-tipped Nike Hercules, initiated in 1953, promised to intercept aircraft at altitudes of more than 19 miles (30 kilometers), at ranges up to 96 miles (155 kilometers).[22]

BOMARC and Nike Hercules, first conceived as complementary programs stressing different defensive concepts (area versus point defense, respectively), instead created friction between the air force and the army as the two sought to control the overall air defense effort and its swelling budget. Because each service's future plans depended on the large-scale successful deployment of its weapon of choice, this rivalry became particularly intense. By fiscal 1960, after the DOD had ignored repeated congressional pleas to choose one system, the House Defense Appropriations Subcommittee and the Senate Armed Services Committee took matters into their own hands. The House subcommittee cut deeply into the BOMARC budget while the Senate committee essentially eliminated Nike Hercules on the grounds that it was "virtually obsolete." Forced to make a decision, the DOD developed a "master plan" that trimmed the overall air defense budget but recommended a mix of both missiles, with Nike Hercules considered the mainstay of the plan.[23]

SAGE became operational in 1958, and the program was completed in late 1961. The massive 275-ton SAGE computers (built by IBM and filling one entire story of a four-story windowless building) were the marvel of the day, with 58,000 vacuum tubes consuming as much electricity as a town of 15,000 people (so great was the waste heat generated by their operation that it was sometimes used to heat the bases on which they were sited). These immense wonders were too vast to deploy in hardened facilities, and their aboveground installation rendered them vulnerable to attack. Each SAGE computer cost roughly $152 million, with directly associated support electronics driving the unit cost beyond $250 million (significantly in excess of the most expensive of today's supercomputers).[24]

committee of the Senate Committee on Armed Services, 86 Cong. 1 sess. (GPO, January 1959), p. 96.

22. Headquarters ARADCOM, "The History of ARADCOM Volume I—The Gun Era—1950–1955," p. 186. A Nike Hercules installation near San Francisco, Site SF-88L, has been restored by the National Park Service and is open to the public. See Tom McNichol, "Cold Warhead," *Washington Post,* November 30, 1997, p. E1, or visit the site on the World Wide Web at http://www.nikemissile.org.

23. Edward Kolodziej, *The Uncommon Defense and Congress, 1945–1963* (Ohio State University Press, 1966), pp. 303–06. This was not the only time the DOD had difficulty selecting systems for production. See, for example, the controversy over the Thor and Jupiter intermediate-range ballistic missiles (chapter 2 in this volume).

24. *Hearings on FY 1958 Department of Defense Appropriations,* House Defense Appropriations Subcommittee, 90 Cong. 1 sess. (GPO, 1957), pp. 312–14. Cray supercomputers, used by DOE nuclear weapons laboratories and the National Security Agency, among others, were typically priced at approximately $30 million in the 1970s and 1980s. See Andrew Pollack, "The Next Generation at Cray," *New York Times,* February 10, 1988, p. D1. But in 1993 the company offered a massively parallel processor machine for a price tag of $60 million. See Sandra Sugawara, "Cray Enters a Parallel Dimension," *Washington Post,* September 28, 1993, p. B1. One

The DEW line, completed in early 1957, consisted of a series of radar sites built about 50 miles (80 kilometers) apart and stretching along the extreme boundary of the North American continent, several hundred miles north of the Arctic circle. It was designed to provide a minimum of two hours of early warning (tracking as well as detecting) of a Soviet supersonic jet bomber attack from all angles of the polar attack route. Further extensions by 1962 stretched the line for 12,000 miles (19,308 kilometers) from Scotland to Midway Island in the Pacific.

The DEW line was but the forwardmost element of a network that blanketed North America under a bristling array of radar antennae. Between the DEW line and the CADIN/Pinetree line was the Mid-Canada Line, and to the south of Pinetree, the Gap Filler network supplemented the Permanent System, numbering 69 sites by the end of 1958. Six squadrons of RC-121 radar aircraft (redesignated EC-121 in September 1963, the forerunner of the Airborne Warning and Control System) patrolled the skies, and these seventy air force aircraft were supplemented by some sixty-seven WV-2s flown by the navy, which had originally developed this derivative of the Lockheed Super Constellation passenger plane to provide radar warning for the fleet.[25]

By 1958 the navy's thirty-six Ocean Picket warning ships with destroyer escort radar (DER) had been joined by sixteen radar-equipped converted Liberty ships on midocean patrol and four radar-equipped ZPG-2W Navy blimps. Three air force "Texas Towers" (so-named because they were based on modified oil-drilling platforms used off the Texas coast) hosted long-range radars on ocean shoals about 100 miles (161 kilometers) off the coast of Boston and New York; their total construction costs came to $200 million, and annual operating costs to more than $20 million.[26] Nonetheless, this impressive array of sensors might still be vulnerable to jamming by Soviet electronic warfare aircraft, in which case they would be incapable of vectoring air defense interceptor aircraft toward incoming Soviet bombers.

early name considered for SAGE was Semiautomatic Air Defense System, with "semiautomatic" denoting a computerized network managed by human beings (to distinguish it from its manual predecessors). But as a physicist working on the program commented, "No one wanted to ask Congress to appropriate more than a billion dollars for something called the SAD network." SAGE ultimately cost several billion (then-year) dollars and by one account "constituted the greatest military research and development outlay since the Manhattan Project." Robert Buderi, *The Invention That Changed the World: How a Small Group of Radar Pioneers Won the Second World War and Launched a Technological Revolution* (New York: Simon & Schuster, 1996), pp. 394–95, 398.

25. Aerospace Defense Command, *Statistical Data Book—Aircraft and Missiles,* vol. 2 (April 1973), p. 159; Navy Department, Office of the Chief of Naval Operations, "Allowances and Location of Navy Aircraft," OPNAV Notice 03110, December 31, 1958, table 2, "Location of Aircraft Inventory and Planned Operating Assignments," pp. 19, 27.

26. Thomas W. Ray, "A History of Texas Towers in Air Defense, 1952–1964," Air Defense Command Historical Study 29, March 1965, p. 22. A total of five Texas Towers were originally planned, although only three were completed. TT-4, which was anchored in much deeper water than the others, was severely battered by Hurricane Donna on September 12, 1960, and collapsed in a subsequent storm on January 15, 1961, with the loss of all twenty-eight maintenance personnel on board. With the advent of radar surveillance aircraft, the remaining two Texas Towers were decommissioned in 1963.

The army's Nike Ajax missile force grew to 242 batteries in 1957 but declined slightly the following year in anticipation of the introduction of the Nike Hercules in 1959.[27] At its peak in 1958, the nearly 120,000 ADC air force personnel operated more than 1,300 combat aircraft at 23 Air Defense Command bases, 27 other air bases with air defense tenant squadrons, 25 control centers, 63 DEW line stations, 155 Gap Filler radar sites, and some 245 other radar stations.[28] These efforts were supplemented by the volunteer Ground Observer Corps, which by 1957 included more than 15,000 observer posts in the United States alone, manned by nearly 350,000 volunteers, who worked with the 80,000 Canadian volunteer ground observers to keep at least 10 percent of the observer posts manned twenty-four hours a day.

U.S. investment in air defense grew even heavier when the Soviet Union unveiled its intercontinental bombers: the jet Bison in 1954 and the turboprop Bear in 1955. Observers in the United States thereupon predicted a "bomber gap," and U.S. funding for strategic bombers as well as air defense soared.

From the safe remove of today, after decades of satellite reconnaissance of the Soviet Union and nearly perfect (or at least extremely adequate) knowledge of Soviet strategic forces, it is difficult to recapture the profound uncertainty that attended intelligence assessments in these early years of the cold war. The Soviet Union, weakened by World War II, sought, by every available means, to conceal this weakness from the West, following the maxim "show the best and hide the rest." In 1955 Americans in Moscow were treated to an inflated display of Soviet airpower, as a handful of bombers made repeated passes over Red Square, creating the impression of strength out of all proportion to reality and reinforcing U.S. estimates of a bomber buildup. Very much alive to the dangers of underestimating the threat, and equally aware of budgetary and bureaucratic disincentives tending in the same direction, the U.S. government—especially the Strategic Air Command—was strongly inclined to believe that the Soviet strategic bomber fleet rivaled the one being feverishly assembled by SAC.[29]

However, technical deficiencies rendered Soviet bombers an unsatisfactory means of delivering nuclear weapons, and they were never

27. *The Emerging Shield,* table 5, pp. 270–71.

28. Aerospace Defense Command, *Statistical Data Book—Budget, Personnel and Air Bases,* vol. 1 (April 1973), n.p.; Aerospace Defense Command, *Statistical Data Book—Aircraft and Missiles,* vol. 2 (April 1973), pp. 43–44, 131; *Department of the Air Force Appropriations for 1958,* Hearings before the Subcommittee of the House Committee on Appropriations, 85 Cong. 1 sess. (GPO, 1957), p. 624.

29. For further details on the origin and resolution of the bomber gap, see Lawrence Freedman, *U.S. Intelligence and the Soviet Strategic Threat,* 2d ed. (Princeton University Press, 1986), pp. 65–67; John Prados, *The Soviet Estimate: U.S. Intelligence Analysis and Russian Military Strength* (New York: Dial Press, 1982), pp. 40–47; Fred Kaplan, *The Wizards of Armageddon* (New York: Simon & Schuster, 1983), pp. 155–61. Prados recounts how when Soviet defense minister Marshal Georgi K. Zhukov told air force chief of staff Nathan Twining during a visit to Moscow in 1956 (as Congress was engaged in extensive hearings on the "bomber gap"), "I think you have the reports too high in estimating our strength," air force and other U.S. officials dismissed his comments as intentionally misleading.

produced in large numbers. Consequently, Soviet priorities soon turned to ballistic missiles. In reality, the bomber gap that finally emerged left the Soviet Union with the numerical inferiority. In contrast to a March 1956 estimate that by 1959 the Soviet Union would deploy 300 Bears and 400 Bisons, the U.S. intelligence community had concluded by 1958 that both programs had been curtailed, with production totaling just 50 to 60 Bears and 85 Bisons (in fact, a recent assessment of intelligence data found that the Soviet Union had a *total* of 85 bombers in 1958 versus 1,769 for the United States, a ratio of nearly 21:1 in favor of the United States!).[30]

When the Soviet Union launched Sputnik in October 1957 and ushered in the age of missiles, the strategic situation changed drastically. With their short flight times and high velocities, missiles rendered virtually the entire investment in air defenses obsolete. Within months of the launch of Sputnik, cracks appeared in a range of air defense plans only recently inaugurated. The volunteer Ground Observer Corps' round-the-clock Operation Skywatch was discontinued in November 1957, and the entire corps disbanded in 1959. Plans for the new trisonic F-108 interceptor aircraft were slowed in 1958, and the program was canceled in September 1959. The air force also scaled back plans for its long-range BOMARC ground-launched antiaircraft missile. In 1957 BOMARC contractors had estimated that the program would eventually entail between 6,200 and 17,300 missiles, at a total cost of between $50 billion and $250 billion (interestingly, the higher cost estimate was for the smaller number of missiles).[31] But the air force reduced the officially approved program from 2,400 missiles at forty bases to 924 missiles at thirty-one sites in June 1958, and reduced it again in 1959.[32] Ultimately, 224 launchers with 392 missiles were deployed at just eight U.S. and two Canadian bases in 1962 and were withdrawn from service a few years later.[33]

30. CIA History Staff, *Intentions and Capabilities: Estimates on Soviet Strategic Forces 1950–1983* (Washington, D.C.: Central Intelligence Agency, 1996), p. 19 (NIE 11-56 for the 1956 estimate) and p. 49 (SNIE 11-7-58 for the revised 1958 estimate); Robert S. Norris and Thomas B. Cochran, *US-USSR/Russian Strategic Offensive Nuclear Forces, 1945–1996,*" NWD-97-1 (Natural Resources Defense Council, January 1997), tables 7 and 8. Available on the World Wide Web at http://open.igc.org/nrdcpro/nudb/dainx.html/.

31. Richard F. McMullen, *Interceptor Missiles in Air Defense, 1944–1964,* ADC Historical Study 30 (February 1965), pp. 59–60.

32. McMullen, *Interceptor Missiles in Air Defense,* p. 62.

33. McMullen, *Interceptor Missiles in Air Defense,* pp. 59–60. On June 7, 1960, a BOMARC missile was destroyed by an explosion and fire at McGuire Air Force Base near Trenton, New Jersey. The missile melted under the intense heat fed by its 100-pound (45-kilogram) detonator of TNT, and the 10-kiloton W40 warhead dropped into the molten mass that was left of the missile and itself melted. The burning of thoriated magnesium in the warhead contributed to the spread of radiation from the accident. About an acre of land surrounding the site was later sealed in concrete to prevent the spread of radioactivity. See Letter from Herbert B. Loper, Assistant to the Secretary of Defense (Atomic Energy), to the Honorable Clinton P. Anderson, Chairman, Joint Committee on Atomic Energy, July 29, 1960, Record Group 128, Declassified General Subject File, Box 1 (Accidents), Document 6391, National Archives; Center for Defense Information, "U.S. Nuclear Weapons Accidents: Danger in Our Midst," *Defense Monitor,* vol. 10, no. 5 (1981), p. 7; Joseph F. Sullivan, "Old Missile Site Is Still Tainted, Kean Says," *New York Times,* July 10, 1985, p. B1; Joseph F. Sullivan, "Jersey Official Says '77 Army Report Urged Cleanup at Site of Missile Fire," *New York Times,* July 12, 1985,

Other air defense programs, however, made it across the threshold of the missile age because of their institutional inertia. The first supersonic air-defense aircraft—the F-106—was delivered to the air force in June 1958, with deliveries of more than 300 aircraft continuing for four years thereafter (the F-106 eventually became the mainstay of the air defense command). Deployment of the army's Nike Hercules antiaircraft missile, which was just entering service in January 1958, continued for four more years, with some 134 batteries and 1,600 launchers ringing American cities and military bases by 1962, shortly after the vulnerable SAGE control system entered service.[34]

Overall, the army's maximum strength of antiaircraft missiles was reached at 245 batteries in 1960, the same year that the Gap Filler radar network peaked at 105 sites. Other long-range radar sites continued to grow in number, peaking at 193 installations in 1962, shortly after the SAGE control centers reached their full 22-site deployment in 1961 (out of 46 originally planned).[35] In 1958 and 1959 the navy began fielding some 300 nuclear-armed Terrier missiles and 300 nuclear-armed Talos missiles aboard some aircraft carriers, cruisers, and destroyers to attack supersonic aircraft.[36] A little noticed consequence of all this effort was the production and deployment of some 10,900 nuclear warheads for the air defense mission, which was equal to 34 percent of the stockpile in 1965 and almost 16 percent of all U.S. warhead production.

By the early 1960s SAGE, the DEW line, and all the other air defense programs could contribute nothing to the destruction of enemy ballistic missiles. In fact, incoming ballistic missiles could quickly obliterate the SAGE and other air defense systems, allowing later arriving bombers an uncontested flight to targets within the United States. The use of ICBMs to suppress air defenses became a central tactic in strategic war plans, and both sides, particularly the Soviet Union, continued to pour resources into this increasingly difficult mission.

Between 1962 and 1967 the United States spent $1.2 billion on the development of the YF-12A interceptor aircraft, an air defense derivative of the Lockheed A-11/SR-71 reconnaissance plane, though none

p. 14. The BOMARC system also had no means of discriminating between friendly and unfriendly aircraft. BOMARC missiles at Suffolk County Air Force Base, positioned to defend New York City, would have fired on bombers using the same flight path as commercial planes flying from Europe. The risk of accidents was therefore not inconsequential.

34. A Nike Hercules battalion was also sent to Formosa (Taiwan) in October 1958, following China's threats against the island of Quemoy several weeks earlier. See Donnelly, *United States Guided Missile Program,* p. 96.

35. Aerospace Defense Command, *Statistical Data Book—Budget, Personnel and Air Bases,* vol. 1 (April 1973); U.S. General Accounting Office, *Air Defense Mission Must Be Clarified before Billions Are Spent on Modernization,* PSAD-78-86 (formerly Secret), May 10, 1978, p. 3; Buderi, *The Invention That Changed the World,* p. 412.

36. The Terrier, armed with a 1-kiloton W45 warhead, was also designed for use against some land targets and had limited cruise missile and antiship capabilities.

were ever deployed. The extensive network of Nike Hercules antiaircraft missiles remained in service in the United States through the mid-1970s (and in Europe until the 1980s), with all but a handful in Florida being deactivated by mid-1975, at an annual savings of about $430 million.[37] With the arrival of the E-3A Sentry (formerly AWACS), a portion of the fleet was allocated to continental air defense, though the bulk of the aircraft were forward deployed in Europe and other theaters. The total cost of AWACS through 1995 was $15.5 billion. However, because only seven of the thirty-three total aircraft deployed were allocated to strategic air defense, only $3.3 billion of this is included in the costs tallied in this chapter.[38]

While the Strategic Defense Initiative proposed by President Ronald Reagan in March 1983 was focused on countering the ballistic missile threat, the Air Defense Master Plan and the Air Defense Initiative concurrently sought to provide similar coverage against air-breathing threats. A continent-ringing network of over-the-horizon backscatter (OTH-B) radars was initiated and deployed in Idaho and Maine, to provide long-range detection of cruise-missile carrying bombers. Spending on the OTH-B program totaled more than $2 billion before the cold war ended and the initiative was derailed.[39] The twenty-five-year-old DEW line was also extensively upgraded under the $6 billion North Warning System initiative. Although these programs were all modest in scope compared with the energetic exertions of the 1950s, in almost every year of the later stages of the cold war the United States continued to spend more on continental air defense than was invested in ballistic missile defense programs such as SDI.

The Costs of Air Defense

Estimating the total costs of these efforts is complicated by the fact that the bulk of strategic air defense expenditures occurred before Secretary of Defense Robert S. McNamara's 1961 inauguration of the Five-Year Defense Program. At that time, annual spending was in excess of $12 billion, but it declined rapidly thereafter and through 1995 totaled only $171 billion, or an average of about $5.2 billion a year.

Available records for spending before 1962 are extremely fragmentary and are displayed at very high levels of aggregation. Thus the costs of many early programs such as Nike Ajax, Lash Up, Pinetree, and the

37. "Scrapping Missiles to Fit the Times," *US News & World Report,* March 4, 1974, p. 42.

38. *Department of Defense Authorization for Appropriations for Fiscal Year 1984,* Hearings before the Senate Committee on Armed Services, 98 Cong. 1 sess. (GPO, 1983), pt. 5, p. 2655; U.S. Air Force, Fact Sheet 96-13, "E-3 Sentry (AWACS)," March 1996.

39. Associated Pres, "Radar Against Soviet Air Attack to Run Part Time," *New York Times,* May 28, 1991, p. A14.

original DEW Line appear to be lost to time. One source does provide some unattributed assessments of annual spending on strategic air defense for the period 1945 through 1982, along with time series data on other strategic defense programs.[40] Comparing these data with figures from other reliable sources provides confidence in the validity of the estimates for strategic air defense. However, these numbers vary substantially from the air defense budgets displayed in the FYDP. Closer examination suggests that the cited air defense budget figures cover only acquisition costs. When personnel levels of Aerospace Defense Command are multiplied by average annual operations and personnel costs and added to the cited estimates, for example, the results are in close agreement with budget displays from the FYDP. Although the resulting estimate is uncertain, it appears to be the best that can be recovered from the available historical record.

According to that estimate, close to $200 billion was expended on strategic air defense in the period 1945 through 1961 (which is consistent with a contemporaneous estimate that some $30 billion [then-year dollars] had been spent as of 1959),[41] bringing the total to more than $371 billion. While details in the earlier period are lacking, from 1962 through 1995 costs included $34.4 billion for strategic air defense aircraft; $19.2 billion for strategic air defense ground-launched interceptor missiles; $7 billion for Nike Hercules battalions (not including warheads); $552 million for Hawk battalions; $6.1 billion for Falcon and Genie air-to-air missiles (not including warheads); $4.9 billion for Talos and Terrier missiles (not including warheads); $49.5 billion for strategic air defense communications, command, and control; and $49.5 billion for strategic air defense radars and other sensors, including $13.9 billion for the North Atlantic Defense System and $6 billion for the North Warning System.

Antiballistic Missile Defense

The American ABM effort began shortly after the Second World War, although initially overshadowed by related air-defense efforts. Early efforts include the short-range Thumper, which was intended to destroy missiles such as the V-2 by direct collision, and the more ambitious Wizard, which was focused on longer-range missiles. These projects received only modest funding.

By the mid-1950s, however, Soviet advances in long-range rocketry led to a dramatic increase in ABM research. In 1955 the army began

40. R. L. Maust, G. W. Goodman, Jr., and C. E. McLain, *History of Strategic Defense,* System Planning Corporation, Final Report SPC 742, Log No. 81-3735, DTIC ADB 066294 (September 1981), p. 3

41. McMullen, *Interceptor Missiles in Air Defense,* p. 87.

work on the ground-based Nike Zeus system, which used four types of mechanically steered radars to guide a long-range, rocket interceptor. Armed with the W50 high-yield (400-kiloton) nuclear warhead, it would intercept missile warheads above the atmosphere. Nike Zeus was vulnerable to relatively simple countermeasures, such as balloon decoys, which could saturate its radar tracking system. This system would have been marginally effective against the small number of early Soviet ICBMs, but it would have been overwhelmed by later Soviet nuclear forces. In the spring of 1958, after the army proposed starting initial production, Secretary of Defense Neil H. McElroy put the project on hold: "We should not spend hundreds of millions on production of this weapon pending general confirmatory indications that we know what we are doing."[42]

Despite intense army and contractor pressure, and the expenditure of more than $3 billion, President Kennedy decided in November 1961 not to deploy Nike Zeus.[43] Research on missile defense continued in the early and mid-1960s under the Nike X program, which focused on extending and refining the Nike rocket and radar systems, and Project Defender (1958–68), which was a broadly based research and technology effort to identify and test a wide variety of more technologically ambitious programs. Under Project Defender, the United States developed the Ballistic Missile Boost Intercept (BAMBI) system, originally conceived as a network of hundreds of satellites with homing missiles employing 400-foot-diameter (122-meter) wire webs to collide with and destroy ballistic missiles during their initial boost phase.

Even with six successful tests (out of a total of seven) in a vacuum chamber provided by the National Aeronautics and Space Administration, BAMBI never progressed beyond studies and laboratory testing. This inaction has been attributed to a variety of factors: from intelligence data showing that the Soviet Union in fact lagged behind the United States in ballistic missile deployments (which meant there was less need for the system) to concern about the system's vulnerability following the discovery of electromagnetic pulse effects in the early 1960s (see footnote 75), to the diversion of resources caused by the Apollo program. Although the costs of BAMBI's individual components was relatively low, Jack Ruina, director of the Advanced Research Projects Agency (ARPA), told Congress in 1963 that deploying the system "would involve costs of the order of $50 billion a year," or $294 billion (more than the entire 1998 military budget).[44]

42. Quoted in Alain C. Enthoven and K. Wayne Smith, *How Much Is Enough?: Shaping the Defense Program, 1961–1969* (New York: Harper & Row, 1971), p. 185.

43. Shortly after taking office, the army lobbied Kennedy to approve a huge system, composed of seventy batteries with 7,000 missiles defending twenty-seven areas throughout the United States and Canada. See Kaplan, *The Wizards of Armageddon*, p. 345.

44. Congressional Research Service Report for Congress, "Project Defender," 87-689 S (July 1987), p. CRS-21.

During this period, the United States and the Soviet Union each made progress on antimissile technology, although neither considered their systems ready for large-scale deployment. In the United States, the Nike X ABM system was at the point where some civilian and military advocates, including the JCS, were lobbying for construction of an ABM system. Knowledge that the Soviet Union was moving forward with its Galosh ABM system around Moscow bolstered their position as did the emerging nuclear and missile capabilities of Communist China amidst the turmoil of the Cultural Revolution.

Since China had frequently derided the efficacy of the American nuclear deterrent and memories of Chinese intervention in the Korean War were still fresh, Americans saw in China's backing of North Vietnam a not implausible, though perhaps overly dire, scenario in which the American nuclear shield might be put to a trial of combat. McNamara's enthusiasm for ABMs was diminishing, but under intense pressure from the army, Congress, and military contractors it was politically impossible to terminate Nike X. He therefore routinely denied production funding but sought to placate ABM advocates by pouring nearly $3 billion a year into research and development.[45] This inevitably increased the program's influence and inertia. In October 1967 McNamara summed up the effort to date: "While we have substantially improved our technology in the field, it is important to understand that none of the systems at the present or foreseeable state of the art would provide an impenetrable shield over the United States. Were such a shield possible, we would certainly want it—and we would certainly build it."[46]

In 1968 the Johnson administration announced plans for the deployment of a thin nationwide system of Nike X interceptors and radars (now known as Sentinel), intended to provide a defense of the nation against so-called light Chinese nuclear attacks (and to defend the Johnson administration from partisan Republican attacks in an election year). However effective Sentinel would have been in protecting the United States from China, it failed to protect the White House from the Republicans, and shortly after assuming office in 1969 President Richard Nixon halted all work on Sentinel, pending a review of the program.[47] Ultimately, the administration proposed a similar but

45. Kaplan, *The Wizards of Armageddon,* pp. 345–46. In January 1964 McNamara was briefed on a study by General Glenn Kent, an air force officer and mathematician, which demonstrated that even with extremely effective ABM systems (with a hypothetical 80 percent success rate in shooting down incoming warheads), "to limit damage so that half the industry (and about 60 percent of the population) survived an attack, the U.S. would have to spend $3.20 for each $1 paid by the U.S.S.R. [to increase its offensive forces]—a losing proposition." The conclusion: not only would a strategy based on damage limitation cost too much, it could not prevent the destruction of the United States. See Kaplan, *The Wizards of Armageddon,* pp. 320–25. The quotation is on p. 322.

46. CRS Report for Congress, "Project Defender," 87-6895, July 1987, p. CRS-24.

47. While the administration was deciding how to reorient Sentinel, there was some confusion over just what rationale was driving the program: "On the same day that his Sec-

more modest program—Safeguard—to replace Sentinel, using political judgments and manipulated intelligence data to justify its case.[48] These systems—Nike X, Sentinel, and Safeguard—were based on similar hardware: they employed two types of large electronic phased-array radars (perimeter acquisition radar and missile site radar), which permitted greatly improved tracking and targeting compared with their mechanical predecessors. A long-range rocket, the Spartan, was designed to use high-yield (5-megaton) nuclear warheads to destroy incoming reentry vehicles above the atmosphere. A high-acceleration short-range rocket, the Sprint, would intercept incoming targets with a low-yield nuclear warhead during reentry into the atmosphere, defeating such simple countermeasures as balloon decoys.

However, the radars of these systems were very expensive and highly vulnerable to direct attack. They were also subject to self-blinding by the explosions of Safeguard's long-range interceptor warheads. As with prior efforts, the cost of the defense was greater than the cost of the offensive buildup needed to overcome the defense. In view of their marginal effectiveness and manifest vulnerability, the decision to deploy Sentinel and Safeguard was a very controversial one (the first phase of Safeguard won Senate approval on August 6, 1969, only with the tie-breaking vote of Vice President Spiro Agnew). The deployment was a political compromise that allowed opposition to the ABM Treaty to be overcome (much as six years earlier underground nuclear testing was allowed to continue as a condition for banning tests in the atmosphere; see chapter 1).

The 1972 ABM Treaty limited the number and location of ABM installations (one within a radius of 93 miles [150 kilometers] of the national capital and one within a radius of 150 kilometers of an ICBM deployment area), reducing Safeguard to at most two sites and bringing to a halt construction at a site near Malmstrom Air Force Base in

retary of Defense [Melvin R. Laird] was telling a television audience that the U.S. had to build Sentinel because 'we do not want to become hostage to the Chinese,' Nixon was explaining that he did not 'buy the assumption' that Sentinel was needed as protection against China." See Freedman, *U.S. Intelligence and the Soviet Strategic Threat,* p. 129.

48. Shortly after Nixon became president, his national security adviser, Henry Kissinger, went to the Pentagon to convey Nixon's orders on ABMs. "First, there will be an ABM; second, it will be cheaper than the Democratic Administration's ABM; third, it will shoot down Soviet missiles, not just Chinese missiles." The orders were transmitted to John S. Foster, Jr., head of DOD research and development. "Foster's conclusion: defending cities would be impossible given the guidelines on how much to spend and who the enemy was; therefore, the ABM must be geared primarily to defending Minuteman ICBM silos." Thus three politically motivated decisions determined not only the creation but the mission of Safeguard. Furthermore, the stated need for the system was predicated on the ability of the Soviet Union to destroy the entire Minuteman force with its SS-9 missile. The intelligence community was not in agreement whether the newly discovered mating of three warheads to the missile indicated the existence of MRVs or MIRVs (each of which could be programmed to strike a separate target). The national intelligence estimate (NIE) issued in June 1969 concluded it was only a MRV. "But under heavy pressure from Henry Kissinger and Defense Secretary Melvin Laird, the CIA changed the NIE to read that the SS-9 was probably a MIRV. Since the CIA had previously noted that the Soviets would have 420 SS-9s by the end of 1975, only if each of the three warheads were MIRVs could they threaten all 1,000 Minuteman ICBMs. Only then would there be a rationale for Safeguard." See Kaplan, *Wizards of Armageddon,* pp. 350–51.

Montana and preliminary work on Whiteman Air Force Base in Missouri. Work proceeded most quickly at Nekoma, North Dakota, with the intention of protecting 150 Minuteman ICBMs at nearby Grand Forks Air Force Base. In 1974, however, the ABM Treaty protocol further restricted the United States and the Soviet Union to one site each. The lone site at Nekoma was completed in 1974 and became fully operational on October 1, 1975.[49]

By this time, the army had already decided to reduce readiness at the site to "below full operational status" as of July 1, 1976. Then, during consideration of the 1976 defense appropriations bill, the House Appropriations Committee voted to deactivate Safeguard immediately, arguing that the limitations of a single ABM site, coupled with the recent Soviet deployment of MIRVS meant "the utility of Safeguard to protect Minuteman will be essentially nullified in the future."[50] (Ironically, U.S. officials publicly justified the development of MIRVs in the 1960s to overwhelm the Soviet ABM system around Moscow.)[51] The committee further complained that the Defense Department had "not demonstrated a willingness to exploit whatever experience may be available" from operating the site at full readiness for one year.[52]

When the measure reached the House floor, North Dakota Republican Mark Andrews, the state's single representative, declared: "Because this ABM site does not have defense capability in today's technology, it does not make much sense for me to stand in the well of the House and argue for the expenditure of another $60 million [the actual amount was $85.3 million, or $238 million in 1996 dollars] just because the expenditure happens to be in my State. I think the committee made the right decision."[53] The House approved the committee's action.

---

49. This and the following five paragraphs are drawn from *Congressional Record,* 94 Cong. 1 sess., vol. 121, pt. 28 (November 14, 1975), pp. 36755–62; *Congressional Record,* vol. 121, pt. 29 (November 18, 1975), pp. 37190–95; and John W. Finney, "Senate Approves Defense Spending of $90.7 Billion," *New York Times,* November 19, 1975, p. 1.

50. *Congressional Record* (November 18, 1975), p. 37193.

51. Privately, officials such as Secretary of Defense McNamara saw MIRVs as an effective way to implement a counterforce strategy *and* limit the number of ICBMs requested by the air force. See Nolan, *Guardians of the Arsenal,* pp. 83–85. In 1974 Kissinger told reporters: "I would say in retrospect that I wish I had thought through the implications of a MIRVed world more thoughtfully in 1969 and 1970 than I did." Quoted in Fred Kaplan, Some Second Thoughts about a First Strike," *Environment,* vol. 26, no. 3 (1984), p. 6. In fact, Kissinger had created a MIRV panel to advise him of the ramifications of deploying MIRVs and was fully aware of the consequences. He decided to approve their deployment (in 1970) for two principal reasons: to gain an advantage over the Soviet Union and to create what he believed would be a significant "bargaining chip" in Strategic Arms Limitation Talks (SALT). In the end, the strategic advantage was short-lived, eventually backfiring and creating the "window of vulnerability" once the Soviet Union deployed its own MIRVed missiles beginning in 1975. As for its use as a bargaining chip, SALT focused exclusively on delivery vehicles. The dilemma created by MIRVs led to calls in the early 1980s for single warhead ICBMs. This missile—dubbed "Midgetman" but formally known as the Small ICBM—was vigorously promoted by, among others, then-Representative Albert Gore, Jr. (Democrat of Tennessee). After seven years of research and development at a cost of $5.6 billion, it was canceled in 1991 following the collapse of the Soviet Union. See Kaplan, *Wizards of Armageddon,* pp. 363–64; Kaplan, "Some Second Thoughts about a First Strike," pp. 6, 8; Donald Mackenzie, *Inventing Accuracy: A Historical Sociology of Nuclear Missile Guidance* (Cambridge, Mass.: MIT Press, 1990), p. 215. The full story of the development of the MIRV is told in Ted Greenwood, *Making the MIRV: A Study of Defense Decision Making* (Cambridge, Mass.: Ballinger, 1975).

52. *Congressional Record* (November 18, 1975), p. 37193.

53. *Congressional Record* (November 18, 1975), p. 37191.

The Senate Appropriations Committee rejected the House position, approving the administration's full request. When the Senate took up the bill on November 14, Senator Edward Kennedy (Democrat of Massachusetts) offered an amendment to terminate immediately Safeguard funding. Kennedy was opposed by, among others, both North Dakota senators and the chairman of the Appropriations Committee. They cited letters from the secretary of the army and the chairman of the Joint Chiefs of Staff, which claimed that ending the program before July 1976 would halt plans to operate and test the various Safeguard systems. But, Kennedy asked, "If this ABM site has real security value, why is the Army reducing its operational state in July of next year?"[54] His amendment was narrowly defeated, 39 to 40.

Kennedy returned four days later with another approach: no cut in funding but immediate termination of the program, with the exception of the new electronic phased-array perimeter acquisition radar (PAR). Now opponents produced a letter from Deputy Secretary of Defense W. P. Clements, Jr., who charged that shutting down Safeguard "would be a direct act of unilateral disarmament on the part of the United States." To this Kennedy responded, "The Army itself is planning to make this non-operational next year. . . . They have to get their story straight over there if they expect anybody in the Senate to understand their position."[55]

This time, Kennedy's amendment passed, 52 to 47. It was incorporated into the final bill, which was approved on January 27, 1976. Secretary of Defense Donald Rumsfeld's *Annual Report* for fiscal 1977 (published January 27, 1976) stated "In accordance with FY 1976 Congressional direction, operation of the Safeguard system has been terminated. . . . PAR will remain fully operational in support of the NORAD warning and attack assessment mission."[56] Safeguard was thus fully operational for less than four months. Its termination marks the *only* time that Congress has successfully voted down a major strategic nuclear weapons program supported by the executive branch.[57]

Safeguard was completely shut down by 1978, although the PAR (renamed PARCS, perimeter acquisition radar characterization system) continued to operate as an early warning radar into the 1990s. Safeguard ultimately cost $21.3 billion from 1968 through 1978 (not including RDT&E and production costs for 115 nuclear warheads for the Sprint and Spartan missiles).

54. *Congressional Record* (November 14, 1975), p. 36762.

55. *Congressional Record* (November 18, 1975), p. 37192.

56. Donald H. Rumsfeld, *Annual Defense Department Report, FY 1977* (GPO, 1976), p. 91.

57. Janne E. Nolan, *Guardians of the Arsenal: The Politics of Nuclear Strategy* (New York: Basic Books, 1989), p. 101. In 1973, the Joint Committee on Atomic Energy terminated the W74 and W75 nuclear artillery shells, and in 1983 Congress canceled the W82 155-millimeter enhanced radiation artillery shell (commonly known as the "neutron bomb"). More recently, in 1992 Congress enacted a conditinoal nine-month nuclear testing moratorium over the strong objection of the Bush administration. See chapters 1 and 9 in this volume.

Immediately following the signing of the ABM Treaty in 1972, American missile defense research focused on improving techniques for defending ICBM silos. The Site Defense Program developed a rapidly deployable radar and interceptor system for this mission, although subsequent congressional restrictions limited the program to component development and precluded prototype testing. Site defense formed the basis for the Low-Altitude Defense System (LoADS) that was considered between 1978 and the early 1980s for defense of the MX ICBM (before the decision to deploy this missile in existing Minuteman silos).

Longer-range interceptors were under development in the overlay program, which in conjunction with LoADS would form a layered defense. These systems used mobile air-based and space-based infrared sensors, such as the airborne optical adjunct and the designating optical tracker, for radars, and nonnuclear "hit-to-kill" kinetic energy interceptors, such as the homing overlay experiment. These were subsequently incorporated into SDI in the 1980s.

The Strategic Defense Initiative

From the time President Reagan unveiled SDI during a nationally televised speech on March 23, 1983, the program changed steadily.[58] It went through three major phases, each marked by less ambitious technical and performance goals, a trend that confirmed skeptics' doubts about the need for and feasibility of antimissile systems. Yet advocates remained undaunted in their quest to deploy defenses against ballistic missile attack.

The Peace Shield

As initially presented, SDI promised to render nuclear weapons "impotent and obsolete." Although this was a somewhat vague and indefinite notion, it was generally taken to mean that SDI would lead to a virtually perfect defense of populations (a study disclosed by the Strategic Defense Initiative Organization [SDIO] in November 1985 called for a

58. In his speech, Reagan also claimed that the Soviet Union possessed nuclear superiority. The following day, Senator Edward Kennedy accused the president of "employing Red-scare tactics and reckless 'Star Wars' schemes" to push through larger military budgets. On the House floor, Representative Ted Weirs (Democrat of New York) criticized Reagan for promoting "futuristic 'Star Wars' schemes." *Congressional Record*, 98 Cong. 1 sess., vol. 129, pt. 6 (March 24, 1983), p. 7312. Several other members of Congress, including at least one Republican, chided the president for making it seem as though the Soviet Union were about to launch a Death Star, or called the plan a naive and dangerous fantasy. The pejorative moniker quickly took hold in the news media. In 1985, writer-director George Lucas even filed a lawsuit to prevent the use of his trademarked film title in two television commercials about missile defenses, but he lost in court. For a useful look at the driving forces behind the evolution of SDI, see Gregg Herken, "The Earthly Origins of Star Wars," *Bulletin of the Atomic Scientists*, vol. 43 (October 1987), pp. 20–28.

seven-layer system of thousands of space-based weapons to defend 3,500 U.S. targets).[59] Certainly the exuberant rhetoric that was used to promote the program would have been difficult to sustain in support of less exalted goals, such as the defense of retaliatory forces.

Reagan's ambitious goal was generally regarded as requiring an implausible level of technical perfection. Although the idea of an impermeable shield over Western civilization (or at least the United States) was appealing, there was little reason to believe that it was attainable, not least because ballistic missiles—the threat mentioned in Reagan's speech—were not the only means of delivering nuclear weapons. Obvious Soviet countermeasures, such as massive numbers of decoy warheads, coupled with the predictable unreliability of battle management computer software, guaranteed that perfection would remain elusive.[60] The Peace Shield would have also required implausible amounts of money, with some critics placing the price tag of the full deployment at $1 trillion or more (in then-year dollars).[61]

Perhaps the greatest accomplishment of these first four years of the SDI program consisted in learning what technologies would not work. At its beginning, the program contemplated a bewildering array of devices that might be of some use in shooting down missiles and warheads. But most of these gadgets, such as railguns, space-based radars, lasers, and particle beams, were found wanting. By 1987 this negative judgment led to the reduction or elimination of support for unpromising technologies, greatly reducing the budgetary demands of the SDI program.

This reduction was a blessing in disguise, as Congress demonstrated a stubborn unwillingness to grant the program more than about $4 billion in annual appropriations (in constant dollars, funding exceeded $4 billion only from 1987 to 1990). Congressional rejection of the administration's attempt to reinterpret the ABM Treaty (to permit activities otherwise prohibited) further constrained the prospects for testing or deployment of exotic systems.

59. Charles Mohr, "Antimissile Plan Seeks Thousands of Space Weapons," *New York Times,* November 3, 1985, p. 1.

60. See especially David Lorge Parnas, "Software Aspects of Strategic Defense Systems," DCS-47-IR (University of Victoria [British Columbia], Department of Computer Science, July 1985). In 1985 Parnas resigned from a DOD panel studying the computing requirements for SDI, calling the effort futile. See also Charles Mohr, "Scientist Quits Antimissile Panel Saying Task Is Impossible," *New York Times,* July 12, 1985, p. A6; David E. Sanger, "A Debate about 'Star Wars,'" *New York Times,* October 23, 1985, p. D1; Michael R. Gordon, "Computers Seen as a Key Hurdle in Missile Shield," *New York Times,* January 18, 1986, p. A1; Charles Mohr, "Expert Doubts Computer System for U.S. Missile Shield Is Feasible," *New York Times,* May 27, 1986, p. A16; Philip M. Boffey, "Software Seen as Obstacle in Developing 'Star Wars,'" *New York Times,* September 16, 1986, p. C1.

61. *Congressional Record,* vol. 132, pt. 6 (April 22, 1986), p. 8253. Senator William Proxmire (Democrat of Wisconsin) totaled the estimated cost of building the various components and concluded that this "will very likely exceed $1 trillion." This figure excluded research and development, transporting elements of the system into space, and future maintenance and modernization. Proxmire also noted that "*Physics Today* has estimated the cost of star wars at roughly $2 trillion." Kaplan, *Wizards of Armageddon,* p. 389; Barry M. Blechman and Victor A. Utgoff, "The Macroeconomics of Strategic Defenses," *International Security,* vol. 11, no. 3 (1986–87), pp. 33–70.

Phase One

The receding dream of technological perfection led to the decision in 1987 to concentrate on those antimissile technologies that could be deployed within about a decade. An actual decision to deploy the system was anticipated in 1993, with the initial operational capability expected in 1997. It was projected to have up to 2,000 ground-based interceptors and 4,000 space-based interceptors, at an estimated cost of between $70 billion and $170 billion.[62]

One mission defined for the system was the protection of American land-based missiles, harkening back to the mission of Safeguard nearly twenty years earlier. In particular, the system was required to demonstrate the ability to intercept 50 percent of the Soviet's force of 308 SS-18 ICBMs, which constituted the core of the Soviet counter silo capability (all such SS-18s are now slated for destruction under the START II Treaty, which has been ratified by the U.S. Senate and awaits ratification by the Russian Duma).

In conjunction with this effort, the air force began looking for practical ways to power large, space-based lasers. Space-based reactors seemed a potential answer, and the SP-100 program was created in 1984. A few years later, in 1988, a highly secret program, code-named TIMBERWIND, was formed to explore whether the thermal power of a reactor could be used for offensive military applications (the technology used was originally developed in the 1950s for the nuclear-powered aircraft program; see chapter 2). The SP-100 consumed a relatively modest amount of funds (more than $425 million) until its expiration in 1994, owing to the lack of interest on the part of two of its sponsoring agencies, the DOE and NASA. TIMBERWIND, rechristened the Space Nuclear Thermal Propulsion program in the early 1990s, cost approximately $132 million since its inception and is no longer active.[63]

Global Protection against Limited Strikes

In 1990 growing disenchantment with the technical and military prospects of a system oriented toward the declining Soviet threat led Congress to endorse, for the first time, significant reductions in the SDI budget (as opposed to reductions to the administration's request), as well as a major restructuring of the SDI program.

---

62. *Cost Estimates for Phase 1 of the Strategic Defense Initiative,* Hearing before the Legislation and National Security Subcommittee of the House Committee on Government Operations, 101 Cong. 1 sess. (GPO, March 21, 1989), p. 10; John M. Broder, "'Star Wars' First Phase Cost Put at $170 Billion," *Los Angeles Times,* June 12, 1988, p. 1.

63. For more on the SP-100, see *The SP-100 Space Reactor Power System Program,* Hearings before the Subcommittee on Investigations and Oversight of the House Committee on Science, Space, and Technology, 102 Cong. 2 sess. (GPO, 1992). For TIMBERWIND, see *The Development of Nuclear Thermal Propulsion Technology for Use in Space,* Hearings before the Subcommittee on Investigations and Oversight of the House Committee on Science, Space, and Technology, 102 Cong. 2 sess. (GPO, 1993).

But the end of the cold war did not mark the end of SDI. By late 1990 it had been reoriented into the Global Protection against Limited Strikes (GPALS) system to defend against tactical and theater missile threats, as well as up to 200 long-range ICBM or SLBM warheads aimed against the United States. The order-of-magnitude reduction in the number of warheads involved in a "strategic" compared with a "limited" attack did not lead to a comparable reduction in the size of the program. The total estimated cost of deploying the GPALS system was in the neighborhood of about $40 billion.[64]

In the wake of the Gulf War and the perceived success of the Patriot missile, Congress passed the Missile Defense Act, which called for the deployment of a ground-based system covering the United States by 1996 and restored the funding cuts imposed the previous year. This congressional enthusiasm was short-lived, however. By mid-1992 it was apparent that the Patriot had been much less successful than originally claimed, though the extent of its shortcomings remained controversial.[65] The Pentagon conceded that there was no prospect of meeting the 1996 deployment target, with the year 2002 representing a more realistic goal. Thus in 1992 the Congress eliminated the target dates for deployment of SDI and declined to increase program's budget.

The Clinton Administration

The Clinton administration in 1993 renamed SDIO the Ballistic Missile Defense Organization (BMDO), but many aspects of the program remain the same as in the Reagan or Bush era. The reason is that the Clinton administration fears that in the future the United States might be deterred from military action against some third world country by the threat of missile retaliation against American troops or the American homeland. Thus to maintain their credibility, American interventionary forces must be able to deploy highly effective theater missile defenses. The administration has also proposed significant revisions to the ABM Treaty to clarify ambiguities between theater and strategic systems and thus pave the way for legally testing and deploying theater systems.

In 1995 the new Republican majority in the 104th Congress strongly endorsed deployment of robust theater missile defenses beyond those contemplated by the Clinton administration, restoring

64. Letter from Robert D. Reischauer, Director, Congressional Budget Office, to the Honorable Joseph Biden, Jr., July 30, 1991.

65. See Theodore A. Postol, "Lessons of the Gulf War Experience with Patriot," *International Security*, vol. 16, no. 3 (1991–92), pp. 119–71; Robert M. Stein, Correspondence: "Patriot Experience in the Gulf War," *International Security*, vol. 17, no. 1 (1992), pp. 199–225; Theodore A. Postol, "Correspondence: The Author Replies," *International Security*, vol. 17, no. 1 (1992), pp. 225–40; Eliot Marshall, "Patriot's Scud Busting Record Is Challenged," *Science*, vol. 252 (May 3, 1991), pp. 640–41; Jock Friedly, "MIT Torn by Bitter Dispute over Missile, *Science*, vol. 271 (February 23, 1996), pp. 1050–52.

the goal of the 1991 Missile Defense Act of deployment of ground-based national missile defenses in the near term (by 2003), testing and deployment of space-based laser weapons soon thereafter, and the extensive modification if not abandonment of the ABM Treaty. For the first time, advocates of the immediate deployment of antimissile systems commanded the congressional majorities needed to realize their long-held goals. As in the past, the "Star Wars" debate encompassed much larger issues, including the overall level of military spending and the importance of arms control as a tool of foreign policy.

Despite intense partisan controversy, there is perhaps less separating the Clinton administration and the Republican Congress than would be assumed by a casual reading of partisan position papers. There is general agreement on continued spending at levels several times greater than those prevailing immediately following the signing of the ABM Treaty ($2.8 billion and $1.8 billion in 1973 and 1974, respectively, versus $3.4 billion and $3.8 billion in 1996 and 1997, respectively). While Congress regularly adds the better part of a billion dollars each year to the administration's request, the DOD has not objected too strenuously to this largesse.

The consensus seems to be that the deployment of a national missile defense may soon prove an appropriate response to current and future missile threats, though members of Congress and the administration disagree on when a decision on such deployment needs to be made. Many also agree that the strictures of the ABM Treaty that served so well during the cold war must be loosened to meet the evolving circumstances of the post–cold war era, though the extent of the loosening needed has not yet been established, nor has the appropriate course of action should Russia fail to see the wisdom of this new course. Yet there is little doubt that the disputes arising despite such broad agreement are continued testament to the fundamental and nearly intractable conundrums posed by the challenges of strategic defense.[66]

The Costs of Missile Defenses

In contrast to air defense expenditures, nearly all antimissile expenditures occurred after the fiscal 1962 creation of the FYDP. Costs incurred before that time are readily documented in the public record. These costs include $3.2 billion for the Nike Zeus program, from 1962 through 1965; $9.2 billion for NIKE X (which included development of components for the Sentinel System) from 1962 through 1969;

66. Tim Weiner, "'Star Wars' System Remains Many Years and Dollars Away," *New York Times,* May 18, 1997, p. A21.

$21.3 billion for Safeguard, and $51 billion for the SDI and subsequent national and theater missile defense programs from 1983 through 1996 (including $2.2 billion for directed energy weapons, see chapter 1) and $13.8 billion for programs not directly related to these major efforts. During the 1983–93 period the accounting was greatly assisted by the fact that virtually all antimissile research (and perhaps a few projects only tangentially related to missile defense, seeking to bask in the warm rays of presidential favor) were aggregated under the budget of the SDIO.[67] With the end of the cold war, the ties that bound these programs were over time insensibly loosened, and increasingly the core antimissile program encompassed by the $4 billion annual BMDO budget has accounted for a declining share of overall antimissile funding, as the military services have taken on the burden of these efforts out of their own accounts, which by the late 1990s amounted to upward of a billion dollars a year. The grand total comes to $100 billion (see figure 4-2).

SDI and the End of the Cold War

In 1993 four former Reagan administration officials, including two military officers, told the *New York Times* that the Army Ballistic Missile Defense Command rigged a key 1984 SDI interceptor test and that other test data were fabricated as part of a program to deceive the Soviet Union. Said one of the officers: "Our adversary was very aware of SDI. It was important to get them to divert their money and technologies."[68]

Six days after this article appeared, Robert C. McFarlane, Reagan's national security adviser from 1983 to 1986, wrote a response for the *Times* dismissing the possibility of a deception program and instead promoting the view that the creation of SDI was designed as a lever "to get the Russians to decrease their numbers of land-based ICBM war-

67. An analysis by the Congressional Research Service in 1995 maintained that at least $70.7 billion had been expended on SDIO programs, with the additional money coming from accounts not officially part of the SDIO budget. See Memorandum, Steven A. Hildreth, Specialist in National Defense, Congressional Research Service, to the Honorable David Pryor, August 1, 1995; Jonathan S. Landay, "Pentagon Hit for Hiding Spending on 'Star Wars'," *Christian Science Monitor*, September 5, 1995, p. 3.

68. Tim Weiner, "Lies and Rigged 'Star Wars' Test Fooled the Kremlin, and Congress," *New York Times*, August 18, 1993, p. A1. Former Secretary of Defense Caspar Weinberger, who had reportedly approved the program, told the *Times* he could not confirm or deny such an effort but said: "You're always trying to practice deception. You are obviously trying to mislead your opponents and to make sure they don't know the actual facts" (p. A1). Nine days later, the *Times* reported that Weinberger, "called the charges fairy tales. He said nothing was done to deceive the Congress or the Soviets about the program or the disputed test. Mr. Weinberger also said that comments he made last week about the frequent use of deception programs by the Pentagon were not meant to confirm the existence of any deception program connected with the [Strategic Defense Initiative] program, or to suggest that the disputed test had been deceptive." Tim Weiner, "General Details Altered 'Star Wars' Test," *New York Times*, August 27, 1993, p. A19. For more on the use of deceptive cover stories by the DOD see John Wagner, "Drafting Rules of Deception—How and When," *Washington Post*, August 6, 1992, p. A23; John Horgan, "Lying by the Book," *Scientific American*, October 1992, p. 20.

FIGURE 4-2. The Cost of U.S. Ballistic Missile Defense Programs, 1962–96[a]

Billions of 1996 dollars

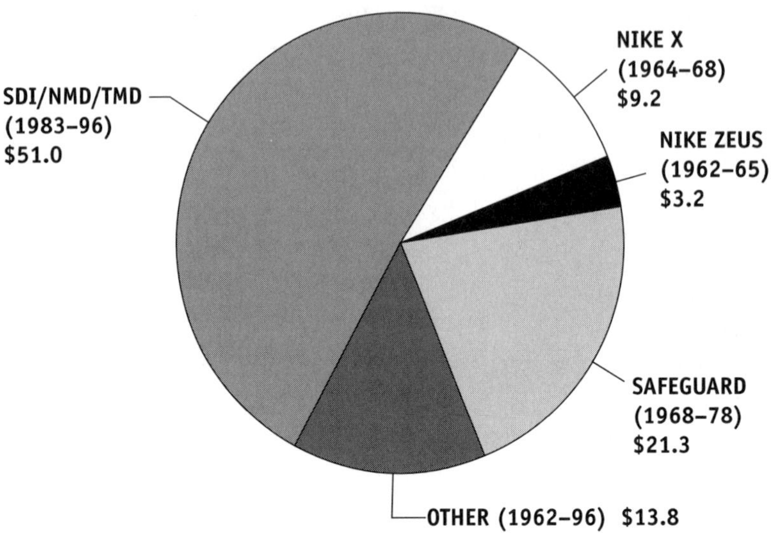

a. Does not include an estimated $1.5 billion in expenditures before 1962. "Other" includes activities not directly associated with any specific major program. SDI = Strategic Defense Initiative; NMD = National Missile Defense; TMD = Theater Missile Defense.

heads." Its military capabilities were not as important as the fact that "such an investment would offer even greater political and economic leverage." This strategy worked, McFarlane concluded, because Mikhail Gorbachev, at the 1985 Geneva summit, agreed to a 50 percent reduction in nuclear warheads. Moreover, a senior Russian official had recently told McFarlane that SDI "accelerated our catastrophe by about five years." Thus, argued McFarlane, SDI "saved us and our allies at least five years of much higher defense budgets—certainly more than $100 billion—not to mention ending an era in which all humankind lived under a balance of terror."[69]

In September 1993 the DOD confirmed the existence of the deception program. A 1994 GAO investigation determined that the plan "was seen as a means of impacting arms control negotiations and influencing Soviet spending," and offered further details, such as the fact

69. Robert C. McFarlane, "Consider What Star Wars Accomplished," *New York Times,* August 24, 1993, p. A15.

that an explosive was placed within the intended target. This could then be detonated by ground observers to create the illusion of a direct impact. The GAO also found that in one test the target vehicle was artificially heated to provide a better infrared signature for the interceptor, a condition that improved the potential for success but deviated from conditions likely to be encountered under actual use. Concerning the explosive designed to simulate a direct hit, the GAO determined that, ironically, the army never activated this deception option because the interceptor vehicle never came close enough to the target to make a rigged explosion appear credible and realistic.[70]

McFarlane's thesis was adopted by a number of observers, eventually ascribing to SDI the pivotal role of triggering the economic collapse of the Soviet Union and, with it, the end of the cold war.[71] But for this view to hold true, two conditions must pertain. First, Soviet military spending (either actual or as a percentage of overall government spending) would had to have shown regular increases, evidence of attempts to match or exceed U.S. expenditures. Second, the USSR would have had to initiate its own SDI, or devise another costly means of countering it. The available evidence indicates neither condition was met.

First, according to CIA data Soviet military spending remained relatively constant throughout the 1980s, actually declining only in 1989 and at a slower rate than the rest of the economy (a slight rise—3 percent overall growth—from 1985 to 1988 can be attributed to programs initiated *before* the Reagan administration, and in any event is far lower than growth levels of the 1970s). Had U.S. spending driven the Soviet Union into bankruptcy (by forcing it to increase spending beyond what it could afford), military spending levels ought to indicate some effort to emulate U.S. plans; they do not.[72] Second, as early as 1983 the CIA predicted that rather than attempting to build its own SDI, the

70. U.S. General Accounting Office, *Ballistic Missile Defense: Records Indicate Deception Program Did Not Affect 1984 Test Results,* NSIAD-94-219 (July 1994). The quotation is on p. 13.

71. In October 1995 Richard V. Allen, Ronald Reagan's first national security adviser, said of SDI: "Actually, it scared the hell out of the Russians. They were not sure whether they should believe it or whether it was a massive hoax. They rolled out all their propaganda tools to counter it, they blustered and threatened, but to little avail. . . . Their antiquated command economy and pitifully weak technological base, at least fifteen years behind in computer technology, could not hope to sustain an effort against a determined and wealthy Western adversary." Richard V. Allen, "The Man Who Changed the Game Plan," *National Interest,* no. 44 (Summer 1996), pp. 64–65. Former CIA director Robert M. Gates wrote in 1996: "By 1983, already panting hard as they tried to keep pace with current and prospective U.S. military deployments, the Soviet leaders were left breathless by one U.S. military initiative that, in its ambition and implications, truly horrified them—Reagan's determination to build a space-based ballistic missile defense." Robert M. Gates, *From the Shadows: The Ultimate Insider's Story of Five Presidents and How They Won the Cold War* (New York: Simon & Schuster, 1996), p. 539.

72. Raymond L. Garthoff, *The Great Transition: American-Soviet Relations and the End of the Cold War* (Brookings, 1994), pp. 506–08, 514–17; Franklyn D. Holzman, "Politics and Guesswork: CIA and DIA Estimates of Soviet Military Spending," *International Security,* vol. 14, no. 2 (1989), pp. 101–31; James E. Steiner and Franklyn D. Holzman, "Correspondence: CIA Estimates of Soviet Military Spending," *International Security,* vol. 14, no. 4 (1990), pp. 185–98; Richard Ned Lebow and Janice Gross Stein, *We All Lost the Cold War* (Princeton University Press, 1994), pp. 369–76.

Soviet Union would "rely principally on a concerted political and diplomatic effort first to force the United States to drop its ballistic missile defense (BMD) plans or, failing that, to negotiate them away."[73] The CIA concluded: "It is highly unlikely that the Soviets will undertake a 'crash' program in reaction to U.S. BMD developments, but rather will seek to counter them by steadily paced efforts over the decades the United States will need to develop and deploy its overall defenses."

This is in fact what occurred. The Soviet Union did conduct some limited research into missile defense technologies (producing some unworkable concepts that generally never proceeded beyond the design phase), but despite numerous accusations of great advances in such technologies by the DOD and U.S. intelligence agencies, its program was a pale imitation of the vigorously funded U.S. effort.[74] Although ample evidence is available to show that military spending placed a tremendous strain on the Soviet economy in general, there are no data supporting the conclusion that efforts to match or counter SDI accelerated the demise of the Soviet Union. If anything, the program was responsible for exacerbating tensions and delaying agreements to reduce nuclear arsenals (McFarlane's stated motivation for backing the program). It thus delayed the eventual end of the cold war and increased U.S. costs.

Antisatellite Programs

The launch of Sputnik not only galvanized work on antimissile systems but spawned an entirely new class of antisatellite (ASAT) weapons

73. Central Intelligence Agency, "Possible Soviet Responses to the U.S. Strategic Defense Initiative," NIC M 83-10017 (September 12, 1983), copy 458 (formerly secret), pp. vii–viii (available on the World Wide Web at http://www.fas.org/spp/starwars/offdocs/m8310017.htm). Nearly two years after this secret report, a senior member of the Soviet general staff told the *Washington Post*: "We are not going to take the path that the U.S. administration is trying to force us onto. We have made it clear that we will not ape the United States." In fact, the "far cheaper, more economic" response would be "an increase in offensive strategic weapons, and . . . certain defensive measures." See Jim Hoagland and Dusko Doder, "Moscow Won't 'Ape' SDI, Top Soviet General Says," *Washington Post*, June 9, 1985, p. A1.

74. For details on the Soviet counterpart to SDI, see Steven J. Zaloga, "Red Star Wars," *Jane's Intelligence Review*, vol. 9, no. 5 (1997), pp. 205–08. A prime example of U.S. mischaracterization occurred from 1984 until about 1990, when the DOD published sketches of a laser facility at Sary Shagan, claiming that the site was the center of an "ominous," highly capable, research effort capable of antisatellite operations and possible missile defense in the future. Yet when the Soviet Union invited a ten-member American team (including three members of Congress and two physicists) to tour the site in July 1989, it was discovered that the facility was capable of only low power operations (about 2 kilowatts) and posed little threat to U.S. military assets. "It's incredible to think that the Pentagon SDI folks probably got an extra $10 billion because of this place," said one visitor. See Bill Keller, "American Team Gets Close Look at Soviet Secret," *New York Times*, July 9, 1989, p. 1; David C. Morrison, "Second Thoughts about Soviet Lasers," *National Journal*, vol. 21 (August 5, 1989), p. 1993; Frank von Hippel and Thomas B. Cochran, "The Myth of the Soviet 'Killer' Laser, *New York Times*, August 19, 1989, p. 23. For a good example of how the DOD portrayed the Soviet space threat in the 1980s, see U.S. Department of Defense, *The Soviet Space Challenge* (GPO, 1987); Hedrick Smith, "Nitze Details U.S. Charges Soviet Has Own 'Star Wars,'" *New York Times*, July 12, 1985, p. A6.

intended to counter the military spacecraft of other nations. The threat of orbiting nuclear weapons, the original impetus for ASAT weapons, mercifully never materialized, for early nuclear-armed ASATs had major operational limitations. Chief among them, the detonation of the ASAT's nuclear warheads would damage American satellites as well as the intended target satellite either by exposure to orbiting debris or from electromagnetic interference. Nuclear explosions in space would have produced large electric fields on the earth's surface and in its airspace, playing havoc with the operations of friendly forces, particularly the sensitive electronic components aboard satellites. High-altitude nuclear tests in the early 1960s—shortly before the enactment of the Partial Test Ban Treaty in 1963—demonstrated that the electromagnetic pulse from an explosion could travel great distances.[75]

Early guidance systems posed another problem. Antisatellite weapons could only count on placing a warhead within a few miles of their target, which meant they had to use a nuclear warhead to achieve a "kill." During the late 1950s and early 1960s several air-launched ASAT systems were tested by the United States as part of the ongoing effort to develop strategic air-launched ballistic missiles. Early ASAT efforts constitute perhaps the most poignant chapter in the history of strategic defense, as they demonstrate the intimate connections between offense and defense, the great dependence of effective defenses on a clear understanding of the characteristics of the offensive threat, and the profound difficulties of planning under conditions of rapidly evolving technology. They also reveal the intense rivalry among the services for primacy in acquiring and deploying novel combat capabilities, as a result of which responsibility for this mission has oscillated between the army and air force.

In the early years of the space age the military potential of this new frontier was limited largely by the imaginings of graphic artists, and no application seemed too fantastic to lie more than a few years in the future. With clouds of American nuclear-armed bombers hovering on continuous airborne alert just outside Soviet airspace, perhaps no great leap of imagination was required to envision swarms of Soviet nuclear-armed spacecraft hovering continuously over American airspace (apart from a few minor details of orbital mechanics). Fortunately, by the mid-1960s it became increasingly apparent that those "minor details," and the frailties of human mechanisms to which bombers on airborne alert proved vulnerable, rendered orbital

75. The "Starfish Prime" nuclear test, a 1.45-megaton warhead detonated at night 248 miles (399 kilometers) above Johnston Island on July 8, 1962, unexpectedly lit up the skies all over Hawaii—hundreds of miles away—for six minutes, shorting out power lines and setting off burglar alarms. Auroras, some lasting as long as fifteen minutes, were seen across the central Pacific. Observers on Kwajalein Island, about 1,600 miles (2,574 kilometers) to the west, witnessed a seven-minute atmospheric light show. See Chuck Hansen, *U.S. Nuclear Weapons: The Secret History* (Arlington, Tex.: Aerofax, 1988), p. 87.

nuclear weapons one of the less attractive modes of strategic attack, early fears notwithstanding. When the threat of orbiting nuclear weapons did not materialize, and their manifest absence of military utility was codified in the 1967 Outer Space Treaty, which banned the stationing of weapons of mass destruction in outer space, the American ASAT deployments were eventually dismantled.

Program 505/MUDFLAP Nike Zeus

As already mentioned, the U.S. Army's Nike Zeus was originally developed as part of an ABM system. After several years of research, it became clear that the missile would be largely ineffective as an ABM, but somewhat effective as an ASAT (with a range of more than 150 miles [241 kilometers]), because a detonation needed to be only within close proximity of a satellite for radiation effects to disable or destroy it. The first successful U.S. space antisatellite intercept under Project Mudflap, or Program 505, took place on May 24, 1963, from Kwajalein Atoll in the Pacific Ocean. Between that date and January 13, 1966, at least eight of the Nike Zeus ground-launched missiles were test-fired.[76] Total costs for the program, which ended in 1967 after the DOD chose to rely instead on Program 437, were a relatively modest $53 million.

Program 437 Thor

The air force also secretly tested and deployed several Thor intermediate-range ballistic missiles, recently returned from active duty in Great Britain (see chapter 2) and modified for the antisatellite mission (the program's existence was only officially revealed in September 1964). This capability grew out of Operation Dominic, a series of high-altitude nuclear tests conducted in the Pacific in 1962. These nuclear-tipped ASATs became operational on Johnston Island in the Pacific in 1964 and could intercept a target at much greater range than Nike Zeus.[77] The Program 437 Thor system was tested at least sixteen times from 1964 to 1970 and was retired in 1976. However, this system could be restored to operational status on six months' notice, since the booster components were stored as part of the Safeguard C program to resume nuclear testing in the event of the demise of the Partial Test Ban Treaty (see chapter 1).[78] Total costs were $917 million.

76. Paul B. Stares, *The Militarization of Space: U.S. Policy, 1945–1984* (Cornell University Press, 1985), pp. 117–20.

77. A contemporaneous document indicates that the program was "directed toward an interim system capable of giving the President the option of destroying an enemy satellite that, for example, might be equipped with a very high yield nuclear device and employed for threat purposes." Letter from Major General A. W. Betts, Director of Military Application, Atomic Energy Commission, to Senator John O. Pastore, Chairman, Joint Committee on Atomic Energy, June 24, 1963, formerly classified Secret, Record Group 128, Declassified General Subject File, Box 1 (Air Force, Department of), Document 7623, National Archives.

78. Stares, *Militarization of Space,* pp. 120–28.

Air-Launched Miniature Vehicle Program

The air-launched miniature vehicle (ALMV) was the primary American ASAT effort in the early 1980s. This weapon, launched from an F-15 fighter by a small two-stage rocket, carried a heat-seeking miniature homing vehicle (MHV) that would destroy its target by direct impact at high speed. The mobility of the system was a significant asset: in contrast to a ground-based system, which must wait for a target satellite to fly over its launch site, an F-15 could bring the ALMV under the ground track of its target.

Plans called for an operational force of more than 100 interceptors. By 1987, however, the program's cost, initially estimated at about $500 million (then-year dollars) had increased roughly tenfold.[79] In an attempt to limit costs, the air force scaled the MHV program back by two-thirds that year. The Reagan administration canceled it in 1988 after its homing guidance system encountered technical problems, testing delays, and significant cost growth. In all, it consumed $2.3 billion.

Kinetic Energy ASAT

Following the cancellation of the ALMV, the army's kinetic energy ASAT became the military's main program for attacking hostile satellites. As with the air force's air-launched project, this ground-based interceptor would destroy satellites by homing in and colliding with them. The three-stage missile would extend a sheet of Mylar plastic, known as a "kill enhancement device," which would strike the target and render it inoperative without shattering the satellite. This interceptor would only be able to reach satellites in low earth orbit, up to ranges of several thousand kilometers. The army planned to start flight-testing its missile in late 1996. There were to be seven flight tests: two actual interceptions of inactive U.S. satellites in orbit and five close passes to orbiting satellites. Deployment was scheduled to begin in June 1998. According to DOD estimates, this ASAT could be built and operated for twenty years for $2 billion to $2.5 billion. With the demise of the Soviet Union, this program languished in the early to mid-1990s, only to be revived by the new Republican majority in Congress, who added tens of millions of dollars to its budget, propelling the program toward an interim operational capability by the end of the decade. From 1989 through 1995 spending for this program totaled more than $300 million, with an additional $205 million from 1996 through 1999

79. "U.S. Funds Killer Satellite Effort," *Aviation Week & Space Technology,* February 6, 1978, p. 18. This article estimated that the program would cost between $400 million and $500 million. The June 1987 Selected Acquisition Report indicated an acquisition cost of $4.2 billion. See "Pentagon Tables Summarize SAR Programs," *Aerospace Daily,* vol. 142, no. 61 (1987), pp. 485–86. Additional operations and maintenance costs of between $1.2 billion and $4.0 billion would also have been required over the life of the program. U.S. General Accounting Office, "U.S. Anti-Satellite Program: Information on Operational Effectiveness, Cost, Schedule and Testing [U]" B-219105, June 11, 1986, unclassified summary.

projected to be necessary to bring the system into operation.[80] However, in October 1997, President Clinton used the line-item veto to eliminate $37 million in funding for the program in 1998.

Directed Energy ASATs

Since the mid-1980s the United States has had at least a latent or residual ASAT capability in the form of the 2-milliwatt Mid-Infrared Advanced Chemical Laser (MIRACL) located at the White Sands Missile Range in New Mexico. Directed energy systems would have the ability to disable large numbers of satellites in a very short period of time, in comparison with the kinetic energy ASAT. In October 1997, MIRACL was fired at an aging air force satellite to gauge the effects various power levels would have on the satellite's operations. When one of the laser's parts melted during the test and computer problems prevented officials from learning to what degree the laser had blinded the satellite, a smaller, 30-watt laser generally used for dry runs was fired instead. In a surprise to army officials, the small laser "adequately" negated operations of the satellite's optical sensor, suggesting that even low-power lasers have the capability to seriously disrupt certain satellites. Future tests are likely to try to refine knowledge of this effect at various power levels, both to disable an adversary's satellites and protect U.S. satellites. Total costs to date have been $600 million.[81]

The Cost of ASATs

Altogether about $14.5 billion was spent on antisatellite weapons and supporting programs, as documented in the FYDP historical database. Some $4.2 billion was expended on ASATs from 1962 through 1995. In that same period $5.3 billion went to space surveillance and related antisatellite C^3I support, more than $4 billion to the air force spacetrack network, and nearly $1 billion to the naval space surveillance system.

Arguably, ASAT programs would have been undertaken whether or not nuclear weapons existed. But Soviet nuclear weapons strongly motivated these programs, and U.S. nuclear weapons were integral to the history of ASAT development. We therefore include only 50 percent of these costs—$7.2 billion—in the overall total for this chapter.

80. U.S. Army, Space and Strategic Defense Command, "Kinetic Energy Anti-Satellite Program (KE ASAT): Background and Overview," November 12, 1996, pp. 14, 20; See also William J. Broad, "In Era of Satellites, Army Plots Ways to Destroy Them," *New York Times,* March 4, 1997, p. C1; Douglas Berenson, "Space Architect Calls on DoD to Explore Various Anti-Satellite Options," *Inside the Pentagon,* June 12, 1997, p. 1.

81. John Donnelly, "Laser of 30 Watts Blinded Satellites 300 Miles High," *Defense Week,* December 8, 1997, p. 1.

Antisubmarine Warfare

Since the Soviet Union first equipped submarines with nuclear-tipped ballistic missiles, cruise missiles, and torpedoes, the United States has sought the ability to detect, track, and sink them. Although not commonly thought of as a component of strategic defense, strategic ASW was explicitly included as a strategic defense mission in the 1960s and has continued to play a major, though less overt, role in the development of the "silent service" ever since. This long-standing mission carries a high price tag.

Antisubmarine warfare is waged with the aid of an extensive array of acoustic and nonacoustic sensors, information processing, attack platforms (mainly aircraft and attack submarines), and conventional as well as (until 1991) nuclear missiles, mines, torpedoes, and depth bombs. As with other strategic defense programs, the development of strategic ASW was largely driven by an offense-defense race between American and Soviet forces. The history of American strategic ASW thus parallels the development of new classes of Soviet missile submarines.

In the late 1950s and early 1960s, the primary threats were Echo-class submarines carrying cruise missiles and Golf and Hotel class submarines carrying ballistic missiles with ranges of hundreds of kilometers. By the late 1960s these coast-hugging submarines were supplanted by the Yankee-class boats, which carried longer-range missiles permitting midocean deployments. These weapons presented the United States with a coastal defense problem, not too unlike that posed by German U-boats during World War II. Lessons learned during the Battle of the Atlantic led the U.S. Navy to rely on proven systems, such as shore-based maritime patrol aircraft and dedicated ASW aircraft carriers, to which were gradually added long-range undersea surveillance sensors made possible by the rapidly improving computers of the time.

In the early 1970s, however, the Soviet Union had introduced the first of a series of Delta-class submarines, which fundamentally altered the strategic ASW challenge. With their cargo of long-range missiles, Deltas were able to remain in bastions near Soviet home waters, where they could be protected from American forces by the Soviet surface fleet and Soviet naval aviation.

Among the numerous sensor arrays deployed to detect Soviet submarines, the workhorse has been an undersea network of acoustic listening devices called the Sound Surveillance System. The navy deployed the first elements of the system in 1954 (under the code name CAESAR) and eventually expanded the arrays to more than 1,000 underwater microphones covering vast regions of the North Atlantic and North Pacific, principally the choke points through which Soviet submarines passed en route to patrol areas near the U.S. coasts (e.g., the so-called Greenland-Iceland-United Kingdom gap), and the patrol areas themselves. The devices report acoustic signals through some 30,000 miles (48,270 kilometers) of undersea cables to (in the 1980s) eighteen navy shore stations for analysis, and their recognition of Soviet submarine noise "signatures" enables ASW forces to localize and track them.

Three large ships—the *Zeus,* the *Neptune,* and the *Albert J. Myer*—were used to maintain and repair the cables (by 1994 only the *Zeus* remained in service). In July 1993 the navy drew back some of the secrecy about SOSUS, allowing civilian scientists to begin using the system to track migrating whales. SOSUS has since been used to listen to an underwater volcano off the coast of Oregon, to catch three boats off the Pacific Northwest coast laying illegal drift nets, to help develop a system to detect nuclear explosions (to verify compliance with the Comprehensive Test Ban Treaty), and to detect and study deep-sea volcanic eruptions. In 1994 the navy began shutting down much of the network, including all but four of the shore stations, citing its high annual operating costs (reported to be $165 million in 1995) as the reason.[82]

Two other systems have been used to augment acoustic search and detection in areas not covered by SOSUS: mobile hydrophone arrays towed by dedicated surface ships, known as the Surveillance Towed Array Sensor System and developed during the late 1970s;[83] aircraft-deployed, submerged buoys designed to transmit their signals to maritime patrol aircraft and satellite, known as the Rapidly Deployable Surveillance System. From the inception of the undersea surveillance program through 1995, the cost has been more than $16 billion.

The performance of these systems depends on a host of factors, and for many years they exploited the fact that Soviet submarines tended to be quite noisy and had to operate in the open oceans because of the limited range of their missiles. These operational constraints were alleviated substantially by the development of quieter submarines (thanks in no small measure to quieting techniques acquired through espionage by the Walker family in the 1970s and 1980s) and long-range submarine missiles.[84] The Soviet Union withdrew its SSBNs

82. William J. Broad, "Long-Secret Navy Devices Allow Monitoring of Ocean Eruption," *New York Times,* August 20, 1993, p. A1; William J. Broad, "Navy Listening System Opening World of Whales," *New York Times,* August 23, 1993, p. A12; William J. Broad, "Scientists Fight Navy Plan to Shut Far-Flung Undersea Spy System," *New York Times,* June 12, 1994, p. 1; Usha Lee McFarling, "Super-Secret Navy System Looks for Work," *Boston Globe,* June 20, 1994, p. 27; William J. Broad, "Anti-Sub Seabed Grid Thrown Open to Research Uses," *New York Times,* July 2, 1996, p. C1; Kathy Sawyer, "From Deep in the Earth, Revelations of Life," *Washington Post,* April 6, 1997, p. A1.

83. U.S. General Accounting Office, *Undersea Surveillance: Navy Continues to Build Ships Designed for Soviet Threat,* NSIAD-93- 53 (December 1992).

84. Personal communication from a U.S. Navy official. See also Jeffrey T. Richelson, *A Century of Spies: Intelligence in the Twentieth Century* (Oxford University Press, 1995), pp. 396–98. For more on the Walker spy family, see John Barron, *Breaking the Ring: The Bizarre Case of the Walker Family Spy Ring* (Boston, Mass.: Houghton Mifflin, 1987); and Howard Blum, *I Pledge Allegiance . . . The True Story of the Walkers: An American Spy Family* (New York: Simon & Schuster, 1987).

to home waters such as the White Sea, the Sea of Okhotsk, and the shallow territorial waters around the Kamchatka Peninsula and Novaya Zemlya, where friendly naval forces could protect them from unfriendly incursions and the submarines could still strike U.S. targets.

The U.S. Navy, however, was slow to exploit this opportunity. Not until the formal enunciation of the controversial forward maritime strategy in early 1986 did it propose using virtually its entire fleet to disable and destroy the Soviet SSBN bastions and their protective forces at the outset of any major conflict.[85] As has too often been the case in the dance of offense and defense, however, by the time the navy began to digest the implications of the forward maritime strategy, the Soviet Union had inaugurated the fourth epoch of American strategic ASW with the introduction of the Typhoon class of ballistic missile submarines. Of unprecedented size, the Typhoons (featured in the book and film *The Hunt for Red October*) were especially designed to operate under the Arctic ice pack and configured to break through this protective shield at the appropriate moment to launch their ICBM-range missiles. While this bold move relegated other naval elements (apart from escorting attack submarines) to the ice-free sidelines, the Typhoon seemingly rendered the entire U.S. Navy irrelevant to the strategic ASW mission, save for American nuclear attack submarines and possibly CAPTOR mines strewn on the seabed.[86]

Undaunted, the silent service proceeded to provide enhanced under-ice capabilities for more than two dozen improved *Los Angeles*–class of attack submarines and initiated the development of the SSN-21 *Seawolf*. The *Seawolf* was designed from the outset to counter the Typhoon. Significantly larger and quieter than its predecessors, the *Seawolf* incorporates a variety of features to optimize its performance under the Arctic ice. The first *Seawolf* set to sea in July 1997, years after the collapse of the Soviet Union, and after a marked decline in the patrol rate of Typhoon and Delta-class submarines (out of an original program of thirty, only three will be built). To date, *Seawolf* has cost $8.5 billion.[87] Looking to the future, the navy is hard at work on the

85. Michael R. Gordon, "Navy Says in a Nonnuclear War, It Might Attack Soviet A-Arms," *New York Times*, January 7, 1986, p. A1; Admiral James D. Watkins, "The Maritime Strategy" (U.S. Naval Institute, January 1986 supplement to *Proceedings*), pp. 2–17. "We can get inside their knickers before they can find us and they don't like it," is how Admiral Watkins, then chief of naval operations, described the offensive role of U.S. attack submarines in congressional testimony in 1985. Quoted in William M. Arkin, "Provocations at Sea," *Bulletin of the Atomic Scientists*, vol. 41 (November 1985), pp. 6–7.

86. This conventional American view of the design and capabilities of the Typhoon has been disputed by Russian specialists, who in private communications with the authors have asserted that, whatever the original intent, in practice the flat deck of the Typhoon proved a convenient lodgement for Arctic pack ice floes, which in sea trials were discovered to remain firmly ensconced athwart the missile launch tube doors.

87. Robert A. Hamilton, "The Stealth of a Seawolf," *New London Day* (Connecticut), July 13, 1997, p. 1; John Mintz, "Navy Floats $2.4 Billion Attack Sub," *Washington Post*, July 19, 1997, p. A1. To pay for the *Seawolf*, the navy will retire 15 *Los Angeles*–class SSNs in 1997 and 1998, some of them well before the end of their projected thirty-year operational lifetimes.

New Attack Submarine Program, which envisions building thirty additional SSNs over the next twenty years at an estimated cost of about $63 billion. Work on the program would be split between two shipyards—General Dynamic's Electric Boat in Connecticut and Newport News in Virginia—in order to satisfy congressional delegations from both states, neither of which want to lose the significant economic impacts of the program at a time when naval shipbuilding orders have diminished significantly.[88]

Nevertheless, the end of the cold war has apparently brought little change to U.S. attack submarine operations, as their crews continue to hone their arcane skills by engaging their former adversaries in games of cat-and-mouse.[89] In late 1996 Rear Admiral Al Konezni, commander of Submarine Group 7 (responsible for submarines operating in the Pacific and Arabian Gulf), told *Defense Daily* that the operating tempo of submarines had increased by 33 percent since the cold war ended.[90] In November 1997, however, the head of the navy's Atlantic fleet submarine force announced that after nearly thirty years it was phasing out submarine patrols under the Arctic ice cap. The decision was made in recognition of a "dramatically smaller number of Russian missile submarines being deployed," according to General Eugene E Habiger, commander in chief of the U.S. Strategic Command. Cuts in the navy's operating budget were also an important factor.[91]

As with bomber, missile, and antisatellite defenses, a massive investment in a defensive system ultimately failed to reduce significantly the nuclear threat, despite occasional high assurances that Soviet strategic missile submarines would be destroyed before they could launch strikes at the American homeland.[92] Nevertheless, SOSUS and other ASW programs contributed substantially to other missions. In particular, they helped protect U.S. ships in the open oceans—especially aircraft carrier battlegroups—from roving Soviet attack submarines.

---

88. Associated Press, "Splitting Contracting of Sub to Raise Cost by $2 Billion, But will Save Jobs," *Washington Post,* September 15, 1997, p. A4.

89. For example, on February 11, 1992, the USS *Baton Rouge* (SSN 689) was tracking a Russian SSN as it entered international waters off the Kola Peninsula. The Russian submarine, apparently unaware of the location of its American counterpart, surfaced directly underneath it, causing minor damage to both vessels. On March 20, 1993, the *USS Grayling* (SSN 646) collided with a Russian Delta-class SSBN as the Russian submarine was on a training run north of the Kola Peninsula (U.S. Navy officials stated they believed the submarine was on a routine missile patrol). Both ships suffered minor damage and returned to their respective home ports. During an April 3, 1993, summit meeting, Russian President Boris Yeltsin listed this accident as one of three continuing "irritants" in U.S.-Russian relations, prompting President Clinton to express regret for the incident. See John H. Cushman, Jr., "U.S. Navy's Periscopes Still Follow Soviet Fleet," *New York Times,* February 23, 1992, p. A14; Michael R. Gordon, "U.S. and Russian Subs in Collision in Arctic Ocean Near Murmansk," *New York Times,* March 23, 1993, p. A13; Thomas L. Friedman, "Clinton Presents Billion to Yeltsin in U.S. Aid Package," *New York Times,* April 4, 1993, p. 1.

90. Bryan Bender, "U.S. Submarine Operations Rise Since End of Cold War," *Defense Daily,* November 1, 1996, p. 183.

91. Patrick J. Sloyan, "Arctic Subs Come in from the Cold," *Newsday,* November 16, 1997, p. A8.

92. David C. Morrison, "Is the Navy Losing Its Edge in ASW?," *National Journal,* April 8, 1989, pp. 870–71.

Costs of the ASW Mission

Estimating the costs of *strategic* antisubmarine warfare is made complicated by several factors.[93] In many cases, systems such as attack submarines are capable of conducting both tactical combat missions—including but not limited to tactical antisubmarine warfare—and strategic antisubmarine operations. Indeed, in the rapidly evolving strategic ASW environment, systems frequently perform missions other than those for which they were originally procured. Furthermore, the silent service more than lives up to its name, practicing a secrecy in operations (and budgeting) approaching that of the intelligence community.

Certainly the greatest conceptual challenge in estimating spending on strategic ASW capabilities is posed by the forward maritime strategy, under which one might not unfairly allocate the bulk of the navy budget from the mid-1980s to the early 1990s to the strategic ASW mission. This would be a trivial calculation, but identifying forces and resources dedicated to the strategic ASW mission is a decidedly nontrivial exercise.

Nuclear attack submarines, maritime patrol aircraft, ocean surveillance sensors, and dedicated ASW aircraft carriers are the primary systems implementing the strategic ASW mission. Since the attack submarine force accounts for the bulk of funds that have been invested in these forces, the most attractive conceptual approach would be to identify that fraction of the attack submarine force that is dedicated to the strategic ASW mission and apply this fraction to the other relevant forces.

This is easier said than done. Though the navy does release information on surface fleet deployments, it has never even hinted at the operational allocations of its attack submarine force. According to one hypothetical reconstruction for the later years of the cold war, the navy included approximately 90 nuclear attack submarines, of which about 75 would be available for combat service (there are currently 80 operational SSNs). Of these some 20 to 30 were nominally allocated to operations in conjunction with carrier battle groups, 5 were deployed in the Mediterranean, at least 40 would be assigned to barrier patrol operations, with the remaining handful assigned to other tasks, such as intelligence gathering and special operations (see chapter 3).[94] A 1990 navy estimate of requirements for an attack submarine force of

93. These complexities are not unique to this present exercise. Throughout the cold war the American intelligence community grappled with the subtleties of assessing the extent and burden of Soviet strategic antisubmarine warfare programs, and while this present exercise is informed by their methodologies, it can claim no greater success, even with slightly more abundant budgetary data. See "Soviet Strategic Defenses," National Intelligence Estimate NIE 11-3-71 25 (February 1971) (formerly Top Secret), table 2, fn. 1, p. 53, National Archives.

94. Linton F. Brooks, "Pricing Ourselves out of the Market: The Attack Submarine Program," *Naval War College Review,* September/October 1979, p. 10.

150 boats allocated 44 boats to barrier patrol and Arctic strategic ASW, with 30 boats assigned to other direct support tasks, 25 dedicated to mine and cruise missile activities, 14 boats as an attrition reserve (to replace submarines damaged or destroyed in battle), and 37 relegated to training and repair status.[95] (The 25 mine and cruise missile boats and the 14 attrition reserve boats essentially represent the gap between what the navy desired and what it could afford and are above and beyond actually realized force levels).

Thus both estimates are consistent with an allocation of approximately half of nuclear attack submarine forces, and thus costs, to the strategic ASW mission. This should be regarded only as a lower limit, as Vice Admiral Henry Chiles, commander of submarine forces in the Atlantic, stated that before 1991 less than 1 percent of the time of the submarines under his command was spent on tasks other than tracking and following Soviet submarines and ships.[96]

The FYDP historical database and other sources suggest that, out of a total of perhaps $10 billion ($6 billion from 1962 to 1974) allocated to strategic nuclear-related operations, $5 billion went to operations by ASW aircraft carriers. Of the estimated $220 billion ($200 billion from 1962 through 1995) spent on attack submarine construction, weapons, and related systems, $110 billion was for strategic ASW-related activities. Out of a total of perhaps $50 billion ($45 billion from 1962 through 1995), $25 billion went to strategic ASW maritime patrol aircraft. About $16 billion out of $20 billion was for strategic-ASW undersea surveillance. In addition, $2 billion went for 600 ASROC missiles (not including warhead costs), and $2.6 billion for 431 SUBROC missiles (not including warhead costs). Two hundred twenty-five (Betty) and 1,000 W34 (Lulu) nuclear depth bombs were also produced and deployed in the mid to late 1950s (costs are included but not broken out in chapter 1). These were gradually replaced by the B57 depth bomb beginning in 1963. Thus total ASW costs amount to some $300 billion, of which $161 billion is counted toward the nuclear weapons-related mission.

Civil Defense

Before the nuclear era, "civil defense" and "strategic defense" were nearly synonymous terms. Early air defense systems extracted a gruesome price from attacking bomber aircrews (whose chances of survival were among the most bleak of any combat specialty during the Second

95. U.S. Senate Committee on Appropriations, "Attack Submarine Requirements," *Department of Defense Appropriations for Fiscal Year 1991,* 101 Cong. 2 sess. (GPO, 1990), pt. 4, p. 267.

96. Patrick Pexton, "Flexible Navy Finds New Uses for Submarines," *Navy Times,* April 19, 1993, p. 10.

World War), as the early airpower maxim that the bomber would get through was largely borne out in the trial of arms. The lavish concentration of interceptor aircraft and ground artillery could render certain highly critical industrial facilities (such as refineries or ball-bearing plants) unappealing targets for bombers, but such active defenses could do little to defend extensive urban areas against strategic bombardment.

Just as early nuclear strategic doctrine was merely the logical extension of prenuclear airpower doctrine writ large, so too was it hoped that the civil defense techniques that had frustrated the pretensions of prenuclear airpower might find useful application in the nuclear era. Initially these hopes were not ill-founded, as nuclear weapons were few in number, threatened imaginable destructiveness, and were delivered on the same slow propeller-driven aircraft that had dropped their conventional antecedents. But by the end of the first decade of the nuclear era, and surely by the end of the second, it became increasingly apparent, in the memorable phrasing of Albert Einstein, that nuclear weapons had indeed changed everything but our mode of thinking. Nuclear arsenals grew to tens of thousands of weapons, dwarfing in number the list of conceivable urban targets. Hydrogen bombs with yields of tens of megatons would wreak genuinely unimaginable destruction and could be delivered on high-speed ballistic missiles. The race would indeed be to the swift, with urban dwellers having but minutes to scramble into deep underground blast shelters for protection.

These uncomfortable facts notwithstanding, the signal successes of civil defense in confounding the expectations of airpower enthusiasts during World War II proved a continual fountain of hope that a solution could be found to the enormous inherent vulnerability of the American population to nuclear attack. While civil defense measures could mitigate the effects of nuclear weapons and save millions of lives, many tens of millions of lives at minimum were at continuous risk during the cold war. Depending on the scale of a nuclear attack, more than 100 million Americans might have been killed outright by a Soviet strike, with millions more injured by fallout and other aftereffects of the attack.[97] That exposure has not changed. The Russian nuclear arsenal is easily sufficient to inflict casualties on the same scale today. Added to that is a relatively new threat: that of nuclear terrorism (see box 4-1).

97. Michael Riordan, ed., *The Day after Midnight: The Effects of Nuclear War* (Palo Alto, Calif.: Cheshire Books, 1982); "Economic and Social Consequences of Nuclear Attacks on the United States," A Study Prepared for the Joint Committee on Defense Production, Published by the Banking, Housing, and Urban Affairs Committee (GPO, 1979); Frank N. von Hippel and others, "Civilian Casualties from Counterforce Attacks," *Scientific American*, September 1988, pp. 36–42.

BOX 4-1

"Looking for a Needle in a Haystack of Needles"

Since the rise in terrorist incidents in the early to mid-1970s, the government has been concerned about the threat of nuclear terrorism.[1] This threat takes two forms: the use or threatened use of a nuclear bomb against a U.S. target by a subnational group, or the use or threatened use of radioactive materials as a radiological poison.

In 1975, after an extortionist threatened to detonate a nuclear device unless he received $200,000, the Nuclear Emergency Search Team (NEST) was created, enlisting volunteers from the Atomic Energy Commission's nuclear weapons complex to train to respond to nuclear terrorist threats. The concept of NEST actually dates to the late 1960s, when teams of laboratory personnel responded to accidents such as the one over Thule, Greenland, in January 1968 (see chapter 5). Since its creation, NEST has been alerted to 110 terrorist threats and responded to about 30; to date, all have been false alarms.

NEST's expertise resides in scientists at the three national nuclear weapons laboratories and an even larger number of volunteers from the Department of Energy's nuclear weapons complex. In 1996 there were more than 1,000 personnel connected to NEST. Some design homemade nuclear devices using off-the-shelf components and then practice disassembling them. Others await the call to leave their regular jobs and join teams of unobtrusive searchers, using sophisticated handheld radiation detectors (hidden inside backpacks, luggage, and even beer coolers) to detect a nuclear device hidden in a city (assumed by the FBI and CIA to be the target of choice in order to cause large numbers of casualties). Because of the large amounts of naturally occurring background radiation in urban areas—emitted by everything from granite and ceramic tiles to cancer therapy machines—locating a bomb's radioactive signature in such settings "is like looking for a needle in a haystack of needles," according to one NEST searcher.

NEST also maintains a computer database that reportedly contains everything publicly available about making a nuclear weapon. Blackmail notes are compared to this database to ascertain the validity and seriousness of such threats. Once a bomb is located, various means are available to disarm it, ranging from freezing it with liquid nitrogen (to disable electronic components) to blowing it up in a way that prevents a nuclear detonation. Should a bomb actually go off, the Methodist Medical Center in Oak Ridge, Tennessee, maintains the Radiation Emergency Assistance Center (REAC), "the only ER in the country dedicated solely to treating nuclear-radiation patients."[2]

NEST conducts regular small-scale exercises annually, participating in full-scale interagency tests less frequently. The last such test, run by the FBI and code-named MIRAGE GOLD, involved between 800 and 1,000 personnel and took place in New Orleans, Louisiana, from October 16 to 21, 1994 (the previous full-scale exercise was in 1986). The premise of MIRAGE GOLD concerned a fictitious domestic terrorist group—the Patriots for National Unity—which assembled and threatened to detonate nuclear weapons within the United States. Postexercise evaluation reports were highly critical of the FBI's management of the drill, noting that the agency had neglected to involve any state or local officials and operated "in an imperial fashion" by failing to communicate with the other involved federal agencies (DOD, DOE, FEMA).[3] The DOE, in particular, condemned the FBI for utterly failing to take

1. This discussion draws on Douglas Waller, "Nuclear Ninjas," *Time,* January 8, 1996, pp. 38–40; U.S. General Accounting Office, *Nuclear Weapons: Emergency Preparedness Planning for Accidents Can Be Better Coordinated,* NSIAD-87-15 (February 1987); *Global Proliferation of Weapons of Mass Destruction,* Hearings before the Permanent Subcommittee on Investigations of the Senate Committee on Governmental Affairs, 104 Cong. 2 sess., pt. 3 (GPO, 1996), esp. pp. 8–12, 67–72, 141–222. Gary Taubes, "The Defense Initiative of the 1990s," *Science,* vol. 267 (February 24, 1995), pp. 1096–1100.

2. Waller, "Nuclear Ninjas," p. 40.

3. Interestingly, the GAO reported in 1987 that the navy had not involved local officials in its emergency planning activities because the

Box 4-1
(continued)

into account how to notify and protect people should a bomb actually go off. "It is a drastic mistake to assume that NEST technology and procedures will always succeed, resulting in zero nuclear yield," wrote the DOE in its report (according to the heavily excised FBI after-action report on the drill, the exercise simulated the actual detonation of a device but no provision was apparently made to simulate fallout from such an event). The DOE also complained that "security procedures for protecting classified materials . . . unnecessarily hampered interagency cooperation."[4] For example, the FBI did not recognize clearances issued by the DOD or the Office of Personnel Management and thus would not share information critical to the successful outcome of the exercise. This problem was first recognized in the mid-1980s, but as of early 1996 it had still not been resolved.

A 1996 Senate investigation into U.S. capabilities to address nuclear terrorism uncovered other problems: NEST exercises allegedly had been conducted "in a manner to 'stack the deck' in favor of unrealistic success."[5] They were said to have allowed "significantly more time to resolve the situation than would be available under realistic conditions," while NEST's ability to respond rapidly to changing situations was inhibited by its bureaucracy. It was also revealed that "some information was inappropriately leaked" to exercise participants, such as "device location [and] type of source" and that "pre-deployment of communications capabilities created optimistic and unrealistic results," allowing pre-staged equipment to be set up "before it could have realistically arrived."[6] Although recent changes made in response to an internal review should improve the program's effectiveness, funding remains low, and many operations, particularly full-scale mobilization exercises, are not yet trouble-free.[7]

From 1980 through 1996, NEST expenditures totaled $443 million. If it is assumed from historical data that an additional $40 million was spent during its first five years of operation, total costs attributable to NEST are about $483 million. In 1997 NEST's budget was $33.9 million.[8] The costs of antinuclear terrorism operations of the FBI, DOD, and FEMA were not made available to this study. Neither were the costs of other agencies involved in preventing proliferation by monitoring the export of selected materials and technologies.[9] These include the U.S. Customs Service (part of the Treasury Department), the Bureau of Export Administration (Department of Commerce), the Center for Defense Trade at the State Department, various offices within the DOD and DOE, and the Nuclear Regulatory Commission.

"Navy believes that the prohibition against either confirming or denying the presence or absence of nuclear weapons at a specific location precludes, in practice, any open communication or planning with state or local governments." General Accounting Office, *Nuclear Weapons,* p. 30. Even concluding a mutual support agreement in the event of an accident "would confirm the existence of such weapons," according to the navy. The army's position was similar to the navy's, though it did coordinate with a selected number of local officials in planning for *conventional* munitions accidents. Given the small number of army installations handling nuclear weapons, officials believed that security would be jeopardized by doing anything to publicly identify their classified functions (p. 33). The air force, by contrast, acknowledged that all its missile and air bases were nuclear-capable and not only recommended a nuclear accident response plan for each one but maintained joint agreements with local officials and shared (unclassified) information with them and allowed them to participate in accident response exercises (pp. 28–29).

4. *Global Proliferation of Weapons of Mass Destruction,* Hearings, p. 9.

5. *Global Proliferation of Weapons of Mass Destruction,* Hearings, p. 142.

6. *Global Proliferation of Weapons of Mass Destruction,* Hearings, p. 9.

7. In May 1997 the DOE conducted "Digit Pace," the largest nuclear weapons emergency response exercise (a simulated transportation accident) in its history, at Kirtland Air Force Base, New Mexico. The exercise involved some 1,500 military and civilian personnel from federal, state, and local agencies and cost more than $9 million. Chris Roberts, "DOE Stages Fake Nuclear Accident," *Albuquerque Journal,* May 21, 1997, p. D2.

8. Data provided by Ed Lasley, U.S. Department of Energy, Office of Stockpile and Facility Transition Programs (DP-41), April 14, 1997.

9. For a list of dual-use items whose export is controlled under 1992 guidelines approved by the Nuclear Suppliers Group, see U.S. Congress, Office of Technology Assessment, *Technologies Underlying Weapons of Mass Destruction,* Background Paper ISC-115 (GPO, 1993), pp. 191–95.

The U.S. civil defense program naturally played a more important role during the early stages of the cold war, before the two sides had amassed the overkill forces they would ultimately acquire. Yet it never expended the amounts of money necessary to be truly effective and was constantly in the shadow of far larger investments in offensive measures. By the 1960s the government had designated tens of thousands of areas to which people could repair for at least limited protection from fallout and invested significant sums in a range of civil defense measures: notification of imminent attack over an emergency broadcast network, stockpiling of emergency provisions (including narcotic painkillers), money supplies, and other resources vital to recovery, plans for the emergency restoration of utilities and facilities, deployment of the national guard, and so forth. A portion of the population took additional precautions at their own expense, such as building personal bomb shelters.

Government civil defense efforts were conducted at a relatively low level until a series of hearings on the issue before the Joint Committee on Atomic Energy in the spring of 1950.[98] The JCAE's proposal for a $32 billion ($280 billion in 1996 dollars) five-year blast-proof population shelter program (fallout was not yet a concern) was considered too costly, as was a scaled-down $16 billion program ($140 billion in 1996 dollars). General Curtis LeMay, presaging the concerns he would later raise about air defenses, argued that such an effort would divert resources away from more vital programs: "I don't think I would put that much money into holes in the ground to crawl into. . . . I would rather spend more of it on offensive weapons systems to deter the war."

On January 12, 1951, President Truman created the Federal Civil Defense Administration (FCDA) and announced a national industrial dispersion policy that was to encourage (and did so with some success) new defense facilities to be built in areas away from likely nuclear targets. Attempts to do the same with government buildings failed. A $938,000 shelter ($6.6 million in 1996 dollars) was designed for the White House but was never built.

The most notable civil defense products of this period were a series of pamphlets, films, and television shows educating the public about the effects of nuclear weapons and potential ways of surviving atomic attack. Out of this effort came the "Duck and Cover" slogan and drills, first demonstrated by a cartoon character named Bert the Turtle in a film produced by the FCDA for elementary school children. The FCDA also printed 20 million cartoon booklets retelling the advice in the film

98. This and the remainder of this section rely heavily on Allan M. Winkler, "A 40-Year History of Civil Defense," *Bulletin of the Atomic Scientists*, vol. 40 (June/July 1984), pp. 16–22; and Bruce Watson, "We Couldn't Run, So We Hoped We Could Hide," *Smithsonian*, April 1994, p. 50.

and distributed 55 million wallet-size cards with instructions on steps to take in case of attack. In late 1951 the FCDA sent three convoys of tractor-trailers across the country under the "Alert America" program. The trucks carried pictorial representations demonstrating an atomic bomb's effect on a typical city and provided information on how civil defense measures could mitigate its effects.

The creation and swift deployment of the immensely powerful hydrogen bomb necessitated a new approach. Underground shelters could no longer survive the blast so the Eisenhower administration endorsed mass evacuation as the only sensible solution. As an FCDA official who served from 1953 to 1957 explained, the focus shifted "from 'Duck and Cover' to 'Run Like Hell.'" The Interstate Highway Act of 1956—which created the modern interstate system—was justified and promoted partly on the basis of its ability to allow swift egress from cities in case of attack.

During a February 21, 1955, meeting with senior members of the House and Senate Public Works and Roads subcommittees, Eisenhower took the unusual step of personally lobbying for the highway bill. Given the anticipated sharp growth in automobile ownership and travel, the proposed bill, he told them, was "vitally essential for national defense." It would also "help the steel and auto spare parts industry" and was therefore "good for America."[99] His greatest concern, however, was that the country's "obsolescent highways, too small for the flood of traffic of an entire city's people going one way, would turn into traps of death and destruction" during an aerial attack or natural disaster.[100]

The interstate highway system, with its 41,000-mile (65,969-kilometer) network of roads connecting nearly every city of 50,000 persons or more, cost several hundred billion dollars (raised largely through a national sales tax on gasoline). Between 1957 and 1963, the period in which national concern over civil defense measures reached its height, these expenditures totaled $60.3 billion. While facilitating mass evacuation from cities in the event of nuclear attack was but one reason for creating this system, it was a critical one (the interstate system, for example, was long referred to as the national defense highway system). To be conservative, we count just 10 percent of the costs over these years, about $6 billion, toward the total costs of government-funded civil defense programs.

During a three-day exercise in June 1955 dubbed "Operation Alert," Eisenhower and senior government officials tested the government's ability to evacuate its offices and reestablish its operations

99. Mark H. Rose, *Interstate: Express Highway Politics, 1939–1989,* rev. ed. (University of Tennessee Press, 1990), pp. 77–78.

100. Dwight D. Eisenhower, *Mandate for Change, 1953–1956: The White House Years* (Garden City, N.Y.: Doubleday, 1963), p. 501.

outside Washington, D.C., in the event of an attack. In this case the hypothetical attack hit Washington, D.C., and fifty-two other cities and promptly killed 8.5 million people, leaving another 8 million injured (with uncounted millions more exposed to varying degrees of fallout) and 25 million homeless. The test—which included a cabinet meeting at a secret location—identified numerous problems and was repeated in succeeding years (during one such exercise, Eisenhower's motorcade, speeding along rural roads to reach the underground command post at Mount Weather before a hypothetical Soviet bomber attack, was waylaid behind a pig farmer's truck).[101] According to his cabinet secretary, Eisenhower's sole comment regarding the exercise was "Staggering."[102] It was around this time that a secret effort was initiated to construct multiple emergency shelters for government officials (see box 3-3). Plans were also formulated to continue essential government functions following a nuclear war (see box 4-2).

During the 1950s, fear of the bomb was never very far away. In keeping with the times (and largely owing to government secrecy about the true effects of nuclear blasts and, until 1954, fallout), optimism about survival was widespread. Popular magazine articles such as "When an Atomic Blast Hits Your Home or Auto," contributed to the notion that with careful planning everything would be okay. Thus in a civil defense film an unflappable father tells his family (gathered in their fallout shelter): "If there's an explosion, we'll wait about a minute. After it's all over, then we'll go upstairs and take a look around, see if it's all right to clean up." *Popular Mechanics* published blueprints for a basic backyard shelter. Still, by 1960 only about 1,500 private shelters had been built.[103]

The effects of fallout, so dramatically presented in the aftermath of the March 1, 1954, "Bravo" 15-megaton thermonuclear test at Enewetak (see chapter 7), changed the debate once again, as officials and the public realized that evacuation alone could not provide adequate protection. Calls for national fallout shelters, paid for largely with federal funds, increased. An FCDA proposal in the spring of 1957 for a comprehensive program of blast shelters with a potential price tag of $20 billion to $40 billion ($138 billion to $277 billion in 1996 dollars) led Eisenhower to appoint a panel of private citizens to study the problem and recommend solutions.

The Gaither Committee (after its chairman, H. Rowan Gaither, Jr.) quickly expanded its focus to the entire range of threats to national security and presented its classified report (titled "Deterrence and Sur-

101. Ted Gup, "How FEMA Learned to Stop Worrying about Civilians and Love the Bomb," *Mother Jones*, January/February 1994, pp. 28–31, 74, 76.

102. Quoted in Richard Betts, *Nuclear Blackmail and Nuclear Balance* (Brookings, 1987), p. 153.

103. Watson, "We Couldn't Run," p. 53.

vival in the Nuclear Age") to the president during a meeting of the National Security Council on November 7, 1957, a little over a month after the launch of Sputnik had startled many in the United States.[104] The report, actually a condensation (drafted largely by Paul Nitze) of a number of detailed subcommittee reports, started by framing the threat: "We have found no evidence in Russian foreign and military policy since 1945 to refute the conclusion that USSR intentions are expansionist, and that her great efforts to build military power go beyond any concepts of Soviet defense."[105]

The report then estimated present and future capabilities on the basis of defense spending, which in the Soviet Union was estimated at 25 percent of GNP, versus 10 percent for the United States. Anticipated growth in the Soviet economy would soon mean actual Soviet spending would exceed that of the United States. Equally worrying, the Soviet nuclear program was allegedly making "spectacular progress," having "produced fissionable material sufficient for at least 1,500 nuclear weapons"[106] and "created from scratch a long-range air force with 1,500 B-29 type bombers."[107] These and other forces posed the gravest threat to the United States, asserted the report, making American strategic forces (at this point composed entirely of bombers) highly vulnerable to a surprise attack, as first observed by Albert Wohlstetter at the Rand Corporation in 1953 (see chapter 2). To rectify this urgent problem, the committee advocated giving top priority to developing an invulnerable second-strike force, one capable of destroying (and hence deterring) the Soviet Union even after a Soviet attack.

While considering the FCDA proposal for shelters, and recognizing that some lives could be saved in this way, the committee concluded

104. The following discussion of the Gaither Committee report relies on Halperin, *National Security Policy-Making,* pp. 47–109. The timing of this briefing was fortuitous, insofar as previous study groups had made important recommendations in this area only to have their work ignored in the absence of an unavoidable need to implement changes. The committee's report might have suffered the same fate "if it had not been for the demonstration of Soviet prowess which accompanied their presentation to the Administration." Samuel R. Huntington, *The Common Defense: Strategic Programs in National Politics* (Columbia University Press, 1961), p. 108. At the start of a November 25, 1957, hearing into the status of U.S. satellite and missile programs following Sputnik, Senator Lyndon B. Johnson declared: "Our country is disturbed over the tremendous military and scientific achievement of Russia. Our people have believed that in the field of scientific weapons and in technology and science, we were well ahead of Russia. . . . It would appear that we have slipped dangerously behind the Soviet Union in some very important fields." U.S. Senate, *Inquiry into Satellite and Missile Programs,* Hearings before the Preparedness Investigating Subcommittee of the Senate Committee on Armed Services, 85 Cong. 1 and 2 sess. (GPO, 1958), pt. 1, pp. 1–2. By contrast, in a paper dated just after President Kennedy took office, science adviser Jerome Wiesner wrote: "Before Sputnik we grossly underestimated Soviet ability; since, we have tended to regard them as scientific supermen who have surpassed us in almost every important area, a fact which is not supported by any known evidence." J. B. Wiesner, "Military Power, Arms Limitation and Foreign Policy" (formerly Secret), January 26, 1961, p. 7, located in Records of Office of Science and Technology, Record Group 359, Box 79, Disarmament-N/T Policy 1961, National Archives.

105. Halperin, *National Security Policy-Making,* p. 78.

106. Halperin, *National Security Policy-Making,* p. 80.

107. In fact, as a recent comprehensive analysis of Soviet force levels demonstrates, the arsenal in 1957 consisted of some 660 stockpile warheads, of which only 160 were strategic, and just 53 strategic bombers. See Norris and Cochran, *US-USSR/Russian Strategic Offensive Nuclear Forces,* tables 8 and 10. On the World Wide Web at http://open.igc.org/nrdcpro/nudb/datab8.htm/;http://open.igc.org/nrdcpro/nudb/datab10.htm/.

Box 4-2

Neither Snow, Nor Sleet, Nor Heat, Nor Fallout . . .

Many government agencies developed and regularly updated plans to resume operations after a nuclear war. Two efforts in particular deserve mention.

Beginning in the early 1950s, the U.S. Postal Service (USPS) developed an emergency planning manual, outlining procedures to allow mail delivery following a nuclear attack. These plans were regularly updated and a complete revision undertaken in 1981. In addition, Executive Order 11490, dated October 28, 1969, as amended by Executive Order 11921, dated June 11, 1976, assigned USPS responsibility for emergency mail service and other duties associated with civil defense programs.

In addition to handling mail delivery, USPS was responsible for distributing and collecting special change-of-address and safety notification cards to facilitate mail delivery and help other government agencies and family members locate survivors. Some 60 million change-of-address cards were printed and stored at about 30,000 post offices (where they perhaps remain). Detailed instructions were also stockpiled, telling people how to fill out the forms and account for any missing persons (and, for postal officials, how to test the cards for radioactivity before processing them). Among the actions outlined in the 1981 revisions, local postmasters were authorized "to burn stamps to prevent their 'falling into enemy hands,' restrict post-attack mail to first-class letters, and place an immediate ban on the issuance of money orders for payment in the country that attacked the United States."[1]

At a 1982 congressional hearing, a USPS official acknowledged that a massive attack would at the very least make implementing the agency's plans difficult, but he defended them by saying the agency must be prepared. Members of Congress questioned the viability of the USPS plans, given their dependence on volunteer mail carriers and the likelihood that major road systems would be destroyed and the availability of gasoline sharply curtailed, if not eliminated. When it was pointed out that not many people would be "left to read or write letters after the nuclear bombs explode," the official remarked: "But those that are will get their mail."[2] The costs of these emergency preparedness efforts, he also noted, were difficult to compile because "plans are not separable

1. Edward Zuckerman, *The Day after World War III* (New York: Viking Press, 1984), p. 6.

2. *Emergency Preparedness Planning of United States Postal Service,* Hearings before the Subcommittee on Postal Personnel and Modernization of the House Committee on Post Office and Civil Service, 97 Cong. 2 sess. (GPO, 1983), p. 18.

that "passive defense programs now in being and programmed for the future will afford no significant protection to the civil population."[108] The committee therefore recommended spending only a few hundred million dollars for shelter research and other nonmilitary defensive efforts. A $22.5 billion ($148.5 billion in 1996 dollars) five-year nationwide program of fallout (as opposed to blast) shelter construction

108. Halperin, *National Security Policy-Making,* p. 81.

Box 4-2
(continued)

from other administrative costs. . . . The initial planning done in the early 1950s involved considerable time. Since then, however, only a nominal amount of time is spent on updating the plans each year."[3]

The Internal Revenue Service (IRS) and the Treasury Department also spent considerable effort developing plans to assess and collect taxes and revive the economy following a nuclear war.[4] During a 1980 postattack exercise, code-named REX-80 ALPHA, economists working at secret relocation sites devised schemes to allow for tax-free cash grants to survivors (tax deductions for losses were deemed impractical because the postattack tax rates would become unreasonably high). To prevent the collapse of the banking system, plans called for the government to step in and purchase destroyed assets, paying off mortgages to the banks over time. For property already paid off, the government would pay the owner over time, allowing some rebuilding to occur.

It is not clear how this scheme would work when most of the records identifying property ownership and mortgage and tax assessments would be destroyed (even though the banks themselves, along with the Federal Reserve, stored critical data in protected underground shelters) and the communications infrastructure shattered. Money to finance these transactions would come from billions of dollars stashed away by the Federal Reserve and, later, from presses stored in shelters by the Bureau of Engraving and Printing (see box 3-3).

As with the Postal Service's plans, these scenarios assume only a limited attack, in this case leaving 75 percent of the country unaffected (except for fallout). To generate new revenue, the existing tax policy would likely be abandoned (all outstanding debts and credits would be erased) and a new system—possibly a national sales tax with rates approaching 30 percent—would be implemented. (An IRS official explained in 1977 that no firm plan had been agreed on, only that proposals and guidelines had been prepared and stored at relocation sites. "Policy choices should be left to be made intelligently by the survivors," said the official.) Government officials were particularly concerned that without some sort of tax system currency would lose all value and people would resort to bartering, which would make postwar reconstruction efforts extremely difficult.[5]

3. *Emergency Preparedness Planning of United States Postal Service,* Hearings, pp. 14, 68.

4. A 1989 study by the Massachusetts Institute of Technology, using a computer model developed by FEMA, found that even a small nuclear attack (239 warheads carrying a combined 77.6 megatons) would either lead to total economic collapse or, at best, a return to one-third of prewar strength within twenty-five years. See M. Anjali Sastry, Joseph J. Romm, and Kosta Tsipis, "Can the U.S. Economy Survive a Few Nuclear Weapons?" *Technology Review,* vol. 92, no. 3 (1989), pp. 23–29.

5. Zuckerman, *The Day after World War III,* pp. 2–5, 286–87.

seemed "the only feasible protection for millions of people"[109] (such shelters it noted, offered "a bonus . . . a significant additional advantage of permitting our own air defense to use nuclear warheads with greater freedom.")[110] Nevertheless, the report stated, the ultimate pro-

109. Halperin, *National Security Policy-Making,* p. 83.

110. Halperin, *National Security Policy-Making,* p. 95. Betraying a troubling ignorance of the effects of even a small-scale nuclear attack (most notably firestorms), the committee asserted: "We are convinced that with proper planning the post-attack environment can permit people to come out of the shelters and survive. It is important to remember that those who survive the effects of the blast will

tection of the United States rested "primarily upon the deterrence provided by SAC."[111]

Eisenhower listened attentively to the presentation, but thought that the cost of the proposed programs was too high a price for the public to bear. (The committee responded that 10 percent of U.S. "productive capacity" was already being devoted to national security programs;[112] in fact, 39 percent and 14 percent of the GNP was devoted to defense during 1944 and 1953, respectively). The military, too, was concerned about the cost, but for the parochial reason that the funds for any additional programs would have to come out of budgets for offensive forces. The air force, in particular, initially rejected the finding that its forces were vulnerable (see chapter 2), although it later used the threat of a "missile gap" to call for large increases in bomber production and the creation of an airborne alert program to ensure that a significant portion of the bomber fleet was in the air at any given time and therefore invulnerable to attack.[113] Secretary of Defense McElroy worried that a massive shelter construction program would alarm American allies and divert funds better spent on foreign aid.

Committee members, anxious to rally the public behind their proposals, pressed the administration to release the report "in the belief that the future security of the United States depends heavily upon an informed and supporting public opinion."[114] Leaks in the press about its recommendations stirred congressional interest, particularly among Democrats who were keen to use it to criticize the president and his spending priorities. But Eisenhower, concerned as always about reining in unnecessary spending and safeguarding the economy, feared that the report would create panic and lead the public to call for increased spending. He thus declined to release the report and con-

---

have adequate time (one to five hours) to get into fallout shelters" (p. 83).

111. Halperin, *National Security Policy-Making,* p. 81.

112. Halperin, *National Security Policy-Making,* p. 87.

113. There was in fact a direct connection between the missile gap and the bomber gap, the subject of much discussion just two years earlier. Just as intelligence analysts at the CIA were concluding—on the basis of improved intelligence data—that actual Soviet bomber production was significantly lower than anticipated, Sputnik was launched. Accordingly, projections in the latest National Intelligence Estimate (a document expressing the consensus of the intelligence community on particular issues) for a large Soviet bomber fleet were discarded. However, "the first NIE ascribing a huge missile arsenal to the Soviet Union was released in November 1957, and projected that the Russians would have 500 ICBMs by the end of 1962 or, if they embarked on a crash program, the end of 1961. There was no solid evidence for this estimate. All the earlier intelligence assumptions had led to the conclusion that the Soviets could have 500 intercontinental bombers by that date. When that projection proved false, Air Force intelligence essentially changed 'bombers' to 'ICBMs,' but retained the original number 500." Kaplan, *Wizards of Armageddon,* p. 161. "Throughout this period," Kaplan continued, "nobody in the Senate knew the origin of the missile gap, knew that it sprang from the failure of the bomber gap to materialize. Nobody knew of the wide disagreements among the intelligence agencies as to the number of ICBMs the Soviets might have in place by the early 1960s. Nobody knew about the U-2 flights. . . . [They] heard only about the Air Force Intelligence estimates, which (next to those of SAC intelligence) were most pessimistic of all" (p. 165). Despite the estimates, the Soviet Union did not deploy 500 ICBMs before 1967; the United States reached that level during 1963.

114. Halperin, *National Security Policy-Making,* pp. 88–89.

tinued to reassure the public that the threat, while serious, could be adequately addressed by existing measures.[115]

The Office of Civil Defense Mobilization (OCDM), which succeeded the FCDA in 1958, supported the Gaither Committee's proposal. Physicist Edward Teller continued to call for deep underground shelters, each with the capacity for 1,000 people. But Eisenhower was ambivalent, averse to the "doomsday" pessimism of the committee's ideas, and concerned as well about the cost of the program given its questionable utility (the secret, smaller-scale program to protect government officials proceeded nonetheless). In the end, he issued a national shelter policy, providing leadership and advice about shelters but stipulating that citizens were responsible for their own protection. OCDM built prototype shelters and distributed free booklets on do-it-yourself shelters. The popular press, including *Good Housekeeping,* supported family shelters, and by the end of 1960 the OCDM estimated that some 1 million were in place across the country.

On July 25, 1961, President Kennedy, just back from his first confrontation with Soviet Premier Nikita Khrushchev in Vienna, gave a nationally televised address concerning the escalating crisis over Berlin. In his speech, Kennedy urged his fellow citizens to undertake preparations to save themselves: "In the event of an attack, the lives of those families which are not hit in a nuclear blast and fire can still be saved if they can be warned to take shelter and if that shelter is available. . . . We owe that kind of insurance to our families and to our country. . . . The time to start is now."[116]

115. In a January 21, 1958, letter to Senator Lyndon Johnson (then chairing a subcommittee examining the state of U.S. satellite and missile programs), Eisenhower refused to even release the report (as well as the 1955 Killian Committee report, which examined strategic weapons programs) to Congress on the grounds that "throughout our history, the President has withheld information whenever he found that what was sought was confidential or that its disclosure would jeopardize the Nation's safety or the proper functioning of our Government." In this case, Eisenhower argued, the committee members were promised their views would remain confidential and that the advisory relationship with him would be jeopardized if he were to violate that confidentially. Furthermore, much of the data contained in the report was considered classified and could not be widely disseminated. Johnson lamented the fact that his subcommittee would not receive even a "desensitized" version of the report inasmuch as he saw no way to force the executive "to disclose information that he does not desire to disclose on the basis that he has received this in confidence." See *Inquiry into Satellite and Missile Programs,* Hearings, pp. 2037–39. Similarly, a year earlier the Eisenhower administration had refused to implement the recommendations of an FCDA panel's report on civil defense, which had concluded that while a massive nuclear attack by the Soviet Union would be devastating, leaving ninety cities "substantially destroyed" and killing 30–35 million people (and leaving another 15 million wounded), with the "proper" psychological preparation, the country could survive a nuclear war. Such conditioning of the population, it noted, would also be valuable to the government in the pre-war period. To educate the public and gird them for the consequences should nuclear war come (but not, it should be noted, to grant them a place in the decisionmaking process), the panel called for a nationwide program of discussion groups, "designed to achieve maximum citizen participation and involvement in the crucial issues raised by the development of nuclear weapons." While the report was well received when presented to the White House (Eisenhower called it "just the kind of thing he had been looking for"), its recommendations were never implemented, out of concern that any education program would generate undue fear in the public, which in turn would undermine U.S. foreign and nuclear policy, which was, after all, based on deterring nuclear war by threatening to wage it. See Wm. F. Vandercook, "Making the Very Best of the Very Worst," *International Security,* vol. 11, no. 1 (1986), pp. 184–95.

116. Quoted in Watson, "We Couldn't Run," p. 47.

Practically overnight, the home shelter business exploded. Outfits with names such as the Peace-O-Mind Shelter Company sold hundreds of units in only a few weeks. The erection of the Berlin Wall on August 13 and the Soviet test of an atomic bomb on September 1 (bringing to an end a three-year bilateral halt in nuclear testing) only heightened the sense that the cold war might get quite hot very quickly. Shortly after his speech, Kennedy requested and received $207.6 million (nearly $1.3 billion in 1996 dollars) for a federal shelter program, with the funds going toward clearly identifying and restocking existing shelters for up to 50 million people (supplemental appropriations brought this to $1.5 billion).[117] *Life* devoted a large portion of its mid-September issue (under the headline "You Could Be among the 97% to Survive If You Follow Advice in These Pages") to fallout shelters, including blueprints, photographs, and step-by-step guides on how to build several different shelters. Kennedy contributed a signed letter to the magazine, urging readers, "to read and consider seriously the contents of this issue."[118]

By the end of the frenzy in December 1961 (after tensions over Berlin eased somewhat), about 200,000 families had taken Kennedy's advice, with many incorporating the shelter into their regular family activities. Heated debates ensued about the morality of turning away or even shooting neighbors who tried to gain access to a shelter during an emergency. Under attack from college professors and others (including Eleanor Roosevelt and the Reverend Billy Graham) for starting the shelter craze and the hysteria that accompanied it, Kennedy sought to restore reason saying, "Let us concentrate more on keeping enemy bombers and missiles away from our shores and concentrate less on keeping neighbors away from our shelters."[119]

The government, faced with the massive cost of protecting the population, eventually resigned itself to a strategic balance built around a condition of mutual vulnerability (at the same time continuing to research active defenses). Kennedy's more ambitious plan (announced in January 1962) for a five-year $3.5 billion ($21 billion in 1996 dollars) effort to safeguard the entire population was not widely supported by his advisers and quickly faltered. One program that did survive was the Emergency Broadcast System, established in 1963 and managed by the Federal Communications Commission, to relay warnings of attack via radio and television (this was reoriented and updated in 1996 to address nonnuclear emergencies).

The public itself lost interest as the threat of nuclear war receded during this period, particularly after the enactment of the Partial Test

117. Winkler, "A 40-Year History of Civil Defense," p. 20.

118. Kaplan, *Wizards of Armageddon,* p. 310.

119. Watson, "We Couldn't Run," pp. 56–57.

Ban Treaty in October 1963, which forced nuclear testing underground and therefore largely out of mind. Although the Cuban Missile Crisis in October 1962 briefly reignited interest in civil defense, few were willing to make the investment, preferring to do nothing or take their chances in government-established shelters. That some shelters proved more vulnerable than expected—a $2,500 steel model built in Dallas collapsed during a rainstorm and an inexpensive version, designed (out of railroad ties and old tires) and promoted by former Manhattan Project chemist and AEC commissioner Willard Libby, burned down in a brushfire—also dampened interest in the idea.[120]

The Carter administration, responding to charges of a civil defense "gap" (by conservative critics evoking the long discredited bomber and missile gaps of the 1950s) rejuvenated the program. Its secret Presidential Directive 41, issued in 1978, was later endorsed by Congress in an amendment to the Federal Civil Defense Act of 1950. The new Carter policy called for, among other measures, a reorganization of the U.S. civil defense bureaucracy through the establishment of the Federal Emergency Management Agency (FEMA) in 1979.

President Reagan further raised the profile and budget of civil defense, proposing a $4.2 billion (then-year dollars), seven-year, civil defense program as a component of his administration's broader strategic modernization plan to develop the capacity to prosecute a protracted nuclear war.[121] Reagan's National Security Decision Directive 26 represented a commitment to a national policy of nuclear war survival. The program to implement the policy contained several ambitious plans: for relocating two-thirds of the American population, constructing blast shelters for essential workers, protecting a significant portion of industrial machinery, and protecting thousands of senior government officials and ensuring the continuity of normal government functions in the event of nuclear war.[122] Even the country's cultural heritage was not overlooked (see box 4-3). These goals seemed, and still seem, far beyond realistic aspiration.

Under FEMA's plan for the crisis relocation of the population, 150 million Americans would be evacuated from about 400 "high-risk" areas to about 2,000 presumably lower-risk "host" areas at least 50 miles

120. When Manhattan Project physicist and arms control advocate Leo Szilard heard of this incident involving his former colleague (which occurred during the Cuban Missile Crisis), he asserted that it proved not only "that God exists, but that He has a sense of humor." Quoted in William Lanouette with Bela Silard, *Genius in the Shadows: A Biography of Leo Szilard* (New York: Charles Scribner's Sons, 1992), p. 460. See also Winkler, "A 40-Year History of Civil Defense," p. 21; and Edward Zuckerman, *The Day after World War III* (New York: Viking Press, 1984), p. 138.

121. Unlike the other elements of his defense program, however, Congress consistently refused to provide more than a modest increase in funding for civil defense. See, for example, George C. Wilson, "Critics Dispute Reagan, Say Soviets Not Superior: Civil Defense Plan Rebuffed in Senate," *Washington Post,* April 2, 1982, p. A1.

122. Bernard Weinraub, "Reagan Asking $4.2 Billion for Buildup of Civil Defense," *New York Times,* March 30, 1982, p. B13; Center for Defense Information, "President Reagan's Civil Defense Program," *Defense Monitor,* vol. 11, no. 5 (1982).

Box 4-3
Protecting America's Cultural Heritage

Unwilling to leave anything to chance, government officials and others implemented a variety of efforts during the cold war to ensure that even if large parts of the country were destroyed, valuable historical documents and precious art would survive.[1]

During the 1950s, a special unit from the National Park Service was responsible for relocating the 2,080-pound (944-kilogram) Liberty Bell from Philadelphia in the event of hostilities. In 1952 and 1953 a "bomb-proof" 55-ton steel and concrete "Charters Vault" was built by the Mosler Corporation of Hamilton, Ohio (which has an ongoing contract to maintain it), at the National Archives to protect the Declaration of Independence, the Constitution, and the Bill of Rights. At the closing of the building each night, the documents and their protective display cases were lowered into the vault.[2] This was also to be done in the event of a nuclear attack. At the request of this project, an archives official searched for the construction and budget records for the vault but was unable to locate any, saying the agency's files on the project do not extend back to 1952. However, a 1953 invoice from the Sheffield Corporation to Mosler for "design and detail" of the vault indicates that this portion of the work cost some $22,800.[3]

To safeguard fine works of art, in 1950 the National Gallery of Art began work on a windowless building at the Randolph-Macon Woman's College in Lynchburg, Virginia. When complete, the $550,000 (in then-year dollars, or about $4.8 million in 1996 dollars) facility would have been able to house sculptures and paintings; the curator would have resided in a fully furnished three-bedroom cottage nearby. For about two decades, large trucks were kept parked and fueled in the gallery's garage and driveways; the museum's security staff started the trucks each week and kept the gas tanks full. When industrial growth made Lynchburg a probable target in the early 1970s, the plan was quietly shelved.

From 1979 to 1981, the General Services Administration (GSA) managed a project called the Cultural Heritage Preservation Group, which worked with government agencies to draw up lists of items to save along with plans to spirit them out of Washington, D.C., in the event of an emergency. Modeled after the successful British effort during World War II to relocate valuable art works from London to Wales, paintings evacuated from the National Gallery of Art were to be taken to the High Point Special Facility at Mount Weather (see box 3-3) and hung on the walls wherever space would allow. However, curators feared humidity would destroy the paintings, so a gallery conservator devised a special rolling box that not only facilitated the swift removal of art from the museum but allowed monitored, airtight storage for an indefinite period. Among the items to be thus saved: paintings by Vermeer, da Vinci, and Raphael. At the request of this project, GSA searched its records but located no cost data for this effort.

1. Ted Gup, "Grab That Leonardo!" in "The Doomsday Blueprints," *Time*, August 10, 1992, p. 37; Gup, "How FEMA Learned to Stop Worrying about Civilians and Love the Bomb," p. 31; Zuckerman, *The Day after World War III*, pp. 238, 292–93.

2. This still takes place, though today the reasons have more to do with reducing costs (leaving the documents in the Rotunda would require full-time security) than with concerns about nuclear attack. Personal communication with Susan Cooper, Public Affairs, National Archives and Records Administration, May 22, 1994.

3. Provided by Richard Gardner, former director of quality and engineering at Mosler.

(80.5 kilometers) away (primarily rural towns).[123] Critics quickly noted that such mass evacuations—regardless of their feasibility—could very well alarm officials in the Soviet Union, perhaps causing them to believe a U.S. attack was imminent and triggering a preemptive strike. In fact, some U.S. officials believed that similar mass evacuations by the Soviet Union would constitute sufficient warning that a nuclear attack could be forthcoming.

Perhaps more than anything else, *Los Angeles Times* reporter Robert Scheer's published interviews with Thomas K. Jones in early 1982 exposed the Reagan administration's views on civil defense and helped foment public and congressional opposition to them. Jones was deputy undersecretary of defense for research and engineering in the office of Strategic and Theater Nuclear Forces at the Pentagon, a former employee of the Boeing Company, and a longtime advocate of civil defense. In his interviews with Scheer, Jones declared that surviving a nuclear attack was not as improbable as commonly believed. Survival was really a simple matter, he explained. All one need do is "Dig a hole, cover it with a couple of doors and then throw three feet of dirt on top. . . . It's the dirt that does it . . . if there are enough shovels to go around, everybody's going to make it."[124] In this fashion, and by protecting industrial facilities from attack, Jones contended not only that much of the U.S. population would survive but that the country could return to more or less normal within two to four years.

While Jones's estimate of two to four years was perhaps optimistic (and glossed over the effects of lingering radioactive fallout on morbidity, not to mention the potential for more catastrophic global effects such as those subsequently identified in various studies on "nuclear winter"), this line of reasoning was not without precedent. The utter devastation of the urban-industrial infrastructure of the Axis powers in World War II had been largely made good with a few decades of peacetime recovery. Economists, particularly those concerned with modeling postwar recovery, were increasingly realizing that the value of a country's human capital dwarfed that of its physical capital. And in no small measure the case for such American efforts was bolstered by the apparent emphasis on blast shelters and evacuation planning in

123. Between 1982 and 1987, FEMA worked with the U.S. Army Corps of Engineers to design and test permanent and transportable blast shelters for key industrial workers. The shelters were sized to handle between 18 and 1,000 workers. See Louis Torres, *A History of Huntsville Division, U.S. Army Corps of Engineers, 1982–1987 Update* (Huntsvlle, Ala.: U.S. Army Corps of Engineers, 1990), pp. 3-4–3-7.

124. Jones was not the only one who held these views. In a series of interviews with Scheer in late 1979 and early 1980, then presidential candidate George Bush said that he did not believe "there is no such thing as a winner in a nuclear exchange": "You have," he said "a survivability of command and control, survivability of industrial potential, protection of a percentage of your citizens, and you have a capability that inflicts more damage on the opposition than it can inflict upon you. That's the way you can have a winner, and the Soviets' planning is based on the ugly concept of a winner in a nuclear exchange." And, he continued, more than 2 or 5 percent would survive. See Robert Scheer, *With Enough Shovels: Reagan, Bush and Nuclear War* (New York: Vintage Books, 1982), pp. 18–26, 261–62.

the Soviet Union, though abundant anecdotal evidence suggested that these efforts inspired no great confidence on the part of the Soviet populace.

After these and other remarks were published, a Senate Foreign Relations subcommittee demanded Jones's appearance to explain views that, in the words of Senator Alan Cranston (Democrat of California), went "far beyond the bounds of reasonable, rational, responsible thinking." But the administration, already under fire for seeming too cavalier about nuclear war, silenced Jones. When after numerous requests he finally did testify, he denied saying that U.S. recovery from a nuclear war could occur in just two to four years (even though Scheer had recorded and transcribed the interviews). Because Jones's views were in large part based on his reading of Soviet civil defense manuals (which advocated similar tactics), the entire notion of civil defense soon fell into disrepute.[125]

Reagan's original lofty vision of civil defense was not realized, and expenditures between 1982 and 1988 amounted to only $1.4 billion. Several cities, most notably New York and Cambridge, Massachusetts, refused to implement FEMA's crisis relocation plans, citing the low probability of success and the immense cost.[126] The only major element of the administration's plan that moved off the drawing boards was the program for ensuring continuity of government during a nuclear war. As discussed in chapter 3, a reported $8 billion was poured into improving the complex of secret bunkers, mobile command posts, and communications networks for the president, his successors, and senior government officials. With the declining salience of the nuclear threat, and in the wake of a series of inadequate responses to natural disasters and various political scandals, FEMA had largely shed its nuclear war-fighting tasks by the early 1990s to concentrate on the more mundane challenges of hurricanes and floods. The Clinton administration mothballed most of the CoG machinery in 1994, though the bunkers and command posts remain in place should the need arise in the future. Increasingly, national security planning at FEMA has focused on the protection of critical national infrastructure against terrorist attack and developing potential responses to terrorist use of weapons of mass destruction. These efforts, however, have attracted neither the funding nor the public attention of their cold war antecedents. Total expenditures for civil defense, from 1951 to 1988 (the last year for which FEMA allocated substantial funds for "radiological protection"), were $13.5 billion.[127]

125. Scheer, *With Enough Shovels,* esp. pp. 18–26.

126. Leslie Bennetts, "City Says No to 'Crisis Relocation,'" *New York Times,* June 10, 1982, p. A1.

127. Department of Defense, Office of Civil Defense, *Annual Statistical Report* (fiscal 1967–72, inclusive; renamed Defense Civil Preparedness Agency in 1972); Office of Management and Budget, *The Budget of the United States Government* (fiscal 1976–1992, inclusive); Maust and others, *History*

Since the end of the cold war, the definition of nuclear defenses has broadened to include such things as controlling the spread of fissile materials and reducing and eliminating nuclear weapons and surplus nuclear materials. These issues are discussed in chapter 5.

of Strategic Defense; U.S. House of Representatives, *Defense Department Authorization and Oversight,* Hearing on H.R. 4180 [H.R. 4428], Department of Defense Authorization of Appropriations for Fiscal Year 1987 and Oversight of Previously Authorized Programs (Civil Defense), before the Committee on Armed Services, 99 Congress, 2 session (GPO, 1986), p. 45; Heritage Foundation, "The New Case for Civil Defense," August 29, 1984.

FIGURE 5-1. The Costs of Dismantling the Bomb[a]

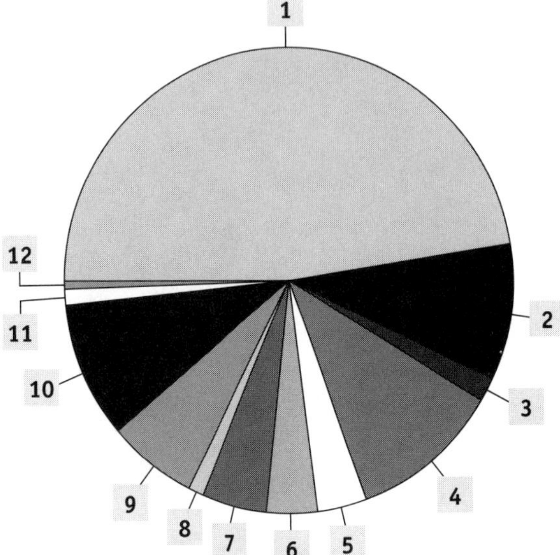

Total: $31.1 billion

1 Plutonium disposition
$14.7 billion / 47.2%

2 Pantex/Y-12 dismantlement activities
$3.0 billion / 9.6%

3 On-Site Inspection Agency
$0.5 billion / 1.6%

4 DOE verification and arms control programs
$3.4 billion / 10.9%

5 International Atomic Energy Agency
$1.1 billion / 3.5%

6 Arms Control and Disarmament Agency
$1.1 billion / 3.5%

7 Comprehensive Threat Reduction Program
$1.5 billion / 4.8%

8 Korean Peninsula Economic Development Organization
$0.3 billion / 1.0%

9 Navy low-level waste disposal
$2.0 billion / 6.4%

10 Submarine retirement/disposal
$3.0 billion / 9.6%

11 Aircraft Maintenance and Regeneration Center
$0.3 billion / 1.0%

12 Other

Kirtland Underground Munitions Storage Complex
$0.5 billion / 0.2%

Minuteman silo destruction
$0.9 billion / 0.3%

a. In constant 1996 dollars. Breakout does not match total because of rounding.

5

Dismantling the Bomb

Arjun Makhijani, Stephen I. Schwartz, and Robert S. Norris

Although large-scale retirement and dismantlement of nuclear weapons did not begin until the early 1990s—as a result of unilateral and bilateral arms reduction measures—this work has always been part of what is done in the U.S. nuclear weapons complex. Weapons have been retired because of obsolescence, revised mission or targeting parameters and, occasionally, safety concerns. The current era of large-scale dismantlement has created a new problem: how and where to store and dispose of tons of surplus fissile materials, notably plutonium-239 and highly enriched uranium.

Summary

—It is not possible at present to estimate with precision the costs of storage, processing for disposal, and actual final disposal of surplus fissile materials from retired warheads. An order of magnitude estimate, based on current assumptions about dismantlement, storage, processing, and repository disposal of surplus plutonium is about $15 billion to $25 billion.

—The Department of Energy is considering two options for disposing of surplus plutonium: "burning" it in reactors as mixed oxide fuel or immobilizing it in glass or other waste forms.

—Securing Russian fissile materials—under bilateral arrangements in effect since 1991—will require additional funds whose magnitude is at present highly uncertain and will depend on policy decisions in the United States and Russia that have not yet been made. These costs could be several billion dollars or even considerably more.

—Costs related to surplus HEU are especially difficult to determine. This is, in theory, a resource with net positive market value, but the actual costs of disposition will be highly dependent on policies pertaining to military fissile materials and the commercial uranium industry.

—The retirement and dismantlement of nuclear delivery vehicles—aircraft, missiles, and submarines—is a relatively straightforward and inexpensive process, costing many times less than the amount required to build and deploy these systems.

—Total expenditures through 1996 for the activities discussed in this chapter are $11 billion. The additional future-year costs associated with the disposal of naval nuclear reactors, the purchase of Russian highly enriched uranium, and the disposal of excess weapons materials could bring this to $40 billion or more, although a great deal of uncertainty surrounds these figures (costs associated with Russian highly enriched uranium are not included in the total for this chapter).

Warhead and Bomb Retirement

The decision to retire nuclear warheads rests on political, military, and technical considerations. A warhead may be retired because it is deemed obsolete and is to be replaced with another warhead. This type of retirement did not create huge surpluses of weapons-usable fissile materials during the cold war. What surpluses arose were held for future use in weapons.[1] Moreover, as a result of the long-standing U.S. and Soviet (now Russian) desire to restrict access to technical design information, no nuclear arms control or reduction agreement has ever required the dismantlement of warheads, much less the actual conversion of fissile materials into forms unusable in weapons.

But attitudes have changed since the late 1980s, and especially since 1991, with the disintegration of the Soviet Union and the large-scale retirement of strategic and tactical warheads by both the United States and Russia. It is now necessary not only to dismantle the warheads but to manage what has become a very large surplus of weapon-grade fissile materials and to put this surplus into forms that cannot be used in weapons.

1. Some observers have dubbed this the ultimate recycling program.

Some 12,800 warheads are expected to be retired and dismantled between 1990 and 2001, when the ongoing large-scale effort will be completed. At the end of this process the U.S. arsenal will number about 10,000 warheads (including 3,450–3,500 strategic warheads, 2,500 to be part of a "shadow stockpile," as a "hedge" against future threats; 950 in the nonstrategic category; and an additional 3,000 in the inactive stockpile, intact but with their tritium reservoirs removed).[2]

Department of Defense Nuclear Weapons Storage

Once a nuclear warhead is retired, the DOD separates it from its delivery vehicle (except in the case of gravity bombs, which are treated as one unit) and transfers it to the custody of the DOE (see chapter 2 for a discussion of the nuclear weapons transportation process). However, because of the limited dismantlement capacity of the Pantex Plant near Amarillo, Texas, there can be considerable periods of time during which the warheads are stored by DOD even after the political or military decision is made to retire or phase them out. That is why many tactical and strategic weapons continue to be stored by DOD even though it was decided in the early 1990s to retire a large percentage of them. The weapons remain in the custody of the DOD until the DOE can take charge of them at Pantex.

The DOD currently stores warheads that are not deployed at eleven locations, in depots previously (and in some cases, currently) used to house weapons also in the active stockpile (table 5-1). The strict secrecy concerning the numbers, location, and movement of nuclear weapons in the arsenal and the inexactness of the DOD's fiscal accounting system make it difficult to determine with certainty how much the DOD has spent or currently expends on the storage of nuclear weapons.[3]

Unlike the $4.4 billion expended between 1962 and 1995 to store and manage U.S. nuclear weapons deployed overseas and accountable to the North Atlantic Treaty Organization (see chapter 2), historical storage costs for weapons based in the United States are not identified. These costs are likely to be somewhat less overall given the fact that tactical weapons outnumbered strategic weapons until 1975 and that many tactical weapons were deployed outside the United States (see figure 1-4). In addition, from the early 1970s onward the majority of strategic weapons were not stored per se but deployed aboard operational ICBMs

2. Robert S. Norris and William M. Arkin, "NRDC Nuclear Notebook—U.S. Nuclear Stockpile, July 1997," *Bulletin of the Atomic Scientists,* vol. 53 (July/August 1997), pp. 62–63.

3. The DOD and the individual services (especially the navy) have a long-standing policy of neither confirming nor denying the presence or absence of nuclear weapons at any given location. This policy sometimes even applies to historical activities, particularly concerning overseas facilities (see chapter 8).

TABLE 5-1. DOD Nuclear Weapons Storage Sites, 1998[a]

Base	*State[a]*
Bangor Naval Submarine Base/Strategic Weapons Facility Pacific	Washington
Barksdale Air Force Base	Louisiana
Fairchild Air Force Base	Washington
Grand Forks Air Force Base	North Dakota
Kings Bay Naval Submarine Base/Strategic Weapons Facility Atlantic	Georgia
Kirtland Air Force Base/Kirtland Underground Munitions Storage Complex	New Mexico
Minot Air Force Base	North Dakota
Nellis Air Force Base	Nevada
North Island Naval Air Station[b]	California
Whiteman Air Force Base	Missouri
Yorktown Naval Weapons Station	Virginia

Sources: William A. Arkin, Robert S. Norris, and Joshua Handler, *Taking Stock: Worldwide Nuclear Deployments, 1998* (Washington, D.C.: Natural Resources Defense Council, March 1998).

a. This list excludes two operational ICBM bases.

b. By summer 1998 all remaining nuclear weapons at North Island are scheduled to be transferred to Bangor Naval Submarine Base. See Lloyd A. Pritchett, "California Nukes Head to Bangor," *Bremerton Sun* (Washington), March 25, 1998, p. A1.

and SLBMs. Such costs, probably numbering in the range of a few tens of millions of dollars today, are included under the counting methodology utilized in chapter 2. In 1992, the DOD began storing a number of nuclear weapons in the new 292,490-square-foot (27,202-square-meter) Kirtland Underground Munitions Storage Complex at Kirtland Air Force Base in New Mexico. The complex, built at a cost of $51.5 million, replaced a storage site inside Manzano Mountain, also on the base, which was opened in the mid-1950s as one of the country's six original National Stockpile Sites (the other five were Bossier Base [now Barksdale Air Force Base], Louisiana; Clarksville Base [Fort Campbell], Tennessee; Killeen Base [Fort Hood], Texas; Lake Mead Base [now Nellis Air Force Base], Nevada; and Medina Base [Lackland Air Force Base], Texas).[4]

Department of Energy Storage and Dismantlement

Some significant details about dismantlement and disposition were raised in an early study by the (now-defunct) Congressional Office of Technology Assessment. Though it made no recommendations, the OTA discussed the safety constraints on dismantlement rates and

4. Lawrence Spohn, "New Arsenal Is Home to Awesome Nukes," *Albuquerque Tribune,* July 21, 1992, p. A1; John Fleck, "Bombs Away," *Albuquerque Journal,* August 2, 1992, p. A1; Robert S. Norris and William M. Arkin, "NRDC Nuclear Notebook: Where the Bombs Are, 1997," *Bulletin of the Atomic Scientists,* vol. 53 (September/October 1997), pp. 62–63.

examined the various options for disposition of surplus HEU and plutonium, such as conversion to reactor fuels or dilution with molten glass, to prevent easy reuse of the material in nuclear bombs.[5]

Dismantlement is essentially the assembly process in reverse (see chapter 1). The first step takes place at the Pantex Plant (except for some warheads containing only highly enriched uranium—such as the W33 8-inch artillery shell—which have been dismantled at the Y-12 Plant at Oak Ridge). Following several inspections and safety checks, the warhead's cover and its nonnuclear components, including all electrical components and other hardware, are removed.[6] Next, the high explosives and the plutonium or uranium core are removed and separated. This work is done in an explosion-proof cell ("Gravel Gertie") to prevent dispersal of fissile materials in case the high explosives accidentally detonate.[7] The conventional high explosives are later burned in an open cage or on special metal trays in an area at Pantex known as the burning ground.[8] Plutonium pits from the primary stage of the warheads are stored in World War II–era concrete bunkers (called igloos) at Pantex. The HEU components and secondaries of the warhead are shipped via specially outfitted trucks to the Y-12 Plant, where they were built, for further processing and storage (many are stored intact).[9] Tritium reservoirs are also removed and shipped back to the Savannah River Site for recycling, purification, and replenishment (see figure 5-2).

5. Office of Technology Assessment, *Dismantling the Bomb and Managing the Nuclear Materials,* OTA-O-572 (GPO, 1993).

6. Safety checks include radiography, "to verify the configuration and condition of warhead components," and tests "to determine actual mass properties, dynamic balance, and center of gravity." Office of Technology Assessment, *Dismantling the Bomb,* p. 38.

7. Although such an accident has not occurred and Pantex has experienced no fatalities in recent years, internal contractor and DOE documents and recent statements by an employee whistleblower have raised concerns that the rigid procedures prescribed for dismantlement are not always followed by Pantex technicians. In late 1993 Victor Rezendes, a senior investigator with the GAO, asserted that Pantex "is probably one of the worst, in terms of occupational safety and health of any of the facilities." See Matthew L. Wald, "Lapses on Nuclear Weapons Raise Questions about Safety," *New York Times,* June 26, 1996, p. A1; Matthew L. Wald, "Study Faults U.S. Program to Dismantle Atomic Arms," *New York Times,* December 1, 1993, p. B8; U.S. General Accounting Office, "Nuclear Weapons: Safety, Technical, and Manpower Issues Slow DOE's Disassembly Efforts," RCED-94-9 (October 1993); U.S. General Accounting Office, "Nuclear Health and Safety: More Attention to Health and Safety Needed at Pantex," RCED-91-103 (April 1991).

8. Due to the powerful adhesives used to secure the explosives to the weapons components, it is not unusual for pieces of depleted uranium, used as a tamper around many warheads and bombs, to remain attached to the HE and, therefore, to be burned along with them. In 1992, the DOE released figures estimating that between 1988 and 1992, 771,000 pounds (350,455 kilograms) of high explosive were burned at Pantex and that the quantity of uranium alloy and depleted uranium attached to this material was 8,170 pounds (3,714 kilograms). Between 1993 through 2000, the DOE anticipated burning an additional 412,000 pounds (191,364 kilograms) of high explosive. See *Department of Defense Authorization for Appropriations for Fiscal Year 1993 and the Future Years Defense Program,* Hearings before the Senate Committee on Armed Services, 102 Cong. 2 sess. (GPO, 1992), pt. 1, pp. 657–58. As this activity is conducted without any filters or indeed containment of any kind, this releases radioactivity downwind of the burning ground, principally on the Pantex site, but also to farm and ranchland directly adjacent to the facility. On March 25, 1997, an ember from one such burn ignited a grassfire, burning 250 acres inside the site boundary in about an hour before being extinguished. For concerns raised by this incident see Don Moniak, "Fire Near Pantex Burning Grounds Raises Questions, Concerns," *Nuclear Examiner,* April 1997, pp. 2–3.

9. Until mid-1965, when HEU fabrication was consolidated at Y-12, the Rocky Flats Plant near Denver, Colorado, also manufactured some HEU components.

Once a warhead's fissile materials are removed, technicians must contend with an aluminum casing filled with electronic and plastic components.[10] Because nuclear weapons were designed specifically *not* to be dismantled (to foil theft and sabotage), disassembling them is not easy. The DOE has experimented with various methods, such as dipping the bomb "carcass" in liquid nitrogen to make it brittle, then dropping a 300-pound weight (136-kilogram) on it to "sanitize" the materials, breaking them down into smaller, indistinguishable pieces. This is necessary not only to prevent the disclosure of classified design information but also to recover valuable recyclable materials: principally gold and silver, but also platinum, copper, and aluminum. Some bomb components are worth as much as $11,000 a ton.[11] In April 1996 the DOE awarded a contract to the Handy and Harman Company of Phoenix, Arizona, to separate these precious metals from sanitized electrical bomb components. The DOE expects to later sell the recovered metals for $1 million and return the proceeds to the U.S. Treasury.[12]

Since 1975, 26,735 warheads have been completely dismantled at Pantex and Y-12.[13] The current rate of dismantlement is about 1,000 to 1,200 warheads a year, or about 4 to 5 per work day.[14] The costs for dismantlement of nuclear weapons are part of the defense programs portion of the DOE budget and are included (but not broken out) in appendix table A-2. In 1988, 1989, and 1990, disassembly work accounted for 34 percent, 42 percent, and 62.5 percent, respectively, of the total workload at Pantex.[15] From 1991 to 1996 the DOE spent nearly $4.6 billion at the Pantex and Y-12 plants, about $3 billion (or two-thirds) of which was largely in support of the dismantlement and storage mis-

10. For example, the B-61 gravity bomb has 5,919 parts. The larger B-83 gravity bomb has 6,619. See *Department of Defense Authorization for Appropriations for Fiscal Years 1992 and 1993,* Hearings before the Senate Committee on Armed Services, 102 Cong. 1 sess. (GPO, 1991), pt. 7, p. 112.

11. Constance Holden, "Breaking Up (a Bomb) Is Hard to Do," *Science,* vol. 261 (September 24, 1993), p. 1673. During the steep rise in gold prices in the early 1980s, a DOE official testified before Congress that one of the advantages to dismantling the W71 warhead (for the retired Spartan antiballistic missile) was that its 5-megaton warhead "is a gold mine." See David C. Morrison, "Gold Plating," *National Journal,* April 26, 1986, p. 1026. According to a physicist quoted in this article, gold is used in warheads to plate certain components, to give them a smooth finish. Plutonium pits might be thus plated to prevent unwanted oxidation, which could eventually affect the bomb's performance. In addition, "when you irradiate gold with X-rays [during the first instants of a nuclear explosion], because it's a high-Z [heavy atomic number] material, you have an electron plasma, which heats up real hot" and contributes to the fusion of isotopes of hydrogen that gives H-bombs their immense power. For fiscal 1981, the DOE requested funds to procure 26,000 troy ounces of gold for the nuclear weapons program.

12. U.S. Department of Energy, press release, "DOE Realizes Post-Cold War Dividend While Meeting 'START' Targets," April 18, 1996.

13. Thousands of additional weapons were disassembled but then reassembled or modified as part of the Stockpile Evaluation Program (see chapter 1 in this volume). In October 1997, the DOE revealed that it could not locate any records documenting the dismantlement of up to 39,000 weapons between 1945 and 1975. See Ralph Vartabedian, "Nuclear Bomb Records Are Lost, Energy Dept. Says," *Los Angeles Times* (Washington edition), October 24, 1997, p. A7; "Washington Insight (Tax Dollars at Work)," *Los Angeles Times* (Washington edition), January 7, 1998, p. A5.

14. In recent years the rate has fluctuated greatly, falling from 1,393 warheads dismantled in 1995 to 1,064 in 1996. The DOE projected just 944 warheads would be dismantled during fiscal 1997. Norris and Arkin, "NRDC Nuclear Notebook"; U.S. Department of Energy, *FY 1998 Congressional Budget Request,* vol. 1: *Atomic Energy Defense Activities,* DOE/CR-0041 (GPO, February 1997), p. 185.

15. Letter from Gloria E. Inlow, Deputy Director Office of Intergovernmental and External Affairs, U.S. DOE Albu-

FIGURE 5-2. DOE Facilities Currently Involved in Nuclear Weapons Dismantlement

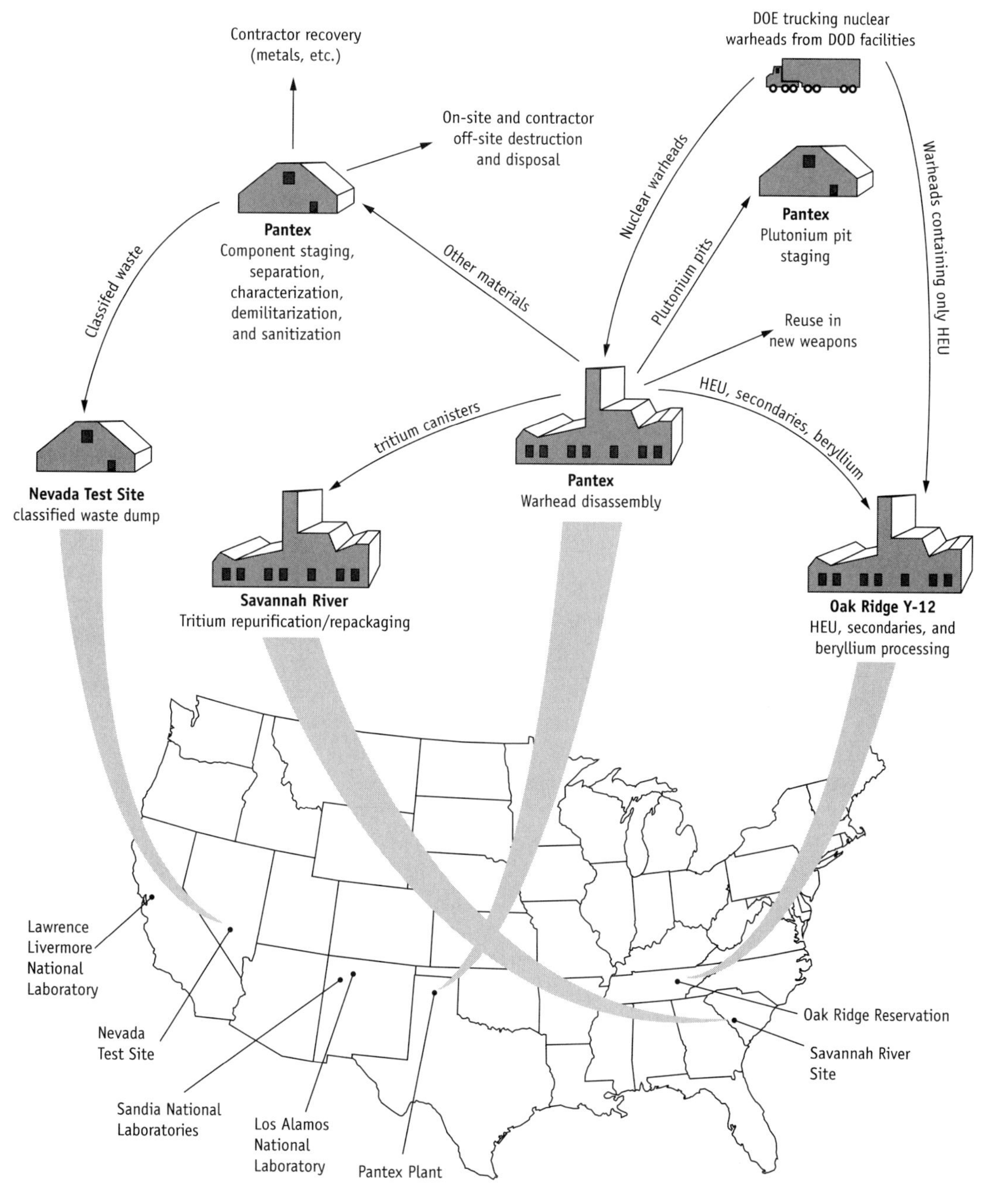

Source: Office of Technology Assessment.

sion (see table 5-2). At an average total cost of about $506 million per year, these expenditures are likely to remain fairly constant through at least 2001, when the current phase of dismantlement is scheduled to end.

The 1993 OTA study, using data supplied by the DOE, found that direct costs for dismantlement at the Pantex and Y-12 plants were an estimated $25 million in 1993 and more than $30 million in 1994. It attributed at least "two-thirds" of these costs to Pantex activities and about "one-eighth" to Y-12. These figures, however, do not include such essential support costs as transportation, security, maintenance, and oversight. Thus they "probably fall short of the totals for the comprehensive mission of dismantlement." The managers of the Pantex and Y-12 plants told OTA that at least two-thirds of their current work was focused on dismantlement, meaning costs for this discrete activity at those two facilities alone "would be almost half a billion dollars." When supporting costs and work at other sites is factored in, "the FY 1993 DOE budget allocated to warhead dismantlement and materials disposition is in the range of $500 million to $1 billion."[16] This would mean that approximately $3 billion to $6 billion was expended on these activities from 1990 through 1996 (to be conservative and avoid double-counting of costs, only the $3 billion for the Pantex and Y-12 plants is included here).

According to current estimates, retired warheads, most plutonium pits, and probably most HEU components from secondaries will remain in storage for two decades or more. The time will depend on the policies adopted to dispose of surplus plutonium and HEU and on the speed with which these policies are implemented.[17] It will also depend on U.S. and Russian policies concerning the acquisition and disposition of surplus fissile materials in Russia. Because of considerable uncertainties in all of these areas, it is not possible at present to make precise estimates of storage costs, other than to say that they will be several billion dollars and could exceed $10 billion if storage extends over several decades.

---

querque Operations Office, to Stephen I. Schwartz, November 21, 1990; and personal communication with Jan Stevenson, Freedom of Information Office, DOE Albuquerque Operations Office, July 3, 1991. An undisclosed portion of the work designated as disassembly involved weapons that were later reassembled (following routine examinations) or modified into other weapons.

16. Office of Technology Assessment, *Dismantling the Bomb*, pp. 44–45.

17. This raises an important issue, inasmuch as the Amarillo area is expanding (the current population is about 200,000, up from 167,567 in 1990), and the northeast portion now extends to within 2.4 miles (3.9 kilometers) of the Pantex Plant. Yet the DOE, in its *Storage and Disposition of Weapons-Usable Fissile Materials Final Environmental Impact Statement*, released in December 1996, favored moving the remaining pits at Rocky Flats to Pantex beginning in the spring of 1997 because of the "proximity of [Rocky Flats] to the Denver metropolitan area." For similar reasons, the DOE decided against storage at Manzano mountain inside Kirtland Air Force Base, which lies outside Albuquerque, New Mexico. Denver's population is 2.2 million; Albuquerque's is 600,000. Both are described by the DOE as "metropolitan." The area around Pantex is described as "sparsely populated." As one Amarillo resident has noted, "At what point is a population 'too large' or not large enough to influence a decision?" Don Moniak, "When Is Amarillo a Metropolitan Area?" *Nuclear Examiner*, March 1997, p. 3.

TABLE 5-2. Weapons Activities and Materials Support Costs at the Pantex and Y-12 Plants, 1991–96

Thousands of dollars

Fiscal year	Operating expenses	Capital equipment	Construction	Total then-year dollars	Total 1996 dollars
Pantex Plant					
1991	153,190	9,070	38,586	200,846	225,164
1992	174,772	8,800	51,627	235,199	258,773
1993	202,900	11,200	33,800	247,900	264,822
1994	213,500	2,000	25,200	240,700	251,095
1995	231,450	2,000	20,410	253,860	259,650
1996				280,031	280,031
Total				1,458,536	1,539,535
Y-12 Plant					
1991	446,168	27,000	52,636	525,804	589,466
1992	518,375	36,555	58,620	613,550	675,097
1993	429,775	30,950	45,720	506,445	541,016
1994	368,248	1,250	30,450	399,948	417,221
1995	348,499	6,475	18,900	373,874	382,402
1996				410,639	410,639
Total				2,830,260	3,015,791
Pantex and Y-12					
1991				726,650	814,630
1992				848,749	933,820
1993				754,345	805,838
1994				640,648	668,316
1995				627,734	642,052
1996				690,670	690,670
Grand total				4,288,796	4,555,326

Sources: Communication from John Trainor, DOE Office of the Chief Financial Officer, Defense Programs Branch, June 9, 1995; and DOE Congressional Budget Estimates for Lab/Exp, fiscal 1992–96; communication from Tom Knight, Office of the Budget, DOE, June 2, 1997. Because the DOE does not segregate dismantlement costs, these figures include expenditures associated with maintaining the current stockpile in addition to costs associated with dismantlement and disposition activities. An estimated two-thirds of the current activities (and presumably the budget) at Pantex and Y-12 concern dismantlement and disposition.

Retirement and Dismantlement of Delivery Vehicles

Not only warheads may have to be retired. Aircraft, missiles and their silos, submarines, and other delivery vehicles all eventually face dismantlement.

Aircraft

After an aircraft is retired, a decision must be made whether to store it or in some cases destroy it, in accordance with an arms control treaty, such as the Strategic Arms Reduction Treaty (START). Most of this work takes place at the Aerospace Maintenance and Regeneration Center (AMARC) at Davis-Monthan Air Force Base, outside Tucson, Arizona.[18] In the dry climate there, aircraft can be stored indefinitely with a minimum of deterioration and corrosion. More than 4,900 air force, army, navy, Marine Corps, and Coast Guard aircraft are currently stored at AMARC.

To comply with START, heavy bombers are flown to AMARC for elimination. To ensure that the plane will never be able to fly again, the rules for destroying such aircraft are spelled out in great detail in the text of the treaty.[19] The procedure is conducted in the open so that Russian reconnaissance satellites will have a clear view of each bomber. Once hazardous fluids, reusable parts, and engines are removed, a 13,000-pound (5,909-kilogram) diamond-edged guillotine blade is hoisted by crane 80 feet (24.4 meters) above the plane and dropped on the tail section, severing it from the fuselage. More than one drop may be needed. The guillotine is also dropped on the wings, separating them from the fuselage. Finally, the remaining fuselage section is sliced in two. What remains is approximately 100,000 pounds (95,955 kilograms) of scrap that is either left at AMARC or sold for about 20 cents a pound (or about $20,000 per bomber). The treaty specifies that the remains shall be visible to satellite observation for ninety days, after which they can be removed. From 1977 to 1995, air force costs for AMARC totaled $333.7 million, largely in connection with strategic bombers.

Missile Silos

Missile silos and their surrounding underground facilities are so enormous that it would be prohibitively expensive to dig them up and restore the countryside to its original condition (they were, after all, designed to survive anything but a direct nuclear attack). Many of the seventy-two Atlas F silos were merely abandoned (see table 2-2 for their locations).[20]

Under the SALT and START treaties, the missiles are removed and stored for later use. The upper part of the silo is blown up and remains

18. For more on AMARC, see Ralph F. Wetterhahn, "Death of the Beast: Saying Goodbye to a Trusty Old Cold Warrior," *Air & Space*, June/July 1995, pp. 24–31.

19. U.S. Arms Control and Disarmament Agency, *START—Treaty between the United States of America and the Union of Soviet Socialist Republics on the Reduction and Limitation of Strategic Offensive Arms* (Washington, D.C., 1991), pp. 33–35.

20. For an excellent overview of the creation of U.S. IRBMS and ICBMs (and air and ballistic missile defenses) and a comprehensive survey of the location and status of silos and launch complexes today, see John C. Lonnquest and David F. Winkler, *To Defend and Deter: The Legacy of the United States Cold War Missile Program,* USACERL Special Report 97/01 (Rock Island, Ill.; Defense Publishing Service, November 1996). On what has become of some abandoned missile silos see—Kelley S. Carpenter, "This Old Silo," *Washington Post,* September 7, 1995, p. D2; "Old Missile Silos: A Burden for Buyers," *New York Times,* June 3, 1987, p. B1; James Brooke, "Swords to Plowshares: A Coda to the Cold War," *New York Times,* October 17, 1995, p. A14; John F. Harris, "The Brawn of an Old Age," *Washington Post,* April 9, 1994, p. A1; Felicia Paik, "Blastoff! Now for Cold War Living," *Wall Street Journal,* October 3, 1997, p. B16.

visible to Russian satellites. After 180 days the silo is filled with earth, leveled, and graded (the launch control capsules are decommissioned by removing all salvageable equipment, filing the elevator shaft with debris and capping it). This was done in the case of 53 of 54 Titan II silos from December 1983 to November 1987.[21] Between 1993 and 1997, 449 Minuteman II silos were destroyed in this manner.[22] To comply with START II (assuming that treaty is ratified by the Russian Duma), another 50 (housing MX missiles) will be blown up until 500 are left for the Minuteman IIIs. The cost to destroy each silo is about $189,220, for a total of about $85 million for the 449 destroyed thus far.[23]

Submarines

Dismantling ballistic missile and attack submarines is a more complicated process, one that occurs at only four locations: Puget Sound Naval Shipyard (PSNS) in Bremerton, Washington; Portsmouth Naval Shipyard in Kittery, Maine; Charleston Naval Shipyard in Charleston, South Carolina; and Pearl Harbor Naval Shipyard in Pearl Harbor, Hawaii. All work is carried out by the Naval Sea Systems Command (NAVSEA).

First, the missiles and other weaponry are unloaded and either dismantled, placed in storage for use on another submarine, or set aside for flight-testing programs. Next, trained crews remove the highly radioactive fuel from the nuclear reactor and prepare it for shipment by rail to the DOE's Idaho National Engineering and Environmental Laboratory, where it is inspected to confirm that it performed as expected and to gather data for improving the performance of future reactor cores. The fuel is then stored at the navy's Expended Core Facility (ECF) at INEEL.[24] Next, all the submarine's systems are shut down and disconnected, including propulsion, armament, communications, water, steering, diving, and ventilation. Any equipment that has been identified for reuse in the fleet is then removed.

If the submarine carried ballistic missiles, the hull section containing the missile compartments will be removed in drydock and the two

21. The fifty-fourth silo (571-7) was turned into a museum, near Green Valley, Arizona, 15 miles (24 kilometers) south of Tucson.

22. The first silo and last silo were blown up at Whiteman Air Force Base on December 9, 1993, and December 15, 1997, respectively. One silo and one launch control capsule at Ellsworth Air Force Base in South Dakota will become a museum.

23. Cost cited in Brooke, "Swords to Plowshares."

24. Until 1992, spent fuel was reprocessed at the Idaho Chemical Processing Plant to recover uranium-235 and krypton-85. According to the navy, the reactor cores present "no environmental problem since the fuel is designed to stringent military standards. In fact, analysis indicates that Naval fuel can be stored in excess of one million years before the protective cladding loses its integrity." See U.S. Navy, Office of the Chief of Naval Operations, Naval Nuclear Propulsion Office, "Disposal of Nuclear Materials and Radioactively Contaminated Materials of Nuclear-Powered Ships," June 1992, p. iv, in U.S. General Accounting Office, *Nuclear-Powered Ships: Accounting for Shipyard Costs and Nuclear Waste Disposal Plans,* NSIAD-92-256 (July 1992), p. 21.

remaining sections of the hull rejoined and made watertight to support a minimum of fifteen years of wet storage (if recycling is not taking place concurrently). In accord with the START I Treaty, the submarine must be visible to reconnaissance satellites for the entire process so that Russia can verify its complete dismantlement. Submarines not inactivated at Puget Sound Naval Shipyard are then towed there. At PSNS, the submarine is placed in drydock and the reactor compartment is removed from the hull and transported by barge up the Columbia River to the Hanford Reservation, where it is disposed of as low-level waste in a large dirt trench.[25] At present, there are more than forty submarine reactor compartments in Trench 94 at Hanford (through 1996, a total of seventy reactors have been disposed of since the inception of the naval propulsion program). All submarine recycling activities take place at PSNS, where all materials are inventoried and anything not reused by the government is sold for scrap.[26]

Between 1969 and 1992 NAVSEA retired more than forty-two submarines, including more than thirty-one since 1986. In 1992, the General Accounting Office estimated that the complete navy goal of decommissioning and dismantling about one hundred submarines and disposing of about 85 reactors by 2000 would cost an estimated $3 billion.[27] For eleven nuclear-powered submarines inactivated between 1988 and 1990, the average cost (in then-year dollars) was $23.6 million.[28] Annual costs are apparently included within the specific program elements for operating and supporting SSBNs, SSNs, nuclear-powered aircraft carriers, and other nuclear-powered ships and are therefore unknown (see chapter 2 for a discussion of the costs of naval reactor maintenance activities at PSNS).

25. In prior years, some submarine reactor compartments were disposed of at the Nevada Test Site. The first reactor compartment was shipped to Hanford in 1986.

26. Until 1992, submarine hulls were only placed in wet storage. In the Soviet Union, from 1959 until 1991 the Murmansk Shipping Company and the Soviet Navy routinely dumped enormous quantities of radiation in the form of reactors, spent fuel, and other radioactive wastes generated from its naval nuclear propulsion program into the Barents and Kara seas and the Arctic Ocean, violating a 1972 international accord—known as the London Dumping Convention—signed by the Soviet Union in 1976. Since 1991, spent fuel has been allowed to remain in reactors aboard docked submarines in and around Murmansk on the Kola Peninsula, and other wastes have accumulated in unsecured warehouses and aboard ships, some of which are intensely contaminated and in danger of sinking. See Thomas B. Cochran, Robert S. Norris, and Oleg A. Bukharin, *Making the Russian Bomb: From Stalin to Yeltsin* (Boulder, Colo.: Westview Press, 1995), pp. 217–52; Office of Technology Assessment, *Nuclear Wastes in the Arctic: An Analysis of Arctic and Other Regional Impacts From Soviet Nuclear Contamination,* OTA-ENV-632 (September 1995); Patrick E. Tyler, "Soviets' Secret Nuclear Dumping Causes Worry for Arctic Waters," *New York Times,* May 4, 1992, p. A1; Walter Sullivan, "Soviet Nuclear Dumps Disclosed," *New York Times,* November 24, 1992, p. C9. Thomas Nilsen, Igor Kudrik, and Alexander Nikitin, *The Russian Northern Fleet: Sources of Radioactive Contamination,* Bellona Report 2 (August 28, 1996) (available on the World Wide Web at http://www.bellona.no/e/russia/nfl/index/html). Fred Barbash, "Nuclear Specter Rises from Naval Graveyard," *Washington Post,* October 11, 1996, p. A1; "U.S. Agrees with Norway to Aid Russia in Atom Plan," *New York Times,* October 8, 1996, p. A12.

27. General Accounting Office, *Nuclear Submarines: Navy Efforts to Reduce Inactivation Costs,* NSIAD-92-134 (July 1992).

28. General Accounting Office *Nuclear Submarines,* p. 11. Decommissioning the USS *Mariano G. Vallejo* (SSBN 658) reportedly cost $29.6 million; an additional $9.2 million was spent reducing the submarine to scrap. See Guy Gugliotta, "Bureaucracy Sinking a Good Idea," *Washington Post,* January 31, 1995, p. A13.

The costs of handling and disposing of the reactor hull compartments at Hanford are paid for by the navy as part of the joint DOE–DOD naval nuclear propulsion program. A 1992 navy report indicates that these costs are relatively small, approximately $8.3 million per reactor compartment.[29] For eight reactor compartment disposals funded in 1991, the total cost was about $60 million. Between 1992 and 2012, the navy expects to spend $99 million to $105 million annually, or about $2 billion total to transport and dispose of low-level waste (including reactor compartments) generated from the retirement of nuclear-powered vessels and to transport reactor cores (by rail) from shipyards to the ECF (the cost of examining and storing the fuel is not included).[30] None of these costs makes any provision for future expenses in the event that shallow land burial is found to be environmentally unsatisfactory.

There are also nine land-based reactors for training naval personnel, five of which are at the Knolls Atomic Power Laboratory sites in Windsor, Connecticut, and Niskayuna, New York, and four at the Naval Reactors Facility at the Idaho National Engineering and Environmental Laboratory (see appendix C). In March 1993 the DOE shut down the reactor at Windsor, Connecticut (two, including a Trident submarine prototype, remain in operation at Niskayuna). Six others were subsequently closed. The Windsor reactor, completed in 1959 at a cost of about $125 million (double the original estimate), has been defueled and will be dismantled and the site restored by 2001. As of August 1996, more than $40 million had been spent removing the reactor's fuel and decommissioning nonreactor areas. Completing this work under the site's preferred option will cost about another $21.1 million.[31]

Monitoring Compliance with Arms Agreements

Between 1988 and 1996 the DOD's On-Site Inspection Agency (OSIA) spent some $445 million implementing and verifying various arms control and reduction measures, including the Intermediate-Range Nuclear Forces Treaty ($233 million), START I ($105 million), START II ($5 million), and the Threshold Test Ban Treaty ($76 million).[32]

29. U.S. Navy, "Disposal of Nuclear Materials," pp. 9–10; By comparison, decommissioning of the first civilian power reactor—the Shippingport Plant—cost $91 million in the 1980s. Dismantling of the Yankee Rowe Plant in Rowe, Massachusetts, the oldest operating civilian power reactor until it was closed in 1992, could cost $370 million. Naval reactors cost considerably less because they "do not require disassembly of the individual radioactive components." See Associated Press, "Officials Raise by $123 Million Estimate of Dismantling Reactor," *New York Times,* November 4, 1994, p. A24.

30. U.S. Navy, "Disposal of Nuclear Materials," p. ii.

31. Matthew L. Wald, "Citing Peace, Navy Will Shut Reactor Prototype," *New York Times,* December 7, 1991, p. 29; Daniel P. Jones, "Sub Reactor's Disposal Raises Questions in Windsor," *Hartford Courant,* August 7, 1996, p. 1.

32. "OSIA Annual Budget Data," table provided by LCDR Tina Tallman, On-Site Inspection Agency Office of Public Affairs, December 4, 1997.

These activities and costs will continue as long as the treaties remain in force. According to the FYDP historical database, the air force and army spent an additional $76 million to support the OSIA's implementation of the INF Treaty. From 1991 to 1995 the services spent another $517 million to implement three arms control agreements, including the INF Treaty (this item does not count toward the total costs discussed in this chapter).[33] Assisting OSIA and other government agencies, the DOE, most recently through its Office of Nonproliferation and National Security, has for many years funded specialized research, development, and testing programs to investigate and design various means of verifying arms control agreements, stemming nuclear proliferation, and countering nuclear terrorism. Verification policy options and costs are also assessed. A 1997 report, for example, estimated that implementing an international warhead dismantlement monitoring regime at the Pantex Plant could cost between $1.5 million and $7 million annually, depending upon the rigorousness of the inspections and the cost of facility modifications. From 1977 to 1996, the DOE expended $3.4 billion on verification and arms control technology programs.[34]

The International Atomic Energy Agency (IAEA) is one of the oldest and largest nuclear nonproliferation agencies, dating back to the Atoms for Peace program (see chapter 8). As an international organization operating under the auspices of the United Nations, the IAEA inspects commercial and research reactors in countries that have agreed to operate open nuclear power programs in accordance with the Nuclear Nonproliferation Treaty. Through such inspections, the IAEA works to prevent the diversion of technology and fissile materials to clandestine nuclear weapons programs. Since the Gulf War, IAEA inspectors have also catalogued the Iraqi nuclear weapons program and overseen the destruction or removal of certain materials and components used in that program.

In an effort to control surplus fissile materials from the United States and Russian nuclear weapons programs, the IAEA is helping to implement a bilateral monitoring program, under which the United States and Russia will each secure 50 metric tons of plutonium and HEU from dismantled warheads. By November 1996, DOE had secured 12 tons of surplus plutonium in special vaults at the Hanford and Oak Ridge reservations and the Rocky Flats Plant. The vaults—

33. The other two agreements are the Chemical Weapons Convention and the Conventional Forces Europe Treaty. Under a reorganization initiative announced by Secretary of Defense William S. Cohen in November 1997, the OSIA—along with the Defense Special Weapons Agency, Defense Technology Security Administration, Cooperative Threat Reduction Program, and other smaller programs—will be consolidated to form a new Threat Reduction and Treaty Compliance Agency.

34. Office of Management and Budget, *The Budget of the United States Government* (fiscal 1979–98, inclusive); Department of Energy, Office of Arms Control and Nonproliferation, "Transparency and Verification Options: An Initial Analysis of Approaches for Monitoring Warhead Dismantlement," Washington, D.C., May 19, 1997, pp. 149–59.

which are outfitted with various antitampering devices and alarms—are visited monthly by IAEA inspectors (a small amount of fissile material at the Pantex Plant is also monitored by the IAEA). In late 1996, the DOE invited ten Russian scientists to visit the vault in Building 371 at Rocky Flats. Russia had not yet initiated its program, citing a lack of funds. However, a storage facility in the Ural Mountains is currently under construction.[35] In December 1997 the IAEA began monitoring the conversion of 3.5 metric tons of HEU at the Portsmouth Gaseous Diffusion Plant in Portsmouth, Ohio. The uranium, a portion of the 174.6 metric tons at ten facilities declared surplus to defense needs by President Clinton on March 1, 1995, will be blended down into low-enriched uranium for use in commercial applications, primarily power reactors. Eventually, IAEA inspectors will be given access to the entire surplus stockpile.[36] From its creation in 1957 through 1996, U.S. contributions to the IAEA have totaled some $1.1 billion.[37]

The Arms Control and Disarmament Agency (ACDA), established in 1961, has spent about $1 billion from 1962 to 1996 on matters related to nuclear weapons negotiations and arms control and reduction agreements.[38] The ACDA currently has four principal missions: managing U.S. participation in arms control negotiations, providing advice and advocacy on arms control matters, helping enforce and implement negotiated agreements, and assessing compliance with existing treaties and the verifiability of proposed agreements.

In an unusual effort in 1967, the ACDA, working with the DOD and the AEC, initiated a field study code-named Project CLOUD GAP to "develop and test inspection procedures to monitor the demonstrated destruction of nuclear weapons." The study was undertaken in conjunction with a proposal by the United States to "transfer 60,000 kilograms of [HEU] and the associated plutonium to nonweapon uses [under international safeguards] if the Soviet Union would be willing to transfer 40,000 kilograms," with the fissile materials to come from dismantled weapons. Utilizing 43 "man-years" of effort (53 percent of which was accountable to DOD), CLOUD GAP personnel inspected forty actual and thirty-two facsimile nuclear weapons at four AEC production facilities, monitored the warhead destruction process (all the real warheads were scheduled for retirement), and assessed attempts by disassembly personnel to evade inspections. The project demonstrated that an inspection regime required disclosing varying amounts

35. Jillian Lloyd, "U.S. Opens Nuclear Doors to Russians," *Christian Science Monitor,* November 26, 1996, p. 4.

36. Matthew L. Wald, "International Team Inspects Ohio Nuclear Processing Plant," *New York Times* (Washington edition), December 2, 1997, p. A26.

37. Marjorie Ann Brown, Congressional Research Service, "United States Financial Participation in the United Nations System," Report 71-248F, November 16, 1971; State Department data.

38. According to ACDA budgetary data and a formula to exclude nonnuclear activities, provided by Matt Murphy, Foreign Affairs Specialist, Public Affairs Office, U.S. Arms Control and Disarmament Agency.

of classified information (with greater access generally producing more accurate assessments by the inspectors) but that careful design and maintenance of a dedicated destruction facility or facilities (and associated equipment) and carefully proscribed inspection procedures would reduce disclosure of such information. Nevertheless, it was felt that only unrestricted assess could provide reasonable certainty that actual weapons were being destroyed. Costs for the effort were shared equally between ACDA and the DOD, with DOD's portion (according to the FYDP historical database) amounting to $4.7 million. The AEC loaned classification officials and provided the nuclear weapons, cooperating fully with the project even though its staff expressed doubts about its value to demonstrate an acceptable inspection regime without revealing sensitive weapons data.[39]

Over the years, the ACDA has played an instrumental role in negotiating the 1963 Partial Test Ban Treaty, the 1967 Outer Space Treaty, the 1967 Treaty of Tlatelolco (also known as the Latin American Nuclear Free Zone Treaty), the 1968 Nuclear Nonproliferation Treaty, the 1971 Seabed Arms Control Agreement, the Strategic Arms Limitation Talks Interim Agreement and the Antiballistic Missile Treaty of 1972, the Threshold Test Ban Treaty of 1974, the SALT II Treaty in 1979, the 1987 INF Treaty, the 1991 START I Treaty, the 1993 START II Treaty, and the 1996 Comprehensive Test Ban Treaty (CTBT). In 1998, in response to pressure from Senator Jesse Helms (Republican of North Carolina) and others in Congress, the ACDA's personnel and operations will be folded into the State Department, and it will cease to be an independent agency. The director (currently John D. Holum) will become the under secretary of state for arms control and international security and will also serve as special adviser to the president and the secretary of state on arms control issues (until Congress finalizes the reorganization Holum will serve as both ACDA director and an under secretary of state).

In October 1994 the United States helped to establish the Korean Peninsula Energy Development Organization (KEDO) as part of an agreement to halt North Korea's nascent nuclear weapons program and prevent it from withdrawing from the Nuclear Nonproliferation Treaty. In exchange for annual shipments of 500,000 metric tons of fuel oil (to generate heat and electricity until the first reactor comes on line) and a commitment by Japan and South Korea to build two light-water power reactors, North Korea agreed to remain subject to the

39. U.S. Arms Control and Disarmament Agency, "Final Report—Volume 1, Field Test FT-34: Demonstrated Destruction of Nuclear Weapons (U)," January 1969 (formerly Secret/Restricted Data, released with deletions under the Freedom of Information Act); U.S. Atomic Energy Commission, Memorandum for Chairman Seaborg and others, through the General Manager, "Project Cloud Gap and CG-34, Demonstrated Destruction of Nuclear Weapons," November 21, 1967 (formerly Confidential, released under the Freedom of Information Act). The authors thank Steven Aftergood of the Federation of American Scientists for providing both of these documents.

NPT, not to separate plutonium from fuel used in its Yongbyon reactor, and to open its facilities to inspection. Since then, the United States has shipped fuel oil to North Korea and has proceeded to encapsulate or "can" more than 8,000 of North Korea's spent fuel rods, a necessary precursor to shipping it abroad (the cost for this activity was some $15 million).[40] In August 1997, KEDO broke ground for the reactors (South Korea and Japan agreed to fund the reactors at an estimated cost of $5 billion, with the United States contributing some $300 million to the effort; however, the financial crisis in South Korea could force a restructuring of these arrangements).[41] Although the agreement is frequently criticized as either a waste of money or as caving in to the demands of a dictatorship, it does appear to be working as far as its immediate nonproliferation goals are concerned, namely, stopping an escalating international crisis, preventing North Korea's withdrawal from the Nuclear Nonproliferation Treaty, and shutting down its plutonium reprocessing program.[42]

Helping to Dismantle the Russian Nuclear Arsenal

Between 1991 and September 1996, Congress provided nearly $1.5 billion to help Russia and the republics of Ukraine, Belarus, and Kazakhstan to dismantle sizable parts of the former Soviet nuclear arsenal and safeguard the remaining nuclear materials.[43] This effort, managed by the DOD, is the bipartisan Cooperative Threat Reduction (CTR) program, commonly known as Nunn-Lugar after its creators and principal sponsors, former Senator Sam Nunn (Democrat of Georgia) and Senator Richard Lugar (Republican of Indiana).[44] Although not all this money has been obligated (as of September 23, 1996, $1.02 billion

40. Stewart Stogel, "N. Korea Lags in Nuclear Cleanup," *Washington Times*, June 4, 1997, p. A20.

41. David E. Sanger, South Korea's Crisis Hinders Nuclear Deal with the North," *New York Times*, February 5, 1998, p. A1; Colum Lynch, "US Cool to Seoul Query on Funding North's Reactors," *Boston Globe*, February 6, 1998, p. A6.

42. James R. Lilley, "Underwriting a Dictatorship," *Washington Post*, July 19, 1996, p. A27; Jessica Mathews, "Score One for Diplomacy," *Washington Post*, February 24, 1997, p. A19; Victor Gilinsky and Henry Sokolski, "Korea: How Long Do We Live with Blackmail?," *Washington Post*, March 27, 1997, p. A27; Victor Gilinsky, *Nuclear Blackmail: The 1994 U.S.—Democratic People's Republic of Korea Agreed Framework on North Korea's Nuclear Program*, Essays in Public Policy 76 (Stanford, Calif.: Hoover Institution on War, Revolution and Peace, 1997); Leon V. Sigal, *Disarming Strangers: Nuclear Diplomacy with North Korea* (Princeton University Press, 1998).

43. "U.S. Security Assistance to the Former Soviet Union," *Arms Control Today*, vol. 26, no. 7 (1996), pp. 25–26. In March 1997 the Defense Department decertified Belarus from participating in the CTR program owing to serious and ongoing human rights violations. While no new funding can be provided, projects in progress were allowed to continue. All remaining SS-25 ballistic missiles and nuclear warheads were removed from Belarus in late November 1996.

44. The need for Nunn-Lugar was first demonstrated by Kurt M. Campbell and others, *Soviet Nuclear Fission: Control of the Nuclear Arsenal in a Disintegrating Soviet Union* (Cambridge, Mass.: MIT Press, 1991); See also Graham T. Allison, Owen R. Coté, Jr., Richard A. Falkenrath, and Steven E. Miller, *Avoiding Nuclear Anarchy: Containing the Threat of Loose Russian Nuclear Weapons and Fissile Material* (Cambridge, Mass.: MIT Press, 1996); Michael R. Gordon, "Nuclear Insecurity—A Special Report; Russia Struggles in Long Race to Prevent an Atomic Theft," *New York Times*, April 20, 1996, p. A1. An excellent overview of the program can be found in Dunbar Lockwood, "The Nunn-Lugar Program: No Time to Pull the Plug," *Arms Control Today*, vol. 25, no. 5 (1995), pp. 8–13.

had been allocated for various projects), efforts to date have yielded significant results. Funds from the program have helped Ukraine deactivate and disable all SS-19 and SS-24 ICBMs based there, all of which were formerly pointed at the United States or its allies. All warheads present in Ukraine, Belarus, and Kazakhstan have been returned to Russia and the missiles have been eliminated.

As of January 1988, U.S. funds had assisted in the deactivation of 4,700 warheads and the destruction of 37 bombers, 95 SLBMs, and 80 SLBM launchers, 293 ICBMs, and 252 ICBM silos. CTR funds were also used to help seal 114 nuclear testing tunnels. In 1995, some members of Congress and others raised strong objections to these efforts, arguing that they are too costly and claiming that the Russians were diverting funds meant to dismantle weapons systems to produce new weapons or using the money "saved" by such aid to fund offensive weapons programs.[45] As a result, funding in 1996 was cut to $300 million. But most observers agree that the long-term security benefits of the program far outweigh its relatively low monetary costs.[46] The 1997 defense authorization bill included $201 million for "Nunn-Lugar II," to expand the existing program and to fund domestic efforts to defend against terrorist attacks involving weapons of mass destruction.

The United States also purchased a quantity of HEU from Kazakhstan to prevent it from being stolen and fabricated into nuclear bombs. In a highly secret operation, code-named Project SAPPHIRE, thirty-one U.S. scientists, technicians, and military personnel flew to Kazakhstan in Air Force C-5 cargo jets in early October 1994, to process and package some 1,320 pounds (about 600 kilograms) of highly enriched uranium stored at the Ulba Metallurgical Facility, about 0.05 percent of the HEU estimated to have been produced by Russia during the cold war. The cost of Project SAPPHIRE was $7 million (paid for with funds from the CTR program), which covered the cost of flights in and out of Kazakhstan on military transport planes, personnel costs, and four separate shipments by the DOE's heavily protected SSTs from Dover Air Force Base in Delaware to the Y-12 Plant at the Oak Ridge Reservation in Tennessee. This figure does not include a payment (in cash and in-kind assistance) to Kazakhstan that the government has not disclosed but is believed to be between $10 million and $30 million (also provided through the CTR program).[47]

45. Bill Gertz, "Russia Uses Pentagon Funds in Constructing New Nukes," *Washington Times*, May 23, 1995, p. A3; Bill Gertz, "Hearings to Probe U.S. Financing of Russian Arms Work," *Washington Times*, May 24, 1995, p. A12.; Baker Spring, "The Defense Budget for Defense: Why Nunn-Lugar Money Should Go to the B-2," Executive Memorandum 424, Heritage Foundation, August 1, 1995; Rich Kelley, "The Nunn-Lugar Act: A Wasteful and Dangerous Illusion," Foreign Policy Briefing 39, Cato Institute, March 18, 1996.

46. See, for example, Zachary Selden, *Nunn-Lugar: New Solutions for Today's Nuclear Threats* (Washington, D.C.: Business Executive for National Security, September 1997).

47. Transcript of a Department of Defense News Briefing with Secretary of Defense William J. Perry, Secretary of State Warren Christopher, and Secretary of Energy Hazel R. O'Leary, November 23, 1994; U.S. Department of Energy,

U.S. Purchases of Russian Highly Enriched Uranium

The cost of international safeguards and dismantlement will be significant in the future. The deterioration of economic conditions in the former Soviet Union means that considerable financial assistance has been and will be required in order to secure warheads and fissile materials and prevent weapons-usable resources from being stolen or sold to third parties.

The first large-scale cost associated with securing Russian materials relates to the purchase of 500 metric tons of highly enriched uranium from Russia under an agreement negotiated in 1992 by the Bush administration and concluded in a contract by President Bill Clinton and Russian President Boris Yeltsin in 1993. The purchase price is reported to be about $8 billion to $12 billion (then-year dollars), somewhat above spot market prices, but below the regulated U.S. domestic price charged by the United States Enrichment Corporation, a government-owned corporation established in 1993 to manage uranium-enrichment activities at the Paducah, Kentucky, and Portsmouth, Ohio, gaseous diffusion plants.[48]

In principle, the purchased uranium can become a resource for use in reactors once it is mixed with slightly enriched, natural, or depleted uranium to make low-enriched uranium for light-water reactors. It could be sold to displace fuel now derived from uranium mines, mills, and enrichment plants and is sufficient for almost eight years of U.S. civilian uranium use.[49]

The ultimate net cost or benefit in purely financial terms of acquiring this uranium is still a matter of some conjecture. The introduction of such a large amount of enriched uranium into the market would cause the price to drop substantially. If that is the approach taken to its use, then the attendant costs such as displacement of workers from the front end of the nuclear fuel cycle would need to be considered. On the other hand, there would be considerable environmental benefits to closing at least portions of the front end of the uranium industry and replacing its output with LEU derived from surplus HEU. As an alternative, the uranium could be held or sold at artificially inflated prices over a long period. This would entail

---

"Costs for Project Sapphire Incurred by the U.S. Department of Energy," n.d.; Jack Anderson and Michael Binstein, "Uranium: Buy It or Else?" *Washington Post,* December 4, 1994, p. C7; Mark Thompson, "Sapphire's Hot Glow," *Time,* vol. 144, no. 23 (December 5, 1994), pp. 38–39. Jack Anderson and Michael Binstein, "O'Leary Calls Project Sapphire a Gem," *Washington Post,* December 12, 1994, p. B14. Kazakhstan's ambassador to the United States has stated that U.S. compensation was "between $20 million and $30 million" in cash and goods. Rowan Scarborough, "Tale Told of How Iran Nearly Got Nuke Gear," *Washington Times,* November 2, 1996, p. A3.

48. Committee on International Security and Arms Control, National Academy of Sciences, *Management and Disposition of Excess Weapons Plutonium* (Washington, D.C.: National Academy Press 1994), p. 130.

49. Arjun Makhijani and Annie Makhijani, *Fissile Materials in a Glass, Darkly,* 2d ed. (Takoma Park, Md.: IEER Press, 1995), p. 77.

a substantial cost. It is not possible at the present time to estimate the net financial cost or benefit of acquiring and using surplus HEU in the commercial nuclear power industry. However, it is clear that the cost of not acquiring it could be incalculable, in that its sale to third parties could create exceedingly deleterious security consequences.

The U.S.-Russian HEU transaction—nicknamed "Megatons to Megawatts"—is being implemented very slowly. Blending down of the HEU into low-enriched uranium is being done in Russia. Through 1997 shipments totaling 1,038 metric tons of LEU (derived from 36 metric tons of HEU) have been made to the USEC. This is equivalent to more than 1,600 nuclear warheads.[50]

As a government-owned corporation producing 40 percent of the world's supply of enriched uranium for commercial power reactors, the USEC has a responsibility not only to taxpayers but also to its shareholders.[51] During 1996 serious concerns were raised about whether the USEC's emphasis on maximizing its profits was jeopardizing its national security mission. In a July 31, 1996, letter to then deputy secretary of energy Charles Curtis, Senator Pete Domenici (Republican of New Mexico) wrote: "I am convinced that the USEC is acting directly contrary to the national-security interests of the United States." This charge was prompted by the disclosure that the USEC had declined repeated offers from Russia to purchase uranium derived from material sufficient to build 400 Hiroshima-size bombs. Curtis conceded the "natural tension between the Enrichment Corporation's commercial interest and its capacity to serve the more fundamental national-security interest" but nevertheless defended the corporation's performance. The DOE subsequently worked with the USEC to ensure that future purchases would not raise such issues. That November, U.S. and Russian negotiators reached agreement on a new five-year contract for

50. Contracted shipments of LEU from 1997 to 2001 (inclusive) will be derived from 132 metric tons of HEU. U.S. Enrichment Corporation, "1995 Year-End Report: Megatons to Megawatts," January 30, 1996; U.S. Enrichment Corporation Fast Facts Sheet (as of December 1997), "Chronology of the Megatons to Megawatts Contract." See also William J. Broad, "Deal for U.S. to Buy Bomb Fuel from Russia Said to Be in Peril," *New York Times,* June 12, 1995, p. A1; Sonni Efron, "Russian Says U.S. Is Not Paying for Uranium From Warheads," *Los Angeles Times* (Washington Edition), June 14, 1995, p. A3; Jessica Mathews, "Undone Deal on Uranium," *Washington Post,* June 19, 1995, p. A19; Peter Passell, "U.S. Goals at Odds in a Plan to Sell Off Nuclear Operation," *New York Times,* July 25, 1995, p. A1; William J. Broad, "Uranium Deal: Is Russia Delivering?" *New York Times,* January 29, 1996, p. A6.

51. In 1998 the government plans to completely privatize the USEC, selling it either to the public through an initial stock offering or to a group of corporations. Two groups have expressed interest in purchasing the USEC. One is an alliance of Allied Signal Inc., Babcock & Wilcox Co., Fluor Daniel Inc., General Atomics Aeronautical Systems Inc., and Lockheed Martin Corp. (currently the operating contractor at Paducah and Portsmouth). The other is an alliance of CH2M Hill Companies Ltd. and the Pleiades Group, an energy acquisition firm headquartered in New York and managed by former secretary of commerce Robert A. Mosbacher and Russian-American entrepreneur Alexander Shustorovich. The sale of the USEC is anticipated to be the largest transfer of a federal government entity to the private sector since the sale to the public of the freight railroad Conrail Inc. in 1987 for $1.6 billion (then-year dollars). See Martha Hamilton, "Uncle Sam's Power Play," *Washington Post,* April 25, 1997, p. D1; John J. Fialka, "U.S. Plans to Sell Uranium-Enrichment Operations," *Wall Street Journal,* August 14, 1997, p. A14; Martha M. Hamilton, "Decision Nears on Date for Sale Of Uranium-Enrichment Agency," *Washington Post,* November 12, 1997, p. C13.

accelerated purchases of uranium derived from dismantled nuclear weapons.[52]

On July 31, 1996, the DOE announced that up to 85 percent of 175 metric tons of surplus HEU from the U.S. weapons program will be blended down into LEU and sold as fuel for commercial reactors. The blending down would occur at up to four sites: the Y-12 Plant, the Savannah River Site, the Babcock and Wilcox Naval Nuclear Fuel Division facility in Lynchburg, Virginia, and the Nuclear Fuel Services, Inc. Plant in Erwin, Tennessee (which also does work for the naval nuclear propulsion program). As a first step in the process, the DOE has transferred ownership of 50 metric tons of the surplus to the USEC.[53]

By the end of 1996 the process of introducing low-enriched uranium made from surplus HEU was proceeding at a rate too low to affect the overall uranium market. Russia is realizing an economic return on its surplus HEU, but so far there has been minimal effect on either the United States budget or utility industry.

Final Disposition Options for Plutonium

The disposition of plutonium will constitute a net cost, despite the fact that it can be used in nuclear reactors as an energy source. Because of fuel fabrication costs, "free" plutonium is more expensive than fully paid-for uranium per unit of energy derived from it in a reactor. In economic terms, therefore, plutonium represents a liability. Storage for an indefinite period is not a realistic option and would be quite costly in any case, as already discussed.

However, plutonium was not always viewed this way. Senator Brien McMahon, chairman of the Joint Committee on Atomic Energy, in a September 18, 1951, speech calling for a massive increase in the production of nuclear weapons materials, confidently told his colleagues that "the atomic material now in our weapon stockpile is far more valuable for peace than is all the gold stored at Fort Knox. The same material which can create a fearful explosion can likewise serve as the fuel for future peacetime industrial power reactors." This "priceless material," he said, "will last thousands of years without deterioration" and "money spent creating it will not be lost." It would be "a splendid physical heritage, usable to bring a better life to all our people."[54]

52. Peter Passell, "Profit Motive Clouding Effort to Buy Up A-Bomb Material," *New York Times,* August 28, 1996, p. A1; Thomas W. Lippman, "5-Year Pact Set for U.S. to Step Up Buying Enriched Uranium from Russia," *Washington Post,* November 24, 1996, p. A20; Peter Passell, "The Sticky Side of Privatization," *New York Times,* August 30, 1997, p. 29.

53. DOE news release, "Clinton Administration Takes Strong Step to Reduce Global Nuclear Danger," July 31, 1996.

54. *Congressional Record,* 82 Cong. 1 sess., vol. 97, pt. 9 (September 18, 1951), p. 11498.

Two reports of the National Academy of Sciences (NAS), one published in 1994 and the other in 1995, have assessed many options for dealing with plutonium, providing cost estimates for each of them.[55] They also discuss each option's merits from other points of view, such as nonproliferation. To prevent the reuse of surplus plutonium in nuclear weapons—either by the weapons states themselves or by subnational groups that might acquire weapons-usable fissile material on the black market—the report advocates the "spent fuel standard" be observed. According to this standard, the plutonium would be mixed with other materials to make it as radioactive as spent fuel from nuclear power plants. This would present a significant physical barrier against theft.[56] It would also deter reuse because the costs of reextracting plutonium would be very high.

The uncertainties in these estimates are so considerable, the NAS noted, that "it is difficult to ascribe much significance to the differences among these [reactor options] cases" as far as costs are concerned. The general range of these costs, including taxes and insurance, would be $2 billion to $10 billion. These costs include a high-level waste disposal fee of 0.1 cent per kilowatt hour (see table 5-3).[57]

The 1995 NAS report on reactor options for excess plutonium disposition also estimated the incremental costs of using MOX (mixed oxide) fuel in comparison with the low-enriched uranium fuel normally used by existing commercial light-water reactors. These would be about 0.3 cents per kilowatt hour electrical.[58] If one-third of the reactor core is loaded with MOX fuel and the burn-up of the fuel is 40,000 megawatt-days thermal per metric ton, the cost of the MOX disposition option amounts to about $300 million for 52.7 metric tons of surplus plutonium.[59] This does not include any costs for modifying reactors using MOX fuel, licensing proceedings, subsidies to electric utilities for using MOX fuel, and long-term waste disposal issues associated with the higher plutonium content of spent fuel resulting from MOX irradiation. In early 1997 two scientists at Los Alamos National Laboratory revealed that plutonium used in U.S. nuclear weapons contains up to

55. Committee on International Security and Arms Control, National Academy of Sciences, *Management and Disposition of Excess Weapons Plutonium*; and Panel on Reactor-Related Options for the Disposition of Excess Weapons Plutonium, Committee on International Security and Arms Control, National Academy of Sciences, *Management and Disposition of Excess Weapons Plutonium—Reactor-Related Options* (Washington, D.C.: National Academy Press, 1995).

56. Spent fuel is highly radioactive, capable of causing a lethal dose in seconds with unshielded exposure. It is therefore handled via remote control.

57. Panel on Reactor-Related Options for the Disposition of Excess Weapons Plutonium, *Management and Disposition of Excess Weapons,* p. 324.

58. Panel on Reactor-Related Options for the Disposition of Excess Weapons Plutonium, *Management and Disposition of Excess Weapons,* p. 302.

59. On March 1, 1995, President Clinton declared 38.2 metric tons of weapon-grade plutonium to be "excess" to national security needs (the DOE has also designated 14.5 metric tons of non-weapon-grade plutonium as surplus). An additional 66.1 metric tons of plutonium is in currently deployed weapons, weapons awaiting disassembly at Pantex, and in pits stored at Pantex. See U.S. Department of Energy, *Plutonium: The First 50 Years* (GPO, February 1996), pp. 20, 75–76.

TABLE 5-3. Estimated Cost of Plutonium Disposition Options[a]

1992 dollars

Disposition option	*Approximate cost estimate for disposition of 50 metric tons of plutonium (dollars)*	*Principal concerns and comments*
Reactor (including taxes)		
New burner reactors (MHTGR), no reprocessing	5.8 billion	Likely to be the most costly among burner reactor options.
Dedicated new ALWRs, no reprocessing	3.2 billion to 5.5 billion, depending on the reactor	Long time frame; requires United States to build MOX facilities.
Completion of WPPSS reactor	2 billion	Long time frame; requires United States to build MOX facilities.
Existing LWRs, United States	300 million (see text)	Requires United States to build MOX facilities.
Existing reactors, foreign countries other than Canada	Comparable to or higher than existing U.S. LWRs	Requires United States to provide MOX to countries that are reprocessing or acquiring commercial plutonium, thereby increasing foreign plutonium.
Existing reactors, Canada	Comparable to existing U.S. LWRs	Requires United States to build MOX facilities actual cost may be higher or lower than other existing reactor options.
ALMR	5.6 billion	Reactor can breed plutonium; requires new reprocessing technology; proliferation concerns; long time frame.
Accelerator		
Subcritical reactor with proton accelerator	High	Technology not yet developed; requires development of new reprocessing techniques and raises proliferation concerns.
Electron accelerator and photofission	Probably high	Feasibility not yet investigated; long time frame.
Waste-treatment		
Vitrification with fission products	Several hundred million to 1 billion	More uncertain geologic disposal cost in comparison with spent fuel.
Vitrification with depleted uranium or thorium-232, with gamma-emitting canisters	Same order of magnitude as vitrification with fission products (IEER estimate)	More uncertain geologic disposal cost in comparison with spent fuel; reextraction less difficult than vitrification with fission products.
Zircon	?	Technology not yet adequately developed, but potentially promising; concerns about possible long time frame.

TABLE 5-3. Estimated Cost of Plutonium Disposition Options[a] (*continued*)

1992 dollars

Disposition option	*Approximate cost estimate for disposition of 50 metric tons of plutonium (dollars)*	*Principal concerns and comments*
Ceramics	?	Technology chosen by the DOE; is being developed.
Other		
Pyroprocessing without ALMR	?	Requires development of new reprocessing technology, raising proliferation concerns; possibly long time frame.
Nuclear explosion in an underground cavity	Relatively low	Grave environmental concerns; conflicts with nuclear testing policy and hence contrary to nonproliferation policy.
Disposal in space	More than 10 billion	Risk of accidents during launching; launch costs could come down in the future.
Direct disposal in a repository	Potentially low	No repository currently available; retrievability and proliferation concerns.
Direct subseabed disposal	Potentially low	No international framework for disposal; may violate the London Dumping Convention; some risk of retireval.
Indefinite storage	High	Highest risk of theft or reuse in warheads.

Sources: Panel on Reactor-Related Options for the Disposition of Excess Weapons Plutonium, Committee on International Security and Arms Control, National Academy of Sciences, *Management and Disposition of Excess Weapons Plutonium—Reactor-Related Options* for reactor options, and Committee on International Security and Arms Control, National Academy of Sciences, *Management and Disposition of Excess Weapons Plutonium* for the remainder, unless noted.

a. Reactor options include taxes. ALMR = advanced liquid metal reactor; ALWR = advanced light-water reactor; LWR = light-water reactor; MHTGR = modular high-temperature gas-cooled reactor; WPPSS = Washington Public Power Supply System (uncompleted commercial reactor at the Hanford Reservation).

1 percent gallium (which was added to make plutonium fabrication easier and to keep the metal stable over a wide range of temperatures). The presence of gallium complicates the fabrication of MOX fuel and therefore it must be removed. This will increase the cost of the DOE's proposal to dispose of between 33 and 42 metric tons of surplus plutonium by using it as fuel in commercial power reactors.[60]

60. James W. Toevs and Carl A. Beard, "Gallium in Weapons-grade Plutonium and MOX Fuel Fabrication," *Science for Democratic Action,* vol. 5, no. 4 (1997), p. 11 (available on the World Wide Web at http://www.ieer.org/ieer/

As of the end of 1996, the DOE's estimate for disposition of 52.7 metric tons of surplus plutonium was $2.3 billion. Stabilizing and storing this material from 1995 to 2000 is estimated by the DOE to cost an additional $8.7 billion.[61] This assumes that about two-thirds of the plutonium would be used in the form of MOX fuel in existing commercial reactors and the rest would be vitrified.[62] The total includes the DOE's estimates for disposal costs for vitrified plutonium, but not for MOX spent fuel. The total costs are estimated to be slightly lower if the government decides to pursue plutonium disposition by vitrification alone, the other option recommended by the NAS.

Vitrification involves the mixing of plutonium with highly radioactive wastes and molten glass and casting the mixture into large glass logs. The intended net effect is to make the plutonium so dilute and to make the glass logs so radioactive that it would be very difficult to steal or to reextract it for use in weapons. There are additional ways of vitrifying plutonium.[63]

The actual costs of plutonium disposition could be substantially higher than DOE now estimates for a number of reasons: (a) repository costs may be higher than now assumed; (b) the costs of disposing of MOX fuel are likely to be far higher than they are for regular spent fuel, and the DOE has not taken this additional cost into account; and (c) licensing costs and other fees to be paid to utilities for taking MOX fuel could be far higher than now assumed by the DOE because the utilities are demanding subsidies and because the MOX option has already provoked widespread opposition.[64]

We can only speculate about the costs of repository disposal at present because of uncertainties in the U.S. repository program (see chapter 6). The estimate offered here is based on an assumption that plutonium would be vitrified in canisters similar to the ones to be produced in the Defense Waste Processing Facility at the Savannah River Site, and that the glass logs will contain about 1 percent plutonium. We also assume that the cost of disposing of a unit weight of vitrified waste would be similar to that of spent fuel.

sdafiles/vol_5/v5n4_1.html); Matthew L. Wald, "An Element Complicates Conversion of Plutonium," *New York Times,* January 27, 1997, p. A14.

61. Disposition activities are estimated by the DOE to last until 2023. See Thomas W. Lippman, "U.S. Decides on Plutonium Disposal Plan," *Washington Post,* December 9, 1996, p. A1; Matthew L. Wald, "Agency to Pursue 2 Plans to Shrink Plutonium Supply," *New York Times,* December 10, 1996, p. A1; General Accounting Office, *Department of Energy: Plutonium Needs, Costs, and Management Programs,* RCED-97-98 (April 1997).

62. Statement by Secretary of Energy Hazel O'Leary at a press conference releasing *Storage and Disposition of Weapons-Usable Fissile Materials: Final Environmental Impact Statement,* December 8, 1996; Department of Energy, *Storage and Disposition of Weapons-Usable Fissile Materials: Final Environmental Impact Statement,* DOE/EIS-0229 (GPO, 1996).

63. See Committee on International Security and Arms Control, *Management and Disposition of Excess Weapons*; Panel on Reactor-Related Options for the Disposition of Excess Weapons Plutonium, Committee on International Security and Arms Control, National Academy of Sciences, *Management and Disposition of Excess Weapons Plutonium—Reactor-Related Options*; and Makhijani and Makhijani, *Fissile Materials in a Glass, Darkly.*

64. For a discussion of subsidies to utilities, which could run into billions of dollars, see Edwin S. Lyman, "Weapons Plutonium: Just Can It," *Bulletin of the Atomic Scientists,* vol. 52 (November-December 1996), pp. 48–52.

This is a very rough assumption based on the following two considerations. Because the amount of heat generated by vitrified plutonium would be far lower than typical spent fuel, even if the plutonium is vitrified with fission products, the canisters could be packed closer together. This would reduce considerably its storage, transportation, and disposal costs. However, criticality considerations (the possibility that a critical mass could be formed within a repository) may prevent close spacing of the canisters, unless the concentration of plutonium is reduced well below 1 percent. This approach, in turn, would increase the amount of vitrified waste and hence the cost of storage, transportation, and disposal. Therefore it is reasonable to assume that the costs of disposing of vitrified plutonium would be roughly the same as that for spent fuel per unit of weight.

Whether plutonium vitrification will create additional glass logs that need to be disposed of depends on whether it is vitrified as part of the high-level waste vitrification program or whether separate logs are cast for the plutonium vitrification program. In the former case, the additional repository costs may be minimal, whereas in the latter case, they would depend on the concentration of plutonium in the glass. At a 1 percent plutonium concentration, 52.7 metric tons of plutonium will produce 5,270 metric tons of glass requiring disposal. In 1990 it was estimated to cost $265,000 (in 1988 dollars) to dispose of a metric ton of spent fuel (with heavy metal content). The assumption was that only one repository would be needed for all the highly radioactive waste other than the transuranic waste slated for the Waste Isolation Pilot Plant (WIPP) in New Mexico.[65]

This amounts to about $330,000 (rounded) in 1996 dollars. On this basis, the cost of the repository disposal of vitrified plutonium would be some $1.7 billion. Thus the overall costs of processing and putting plutonium into nonweapons-usable forms and disposing of it could range from a few billion dollars to tens of billions of dollars, depending on the duration of storage, the choice of disposition options, and the cost of the repository. Related issues, such as the management and disposal of nuclear waste from weapons protection activities, are considered in chapter 6.

65. Arjun Makhijani and Scott Saleska, *High-Level Dollars and Low-Level Sense: A Critique of Present Policy for the Management of Long-Lived Radioactive Wastes and Discussion of an Alternative Approach* (New York: Institute for Energy and Environmental Research, 1992), pp. 66–68.

6

Nuclear Waste Management and Environmental Remediation

Arjun Makhijani, Stephen I. Schwartz, and William J. Weida

We have recently held a symposium or seminar on the problems involved in waste disposal and storage, the proper disposition and storage of these very hot and radioactive waste materials, and are getting the benefit of the best judgement in the country, we believe, in that field. In summary, there appears to be nothing to be alarmed about, but a great deal of persistent effort will be required.

—*David E. Lilienthal, first chairman of the Atomic Energy Commission, February 2, 1949*

As discussed in chapter 1, it was not until the late 1980s that the government began to pay serious attention to the back end of the arms race, the enormous quantities of long-lived, dangerous wastes generated as a result of large-scale nuclear weapons production activities. The consequences of this inattention, the Department of Energy's difficulties in assessing the magnitude of the problem, and the costs of trying to "clean up" highly polluted sites and manage more than five decades of accumulated nuclear waste are the subject of this chapter.

In 1995 the DOE (at the direction of Congress) produced its first comprehensive report (*Baseline Environmental Management Report*) on the cleanup liabilities accumulated over five decades of nuclear weapons production. It was compiled by the DOE's Office of Strategic Planning and Analysis in its Environmental Management Division and was updated in 1996. Though many gaps, uncertainties, and methodological problems remain, it represents great progress over previous piecemeal efforts at estimating cleanup costs. The costs presented here are based on the most recent version of that report.[1] Unfortunately, the DOE has discontinued its previously planned (and congressionally required) annual updates of this study. We have not used these costs in

1. U.S. Department of Energy, Office of Environmental Management, *The 1996 Baseline Environmental Management Report,* DOE/EM-0290 (GPO, June 1996).

FIGURE 6-1. The Costs of Nuclear Waste Management and Environmental Remediation[a]

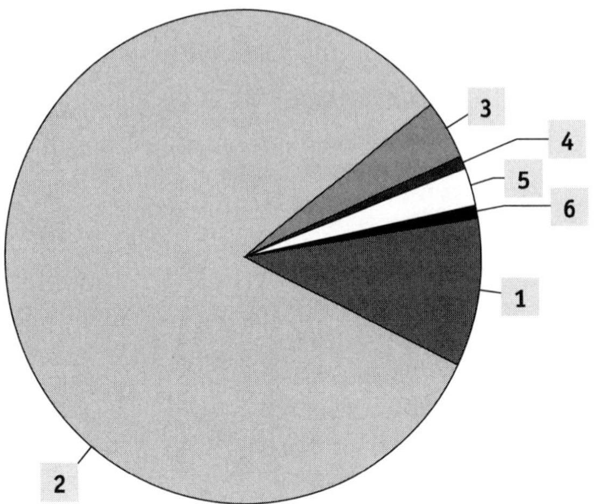

Total: $365.1 billion

1 DOE ERWM (1972–95)
$35.7 billion / 9.8%

2 DOE ERWM (1996–2070)
$300.0 billion / 82.2%

3 DOE site risk-reduction programs
$15.0 billion / 4.1%

4 Uranium Mill Tailings Remedial Action Program
$2.5 billion / 0.7%

5 DOD nuclear base cleanup
$8.7 billion / 2.4%

6 Other

Formerly Utilized Site Remedial Action Program
$1.0 billion / 0.3%

Environment, safety, and health programs
$0.2 billion / <0.1%

Yucca Mountain Project (defense waste only)
$0.6 billion / 0.2%

Bikini/Enewetak cleanup
$0.3 billion / <0.1%

DOE legal costs (incomplete)
$0.1 billion / <0.1%

Public health service
$0.9 billion / 0.2%

Environmental Protection Agency
$0.4 billion / <0.1%

Defense Nuclear Facilities Safety Board
$0.1 billion / <0.1%

a. In constant 1996 dollars. Breakout does not match total because of rounding.

the more recent *Accelerating Cleanup* report because it is an incomplete account that omits huge costs that will occur after 2006.[2]

Summary

—The nuclear weapons establishment created enormous long-term environmental liabilities without significant investment in or planning for the return of the sites to unrestricted use if and when they were no longer needed.

—The DOE's best estimate of cleanup costs as of mid-1996 is $227 billion. After examining the department's environmental management report, we estimate the costs to range from $216 billion to $410 billion (in undiscounted 1996 dollars). These estimates exclude certain cleanup problems, such as those for currently operating facilities and those arising from underground nuclear testing, and therefore may well understate the total cost. From 1989 through 1996 the DOE spent $33 billion on environmental remediation and waste management programs. The government is now considering new, controversial strategies for reducing estimated costs, one of which would be to relax cleanup guidelines and revise compliance agreements with states.

—The potential cost of waste management and environmental remediation is roughly comparable to the cost of building the bombs and warheads (excluding most DOD-related costs, such as those connected with delivery vehicles). It might even be greater, depending on the ultimate extent of cleanup and the costs of waste management and disposal.

—There are currently no provisions for meeting the long-term costs of residual contamination; enforcing restrictions on site use where they are needed; or taking remedial measures in the event that waste disposal systems fail in ways not now anticipated (as they have done in the past).

—The DOE policy of relying mainly on reprocessing to dispose of surplus irradiated nuclear fuel and target rods) other than those at the Hanford Reservation) that are now corroding in underwater storage is the least acceptable option from the standpoint of environmental and nonproliferation concerns.

—The DOE has pressured the Environmental Protection Agency (EPA) to discontinue its efforts to issue comprehensive cleanup standards for radioactively contaminated sites. Cleanup is now proceeding

2. U.S. Department of Energy, Office of Environmental Management, *Accelerating Cleanup: Paths to Closure* (Draft), DOE/EM-0342 (GPO, February 1998).

without such standards, meaning that cleanup goals will likely be determined on an ad hoc local basis.[3]

Production versus the Environment

As a crash wartime effort, the Manhattan Project was conducted with little thought to its long-term consequences for the environment. The main concern was to produce the materials required for atomic weapons that could, if they worked, be used in World War II. The uranium was acquired from abroad, but the remainder of the production and processing was done in the United States.

Not until 1947 did the Atomic Energy Commission charge a committee of environmental, safety, and health experts with assessing the effects of the radioactive and toxic materials used in weapons production. This committee reported that the disposal of contaminated waste, "if continued for decades, presents the gravest of problems. This is one of the areas of research that cannot be indefinitely postponed."[4] Yet the recommendations were ignored. Four decades would pass before the government began to address seriously the consequences of placing bomb production ahead of environmental concerns.

During the 1950s, military requirements for and production of nuclear weapons grew so rapidly that the AEC, which owned the nuclear weapons complex, became one of the largest industrial enterprises in the United States. In 1953 the work force in this complex totaled about 149,000, of which all but 6,900 were contractor employees. Some 70,000 were construction workers and about 72,000 were permanent workers who designed, tested, and produced nuclear weapons and did all the supporting and managerial work required (figure 6-2). They included some of the most qualified scientists in the country. The AEC's activities (largely uranium enrichment) consumed 5.5 billion kilowatt-hours of electricity in 1951 and peaked in 1956 at 60.7 billion kilowatt-hours, which represented 12 percent of the country's total (the gaseous diffusion plants together—in Oak Ridge, Tennessee, Paducah, Kentucky, and Portsmouth, Ohio—consumed more electricity daily "than is produced by the Hoover, Grand Coulee, and Bonneville dams plus the entire original TVA system combined"). By the mid-1950s, total capital investment in atomic energy had reached nearly $9 billion (in then-year dollars), "which well exceeds the com-

3. For instance, the guideline that the DOE is proposing for the Rocky Flats Environmental Technology Site buffer zone would allow plutonium contamination as high as 651 picocuries per gram, which is almost forty times higher than the cleanup guideline used for Johnston Island and Rongelap Atoll in the Pacific Ocean. See Marc Fioravanti and Arjun Makhijani, *Containing the Cold War Mess: Restructuring the Environmental Management of the U.S. Nuclear Weapons Complex* (Takoma Park, Md.: Institute for Energy and Environmental Research, October 1997), pp. 3, 55.

4. Quoted in Douglas Pasternak, with Peter Cary, "A $200 Billion Scandal," *U.S. News & World Report,* December 14, 1992, pp. 34–47.

bined capital investment of General Motors, U.S. Steel, Du Pont, Bethlehem Steel, Alcoa, and Goodyear."[5]

Although the AEC was a governmental institution with enormous financial, legal, and de facto judicial and regulatory power (thanks to the Atomic Energy Act of 1946; see chapters 1 and 9), there was little sustained congressional oversight of health and environmental issues until the 1970s. There was also a distinct lack of interest in nuclear waste and environmental management within the AEC itself. As Carroll L. Wilson, the first general manager of the AEC, explained:

> Chemists and chemical engineers were not interested in dealing with waste. It was not glamorous; there were no careers; it was messy; nobody got brownie points for caring about nuclear waste. The Atomic Energy Commission neglected the problem. . . . [T]here was no real interest or profit in dealing with the back end of the fuel cycle.[6]

Another reason for the lack of external scrutiny was that the AEC did not actually operate the nuclear weapons complex, but only supervised it. The production of nuclear weapons was considered so complex and difficult that only corporations were presumed to have the expertise to carry it out. This government-owned, contractor-operated system was inherited from the Manhattan Project, when the immense engineering capabilities of large corporations (such as Du Pont and General Electric) and universities (such as the University of California) were used to design the weapons and to build and operate the factories that created and processed the materials used for the first atomic bombs (see appendix C for a list of facilities and contractors).

Before corporations agreed to do the job, they insisted that they be completely free of liability for their actions, even when these actions were negligent. In the case of General Electric's contract to manage the Hanford Reservation and the Knolls Atomic Power Laboratory, company president Charles Wilson "qualified his acceptance with two stipulations. He required that the contract contain a provision freeing the company of its obligations in case the atomic energy legislation imposed conditions that in GE's 'sole judgment' the company considered 'unacceptable.' In addition, General Electric expected full recovery of all costs incurred in connection with the contract and protection against any liabilities, since hazards of 'an unusual and unpredictable nature' were involved."[7]

5. Thomas B. Cochran and others, *Nuclear Weapons Databook,* vol. 2: *U.S. Nuclear Warhead Production* (Cambridge, Mass.: Ballinger, 1987), p. 14; David Shea Teeple, *Atomic Energy* (New York: Duell, Sloan, & Pierce, 1955), pp. 65–66, 85, 87; Harold Orlans, *Contracting for Atoms* (Brookings, 1967), pp. 3–4; Gordon Dean, *Report on the Atom: What You Should Know about Atomic Energy* (London: Eyre & Spottiswoode, 1954), pp. 66–67.

6. Carroll L. Wilson, "Nuclear Energy: What Went Wrong?" *Bulletin of Atomic Scientists,* vol. 35 (June 1979), p. 15.

7. See Rodney P. Carlisle with Joan M. Zenzen, *Supplying the Nuclear Arsenal: American Production Reactors, 1942–1992* (Johns Hopkins University Press, 1996), p. 54. According to Robert R.

Figure 6-2. Employment Levels in the U.S. Nuclear Weapons Production Complex, 1949–71

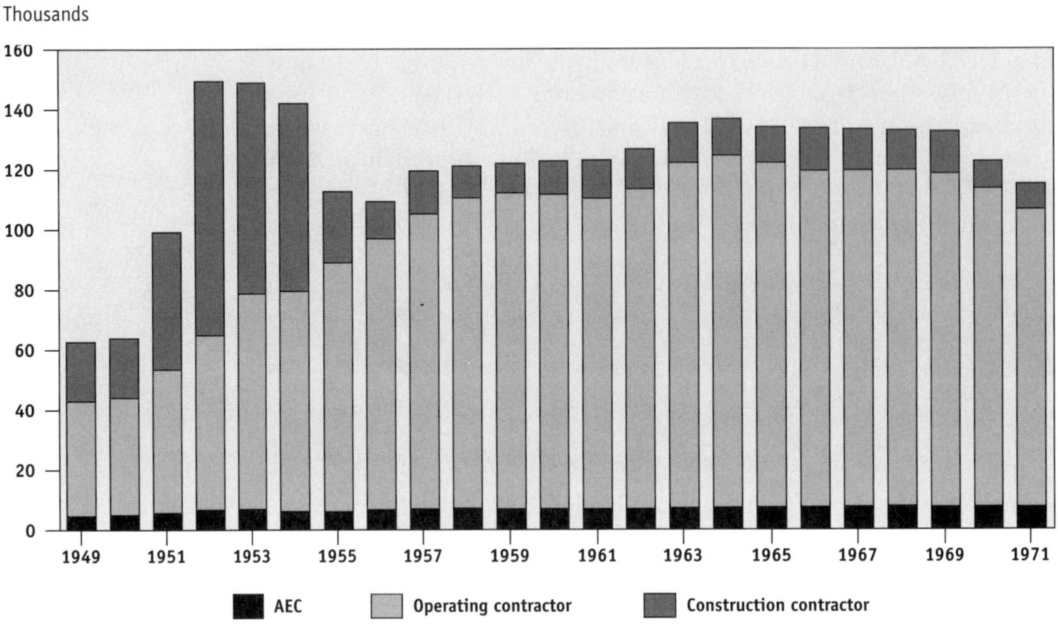

Source: Cochran and others, *Nuclear Weapons Databook*, vol. 2, p. 14.

High-Level Radioactive Waste Tanks

A prime example of an urgent and long-term environmental problem is that created by the mismanagement of high-level radioactive wastes. At the Hanford Reservation and the Savannah River Site, plutonium production and processing resulted in large quantities of highly radioactive liquid wastes (today approximately 55 million gallons [208 million liters] are stored at Hanford; 33 million gallons [125 million liters] at SRS; and 580,000 gallons [2.2 million liters] at INEEL). During World War II, Manhattan Project officials decided to store these wastes in carbon steel tanks rather than stainless steel tanks.

Nordhaus, DOE general counsel, since the mid-1940s the DOE "agreed to reimburse almost all legal costs and court judgements incurred by M&O [management and operating] contractors arising out of the performance of their contract work. Subject to exceptions for bad faith and willful misconduct by senior contractor officials, contracts written before 1991 generally treated as an 'allowable cost,' reimbursable by the Department, all litigation expenses, including reasonable attorneys' fees, judgements, and any settlements approved by the Department, arising out of third-party suits against a contractor. . . . In the case of litigation arising out of nuclear risks, the Price Anderson Act imposes indemnification requirements on the Department that are even broader than those assumed by the traditional M&O contract. (For example, there is no bad faith or willful misconduct exclusion)." See *DOE and Contractor Litigation Costs,* Hearings before the Subcommittee on Oversight and Investigations of the House Committee on Energy and Commerce, 103 Cong. 2 sess. (GPO, 1994), pp. 70–71.

Stainless steel was in short supply and carbon steel was less expensive, but the acidic wastes first had to be neutralized to prevent them from dissolving the tanks (and leaking out of them). This neutralization process, which involved adding lye and water to the wastes, substantially increased their volume and created large quantities of sodium nitrate; it also caused most of the radionuclides to precipitate to the bottom of the tanks, where they formed a hot and hard-to-handle sludge. Other materials, including flammable and explosive chemicals, were also dumped into the tanks at Hanford at various times, often with little or no thought to the long-term consequences.

Several dozen tanks at Hanford present some risk of explosion or fire.[8] Wastes in some tanks at both Hanford and Savannah River generate hydrogen and other explosive gases. The tanks must therefore be ventilated to prevent these gases from building up to explosive levels. Some tanks contain solid and liquid flammable materials. The danger of fire and explosion from a variety of potential causes as well as the threat of leaking of highly radioactive waste makes Hanford tank remediation the most urgent problem in the nuclear weapons complex. Estimates for the cost of this effort run into the tens of billions of dollars with completion estimated by the DOE in 2032. The current annual cost just to monitor and maintain these tanks is some $300 million, making them one of the largest waste management projects in the country.

To reduce the risk and empty the tanks at both Hanford and SRS, the DOE has embarked on an ambitious plan to vitrify the waste.[9] A vitrification plant with a number of associated waste-processing facilities, known as the Defense Waste Processing Facility and costing more than $4 billion in all, has been built at the Savannah River Site. In March 1996, seven years behind schedule, one section of the DWPF was opened.[10] It vitrifies the sludge that contains the bulk of the radioactivity. (DOE's original 1983 cost estimate was $1.53 billion, or $2.3 billion in 1996 dollars, with a projected start-up date in mid-1989.)[11]

8. *Accident and Explosion Risks at Department of Energy High-Level Radioactive Waste Facilities,* Hearings before the Senate Committee on Governmental Affairs, 101 Cong. 2 sess. (GPO, 1990); General Accounting Office, *Nuclear Energy: Consequences of Explosion of Hanford's Single-Shell Tanks are Understated,* RCED- 91-34 (1990); General Accounting Office, *Nuclear Waste: Hanford Tank Waste Program Needs Cost, Schedule, and Management Changes,* RCED-93-99 (March 1993); Fioravanti and Makhijani, *Containing the Cold War Mess,* pp. 165–78.

9. Vitrification is the process of mixing liquid wastes with molten sand to form a solid, stable (albeit intensely radioactive) glass waste. This waste is poured into 1,100-pound (500-kilogram) stainless steel canisters (weighing 3,700 pounds [1,682 kilograms] each when full). More than 5,500 such canisters are expected to be created over the next quarter century; as of mid-January 1998, more than 300 had been filled and welded shut at the DWPF. Author's telephone communication with James D. Werner, Office of Environmental Management, Department of Energy, January 15, 1998.

10. Ralph Vartabedian, "Plant to Clean Up Nuclear Weapons Waste to Open," *Los Angeles Times,* March 12, 1996, p. A6; Gary Lee, "Nuclear Waste Plant Opens," *Washington Post,* March 13, 1996, p. A3; Matthew L. Wald, "Factory is Set to Process Dangerous Nuclear Waste," *New York Times,* March 13, 1996, p. A16.

11. U.S. General Accounting Office, *Nuclear Waste: Defense Waste Processing Facility—Cost, Schedule, and Technical Issues,* RCED-92-183 (June 1992), pp. 14–20.

Before vitrification, however, the liquids and salts containing almost all the waste and the radioactive cesium-137 must be greatly reduced in volume. The DWPF uses an "in-tank" precipitation process to accomplish this concentration, but the method has a toxic and flammable by-product, benzene, which it generates in substantial quantities. The technical issues surrounding benzene generation, management, and incineration proved to be too complex and the process was abandoned in January 1998. The bulk of the waste cannot be removed from the tanks until a new process is developed. The problem of the Hanford tanks is even more difficult than at SRS because Hanford wastes are more complex and less well understood. No safe way has yet been devised to put Hanford wastes into a form suitable for vitrification (a plan to construct a plant similar to DWPF at Hanford was postponed in 1993 pending the resolution of critical technical issues).[12] The DOE currently plans to privatize the project and see whether contractors can successfully process wastes from two of the 177 tanks.

The history of the problematic high-level waste tanks is instructive. At first, the tanks were intended only as a temporary expedient.[13] But following World War II, no safer method of long-term storage was adopted, and the wastes kept accumulating. The significant increase in plutonium production in the 1950s (see chapter 1) only exacerbated the problem, yet the AEC's "solution" was merely to construct additional tanks to accommodate the newly generated wastes. Different, more expensive approaches were considered uneconomical and a potential drain on Hanford's main mission: to produce fissile materials. It was not as if a solution was unavailable. In Idaho, the AEC decided to calcine most high-level wastes from the Idaho Chemical Processing Plant—that is, to heat them and turn them into a dry, stable powder in oxide chemical form, suitable for extended storage in large stainless steel bins. (The ICPP recovered highly enriched uranium from irradiated naval reactor fuel.)

Another proposed remedy had more serious consequences. Beginning in 1954, potassium ferrocyanide was added to the tanks at Hanford to precipitate cesium-137 from the solution, so that the resulting concentrated liquid could be drained off to make more room for fresh wastes. Three years later, it was discovered that the ferrocyanide at the bottom of the tanks, in combination with nitrates and nitrites, was explosive at high temperatures. This was a serious concern because the radioactive decay in tank wastes generates a great deal of excess heat. The practice was stopped, but no action was taken to remove the wastes from these tanks or otherwise eliminate the risk of explosions. When

12. General Accounting Office, *Nuclear Waste: Hanford Tank Waste Program.*

13. A compelling account of the reasoning of Manhattan Project officials on this point can be found in Peter Bacon Hales, *Atomic Spaces: Living on the Manhattan Project* (University of Illinois Press, 1997), pp. 139–43.

the situation did finally become public in 1989, it was discovered that most of the tank temperature sensors were not in working order.[14] The DOE recently declared that the ferrocyanides have apparently degraded with time and no longer pose a threat.

Another problem was that numerous tanks developed leaks. Of the first sixteen tanks built at SRS, nine developed leaks in the primary containment. There were several substantial leaks from tanks and pipes into the soil and groundwater on the site. At Hanford, at least 750,000 gallons (2.8 million liters) of high-level radioactive wastes leaked into the soil, mainly in the first thirty years of operation.[15] Sixty-seven of 149 single-shell tanks at Hanford are confirmed or suspected leakers. Fortunately, the leaks eventually sealed themselves because of salts in the wastes that deposited on the cracks. More significant, between 1946 and 1966, in excess of 120 million gallons (454 million liters) of liquid wastes were *intentionally* discharged from the Hanford tanks directly to the ground. Most of these discharges occurred between 1946 and 1958 in conjunction with early efforts to recover uranium and plutonium from spent fuel generated during several expansion programs undertaken by the AEC in the 1950s.[16] With the buildup of pockets of high temperature and pressure in the tanks, there have also been violent releases of steam, which in a case in 1965 was radioactive.[17]

Despite these problems, the AEC and its successor agencies continued to believe that waste could be stored in tanks indefinitely, without serious environmental consequences, provided new tanks were built every few decades. The one problem that the AEC did address was the tank leaks, which had an adverse effect not only on health and the environment but also on plant operations, and maintenance. Since the

14. General Accounting Office, *Nuclear Energy*, pp. 3–4.

15. U.S. General Accounting Office, *Nuclear Waste: DOE's Management of Single-Shell Tanks at Hanford, Washington*, RCED-89-157 (1989), pp. 2, 16–18; U.S. General Accounting Office, *Nuclear Waste: Hanford Single-Shell Tank Leaks Greater Than Estimated*, RCED-91-117 (1991), p. 2. A forthcoming report by Los Alamos National Laboratory will reportedly conclude the above figure is a substantial underestimate and that the total is closer to 1.5 million gallons (5.7 million liters). See James Long, "Tanks at Hanford Pollute Water," *Portland Oregonian*, November 25, 1997, p. D1. The 1991 GAO report documents how an additional 50,000 to 800,000 gallons (189,000 to 3 million liters) of cooling water added to just one tank leaked into the ground. Westinghouse Hanford Company, the DOE contractor, did not include the cooling water figure in its initial leak estimate of 750,000 gallons in 1989 on the grounds that the water was uncontaminated when it was added to the tank.

16. J. L. Waite, Westinghouse Hanford Company, *Tank Wastes Discharged Directly to the Soil at the Hanford Site*, WHC-MR-0227 (April 1991), p. 7. In the Soviet Union, following a 1957 explosion of a waste tank at Chelyabinsk-65 (which led to widespread radioactive contamination severe enough to kill whole forests) and concerns about contamination from releasing reprocessing wastes directly into open ponds and reservoirs, the government decided to inject wastes directly into the ground at Tomsk-7 in 1963 and at Krasnoyarsk-26 in 1967 (geologic conditions did not permit this option at Chelyabinsk-65). Deep-well injection also takes place at the All Russian Institute of Atomic Reactors at Dimitrovgrad, near the Volga River. According to Russian officials, deep-well injection places the wastes 984 to 2,300 feet (300 to 700 meters) underground, beneath layers of shale and clay that contain the liquids. The injection sites at Tomsk and Krasnoyarsk, both in Siberia, are near rivers that empty into the Arctic Ocean. This practice continues today, with the result that about half of all Soviet and Russian reprocessing wastes have been disposed of in this manner. The long-term environmental consequences of this remain unknown. See Thomas B. Cochran, Robert S. Norris, and Oleg A. Bukharin, *Making the Russian Bomb: From Stalin to Yeltsin* (Boulder, Colo.: Westview Press, 1995), pp. 54–55; Glenn Zorpette, "Down the Drain," *Scientific American*, December 1996, pp. 20, 24.

17. International Physicians for the Prevention of Nuclear War and the Institute for Energy and Environmental Research, *Plutonium: Deadly Gold of the Nuclear Age* (Cambridge, Mass.: International Physicians Press, 1992), pp. 106–07.

AEC developed the "double-shell tank," consisting of a steel tank and a full outer steel liner, the leaks have ceased (but only in those tanks).

Spent Fuel Management and Reprocessing

The DOE manages about 2,700 metric tons of spent fuel, from which it originally intended to extract weapons-usable nuclear materials mainly for use in various nuclear weapons programs (by comparison, spent fuel thus far generated by U.S. commercial power reactors amounts to about 33,000 metric tons). In 1992, however, the reprocessing of spent fuel was suspended owing to large surpluses of plutonium and highly enriched uranium and the environmental and safety threat posed by aging reprocessing and waste management facilities. Reprocessing was resumed on a limited scale in 1996—at a cost of about $300 million a year—after DOE officials concluded that much of the spent fuel at SRS was a serious risk to health and safety.[18]

About 90 percent of DOE's spent fuel is stored underwater in twenty-nine pools at Hanford, the SRS, and the Idaho National Engineering and Environmental Laboratory.[19] The oldest pools were built more than forty years ago and many do not meet current seismic safety standards. Because some spent fuel was only designed to be stored underwater for about eighteen months, some of it is corroding, releasing radioactivity into the cooling water and taxing filtration systems (the navy maintains that its reactor fuel is far more durable; see chapter 5, footnote 24). The problems of corrosion can be mitigated by various means, such as better underwater storage (for instance, in sealed canisters) and dry cask storage. After initially proposing in 1989 to reprocess more than 2,100 metric tons of spent fuel at Hanford, the DOE finally decided to store it in dry casks. At the same time, the DOE has chosen to reprocess the spent fuel at SRS. An independent analysis by the Institute for Energy and Environmental Research (IEER) concluded that this approach was the most damaging from the point of view of high-level waste generation, worker and off-site radiation doses, and implementation of U.S. nonproliferation policy.[20] For that reason, it appears to be more a pork-barrel project designed to keep aging and otherwise inactive facilities open rather than a way to

18. Matthew L. Wald, "U.S. to Resume Reprocessing of Nuclear Fuel," *New York Times,* January 5, 1996, p. A11; U.S. Department of Energy, *Spent Fuel Working Group Report on Inventory and Storage of the Department's Spent Nuclear Fuel and Other Reactor Irradiated Nuclear Materials and Their Environmental, Safety and Health Vulnerabilities,* vols. 1 and 2 (GPO, 1993).

19. Noah Sachs, *Risky Relapse into Reprocessing: Environmental and Non-Proliferation Consequences of the Department of Energy's Spent Fuel Management Program* (Institute for Energy and Environmental Research, 1995) (available on the World Wide Web at http://www.ieer.org/ieer/reports/risky.html). The remainder is stored in dry casks or was buried years ago in carbon steel tubes or dirt trenches. The carbon steel tubes are almost certainly rusting by now. Because of poor record-keeping, the DOE is not certain exactly where the spent fuel in unlined dirt trenches is buried.

20. Sachs, *Risky Relapse into Reprocessing.*

address environmental and technical concerns related to the management of corroding spent fuel.

Repository Programs

The troubled history of selecting repository sites for high-level and transuranic (TRU) nuclear wastes is another clear example of the lack of attention to environmental issues related to nuclear weapons production.[21] The AEC first tried to create a repository in a salt mine in Lyons, Kansas. When the project was begun in 1963 (under the name Project Salt Vault), it was to concentrate on waste disposal research. Studies demonstrated that salt corroded the experimental stainless steel canisters and electrical conduits in the test location, and the project was halted in 1967. Future accidental intrusions in the site should have been a concern in any event, since the public record showed that the area had also been the location of oil and gas exploration.[22]

On May 11, 1969, a serious fire broke out at the Rocky Flats Plant near Denver, at the time the worst industrial fire in the United States.[23] The cleanup from that fire generated a large amount of plutonium-contaminated TRU waste, which for safety and political reasons could not be disposed of on-site by the then standard method of shallow land burial. It was sent to the INEEL, on the understanding that all TRU waste would be removed from Idaho by 1980.[24] This, rather than a rigorous scientific evaluation, was the reason that Lyons was reconsidered as a candidate repository for TRU waste.

In early 1971, without careful investigation, the AEC declared the Lyons site "equal to or superior to the others" and established the National Radioactive Waste Repository program there. It asked the Joint Committee on Atomic Energy to provide the entire $25 million budget ($90 million in 1996 dollars) in advance, so that it would be available within three months as opposed to the usual twelve months, to ensure that the repository would become a reality.[25] Yet, despite fif-

21. TRU waste contains materials, usually plutonium, heavier than uranium. It results from weapons production activities and includes molds for weapons components, contaminated tools, and clothing, and scrap metal and plastic contaminated with plutonium.

22. Ronnie D. Lipschutz, *Radioactive Waste: Politics, Technology and Risk* (Cambridge, Mass.: Ballinger, 1980), p. 118.

23. The fire occurred in Building 776-777, which was used "for manufacturing plutonium parts for weapons and for test devices." Approximately 2,100 pounds (950 kilograms) of plutonium was in the area affected by the fire. A great deal of equipment was destroyed and the building was heavily contaminated. In August 1969 the AEC estimated the financial loss from the fire (including plutonium recovery and building decontamination costs) at $70.7 million ($296.8 million in 1996 dollars). Warhead production, specifically of the B61, W62 (Minuteman III), and W68 (Poseidon), was delayed six to twelve months. Between September 1955 and November 1965, Rocky Flats experienced six major fires causing a total of $6.3 million in damage. See U.S. Atomic Energy Commission, *Report on Investigation of Fire, Building 776-777, Rocky Flats Plant,* vol. 1 (GPO, August 1969), pp. 1–4, 97–104 (formerly classified Secret, released, with deletions, by DOE on June 27, 1994).

24. Lipschutz, *Radioactive Waste,* p. 119.

25. H. Peter Metzger, *The Atomic Establishment* (New York: Simon & Schuster, 1972), p. 155–57; Milton Shaw, Director of AEC Reactor Development, quoted in Lipschutz, *Radioactive Waste,* p. 119. Metzger speculates that newspaper articles about

teen years of prior studies at the Lyons site and other salt sites similar to it and an expenditure of more than $100 million (about $600 million in 1996 dollars), the AEC still did not have a clear grasp of the problems with the site.

It was the Kansas Geological Survey that had warned from the beginning that the site was as leaky as a sieve and pronounced it unsuitable. Water seepage was an obvious problem, as confirmed by independent geologists and even an AEC staff report described water leaking into the mine because of oil and gas exploration holes, which had been drilled in the area but not recorded on any maps.[26] The project was abandoned in 1973 and the AEC turned its attention elsewhere.[27]

The Waste Isolation Pilot Plant

The Waste Isolation Pilot Plant is now the designated repository site for TRU wastes, but it is not large enough to dispose of all the transuranic waste known to currently exist in the weapons complex.[28] Current official estimates almost certainly understate the problem, because until 1970 such waste was dumped into trenches as "low-level waste." This practice stopped after the damage from the 1969 fire at Rocky Flats was assessed. Hence, after twenty-five years of burying TRU-contaminated wastes in shallow, unlined dirt trenches, the AEC decided that they were too dangerous to be disposed of in this manner, since they contained large concentrations of long-lived radionuclides.[29]

WIPP is located in the salt beds of southeastern New Mexico, 26 miles (42 kilometers) east of the town of Carlsbad. Originally conceived as a pilot disposal facility for commercial and government-generated high-level waste, it has since 1979 been designated a disposal site for only DOE TRU wastes. As a DOE project, WIPP is not subject to licensing by the Nuclear Regulatory Commission (NRC), but the DOE has agreed with New Mexico that it should be subject to EPA standards.

In October 1996, the DOE submitted its compliance application to the EPA, with a planned opening date for WIPP of April 1998 (the

sloppy AEC waste disposal practices, and the publication in January 1971 of photographs of radioactive waste from Rocky Flats being disposed of in flimsy cardboard boxes at INEEL—known at that time as the National Reactor Testing Station—prompted the AEC to rush the selection of the Lyons site.

26. Lipschutz, *Radioactive Waste,* p. 119; and Metzger, *The Atomic Establishment,* p. 158

27. Lipschutz, *Radioactive Waste,* pp. 118–20; Keith Schneider, "Leaky Mine Threatens A-Waste Storage Plan," *New York Times,* February 1, 1988, p. A18.

28. Except where noted, adapted with permission from Arjun Makhijani and Scott Saleska, *High-Level Dollars, Low-Level Sense: A Critique of Present Policy for the Management of Long-lived Radioactive Waste and Discussion of an Alternative Approach* (New York: Apex Press, 1992).

29. For an extensive discussion of the TRU waste problem see Fioravanti and Makhijani, *Containing the Cold War Mess,* pp. 50–147.

General Accounting Office, commenting on the department's draft application in a report three months earlier, questioned the ability of the DOE to meet this deadline, given the need to complete several outstanding tasks and the uncertainty that all the required permits would be issued on time).[30] Also in October 1996, an advisory committee with the National Research Council released a report on WIPP, endorsing the project's design and asserting that as long as the site remains sealed off from all human activity, it "has the ability to isolate transuranic waste for more than 10,000 years."[31] The states of Texas and New Mexico and concerned environmental organizations, contending that human intrusion into WIPP was a serious risk, filed a lawsuit charging that current EPA compliance standards are inadequate; the latter two also submitted comments to EPA claiming that the DOE's application was substantially incomplete and should therefore be rejected.

In June 1997, the DOE, calling WIPP a "cornerstone" to its overall cleanup strategy, delayed the facility's opening date to May 1998, a decade behind schedule. That same month, the Circuit Court of the District of Columbia ruled in favor of the EPA in the compliance standards lawsuit. On May 13, 1998, the EPA approved the DOE's application and licensed WIPP to begin operations. The state of New Mexico and environmental organizations intend to file additional lawsuits challenging the legality of EPA's and DOE's actions. It is therefore unclear when or whether WIPP will ever open.[32]

Unlike the DOE's program at Yucca Mountain, WIPP is by and large complete. Located 2,150 feet (655 meters) below the surface, it can hold about 880,000 55-gallon drums, enough to contain slightly less than 5.6 million cubic feet (160,000 cubic meters) of waste. However, many technical and regulatory issues related to the geology and hydrology of the WIPP site cast doubt on its suitability.

—*Pressurized water pockets below WIPP.* A 1987 DOE study showed that a pressurized brine reservoir may be present 800 feet (244 meters) below the current repository location. At some point in the future, brine could breach the repository and carry radioactivity to the surface.[33]

—*Water leakage into WIPP.* The DOE first encountered water seepage into WIPP excavations in 1983. The public was unaware of it until the fall of 1987, when a group of New Mexico scientists concluded that

30. U.S. General Accounting Office, *Nuclear Waste: Uncertainties about Opening Waste Isolation Pilot Plant,* RCED-96- 146 (July 1996).

31. Joby Warrick, "Nuclear Burial Site Endorsed," *Washington Post,* October 24, 1996, p. A19.

32. Department of Energy, Office of Environmental Management, *Accelerating Cleanup,* p. ES-3; Case No. 96-1107, *State of New Mexico* v. *EPA,* U.S. Court of Appeals for the District of Columbia Circuit, June 6, 1997; Matthew L. Wald, "New Mexico Site Is Approved for Storage of Nuclear Waste," *New York Times,* May 14, 1998, p. A1.

33. Statement of Lokesh Chaturvedi, Deputy Director, New Mexico Environmental Evaluation Group, in *Status of the Waste Isolation Pilot Plant Project,* Hearings before a Subcommittee of the House Committee on Government Operations, 100 Cong. 2 sess. (GPO, 1989), pp. 92–93.

over a period of time, brine seeping into the repository could corrode the waste drums, forming a "radioactive waste slurry" consisting of a mixture of brine and nuclear waste that might eventually reach the surface.[34]

—*Wall cracking and ceiling collapse.* Cracks have appeared in the ceilings and floors of several large waste storage rooms, and in three areas the ceiling has also collapsed. The cause, it seems, is that the rate of room closure is two to three times faster than was anticipated.[35]

—*Natural resource issues.* Natural resources, especially reserves of oil and gas, exist in the region of the WIPP repository. These resources could invite future accidental intrusion into the site.[36]

—*Compliance with hazardous waste law.* More than half of TRU waste slated for disposal in WIPP is contaminated with hazardous chemicals. These transuranic wastes are therefore also classified as mixed waste and fall under the Resource Conservation and Recovery Act (RCRA), which stipulates that hazardous wastes must be characterized in detail.[37] According to the DOE, however, "a large volume of TRU-mixed wastes to be sent to WIPP was generated from defense programs in the distant past. Documentation on the chemical constituents of these wastes . . . is often inadequate or does not exist."[38]

Other problems are related to the waste capacity of WIPP and to DOE's priorities. In another twenty years or so, the net accumulation of this retrievable waste is expected to be almost 4 million cubic feet (112,000 cubic meters), and WIPP's projected capacity is expected to accommodate this amount. However, it does not include an estimated 5 million cubic feet (140,000 cubic meters) of buried transuranic wastes, or large quantities of transuranic-contaminated soil also present at various sites, some or all of which may be removed during cur-

34. General Accounting Office, testimony by Keith O. Fultz, Senior Associate Director, Resources, Community, and Economic Development Division, *Status of the Department of Energy's Waste Isolation Pilot Plant,* T-RCED-88-63 (1988), pp. 8–9, as contained in *Status of the Waste Isolation Pilot Plant Project,* Hearings, pp. 13–14. Water currently leaking into WIPP is mixing with lead used during the repository's construction. This contaminated water is classified as a hazardous waste and is being pumped out of WIPP for off-site disposal. Thus WIPP is actually generating one form of waste before it is even approved to dispose of another.

35. The principle behind WIPP is that, once filled, the salt walls of the repository will slowly "creep" over the waste packages, entombing and sealing them off from the surface and the rest of the environment. As the wall and ceiling collapses demonstrate, however, the rate of movement is substantially faster than originally predicted, calling into question DOE's timetable for emplacing the waste. In theory, waste buried in WIPP is supposed to be recoverable if serious problems are discovered before the repository is filled and sealed. See Keith Schneider, "Nuclear Waste Dump Faces Another Potential Problem," *New York Times,* June 3, 1989, p. 8.

36. The DOE has expended considerable effort in devising schemes to ward off human intrusion into WIPP. See Kathleen M. Trauth, Stephen C. Hora, and Robert V. Guzowski, *Expert Judgement on Markers to Deter Inadvertent Human Intrusion into the Waste Isolation Pilot Plant,* SAND92-1382 (Albuquerque, N.M.: Sandia National Laboratories, 1993); T. R. Reid, "Warning Future Earthlings about Nuclear Waste," *Washington Post,* November 11, 1984, p. A1; T. R. Reid, "New Atomic Dump Poses Unprecedented Challenges," *Washington Post,* July 5, 1989, p. A4.

37. Regulations pursuant to RCRA are incorporated into 40 CFR Part 264.

38. U.S. Department of Energy, *RCRA Compliance at the Department of Energy's Waste Isolation Pilot Plant,*" DOE/WIPP 88-018 (June, 1988), p. 12, as contained in *Status of the Waste Isolation Pilot Plant Project,* Hearings, pp. 133–55.

rent and projected environmental remediation programs. A recent independent analysis showed that the DOE does not have reliable estimates of the volume of buried TRU waste, TRU contaminated soil, or the amount of radioactivity contained in them. The actual amounts of radioactivity in the wastes may be far larger than the official estimates, based on the one incomplete investigation on TRU wastes done at INEEL.[39]

DOE estimates of the quantities of TRU-contaminated soil have become increasingly vague over the years, even as the department spends increasing sums on environmental management programs, some of which are designed to quantify the amount of wastes destined for removal and repository disposal. In fact, the DOE's *Integrated Database* on wastes has now stopped reporting quantities of contaminated soil altogether. In 1990, most sites with large quantities of TRU waste made estimates of contaminated soil. The reported total for all sites was between 5 million and 10.3 million cubic feet (140,000 and 289,000 cubic meters). In 1995 only Hanford reported a figure—1.1 million cubic feet (32,000 cubic meters) of soil contaminated by liquid waste under the contaminated soil category of TRU—about the same as its reported total for 1990. Other facilities provided no data, so that the reported total is now simply and misleadingly recorded as more than 32,000 cubic meters.[40] The total contaminated soil in the TRU waste category is likely to be very large, however, on the order of 10.7 million cubic feet (300,000 cubic meters) and perhaps much more, roughly double the capacity of WIPP. The quantity of TRU waste is now so vast partly because the soil around its disposal sites has become contaminated owing to the poor waste management practices of the past.

There remains some uncertainty as to whether wastes not now classified as TRU might be reclassified as such. The DOE has thus far failed to decide what it plans to do with this buried transuranic waste and transuranic-contaminated soil, yet it is this waste, and not the retrievable waste stored in monitored facilities, that poses the greatest short- and medium-term environmental risk.

Thus DOE's current transuranic waste policy is something of a paradox. On the one hand, transuranic waste is considered so dangerous that it needs to be stored in a repository 2,150 feet (655 meters) underground to isolate it from the environment. On the other hand, little has been done to permanently dispose of the transuranic waste contaminating the ground or lying in shallow pits and disposal cribs. WIPP will not have the capacity to dispose of many of the transuranic

39. Fioravanti and Makhijani, *Containing the Cold War Mess,* esp. pp. 52, 76–86.

40. U.S. Department of Energy, *Integrated Data Base for 1990: U.S. Spent Fuel and Radioactive Waste Inventories, Projections, and Characteristics,* DOE/RW-0006 (GPO, 1990), rev. 6, p. 82. Also see rev. 11 of the same publication published in September 1995, p. 107.

wastes that are causing the greatest contamination problems, and no additional repository plans are at present under consideration.

From 1976 to 1995 WIPP cost $2 billion.[41] The DOE expects to spend a total of $8.4 billion on construction and operation of the repository for twenty-five to thirty-five years. In 1979 it estimated that the *total* cost of WIPP would be $1.1 billion ($2.2 billion in 1996 dollars). This figure doubled to about $2 billion in the late 1980s and doubled again in 1991, to $4.4 billion ($4.9 billion in 1996 dollars). The DOE has blamed the cost increases on additional requirements imposed by Congress. In August 1993 it released a chart showing the actual and expected cumulative costs of the program from the 1970s through 2028, when WIPP is officially expected to close. The chart indicated that operating WIPP would cost less than testing it. Asked to explain, DOE officials said that full-scale disposal operations would cost less than the test phase because "the department wouldn't need to hire as many top-drawer scientists for the final burial of wastes." A Republican staffer with the House Energy and Commerce Committee remarked that the chart was unlike any "cost curve" he had ever seen for a federal project.[42]

Recently the DOE has been making more careful estimates of both the volume and radioactivity of buried waste TRU and soil contaminated by TRU. Preliminary findings suggest that the problem may be far more serious than previously thought and that considerable effort and expense will be needed to address it. For all these reasons, the ultimate cost of storing and disposing of TRU waste is likely to exceed the DOE's estimate.

Another point to consider is that the estimate of $8.4 billion for WIPP applies to the repository costs alone. When all the costs of the currently preferred method of cleanup and management are taken into account, the amount required to handle, treat, and dispose of TRU wastes will be about $20 billion. The additional costs are included in the cleanup totals provided here. However, the current program is expected to disregard a large quantity of buried TRU wastes from the repository program. If all transuranic waste were to be treated and disposed of in a repository, the overall transuranic waste disposal costs would rise to more than $59 billion. This last figure represents a threefold increase in TRU management costs and would cause the DOE's overall cleanup estimate of $227 billion to increase by about 18 percent.[43]

41. Data provided by Christine Gelles, DOE Office of Budget, June 30, 1995.

42. See Tony Davis, "Doubled Price Tag for WIPP Catches Opponent by Surprise," *Albuquerque Tribune*, August 5, 1993, p. A1; DOE Office of Environmental Management, *The 1996 Baseline Environmental Management Report*, vol. 3, p. New Mexico-79.

43. DOE Carlsbad Area Office, *Waste Isolation Pilot Plant Disposal Phase Draft Supplemental Environmental Impact Statement*, DOE/EIS-0026-S-2 (GPO, 1996), p. S-59. We have converted the 1994 dollar figures in this document to 1996 dollars.

Yucca Mountain Project

The problems surrounding the long-term disposal of high-level waste from plutonium production are perhaps even worse. In 1985 the Reagan administration decided that such wastes would be disposed of in the same repository as spent fuel from commercial nuclear reactors. But that program—like other radioactive waste repository programs before it—has been driven more by political expediency than sound science, which has been a prominent casualty of these programs.

Since 1988 the only designated site to be investigated as a suitable repository is Yucca Mountain, a volcanic outcropping adjacent to the Nevada Test Site. Prior to 1988 the DOE, operating under the Nuclear Waste Policy Act of 1982 (P.L. 97-425), was studying nine sites in Louisiana, Mississippi, Texas, Nevada, Utah, and Washington as potential candidates for the first high-level waste repository (then scheduled to open in 1998).[44] Beginning in January 1986, twelve additional sites in Georgia, Maine, Minnesota, New Hampshire, North Carolina, Wisconsin, and Virginia for a second repository (scheduled to open in 2003) were under consideration. By May 1986, however, the DOE's plans had engendered significant local opposition and secretary of energy John S. Herrington announced that his department had narrowed the list for the first repository to just three sites: Yucca Mountain, the Hanford Reservation, and Deaf Smith County, Texas. Herrington also announced an indefinite suspension on the search for a second repository site, a decision based in no small measure on political considerations.

By 1987 the estimated cost of the site characterization program alone had grown to nearly $5 billion, from initial estimates in 1981 of $180 million to $240 million (all figures in then-year dollars). The House Interior Committee approved a bill in October 1987 calling for an independent review commission to reevaluate the waste repository program. Meanwhile in the Senate, J. Bennett Johnston (Democrat of Louisiana) and James McClure (Republican of Idaho), concerned about the sharply rising cost and eager to keep the process on track, introduced legislation requiring the DOE to select just one site for investigation. This bill, backed by President Ronald Reagan, passed as part of the annual energy and water appropriations bill. In conference committee, this approach quickly gained favor over the idea of an independent commission, especially when it was suggested that Yucca Mountain be designated the sole candidate site, setting aside the objective scientific and technical criteria underlying the original act. When

44. This and the following paragraph are drawn from Scott Saleska, *Nuclear Legacy: An Overview of the Places, Problems, and Politics of Radioactive Waste in the United States* (Washington, D.C.: Public Citizen Critical Mass Energy Project, September 1989), pp. VII-1–VII-5.

the legislation returned to the House and Senate floors for final passage, members eagerly supported the Nuclear Waste Policy Amendments Act of 1987 (P.L. 100-203), which eliminated their states or districts from consideration and isolated the relatively weak four-member Nevada congressional delegation.

Unfortunately, geological and technical conditions suggest that Yucca Mountain is a poor site and that its characteristics will be difficult to predict. For instance, plutonium has been migrating far more rapidly than expected from a test location at the nearby Nevada Test Site. Volcanic and seismic activity at the site is also a concern. As another example, two Los Alamos scientists have theorized that conditions are such that once entombed the fissile materials may become concentrated into a critical mass and may perhaps even explode with considerable force after the waste canisters have given way.[45] Although this theory has been discounted by most reviewers so far, the issue is not yet settled.[46] That such a theory could be advanced seriously after four decades of considering repositories as a suitable means of radioactive waste disposal shows not only that insufficient scientific resources have been invested in the work, but that it is exceedingly difficult to try to predict the behavior of long-lived fission products and fissile materials for tens of thousands of years, which is longer than all of recorded history. Adding to the problems at the site and reminiscent of the earlier surprises at Project Salt Vault and WIPP, rainwater has traveled some 800 feet (244 meters) from the surface down into the area where the repository would be built. This has taken place in just forty years, rather than the hundreds or thousands of years predicted. Although the amount of water is relatively small, it raises serious questions about whether the repository will be able to effectively contain high-level radioactive wastes.[47]

The fact is that the DOE failed to utilize preexisting scientific data and analyses. A 1983 study on geologic disposal, done by the National Academy of Sciences (NAS) and commissioned by the DOE itself, included some cautionary calculations about Yucca Mountain. It concluded that, because of the small volume of groundwater and the absence of surface water in the area, an individual (defined as a subsistence farmer) experiencing maximum exposure by using groundwater contaminated by long-term high-level waste leakage could expect

45. William J. Broad, "Scientists Fear Atomic Explosion of Buried Waste," *New York Times*, March 5, 1995, p. A1; William J. Broad, "Theory on Threat of Blast at Nuclear Waste Site Gains Support," *New York Times*, March 23, 1995, p. A18; "Nuclear Waste Storage at Yucca Mountain," *Science*, vol. 269 (August 18, 1995), pp. 906–07. A recent review of the issue by a team at the University of California, Berkeley, concluded: "There don't appear to be any geochemical or geophysical mechanisms for these supercritical scenarios to happen." See Gary Taubes, "Yucca Blowup Theory Bombs, Says Study," *Science*, vol. 217 (March 22, 1996), p. 1664.

46. See, for example, Richard L. Garwin, "Comment on the Bowman and Venneri Analysis," *Science & Global Security*, vol. 5 (1996), pp. 333–36.

47. Matthew L. Wald, "Doubt Cast on Prime Site as Nuclear Waste Dump," *New York Times* (Washington edition), June 20, 1997, p. A12.

the doses to range from 1 rem to 1,000 rem per year.[48] These doses are 40 to 40,000 times greater than the EPA dose limit for the general population of 25 millirem (0.025 rem) per year from nuclear fuel-cycle facilities. More recent DOE-sponsored studies also indicate that doses could be hundreds of times above allowable limits.[49]

Responding to such calculations, the nuclear power industry—which would also dispose of its spent fuel at Yucca Mountain, should it be licensed—advocates a new method of dose calculation that would abandon the conservative approach of protecting future populations by limiting radiation doses to the maximally exposed individual, generally defined in such circumstances to be a subsistence farmer. A 1995 report by a NAS panel also recommended (with one dissent) a new method of calculating doses that could result in a severe relaxation of radiation protection standards.[50]

The DOE seems to have created a kind of "Murphy's law" of nuclear waste repositories: the more money it spends on opening a repository, the further away the opening date. The estimated time for opening a repository increased from about ten years in the mid-1970s to twenty-one years by 1989.[51] From 1983 to 1996 the DOE spent more than $6 billion on the high-level waste nuclear repository program (including nearly $4 billion on Yucca Mountain since 1988), and with an official opening date set for 2010 at the earliest, the uncertainty remains as great as ever.[52] Only a portion of the costs of the repository program and Yucca Mountain can be attributed to the nuclear weapons program, because most of the repository (if it opens) will be devoted to waste from commercial nuclear power plants. The percentage of space dedicated to storing military nuclear waste is difficult to estimate and will depend on several factors, including final decisions on the processing of wastes at the Hanford Reservation and the ultimate disposition of surplus plutonium (see chapter 5). For the pur-

48. National Research Council—Waste Isolation Systems Panel, Board on Radioactive Waste Management, National Research Council, *A Study of the Isolation System for Geologic Disposal of Radioactive Wastes* (Washington, D.C.: National Academy Press, 1983). By way of comparison, a chest X ray involves a dose of a small fraction of a rem.

49. For various dose estimates from a Yucca Mountain repository see "A Centerfold for Technoweenies," *Science for Democratic Action,* Institute for Energy and Environmental Research, vol. 4. no. 4 (1995), pp. 8–9.

50. For a discussion of the industry report, see Arjun Makhijani, "Calculating Doses from Disposal of High-Level Radioactive Waste: Review of a National Academy of Sciences Report," *Science for Democratic Action,* vol. 4. no. 4 (1995), p. 1, and associated table and graphs on pp. 8–9 of the same issue; Committee on the Technical Bases for Yucca Mountain Standards, Board on Radioactive Waste Management, National Research Council, *Technical Bases for Yucca Mountain Standards* (Washington, D.C.: National Academy Press, 1995); Thomas H. Pigford, "The Yucca Mountain Standard: Proposals for Leniency," University of California, Berkeley, Department of Nuclear Engineering, UCB-NE-9525 (November 1995). Also in *Proceedings of the Materials Research Society, Scientific Basis of Nuclear Waste Management,* November 1995.

51. Makhijani and Saleska, *High-Level Dollars, Low-Level Sense,* p. 66. Unlike WIPP, most of the funding for Yucca mountain comes from a 1/10 of a cent per kilowatt-hour fee imposed upon nuclear-generated electricity by the Nuclear Waste Policy Act. The balance is to be paid by DOE for the disposal of high-level wastes generated as a result of nuclear weapons production.

52. Department of Energy, Office of Civilian Radioactive Waste management, Monthly Summary of Program Financial and Budget Information, as of December 31, 1996"; U.S. General Accounting Office, *Nuclear Waste: Impediments to Completing the Yucca Mountain Repository Project,* RCED-97-30 (January 1997).

poses of this accounting, we include just $612.8 million, the amount of funding allocated to Yucca Mountain between 1993 and 1996 from the defense nuclear waste disposal fund.

Depleted uranium (DU), a by-product of uranium enrichment, is yet another nuclear waste that continues to pile up. The United States has about 1.2 billion pounds (560,000 metric tons) of depleted uranium hexafluoride stored around the country, but mainly at the three uranium enrichment plants (two of which—Portsmouth, Ohio, and Paducah, Kentucky—were privatized in 1993, and one of which, Oak Ridge, is closed). The DOE spent more than $30 million in 1996 just to store and monitor this material, which is kept in 46,422 large steel cylinders, most of which are outdoors and are therefore corroding.[53] This material has not yet been officially designated a waste, because the DOE and private industry have been selling some of it, for instance, to Department of Defense contractors for use in artillery shells and tank armor.[54] Senior military officials, however, appear unwilling to acknowledge the health risks associated with exposure to depleted uranium, which is radioactive. No practical measures have been taken to protect exposed armed forces personnel, nor to assess the doses in general.[55] Suspicions that exposure to depleted uranium may be a contributing factor to some cases of "Gulf War Syndrome" have not yet been put to rest. Since the market for DU has collapsed and is unlikely to revive, this material may have to be declared a waste.

The DOE is only now beginning to evaluate its options for dealing with this enormous quantity of radioactive material. Even these activities, however, seem to be setting the stage for failure. In its "Notice of Intent to Do a Programmatic Environmental Impact Statement" on the disposition of depleted uranium, the DOE seems to have overlooked key scientific facts.[56] One is that except for nomenclature, both the specific activity of radioactivity of depleted uranium and the nature of the radiation it emits fit the regulatory definition of transuranic waste. Because transuranic waste must be disposed of in a geologic repository, it would appear reasonable to consider geologic disposal under the same rules that govern TRU waste as one alternative for DU. But the

53. Matthew L. Wald, "Danger From Uranium Waste Grows as Government Considers Its Fate," *New York Times* (Washington edition), March 25, 1997, p. A14.

54. Bob Davis, "Dubious Defense: Law Forces Pentagon to Purchase and Store Metal It Doesn't Want," *Wall Street Journal,* June 10, 1991, p. A1.

55. Exposure is possible in two ways—when in close proximity to DU weapons or armor plating (such as in the interior of a tank) or by inhaling uranium particles after a DU shell has exploded. Doug Rokke, a health physicist and former director of DOD's Depleted Uranium Project who surveyed postwar contamination in the Gulf and prepared training materials for the army on the hazards of DU ammunition *after* the war (on the basis of testing in Nevada), asserts that senior military officials "have made a political decision and are totally unwilling to recognize that there are health consequences of the use of depleted uranium in the Gulf War. . . . The Pentagon thinks that the problems . . . will just go away if it doesn't talk about it." See U.S. General Accounting Office, *Operation Desert Storm: Army Not Adequately Prepared to Deal with Depleted Uranium Contamination,* NSIAD-93-90 (January 1993), p. 3; Bill Mesler, "The Gulf War's New Casualties," *Nation,* July 14, 1997, pp. 19–20; Kathleen Sullivan, "New Link to Gulf War Ills: Bullets of Uranium," *San Francisco Examiner,* August 17, 1997, p. A1.

56. *Fed. Reg.* (January 25, 1996), pp. 2239–42.

DOE has not yet done so, and it has instead chosen to ignore public comments supporting this course of action.[57]

Overview of Waste and Contamination

The sources of waste and contamination extend far beyond those just described.[58] There are in the United States today vast amounts of contaminated water and soil, millions of pounds of surplus chemicals and 9 million pounds (4.1 million kilograms) of lead,[59] thousands of contaminated buildings and facilities,[60] highly contaminated processing equipment, abandoned equipment and buildings, and disposal areas where dangerous wastes were improperly discharged or dumped. In addition, environmental awareness has brought new problems to light. It was once thought that plutonium could be disposed of in soil, where it would become trapped through "ion exchange." Hence large amounts of low-level wastes were dumped directly into dirt trenches at many facilities, including Hanford, SRS, Oak Ridge, INEEL, and Los Alamos. Yet subsequent analysis determined that in some cases plutonium migrated into the groundwater in as little as twenty years, possibly because of the presence of solvents or other factors that released it from the soil.[61]

Scientifically sound assessments of environmental problems in the nuclear weapons complex have only recently begun and are by no means complete. It will be many years before even the scope of these problems is clearly defined, although some of the more urgent issues—such as potential waste tank fires or explosions—have been identified and are now much better understood than a decade ago. To complicate matters, many of the DOE's facilities are vulnerable to earthquakes, tornadoes, or floods, all of which could damage buildings and equipment and potentially release hazardous materials. Despite longtime knowledge of these natural threats—for example, both the Paducah Gaseous Diffusion Plant and the Savannah River Site are located in earthquake zones—no systematic study of the danger or the best means of addressing it was undertaken until the Clinton administra-

57. Annie Makhijani and Arjun Makhijani, "Comments of the Institute for Energy and Environmental Research on the Department of Energy Notice of Intent Addressing the Alternative Strategies for the Long-Term Management and Use of Depleted Uranium Hexafluoride, *Federal Register*, Thursday, January 25, 1996," March 22, 1996.

58. For an overview of the vast quantity of materials currently in the DOE's inventory, see U.S. Department of Energy, *Taking Stock: A Look at the Opportunities and Challenges Posed by Inventories from the Cold War Era*, EM-0275, vol. 1 (GPO, 1996).

59. Department of Energy, *Taking Stock*, pp. 20–21.

60. At Rocky Flats, for example, workers have dubbed more than two dozen areas "infinity rooms" because radiation monitors go off the scale inside them. These rooms—one of which measures 100 yards long by 50 yards wide (91 meters by 46 meters)—have been sealed and are off-limits. One has not been entered since the early 1970s. Author's telephone conversation with reporter Mark Obmascik of the *Denver Post*, May 8, 1997.

61. Arjun Makhijani, Robert Alvarez, and Brent Blackwelder, *Deadly Crop in the Tank Farm* (Washington, D.C.: Environmental Policy Institute, 1986), p. 78; see also Fioravanti and Makhijani, *Containing the Cold War Mess*, pp. 121–27.

tion. A report, scheduled for release in December 1998, will recommend risk reduction measures likely to cost tens of billions of dollars.[62]

Table 6-1 itemizes the radioactive waste created during the production of nuclear weapons for the U.S. arsenal. These wastes do not include uranium mining wastes in other countries, or the substantial wastes that will be created during the DOE's ongoing environmental restoration program, principally from the decontamination and decommissioning of surplus buildings and equipment. Nor do they include the large volume of soil and water contaminated during nuclear weapons production and testing from 1943 through 1992 at Hanford, SRS, Oak Ridge, INEEL, the Nevada Test Site, and elsewhere.

The Cost of "Cleanup"

No amount of money can return all the land and water under DOE facilities to their original condition, though this may prove feasible in some cases. Once long-lived radioactive wastes are created, nothing practical can be done to make them "go away." In many cases the only feasible action is to isolate them from the human environment for periods comparable to 10 to 20 half-lives of the radioisotope in question (for example, 240,000 to 480,000 years for plutonium-239). From 1989 through 1996, the DOE expended $33 billion on environmental management activities (see table 6-2). However, only about one-fourth of this has actually gone toward environmental restoration; the remainder was used to maintain buildings and other facilities and to store, monitor, and stabilize past and ongoing wastes.

Another problem is that a sizable amount of the soil and groundwater contamination is highly dispersed. It will be very difficult and expensive to clean this up, and in many cases the technology simply does not exist (although the DOE has initiated a technology development program to investigate some of these problems). Moreover, the environmental costs and health risks of such cleanup could be quite large, principally because all it can do is transfer low levels of contamination from one location to another, sometimes contaminating new areas in the process and creating additional risks during transportation between sites. If the soil is disturbed and excavated on a large scale, the cleanup may also render some areas barren, or nearly so. Equally serious, there appears to be no way at present to gather together the dispersed but highly radioactive wastes from underground nuclear weapons testing in Nevada and elsewhere.[63]

62. Richard Cole, "Elements Threaten Nuclear Arms Plants," *Washington Post*, July 15, 1996, p. A7.

63. In addition to these locations, tests for weapons development and effects purposes, as well as for the Plowshare and VELA

TABLE 6-1. Volume and Radioactivity of Waste Created during U.S. Nuclear Weapons Production[a]

Measurement	*Mining*	*Milling*	*Low-level*	*High-level*	*Transuranic*
Radioactivity curies	10,000	100,000	15 million	1 billion	Information not available
Quantity	100 million metric tons	100 million metric tons	3 million cubic meters	400,000 cubic meters	More than 200,000 cubic meters

Sources: *Integrated Data Base Report—1995: U.S. Spent Fuel and Radioactive Waste Inventories, Projections, and Characteristics,* DOE/RW-0006 Rev. 12 (Washington, D.C.: U.S. Department of Energy, 1996), p. 13, except for mining and milling wastes. For uranium mining and milling volume and radioactivity we have used the coefficients in Howard Hu and Arjun Makhijani, "The Global Picture: Summary and Recommendations," in Howard Hu, Arjun Makhijani, and Katherine Yih (eds.), *Nuclear Wastelands: A Global Guide to Nuclear Weapons Production and Its Health and Environmental Effects* (Cambridge, Mass.: MIT Press, 1995), table 12.2, p. 581, and applied them to the 994 metric tons of HEU produced in the United States.

a. All numbers are rounded to one significant figure, except as indicated.

An economic question arises directly from the reality that no remedial effort can be perfect: What will it cost to protect the affected communities and future generations there by maintaining site restrictions and other safeguards such as monitoring the site and educating the communities, essentially in perpetuity in many cases? At this point, no one knows. Between 1994 and 1996, the DOE spent some $6 million to support eleven citizen advisory boards. These boards, on which community activists, plant workers, health professionals, teachers, and government officials serve, are part of the DOE's approach to its cleanup mission, providing advice and feedback to the DOE on various aspects of its remediation and waste management programs, potentially creating a useful means of access to vital information for citizens in surrounding communities.

Toxic nonradioactive materials can be destroyed in a variety of ways. Incineration is the most common method used, but it creates its own problems in the form of emissions of dioxins and other pollutants. Advanced treatment methods that could reduce such pollutants are in the development stage One complication of treating wastes in which radioactive and hazardous nonradioactive materials are mixed ("mixed wastes") is that the requirements for managing the radioactive portion of the wastes can be in conflict with those for dealing with the nonradioactive portion. For instance, incineration does not destroy radioactivity and can result in increased air emissions of radioactive materi-

Uniform programs (see chapters 1 and 3, respectively), were conducted in Alaska (three tests), Colorado (two tests), Mississippi (two tests), and New Mexico (three tests). For information on current monitoring and remediation activities at some of the sites, see DOE Office of Environmental Management, *1996 Baseline Environmental Management Report,* vol. 2, pp. Alaska 1–Alaska 6, Mississippi 1–Mississippi 6, Nevada 31–Nevada 36, and vol. 3, pp. New Mexico 91–New Mexico 94.

TABLE 6-2. DOE Environmental Restoration and Waste Management Programs, 1989–96

Millions of 1996 dollars

Year	Obligation
1989	1,909.4[a]
1990	2,318.3
1991	3,490.4
1992	3,957.8
1993	5,094.5
1994[b]	5,330.8
1995	5,142.7
1996	5,735.0
Total	32,978.9

Source: U.S. Congressional Budget Office, *Cleaning Up the Department of Energy's Nuclear Weapons Complex,* p. 7 (for 1989); Office of Management and Budget, *Budget of the United States Government* (fiscal 1992–98, inclusive, for 1990–96).

a. Congressional appropriation.

b. Figures for fiscal 1994–96 exclude the uranium enrichment decontamination and decommissioning program.

als.[64] As another example, chemical treatment of the hazardous component of mixed waste can increase the volume of radioactive waste requiring disposal. Table 6-3 shows the pollutants found in various media at the Hanford Reservation, which is possibly the most contaminated site in the weapons complex.[65]

One of the most expensive long-term tasks will be to decontaminate and decommission buildings involved in weapons production. Long after their missions have ended, these structures will remain hazardous. In early 1992, DOE field offices estimated that some 1,700 facilities might close over the next thirty years, at a projected cost of $54 billion ($59 billion in 1996 dollars), but subsequent plans suggest that as many as 7,000 facilities may close.[66]

Tending to Abandoned Facilities

Two separate programs address problems of defunct facilities. The first, the Formerly Utilized Site Remedial Action Program (FUSRAP),

64. For more on incineration, see David Kershner, Scott Saleska, and Arjun Makhijani, "Radioactive Mixed Waste Incineration," Institute for Energy and Environmental Research, June 1993.

65. Arjun Makhijani and others, "The United States," in Arjun Makhijani, Howard Hu, and Katherine Yih, eds., *Nuclear Wastelands: A Global Guide to Nuclear Weapons Production and Its Health and Environmental Effects* (Cambridge, Mass.: MIT Press), p. 223.

66. U.S. General Accounting Office, *Department of Energy: Cleaning Up Inactive Facilities Will Be Difficult,* RCED-93-149 (June 1993), pp. 4–5.

TABLE 6-3. Summary of Hazardous Substances Released to the Environment at Hanford Reservation

Contaminant	*Air*	*Soil*	*Surface water*	*Groundwater*
Radionuclides	Argon-41[a] Radon-222[a] Strontium-90[a]	Cesium-137 Ruthenium-106		Cesium-137 Gross alpha Gross beta Iodine-129 Plutonium-239 Plutonium-240 Radium Strontium-90 Tritium
Metals				Barium Cadmium Chromium Mercury
Ionrganic compounds	Ammonia[a,b]			Fluorides Nitrates
Volatile organic compounds (VOCs)	Carbon tetrachloride[a]			Carbon tetrachloride[a] Chloroform Dichloromethane[a] Hexone[a] Methylcyclohexane[a] Perchloroethylene[c] Phthalates[a] 1,1,1-Trichloroethane
Miscellaneous		Pesticide rinsate[a] Untreated wastewater[a,d]	Untreated wastewater[a,d]	Coliform Kerosene[a] Oil Pesticide rinsate[a] Temperature[e] Untreated wastewater[a,d]

Source: Makhijani and others, *Nuclear Wastelands*, "The United States," p. 221.

a. The present or potential contamination associated with current and past discharges of this pollutant has not been fully determined.

b. Ammonia was released into the air by the plutonium uranium extraction (PUREX) facility located at the Hanford Reservation.

c. This VOC is also known as tetrachloroethylene or tetrachloroethene.

d. The direct discharge of untreated sanitary wastewater and of process wastewaters containing radioactive and nonradioactive hazardous materials into the soil may have contaminated the soil and groundwater at the site.

e. Changes in ambient groundwater temperatures have been caused by effluent cooling waters.

was established in 1974. Managed by the DOE until 1998 (when Congress transferred management responsibilities to the U.S. Army Corps of Engineers), it covers forty-six sites in more than a dozen states, most rather small, that at one time handled nuclear materials. These range from the Combustion Engineering Site in Windsor, Connecticut, which did work for the aircraft nuclear propulsion program (see chapter 2), to the Alba Craft shop in Oxford, Ohio, which machined uranium for the Fernald Plant, or Grand Valley, Colorado, site of a Project Plowshare test to study the use of nuclear explosives to stimulate natural gas production. As of the end of 1997, remedial work had already been completed at twenty-five FUSRAP sites.

The second program, overseen by the DOE, is the Uranium Mill Tailings Remedial Action Program (UMTRA), which manages sites formerly involved in mining and processing uranium ore. For every metric ton of uranium extracted from ore, hundreds of metric tons of waste were produced in the form of mill tailings—a finely ground radioactive material with the consistency of sand.[67] The DOE shares responsibility for cleaning up these sites with private energy companies under the Uranium Mill Tailings Radiation Control Act of 1978.[68] There about twenty-four UMTRA sites, principally former mines and factories in Colorado, Montana, and Utah. As of February 1996, surface contamination at sixteen UMTRA sites had been fully cleaned up.

The costs for both FUSRAP and UMTRA through 1996 are included in DOE's overall (nondefense) environmental restoration and waste management (ERWM) budget. According to GAO testimony in 1996, UMTRA's costs have increased 37 percent since its creation in 1979, and the program is currently behind schedule.[69] If the surface cleanup is completed in 1998, eight years later than anticipated, it will likely cost $2.4 billion. The groundwater cleanup, for which preparatory work began in 1991, could be completed by 2014, at a cost of at least $147 million, depending on the method selected by the DOE and whether states in which the sites are located elect to pay their share of the costs.[70] FUSRAP activities have cost more than $499 million since 1981. Total projected costs through 2016 are estimated by the DOE at more than $1 billion.

67. Lax oversight on the part of the AEC allowed significant amounts of tailings to be used in construction projects, including homes and schools, during the 1950s and 1960s, exposing unsuspecting people to highly elevated levels of radon. See Metzger, *The Atomic Establishment,* pp. 161–92.

68. Under the act, P.L. 95-604, the DOE is responsible for mines and processing plants involved in the nuclear weapons program while the private companies, under the oversight of the NRC, handle activities at sites that produced materials for the civilian nuclear power program.

69. Despite this, the Congressional Budget Office in May 1994 characterized UMTRA as, "perhaps the brightest spot in DOE's cleanup record." U.S. Congressional Budget Office, *Cleaning Up the Department of Energy's Nuclear Weapons Complex,* May 1994, p. 12.

70. General Accounting Office, "Uranium Mill Tailings: Status and Future Costs of Cleanup," Statement of Bernice Steinhardt, Associate Director, Energy, Resources, and Science Issues,

Bikini and Enewetak

Atmospheric and underwater nuclear tests in the Pacific severely contaminated the coral atolls of Bikini and Enewetak.[71] In the 1960s, more than twenty years after being evacuated from their home, the Bikini islanders petitioned to be allowed to return home, and President Lyndon Johnson ordered the DOD and AEC to make Bikini habitable. On February 11, 1969, the Defense Atomic Support Agency and the AEC entered into an agreement to clean up the atoll, whereby DASA would do the physical work and the AEC would determine "the radiological health and safety requirements." However, a three-page Memorandum of Understanding concerning the cleanup explicitly stipulated that the effort "will not interfere significantly with the maintenance of the test readiness posture," the program known as Safeguard C, initiated in 1963 to permit the immediate resumption of atmospheric testing should the United States choose to withdraw from the Partial Test Ban Treaty (see chapter 1). Because the logistical and support requirements for operating in the Marshall Islands were to be shared between the two programs, the DOD and AEC (and later the DOE) sought to ensure that Safeguard C would always be the first priority. The costs to DASA, the AEC, and the Department of Interior for this effort totaled $10.7 million through 1975.[72]

In 1972 the United States returned the people of Bikini to their atoll, even though it was understood that the consumption of native foods would increase internal doses of radiation (the AEC believed that advice on what to eat and steady supplies of imported foods would keep the risk low). Within several years, however, a monitoring program showed increases in radiation doses and by 1978 the government was forced to reevacuate the atoll and undertake another cleanup. Although the islanders have returned for several visits in the intervening years, the cleanup continues and the atoll is still deemed uninhabitable. As a result, the Bikinians continue to live in exile, most of them in shacks on a desolate island called Kili, some 400 miles (644 kilometers) from their home. At Bikini, as on the other atolls, massive steel and concrete bunkers (some still contaminated) dot the landscape,

Resources, Community, and Economic Development Division, T-RCED-96-85, February 28, 1996; General Accounting Office, *Uranium Mill Tailings: Cleanup Continues, but Future Costs Are Uncertain*, RCED-96-37 (Decmber 1995).

71. The following section relies on International Physicians for the Prevention of Nuclear War and the Institute for Energy and Environmental Research, *Radioactive Heaven and Earth: The Health and Environmental Effects of Nuclear Weapons Testing in, On, and Above the Earth* (New York: Apex Press, 1991), pp. 79–81. In the late 1970s, the Defense Nuclear Agency estimated that some 154 acres, or about 8 percent of Enewetak's land area, was vaporized as a result of testing activities. Testing at Bikini, which occurred principally in the lagoon, did not result in such land loss. See U.S. General Accounting Office, *Enewetak Atoll—Cleaning Up Nuclear Contamination*, PSAD-79-54 (GPO, May 8, 1979), p. 13.

72. Data compiled by Tom Bell, Office of Health Studies, U.S. Department of Energy, July 1996, from Defense Nuclear Agency, *The Radiological Cleanup of Enewetak Atoll* (Alexandria, Va.: Defense Nuclear Agency, 1980). The original estimated cost in 1969 was $5.8 million.

silent testimony to the huge scale of the atmospheric testing program carried out on their islands from 1946 to 1958.

During 1972 and 1973, the AEC surveyed radiation levels on Enewetak, concluding in 1974 that any cleanup program must address plutonium-239 contamination, and deciding to apply more stringent standards than those used for Bikini and Rongelap (see chapter 7). As part of the cleanup effort, 1,000 personnel from the army, navy, and air force transported 111,000 cubic yards (84,927 cubic meters) of radioactive soil and debris to Runit Island, where it was placed in a 30-foot-deep (9-meter), 350-foot-wide (107-meter) crater left by the May 5, 1958, "Cactus" test. The material was then entombed beneath a dome composed of 358 concrete panels, each 18 inches (45.7 centimeters) thick. The unprecedented job, which took three years, was completed in 1980 at a cost of about $239 million.[73]

The Government's Moral Obligation

By building and operating nuclear production and testing facilities, the government incurred moral obligations both to the workers at these facilities and the communities that coalesced around them. In partial recognition of these obligations, the DOE and individual states have entered into legal agreements on cleanup, and the federal government has retained liability for past pollution and waste problems at the Paducah and Portsmouth gaseous diffusion plants even as those sites are privatized as the United States Enrichment Corporation.

However, most of the government's obligation is not based on statutory law, and the extent to which communities can depend on the DOE to clean up past (and future) contamination from weapons production is unclear. For example, during his official exit interview as under secretary of energy in the Bush administration, John Tuck declared that the DOE signed numerous cleanup agreements to allow the continued production of nuclear weapons, not to meet environmental needs, and that it did so knowing there would not be enough money to fulfill the terms of the contracts.[74] In addition, from fiscal 1990 through 1995, the DOE spent more than $97 million in legal fees defending contractors at its nuclear sites against citizen lawsuits relating to DOE's past and ongoing operations.[75]

---

73. Tabular data compiled by Tom Bell, Office of Health Studies, U.S. Department of Energy from a 1980 Defense Nuclear Agency report. These data indicate costs of about $188 million. An appendix in the DNA report indicates total then-year costs of $100 million, or about $239 million in 1996 dollars. The difference (amounting to $51 million in 1996 dollars) between this figure and the tabular data is not explained. However, the $100 million then-year cost is confirmed in General Accounting Office, *Enewetak Atoll—Cleaning Up Nuclear Contamination,* p. 3.

74. Mark Obmascik, "DOE 'Knew' Cleanup Pacts Doomed," *Denver Post,* March 1, 1994, p. A1.

75. Memorandum, Jane Taylor, U.S. DOE, Office of General Counsel, for Karen Rosenthal, May 22, 1995; *DOE and Contractor Litigation Costs,* Hearings, pp. 20–32, 84–104. According to Taylor,

Pollution created by the DOE and its predecessors while producing nuclear weapons imposes real economic costs on communities around nuclear production sites and shifts part of the true cost of nuclear weapons production to workers at the facilities. In *Silkwood* versus *Kerr-McGee Corporation,* the Supreme Court wrote: "The promotion of nuclear power is not to be accomplished 'at all costs.' . . . Congress therefore disclaimed any interest in promoting the development and utilization of atomic energy by means that fail to provide adequate remedies for those who are injured by exposure to hazardous nuclear materials."[76]

That the government and its contractors knew defense nuclear facilities could present health hazards is well established.[77] It is also well established that the federal government has continually underestimated the extent of these hazards and the cost of their remediation (see table 6-4 for the history of "cleanup" estimates).[78] Table 6-2 shows the rapid increase in spending for cleanup and waste management from 1990 to 1995. Annual obligations in 1996 were $5.7 billion (see also figure 6-3).

In its 1994–98 *Five-Year Plan,* the DOE stated that the plan "expresses the DOE commitment to a 30-year goal for . . . cleanup."[79] The 1995 DOE "base-case" estimate for site cleanup "assumes program activities through the year 2070," more than doubling the time thought necessary just one year earlier.[80] These statements indicate the long duration and difficulty of the cleanup program.[81]

"No cost information exists for fiscal years prior to FY 90," although such costs were certainly incurred. This total does not include DOE payment of fines levied upon contractors or the tens of millions of dollars expended in challenges to workers compensation lawsuits. Nor does it include more than $27 million spent by DOE to establish and maintain a litigation support database to assist in handling current and future litigation against current and former contractors. See U.S. General Accounting Office, *Managing DOE: The Department's Efforts to Control Litigation Costs,* T-RCED-96-170 (1996), p. 7.

76. *Silkwood* v. *Kerr-McGee Corporation* (104 S. Ct. 615 [1984]), p. 626.

77. See for example, *Early Health Problems of the U.S. Nuclear Weapons Industry and Their Implications for Today,* S. Rpt. 101-63, 101 Cong. 1 sess. (GPO, 1989); Metzger, *The Atomic Establishment,* especially pp. 115–44.

78. See also, Keith Schneider, "Cost of Cleanup at Nuclear Sites Is Raised by 50%," *New York Times,* July 4, 1990, p. A1; Matthew L. Wald, "U.S. Raises Estimates of Weapons Sites Cleanup," *New York Times,* September 6, 1991, p. A18; U.S. General Accounting Office, *Nuclear Health and Safety: More Can Be Done to Better Control Environmental Restoration Costs,* RCED-92-71 (April 1992).

79. DOE, *Environmental Restoration and Waste Management Five Year Plan, FY 1994–1998,* DOE/S-00097P, vol. 1 (GPO,), p. 1.

80. Thomas P. Grumbly, Assistant Secretary of Energy for Environmental Management, "Statement to the Committee on Armed Services," U.S. Senate, April 25, 1995, p. 7.

81. Even DOE studies of how best to handle the problem have gone over budget and beyond schedule. The Waste Management Programmatic Environmental Impact Statement, an unprecedented effort to assess the quantities and types of waste produced by the weapons complex and recommend solutions, was initiated in 1990 in response to a citizens' lawsuit. It was supposed to take three years and cost $8 million. The final report was not completed until six years later, at a cost of $59 million (both figures in then-year dollars). See Peter Eisler, "'Tragedy of Errors' Engulfs Toxic Material," *USA Today,* February 15, 1996, p. 1A. At least through the mid-1990s, the DOE reportedly spent significantly more than the private sector and other government agencies for equivalent environmental management projects (32 percent and 15 percent, respectively). These higher costs were said to be a function of DOE management practices, DOE cost overruns (48 percent on average), and schedule slippages (52 percent from initiation to completion), and were attributed to poor project definition. See Independent Project Analysis, Inc., *The Department of Energy, Office of Environmental Restoration & Waste Management: Project Performance Study* (November 1993), pp. iii–vii.

TABLE 6-4. Official Cost Estimates to "Clean Up" the DOE's Nuclear Weapons Production Complex, 1988–96

Billions of dollars

Date	*Estimate*	*Constant 1996 dollars*	*Completion date*	*Agency*
March 10, 1988	100	126	Unstated	GAO[a]
July 1, 1988	66–110	83–138	2025–45	DOE[b]
July 6, 1988	80–110	100–138	2013	GAO[c]
December 1988	53–92	64–111	Unstated (after 2010)	DOE[d]
December 1988	53.4	65	2010	DOE[e]
January 20, 1989	91–200	110–242	2040 (or longer)	DOE[f]
May 20, 1993	400	427	Unstated	DOE[g]
April 3, 1995	175–500	179–511	2070	DOE[h]
June 1996	200–400	200–400	2070	DOE[i]

a. "$100 Billion Seen for Atom Cleanup," *New York Times,* March 12, 1988, p. 30. J. Dexter Peach, GAO assistant comptroller general, offered this estimate in testimony before the Transportation, Tourism, and Hazardous Materials Subcommittee of the House Energy and Commerce Committee. At the same hearing, Joseph Salgado, undersecretary of energy, concurred that Peach's estimate "is probably in the ballpark."

b. U.S. Department of Energy, *Environment, Safety and Health Report for the Department of Energy Defense Complex,* July 1, 1988, pp. 34–35. This estimate excludes the following sites: Ames Laboratory, Argonne National Laboratory, Oak Ridge Gaseous Diffusion Plant (K-25), Paducah Gaseous Diffusion Plant, Portsmouth Gaseous Diffusion Plant, and the Waste Isolation Pilot Plant. It also does not include the costs of DOE naval nuclear propulsion facilities (Bettis Atomic Power Laboratory, Knolls Atomic Power Laboratory, and the Naval Reactors Facility at INEEL), FUSRAP or UMTRA.

c. General Accounting Office, *Nuclear Health and Safety: Dealing With Problems in the Nuclear Defense Complex Expected to Cost Over $100 Billion,* RCED-88-197BR (GAO, July 1988), pp. 1-6, 16–22. These figures are based on DOE data and do not include day-to-day operations costs. The report cautions that, with regard to disposing of radioactive wastes and cleaning up contaminated facilities, "DOE data indicate the eventual cost could easily exceed $45 billion." It also notes that "this cost information is not budget quality and should be used only to illustrate the magnitude of effort needed to address these problem areas over the next 25 years."

d. U.S. Department of Energy, *Environment, Safety, and Health Needs of The U.S. Department of Energy,* vol. 1 (GPO, 1988), p. 2. This estimate excludes the following sites: Bettis Atomic Power Laboratory, Knolls Atomic Power Laboratory, and the Naval Reactors Facility at INEEL). "Base program" costs (for day-to-day activities) are included only through 2010.

e. Report to Congress by the President, "United States Department of Energy Nuclear Weapons Complex Modernization Report" (2010 Report), December 1988, pp. 28–29. This estimate includes projected funding for "Defense Waste Management" (the storage, treatment, processing, and disposal of radioactive wastes) and "Environment, Safety, and Health" (to comply with current federal and state standards). The report states that the total estimated cost (up to and beyond 2010) for the environmental restoration program, "ranges from $40 to $70 billion."

f. "Cleanup Put at $57 Billion," *New York Times,* January 21, 1989, p. 11.

g. Paul Grimm, Acting Assistant Secretary for Environmental Restoration and Waste Management, U.S. Department of Energy, Speech to Stakeholder's Meeting, Boise, Idaho, May 20, 1993.

h. U.S. Department of Energy, *Estimating the Cold War Mortgage: The 1995 Baseline Environmental Management Report,* vol. 1, DOE/EM-0232 (GPO, 1995), pp. i, ix, xvi, 4.1–4.7. This estimate assumes significant productivity increases that will (in theory) reduce costs in future years. It excludes sites where cleanup is not feasible (for example, test shafts at the Nevada Test Site and contaminated groundwater), all currently active facilities (that is, Livermore, Los Alamos, Sandia, National Laboratories, and the Pantex Plant) and all naval nuclear propulsion facilities. It also excludes $23 billion (then-year dollars) expended for environmental restoration and waste management between fiscal 1989 and fiscal 1994 and all "cleanup" costs before 1989. Long-term surveillance and maintenance costs beyond 2070 ($50 million to $75 million annually) are also not included.

i. DOE Office of Environmental Management, *The 1996 Baseline Environmental Management Report.*

Because total and annual cleanup costs are so high, many people have seriously discussed the possibility of leaving polluted DOE sites as "sacrifice zones"; that is, they could simply be fenced off and left as unusable land. Mark Silverman, the former manager of Rocky Flats, suggested that buildings at that site should be buried, not cleaned up, and preserved as "a monument to the Cold War."[82] In 1993 both Senator John Glenn (Democrat of Ohio) and Peter A. Johnson, the project director of a comprehensive 1991 Congressional Office of Technology Assessment report on the cleanup program,[83] suggested that one way to deal with the most heavily contaminated parts of the Fernald plant in southwestern Ohio might be to "put a fence around it." The *Washington Post* editorialized in mid-1994 that the high costs of the cleanup program were acceptable "only if the money is buying more health protection than it could if aimed at other kinds of pollution. . . . [I]n some of these cases it may be wiser and safer as a matter of environmental policy to leave them alone for another half-century."[84]

Aside from the potential health hazards, land-use problems, community problems, and tax base problems these so-called "national sacrifice zones" would create, they would violate the government's moral obligation to ensure the health and safety of its citizens. Fencing off parcels of contaminated land will not halt the migration of contaminated groundwater or surface water. Such a policy, moreover, offers no guarantee at all that the long-lived contaminants on site will not have an impact on generations far into the future. Finally, considerable expenditures must be incurred in any case to safeguard plutonium and plutonium-contaminated materials at various sites that could be used to make weapons. Thus, even apart from any moral obligations and cleanup, large costs at shutdown DOE facilities are unavoidable (see chapter 5).

Assessing the DOE's Cost Assumptions

Before 1989 the DOE allocated very little specific funding to long-term environmental remediation. The typical methods of waste disposal simply created more long-term cleanup problems. For instance, for decades large quantities of radioactive waste were routinely placed in cardboard boxes and dumped into shallow, unlined dirt trenches, a practice that is prohibited today. Moreover, the assumption was that

82. "Don't Clean Up Flats Buildings, Bury Them, Plant Manager Says," *Gazette Telegraph* (Colorado Springs), February 20, 1994, p. B6.

83. U.S. Congress, Office of Technology Assessment, *Complex Cleanup: The Environmental Legacy of Nuclear Weapons Production* OTA-O-484 (GPO, 1991); U.S. Congress, Office of Technology Assessment, *Long-Lived Legacy: Managing High-Level and Transuranic Waste as the DOE Nuclear Weapons Complex,* Background Paper OTA-BP-O-83 (GPO, 1991).

84. Paul Barton, "Possible Fernald Fix: 'Put a Fence Around It'," *Cincinnati Enquirer,* November 2, 1993, p. B2; "Cleaning Up the Nuclear Sites," *Washington Post,* June 16, 1994, p. A24.

nuclear weapons production on a large scale would continue indefinitely, so that the question of the remediation of the sites and their return to the public, either on a restricted or unrestricted basis, did not arise with any particular urgency.[85]

Today it is clear that most sites and most facilities will be shut forever, and that there will be little if any new nuclear weapons production in past facilities (the principal exception will be the TA-55 facility at Los Alamos, which is being upgraded to produce a small number of plutonium pits; see chapter 1). The main activities at most locations will be related to waste management and cleanup, though the ultimate scale of and funding for those activities remains uncertain.

In presenting estimates for the cost of waste management and cleanup, we have focused primarily on activities specifically designated as such since 1989, when Secretary of Energy James D. Watkins created a separate office and budget category for this work. There were, of course, expenditures on waste management before 1989. However, these were primarily oriented to maintaining ongoing operations and before 1978 were generally subsumed within the overall production budget (except for obligations of $15.3 million, $22.6 million, and $59.4 million in 1971, 1972, and 1974, respectively). Cleanup-related activities as currently defined were more or less minimal, with $8.5 billion in funding from 1971 to 1998 supporting the WIPP, the DWPF at the Savannah River Site, and the operation of the Hanford tanks (see figure 6-3). In some cases the DOE was in compliance with regulations that would have applied to nonnuclear, nonmilitary industries, whereas in others it was not. Such compliance issues took on greater budgetary importance in the mid- to late-1980s, when the courts, in response to challenges by environmental organizations such as the Natural Resources Defense Council, required the DOE to comply with environmental laws. These interpretations of environmental statutes were followed by similar requirements from the states and by new laws passed by Congress, most specifically the Federal Facilities Compliance Act (FFCA) of October 6, 1992.

For these reasons, for the period 1946–70, we have counted all DOE-related waste management and similar expenditures under production costs in chapter 1. The costs of waste management and environmental remediation from 1971 onward fall under "environmental management" and are discussed in this chapter. We also include a portion of environment, safety, and health (ES&H) costs under cleanup costs. ES&H costs are allocated by prorating them according to the size of the defense programs budget in relation to the EM budget. The

85. For example, in April 1997, Jim McGrail, director of DOE's stockpile stewardship program at the Nevada Test Site, told the Associated Press that "in 1983, we were projecting the nuclear weapons program would double in the next 20 years." Robert Macy, "Nearly Completed Nuclear Test Site in Need of Mission," *Philadelphia Inquirer*, April 6, 1997, p. A2.

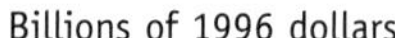

FIGURE 6-3. DOE Spending on Environmental Remediation and Waste Management Programs, 1978–96[a]

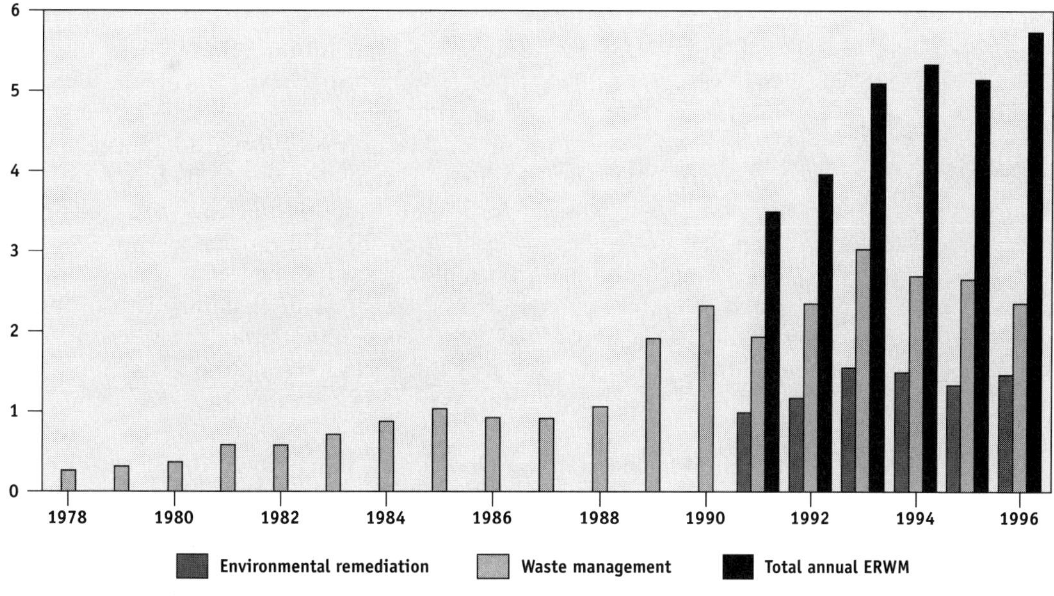

a. Breakout between ER and WM categories not provided in budget documents until 1991. From 1978 to 1989, essentially all funding went toward waste management activities. ER and WM categories do not equal total EM spending because of additional expenditures (not shown) for corrective activities, stabilization efforts, technology development, transportation management, and program direction.

ES&H costs add about 1 percent to the cost of waste management and cleanup, as determined from official budget data for 1992–96. For 1995–2070, we have added 1 percent to the DOE cost estimates.

As already noted, in 1995 the DOE issued its first *Baseline Environmental Management Report*. The DOE issued revised, lower estimates for cleanup costs in the June 1996 update of this report. Unlike the 1995 report, however, the 1996 version does not provide the full range of estimates for all the sites considered, but only for the most expensive five sites that represent 70 percent of all estimated cleanup costs. The range for these five sites is stated to be \$150 billion to \$284 billion.[86] By extrapolating these costs on a proportional basis to cover all reported sites, we calculated that cleanup costs range from \$214 billion to \$406 billion. Adding 1 percent for ES&H costs brings this to \$216 billion to \$410 billion. We have rounded these off and use the range of

86. DOE Office of Environmental Management, *The 1996 Baseline Environmental Management Report*, Executive Summary, p. xxiii.

$200 billion to $400 billion for total estimated cleanup costs, or a midrange cost of $300 million. The lower range of costs corresponds to a minimal caretaker function known as the "Iron Fence" scenario. The 1996 upper-limit estimate is about $100 billion lower than that given in the 1995 report.

It is important to understand what the minimal end of the cost range represents. The DOE estimates that just to keep the dangers posed by existing wastes and contamination from getting worse would require an expenditure of $175 billion over a period of seventy-five years from 1995 onward. The principal costs would be for converting high-level waste to solid form and disposing of it, for treating plutonium that now exists in unstable forms, and for managing spent fuel that is deteriorating. All buried wastes would be left in place. Contaminated sites for which no method of remediation currently exists (encompassing problems likely to pose the highest future costs) were essentially assigned a null cost and excluded from the assessment. This practice further distorts the magnitude of the problem.[87]

In the summer of 1996 the DOE examined further measures for reducing estimated cleanup costs. One suggestion was to accelerate the cleanup of certain sites so as to reduce landlord function costs, and to change cleanup goals from those in existing compliance agreements. This effort is called *Accelerating Cleanup: Paths to Closure.* It remains highly controversial because it includes proposals to accelerate waste disposal and implies relaxed cleanup guidelines in many cases by restricting future site uses to larger areas than previously assumed. Even with an accelerated effort, the majority of costs in the EM program will be incurred after 2006, and those sites "completed" by that time will require institutional controls and long-term monitoring, the costs of which are not factored into the current program.

The DOE's latest estimates do not include the costs of cleaning up facilities currently in operation—such as the Pantex Plant in Amarillo, Texas; the weapons laboratories in Livermore, California, and Los Alamos and Albuquerque, New Mexico; or various naval nuclear propulsion facilities in Idaho, New York, Connecticut, and Pennsylvania[88]—or the long-term costs to the communities for monitoring environmental impacts and enforcing site-use restrictions. Nor do they include the $27 billion that was obligated from 1989 through 1995 (48 percent for waste management, 26 percent for environmental remediation, and 26 percent for corrective activities, facility stabilization, technology development, transpiration management, and program direction).

87. U.S. Department of Energy, Office of Environmental Management, *Estimating the Cold War Mortgage: The 1995 Baseline Evnvironmental Management Report,* DOE/EM-0232, vol. 1 (GPO, 1995), p. 5.6.

88. U.S. Department of Energy, *Estimating the Cold War Mortgage,* pp. ix–xi.

One of the most critical omissions in the DOE estimates is the cost of handling situations in which contamination is so severe that there is no foreseeable technical means of cleaning it up. The most important site in this regard is the Nevada Test Site, where testing has left millions of curies of fission products and thousands of kilograms of unfissioned plutonium at and around the 804 underground test locations. According to the DOE, "No cost-effective technologies exist for restoring these sites."[89] In addition, in September 1996 the National Research Council criticized DOE's plans for the Hanford Reservation stating, "Not enough information is currently available for choosing the best long-term cleanup" plan. Noting that DOE's final environmental impact statement for the site only addresses what should be done with the tens of millions of gallons of high-level waste, "not what should be done with the tanks themselves or waste that has leaked into the surrounding environment," the Council concluded that, "significant uncertainties exist in the areas of technology, costs, performance, regulatory environment, future land use and health and environmental risks."[90]

The DOE estimate of cleanup costs is not merely incomplete; it also fails to suggest how those costs might be used to establish specific standards of cleanup. Nor is it oriented to any specific reduction of risk. Indeed, the EPA, acting on a DOE request, has abandoned plans to issue cleanup standards, although it retains the theoretical option of continuing to formulate them. The overall figures are derived from a compilation of costs made by its contractors and its field offices. These parties clearly have a vested interest in keeping cost estimates high. The fact that just five major contractors are at present responsible for waste management and remediation efforts at the complex's ten most contaminated sites—with the Lockheed Martin Corporation alone in charge of four major sites—tends to exacerbate this problem (see appendix C). To counter this tendency and to take into account past misdirected spending and waste, DOE headquarters applied a set of factors to reduce costs submitted by the field offices. The resulting figures are presented as estimates savings owing to various unspecified efficiency improvements. In reality, these are by and large arbitrary factors that are not based on DOE experience. Despite a greater degree of detail, it is therefore difficult to treat these new cleanup cost estimates as significantly more accurate than previous ones. The draft *Accelerating Cleanup* plan does not utilize these arbitrary factors, although it does compound the DOE's earlier problems by omitting long-term costs and implicitly assuming less stringent remediation standards.

89. DOE Office of Environmental Management, *1996 Baseline Environmental Management Report,* vol. 2, pp. Nevada 3–Nevada 29.

90. Associated Press, "Hanford Cleanup Plan Too Limited, Panel Says," *Washington Post,* September 9, 1996, p. A17.

What the baseline report does underscore is that solutions will be expensive and will take many years to implement. At this stage, the *Baseline Environmental Management Report* provides the most comprehensive look at the problem. For that reason we have used its estimates here, though they will undoubtedly have to be revised again, not least because the scope and duration of this undertaking is truly unprecedented. The DOE's track record with far smaller projects is not reassuring. From 1980 through 1996, out of eighty projects designated as "major system acquisitions," only fifteen have been completed, with many of these behind schedule and over budget. Thirty-one other projects were terminated before completion (after expenditures of more than $10 billion in then-year dollars) and the remaining thirty-four are still in progress. But many of these have experienced cost overruns and are behind schedule.[91]

In a possible portent of things to come, in April 1997 a contractor working on what was supposed to be DOE's showcase effort to lower costs by shifting remediation work to private contractors requested an additional $157 million (on top of an original fixed-price contract of $200 million) to retrieve buried transuranic waste from a heavily contaminated 1-acre plot at INEEL, known as Pit 9. Although $54 million (then-year dollars) had been expended studying the problem and building the retrieval technology, no actual work had started. Idaho state officials blamed the DOE for the problems, the DOE blamed the contractor (Lockheed Martin Advanced Environmental Systems Co.) for basing its plans on an untested technology, and the contractor blamed the DOE bureaucracy and greater-than-expected wastes at the site (and asked for its contract to be revised to the more traditional DOE cost-reimbursement formula). The DOE has been working since 1993 to overhaul its archaic contracting system to ensure greater accountability. The contract for this particular project is part of that effort and allowed Lockheed considerable leeway, as part of a bargain to pay a fixed price for cleanup. Now, in the face of increased costs, the project is running into a conflict between the DOE, Lockheed Martin, and the overall site contractor, which is another subsidiary of Lockheed Martin. DOE spokesman Brad Bugger simply stated that the department, despite owning the site, had no managerial control over its contractor. "You have to understand the nature of the contract," he told the Associated Press. "We can't dictate how they do their work."[92]

91. U.S. General Accounting Office, *Department of Energy: Opportunity to Improve Management of Major System Acquisitions*, RCED-97-17 (November 1996).

92. Associated Press, "Lockheed Ups Tab for Nuclear Cleanup in Idaho," *Washington Times*, April 22, 1997, p. A8; Mark Maremont, "DOE's Pilot Plan to Privatize Cleanup of Nuclear Waste May End at Pit 9," *Wall Street Journal*, July 28, 1997, p. A20; Fioravanti and Makhijani, *Containing the Cold War Mess*, pp. 131–47; General Accounting Office, *Nuclear Waste: Department of Energy's Project to Clean Up Pit 9 at Idaho Falls Is Experiencing Problems*, RCED-97-80 (July 1997); John Mintz, "Lockheed Martin Mired in Toxic Mess Cleanup," *Washington Post*, October 5, 1997, p. A14.

Table 6-5 shows a summary of EM costs and associated ES&H costs for the five most expensive sites in the DOE complex. The unadjusted figures are based on data obtained from the sites themselves before being adjusted by DOE headquarters staff. In brief, cleanup costs from 1989 to the year 2070 could range from a low of about $200 billion, which would leave a trail of highly contaminated and dangerous sites for future generations to deal with, to $400 billion or more when all sites are taken into account.

Department of Defense Nuclear Cleanup

The DOD also expends funds for cleaning up nuclear weapons sites, although on a much smaller scale than the DOE.[93] (On the work of other agencies in nuclear waste matters, see box 6-1.) This is principally because the deployment, storage, and maintenance of nuclear weapons typically generates significantly less waste than their testing and production. DOD's environmental burden is thus largely one of toxic chemicals and retired facilities. DOD funding falls within two programs, the Defense Environmental Restoration Account (DERA) and the Base Realignment and Closure account (BRAC). DERA funds work at operational facilities, while a portion of the BRAC program addresses problems at recently closed bases. The entire effort is part of the Defense Environmental Restoration Program (DERP). In 1991 the DOD estimated the total cost of cleaning up its facilities (nuclear weapons–related and otherwise) to be $25 billion; by 1996 this figure had risen to nearly $30 billion. In 1993 the DOD identified 11,000 individual polluted sites at 900 facilities but only completed work at 372 of the sites; by 1996 some 26,500 sites had been identified, with work completed at 1,700. Unlike the larger ERWM program managed by the DOE, DERP receives about $2 billion a year.

Some of the facilities included under DERP are the hundreds of bases established for the air defense mission in the 1950s and 1960s, nuclear weapons depots, and air and missile bases. The DOD has also identified some "potentially contaminated" sites. The following list identifies these sites and the cause of contamination:[94] Barksdale Air

93. *Radiological Contamination in the United States,* Hearings before the Senate Committee on Governmental Affairs, 102 Cong. 2 sess. (GPO, 1993), pp. 182–91, 226–72; Daryl Kimball, Lenny Siegel, and Peter Tyler, *Covering the Map: A Survey of Military Pollution Sites in the United States* (Washington, D.C.: Physicians for Social Responsibility, and the Military Toxics Project, May 1993).

94. U.S. Senate 1992, *Radiological Contamination in the United States,* pp. 259–72. The effort to characterize radioactively contaminated sites has been complicated by the paucity of basic data maintained by the various services regarding the amount and types of radioactivity at any given location. At Johnston Island, for example, air force data failed to mention significant plutonium contamination from launch pad accidents. Since August 1993, the Defense Special Weapons Agency has operated (a specially built plant on Johnston Island to clean 180,000 metric tons of plutonium-contaminated soil by scanning it for radioactivity and extracting the plutonium. A of March 1997, about 110,000 metric

TABLE 6-5. The DOE's Five Most Expensive Contaminated Sites

Billions of undiscounted 1996 dollars

Site	*Estimated cleanup cost*
Hanford Reservation	50.2
Savannah River Site	48.8
Oak Ridge Reservation	25.1
Idaho National Engineering and Environmental Laboratory	18.6
Rocky Flats Environmental Technology Site	17.3
Total	160.0

Source: U.S. Department of Energy, Office of Environmental Management, *The 1996 Baseline Environmental Management Report,* table 4-2, p. 4-14.

Force Base (Louisiana), contaminated soil and debris from July 6, 1959 C-124 crash (Broken Arrow); Davis-Monthan Air Force Base (Arizona), fission products from nuclear-cloud-sampling aircraft missions (washdown debris); Grissom Air Force Base (Illinois), B-58 remains, magnesium-thorium alloy; Holloman Air Force Base (New Mexico), fission products from nuclear-cloud-sampling aircraft missions (washdown debris); Johnston Island (Pacific Ocean), plutonium-contaminated lagoon and contaminated launcher facility (from accidents on June 4, July 25, and October 15, 1962); Kirtland Air Force Base (New Mexico), contaminated animal carcasses from radiation experiments; McGuire Air Force Base (New Jersey), plutonium-239 from June 7, 1960, BOMARC explosion and fire;[95] Nellis Air Force Base (Nevada), fission products from nuclear-cloud-sampling aircraft missions (washdown debris); Vandenberg Air Force Base (California), BOMARC missile remains.

Because allocating DOD cleanup costs to the nuclear weapons program on a site-by-site basis is beyond the scope of this project, we adopt a more general yet conservative approach. Assuming that the DOD's estimate of $30 billion for the total effort is correct, and finding that DOD nuclear weapons spending has accounted for about 29 percent of all military-related spending since World War II (not including funds to be spent in the future for the deferred costs of cleaning up the DOE weapons production complex and dismantling weapons), we estimate that some $8.7 billion (29 percent of the total projected cost) will

tons had been cleaned, and the work was expected to continue for an additional five years. See, U.S. General Accounting Office, *Environmental Cleanup: Better Data Needed for Radioactively Contaminated Defense Sites,* NSIAD-94-168 (August 1994), esp. pp. 3–4; Defense Special Weapons Agency, "Plutonium-Contaminated Soil Cleanup Plant," fact sheet, March 1997.

95. For more details on this accident, see chapter 4, fn. 33, in this volume.

be needed to address radioactive and toxic waste problems attributable to supporting nuclear forces. However, if DOD's estimating experience is anything like DOE's, actual costs are likely to be much higher. Through 1996, DERA had spent more than $15 billion, of which (under the preceding formula) some $4.4 billion is potentially attributable to the nuclear weapons mission).

The enormous financial costs of waste management and cleanup are only part of the legacy of nuclear weapons production during the cold war. Past and future health-related costs have been and will continue to be incurred far into the future. These issues are addressed in the next chapter.

Box 6-1

Other Key Agencies

Some of the other key agencies that play a role in environmental remediation and nuclear waste decisions are the Public Health Service, the Environmental Protection Agency, the Defense Nuclear Facilities Safety Board, and the Nuclear Waste Technical Review Board.

Public Health Service and Environmental Protection Agency

Starting in 1948, the AEC worked with the Public Health Service (PHS) to provide baseline environmental surveys around the Hanford Reservation and the Savannah River Plant before the start of production efforts, to monitor the health effects of radiation exposure at uranium mines and mills in Colorado, and to study the discharge of radioactive wastewater at Hanford and the Oak Ridge Reservation. These activities continued through 1970, at a total cost of $997 million. Through 1960, the AEC transferred funds to PHS to cover the costs of this work (they are therefore subsumed, in whole or in part, under production-related costs in chapter 1). The total cost to the PHS from fiscal 1961 to 1970 was $942 million.[1] In January 1971, the PHS off-site radiological monitoring effort was transferred to the newly created Environmental Protection Agency (EPA). EPA continues this work today at both operational and proposed facilities. It is also involved in setting standards for contamination and radiation exposure arising from waste disposal at proposed repositories. EPA's costs for this work from 1971 to 1991 were about $400 million. Between 1991 and 1996 it spent an estimated $16 million to oversee environmental compliance at DOE facilities. Adding in DOD facilities brings the total to approximately $137 million over this period.[2]

---

1. Letter with enclosures, Lynn Page Snyder, Staff Historian, Public Health Service, to Stephen I. Schwartz, March 25, 1995.

2. Calculations based on budget data provided by Melba Meador, Environmental Protection Agency, Public Liaison Division, March 17, 1997, and U.S. Environmental Protection Agency, *The State of Federal Facilities: A Comprehensive Overview of the Environmental Compliance Status of Federal Facilities through the End of FY 1992*, EPA 300-R-94-001 (GPO, 1994); and U.S. Environmental Protection Agency, *The State*

BOX 6-1
(continued)

Defense Nuclear Facilities Safety Board

In the late 1980s Congress established two organizations to provide it and the DOE with advice on nuclear weapons and nuclear waste matters. The Defense Nuclear Facilities Safety Board (DNFSB) was created to provide some independent oversight of the DOE's weapons complex (earlier bills to provide even greater authority and jurisdiction were watered down by members of the House and Senate Armed Services Committees who acted after DOE officials criticized the proposals as unwarranted and burdensome). The DNFSB currently has jurisdiction over most nuclear weapons facilities (except the naval nuclear sites) and conducts inspections, holds hearings, and provides regular advice to the secretary of energy. It has no regulatory authority to enforce its recommendations. Through 1996, its costs totaled $102 million.[3]

Nuclear Waste Technical Review Board

The Nuclear Waste Technical Review Board (NWTRB) was established in 1987 (although it did not begin operating until fiscal 1989) as an independent, eleven-member review board appointed by the president to "evaluate the technical and scientific validity of activities undertaken" under the Nuclear Waste Policy Amendments Act of 1987 in support of the national geologic repository for high-level radioactive waste. The board may hold hearings and is required to submit semiannual reports to Congress and the secretary of energy on its "findings, conclusions, and recommendations." Since fiscal 1989, the NWTRB's operations have cost some $21 million. The board is to remain in existence until the commencement of radioactive waste disposal in a repository.[4]

---

of Federal Facilities: An Overview of Environmental Compliance at Federal Facilities, FY 1993–94, EPA 300-R-96-002 (GPO, 1995).

3. Data provided by Carole Morgan, Defense Nuclear Facilities Safety Board, May 24, 1995.

4. Data provided by Frank Randall, Nuclear Waste Technical Review Board, May 22, 1995. All NWTRB funding comes from the nuclear waste fund administered by the DOE's Office of Civilian Radioactive Waste Management.

FIGURE 7-1. The Costs of Victims of the Bomb[a]

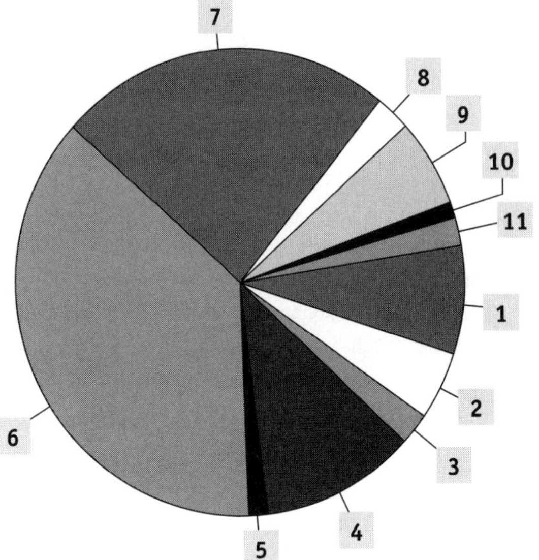

Total: $2.05 billion

1. Nuclear Test Personnel Review
   $158 million / 7.7%
2. Fernald residents' lawsuit settlement
   $94 million / 4.6%
3. Fernald workers' lawsuit settlement
   $50 million / 2.4%
4. Radiation Exposure Compensation Act payments
   $225 million / 11.0%
5. U.S. Transuranium and Uranium Registries
   $30 million / 1.5%
6. Marshall Islands compensation
   $759 million / 37.0%
7. Radiation Effects Research Foundation
   $500 million / 24.4%
8. Dose reconstruction studies
   $51 million / 2.5%
9. Palomares accident cleanup and settlement
   $120 million / 5.9%
10. Advising Committee on Human Radiation Experiments/DOE support
    $23 million / 1.1%
11. Other
    - Thule accident cleanup
      $9 million / 0.4%
    - *Fukuyru Maru* compensation
      $15 million / 0.7%
    - Human radiation experiments (University of Cincinnati only)
      $5 million / 0.2%
    - Plutonium injections lawsuit settlement
      $7 million / 0.3%

a. In constant 1996 dollars. Breakout does not match total because of rounding.

7

Victims of the Bomb

Arjun Makhijani and Stephen I. Schwartz

Although nuclear weapons have not been used in war since the bombing of Nagasaki on August 9, 1945, the nuclear arms race has had many casualties.[1] As a result of fallout from U.S. atmospheric testing between 1945 and 1963, an estimated 70,000 to 800,000 people in the United States and around the world have died or will die prematurely from a fatal cancer attributable to the testing (a comparable number of fatalities would be attributable to the Soviet testing program).[2] Many of the 500,000 to 600,000 people who have worked in the nuclear weapons production complex over the past five decades, especially in the 1940s and 1950s, may have been exposed to significant doses of radiation, along with toxic chemicals used in the manufacturing process. In many cases, however, poor or fraudulent record-keeping

1. Parts of this chapter first appeared (in a different format) in Arjun Makhijani, "Energy Enters Guilty Plea," *Bulletin of the Atomic Scientists,* vol. 50 (March/April 1994), pp. 18–28; and Arjun Makhijani, Howard Hu, and Katherine Yih, eds., *Nuclear Wastelands: A Global Guide to Nuclear Weapons Production and Its Health and Environmental Effects* (Cambridge, Massachusetts: MIT Press, 1995). They are reprinted here with the kind permission of the original publishers.

2. See discussion beginning on p. 428. Figures based on "A Report of the IPPNW International Commission to Investigate the Health and Environmental Effects of Nuclear Weapons Production"; and the Institute for Energy and Environmental Research, *Radioactive Heaven and Earth: The Health and Environmental Effects of Nuclear Weapons Testing in, on, and above the Earth* (New York: Apex Press, 1991), pp. 33–47. See also the cancer risk coefficients in Committee on the Biological Effects of Ionizing Radiation, Board on Radiation Effects Research, Commission on Life Sciences, National Research Council, *Health Effects of Exposure to Low Levels of Ionizing Radiation: BEIR V* (Washington, D.C.: National Academy Press, 1990).

prevents an accurate assessment of their actual doses.[3] At least some of the 220,000 military personnel who took part in atmospheric nuclear tests in the 1940s–60s have died or developed serious health ailments attributable to their participation.

Over the years, the government (often only after years of prodding and litigation) has provided modest financial compensation to some victims, although many maintain the sums are inadequate. In December 1993 the Department of Energy admitted that for many years it conducted radiation experiments on largely unsuspecting populations, an admission that provoked widespread outrage and further diminished public trust in the government and government nuclear activities in particular. Although these human costs resist quantification, any discussion of the costs to date of nuclear weapons must attempt to take them into account. The directly quantifiable costs associated with victims of U.S. nuclear weapons and weapons-related programs since 1945 totals almost $2.1 billion (figure 7-1).

Exposed Populations

Broadly speaking, the manufacture and deployment of nuclear weapons has exposed seven groups of people to environmental and health dangers: (1) workers in uranium mines and mills and in nuclear weapons design, production, and testing facilities; (2) armed-forces personnel who participated in atmospheric weapons testing; (3) people living near nuclear weapons sites; (4) human experiment subjects; (5) armed forces personnel and other workers who were exposed during deployment, transportation, and other handling and maintenance of weapons within the Department of Defense; (6) residents of Hiroshima and Nagasaki in August 1945;[4] and (7) the world's inhabitants for centuries to come.

The first three categories include more than 1 million people. Assessing the number of people in the fourth, fifth, and seventh categories is fraught with methodological difficulties, as this chapter makes clear. (The members of category six are addressed in box 7-1.)

Workers in Nuclear Weapons Facilities

Workers in nuclear weapons production and testing facilities have been among the most heavily exposed populations (along with mem-

3. For instances of fabricated data and poor records, see Institute for Energy and Environmental Research, *Science for Democratic Action,* vol. 5, no. 3 (1996).

4. An estimated 210,000 persons were killed by the bombings or died from injuries suffered in the immediate aftermath (through the end of 1945). The survivors received varying doses of radiation. See Richard Rhodes, *The Making of the Atomic Bomb* (New York: Simon & Schuster, 1986), pp. 733–34, 740, 742.

Box 7-1

Monitoring the Aftermath of Hiroshima and Nagasaki

Since 1946, the United and Japan have jointly supported a program to conduct detailed studies of the survivors of the bombings of Hiroshima and Nagasaki. From 1946 to 1975, this effort was called the Atomic Bomb Casualty Commission (ABCC). It was directed by the National Research Council of the National Academy of Sciences (under contract with the AEC) and the Japanese National Institute of Health. From 1975 onward it has been known as the Radiation Effects Research Foundation (RERF) and managed by the National Academy of Sciences and the Japanese Ministry of Health and Welfare. It is still funded in the same way, except that the DOE is now the source.

Estimates of the health risks of low-level radiation have been based in large part on data from this program. It has also been used to establish criteria for radiation exposure for nuclear plant workers and (in all likelihood) contributed to military efforts during the 1950s to 1970s to understand some potential effects of the nuclear battlefield. In mid-March 1954, following the return of the *Daigo Fukuryu Maru* and its fallout-dusted crew (see page 421), American doctors in Japan working with the ABCC, volunteered to treat the twenty-three fishermen. An annual survey of adults in Hiroshima in 1993 examined 4,003 persons (approximately 80 percent of the survivors there).

Because RERF's overall budgetary data are maintained in Japan, a detailed reconstruction of its historical costs is beyond the means of this study. However, an official connected with the program provided some general guidelines for estimating costs.[1] On that basis, it appears that from 1946 to 1996 the ABCC/RERF has cost the United States $500 million. Part of this cost, however, is attributable to the military uses of atomic energy. Other parts, which cannot be separated, must be attributed to radiation standard-setting and risk assessment in general.

1. Radiation Effects Research Foundation, *Annual Report, 1 April 1993—31 March 1994*; personal communication, Al Lazen, RERF (National Research Council), April 21, 1995.

bers of the armed forces, some victims of human experimentation, and some people living downwind of nuclear weapons facilities). However, the extent of exposure and health damage varies considerably within the populations of workers and depends greatly on the specific nature of their duties and length of service. Generally speaking, workers who served in the first two decades of nuclear weapon production, that is until the mid-1960s or so, were the most heavily exposed.[5]

5. Conditions were even worse for their Soviet counterparts. In May 1996, at a conference in Dubna, Russia, more than 300 people—mostly Russian—gathered to discuss the history of the Soviet nuclear weapons program. A chemist, Liya Sokhina, recalled that in 1948, at age twenty-three, she worked in the Mayak complex (then known as Chelyabinsk-40 and subsequently as Chelyabinsk-65) collecting plutonium oxide from the rafters using a dust broom and bag. Sokhina worked without gloves or a mask. The plutonium was in the rafters because of a pyrophoric explosion (metallic plutonium exposed to air can spontaneously ignite and burn). Such explosions were apparently all too routine, necessitat-

Workers faced the hazards not only of radioactive exposure but also of a large number of nonradioactive toxic materials, including fluorine gas, hydrofluoric acid, nitric acid, organic compounds (for example, carbon tetrachloride, trichloroethylene, EDTA, and HEDTA), and toxic metals such as beryllium, mercury, and chromium. Records of exposures to radioactivity dating back to the Manhattan Project still exist. Even though these records are seriously deficient in a number of ways, they can be used to assess collective exposures and hence risks to groups of workers. Individual assessments of health damage and risk are far more difficult. In contrast, there are practically no records of worker exposure to nonradioactive toxic materials. Even routine measurements of most of these materials in the air at the plants were not made. Almost no reliable data are available on the potential synergistic effects on human beings of combined exposures to radiation and nonradioactive toxic materials.[6]

Until 1994, the government insisted that worker exposures were generally low and that there were no significant, large-scale, adverse health effects on the 500,000 to 600,000 people who have worked in the U.S. nuclear weapons complex since its creation in 1942 (notwithstanding evidence and warnings from the Atomic Energy Commission's own contractors as early as 1947 that, for example, radioactive particles emitted by facilities at the Hanford Reservation "can produce radiation damage," and "the theoretical possibility of injury developing 10 to 15 years from now poses a serious problem.")[7] But in March 1994, the DOE admitted the following serious problems in its worker dosimetry record:[8] (1) there was little information on nonradioactive hazardous materials and essentially no records on worker dose; (2) records for exposure to external radiation were incomplete, unreliable, and misleading, in part because of poorly calibrated measuring devices, the issuance of multiple badges, and poor placement of dosimeters; (3) internal exposure records were unreliable; (4) the electronic version of radiation records "did not accurately reflect the data on the original record"; and (5) methods for measuring and calculating doses varied considerably from one facility to another, so that

---

ing frequent cleanups, even outside the building on the roof, in subzero temperatures. "Most of the plutonium went out in waste or ended up on the ceiling as dust . . . only 40% of the metallic Pu made it through fabrication. . . . Typical radiation doses were 100 rad per year," she said. "We were constantly breathing radioactive aerosols . . . respiratory diseases were widespread . . . many colleagues died in the 1950s . . . the doctors worked heroically . . . but the country depended on us." Thomas Reed and Arnold Kramish, "Trinity at Dubna," *Physics Today*, vol. 49 (November 1996), pp. 32–33.

6. The only reasonably well-documented synergism is that between smoking and radon exposure (in uranium mines and other locations), but smoking involves exposure to both radioactive and nonradioactive toxic materials.

7. *Early Health Problems of the U.S. Nuclear Weapons Industry and Their Implications for Today*, S. Rept. 101-63, 101 Cong. 1 sess. (GPO, 1989), pp. 4, 6.

8. U.S. Department of Energy, "Deficiencies in Reporting of Worker Exposure to Radiation and Toxic Material," Submitted to the Subcommittee on Oversight and Investigations, Committee on Energy and Commerce, U.S. House of Representatives, March 17, 1994.

it was not possible to reliably pool information from various plants for epidemiological studies.

Jim Wells, an associate director of the General Accounting Office, stated at a March 1994 congressional hearing that in some cases when dosimeters were not returned, zeros were entered into the dose record of the worker.[9] In effect, this means that a part of the historical external dosimetry record is fabricated, in that the zeros entered into the records have no connection with any measurements that were actually made or, indeed, any actual exposures.

Other deficiencies also exist in at least part of the dosimetry record. A review of raw data of worker records at the Fernald Plant (formally the Feed Materials Production Center) in southwestern Ohio—where uranium was processed into fuel and target elements for the production reactors at the Savannah River Plant—made available to the Institute for Energy and Environmental Research as a result of a class-action lawsuit filed by workers against the former contractor of the plant, National Lead of Ohio (from 1981 to 1985)—turned up many problems with the dose records and calculations. During one period in the 1980s, when a new type of dosimeter was introduced, problems with dosimeter readings led National Lead officials to use a "correction factor" that in some cases yielded *negative* radiation dose estimates, a physical impossibility. There remains no clear, official statement about what was entered into the dose records of workers in such cases, or how the use of such factors could be justified even when they did not yield impossible results.

Many Fernald workers also suffered exposure to other radioactive materials, such as thorium-232, along with nonradioactive toxic materials such as hydrofluoric acid. Mortality data for workers at the plant indicate there was an overall loss of life expectancy of roughly four or five years among these workers for deaths from all causes. A definitive epidemiological conclusion is not yet possible because dose and health data have not been correlated and analyzed in detail.

The plant's authorities did not calculate at all internal radiation doses due to inhalation of uranium and other radioactive materials, even though urine samples and (after the late 1960s) lung-burden data were collected. In the 1950s and 1960s, workers were told, on the basis of urine data, that they had not been overexposed, when in fact the model underlying these statements—which related the uranium content of urine to internal radiation dose—was inappropriate and yielded gross underestimates in many cases.

9. Jim Wells, *Protecting Department of Energy Workers Health and Safety*, Testimony before the House Subcommittee on Oversight and Investigations, T-RCED-94-143 (March 17, 1994).

In 1994 IEER presented its own calculations of internal doses to Fernald workers—the only such independent calculations that have ever been based on raw data collected by a nuclear weapons contractor. Figure 7-2 shows the number of workers who, averaged over an entire year, had uranium in their lungs in quantities that would result in radiation exposure above then-prevailing limits.

In this evaluation, more than half the workers were exposed to more than the then-prevailing standards for workers for lung doses of 15 rem a year in every year but one in the 1950s and early 1960s. In the worst year—1955—about 90 percent of the workers were overexposed. Cumulative average individual lung doses were several hundred rem (a chest x ray involves a dose of a small fraction of a rem), which meant a significant increase in lung cancer risk.[10]

After the new radiation dose estimates were presented to the jury during the trial in July 1994, the DOE settled the lawsuit. It agreed to provide all surviving workers who had worked at Fernald for more than two weeks with medical monitoring for life; renounce the right to go to court to fight workers' compensation claims and to agree to the judgment of a panel of three doctors on such claims; and to provide a cash compensation fund of $15 million (then-year dollars) in addition to the above.[11] It is difficult to assess the total monetary value of the settlement, but it could be on the order of $50 million. Fernald had about 6,000 workers over its operating life, and about 4,000 of them were still alive at the time of the settlement. Fernald workers thus represent about 1 percent of the total historical work force in the U.S. nuclear weapons complex. A broadly similar settlement for all workers would cost several billion dollars.

The DOE now admits that it did not integrate internal body burden information in the dose records of any of its workers until 1989.[12] Studies that reevaluate worker doses according to these methods and couple them with health data have not yet been done for any other weapons plant. The Fernald estimates and DOE's admission regarding its failure to integrate internal dose data raise the question of what degree of overexposure might be found at other plants and the expense that would be incurred in providing medical monitoring, health care, and compensation to nuclear weapons plant workers, including those who have worked at test sites.

---

10. Bernd Franke, and K. R. Gurney, *Estimates of Lung Burdens for Workers at the Feed Materials Production Center, Fernald, Ohio* (Takoma Park, Md.: Institute for Energy and Environmental Research, July 1994). Unfortunately, the data are too unreliable to permit accurate reestimation of individual doses. As a result, only group exposures and risks can be reestimated. Even so considerable uncertainties will remain. Arjun Makhijani, participated in the review of this analysis and helped perform some of the early calculations.

11. "Energy Department Settles Lawsuit with Workers," *New York Times*, July 27, 1994, p. A18.

12. Arjun Makhijani and Bernd Franke, "Worker Radiation Dose Records Deeply Flawed," *Science for Democratic Action*, vol. 6 (November 1997), pp. 1, 4–7; Matthew L. Wald, "Tracking of Radiation Exposure in Bomb Work Is Questioned, *New York Times*, November 9, 1997, p. 23.

FIGURE 7-2. Percentage of Fernald Workers with Lung Doses of Uranium Exceeding Prevailing Limits, 1952–80[a]

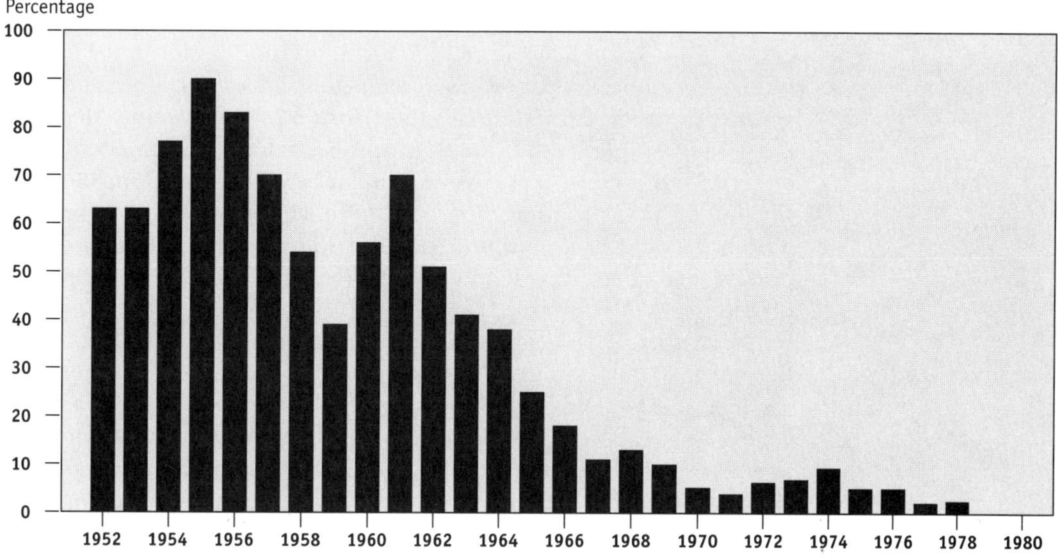

Source: Institute for Energy and Environmental Research.

a. Inferred annual average uranium lung burden corresponding to a lung dose of 15 rem or more.

Uranium Miners

Uranium miners were another highly exposed group. During the 1950s, it was well known (in part through definitive studies in Europe in the 1940s) that exposure to radon and its decay products in unventilated or poorly ventilated mines was a health hazard, increasing the risk of lung cancer. Nevertheless, the AEC did not require that the mines be ventilated, choosing instead to emphasize production.[13] The AEC also systematically derailed efforts to alert the miners or remedy the problem.

In the late 1940s, for example, an AEC commissioner ordered the commission's own Health and Safety Laboratory to "keep away from"

13. For a concise overview of the history of this issue, see H. Peter Metzger, *The Atomic Establishment* (New York: Simon & Schuster, 1972), pp. 115–44; James N. Baker and others, "Keeping a Deadly Secret," *Newsweek,* June 18, 1990, p. 20. For the history and subsequent court battles to win compensation for the miners, see Stewart L. Udall, *The Myths of August: A Personal Exploration of Our Tragic Cold War Affair with the Atom* (New York: Pantheon Books, 1994), pp. 183–202. The Joint Committee on Atomic Energy (JCAE) and others in Congress also worked to protect the uranium industry. In 1962 Senator Robert S. Kerr (Democrat of Oklahoma), not a member of the JCAE, was reported to have personally benefited from uranium pricing and supply policies that he helped to maintain. In an era before strict conflict-of-interest laws, Kerr simultaneously served as chairman of Kerr-McGee Oil Industries, whose mines were the largest supplier of uranium to the AEC. See Harold P. Green and Alan Rosenthal, *Government of the Atom: The Integration of Powers* (New York: Atherton Press, 1963), p. 47; Harold Orlans, *Contracting for Atoms* (Brookings, 1967), p. 163.

the issue. At about the same time, Shields Warren, M.D., head of the AEC's Division of Biology and Medicine, learned about a proposed study of the mining problem by the National Cancer Institute and, concerned that it would receive widespread publicity and alarm the miners, used his influence to prevent it from getting under way. In 1954, even as it publicly dismissed the connection between cancer and radiation exposure from radon gas, the Division of Biology and Medicine proposed to secretly study the body tissues of deceased miners for "the effect of radioactive materials on human beings" (for the present-day version of this program, see box 7-2). This "unique opportunity" was abandoned in its early stages when some pathologists and others outside the AEC were made aware of it and raised serious ethical objections.[14]

More than 4,100 miners—including more than 1,500 Navajos—became the subject of what was essentially an experiment to determine the health effects of exposure to high levels of radon in such mines.[15] These workers received a formal apology from the government in 1990 and are eligible for compensation up to $100,000 under the Radiation Exposure Compensation Act (signed by President George Bush on October 15, 1990).[16] As of January 13, 1998, 1,341 miners (or their widows) had received $139.6 million in compensation, although 1,357 applicants had their claims denied.[17] There have been problems in actually obtaining compensation, however, especially among Native Americans, who often do not have the written documentation, such as marriage licenses, required by the Department of Justice to establish their claims.[18]

Not all lawsuits have been successful. A lawsuit by workers claiming damages due to exposure from work at the Nevada Test Site was rejected by a federal district court in July 1994, fifteen years after the suit was first filed. Judge Philip M. Pro ruled that the plaintiffs (six former test site workers, only one of whom was still alive) did not present enough evidence to prove that their cancers were caused by work-site radiation exposures or that the government was negligent in its man-

14. Udall, *Myths of August*, pp. 190–92, 196.

15. Conditions in the Soviet Union were even harsher. During the late 1940s and early 1950s, authorities there rounded up workers for the mines in the Soviet zone of Germany because not enough volunteers were willing to endure the abominable conditions. Police were instructed to "enlist" people who were not regularly employed. Prisoners of war and refugees in Poland were sent to the mines and youth brigades were created. According to the CIA, by 1950 the uranium industry in Soviet-controlled Germany employed 150,000 to 200,000 people. Many of these workers lived in barracks guarded by barbed wire and troops. Escapees were caught and punished, and "little attention was paid to medical consequences of working with uranium: protective clothing was inadequate, and many of the miners contracted lung cancer from exposure to radon gas. There is no reason to suppose that conditions in Soviet mines were any better." See David Holloway, *Stalin and the Bomb: The Soviet Union and Atomic Energy, 1939–1956* (Yale University Press, 1994), pp. 193–94.

16. Keith Schneider, "U.S. Fund Set Up to Pay Civilians Injured by Atomic Arms Program," *New York Times*, October 16, 1990, p. A1.

17. "Radiation Exposure Compensation System—Claims to Date Summary," provided by Magaly Carter Bernazky, Torts Branch, Civil Division, Department of Justice, January 13, 1998.

18. Keith Schneider, "Valley of Death: Late Rewards for Navajo Miners," *New York Times*, May 3, 1993, p. A1.

Box 7-2
The U.S. Transuranium and Uranium Registries

In 1949 scientists with the AEC embarked on "a modest program of postmortem tissue sampling at autopsy" at the Hanford Reservation.[1] By radiochemically analyzing bone, lung, liver, and occasionally other tissues of Hanford workers and residents of nearby Richland, they hoped to learn how and where plutonium is deposited in the body upon ingestion or inhalation. In 1968 the effort was renamed the National Plutonium Registry and the goal broadened to include accidental intakes of plutonium and to correlate them to an individual's health records over the remainder of his or her life. It became the United States Transuranium Registry in 1970, in order to encompass all transuranic (heavier than uranium) elements. In 1978 the United States Uranium Registry was created, with a similar mission. Both of these agencies were combined in February 1992 to form the United States Transuranium and Uranium Registries (USTUR), now managed by Washington State University and housed in Richland, Washington.

Individuals are normally recruited for the registries by their employers, in this case primarily DOE weapons plant contractors. Participation is voluntary and may be withdrawn at any time. Scientists with the registries are especially interested in persons with a documented history of exposure to elements such as plutonium or americium-241 (a by-product of plutonium decay).

By 1978, 15,000 candidate workers had been identified. Nearly half of them were from Hanford, with most of the remainder split between Rocky Flats, Los Alamos National Laboratory, and the Savannah River Plant. This also included 100 persons who were identified at private facilities. Permission for one thousand autopsies had been authorized, and ninety-three performed by mid-1978. Until 1994, radiochemical tissue analysis was performed at several DOE facilities (Rocky Flats; Battelle Pacific Northwest Laboratory, until September 30, 1978; and Los Alamos), but most of the work—except for cases originating at Rocky Flats—took place at Los Alamos. In February 1994, responsibility for this work was transferred to Health Physics and Radiation Biology Research Program at Washington State University (the previous contractor was the Hanford Environmental Health Foundation).

Upon being notified of a registrant's death (the registries do not routinely monitor the status of their participants), consent is obtained from the next of kin for an autopsy. If consent is given, arrangements are made with a qualified pathologist (except for persons who are HIV-positive or have Hepatitis B, who are rejected for safety reasons), who collects selected tissue samples and slides and forwards them to the registries for analysis.

Data and specimens from the registries are archived at the National Human Radiobiology Tissue Repository in Spokane, Washington. Included in the collection are tissue slides and solutions from persons who have participated in the program. In 1996 the collection of the U.S. National Radiobiology Archives was transferred from Pacific Northwest Laboratory to Washington State University; it included data and tissues of animals injected with or exposed to various radioactive elements in studies dating to the 1940s. As of September 30, 1996, there were 886 registrants (292 "active" and 350 deceased; the remaining 243 people were classified as "inactive" or no longer part of the program), with nearly all being for the Transuranium Registry. Funding for the effort comes from the DOE and from 1968 to 1996 totaled about $30 million.

1. U.S. Transuranium and Uranium Registries, *Annual Report of the United States Transuranium and Uranium Registries, April 1992—September 1993,* USTUR-0015-94 (Washington State University, September 1993); U.S. Transuranium and Uranium Registries, "Questions and Answers about the United States Transuranium and Uranium Registries," May 1994.

agement of the site.[19] Although some individual workers have received compensation, no other class action suit for workers has won settlement following the Fernald case. As of January 13, 1998, 155 "on-site" participants in tests at NTS—a category that consists by and large of nonmilitary test-site employees—had received $11.8 million under the Radiation Exposure Compensation Act; 659 claims were denied.[20]

Armed Forces Personnel

Approximately 220,000 armed forces personnel participated in the U.S. atmospheric testing program from 1946 to 1963 (see chapter 1).[21] There are some external dose records for these personnel, but a large number of them were destroyed in 1978 when a fire broke out in a St. Louis records repository. This occurred just about the time some atomic veterans and downwinders were raising questions about whether their cancers were related to their exposures during nuclear weapons testing.

Since 1978 the Defense Special Weapons Agency (formerly the Defense Nuclear Agency) has been conducting a Nuclear Test Personnel Review (NTPR). As of July 1996, approximately 210,000 DOD military, civilian, and contract personnel who participated in atmospheric nuclear tests had been identified. Since 1988, an additional 195,000

19. Keith Schneider, "Atom Tests' Legacy of Grief: Workers See Betrayal on Peril," *New York Times*, December 14, 1989, p. A1; Michael Janofsky, "After Years of Suing U.S., Hope for A-Bomb Worker," *New York Times*, January 6, 1994, p. D20; Associated Press, "Lawsuit by Nuclear Test Site Workers Fails," *New York Times*, July 23, 1994, p. A26. When this case originated in 1980, there were 216 plaintiffs.

20. "Radiation Exposure Compensation System—Claims to Date Summary," January 13, 1998.

21. An especially engrossing personal account of this program can be found in Thomas H. Saffer and Orville E. Kelly, *Countdown Zero* (New York: Penguin Books, 1982). The Soviet Union conducted similar exercises. For a September 14, 1954, test (the ninth Soviet test ever conducted), 45,000 soldiers were sent to a site near the village of Totskoye (some 600 miles [964 kilometers] southeast of Moscow) and divided into two groups. A 40-kiloton bomb dropped from a Tu-4 bomber was detonated at 9:33 A.M., 1,150 feet (350.5 meters) in the air between them, with troops as close as 2 miles (3.2 kilometers) to ground zero (an additional 1 million people lived within 100 miles [161 kilometers] of the site; many fell ill after the test). Following the blast, a mock battle ensued, lasting the remainder of the day. Many of the troops were not issued protective equipment or even informed of the dangers. Some of those who had gas masks removed them in the oppressive 115-degree Fahrenheit (46-degree Celsius) temperatures. Exposure levels, by one account, were ten times the maximum level allowable for American troops for an entire year. By 1992, 1,000 veterans of this test were still alive, although none were reportedly healthy. Convinced that their exposure that day caused their illnesses, they met with Russian generals to complain and seek adequate medical care. Yet even thirty-eight years later, the generals tried (without success) to persuade the Totskoye survivors that the bomb used that day was an "imitation" and therefore not responsible for their condition (this despite the existence of an official Soviet Army film documenting the event). In September 1994, the first joint Russian-U.S. army exercise took place on the Totsk testing ground. See Marlise Simons, "Soviet Atom Test Used Thousands As Guinea Pigs, Archives Show," *New York Times*, November 7, 1993, p. 1; John-Thor Dahlburg, "1954 War Games Used Real Nuclear Bomb," *Los Angeles Times* (Washington edition), September 3, 1992, p. A6; Fred Hiatt, "Survivors Tell of '54 Soviet A-Blast," *Washington Post*, September 15, 1994, p. A30. Ministry of the Russian Federation for Atomic Energy and the Ministry of Defense of the Russian Federation, *USSR Nuclear Weapons Tests and Peaceful Nuclear Explosions: 1949 through 1990* (Sarov, Russia: RFNC-VNIIEF,

military personnel who took part in the postwar occupation of Hiroshima and Nagasaki have been identified.[22]

The National Academy of Sciences has examined these data in two studies of the mortality of test participants. The first, in 1985, covered 46,000 participants in five separate test series, and the second, in 1996, focused on 42,000 participants in two 1946 tests known as "Operation Crossroads."[23] The 1985 study found the incidence of leukemia and prostate cancer to be higher than expected among the participants but could not link this to radiation exposure (one of the study's coauthors stressed that limitations in the study design might have affected its conclusions). Similarly, the 1996 study found the mortality rate for Crossroads participants higher than expected but saw no link to ionizing radiation. The total costs of the NTPR through 1996 were $157.6 million, with at least $18 million of this going toward dose reconstruction studies .[24]

Some of the personnel taking part in these tests were subjected to experiments. Pilots, for example, were ordered to fly though mushroom clouds shortly after a test explosion to ascertain whether they would be able to fight in a nuclear war environment (and also to study the safety of cloud-sampling missions to collect bomb debris for scientific analysis). The degree of internal radiation was measured by having the pilots swallow a Vaseline-coated film badge sensitive to radiation attached to a string that hung out of their mouths. That military personnel were deliberately exposed to radiation in such exercises is clear from extensive records compiled by the Presidential Advisory Committee on Human Radiation Experiments.[25]

Data from these film badges proved inadequate in any case because only a small number of personnel were provided with badges. Furthermore, the level of exposure right after a test depended greatly on an individual's exact location and activity. The level would be high, say, for troops who marched into or near ground zero shortly after a test or those who worked with equipment rendered radioactive by the atomic blast. Thus the assumption that doses received by a small number of

1996), p. 11.

22. Defense Special Weapons Agency, "Nuclear Test Personnel Review (NTPR)," fact sheet, n.d. (circa 1996).

23. Institute of Medicine, *Mortality of Veteran Participants in the Crossroads Nuclear Test* (Washington, D.C.: National Academy Press, 1996); Associated Press, "Higher Death Rate in A-Test Witnesses Is Not Tied to Radiation," *New York Times*, October 31, 1996, p. A17.

24. Letter from General Kenneth L. Hageman, Director, Defense Nuclear Agency, to Patricia Broudy, Legislative Director, National Association of Atomic Veterans, March 3, 1995, reprinted in *Effects to Veterans of Exposure to Ionizing Radiation, Subsequent Treatment, and Compensation*, Hearings before the Subcommittee on Compensation, Pension, Insurance and Memorial Affairs of the House Committee on Veterans Affairs, 104 Cong. 2 sess. (GPO, 1996), pp. 56–58; data for 1995–96 provided by the Defense Special Weapons Agency, August 15, 1997.

25. Advisory Committee on Human Radiation Experiments, Final Report (GPO, 1995), pp. 454–505. An extensive catalog and description of 2,389 radiation experiments conducted on military personnel from 1944 to 1994 an be found in Department of Defense, Assistant to the Secretary of Defense for Nuclear and Chemical and Biological Defense Programs, *Report on Search for Human Radiation Experiment Records*, vols. 1 and 2 (GPO, June 1997) (available on the World Wide Web at http://www.defenselink.mil/pubs/dodhre/index.html).

personnel wearing film badges could be taken as representative of all other personnel was questionable. Data on internal doses in such cases are sparse or nonexistent. Nevertheless, official evaluations have concluded that armed forces personnel had insignificant internal exposures.[26] According to an analysis of Operation Crossroads, however, at least some of the personnel were likely to have experienced high internal exposures because of the widespread contamination, poor safety practices, and "hairy-chested" attitudes of naval officers.[27] It is now by and large impossible to identify the individuals who were highly exposed. In 1988 Congress passed legislation enabling 62,000 veterans (or their widows) who participated in nuclear test exercises at the Nevada Test Site from 1951 until 1962 to apply for compensation (up to $75,000 per person) if they had contracted any of thirteen types of cancer. However, many veterans believe the compensation is inadequate.[28]

Other Armed Forces Personnel

Personnel involved in handling, transporting, and working in close proximity to nuclear weapons or naval propulsion reactors have been exposed to some radiation.[29] So have those who helped clean up plutonium and other radioactive materials dispersed during several major nuclear weapons accidents (see box 7-3).[30] No estimates of cumulative

26. Out of an exposed population of about 220,000 personnel, "one might anticipate approximately 106 excess cancer deaths attributable to participation in the nuclear tests." Advisory Committee on Human Radiation Experiments, Final Report, pp. 481–82

27. Jonathan M. Weisgall, *Operation Crossroads: The Atomic Tests at Bikini Atoll* (Annapolis, Md.: Naval Institute Press, 1994), p. 236; Arjun Makhijani, and David Albright, *Irradiation of Personnel During Operation Crossroads: An Evaluation Based on Official Documents* (Washington, D.C.: International Radiation Research and Training Institute, 1983).

28. Inquiries to the Department of Veterans Affairs to ascertain how much has been paid out to veterans since 1988 and how many have applied for and received compensation (or been denied same) yielded a surprising result: the department does not know because its accounting systems are not designed to provide such information on an aggregate basis, only for individual claims (with an appropriate claim number). Author's telephone communication with Joyce Greaving, consultant to the Department of Veterans Affairs (budget division and administration), July 28, 1997.

29. Also exposed were an estimated 8,000 to 20,000 personnel, primarily pilots and submariners, who were given nasopharyngeal irradiation treatments: capsules of radium inserted into the nostrils under a local anesthetic for about six to twelve minutes repeatedly over a number of months to shrink tissue around the eustachian tubes, relieving pain in the inner ear caused by changes in air pressure. An unknown number of military dependents also received such treatments, along with an estimated 500,000 to 2 million civilians from 1940 until the mid-1960s (although the practice began in the 1920s, treating such conditions as deafness, infections, asthma, and recurrent tonsillitis). The advent of pressurized cabins and antibiotics as well as medical studies in the 1950s and 1960s on the cancer risk associated with this form of therapy led the military to discontinue its use in the 1960s. See Department of Defense, *Report on Search for Human Radiation Experiment Records,* vol. 1, pp. 37–44.

30. The most well known of these are the accidents over Palomares, Spain, on January 17, 1966, and Thule, Greenland, on January 21, 1968 (see box 7-2). Some other known accidents involved significant cleanup efforts as well. A May 22, 1957, accidental jettison of a bomb from a B-36 over Kirtland Air Force Base produced a high-explosive detonation and completely destroyed the bomb's components; a January 31, 1958, B-47 crash and fire occurred at an overseas base (possibly French Morocco or Libya); a November 4, 1958, B-47 crash over Dyess Air Force Base in Texas, caused a high-explosive detonation and produced a crater 35 feet in diameter and 6 feet deep (11 meters in diameter and 1.8 meters deep); a November 26, 1958, B-47 ground fire at Chennault Air Force Base in Louisiana destroyed a single nuclear

doses are available, however, except for navy personnel working on or near nuclear propulsion reactors.[31]

Downwinders

The third group of victims, often called "downwinders," are people who live near nuclear weapons facilities. At times, "near" may mean hundreds of kilometers downwind, especially for atmospheric nuclear tests (until 1963) and large intentional or accidental releases, as at Hanford between 1944 and 1964 (see box 8-3). In the case of hot spots caused by the rain-out of radioactive particles, the downwind areas might be thousands of kilometers away for iodine-131, yet the people in those areas may experience the same level of exposure as others far closer to the tests.[32] A recent assessment by the National Cancer Institute—requested by Congress in 1982 but only released in 1997—found that ninety atmospheric nuclear tests conducted at the Nevada Test Site from January 27, 1951, until July 17, 1962, deposited high levels of radioactive iodine-131 (150 million curies) across much of the United States (mainly in 1952, 1953, 1955, and 1957; see figure 7-3), in doses large enough to produce 10,000 to 75,000 cases of thyroid cancer, some 10 percent of which might be fatal. Children, particularly those under five years of age, were especially vulnerable. A comprehensive analysis of all the radioactive elements in fallout—including plutonium, cesium, and strontium-90—could take years.

Downwinders were certainly exposed to iodine-131 during the Hanford Plant's first two decades of operation and during nuclear testing in the Marshall Islands. Exposures to releases from other plants were likely high as well.[33] The situation is unclear because official estimates

weapon; a July 6, 1959, C-124 crash and fire at Barksdale Air Force Base in Louisiana destroyed one nuclear weapon; a June 7, 1960 fire at McGuire Air Force Base in New Jersey destroyed a BOMARC missile and its warhead; on July 25, 1962, a Thor missile and its test warhead on Johnston Island were destroyed in the North Pacific; and a December 8, 1964, B-58 crash and fire at Bunker Hill (now Grissom) Air Force Base in Indiana burned parts of five nuclear weapons. For further information, see chapter 4, footnote 33, and chapter 6 in this volume. See also, "U.S. Nuclear Weapons Accidents: Danger in Our Midst," *Defense Monitor,* vol. 10, no. 5 (1981).

31. We have not considered armed forces personnel exposed to depleted uranium from "conventional" munitions in this report. Such munitions, though radioactive, do not produce nuclear explosions and hence cannot be regarded as part of the U.S. nuclear arsenal. However, depleted uranium is a by-product of uranium enrichment for nuclear weapons. Costs associated with its use could be considered a part of a disposal scheme (see chapter 6).

32. National Cancer Institute, *Estimated Exposure and Thyroid Doses Received by the American People from Iodine-131 in Fallout Following Nevada Atmospheric Nuclear Bomb Tests,* NIH 97-4264 (GPO, October 1997); Peter Eisler and Steve Sternberg, "Nuke Fallout Questions Get More Air Time," *USA Today,* October 1, 1997, p. 4A; Curt Suplee, "40 Years Later, Bomb Test Fallout Raises Health Alarm," *Washington Post,* October 2, 1997.

33. At the Savannah River site, for example, 16.4 million curies of tritium were routinely or accidentally released from three processing buildings between 1955 and 1993 (this is equal to about 3.7 pounds [1.7 kilograms] of pure tritium). Significant amounts were also released from the SRS production reactors. Fourteen percent of this total—2.36 million curies—was released in one year of operation, 1958. Historically, the majority of tritium releases from the weapons complex occurred at SRS. Human error has been the primary

Box 7-3

Broken Arrows: The Palomares and Thule Accidents

On January 16, 1966, a B-52G bomber, returning to its North Carolina base following a routine airborne alert mission, collided with the fueling boom of a KC-135 tanker 30,000 feet (9,144 meters) above the coast of Spain while attempting to refuel.[1] Both aircraft broke up and the 40,000 gallons (151,000 liters) of jet fuel in the KC-135 exploded, killing its four-man crew. Four members of the B-52's seven-man crew were able to parachute to safety. Of the four unarmed B28 hydrogen bombs carried by the B-52 (a weapon with yields ranging from 70 kilotons to 1.45 megatons), three crashed on the ground in the vicinity of Palomares, a poor farming community 1 mile (1.6 kilometers) off the coastal highway. The fourth sank off the coast and was missing for nearly three months before being located by the submersible *Alvin* 5 miles (8 kilometers) offshore in 2,850 feet (869 meters) of water.[2] The high explosives in two of the bombs that fell on Palomares detonated, digging craters 6 to 10 feet (1.8 to 3 meters) deep and scattering plutonium and other debris 100 to 500 yards (91 to 457 meters) away from the impact area (the third bomb was recovered relatively intact from a dry riverbed).

For three months, 1,700 U.S. personnel and Spanish civil guards worked to decontaminate the area. An estimated 1,400 tons of radioactive soil and vegetation was excavated and sent to the United States for disposal (at the Savannah River Plant) and crops of tomatoes were buried or burned. Through all this, U.S. personnel wore protective clothing and underwent regular radiation checks; such measures were not taken for the Spanish workers. (The air force commander in charge later stated: "The U.S. Air Force was unprepared to provide adequate detection and monitoring for its personnel when an aircraft accident occurred involving plutonium weapons in a remote area of a foreign country.")

A radiation survey conducted jointly by the Defense Nuclear Agency and the Junta de Energia Nuclear (JEN) found that no less than 650 acres (more than 1 square mile [2.59 square kilometers]) of village, crops, and farms were contaminated; however, during the survey winds picked up and scattered the plutonium dust, and the DNA's subsequent report noted: "The total extent of the spread will never be known." Yet there was only sporadic monitoring of villagers and no effort to determine what level of contamination was acceptable. As the DNA's report later noted, "The Spanish government had not established criteria for permissible levels, which is completely understandable because plutonium-producing facilities and nuclear weapons were non-existent in Spain. Significantly, there were no criteria in the United States for accident situations. The available criteria pertained only

1. This discussion draws on Chuck Hansen, *The Swords of Armageddon*, vol. 8 (Sunnyvale, Calif.: Chuckelea Publications, 1995), appx. 3, pp. 135–41; Tad Szulc, *The Bombs of Palomares* (New York: Viking Press, 1967); Flora Lewis, *One of Our H-Bombs Is Missing* (New York: McGraw-Hill, 1967); John May, *The Greenpeace Book of the Nuclear Age: The Hidden History, the Human Cost* (New York: Pantheon Books, 1989), pp. 148–54, 162–68; Edward Schumacher, "Where H-Bombs Fell in '66, Spaniards Still Worry," *New York Times*, December 28, 1985, p. 2; Letter from Myron B. Kratzer, Assistant General Manager for International Activities, U.S. Atomic Energy Commission, to Jose M. Otero, President, Nuclear Energy Board, Madrid, Spain, December 2, 1968, located in the Department of Energy Archives, Record Group 326, DOS McCraw Collection, Box 17, Job 1320, Folder MHS 3-9 (1968) March, Thule Incident; *USAF Nuclear Safety*, AFRP 122-1 Jan/Feb/Mar 1970, vol. 65, Special Edition (on Project Crested Ice), pt. 2, pp. 2–97; Peter B. De Selding, "A Broken Arrow's Dark Legacy," *Nation*, June 25, 1988, pp. 888–91.

2. Thirty-eight U.S. Navy ships participated in the search for this bomb. Despite the fact that news of the missing bomb and the recovery effort became well known, the DOD refused for forty-four days to admit it had been lost. This led to absurd exchanges between the press and DOD officials in which the latter would make statements such as "I don't know of any missing bomb, but we have not positively identified what I think you think we are looking for." Quoted in Anthony Lake, "Lying around Washington," *Foreign Policy*, no. 2 (Spring 1971), p. 93.

Box 7-3
(continued)

to plutonium processing plants." Thus, the DNA applied guidelines governing fallout from tests at the Nevada Test Site.

Following the cleanup effort, the AEC and JEN established a monitoring program for the villagers and their land, with the AEC providing the funds and JEN conducting the surveys. In November 1971, Wright Langham with Los Alamos laboratory visited Palomares to assess the program. He found that only 100 villagers (about 6 percent of the population at the time of the accident) had undergone lung and urine testing: 29 tested positive but the results were deemed "statistically insignificant." Air monitoring for plutonium dust had ceased two years after the accident, even though high counts were occasionally obtained during periods of strong winds. Soil sampling was hampered by the fact that JEN had only one alpha spectrometer, which did not always work well. Langham reported that morale among the JEN staff assigned to the task had diminished since the accident and that the United States ought to provide more money and equipment to keep the effort going. A DNA report completed in 1975 concurred: "Palomares is one of the few locations in the world that offers an on-going experimental laboratory, probably the only one offering a look at an agricultural area."

The monitoring program apparently continued at least through 1986. In 1985, at the instigation of Palomares's mayor Antonia Flores (who witnessed the accident as a child), the villagers who had been monitored were finally allowed access to their medical records, which, according to Francisco Mingot, the director of JEN's Institute of Radiobiological and Environmental Protection, were kept secret under pressure from the United States and, later, from the Franco dictatorship, which sought to avoid excessive concern. The cost of the AEC-funded monitoring effort from 1966 through 1986 totaled some $5 million. The total cost of the accident—excluding the aircraft but including the search and decontamination effort and the settlement of more than 500 claims brought by the residents of Palomares—was officially estimated at more than $120 million.[3]

A little more than two years after the Palomares accident, on January 21, 1968, a B-52G bomber on a secret early-warning mission crashed on the ice near Thule Air Base, Greenland, following an uncontrollable on-board fire that quickly cut off the plane's electrical power.[4] Six of the seven crew members were able to eject safely. After passing directly over the base, the plane hit the ice-covered North Star Bay at a speed of 560 miles (900 kilometers) per hour. The impact destroyed the B-52, triggering the explosion of its 35,000 gallons (132,500 liters) of jet fuel, as well as detonating the high explosives in all four of the B28 bombs it carried. That explosion propelled parts of the bombs—including plutonium, uranium, and tritium components—into the inferno. Bomb debris and plane wreckage burned for at least twenty minutes and covered an area 1,000 to 2,000 feet (305 to 610 meters) wide. The heat of the fire melted the ice, which later froze, encapsulating some of the debris. One B28 secondary assembly (the thermonuclear part of the bomb) apparently melted through the ice and was later retrieved during an underwater survey.

---

3. Strategic Air Command, History and Research Division, *Project Crested Ice: The Thule Nuclear Accident,* vol. 1, SAC Historical Study 113 (1969), p. 39. However, Randy Maydew, a retired employee of Sandia National Laboratories who participated in the recovery effort of the missing bomb, has stated that this effort alone "cost more than $50 million" ($262 million in 1996 dollars). See John German, "Palomares 'Bomb Number Four'—It Crashed, It Fell, It Sank, but (Whew!) It Never Blew Up," *Scandia LabNews,* January 19, 1996 (available on the World Wide Web at http://sandia.gov/LabNews/LN01-19-96/palo.html).

4. Scott D. Sagan, *The Limits of Safety: Organizations, Accidents, and Nuclear Weapons* (Princeton University Press, 1993), pp. 156– 203.

Box 7-3
(continued)

A massive cleanup effort dubbed Project Crested Ice (but known informally among workers as "Dr. Freezelove") was carried out by more than 700 U.S. servicemen and Danish civilian workers from Thule, including U.S. specialists from more than seventy government agencies. Despite nearly impossible working conditions—total darkness until February, winds of up to 85 miles (137 kilometers) per hour, temperatures 28 to 70 degrees Fahrenheit below zero (-33 to -57 degrees Celsius), equipment that functioned poorly (if at all) in the subzero temperatures, and intense pressure to finish the recovery before the spring thaw—within eight months of the accident, 10,500 tons (237,000 cubic feet [6,700 cubic meters]) of contaminated snow, ice, and debris had been collected in barrels and shipped to the Savannah River Plant for disposal (aircraft debris was sent to Oak Ridge for burial). Residual waste was allowed to melt into the bay with the spring thaw, on the theory that the large volume of water would sufficiently dilute the radiation to safe levels. The entire effort is estimated to have cost some $9.4 million.[5]

Within twenty years of the accident, some of the 500 Danish workers reported a range of debilitating ailments, including cancer and sterility, which they associated with their work on Crested Ice. Wearing no radiological protective clothing (face masks were often discarded because they restricted breathing in the harsh conditions), search teams (initially all American, later a mix of American and Danish workers) used radiation monitors to locate the debris and then retrieved it by hand. While Air Force personnel drove ice scrapers and loaders, the Danes filled barrels and other containers with debris, which were later dumped into a total of sixty-seven spare 25,000-gallon (95,000-liter) fuel tanks. Spills were all but unavoidable. After their shifts, workers and equipment were decontaminated "by simply brushing the snow from garments and vehicles," according to the official

5. Strategic Air Command, *Project Crested Ice,* p. 39.

of releases of radiation—where they exist—tend to be low, especially in the case of airborne releases.

Waterborne releases also posed serious hazards, at many sites such as Savannah River and Oak Ridge. The hazards were especially high from the reactors at Hanford, where local river water was used to cool reactors and then discharged directly into the Columbia River. Eight of nine production reactors at Hanford used this method, known as once-through cooling. For instance, the water contained high levels of phosphorous-32, which remains hazardous for some 140 days and could therefore rise through the food chain and pose a threat to the surrounding human population. Although at least one Du Pont official was evidently concerned about certain environmental

cause of accidental releases. See U.S. Department of Energy, Assistant Secretary for Environment, Safety and Health, *Report of the Task Group on Operation of Department of Energy Tritium Facilities,* DOE/EH-0198P, October 1991; U.S. Department of Energy, "Openness Press Conference Fact Sheets," June 27, 1994, pp. 118–25.

Box 7-3
(continued)

air force report. In only a few instances was clothing deemed too contaminated for continued use; in these cases it was discarded. To save time, nasal swabs were often used in lieu of urine samples, even though, noted an air force health physicist, "since everyone's nose ran profusely in this climate, there was a reasonable doubt as to the validity of this check."

In the years following Project Crested Ice, the wife of the Danish personnel manager at Thule began collecting the names and medical histories of about eight hundred of the Danes involved in the effort. Many reported a broad array of ailments, including ninety-eight cancers. In December 1986 Denmark's prime minister Poul Schlueter stated that surviving Thule workers would be examined by radiological experts. Eleven months later, the Danish Institute for Clinical Epidemiology reported that Thule workers who had participated in Crested Ice experienced a 40 percent greater cancer diagnosis than a cohort of 3,000 Thule workers who were at the base before and after the accident and did not take part in the cleanup. A report released the same month by the Institute of Cancer Epidemiology found the cancer rate for Crested Ice workers 50 percent higher than that for the general population, but this study concluded that radiation exposure was not the cause.

In late 1987 nearly two hundred of the Danish workers sued the United States under the Foreign Military Claims Act for damages caused by their work during Crested Ice. This suit was disallowed by the air force, but the discovery process did dislodge hundreds of secret documents. While these shed no light on the workers' health problems, they revealed that U.S. Air Force personnel who worked alongside the Danes had not undergone any long-term monitoring, even though many of them may have been more highly exposed than the Danes. To date, the air force's refusal to release any information concerning the toxic or radioactive inventory of the bombs or the B-52 continues to stymie Danish hopes of pinpointing the cause of the workers' illnesses.

impacts shortly after the site for Hanford was selected in December 1942, the government's view of contamination risks was more problematic.[34]

In 1944 the Army Corps of Engineers built a laboratory on the Columbia River to help assess the impact of radiation on the river. Under the direction of Herbert Parker, Hanford's health scientists found radiation contaminating bacteria, algae, mussels, fish, and birds. The river water itself, used for drinking and irrigation, was also contaminated. Among those at risk were eight Indian tribes who relied on the river for food for part of the year. As more reactors were built in

34. In 1942 Crawford Greenewalt, manager of Du Pont's Technical Division Explosives Department, studied meteorological data to determine the best siting for Hanford facilities in the event "a pile [reactor] blew up." After examining potential radiological levels in the Columbia for their effect on people and fish, he eventually decided to build cooling ponds to allow some of the radiation in the effluent to decay before being released to the river. This mitigated but by no means eliminated the problem. See Rodney P. Carlisle, with Joan M. Zenzen, *Supplying the Nuclear Arsenal: American Production Reactors, 1942-1992* (Johns Hopkins University Press, 1996), pp. 19, 30–32.

FIGURE 7-3. Average Per Capita Thyroid Doses of Iodine-131 from U.S. Nuclear Testing Fallout, by County, 1951–62

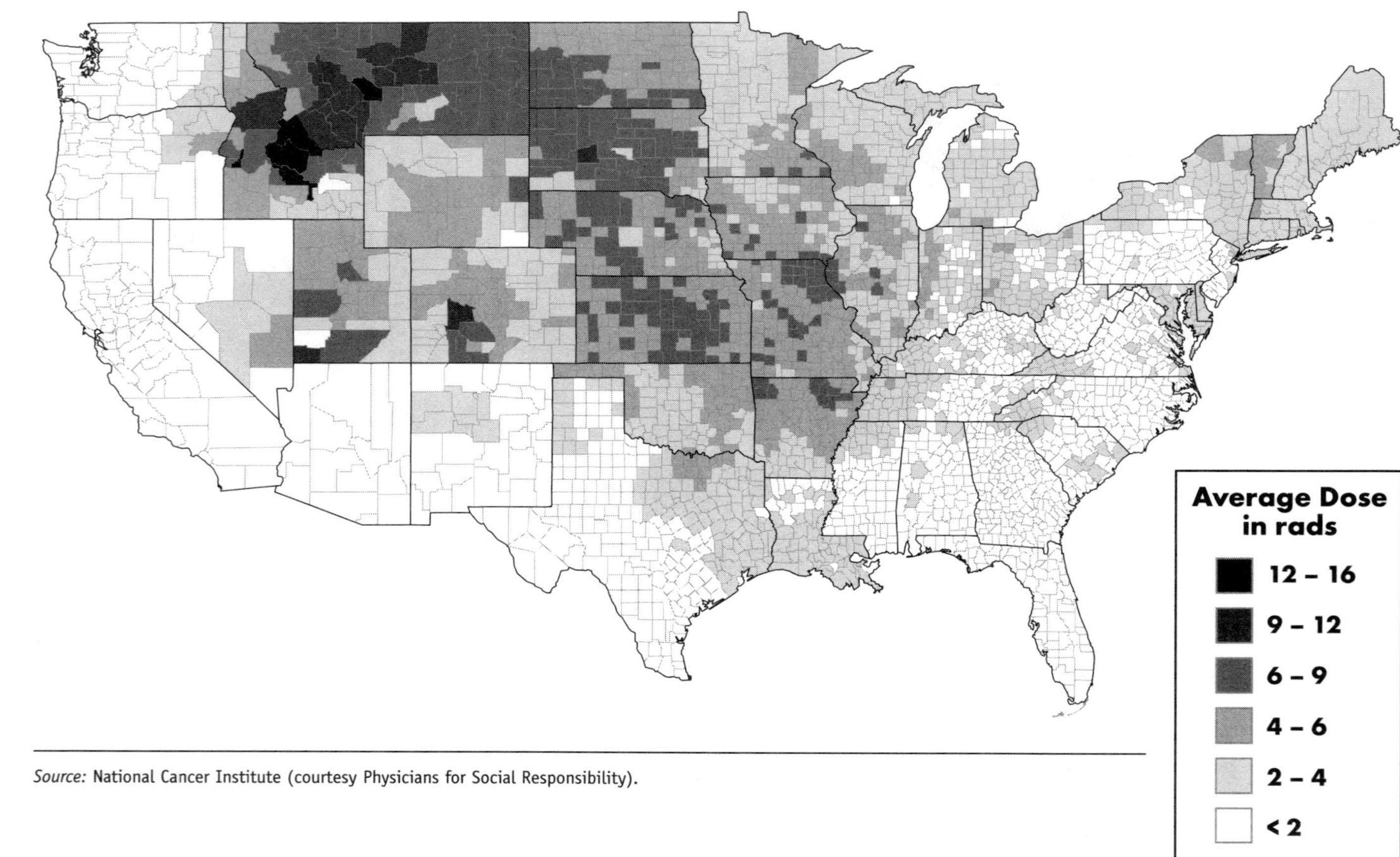

Source: National Cancer Institute (courtesy Physicians for Social Responsibility).

the 1950s, discharging an ever larger amount of radioactive water into the Columbia, the problem became more serious.

In 1954 the AEC discussed the issue at a secret meeting, and that summer AEC chairman Lewis Strauss visited Hanford to assess the situation. There, Parker (who had become an employee of General Electric, then the principal Hanford operating contractor) informed him that radiation measurements in some fish, especially whitefish, were so high that Hanford officials were considering prohibiting sport fishing for many miles downstream. Furthermore, ducks, geese, and local crops irrigated with water from the river were also a potential source of radiation. Nevertheless, the AEC decided not to publicize the risk. In an August 19, 1954, memorandum, Parker argued that because the measured radiation still met safety guidelines, the potential threat should remain a secret. Moreover, restricting sport fishing would have compelled the AEC to address the issue publicly, which would have been anathema to the agency because it would have been accused of placing its production goals ahead of public health and safety. "The public relations impact would be severe," he wrote.[35] No fishing ban was ever imposed, even though continual monitoring indicated that radiation in the Columbia exceeded the level that had triggered Parker's concern in 1957, 1958, 1960, 1961, 1963, and 1964.[36]

The most closely studied weapons facility so far is Fernald. According to the DOE's official estimates announced in 1987, the cumulative release of uranium to the air amounted to 136 metric tons (300,000 pounds). Earlier estimates were even lower. IEER's 1989 analysis, as part of a class-action suit, claimed that releases ranged from 270 to 1,400 metric tons (595,000 to 3.1 million pounds), with a best estimate of 390 metric tons (860,000 pounds). A later, more complete study commissioned by the Centers for Disease Control and Prevention, and whose authors had access to all the relevant documents, concluded in 1993 that the releases were probably in the range of 270 to 360 metric tons (595,000 to 794,000 pounds) with a best estimate of 310 metric tons (684,000 pounds), or about two-and-half times the DOE's 1987 estimate. In general, the CDC and IEER put forth similar reasons for the official underestimation of releases. The CDC study also found that

35. This was not the last time that public relations concerns overrode public safety. In 1956 H. V. Clukey, a Hanford scientist, concerned about tugboat crews who drank water directly from the river, remarked: "Restrictions on its use are not essential, but might cause little inconvenience. However, public relations might suffer from such restrictions." Jim Thomas, "Did They Know?" *Hanford Education Action League Perspective,* vol. 1, no. 3 (1990), pp. 3–4.

36. Jim Thomas, "Atomic Deception: Oh What a Tangled Web!" *Hanford Education Action League Perspective,* no. 10/11 (Summer/Fall 1992), pp. 4–7, 17, 20; Keith Schneider, "Nuclear Complex Threatens Indians," *New York Times,* September 3, 1990, p. A9. Schneider recounts an incident in the 1960s when a Hanford worker tripped radiation alarms upon arriving for work. "An investigation revealed that the day before he had eaten a can of oyster stew contaminated with radioactive zinc. The oysters had been harvested in Willapa Bay, along the Pacific Coast in Washington State, 25 miles north of Astoria," and nearly 300 (483 kilometers) miles downstream from Hanford.

radon-222 gaseous releases from wastes stored in large on-site tanks were responsible for the highest exposures and that the risk of lung cancer among the off-site residents experiencing the greatest exposure was likely to be comparable to that posed by smoking.[37]

Uranium releases were grossly underestimated for a variety of reasons. Among the most important was the fact that the official calculations did not take into account many sources of emissions and pollution control equipment, notably scrubbers, was inefficient.[38] Furthermore, some official data were fabricated. Over a period of thirteen years, from 1969 to 1982, zeroes were often entered for uranium releases when no measurements had been manually made. In another instance, the entire set of estimates of releases from scrubbers used what one internal document called an "inherently deceptive" method of estimating releases.[39] These disclosures followed a class-action lawsuit against the site's contractor, filed in 1985 by a group of residents living in the vicinity of Fernald for excessive and unnecessary exposure to uranium from the plant. The suit was triggered by publicity surrounding a November 1984 accident and the discovery by Lisa Crawford, a neighbor of the plant, that her well was contaminated by uranium and that officials had known about the pollution since 1981 but failed to notify her and her family. In 1989 the DOE settled the case for an unprecedented $78 million ($94 million in 1996 dollars).[40] Although the suit was against National Lead of Ohio, under the terms of its contract (see chapter 6, footnote 7), the DOE (and hence the taxpayer) was obligated to pay all legal expenses and damages, including those arising from contractor negligence (none was admitted to in the settlement, however). Dose reconstruction efforts have also been completed or are under way at many other sites, including Hanford, Rocky Flats, and Oak Ridge. These studies confirm that the DOE generally underestimated exposures to off-site populations and did not measure many radioactive and nonradioactive pollutants (see box 7-4).[41]

People living downwind of the Nevada Test Site were included in the compensation legislation passed by Congress. Like the armed forces personnel, many victims see the legislation as inadequate.[42]

37. Killough and others, "Fernald Dosimetry Reconstruction Project: Task 6: Radiation Doses and Risks to Residents from FMPC Operations from 1951–1988," Draft Report (Neeses, South Carolina: Radiological Assessments Corporation, 1996), p. xiii.

38. A series of special filters designed to "scrub" the air from inside a building and remove most particulate contaminants before release to the environment.

39. Arjun Makhijani and Bernd Franke, *Addendum to the Report: Release Estimates of Radioactive and Non-Radioactive Materials to the Environment by the Feed Materials Production Center 1951–85* (Takoma Park, Md.: Institute for Energy and Environmental Research, 1989).

40. Matthew L. Wald, "Energy Dept. to Pay $73 Million to Settle Uranium Case in Ohio," *New York Times,* July 1, 1989, p. 1. Under the terms of the settlement, $73 million would be divided among the residents, and an additional $5 million would be paid to local businesses for any decline in property value as a result of the contamination.

41. "Status of Health Studies," *Physicians for Social Responsibility Health Research Bulletin,* vol. 3 (Fall/Winter 1996), pp. 6–18.

42. Thomas W. Lippman, "For Utah Fallout Victims, Money Is of Little Comfort," *Washington Post,* May 18, 1993, p. A1.

Under the Radiation Exposure Compensation Act, 1,375 of these downwinders in the United States have received $72.1 million as of January 13, 1998, although 1,121 have had their claims denied.[43] These downwinder families are eligible for up to $50,000. An additional twenty-two people have received $1.2 million for childhood leukemias linked to atmospheric nuclear tests (nineteen other claims were denied).[44]

In addition to the major weapons factory sites, there are hundreds of smaller sites where subcontractors did work for the prime contractors. The former Alba Craft Site in Oxford, Ohio, is but one example (see chapter 6). This small workshop machined uranium. It was located in a residential neighborhood, adjacent to homes and backyards where children played. No warning signs were posted to indicate the presence of radioactive and toxic materials, and workers were told not to talk about what they did. Uranium chip fires were frequent. There was no pollution control system, not even a stack; uranium dust was simply vented out the window with a fan; contaminated water was discharged to an open outside drain.

Because the smaller facilities were often located within residential areas and failed to impose even the modest pollution control and monitoring measures adopted at the major plants in the early years, the potential damage to the health of exposed people at such sites could be significant, even though the amounts of material processed were not large.

Pacific Downwinders

The downwinders and other affected populations in the Marshall Islands have also suffered damage, most notably, an increase in thyroid problems. Bikini and Enewetak were the sites of sixty-six tests between 1946 and 1958, even though since at least 1948 the weather patterns in the Marshall Islands were known to be unsuitable for weapons testing.[45] Many exposed people had their thyroids removed to prevent cancer from occurring. Even so, ongoing medical surveys suggest that the Marshallese exposed to atmospheric testing experienced an increase in thyroid cancer and nodules. Still-births and miscarriages

43. "Radiation Exposure Compensation System—Claims To Date Summary."

44. By way of comparison, under the Civil Liberties Act of 1988, more 81,000 Japanese-Americans who were illegally interned, evacuated, or relocated during World War II have received $20,000 each, for a total of more than $1.8 billion since 1991 (by law, payments will end on August 10, 1998). See Memorandum, Joanne M. Chiedi, Director of Operations, Office of Redress Administration, U.S. Department of Justice, Civil Rights Division, to Stephen Schwartz, July 7, 1995; author's telephone communication with Lisa Johnson, Office of Redress Administration, January 22, 1998.

45. Institute for Energy and Environmental Research, *Radioactive Heaven and Earth,* p. 72.

Box 7-4
Dose Reconstructions and Health Assessments

Beginning in 1992, the DOE—under pressure from citizens' organizations and members of Congress—initiated a series of wide-ranging health studies to document the damage and potential damage caused by nearly fifty years of nuclear weapons production and testing activities. Before 1992 the only extensive work in this area was a dosimetry reconstruction project at the Fernald Plant and a worker mortality study at the Hanford Reservation dating to 1965. As of November 1997, some twelve studies had been completed covering both workers and neighboring communities at nine sites. An additional twenty-one projects were under way.[1] From 1990 through 1996, seventeen of these studies had cost the DOE $50.6 million (costs for five studies managed by the Agency for Toxic Substances and Disease Registry, ATSDR, were not available). Through 1996, the most money had been spent at Rocky Flats ($13.2 million), followed by Hanford ($9 million), Oak Ridge ($8.4 million), Savannah River ($7.7 million), the Idaho National Engineering and Environmental Laboratory ($4.8 million), and Fernald ($4.2 million). [2]

The studies vary in their design and purpose. During 1994–95, the Centers for Disease Control and Prevention spent nearly $583,000 assessing the incidence of thyroid cancer in Marshall Islanders exposed to fallout from U.S. atmospheric nuclear testing in the Pacific. At the Hanford Reservation, studies have tracked worker mortality and attempted to painstakingly reconstruct the possible downwind doses caused by deliberate or accidental releases of radiation, notably iodine-131. In March 1997 one of these studies urged the DOE to locate the approximately 14,000 people whose thyroids would have received significant doses from Hanford operations between 1945 and 1951. It further called on the DOE to establish an ongoing medical monitoring program for these individuals to screen for thyroid cancer and other abnormalities associated with the radiation received. The ATSDR estimated it would cost $4 million to establish the effort and $9.6 million to operate it for one year, assuming the maximum possible enrollment of affected individuals (as of January 1998, the DOE has refused to provide funding for such a program).[3]

1. For a concise and highly readable overview of these studies, see *Physicians for Social Responsibility Health Research Bulletin,* vol. 4 (Winter 1997–98), pp. 6–9.
2. Data provided by Lori Azim, Office of Environment, Safety, and Health, U.S. Department of Energy, August 7, 1996.
3. Warren E. Leary, "Exams Urged for Neighbors of 1945–51 Atomic Leaks," *New York Times* (Washington edition), March 22, 1997, p. A8; Steve Sternberg, "Who Pays for Plutonium Risk? $12.9 Million for Screening vs. 'Gigabucks' for Cleanup," *USA Today,* January 15, 1998, p. 1A.

also increased among women on Rongelap during the first four years after exposure.[46]

Following the 15-megaton "Bravo" nuclear test on March 1, 1954 (the largest U.S. test ever; the anticipated yield was 6 megatons), Rongelap was showered with fallout (its eighty-six inhabitants suffered

46. T. Takahasi and others, "An Investigation Into the Prevalence of Thyroid Disease on Kwajalein Atoll, Marshall Islands," *Health Physics,* vol. 73, no. 1 (1997), pp. 199–213; Merill Eisenbud and Thomas Gessel, *Environmental Radioactivity* (San Diego: Academic Press, 1997), p. 386.

severe radiation sickness, including nausea, radiation burns, and progressive hair loss). At first, the AEC tried to keep the incident a secret; later it attempted to downplay the risks of fallout.[47] In 1957 the government returned the inhabitants of Rongelap to their homes, even though radiation levels in food were greater than considered acceptable for U.S. citizens. AEC scientists considered this a valuable opportunity to study the uptake of radioactive particles in a contaminated environment. At a January 1956 presentation before the AEC's Advisory Committee on Biology and Medicine, an official supporting this approach noted that the northern Marshall Islands, where Rongelap is located, "is by far the most contaminated place in the world," adding, "while it is true that these people do not live, I would say, the way Westerners do, civilized people, it is nevertheless true that they are more like us than the mice."[48]

By 1962 the inhabitants of Rongelap were noticing a growing incidence of thyroid nodules, and among the exposed children, one died of leukemia. When the people of Utirik (a nearby atoll) began developing thyroid cancer in the 1970s (despite being further away from the Bravo blast and experiencing lower exposure rates than those on Rongelap), the DOE's resident physician in the Marshall Islands, Konrad Kotrady, disputed earlier assumptions about a weak linkage between low doses and cancer rates. He also took issue with the medical care provided to the islanders (largely through the DOE's Brookhaven National Laboratory), which treated the islanders more like guinea pigs in a research program than patients. But the doctor's concerns—voiced in 1977—apparently went unaddressed.

A November 1982 bilingual DOE report on contamination on Rongelap included a map (figure 7-4) indicating that some inhabited parts

47. Institute for Energy and Environmental Research, *Radioactive Heaven and Earth,* pp. 81–85. This and the following three paragraphs rely heavily on this account. The islanders, having never seen snow, believed it was snowing; children played in this "snow." The people of Rongelap were evacuated some about fifty hours after the test; the residents of Utirik were evacuated about twenty-four hours later. The average exposure of the people on Rongelap was about 190 rems. On Alinganae it was 69 rems. (This is equivalent to about 19,000 and 6,900 chest x-rays *per person,* respectively). Doses to the thyroid were up to 2,000 rem (Eisenbud and Gessel, *Environmental Radioactivity,* p. 386). All the inhabitants of the two islands were evacuated to Kwajalein and placed under "continuous and competent medical supervision," as described by AEC chairman Lewis Strauss in his memoirs. He also said medical follow-ups later in the year showed the Marshall Islanders "had continued in excellent health, their blood counts were approximately normal, and a few skin lesions had healed." In fact, a study by Brookhaven National Laboratory found that white blood cell and lymphocyte counts fell by half and did not return to normal for one and two years, respectively. Platelet counts fell by one-third and did not rebound for more than two years. Nevertheless, Lewis stated: "A check made three years later (1957) indicated that no deaths had occurred among the Rongelap people . . . in any way related to radiation effects." Lewis L. Strauss, *Men and Decisions* (Garden City, N.Y.: Doubleday, 1962), pp. 412–13; Institute for Energy and Environmental Research, *Radioactive Heaven and Earth,* pp. 76, 78. See also *Radiation Exposure from Pacific Nuclear Tests,* Hearings before the Subcommittee on Oversight and Investigations of the House Committee on Natural Resources, 103 Cong. 2 sess. (GPO, 1994).

48. U.S. Atomic Energy Commission, Minutes of the Advisory Committee on Biology and Medicine meeting on January 13–14, 1956, Record Group 326, Division of Biology and Medicine, Box 3218, Folder (ACBM meeting), formerly Secret, p. 232, Department of Energy Archives. "The mice" refers to experimental mice mentioned by the speaker earlier in the meeting.

of the atoll were as contaminated as those forbidden to humans.[49] In August 1983 Parliament of the Marshall Islands passed a unanimous resolution calling on the United States to evacuate the people on Rongelap. The DOE asserted the atoll was safe, despite the data from its own map (which it refrained from discussing). Disturbed by the government's inaction in the face of acknowledged danger, the environmental organization Greenpeace in 1985 evacuated some 320 people aboard its flagship, the *Rainbow Warrior,* relocating them to Majetto, an island in the Kwajalein Atoll.[50] In 1988 an independent study authorized by the U.S. Congress recommended that the northern part of Rongelap be considered "forbidden territory." In testimony before Congress the following year, the author admitted that the safety of people living on the remainder of the atoll could only be ensured if they relied on imported foods for the next thirty to fifty years.

In 1992 the DOE, the Department of Interior, and the government of the Marshall Islands agreed to sponsor a new study of the habitability of Rongelap Atoll, to be done by a three-person international scientific management team headed by Keith Baverstock of the World Health Organization (IEER's executive director, Bernd Franke, and health physicist Steve Simon, were the other members of that team). At the end of the project, participants concluded that if people returned to Rongelap, maximally exposed individuals eating only local food would receive doses in excess of 100 millirem per year, which was the maximum exposure agreed to by the DOE, the Department of the Interior, Marshall Islands officials, and the Rongelap Atoll local government that would trigger cleanup and resettlement and compensation.[51]

The Marshall Islanders have received four compensation packages to redress the damage from U.S. nuclear tests. Following their forced relocation from Bikini to Rongerik atoll in 1946, the Bikinians in mid-1948 moved again, to Kili, an island 400 miles (644 kilometers) south of Bikini. Because of the island's small size, lack of a lagoon and sheltered fishing grounds, and poor accessibility from the sea between November and May (owing to heavy surf caused by seasonal trade winds), conditions there worsened and food supplies ran critically low.

In 1956, the U.S. government gave the Bikinians $25,000 in one dollar bills (about $134,900 in 1996 dollars) and a $3 million trust fund

49. U.S. Department of Energy, *Melelen Radiation Ilo Ailiñ ko Ituiōñ Ilo Majōjl, ko Rar Etali Ilo 1978* (The meaning of radiation for those atolls in the northern part of the Marshall Islands that were surveyed in 1978), PNL-SA-10885/DE84 008308, 1979, pp. 8–9.

50. It was shortly after this voyage that French commandos placed a bomb on the *Rainbow Warrior* while it was docked in Auckland harbor, killing a photographer and sinking the ship. The French government took this unprecedented and widely condemned action to prevent Greenpeace from protesting continued nuclear testing at the French test site in Mururoa.

51. Republic of the Marshall Islands, Rongelap Atoll Local Government, U.S. Department of Energy and U.S. Department of the Interior, "Memorandum of Understanding for the Rongelap Resettlement Project," February 1992.

FIGURE 7-4. Northern Marshall Islands

Aerial Radiation Survey September–November 1978

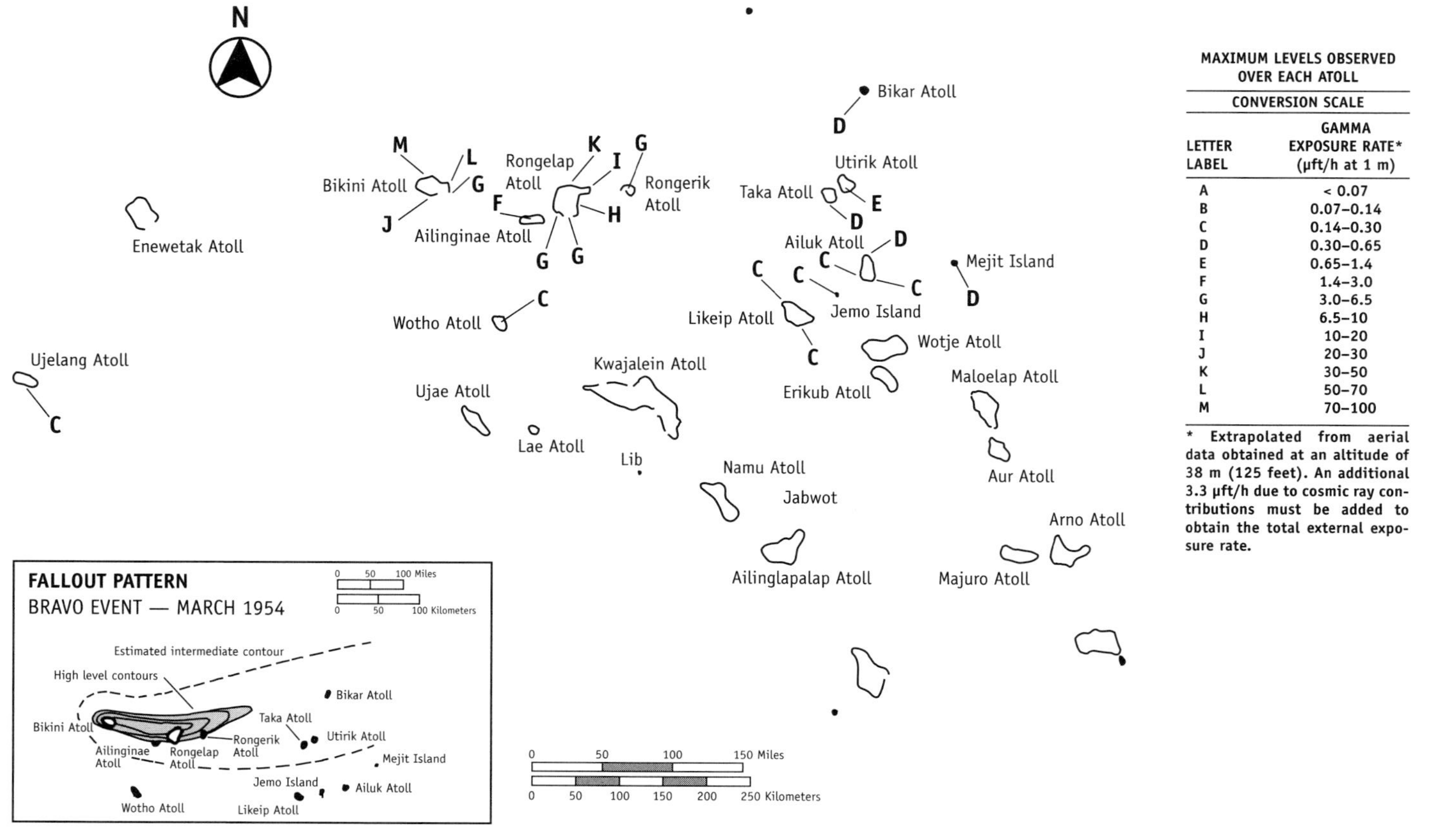

MAXIMUM LEVELS OBSERVED OVER EACH ATOLL

CONVERSION SCALE

LETTER LABEL	GAMMA EXPOSURE RATE* (μft/h at 1 m)
A	< 0.07
B	0.07–0.14
C	0.14–0.30
D	0.30–0.65
E	0.65–1.4
F	1.4–3.0
G	3.0–6.5
H	6.5–10
I	10–20
J	20–30
K	30–50
L	50–70
M	70–100

*** Extrapolated from aerial data obtained at an altitude of 38 m (125 feet). An additional 3.3 μft/h due to cosmic ray contributions must be added to obtain the total external exposure rate.**

This map documents the levels of radioactive contamination in the Northern Marshall Islands more than 20 years after the end of U.S. atmospheric nuclear testing there. its publication in 1978 generated controversy because it showed that certain inhabited areas of Rongelap Atoll were as contaminated as those deemed unsafe for human habitation.

Credit: U.S. Department of Energy (courtesy Jonathan M. Weisgall)

($23.8 million in 1996 dollars), which provided them with annual payments of about $15 (then-year) per person.[52] Additional compensation came in the form of an ex gratia (admitting no guilt) payment from Congress in 1964 for $950,000 ($4.4 million in 1996 dollars) for high exposures caused by Bravo, and Congress established a $150 million trust fund for the Marshall Islands established in 1986, supplemented by an additional $90 million in 1992 (for a total of $304.3 million in 1996 dollars).[53]

The DOE also "currently provides high-quality medical care for 137 of the 54,000 inhabitants of the Marshall Islands." These 137 people (out of 253 initially exposed, 131 are still living) were deemed to have experienced "a relatively high level of radiation" from the Bravo test.[54] This program, which has been under way since the late 1970s, at present costs $2.5 million annually ($18,248 per person). A separate program managed by Brookhaven National Laboratory and dating to 1955 monitors the health of Marshall Islanders exposed to fallout from tests in the 1950s and 1960s. It has expended more than $20.2 million since 1986 and at present spends some $1.6 million a year.[55] The Department of Interior, under the 1986 "Compact of Free Association" (48 U.S.C. § 1931) granting independence to the Marshall Islands, provides more general medical care for about 11,000 islanders from Bikini, Enewetak, Rongelap, and Utirik. All told, since 1980, at least $134.5 million has been spent on radiological surveillance and health care for these islanders. Additional efforts to manage dose assessments, monitor the environment, and conduct agricultural research are managed by the Department of the Interior and have cost the government some $292 million, with the bulk of this—about $192 million—going to Bikini.[56] In addition, since the mid-1950s the Department of the Interior and the Department of Agriculture have been providing surplus food to the Marshall Islands and overseeing various resettlement and rehabilitation efforts.[57] To date the total compensation costs relating to the Marshall Islanders have been at least $759 million.

52. Weisgall, *Operation Crossroads*, p. 312–13.

53. Barton C. Hacker, *Elements of Controversy: The Atomic Energy Commission and Radiation Safety in Nuclear Weapons Testing, 1947–1974* (University of California Press, 1994), pp. 270–71; Jeffrey Davis, "Bikini's Silver Lining," *New York Times Magazine*, May 1, 1994, pp. 42–48, 68, 72–73.

54. Letter from Dr. Tara O'Toole, Assistant Secretary for Environment, Safety and Health, U.S. Department of Energy, to the Honorable Ted Stevens, Chairman, Committee on Governmental Affairs, U.S. Senate, March 26, 1996, reprinted in *Human Radiation Experiments*," Hearings before the Senate Committee on Governmental Affairs, 104 Cong. 2 sess., S. Hrg. 104-588. (GPO, 1996), pp. 347–49.

55. Letter from Kara Villamil, Public Affairs, Brookhaven National Laboratory, to Stephen I. Schwartz, July 2, 1997. Data for years before 1986 "are not readily available."

56. Letter from Dr. Tara O'Toole to Honorable Ted Stevens, March 26, 1996; author's telephone communication with Tom Bell, program manager for the Marshall Islands Project Office, Office of International Health (EH-63), U.S. Department of Energy, June 12, 1997; author's telephone communication with Holly Barker, senior adviser, Embassy of the Marshall Islands, August 5, 1997.

57. Data provided by Joseph H. McDermott, Marshall Islands—Federated States of Micronesia—Palmyra and Wake Atolls—Navassa Island Desk Officer, Policy Division, Office of Insular Affairs, U.S. Department of the Interior, June 12, 1997.

Perhaps the most widely known downwinder case concerns the Japanese fishing boat *Daigo Fukuryu Maru* (the No. 5 Lucky, or Fortunate, Dragon) and its crew of twenty-three, who were exposed to extremely high levels of fallout hours after the Bravo test while trawling for tuna 100 miles (161 kilometers) east of Bikini and outside the restricted area established for the test (an American tanker, the *Patapsco*, was also caught under the cloud when it was misguided by a search plane sent to ensure the restricted area was clear before the test). Startled by the test and its aftermath, the crew decided to return home. By the time they reached their homeport of Yaizu southwest of Tokyo less than two weeks later, they were suffering the effects of radiation sickness. But before the danger had been recognized, much of the several tons of tuna and shark in the ship's hold had been sold. Panic gripped Japan, fish prices collapsed, and authorities tried to track down the contaminated fish (this fear spread to the United States two weeks later, where much Japanese tuna would normally have been sold, and substantial efforts were mounted to monitor fish for contamination and calm the public).

On September 23, 1954, one of the *Fukuryu Maru's* crewmen died of liver disease.[58] Attempting to contain the negative publicity, the U.S. State Department quickly drew on its emergency funds to issue a payment of 1 million yen to his widow ($2,778 at the prevailing rate of exchange and more than $21,000 in 1996 dollars). In late 1954 the U.S. government, seeking to avoid legal liability while accepting moral responsibility, issued a $2 million ex gratia payment to the Japanese government for damages caused by the Bravo test ($15.3 million in 1996 dollars). Much of the money went to the tuna industry and agencies that dealt with the aftermath of the test, although $151,000 (about $1.2 million in 1996 dollars) was shared among the twenty-two surviving crew members, who left the hospital in May 1955 following fourteen months of treatment.[59] (For the government's handling of another testing-related case, see box 7-5.)

Human Radiation Experiments

From the 1940s into the 1970s, more than 23,000 people were subjected to 1,400 different radiation experiments, many without their informed consent. The subjects were diverse in terms of gender, race, and age, but in general they were chosen from vulnerable populations such as the poor and prisoners. As already mentioned, some experiments involved workers and armed forces personnel; downwinders were also exposed owing to deliberate releases of radioactivity.

58. Subsequent analysis of the liver indicated a relatively high radioiodine burden. See Eisenbud and Gessell, *Environmental Radioactivity*, pp. 384–85.

59. Hacker, *Elements of Controversy*, pp. 157–58.

Box 7-5
A Kodak Moment

Although the AEC had few compunctions about keeping the public in the dark about the hazards of the nuclear testing program, it adopted a different policy for the Eastman Kodak Company of Rochester, New York.[1] On January 27, 1951, the AEC inaugurated its newly established continental test site—the Nevada Proving Ground (now the Nevada Test Site)—by secretly detonating a 1-kiloton nuclear device, code-named Able. Two days later, Geiger counters at Kodak's film plant on the shores of Lake Ontario detected high levels of radiation as heavy snow blanketed the city. Kodak officials became worried that the radiation would damage film stocks and cause significant financial losses.

Having experienced a similar occurrence nearly six years earlier, following the Trinity test, Kodak executives had little doubt that fallout from a nuclear test was responsible.[2] Kodak registered a complaint with the National Association of Photographic Manufacturers, who in turn telegrammed the AEC: "Tests snowfall Rochester Monday by Eastman Kodak Company give ten thousand counts per minute, whereas equal volume snow falling previous Friday gave only four hundred. Situation serious. Will report any further results obtained. What are you doing?" The following day, the AEC released a statement to the Associated Press that it was "investigating reports that snow that fell in Rochester was measurably radioactive. The reports . . . indicate that there is no possibility of harm to humans or animals. . . . All necessary precautions, including radiation surveys and patrolling, are being undertaken to insure that safety conditions are maintained."

1. Atomic Energy Commission, Report by the Director of Military Application, "Summary of Relations between the AEC and the Photographic Industry Regarding Radioactive Contamination from Atomic Weapon Tests, from January through December 1951," January 17, 1952, Record Group 325, Secretariat Collection, Box 1258, Folder MH&S 3-3 Contamination & Decontamination, formerly Confidential, declassified March 28, 1983, Department of Energy Archives; Richard L. Miller, *Under the Cloud: The Decades of Nuclear Testing* (New York: Free Press, 1986), pp. 58–59, 90–91; Peter Pringle and James Spigelman, *The Nuclear Barons* (New York: Holt, Rhinehart & Winston, 1981), pp. 179–80.

2. As the radioactive cloud from Trinity crossed the country, fallout was washed out by rainfall into the Wabash River in Indiana, more than 1,000 miles (1,609 kilometers) from Alamogordo, New Mexico. The river water, in turn, contaminated some materials such as corn husks later used to package Kodak industrial X-ray film. The film was damaged by the radiation.

On December 7, 1993, Secretary of Energy Hazel O'Leary broke with her predecessors and made a stunning admission: for the first time, the head of a nuclear weapons establishment stood before the people it was pledged to protect and admitted that it had been experimenting upon them in ways that might have harmed them. Upon learning in late 1993 of a particularly troubling series of experiments involving the injection of plutonium and uranium into unknowing subjects, O'Leary remarked, "The only thing I could think of was Nazi Germany."[60] It soon became apparent that other agencies, including the

60. Russell Watson with Daniel Glick and Mark Hosenball and others, "America's Nuclear Secrets," *Newsweek*, December 27, 1993, p. 15.

Box 7-5
(continued)

Kodak's general manager also telephoned AEC Commissioner Sumner Pike to notify him of the situation. The AEC eventually replied that a test had in fact taken place and that while it appreciated the company's and the industry's concerns, it could provide no assurances that fallout from future tests would not be carried across the country by the prevailing winds. Kodak president T. J. Hargrave warned the AEC that if the company's costs to deal with the radioactivity should mount it would "very likely" have to sue the government for damages. The AEC, which took this threat very seriously, countered with an extraordinary offer. Foregoing the strict secrecy rules it enforced everywhere else, the AEC decided to send Kodak, before and after each future test, a series of classified maps—updated daily—delineating areas of potentially heavy fallout (along with general information on the type of test, for example, tower shot or air drop). A Kodak executive and representatives of several other photographic companies were granted "Q" clearances (see chapter 8) to receive and make use of the information to alter plant operations and otherwise avoid contact with contaminated materials. Thus beginning with the Operation Greenhouse series of tests in 1951 at Enewetak (and continuing presumably until the end of atmospheric testing in 1962), this industry knew in advance when a test would occur, where the fallout was expected to go, and, most important, where it went. Yet citizens living downwind of (and in closer proximity to) the test site, particularly in Nevada and Utah, were never given any such detailed early warnings. Whatever fallout did drift away from the test site—the AEC assured the public in *Atomic Tests in Nevada,* a booklet it distributed widely in Nevada and southern Utah in the mid-1950s—was exceedingly minimal: "Your potential exposure . . . will be low . . . made possible by very close attention to a variety of on-site and off-site procedures." By staying indoors for a few hours following a test or, if outside, taking a bath and dusting off clothes and shoes, the AEC noted, they could avoid harm from fallout. [3]

3. A. Costandina Titus, "Selling the Bomb: Public Relations Efforts by the Atomic Energy Commission during the 1950s and Early 1960s," *Government Publications Review,* vol. 16 (January/February 1989), pp. 15–29. For compelling documentary evidence of the consequences of this indifference, see Carole Gallagher, *American Ground Zero: The Secret Nuclear War* (Cambridge, Mass.: MIT Press, 1993).

DOD, the National Aeronautics and Space Administration, and the Department of Veterans Affairs had been involved in human radiation experiments. The same month, the GAO revealed for the first time that the DOD and the AEC deliberately released radionuclides into the air from 1948 to 1952 in order to design and test radiation weapons.[61] Such weapons, discussed as far back as the Manhattan Project, are designed to create temporarily high radiation fields to kill or debilitate enemy soldiers.[62]

61. U.S. General Accounting Office, *Nuclear Health and Safety: Examples of Post World War II Radiation Releases at U.S. Nuclear Sites,* RCED-94-51FS (November 1993).

62. Barton J. Bernstein, "Radiological Warfare: The Path Not Taken," *Bulletin of the Atomic Scientists,* vol. 41 (August 1985), pp. 44–49; International Physicians for the Prevention of Nuclear War and the Institute for Energy and Environmental Research, *Plutonium: Deadly Gold of the Nuclear Age* (Cambridge, Mass.: International Physicians Press, 1992), pp. 141–45.

There were at least five kinds of experiments, classified according to purpose: to design instrumentation for spying on the Soviet Union, to design radiation weapons, to test the ability of soldiers and astronauts to withstand radiation on battlefields and in space, to study occupational exposure to radiation, and to study the metabolism of radioactive materials (see table 7-1).[63] Some experiments may have had more than one purpose. In several, external doses were given to sick people supposedly to treat cancer. The full objectives of the experiments cannot be determined accurately without additional documentation.

The legal aspects of these experiments are revealing. As discussed in chapter 6, the U.S. nuclear weapons establishment was so concerned about liability that contractors to the AEC demanded and were granted complete immunity for actions relating to radiation, even for negligence. Apprehension about liability seems to have carried over to the human experiments. As early as 1947, an official of the experimentation program suggested documents on the matter be withheld in order to avoid "adverse effect on public opinion or . . . legal suits" (see figure 8-1). When Charles Edington, a reviewer of the proposal, approved the irradiation of the testicles of prisoners in Washington and Oregon State prisons from 1963 to 1971, he explained:

> All of our mammalian work has been carried out to get a better idea of radiation effects on germ cells and spermatogenesis, etc., with the hope of extrapolating the results to man. This proposal is a direct attack on our problem. I'm for support at the requested level as long as we are not liable. I wonder about possible carcinogenic effects of such treatments.[64]

Despite the protestations that the doses were low and would not cause harm, many such experiments were specifically designed to induce harm. The irradiation levels in this particular case reached 600 rads, known to be very dangerous even during the Manhattan Project. In another experiment, conducted in 1946–47, uranium salts were injected into subjects at the University of Rochester at levels that would produce injury to the kidneys.[65]

In December 1993 Secretary O'Leary acknowledged that the government had conducted human experiments and that some of these

---

63. In an experiment unrelated to any of these goals, the Air Force's Arctic Aeromedical Laboratory, from August 1955 to September 1957, gave trace elements of iodine-131 to eighty-five Inupiaq (Eskimo) and seventeen Athapascan Indians (all Alaskan natives) and nineteen military personnel to study the role of the thyroid gland in acclimatization of human beings to cold and improve U.S. military operations in cold weather environments. See National Research Council, *The Arctic Aeromedical Laboratory's Thyroid Function Study: A Radiobiological Risk and Ethical Analysis* (Washington, D.C.: National Academy Press, 1996); Department of Defense, *Report on Search for Human Radiation Experiment Records,* vol. 1, pp. 45–48.

64. Charles W. Edington, handwritten review comments as summary of Review of Recent Proposal, Division of Biology and Medicine, U.S. Atomic Energy Commission, April 14, 1963, at the Institute for Energy and Environmental Research.

65. *American Nuclear Guinea Pigs: Three Decades of Human Radiation Experiments on U.S. Citizens,* House Report prepared by the Subcommittee on Energy Conservation and Power of the Committee on Energy and Commerce, 99 Cong. 2 sess. (GPO, 1986).

TABLE 7-1. Examples of U.S. Radiation Experimentation on Humans[a]

Date and purpose	*Description*	*Institution*[b]
Develop instrumentation for spying on the Soviet nuclear weapons complex		
1949	Intentional release of iodine-131 to environment	AEC, air force
1950	Intentional release of radioactive material to the environment	Los Alamos Scientific Laboratory, air force
Develop radiation weapons		
1948	Intentional release of lanthanum-140 to environment	AEC
1949–52	Intentional release of tantalum-182 and possibly other radioactive material to the environment	Army, AEC, air force
Determine the effects of radiation on the ability of military personnel to function on the nuclear battlefield and/or effects of radiation on astronauts		
1943–44	Whole-body irradiation by X rays	University of Chicago
1953	Exposure of hands to radioactive material	Foster D. Snell (consulting firm), Monsanto
1960–71	Whole-body irradiation by X rays	University of Cincinnati
1960–74	Whole-body gamma irradiation	Oak Ridge Institute of Nuclear Studies
Early 1970s	Neutron and ion beam irradiation	Lawrence Berkeley Laboratory
Occupational exposure to external radiation		
1945	Exposure of skin to beta rays	Clinton Laboratory (Oak Ridge)
1947	Exposure of fingers to radioactive material	University of Chicago
1955	Exposure of skin to radium-224	New York University
1963–71	Irradiation of the testicles of prisoners by X rays	Pacific Northwest Research Foundation, University of Washington[c]
Determine metabolism of radioactive materials[d]		
1943–47	Polonium injections	University of Rochester
1945–47	Plutonium injections	Manhattan District Hospital (Oak Ridge), UCSF, University of Rochester, University of Chicago
1946–47	Injections of U-234 and U-235 uranium nitrate to induce renal injury	University of Rochester
Late 1940s	Administration of radioactive iron to pregnant women	Vanderbilt University
1946–56	Ingestion of radioactive iron and calcium	MIT, Harvard
1950, 1952	Exposure of skin to tritium; also some by ingestion and inhalation	Los Alamos Scientific Laboratory

TABLE 7-1. Examples of Radiation Experimentation on Humans[a] *(continued)*

Date and purpose	*Description*	*Institution*[b]
1953–57	Uranium injections	Massachusetts General Hospital (Boston), ORNL
? (results published 1959)	Calcium-45 and strontium-85 injections	Columbia University, Montefiore Hospital (Bronx, New York)
1960s	Uranium-235 and manganese-54 ingestion	Los Alamos Scientific Laboratory
1961–63	Ingestion of real and simulated fallout from nuclear tests	University of Chicago, Argonne National Laboratory
1961–65	Radium and thorium injections/ ingestion	MIT
? (results published 1962)	Ingestion of lanthanum-140	Oak Ridge Institute of Nuclear Studies
1963	Phosphorus-32 injections	Battelle Memorial Institute (Richland, Washington)
1962–65	Intentional release of iodine-131 to environment/ingestion	ORNL, National Reactor Testing Station (ID)
1965	Technetium-95 (metastable) and technetium-96 injections/ingestion	Pacific Northwest Laboratory
1965–73	Inhalation of argon-41/ingestion of various radioactive isotopes	AEC
1967	Promethium-143 injections/ingestions	Hanford Environmental Health Foundation, Battelle Memorial Institute
? (results published 1968)	Lead-212 ingestions/injections	University of Rochester

Source: Makhijani and others, *Nuclear Wastelands,* pp. 180–81.

a. Categories are those considered most appropriate from publicly available evidence. The purpose is not always explicitly stated and in this case represents judgments made by IEER staff.

b. AEC = U.S. Atomic Energy Commission; UCSF = University of California, San Francisco; MIT = Massachusetts Institute of Technology; ORNL = Oak Ridge National Laboratory.

c. These experiments were possibly related to radiation weapons development.

d. Some of these experiments may fit into other categories, and some may have had military applications.

may have been done without proper informed consent.[66] A presidential commission appointed to review the entire range of human experiments by the government reported in October 1995 that although the consent of some subjects was obtained, it was not until 1974 that the government introduced "comprehensive policies requiring the consent of *all* subjects of research, including both healthy subjects and

66. H. Josef Hebert, "Radiation, Arms Tests Concealed," *Seattle Post-Intelligencer,* December 8, 1993, p. A1; R. Jeffrey Smith, "U.S. Discloses 204 Secret Nuclear Tests," *Washington Post,* December 8, 1993, p. A1; "Experiments on Humans," *Washington Post,* December 30, 1993, p. A22.

patient subjects" and that it "did not generally take effective measures to implement [its] requirements and policies on consent to human radiation research." In fact, the commission had difficulty finding evidence that proved that consent had been obtained in most cases. It also estimated that 2,000 to 3,000 of the armed services personnel who participated in nuclear weapons tests "were research subjects."[67]

In a controversial finding, the commission determined that only about thirty individuals in three sets of experiments deserved financial compensation for being subjected to dangerous experiments without their knowledge. However, apologies were owed to a large number of experiment subjects to whom no direct benefit accrued from the experiment (formal apologies were issued by President Bill Clinton and Secretary O'Leary in March 1997).[68] Costs for the experiments themselves are difficult to obtain, but the principal researcher of one long-running series of experiments on eighty-eight patients at the University of Cincinnati College of Medicine from 1960 to 1972 estimated that it cost more than $1 million in then-year dollars, or approximately $5 million in 1996 dollars.[69] The presidential commission's work over two years cost $6.3 million. The DOE spent an additional $16.2 million for administrative support, document retrieval, and declassification expenses associated with the study.[70]

In March 1997 the DOE reached an out-of-court settlement of $6.5 million with seventeen of the nineteen subjects of the plutonium and uranium injection experiments (one family refused compensation and one subject was never located). In December 1997 the Massachusetts Institute of Technology and the Quaker Oats company agreed to settle a class action lawsuit arising from an AEC-sponsored experiment in the late 1940s and early 1950s at the Walter E. Fernald State School in Waltham, Massachusetts, where more than 100 boys between the ages of twelve and seventeen (many of whom were inaccurately labeled retarded) were fed oatmeal containing radioactive trace elements of iron and calcium in an effort to study the absorption of nutrients throughout the body. A consent form sent to parents by the school in 1953 described the experiment only in vague terms and failed to mention the ingestion of radioactive materials. As an incentive to participate, the boys were told they would be part of a "science club" and

67. Advisory Committee on Human Radiation Experiments, Final Report, pp. 780-782, 789.

68. Advisory Committee on Human Radiation Experiments, Final Report, pp. 801–03; Joby Warrick, "U.S. Moves to Shield Subjects of Human Medical Research," *Washington Post,* March 29, 1997, p. A4. The experiments, said Clinton, "failed both the test of our national values and the test of humanity."

69. Advisory Committee on Human Radiation Experiments, Final Report, pp. 385–89; Department of Defense, *Report on Search for Human Radiation Experiment Records,* vol. 1, pp. 30–32; and *Radiation Experiments Conducted by the University of Cincinnati Medical School with Department of Defense Funding,* Hearings before the Subcommittee on Administrative Law and Governmental Relations of the House Judiciary Committee, 103 Cong. 2 sess. (GPO, 1994), p. 174.

70. Paul Barton, Radiation Study Fallout Debated," *Cincinnati Enquirer,* December 25. 1995, p. A26.

would receive special treatment, such as trips to baseball games and extra portions of milk at meals. As of this writing the settlement of $1.85 million (with the bulk of the money coming from MIT) was awaiting approval by the plaintiffs in April 1998. As the settlement payment will come from nongovernmental sources, its costs are not included here.[71]

Cases still pending include testicular irradiation experiments at Oregon State Prison and Washington State Prison between 1963 and 1971 (to determine what doses induced sterility); a lawsuit involving 820 women who between 1945 and 1947 were given small doses of radioactive iron by Vanderbilt University while pregnant; and the whole body of irradiation experiments at the University of Cincinnati.[72]

Fallout from Atmospheric Nuclear Testing

A concern of global proportions is the effect of atmospheric nuclear-weapons testing and of releases of krypton-85, carbon-14 dioxide, and other gaseous radionuclides from plutonium production. Given the long-lived nature of some of the radionuclides involved, notably carbon-14, these exposures will persist for thousands of years.

It is possible to make rough estimates of the number of fatal cancers that have been and will be caused globally as a result of all atmospheric testing (528 tests since 1945, with the United States responsible for 215, or 41 percent of these)[73] from its inception in 1945 to its halt in 1980 (when China conducted the last atmospheric nuclear test). From the data compiled by the United Nations Scientific Committee on the Effects of Atomic Radiation, doses appear to amount to a few millirem per year.[74]

The main radionuclides of concern are carbon-14, cesium-137, zirconium-95, and strontium-90. Though the increase in risk for any individual (except many downwinders) is small, it has been estimated that fallout has caused and will cause 430,000 fatal cancers until the end of the next century owing to radiation exposures in this century alone. Perhaps a third of these (roughly 140,000) may be due to U.S. atmospheric testing (see footnote 73).[75] Thereafter, carbon-14, with a half-

71. Associated Press, "Radioactive Oatmeal Suit Settled for $1.85 Million," *Washington Post,* January 1, 1998, p. A17.

72. Warrick, "U.S. Moves to Shield Subjects of Human Medical Research"; Matthew L. Wald, "Rule Adopted to Prohibit Secret Tests on Humans," *New York Times* (Washington edition), March 29, 1997, p. 7.

73. Megatonnage expended in atmospheric testing is a better measure of the quantities of fissile materials thus dispersed. The United States accounts for 141 out of 427.9 megatons, or 33 percent of the total. See Robert S. Norris, and William M. Arkin, "NRDC Nuclear Notebook—Known Nuclear Tests Worldwide, 1945–1995," *Bulletin of the Atomic Scientists,* vol. 52 (May/June 1996), pp. 61–63.

74. Institute for Energy and Environmental Research, *Radioactive Heaven and Earth,* pp. 33–47.

75. See Institute for Energy and Environmental Research, *Radioactive Heaven and Earth,* pp. 33–47.

life of 5,730 years, will be the overwhelming component of doses from fallout. Including carbon-14 exposures through infinity yields approximately 2.4 million cancer fatalities, with some 800,000 potentially attributable to U.S. atmospheric tests (to put this in perspective, 617,389 U.S. military personnel were killed in World Wars I and II, the Korean War, the Vietnam War, and the Gulf War combined).[76] All of these fatalities are, of course, estimates of premature deaths, each of which results in the loss of life expectancy. The rate of cancer incidence is, on average, about 50 percent higher than cancer fatalities.

It is important to note that these calculations are based on the hypothesis that all radiation doses below the ones that produce immediate observable effects (that is, all radiation levels that go under the rubric of "low-level" doses) produce proportional increases in cancer risk. This is known as the linear, no-threshold hypothesis and is the accepted basis of public health protection and environmental regulations. There is some controversy as to the effects of radiation at very low doses because the increase in individual risk is very low and difficult to observe. Clouding the issue are the far larger number of cancers from all other causes and higher doses from other sources, including natural background radiation, which tend to mask the proportionally smaller number of concerns attributable to fallout. The estimates just cited were calculated assuming that the risk from very low doses is the same per unit of dose as higher doses (as in the case of Hiroshima and Nagasaki survivors). The estimates of cancers would be lower by a factor of two (70,000 to 400,000 attributable to U.S. testing) if the risk of low doses delivered at low dose rates is assumed to be a factor of two lower than sudden doses, as is common regulatory practice.

By comparison, while doses from atmospheric testing fallout of a few millirem per year are lower than natural background (which is about 100 millirem at sea level), they are qualitatively different from a political and moral standpoint.[77] Inflicting a known harm on fellow human beings without their informed consent cannot be reasonably compared to cancer arising from natural causes or even one's normal living arrangements and choices. In a very real sense, more Americans have been harmed by the nuclear weapons that were supposed to *protect* them than were the peoples of the former Soviet Union, China, and other countries against whom these weapons were targeted. The same was true for the people of the Soviet Union, since the Soviet government paid even less attention to environmental and safety concerns.[78]

76. Department of Defense, "Conflicts and Casualties" (table), *Defense 96 Almanac,* Issue 5, pp. 43–44.

77. This natural background estimate does not include exposure to indoor radon-222. That exposure level is mainly an artifact of home construction. It averages 200 milliram per year in the United States.

78. See, for example, Daniel Williams, "Legacy of Soviet Nuclear Tests Haunts Kazakhstan," *Washington Post,* November 7, 1997, p. A1.

The potential for radiation damage was understood by U.S. government officials at the time the tests were conducted (see box 1-1). In 1960 an editorial in a University of California engineering alumni magazine proclaimed such damage to be acceptable. It was reprinted without comment in 1990. Here is an excerpt:

> The increase in radiation one receives from fallout is about equal to the increase one receives from cosmic rays when moving from sea level to the top of a hill several hundred feet high. . . . It means, though, your baby's chances of having a major birth defect are increased by one part in 5,000 approximately. Percentagewise, this is insignificant. When applied to the population of the world, it means that nuclear testing so far has produced about an additional 6,000 babies born with major birth defects. Whether you choose to look at 'one part in 5,000' or '6,000 babies,' you must weigh this acknowledged risk with the demonstrated need of the United States for a nuclear arsenal.[79]

One of the heaviest costs, but also among the most resistant to quantification, has been the loss of trust occasioned by revelations of human experimentation, poor or nonexistent data on doses received, fabricated data on releases to the environment, and other cases of deception associated with nuclear weapons production and testing (see chapter 8). Despite its knowledge of the dangers of fallout, the AEC consistently deceived U.S. citizens living in the vicinity of the Nevada Test Site, assuring them the danger was minimal even as it undertook secret studies of fallout in milk, water, and foodstuffs to better track the path of the clouds. The AEC also engaged in self-described "body-snatching" to study fallout's effect on people.[80] The nuclear weapons establishment was not the only government body to engage in such practices. Two others that come readily to mind are the U.S. Public Health Service and the Centers for Disease Control, which ran the infamous Tuskeegee syphilis experiment from 1932 to 1972, and the CIA, which conducted the MKULTRA drug-induced mind-control experiments in the 1960s. However, the scope and extent of the AEC's power, the grave violations of trust in human experimentation, and negligent management of the weapons complex stand out as among the more egregious government actions in post–World War II U.S. history.

Many of the costs itemized in this chapter, quantifiable and otherwise, could have been avoided or at least significantly reduced had gov-

79. Editorial in *California Engineer,* April 1960, reprinted in *California Engineer,* vol. 68, no. 3 (1990), p. 23.

80. H. Josef Hebert, "Agency Sought Cadavers for Its Radiation Studies," *Washington Post,* June 22, 1995, p. A3. More than 15,000 subjects were involved in studies such as this. A useful overview of nearly sixty past and ongoing (as of mid-1995) human tissue studies by the DOE and its predecessors can be found in U.S. General Accounting Office, *Department of Energy: Information on DOE's Human Tissue Analysis Work,* RCED-95-109FS (May 1995).

ernment officials been more candid about the nature of the nuclear weapons program and the risks involved. That they were not is a direct result of the secrecy surrounding nuclear weapons since the beginning of the Manhattan Project. The costs and consequences of this secrecy are explored in chapter 8.

FIGURE 8-1. "It is desired that no document be released . . ."[a]

SECRET THIS DOCUMENT CONSISTS OF 1 PAG
NO. 1 OF 2 SERIES

SECRET

UNITED STATES
ATOMIC ENERGY COMMISSION
WASHINGTON 25, D. C.

* 19940000081 *
DOE-OR

4234

April 17, 1947

U. S. Atomic Energy Commission
P. O. Box E
Oak Ridge, Tennessee

Attention: Dr. Fidler

Subject: MEDICAL EXPERIMENTS ON HUMANS

1. It is desired that no document be released which refers to experiments with humans and might have adverse effect on public opinion or result in legal suits. Documents covering such work field should be classified "secret". Further work in this field in the future has been prohibited by the General Manager. It is understood that three documents in this field have been submitted for declassification and are now classified "restricted". It is desired that these documents be reclassified "secret" and that a check be made to insure that no distribution has inadvertantly been made to the Department of Commerce, or other off-Project personnel or agencies.

2. These instructions do not pertain to documents regarding clinical or therapeutic uses of radioisotopes and similar materials beneficial to human disorders and diseases.

ATOMIC ENERGY COMMISSION

O. G. HAYWOOD, JR.
Colonel, Corps of Engineers.

RESTRICTED DATA

CLASSIFICATION CANCELLED
AUTHORITY: DOE/SA-20
BY H. R. SCHMIDT, DATE:
HRSchmidt 2/22/94

SECRET

a. This 1947 memorandum to a physician at the Atomic Energy Commission's Oak Ridge, Tennessee, facility, indicates that from an early date officials sought to withhold information on human radiation experiments not for legitimate security reasons but to avoid generating public controversy or legal action. This document was only declassified in February 1994.

8

The Costs and Consequences of Nuclear Secrecy

William Burr, Thomas S. Blanton, and Stephen I. Schwartz

To all the costs discussed in the preceding chapters must be added one more: the costs of keeping nuclear weapons information secret and secure.

The atom had us bewitched. It was so gigantic, so terrible, so beyond the power of imagination to embrace that it seemed to be the ultimate fact. It would either destroy us or bring about the millennium. . . . Our obsession with the atom led us to assign to it a separate and unique status in the world. So greatly did it seem to transcend the ordinary affairs of men that we shut it out of those affairs altogether; or rather tried to create a separate world, the world of the Atom.

—David E. Lilienthal, first chairman of the Atomic Energy Commission, 1963

Summary

—The costs of nuclear secrecy are so difficult to measure that only a minimum estimate can be made, in the neighborhood of $3.4 billion. This is the total measurable cost of Department of Energy (and its predecessors) security clearance operations since 1948, one-third of the known costs of Department of Defense for information security from 1990 through 1995, and two relatively small charges relating to AEC clearances in 1948 and 1953. Using the DOE's rule of thumb that secrecy and security measures constitute about 20 percent of total program costs, nuclear secrecy may have cost the AEC/ERDA/DOE weapons production complex some $70 billion, with tens of billions more spent by the DOD and the intelligence community. But these are not included in this study's total estimated costs because military expenditures on secrecy and security cover both nuclear and nonnuclear efforts. Moreover, nuclear secrecy expenditures cannot easily be disaggregated, and a great deal of nuclear budget data remain classified.

—U.S. nuclear secrecy policy was founded on the unprecedented concept of "restricted data," which treated nuclear weapons information as classified from inception—or "born secret."

—The intangible costs of secrecy, particularly the political costs, may be more significant than the budgetary costs: the nuclear secrecy system has had adverse implications for informed congressional and public debate over nuclear policy, constitutional guarantees, government accountability, and civilian control over the military.

—Nuclear secrecy can aid or impair efforts to stem nuclear proliferation. At best, it helps slow proliferation by raising the costs to would-be nuclear states; at worst, it complicates and delays efforts to develop international safeguards.

—Even without changes in the secrecy system, stronger congressional oversight of nuclear weapons programs and more robust internal accountability within the executive branch could have mitigated the effects of extreme secrecy by protecting public interests. But normal checks and balances in the constitutional system failed in part because of nuclear secrecy.

The Beginnings of Nuclear Secrecy

Since the days of the Manhattan Project, secrecy has been the U.S. government's preferred strategy for preventing the proliferation of nuclear weapons technologies among actual or potential adversaries. Even before the government had invested substantial financial resources in an atomic bomb project, civilian scientists who sought to check Nazi Germany's atomic program tried to restrict access to data on recent scientific breakthroughs.[1] More than half a century later, secrecy remains necessary because it raises the costs of weapons development (for example, to avoid arousing suspicions in the United States and elsewhere, Iraq has spent billions of dollars of oil revenue on obsolete, though effective, electromagnetic uranium-enrichment technology rather than seeking to acquire more widely used enrichment technologies). Nuclear secrecy has incurred substantial—yet until now largely unrecognized—budgetary, economic, and political costs. Though each of these costs has been significant, the political costs are especially troubling because of their implications for constitutional democracy in the United States. As long as the principle of openness and accountability is central to American political life, the costs of nuclear secrecy must be acknowledged and assessed.

1. For initial voluntary censorship efforts, see Lillian Hoddeson, with contributions from Gordon Baym and others, *Critical Assembly: A Technical History of Los Alamos during the Oppenheimer Years, 1943–1945* (Cambridge University Press, 1993), p. 20.

The concept of government-mandated secrecy arose from the desire to limit the potential threat to the United States posed by atomic energy. When the bombings of Hiroshima and Nagasaki became public knowledge, Western leaders declared that American and British allies had unlocked the "secrets of nature." Although these same leaders did not believe their governments could indefinitely monopolize the scientific knowledge that made atomic weapons possible, they took it for granted that information controls could slow nuclear proliferation. Accordingly, they established a disciplined bureaucracy and tight limits on the distribution of nuclear weapons information to those with a "need to know." With the passage of time, the Atomic Energy Commission and its successor organizations—the Energy Research and Development Administration (1975–77) and the Department of Energy (1977–present)—have released more and more formerly restricted data, but the most vital secrets, such as weapons design information, necessarily remain classified. Government concerns on the whole have been reasonable—to prevent further proliferation of these enormously dangerous and destructive weapons—but too often have been translated into unreasonably broad measures that result in the overclassification of huge quantities of data and prevent the timely declassification of important historical information.

Even before the advent of Secretary of Energy Hazel R. O'Leary's openness initiative in 1993–97, the DOE and its predecessors had released significant information on nuclear weapons (such as which were uranium "gun" types and which were plutonium implosion designs), and the Department of Defense had declassified information on early nuclear war plans, including details of the first Single Integrated Operational Plan.[2] What the DOE and DOD have guarded so assiduously over the decades are not the fundamentals of nuclear physics, which cannot be kept secret, or even basic applications of nuclear science to power plant technology, but the practical applications of nuclear weapons and weapons delivery systems. Too often, however, secrecy has been used to withhold information that concerns not sensitive technology or war plans, but embarrassing or controversial government actions, such as human radiation experiments (see figure 8-1).

Thus the veil of secrecy covers fissile materials production technology and output levels,[3] nuclear weapons design and technology, specific data on certain weapons effects, nuclear power for submarines (includ-

2. See, for example, Thomas H. Etzold and John Lewis Gaddis, *Containment: Documents on American Policy and Strategy, 1945–1950* (Columbia University Press, 1978), pp. 315–34; David A. Rosenberg, "The Origins of Overkill: Nuclear Weapons and American Strategy, 1945–1960," in Steven E. Miller, ed., *Strategy and Nuclear Deterrence* (Princeton University Press, 1984), pp. 113–181; Scott D. Sagan, "SIOP-62: The Nuclear War Plan Briefing to President Kennedy," *International Security,* vol. 12, no. 1 (1987), pp. 22–51.

3. Between 1993 and 1996 the DOE released the total and annual production figures for plutonium and the total production figure for HEU. Annual HEU production rates and nearly all data concerning tritium production

ing the total amount of highly enriched uranium used by naval reactors and currently in navy custody), historical and current weapons deployments, characteristics of nuclear weapons delivery systems (for example, range and accuracy), nuclear war plans and projected nuclear operations in wartime, and intelligence sources and methods of detecting overseas nuclear developments. Even the number of nuclear weapons in the U.S. nuclear stockpile at present remains an official secret, although the historical numbers from 1945 to 1961, along with other selected stockpile data, were declassified in 1994.[4]

Information controls necessarily extend beyond the documents containing secrets. To ensure high levels of secrecy and to prevent leaks, personnel seeking "Q" clearances (required to work on nuclear weapons or with nuclear materials) from the DOE must undergo extensive background investigations (and occasional reinvestigations) and comply with elaborate security measures. Military personnel must undergo similar procedures to get CNWDI (critical nuclear weapon design information) clearances (see box 8-1 for the various types of nuclear security clearances). Moreover, elaborate security systems guard the various facilities that house classified documents, nuclear weapons production and testing sites, and weapons systems.[5]

Nuclear security is necessarily expensive. The DOE alone possesses at least 280 million pages of classified documents.[6] Maintaining security for this document stockpile means paying for guards, guns, safes, investigators, specially trained office personnel, electronic security systems, and the officials who preside over and monitor the security system, not to mention the "secure" facilities needed for work on classified documents or the technical support for ultimately declassifying them. It also means paying for the secure transport or transmission of classified material, such as special couriers and secure telephone and fascimile lines, and the required periodic inventories of top secret material. These costs can be thought of as a permanent "mortgage" imposed by the creation of classified documents. Indeed, security has been enforced at the DOE long enough for its officials to have developed routine methods for measuring its costs. A long-standing rule of thumb has been that security adds about 20 percent to the cost of

(except for the fact that 13 kilograms were produced at the Hanford Reservation) remain classified.

4. U.S. Department of Energy, "Openness Press Conference Fact Sheets," June 27, 1994, pp. 162–73.

5. For CNWDI clearances and the information encompassed by them, see Department of Defense, "Access to and Dissemination of Restricted Data," Directive 5210.2, January 12, 1978.

6. This is only an estimate. See Committee on Declassification of Information for the Department of Energy Environmental Remediation and Related Programs, *A Review of the Department of Energy Classification Policy and Practice* (Washington, D.C.: National Academy Press, 1995), p. 7. Of these, 230 million are more than twenty-five years old and thus subject to Executive Order 12958 (see p. 531 of the order). See *Report of the Commission on Protecting and Reducing Government Secrecy*, S. Doc. 105-2 (GPO, 1997), p. 74.

a program involving classified activities (excluding special access programs).[7]

The costs of the various activities surrounding nuclear secrecy are extremely elusive. The only hard figure we have been able to calculate is $1.97 billion for AEC, ERDA, and DOE personnel security investigations from 1952 to 1996 (see the next section and footnote 64). But even that number is incomplete. Because personnel security expenditures have only been one component of the budgetary cost of secrecy, the historical costs must stretch into multiple billions. Other costs, such as political and technological, are not readily amenable to fiscal quantification but are even more important than budgetary costs because of their implications for constitutional democracy. These intangible costs include circumscribed public debate over U.S. military policy, weakened civilian control over the military, and reduced effectiveness of U.S. nonproliferation policy.

Nuclear Secrecy: Historical Background

Ironically, the impetus for nuclear secrecy and the original means of imposing it did not come from the military officers who administered the Manhattan Project.[8] Rather, the leadership came from the private sector, from the world of civilian physicists who believed that the only way to arrest Germany's wartime atomic weapons program was to restrict the circulation of scientific breakthroughs, such as the discovery of transuranic elements (the basis for the discovery of plutonium) and carbon's potential as a moderator for producing chain reactions. During 1939 and 1940 these scientists developed a voluntary system of self-censorship to prevent the publication of these developments. This led *Time* magazine in May 1942 to remark on the utter absence of chemistry and physics papers at a recent meeting of the American Philosophical Society: "Such facts as these add up to the biggest scientific news of 1942; that there is less and less scientific news. Today's momentous achievements will not be disclosed until the war's end."[9]

7. Conversation with Roger Heusser, Deputy Director, NN-52, Office of Declassification, U.S. Department of Energy, February 6, 1995. Special access programs impose access controls on "need to know" requirements stricter than those normally required for access to a classified program. In a 1954 book, former AEC chairman Gordon Dean wrote that "one out of every four employees in the Atomic Energy Commission, one out of every twenty-five of our contractors' employees, and probably one out of every twenty dollars spent on operation of the atomic energy program are devoted in one way or another to maintaining [security]." This rough percentage appears to be fairly constant over time. Gordon Dean, *Report on the Atom: What You Should Know about Atomic Energy* (London: Eyre & Spottiswoode, 1954), p. 203.

8. One of the best accounts of the historical development of nuclear secrecy in the United States remains Arvin S. Quist, *Security Classification of Information,* vol. 1: *Introduction, History, and Adverse Impacts* (U.S. Department of Energy, Oak Ridge Gaseous Diffusion Plant, 1989), esp. pp. 46–52.

9. Quoted in Herbert N. Foerstel, *Secret Science: Federal Control of American Science and Technology* (Westport, Conn.: Praeger, 1993), pp. 49–50. Ironically, it was this very action

Box 8-1

Types of Classified Information and Nuclear Clearances

The Government classifies nuclear weapons information in various ways and maintains a number of different clearances to control acces to it.

National Security Information (NSI): Information relating to U.S. foreign relations or military policy that requires protection against unauthorized disclosure and that has been determined to be classified in conformity with presidential executive order.

Unclassified Controlled Nuclear Information (UCNI): Used by the DOE to prevent the unauthorized dissemination of unclassified information on physical security for special nuclear material, critical installations, and equipment.

Restricted Data (RD): All data concerning the design, manufacture, and use of nuclear weapons; the production of special nuclear material; and the use of special nuclear material in the production of energy. According to the Atomic Energy Act, RD can be declassified as long as there is no "undue risk" to national security.

Formerly Restricted Data (FRD): Information relating to the military use of nuclear weapons protected under joint agreements by the DOE and DOD and information that the DOE has removed from the restricted data category. The two agencies protect it as classified national security information; in any releases to foreign governments, FRD are treated as restricted data. Declassification requires a determination that release of the information will not cause unreasonable risk to national security.

Q Sensitive: The highest clearance for access to restricted data. "Q Sensitive" provides individuals with access to the most sensitive categories of special nuclear materials (SNM)—those materials that are most readily weaponized, such as plutonium, uranium-233, or uranium-235. Individuals with this clearance have access to nuclear weapons design, manufacture, and use data. When working with this information, they have armed guards nearby because disclosure "could cause exceptionally grave danger to the nation." These individuals routinely have access to national security information and top secret formerly restricted data.

Q Nonsensitive: Individuals holding this clearance have access to less sensitive types of SNM. Individuals working with Q nonsensitive clearances also have armed guards stationed nearby.

L Clearances: Individuals with L clearances have access to secret national security information as well as confidential RD and secret formerly restricted data.

Sigma Categories: Within the RD and FRD categories, Sigma designates differing degrees of access to information concerning the design, manufacture, or utilization of nuclear weapons or nuclear explosive devices:

—Sigma 1. Theory of operation (hydrodynamic and nuclear) or complete design of thermonuclear weapons or their unique components.

—Sigma 2. Theory of operation or complete design of fission weapons or their unique components. This includes the high-explosive and nuclear initiation systems as they pertain to weapon design and theory.

—Sigma 3. Manufacturing and utilization information not comprehensively revealing the theory of operation or design of the physics package. Complete design and operation of nonnuclear components, but only information

Box 8-1
(continued)

as prescribed below for nuclear components. Utilization information necessary to support the stockpile to target sequence. Information includes (a) general external weapon configuration, including size, weight, and shape; (b) environmental behavior, fuzing ballistics, yields, and effects; (c) nuclear components or subassemblies that do not reveal theory of operation or significant design features; (d) production and manufacturing techniques relating to nuclear parts or subassemblies; (e) anticipated and actual strike operations.

—Sigma 4. Information inherent in preshot and postshot activities necessary in the testing of atomic weapons or devices. Specifically excluded are the theory of operation and the design of such items. Information includes (a) logistics, administration, other agency participation; (b) special construction and equipment; (c) effects, safety; and (d) purpose of tests, general nature of nuclear explosive tested (including expected or actual yields), and conclusions derived from tests outside of design features.

—Sigma 5. Production rate and stockpile quantities of nuclear weapons and their components.

—Sigma 9. General studies not directly related to the design or performance of specific weapons or weapon systems such as reliability studies, fuzing studies, damage studies, and aerodynamic studies.

—Sigma 10. Chemistry, metallurgy, and processing of materials peculiar to the field of atomic weapons or nuclear explosive devices.

—Sigma 11. Information concerning inertial confinement fusion that reveals or is indicative of weapon data.

—Sigma 12. Complete theory of operation, complete design, or partial design information revealing either sensitive design features or how the energy conversion takes place for the nuclear energy converter, energy director, or other nuclear-directed energy weapon systems or components outside the envelope of the nuclear source within the envelope of the nuclear-directed energy weapon.

—Sigma 13. Manufacturing and utilization information and output characteristics for nuclear energy converters, directors, and other nuclear-directed energy weapon systems or components outside the envelope of the nuclear source, not comprehensively revealing the theory of operation, sensitive design features of the nuclear-directed energy weapon, or how the energy conversion takes place. Information includes (a) general external weapon configuration and weapon environmental behavior characteristics, yields, and effects; (b) component and subassembly design that does not reveal theory of operation or sensitive design features of nuclear-directed energy weapons categorized as Sigmas 1, 2, or 12; and (c) production and manufacturing techniques for components or subassemblies of nuclear-directed energy weapons that do not reveal information categorized as Sigmas 1, 2, or 12.

Critical Nuclear Weapons Design Information (CNWDI): A DOD category of weapons data that is analogous to "top secret" or "secret restricted data." Disseminated within the department and the armed services on a need-to-know basis, it includes information relating to the theory of operation or design of the components of a nuclear weapon. CNWDI excludes a number of categories of less sensitive information related to the maintenance and operation of nuclear weapons.

To win military support for an atomic program, scientists on the newly created National Defense Research Committee strove to impress the military with their seriousness by taking oaths of allegiance, by requiring army or navy security clearances, and by establishing a classification system that compartmentalized information. Applying it to research and development activities, scientists limited the circulation of data on a strict "need-to-know basis" to ensure that few would ascertain the big picture through access to all data.[10]

Security and secrecy were tightened even further when the U.S. Army Corps of Engineers took charge of the nuclear program in 1942 through the Manhattan Engineer District, commonly known as the Manhattan Project. MED director General Leslie Groves had three security priorities, two of which were self-evident: to prevent the Axis powers from discovering the atomic project and to ensure "complete surprise" when atomic weapons were first used. But Groves also worried about Soviet espionage and wanted to "keep the Russians from learning of our discoveries."[11] To meet those goals, the MED centralized control over program security policy and by 1944 had consolidated intelligence, counterintelligence, and security functions into an Intelligence and Security Section, establishing an organizational routine that the AEC would institutionalize during the postwar era.[12]

In keeping with General Groves's thinking that compartmentalization was the "very heart of security," the army aggressively applied this principle by limiting the information available to individuals and groups. Army procedures went beyond the civilian standards, applying compartmentalization not only to research and development but to every type of project activity (such as breaking down the blueprints of production plants). The special weapons laboratory at Los Alamos epitomized compartmentalization by segregating weapons research and development from other project areas. In addition, the MED security office began investigations supplementing the more perfunctory clearance procedures initially required to expedite project work. With mixed success—Klaus Fuchs, David Greenglass, and Theodore Alvin Hall all evaded Los Alamos security—the MED's Counterintelligence Corps Detachment ini-

that alerted the Soviet Union to the fact that the United States had undertaken a large and secret project to make use of atomic energy. See David Holloway, *Stalin and the Bomb: The Soviet Union and Atomic Energy, 1939–1956* (Yale University Press, 1994), pp. 78–79.

10. For further background on the early secrecy program, see Vincent C. Jones, *Manhattan: The Army and the Atomic Bomb* (Washington, D.C.: Center of Military History, U.S. Army, 1985), pp. 253–54, 268. Opposition to compartmentalization by some scientists is recorded in Richard G. Hewlett and Oscar E. Anderson, Jr., *A History of the United States Atomic Energy Commission*, vol. 1: *The New World, 1939–1946* (University Park, Pennsylvania, 1962), pp. 227–28. For a suggestive analysis of social considerations that may have made nuclear weapons scientists proponents of strict secrecy rules, including compartmentalization, see Hugh Gusterson, *Nuclear Rites: A Weapons Laboratory at the End of the Cold War* (University of California Press, 1996), pp. 68–100.

11. Charles A. Ziegler and David Jacobson, *Spying without Spies: Origins of America's Secret Nuclear Surveillance System* (Westport, Conn.: Praeger, 1995), p. 9.

12. Jones, *Manhattan*, pp. 253–79; Hewlett and Anderson, *New World*, pp. 227–29.

tiated campaigns to detect and combat espionage and sabotage.[13] To prevent the amplification of leaks, the MED enjoined the press not to publish or broadcast stories about secret weapons projects, a practice that presaged later attempts to encourage media self-censorship.[14] Despite this effort—overseen by the government's Office of Censorship and in effect from early 1943 until thirty minutes after the White House announced the dropping of the "Little Boy" atomic bomb on Hiroshima on August 6, 1945—there were a number of published stories disclosing the existence of the MED and its facilities at Los Alamos, Oak Ridge, and Hanford.[15]

By detonating two atomic bombs over Hiroshima and Nagasaki in early August 1945, the government declassified dramatically the existence of the Manhattan Project. Although Soviet physicists knew that an atomic bomb project was under way in the United States and had enough intelligence information on the Manhattan Project to accelerate their own atomic research near the end of the war, Hiroshima and Nagasaki demonstrated that the deadly new weapons were eminently practicable and that competent physicists could design them. Only days later, Washington took its second major declassification step by releasing physicist Henry D. Smyth's report, *Atomic Energy for Military Purposes,* which provided basic information on the Manhattan Project without compromising weapons physics and technology secrets. This was done both to give credit to MED personnel—and thus avoid disgruntlement among the scientists and future leaks—and to allow the public to have a "reasonable understanding" of what happened without providing any data that "competent scientists" would not already understand or easily deduce.[16]

---

13. Michael Dobbs, "Code Name 'Mlad,' Atomic Bomb Spy," *Washington Post,* February 25, 1996, p. A1; Michael Dobbs, "New Documents Name American as Soviet Spy," *Washington Post,* March 6, 1996, p. A1. Theodore Hall's story is told in Joseph Albright and Marcia Kunstel, *Bombshell: The Secret Story of America's Unknown Atomic Spy Conspiracy* (New York: Times Books, 1997). Soviet intelligence intercepts also indicate the existence of at least two other Soviet sources within the Manhattan Project: "Fogel"/"Pers" and "Quantum." Anatoly Yatskov, the former Soviet intelligence officer who controlled most of the atomic spies in the United States, boasted to the *Post* in 1992 that the FBI had unmasked "only half, or less than half" of his atomic spies. Thus, the Manhattan Project was truly kept secret from everyone *except* the Soviet Union.

14. For a discussion of the pros and cons of compartmentalization, see Quist, *Introduction, History, and Adverse Impacts,* pp. 50–51; and Jones, *Manhattan,* pp. 270–72. Some participating scientists conceded the necessity for compartmentalization but believed that it came at a "stiff price" because of the "wasting of talent and scientific manpower and the loss of precious time." For compartmentalization's central role in maximizing project security, see Robert S. Norris with Stanley Goldberg, "A Biography of General Leslie R. Groves" (in progress).

15. Foerstel, *Secret Science,* pp. 50–58. So zealous was the government in censoring *anything* having to do with atomic energy that the plot of a Superman comic strip appearing on April 14, 1945, showing the Man of Steel about to confront a cyclotron, or atom smasher, was hastily rewritten following a complaint from the Office of Censorship's Press Division (p. 55).

16. Quist, *Introduction, History, and Adverse Impacts,* pp. 63–64; Jones, *Manhattan,* pp. 556–62. For indirect knowledge of the Manhattan Project in the Soviet Union and the impact of Hiroshima on Soviet decisionmaking, see Holloway, *Stalin and the Bomb,* pp. 78–79, 133. Although the Smyth report did not reveal any secrets, Soviet scientists nonetheless found it useful. A Russian translation of 30,000 copies was published in early 1946. Together with information obtained from its spies, Holloway notes, the report helped guide subsequent Soviet technical decisions by explaining what general processes the United States had used to manufacture nuclear materials (pp. 173, 178, 180, 187, 192–93).

The declassification of the Smyth report was controversial—in 1952 President-elect Dwight Eisenhower considered it a breach of security—but it set limits for the official release of atomic energy information. However, MED scientists charged with reviewing information security policy and developing some basis for selective declassification worried that nuclear secrecy could impose damaging costs on scientific progress. Although the scientists believed that much data needed to be withheld, they were profoundly skeptical about the feasibility of controlling information derived from scientific investigation. Thus the MED's 1945 Committee on Declassification, chaired by scientist Richard Tolman, held that security controls were necessary if "there is a likelihood of war within the next five or ten years," but that more permanent controls would "weaken us disastrously for the future—perhaps twenty years hence." The Committee of Senior Responsible Reviewers, which declassified 500 MED documents in 1946, was even more doubtful about the efficacy of controls: "The facts of nature cannot long be kept as classified information . . . to attempt to do so even for the relatively short time of a year or two is not conducive to the national welfare."[17]

Restricted Data

When politicians and policymakers began debating the framework for postwar control of atomic energy, information on the potential for overseas nuclear proliferation, especially prospects for the Soviet atomic program, was tightly controlled. Although those with access to these data did not suffer from the illusion that the United States could indefinitely monopolize atomic information, they wanted a policy system that would prevent leaks of information useful to weapons production and development. Therefore when Congress passed the Atomic Energy Act of 1946 creating the AEC (and the Joint Committee on Atomic Energy, see chapter 9), it codified the MED's highly restrictive secrecy system. More than half a century later, the Atomic Energy Act (as amended in 1954) regulates the classification and declassification of nuclear weapons information. Significantly, this system is entirely separate from, but parallel to, the classification system

17. During one of his first AEC nuclear briefings, President-elect Eisenhower told the commission, including Smyth, that the "Smith report" had given away too much information on the atomic project, such as the locations of production plants. For an account of this meeting in November 1952, see Richard G. Hewlett and Jack M. Holl, *Atoms for Peace and War, 1953–1961, Eisenhower and the Atomic Energy Commission* (University of California Press, 1989), p. 14; and Quist, *Introduction, History, and Adverse Impacts,* pp. 65–70. For a stronger critique of secrecy and compartmentalization prepared by Oppenheimer and his associates, see Peter Galison and Barton Bernstein, "In Any Light: Scientists and the Decision to Build the Superbomb, 1952–1954," *Historical Studies in the Physical Sciences,* vol. 19 (1989), p. 275.

for national security information (NSI) governed by presidential executive orders.[18]

The Atomic Energy Act's crucial and unprecedented innovation was the concept of "restricted data" (RD), which has seen no fundamental change since 1946. The act treated as RD all information relating to the "design, manufacture, or utilization of nuclear weapons," the "production of special nuclear material," or "the use of special nuclear material in the production of energy." Although the 1946 act endorsed the free circulation of scientific and technical information as a condition for social progress and tried to separate "basic scientific information" from "technical information" relating to atomic energy applications, it rigorously classified nearly all atomic energy information as RD.[19]

The novelty of the 1946 act was that it created an aura of "born classified" around nuclear weapons information. Because this information was the product of secret government activity of a highly significant nature, no one was required to certify its status as restricted data; the information was classified from its inception and no one could see RD without authorization. In other words, its special status removed any need for an affirmative classification decision by a responsible authority. Moreover, because it was automatically classified, RD information would remain classified until government officials made a positive decision to declassify it.[20]

Another oddity of RD was its ability to originate outside the government through the thinking and research of private parties. Although the act does not outlaw this activity, it enjoins those same parties from disclosing private RD to unauthorized persons. Although the 1954 act forbade the AEC to provide RD to foreign countries, other language permitted circulation of information needed to "assure the common defense and security;" soon that provided leeway for limited technical exchanges with the British under the 1948 "modus vivendi."[21]

18. For basic information on the provisions of the Atomic Energy Act, see Quist, *Introduction, History, and Adverse Impacts,* pp. 52–59. Rather than relying on nuclear secrecy as such, American leaders were sanguine that a putative U.S. monopoly of high-grade uranium ore would restrict Soviet nuclear development. See Ziegler and Jacobson, *Spying without Spies,* pp. 21–31. See chapter 1, fn. 65, in this volume.

19. Quist, *Introduction, History, and Adverse Impacts*; Hewlett and Anderson, *New World,* p. 514. See also Allan Robert Adler, "Public Access to Nuclear Energy and Weapons," in David P. O'Very, Christopher E. Paine, and Dan W. Reicher, eds., *Controlling the Atom in the 21st Century* (Boulder, Colo.: Westview Press, 1994), pp. 73–106.

20. In December 1997, Secretary of Energy Federico F. Peña announced an end to the concept of "born classified." This important change, and others concerning how the DOE classifies and declassifies information, will formally occur on June 29, 1998, when new regulations (available on the World Wide Web at http://www.doe.gov/html/osti/opennet/fin-reg.html) published in the *Federal Register,* vol. 62, no. 250 (December 31, 1997), pp. 68501–17, take effect. However, full implementation of these changes will not occur until Congress amends the Atomic Energy Act.

21. Quist, *Introduction, History, and Adverse Impacts,* p. 55, discusses examples of government efforts to suppress the disclosure of privately created RD, the most famous being the *Progressive* case (discussed later in this chapter). For background on the "modus vivendi," see Richard G. Hewlett and Francis Duncan, *A History of the United States Atomic Energy Commission,* vol. 2: *Atomic Shield, 1947–1952* (Pennsylvania State University Press, 1962), pp. 273–314.

Secrecy and Security Procedures

As already mentioned, the concept of "born secret" has profound implications for a free society, but its creation went unchallenged.[22] To ensure tight control over RD, the AEC created a sizable bureaucracy charged with developing policies and standards for information and physical security, monitoring the implementation of standards, and otherwise enforcing security regulations. To enforce secrecy, the AEC's Security Division was given the power to grant classification authority, as well as to manage personnel security clearances, physical security, internal security, and security for Washington headquarters. Physical security alone meant developing protective systems for more than 1,200 sites around the country, not only the "atomic cities" at Hanford, Los Alamos, and Oak Ridge but also the nuclear weapons stockpile (over which the AEC maintained exclusive control until 1951 and majority control until 1958)[23] and the numerous contractor facilities. It also meant developing systems for the protection of classified information (for example, systems for delineating security areas, storing the information, identifying personnel with security clearance, and transporting documents).[24] These were exacting and costly tasks, and the demands of the Republican Eightieth Congress added to the pressure for strict safeguards.[25]

Although the Security Division was seemingly in charge of only technical and administrative problems, the press and the Republican-controlled Congress politicized its activities by accusing the AEC of losing or otherwise mishandling classified material. What had in fact happened was the army had bequeathed millions of partly inventoried documents to the AEC; to complicate matters, certificates of destruction did not exist for routinely destroyed items. To gain control over the mountains of classified paper at its installations, the AEC developed procedures to track documents in its possession. Thus by early 1949 it could report that it was generating 10,000 secret documents a month and routing an addi-

22. For further consideration of problems raised by the restricted data concept, see A. DeVolpi and others, *Born Secret, The H-Bomb, the Progressive Case, and National Security* (New York: Pergamon Press, 1981), pp. 132–37.

23. Robert S. Norris and William M. Arkin, "Nuclear Notebook (U.S. Weapons Secrets Revealed)," *Bulletin of the Atomic Scientists,* vol. 49 (March 1993), p. 48. AEC control over the stockpile diminished to low levels by the mid-1960s. On February 10, 1967, President Lyndon Johnson directed the AEC to deliver all its remaining reserve weapons to the DOD.

24. For the responsibility and early activities of the Security Division, see *Fifth Semiannual Report of the Atomic Energy Commission,* January 1949 (GPO, 1949), pp. 120–29. See also Atomic Energy Commission, "Revised Delegations of Authority to Director of Security," AEC 214/3, September 22, 1953, Record Group 324, Atomic Energy Commission, Office of the Secretariat, Box 60, National Archives.

25. On the pressure from Congress, see *Investigation into the United States Atomic Energy Project,* Hearings before the Joint Committee on Atomic Energy, 81 Cong. 1 sess. (GPO, 1949), pts. 1–24. The demands of physical security were sometimes extreme and wasteful. For example, the requirement that all non-AEC workers on site have an escort could lead to a situation, in AEC Chairman David Lilienthal's words, where one had "one man to work and one man to watch him work." For this and examples of congressional pressures causing unjustifiable expenditures, see David Lilienthal, *The Journals of David E. Lilienthal,* vol. 2: *The Atomic Energy Years, 1945–1950* (New York: Harper & Row, 1964), pp. 361–62, 426–27, 461 (the quotation is on p. 426).

tional 10,000 items between facilities. To keep track of each top secret document, the Security Division developed an elaborate system of inventories. By the fall of 1953 it had compiled accountability records for 60,000 "top secret" items.[26]

The political costs of secrecy were strikingly evident in the area of security clearances, which had grown tighter than ever under the intensifying pressures of the cold war. This problem quickly took on massive proportions: during the first three fiscal years of operation, the AEC had to clear more than 147,000 individuals, many of them contract employees.[27] The commission also initiated a security review of MED employees who had remained with the atomic project. Although organizational responsibilities for clearances would shift over time, each new and old employee would have to undergo an extensive background check, which the FBI would be asked to handle if an individual was politically suspect or the position was particularly sensitive (as in the case of nearly all AEC positions). AEC chairman David Lilienthal worried about relying on anonymous informants and the FBI's dubious investigative techniques, which he felt threatened an individual's civil liberties and personal freedom. He was also uncomfortable "play[ing] God and decid[ing] on *ex parte* evidence of FBI detectives" when the commission itself ruled on more difficult cases. Yet the demands of other business and Republican pressure for strict security reduced accountability to a low priority.[28]

By January 1949 incessant congressional pressure fueled by the cold war atmosphere had decisively shaped the criteria that security personnel used for vetting AEC employees, potential or otherwise. These criteria would exclude from employment any individuals (including their spouses) who belonged to a proscribed organization on the attorney general's list, who advocated violent revolution, or had a "sympathetic interest" in fascist or communist ideologies, and who had shown "sympathy" for various front organizations or had associated with people with "subversive" interests. By 1956 the AEC had dismissed or denied clearances to about 500 scientists, representing about 5 percent of the total number of AEC scientists for any given year during the period. The

26. As impressive as this sounds (especially before the widespread introduction of computers into the workplace), former AEC chairman Gordon Dean wrote in 1954 (referring to late 1952) that the AEC had "more than a million classified documents." Even assuming that not all of these were considered "top secret," this figure appears to indicate a rather substantial backlog. See Dean, *Report on the Atom,* p. 215. Hewlett and Duncan, *Atomic Shield,* pp. 94–95; *Fifth Semiannual Report of the U.S. Atomic Energy Commission,* p. 127; U.S. Atomic Energy Commission, "Revised Delegations of Authority to Director of Security," AEC 214/3, September 22, 1953, Record Group 324, Atomic Energy Commission, Office of the Secretariat, Box 60.

27. Between fiscal 1947 and 1963, the AEC conducted nearly 717,000 full background investigations. See Harold P. Green, "Q-Clearance: The Development of a Personnel Security Program," *Bulletin of the Atomic Scientists,* vol. 20 May (1964), pp. 9–15. From January 1947 to April 1949, personnel security matters consumed one-third of the AEC's meeting time. See Harold P. Green and Alan Rosenthal, *Government of the Atom: The Integration of Powers* (New York: Atherton Press, 1963), p. 7, fn. 4.

28. Lilienthal, *The Atomic Energy Years,* pp. 189, 233, 415. For security clearance program developments, see *Fifth Semiannual Report of the U.S. Atomic Energy Commission,* pp. 120–21; and Hewlett and Duncan, *Atomic Shield,* pp. 23–26, 88, 92, 332–33, 351–52, 475–76.

Oppenheimer case (discussed later; see also chapters 1 and 4) was only the most famous (or infamous) example of the role of political criteria in revoking "Q" clearances.[29]

The overall expense of early atomic secrecy remains obscure because the published budgets of the AEC do not identify security costs. The only available figure from the 1940s is a $6.3 million charge ($62.4 million in 1996 dollars) by the FBI for security investigations during 1948. Expenditures on security investigations were not even regularly itemized in the U.S. budget until the early 1950s, when annual spending averaged about $12 million to $13 million in then-year dollars ($87 million to $94 million in 1996 dollars). These expenditures represented a formidable workload. By the fall of 1953, the 230 employees at AEC headquarters and field offices responsible for handling nuclear clearances had processed 400,000 cases.[30]

At the same time that the AEC was trying to control access to restricted data, it had to respond to DOD demands and make nuclear information available to military personnel with a "need to know." The Eighth Air Force, one of the early components of the newly organized Strategic Air Command, may have initiated this process in May 1947, when it asked AEC to grant its personnel a "blanket" atomic clearance.[31] In response, during 1947 and 1948 the AEC developed procedures for providing military personnel with certain classes of RD—such as weapons characteristics—needed to plan and implement atomic strike capabilities.[32]

The simultaneous unfolding of the Fuchs and Rosenberg espionage cases and the outbreak of the Korean War during mid-1950 produced conflicting pressures for stronger secrecy and for expediting the military's access to RD. Although the AEC tightened up on the release of technical information to Britain and Canada, it sanctioned wider dissemination of classified information on a need-to-know basis. (For an unusual need-to-know case, see box 8-2.) Simply to expedite extensive construction projects under way in Tennessee and Washington state as part of the crash program to develop the hydrogen bomb (see chapter 1), the AEC had to clear more people and release more information.

29. *Fifth Semiannual Report of the U.S. Atomic Energy Commission*, pp. 120–22, 188–90; David Caute, *The Great Fear: The Anti-Communist Purge Under Truman and Eisenhower* (New York: Simon & Schuster, 1978), pp. 463–66.

30. *Budget of the United States Government, Fiscal Year 1950*, p. 76; Atomic Energy Commission, "Revised Delegations of Authority to Director of Security."

31. Lilienthal, *The Atomic Energy Years*, p. 184. Not long after this request, the Eighth Air Force had twenty-five atomic-capable aircraft on hand, but only seven trained crews. See also Leonard Wainstein and others, *The Evolution of U.S. Strategic Command and Control and Warning, 1945–1972*, Institute for Defense Analyses Study S-467 (June 1975), pp. 72–73.

32. Instead of "Q" clearances, the Commission allowed the services to issue "M" clearances as well as make available limited types of RD to other military personnel and contractors without special clearances. By early 1950, 30,000 military personnel had access to atomic weapons information, but owing to time-consuming clearance procedures, incoming cases and the backlog of older cases mounted by the thousands. Hewlett and Duncan, *Atomic Shield*, pp. 472–73. For AEC efforts to provide special clearances to military personnel see Quist, *Introduction, History, and Adverse Impacts*, pp. 71–72.

Box 8-2

Moses Gets Clearance

In 1989 the DOE acknowledged that Charlton Heston, best known for his roles in *The Ten Commandments* and *Ben Hur,* had been granted a Q clearance in 1983 to provide narration for top secret films and videotapes discussing various aspects of the nuclear arsenal. Heston worked on six productions through 1989, including one titled *Trust but Verify,* about the 1974 Threshold Test Ban Treaty. Heston got the job after Charles Barnett, the head of film and video production at Los Alamos National Laboratory and an old friend of Heston's, in a discussion with a colleague over the poor quality of narration in a recent production, blurted out, "Who in the hell do you want? Charlton Heston?" Although not serious at first, Barnett felt strongly about the projects he produced and eventually contacted Heston to sound him out on the idea. To his surprise, Heston agreed to help (and declined to be paid for his work).

Asked by the *Los Angeles Times* about his secret work, Heston responded, "I'm not trying to be dramatically secretive or anything, but I can't get into that. I do work for other agencies from time to time. Most of the stuff that [I] do in this area is not designed for public consumption." The DOD and CIA refused to divulge if either had granted separate clearances for Heston for similar work.[1]

1. Allan Parachini, "For Top Secret Narration, Call Charlton Heston," *Los Angeles Times,* November 9, 1989, p. F1.

Moreover, to accelerate the processing of military clearances, in November 1950 Gordon Dean, the AEC's new chairman, authorized the DOD to abolish the "M" clearance. From that point onward, the military's own security classification procedures governed the distribution of atomic weapons information within the services.[33]

Within the limits of tight security controls, the AEC nevertheless declassified some information during its early years. Aware of the costs imposed by secrecy and concerned that efforts to suppress nonweapons information could lead to public hysteria, David Lilienthal was personally committed to maximum feasible openness. However, most of the early declassifications were limited to basic, descriptive information of AEC facilities or to basic science (primarily pure and applied mathematics and basic physics), and as such were not controversial. Yet even this minimalist approach to openness had powerful adversaries on the Joint Committee on Atomic Energy. Senator Millard Tydings (Democrat of Maryland) roundly criticized the AEC's *Fifth Semiannual Report,* arguing against identifying even the location of AEC facilities on the grounds

33. Hewlett and Duncan, *Atomic Shield,* pp. 474–76; Hewlett and Holl, *Atoms for Peace and War,* p. 118.

that such information would provide target intelligence to America's adversaries. When Senator Tom Connally (Democrat of Texas) asked: "Why is it necessary, because you spend public money, to go out and blah, blah all over the country?" Lilienthal responded: "It is the general principle of public accountability of reporting within the limits of security. . . . [E]xpansion of production is something that obviously cannot be concealed because it is on a very large scale, involving tens of thousands of people."[34] Although one venturesome senator, JCAE cochairman Brien McMahon (Democrat of Connecticut) proposed giving careful consideration to releasing the size of the weapons stockpile, his interest in greater openness found no support in Congress or the White House.[35]

Although successful Soviet development of the atomic bomb in August 1949 demonstrated the limits of U.S. secrecy programs, the line that Truman and the Congress drew against the release of weapons information remained in place for many years.[36] Indeed, in early 1950 the government revealed the lengths to which it would go to control nuclear data: it threatened an injunction against *Scientific American* to compel it to stop publication of an article in its April issue on the hydrogen bomb. Even though author and physicist Hans Bethe had drawn upon publicly available and *previously published* material, the AEC insisted that publication was a violation of the Atomic Energy Act. The commission forced the journal to excise material it deemed objectionable and then ordered it to destroy the plates and burn all 3,000 copies of the issue containing the original article that it had already printed (an AEC security officer was dispatched to the printing plant to oversee this process). In the May issue of the magazine, publisher Gerard Piel wrote: "We consider that the Commission's action . . . raises the question of whether the Commission is thus suppressing information which the American people need in order to form intelligent judgements on this major problem."[37]

34. Despite Lilienthal's defense of the AEC's report, the JCAE's criticism took its toll. *Time* compared the *Sixth Semiannual Report* to a Soviet five-year plan: "There is not a firm figure to inform, alarm, or comfort the nation's potential foes or friends," said the magazine. Quoted in Green and Rosenthal, *Government of the Atom,* pp. 200–01.

35. Quist, *Introduction, History, and Adverse Impacts,* p. 74; Hewlett and Duncan, *Atomic Shield,* pp. 352–53; *Atomic Energy Report to Congress,* Hearings before the Joint Committee on Atomic Energy, 81 Cong. 1 sess. (GPO, 1949), pp. 8, 15–16. Apparently Lilienthal was open to discussing the pros and cons of releasing stockpile figures, but Truman dismissed the idea; see Lilienthal, *The Atomic Energy Years,* pp. 192, 361, 453, 463–65, 468. For a catalog of all known AEC and DOE declassifications from 1946 through 1995, organized by information type, see U.S. Department of Energy, Office of Declassification, *Drawing Back the Curtain of Secrecy, Restricted Data Declassification Decisions, 1946 to the Present (RDD-3)* (GPO, 1996).

36. Moreover, whatever weapons information the AEC released during the 1950s and 1960s was not made available publicly but declassified to ease discussion among scientific experts. See U.S. Department of Energy, *Drawing Back the Curtain of Secrecy,* p. iii.

37. DeVolpi and others, *Born Secret,* pp. 135–36; Foerstel, *Secret Science,* pp. 79–80; *Impact of National Security Considerations on Science and Technology,* Hearings before the Subcommittee on Science, Research, and Technology and the Sub-

Atomic Energy Act Revision and Declassification

By the mid-1950s Congress had begun to relax controls over nuclear information: it amended the Atomic Energy Act and abolished the commission's monopoly over atomic energy. In line with Eisenhower's "Atoms for Peace" program promoting civilian uses of nuclear energy in the United States and overseas (announced in a United Nations speech on December 8, 1953), the Atomic Energy Act of 1954 relaxed controls over RD so that atomic energy information could be made available to the public, U.S. businesses, and friendly foreign governments. While Atoms for Peace could make participants nuclear-capable, the administration believed that appropriate safeguards—including monitoring by the newly created International Atomic Energy Agency—would channel overseas nuclear developments away from military applications.[38]

To ease declassification of RD, the 1954 act lowered the threshold set in 1946 for downgrading RD. Instead of a strict "adverse effect" test, declassifiers could release RD if it would not cause "undue risk" to U.S. national security. To ensure that atomic energy information was not subject to unnecessary controls, the act provided for continuous review of RD. To facilitate the development of commercial nuclear power, the act created a special "L" clearance, based on the relatively lenient "national agency check," allowing corporate officials access to confidential RD. To expedite the military's access to nuclear weapons, the act established a new category of nuclear information: formerly restricted data (FRD). Specific data about the military application of nuclear weapons, formerly classified RD, would be transclassified as FRD and subject to rou-

committee on Investigations and Oversight of the House Committee on Science and Technology, 97 Cong., 2 sess. (GPO, 1982), pp. 227–28. Interestingly, during the years before 1950, the *Bulletin of Atomic Scientists* censored itself by not publishing articles on the H-bomb "lest they encourage the Soviets to enter the race." See Galison and Bernstein, "In Any Light," p. 282.

38. For background on "Atoms for Peace" and ensuing revisions of the Atomic Energy Act, see Quist, *Introduction, History, and Adverse Impacts,* pp. 55–59, 75–76; and Hewlett and Holl, *Atoms for Peace,* pp. 71–72, chap. 5. For the assumptions of Atoms for Peace, see Myron B. Kratzer to Chairman Seaborg and others, "Review of Atoms for Peace Policy," November 13, 1964, copy at the National Security Archive, Washington, D.C. The promulgation of Atoms for Peace clearly illustrates "how the desire to foster complacent pubic acceptance of [the doctrine of] massive retaliation undercut the nation's capacity to rationally consider the long-term dangers of the nuclear age." The idea behind the program, according to Secretary of State John Foster Dulles was that "U.S. and Soviet donations to an international agency (for the purposes of supplying reactors around the world) would actually *decrease* the amount of fissionable material available for weapons." Even when Soviet foreign minister Vyacheslav Molotov pointed out that reactors could potentially be used to "increase the production of material needed to produce atomic bombs," Dulles failed to grasp that, "in effect, the United States had undertaken a major commitment to the global dissemination of nuclear energy with no prior effort by the administration to acquire even a rudimentary understanding of the risks." Under Atoms for Peace and subsequent cooperation agreements, the United States eventually exported 25.9 metric tons of highly enriched uranium fuel and 1,647.4 pounds (748.8 kilograms) of plutonium for use in power, research, and test reactors and other research programs. See David Goldfischer, *The Best Defense: Policy Alternatives for U.S. Nuclear Security from the 1950s to the 1990s* (Cornell University Press, 1993), pp. 136–37; David Albright, Frans Berkhout, and William Walker, *Plutonium and Highly Enriched Uranium 1996: World Inventories, Capabilities and Policies* (Oxford University Press, 1997), pp. 248–53; U.S. Department of Energy, *Plutonium: The First 50 Years—United States Plutonium Production, Acquisition and Utilization from 1944 through 1994,* DOE/DP-0137 (1996), pp. 68–73.

tine military secrecy procedures. Thus cleared military personnel with a "need to know" could obtain information they needed without having to receive additional clearances.[39]

In the years that followed the 1954 act, the AEC released a volume of information for the use of the U.S. nuclear power industry, including data on reactor design, reactor materials, chemical engineering, and controlled thermonuclear research. Between 1946 and 1974 it declassified 1.6 million documents, after reviewing 2.9 million of them.[40]

Over the years, the AEC and its successor organizations also released masses of secondary information on the nuclear weapons program: yields of the weapons dropped on Japan, dates of nuclear weapons tests, types of nuclear weapons, nuclear weapons test yields through 1958, nuclear weapons effects, "the fact that reactor grade plutonium can be used to make nuclear weapons," the "fact of boosting," and the "fact" that the United States had deployed "thousands of tactical nuclear weapons" in Western Europe. Nevertheless, in keeping with its congressional mandate, the AEC withheld any significant information on nuclear weapons design and stockpile data, "with no exception even for primitive or obsolete weapons." By the early 1970s three programs remained classified to a great degree: weapons, naval nuclear propulsion, and the various isotope separation technologies for enriching uranium.[41]

The AEC also maintained control over information on potentially controversial issues, primarily the threat to worker safety and public health posed by nuclear weapons production facilities and the nuclear testing program (see box 8-3). While recognizing public concerns about health hazards, AEC officials would provide only minimal (or incomplete or false) information about production and testing, particularly concerning the hazards from production processes and fallout levels after weapons tests, overruling employees in the field who favored more candor about the risks. From the confines of "a secrecy-shrouded program" it was "all too easy to deny, dissemble, or mislead," rather than inform the public.[42]

39. Quist, *Introduction, History, and Adverse Impacts,* p. 75.

40. Quist, *Introduction, History, and Adverse Impacts,* pp. 76–80. For examples of information on nuclear reactors declassified after 1954, see U.S. Department of Energy, *Drawing Back the Curtain of Secrecy,* pp. 44–60.

41. Quist, *Information, History, and Adverse Impacts,* p. 77. For great detail on what has been declassified and what remains classified, see U.S. Department of Energy, "Draft Public Guidelines to Department of Energy Classification of Information," Washington, D.C., June 27, 1994, pp. 8–39; and U.S. Department of Energy, *Drawing Back the Curtain of Secrecy.*

42. Barton C. Hacker, *Elements of Controversy, The Atomic Energy Commission and Radiation Safety in Nuclear Weapons Testing, 1947–1974* (University of California Press, 1994), p. 278; for an example of misleading information, see the discussion of the 1954 Bravo shot and the Marshall Islanders (pp. 147–48). See also chapter 7 in this volume. For withholding of fallout levels, see DeVolpi and others, *Born Secret,* p. 154. See also *Radiation Exposure from Pacific Nuclear Tests,*

Freedom of Information and Restricted Data

The Freedom of Information Act (FOIA), passed by Congress in 1966 and strengthened in 1974 through amendments, sanctioned the restricted data system. Section (b)(3) of the act allows federal agencies to withhold information "specifically exempted from disclosure by statute" when such statute provides no discretion to the agency in releasing the information or where the statute "establishes particular criteria for withholding." This phrasing enables the DOE to use the Atomic Energy Act's "undue risk" provisions to deny restricted data to FOIA requesters.[43] In addition, the DOE and the armed services often deploy the FOIA's (b)(1) national security exemption to deny the release of FRD and other information relating to nuclear weapons (for example, nuclear stockpile numbers, historical deployment information, war plans, control arrangements, and the extent of nuclear accidents).[44]

Despite FOIA's (b)(3) provision protecting RD, during the early 1980s Congress tightened controls over nuclear information by creating the category of unclassified controlled nuclear information (UCNI) in an amendment to the Atomic Energy Act. Concerned about nuclear proliferation and nuclear terrorism, Congress decided to regulate access to certain unclassified details on "atomic energy defense programs," such as the design of, and security measures for, various nuclear facilities. That would allow the information to be made available to uncleared local authorities who might need it in an emergency but would constrain public release. Although some of this information was *already* in the public domain, the DOE could treat it as UCNI (thus retroactively classifying it) and exempt it from disclosure under the FOIA's (b)(3) provision, if the information was contained in documents under its control. So as not to reveal that it was treating some publicly available information as UCNI, the DOE could further apply the UCNI restriction to "the fact that a document that has been widely disseminated into the public domain . . . contains information that would be controlled as UCNI."[45]

Oversight Hearing before the House of Representatives Subcommittee on Oversight and Investigations of the Committee on Natural Resources, 103 Cong., 2 sess., serial no. 103-68 (GPO, 1994).

43. Occasionally, however, other tactics are used, as in the case of a coalition of Idaho environmental organizations that in 1989 sought information on radioactive and chemical releases to the environment at the Idaho National Engineering and Environmental Laboratory. This group was informed by the DOE's Idaho Operations Office that its fee waiver had been denied and the request would cost $1.2 million for search and photocopying costs. A request by the same group two years later for records on worker radiation exposures was effectively denied with a notification that the charge for processing would be $10,400. See Chuck Broscious, "Gaining Information on the Legacy of Nuclear Weapons Production," *Gonzaga Law Review*, vol. 31, no. 1 (1995/96), pp. 141–42.

44. Allan Robert Adler, ed., *Litigation under Federal Open Government Laws*, 18th ed. (Washington, D.C.: American Civil Liberties Union Foundation, 1993), p. 61.

45. U.S. Department of Energy, "Openness Press Conference Fact Sheets," June 27, 1994; U.S. Department of Energy, "Topical Guidelines for New Production Reactors," TG-NPR-2, 1983, p. 1; U.S. Department of Energy, "Topical Guidelines for

Box 8-3
The Green Run

Following the successful detection of "Joe-1," the first Soviet atomic bomb test, in September 1949, Admiral Roscoe Hillenkoetter, director of central intelligence, wrote to the Joint Chiefs of Staff on October 28, 1949, requesting a change in the charter for the air force agency involved in the detection effort.[1] At that time AFOAT-1 (see text, footnote 58) was responsible for detecting and identifying atomic bomb explosions. Hillenkoetter argued for increasing the scope of the agency's efforts to include other aspects of the Soviet nuclear program, including the location and output of key production facilities. Air force chief of staff Hoyt Vandenberg responded on November 2 that an expanded air force detection program could yield the information and data sought by Hillenkoetter.[2]

One month later, AFOAT-1 and the AEC conducted a secret experiment to test the air force's ability to detect nuclear weapons production facilities. At the Hanford Reservation in Washington, 1 ton of freshly irradiated uranium fuel from one of Hanford's reactors was reprocessed in the T Plant just sixteen days after being removed from the reactor (it appears that officials with General Electric, Hanford's operating contractor, may have initially had reservations about the experiment but acquiesced at the urging of the air force). At the time, reprocessing normally occurred ninety days after defueling, which allowed the most dangerous radioactivity to decay to lower levels. Officials assumed that the Soviet Union was reprocessing fuel more quickly and wanted to ascertain how best to detect it. Because of the fresh nature of the fuel, the experiment was dubbed the "Green Run."[3]

As the fuel was dissolved in acid (an early and essential step in the reprocessing process) it released enormous quantities of radiation. Because of problems with detection equipment and the contamination of the monitoring laboratory by the radioactive plume, the exact amount is unknown, but historical documents indicate a range from 4,000 to 7,800 curies of iodine-131 (iodine-131 is a particularly dangerous isotope because it is easily absorbed by the thyroid) and 20,000 curies of xenon-133. In all, two to three times more radiation was released than expected. A dose reconstruction effort in the 1980s (following the release of documents in 1986 revealing the experiment) estimated that 11,000 curies of iodine-131 were released.

Earlier experiments at Hanford and at the Oak Ridge Reservation in the spring of 1949 attempted to detect emissions from routine operations via specially outfitted B-29 bombers (under the code name Operation Fitzwilliam). Finding that their equipment was not sensitive enough, the researchers recommended in April 1949 that the test at Hanford be repeated, but that the radiation filters in the high stacks at the T Plant be disconnected, to allow larger and more readily detectible amounts of radiation to be released into the atmosphere.

1. The test itself occurred on August 29, 1949.

2. Charles Ziegler, "Waiting for Joe-1: Decisions Leading to the Detection of Russia's First Atomic Bomb Test," *Social Studies of Science*, vol. 18, no. 2 (1988), p. 223.

3. *Early Health Problems of the U.S. Nuclear Weapons Industry and Their Implications for Today,"* S. Rpt. 101-63 (GPO, December 1989), pp. 8–9; Jim Thomas, "New Details of Green Run's Sorcery," *Hanford Education Action League Perspective*, no. 10/11 (Summer/Fall 1992),

Hazel O'Leary and the Culture of Openness

It was not until the Clinton administration, and the 1993 confirmation of Hazel O'Leary as secretary of energy, that the DOE released signifi-

High Explosives," Unclassified Controlled Nuclear Information, TG-HE-1, 1992, p. I-3. For background on UCNI's origins, see Allan Robert Adler, "Unclassified Secrets," *Bulletin of the Atomic Scientists*, vol. 41 (March 1985), pp. 26–28.

Box 8-3
(continued)

As a result of the experiment, large amounts of iodine-131—the largest single release at Hanford—were spread by the winds over parts of eastern and southern Washington, northern Oregon, and western Idaho. The AEC sent out personnel to secretly gauge the results (the official report noted that "a significant increase in the I-131 activity on vegetation occurred immediately after the dissolving of the green run on Dec. 3"), but it never informed the public about the danger. As a result, thousands of people living downwind of Hanford, especially infants, were exposed to very high levels of radiation, with contamination levels exceeding by twenty times the existing "tolerance level." After the story broke in 1986, a retired radiation control manager at Hanford told a local reporter that the original intent was to disperse radiation great distances, possibly as far as Minneapolis, but that adverse weather and rain limited the spread. "We really plastered the Columbia Valley," he said. Compounding matters, grasses and other feed consumed by cows concentrated the iodine in cow's milk, which was then consumed by unsuspecting citizens. Today, following several dose reconstruction efforts, the government is recommending routine health screenings for those exposed (see box 7-4). Nearly fifty years after it occurred, much of the documentation concerning the Green Run remains classified.

Although there is no evidence that the Green Run was repeated, AFOAT-1 continued to monitor U.S. production plants. On February 16, 1956, the AEC notified the JCAE that "the AEC has accepted a proposal that the Air Force conduct regular flight tests with specially instrumented USAF aircraft over certain AEC installations. The project includes the testing of certain technical radiation detection aids as recommended by Dr. E. O. Lawrence of the University of California Radiation Laboratory."

In fact, the program had begun earlier that month and was expected to run through mid-March, although weather conditions could prolong the testing through April 30. As described by the AEC, the program "essentially consists of a number of flight runs over AEC installations at varying altitudes and embraces three categories of tests: (1) infra-red (and black and white) photography, (2) radioactive [*sic*] radiation detection by special instrumentation, and (3) magnetic radiation." The AEC installations to be studied were Oak Ridge, the Savannah River Plant, the Fernald Plant, Hanford, the Rocky Flats Plant, the National Reactor Testing Station (now the Idaho National Engineering and Environmental Laboratory), and a uranium "feed materials" plant in St. Louis, Missouri.[4]

---

pp. 21, 26; Michael D'Antonio, *Atomic Harvest: Hanford and the Lethal Toll of America's Nuclear Arsenal* (New York: Crown, 1993), pp. 119–26; Department of Defense, Assistant to the Secretary of Defense for Nuclear and Chemical and Biological Defense Programs, *Report on Search for Human Radiation Experiment Records* (GPO, June 1997), vol. 1, pp. 49–54.

4. Letter from K. E. Fields, General Manager, U.S. Atomic Energy Commission, to the Honorable Clinton P. Anderson, Chairman, Joint Committee on Atomic Energy, February 16, 1956, Record Group 128, Declassified General Subject File, Box 1 (AEC), Document 4802, National Archives.

cant quantities of new information on the U.S. nuclear weapons program and its history. The DOE "openness" initiatives, however, did not emerge in a political vacuum; they were the result of years of political pressure and lobbying by citizens' groups, public interest organizations, members of Congress, environmentalists, health professionals, and historians, as well as some measures taken by the Bush administration. The result of these combined efforts was a plethora of data on such issues as production rates of weapon-grade plutonium at Savannah River Site and Hanford Reservation between 1945 and 1993; total production of HEU; the total megatonnage of the nuclear weapon stockpile 1945 to date; the size of the U.S. nuclear stockpile through 1961; annual and cumulative atmospheric tritium releases at Savannah River (see chapter 7); serious accidents, such as the fires at Rocky Flats in 1957 and 1969 (see chapter 6); the total number of nuclear tests and total quantity of plutonium expended in them; previously unannounced atmospheric test yields; tests in the Marshall Islands; and atmospheric fallout.[46]

The DOE's openness initiative sprang from a recognition that startlingly low public confidence in the department and the need to rebuild trust to carry out its new cleanup mission required a new approach to classified information that took into account an overriding public interest in the agency's programs and policies. Nevertheless, arms control and nonproliferation obligations required DOE officials to enforce strictly controls over what they saw as the most vital secrets. Thus elements of nuclear weapons design and sensitive isotope separation processes remain classified. Moreover, owing to strong resistance from many within the DOD, the declassification of the size of the nuclear stockpile since 1962 and information on the yields of some atmospheric nuclear weapons tests during 1962 have been obstructed.[47]

The continuing focus on protecting nuclear weapons information as well as the flaws of official secrecy are revealed in DOE declassification decisions concerning a 1967 report on the Lawrence Radiation Laboratory's (now Lawrence Livermore National Laboratory) "Nth Country" experiment during the 1960s. Concerned about what today is called nuclear proliferation, Livermore had asked two postgraduate physicists with no expertise in nuclear weapons or any security clearances to work together to see if they could produce a "credible weapon design." Later joined by a Livermore army research associate, the team used the open literature and their own knowledge to design an implosion-type weapon. The degree to which the experiment was a success remains classified, but

46. For much of the new information, see the DOE's "Declassification of Pre-1961 Nuclear Test Yields" and "Summary List of Previously Unannounced Tests," both December 7, 1993; and "Openness Press Conference Fact Sheets," June 27, 1994. Although President Clinton's 1995 Executive Order 12958 on national security information (discussed later in this chapter) reaffirms current rules on restricted data, it may have important implications for the release of historical information on delivery systems, war plans, and related data.

47. For delays in declassification of stockpile numbers and yields, see Committee on Declassification of Information, "DOE Classification Policy and Practice," pp. 53–59. For the eight classified yields from 1962, see U.S. Department of Energy, "Openness Press Conference Fact Sheets," June 27, 1994, p. 175. One of the classified yields is for the "Frigate Bird" test on May 6, 1962, when the USS *Ethan Allen* (SSBN-608) launched a Polaris A-2 missile while submerged about 1,500 nautical miles (2,777 kilometers) east-northeast of Christmas Island in the Pacific Ocean. The missile's reentry vehicle traveled about 1,020 nautical miles (1,889 kilometers) toward the island, detonating at an altitude of 8,300 feet (2,530 meters). The yield of the W47Y1 warhead is estimated at 1.2 to 1.5 megatons (this warhead was retired in 1974). "Frigate Bird" was the first and only operational test of a U.S. SSBN/SLBM weapon system. See Robert S. Norris and Thomas B. Cochran, "United States Nuclear Tests, July 1945 to 31 December 1992," Nuclear Weapons Databook Working Paper 94-1, Natural Resources Defense Council, Washington, D.C., 1994, p. 33.

the heavy excisions in the report (including its bibliography of open literature) imply that the team's design work was credible. Plainly, the DOE does not want to abet any efforts at imitation (though given the apparent results, such an approach is unlikely to thwart a determined proliferant).[48]

The recognition that old standards for classifying nuclear weapons information were partly outmoded led Secretary O'Leary to initiate a Fundamental Classification Policy Review in February 1993, the first effort since 1946 to reevaluate in a comprehensive way nuclear secrecy guidelines. A draft report issued in early 1996 took a rather conservative stance but showed, nevertheless, the strong influence of O'Leary's general approach. Asserting that by its very nature, the idea of "born secret" promotes overclassification, the report recommended modifying the Atomic Energy Act and introducing a new classification system based on defensible judgments "unambiguously related to national policy." In the post–cold war era, it argued, classification decisions "must be based on explainable judgments of identifiable risk to national security and no other reason." Drawing upon these and related principles, the report made cautious but clear recommendations for continued classification of nuclear weapons design information. It also proposed that the DOE divest itself of the responsibility that it now shares with the DOD for classification policy on such critical issues as weapons stockpile information. The implication is that even if the DOE establishes a more justifiable classification system, the DOD could continue with business as usual unless it decided to undertake its own "fundamental review."[49]

Paralleling and informing Secretary O'Leary's openness program was the complex effort from 1993 to 1995, mandated by President Bill Clinton, to frame a new executive order on classified information policy. The result was Executive Order 12958 signed in April 1995. This order has important implications for declassifying information on nuclear weapons policy, especially that contained in historical documents. Not only is its tone more favorable to releasing information but it establishes more liberal criteria for declassifying historical documents more than twenty-five years old. Nevertheless, statutory requirements compel E.O. 12958 to leave the heart of the nuclear secrecy system in place.

In December 1997, the DOE announced the issuance of new regulations, including new guidelines shifting the focus from "born classified"

48. W. J. Frank, ed., *Summary Report of the Nth Country Experiment,* UCRL-50249, Lawrence Radiation Laboratory (March 1967), released by Department of Energy under the Freedom of Information Act to the National Security Archive, February 3, 1995. The less than foolproof nature of secrecy controls is indicated by the DOE's decision to wholly excise a section in the report entitled, "A Possible Security Leak in the Literature."

49. U.S. Department of Energy, "Fundamental Classification Policy Review," Draft Report for Public Comment, February 1, 1996. Also open to criticism are recommendations for providing authority to the secretary of energy to reclassify specific information and against releasing data on the tritium stockpile.

to "born unclassified," except where strictly necessary (see footnote 20). At the same time the DOE and DOD announced broad agreement on the general recommendations contained in the Fundamental Classification Policy Review along with a number of specific recommendations. Even if one takes exception to some of the particulars, the rules constitute an innovative effort to institutionalize accountability into the nuclear secrecy system. However, only about one-third of the more than three hundred changes in DOE classification policy recommended by the review were accepted by the DOD (and some of these increase the classification level for certain categories of information, such as weapon design data). It would therefore appear that effecting deeper and more permanent change will require wholesale revisions by Congress of the Atomic Energy Act.[50]

Budgetary Costs

A 1994 report to the secretary of defense and the director of central intelligence found that "no one has a good handle on what security really costs. Our accounting systems are not designed to collect security cost data and do not provide the analytic tools necessary to support resource decision-making."[51] Even today, the DOD does not know how much it spends on maintaining secrecy for nuclear-related activities.[52] Surprisingly, the Pentagon does not even know how many civilian or uniformed personnel have nuclear weapons clearances. Although the DOD has a standardized clearance system for nuclear information—critical nuclear weapons design information—no one in the government knows how many such clearances are active at any given time. Centralized authority provides the rules for CNWDI clearances, but the system operates on an entirely decentralized basis, at the command level or lower, with clearance granted on a need-to-know basis to personnel who already have military clearances; no additional investigations are necessary. Accountability is sacrificed in the name of operational flexibility.[53]

Therefore, at the level of security clearances, the costs of nuclear secrecy blend in with other costs. The military's security costs for nuclear programs are equally difficult to discern. For example, a

50. "Joint Statement by the Department of Energy and the Department of Defense on the Joint Disposition of the Recommendations of the Fundamental Classification Policy Review," December 22, 1997; Department of Energy, "Department of Energy and Department of Defense Approve Major Changes in Classification Policy," fact sheet, December 22, 1997.

51. Joint Security Commission, *Redefining Security: A Report to the Secretary of Defense and the Director of Central Intelligence* (Washington, D.C., February 28, 1994), p. 115. For the full discussion on costs, see pp. 115–22 of this report.

52. Telephone conversation with David Whitman, Office of the Assistant Secretary of Defense for Command, Control, Communications, and Intelligence, February 13, 1995.

53. Telephone conversation with Pete Nelson, Security Branch, Office of Assistant Secretary of Defense for Command, Control, Communications, and Intelligence, October 20, 1994.

nuclear weapons officer on a ballistic missile submarine may have security duties in addition to other responsibilities, obfuscating the DOD's contribution to the budgetary costs of nuclear secrecy.

Although nuclear secrecy costs cannot be readily disaggregated, newly available data shed light on the volume of DOD secrecy spending in general. In recent years, the DOD has been tracking some secrecy-related spending under the category of "information systems security program."[54] According to DOD's Future Years Defense Program historical database, during fiscal 1992–95, spending in that category alone was nearly $1.7 billion. Another series of expenditures during 1990–95 were directly or indirectly related to secrecy: $533 million for industrial security and $195 million for physical security, bringing total identified secrecy-related spending during that time to $2.4 billion. Absent any more reliable data, we have attributed one-fifth of this figure, or $480 million to the nuclear weapons program, although the true cost is possibly higher.

However, even these figures are substantially incomplete. Whereas the FYDP shows $178 million in spending for all three categories during 1993, an Office of Management and Budget analysis done at the request of Congress indicates that in 1993 alone the DOD spent more than $2 billion on electronic security, personnel clearances, management of classified documents, and the like. A work force of more than 30,000 people managed and operated this secrecy system.[55] A 1993 General Accounting Office report found that the DOD spends about $3 billion (then-year dollars) annually on physical security, with a large portion of that devoted to guard forces. Some $72 million (then-year dollars) was expended between fiscal 1990 and 1992 for special safes and file cabinets. While a typical five-drawer legal size file cabinet with lock might cost $174, a five-drawer cabinet designed to meet classified document storage standards, including electromechanical combination locks, can cost $2,160 on average, which amounts to a unit cost differential of $1,985. The government also purchased more than 252,000 special secure telephones at an initial cost of $3,000 per phone (later dropping to $1,660 per phone).[56] Given the complex security arrangements regulating nuclear weapons information, it is plausible

54. This category covers spending by all offices of the Department of Defense—including intelligence agencies—and "includes resources, manpower, authorizations, necessary facilities and equipment required to perform INFOSEC [Information Security] research and development, to provide INFOSEC services, to procure INFOSEC products required to secure telecommunications and information systems when such products are separately procurable from host systems, and to provide INFOSEC maintenance and support. Also includes costs associated with the protection afforded to telecommunications and information systems which process sensitive data and efforts to ensure authenticity, integrity, and availability of the information and the system." U.S. Department of Defense, Office of the Comptroller, *FYDP Program Structure,* DOD 7045.7-H (Springfield, Va., National Technical Information Service, 1993), p. 3-22.

55. See Letter and enclosures from Leon L. Panetta, Director, Office of Management and Budget, to Honorable Steny Hoyer, April 13, 1994.

56. U.S. General Accounting Office, *Classified Information: Costs of Protection Are Integrated with Other Security Costs,* NSIAD-94-55 (October 1993), pp. 15, 19.

that hundreds of millions of dollars of the $2 billion identified by the OMB in fiscal 1993 directly supported nuclear secrecy programs.[57]

Intelligence programs and activities have also been an important factor in nuclear secrecy spending over the years. During the cold war, monitoring nuclear weapons developments in the Soviet bloc and China was an important activity, involving the Central Intelligence Agency, Defense Intelligence Agency, the air force, and the AEC and later its successors. This effort dates to the 1940s, when U.S. intelligence first monitored German nuclear potential and then established, in 1947, AFOAT-1, the once-secret air force organization responsible for using advanced technology to detect foreign nuclear weapons tests (known today as the Air Force Technical Applications Center; see chapter 3).[58] Nuclear intelligence came to subsume a variety of "black" or special-access code-word programs involving communications intelligence, radar intelligence, signals intelligence, and satellite photography. Except for the U-2 and SR-71 flights and satellite photography, most of these activities remain officially secret, their existence neither confirmed nor denied by the government.[59] The cumulative costs of maintaining tight controls over these programs must be staggering—one direct participant for many years estimated that "a classified program increases a manufacturer's costs up to 25 percent"—but those expenditures are as elusive as their aggregate costs.[60]

Unlike the DOD and the intelligence agencies, the DOE makes available budgetary information on more recent nuclear secrecy costs, but details on historic costs are scarce. An AEC document prepared for congressional oversight purposes in 1953 shows that secrecy spending was substantial during the early 1950s but also demonstrates why the details are sparse. That year the AEC spent $55.7 million on security (nearly $410 million in 1996 dollars). The bulk of the expenditures—more than $235 million—was for guards, while $92 million was for personnel investigations and another $12.5 million was for maintaining control over documents. However, the AEC could provide such detail only by examining primary sources—"payrolls, invoices and work orders"—because its accounting system did not specify all secrecy and

57. R. Jeffrey Smith, "32,400 Workers Stockpiling U.S. Secrets," *Washington Post,* May 15, 1994, p. A1; Analysis of FYDP historical database.

58. AFOAT-1 was an acronym for Air Force Deputy Chief of Staff for Operations, Atomic Energy Office, Section One.

59. One notable exception was the Air Force's 1994 acknowledgment of the existence of Project Mogul, an effort from 1946 to 1950 to use high-altitude balloons rigged with special acoustic sensors to detect Soviet atomic bomb tests. See chapter 3. The existence of photo-reconnaissance satellites was only officially declassified by President Jimmy Carter on October 1, 1978. See Jeffrey T. Richelson, *America's Secret Eyes in Space: The U.S. Keyhole Spy Satellite Program* (New York: Harper & Row, 1990), pp. 139–43.

60. Ben R. Rich and Leo Janos, *Skunk Works: A Personal Memoir of My Years at Lockheed* (New York: Little, Brown, 1994), p. 333. According to a communication dated February 8, 1995, from U.S. Air Force Technical Applications Center, Patrick Air Force Base, Florida, AFTAC "does not have a mechanism in place to track costs related to security supporting [its] mission." For nuclear intelligence during the 1940s and the early years of AFOAT-1, see Zeigler and Jacobson, *Spying without Spies.*

RC-135S COBRA BALL aircraft are used to collect optical and electronic intelligence data from foreign missile launches to help verify compliance with arms control agreements. They operate in international airspace in conjunction with the COBRA DANE phased-array radar at Shemya Air Force Base, Alaska, and the floating COBRA JUDY radar to track missile trajectories and reentry vehicles.

Credit: U.S. Air Force

Engineers with TRW inspect one of the company's Defense Support Program satellites. These are deployed in geostationary orbits to detect the infrared heat signatures accompanying the launch of ballistic missiles and relay that information to U.S. military command centers. Other optical and electronic sensors are also carried aboard the satellites.

Credit: TRW

During President Ronald Reagan's visit to Moscow in May 1988, Lieutenant Commander Woody Lee stands in Red Square with the "Football" attached to his wrist by a leather strap while the president tours the square with General Secretary Mikhail Gorbachev. Inside the briefcase is a notebook containing details of the U.S. nuclear war plan and available strike options. A military aide carrying this briefcase accompanies the president at all times.

Credit: UPI/Corbis-Bettman

Based at Offutt Air Force Base in Omaha, Nebraska, the National Airborne Operations Center is the president's airborne command post in the event of nuclear war. At least one aircraft (there are four in all) is always on alert with full battle staff, ready for takeoff on fifteen minutes' notice. The aircraft is specially shielded against the effects of electromagnetic radiation and is capable of transmitting nuclear launch orders. This 1973 photograph shows the E-4A configuration of the plane; it has since been upgraded to an E-4B.

Credit: U.S. Air Force

The COBRA JUDY phased-array radar aboard the USNS *Observation Island* is 35 feet (10.7 meters) high. It operates in international waters to monitor the launch and flight path of foreign ballistic missiles.

Credit: Raytheon Company (courtesy Jeffrey Richelson)

This August 20, 1966 photograph from a CORONA photoreconnaissance satellite shows Dolon airfield in the Soviet Union. Photographs such as this provided a wealth of information on Soviet military capabilities (in this example, bombers can be distinguished from transport aircraft), helping to allay fears of a "missile gap" but also supplying important targeting information to the military, particularly the Strategic Air Command.

Credit: National Reconnaissance Office (courtesy Federation of American Scientists)

This 1959 photograph of the Soviet Union's missile launching complex at Tyuratam (in what is now Kazakhstan) was taken by a U-2 spy plane flying at about 70,000 feet (21,336 meters). The large triangular-shaped area is a flame pit to direct hot exhaust away from the launch pad (photo-interpreters carefully measured the shadows cast in the pit and by the nearby buildings to determine the size of these structures). U-2s flew regularly over this facility to gather intelligence on the latest advances in Soviet rocketry. Sputnik was launched from this complex in October 1957, as were all subsequent Sputniks, all manned spaceflights, and all lunar and planetary flights.

Credit: Central Intelligence Agency (courtesy Federation of American Scientists)

This 139,800-square-foot (13,001-square-meter) radiation hardened facility built into Mount Pony near Culpeper, Virginia, was designed to protect more than 500 senior Federal Reserve officials in the event of nuclear war and to help restore the economy following one. Preplanned freeze-dried menus were kept on hand for the first thirty days of occupation. Until 1988, several billion dollars of U.S. currency were stored in the site's large, high-security vault.

Credit: Don Eiler's Custom Photography (courtesy U.S. Federal Bank of Richmond)

Workers at the Mosler Safe Company circa 1960 stand by one of the two giant blast doors they built for vehicular entrances to the secret fallout shelter for Congress located underneath the Greenbrier resort in White Sulphur Springs, West Virginia. The door is 19.5 inches (49.5 centimeters) thick and weighs more than 20 tons.

Credit: Mosler Safe Company (courtesy Richard Gardner)

The High Point Special Facility, located inside Mount Weather, Virginia, is an unacknowledged continuity-of-government facility operated by the Federal Emergency Management Agency. Completed in 1958, it was designed to accommodate the president, his cabinet, the Supreme Court, and several thousand additional people, and includes a hospital, crematorium, dining and recreation areas, reservoirs, a power plant, and radio and television studios. The entrance to the facility is through the gated tunnel at the lower left (box).

Credit: William Campbell for Time

Twenty-four conventionally-armed Nike Ajax antiaircraft missiles stand on alert at Lorton, Virginia (south of Washington, D.C.) on October 28, 1956. By 1958, nearly 200 such batteries had been deployed across the United States. Shortly thereafter, the Army began to gradually replace these with the longer-range, nuclear-capable Nike Hercules missile and the last Nike Ajax battery was deactivated in late 1963.

Credit: U.S. Army

To protect the new underground headquarters of the North American Air Defense Command (NORAD) from shockwaves caused by nuclear explosions, workers (circa 1963) install the first of more than 1,300 giant metal springs on which buildings were later constructed. Each spring was approximately 4 feet (1.2 meters) long and 20 inches (50.8 centimeters) in diameter, and could withstand a maximum pressure of 65,000 pounds (29,545 kilograms).

Credit: U.S. Air Force (courtesy U.S. Army Corps of Engineers)

An F-106 Delta Dart fires a training version of the Genie air defense missile. More than 10,000 such missiles were deployed between 1957 and 1984. An estimated 5,000 1- to 2-kiloton warheads were produced for the Genie.

Credit: U.S. Air Force (courtesy Natural Resources Defense Council)

An aerial view of the Stanley R. Mickelsen Safeguard complex in Nekoma, North Dakota, the only operational antiballistic missile system ever deployed by the United States. The pyramid-shaped building is the missile site radar, used to track incoming missiles and guide Spartan and Sprint missiles to their targets. A separate long-range detection radar was located further north at Concrete, North Dakota. The missile field in the foreground contains reinforced underground launchers for thirty Spartan and sixteen Sprint missiles (an additional fifty or so Sprint missiles were deployed at four remote launch sites). The complex was deactivated in 1976 after being operational for less than four months.

Credit: U.S. Army

The navy's P-3 Orion antisubmarine warfare plane (shown here as a prototype model in December 1960) is deployed from coastal bases to locate and if necessary destroy enemy submarines. Its unusual tail houses a magnetic anomaly detector, to locate large metallic objects underwater. In addition to conventional armament, the aircraft could carry two B57 nuclear depth bombs (these weapons were retired in 1993).

Credit: U.S. Navy

The nuclear-powered attack submarine USS *Thresher* under way on July 24, 1961. On April 10, 1963, while undergoing postoverhaul sea trials, the *Thresher* imploded and sank in approximately 8,500 feet (2,591 meters) of water 100 miles (161 kilometers) east of Cape Cod, Massachusetts, killing all 129 people aboard, including 17 civilian observers. The submarine was never recovered.

Credit: U.S. Navy

A radioactive spray plume rises above the destroyer USS *Agerholm,* following the underwater detonation of a 10-kiloton warhead carried by an antisubmarine rocket (ASROC) launched from the ship only seconds earlier. This May 11, 1962, full-scale proof test, code-named Operation Swordfish, took place about 370 nautical miles (685 kilometers) west-southwest of San Diego, California. Detonation occurred 650 feet (198 meters) underwater. It was the last of only five underwater U.S. nuclear weapons tests.

Credit: U.S. Navy (courtesy Natural Resources Defense Council)

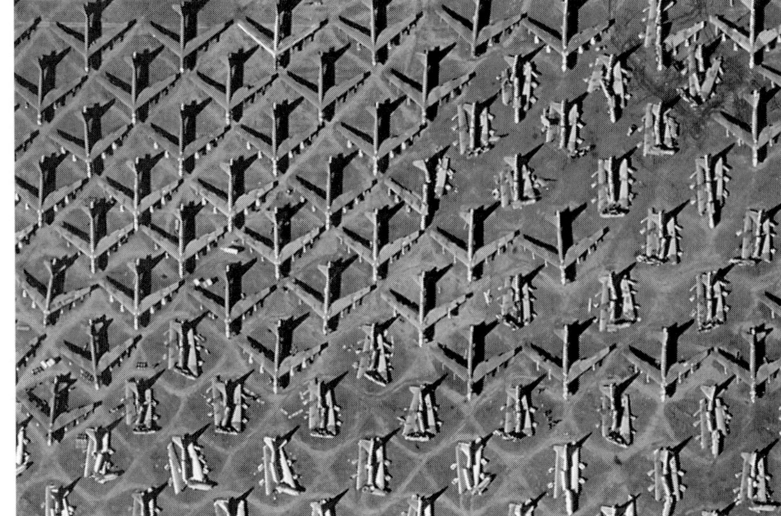

Upon retirement, B-52 bombers are flown to the Aerospace Maintenance and Regeneration Center (informally known as "The Boneyard") at Davis-Monthan Air Force Base near Tucson, Arizona. There, the aircraft are cut apart with a diamond-edged guillotine blade and left in the open for ninety days, so that Russian photo-reconnaissance satellites can verify they have been destroyed. The remains are then sold as scrap. This is how a portion of the site looked in December 1994.

Credit: Chad Slattery

At the Pantex Plant near Amarillo, Texas, nuclear weapons and weapons components are stored in highly secured earth-covered bunkers known as "igloos." There are sixty such igloos at Pantex (some more than fifty years old), currently holding more than 10,000 plutonium pits and an indeterminate number of weapons awaiting disassembly.

Credit: Department of Energy

As a result of the 1987 Intermediate-Range Nuclear Forces or INF Treaty, all Pershing II missiles (minus their nuclear warheads) were retired and destroyed. Here, a defueled Pershing rocket motor stage is crushed at the Longhorn Army Ammunition Plant in Karnack, Texas, September 8, 1988. This was the first of more than 200 Pershing IIs destroyed under the treaty.

Credit: U.S. Army/U.S. Air Force (courtesy Natural Resources Defense Council)

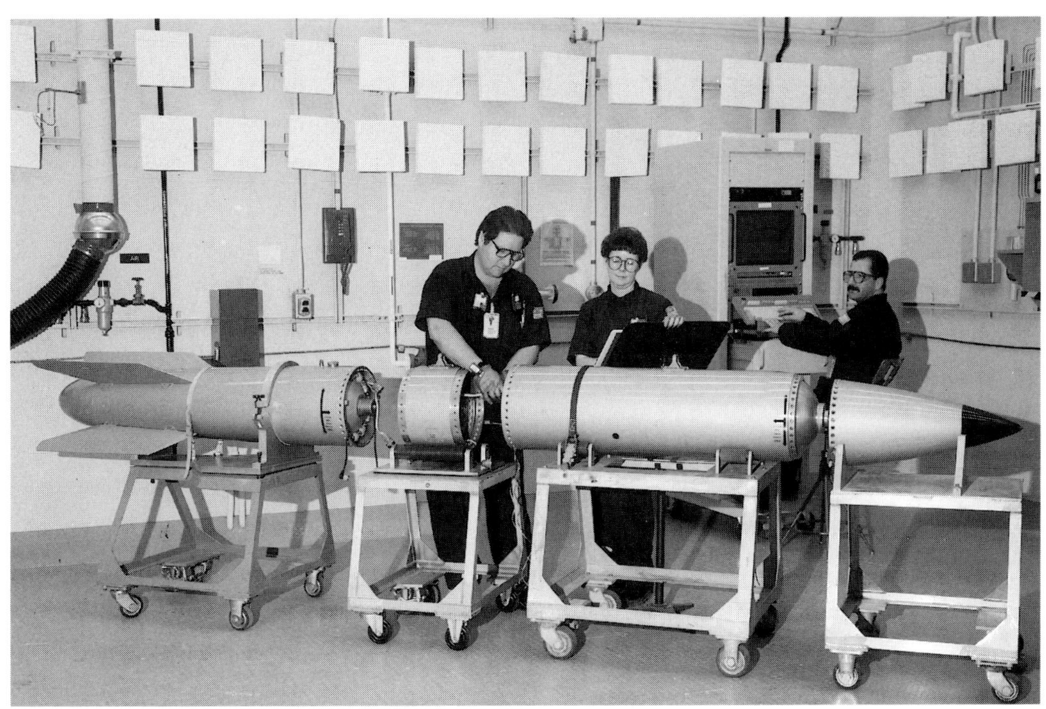

Workers at Pantex begin disassembling a B61 gravity bomb by separating it into its major subcomponents. The bomb's warhead is in the section directly behind the nose.

Credit: Department of Energy

As part of the dismantlement process, submarines are brought into drydock, where they are defueled, their reactor compartments are removed, and all usable equipment and materials are removed and recycled. All weapons are removed before this stage. This 1993 photograph taken at Puget Sound Naval Shipyard in Washington shows two ballistic missile submarines, each of which carried sixteen Poseidon C-3 ballistic missiles.

Credit: Ralph Wasmer, U.S. Navy

A defueled reactor compartment (right) is shown separated from the rest of the submarine. Once separated, special steel bulkheads are attached to both ends of the compartment and welded into place. After their radioactive fuel is removed, the compartments are classified as low level waste.

Credit: Ralph Wasmer, U.S. Navy

Once sealed off, the reactor compartments are shipped by barge out of Puget Sound, down the coast and along the Columbia River to the port of Benton, south of the Hanford Reservation. There the compartments are transferred to special multiwheeled high-load trailers for transport to Trench 94 in the Hanford Reservation's 218-E-12B burial ground (near the center of the site), raised onto support columns, and welded into place. In this November 1994 photograph of Trench 94, forty-three reactor compartments are visible and foundations are being prepared for a forty-fourth. Once full, the trench will be filled with dirt and buried. The compartments are expected to retain their integrity for more than 600 years.

Credit: U.S. Navy

This photograph shows eleven high-level waste tanks under construction at the Hanford Reservation circa 1943. Once completed, these tanks, built of reinforced concrete and carbon steel, were buried underground. Workers on the tank at right show the scale. Of the sixteen tanks built at Hanford during the Manhattan Project, twelve were 75 feet (22.9 meters) in diameter. Intended only as an interim measure, they began to leak within only a few years of being completed and remain in existence today.

Credit: Department of Energy

Until 1970, solid low-level and transuranic waste at the Atomic Energy Commission's nuclear weapons facilities (shown here is Hanford Reservation, circa 1950s) was frequently disposed of in cardboard boxes. Once filled, this unlined trench would have been covered with dirt, leaving the cardboard to deteriorate and allowing the waste to contaminate the soil and leach into the groundwater.

Credit: Department of Energy

Thousands of drums of transuranic waste sit in temporary buildings at the Idaho National Engineering and Environmental Laboratory awaiting shipment to the Waste Isolation Pilot Plant in New Mexico, March 1994.

Credit: Robert Del Tredici

The Feed Materials Production Center is located near Fernald, Ohio, and is 20 miles (32 kilometers) northwest of Cincinnati. This 1.6-square-mile (4.1-square kilometer) facility converted a variety of uranium "feed materials" into uranium metal, primarily for use as target and fuel elements in the production reactors at the Department of Energy's Savannah River Site in South Carolina. Production operations ceased in 1989, and the plant is currently undergoing extensive decontamination and decommissioning.

Credit: Department of Energy

Beneath this concrete dome on Runit Island (part of Enewetak Atoll), built between 1977 and 1980 at a cost of about $239 million, lie 111,000 cubic yards (84,927 cubic meters) of radioactive soil and debris from Bikini and Rongelap atolls. The dome covers the 30-foot (9 meter) deep 350-foot (107 meter) wide crater created by the May 5, 1958, Cactus test. Note the people atop the dome.

Credit: Defense Special Weapons Agency

VIP observers sitting on the patio of the Officer's Beach Club on Parry Island are illuminated by the 81 kiloton Dog test, part of Operation Greenhouse, at Enewetak Atoll, April 8, 1951.

Credit: Defense Special Weapons Agency

Private First Class Carl Lacinski (right) hands his film badge to Lieutenant Pearle W. Mack in preparation for the Charlie test at the Nevada Proving Ground, April 22, 1952. Badges such as these, which could measure only external radiation exposure, were distributed to just a small number of participating troops.

Credit: National Archives

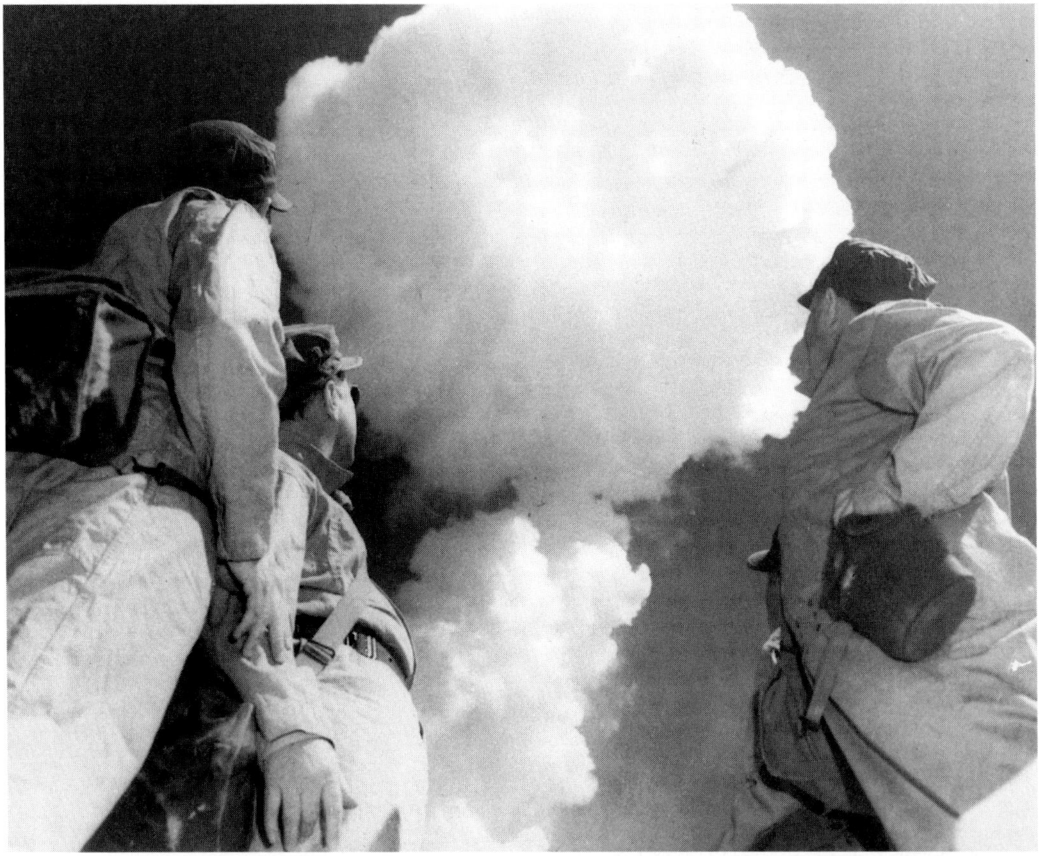

(Left to right) Representatives Chet Holifield, Sterling Cole, and Melvin Price, all members of the Joint Committee on Atomic Energy, observe the results of the 31-kiloton Charlie test, which was detonated at a height of 3,447 feet (1,051 meters). This test was broadcast live on national television.

Credit: National Archives

Troops participating in exercises at "Camp Desert Rock" (Nevada Proving Ground) observe the formation of a mushroom cloud following the detonation of the Dog test (part of Operation Buster-Jangle), a 21-kiloton device dropped from a B-50 bomber that exploded at a height of 1,417 feet (432 meters) on November 1, 1951.

Credit: Defense Special Weapons Agency

Demonstrating a common decontamination procedure, Lieutenant Colonel Robert Cassidy uses a broom to remove radioactive dust from Lieutenant Colonel Glover Johns following the 1952 Charlie test at the Nevada Proving Ground. Johns had toured the blast area shortly after the test along with other troops at "Camp Desert Rock." If his clothes were in fact contaminated, this procedure would have returned some of the contamination to the air, where it could be inhaled or ingested. Radioactive particles would also adhere to the broom, possibly spreading contamination to those who may not have been initially affected.

Credit: National Archives

Eighty days after it fell into the ocean following the January 1966 midair collision between a nuclear-armed B-52G bomber and a KC-135 refueling tanker over Palomares, Spain, this B28RI nuclear bomb was recovered from 2,850 feet (869 meters) of water and lifted aboard the USS *Petrel*. This photograph was among the first ever published of a U.S. hydrogen bomb. Left to right are Sr. Don Antonio Velilla Manteca, chief of the Spanish Nuclear Energy Board in Palomares; Brigadier General Arturo Montel Touzet, Spanish coordinator for the search and recovery operation; Rear Admiral William S. Guest, commander of U.S. Navy Task Force 65; and Major General Delmar E. Wilson, commander of the Sixteenth Air Force. The B28 had a maximum yield of 1.45 megatons.

Credit: U.S. Navy (courtesy Natural Resources Defense Council)

Left to right are Representatives Carl Hinshaw, Melvin Price, Sterling Cole, Paul Kilday, and Chet Holifield, during their visit to the Nevada Proving Ground to observe the Charlie test (which involved a nuclear device dropped from a B-50 bomber), April 22, 1952.

Credit: National Archives

Senator Brien McMahon, chairman of the Joint Committee on Atomic Energy, talking with reporters on January 27, 1950, after meeting with the Atomic Energy Commission to hear about "all kinds of bombs." This meeting occurred four days before President Harry S Truman ordered the AEC "to continue its work on all forms of atomic weapons, including the so-called hydrogen or superbomb."

Credit: U.S. Senate Historical Office

security expenditures. The implication of this apparently unique compilation is that a documentary basis for a retrospective accounting of the early years of the AEC secrecy system would be exceedingly difficult and perhaps impossible to produce.[61]

In contrast to the early years of the nuclear weapons program, the DOE now tracks information security spending under its safeguards and security program, which includes everything from guards and guns to classification and declassification activities. However, program costs include spending on security for fissionable material, which exceed the expenditures on information controls and related personnel security. Nevertheless, direct costs for classification-related work at the DOE can be readily specified; in recent years, they have consumed an average of about $100 million a year.[62]

Indirect costs may increase DOE's average; for example, personnel security investigations are in some ways the bedrock of nuclear secrecy because they determine who can (and cannot) work with classified information.[63] The costs of those investigations are the only secrecy-related expenses for which a more or less consistent historical time series exists, although the *Budget of the United States Government* (compiled annually by OMB) did not begin to tally them until 1952; thus costs for the first ten years of the atomic program are unrecorded. However, compiling these line items yields a total of $1.97 billion for AEC, ERDA, and DOE expenditures on security investigations from 1952 to 1996. Factoring in the AEC's and DOE's cost for processing and reviewing investigative materials—an additional 10 percent—brings the total to nearly $2.2 billion.[64]

61. U.S. Atomic Energy Commission, "Atomic Energy Commission Security Costs, Note by the Secretary," AEC 611/6, December 4, 1953, copy obtained from the Presidential Advisory Commission on Human Radiation Experiments. Former AEC chairman Gordon Dean stated that at the end of 1952, "Of the 7,300 people employed directly by the Atomic Energy Commission . . . 1,700 of them [23 percent] were engaged in security work—as guards, supervisors, investigators, or evaluators. Among the Commission's contractors, about 6,000 people were engaged in security work of one kind or another [about 10 percent of the total operating contractor work force of 58,101 people]. Nearly 200 people were engaged, either part or full-time, in the review of documents to determine what needed to be held secret and what did not. About 300 people were involved directly and on a full-time basis keeping tabs on the whereabouts of the commission's more than 1 million classified documents. More than 400 people were engaged in keeping the most precise kind of records on the fissionable materials—uranium-235 and plutonium—in the possession of the commission and its contractors. The cost of this 'fissionable material accountability' runs in excess of $2,000,000 per year [$14.4 million in 1996 dollars]." Dean, *Report on the Atom,* pp. 214–15.

62. Committee on Declassification of Information, "DOE Classification Policy and Practice," p. 18. From 1993 through 1995, DOE headquarters and components spent nearly $300 million dollars on classification and declassification activities. In fiscal 1993 alone, direct costs for were more than $98 million. See Letter and enclosures from Leon L. Panetta, Director, Office of Management and Budget, to Honorable Steny Hoyer, April 13, 1994; personal communication with Karen Rosenthal, Department of Energy, Office of Consumer and Public Liaison, April 10, 1995.

63. The workings of the investigation/reinvestigation system are beyond the scope of this study, but it was by no means infallible. For congressional concerns during the 1980s, see U.S. Congress, *Review of the Department of Energy's Personnel Security Clearances Program,* Hearing before the House Committee on Government Operations, Subcommittee on Environment, Energy, and Natural Resources, 100 Cong. 1 sess. (GPO, 1987). Evidence about substantial investigative backlogs provided in this hearing, for example (see p. 27), suggests that given the security clearance program's objectives, the Energy Department was not spending enough on this component of the secrecy program.

64. For the security investigation lines, see *The Budget of the United States Government for Fiscal Year 1954,* p. 95, and successive volumes. Incomplete data on security investigations

During fiscal 1994–96 alone, security investigations cost more than $112 million, averaging more than $37 million a year and bringing the average cost of DOE secrecy spending to well over $130 million a year.[65] (For more on security investigations, see box 8-4.)

Notwithstanding these expenditures, six reports issued by the GAO between 1987 and 1995 documented serious deficiencies in the DOE's safeguards and security program. In 1987, for example, the department did not routinely reinvestigate 12,000 employees with high-level clearances or especially sensitive positions. In 1991 the GAO assessed the DOE's own data and identified more than 2,100 security lapses at thirty-nine facilities, including violation of the two-person rule for access to nuclear materials, excessive rates of false alarm for intrusion detection and alarm systems, and the inability of security forces to demonstrate such basic skills as apprehending and arresting individuals posing a threat to security.[66]

Even if specific budgetary data on spending by the DOE and its predecessors is limited to security investigations, it is nevertheless possible

---

during the late 1970s can be found in *1976 ERDA Authorization,* Hearings before the House Committee on Science and Technology, Subcommittee on Energy Research, Development, and Demonstration (Fossil Fuels), 94 Cong. 1 sess. (GPO, 1975), pp. 395–97; and *ERDA Authorizing Legislation Fiscal Year 1976,* Hearings before the Joint Committee on Atomic Energy, 94 Cong. 1 sess. (GPO, 1975), p. 26. For more recent fiscal years, see Department of Energy annual budget requests, beginning with U.S. Department of Energy, Assistant Secretary, Management and Administration, Office of the Controller, *Congressional Budget Request, Fiscal Year 1990* (GPO, January 1989). The only recorded pre-1952 expenditure is a $6.3 million payment to the Federal Bureau of Investigation, noted in the *Budget of the United States Government for Fiscal Year 1948,* p. 83. The 10 percent processing and reviewing cost figure comes from a telephone conversation by the author (Burr) with Lynn Gebrowsky, Department of Energy, Personnel Security Office, February 27, 1997.

65. Communication with Karen Rosenthal, U.S. Department of Energy, Office of Consumer and Public Liaison, April 10, 1995, and Thomas Knight, Department of Energy Budget Office, December 3, 1996.

66. See the following publications by the U.S. General Accounting Office: *Nuclear Security: DOE's Reinvestigation of Employees Has Not Been Timely,* RCED-87-72 (March 1987); *Nuclear Security: Safeguards and Security Weaknesses at DOE's Weapons Facilities,* RCED-92-39 (December 1991); *Nuclear Security: Weak Internal Controls Hamper Oversight of DOE's Security Program,* RCED-92-146 (June 1992); *Nuclear Security: Safeguards and Security Planning at DOE Facilities Incomplete,* RCED-93-14 (October 1992); *Nuclear Security: Improving Correction of Security Deficiencies at DOE's Weapons Facilities,* RCED-93-10 (November 1992); and *Department of Energy: Procedures Lacking to Protect Computerized Data,* AIMD-95-118 (June 1995). In late 1990 an FBI investigation reportedly determined the following security lapse: Chinese intelligence agents, visiting Lawrence Livermore National Laboratory in the 1980s under a DOE program, had acquired plans for the neutron bomb from documents obtained at the laboratory. See Michael Wines, "Chinese Atom-Arms Spying in U.S. Reported," *New York Times,* November 22, 1990, p. A5. A 1991 GAO audit of 600,000 classified documents at Livermore found that about 10,000 were missing. They covered "a wide range of subject matter, including nuclear weapons design, X-ray laser design, special nuclear materials such as plutonium, and photographs of nuclear weapons and nuclear weapons tests." Although LLNL and the DOE "believe that the missing documents are the result of administrative error, such as inaccurate record keeping," there is no certainty they were not stolen and the data they contained compromised. See U.S. General Accounting Office, *Nuclear Security: Accountability for Livermore's Secret Classified Documents Is Inadequate,* RCED-91-65 (February 1991), p. 3. These reports directly contradicted earlier DOE assertions that security lapses involving thousands of foreign visitors to LLNL and other nuclear facilities had not definitively resulted in the disclosure of classified information. See Michael R. Gordon, "Officials Concede Lapses in Security," *New York Times,* October 12, 1988, p. A14; U.S. General Accounting Office, *Nuclear Nonproliferation: Major Weaknesses in Foreign Visitor Controls at Weapons Laboratories,* RCED-89-31 (October 1988). In September 1996 the GAO reported that foreign visitors to the nuclear weapons laboratories had increased by 55 percent over 1986–87 levels (to 5,878 visitors annually), with visitors from countries designated as "sensitive" by the DOE (primarily China, India, Israel, Taiwan, and the states of the former Soviet Union) increasing at a rate of 225 percent over the same period (to 1,679 visitors annually). See U.S. General Accounting Office, *DOE Security: Information on Foreign Visitors to the Weapons Laboratories,* T-RCED-96-260 (September 26, 1996).

Box 8-4

Typical Costs of Security Investigations

In fiscal 1993, the cost of a security investigation for a DOE employee could be as low as $1,550 but might exceed $4,500.[1] Limited background investigations by the Office of Personnel Management (OPM)—for individuals needing "secret" or "L" clearances—were the least expensive; they cost $1,825. Initial background investigations performed by OPM cost $2,838; they are for employees who occupy "critical sensitive" positions but do not have access to classified material. Presumably, this category includes executive secretaries, administrative assistants, and the like wherever job performance requires discretion. Both OPM and the FBI conduct "single-scope background investigations"—full investigations of the previous ten years of an individual's life—for individuals seeking "Q" and top secret clearances or access to sensitive compartmented information (SCI). These investigations cost $3,225, and more than 10,000 were performed. The FBI conducts them when they are for positions of a "high degree of importance or sensitivity." The FBI also conducts some initial background investigations and some reinvestigations, apparently for more sensitive positions. These cost $4,627 per case. About twenty were carried out in 1993.

1. U.S. Department of Energy, *FY 1995 Congressional Budget Request: Atomic Energy Defense Activities*, vol. 1 (1994), pp. 464–68.

to develop a rough estimate of their overall secrecy-related spending. Using the rule of thumb mentioned earlier—that security adds about 20 percent to the costs of classified nuclear programs—it is possible to develop a tentative figure for those expenditures. Given this study's estimate that historical expenditures on nuclear weapons design, development, testing, and production totaled about $409 billion (see figure 1-1), then 20 percent of that sum equals $82 billion. Assuming the same 20 percent added cost for the $5 trillion in programs discussed in chapters 2, 3, and 4, it is quite possible that total cold war, nuclear-related secrecy expenditures exceed $1 trillion. To be conservative and avoid double counting, however, we do not include any of these possible costs in the overall total for this chapter or book.

Secrecy's Intangible Costs

In addition to specific budgetary expenditures, nuclear secrecy has entailed other costs that are intangible but even more significant.[67] One

67. Quist, *Introduction, History, and Adverse Impacts*, pp. 85–99, remains the essential starting point for any consideration of the nonbudgetary costs of nuclear secrecy. For an extraordinary discussion of the negative impact that nuclear

is the burden that secrecy places on informed public debate in a constitutional democracy. As Senator Brien McMahon remarked nearly fifty years ago, it runs "counter to [our] democratic traditions." Although a powerful and vocal proponent of nuclear weapons who supported high levels of secrecy, McMahon suggested that as long as nuclear stockpile numbers were secret, "Congress would have to . . . vote on appropriations without knowing . . . basic and fundamental facts in our war policy."[68] *Life* magazine, in a February 1950 primer on the atomic bomb, strongly criticized this practice:

> It must be assumed [on the basis of public statements and data] that the approximate size of the U.S. stockpile of bombs is no secret. Nevertheless, this information, so vitally necessary to the making of policy, is denied to the people who are finally responsible for determining what policy shall be: the citizens of the U.S. and their elected representatives. There is no possible justification for this kind of overextended secrecy.[69]

McMahon's implication may be as valid now as it was then. After all, even if much information on nuclear weapons design is properly classified, a blackout on the numbers of weapons, as well as overall spending levels, impairs informed debate on the direction, dimensions, and consequences of the central element of U.S. military posture.

Despite the significance of the stockpile figures, some high-level officials preferred to be kept in the dark or received the information with some trepidation. Sometime before he actually learned the size of the stockpile, President Harry S Truman told his cabinet that he did not want to know the figures. He ought to have been more interested because when informed on April 3, 1947, he was reported to be visibly shocked that only seven weapons were available for immediate use. Just fourteen months earlier, when he had authorized Operation Crossroads (see chapter 1), Truman had (unknowingly) approved the detonation of one-third of the total U.S. stockpile! Surprisingly, for more than five years McMahon and the Joint Committee declined the AEC's offers for a briefing on the nuclear stockpile. McMahon finally accepted and was informed on September 19, 1951, the day after delivering a major Senate speech calling on the United States to "go all-out in atomic development and production" (see the introduction to this volume and chapter 9).[70]

---

secrecy can have on the lives of holders of "Q" clearances—from marriages to ethical choices, see Gusterson, *Nuclear Rites*, pp. 70–100.

68. Minutes of an Executive Meeting of the Joint Committee on Atomic Energy, April 6, 1949, Records of Joint Committees of Congress, Record Group 46, Box 202, JCAE Document 1059, National Archives. For background on McMahon, see Spencer R. Weart, *Nuclear Fear: A History of Images* (Harvard University Press, 1988), pp. 141–42.

69. "The Atomic Bomb," *Life*, February 27, 1950, p. 100.

70. When the newly created Atomic Energy Commission took over responsibility from the Manhattan Engineer District on January 1, 1947, commissioner and physicist Robert F. Bacher was "very deeply shocked" to learn that the stock-

Having set a precedent with the Manhattan Project, the government continued to make key decisions on the nuclear program with minimal, if any, public airing of the issues. When the Truman administration made its decisions on the hydrogen bomb program, for instance, policymakers did not publicly address the implications of putting such an immensely powerful weapon in the U.S. arsenal, much less the prospect of the massive and costly atmospheric testing that thermonuclear weapons would require or the economic and environmental implications of a huge expansion of the nation's capacity to produce fissile materials.[71] Although some of the principals, such as Lilienthal and Oppenheimer, wanted a frank discussion of the issues, that never occurred, and the public health and environmental, much less military and diplomatic, implications of the "Super" did not come to the public's attention until the bomb was a fait accompli.[72] Until the present study, the fiscal implications of this decision and others taken in the 1950s to expand significantly the nuclear arsenal have gone largely unexamined.

Governmental Obfuscation

Nuclear secrecy had the potential to obstruct congressional understanding of U.S. nuclear policy as much as that of the public. This became evident in the late 1960s when DOD and air force officials began making public statements about the advantages of equipping ICBMs with highly accurate multiple independently targeted reentry vehicles that could "kill" hard targets—such as missile silos and underground command posts—in the Soviet Union. Because such statements did not coincide with the retaliatory emphasis of publicly stated national policy, some

---

pile "did not have anything like as many weapons" as he believed it should have. As late as February 1947, both Secretary of the Navy James Forrestal and Chief of Naval Operations Chester Nimitz were unaware of the stockpile's size or the current rate of production, but each assumed that the other was. Asked to provide recommendations on bomb production, they advised continuing current production rates until a thorough analysis of U.S. nuclear requirements could be completed. War planners for the Joint Chiefs of Staff, including Major General Curtis LeMay, were not allowed access to stockpile information until the winter of 1947, a delay that severely hindered the formulation of early nuclear war plans. See David Alan Rosenberg, "U.S. Nuclear Stockpile, 1945 to 1950," *Bulletin of the Atomic Scientists*, vol. 38 (May 1982), pp. 25–30; Roger M. Anders, ed., *Forging the Atomic Shield: Excerpts from the Office Diary of Gordon E. Dean* (University of North Carolina Press, 1987), p. 8; Hewlett and Duncan, *Atomic Shield*, pp. 47–48, 557; Jonathan M. Weisgall, *Operation Crossroads: The Atomic Tests at Bikini Atoll* (Annapolis, Md.: Naval Institute Press, 1994), pp. 8–9, 31.

71. The Eisenhower administration continued this practice. According to the minutes of a May 27, 1953, National Security Council meeting, President Eisenhower "thought it was unwise to make any distinction between fission and fusion weapons. Indeed, he thought we should suppress in all future official statements any reference to the term 'thermonuclear.'" The NSC duly "noted the President's desire that reference in official statements to 'thermonuclear' weapons be discontinued for security reasons, and that such weapons be included within the term 'atomic' weapons." AEC chairman Gordon Dean, a participant in this meeting, added, in his diary, "Also 'fusion' and 'hydrogen.' . . . The President says 'keep them confused' as to 'fission' and 'fusion.'" See Goldfischer, *The Best Defense*, p. 132; Stephen Hilgartner, Richard C. Bell, and Rory O'Connor, *Nukespeak: The Selling of Nuclear Technology in America* (New York: Penguin Books, 1983), pp. 217–18.

72. DeVolpi and others, *Born Secret*, pp. 29–30, 55. For the largely secret debate over the H-bomb, see Galison and Bernstein, "In Any Light," pp. 267–347.

members of Congress worried that the Pentagon was planning for a first strike, an approach that could exacerbate the U.S.-Soviet strategic competition (in fact, during the 1950s, SAC anticipated striking first upon receiving confirmation that an attack was imminent; see chapter 3). The Nixon administration turned double talk into a fine art by denying that the DOD's statements signaled a policy change, even as pro-accuracy statements and budget requests continued to surface. Although Congress temporarily contained accuracy programs, the difficulty it experienced in obtaining credible information on strategic weapons developments demonstrates how secrecy can frustrate intelligent discussion of nuclear strategy even at the highest levels of government.[73]

Occasionally, members of Congress did chafe against secrecy provisions. During an April 1973 hearing before the JCAE's subcommittee on military applications, Air Force Major General Edward Giller was briefing members on nuclear weapons installations in Europe when Representative Manuel Lujan (Republican of New Mexico) asked him if the Soviet side knew where all of these were. When Giller responded that they probably did, since "most of our stockpile sites have characteristic fencelines, lighting, and communication facilities," he was asked why the chart he was using was marked "Secret," then, to which he replied: "The numbers they do not know, I believe."[74] At a follow-on hearing on May 22, Senator Stuart Symington (Democrat of Missouri) recounted a trip he had made to Europe in 1967:

> I saw one of our missiles, either the Honest John or Pershing . . . and they emphasized how secret it was. They had it all done right up to the actual firing for me, including the whistle. Everybody came in and went to their post, you might say, under the alert immediately. Like a pilot running for a plane under an Air Force alert. I suddenly looked up and I saw scores of civilians standing around a sort of punch bowl in which all of this was located. I said, "Who are those people?" He said, "They are the people living around here." I said, "They are looking at everything you are doing. You said it is highly classified. How about it?" The General in charge said, "The [deleted] are a very homogenous people." That was the answer.[75]

(For more on the "arbitrary" aspects of secrecy policy, see box 8-5.)

Completely removed from both public and congressional scrutiny were (and are) the nuclear war plans developed by military organiza-

73. Alton Frye, *A Responsible Congress: The Politics of National Security* (New York: McGraw-Hill, 1975), pp. 67–96; conversation with Lynn Eden, Center for International Security and Arms Control, Stanford University, May 8, 1995. For further discussion of the use of obfuscation by the military to prevent civilian interference, see Peter Douglas Feaver, *Guarding the Guardians: Civilian Control of Nuclear Weapons in the United States* (Cornell University Press, 1992), pp. 242–46. See also DeVolpi, *Born Secret,* p. 36. For a history of the development of highly accurate ballistic missiles, see Donald Mackenzie, *Inventing Accuracy: A Historical Sociology of Nuclear Missile Guidance* (Cambridge, Mass.: MIT Press, 1990).

74. *Military Applications of Nuclear Technology,* Hearings before the Subcommittee on Military Applications of the Joint Committee on Atomic Energy, 93 Cong. 1 sess. (GPO, 1973), pt. 1, p. 31.

75. *Military Applications of Nuclear Technology,* Hearings, pt. 2, p. 26.

tions. Although the existence of the SIOP—the comprehensive war plan first developed in 1960—has been known for many years, its details have remained almost wholly secret. To restrict access to data on nuclear war plans to only those with a "need to know," the DOD developed a special "compartment" of "extremely sensitive information" (or SIOP-ESI) for the most sensitive SIOP data, such as operational details of nuclear strike options.[76] Although some such secrecy was justifiable to preserve military operational security, comprehensive plans that would kill tens or hundreds of millions of people remained outside the sphere of public, democratic accountability.[77]

Indeed, the military officials responsible for devising targeting plans have been so antagonistic to civilian interference and so zealous about preserving SIOP secrecy that even civilian policymakers with a clear "need to know" have had great difficulty in ascertaining details of plans for nuclear war. This degree of secrecy has impeded civilian control of nuclear weapons by making it more difficult for political authorities to determine whether nuclear war plans are consistent with public policy goals (whether, for example, they entail excessive levels of destruction and fallout). Even senior military officials were often not trusted with access to nuclear war plans before the creation of the SIOP. After 1951 SAC's commander in chief General Curtis LeMay, for one, did not submit his annually updated Basic War Plans as required for Joint Chiefs of Staff review, "believing that the details of operational planning should be closely guarded."[78]

Ironically, secrecy also served to protect from prosecution those who stole atomic secrets. During World War II, U.S. cryptanalysts working for the Army Security Agency (ASA) succeeded in breaking the code used by the Soviet Union for cables sent from its New York consulate to Moscow. By doing so, they discovered that Soviet spies were funneling information from the Manhattan Project to Moscow.

Yet the extreme secrecy surrounding this effort (known by the codename Venona) and the Manhattan Project thwarted U.S. efforts to halt

76. JCS telegram 986357, to Director, Joint Strategic Target Planning Staff, November 25, 1960, Records of the Joint Chiefs of Staff, Record Group 218, 3205 (August 17, 1959), National Archives.

77. Despite all the elaborate justifications for deterrence proffered over the decades, as well as the obvious desire on the part of nearly all military and civilian leaders not to use nuclear weapons, the nuclear arsenal is designed to inflict swift and devastating destruction and continues to be maintained and routinely tested to do just that. That these weapons have not been used in war in more than fifty years does not automatically justify either the policy or the secrecy that surrounds them. As discussed in chapter 3, the policy of basing national security on the threat of widespread nuclear destruction could easily have turned out far differently, as the recent declassification of once secret documents makes all too clear.

78. For the early development of the SIOP and some of the few details that have been declassified, see David Alan Rosenberg, "'A Smoking Radiating Ruin at the End of Two Hours:' Documents on American Plans for Nuclear War with the Soviet Union, 1954–1955," *International Security,* vol. 6, no. 3 (1981–82), pp. 3–38; Rosenberg,"The Origins of Overkill." For the secrecy of nuclear targeting and the SIOP, see Feaver, *Guarding the Guardians,* pp. 57–60; and Bruce G. Blair, *The Logic of Accidental Nuclear War* (Brookings, 1993), pp. 44–45. For the problem of nuclear planning in a democracy, see Robert Dahl, *Controlling Nuclear Weapons, Democracy versus Guardianship* (Syracuse University Press, 1985).

Box 8-5
Secrecy Run Amok

While chairman of the Atomic Energy Commission from 1961 to 1971, Glenn T. Seaborg (the co-discoverer of plutonium) kept a daily journal that he hoped would provide "for historians and other scholars a record that might not be available elsewhere of what occurred at high levels of government regarding the AEC's important area of activity."[1] Seaborg's journal included personal thoughts, correspondence, minutes of meetings, and other supporting documentation, but he diligently excluded "any subject matter that could be considered classified under standards of the day." Before leaving the AEC, Seaborg had the journal reviewed by the AEC's Office of Classification: "It was cleared, virtually without deletions." Two copies were shipped to California—to Seaborg's office at the University of California at Berkeley and to Livermore Laboratory (and soon after to his home). Neither his office nor his home were outfitted to store classified materials, indicating to Seaborg that "the AEC regarded the journal as an unclassified document."

In July 1983, the DOE's chief historian asked to borrow a copy of the journal to help write the volume of the AEC's official history covering Seaborg's tenure, promising to return it within three weeks once copies had been made. Nineteen months later, Seaborg was informed that the journal contained classified information. The DOE placed his second copy at home in a locked safe (with an alarm). Three months later, it ordered a classification review of this copy; because Seaborg had no written verification and the DOE could not locate any records from the AEC's Office of Classification 1971 action clearing the journal, he could not "prove" it was unclassified.

Demonstrating the arbitrary and often capricious nature of classification and declassification actions, the reviewer (working for several weeks at Seaborg's home) made 162 deletions affecting 137 documents. One year later, Seaborg learned that his first copy (borrowed by the DOE historian) was also undergoing a review. That review—of the identical document—later resulted in 327 deletions and the removal of 530 documents pending further review. In October 1986 the DOE ordered a second review of Seaborg's journal, this time to "sanitize" it. The process took two months and involved up to a dozen people. When this copy was returned to Seaborg, it had been subject to some 1,000 deletions, and about 500 documents had been removed. An additional review was made of portions of the journal provided to an author collaborating with Seaborg on a book about arms control. Numerous deletions were made and documents confiscated (some not returned for nearly four years). The DOE then sent another team of twelve people to Seaborg's office and home to itemize all of his personal correspondence and papers, including those from the twenty-five years prior to his work with the AEC. Additional classified material was discovered. As Seaborg later remarked, "My grammar and high school and university student papers stored in another part of my home, overlooked by the DOE classification teams, have so far escaped a security review."

Among the items deleted from his journal were a "description of one of the occasions when I accompanied my children on a 'trick or treat' outing . . . and my account of my wife Helen's visit to the Lake Country in England." The reviewers also removed "many items that were already part of the public record," including material

1. Glenn T. Seaborg, "Secrecy Runs Amok," *Science,* vol. 264 (June 3, 1994), pp. 1410–11.

Box 8-5
(continued)

from Seaborg's 1981 book (with Benjamin S. Loeb) *Kennedy, Khrushchev, and the Test Ban,* and the "code names of previously conducted nuclear weapons tests," which the DOE itself had published in 1985.

Reflecting on the process, Seaborg stated: "I would go so far as to contend that hardly any of the approximately 1,000 classification actions . . . taken so randomly by the various reviewers could be justified on legitimate national security grounds."[2]

Other examples abound. In 1993, Alex DeVolpi, a researcher at DOE's Argonne National Laboratory near Chicago, visited Russia and met with Russian nuclear scientists. They showed him their superbomb, a 150-megaton weapon, of which six had actually been built. Returning home, DeVolpi decided to include the information in a revised version of entries on the "atomic bomb" and the "hydrogen bomb" that he had written a decade earlier for a scientific encyclopedia. When Argonne security officials read about the 150-megaton bomb, they demanded he delete it, along with other data first used in the decade-old published version. When DeVolpi produced his original copy of the encyclopedia entries and showed them it was stamped "unclassified," the officials confiscated the document, his computer, and his security clearance. Only the direct intervention of Secretary of Energy O'Leary allowed DeVolpi to regain his computer, materials, and clearance.[3]

Equally troubling is the case of Hugh DeWitt, a physicist who has spent more than four decades working on unclassified matters at Lawrence Livermore National Laboratory. In 1991 DeWitt wrote an article for Stanford University's alumni magazine about the politics of selling the X-ray laser, the centerpiece of the Strategic Defense Initiative. In the article, based entirely on open sources, he discussed well-known instances of senior laboratory officials leaking classified information to promote the laser, which by that time was no longer an active program (see chapter 1). Two months after it was published, lab security officials told DeWitt that his article constituted a "Class A security infraction."

Two years later, DeWitt happened to mention this incident to journalist Robert Scheer, adding that officials said he had disclosed nine "items" of classified information. When Scheer related this story in summarized form in a May 2, 1993, article in the *San Francisco Examiner,* security officials notified DeWitt a week later that the number of classified items was itself classified. Ten months after this, on March 8, 1994, DeWitt's security clearance was revoked and his office moved 30 feet (9 meters), from inside a fenced-in area to an unclassified area. In April 1994, he appealed to Secretary O'Leary citing the apparently retaliatory nature of the lab's action against him. One month later, O'Leary announced that DeWitt's clearance had been restored.[4]

---

2. Seaborg, "Secrecy Runs Amok," p. 1411. The head of the DOE Office of Declassification stated in April 1997: "Although Mr. Seaborg believes his papers were reviewed before he left the Atomic Energy Commission in 1971, we have been unable to confirm this, either through a search of the files or from interviews with people who were here at the time. In any event, we were obliged to remove classified information from these papers, some of which were from other agencies and governments. Mr. Seaborg has requested a re-review of 71 documents. All of these documents have been declassified except one, which is pending action at another agency." See A. Bryan Siebert, "The DOE's Declassification Program," Letter to the Editor, *Washington Post,* April 16, 1997, p. A16.

3. Transcript of report by Dan Charles, KQED-AM (San Francisco), May 5, 1994.

4. Letter from Hugh E. DeWitt to Secretary Hazel O'Leary, April 4, 1994; Hugh DeWitt, "The Selling of a Wonder Weapon," *Stanford,* March 1991, pp. 28–33; Keay Davidson, "Nuke Lab Scientist Regains Security Status," *San Francisco Examiner,* May 6, 1994, p. A2.

the espionage. As prominent an official as FBI director J. Edgar Hoover reportedly knew nothing about the Manhattan Project until a senior member of the U.S. Communist party inadvertently informed him of it in the spring of 1943. The ASA was reluctant to pass on even paraphrased versions of the Venona intercepts for fear that doing so would reveal the source and compromise the operation (even though the Soviet Union was made aware as early as 1947—by a mole in the Armed Forces Security Agency, successor to the ASA—that its cables were being decoded, and U.S. officials discovered that the Soviet Union knew about VENONA three years later). Thus Theodore Alvin Hall and other *known* spies were questioned by the FBI in 1951 on the basis of material gleaned from such intercepts but were never prosecuted because doing so would have forced the agency to disclose Venona's existence:

> The tacit decision to keep the translated messages secret carried a political and social price for the country. Debates over the extent of Soviet espionage in the United States were polarized in the dearth of reliable information then in the public domain. Anti-communists suspected that some spies—perhaps including a few who were known to the U.S. Government—remained at large. Those who criticized the government's loyalty campaign as an overreaction, on the other hand, wondered if some defendants were being scapegoated. . . . With the Korean war raging and the prospect of war with the Soviet Union a real possibility, military and intelligence leaders almost certainly believed that any cryptologic edge that America gained over the Soviets was too valuable to concede—*even if it was already known to Moscow.*[79] (emphasis added)

Environmental and Health Implications

Official secrecy also hampered public discussion of the environmental and public health implications of AEC and DOE programs. For activities such as plutonium production or nuclear tests, federal agencies withheld information that could have helped nongovernmental scientists and affected communities determine whether a hazard existed.[80] Other activities, such as the wide-ranging human radiation experiments program, while not entirely secret, remained by and large unknown until the mid-1980s (see chapter 7). Some of the experiments (such as intentional releases into the atmosphere) involved

79. Robert Louis Benson and Michael Warner, *Venona: Soviet Espionage and the American Response, 1939–1957* (Washington, D.C.: National Security Agency and Central Intelligence Agency, 1996), pp. xviii, xxi, xxvi, xxix; Michael Dobbs, "Unlocking the Crypts: Most Spies Code Revealed Escaped Prosecution," *Washington Post,* December 25, 1996, p. A18.

80. Even when community groups litigated, they found a wall of secrecy; for example, during the 1970s, Federal courts backed the Navy Department when it refused to provide an environmental impact statement on nuclear weapons facilities located near Honolulu International Airport. See DeVolpi and others, *Born Secret,* p. 155.

restricted data and national security issues, but other concerns kept them out of public view; AEC officials and their successors simply wanted to minimize the government's exposure to embarrassing publicity and litigation from unsuspecting populations. Thus, although the AEC was releasing information about nuclear power during the 1950s, it kept quiet about the experiments. With such policies in place, worker safety and public health issues "could not . . . emerge as subjects of public debate."[81] Neither could the enormous environmental and safety costs of nuclear weapons production.

Even the strongest advocates of nuclear secrecy must acknowledge that for the most part both Congress and the executive branch failed in their responsibilities to meet important public interests in a safe and healthy environment. Indeed, some of the worst effects of nuclear secrecy could have been mitigated if Congress had pursued more aggressively its oversight responsibilities and ensured that the AEC conducted tests and constructed and operated fissile materials production and storage facilities in ways that minimized risks to the public. The JCAE could have protected public interests by prodding the AEC and DOD to bear in mind more fully the environmental and health effects of nuclear weapons. In this way, Congress could have strengthened the constitutional system of checks and balances instead of allowing them to atrophy. Then the JCAE could have simultaneously preserved nuclear secrecy on the one hand, while protecting local community interests in a healthy and safe environment on the other. Instead it used its extraordinary powers to collaborate with the AEC to place the production of nuclear weapons and weapons materials ahead of environmental, health, and safety considerations (see chapter 9).

Admittedly, it may be too much to expect Congress to have been alert to the environmental costs of the nuclear weapons program when public interest in such issues was politically inconsequential and the presidents who approved major investments in weapons production during the 1940s and 1950s seemingly had no interest in or understanding of their long-run environmental impact.[82] Nevertheless, the JCAE conspicuously avoided most opportunities to probe into the public health or environmental implications of AEC activities and instead generally played the role of the AEC's unquestioning advocate, particularly during the 1950s.

---

81. The quotation is from Hacker, *Elements of Controversy*, p. 118. Hacker was writing about nuclear test secrecy, but the point is valid for other issues. For AEC decisions to keep documents "confidential" to avoid "administrative embarrassment," see Memorandum, Advisory Committee Staff to Members of Advisory Committee on Human Radiation Experiments, "Official Classification Policy to Cover Up Embarrassment," May 1, 1995, copy at the National Security Archive, Washington, D.C.

82. During a critically important discussion of new investments in fissile material production capacity, when told that the materials "would not be dissipated . . . even after five thousand years," President Truman reportedly said, "None of us need worry about conditions after five thousand years." Memorandum for the President, January 17, 1952, President's Secretary's Files, Harry S Truman Library.

The JCAE did hold hearings on radioactive fallout from nuclear testing in 1957, 1959, and 1962 to educate itself on the issue and to pressure the AEC to be more forthcoming on the risks associated with fallout. Equally important, the JCAE convened hearings to protect its legislative turf when a subcommittee of the Senate Foreign Relations Committee announced hearings of its own. (An earlier effort to hold a joint hearing was abandoned after JCAE members objected.) The 1957 hearings apparently grew out of a constituent request made to Senator Alan Bible (Democrat of Nevada) for information about the consequences of nuclear testing in Nevada. Bible forwarded the letter to the JCAE, and its chairman, Senator Clinton Anderson (Democrat of New Mexico), in turn forwarded it to the AEC. The AEC responded to Anderson, but its letter was classified "Secret," and Anderson could not divulge its contents to his colleague. Anderson, a staunch opponent of AEC secrecy—especially where it affected business interests—convened eight days of hearings in May 1957 before a Special Radiation Subcommittee chaired by Representative Chet Holifield (Democrat of California). During these hearings, the AEC was accused of being "grossly tardy and negligent" in disclosing the "harsh realities" of the effects of nuclear testing and of intentionally downplaying the risks of radiation. The 1959 hearings came about after the DOD leaked information about Operation Argus, a series of three very high altitude (about 300 miles [483 kilometers]) low-yield (1.7 kiloton) nuclear tests in the South Atlantic between August 27 and September 6, 1958, for the purpose of studying how high-altitude detonations affected the magnetic field. The DOD sought to prove that nuclear tests could not be readily detected, apparently in an effort to head off a testing moratorium. The JCAE was not persuaded of this view, and Anderson used the occasion to charge that the DOD had revealed classified information yet "was gagging the Joint Committee on an unclassified but most important bit of information on fallout": whereas the AEC had insisted that fallout injected into the stratosphere remained there for seven years, the DOD had found it remained aloft for just two. "In layman's language, it looks like strontium 90 isn't staying up there as long as the AEC told us it would, and the fallout is greatest on the United States."[83]

The degree to which nuclear secrecy and the compartmentalization of nuclear information served to enervate congressional oversight is a question for sociologists and historians to investigate and is outside the scope of this study. No doubt secrecy played a role, if only to discourage non-JCAE members from pressing the Joint Committee on behalf of their constituents. It was this failure of congressional oversight that prompted community organizations and public interest

83. See Green and Rosenthal, *Government of the Atom*, pp. 40, 204–06, 220–21.

groups to fill the vacuum during the 1970s and 1980s and press for the changes in the secrecy system pioneered by Secretary O'Leary during the mid-1990s.

A parallel breakdown of oversight and accountability took place in the executive branch. Here, too, some of the worst effects of secrecy could have been mitigated if presidents had established rigorous systems of accountability that provided more comprehensive knowledge of nuclear weapons costs. It remains startling that presidents as fiscally prudent as Truman or Eisenhower did not insist that methods be developed to ensure better understanding of or control over nuclear weapons costs, especially as nuclear weapons were considered capable of providing a more cost-effective defense than a large conventional buildup and were promoted on that basis. Although Eisenhower was willing to limit spending on questionable programs such as the nuclear-powered bomber, the lack of comprehensive accountability was evident at the end of his administration when he realized that the United States had fielded far greater nuclear capabilities than were necessary to deter an attack by the Soviet Union.[84]

Secretary O'Leary's decisions to release information about once-secret AEC and DOE activities enriched public debate and restored greater accountability to the political system. Unfortunately, revelations about human radiation experiments and intentional radiation releases may also have contributed to already high levels of public mistrust toward, and cynicism about, the government. It is an irony that greater disclosure of classified information can have the immediate impact of increasing mistrust, but the many revelations over the years of secret government abuses of power—from Watergate to Cointelpro to ABSCAM and the Iran-Contra scandal and the ongoing controversy over presidential and congressional campaign financing—have clearly eroded public trust in the government.[85] Scandals create the impression that the government is hiding even more serious misdeeds. Thus, even when secrecy serves legitimate public interests, the public continues to believe, and not without reason, that it is excessive. In 1997 prominent members of Congress from across the political spectrum called for an overhaul of the government's classification system. Until

84. For funding limits on nuclear-powered bombers, see Peter Roman, "Strategic Bombers over the Missile Horizon, 1957–1963," *Journal of Strategic Studies,* vol. 18 (March 1995), pp. 208–10. For Eisenhower's conclusions about U.S. "overkill" capabilities, see Rosenberg, "The Origins of Overkill," p. 188. Whether nuclear secrecy had an adverse effect on direct monitoring of costs by, for example, the Bureau of the Budget (the Office of Management and Budget's forerunner) remains to be determined because relevant records on nuclear weapons budgets are still classified.

85. Although not an example of the abuse or misuse of power, the 1960 U-2 affair "was the first time many Americans discovered that their government was not always candid. During the Eisenhower Presidency, it was said that if Diogenes were still searching for an honest man, he should be taken to the Oval Office. It was ironic that Eisenhower should be the first American President to confess his administration had lied to the public. . . . The U-2 alerted many Americans for the first time to the existence of the CIA and American espionage." Michael R. Beschloss, *Mayday: Eisenhower, Khrushchev and the U-2 Affair* (New York: Harper & Row, 1986), pp. 394–95.

nuclear secrecy, like government secrecy in general, becomes more defensible, one of its significant intangible costs will be low public confidence in government.[86]

Damage to Constitutional Rights

Another cost of nuclear secrecy was the damage to Constitutional rights caused by the loyalty investigations that accompanied the AEC's personnel security reviews during the anti-communist purges of the early cold war. During the period 1947–55, 494 scientists lost their clearances—and presumably their jobs—in the course of the review process. Certainly, the case of J. Robert Oppenheimer is the most famous of them but also the most extraordinary. As the éminence grise in the early history of the atomic bomb, up to the time when the AEC revoked his clearance, Oppenheimer had received decidedly special treatment from the security bureaucracy. What other senior AEC official had a wife or brother who had once belonged to the U.S. Communist party! Yet in the McCarthyite frenzy of the early 1950s, the charges of disloyalty and espionage brought against Oppenheimer in 1953 made it possible for President Eisenhower, a critic of McCarthy, to abrogate Oppenheimer's privileged treatment and support proceedings against him, despite the lack of evidence of any kind of espionage. As Lilienthal remarked at the time, "There hasn't been a proceeding like this since the Spanish Inquisition."[87]

A key issue was Oppenheimer's evasive responses to questions about contacts with Communist party members during the early 1940s, equivocations that in the supercharged atmosphere of the period were enough to bring him down. While AEC rules stipulated that security review proceedings not be adversarial, through the influence of AEC chairman Lewis Strauss the commission handled the proceedings essentially as a prosecution in which Oppenheimer was "left without the normal protections guaranteed by a trial but with virtually all of the disadvantages."[88] When one considers the way in which the AEC han-

86. See 1994 survey ("Public Favors Security, Questions Secrecy") cited in *Secrecy and Government Bulletin*, Issue 48 (May 1995); E. J. Dionne, Jr., "Tight Lips Sink Ships," *Washington Post*, March 7, 1997, p. A21; Tim Weiner, "Bill Seeks to Ease Secrecy Overload," *New York Times* (Washington edition), May 8, 1997, p. A29; For contributions to the discussion on the need for a defensible nuclear secrecy policy, see Committee on Declassification of Information, "DOE Classification Policy and Practice"; and Council on the Department of Energy's Nuclear Weapons Complex, *Official Use Only: Ending the Culture of Secrecy in the U.S. Nuclear Weapons Complex* (Seattle, Wash.: Tides Foundation, July 1995).

87. Caute, *The Great Fear*, p. 364. Lilienthal is quoted in Stephen J. Whitfield, *The Culture of the Cold War* (Johns Hopkins University Press, 1991), p. 181. For more on the Oppenheimer case, including full citations to the literature, see Barton J. Bernstein, "The Oppenheimer Loyalty-Security Case Reconsidered," *Stanford Law Review*, vol. 342 (July 1990), pp. 1383–1484. See also Philip M. Stern with the collaboration of Harold P. Green, *The Oppenheimer Case: Security on Trial* (New York: Harper & Row, 1969).

88. Bernstein, "The Oppenheimer Loyalty-Security Case Reconsidered," pp. 1387, 1461–65.

dled the Oppenheimer case, one wonders how it dealt with the 494 others. By equating disagreements with disloyalty, by using star chamber proceedings, and by relying on anonymous testimony, the AEC proceeded under different rules from those established by the Constitution for protecting the accused.

One of the most extraordinary examples of the potential dangers posed by nuclear secrecy to Constitutional rights was the government's lawsuit against the *Progressive* for its plans to publish in 1979 an article by Howard Morland on the "secret" of the hydrogen bomb. Because Morland's research in unclassified sources had led him to deduce several concepts relevant to developing, if not actually designing, hydrogen bombs, the Carter administration tried to suppress publication of his article by deploying the Atomic Energy Act.[89] That is, it treated Morland's research as privately generated restricted data and therefore subject to control. Although the government later dropped the case, it went beyond its earlier action against *Scientific American* by using the Atomic Energy Act as the basis for an injunction against a publication.

Because the lawsuit was abandoned (and the article later published in full), the courts did not have an opportunity to test the constitutionality of the "born secret" concept. Nevertheless, the *Progressive* case indicated the dangers posed by nuclear secrecy to First Amendment rights, not least because the government argued that scientific or "technical" information was not political expression and therefore not protected under the First Amendment.[90] As two legal scholars later wrote:

> The government did seem to argue, amazingly, that scientific knowledge plays no vital role in discussions of current events and political choices, and for that reason deserves little or no First Amendment protection. . . . What sort of information would the government next claim deserved no greater protection than this? Even if such claims were confined to information bearing only on matters of science and technology—a dubious prospect, at best—their sweep would be breathtakingly broad in an era when science and society, technology and culture, are pervasively and powerfully linked.[91]

During a trial in which the magazine sought an end to the government's injunction against publication, Morland's basic college physics textbook, cited as one of his public sources of information, was declared secret on the basis of certain underlined passages. The fact

89. DOE and GAO investigations later determined that some of these documents were erroneously declassified owing to "simple administrative and clerical errors" during a large-scale AEC declassification review of inactive files from 1971 to 1976. See Letter from Comptroller General of the United States to Senator John Glenn, September 21, 1979, B-165546, U.S. General Accounting Office.

90. The most comprehensive study of the *Progressive* case and its implications remains DeVolpi and others, *Born Secret.* See also Howard Morland, *The Secret That Exploded* (New York: Random House, 1981).

91. Quoted in Foerstel, *Secret Science,* pp. 88, 92.

that Morland had done the underlining in college years earlier preparing for an exam was deemed irrelevant. A 1975 article by Edward Teller in the *Encyclopedia Americana* introduced as evidence was also declared secret, along with the affidavits introducing it and the court's opinion about these matters. (When several physicists at Argonne National Laboratory wrote to Senator John Glenn that Teller's article revealed the "secret" of hydrogen bomb design, the DOE classified their letter as secret/restricted data. The public release and widespread publication of this letter served to undermine the government's case.)[92]

Adverse Effects on Foreign Policy

Nuclear secrecy has, at times, complicated U.S. foreign relations by upsetting relations with close allies. Moreover, it has occasionally interfered with a key U.S. policy objective: preventing the further spread of nuclear weapons. One secrecy policy that has occasionally conflicted with U.S. diplomacy has been the DOD's "neither-confirm-nor-deny" posture concerning the presence or absence of U.S. nuclear weapons at any specific location, whether at home or abroad, in the past or at present.[93] Although allied governments have often known of the movement and locations of U.S. nuclear weapons on or through their territories, the information was not always certain, especially when the weapons were carried aboard navy ships. No doubt, foreign leaders sought the tightest of control over knowledge of nuclear transit and storage because they wanted to avoid leaks that could cause domestic and foreign policy difficulties.[94]

Most governments cooperated easily with the neither-confirm-nor-deny policy, facilitating U.S. nuclear weapons operations by insulating them from public visibility and thus potential controversy. The policy nevertheless contributed to the spread of "nuclear allergies" during the cold war, when some allies or their publics raised concerns about nuclear weapons deployments. Although uncertainty and suspicion about U.S. weapons locations were prevalent in Japan—where the "nuclear allergy" first developed—and in the Scandinavian countries,

92. Foerstel, *Secret Science,* pp. 82–92.

93. In 1995, for example, Secretary of Defense William Perry refused to publicly discuss whether the United States had ever stored nuclear weapons in Greenland. See "Perry Has No Comment on Nukes in Greenland," *Washington Times,* July 2, 1995, p. A7. See also David C. Morrison, "Bombs? What Bombs?," *National Journal,* April 25, 1987, p. 1036.

94. In 1957, when the U.S. Air Force made arrangements to store nuclear weapons at Thule Air Force Base in Greenland, Denmark's prime minister was "adamant" that there "be no publicity of any kind about this matter;" indeed, he "restricted knowledge of it to himself" because he worried that disclosure "would be highly damaging both to the Danish Government and to [America's] defense relationship with Denmark." See Danish Institute of International Affairs, *Grønland Under den Kolde Krig* (Greenland during the Cold War) (Copenhagen: Dansk Udenrigspolitisk Institut, 1997), p. 284. This is an authoritative account of U.S. nuclear weapons activity in and over Greenland from 1951 to 1968.

the most dramatic case was in New Zealand in the mid-1980s.[95] Stonewalled by the navy's neither-confirm-nor-deny policy, the New Zealand Labor government in 1987 passed the world's first statute barring entry to all nuclear-powered and nuclear-armed naval vessels on the basis of the responses a ship's captain gave to questions about the nature of the ship's propulsion and armament. Because the United States refused to compromise its position even for vessels known not to be nuclear powered (a ship's designation reveals its mode of propulsion; for example, CVN denotes a nuclear-powered aircraft carrier; its conventionally powered counterpart is CV) or capable of carrying nuclear weapons, this effectively banned port visits by all U.S. Navy ships. This unfortunate antagonism of allies has largely abated, thanks largely to President George Bush's unilateral 1991 decision to retire most nonstrategic naval weapons (see chapter 2).[96] While tensions have eased, the policy remains in effect.[97] As a result of the 1994 Nuclear Posture Review, the DOD pledged to review the policy, but it is not apparent that any changes have been made.[98] As late as February 1996 the United States continued to oppose the 1986 South Pacific Nuclear Free Zone Treaty (also known as the Treaty of Rarotonga) on the grounds that it would impede the passage of nuclear-powered and nuclear-armed U.S. naval vessels (although the government signed the three protocols to the treaty the following month, it has yet to submit the treaty to the Senate for ratification).[99]

95. Other countries that challenged or considered challenging the neither-confirm-nor-deny policy included Fiji and the Philippines, both during 1987. Philippine nationalists opposing the U.S. bases at Subic Bay and Clark Field proposed strengthening the antinuclear provisions in the Philippine Constitution to prohibit both the storage of weapons and their transit through Philippine territory. These measures complicated U.S. efforts to extend the leases for American bases and were strongly opposed by Secretary of State George Shultz. Philippine attitudes toward nuclear weapons and the uncompromising U.S. position on the issue no doubt influenced the Philippine Senate's decision in 1991 not to renew the leases for the bases, leading to the U.S. withdrawal in November 1992. See Nicholas D. Kristof, "Fiji's Leaders Weigh Curbs on Nuclear Ships," *New York Times,* April 30, 1987, p. A16; William E. Berry, Jr., *U.S. Bases in the Philippines: The Evolution of the Special Relationship* (Boulder, Colo.: Westview Press, 1989), pp. 289–91.

96. Bush's national security adviser, Brent Scowcroft, reportedly "leaned on" Secretary of Defense Dick Cheney for a year to remove the weapons in a deliberate effort to quell growing opposition to port calls by U.S. ships in Japan, Scandinavia, and the South Pacific. Senior aides to Cheney who opposed the removal of nonstrategic weapons assigned to submarines were overruled when chief of naval operations Admiral Frank Kelso voiced no objection to the proposed change. See R. Jeffrey Smith, "6th Fleet at Ease on A-Arm Loss," *Washington Post,* October 17, 1991, p. A40.

97. For background on "nuclear allergies" during the 1980s, see *Bulletin of the Atomic Scientists,* vol. 41 (June/July 1985), especially William M. Arkin and Richard W. Fieldhouse, "Focus on the Nuclear Infrastructure," pp. 11–15, and David C. Morrison, "Japanese Principles, U.S. Policies," pp. 22–24; Geoffrey Murray, "Japan Reels under Reischauer's Nuclear 'Bombshell,'" *Christian Science Monitor,* May 19, 1981, p. 5; Geoffrey Murray, "Nuclear 'Facts of Life' Intrude into Japan Defense Furor," *Christian Science Monitor,* June 3, 1981, p. 9. See also chapter 2, fn. 126, in this volume. For the Swedish case, see Hans M. Kristensen, William M. Arkin, and Joshua Handler, *U.S. Naval Nuclear Weapons in Sweden,* Neptune Papers 6 (Washington, D.C.: Greenpeace, September 1990). For the U.S.–New Zealand confrontation, see David Lange, *Nuclear Free: The New Zealand Way* (New York: Penguin Books, 1990). For a detailed history of the neither-confirm-nor-deny policy, see Hans M. Kristensen, "The Neither Confirm Nor Deny Policy: A Chronology," unpublished working paper, January 1996.

98. *U.S. Nuclear Policy,* Hearings before the House Committee on Foreign Affairs, 103 Cong. 2 sess. (GPO, 1994), p. 19.

99. *U.S. Nuclear Policy,* Hearings, pp. 19–21; "U.S. Won't Support Nuclear-Free Zone in Southeast Asia," *Baltimore Sun,* February 9, 1996, p. A13.

Secrecy and Nonproliferation

Nuclear secrecy went hand in hand with the another cold war phenomenon: aggrandizement of executive power at the expense of congressional authority. To cite one example, beginning with the Nixon administration, the AEC secretly and illegally provided restricted data on the design of nuclear weapons to the French government. Intended to strengthen French nuclear forces, this cooperation violated Atomic Energy Act provisions requiring congressional approval for any nuclear weapons assistance to other governments. President Richard Nixon did not tell Congress about this cooperation—which continues to this day—because he understood that congressional concern over nonproliferation and hostility toward France were likely to thwart it. In this episode, nuclear secrecy, like foreign policy secrecy as a whole, contributed to the general erosion of congressional authority during the cold war.[100]

In a similar manner, the Reagan, Bush, and Clinton administrations used secrecy to transfer sensitive plutonium-processing technology and data to Japan, contravening both the Nuclear Nonproliferation Act of 1978, which bars the export of such technology, and repeated reassurances to Congress in the late 1980s that a U.S.–Japan nuclear cooperation agreement specifically excluded the transfer of such technology and the restricted data necessary to make it work. When the environmental organization Greenpeace exposed the program in September 1994—citing documents obtained under the FOIA—the DOE immediately announced it would let the cooperation agreement lapse. DOE officials later justified the exports on the grounds that they were "permissible exercises of its statutory authorities" and that because Japan had a high level of indigenous nuclear technology, U.S. transfers of otherwise restricted equipment and data were legal.[101]

---

100. To bypass the Atomic Energy Act, U.S. officials have met annually with French nuclear officials and, in a carefully structured series of questions and answers, indicate *without explicitly saying so* the best means to resolve a problem. This process is called "negative guidance" or "Twenty Questions" and involves the use of winks, head shakes, silences, and other nonverbal cues that U.S. officials use to guide their French counterparts to the answers they seek. This cooperation was formalized in 1985. See Richard H. Ullmann, "The Covert French Connection," *Foreign Policy*, no. 75 (Summer 1989), pp. 3–33; Robert S. Norris, Andrew S. Burrows, and Richard W. Fieldhouse, *Nuclear Weapons Databook*, vol. 5: *British, French, and Chinese Nuclear Weapons* (Boulder, Colo.: Westview Press, 1994), pp. 189–93; William Drozdiak and R. Jeffrey Smith, "French Nuclear Program Closely Tied to U.S.," *Washington Post*, September 19, 1995, p. A1. On June 4, 1996, U.S. and French officials signed a secret accord expanding this cooperation to include the sharing of computer modeling data for the fission triggers in U.S. nuclear weapons. The United States largely took the action to secure French support for the Comprehensive Test Ban Treaty. See R. Jeffrey Smith, "France, U.S. Secretly Enter Pact to Share Nuclear Weapons Data," *Washington Post*, June 17, 1996, p. A9.

101. Matthew L. Wald, "U.S., Criticized for Helping Japan over Plutonium, Will Stop," *New York Times*, September 9, 1994, p. A12; Thomas W. Lippman, "U.S. Illegally Sent Plutonium Technology to Japan, According to Greenpeace Study," *Washington Post*, September 13, 1994, p. A19; Greenpeace International, *The Violation of International Nuclear Export Controls: Supergrade Plutonium, The United States, and Japan* (Washington, D.C., April 1995).

Executive branch nuclear secrecy also undermined U.S. nonproliferation policy during the 1980s, particularly congressional efforts to curtail Pakistan's nuclear weapons program. Under the 1985 amendment to the Foreign Assistance Act of 1961, known as the Pressler amendment after Senator Larry Pressler (Republican of South Dakota), Congress required the executive branch to certify that Pakistan did not "possess" a nuclear device as a condition for receiving U.S. military aid.[102] As early as 1986, the Department of State privately acknowledged that the Karachi nuclear facility was producing weapon-grade plutonium. However, President Reagan continued to certify Pakistan's nonnuclear weapons status in requests for economic and military assistance funding, and Congress (not without some debate) supported the executive branch. Anxious to avoid complicating its efforts to sustain Pakistani support for covert U.S. operations against Soviet forces in Afghanistan, the Reagan and Bush administrations deemphasized warning signs on Pakistan's nuclear status and creatively interpreted the triggering language in the Pressler amendment until 1990, when overwhelming evidence forced the White House to terminate aid. A CIA analyst who told his superiors in the late 1980s that other executive branch officials were misleading Congress about Pakistan's capabilities was barred by his superiors from communicating his concerns to congressional staff and shortly thereafter dismissed.[103]

Revelations in 1995 and 1996 that China had secretly shipped missiles and nuclear weapons technology to Pakistan similarly put the Clinton administration in a bind over whether and how to penalize China. In the end, the administration moved to suppress confirmation of the transfers to avoid having to invoke sanctions and risk a backlash from China. Eventually, officials confirmed the transfers but resisted efforts to impose sanctions and negotiated secretly with China to avoid a public confrontation.[104]

The costs of U.S. nuclear secrecy for establishing an effective nonproliferation regime remain high. The government has, for example,

102. Robert D. Shuey, Steven R. Bowman, and Zachary S. Davis, "Proliferation Control Regimes: Background and Issues," Congressional Research Service, 97-343F, March 19, 1997, p. 3.

103. Virginia Foran, "Strategic Non-Proliferation: Balancing Interests and Ideals," in Foran, ed., *U.S. Nuclear Non-Proliferation Policy, 1945–1991* (Alexandria, Va.: Chadwyck-Healey, 1992), pp. 29–31; John Glenn, "This Country Encouraged the Spread of Nuclear Weapons," *Washington Post*, June 24, 1992, p. A19; Jeff Gerth, "Criticism of C.I.A. Analyst's Dismissal Bolsters a Fight for Whistle-Blower Protections," *New York Times* (Washington edition), July 20, 1997, p. 14.

104. R. Jeffrey Smith, "An M-11 Missile Violation by Any Other Name . . . ," *Washington Post*, August 3, 1995, p. A29; Elaine Sciolino, "Despite Nuclear Fears, Senate Acts to Life Pakistan Curbs," *New York Times*, September 22, 1995; R. Jeffrey Smith, "China Aids Pakistan Nuclear Program," *Washington Post*, February 7, 1996, p. A1; Tim Weiner, "Atom Arms Parts Sold to Pakistan by China, U.S. Says," *New York Times*, February 8, 1996, p. A1; R. Jeffrey Smith and Ann Devroy, "U.S. Asks China to End Shipments," *Washington Post*, February 28, 1996, p. A23; Steven Erlanger, "U.S. Studying Limited Penalties for Chinese Sale," *New York Times*, March 29, 1996, p. A6; Steven Erlanger, "U.S. Won't Punish China over Sale of Nuclear Gear," *New York Times*, May 11, 1996, p. A1; Bill Gertz, "Beijing Flouts Nuke-Sales Ban," *Washington Times*, October 9, 1996, p. A1; Bill Gertz, "State Department Mum on Chinese Nuke Sale to Pakistan," October 10, 1996, p. A3.

withheld information from the IAEA on critical technologies necessary to construct nuclear weapons. To the extent that the United States eschews safeguards on its own nuclear materials stockpiles or otherwise restricts the IAEA's analytic capabilities by withholding significant data, it weakens the IAEA's moral authority and its ability to monitor effectively nuclear developments. After all, if the United States limits its cooperation with the IAEA, other countries will feel less disposed to cooperate. Thus secrecy runs directly counter to the government's own professed antiproliferation policy.[105]

Impacts on Technological Advancement

Another qualitative, unmeasurable cost of nuclear secrecy merits attention: its possible impact on technological progress. Given that scientific and technological advancement has always depended on the widest possible exchange of information, one might ask whether nuclear secrecy has had an impact, important or otherwise, on technological development. But because nuclear weapons technology remains secret, any question about the impact of nonsecrecy is counterfactual, perhaps impossible to answer. We do not know what kind of difference a lack of secrecy would have made for research work in science-based industry. When in the early 1980s the DOE had more than 1,000 secret patents, mostly for government-sponsored inventions, would the secrecy of some, say, exotic nuclear weapon have slowed or prevented the development of some beneficial application (see chapter 10)?[106] As Steven Aftergood, director of the Federation of American Scientists's Project on Government Secrecy has said: "We don't know what we don't know, so it's hard to be too definitive about what buried treasures might be in the various archives. On the other hand, the government has spent many millions of dollars on classified research and development over the past few decades, and you would think there would be one or two things in there that would be useful, that would have commercial value."[107]

Granting the difficulty of the question, it should be noted that since the final days of the MED, scientists and military leaders have assumed that nuclear secrecy had the potential to retard technological progress by cutting off formal and informal communications between scientists.

105. Presentations by Steven Aftergood, Federation of American Scientists, and David Albright, Institute for Science and International Security, at Department of Energy, "Fundamental Review of the Department of Energy's Classification Policy Kickoff Meeting," March 16, 1995.

106. DeVolpi and others, *Born Secret,* p. 141.

107. See Committee on Declassification of Information for the Department of Energy Environmental Remediation and Related Programs, *A Review of Department of Energy Classification Policy and Practice* (Washington, D.C.: National Academy Press, 1995), p. 18; Daniel G. Dupont and Richard Lardner, "Needles in a Cold War Haystack," *Scientific American,* November 1996, p. 41.

General Groves referred to this problem during congressional testimony in 1946: "The more that a scientist knows in his own field and related fields, the better job he can do." With atomic information classified, "we are in effect decreasing . . . his ability to do his best work in his scientific research because there are certain things he doesn't know that if he did know he would be able to do better."[108]

The nuclear secrecy system created a situation unparalleled in modern history: the fruits of scientific research and development could become classified on a virtually automatic basis. Before World War II it would have been extraordinary for scientists to participate on a large scale and for many years in secret research and development. But the Manhattan Project and other wartime projects (such as the development of radar) eroded the long-standing assumption that the results of scientific research required the widest possible dissemination as a basis for further advancement of knowledge and progress in research. Consequently, during the postwar era, many scientists became habituated to doing classified work.[109]

The potential drawbacks of classified research in the nuclear field, or any other research field, are many. Security classification can keep "others ignorant of information already discovered, results in needless duplication of effort and delays scientific and technological advances." In addition, compartmentalized secrecy within a government organization can lead to inefficiencies. As long as only those scientists and technicians with a need to know can participate in a research program, they cannot benefit from the insights of colleagues in other "compartments."[110]

Secrecy created other inefficiencies in the nuclear weapons complex and possibly discouraged scientific workers from participating in government-sponsored scientific research programs. In any given year during the 1950s, the skills of thousands of scientists, technicians, and engineers were wasted because they were unemployed or underemployed while waiting for security clearances. The obstacles to getting and keeping clearances and the restrictions related to secret work in the sciences led many young scientists to avoid government work or fields in which secrecy restrictions were prevalent, such as radiobiology and radiochemistry.[111]

On the boundary between intangible and tangible costs is the impact of secrecy on nuclear weapons programs that could not survive

108. Quist, *Introduction, History, and Adverse Impacts,* p. 91.

109. Quist, *Introduction, History, and Adverse Impacts,* pp. 89–90.

110. Quist, *Introduction, History, and Adverse Impacts,* pp. 92–98; DeVolpi and others, *Born Secret,* p. 157. For examples of how compartmentalization led to duplication in classified research, see Ziegler and Jacobson, *Spying without Spies,* pp. 108–09.

111. Caute, *The Great Fear,* pp. 461–62. For the intrusive nature of investigations for nuclear clearances, see Gusterson, *Nuclear Rites,* pp. 72–75.

if exposed to public scrutiny. The most prominent recent example is the Strategic Defense Initiative's TIMBERWIND program for a nuclear-powered rocket (see chapter 4). Apparently designed to carry particle beams, lasers, and homing rockets for missile defense purposes, until the early 1990s TIMBERWIND was a compartmentalized program whose existence was secret except to those with special access security clearances. In fact, its technology was derived from a largely secret nuclear-powered aircraft program, which ran from 1946 until 1961 (see chapter 2).

This program received special treatment precisely because its architects feared that public discussion of the dangers of nuclear-powered rockets would create difficult political and public relations problems. Indeed, a leak to the Federation of American Scientists in the spring of 1991 brought TIMBERWIND to the front page of major newspapers and ignited the debate that Pentagon officials had sought to avoid. By the end of 1992 a Pentagon audit had concluded what the critics had already argued, that TIMBERWIND's special access status was unjustified. Within a few months, the DOD canceled this program.[112] TIMBERWIND may be exceptional because few nuclear programs ever reached "special access" status. Nevertheless, it raises the question of whether government secrecy prolonged the existence of other programs that otherwise would not have survived open discussion.

What Price Secrecy?

The historic and current costs of nuclear secrecy fall into various categories—budgetary, political, and possibly technological. Although the budgetary costs have been high and are troubling on that account, the political costs raise questions about governmental accountability in a liberal democracy.[113] As long as the secrecy system concealed as much as it did about the U.S. nuclear weapons complex, American citizens could not be sure that it was operating in ways that met, or obstructed, the public interest in matters of national security, worker and community safety, environmental protection, or fiscal responsibility. Although citizens should have been able to trust their representatives in Congress to safeguard their interests, the responsible committees failed to do their job, allowing constitutional checks and balances to atrophy, while the financial, environmental, and public health costs of

112. William J. Broad, "Rocket Run by Nuclear Power Being Developed for 'Star Wars,'" *New York Times*, April 3, 1991, p. A1; Joseph Lovece, "Pentagon Audit Blasts SDI Nuclear Rocket Classification," *Defense Week*, January 11, 1993, p. 1; Vincent Kiernan, "DoD Cancels Plans for Nuclear Rocket," *Space News*, May 17–23, 1993, p. 6.

113. As Senator McMahon once noted, "I want to make sure we are not paying a reckless price for [secrecy]." Minutes of an Executive Meeting of the Joint Committee on Atomic Energy, April 6, 1949, Records of Joint Committees of Congress, Record Group 46, Box 202, JCAE Document 1059, National Archives.

the nuclear program mounted, in no small measure because of inadequate oversight (see chapters 6 and 9). Recent years have seen much progress in oversight, due largely to the activity of citizens' organizations, but other political costs continue to climb. As long as data concerning the size of the weapons stockpile remain secret, the ability of citizens to raise basic questions about the direction and cost of U.S. nuclear policy will be restricted.

The high costs of secrecy deserve to be questioned, as can the absolute value of nuclear secrecy itself. It might be argued that nuclear secrecy as practiced in the United States has had limited value because of its failure to meet a major stated goal: to prevent nuclear proliferation (although secrecy in conjunction with other measures such as export controls has helped to slow the pace of the proliferation and perhaps even limited the number of proliferants). Manhattan Project scientists recognized the ultimate limits of secrecy when they wrote in 1946 that "the facts of nature cannot long be kept as classified information"; the implication was that, given time and sufficient resources, competent physicists could design nuclear weapons. Thus official secrecy notwithstanding, America's major cold war adversaries, the Soviet Union and the People's Republic of China, acquired nuclear weapons quickly enough (in 1949 and 1964, respectively). David Holloway—author of the most authoritative study on the Soviet atomic program's early years—concludes that successful spying only sped up the Soviet program by one or two years and that even without spying the Soviets quickly developed their own designs for atomic and thermonuclear weapons.[114] That other countries—such as Israel, India, Pakistan, and South Africa—designed and produced nuclear weapons, in spite of U.S. information controls, confirmed the limits of secrecy.[115]

While the intangible costs of nuclear secrecy have been high and the system has had significant failures, the serious dangers of further nuclear proliferation cannot be overlooked. In this respect, secrecy is a necessary component of an effective counterproliferation strategy because of its potential, as already mentioned, for raising the costs of nuclear weapons development. Analysts have emphasized the slowing impact that nuclear secrecy had on the Iraqi nuclear program before the Gulf War. According to this argument, even if persistent physicists and governments can readily deduce general concepts of nuclear weapons production and design, other important categories of information—for example, certain uranium enrichment technologies, fabrication methods, and precise arrangement of weapons parts—are not

114. Holloway, *Stalin and the Bomb,* pp. 222–23. See also German A. Goncharov, "Thermonuclear Milestones," *Physics Today,* vol. 49 (November 1996), pp. 46–61.

115. Quist, *Introduction, History, and Adverse Impacts,* p. 70. That nations have the capacity to develop nuclear weapons does not mean that they will do so. See William H. Kincade, *Nuclear Proliferation: Diminishing Threat?* (Boulder, Colo.: Institute for National Security Studies, U.S. Air Force Academy, 1995).

readily deducible and their continued secrecy can obstruct the development of nuclear weapons. Thus, while a sunset principle can be applied to almost all government secrets, nuclear weapons blueprints are not among them. Moreover, U.S. obligations under the Nuclear Nonproliferation Treaty preclude openness in such areas as weapons design.[116]

In keeping with the idea that secrecy can make a contribution to nonproliferation policy, the DOE's Fundamental Classification Policy Review strongly argues that proliferation cannot be curbed without tight control over design information. But even this report agrees with Manhattan Project scientists that secrecy is not enough to curb proliferation: it "may delay, but cannot prevent, acquisition of a first generation nuclear weapon."[117]

The effectiveness of secrecy in halting the spread of nuclear weapons technology may even steadily diminish over time as more and more information seeps into the public domain from government, nongovernment, and foreign sources. The availability of both nominally classified information and sensitive technologies in illegal markets also weakens nuclear secrecy. These trends could make RD of little consequence in decades to come. The erosion of secrecy in the area of nuclear weapons science may be regrettable, but it is a fact.

In 1970 the Defense Science Board's Task Force on Secrecy remarked:

> Overclassification has contributed to the credibility gap that evidently exists between the government and an influential segment of the population. A democratic society requires knowledge of the facts in order to assess its government's actions. An orderly process of disclosure would contribute to informed discussions of issues. When an otherwise open society attempts to use classification as a protective device, it may in the long run increase the difficulties of communications within its own structure so that commensurate gains are not obtained. Experience shows that, given time, a sophisticated, determined and unscrupulous adversary can usually penetrate the secrecy barriers of an open society. . . . The barriers are apt to be far more effective against restrained friends or against incompetents, and neither pose serious threats.[118]

In the end, halting the spread of nuclear weapons may necessitate a mix of secrecy and openness. Indeed, an effective antiproliferation

116. Presentations by Wolfgang Panofsky and David Albright at panel on nonproliferation and nuclear secrecy, "Fundamental Review of the Department of Energy's Classification Policy Kickoff Meeting," March 16, 1995. For the distinction between deducible and nondeducible nuclear secrets, see DeVolpi and others, *Born Secret,* pp. 127–28.

117. U.S. Department of Energy, "Fundamental Classification Policy Review," p. 18. For a critique of U.S. nonproliferation policy as of 1980 and the failure of secrecy to inhibit proliferation, see DeVolpi and others, *Born Secret,* pp. 110–30.

118. Office of the Director of Defense Research and Engineering, *Report of the Defense Science Board Task Force on Secrecy* (July 1, 1970), p. 6.

system may require substantially more transparency than we have now. If the United States is to achieve its nonproliferation goals through cooperation rather than unilateral efforts, it will need to make more information available to international regulators. Some of the information, particularly details on weaponization, may require special controls for dissemination among the regulators at the IAEA. However, some argue that a nonproliferation regime can only be effective if the nuclear weapons states take part in a United Nations–sponsored international registry that identifies the numbers, types, and locations of nuclear weapons, although the general parameters are well known. Much of this information is now secret but the transparency created by such a catalog would add to the legitimacy of nonproliferation goals by requiring all states, those with nuclear weapons and those without, to participate in an open system of accountability.[119]

Even if nuclear secrecy has some utility, the current system's excessive financial and political costs make it necessary to replace the "born secret" concept with a more defensible system, an approach finally agreed to by the DOE and DOD in late 1997. The DOE's Fundamental Classification Policy Review may well provide a basis for reform precisely because it challenges the notion of "born classified," although some of its specific proposals (such as granting authority to the secretary of energy for reclassifying information) are problematic.

The DOE initiatives may go far in improving the system's credibility, but the nuclear secrecy problem cannot and will not be settled there. The lack of accountability and overclassification will remain endemic to the U.S. nuclear secrecy system unless and until the DOD initiates a comparable reform of its secrecy programs. Nevertheless, even if a more defensible nuclear secrecy system emerges, it will continue to have significant financial costs and an uneasy relationship with a democratic society. Future generations will continue to bear the political, environmental, and financial costs of cold war nuclear secrecy.

119. For an overview of the nuclear weapons registry concept, see Harald Mueller, "Transparency in Nuclear Arms: Toward a Nuclear Weapons Register," *Arms Control Today,* October 1994, pp. 3–7.

FIGURE 9-1. The Costs of Congressional Oversight of the Bomb[a]

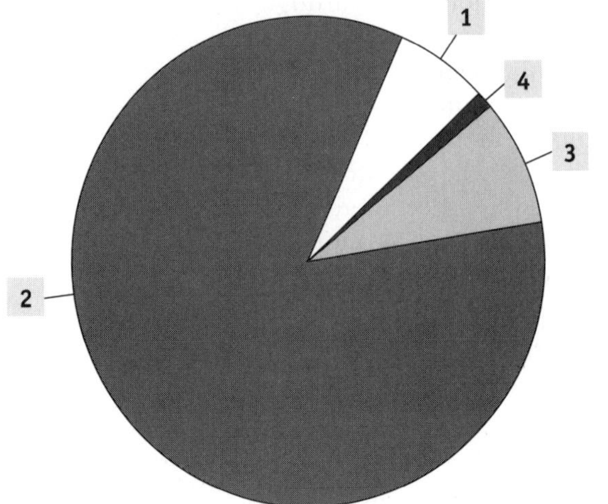

Total: $901 million

1 Joint Committee on Atomic Energy
$56 million / 6.2%

2 Assorted oversight committees, 1978–97
$760 million / 84.4%

3 General Accounting Office
$75 million / 8.3%

4 Office of Technology Assessment
$10 million / 1.1%

a. In constant 1996 dollars.

9

Congressional Oversight of the Bomb

Stephen I. Schwartz

Evidence currently available indicates that Congress has done a less than satisfactory job in overseeing nuclear weapons programs. Structurally, Congress is hindered by its committee system, which parcels out portions of these programs to several dozen committees and prevents any one of them from overseeing the entire effort. In addition, the persistent emphasis on the annual authorization and appropriations bills for the defense budget leaves members little time to assess the overall strategy into which the current year's budget is designed to fit (the cost of congressional oversight is summarized in figure 9-1). Most members of Congress have found nuclear weapons issues extraordinarily complex. Out of necessity and later by default, they defer judgment on such matters to their colleagues on the few committees having jurisdiction over the programs. A further problem is that the pressure of other business, constituent meetings, fund raising, biannual campaigns (for House members), and other time-consuming matters leaves little time for most members, even those with an interest in the subject, to devote more than a fraction of their time to nuclear weapons policy and budget matters.

For all these reasons, Congress has not given nuclear weapons the focused attention they require. It has tended to use occasional international and domestic crises to conduct brief but wide-ranging inquiries (such as the 1956 airpower hearings following the disclosure of the bomber gap, the 1957–58 missile hearings following Sputnik, and the 1988–90 hearings on nuclear weapons production following the collapse of DOE's production complex) and, especially during the 1950s and 1960s, sought to promote largely unrestrained weapons development at the expense of appropriate fiscal controls.

Congress and the Bomb

For thirty years, congressional control over nuclear weapons was vested in large measure in the Joint Committee on Atomic Energy. The JCAE wielded enormous power, not only because it had this control over nuclear weapons programs (through its ability to authorize funding) but also because it had a large say in what information was released to Congress and thus could limit debate of these programs. Congress itself, as discussed previously, knew little about the Manhattan Project (see chapter 1). Only a handful of members were privy to the program and to the vast sums being expended on it, and they were uniformly supportive, which is hardly surprising in the context of wartime. Once the secret was revealed in August 1945 with the successful detonation of two atomic bombs over Hiroshima and Nagasaki, attention turned toward the role Congress should play in overseeing the future of the program.

Despite the enormous sum spent developing the bomb, there are no indications that anyone in Congress pressed the executive branch for an accounting (perhaps because the obvious success of the effort made such an examination seem irrelevant). Nor did anyone apparently question the decision to keep the weapons complex in operation after the war (owing to the successful use of atomic bombs, the inertia of the multibillion program, and the assumption that more weapons would be needed). The program remained quite secret and discussions were limited to rather general terms. Perhaps most significant, few members of Congress could understand in more than a general way the daunting scientific and technical nature of nuclear weapons production and its implications for warfare and diplomacy, and many were reluctant to raise questions about the program.[1]

1. In an unusual display of candor, Representative Chet Holifield (Democrat of California) told his colleagues on a JCAE subcommittee during a 1973 hearing on nuclear weapons developments that some things about nuclear strategy and plans to use nuclear weapons "never have made sense to me. I did not feel it was my responsibility to sit in judgment on them. Maybe I am wrong. Maybe all of us are wrong." Elected in 1942, Holifield joined the JCAE at its creation in 1947 and, along with his seventeen colleagues on the committee, had greater access to nuclear weapons information than anyone else in Congress. He was the JCAE's chairman from 1961 to 1962, 1965 to 1966, and 1969 to 1971 and retired in 1974. *Military Applications of Nuclear Technology*, Hearings before the Subcommittee on Military Applications of the Joint Committee on Atomic Energy, 93 Cong. 1 sess. (GPO, 1973), pt. 1, p. 20. For more on Holifield, see Richard W. Dyke, *Mr. Atomic Energy: Congressman Chet Holifield and Atomic Energy Affairs, 1945–1974* (New York: Greenwood Press, 1989); and Richard W. Dyke and Francis X. Gannon, *Chet Holifield: Master*

The procedures Congress used to examine military spending from 1945 to 1950 were little different from those in use since before World War II: "Congress concentrated principally on an item by item review,"trying to economize spending and improve efficiency. Under this approach, it "interested itself essentially in the *how,* and not in the *why,* of military spending."[2] During this period, Congress generally ignored the possible mismatch between U.S. foreign policy objectives and military power and failed to scrutinize how the weapons systems requested by the administration would be used to meet potential military contingencies. Discussion and debate on strategic policy were negligible. No effort was made to assess the long-term costs of containment or precisely what Soviet actions were supposed to be contained. Instead, members spent their time and energy poring over the numerous items in the budget request; in assessing the fiscal 1947 budget, for example, the House Subcommittee on War Department Appropriations deliberately avoided exploring the underlying justification for the military budget and spent copious time investigating proposed expenditures on hospital beds and eating utensils.[3]

As a result, the Congress authorized the production of an enormous fleet of strategic bombers (see chapter 2) without any clear understanding of how these aircraft would be used or how the administration arrived at its funding request for a given number of planes. While airpower was obviously important, the focus was only on how many aircraft to purchase, not on why *X* number would deter a war better than *Y* number, or how they would contribute to anything less than an all-out war with the Soviet Union. The remarks of Representative John E. Rankin (Democrat of Mississippi), during House consideration of the air force budget in the early 1950s, embody the "deep contradictions and startling strategic myopia" of the debate:

> This movement to increase our Air Force is to me the most encouraging step that has yet been taken on this floor. We have reached the time when our Air Force is the first line of defense. The next war will be an atomic conflict. It will be fought with airplanes and atomic bombs. It may mark the end of our civilization. I shall vote for the top amount offered here [$822 million, $9.3 billion in 1996 dollars].[4]

The start of the Korean War in June 1950 signaled to many in Congress that the Soviet Union was determined to use force to dominate independent nations. It also led them to abandon the arbitrary ceiling on military spending that President Truman had imposed to control

Legislator and Nuclear Statesman (Lanham, Md.: University Press of America, 1966).

2. Edward A. Kolodziej, *The Uncommon Defense and Congress, 1945–1963* (Ohio State University Press, 1966), p. 36.

3. Kolodziej, *The Uncommon Defense and Congress,* p. 41.

4. Quoted in Kolodziej, *The Uncommon Defense and Congress,* pp. 80–81.

all government spending and ushered in a series of large increases to the military budget, much of which went toward additional strategic bombers and increased nuclear weapons production (even though no appreciable effect from this funding was expected for several years, see the introduction to this volume). These additions to nuclear forces were made at the expense of conventional forces, a trend accelerated by President Dwight Eisenhower's "New Look" program instituted in 1954. As would happen three decades later under President Ronald Reagan, Congress was persuaded by external events and strong presidential leadership to accept and enact progressively higher military budgets (which rose from $131 billion in 1949 to $448 billion in 1953). In contrast to the 1980s buildup, however, the increases here were seen as a response to a national emergency and not as a down payment on an overall plan. Although the budgets eventually fell following the armistice agreement in 1953, they never returned to pre-1950 levels (see figure 9-2).

Following the Korean war and Eisenhower's election, the new administration attempted once again to contain military spending. Congress, conditioned by the high budgets during the war and by Truman's emphasis on strategic airpower, was reluctant to do anything that might be seen as diminishing America's strength. A formidable airpower coalition had developed in Congress. and it chafed at cuts in what was considered the linchpin of nuclear deterrence. During a 1953 floor debate, the focus was therefore on whether the 120 wings of aircraft proposed by Eisenhower were adequate, compared with the 143 wings championed by Truman. Why a bigger force was needed was unexplained: it was simply better. The underlying strategy governing the use of the planes was similarly ignored, along with the growing emphasis on nuclear weapons as the principal means of deterring attack and fighting a war should deterrence fail (even though all Soviet threats to that date—such as Berlin and Korea—had been met by *conventional* forces).[5] The developing Soviet atomic capability and the potential threat it would pose to U.S. forces went unexamined. As in previous years, the primary concern was the equipment necessary to support deterrence and to maintain U.S. strategic superiority.

The disclosure of an apparent "bomber gap" in 1955 launched a series of congressional investigations, especially in the Senate, into how the United States could have fallen behind the Soviet Union. It also triggered an increase in bomber production and procurement. But as

5. This is illustrated most dramatically in the congressional response to the 1954 testimony of General Matthew B. Ridgway, chief of staff of the army. Testifying before the army appropriations subcommittee, Ridgway stated that one effect of the arbitrary budget ceilings imposed by the New Look was that "the military power ratio between western defensive capability and the Soviet bloc's offensive capability is *not* changing to our advantage." Even though this statement was the exact opposite of what the administration was claiming, it received no special attention from the subcommittee. See Kolodziej, *The Uncommon Defense and Congress,* pp. 204–07.

FIGURE 9-2. U.S. Expenditures for National Defense, 1940–96[a]

Billions of 1996 dollars

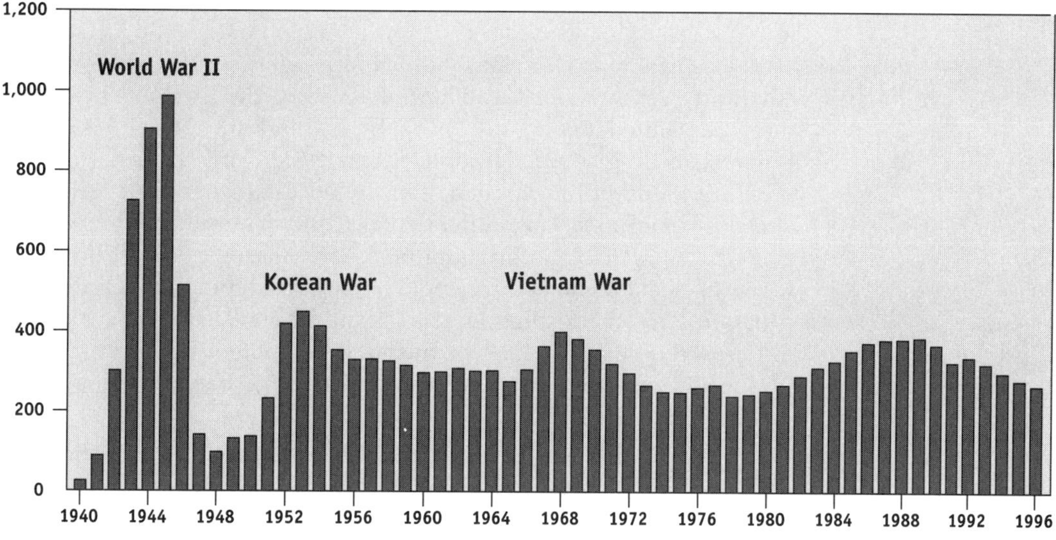

Source: Office of Management and Budget, *Budget of the United States Government, Fiscal Year 1998, Historical Tables,* pp. 42–49 (GPO, 1997). This accounting excludes $1.8 trillion in spending for veterans' benefits and services and $1.2 trillion for international affairs. These expenditures are directly related to overall U.S. foreign policy objectives, and thus defense spending, but are accounted for separately by the government.

a. Total equals $18.683 trillion.

in prior debates, the emphasis was on numbers of weapons to be built and not on the strategy behind the forces. In addition, the fear of falling behind the Soviet Union in numbers of deployed bombers drove Congress to authorize construction of more aircraft without analyzing how more aircraft necessarily translated into more security.

Favoring a focus on numbers of weapons over an exploration of nuclear strategy and policy, and choosing to address only a single year's budget rather than taking a longer view, Congress also failed to examine closely issues that fell outside the confines of the traditional budget debate. In particular, it glossed over the question of how tactical nuclear weapons would be used in a conflict and the pace of research into ballistic missiles. On the former, testimony revealed that the army and the Defense Department had distinctly different views on how wars would be fought. Army chief of staff General Maxwell D. Taylor insisted that despite the atomic thrust of the New Look, the army was "not overly committed in the atomic weapons field" and was prepared to use conventional weapons because "the big atomic bang would not be applicable to all situations." Defense secretary Charles E. Wilson, on the other hand, was "quite certain that if we get involved in another war it would be an atomic war." The difference between these two views was not trivial and its implications—for force structure (and hence budgets) and for strategy—were profound. Yet discussion of these issues appears to have been minimal.[6] Concerning ballistic missiles, the lack of interest would be sharply reversed following the launch of Sputnik in October 1957 (see chapter 2). Curiously, the House defense appropriations subcommittee reported earlier in 1957 (regarding the fiscal 1958 budget) that the United States was "probably behind the Soviet Union in progress made in the perfection of the IRBM" and claimed (without presenting any evidence) that the United States was "very probably ahead of the Soviets" in producing an ICBM. The subcommittee concluded: "All available information makes it clear that there is no room for complacency among our people in the consideration of our defense program." Yet, the leading Democrat and Republican on the subcommittee agreed that funding for missile development was too high and no specific warnings or statements of concern were forthcoming about the implications of falling behind the Soviet Union.[7]

Following Sputnik, numerous hearings were convened to ask how the Soviet Union was able to launch an ICBM and a satellite before the United States, the presumptive leader in high technology. The nuclear status quo—the assumption that the United States would always remain ahead of and thus more powerful than the Soviet Union—was shattered. New committees were established to oversee the developing missile and space programs. Most important, Congress added $3.6 billion (roughly $22 billion in 1996 dollars) more than the administration thought necessary to the defense budget from 1958 to 1962 specifically for offensive and defensive strategic forces, allocating $2.7 billion ($16.5 billion) for offensive weapons and $914 million ($5.6 billion) for defensive weapons and early warning and intelligence systems. It seemed that "Congress' contribution to defense policy was not primarily in strategic conceptualization" but in "its more established concern for the specific force levels and weapons systems proposed by the administration."[8]

Eisenhower's reluctance to view Sputnik and the newly christened "missile gap" as a crisis (because he wanted to avoid calls for unrestrained spending and, later, because U-2 intelligence photographs disproved it) troubled congressional Republicans. Congressional Democrats, especially Senator Lyndon Johnson of Texas, filled the vacuum left by the president and, in response to public concerns, pushed for greater military spending. Fellow Texan and Speaker of the House Sam Rayburn summed up the prevailing mood on Capitol Hill when

6. Kolodziej, *The Uncommon Defense and Congress,* pp. 246–48.

7. Kolodziej, *The Uncommon Defense and Congress,* pp. 249–50.

8. Kolodziej, *The Uncommon Defense and Congress,* pp. 264–66, 271.

he told the *Washington Post* in March 1959, "We just cannot afford to take any risks. The times in which we are living are just too perilous to permit even the slightest let-up in our preparedness program."[9]

When the Kennedy administration took office in January 1961, the missile gap was still a powerful budgetary driving force. Indeed, Kennedy had used the issue against Eisenhower to great effect. Although Kennedy and Secretary of Defense Robert S. McNamara quickly ascertained that the gap in fact favored the United States, it proved politically impossible to disavow it, at least immediately.[10] The result was the unprecedented buildup of U.S. strategic forces, including the deployment of 1,000 Minuteman and 54 Titan II ICBMs, the continued deployment of Polaris submarines, and additional purchases of B-52 bombers. By the late 1960s the nuclear arsenal had assumed the size and character it would maintain for the next quarter century. Along the way, some highly popular projects such as the nuclear-powered aircraft and the B-70 bomber were canceled. These decisions were strongly opposed by important segments of Congress, but in the end they stood. The size and pace of the overall strategic buildup no doubt made the termination of a handful of programs more palatable.

Although the completion of the programs initiated under Kennedy preoccupied Congress during the mid-to-late 1960s, the growing involvement in the Vietnam War garnered increasing attention and funding. The principal strategic debate during this period and the mid-1970s concerned the deployment of antiballistic missile defenses (see chapter 4). McNamara had decided in 1968 that the technology was not yet mature enough to warrant such a move. Furthermore, he recognized that building an ABM system would likely force the Soviet Union to respond, not just by deploying a system of its own but by building even larger numbers of offensive missiles. While expensive, such a policy was far more cost-effective for the Soviet Union than for the United States.

9. Kolodziej, *The Uncommon Defense and Congress,* p. 300.

10. On February 6, 1961, just two weeks after Kennedy's inauguration, McNamara and his deputy Roswell Gilpatric held a not-for-attribution briefing to discuss ongoing studies at the DOD and their possible ramifications for the fiscal 1962 budget. Asked whether the Soviet Union had more deployed ICBMs than the United States, McNamara, when pressed, stated that there were "no signs of a Soviet crash effort to build ICBMs" and that both countries had "about the same number of ICBMs at present—not a very large number." McNamara added that these were only preliminary estimates. The front pages of next morning's newspapers reported that Kennedy's advisers had found no missile gap. That afternoon, White House press secretary Pierre Salinger issued a statement (with Kennedy's approval) asserting that these reports were "absolutely wrong" because a final assessment on the matter was still pending. At a press conference on February 8, Kennedy said he had spoken with McNamara the previous afternoon and that McNamara had "stated that . . . no study had been concluded in the Defense Department which could lead to any conclusion at this time as to whether there is a missile gap or not. . . . [T]herefore it would be premature to reach a judgment as to whether there is a gap or not a gap." The issue became a major political imbroglio for the new administration, with congressional Republicans demanding that Kennedy apologize to Eisenhower for "slander" by promoting the missile gap and Democrats responding that the Eisenhower administration had withheld important information on the defense program from Kennedy. See Desmond Ball, *Politics and Force Levels: The Strategic Missile Program of the Kennedy Administration* (University of California Press, 1980), pp. 89–92.

When Richard Nixon became president, however, he reversed this policy and reconfigured the existing program for early deployment. The decision was extremely controversial, and although the Safeguard ABM system was eventually deployed in 1975, during the Ford administration, the ABM Treaty of 1972 had rendered it too expensive to maintain. The army decided to shut it down after a year of operation, but Congress voted to terminate it immediately, marking the only time in the entire history of the nuclear weapons program that the Congress canceled a strategic nuclear weapons system supported by the executive branch (see chapter 4). While détente eased the tensions of previous years and sought to make the arms race more manageable, the move to modernize nuclear weapons continued, principally in the form of multiple independently targeted reentry vehicles deployed atop Minuteman III ICBMs and Poseidon SLBMs.

President Jimmy Carter came into office determined to cut military spending. He promptly canceled the B-1 bomber, which angered the airpower coalition in Congress. More ambitious plans to enact a comprehensive test ban and a second SALT Treaty were shelved in the face of growing concern about a newly resurgent Soviet Union. The invasion of Afghanistan in 1979 served as a reminder that détente, notwithstanding the cold war, was not yet over and led Congress to support new, less vulnerable weapons systems such as the MX and Trident II missiles. In 1980 Carter responded to strident attacks on his policies by requesting a substantial increase in the defense budget, paving the way for the even larger increases requested by the Reagan administration.

During this period, Carter delved into U.S. nuclear strategy and implemented a number of programmatic and policy changes. The most well known of these is Presidential Directive 59 (PD-59), signed by Carter in July 1980 (over the objections of Secretary of State Cyrus Vance and his successor Edmund Muskie), which stated that U.S. nuclear forces must be able to respond in a flexible manner to Soviet strikes and to fight, if necessary, a protracted nuclear war. At a top secret hearing before the Senate Foreign Relations Committee that September, Secretary of Defense Harold Brown carefully explained the purpose and ramifications of the new policy, but Senator John Glenn (Democrat of Ohio) found it frustrating and confusing:

> SENATOR GLENN: I don't understand why we telegraph our punches on this. I want the Soviets to think we have every option. I know your point is that this leads to every option, but I don't see why we need to give more credibility to the fact that we might be willing to consider a limited exchange. . . . I don't think it is in our best interests to shift the emphasis from massive retaliation to a more limited retaliation. . . .
>
> SECRETARY BROWN: What you said was that you thought that perhaps the best posture to take was that no matter what they do to us, we go all out in return?

SENATOR GLENN: I think that is the greatest deterrence. It would be for us if the shoe were on the other foot.

SECRETARY BROWN: If they knew we would do so.

SENATOR GLENN: Why do we tell them we won't do it?

SECRETARY BROWN: I am saying we keep all the options open and they should not think that we would give no response, because we have no credible response.

SENATOR GLENN: I get lost in what is credible and not credible. This whole thing gets so incredible when you consider wiping out whole nations, it is difficult to establish credibility.

SECRETARY BROWN: That is why we sound a little crazy when we talk about it.

SENATOR GLENN: That is the best statement of the day. I agree with you.[11]

The election of Ronald Reagan in 1980 brought into the White House and Capitol Hill a large number of conservative policymakers with a deep dislike of arms control, a strong distrust of the Soviet Union, and a desire to rebuild American military strength following what they considered a period of laxity and weakness in the 1970s. To that end, the administration proposed the largest peacetime military program in U.S. history, calling for the deployment of entire new classes of ICBMs and SLBMs, and reviving the B-1 bomber (although most of these programs were in fact begun under Carter).

Flush with victory and sensing a mandate from the public, a bipartisan majority of Congress wholeheartedly endorsed the Reagan program, even though the justification for the large increase in spending was, at best, ill-defined (see the Introduction). "Peace through strength" became a shorthand rationale for the program, but as in the 1950s, few in Congress asked how more weapons would support deterrence. Complicating matters, the administration leaked word of a new strategy to fight and prevail in a protracted nuclear war with the Soviet Union. Although this thinking was actually an extension of previous operational policies (especially Carter's PD-59), it clashed with the public's understanding of U.S. policy and precipitated widespread antinuclear demonstrations and the creation of the nuclear freeze movement. This in turn encouraged similar sentiments in Congress and by 1985 support for increasing defense budgets had fallen off.

Throughout this period, there were almost annual debates about funding the MX missile, but these were less about nuclear strategy in general and more about this one program, which was originally pro-

11. *Nuclear War Strategy,* Hearings before the Senate Committee on Foreign Relations, 96 Cong. 2 sess. (GPO, 1981), pp. 21–22.

posed as the mobile solution to theoretically vulnerable (and stationary) Minuteman ICBMs but was eventually deployed in existing ICBM silos after the mobile basing schemes were ridiculed and rejected by significant segments of Congress and the public (especially ranchers in Nevada and Utah whose land was considered ideal for the mobile MX). Equally important was the declaration in April 1983 by the president's Scowcroft Commission that the "window of vulnerability" was essentially nonexistent when the survivability of all the elements of the strategic triad (ICBMs, SLBMs, and bombers) were considered collectively and not in isolation.[12]

Congress did finally cap the MX program at fifty deployed missiles, but every other strategic nuclear program—the Trident II/D-5 SLBM, the B-1B, and B-2 bombers, the air-launched cruise missile, and the Trident Ohio-class SSBNs—along with a number of nonstrategic programs (the ground-launched cruise missile, the Pershing II missile, new nuclear depth bombs, SSNs, and artillery shells, among others) and an overhaul of the nuclear command, control, and communications network, proceeded largely as planned. The Strategic Defense Initiative also received significant funding throughout the 1980s despite widespread skepticism that the program would work as designed (see chapter 4).

Although there is evidence that the administration viewed the entire $2.8 trillion buildup (total obligations for national defense from 1982 through 1989) less as a means of restoring American military strength than as a tool to bankrupt the Soviet Union, that is not how the program was consistently characterized to Congress or the public (see the introduction). A great deal of effort went into describing the nature of the weapons to be purchased and the threat they were designed to counter. In 1981 the DOD produced *Soviet Military Power,* a glossy booklet lavishly illustrated with charts, drawings (some based on reconnaissance satellite photographs), and photographs that portrayed the Soviet military in the most menacing light possible and largely without reference to counterpoising U.S. military forces.[13] By 1983, 300,000 copies were being published, at a cost of more than $860,000.[14] Like past weapons buildups, this one was sold to the public as necessary to counter the Soviet threat. During a March 31, 1982, press conference, President Reagan even declared the Soviet Union to be militarily superior to the United States in terms of strategic offensive forces (an argument first raised during the 1980 campaign), an assessment at odds with the views of, among others, his own secretaries

12. *Report of the President's Commission on Strategic Forces,* April 6, 1983.

13. For an instructive analysis of the 1987 version of this document, see Tom Gervasi, *Soviet Military Power: The Pentagon's Propaganda Document, Annotated and Corrected* (New York: Vintage Books, 1988).

14. Gervasi, *Soviet Military Power,* p. v.

of defense and state. and the chairman of the Joint Chiefs of Staff.[15] It was during this period that military spending came to be widely seen as a significant economic program. To be sure, past programs had often been supported by Congress in part because of their ability to bring (and retain) jobs at home. But never before had so much money been made available when the country was not at war. California, in particular, experienced a significant economic boost. Thus, when spending began to tail off in the mid-1980s, members of Congress sought to retain what they could in no small measure because the economic effects were so large.

The Bush administration initially sought to continue the Reagan-era buildup, but the collapse of the Berlin Wall in November 1989 and subsequent events in Eastern Europe and the Soviet Union signaled, if not the end of the cold war, at least the unfolding of a dramatically different era.[16] Iraq's invasion of Kuwait in August 1990 and the Gulf War the following January reinforced the notion that military strength was still needed, but it also demonstrated that nuclear weapons were by and large irrelevant to what George Bush would come to call the "new world order."[17] The START agreement was signed in 1991 and deep unilateral reductions in tactical nuclear weapons were initiated by Bush and Mikhail Gorbachev later that year. As a result—and owing to the collapse of DOE's nuclear weapons production complex—Congress questioned the need for new nuclear weapons and new production facilities, including the B90 nuclear depth/strike bomb, the Short-Range Attack Missile II, and its tactical variant SRAM-T. This opposition played a key role in the administration's decision to forgo building these weapons.

In addition, public and congressional support for a halt in nuclear testing led Congress—over the administration's objections—to impose a nine-month moratorium on testing in September 1992. This moratorium was subsequently extended by the Clinton administration (over the

15. "The truth of the matter is that on balance, the Soviet Union does have a definite margin of superiority, enough so that there is risk and there is what I have called, as you all know, a 'window of vulnerability.' And I think that a freeze would not only be disadvantageous—in fact, even dangerous to us with them in that position—but I believe that it would also militate against any negotiations for reduction. There would be no incentive for them, then, to meet with us and reduce." In making this assertion, Reagan, as he had previously, was comparing only numbers of ICBMs and SLBMs (1,569 for the United States versus 2,388 for the Soviet Union). Comparing total actual deliverable warheads (including those on bombers) would have demonstrated U.S. superiority (10,291 versus 8,716). Ronald Reagan, *Public Papers of the Presidents of the United States: Ronald Reagan, 1982—January 1 to July 2, 1982* (GPO, 1993), p. 399; Robert G. Kaiser, "Critics Dispute Reagan, Say Soviets Not Superior," *Washington Post,* April 2, 1982, p. A1; Judith Miller, "Reagan's View on Lag in Arms Being Disputed," *New York Times,* April 2, 1982, p. A1.

16. See, for example, Michael R. Gordon, Stocking the Atomic Arsenal: How Much Deterrence to Buy" *New York Times,* May 23, 1990, p. A1.

17. Although there is a strong belief in certain quarters that the threat of using nuclear weapons deterred Iraq from using chemical and biological weapons during the Gulf War, it appears more likely that the short duration of the war prevented Iraq from using such weapons. Moreover, before the start of the war, President Bush privately decided that U.S. forces would not retaliate with nuclear weapons even if Iraq attacked with chemical weapons. See William M. Arkin, "Nuclear Excuses," *Bulletin of the Atomic Scientists,* vol. 52 (May/June 1996), p. 64; William M. Arkin, "Calculated Ambiguity: Nuclear Weapons and the Gulf War," *Washngton Quarterly,* vol. 19 (August 1996), pp. 3–18.

objections of many in the nuclear weapons laboratories and a vocal minority in Congress) and helped lead to the Comprehensive Test Ban Treaty in 1996, which was submitted to the Senate for ratification in September 1997. The administration also signed START II in 1993, which was finally ratified by the Senate in January 1996 and awaits ratification by the Russian parliament. Current congressional interest in nuclear weapons is focused on DOE's stockpile stewardship program to maintain the nuclear arsenal in the absence of underground testing, on deploying defenses against ballistic missile attack, and on attempting to procure additional B-2A bombers beyond the twenty-one already ordered.

DOE's Collapse: Why Congress Missed the Warning Signs

One consequence of the Reagan administration's military buildup was a renewed emphasis on nuclear weapons production and testing. Facilities that had been operating at relatively low levels were put back into full production, and new facilities were authorized. But the nuclear weapons complex, parts of which were at that point more than thirty years old, could not cope with the strain. Because the AEC and DOE invested very little in infrastructure maintenance—preferring to devote the bulk of annual funding to warhead and bomb production—the production complex was allowed to deteriorate to the point that it essentially collapsed under the weight of these new programs in the mid- to late-1980s.

Ironically, it was the reactor explosion and meltdown in Chernobyl on April 26, 1986, that first brought the precarious state of the DOE complex to national attention. Less than one month after the accident, a House subcommittee held a field hearing near the Hanford Reservation to investigate charges that critical safety issues at the Hanford N-reactor had been overlooked and that distinct similarities between the N-reactor and Chernobyl Unit 4, including the lack of a steel and concrete containment vessel required on all commercial reactors, made an accident a distinct possibility. In early January 1987 the DOE shut down the N-reactor for six months for an unexpected $63 million safety upgrade. Just one year later, after spending $88 million (with plans to spend an additional $38 million), the DOE announced it would not restart the reactor because plutonium requirements could be met with existing stockpiles.[18]

Also in January 1987, the DOE effectively retired the thirty-two-year-old C-reactor at the Savannah River Plant after discovering radiation-induced cracks in the reactor vessel. In March 1987 the General

18. Matthew L. Wald, "U.S. Won't Reopen Plutonium Plant," *New York Times*, February 17, 1988, p. A11.

Accounting Office reported to the Senate Governmental Operations Committee that from 1979 until late 1986 (during the resurgence of production initiated by the Reagan administration), all the reactors at the Savannah River Plant had been operating at power levels higher than their emergency core cooling systems could handle. The GAO cited the contractor, E. I. Du Pont de Nemours, for a mathematical error that led to an overestimation of the efficiency of the cooling systems. After discovering the error, Du Pont cut power levels in the reactors. About a week later, the DOE reduced the power levels still further, in response to expressions of concern from the GAO, the National Academy of Sciences, and members of Congress.[19] Between April 10 and August 17, 1988, the K-, L-, and P- reactors at Savannah River were shut down for routine refueling and maintenance.[20] On August 10, the P-reactor experienced a dangerous power surge during an attempted restart. Although the reactor operators noticed the surge, they failed to determine the cause. Rather than stopping, they ignored safety procedures and continued until the reactor automatically shut down.[21]

Additional developments kept the DOE in the news and under congressional scrutiny. In mid-September it indefinitely delayed the opening of the Waste Isolation Pilot Plant owing to safety concerns (see chapter 6). On September 29 two workers and an inspector in Building 771 (the main plutonium-processing facility) at Rocky Flats were contaminated with plutonium (the DOE shortly thereafter halted operations in the building).[22] On September 30 documents released at a joint congressional hearing revealed more than thirty serious accidents at the Savannah River reactors—including power spikes, discharges of radioactive water, and a partial meltdown of the C-reactor in 1970—which were kept secret by Du Pont and the AEC and DOE (although former AEC commissioners quickly came forward to say they were never informed of accidents that happened during their tenure).[23]

By now, the *New York Times* was on top of the exploding story. Almost daily news stories, many on the front page, brought new problems to light, alarming the public and Congress alike. In addition to voicing health and safety concerns, some people questioned the DOE's ability to

19. Matthew L. Wald, "G.A.O. Says 4 Government Reactors Operated at an Unsafe Power Level," *New York Times,* March 13, 1987, p. A15, and "U.S. Will Cut Power at Bomb Fuel Reactors amid Concern about Safety," *New York Times,* March 21, 1987, p. 6.

20. Rodney P. Carlisle, with Joan M. Zenzen, *Supplying the Nuclear Arsenal: American Production Reactors: 1942–1992* (Johns Hopkins University Press, 1996), p. 191.

21. Cass Peterson,"Reactor Runs Out of Control Briefly," *Washington Post,* August 18, 1988, p. A1, and "Top Managers Not Notified of Reactor's Startup Problems," *Washington Post,* August 19, 1988, p. A2.

22. Keith Schneider, "2D Nuclear Plant Is Ordered Closed by Energy Dept.," *New York Times,* October 11, 1988, p. A1.

23. Keith Schneider, "Ex-Nuclear Aides Deny Being Told of Plant Mishaps," *New York Times,* October 5, 1988, p. A1; *Nuclear Reactor Safety at the Department of Energy's Savannah River Plant,* Joint Hearing before a House Committee on Government Operations and a Senate Committee on Governmental Affairs, 100 Cong. 2 sess. (GPO, 1988).

maintain production of the arsenal. Attempting to turn a deteriorating situation (and weapons complex) to its advantage, senior DOE officials leaked information about additional problems to the *Times* and other media outlets, at the same time requesting billions of dollars from Congress to rebuild the complex. It was a calculated effort, and it failed.[24] The question of the fate of the arsenal was eclipsed by mounting health, safety, and environmental issues. Despite dire warnings from a handful of DOD officials that unilateral disarmament would result if production was not restored quickly (see chapter 1), Congress and the public quickly lost trust in the DOE and demanded to know how and why things had been allowed to get so far out of control.

Of course, the problems did not develop overnight. They were the natural result of a combination of factors, including AEC and DOE arrangements with the contractors who actually operated the weapons facilities, pervasive secrecy, and the inclination of the DOE and congressional overseers to put weapons production ahead of everything else in order to meet the military's requirements for more and more powerful nuclear weapons (see chapters 1 and 6).

In a revealing November 28, 1988, *Times* article, members of Congress discussed where they went wrong.[25] Representative Albert Bustamante (Democrat of Texas), a member of the Armed Services Committee, said the issues were too complex: "Anytime we get into a problem like now, nobody on the committee knows what is what. We just delegate things to the Department of Energy." Senator James Exon (Democrat of Nebraska), a senior member of the Armed Services Committee, agreed. The issues, he said, "are not easily understood by those of us who are not scientists." A spokesman for House Armed Services chairman Les Aspin (Democrat of Wisconsin) noted that the weapons complex was not considered on an equal basis with the weapons systems that the committee normally spent a great deal of time debating. "It has been a poor stepchild. It just doesn't fit in around here." An aide to Senator Sam Nunn (Democrat of Georgia), chairman of the Senate Armed Services Committee, admitted that "for a long time Congress just rubber stamped the Department of Energy" and that as a result the complex suffered from "benign neglect." Ironically, despite the frankness of these comments, congressional micromanagement of defense programs increased in the 1970s and 1980s, and the overall portion of the defense budget that had to be authorized in any given year rose from 31 percent in 1971 to 100 percent by 1983.[26] Yet DOE issues languished.

24. See William Lanouette, *Tritium and the Times: How the Nuclear Weapons-Production Scandal Became a National Story* (Cambridge, Mass.: Joan Shorenstein Barone Center, Harvard University, May 1990).

25. Fox Butterfield, "Trouble at Atomic Bomb Plants: How Lawmakers Missed the Signs," *New York Times*, November 28, 1988, p. A1.

26. John O. Marsh, Jr., *Congressional Oversight of National Secu-*

Surprisingly few members availed themselves of the opportunity to learn more by visiting the facilities they oversaw. For example, although congressional visitors to the Nevada Test Site were frequent in the 1950s, following the cessation of atmospheric nuclear testing in 1963 interest in touring the site and meeting with site officials declined even as the cost of nuclear testing increased (see appendix table A-2). Aside from members of the Nevada delegation, the only other visitors were Representative Barry M. Goldwater, Jr. (Republican of Arizona) in 1980, Representatives James V. Hansen and Douglas W. Owens (Republicans of Utah) in 1987, Representative Rick Boucher (Democrat of Virginia) in 1990, and Representative Michael J. Kopetski (Democrat of Oregon) in 1992. Senator Exon also visited the site in May 1992, becoming the first non-Nevada Senator to do so in more than three decades.[27]

During this visit, conducted while Congress was considering enacting restrictions on nuclear testing, Exon was reportedly amazed at the large number of craters from past tests dotting the site, despite his years of service on the Armed Services Committee, which has jurisdiction over the testing program and holds regular hearings on it. Impressed by what he saw and heard, Exon persuaded four of his committee colleagues—Jeff Bingaman (Democrat of New Mexico), Carl Levin (Democrat of Michigan), Harry Reid (Democrat of Nevada), and Strom Thurmond (Republican of South Carolina)—to accompany him on a return visit two months later for briefings from the directors of the Los Alamos and Livermore laboratories and head of the Defense Nuclear Agency. Exon, who before these visits was generally if not strongly in favor of nuclear testing, came away convinced that a testing moratorium was a useful step in achieving a permanent test ban. Other facilities received even less attention. At the Pantex Plant in Texas, members of that state's delegation paid occasional visits, but it was not until 1992 that Senator Exon became the first out-of-state member to tour the site.[28]

Members did not even appear interested when the AEC and DOE wasted prodigious amounts of money. Following a major fire in 1969 at the Rocky Flats Plant (see chapter 6), the AEC began planning a new plutonium-processing building. The original cost for Building 371 was $63 million ($248.8 million in 1996 dollars). By the time the building was authorized in April 1971, the cost had risen to $113 mil-

---

rity: A Mandate for Change (Washington, D.C.: Center for Strategic and International Studies, October 1992), pp. 12–16.

27. The only president in or out of office to visit the NTS was John F. Kennedy in 1962 (where he toured the Nuclear Reactor Development Station, then developing nuclear propulsion systems for space missions and the PLUTO nuclear-armed cruise missile (see box 2-2). Electronic mail communications with Derek Scammell, Office of Public Affairs, Department of Energy Nevada Operations Office, September 2 and 10, 1997.

28. Electronic mail communications with Derek Scammell, September 2 and 10, 1997; author's communication with congressional sources.

lion ($446.3 million in 1996 dollars). This was revised again in 1977 to $187 million ($522.5 million in 1996 dollars). When finally completed in March 1980, the total cost had soared to $215 million ($559.5 million).[29]

Once production started, however, it was discovered that solvents used in the processing of plutonium destroyed the seals on the glove boxes, making large parts of the building unusable and forcing DOE to close the plant a month later. Despite this expensive and controversial failure, Representative Samuel Stratton (Democrat of New York), chairman of the Procurement and Military Nuclear Systems subcommittee, told the *New York Times* that his committee "never really got into" the Building 371 fiasco because "we felt it was a little out of our purview. We had enough problems already, so we never went out there to look at it." Representative John M. Spratt, Jr. (Democrat of South Carolina), a member of the subcommittee, added: "In truth, most of our time is spent on the annual budget process and we have little left for oversight."[30]

One key reason why House members in particular professed little concern about Building 371 and other DOE problems was that their staff expert did not find these issues troubling. Representative Stratton's subcommittee at that time had but one staff member, Robert Schafer, considered supportive of DOE by many of his colleagues.[31] In an interview with the *Times,* Mr. Schafer discounted the significance of

29. U.S. Department of Energy, "Plutonium Recovery Modification Project (PRMP), Historical Overview and Baseline Establishment," Briefing to Secretary of Energy James D. Watkins, March 6, 1990. Such cost overruns and design failures were unfortunately fairly routine. In addition to Building 371, they include the Clinch River Breeder Reactor, the Fast Flux Test Facility at the Hanford Reservation, and the Gas Centrifuge Enrichment Plant at the Portsmouth Gaseous Diffusion Plant. Unadjusted costs for these efforts total $5.5 billion. See Keith Schneider, "U.S. Spent Billions on Atom Projects That Have Failed," *New York Times,* December 12, 1988, p. A1; Keith Schneider, "A Fifth of Nuclear Arms Spending Is Termed Wasteful or Unneeded," *New York Times,* May 20, 1991, p. A1. In late 1996 the GAO reported that from 1980 through 1996, thirty-one of eighty major projects were terminated before completion after expenditures totaling more than $10 billion (in then-year dollars). Only fifteen of the projects were completed, mostly behind schedule and above cost. See U.S. General Accounting Office, *Department of Energy: Opportunity to Improve Management of Major System Acquisitions,* RCED-97-17 (November 1996).

30. In a similar vein, Senator Nunn, a member of the Senate Armed Services Committee since 1972, told a reporter in early 1984: "The budget cycle drives the Congress, and the Congress drives the executive branch to such an obsession that we don't have time to think about strategy. We never had a strategy hearing since I've been in the Senate." Michael R. Gordon, "Sam Nunn for the Defense—Georgia Boy Makes Good as Gentle Pentagon Prodder," *National Journal,* March 31, 1984, p. 614. In fact, a 1985 study on reforming the congressional budget process (in which sixteen current members of Congress participated) reported: "The Congress is so immersed in the fine points of the defense program that it lacks the time, the resources, and the orientation to execute its oversight role effectively by engaging in a substantive dialogue with the executive branch on fundamental policy decisions. It is lost in the trees of defense decisionmaking, unable to make out—far less influence—the broad outlines of the policy forest. The executive branch reinforces this tendency by avoiding discussion of major long-run defense issues with the Congress, while simultaneously bemoaning congressional micromanagement." See Alice M. Rivlin and others, "Report of the Working Group on the Congressional Defense Budget Process," in Barry M. Blechman and William J. Lynn, eds., *Toward a More Effective Defense: Report of the Defense Organization Project* (Cambridge, Mass.: Ballinger, 1985), pp. 106–07.

31. The lack of adequate staff is unfortunately not a new phenomenon. In 1951 the Senate military appropriations subcommittee employed one staff member to handle the entire $419 billion defense appropriations bill. In 1952 the House defense appropriations subcommittee had two people on its staff. During 1959–60 that figure had risen to six, with four staff for its Senate counterpart. See Kolodziej, *Uncommon Defense and Congress,* pp. 481–82.

the 1988 reactor incidents at the Savannah River Plant and accused the committees who released information about them of "sensationalism for a political purpose."[32] Schafer also stated that water leakage into WIPP (a situation about which even DOE's own inspectors were worried) was "not much of a problem" and that the DOE was guilty of "an inappropriate overreaction" for shutting down a building at Rocky Flats following the September 29, 1988, contamination incident.[33] Thus it is not surprising that members of the House Armed Services Committee—admittedly confused by the apparent complexity of the issues, but assured by their own staff that there was little to worry about and preoccupied with the annual budget exercise—found little to be concerned about in DOE's operations. That DOE itself had also ignored the warning signs of impending trouble further contributed to this situation. The thinking in the Senate Armed Services Committee was no doubt similar. If the members of Congress with jurisdiction over these issues (and access to the information necessary to make informed decisions) felt no concern, the rest of Congress, which traditionally relied on their more knowledgeable colleagues for advice on arcane military matters, was certainly in no position to question their judgment. As the *New York Times* noted: "Mr. Schafer's views about the Energy Department's safety record are important, many legislators say, because he largely controls the work of the subcommittee. A staff aide to another committee member said Mr. Schafer routinely excluded legislative assistants from subcommittee discussions of money for the weapon plants."[34]

This was the situation until late 1988. In early 1989, the House Armed Services Committee, acknowledging its past failures, established the Department of Energy Defense Nuclear Facilities panel, chaired by Representative Spratt. Although not a formal subcommittee, the panel had clout and reported directly to the Procurement and Military Nuclear Systems Subcommittee, which had jurisdiction over the DOE's budget. Between February and July, it held fifteen public hearings on the state of the weapons complex.[35] A large number of hearings were also held between 1990 and 1992. Since then, interest in the issue has diminished, even as billions of dollars a year are appropriated to maintain and clean up the complex (see chapter 6). The crisis has passed and with it the sense that the problem requires high levels of regular attention. Following their ascension to power in the 1994 elections, the newly empowered Republican majority in the House, as

32. In fact, DOE officials provided the documents to the committee. See Lanouette, *Tritium and the Times,* pp. 11–14.

33. Butterfield, "Trouble at Atomic Bomb Plants."

34. Butterfield, "Trouble at Atomic Bomb Plants."

35. *National Defense Authorization Act for Fiscal Year 1990—H.R. 2461 and Oversight of Previously Authorized Programs,* Hearings before the House Committee on Armed Services, 101 Cong. 1 sess. (GPO, 1990). The Senate Armed Services Committee, while not creating a new subcommittee or panel, expanded the operations of its subcommittee on strategic forces, which held a large number of hearings on DOE issues between 1989 and 1992.

I think in the past the members of this committee . . . have never tried to become military planning experts, strategic, tactical or any other kind of experts. The way the Atomic Energy Act was written was that the Defense Department, working with the President, asked for a certain number of weapons of certain kinds and the facilities to manufacture them. The members of the Joint Committee have never tried becoming war strategists, war planners. We more or less considered that was the job of the Armed Services Committee if they wanted to go into that part. Our function has really been to develop in our laboratories weapons asked for by the military and directed by the President, and we have never applied ourselves to war planning and war gaming and setting ourselves up as Chief of Staff to exercise judgment over how a war should be fought.[36]

—*Representative Chet Holifield, April 16, 1973*

part of an overall effort to streamline congressional operations, eliminated the panel, folding its operations back into a larger subcommittee. Today, although weapons production has ceased and cleanup operations are under way, most members of Congress remain ill informed about the DOE. Many of the members who took it upon themselves to become educated in nuclear arcana in the aftermath of the DOE's collapse—including Senators Exon and Nunn—lost subsequent reelection bids or have retired.

Joint Committee on Atomic Energy, 1946–77

In his first announcement on the atomic bomb on August 6, 1945, President Truman asked Congress to "consider promptly the establishment of an appropriate commission to control the production and use of atomic power."[37] After several false starts and jurisdictional disputes, the Senate in late October finally appointed an eleven-member special committee with full jurisdiction over the field of atomic energy. During November and December hearings were held before the committee to consider how best to administer this new program and, particularly, what role the military should play in its development. Draft legislation followed, which ultimately became the Atomic Energy Act of 1946 and was signed by Truman on August 1, 1946.

Under the act, the government was granted more or less a monopoly over atomic power, on the grounds that only the government should be able to control fissile materials and the facilities that produce them. In addition, tight controls were imposed on information about atomic energy, and on the sharing of information and technology with allies (see chapter 8). To oversee the entire program, a five-man Atomic Energy Commission was created, along with a Military Liaison Committee and a General Advisory Committee (composed of scientists) to provide assistance and advice. To ensure a strong congressional role in overseeing the program, the act created the JCAE, the only committee to be brought into being by an act of legislation (and thus held to have rights under that law) and the only joint committee to have full legislative powers.[38] Not only could the JCAE hold investigative hearings and undertake studies of issues, all bills, or other

36. *Military Applications of Nuclear Technology*, Hearings, pt. 1, p. 19.

37. Robert C. Williams and Philip L. Cantelon, eds., *The American Atom: A Documentary History of Nuclear Policies from the Discovery of Fission to the Present, 1939–1984* (University of Pennsylvania Press, 1984), p. 70.

38. An account of the development of the Atomic Energy Act may be found in Richard G. Hewlett and Oscar E. Anderson, Jr., *A History of the United States Atomic Energy Commission*, vol. 1: *The New World: 1939/1946* (Oak Ridge, Tennessee: U.S. AEC Technical Information Center, 1972), pp. 408–530.

matters pertaining to atomic energy in both the House and the Senate had to be referred to the JCAE.

In 1954 the JCAE gained the power to authorize funds for the Atomic Energy Commission.[39] Its joint nature was especially important, as it helped to minimize differences between the House and Senate and bolstered its authority with the executive branch, which could not pit one committee against the other in an effort to either kill or delay undesirable legislation or achieve an agreeable compromise: "If an AEC proposal were defeated by the Joint Committee, it could not be resurrected by another committee. Alternatively, if a JCAE proposal were unpalatable to the Executive, there was no possibility of having it buried in a committee of the other house. Any battle the Executive lost within the Joint Committee would have to be fought on the floor of each house, and here . . . the JCAE would have considerable advantages."[40] No other committee, before or since, has been granted such unique and far-reaching powers. The pace and scale of the nuclear weapons program, especially in the 1950s, is in no small measure attributable to the considerable influence of the JCAE and, in particular, to Brien McMahon, who as a freshman senator from Connecticut was quick to grasp the potential of atomic energy and sought to make the issue his own.[41]

The Atomic Energy Act stipulated that the committee consist of eighteen members, equally divided between the House and the Senate. The committee was to be vested with full jurisdiction over "all bills, resolutions, and other matters in the Senate or the House of Representatives relating primarily to the [Atomic Energy] Commission or to the development, use and control of atomic energy."[42] The AEC was explicitly required to keep the JCAE "fully and currently informed with respect to all of the Commission's activities," giving the JCAE "a unique capacity for legislative surveillance." (This was expanded in 1954 to cover all atomic energy matters of the Department of Defense as well.) This arrangement allowed the committee to function largely as a coequal of the AEC, leading Representative Henry M. Jackson (Democrat of Washington) to boast to his colleagues in July 1952 that with regard to "two vital policy matters [almost certainly the crash development of the hydrogen or "Super"

39. The quest for this authority, which began in 1949, and the conflicts it created with the House Appropriations Committee, are discussed in Harold P. Green and Alan Rosenthal, *Government of the Atom: The Integration of Powers* (New York: Atherton Press, 1963), pp. 169–72, 222–31.

40. Green and Rosenthal, *Government of the Atom,* p. 27.

41. In theory, the JCAE was supposed to provide greater accountability for the nuclear weapons (and later nuclear energy) program. In reality, by giving the committee the sole authority to both oversee and authorize funds for the AEC, the Atomic Energy Act created an unworkable system, in which accountability and regulation quickly took secondary importance to the vigorous promotion of the nuclear program.

42. This, of course, included nuclear power for civilian purposes. The JCAE's influence in this area was equal to, if not greater than, that for nuclear weapons. However, this subject is outside the scope of this study.

bomb and the 50-150 expansion program to boost uranium and plutonium production, see chapter 1], the drive and the urging from the Committee played so powerful a role that in a very real sense it can be said that the Committee made the decision with the advice and consent of the Executive Branch."[43] This statutory authority, and the rigor with which it was enforced, allowed the JCAE in effect to function as part of the executive branch. Moreover, by gaining access to predecisional documents, the committee not only could respond to but could shape administration policy with regard to nuclear weapons.[44]

The JCAE was also authorized to appoint staff and use personnel and services (including those of the executive branch) as was deemed necessary to carry out its mission. This staff, which served members of both parties on the JCAE, was the source of much of the committee's power because it developed close and continuing relationships with the personnel at AEC headquarters and key field facilities, with the result that members often came to know more about AEC operations than the commissioners themselves.[45]

Members of the JCAE were chosen on the basis of a variety of factors, including geography, seniority, and membership on other committees.[46] Interest in the atomic energy field and the existence of a nuclear weapons facility in one's state or district was also important. Hence Argonne and Los Alamos (and later Livermore) laboratories, Hanford, Oak Ridge, Pantex, the Nevada Test Site, and uranium mining facilities in the mountain states were usually represented on the committee (for the representation of these and nuclear weapons production facilities in the Senate, see box 9-1). Representative Craig Hosmer (Republican of California) quit his job with an AEC field office to run for Congress in 1948 with the explicit intention of serving on the

43. Jackson added: "In this atomic energy business, the simple right to know the highly secret facts in and of itself confers immense powers of moral suasion. Here, in a most literal sense, knowledge is power." Quoted in Green and Rosenthal, *Government of the Atom,* pp. 103–04.

44. Green and Rosenthal, *Government of the Atom,* pp. 89–103.

45. Green and Rosenthal, *Government of the Atom,* pp. 66–68. Probably the most dramatic example of staff influence was William L. Borden's November 7, 1953, letter to FBI director J. Edgar Hoover accusing J. Robert Oppenheimer of being a Communist spy. AEC commissioner Henry Smyth, the only commissioner to vote in 1954 not to revoke Oppenheimer's security clearance, wrote to AEC chairman Lewis Strauss: "Borden's letter of accusation is important not because it brings forward new evidence of any consequence [in fact it did not] but because of the position he has held [until June 1, 1953] as head of the staff of the Joint Congressional Committee on Atomic Energy." Smyth, Strauss later wrote, added that "to ignore the Borden letter and to continue clearance were obviously unwise." See Lewis L. Strauss, *Men and Decisions* (New York: Doubleday, 1962), p. 275.

46. Because House and Senate rules limit the number of committees on which a member can serve, committee slots are chosen very carefully. The JCAE, however, was exempted from these rules and thus members could and did serve on it as well as on two or three other committees. Thus Senate Armed Services Committee chairman Richard Russell (Democrat of Georgia) was also a senior member of both the Appropriations Committee and the JCAE (although he rarely attended JCAE hearings). Senator Clinton Anderson (Democrat of New Mexico) simultaneously served on the Aeronautical and Space Sciences, Finance, and Interior and Insular Affairs committees in addition to the JCAE. Such arrangements multiplied the power of the JCAE by allowing members to use their knowledge and influence from serving on the JCAE on related matters (for example, mining issues, or missile development) before other committees. Green and Rosenthal, *Government of the Atom,* pp. 32, 34, 36.

JCAE (he had to wait for ten years, however, because open seats were awarded to members with more seniority).[47]

Although the JCAE expended considerable effort on investigating security matters—for example, an exhaustive series of hearings was held in 1949 on purported AEC mismanagement, including security lapses[48]—and even as the stringent secrecy surrounding all aspects of atomic energy in the late 1940s and early 1950s served to foster a sense of camaraderie among JCAE members, they breached these rules from time to time. For example, shortly after President Truman announced the first Soviet atomic test on September 23, 1949, JCAE member Senator Edwin Johnson (Democrat of Colorado) "unwarily blurted . . . out on a national television program" the highly sensitive fact (classified as top secret) that it was a plutonium bomb with a natural uranium tamper, information that revealed the nature and accuracy of a monitoring program run by a secret air force organization (see chapter 8). Senator McMahon infuriated the AEC and the president by leaking word of the AEC's 50-150 expansion program immediately after emerging from a January 17, 1952, meeting with Truman. And in 1959, Senator Clinton Anderson released information on the deposition of fallout across the United States that was considered secret by the DOD because he felt the JCAE was being "gagged" by the DOD (see chapter 8).[49]

Despite these occasional lapses, the JCAE took secrecy very seriously, so seriously that "almost no information of substance was communicated to the rest of Congress" from 1947 through 1953.[50] In fact, the committee itself refused to be briefed on the size of the stockpile, apparently believing that even it could not be trusted with such a vital

47. In a reverse move, the JCAE in 1962 used its considerable influence to force the Kennedy administration to nominate its longtime executive director, James T. Ramey, as an AEC commissioner. Ramey, who had engineered the policies that led to the JCAE's dominance over the AEC in the mid- to late-1950s, had many foes inside the commission (several of whom announced that they would resign if Ramey were appointed). The administration also had serious doubts about the wisdom of nominating someone who had worked so vigorously to render the executive branch subordinate to the legislative. The JCAE forced the issue by refusing to consider the nominations of anyone else. At the time, there were two vacancies on the five-man commission, making it difficult to assemble a quorum and thus delaying important work. Eventually, the administration gave way and Ramey was nominated and confirmed by his former employers. See Green and Rosenthal, *Government of the Atom,* p. 107.

48. *Investigation into the United States Atomic Energy Project,* Hearings before the Joint Committee on Atomic Energy, 81 Cong. 1 sess. (GPO, 1949), pts. 1–24.

49. Charles Ziegler, "Waiting for Joe-1: Decisions Leading to the Detection of Russia's First Atomic Bomb Test," *Social Studies of Science,* vol. 18, no. 2 (1988), pp. 220, 228 (note 70); Roger M. Anders, ed., *Forging the Atomic Shield: Excerpts from the Office Diary of Gordon E. Dean* (University of North Carolina Press, 1987), p. 197. During an October 28, 1949, symposium on Geiger counters hosted by the Naval Research Laboratory (whose work was integral to the detection of the first Soviet bomb), AEC commissioner Sumner Pike offhandedly revealed that the bomb was a plutonium device. Despite the highly public circumstances, including the presence of reporters, the critical information "failed to register with the 'outsiders,'" although three laboratory scientists present that evening "had our hearts in our throats." Herbert Friedman, Luther B. Lockhart, and Irving H. Blifford, "Detecting the Soviet Bomb: Joe-1 in a Rain Barrel," *Physics Today,* vol. 49, no. 11 (1996), p. 41. These authors appear unaware of Senator Johnson's (apparently) earlier revelation of this same information to a much larger audience.

50. This is particularly evident in the questioning by other members of Senator McMahon and Representative Jackson following their respective floor speeches arguing for the expansion of nuclear weapons production on September 18, and October 9, 1951, respectively. See *Congressional Record,* 82 Cong. 1 sess., vol. 97, pt. 9 (1951), pp. 11496–501, and pt. 10, 12866–73.

Box 9-1

Representation of Selected Nuclear Weapons Production Facilities in the U.S. Senate, 1945–97

As can be seen from table 9-1, the turnover in Senate seats has been fairly low for those states with one or more major DOE nuclear weapons facilities.[1] These long tenures are in marked contrast to the short service of DOE secretaries (an average of less than three years since 1977) and AEC commissioners (totaling twenty-six by May 1965 and serving slightly more than three years on average), and they demonstrate the tendency for experience and hence power to accumulate in the Congress. In the JCAE, for example, from 1947 to 1962 fourteen members had served for a decade or more.[2] Senator Richard B. Russell (Democrat of Georgia) served on the JCAE from its creation until his death in office in 1971, a total of twenty-three years (during the same period, he was chairman of the Armed Services Committee). Senator (earlier Representative) Henry M. Jackson served on the JCAE for twenty-two years and was one of its more active members, serving as its vice chairman in its final year of existence. Senator John O. Pastore (Democrat of Rhode Island) also served on the JCAE for twenty-two years, eight of them as chairman. An asterisk denotes members who served on the JCAE during some phase of their Senate career.

Table 9-1. Representation of Nuclear Weapons Facilities in the U.S. Senate, 1945–97

Senator and facility	*Period of service*	*Length of service (years)*
California: Lawrence Livermore National Laboratory, 1952–present		
Barbara Boxer (D)	1993–	6
Dianne Feinstein (D)	1992–	7
John Seymour (R)	1991–92	1
Pete Wilson (R)	1983–91	8
S.I. Hayakawa (R)	1977–83	6
John V. Tunney* (D)	1971–77	6
Alan Cranston (D)	1969–93	25
George Murphy (R)	1965–71	6
Pierre Salinger (D)	1964[a]	<1
Clair Engle (D)	1959–64	5
Thomas H. Kuchel (R)	1953–69	16
Richard M. Nixon (R)	1950–57	7
William F. Knowland (R)	1945–59	14
Average length of service:		8.9
Colorado: Rocky Flats Environmental Technology Site, 1952–present		
Wayne Allard (R)	1997–	1
Ben Nighthorse Campbell (R)[b]	1993–	4
Hank Brown (R)	1991–97	6
Timothy E. Wirth (D)	1987–93	6
William L. Armstrong (R)	1979–91	12
Gary W. Hart (D)	1975–87	12
Floyd Haskell (D)	1973–79	6

1. Data provided by Michele Manon, U.S. Senate Historical Office, May 22, 1997.

2. Green and Rosenthal, *Government of the Atom,* pp. xiv–xv; Orlans, *Contracting for Atoms,* pp. 159–60.

Box 9-1 *(continued)*

Table 9-1. Nuclear Facility Representation in the U.S. Senate, 1945–97

Senator and facility	*Period of service*	*Length of service (years)*
Gordon Allot (R)	1955–73	18
Peter H. Dominick* (R)	1963–75	12
John A. Carroll (D)	1957–63	6
Eugene D. Millikin* (R)	1941–57	16
Edwin C. Johnson* (D)	1937–55	18
Average length of service:		9.8
Idaho: Idaho National Engineering and Environmental Laboratory, 1949–present		
Dirk Kempthorne (R)	1993–	4
Larry Craig (R)	1991–	6
Steven D. Symms (R)	1981–93	12
James McClure (R)	1973–91	18
Frank Church (D)	1957–81	24
Leonard B. Jordan (R)	1962–73	11
Herman Welker (R)	1951–57	6
Bert H. Miller (D)	1949	<1
Henry C. Dworshak* (R)	1946–49; 1949–62[c]	17
Glen H. Taylor (D)	1945–51	6
Average length of service:		11.6
Kentucky: Paducah Gaseous Diffusion Plant, 1951–present		
Mitch McConnell, Jr. (R)	1985–	12
Wendell Ford (D)	1974–	23
Walter D. Huddleston (D)	1973–85	12
Marlow W. Cook (R)	1968–74	6
Thurston B. Morton (R)	1957–68	11
John Sherman Cooper (R)	1956–73	17
Robert Humphreys (D)	1956[d]	<1
Alben W. Barkley (D)	1927–51; 1955–56	25
John Sherman Cooper (R)	1952–55	3
Thomas R. Underwood (D)	1951–52[e]	1
Earle C. Clements (D)	1950–57	6
Virgil M. Chapman (D)	1949–51	3
Garrett L. Withers (D)	1949–50	1
Average length of service:		9.2
Nevada: Nevada Test Site, 1951–present		
Richard H. Bryan (D)	1989–	8
Harry M. Reid (D)	1987–	10
J. Chic Hecht (R)	1983–89	6
Paul Laxalt (R)	1974–87	13
Howard W. Cannon (D)	1959–83	26
Alan Bible* (D)	1954–74	20
Ernest S. Brown (R)	1954[f]	<1
George W. Malone (R)	1947–59	12
Patrick A. McCarran (D)	1933–54	21
Average length of service:		12.9

Box 9-1
(continued)

Table 9-1. Nuclear Facility Representation in the U.S. Senate, 1945–97

Senator and facility	*Period of service*	*Length of service (years)*
New Mexico: Los Alamos National Laboratory, Sandia National Laboratories, 1943–present		
Jeff Bingaman (D)	1983–	14
Harrison H. Schmitt (R)	1977–83	6
Pete V. Domenici* (R)	1973–	24
Joseph M. Montoya* (D)	1964–77	13
Edwin L. Mechem (R)	1962–64	2
Clinton P. Anderson* (D)	1949–73	24
Dennis Chavez (D)	1936–62	26
Carl A. Hatch (D)	1934–49	15
Average length of service:		15.5
Ohio: Ashtabula Plant, Fernald Plant, Mound Laboratory, Portsmouth Gaseous Diffusion Plant, 1947–present		
Michael DeWine (R)	1995–	2
John Glenn (D)	1974–	23
Howard M. Metzenbaum (D)	1974;[g] 1976–95	19
Robert Taft, Jr. (R)	1971–76	5
William B. Saxbe (R)	1969–74	5
Stephen M. Young (D)	1959–71	12
Frank J. Lausche (D)	1957–69	12
George H. Bender (R)	1954–57	3
Thomas A Burke (D)	1953–54	1
John W. Bricker (R)	1947–59	12
Robert A. Taft (R)	1939–53	14
Average length of service:		9.8
South Carolina: Savannah River Site, 1950–present		
Ernest Hollings (D)	1966–	31
Donald S. Russell (D)	1965–66	1
Thomas A. Wofford (D)	1956	<1
Strom Thurmond (R)[h]	1954–56;[i] 1956–	43
Charles E. Daniel (D)	1954[j]	<1
Olin D.T. Johnston (D)	1945–65	20
Burnet R. Maybank (D)	1941–54	13
Average length of service:		18
Tennessee: Oak Ridge Reservation, 1942–present		
Bill Frist (R)	1995–	2
Fred Thompson (R)	1994–	3
Harlan Mathews (D)	1993–94	1
Albert A. Gore, Jr. (D)	1985–93	8
James R. Sasser (D)	1977–95	18
William E. Brock III (R)	1971–77	6
Howard H. Baker, Jr.* (R)	1967–85	18
Ron Bass (D)	1964–67	3
Herbert S. Walters (D)	1963–64	1
Albert A. Gore, Sr.* (D)	1953–71	18

Box 9-1
(continued)

Table 9-1. Nuclear Facility Representation in the U.S. Senate, 1945–97

Senator and facility	*Period of service*	*Length of service (years)*
C. Estes Kefauver (D)	1949–63	14
A. Thomas Stewart (D)	1939–49	10
Kenneth D. McKellar (D)	1917–53	36
Average length of service:		10.6
Texas: Pantex Plant, Medina Modification Center, 1952–present		
Kay Bailey Hutchison (R)	1993–	4
Phil Gramm (R)	1985–	12
Robert C. Kruger (D)	1993[k]	<1
Lloyd M. Bentsen, Jr. (D)	1971–93	22
Ralph W. Yarborough (D)	1957–71	14
John Tower (R)	1961–85	24
William A. Blakley (D)	1957; 1961[l]	<1
M. Price Daniel (D)	1953–57	4
Lyndon B. Johnson* (D)	1949–61	12
Thomas T. Connally* (D)	1929–53	24
Average length of service:		14.5
Washington: Hanford Reservation, 1942–present		
Patty Murray (D)	1993–	4
Slade Gorton (R)	1981–87; 1989–	14
Brock Adams (D)	1987–93	6
Daniel J. Evans (R)	1983–89	6
Henry M. Jackson* (D)	1953–83	30
Harry P. Cain (R)	1946–53	7
Warren Magnuson (D)	1945–81	36
Hugh B. Mitchell (D)	1945–47	2
Monrad C. Wallgren (D)	1941–45	4
Average length of service:		12.1

* Served on the JCAE.

a. Appointed by California's governor to fill the unexpired term of Senator Engle, who died on July 30, 1964.

b. Campbell changed party affiliation from Democrat to Republican in 1994.

c. Appointed by Idaho's governor to fill the unexpired term of Senator Miller, who died on October 8, 1949.

d. Appointed by Kentucky's governor to fill the unexpired term of Senator Barkley, who died on April 30, 1956.

e. Appointed by Kentucky's governor to fill the unexpired term of Senator Chapman, who died on March 8, 1951.

f. Appointed by Nevada's governor to fill the unexpired term of Senator McCarran, who died on September 28, 1954.

g. Appointed by Ohio's governor to fill a vacancy left by the resignation of Senator Saxbe on January 3, 1974.

h. Thurmond changed party affiliation from Democrat to Republican in 1964.

i. Senator Thurmond resigned from office on April 4, 1956, to fulfill a campaign pledge made in 1954, when he was elected as a write-in candidate. He was reelected as a Democrat on November 6, 1956.

j. Appointed by South Carolina's governor to fill the unexpired term of Senator Maybank, who died on September 1, 1954.

k. Appointed by the governor of Texas to fill the vacancy left by Senator Bentsen's resignation on January 20, 1993.

l. Appointed by the governor of Texas to fill the vacancy left by Senator Daniel's resignation on January 14, 1957, and again to fill the vacancy left by Senator Johnson's resignation on January 3, 1961 (to become vice president).

national secret.[51] Nearly 75 percent of the committee's hearings from 1947 to 1951 were in executive session, and through 1953 only a few committee reports were ever submitted to Congress.[52] By 1954 these practices began to change, both because the Soviet Union had demonstrated that it, too, could develop nuclear weapons and because greater openness was required to promote the civilian uses of atomic power. However, for eight crucial years of the atomic program, the eighteen-member JCAE represented the entire Congress when it came to overseeing the AEC and its multibillion-dollar budget.

But the members and staff of the JCAE did not merely oversee the nuclear program; they played a very active role in directing and promoting it.[53] Although the committee was generally passive from 1946 through most of 1949, from late 1949 onward it "generally encouraged and exhorted the willing but cautious AEC to expand programs which the JCAE regarded as important and functioned as a 'big brother,' cooperating with and protecting the AEC against its critics and those who favored curtailment of its program."[54]

One strong proponent of these programs was Senator McMahon, author of the Atomic Energy Act and the JCAE's third chairman.[55] In September 1951 he offered a Senate resolution noting that atomic energy had revolutionary potential, that "only 3 cents out of each American dollar paid for military defense has been spent upon atomic weapons" (though how he reached this conclusion is questionable), that "the allocation of 3 cents in each military dollar for our best and cheapest weapon is unreasonably and imprudently small," and that therefore "the United States must go all-out in atomic development and production."[56] Although McMahon's resolution never came up for

51. McMahon was eventually briefed by the JCAE on the size of the stockpile on September 19, 1951, as noted in chapter 8, under "Secrecy's Intangible Costs." See also Richard G. Hewlett and Francis Duncan, *A History of the United States Atomic Energy Commission,* vol. 2: *Atomic Shield: 1947/1952* (Oak Ridge, Tenn.: U.S. AEC Technical Information Center, 1972), pp. 557; Anders, *Forging the Atomic Shield,* p. 112.

52. Green and Rosenthal, *Government of the Atom,* pp. 199–200.

53. It can even be argued that the JCAE began to look upon the nuclear weapons complex as its own. In 1974 the staff of the committee unilaterally renamed Oak Ridge National Laboratory the Holifield National Laboratory to honor their retiring chairman, Chet Holifield. Congress, at the behest of the dismayed Tennessee congressional delegation and Oak Ridge community leaders, took action to restore the site's original name in late 1975. Leland Johnson and Daniel Schaffer, *Oak Ridge National Laboratory: The First Fifty Years* (University of Tennessee Press, 1994), pp. 158–59. For a discussion of the JCAE's promotion of the Aircraft Nuclear Propulsion program, see also chapter 2 in this volume.

54. The first Soviet test of an atomic bomb on August 29, 1949, the establishment of the People's Republic of China on October 1, 1949, and the start of the Korean War on June 25, 1950, were three critical reasons for this change in attitude. Green and Rosenthal, *Government of the Atom,* p. 5.

55. McMahon was also the first chairman of the JCAE, selected by its new members on August 2, 1946, the day after President Truman signed the Atomic Energy Act of 1946 and just before Congress adjourned for the first postwar elections. When the JCAE reassembled in January 1947 under Republican control, it selected Senator Bourke B. Hickenlooper (Republican of Iowa) as its chairman. McMahon was restored as chairman after the 1949 elections returned the Democrats to power. Green and Rosenthal, *Government of the Atom,* pp. 5, 8.

56. Sometime in late 1949 or early 1950, Senator McMahon became concerned about press reports that nuclear weapons were consuming upward of $1 billion annually ($8.7 billion in 1996 dollars). On January 10, 1950, AEC chairman Gordon Dean expressed similar concerns to William Borden "about the publication of false reports about the *billions* of dollars estimated [for the proposed program to develop the hydrogen bomb]." See Anders, *Forging the Atomic Shield,* p. 56. The JCAE staff, after look-

a vote, his sentiments were translated into dramatically increased funding for the 50-150 program.

At the same time, the JCAE submitted a report to Congress highlighting its own "strenuous efforts" to expedite the work of the hydrogen bomb program before Truman's January 31, 1950, announcement authorizing a crash program and renewing "its urgings that no stone be left unturned to attain necessary objectives in the shortest space of time." The report also mentioned the committee's role in encouraging the increased exploitation of new sources of uranium and suggested that "there are opportunities for faster advancement which need to be vigorously exploited."[57]

The JCAE also exerted considerable influence on the budget process. Not content to merely act on the annual requests submitted by the AEC, it routinely questioned AEC officials to elicit information on funding requests that had been submitted to the president only to be reduced or eliminated by the Bureau of the Budget before submission to Congress. Then, using its wide-ranging authority under the Atomic Energy Act, it asked the AEC for the details of those programs, often adding funds back into the AEC budget for those programs that it deemed necessary (but that were often opposed by the AEC). The JCAE appeared to be "the only Congressional committee which systematically reviews the internal budget-making process of an executive agency and the Bureau of the Budget in this manner," in effect becoming "an important participant and pleader in the formulation of the atomic-energy budget," and what it could not obtain by "negotiation," it sought "to impose through authorization legislation."[58]

ing into the matter, reported to McMahon that "less than 1/40th of our total military spending since the war has been devoted directly to atomic weapons and that only 1 percent or less of our budget as a whole since the war has been devoted directly to atomic weapons." Subsequent research and memoranda refined this estimate in May 1950, although the overall figure remained the same. However, this low figure was derived by excluding from the accounting *all* costs associated with the delivery of nuclear weapons, thus making the entire effort appear abnormally small (in 1950, for example, at least $39.2 billion—34 percent of the total DOD budget—was dedicated to "atomic energy activities." Total AEC and DOD nuclear weapons–related spending that year was 40 percent of the defense budget and 11 percent of the total federal budget). Ironically, in later years (see chapter 11) the cost of the bombs and warheads would be excluded by others to make the overall costs appear lower than they actually were. Nevertheless, McMahon used the 1/40th figure in speeches and Borden provided the figures (on a not-for-attribution basis and without explaining what they excluded) to the *Washington Post* after that newspaper ran an editorial on June 15, 1950, stating that atomic energy was costing "about three quarters of a billion dollars annually." See Memorandum, Bill Borden, February 25, 1950, to Senator McMahon; Memorandum, Walter Hamilton to Bill Borden, February 22, 1950; Memorandum, Walter Hamilton to Bill Borden, May 23, 1950 (with attachment); Memorandum, Committee Staff to the Joint Committee on Atomic Energy, "The Scale of our Atomic Weapons Effort," May 23, 1950; copy of letter from William L. Borden to Alan Barth, Editorial Department, *Washington Post,* June 17, 1950. All these documents are in JCAE General Correspondence Files, Record Group 128, Box 17, AEC Budget (Folder 2), National Archives. McMahon's speech can be found in *Congressional Record,* 82 Cong. 2 sess., vol. 97 (1951), pt. 9, pp. 11496–501. For details on early DOD and Air Force expenditures for nuclear weapons, see Lee Bowen and Robert D. Little, A History of the Air Force Atomic Energy Program, 1943–1953, vol. 3: *Building an Atomic Air Force, 1949–1953* (Washington, D.C.: U.S. Air Force Historical Division, 1959), pp. 460–96 (formerly Top Secret, declassified in 1980).

57. Green and Rosenthal, *Government of the Atom,* pp. 10–11.

58. Green and Rosenthal, *Government of the Atom,* p. 110.

In fact, the JCAE strongly questioned the BoB's role in the budget-making process, accusing it of meddling in scientific and technical matters about which it knew little. Although this practice raised important questions concerning the separation of powers, the Truman and Eisenhower administrations were by and large indifferent to it, tacitly ceding significant authority to the JCAE. Indeed, in terms of its sustained influence and accomplishments, the JCAE has been called "probably the most powerful Congressional committee in the history of the nation."[59]

The JCAE's modus operandi can best be summed up in its own words from a 1951 report to Congress: "Greater boldness and more scientific and technical daring should be brought to bear upon the program." From late 1949 onward, the JCAE encouraged a more or less unrestrained nuclear weapons program, supporting several massive expansions of AEC fissile material production and calling for the deployment of large numbers of nuclear weapons. Nuclear-powered submarines and aircraft were also strongly supported. For the most part, the programs the committee had in mind exceeded the bounds of what the Executive "deemed prudent or economical," and in its negotiations with the AEC it sometimes acted like a "sovereign" body.[60]

Despite the JCAE's enormous power and legal authority to employ an unlimited number of staff and conduct wide-ranging investigations, its operating costs were relatively modest, totaling a little more than $56 million for just over three decades of activity (including the operations of the Senate Special Committee on Atomic Energy during 1945–46, which drafted the Atomic Energy Act).[61] Nevertheless, the impact of the JCAE—both what it did and, perhaps more significantly, what it did not do—on the growth and operations of the nuclear weapons complex and the acquisition of nuclear weapons cannot be underestimated. (For the JCAE's important contribution to nuclear weapons safety, see box 9-2.) If in 1946 Congress had put the atomic-energy program under the control of conventional committees of Congress, "almost certainly, the national investment in atomic energy would have been substantially less and the present level of technology considerably lower."[62]

59. Green and Rosenthal, *Government of the Atom,* pp. 85–87, 110–13, 266.

60. Green and Rosenthal, *Government of the Atom,* p. 105.

61. This figure does not include the salaries or office-related costs of the members of the JCAE over its thirty-one-year history. The staff, while larger than many other committees, does not appear to have been excessively large. In March 1964, for example, it comprised seven professional and sixteen clerical and secretarial workers. See Joint Committee on Atomic Energy, General Correspondence, Record Group 128, Box 158, Folder Committee Budget 1946–55, National Archives; *U.S. Statutes at Large* (1950–77, inclusive); Harold Orlans, *Contracting for Atoms: A Study of Public Policy Issues Posed by the Atomic Energy Commission's Contracting for Research, Development, and Managerial Services* (Brookings, 1967), p. 159.

62. Green and Rosenthal, *Government of the Atom,* p. 266. "The vast expansion of plant for the production of nuclear materials . . to implement Truman's decision [on the Super bomb] and to outproduce the Russians, has been the single most important achievement that can be credited to the JCAE. For it led before long to the era of nuclear plenty with the diversification of

Nuclear Weapons Oversight, 1977–97

Following the dissolution of the JCAE in 1977 (approved by members of Congress frustrated with the committee's stranglehold on nuclear policy matters and carried out in conjunction with a broader reorganization of congressional committees in the wake of Watergate), its nuclear weapons responsibilities devolved principally to two sets of committees: the House and Senate Armed Services committees and the House and Senate Energy and Water Development subcommittees.[63] The Armed Services committees authorized funding and generally concentrated on delivery systems, while the Appropriations subcommittees handled funding for the newly created DOE. Over the years, a number of other committees and subcommittees have carved out responsibilities for overseeing one or more aspects of the nuclear infrastructure. At present, more than thirty are involved, as outlined in table 9-2. The costs of this oversight are estimated at $40 million a year, for a total of $760 million since the breakup of the JCAE.

Despite the number of committees and subcommittees with jurisdiction over various elements of the infrastructure, the bulk of interest and time in any given year (except from 1988 to 1992) tends to be devoted to the annual budgets for nuclear weapons programs. The occasional scandal, accident, crisis, or arms agreement may generate a period of intense interest, but this has always subsided. For example, during the 104th Congress, the Oversight and Investigations Subcommittee of the House Commerce Committee held five hearings and expended countless hours investigating the travel habits and expenses of Secretary of Energy Hazel R. O'Leary, calling into question some $5 million in costs.[64] By contrast, the status of the more than $5 billion being spent by the DOE on an annual basis to clean up half a century of accumulated radioactive and toxic waste from the nuclear weapons production complex generated comparatively little interest.[65]

nuclear weapons and strategies, the promotion of other major military and civilian uses for nuclear materials, and all the problems of subsidies, embarrassingly large hoards, and eventual economic dislocation characteristic of other too-successful government critical commodity stockpiling programs." See Orlans, *Contracting for Atoms,* pp. 160–61.

63. Bob Rankin, "House Quietly Strips Atomic Energy Committee of Legislative Powers," *Congressional Quarterly,* vol. 35 (January 8, 1977), pp. 44–45.

64. See, for example, *Department of Energy: Travel Expenditures and Related Issues,* Hearings before the Subcommittee on Oversight and Investigations of the House Committee on Commerce, 104 Cong. 2 sess. (GPO, 1996).

65. Congressional efforts in 1995 to eliminate the Department of Energy—in the interest of reducing the size of the federal bureaucracy—also demonstrated a profound lack of understanding on the part of many representatives and some senators of the current mission of the DOE. Few realized that more than 65 percent of its budget goes to the management of the nuclear stockpile and remediation and management of radioactive and toxic waste from weapons production, two activities that cannot be eliminated. These efforts were eventually shelved when proponents were unable to demonstrate that the proposed solution—creating a new agency within the DOD to handle weapons activities and transferring all cleanup work to the Environmental Protection Agency—would actually save money or improve performance. Nevertheless, presidential candidate Robert J. Dole supported the idea during the 1996 campaign and in May 1997, House and Senate Republicans reintroduced legislation to abolish the agency and transfer its nuclear weapons activities to the Department of Defense. See Associated Press, "Republicans Vow Again to Pull the Plug on Energy," *Washington Post,* May 9, 1997, p. A23.

Box 9-2
The JCAE and the Development of the Permissive Action Link

Although the JCAE took credit for creating the permissive action link (PAL) and claimed that its executive director, James T. Ramey, originated the idea, several people suggested the concept (and later the physical apparatus) of "locking" nuclear weapons to prevent unauthorized use (for further information on PALs, see chapters 1 and 3).[1] Fred Iklé, then an analyst with the Rand Corporation, is said to be the intellectual "father" of the PAL by virtue of a paper he wrote in 1957–58 on accidental nuclear war in which he suggested a mechanical lock for weapons. However, there is no evidence to suggest that Iklé or Rand ever promoted this concept or pushed for its implementation. At about the same time, scientists at Livermore, Los Alamos, and Sandia laboratories began investigating methods of controlling the use of nuclear weapons. Concepts were refined, and a prototype built at Livermore was demonstrated in the fall of 1960 before a military audience in Washington and in December 1960 for incoming Secretary of Defense Robert S. McNamara. The military officers were unimpressed and considered the device redundant in light of what they considered adequate nonmechanical controls already in effect. McNamara's response is unknown, but apparently he did not consider it an urgent matter.

During the summer of 1960 Senator Clinton Anderson, chairman of the JCAE, authorized a staff study of security at NATO bases. Ramey traveled to Sandia National Laboratories to hear firsthand about use-control measures. While there, he came across a remote control for the television in his quarters and had a brainstorm: could a similar device control the use of nuclear weapons from a central location? Returning to Washington, Ramey asked Los Alamos scientist and JCAE consultant Harold Agnew to assess the prospects for such a device (unbeknownst to Agnew, work was already well under way at Sandia). Ramey and the JCAE staff also prodded the air force to consider use-control technology for its weapons.

In November and December, a special ad hoc JCAE subcommittee on nuclear weapons security in NATO chaired by Representative Chet Holifield traveled to fifteen nuclear installations in eight countries, including Britain, Germany, Italy, and Turkey.[2] During their tour, committee members, staff, and consultants (including Ramey and Agnew) were struck by the lax protection at some sites. At one base, they were amazed to find an aircraft on quick reaction alert armed with fully operational U.S. nuclear weapons and under the control of a foreign pilot.[3] "The only evidence of U.S. control was a lonely 18-year-old sentry armed with a carbine and standing on the

1. Jack Raymond, "U.S. to Install Locks on Atom Weapons as Extra Safeguard," *New York Times,* July 6, 1962, p.1; *Congressional Record,* 87 Cong. 2 sess., vol. 108, pt. 10 (July 10, 1962), pp. 13056–58; Green and Rosenthal, *Government of the Atom,* pp. 68–69; Peter Stein and Peter Feaver, *Assuring Control of Nuclear Weapons: The Evolution of Permissive Action Links,* Center for Science and International Affairs, Harvard University, CSIA Occasional Paper 2 (Lanham, Md.: University Press of America, 1987), esp. pp. 23–51.

2. Letter from Representative Chet Holifield, Joint Committee on Atomic Energy, to President John F. Kennedy, February 15, 1961 (formerly Secret/Restricted Data, National Security Archive). In yet another display of the frequently arbitrary nature of classification and declassification decisions, a copy of this letter declassified by the Department of Energy in 1996 and released to the National Security Archive the following year deleted as sensitive national security information the words "Turkey" and "Italy" in the sentence:"In particular, the problems with Jupiter missile bases in [deleted] . . . should be considered." Given that Jupiter missiles were only ever deployed in Turkey and Italy—a well-known unclassified fact—and that all the missiles were withdrawn from service thirty-five years ago, it is difficult to understand the basis for such a deletion. Another copy of this letter located in the JCAE's files at the National Archives (Record Group 128, Box 10, Executive Session, February 20, 1961) and declassified sometime in fiscal 1988 contains no such deletions.

3. Quick-reaction alert aircraft (and later, missiles) were deployed at a number of European bases in an effort to ensure that a surprise Soviet attack would not destroy all U.S. and NATO forces before they could be used.

Box 9-2
(continued)

tarmac."[4] Alarmed that this was the only thing standing between the pilot and an unauthorized launch, the JCAE came away convinced that a better means of control had to be devised and implemented.[5]

On February 15, 1961, the JCAE sent a summary of its inspection report to President John F. Kennedy, describing "the fictional weapons custody system now in use" at NATO bases in Italy and Turkey and offering recommendations for improving NATO security. For the remainder of the year and through mid-1962, the committee held hearings to monitor the administration's progress in fixing what it viewed as a critical security problem and to examine (and try) various PAL prototypes. In June 1960 Kennedy signed National Security Action Memorandum 160 mandating the use of PALs on selected U.S. nuclear weapons. On July 5, 1962, he publicly announced he was requesting $23.3 million ($137 million in 1996 dollars) to supplement the AEC's budget and allow it to manufacture and install PALs on nuclear weapons. By September 1962, five-digit mechanical lock PALs were in place on Nike Hercules and Honest John missiles, atomic demolition munitions, the Davy Crockett, and W33 and W48 artillery shells. Early PALs were little more than mechanical locks that could have been defeated given enough time and a hacksaw. Later versions were more sophisticated, employing multiple-digit coded switches and allowing only a limited number of tries before disabling the weapon (whereupon it had to be returned to the AEC or DOE for refurbishment).

The air force and especially the navy strongly opposed PALs, arguing that they would impede operational effectiveness and thus compromise deterrence. The air force eventually acquiesced after determining that PALs would actually increase the flexibility of its operations (by allowing, for example, bombers to be scrambled on alert with the knowledge that their load of nuclear weapons could not be used accidentally). Navy tactical weapons were also slow to acquire PALs, and PALs for submarine-launched ballistic missiles were only installed in 1997.

Although PALs might eventually have been developed and deployed with U.S. nuclear weapons (given increasing security concerns as the stockpile grew from a few hundred weapons between the late 1940s and early 1950s to more than 20,000 weapons by 1962), DOD intransigence could have delayed this for many years, as in the case of the navy and its SLBMs.[6] That they were deployed when they were, and that the issue received sustained congressional and presidential attention is attributable in no small measure to the JCAE's decision to tour NATO bases in 1960 and its persistence in pressing the issue and pointing out the rather wide discrepancy between presumed and actual security measures for U.S. nuclear weapons in Europe.

---

4. Stein and Feaver, *Assuring Control of Nuclear Weapons*, pp. 30–31.

5. Interestingly, a trip in 1962 by Secretary McNamara and State Department officials Paul Nitze and Henry Rowen uncovered equally alarming problems. For example, "A road mobile German 'Honest John' unit was visited—a 'battlefield' nuclear delivery system. The warhead was with the unit, accompanied by two U.S. custodians who, Harry Rowen said, looked 'rather lonely.' They kept the secrets of their trade in what seems to be a wooden safe. . . . A Mace unit was visited. These fixed, 'soft,' air breathing, U.S.-manned 600–1200 mile ground-to-ground missiles are regularly maintained in a condition that permits them to be fired by the crews at 6 minutes' notice. They are aimed at Eastern European airfields. The warheads are kept on the missiles. Harry Rowen felt that these were the most dangerous delivery systems now in Europe, both because they could be fired so readily and because their vulnerability would create great pressure to fire them in a period of tension or limited hostilities. . . . A German strike air squadron was visited. Warheads were, of course, stored aboard those aircraft on alert status. The assumption that the German pilots do not know how to arm these warheads turns out to be fictional; on request, one of the pilots showed the U.S. visitors how this was done." Memorandum (Secret), Henry Owen, State Department, European Office, to Mr. Johnson, October 10, 1962, National Security Archive.

6. DOD officials even balked at the original wording for PALs coined by a Sandia scientist: prescribed action link. They apparently felt that the phrase connoted too much in the way of negative control and might be confused with "proscribed," implying a desire to never use the weapons. Permissive action link was the accepted compromise. Stein and Feaver. *Assuring Cntrol of Nuclear Weapons*, pp. 36–37.

TABLE 9-2.

House and Senate Committees and Subcommittees with Jurisdiction over Nuclear Weapons Programs, 1998[a]

Appropriations	*Appropriations*
Defense	National Security
Energy and Water Development	Energy and Water Development
Military Construction	Military Construction
Armed Services	*Budget*
Strategic Forces	*Commerce*
Budget	Oversight and Investigations
Energy and Natural Resources	Energy and Power
Energy Research and Development	*Government Reform and Oversight*
Production and Regulation	*International Relations*
Environment and Public Works	International Operations and Human Rights
Clean Air, Wetlands, Private Property, and Nuclear Safety	*National Security*
Foreign Relations	Military Acquisition
Governmental Affairs	Research and Technology
Select Committee on Intelligence	Oversight and Investigations
	Resources
	Science
	Energy and Environment
	Oversight and Investigations
	Select Committee on Intelligence

a. Committees are in italics.

Although it may be easier for members of Congress to understand a matter such as travel expenses (and, of equal if not greater importance, to turn such matters into political scandals that resonate with the news media and the electorate), the amount of attention devoted to minor issues such as this is, and has been, completely out of proportion to their cost and long-term import for the country at large.

Even members of Congress recognize that oversight of nuclear weapons matters is less than rigorous. Senator John Kyl (Republican of Arizona) complained: "It's perplexing when most Senators don't take as seriously as they should their constitutional responsibilities [concerning nuclear weapons oversight]." Senator Robert C. Smith (Republican of New Hampshire), chairman of the Senate Armed Services Committee's subcommittee on strategic forces was remarkably candid. "We're very lax in our oversight responsibilities in this area.

We're falling well short of the mark," he told a reporter for *Congressional Quarterly*.[66]

In conclusion, congressional oversight of the nuclear weapons program since the late 1940s can be considered a study in extremes. Periods of intense scrutiny of matters broad and narrow are interspersed with periods of relatively little attention. As with many government programs, consistent annual scrutiny of budgets, plans, and operations—when practiced at all—rarely proceeds beyond the staff level. This and the relatively high levels of secrecy surrounding most nuclear programs have allowed the nuclear weapons program to oversee itself to a large extent, a practice that unfortunately is not conducive to efficient government (some of the other agencies involved in the program's operations are discussed in box 9-3). As the twenty-first century approaches and the future size and role of the nuclear arsenal become a subject of increasing debate, Congress must devise and implement mechanisms to improve its vital oversight functions. Failure to do so will inevitably lead to the wasteful expenditure of billions of dollars and the perpetuation of unnecessary or unwise programs. Chapter 10 examines the economic implications of nuclear weapons and nuclear deterrence. A proposal to improve congressional understanding of the overall nuclear weapons budget is taken up in chapter 11.

66. Jonathan Weisman, "Who's Minding the Store?" *Bulletin of the Atomic Scientists*, vol. 53 (July/August 1997), pp. 33–34.

Box 9-3
Other Agencies and Organizations with Oversight Functions

A number of government agencies have contributed to the oversight of the nuclear weapons program. Previous chapters have detailed the costs incurred by the most important of these. Following are short descriptions of three other agencies that have been involved in the program in significant ways at one time or another.

Office of Management and Budget

The Office of Management and Budget (formerly the Bureau of the Budget) is responsible for formulating the annual budget, reconciling differences between a president's goals and executive agency requests. The OMB also monitors budgetary performance. Its total costs with respect to the nuclear weapons program are estimated to be in the low tens of millions of dollars.

General Accounting Office

The General Accounting Office is the government's auditor, examining the spending and management of government programs. Most of its work is done in response to congressional requests. Two divisions—Resources, Community, and Economic Development and National Security and International Affairs—conduct most of the audits on DOE and DOD nuclear weapons programs. The GAO issues frequent reports (in classified and unclassified versions) to government officials and the public. In 1994 the GAO had a $443 million budget, with nearly 4,600 employees and twenty-six field offices. It issued 1,115 reports and 4,200 legal rulings.[1] More germane to this study, between 1987 and 1997 the GAO issued more than 100 reports on various problems with DOE's management of the nuclear weapons complex and another several hundred on nuclear delivery systems. Although the agency is not able to provide a calculation of its discrete work related to nuclear weapons activities—which varies from year to year, depending upon congressional requests—it estimates that the average cost per report is $150,000.[2] On this basis, we estimate its historical costs related to the nuclear infrastructure to be at least $75 million.

Office of Technology Assessment

The Office of Technology Assessment was created in 1972 as an analytical arm of Congress, helping members of Congress assess technological changes and their consequences for society. In 1995, in an effort to cut costs, Congress terminated the operations of the OTA, charging that its functions duplicated those of the GAO and the Congressional Research Service. Between 1990 and 1993 the OTA produced four major reports on nuclear weapons issues: two on the environmental restoration and waste management program, one on dismantling and disposing of nuclear weapons and weapons materials, and one on proliferation issues. The total cost for these reports (including salaries and overhead) was $3.1 million.[3] Using this period as a guide, we estimate total OTA expenses related to the nuclear weapons program to be approximately $10 million.

1. Robert Pear, "Study Criticizes Objectivity of U.S. Accounting Agency," *New York Times*, October 17, 1994, p. B10.

2. Personal communication, Vic Rezendes, Director, Energy Issues, Resources, Community, and Economic Development Division, General Accounting Office, June 9, 1995.

3. Letter from Peter A. Johnson, Senior Associate, Office of Technology Assessment, to Stephen I. Schwartz, March 21, 1995. Six other significant reports were produced from 1984 to 1990. An electronic collection of every OTA report ever produced is available on the World Wide Web at http://www.wws.princeton.edu:80/~ota/.

10

The Economic Implications of Nuclear Weapons and Nuclear Deterrence

William J. Weida

The previous chapters of this book have dealt largely with the direct, measurable costs and benefits of specific nuclear arms and programs. The other costs and benefits associated with employing these weapons are much less apparent but equally important. They emanated in part from the concept of deterrence, whose rationale was partly economic. Basing the nation's defenses on nuclear weapons appeared to be less expensive because it was considered easier to implement than alternative strategies for deterring the Soviet threat, principally the perceived imbalance of conventional forces in Europe. Indeed, "by guaranteeing great damage to an aggressor" deterrence was thought to be "very much less difficult than erecting a nearly airtight defense of cities in the face of full-scale thermonuclear surprise attack."[1]

It is important to remember that deterrence was regarded as "very much less difficult" and hence less expensive than other methods of dealing with Soviet strategic forces during the cold war, when U.S. defense policy was complicated by great uncertainty regarding both Soviet intentions and the mechanics of waging nuclear war. Additional uncertainties about planning and cost factors, the strategic context,

Until the latest of our world conflicts, the United States had no armaments industry. American makers of plowshares could, with time and as required, make swords as well. But now we can no longer risk emergency improvisation of national defense; we have been compelled to create a permanent arms industry of vast proportions. . . . This conjunction of an immense military establishment and a large arms industry is new in the American experience. The total influence—economic, political, even spiritual—is felt in every city, every State house,

1. Charles J. Hitch and Roland N. McKean, *The Economics of Defense in the Nuclear Age* (Harvard University Press, 1960), pp. 339–44.

every office of the Federal government. We recognize the imperative need for this development. Yet we must not fail to comprehend its grave implications. Our toil, resources and livelihood are all involved; so is the very structure of our society.

In the councils of government, we must guard against the acquisition of unwarranted influence, whether sought or unsought, by the military-industrial complex. The potential for the disastrous rise of misplaced power exists and will persist. We must never let the weight of this combination endanger our liberties or democratic processes. We should take nothing for granted. Only an alert and knowledgeable citizenry can compel the proper meshing of the huge industrial and military machinery of defense with our peaceful methods and goals, so that security and liberty may prosper together.

—*President Dwight D. Eisenhower, Farewell Radio and Television Address to the American People, January 17, 1961*

technology, the Soviet Union and its reactions to U.S. strategies, and even chance events, created a volatile defense budgeting environment.[2] Deterrence had the potential to reduce at least some of the uncertainty and hence some of the costs. Such benefits, if real, were well worth pursuing. The trouble was that the benefits of a sufficient level of deterrence were (and are) close to impossible to calculate. Estimates of the costs varied almost as widely as the number of nuclear warheads said to be required for deterrence, which have ranged from tens of weapons to tens of thousands, depending on whose view was being propounded (see figure 3 in the introduction and chapter 2).[3]

Although the benefits of deterrence could be evaluated in terms of avoiding the costs of a nuclear war, such benefits consisted of avoiding human and other losses that cannot be adequately measured in dollars; one cannot scientifically assess the consequences of events that did not occur. Furthermore, in attempting to weigh the costs and benefits of nuclear weapons one must understand that the nuclear forces amassed by the United States during the cold war were not necessarily the sole or even the major reason for the absence of direct conflict with the Soviet Union or China. As previously explained (see the introduction), far greater sums were spent on nonnuclear forces, and these forces certainly played some part in the avoidance of nuclear war. Nor can one ignore the fact that the creation and maintenance of large nuclear arsenals on hair-trigger alert could have unleashed (and in several instances nearly did) the very conflict they were ostensibly deployed to avoid (see chapter 3).

However, the indirect costs and benefits from the production and maintenance of deterrent forces can be measured. This is partly because they do not differ substantially from any other kind of military spending and partly because they are important for political and economic reasons and thus are subject to considerable research and better record-keeping. Indirect costs and benefits include regional economic gains, employment, domestic political power, and other nonmilitary benefits. Even though indirect benefits had little to do with deterrence or other possible military uses of nuclear weapons, they frequently influenced the allocation of resources to nuclear forces.

Such allocations were further complicated by the fact that nuclear weapons were usually developed in response to the Nuclear Weapons Stockpile Memorandum (now called the Nuclear Weapons Stockpile Plan), a classified annual report by the DOD and DOE to the president on current and anticipated nuclear weapons and weapons materials requirements. Even in the defense arena, classification barriers

2. Hitch and McKean, *Economics of Defense in the Nuclear Age,* pp. 188–92.

3. See, for example, Robert Holzer, "Report Urges Deep Nuclear Cuts," *Defense News,* August 16–23, 1993, p. 8.

allowed this document to bypass most of the normal review processes, including congressional oversight.[4] As a result, it was not required to meet the normal cost-benefit criteria to which other defense documents were subjected. In addition, the vast majority of the costs for nuclear warhead research, development, testing, and production were recorded in the AEC, ERDA, and DOE budget, not the Defense Department budget.[5] This meant that the resources allocated to nuclear weapons were not obvious to the average citizen or even to many in Congress, where different committees consider separately annual funding requests for nuclear warheads and their delivery vehicles.

As patterns of resource allocation for nuclear forces evolved from this complex set of conditions, domestic political and economic criteria often played decisive roles, as they did in the case of the Strategic Defense Initiative, the *Seawolf* submarine program, and the B-2A bomber. This mix of political, military, and economic motives, coupled with the firm belief of the key participants in the validity of the concept of deterrence, shaped the future course of spending for nuclear weapons.

The Allocation of Resources to Deterrence

Deterrence was initially viewed as a "pure public good" because no one, whether or not they shared in its cost, could be excluded from its benefits. If nuclear war occurred, however, the value of deterrence as a public good might be unevenly distributed or disappear altogether. Thus deterrence was clearly a public good only as long as it did not fail—and the necessity of ensuring nonfailure created additional economic burdens.

Efficient deterrence could theoretically be achieved through actions of the free market, but the free market is notoriously bad at allocating money for public goods. Furthermore, relying on free-market mechanisms requires perfect information, but in matters of high policy such as this, "the critical elements of the problem have to be protected by secrecy."[6] Thus U.S. policymakers were forced to pursue deterrence utilizing imperfect data, perceptions, and expectations. Expectations were particularly difficult to discern because in many cases it was impossible to distinguish between "individuals' true beliefs

4. For a description of this process, see Thomas B. Cochran and others, *Nuclear Weapons Databook*, vol. 2: *U.S. Nuclear Warhead Production* (Cambridge, Mass.: Ballinger, 1987), pp. 102–20.

5. Although AEC, ERDA, DOE, and DOD funding are ultimately grouped together within the overall government budget under the rubric of "national defense," Congress has always considered them separately. For an interesting, early example of how only AEC costs were considered when calculating the nuclear weapons budget, see chapter 9.

6. Hitch and McKean, *Economics of Defense in the Nuclear Age,* pp. 339–44.

of what the future holds in store and the rosy or bleak futures that they paint to support the policy positions they advocate."[7] Hence the case for various nuclear options was frequently overstated or understated (for an early example of this, see the discussion of the bomber gap in chapter 4).

In this environment of uncertainty, policymakers had to rely on alternative, nonmarket methods for allocating economic resources to nuclear weapons, and this approach increased the costs of those weapons. Resources are most efficiently allocated when information is perfect, but the atmosphere of the cold war made good information nearly impossible to acquire. As a result, the United States often incorrectly estimated both the requirements for and the full costs of its nuclear forces. This in turn meant that many resources allocated to nuclear weapons could have been spent on other military or nonmilitary products, services, or investments or not spent at all. The effect of these alternatives would have been to decrease taxes and stimulate the private economy.

The Public and Private Impacts of Resource Misallocation

Within the federal budget, economic choice entails using limited resources for either defense or nondefense goods after considering present and future effects of this choice on the U.S. economy. When a decision is made to devote a given amount of national resources to defense, the federal government tries to rationally choose between more defense and less of other things, or vice-versa. However, "national security" is such a vague concept that a decision to increase national security usually presents no clear choice between defense or nondefense spending.

For example, the financial resources required to purchase one B-1B bomber at a cost of $333 million may imply a decision to forgo building new schools in more than twenty cities; two electric power plants, each serving a town of 60,000 people; two fully equipped hospitals; or some 30 miles (48 kilometers) of interstate highway.[8] This represents a choice with long-term security implications because federal money directed toward building infrastructure or promoting economic activity may create more economic growth than defense-related spending, and, in the long run, this may increase national security.

Because private enterprises do not rely on revenues generated from taxes, they usually create more economic activity than any form of gov-

7. Albert Carnesale, "Introduction: Framework for Analysis," in Albert Carnesale and Richard Haass, eds., *Superpower Arms Control: Setting the Record Straight* (Cambridge, Mass.: Ballinger, 1987), p. 2.

8. Author's calculations.

ernment spending. And when compared with most civilian products, the military products associated with strategic nuclear weapons have a smaller multiplier effect on the overall economy. After an ICBM is constructed, for example, it sits in its silo consuming additional resources as it is operated, manned, and supported throughout its general life. It cannot, however, be used to stimulate directly additional economic growth. Conversely, as various scholars have shown, the commercial market provides capabilities superior to defense producers.[9] For example, a newly constructed civilian tractor may be used to build roads, raise crops, or engage in other activities that increase the general level of the economy. Consequently, if imperfect information causes misallocations of the government's budget that result in higher taxes, this levies a substantial economic cost on the United States.

In sum, purchases of nuclear weapons do not enhance production capacity in the United States or increase the quantity of consumer goods. They do create a demand for additional resources to support themselves, but they do not generate new goods that can be used to offset their operating costs. Because they do not create additional goods, they also do not make additional jobs. They are end items, representing a nonrecoverable sunk cost. This means that the decision to spend money on nuclear weapons instead of something else carries a greater cost than absolute dollar amounts might imply. These economic "penalties" for spending on nuclear weapons do not mean that no such spending should occur. They simply mean one should not spend more on nuclear forces than is necessary for security reasons. Unfortunately, such an outcome is the logical consequence of believing that nuclear forces are less expensive than they actually are, of being required to make critical budgetary decisions without access to essential information—as was prevalent during the cold war—and of basing national security on the indeterminate and largely unmeasurable concept of nuclear deterrence.

Regional Economic Impacts

When defense and nondefense programs are debated on their own merits based on their contributions to national priorities, trade-offs between defense and nondefense programs are a natural consideration. When defense programs are sold by appealing to regional economic interests, however, trade-offs are difficult to discern because the opportunity costs of a national decision cannot be evaluated within a regional framework.

9. See, for example, Jay Stowsky, *The Employment Effects of International Trade in the Telecommunication Equipment Industry*, U.S. Congress Office of Technology Assessment (GPO, 1985).

Many regions in the United States derive economic benefits from the production, deployment, operation, and maintenance of nuclear forces. In the 1980s, California came to depend more than any other state on military spending, the majority of which went toward nuclear programs such as the B-1 and B-2 bombers, the Trident I, Trident II, and MX missiles, the Strategic Defense Initiative, and various satellite programs such as MILSTAR.[10] Individuals and organizations in these regions often oppose reductions in nuclear weapons or weapons-related spending not on security grounds but out of fear that it would adversely affect their economies.[11] In fact, some special interest groups and regional political forces have advanced their short-term economic interests even when those interests did not coincide with the good of the nation as a whole (and sometimes even when their own health and safety might be threatened).[12]

As a result of decisions made during the Manhattan Project and the expansion of the nuclear weapons production complex during the 1950s, nuclear weapons facilities—for reasons of security and land requirements—were usually located in isolated regions of the country. This action has had two economic consequences. First, because most components used to make nuclear weapons cannot be produced in the isolated regions that host nuclear facilities, the regional economic impact of nuclear spending is significantly reduced. Those who benefit economically from nuclear production are often far removed from the areas in which the production occurs (and thus from the costs incurred in the process).

Second, the high wage levels at nuclear facilities both help the local economy and create problems for competing employers by inflating the local wage structure.[13] Nondefense employers who cannot afford to pay what the government and its contractors pay are unable to retain skilled workers because nearly everyone desires to join the nuclear plant work force.[14] This effect is present to one degree or

10. In 1986 defense contractors based in California received 20 percent of DOD prime contract awards. The next three states combined—New York, Texas, and Massachusetts—received 21 percent. See Ricardo Pimentel, "With Jobs as Bait, It's Hard Not to Bite," *Sacramento Bee*, June 28, 1987, p. A27.

11. For evidence to support this contention see William J. Weida and Frank L. Gertcher, *The Political Economy of National Defense* (Boulder, Colo.: Westview Press, 1987).

12. Associated Press, "Iowans Debate Jobs vs. Nuclear Bomb Plant," *New York Times*, March 27, 1983, p. A27; Mark Obmascik, "DOE 'Knew' Cleanup Pacts Doomed," *Denver Post*, March 1, 1994, p. A1; United Press International, "Consultant Says Closing Pantex Would Damage Amarillo," August 3, 1993; Mike Rupe, "Pantex Fuels Economy," *Amarillo Sunday News-Globe*, December 26, 1993, p. 25A; Kenneth J. Garcia and David Perlman, "Fighting for Lethal Leftovers," *San Francisco Chronicle*, April 13, 1995, p. 1.

13. In 1997 four U.S. Air Force Minuteman ICBM bases spread across Colorado, Nebraska, North Dakota, Montana, and Wyoming employed 11,000 people and spent approximately $1 billion a year on operations and support. This "has the impact of a Fortune 500 company in a region where jobs are scarce." See James Brooke, "Counting the Missiles, Dreaming of Disarmament," *New York Times* (Washington edition), March 19, 1997, p. A16. Los Alamos National Laboratory, with an annual budget of more than $1 billion reportedly generates more than $3.4 billion in economic activity in New Mexico each year. See "From Armageddon to Animation," *Economist*, vol. 342 (January 11, 1997), p. 25.

14. For example, see James Brooke, "Atomic City Ponders Its Future after Bomb," *New York Times*, November 29, 1995, p. A20.

another around most defense nuclear sites, and it tends to drive other, nonnuclear firms out of the region, increasing economic dependency on the nuclear facility.

For the citizens of the region, the potential risk to human health is a negative "externality," which shifts part of the true cost of nuclear weapons production to the employees at the facility and to nearby residents.[15] Just such an effect can be seen at the Rocky Flats Plant near Denver, Colorado. Since the plant stopped producing plutonium triggers in 1990, many workers have been laid off, but because the potential medical risks associated with their nuclear weapons work are so great they have had difficulty finding jobs because other employers cannot afford to have them in their health insurance pools.[16] Negative externalities associated with nuclear weapons production can also place entire communities at risk when pollution makes a site (or region) unsuitable for other purposes and shifts to the community the economic costs incurred in closing a facility or converting it incorrectly. However, some DOE facilities, notably the Hanford Reservation, have experienced a significant economic boom as a result of halting production and embarking on massive cleanup programs; Hanford's program is the largest within the DOE weapons complex and therefore the country. Its ultimate cost could reach $50 billion to $100 billion.[17]

Pork Barrel Spending

The use of federal funds to create regional economic benefits is as old as the United States itself (the process is sometimes referred to as "distributive politics"). Early in the country's history, most federal pork barrel funds were allocated to the construction of infrastructure. Roads, bridges, canals, and the like were chosen because they provided an easy way to target specific areas and because they were defensible projects for every congressional district. New infrastructure enhanced economic development and increased the standard of living for the residents of the region where the funds were spent.

After World War II, large nuclear facilities became attractive to politicians who sought to use federal funds to stimulate the economy of an isolated region. To host new nuclear facilities, however, the regions had to incur substantial bonded debt to build infrastructure

15. An externality is a cost (or benefit) that is not accounted for in the normal course of operation but is, nonetheless, very real.

16. Minard Hamilton, "Countdown in the Bomb Factories," *Progressive,* March 1990, pp. 30–33; William J. Weida, Testimony in Hearings before the House Armed Services Committee on Worker Transition, June 29, 1994.

17. Bill Richards, "Nuclear Site Learns to Stop Worrying and Love the Boom," *Wall Street Journal,* August 28, 1992, p. A1; Jim Lynch and Karen Dorn Steele, "River of Money," *Spokane Spokesman-Review,* November 13, 1994, p. A1; Timothy Aeppel, "Mess at A-Bomb Plant Shows What Happens If Pork Gets into Play," *Wall Street Journal,* March 28, 1995, p. A1.

and provide amenities, debt that could not be repaid if the facility closed or reduced its work force. This made the region highly dependent on the employment provided by the facility, and it often meant that further economic growth was linked, in the minds of the citizens of the region, to new nuclear projects. Continually justifying a series of these projects required ever-increasing weapons requirements (see chapter 2). Unfortunately, the negative externalities (pollution, inflated wage structures, health hazards, and the like) accompanying many nuclear weapons facilities depressed other regional economic activity and made host regions even more dependent on federal funds. This, in turn, increased each region's efforts to retain existing defense projects and to secure new ones.

The use of nuclear weapons to channel federal funds into regions was a logical step in the evolution of pork barrel spending. Deterrence is an elusive concept, depending not only on what one considers a deterrent but what one believes one's opponent considers a deterrent, judgments that are necessarily highly subjective and thus capable of supporting a broad range of potential programs. But deterrence was also viewed as being absolutely essential to the survival of the United States, especially during the first two decades of the cold war. Such "clarity of need," when coupled with "fuzziness of purpose," made nuclear weapons ideal candidates for political and economic justification. In a political sense, deterrence-based projects are easier to defend precisely because their performance requirements are so uncertain. In an economic sense, the tie between regional economic benefits and nuclear weapons created a powerful force for continued weapons production and an economic inertia that made it difficult to wean a region away from nuclear weapons or to stop a production process.

Thus, when the Johnson administration decided in January 1964 to reduce the production of plutonium and end the enrichment of uranium for the weapons program, "the cutbacks were announced and carried out in a piecemeal fashion, with closure of a few major facilities at a time, over a period of 6 years." This was done because the AEC "hoped to mitigate the economic impact by spacing out the shutdowns" (even though President Lyndon Johnson, in announcing the cutbacks, asserted that the reactors should not be a "WPA nuclear project, just to provide employment when our needs have been met.") Yet the Atomic Energy Commission never publicly announced its policy, and the decision to stretch out the shutdown only prolonged local anxieties and led to the creation of formidable political coalitions that sought to keep the reactors open.[18]

18. Rodney P. Carlisle with Joan M. Zenzen, *Supplying the Nuclear Arsenal: American Production Reactors, 1942–1992* (Johns Hopkins University Press, 1996), pp. 147–51, 161. The AEC complicated its own efforts and fed this anxiety by never publicly stating that the reason for the shutdown of the plutonium reactors and the end to HEU production was that a

Employment and Economic Stimulation

Like all forms of spending, nuclear weapon spending boosts employment. At the start of the Reagan administration's military buildup, $1 billion in defense spending created about 35,000 jobs. By 1985 this figure had dropped to about 25,000 jobs, because of changes in the nature of military spending.[19] In the mid-1980s DOD weapons operations directly employed between 115,000 and 120,000 people, most of whom were military personnel at about 50 bases in the United States and 160 bases in Europe and elsewhere.[20] At the same time, the DOE employed about 65,000 people to design and build nuclear weapons: 20,000 at three national laboratories and about 45,000 at as many as seventeen facilities producing nuclear warheads and processing nuclear materials.[21] In addition, between one-third and one-half of U.S. aircraft production and almost all missile production was for nuclear-capable delivery systems.[22] The aerospace industry employed about 550,000 production workers and a total work force of about 1,151,000, including management, research and development, and support staff.[23]

Defense spending is one tool of fiscal policy, and the Reagan administration's military buildup in the early to mid-1980s clearly demonstrated how defense spending can stimulate the economy. When viewed from the perspective of past military buildups, however, both the nuclear and conventional defense spending increases of the Reagan administration were small enough that the initial Keynesian effects were roughly comparable to those experienced in recent non-

large surplus of both materials had been achieved and that no further production was required. Instead, it explained that some of the reactors would be placed on "standby," leaving the distinct impression that the closures might be only temporary. The AEC's refusal to cease immediately plutonium production once requirements were met also led to unnecessary economic waste in that the material was not actually needed, and long-lived nuclear waste resulted from processing activities that would not otherwise have been carried out. Russia faces a similar problem, running two plutonium production reactors solely to keep people employed. "This is economically ruinous for the country, not just because no one needs more plutonium but because it is expensive to store," said physicist Yuri I. Yershov of the Obninsk Institute of Atomic Energy. "But to shut down the main source of employment in a city of 100,000 is a tall order. For social reasons, the plants keep producing." Quoted in Carol J. Williams, "Experts Troubled by Russia's Lax Nuclear Security," *Los Angeles Times* (Washington edition), April 8, 1996, p. A3. In September 1997 Russian president Boris Yeltsin announced that production of weapon-grade plutonium would cease by 2000. See Carol J. Williams, "Russia Vows Not to Make Plutonium for Bombs," *Los Angeles Times* (Washington edition), September 24, 1997, p. A1. For a more detailed treatment of this issue see Oleg Bukharin, "The Future of Russia's Plutonium Cities," *International Security*, vol. 21, no. 4 (1997), pp. 126–58.

19. DOD figures, David Blond, Program Analysis and Evaluation, Washington, D.C., 1985.

20. Donald R. Cotter, "Peacetime Operations: Safety and Security," in Ashton B. Carter, John D. Steinbruner, and Charles A. Zraket, eds., *Managing Nuclear Operations* (Brookings, 1987), p. 18.

21. Cotter, "Peacetime Operations," pp. 20–21.

22. Frank L. Gertcher, and G. T. Kroncke, *U.S. Aerospace Industry Space Launch Vehicle Production,* a preliminary research report for the National Defense University by R&D Associates, RDA-TR-301200-001, Colorado Springs, Colo., December 1985.

23. Gertcher and Kroncke, *U.S. Aerospace Industry Space Launch Vehicle Production.* See also U.S. Department of Commerce, *U.S. Industrial Outlook* (GPO, 1987).

defense programs.[24] This is further confirmed by a 1982 study that found that the effects of defense spending on the U.S. economy were similar to those of nondefense spending.[25] For these reasons, one could stimulate employment and the economy with any type of government expenditure. However, for the reasons stated earlier in this chapter, defense spending to support economic rather than security objectives is generally an inefficient way to accomplish national fiscal objectives or to generate "spin-off" civilian products.[26]

The Special Nature of Nuclear Weapons Contracts

The decision to award a contract for a missile or bomber is, by definition, a decision to award that contract to a single producer and its subcontractors, just as it is also a decision to spend the allocated amounts for that program in one or more well-defined regions of the United States. In the case of nuclear warhead production, a decision to purchase additional warheads avoided even the risk of competing for contracts. Warheads were produced in established government-owned facilities and the decision to build them was a decision to spend money in places such as Broomfield, Colorado (the Rocky Flats Plant), Aiken County, South Carolina (the Savannah River Site), and Amarillo, Texas (the Pantex Plant). From an economic standpoint, a monopoly producer was both created and perpetuated. As a semiofficial history of the AEC/DOE production reactor program notes:

> Not only was production of plutonium and tritium controlled by the government as a monopoly, but consumption was all taken by the government, a single-consumer situation that economists call a "monopsony." This unique arrangement . . . represented an anomaly in the American industrial world. . . . None of the operating contractors . . . risked major capital investments in the enterprises; the contracts provided for cost reimbursement. Demand was not driven by a free or even by a regulated economic market but by the

24. National Research Council, *The Impact of Defense Spending on Non-defense Engineering Labor Markets* (Washington, D.C.: National Academy Press, 1986), pp. iii, 3, 5.

25. Data Resources, Inc./McGraw-Hill, "Defense Spending and Jobs," *Defense Economics Research Report,* vol. 2, no. 11 (1982), p. 4.

26. This was recognized as early as 1950, in a critique of NSC 68 by the Bureau of the Budget: "It is neither necessary nor desirable to regard military expenditures per se as a method of maintaining high employment. Large and growing military expenditures not only would divert resources from the civilian purposes to which they should be put but also would have more subtle effects on our economic system. Higher taxes, if necessary, would have a proportionately dampening effect on incentives and on the dynamic nature of the economy, without any offsetting productive impact from the expenditures. The rate of private investment might be slowed down unless special measures or controls were undertaken. There would be a continuing tendency to reduce public expenditures for developmental purposes which are highly desirable for the continual strengthening of our economy." Memorandum, Deputy Chief of the Division of Estimates, Bureau of the Budget (Schaub) to the Executive Secretary of the National Security Council (Lay), "Comments of the Bureau of the Budget [on NSC 68]" (Top Secret), May 8, 1950, reproduced in Everett S. Gleason and Fredrick Aandahl, eds., *Foreign Relations of the United States, 1950,* vol. 1: *National Security Affairs: Foreign Economic Policy* (GPO, 1977), p. 305.

> single customer's weapons policy. . . . As a result of the Cold War and the imperatives of the nuclear standoff, this aspect of the American economy resembled the economy of the Soviet Union, in which decisions were made on a planned basis by a remote government, without reference to market forces, behind closed doors, for reasons that would not be made public.[27]

Nuclear weapon contracts can be precisely targeted at a region only with the support of a broad group of politicians, all of whom are advancing their own favorite programs. In 1995 nearly half a billion dollars in additional funding for B-2A bombers was allocated out of a tight federal budget and over the objections of the air force. To comprehend why this was done, it helps to understand that Los Angeles county, which was just starting to recover from a major recession caused by earlier cuts in defense contracts, discovered that 59 percent of all remaining defense work in the region was based on just two military aircraft contracts, the B-2 and the C-17.[28] With 1996 an election year and California being an important political battleground, forcing the air force to take unwanted B-2s was an obvious pork barrel solution to a difficult regional economic problem.

During this process, specific military requirements for additional B-2s did not exist. Northrop, the B-2A contractor, tried to convince air force officials that the aircraft had a valid conventional war mission, but in the eyes (and words) of the populace and its elected representatives, the purpose of the new contract was clearly to stimulate the regional economy.[29] When a contract is sold on its economic benefits, people attempt to retain that contract in their community for the same reasons. When people are not convinced of the purpose or operational necessity of the weapon produced by the contract (but see it primarily or entirely in economic terms), it is equally understandable that arguments about obsolescence and lack of military requirements carry little weight.

Related Costs of Nuclear Weapons

Nuclear weapons impose a number of related but often intangible economic costs that can be divided in several kinds as they relate

27. Carlisle and Zenzen, *Supplying the Nuclear Arsenal,* pp. 160–62.

28. Daniel Flaming, Mark Drayse, and Michael Beltramo, "Seven Years into the Meltdown: Defense Conversion in Los Angeles," Presentation at the American Economic Association, San Francisco, Calif., January 7, 1996; Patt Morrison, "Payloads, Paydays, and Palm Trees," *Los Angeles Times,* December 5, 1993, p. A1.

29. James F. Pelz, "No Need for More B-2's Clinton Says," *Los Angeles Times* (Washington edition), February 9, 1996, p. 1; Bradley Graham, "U.S. to Add One B-2 to 20 Plane Fleet," *Washington Post,* March 22, 1996, p. A20; Robert Scheer, "Why Worry? Learn to Love the Bomber," *Los Angeles Times* (Washington edition), July 11, 1995, p. 11. During an earlier congressional debate in 1994, when the issue concerned whether or not to cap production at twenty bombers, Senator Dianne Feinstein (Democrat of California) proclaimed on the Senate floor that the B-2 was essential because it carried a heavy "payroll." Her remarks were later revised in the *Congressional Record* to read "payload." See Lawrence J. Korb, "Peace without Dividend: Why We Can't Seem to Cut the Defense Budget," *Washington Post,* July 9, 1995, p. C1.

to opportunity, performance, capital, resource consumption, and inflation.

Opportunity Costs

Among the most important costs of nuclear weapons are opportunity costs. These refer to what one gives up by making an economic choice. They occur at three major points: first, when the weapon is built and purchased and the significant radioactive and hazardous waste involved in this process is safely disposed of (although this latter activity may not occur until decades after a weapon is built); second, when the weapon is deployed and maintained; and third, when the weapon is decommissioned and the additional nuclear waste generated by decommissioning must be safely stored.

The more transparent resource allocations are, the more closely the stated costs of a nuclear weapon (or any defense project) will approximate its true costs because the opportunity costs will be more fully expressed. For example, the costs of nuclear weapon-related waste have generally been hidden by federal government subsidies that either ignored the magnitude of the pollution problems or sought storage methods that placed the material out of sight in isolated regions of the United States (see chapter 6). This practice kept the opportunity costs incurred in waste generation from being fully expressed and artificially depressed the stated costs of the weapons involved.

Efficiency versus Effectiveness

A major difference between military and civilian projects is that military projects are, by necessity, concerned principally with performance, not economic efficiency. This is particularly true of nuclear weapons. Design follows philosophy, and this key difference creates production methodologies that often lead to higher costs (see "What Do Nuclear Bombs Cost" in chapter 1). However, these higher costs do not translate to more jobs. Manufacturing nuclear weapons is a capital-intensive activity, and since nuclear jobs tend to be more highly paid, few direct jobs are created. For the defense industry as a whole, a study by the Congressional Research Service estimates that nondefense spending produces 16 percent more jobs than defense spending.[30]

30. Linda Levine, "Defense Spending Cuts and Employment Adjustments," Congressional Research Service Report for Congress 90-55E, Library of Congress, 1990.

The Cost of Capital

Government borrowing to finance a deficit tends to raise the general level of interest rates and "crowd out" other potential investments. This condition is further exacerbated when interest rates are kept high to entice foreign lenders to invest in U.S. debt. To the extent that demand for investment in nuclear defense has crowded out other, valid investment requirements in the economy in general, the share of the gross domestic product (GDP) allocated to nuclear weapons has potentially lowered both the productivity and competitiveness of the U.S. economy (the same situation attains in Russia, although deeper structural problems exacerbate the problem there).

Resource Consumption

Research in the United States and Britain on the general tendency of military spending to consume resources required for other, nonmilitary manufacturing (called the depletionary effect) has suggested that the demand for human and physical resources to develop and build nuclear weapons crowds out other potential users of these resources. This and other work depicts these capital outlays as unproductive investments.[31] However, depletionist arguments await further testing.

Inflationary Effects

Because nuclear weapons are not available for sale to absorb the extra income generated by their production, the government may have to increase taxes to absorb the added purchasing power it has created. If such measures fail to absorb the added purchasing power on a large scale and the large-scale budget deficits this implies, the effect will usually be inflationary.[32] Since the late 1960s, however, citizens of the United States have generally been unwilling to support increased taxes to finance any federal spending.[33]

Capital Misallocation and Other Investment Implications

Private capital raised by defense companies in open markets is subject to the normal forces of those markets. To the extent that the produc-

31. For example, see Seymour Melman, *The Pentagon and the National Debt: The Consequences of the Global Military Mission of the United States* (Northampton, Mass.: Aletheia Press, 1994); Lloyd J. Dumas, ed., *The Socio-economics of Conversion From War to Peace* (Armonk, N.Y.: M. E. Sharpe, 1995); Keith Hartley, *NATO Arms Cooperation: A Study in Economics and Politics* (London: George Allen & Unwin, 1983); Kenneth E. Boulding, *The Structure of a Modern Economy: The United States 1929–1989* (New York University Press, 1993).

32. Charles L. Schultze, Testimony before the Subcommittee on Economic Goals and Intergovernmental Policies, Joint Economic Committee, Congress of the United States, Washington, D.C., October 13, 1981, p. 3.

33. Weida and Gertcher, *The Political Economy of National Defense,* p. 18.

ers of nuclear weapons receive government subsidies, however, profits in these industries may be inflated.[34] One such subsidy relieved defense nuclear site managers of all liability for activities that occurred at their plants.[35] Allocation of capital to companies that are subsidized in this manner may be significantly increased because the risk of investment has been lowered. The fact that during the cold war many companies (such as General Dynamics, FMC, Singer) left the nondefense market and concentrated on defense business provides evidence that higher profits were available in defense contacting. Many others, while still engaged in nondefense pursuits, became heavily dependent on military-related contracts (Westinghouse is a notable example). A study by the DOD confirmed that higher profits were earned by defense contractors than by comparable durable goods industries in the period 1980–83.[36] This tends to crowd nondefense industries out of the market and it may raise the cost of capital in these industries.

Empirical work suggests large trade-offs between military spending and investment in Europe. It appears that from 1949 to 1971 U.S. military spending was inversely related to investment (as spending increased, investment decreased), as a result of two wartime buildups in an economy close to full capacity.[37] Since 1971 there seems to have been a trade-off between consumption and military spending, which implies a decline in living standards and in key human capital expenditures.[38] Military spending, it has been suggested, has a depressing effect on investment, trade, and productivity when feedback effects are taken into account.[39]

General Wage Effects: Two Competing Hypotheses

A 1980 report to the House Armed Services Committee, along with other studies, claimed that because unemployment was low among skilled technical and professional workers before the start of the Reagan military buildup, the demand for engineers was so great that salaries would rise dramatically.[40] Hence military spending during the first two years of the Reagan presidency may have caused inflation in

34. For numerous examples of subsidies to the defense industry see Weida and Gertcher, *The Political Economy of National Defense,* chap. 8, pp. 135–44.

35. The contract under which Du Pont managed the Hanford Reservation during the Manhattan Project protected the company from any and all losses it might incur (in addition to reimbursing it for *all* costs). See chapter 6.

36. U.S. Department of Defense, "Defense Financial and Investment Review," Washington, D.C., June 1985.

37. David Gold, "The Impact of Defense Spending on Investment, Productivity, and Economic Growth," Defense Budget Project, Washington, D.C., 1990.

38. See, for example, Boulding, *The Structure of a Modern Economy;* and Michael Edelstein, *What Price Cold War? The Accumulation of Physical Capital, and Economic Growth: the United States, 1890–1980* (Canberra: Australian National University, 1986).

39. Michael Dee Oden, "Military Spending Erodes Real National Security," *Bulletin of the Atomic Scientists,* vol. 44 (June 1988), pp. 36–42.

40. Robert W. DeGrasse, *Military Expansion, Economic Deadline: The Impact of Military Spending on U.S. Economic Performance* (Armonk, N.Y.: M. E. Sharpe, 1980), p. 12; *The Ailing Defense Industrial Base: Unready for Crisis,* House Rpt., Defense Industrial Base Panel of the Committee on Armed Services (GPO, December 31, 1980), p. 13.

high technology sectors while the rest of the economy remained depressed, and it may have taken a disproportionate number of engineers and scientists out of the civilian sector and placed them in military projects. Furthermore, engineering talent could become more expensive for all firms, diminishing the competitiveness of nondefense firms that could not employ enough engineers and scientists.

However, a 1986 study by the National Academy of Engineering could identify none of these problems.[41] Instead, the NAE study found:

1. "In the mid 1980s, when defense production was rising sharply, the companies included in the [wage/employment] Index [for electrical and aerospace engineers] did not find it difficult to fill scientific and technical positions."
2. "There is no evidence that the defense program seriously depleted the supply of Ph.D.-level engineers and scientists available for non-defense work."
3. "There is no evidence at present that either the defense sector or the commercial sector is lacking in appropriate representation of the 'best' of our engineers."

These statements, when coupled with the fact that "average salaries were almost identical for those entering commercial work as for those entering government contract work (mostly defense) in 1983–84," indicate that the supply of engineers and scientists easily filled the needs of both the defense and nondefense sectors.

National Costs

According to the Organization for Economic Cooperation and Development (OECD), public expenditures, particularly for social programs, have increased much faster than economic output in all major industrialized nations.[42] This means that U.S. social and economic programs were not an either/or proposition when compared with nuclear weapon spending and goes a long way toward explaining the ultimate scale and pace of the U.S. nuclear weapons program: the underlying strength of the economy allowed several large crash programs and rapid buildups in the 1950s and 1960s and provided for general economic growth at the same time.

From the evidence on the relationship between long-term spending and GDP,[43] it seems that nonbasic military spending in R&D and other "support" areas has little impact on increasing productivity. Congres-

41. *Impact of Defense Spending on Non-defense Engineering Labor Markets,* pp. 8, 10–11.

42. "The Rise in Public Expenditure—How Much Further Can It Go?" *OECD Observer,* no. 72 (May 1978), p. 8.

43. See Richard Meyer, "Of Swords and Ploughshares," *Financial World,* vol. 162, no. 12 (1993), pp. 20–22; and Oden, "Military Spending Erodes Real National Security."

sional Budget Office models suggest that only publicly funded agricultural research has been productive, and there is little return on other types of public spending. Even where there appears to be a long-term, positive relationship between growth and spending on public infrastructure, military capital spending does not contribute to growth.[44] There is also some evidence to suggest a tradeoff between military spending and civilian public investment in areas such as infrastructure.

Conversion from Defense to Civilian Production

Resources devoted to nuclear weapons are a sunk cost. The inability to reuse the resources dedicated to nuclear weapons production differs markedly from the ability to convert many other defense facilities because:

1. Conversion was never an objective when nuclear facilities were built—security and isolation were.
2. The technologies used in manufacturing nuclear weapons are significantly different from those used in normal manufacturing.[45] Many of the skills necessary to produce nuclear weapons are unique.[46] Conversion is difficult in facilities constructed to build esoteric weapons and especially when the government wants to retain nuclear weapons and the capability to remanufacture them indefinitely, and thus places both technologies and facilities off-limits.[47]
3. Buildings and other facilities have been highly contaminated.
4. The land on which production plants sit is usually isolated, and large parts of it are contaminated.

---

44. David Alan Aschauer, "Genuine Economic Returns to Infrastructure Investment," *Policy Studies Journal,* vol. 21, no. 2 (1993), pp. 380–90.

45. For example, "the unique heavy-water design of the reactors at Savannah River eventually led to another problem, not apparent at first. In 1955, when all five reactors were operating, there was no commercial reactor industry in the United States. . . . By the 1980s, about a hundred had been built. Almost all of the power reactors used either pressurized or boiling water for cooling and moderating. . . . This meant that the state of the art of reactor operation at Savannah River grew and changed in considerable isolation from the practices and methods in the burgeoning reactor industry. As time went on, that technological and cultural isolation became more pronounced." A similar issue became apparent at Hanford following President Johnson's 1964 decision to scale back plutonium production. In an effort to keep the reactors operating, local civic boosters proposed a number of alternative uses, including "using one of the older reactors as a test reactor or as a training unit for reactor operators." But the "reactors were of unique design. Their light-water cooling and graphite moderation were not suited to power production. . . . Training on a once-through water-cooled graphite-moderated reactor had little bearing on the operational needs of the new pressurized water and boiling water reactors that were emerging as the standards for American commercial power production through the 1960s." See Carlisle and Zenzen, *Supplying the Nuclear Arsenal,* pp. 90–91, 157.

46. "Many [nuclear weapons complex workers] have no counterparts in private industry, for example, those engaged in fabrication of plutonium and enriched uranium or the assembly of high explosives and plutonium." See *Report of the President's Blue Ribbon Task Group on Nuclear Weapons Program Management, Appendix 3: Cost Issues,* July 1985 (formerly Sigma 3/Restricted Data), p. 2.

47. See, for example, Stephanie Simon, "Marketing a Nuclear Wasteland," *Los Angeles Times* (Washington edition), February 4, 1998, p. A1.

5. Much on-site groundwater at nuclear production sites is contaminated. In many cases there is little or no prospect of cleaning up or even containing this contamination.
6. The scientific and technical personnel who for decades have seen their vital mission as building nuclear weapons are often reluctant to engage in other types of work or have difficulty applying their specialized and highly classified skills to the commercial sector.[48]

These factors create additional costs when nuclear weapons facilities are decommissioned. Although cleanup and decommissioning produces jobs, the burden of paying for decommissioning remains with the taxpayers. Thus resources devoted to nuclear weapons can be considered to have a "future negative" value: countries that spend the most for nuclear weapons suffer the largest "future negative" resource loss, especially if their programs downplay or ignore important environmental or safety issues, as is starkly apparent in the emerging history of the Soviet nuclear program.[49]

Federal Research and Development Funding

In the United States, military R&D consumed more than 80 percent of all federally funded R&D from 1955 to 1960, dropping to about 50 percent between the mid-1960s and the mid-1980s before rising again to 70 percent of all federally funded R&D and 30 percent of total R&D in the early 1980s.[50] By 1994 federally funded military R&D still consumed 55 percent of all federal R&D funding, and the percentage was expected to remain roughly the same in 1995–96.[51] Nuclear weapons

48. Christopher Anderson, "Weapons Labs in a New World," *Science,* vol. 262 (October 8, 1993), pp. 168–71; Robert Lee Hotz, "Learning to Live without the Bomb," *Los Angeles Times,* December 22, 1994. p. A1; Jane Meredith Adams, "Cold War's Demise Has Makers of Nuclear Weapons Scrambling," *Dallas Morning News,* April 17, 1995, p. 1. For a more detailed discussion of the potential contributions of the nuclear weapons laboratories after the cold war, see Office of Technology Assessment, *Defense Conversion: Redirecting R&D,* OTA-ITE-522 (GPO, 1993), esp. pp. 73–120.

49. For example, high-level nuclear waste from processing operations at Chelyabinsk-65 has been discharged directly into Lake Karachay, a 65.5-acre natural lake, for decades, making it the most polluted place on Earth. In 1967 a severe drought exposed the radioactive sediments on the lake bottom, causing them to be dispersed by winds over an area larger than the state of Maryland. In 1990 a site visit and analysis by Western observers found that radiation exposure in the area where waste is discharged into the lake "is about 600 rem per hour, sufficient to provide a lethal dose within an hour." Thomas B. Cochran, Robert S. Norris, and Oleg A. Bukharin, *Making the Russian Bomb: From Stalin to Yeltsin* (Boulder, Colo.: Westview Press, 1995), pp. 103–08. See also chapter 6 of this volume and Michael R. Gordon, "Siberian Village Rethinks Cost of Nuclear Projects," *New York Times,* August 19, 1994, p. A10; John-Thor Dahlburg, "The Atom Sows Crop of Sadness," *Los Angeles Times* (Washington edition), September 2, 1992, p. A1; John-Thor Dahlburg, "Soviet Nuclear Bomb Drive Took a Vast Human Toll," *Los Angeles Times* (Washington edition), September 3, 1992, p. A1; John-Thor Dahlburg, "A Nuclear-Tainted Russia Hunts for Affordable Cure," *Los Angeles Times* (Washington edition), September 4, 1992, p. A1; Tara Sonenshine and Jay LaMonica, "The Most Polluted Spot on Earth," *New York Times,* February 15, 1992, p. A23; Michael Dobbs, "In the Former Soviet Union, Paying the Nuclear Price," *Washington Post,* September 7, 1993, p. A1.

50. David Holloway, *The Soviet Union and the Arms Race,* 2d ed. (Yale University Press, 1984), p. 134.

51. National Science Foundation, *Federal R&D Funding by Budget Function: Fiscal Years 1994–1996,* NSF 95-342 (Arlington, Va., 1995), pp. 7, 11–12.

were, and are, large consumers of this R&D funding. Taken together, DOE nuclear defense programs, DOD research operations, and the National Institutes of Health in 1995 accounted for two-thirds of all federal support for academic R&D.[52] Military R&D has two unique characteristics: it distorts new technology and encourages expensive applications with little marketability, and it may lead to military or government control of scientific and technological information, which may prove to be detrimental to scientific and technological progress in the civilian sector.[53]

Most military R&D, and most of the R&D performed by the nuclear weapons laboratories, is applied research. Little funding goes toward basic research. In the 1980s, only 12 percent of the budget for military R&D was spent on basic technology.[54] Whereas total military research and development in the United States rose from $27 billion in 1981 to $47 billion in 1989, the amount spent on basic research fell from $4.27 billion to $3.97 billion over the same period.[55]

The decision to allocate federal R&D funds to programs that generate little basic research has serious long-term implications. According to some, it set U.S. technology back twenty years.[56] In the 1990s, the nuclear weapon laboratories have engaged in increasing competition with other users of government research money (private labs, colleges, universities) for a shrinking pool of research assets. National support for federally funded research and development is declining, and spending for this category of R&D has fallen 7 percent in real terms since 1988.[57] This competition will make it more difficult for productive civilian projects to receive federal funding and thus raises the overall cost of such projects.

Because of the length of time over which cold war funding for R&D occurred, it is now possible to view the results and to evaluate their

52. Irwin Goodwin, "Washington Reports," *Physics Today,* June 1995, pp. 43–44.

53. DeGrasse, *Military Expansion, Economic Deadline,* p. 12. A 1970 Defense Science Board report was especially critical on this point: "The Task Force emphasizes that there are very great disadvantages to extensive reliance on secrecy in our society. . . . [C]lassification of technical information impedes its flow within our own system, and may easily do far more harm than good by stifling critical discussion and review or by engendering frustration. There are many cases in which the declassification of technical information within our system had a beneficial effect and its classification has had a deleterious one." The examples cited for beneficial effects were the U.S. lead in microwave electronics and computer technology, the peaceful uses of nuclear reactors, and transistor technology. "As a result of considerations of this kind, the Task Force believes that much of research and exploratory development . . . should generally be unclassified." See Office of the Director of Defense Research and Engineering, *Report of the Defense Science Board Task Force on Secrecy,* July 1, 1970, p. 9.

54. Judith Reppy, "Conversion From Military R&D: Economic Aspects," Paper prepared for the 38th Pugwash Conference, Dagomys, USSR, August 29–September 3, 1988, p. 2.

55. Mark Thompson, "Research, Development for Defense Takes Beating," *Gazette Telegraph,* Colorado Springs, Colo., April 3, 1988, p. A15.

56. Robert DeGrasse Jr. and Paul Murphy, "The High Cost of Rearmament," *Bulletin of the Atomic Scientists,* vol. 37 (October 1981), p. 20. See also Rosy Nimroody, "The Trillion Dollar Brain Drain," *Science Digest,* August 1986, pp. 51–57; Ken Garcia, "The 'Star Wars' Drain," *San Jose Mercury News,* June 15, 1986, p. 1A; and Don Shannon, "'Star Wars' Would Absorb New Research Funds, Provide Few Benefits, Study Says," *Los Angeles Times,* October 27, 1984, p. A18.

57. Linda R. Cohen and Roger G. Noll, "Privatizing Public Research," *Scientific American,* September 1994, pp. 72–77.

effect on the U.S. economy. If benefits from government-funded R&D outweighed costs, one would expect growing technological superiority in the United States.[58] However, American firms experienced their greatest losses to foreign industries during this period in areas such as aircraft, electronics, and machine tools, where military R&D predominated. There is little evidence that the United States received any benefits that could not have been achieved more cheaply through normal, nonmilitary research and development.

The nuclear weapons labs are generally involved in applied science: in fiscal 1992, just 17.4 percent of R&D funding for all the DOE's national laboratories was spent on basic research, versus 27.2 percent on applied research. While 52.4 percent ($2 billion in then-year dollars) of all DOE R&D funding was spent on research related to commercial product development, most of this was performed at the principal nuclear weapons laboratories (Lawrence Livermore, Los Alamos, and Sandia) and was supported by the DOE's defense and nuclear energy programs.[59] At present, little research in applied science is done at U.S. universities because the National Science Foundation prefers nonapplied work, and the DOD generally only funds work with specific mission or hardware applications. Thus the three nuclear weapons labs now occupy a niche served by no other segment of the research community.

Unfortunately, the classified nuclear work at the three labs seriously hampers their ability to conduct good applied research in useful civilian fields.[60] The labs have had difficulty successfully juggling the demands of classified and nonclassified research, and it is clear that if applied research for civilian projects is actually a goal of federally funded research, it could be achieved faster and more cheaply in facilities removed from the control of nuclear weapons developers.[61]

The federal government has increased the numbers of scientists and engineers through various programs associated with defense and nuclear weapons activities. The National Academy of Engineering has confirmed that an "effective policy [for increasing the numbers of

58. DeGrasse, *Military Expansion, Economic Deadline,* pp. 13–14.

59. General Accounting Office, *National Laboratories: Are Their R&D Activities Related to Commercial Product Development?,* PEMD-95-2 (November 1994), pp. 1–17. The above figure and this report concern the ten multiprogram DOE laboratories: Argonne National Laboratory, Lawrence Berkeley Laboratory, Oak Ridge National Laboratory, Battelle Pacific Northwest Laboratory, Idaho National Engineering and Environmental Laboratory, Lawrence Livermore National Laboratory, Los Alamos National Laboratory, Sandia National Laboratory, Brookhaven National Laboratory, and the National Renewable Energy Laboratory. All but the NREL are involved—to varying degrees—in the nuclear weapons and nuclear waste programs.

60. See, for example, Stephen Budiansky, "Keeping Research Under Wraps," *U.S. News & World Report,* March 22, 1993, pp. 48–50.

61. Office of Technology Assessment, *Defense Conversion: Redirecting R&D,* pp. 97–120. In 1996 the DOE, under pressure from congressional Republicans and citing a lack of funds, sharply scaled back its program (which started in 1990) of encouraging cooperative research and development ventures between its national laboratories and private industry. See Andrew Lawler, "DOE to Industry: So Long, Partner," *Science,* vol. 274 (October 4, 1996), pp. 24–26; Claudia Deutsch, "The Private Sector Life of a Government Lab," *New York Times,* August 23, 1997, p. 25.

engineers] after World War II was federal direct support for research grants and contracts in such areas as military, nuclear, space, energy, environmental technology and medical research, as well as in basic scientific research."[62] This same goal could conceivably have been achieved as a matter of national education policy without relying on nuclear or military-related funding.

Direct By-Products or Benefits of Nuclear Weapons Production

Military R&D creates both civilian and military technologies, some of which are generated as an indirect result of the original research activities. These "spin-offs" are often used to justify the existence of the program from which they originated.[63] Government agencies such as the National Aeronautics and Space Administration, which were open to public scrutiny, often justified their levels of funding with lists of the spin-offs they created. In other, more secretive programs such as nuclear weapons, there were fewer reasons to justify expenses and hence fewer spin-offs were publicized.

Proponents of military R&D as an effective economic stimulus believe spin-offs from military technology affect all sectors of the economy and thus enable the United States to recoup money spent on defense-related R&D. They cite spin-offs from early military spending that resulted in the concepts of mass production, interchangeable parts, and the use of semiautomatic and automatic milling machines. In addition, they note that military research and development created the ENIAC computer and was responsible for most early microchip development.[64]

However, more recent experience with spin-offs has not been good. A 1984 study by the House of Representatives Budget Committee's Task Force on Economic Policy and Growth found that despite the claims of defense advocates, recent military research and development did not generate many "spin-off" benefits to the civilian economy.[65] Commercial spin-offs entail a choice: are they a justification for mili-

62. *The Impact of Defense Spending on Non-defense Engineering Labor Markets,* p. 4.

63. See, for example, Malcolm W. Browne, "The Star Wars Spinoff," New York Times Magazine, August 24, 1986, p. 19; David C. Morrison, "Star Wars' Healing Spin-Offs," *National Journal,* vol. 23 (May 11, 1991), p. 1140.

64. Bill Thomas, "Military Spin-offs, Engines of Change," *Best of Business Quarterly,* Spring 1987, p. 45. There is occasionally confusion, however, over what begat what. For example, journalist and author Martin Walker claims that Boeing's venerable 707 aircraft "began life as a military [KC-135] refueling tanker for the Strategic Air Command." Martin Walker, *The Cold War: A History* (New York: Henry Holt, 1993), p. 140. In fact, "The Boeing Military Airplane Company's model 367-80 was the basic design for the commercial 707 passenger plane as well as the KC-135A Stratotanker." U.S. Air Force Fact Sheet 92-21, "KC-135 Stratotanker," October 1992.

65. Gerald F. Seib, "Defense Buildup Threatens Long-Term Economic Growth, House Report Asserts," *Wall Street Journal,* April 24, 1984, p. 62.

tary spending, or should they be regarded as a natural, albeit infrequent, result of spending military funds? Both common sense and economic theory indicate that deliberately targeted resources are more likely to produce desired research results at a lower cost and, once classification rules are factored in, perhaps in a shorter period of time as well. Indeed, one can argue that if spin-offs are an important economic consequence of spending for research and development, spin-offs from the much larger civilian sector of the U.S. economy should have had such a profound effect on the development of military goods that they significantly lessened the need for military R&D. That this has not occurred demonstrates that relying on spin-offs from military programs is an inefficient way to support civilian research in comparison with direct funding of civilian projects.[66]

Nuclear weapons were developed during an era of dramatic technological advancement in virtually all fields. How many of the products derived from these advances were specifically due to funding and research in the military sector as opposed to the general inertia in the field itself will never be known. In all probability, they could have been realized at less cost by directly investing in their research. However, whether such products and processes would have been developed at all is a complicated issue. According to economic theory, if demand exists, supply will follow in a free market. But military research and procurement are not part of a free market and are not responsive to normal consumer decisions. Instead, a potential product is generated through a subsidized federal research program with little or no thought given to whether it has other, peaceful uses. Often, this product is then "sold" to a defense establishment that had no idea of its existence or potential uses until a defense contractor or researcher explained the product's possibilities (for how this was done with warheads, see chapter 1). Long after it is sold to the government, a search for market-driven civilian demand is conducted as a way to use the already developed article. In recent years, NAVSTAR satellites, originally developed to provide pinpoint accuracy for ballistic missiles and other weapons systems (see chapter 3), have gained wide commercial use as providers of data to on-board automobile electronic atlases and hand-held directional finders. Technology first developed to detect warheads for the SDI is now used to detect breast cancer.

As a result of this complicated, nonmarket approach, determining a value for these articles, or determining the percentage of their value that was added by nuclear weapon research, is impossible. Many items related to nuclear weapons never survived the search for a civilian

66. For a description of these problems see Daniel Charles, "Labs Struggle to Promote Spin-offs," *Science*, vol. 240 (May 13, 1988), pp. 874–76.

market. Without judging their merits or utility, one can say that the items listed in box 10-1 do appear to have valid uses in a peacetime economy.

Conclusion

Important defense interests such as deterrence must be funded in a way that preserves the strength inherent in the U.S. economy. When defense programs are easy to define and specify, a routine allocative process provides all the accountability necessary to accomplish this. However, if a program is difficult to define clearly, as deterrence was (and is), and if the allocation must be done in a cold war political environment, a rational allocative process is almost impossible to sustain.[67] Instead, what is likely to happen is exactly what the United States experienced: the urgency, classification, and politics of spending for nuclear deterrence often proceeded with grossly insufficient congressional and public scrutiny to allow it to be compared accurately with other uses of national resources.

The penalty paid by the United States for procuring nuclear forces in this manner was substantial. The allocation of resources to nuclear weapons sometimes had little discernible relationship to the levels of threat these weapons were supposed to counter. Furthermore, the indirect costs outlined in this chapter were undoubtedly increased by the immunity nuclear spending had from strict accountability, especially at the height of power of the Joint Committee on Atomic Energy. This leads to the presumption that the United States allocated more resources than it should have to nuclear weapons, though exactly how much more can never be precisely quantified.

The key lesson from this history is that standardized procedures for allocating government funds are unlikely to prove satisfactory in circumstances that are both new and threatening to the nation. History offers compelling evidence of the impossibility of adequately predicting the future for either military or economic planning. This implies a need for a flexible and diverse economy to adequately support political or military alternatives such as deterrence that our country elects to pursue. But the economy cannot achieve flexibility

67. For example, "No one can 'prove' how many nuclear weapons are appropriate, excessive, or inadequate, but, given the limited potential savings from reducing nuclear forces and the serious consequences of being wrong, we should not try to find the right level essentially by trial and error." Brent Scowcroft and Arnold Kanter, "Which Nuke Policy?" *Washington Times,* March 24, 1997, p. A15. Brent Scowcroft and Arnold Kanter were arguing against calls to reduce the U.S. nuclear arsenal, but their reasoning works equally well in the opposite direction. As already demonstrated (see chapter 2 in this volume), a process akin to "trial and error" was indeed largely responsible for the ultimate size of the nuclear arsenal, as well as the size of the individual weapons programs comprising it.

and diversity unless ways are found to allocate rationally national resources in a manner that allows reasonable economic trade-offs between defense and nondefense spending. The attempt to fund deterrence in a cold war environment has shown that even for the most worthwhile programs, reasonable economic trade-offs cannot occur if regional economic concerns, spurious political motivations, or unrealistic assessments of needs and threats are allowed to dominate spending decisions. Chapter 11 offers some recommendations for improving our understanding of the comprehensive costs of U.S. nuclear weapons programs along with some conclusions from this study.

Box 10-1

Items Developed in Connection with the U.S. Nuclear Weapons Program with Actual or Potential Nonmilitary Uses

End products

Nuclear power reactors[1]

NAVSTAR global positioning system (GPS): satellite mapping and location[2]

Space launch vehicles: using retired Atlas, Titan, and Minuteman ICBMs and Thor IRBMs[3]

Ablative technology: ceramic materials for high heat

Insensitive explosives: makes explosives safer

Shock-absorbing materials: for packing and insulation

Composite materials: high strength and low weight

Flat panel displays: for computer use in rugged conditions

Improved computers

Component chips, boards, and the like

The Internet[4]

Hard copy technology

Information storage

Human interface and visualization technologies

Database systems

Networks and communications

Portable telecommunications equipment and systems

Human genome research

Brilliant products: for robotics and monitoring uses

Semiautonomous or integrated local systems: sense environmental facts and react accordingly[5]

Intelligent vehicles

Advanced structural materials: providing new flexibility, strength, and lightness

Electronic and photonic materials: improved conductivity

Electronic components: for miniaturized uses

Sources: The following have identified one or more of these products/processes as potentially useful for civilian economic activities: Susan Strong, Council for Economic Conversion, 1994; Council on Competitiveness, *Gaining New Ground: Technology Priorities for America's Future* (Washington, D.C., 1992); Greg Mello and Lisa Oberteuffer, "The Conversion of Los Alamos National Laboratory to a Peacetime Mission: Barriers and Opportunities," Los Alamos Study Group, Santa Fe, New Mexico, November 1, 1992, pp. VI-7, 8; Letter from Greg Mello and Marylia Kelley, to Dr. Carl Anthony, Chairman, East Bay Conversion and Reinvestment Commission, December 14, 1993; and Greg Mello, unpublished paper, January 22, 1994.

1. Commercial nuclear power reactors are a direct spin-off of the navy's nuclear propulsion reactor program. The first commercial nuclear power reactor, built at Shippingport, Pennsylvania, between 1954 and 1957, was based on a scaled-up version of a discontinued aircraft carrier reactor designed by Westinghouse's Bettis Atomic Power Laboratory. The reactor achieved criticality on December 2, 1957. While a technical success, the cost of the plant's 60 megawatts of electricity was ten times higher than the prevailing rate. See Jack Dennis, ed., *The Nuclear Almanac: Confronting the Atom in War and Peace* (Reading, Mass.: Addison-Wesley, 1984), pp. 70–72. The total cost for constructing Shippingport and R&D (borne by the Atomic Energy Commission) was $210 million ($1.5 billion in 1996 dollars). Richard G. Hewlett and Francis Duncan, *Nuclear Navy: 1946–1962* (University of Chicago Press, 1974), p. 402.

2. John Mintz, "U.S. Opens Satellites to Civilians," *Washington Post*, March 30, 1996, p. A1. In April 1996, South Carolina legislator David Thomas proposed using the GPS system to track parolees, who would wear special electronic bracelets subject to constant monitoring. "Spy in the Sky," *USA Today*, April 2, 1996, p. A3.

3. Edmund L. Andrews, "New Careers for Cold War Relics," *New York Times*, April 15, 1994, p. D1.

4. The Internet was originally a program sponsored by the Defense Department's Advanced Research Projects Agency to provide a survivable communications link between military bases in the event of nuclear war. The concept was first posited by researcher Paul Baran at the Rand Corporation, the air force think tank. Baran's specific concern was to provide a secure means for civilian and military officials to order a retaliatory nuclear strike, thus reducing the incentive to resort to launch-on-warning out of fear that the communications network would not survive an attack. A limited network connecting four universities—called ARPANET—was created in 1969; by 1971 there were fifteen nodes in the network. By the end of 1992 there were one million computers connected to what had become the Internet. See Peter Grier, "In the Beginning, There Was ARPANET," *Air Force Magazine*, January 1997, pp. 66–69; Mike Mills, "A Pentagon Plan Became the Internet," *Washington Post*, July 2, 1996, p. A6.

5. Environmental sensing devices (ESDs) were originally developed for the nuclear weapons program in the late 1950s to prevent the accidental or unauthorized detonation of a warhead. ESDs are an integral

BOX 10-1
(continued)

Microelectronics
Electronic controls
Opto-electronic components
Electronic packaging and interconnection
Displays
Energy: generation and storage
Hydrogen fuels
Direct solar
Thermal
Photovoltaics
Meteorology and geodesy: for predicting global-warming trends, violent storms, earthquakes[6]

Technology development for current and future commercial use
Battery technology
Nanoelectronics
Electro-optics[7]
Advanced materials
Aeronautical technology
Global positioning systems

Production processes: improvements to existing commercial methodologies
Precision machining
Command and control information systems
Improved electronic design and manufacturing
Improved mechanical design and manufacturing
Improved materials processing
Atomic scale manipulation of materials

Targeting technology: location, analysis, and guidance technologies
Geological surveying
Precision mapping
Precision photography (for targeting)
Pollution monitoring devices (from surveillance)

Fission by-products
Tritium: commercial uses such as replacing radium in watches, self-illuminating exit signs
Americium-241, a radioactive decay by-product of plutonium used in most ionizing smoke detectors
Depleted uranium (uranium-238)—for armor-piercing shells and armor and shielding
Cesium-137: used in commercial source applications (for example, radiography and food and medical irradiation)
Cobalt-60: commercial and medical irradiation.

---

part of the warhead. They measure certain environmental parameters such as acceleration, rate of spin, and free fall (which ones depend on the type of warhead), and they arm the warhead only if the measured parameters correspond to those encountered under conditions of normal use. Thus an ESD aboard a warhead that falls off a missile would not register the appropriate conditions necessary to arm itself and the warhead would not explode (additional design features also ensure that this does not occur). These devices also prevent an unauthorized user from attempting to use a warhead for a purpose other than that for which it was designed (for example, a terrorist could not simply steal a missile warhead and detonate it). An important exception to this, however, was atomic demolition munitions, essentially nuclear land mines, which by design did not experience any environmental stresses before detonation.

6. For example, see William J. Broad, "U.S. Will Deploy Its Spy Satellites on Nature Mission," *New York Times*, November 27, 1995, p. A1.

7. In 1996 an underwater laser scanner originally developed to study sunken Soviet submarines was used to scan the Long Island Sound for debris from TWA Flight 800. Previous nonmilitary uses included scanning an underwater sewage pipe for a leak and producing photographic quality images of rare clams and worms on the floor of the Gulf of Mexico. See Andrew C. Revkin, "Cold-War Laser Aids T.W.A. Hunt," *New York Times*, August 1, 1996, p. B1.

11

Strengthening Atomic Accountability

Stephen I. Schwartz

> **I believe that in a democracy, where the affairs of government are the business of all the people . . . that the people can be depended upon to make the proper decision—if they have the facts. I don't believe that any other position is defensible in a democracy.**
>
> —*Governor Val Peterson, Director, Federal Civil Defense Administration, September 1953*

U.S. nuclear weapons clearly played a major role in the prosecution of the cold war. Yet the tit-for-tat escalation in weaponry and the remaining uncertainties regarding Soviet policies make it impossible to know exactly which threats or crises were avoided, what risks were incurred in producing and deploying large numbers of weapons, and what risks will arise in the future as a result of past nuclear policies. The evidence assembled here indicates that with more effective and consistent oversight by Congress and the executive branch, deterrence could have been achieved and maintained at much less expense and with significantly less danger of exacerbating global tensions or triggering the very conflict we sought to avoid. One need only examine the impact of public pressure in the 1950s and 1960s to end atmospheric nuclear testing, and of efforts in the 1980s to curtail hazardous nuclear weapons production activities, to realize that more widespread knowledge of the costs and risks associated with the U.S. nuclear weapons program would likely have led the public (and many in Congress) to demand similar changes. That such a debate on costs never occurred is directly attributable to the government's own failure to understand the costs and the use of secrecy to impede discussion where costs were known.[1]

1. For example, beginning in 1986 the DOD restricted the release of *unclassified* information concerning the costs of particular elements of the strategic defense initiative in an effort to curb public discussion of the program. See Michael R. Gordon, "Pentagon Curbing Public Data on 'Star Wars,'" *New York Times*, January 26, 1987, p. A25.

The nuclear weapons complex was given a virtual blank check—or blank checkbook—and allowed to spend public money with remarkably little fiscal oversight, congressional or otherwise. That is to say, the government made almost no effort to ensure that deterrence was achieved at the least possible cost and burden to American taxpayers. The great fear of war—nuclear or otherwise—through much of this period helps to explain, but does not adequately justify, this abandonment of fiscal responsibility.[2] Indeed, the threat of deliberate or accidental nuclear war may well have been aggravated by the intensity of the nuclear arms race. Certainly, the costs and dangers facing the post–cold war world arising from large stockpiles of nuclear weapons and fissile materials are far greater than they would have been had the number of warheads and quantities of materials produced been significantly lower.

Exactly how much of this country's $5.5 trillion investment in nuclear weapons to date was "wasted" as a consequence of this inattention will remain a matter of debate, both because there has never been a fixed or even approximate numerical goal or endpoint for deterrence and because "waste" is in the eye of the beholder. Many observers would classify the nuclear-powered aircraft program as a waste of $7 billion because it never produced anything approaching a workable concept and diverted critical resources away from more urgent programs such as the development of ICBMs. But what about the more than $1.6 billion expended on Safeguard C, the thirty-year effort to ensure that the United States was able to resume atmospheric nuclear testing on short notice? Or the more than $400 billion expended on air defense, in part after it was understood that the Soviet bomber program posed no large-scale threat to the United States? Or the estimated 16,500 tactical nuclear-weapons produced and deployed under the New Look on the faulty and unquestioned assumption that they were a less expensive form of deterrence than conventional weapons? What we can say is that, at a minimum, hundreds of billions of dollars were expended on programs that contributed little or nothing to deterrence, diverted limited resources and effort away from those that did, or created long-term costs that exceeded their benefits (as in the case of the overproduction of fissile materials).

Moreover, the desire to quantify precisely what was "required" for deterrence diverts attention from the fundamental point that the way in which nuclear weapons programs were managed violated the core principles and practices of fiscally sound democratic governance. The

2. In 1989, during the first public congressional debate on the B-2 bomber, Representative Floyd Spence (Republican of South Carolina) argued that the cost of the B-2 bomber was irrelevant in light of the plane's contribution to national defense. "If the B-2 bomber can help keep us free then it is one of the most cost effective programs we have. Cost? What price tag do you put on freedom?" he asked his colleagues. Representative David Dreier (Republican of California) added, "If we spend too much for our national security, what do we lose? We lose something very important, some money. If we spend too little. . . . We violate our oath of office to 'provide for the common defense.'" *Congressional Record,* 101 Cong. 1 sess., vol. 135, no. 2 (July 26, 1989), p. H4309.

notion of the 1950s that nuclear weapons provided "a bigger bang for a buck" was accepted despite contemporary evidence that this assumption would not hold up to careful scrutiny. The appropriate question to ask today is not how much or how little should have been spent (to which there will never be a single, unambiguous answer), but rather why have numerous government officials over more than fifty years failed consistently to ensure that what was expended on nuclear weapons was spent wisely and in the most efficient manner?

Although it can be argued that excessive or wasteful spending is a perennial problem in the United States, and while it may be tempting to compare the nuclear weapons program to welfare or agricultural subsidies or other entitlement programs in this regard, nuclear weapons are different in one critical respect: the costs of nuclear weapons programs are largely unknown, as evidenced by the extensive analysis in the preceding chapters. In contrast, the costs of entitlement programs are frequently debated in Congress and are readily available in government documents to anyone who cares to look. Whatever problems have been encountered in managing and disbursing entitlements, they are at least well understood; indeed, the well-known failures and abuses of the system have led to frequent and sustained calls and periodic legislation to either pare back or eliminate particular programs, most recently in 1996. But the costs of nuclear weapons have never been fully understood or compiled by the government, and in more than half a century Congress has taken action to terminate nuclear weapons programs only a handful of times. Indeed, it has never held a hearing, debate, or vote on the cost, scale, pace, or implications of the overall program, even though the potential for waste, fraud, and abuse is at least equal to that for entitlement programs.[3]

This study represents the most comprehensive review to date of the costs and consequences of the U.S. nuclear weapons program and infrastructure. Still, time, resources, and the continued classification of crucial data have prevented a truly definitive accounting. That vital task we leave to future historians and scholars, and to the government officials we hope will assist them in their efforts. Before doing so, we offer some comments about the unfinished research agenda and several recommendations derived from our findings.

Paths for Future Research

The most obvious and important gap in our knowledge concerns the discrete costs of the sixty-five types of nuclear warheads and bombs

3. This is evident in that both programs consumed roughly equivalent amounts of public funding over the same period of time (see figure 2 in the introduction).

manufactured between 1945 and 1990. Although there remain valid reasons for withholding information on the precise amount of nuclear materials in each weapon, we believe strongly that the continued classification of *all* costs related to specific nuclear warheads—including the aggregate cost of nuclear materials in most weapons—is both misguided and counterproductive.[4] It is misguided because the "secret" of the bomb was revealed decades ago. Even the amount of material required to achieve a chain reaction is well known.[5] While official budget data would be a valuable resource for historians and scholars, in terms of assessing the trends in warhead costs over time and the relation of these costs to particular missions, they would be of little use to anyone attempting to ascertain exactly how U.S. nuclear weapons were assembled or what they contain(ed).[6] The continuing classification is counterproductive because it wastes scarce government resources, and because the data could help constrain future nuclear proliferation by revealing the relatively high cost of even crude nuclear weapons.

It is also unfortunate that the budgetary data compiled by the DOE and its predecessors do not clearly indicate how much was spent per element to produce the estimated 825 metric tons of highly enriched uranium, 103.5 metric tons of (weapon and fuel-grade) plutonium and estimated 495 pounds (225 kilograms) of tritium for the weapons and naval nuclear propulsion programs since the mid-1940s. Such figures would be especially useful in understanding how funds for the various expansion programs of the 1950s were utilized. Given that huge surpluses of plutonium and HEU were generated as a result of these efforts, it is important to know exactly how these funds were expended. While it may be the case that the data do not actually exist (time and resources precluded this study from undertaking a comprehensive review of historical documents at each DOE production facility), and while DOE would likely argue that releasing costs would allow someone to calculate the per unit cost of each material, the release of the

4. Because certain nuclear weapons (principally artillery shells), now retired, used only highly enriched uranium, even the aggregate cost of nuclear materials in these weapons could possibly provide enough information to calculate the total amount of material they used. If so, we would support releasing only the total cost of such weapons without providing a breakdown on the cost of the individual components.

5. The weight of the plutonium core of the first nuclear device—nicknamed the Gadget—detonated on July 16, 1945, was actually declassified and published in 1975; it was about 13.5 pounds (6.1 kilograms). This device was essentially identical to the Fat Man bomb detonated over Nagasaki. The Little Boy bomb dropped on Hiroshima reportedly used about 132 pounds (60 kilograms) of HEU. Modern weapons are much more efficient. Nongovernmental experts have argued that current international safeguards for plutonium and HEU be tightened, so that the minimum amount considered dangerous from the standpoint of being able to construct a nuclear weapon would be lowered from 17.6 pounds (8 kilograms) of plutonium to 2.2 pounds (1 kilogram) and from 55.1 pounds of HEU (25 kilograms) to 6.6 pounds (3 kilograms), but the International Atomic Energy Agency has refused. See Thomas B. Cochran, William M. Arkin, and Milton M. Hoenig, *U.S. Nuclear Forces and Capabilities,* vol. 1: *U.S. Nuclear Weapons Databook* (Cambridge, Mass.: Ballinger, 1984), pp. 31–32; Thomas B. Cochran and Christopher E. Paine, "The Amount of Plutonium and Highly-Enriched Uranium Needed for Pure Fission Nuclear Weapons," Natural Resources Defense Council, Washington, D.C., April 13, 1995; William J. Broad, "A Smuggling Boom Brings Calls for Tighter Safeguards," *New York Times,* August 21, 1994, p. A1.

6. For more on this point, see the discussion beginning on p. 93.

total cost for the entire program per element (as opposed to a year-by-year accounting) would eliminate this potential problem. In any event, if these costs are as crudely calculated as weapon costs, the DOE's concerns are moot (see chapter 1).

In addition, a better understanding of U.S. nuclear history requires detailed information about the cost of every nuclear weapons test. We have included data that we have been able to locate with a reasonable amount of effort, but we know that more remains to be uncovered. For every test, a detailed report, usually including a separate section on costs, was prepared. These data would shed light on the scale of the testing effort, especially the enormous costs involved in testing at Enewetak and Bikini. Some of the reports reside in the DOE's Coordination and Information Center in Las Vegas; many more apparently remain at the weapons laboratories. The DOE ought to provide scholars a means of access to the cost portions of the test reports (along with other unclassified portions). Access to the full set of data would allow a detailed assessment of the costs associated with weapons development, versus weapons effects, versus safety and reliability testing. Although mostly of historical importance, these data could be helpful in assessing the scale of weapons development in other countries.[7]

Turning to nuclear delivery systems, we find great disparity in the information on the annual operations and support costs for these weapons. Several figures currently exist and each is different. Because these are current rather than historical costs, it remains disturbing that there is no agreed upon figure: these data have considerable impact on current and future budget debates and on assessments of what it will cost to maintain various levels of nuclear forces in the future. Although this issue must ultimately be resolved by the various government agencies involved, researchers in and out of the government can provide valuable input on the matter.

Perhaps the murkiest expenditure data relating to nuclear weapons concern the costs borne by U.S. intelligence agencies to support nuclear weapons operations. Notwithstanding the recent decisions by the CIA to declassify the total U.S. intelligence budget for fiscal 1997 and 1998, the time is long overdue for the routine disclosure of the

7. Ironically, Russia has already provided a great deal of this information to the United States. From December 1992 through December 1995, the Defense Special Weapons Agency paid 200 senior Russian nuclear weapons designers more than $300,000 to write a secret history of the Soviet Union's nuclear testing program from 1949 until 1990 (each author was actually provided only about $500, with the remainder covering expenses and taxes). The resulting seventeen chapters, with illustrations, provided unprecedented details of specific tests that the United States expended tens of billions of dollars to uncover during the cold war (see chapter 3). Although it did not discuss specific weapons designs or deployment information (concentrating instead on scientific analyses of the test results and their impact on people and the environment), DSWA has thus far refused to release the document, citing Russian claims that the information is sensitive and should only be made available to properly cleared government and contractor employees. Others (including one of the authors of this book) argue that if the information is not secret it should be made available to the public, especially since public funds paid for it. See David Hoffman, "Russians Wrote Atomic History for Pentagon," *Washington Post*, October 27, 1996, p. A1.

aggregate annual intelligence budget; indeed, the open secret of the annual figure makes a mockery of the entire classification system (see chapter 3). While recognizing the need to keep secret certain aspects of the overall intelligence effort, we strongly support breaking down the annual intelligence budget into functional components (or at least segregating nuclear weapons-related expenditures from all others) so that lawmakers, scholars, the media, and the public can better comprehend how funds are being expended. Although some categories might necessarily overlap (for example, SIOP target analysis and selection and counterproliferation), such a functional approach would offer significant benefits while safeguarding the costs and operational details of any particular program or agency.

We have attempted such an approach with regard to the nuclear side of the equation, though it is admittedly less detailed than we would have preferred. Nevertheless, if extended across the spectrum of intelligence programs, it would go a long way toward demystifying the intelligence budget and community. This should be seen not as an effort to expose programs or to eliminate them, but as a way of furthering democratic debate about a crucial aspect of U.S. national security at a time when it is buffeted by charges of incompetence and mismanagement. Such scrutiny is sorely needed to properly inform the calls and proposals for reform.

Now that much of the historical data detailing the cost of building and deploying the nuclear arsenal have been assembled, new attention should be focused on the costs associated with maintaining and dismantling that arsenal. These should include the costs of day-to-day operation and support, of taking apart the warheads (and storing or disposing of their fissile materials), and of dismantling missiles and missile silos, strategic bombers, and ballistic missile submarines. Verification measures under the INF, START, and test ban treaties should also be assessed and tracked. Although such costs historically have been relatively small compared with those of the buildup of nuclear weapons, they assume increasing importance with the end of the cold war and the pursuit of deeper cuts in the arsenal. Quantifying the historical and current trends can help improve fiscal planning for the future.

The environmental aftermath of nuclear weapons production and deployment also requires careful attention. Although the DOE began monitoring its expenses and providing detailed annual assessments through its *Baseline Environmental Management Reports,* this effort has now been terminated in favor of a far less comprehensive one. Furthermore, most of the DOD costs pertaining to nuclear base cleanups, while significantly smaller than the DOE's obligations, remain unknown because of their aggregation within the overall defense environmental restoration budget. More effort should be made to understand the costs related to decontaminating former nuclear bases, both to assess the complete budgetary implications of the overall program and to provide sound guidance for the future.

Much also remains to be done in assessing the full costs of exposure to radiation and fallout from mining, production, and testing. In the past several years, various programs have been established (or are in the process of being established) to monitor the health of some plant workers and civilians living downwind of production and test sites (see chapter 7). These studies are generating valuable data about the long-term consequences of the U.S. nuclear weapons program and its relative indifference to the impact of nuclear weapons production on health. Such programs are of concern not only to the people who were adversely affected but also to scholars seeking to understand the total impact of the U.S. program. They should be of interest to policymakers as well, insofar as many of the costs may ultimately be borne by taxpayers.

Recommendations

The overall sum expended to date by American taxpayers for nuclear weapons is significant: nearly $5.5 trillion. More telling, however, is the fact that taxpayers and government decisionmakers had no idea what that figure was (and is) or how it came to be so large. This lack of knowledge and, perhaps more important, the lack of understanding about the history of the overall program, has important ramifications for ongoing debates about nuclear weapons.

For example, during 1996 and 1997 several members of Congress supporting legislation mandating the deployment of a nationwide missile defense system by 2003 argued that such a measure was required in part because until the advent of the Strategic Defense Initiative in 1983 little had been spent on missile defense programs; nor had any such system ever been deployed. In fact both of these assertions were false, and their promulgation contributed to the failure to pass the legislation when it became known to the Congress at large and the public that nearly $100 billion had already been spent on such programs with little tangible benefit.[8]

8. Joseph Cirincione, "Why the Right Lost the Missile Defense Debate," *Foreign Policy*, No. 106 (Spring 1997), pp. 39–55. For example, Representative Curt Weldon (Republican of Pennsylvania) wrote: "In the mid-1970s and early 1980s, Congress funded, without controversy or fanfare, programs that researched potential defenses against missile threats. However, these programs received minimal funding and little attention from members of Congress. Not until President Ronald Reagan's 'Star Wars' speech on March 23, 1983, did the concept of missile defenses receive national attention." ("Why We Must Act at Once," *Orbis*, vol. 40/1 [Winter 1996], pp. 63–69). Senator John McCain (Republican of Arizona) similarly wrote: "This country has spent 13 years and $38 billion to develop capabilities to defend effectively our citizens and our troops overseas from ballistic missile attack. It is time we deployed a system that will defend Americans at home." ("The Missile Threat the White House Ignores," *Wall*

In late 1996, the Department of Energy announced that at an average projected cost of $4.0 billion a year (revised to $4.5 billion in September 1997, equal to $4.3 billion in 1996 dollars), its stockpile stewardship and management program to maintain nuclear weapons in the absence of nuclear testing would cost less on an annual basis than what was spent during the cold war to produce and test new nuclear weapons. Yet data analyzed for this book demonstrate that from 1948 to 1991 average annual spending for the activities now called stockpile stewardship was $3.6 billion, $700 million *less* per year than the DOE's proposed program (see chapter 1). The release of these data prompted immediate questions in Congress and elsewhere about how the DOE's program of extremely limited weapons production and simulated testing could exceed cold war–era costs encompassing large-scale production and testing.

Although the costs of nuclear weapons have declined dramatically in recent years with the cancellation of modernization programs and the dismantlement of many weapons systems, current costs remain significant: amounting to some $35 billion a year, or about 14 percent of the annual defense budget. Without a full understanding of the present and future costs, policymakers are ill equipped to assess the budgetary ramifications of decisions concerning the nuclear stockpile, including the costs of retaining forces scheduled to be dismantled under the START II Treaty should it not be ratified by the Russian Duma.[9]

We therefore recommend that Congress pass legislation requiring the president to prepare and submit annually with each year's budget request a report detailing the comprehensive costs of all nuclear weapons–related government programs. The Office of Management and Budget should be designated the lead agency for assembling this report, which in addition to the costs for the budget being submitted should include the actual costs for the prior year and the estimated costs for the following year. If data were assembled on an annual basis, lawmakers, executive branch officials, policy analysts, journalists, and

Street Journal, May 22, 1996, p. A22). Representative Robert Erlich (Republican of Maryland) asked the readers of a column he wrote when the United States completed construction of a national ballistic missile defense system—1958, 1963, 1971, or 1985—and then provided the answer: "none of the above. In fact, the real answer is never." In reality, the answer is 1975, the year the Safeguard system became operational (see chapter 4). Robert Erlich, "Missile Vulnerability Grows," *Defense News,* January 13–19, p. 21.

9. Demonstrating the great uncertainty surrounding the current costs of nuclear weapons, in 1996 and 1997 DOD officials estimated that maintaining strategic forces at START I levels would cost either an additional $10 billion beginning in 2000, $6 billion to $8 billion between 1998 and 2002, $5 billion between 1998 and 2004, or $1 billion annually beginning in 1998. To address this potential funding shortfall (and avoid spending billions of dollars on weapons due to be retired), the DOD is considering retaining those weapons but foregoing planned upgrades. See Elaine M. Grossman, "Russian Failure to Ratify Start II Would Cost U.S. $10 Billion After FY-00," *Inside the Pentagon,* April 25, 1996, p. 1; R. Jeffrey Smith, "U.S. Studies Deeper Nuclear Warhead Cuts," *Washington Post,* January 23, 1997, p. A4; Jeff Erlich, "Safety in Nuclear Numbers," *Defense News,* February 3–9, 1997, p. 1; Elaine M. Grossman, "To Save Funds, Pentagon May Let Some Start I Nuclear Forces Age Out," *Inside the Pentagon,* May 29, 1997, p. 1.

the public would be better able to track nuclear weapons–related spending and discern trends in such spending. The DOE and DOD, which together are responsible for nearly all of this spending, would also benefit by obtaining a clearer understanding of their respective programs. With more than 60 percent of its annual budget allocated to "atomic energy defense activities" and related programs at present, the DOE's budget submissions already contain much of the necessary data. What remains to be done, however, is to demarcate clearly the costs of those items that are not fully part of the weapons program, such as naval nuclear propulsion, environment, safety and health, intelligence, and so forth. The amount of effort required to accomplish this should be relatively modest.

Since 1995 the DOD has produced several charts in its annual reports showing spending for strategic nuclear forces based on funding levels for Major Force Program 1 (Strategic Forces). This welcome step is far from adequate. The data in these charts can be (and already have been) assumed to represent the sum total of nuclear weapons spending by the DOD or, worse, the entire government. This assumption prompts the misleading conclusion that nuclear weapons currently consume less than 3 percent of the defense budget.[10] What is needed is a comprehensive accounting of *all* nuclear-related costs in the budget (as delineated in this book). Owing to dual-capable systems and uncertainties about true operations and support costs, assumptions will have to be made about what percentage of certain programs to allocate to the nuclear side of the ledger (much as we have already done here; see chapters 2, 3, and 4). Since intelligence-related costs are formally included in the defense budget, the nuclear-related portion of these should be reported as well. As explained earlier, there are ways to accomplish this that will not jeopardize sources and methods yet allow for a clearer understanding of how the intelligence community at present supports the nuclear weapons program.

The OMB should include the nuclear weapons–related programs and costs of all other government agencies. These include the Commerce Department (Bureau of Export Administration, National Oceanic and Atmospheric Administration); Defense Nuclear Facilities Safety Board; Department of Health and Human Services (Centers for Disease Control and Prevention, Agency for Toxic Substances Disease Registry); Department of Veterans Affairs; Environmental Protection Agency; Executive Office of the President (National Security Council, Office of Management and Budget, Office of Science and Technology Policy, White House Military Office, White House Communications

10. See, for example, James Brooke, "Former Cold Warrior Has a New Mission: Nuclear Cuts," *New York Times*, January 8, 1997, p. A12; Brent Scowcroft and Arnold Kanter, "Which Nuke Policy?" *Washington Times*, March 2, 1997, p. A15.

Agency); Federal Emergency Management Agency; Interior Department (Office of Insular Affairs/Marshall Islands, U.S. Geological Survey, Military Geology Project); Justice Department (representing the government in weapons-related lawsuits against the DOE and DOD, Federal Bureau of Investigation, compensation paid by the Torts Branch/Civil Division, under the Radiation Exposure Compensation Act); Labor Department (Occupational Safety and Health Administration); National Aeronautics and Space Administration (space shuttle operations); National Archives (storage of classified nuclear weapons documents and declassification of historical documents); State Department (including the Arms Control and Disarmament Agency, soon to become the Assistant Secretary for Arms Control and Disarmament); and the Treasury Department (U.S. Customs Service). The costs attributable to legislative branch agencies, including the Congressional Budget Office Congressional Research Service, General Accounting Office, and Congress itself, should also be included.

The president should also play a more active role in formulating nuclear weapons policy and requirements. The last (and only) president to immerse himself in the nuclear planning process was Jimmy Carter, a former nuclear submariner. His successors have not been as engaged or attentive. In fact, President Bill Clinton's repeated and misleading assertions during the 1996 campaign that nuclear missiles were no longer pointed at "the children of the United States" betrayed a flawed understanding of the largely symbolic 1994 ICBM detargeting measure jointly undertaken by Russia and the United States.[11]

The president currently signs off on the annual Nuclear Weapons Stockpile Plan, which determines the overall size of the stockpile and the number of weapons to be built and dismantled, but presidents typically have provided little input or guidance to this plan before it reaches the Oval Office. With nuclear weapons currently consuming a sizable percentage of the overall military budget, it is vital to understand how the figures in the plan were derived. Moreover, these costs (except for those associated with environmental remediation and waste management programs) are linked to the Single Integrated Operational Plan, historically and today the most important factor driving the maintenance and deployment of the nuclear stockpile.

We do not intend to suggest that the president personally dictate the composition of the nuclear stockpile, select targets, or otherwise manage the preparation of the SIOP. But as the legally designated offi-

11. See Bruce G. Blair, "Where Would All the Missiles Go?," *Washington Post,* October 15, 1996, p. A15; J. Michael Waller, "The Missiles Pointed at America," *Washington Times,* September 2, 1996, p. A15; Douglas Berenson, "DOD Concedes Strategic Missile Detargeting Deal Is Easily Reversed," *Inside the Pentagon,* May 29, 1997, p. 1.

cial with the authority to order the use of nuclear weapons, he should participate in some fashion in the detailed planning process for the plan he may one day be called upon to execute. After all, even today the SIOP concerns the lives and potential deaths of hundreds of millions of people.[12]

Because of the singular importance of the SIOP, we recommend that the president authorize an independent review of the current SIOP and the process by which it was devised. The review committee could include current and former military and civilian officials with nuclear planning responsibilities, as well as nongovernmental experts, and it should be given access to all relevant classified materials in order to enable it to render a truly informed judgment. This committee should also review the most recent nuclear weapons stockpile plan, which contains provisions for maintaining large numbers of nuclear weapons in inactive storage, as a hedge against sudden reversals in the current international climate.

We also encourage the DOE to continue the openness initiative started by Secretary Hazel R. O'Leary in late 1993. It has already brought important dividends: increased trust in the department and improved public understanding of its nuclear weapons missions. Further steps are needed, however, to ensure the release of all relevant historical data pertaining to nuclear weapons development, production, and testing. The DOD and the various nuclear agencies under its aegis should initiate similar efforts and Congress should amend the Atomic Energy Act to make permanent the reforms recommended by the Fundamental Classification Policy Review. A complete history of the nuclear age cannot be compiled—nor the costs and consequences fully understood—without better and broader access to the original documentation held by these agencies. In particular, the detailed annual and semiannual histories by the Defense Special Weapons Agency and its predecessors are likely to prove an uncommonly valuable resource to future scholars.

Last but not least, we urge Congress to strengthen its oversight of nuclear weapons programs by focusing not just on the most expensive or most controversial items in the budget in any given year but rather on the larger strategic picture of how nuclear weapons would be used, how the various elements of the program contribute to deterrence, and what constitutes deterrence in the post–cold war era. Congress has begun emphasizing the broader picture to some extent in its scrutiny of the DOE's environmental remediation and waste management program (especially from 1990 through 1994): it examined the overall

12. For a more detailed discussion of this point, see Janne Nolan, *Guardians of the Arsenal* (New York: Basic Books, 1989), esp. pp. 263–70.

goals and cost of the effort in great detail, but the individual programs at facilities throughout the country generally received less attention. Clearly, a mixture of the two approaches is needed to ensure a full and fair treatment of the budget. Yet with strikingly few exceptions, the annual congressional debate usually focuses on the minute details of a few programs at the expense of the overall effort those programs are supposed to support. This approach can be compared to building a house by carefully examining the cost of only a few of the obvious elements and rarely pausing to consider what the house will actually cost or look like, or if it will even meets one's needs.[13]

Given the structure of our representative democracy—particularly its myriad constituent groups and their ability to pull policy in many conflicting directions simultaneously—decisions about nuclear weapons budgets or any other item of public spending will never be entirely coherent. Nevertheless, the record to date (see chapter 9) demonstrates that Congress has been less than diligent in exercising its oversight responsibilities with regard to the nuclear weapons budget. Armed with the data that we have provided, and with data that we hope the executive branch (with Congressional prodding) will continue to provide on an annual basis, Congress will finally be able to make truly informed decisions, not just about individual weapons, but about the arsenal as a whole and about the sometimes hidden or overlooked costs (such as waste management, command and control, and intelligence support) that inevitably accompany decisions about which missile, aircraft, or submarine to purchase. The fact that much of the current arsenal was acquired on the basis of arbitrary or strategically irrelevant decisions and justified by post hoc rationales should serve as an important reminder that programs, policies, and weapons levels frequently cited as sacrosanct did not necessarily originate from an objective, clearly defined military purpose (see chapter 2).

More than half a century after the advent of nuclear weapons, almost a decade after the fall of the Berlin Wall, and with the cold war receding into history and the future of nuclear deterrence the subject of increasing debate, the time has come to consider carefully the costs and consequences to the United States, and the world, of producing tens of thousands of nuclear weapons and basing national security on the threat of nuclear annihilation. We have provided what we hope will be a starting point for such an assessment, focusing on the one aspect of the endeavor that until now has been largely ignored. As we anticipate the end of the twentieth century and the beginning of the twenty-first, we cannot rectify our mistakes or build on our achievements if such a crucial part of our nuclear history remains incomplete or

13. For a similar perspective on this issue, see Nolan, *Guardians of the Arsenal,* pp. 274–78.

unwritten. Neither can we hope to prevent other countries from acquiring nuclear weapons if we do not fully comprehend the forces that have driven our own program and affect it still. Given the enormous sums expended and the substantial risks incurred, we owe it to ourselves and future generations to seek answers to these questions, to fill the gaps in the atomic ledger.

A

U.S. Nuclear Weapons Production Costs, 1948–96

TABLE A-1. Estimated Annual AEC/ERDA/DOE Spending on Nuclear Weapons Materials Production, 1948–96[a]

Millions of dollars

Fiscal year	Then-year operating expenses	Constant 96 operating expenses[b]	Then-year source materials procurement	Constant 96 source materials procurement	Then-year construction and capital equipment	Constant 96 construction and capital equipment	Then-year annual total	Constant 96 annual total
1948							262.7	2,550.7
1949	108.7[c]	1,055.0[c]			158.5	1,492.5	267.2	2,547.5
1950	81.8	716.3	38.6	338.0	68.3	598.1	188.7	1,652.4
1951	90.8	640.8	47.5	335.2	1,247.5	8,803.8	1,385.8	9,779.8
1952	145.5	1,058.2	72.5	527.3	284.1	2,066.2	502.1	3,651.7
1953	198.8	1,489.1	82.2	615.7	2,591.6	19,412.7	2,872.6	21,517.5
1954	274.8	2,175.8	142.8	1,130.6	410.4	3,249.4	828.0	6,555.8
1955	443.3	3,269.2	193.6	1,427.7	159.0	1,172.6	795.9	5,869.5
1956	553.0	3,824.3	281.0	1,943.3	46.2	319.5	880.2	6,087.1
1957	581.6	3,906.0	397.8	2,671.6	66.0	443.3	1,045.4	7,020.9
1958	547.7	3,535.8	598.6	3,864.4	35.7	230.5	1,182.0	7,630.7
1959	541.3	3,366.3	705.3	4,386.2	76.5	475.7	1,323.1	8,228.2
1960	553.3	3,409.1	715.9	4,411.0	101.3	624.2	1,370.5	8,444.3
1961	560.3	3,369.2	634.6	3,816.0	76.3	458.8	1,271.2	7,644.0
1962	491.1	2,926.7	537.2	3,201.4	53.4	318.2	1,081.7	6,446.3
1963	477.9	2,796.4	477.7	2,795.2	111.6	653.0	1,067.2	6,244.6
1964	463.7	2,616.8	326.2	1,840.9	36.7	207.1	826.6	4,664.8
1965	393.0	2,154.6	267.5	1,466.6	34.9	191.3	695.4	3,812.5
1966	373.2	1,889.6	[d]	[d]	36.5	184.8	409.7	2,074.4
1967	209.3	1,018.5[e]	[d]	[d]	31.6	153.8	240.9	1,172.3
1968	206.5	966.8	[d]	[d]	20.3	95.0	226.8	1,061.8
1969	209.4	937.3	[d]	[d]	35.5	158.9	244.9	1,096.2
1970	207.7	871.6[f]	50.4	211.5	42.4	177.9	300.5	1,261.0
1971	200.8	793.0	16.9	66.7	39.6	156.4	257.3	1,016.1
1972	196.0	707.8[g]	1.5	5.4	111.6	403.0	309.1	1,116.2
1973	209.5	696.9	1.8	6.0[h]	105.6	351.3	316.9	1,054.2
1974	257.7	788.6	2.6	8.0	233.2	713.6	493.5	1,510.2
1975[i]	280.1	782.6	5.7	15.9	262.4	733.2	548.2	1,531.7
1976[j]	338.1	879.8	14.0	36.4	64.9	168.9	417.0	1,085.1
1976T	93.8	244.1	4.6	12.0	16.1	41.9	114.5	298.0
1977	350.0	837.7			103.9	248.7	453.9	1,086.4
1978[k]	400.7	888.1			202.1	447.9	602.8	1,336.0
1979	321.3	656.1[l]			121.7	248.5	443.0	904.6
1980	347.9	636.1[l]			156.6	286.3	504.5	922.4
1981	461.3	761.0[l]			196.1	323.5	657.4	1,084.5
1982	647.7	992.2			308.0	471.8	955.7	1,464.0
1983	830.9	1,224.8			280.0	412.7	1,110.9	1,637.5
1984	1,044.0	1,492.3			351.6	502.6	1,395.6	1,994.9
1985	1,238.1	1,704.0			364.5	501.7	1,602.6	2,205.7
1986	1,276.9	1,714.0			321.0	430.9	1,597.9	2,144.9

TABLE A-1. Estimated Annual AEC/ERDA/DOE Spending on Nuclear Weapons Materials Production, 1948–96[a] (*continued*)

Millions of dollars

Fiscal year	*Then-year operating expenses*	*Constant 96 operating expenses*[b]	*Then-year source materials procurement*	*Constant 96 source materials procurement*	*Then-year construction and capital equipment*	*Constant 96 construction and capital equipment*	*Then-year annual total*	*Constant 96 annual total*
1987	1,271.3	1,656.0			400.1	521.2	1,671.4	2,177.2
1988	1,334.9	1,676.8			322.1	404.6	1,657.0	2,081.4
1989	1,448.0	1,749.8			385.7	466.1	1,833.7	2,215.9
1990	1,758.2	2,063.9			405.0	475.4	2,163.2	2,539.3
1991	1,882.7	2,110.7			382.5	428.8	2,265.2	2,539.5
1992	1,580.2	1,738.6			456.3	502.0	2,036.5	2,240.6
1993	1,562.0	1,668.6			307.9	328.9	1,869.9	1,997.5
1994	132.0	137.7			2.8	2.9	134.8	140.6
1995	115.6	118.2			1.0	1.0	116.6	119.2
1996[m]								
Total[n]	27,292.4	76,712.8	5,616.5	35,133.0	11,626.6	51,061.1	44,798.2	165,457.6

a. For obligations for operating expenses between 1948 and 1960, source material procurement costs between 1956 and 1965, and construction costs between 1948 and 1964, see U.S. Bureau of the Budget, *The Budget of the United States Government* (fiscal 1950–66, inclusive); for source material procurement obligations between 1950 and 1955, see *AEC Semi-Annual Report for Fiscal Year 1964*, p. 395; for budget authority for operating expenses between 1961 and 1995 and for construction and capital equipment obligations between 1965 and 1995, see U.S. Congress, Joint Committee on Atomic Energy and House Energy and Water Appropriations Subcommittee, *AEC/ERDA/DOE Annual Budget Requests to Congress* (fiscal 1963–96, inclusive).

b. Does not include an estimated $9.4 billion for uranium enrichment between 1967 and 1993, largely if not entirely for naval nuclear propulsion reactors.

c. Includes source material procurement obligations. See U.S. Bureau of the Budget, *The Budget of the United States Government, Fiscal Year 1951*, p. 71.

d. Data for 1966–69 are not available and are therefore not included in the annual totals for these years.

e. Does not include an estimated $140 million for uranium enrichment. Estimate based on trend through 1968 and 1969 (estimated and requested) budget authority for the line-item in the same table. See U.S. Congress, Joint Committee on Atomic Energy, *AEC Budget Request to Congress for Fiscal Year 1969*, p. 2026.

f. Does not include $113.7 million for uranium enrichment. See U.S. Congress, Joint Committee on Atomic Energy, *AEC Budget Request to Congress for Fiscal Year 1972*, p. 2555 (for actual budget authority), and U.S. Congress, Joint Committee on Atomic Energy, *AEC Budget Request to Congress for Fiscal Year 1971*, p. 1755 (for estimated allocation for enrichment).

g. Does not include $179.4 million for uranium enrichment. See U.S. Congress, Joint Committee on Atomic Energy, *AEC Budget Request to Congress for FY 1973*, p. 486.

h. Nixon administration's budget request. See U.S. Congress, Joint Committee on Atomic Energy, *AEC Budget Request to Congress for FY 1973*, p. 486.

i. Congressional appropriation. See U.S. Congress, Joint Committee on Atomic Energy, *AEC Budget Request to Congress for Fiscal Year 1976*, p. 575.

j. For 1976 and for Transition Quarter, Ford administration's request. See U.S. Congress, House Energy and Water Appropriations Subcommittee, *ERDA Budget Request to Congress for Fiscal Year 1976*, p. 575.

k. Congressional Appropriation. See U.S. Congress, House Energy and Water Appropriations Subcommittee, *DOE Budget Request to Congress for Fiscal Year 1979*, p. 1077.

l. Does not include approximately $6 million per year for the enrichment of scrap uranium at weapons complex facilities. See U.S. Congress, House Energy and Water Appropriations Subcommittee, *DOE Annual Budget Request to Congress for Fiscal Year 1981*, p. 2322.

m. Materials production was reclassified as part of the stockpile stewardship program beginning in fiscal 1996.

n. Breakout does not match total due to a $2.5 billion difference in expenditures in fiscal 1948, which was not expressed in detail in the source document.

TABLE A-2. Estimated Annual AEC/ERDA/DOE Spending on Nuclear Weapons Research, Development, Testing and Production, 1948–1996[a]

Millions of dollars

Fiscal year	Then-year R&D[b]	Constant 96 R&D	Then-year testing[c]	Constant 96 testing	Then-year production[d]	Constant 96 production	Then-year total operating expenses	Constant 96 total operating expenses	Then-year construction and capital equipment	Constant 96 construction and capital equipment	Then-year annual total	Constant 96 annual total
1948											146.8	1,425.5
1949							90.7	854.0	85.2	802.3	175.9	1,656.3
1950							85.8	751.3	79.0	691.8	164.8	1,443.1
1951							141.5	998.6	103.6	731.1	245.1	1,729.7
1952							206.2	1,499.6	108.0	785.5	314.2	2,285.1
1953							228.0	1,707.9	42.7	319.9	270.7	2,027.8
1954							218.1	1,726.8	41.0	324.6	259.1	2,051.4
1955							238.2	1,756.6	30.1	222.0	268.3	1,978.6
1956[e]	105.1	727.1	48.6	337.5	103.7	717.2	257.4	1,780.8	42.9	296.7	300.3	2,077.5
1957	121.4	815.5	51.1	343.2	150.8	1,012.8	323.3	2,171.5	62.3	418.4	385.6	2,589.9
1958	126.4	816.1	73.5	474.5	233.4	1,506.8	433.3	2,797.4	48.4	312.5	481.7	3,109.9
1959	152.3	947.4	50.4	313.4	282.2	1,755.0	484.9	3,015.8	36.8	228.9	521.7	3,244.7
1960	169.0	1,041.3	29.1	179.3	301.5	1,857.7	499.6	3,078.3	28.3	174.4	527.9	3,252.7
1961	174.9	1,051.5	20.6	123.9	322.2	1,937.5	517.7	3,112.9	25.4	152.7	543.1	3,265.6
1962							652.8	3,890.3	98.1	584.6	750.9	4,474.9
1963[f]			133.2	779.4	511.9	2,995.3	645.1	3,774.7	125.6	734.9	770.7	4,509.6
1964			212.6	1,199.8	542.2	3,059.8	754.8	4,259.6	109.7	619.1	864.5	4,878.7
1965			218.5	1,197.9	488.5	2,678.2	707.0	3,876.1	120.4	660.1	827.4	4,536.2
1966	214.8	1,087.6	206.7	1,046.6	248.8	1,259.7	670.3	3,393.9	109.6	554.9	779.9	3,948.8
1967	220.5	1,073.0	198.5	965.9	242.2	1,178.6	661.2	3,217.5	92.1	448.2	753.3	3,665.7
1968	225.2	1,054.3	248.2	1,162.0	243.2	1,138.6	716.6	3,354.9	170.7	799.2	887.3	4,154.1
1969	240.8	1,077.9	310.4	1,389.4	265.1	1,186.7	816.3	3,654.0	251.0	1,123.5	1,067.3	4,777.5
1970	250.7	1,052.0	251.9	1,057.1	304.9	1,279.5	807.5	3,388.6	168.0	705.0	975.5	4,093.6
1971	250.5	989.3	218.3	862.2	359.1	1,418.2	827.9	3,269.7	120.4	475.5	948.3	3,745.2
1972	247.7	894.5	196.5	709.6	398.6	1,439.5	842.8	3,043.6	172.3	622.2	1,015.1	3,665.8
1973	269.8	897.5	184.4	613.4	403.9	1,343.6	858.1	2,854.5	157.9	525.3	1,016.0	3,379.8
1974[g]	280.0	856.8	168.4	515.3	374.4	1,145.7	822.8	2,517.8	128.9	394.4	951.7	2,912.2
1975	299.0	835.4	187.8	524.7	377.2	1,053.9	864.0	2,414.0	169.8	474.4	1,033.8	2,888.4
1976	336	874.1	216.8	564.1	349.3	908.9	902.0	2,347.1	153.8	400.2	1,055.8	2,747.3
1976T	100.9	262.6	57.5	149.6	93.9	244.3	252.3	656.5	38.9	101.2	291.2	757.7
1977	344.1	823.6	219.6	525.6	398.2	953.1	961.9	2,302.3	149.6	358.1	1,111.5	2,660.4
1978	366.4	812.1	225.2	499.1	503.5	1,115.9	1,095.1	2,427.1	191.3	424.0	1,286.4	2,851.1

1979	396.3	809.3	207.2	423.1	614.0	1,253.8	1,250.8[h]	2,554.2	236.3	482.5	1,487.1	3,036.7
1980[i]	527.2	964.0	198.0	362.0	748.0	1,367.7	1,510.3[h]	2,761.6	318.1	581.6	1,828.4	3,343.2
1981[j]	604.0	996.4	297.8	491.3	982.0	1,619.9	1,930.6[h]	3,184.8	424.1	699.6	2,354.7	3,884.4
1982[k]	696.5	1,066.9	361.0	553.0	1,278.4	1,958.3	2,383.2[h]	3,650.7	645.7	989.1	3,028.9	4,639.8
1983[l]	781.5	1,152.0	408.3	601.9	1,472.1	2,170.0	2,716.3[h]	4,004.0	679.3	1,001.3	3,395.6	5,005.3
1984	722.7	1,033.0	490.4	701.0	1,665.7	2,380.9	2,937.6[h]	4,199.0	644.9	921.8	3,464.5	4,952.1[m]
1985	975.4	1,342.4	531.2	731.1	1,806.3	2,486.0	3,370.4[h]	4,638.6	836.7	1,151.5	3,992.1	5,494.2[m]
1986	961.7	1,290.9	522.4	701.2	1,741.3	2,337.3	3,328.1[h]	4,467.2	808.8	1,085.6	3,867.0	5,226.5[m]
1987	1,007.3	1,312.1	531.9	682.8	1,799.6	2,344.1	3,408.8[h]	4,440.3	700.6	912.6	3,792.4	4,940.0[m]
1988	1,039.8	1,306.1	509.0	639.4	1,853.8	2,328.6	3,477.4[h]	4,368.0	659.4	828.3	3,857.8	4,845.8[m]
1989	1,022.7	1,235.9	409.2	494.5	1,793.8	2,167.7	3,307.9[h]	3,997.5	579.6	700.4	3,632.5	4,389.7[m]
1990	1,027.0	1,205.5	504.5	592.2	2,059.1	2,417.1	3,687.6[h]	4,328.7	619.3	727.0	4,140.9	4,860.8[m]
1991	1,032.2	1,157.2	457.3	512.7	2,492.7	2,794.5	4,086.9[h]	4,581.7	656.6	736.1	4,652.8	5,216.1[m]
1992	1,172.6	1,290.1	457.6	503.5	2,321.3	2,554.0	4,134.3[h]	4,548.7	554.5	610.1	4,688.8	5,158.8
1993	1,279.4	1,366.7	375.0	400.6	2,142.6	2,288.9	4,122.9[h]	4,404.3	539.5	576.3	4,662.4	4,980.6
1994	1,138.0	1,187.1	371.7	387.8	1,634.8	1,705.4	3,320.9[h]	3,464.3	329.1	343.3	3,650.0	3,807.6
1995	1,178.3	1,205.2	166.5	170.3	1,527.6	1,562.4	3,029.7[h]	3,098.8	301.0	307.9	3,330.7	3,406.7
1996[n]	1,375.4	1,375.4	0.0	0.0	1,727.6	1,727.6	3,427.8[h]	3,427.8	233.5	233.5	3,661.3	3,661.3
Total	21,433.4	39,285.8	10,526.8	24,481.9	37,159.4	70,650.7	73,014.7	150,013.9	13,028.8	28,354.1	84,479.7	177,634.4

a. For obligations for operating expenses between 1948 and 1960 and for construction and capital equipment, see U.S. Bureau of the Budget, *The Budget of the United States Government* (fiscal 1950–66, inclusive); for budget authority for operating expenses between 1961 and 1996 and for construction and capital equipment costs between 1965 and 1996, see U.S. Congress, Joint Committee on Atomic Energy and House Energy and Water Appropriations Subcommittee, *AEC/ERDA/DOE Annual Budget Requests to Congress* (fiscal 1963–96, inclusive).

b. Includes inertial confinement fusion programs. R&D reclassified as stockpile stewardship program beginning in fiscal 1996.

c. Does not include Project Plowshare expenses. Testing was reclassified as part of the stockpile stewardship program beginning in fiscal 1996.

d. Includes surveillance, storage, and dismantling expenditures. Production was reclassified as part of the stockpile management program beginning in fiscal 1996.

e. For 1956–61, R&D and testing expenses are provided in a memorandum from General Delmar Crowson, AEC Director of Military Application, to John Conway, JCAE Executive Director, May 10, 1966. Total operating expenses are listed in U.S. Bureau of the Budget, *The Budget of the United States Government* (fiscal 1958–62, inclusive) for operating expenses for 1956–60, and in U.S. Congress, Joint Committee on Atomic Energy, *AEC Annual Budget Request to Congress for Fiscal Year 1963*, p. 504 (for operating expenses for 1961). Annual production operating expenses are estimated by subtracting R&D and testing from the total.

f. For 1963–65, production expenses include R&D. See U.S. Congress, Joint Committee on Atomic Energy, *AEC Annual Budget Request to Congress for Fiscal Years 1965, 1966, and 1967*.

g. For 1974–76 (and 76T), R&D operating expenses include national security program estimates for the laser fusion program. See U.S. Congress, House Energy and Water Appropriations Subcommittee, *ERDA Budget Request to Congress for Fiscal Year 1976*.

h. Includes program direction expenses.

i. R&D and testing expenses are the Carter administration's request. See U.S. Congress, House Energy and Water Appropriations Subcommittee, *DOE Budget Request to Congress for Fiscal Year 1980*, p. 2286. R&D expenses also include actual expenditure for inertial confinement fusion, which was accounted for separately from other R&D programs. See U.S. Congress, House Energy and Water Appropriations Subcommittee, *DOE Budget Request to Congress for Fiscal Year 1982*, p. 1575.

j. R&D and testing expenses are congressional appropriation amounts. See U.S. Congress, House Energy and Water Appropriations Subcommittee, *DOE Budget Request to Congress for Fiscal Year 1982*.

k. R&D and testing expenses are from the Reagan administration's request. See U.S. Congress, House Energy and Water Appropriations Subcommittee, *DOE Budget Request to Congress for Fiscal Year 1982*.

l. For 1983–85, R&D and testing operating expenses are the congressional appropriation. See U.S. Congress, House Energy and Water Appropriations Subcommittee, *DOE Budget Request to Congress* (for fiscal 1984–86, inclusive).

m. Excludes Strategic Defense Initiative related expenditures as follows: $168.7 million (1984), $295.9 million (1985), $326.3 million (1986), $412.9 million (1987), $350.5 million (1988), $308.2 million (1989), $194.9 million (1990), $101.7 million (1991).

n. Beginning in fiscal 1996, research, development, and test readiness programs were reclassified by DOE as stockpile stewardship. Production costs (including assembly/disassembly activities and tritium research) were reclassified as stockpile management.

TABLE A-3. DOD Expenditures for Nuclear Weapons Research, Testing, and Development, 1962–95

Millions of dollars

Fiscal year	*Then-year research and testing*	*Constant 96 research and testing*[a]	*Then-year development*	*Constant 96 development*[b]	*Then-year overhead*	*Constant 96 overhead*[c]	*Then-year annual total*	*Constant 96 annual total*
1962	227.2	1,365.5	11.4	68.4	46.7	280.7	285.3	1,714.6
1963	340.0	1,998.8	19.0	111.9	39.9	234.4	398.9	2,345.1
1964	260.0	1,466.4	17.3	97.6	39.2	221.1	316.5	1,785.1
1965	301.6	1,653.4	13.8	75.5	35.8	196.4	351.2	1,925.3
1966	270.2	1,367.9	17.0	86.0	34.9	176.7	322.1	1,630.6
1967	252.6	1,229.5	14.3	69.7	39.8	193.6	306.7	1,492.8
1968	264.6	1,238.7	10.8	50.6	38.9	182.2	314.3	1,471.5
1969	266.6	1,193.2	7.7	34.6	41.1	184.0	315.4	1,411.8
1970	283.4	1,189.4	12.8	53.8	35.7	149.8	331.9	1,393.0
1971	262.9	1,038.3	12.6	49.8	23.5	92.7	299.0	1,180.8
1972	281.6	1,017.0	18.4	66.4	18.9	68.1	318.9	1,151.5
1973	283.6	935.3	12.8	42.7	12.8	42.5	309.2	1,020.5
1974	266.2	814.4	9.1	27.8	18.5	56.6	293.8	898.8
1975	268.7	750.7	10.3	28.8	21.8	60.9	300.8	840.4
1976	276.2	718.8	14.9	38.8	24.5	63.8	315.6	821.4
1977	297.4	712.5	15.4	36.9	41.0	98.3	353.8	847.7
1978	338.3	749.7	13.5	29.8	19.7	43.7	371.5	823.2
1979	387.8	791.9	19.3	39.3	23.0	47.0	430.1	878.2
1980	393.4	719.2	26.6	48.6	25.1	45.9	445.1	813.7
1981	321.9	382.6	18.2	30.1	24.7	40.7	364.8	453.4
1982	297.1	455.1	38.7	59.3	28.3	43.4	364.1	557.8
1983	358.2	528.0	36.5	53.9	31.2	46.0	425.9	627.9
1984	377.7	539.9	35.8	51.2	44.0	63.0	457.5	654.1
1985	382.5	526.4	26.8	36.9	43.5	59.8	452.8	623.1
1986	390.3	523.9	38.8	52.1	44.4	59.6	473.5	635.6
1987	365.0	475.4	39.7	51.7	59.0	76.8	463.7	603.9
1988	395.0	496.1	30.2	37.9	72.0	90.4	497.2	624.4

TABLE A-3. DOD Expenditures for Nuclear Weapons Research, Testing, and Development, 1962–95 (*continued*)

Millions of dollars

Fiscal year	*Then-year research and testing*	*Constant 96 research and testing*[a]	*Then-year development*	*Constant 96 development*[b]	*Then-year overhead*	*Constant 96 overhead*[c]	*Then-year annual total*	*Constant 96 annual total*
1989	343.2	414.7	25.9	31.3	71.1	86.0	440.2	532.0
1990	332.7	390.5	26.6	31.2	74.4	87.3	433.7	509.0
1991	386.3	433.1	17.3	19.4	85.1	95.4	488.7	547.9
1992	395.5	435.2	15.2	16.7	97.6	107.3	508.3	559.2
1993	398.8	426.0	16.2	17.3	296.4	316.7	711.4	760.0
1994	239.7	250.0	10.4	10.8	75.9	79.2	326.0	340.0
1995	224.8	230.0	6.2	6.3	57.5	58.8	288.5	295.1
Total	10,731.0	27,457.2	659.5	1,563.1	1,685.8	3,748.8	13,076.3	32,769.1

a. Because the FYDP historical database does not provide annual spending totals for the Defense Nuclear Agency (DNA) before 1981, figures provided by the DNA's successor, the Defense Special Weapons Agency (DSWA), for 1962–80 were added to this column. However, because some components of DNA spending were apparently carried out under more than one program element, it is possible that this approach has resulted in the double counting of as much as $8.9 billion between 1962 and 1980. In addition, a portion of DNA expenditures (such as routine stockpile surety inspections) are more appropriately counted under chapter 2 of this volume. Because the FYDP and DNA/DSWA provide no detailed breakdown of historical annual spending, all known DNA/DSWA costs are counted here. This estimate is derived by calculating total adjusted expenditures for program elements 0602118A (nuclear weapons effects research and test); 0602713H (nuclear weapons survivability and security); 0602701 (nuclear monitoring research); 0602704H (nuclear weapons effects development); 0602710H (nuclear weapons effects test); 0602715 (Defense Nuclear Agency); and 0603714H (nuclear vulnerability and survivability). Additional data come from "DNA Funding Profile, 1963–1994," Defense Special Weapons Agency, August 15, 1997.

b. These are programs funded by the different armed services in support of weapons development programs in conjunction with the Department of Energy and its predecessor agencies. These figures are derived by calculating total adjusted figures from program elements: 0602117A (nuclear munitions and radiacs); 0602615A (nuclear munitions); 0603604A (nuclear munitions–advanced development); 0603634N (electromagnetic effect protection development); 0603638A (nuclear hardening–advanced technology); 0604222F (nuclear weapons support); and 0604603A (nuclear munitions–engineering and development).

c. These costs are derived by calculating the total adjusted expenditures for program element 0305115H (nuclear weapons operations). According to DOD, this program element funds "peculiar and support equipment, necessary facilities and the associated costs specifically identified and measurable to the following: Field Command, DNA, the Joint Atomic Information Exchange Group Support, and the management headquarters and operational elements of the DNA." See U.S. Department of Defense, Office of the Comptroller, *FYDP Program Structure*, DOD7045.7-H (Springfield, Va.: National Technical Information Service, October 1993), pp. 3-38–3-39.

B

Selected DOD Nuclear Weapons Program Costs, 1962–95

The following budgetary data come from the Department of Defense's Future Years Defense Program historical database and include most but not all of the programs pertaining either wholly or partly to nuclear weapons (most programs concerning intelligence-related activities are notably missing). These data cover the period 1962–95. They were declassified by the DOD at the request of this study's authors and made available in March 1996. The entire database, which is substantially larger and includes detailed annual figures on force and personnel levels (including future-year projections), remains classified.

Attached to each program element number is a letter designating a particular component of the Department of Defense. The following are found in this database: A = Army; B = Defense Mapping Agency; C = Ballistic Missile Defense Organization; D = Office of the Secretary of Defense; F = Air Force; H = Defense Nuclear Agency; J = the Joint Staff (including unified and specified commands); K = Defense Information Service Agency; L = Defense Intelligence Agency; M = Marine Corps; N = Navy; V = Defense Investigative Service. Program element titles followed by "(H)" are considered historical. Such programs have not expended funds for at least two fiscal years.

Full definitions and descriptions of many of the following programs can found in U.S. Department of Defense, Office of the Comptroller, *FYDP Program Structure,* DOD 7045.7-H (Springfield, Va.: National Technical Information Service, October 1993).

A searchable on-line version of this database (including program descriptions) can be found at: http://www.brook.edu/fp/projects/nucwcost/weapons.htm.

Table B-1. Department of Defense Future Years Defense Program Database, 1962–95

Thousands of dollars

Program element number	Program element title	Years active	Total then-year cost	Total adjusted cost (1996 dollars)
0101111F	B-47 Squadrons (H)	1962–66	906,544	5,257,632
0101112F	EB-47 Squadrons (H)	1962–65	29,087	165,859
0101113F	B-52 Squadrons	1962–95	37,680,117	93,634,836
0101114F	B-58 Squadrons (H)	1962–70	688,455	3,709,840
0101115F	FB-111 Squadron (H)	1966–92	3,690,680	10,246,812
0101116F	SKYBOLT (H)	1962–63	277,440	1,650,126
0101117F	HOUND DOG (AGM-28) (H)	1962–76	379,419	1,963,212
0101118F	Short Range Attack Missile (AGM-69)	1965–95	2,188,229	6,152,235
0101120F	Advanced Cruise Missile	1986–95	3,644,844	4,507,369
0101121F	B-1 Squadrons (H)	1974–78	394,371	958,449
0101122F	Air-Launched Cruise Missile (ALCM)	1977–95	3,554,104	5,462,328
0101126F	B-1B Squadrons	1982–95	30,137,905	40,782,701
0101127F	B-2 Squadrons	1988–95	14,966,462	16,830,988
0101131F	RB-47 Squadrons (H)	1962–67	85,598	485,893
0101133F	SR-71 Squadrons (H)	1963–91	5,502,865	14,866,301
0101135F	Aircraft Survivability Enhancements (H)	1985–89	46,761	61,907
0101141F	KC-97 Squadrons (H)	1962–66	419,060	2,439,060
0101142F	KC-135 Squadrons	1962–94	26,022,127	50,585,112
0101211F	ATLAS Squadrons (H)	1962–65	1,427,759	8,434,443
0101212F	TITAN Squadrons (H)	1962–88	3,926,596	18,492,496
0101213F	Minuteman Squadrons	1962–95	30,904,996	101,698,710
0101214F	MINUTEMAN Integrated Command and Control System (H)	1970	19,999	83,924
0101215F	Peacekeeper Squadrons	1980–95	9,467,608	12,414,946
0101216F	Strategic Update (H)	1982–89	8,043,871	10,758,417
0101217F	Special Support Projects (H)	1984–86	336,005	464,532
0101218F	Short Range Attack Missile II (SRAM II) (H)	1990–91	20,290	23,311
0101219F	Small ICBM Squadrons (H)	1991–92	3,618	4,029
0101220N	Peacekeeper Financing (H)	1983–84	733,634	1,071,051
0101221N	Strategic Sub & Weapons System Support	1962–95	46,883,280	123,034,376

0101222N	Support Ships (FBMS)	1962–95	6,120,562	12,928,902
0101223N	REGULUS Missile System (H)	1962–65	37,299	214,354
0101224N	SSBN Security Technology Program	1970–95	933,001	1,486,189
0101225N	Navy Navigation Satellite System Improvement (H)	1971	3,000	11,848
0101226N	Submarine Acoustic Warfare Development	1991–95	123,128	133,888
0101228N	Trident I	1973–95	53,775,050	82,789,310
0101229N	Strategic Cruise Missile	1979–80	5,196	9,503
0101235F	ICBM Helicopter Support	1992–95	42,963	44,525
0101310F	Strategic Automated Command and Control System (SACCS)-ADP	1962–93, 1995	864,505	3,814,337
0101312F	PACCS and WWABNCP System EC-135 Class V Mods	1962–95	3,076,974	6,398,272
0101313F	Strat War Planning System—USSTRATCOM	1984–95	811,042	945,506
0101315N	FBM Control System—Communications	1964–95	5,158,996	7,739,291
0101316F	USSTRATCOM Command and Control	1962–95	2,576,433	4,997,966
0101316N	USSTRATCOM Command and Control	1993–95	12,474	13,014
0101317F	Post Attack Command and Control System (PACCS) Communications	1962–95	162,523	284,486
0101321F	Special Purpose Communications	1963–95	100,044	355,141
0101321N	Special Purpose Communications (H)	1965–71	10,446	48,754
0101322F	Titan Communications (H)	1962–88	78,354	195,979
0101323F	MINUTEMAN Communications	1962–95	361,711	679,787
0101401N	Extremely Low Frequency (ELF) Communications	1972–79, 1981–91	309,368	544,399
0101402N	Navy Strategic Communications	1967–95	983,642	1,667,623
0101403N	HYDRUS	1969–79, 1981–82	45,591	144,994
0101812F	Satellite Basing (H)	1970–77	99,396	328,046
0101815F	Advanced Strategic Programs	1990–93	183,820	202,943
0101820F	Mission Evaluation Activities (Offensive)	1977–95	269,743	361,841
0101830F	Operational Headquarters (Offensive)	1970–95	778,472	1,195,041
0101830N	Operational Headquarters (Offensive)	1962–95	376,095	651,205
0101856F	Environmental Compliance	1991–95	243,460	260,589
0101856N	Environmental Compliance	1992–95	20,265	21,195
0101876F	Minor Construction (RPM) (Offensive)	1992–95	24,988	26,458
0101876N	Minor Construction (RPM) (Offensive)	1992–95	45,213	47,267
0101878F	Maintenance and Repair (RPM) (Offensive)	1992–95	965,096	1,027,244
0101878N	Maintenance and Repair (RPM) (Offensive)	1992–95	216,889	231,381
0101894F	Real Property Maintenance (Offensive) (H)	1962–92	10,307,762	20,722,388
0101894N	Real Property Maintenance (Offensive) (H)	1979–91	734,030	974,011
0101895F	Base Communications, Offensive	1962–95	1,241,274	2,215,674
0101895N	Base Communications, Offensive	1979–95	77,527	92,543

TABLE B-1. Department of Defense Future Years Defense Program Database, 1962–95 (*continued*)

Thousands of dollars

Program element number	*Program element title*	*Years active*	*Total then-year cost*	*Total adjusted cost (1996 dollars)*
0101896F	Base Operations (Offensive)	1962–95	25,905,308	65,203,234
0101896N	Base Operations (Offensive)	1962–95, 1976–95	1,517,012	2,016,782
0101897F	Training (Offensive)	1962–95	2,974,584	5,855,748
0101897N	Training (Offensive) (H)	1962–74	157,857	804,488
0101898F	Management Headquarters, USSTRATCOM	1962–95	3,386,902	8,492,786
0101898N	Management Headquarters, USSTRATCOM	1993–95	31,438	32,754
0102111F	F-101 Squadrons (H)	1962–78	887,254	4,662,153
0102112F	F-102 Squadrons (H)	1962–70	350,410	1,942,291
0102113F	F-104 Squadrons (H)	1963–70	66,220	339,267
0102114F	F-106 Squadrons (H)	1962–87	2,441,762	8,592,193
0102115N	F-6 Squadrons (H)	1962–63	5,626	33,617
0102116F	Air Defense F-15	1979–93	933,691	1,237,081
0102120F	F-16 Interceptor Squadrons (H)	1990, 1994	1,269	1,448
0102211F	BOMARC Squadrons (H)	1962–73	175,554	891,756
0102212A	NIKE-HERCULES Battalions (H)	1962–79	1,391,017	7,043,221
0102213A	HAWK Battalions (H)	1963–70	106,282	552,128
0102215N	ABM Support (H)	1969–71	17,000	71,503
0102310F	NCMC—TW/AA Systems (H)	1974–94	1,376,039	1,722,449
0102311F	NCMC—Space Defense Systems (H)	1962–92	1,337,452	2,964,969
0102312F	C3 Power Reliability Program	1986–89	50,440	63,256
0102313F	Ballistic Missile Tactical Warning/Attack Assessment System (H)	1982–92	219,942	278,594
0102314F	Back-Up Interceptor Control (BUIC) System (H)	1962–86	410,119	2,143,875
0102315A	Surface-to-Air Missile Fire Coordination Centers (H)	1962–75	227,148	1,157,333
0102317F	Joint Control Centers (H)	1970	98	411
0102318F	Region Control Centers (H)	1962–85	561,118	1,862,539
0102319F	Manual NORAD Control Centers (H)	1962–84	670,151	3,534,700
0102322F	AAC Integrated Command & Control System (H)	1983–89	13,723	18,109
0102323F	TW/AA Interface Network (H)	1962–92	377,836	847,021
0102324F	ADC Command and Control System (H)	1962–75	2,302	8,257

0102325F	Joint Surveillance System	1974–95	2,349,326	3,035,445
0102331F	Communications, 416L	1962–95	1,042,289	3,112,183
0102333A	Air Defense Communications (H)	1971–76	31,003	105,607
0102410F	Airborne Warning and Control System (AWACS) (H)	1973–75	761	2,284
0102411F	North Atlantic Defense System	1962–95	4,169,853	13,856,946
0102412F	North Warning System (NWS)	1962–95	2,915,341	6,006,425
0102413F	Airborne Early Warning and Control Systems (H)	1962–79	695,777	3,293,908
0102414N	Airborne DEW-Line Extension (H)	1962–66	101,467	584,121
0102415N	Picket Ships, DEW-Line Extension (H)	1962–65	610	3,498
0102416N	Picket Ships, Offshore Radar (H)	1962–65	105,099	607,449
0102417F	Over-the-Horizon Backscatter Radar	1968, 1970-74, 1979–95	1,590,898	2,099,979
0102421F	Program 437 (H)	1963–77	181,976	911,896
0102422A	Program 505 (H)	1963–67	9,408	52,712
0102423F	Ballistic Missile Early Warning System (BMEWS)	1962–92	2,113,609	5,818,807
0102424F	SPACETRACK	1962–93	1,656,836	3,816,607
0102425F	Over-the-Horizon (OTH) Radar System (H)	1963–76	186,650	834,303
0102426F	Bomb Alarm System (H)	1963–70	39,636	199,423
0102427N	Naval Space Surveillance	1962–95	497,430	952,307
0102428N	Space Systems Control	1971–76, 1978, 1984–95	96,489	116,728
0102429F	NIKE Targets (H)	1962–71	67,074	331,113
0102431F	Defense Support Program (H)	1962–92	8,541,254	16,587,535
0102432F	Submarine-Launched Ballistic Missile (SLBM) Radar Warning System (H)	1974–92	1,052,241	1,629,069
0102433F	NUDET Detection System (H)	1981–92	378,967	493,324
0102434F	Perimeter Acquisition Radar-Attack Characterization System (PARCS) (H)	1977–81, 1991	211	383
0102435F	PARCS Communications (H)	1979–82	881	1,530
0102436F	Command Center Processing and Display System (H)	1979–92	200,343	265,215
0102441F	Program 437 Communications (H)	1966–71	1,034	4,744
0102443F	Space Defense Interface Network	1962–92	45,013	105,851
0102444F	Over-the-Horizon Radar System Communications	1962–82, 1985–94	13,826	47,544
0102449F	Space Shuttle (H)	1978–86	1,592,474	2,591,007
0102450F	Space Defense Operations (H)	1981–89	142,147	199,943
0102496F	Base Operations–SPACECOM (H)	1983–92	844,474	1,070,155
0102498F	Management Headquarters (Space Command) (H)	1982–92	415,627	525,441
0102498N	Management Headquarters (Space Command)	1983–95	93,074	109,778
0102514A	SAFEGUARD Defense System (H)	1968–77	5,033,217	19,616,983
0102516A	SAFEGUARD Communications (H)	1969–77	78,183	270,674
0102517A	SAFEGUARD Logistic Support (H)	1969–78	332,492	1,060,170

TABLE B-1. Department of Defense Future Years Defense Program Database, 1962–95 (*continued*)

Thousands of dollars

Program element number	*Program element title*	*Years active*	*Total then-year cost*	*Total adjusted cost (1996 dollars)*
0102518A	SAFEGUARD Training (H)	1969–73	34,582	133,837
0102519A	SAFEGUARD Construction Supervision (H)	1969–75	4,024	15,125
0102520A	SAFEGUARD Base Support (H)	1973–77	32,836	93,913
0102802A	Service Support to DCPA (H)	1974–75	19	56
0102802F	Service Support to DCPA (H)	1974–80	177	423
0102802N	Service Support to DCPA (H)	1977–79	62	135
0102811A	Military Survival Measures (H)	1968	207	969
0102812A	JCS Directed and Coordinated Exercises (H)	1966–74	7,108	29,958
0102813N	Barrier Communications Network (H)	1962–64	1,204	7,062
0102814A	Special Programs	1981–93	2,055,438	2,746,121
0102815A	Joint Continental Defense Systems Integration Planning Staff (H)	1969–73	723	2,834
0102815F	Joint Continental Defense Systems Integration Planning Staff (H)	1968–74	6,396	24,956
0102815M	Joint Continental Defense Systems Integration Planning Staff (H)	1969–71	42	175
0102815N	Joint Continental Defense Systems Integration Planning Staff (H)	1969–72	381	1,538
0102816F	Operational Headquarters (Defensive)	1969–95	493,980	797,775
0102820F	Mission Evaluation Activities (Defensive)	1977–95	137,559	204,663
0102821A	Classified Program	1983–87	135,581	180,756
0102822F	LEO (H)	1986–87	260,898	341,599
0102827F	Industrial fund and stock fund support (H)	1987, 90	(546,071)	(711,488)
0102856F	Environmental Compliance	1991–95	52,542	57,658
0102876F	Minor Construction (RPM) (Defensive)(H)	1992–93	3,039	3,343
0102878F	Maintenance and Repair (RPM) (Defensive)	1992–95	26,818	29,142
0102890F	Visual Information Activities, Strategic	1981–95	184,451	230,987
0102890N	Visual Information Activities, Strategic	1981–91	3,131	4,163
0102894F	Real Property Maintenance (Defensive) (H)	1962–92	4,417,086	9,011,420
0102895F	Command and Base Communications, Air Defense	1962–95	337,501	656,405
0102896A	Base Operations (Defensive) (H)	1962–75	601,356	2,868,007
0102896F	Base Operations (Defensive)	1962–95	7,347,885	21,973,955
0102896N	Base Operations (Defensive) (H)	1962–64	2,913	14,948

0102897A	Training (Defensive) (H)	1962–74	16,855	70,958
0102897F	Training (Defensive)	1962–95	1,852,510	4,282,302
0102897N	Training (Defensive) (H)	1962–65	9,588	55,406
0102898A	Management Headquarters (Strategic Defensive Forces) (H)	1962–75	174,984	810,195
0102898F	Management Headquarters (Strategic Defensive Forces)	1962–95	1,343,485	4,787,558
0102898N	Management Headquarters (Strategic Defensive Forces) (H)	1962–71	46,297	263,640
0102998F	Management Headquarters, ADP Support (H)	1981–94	3,632	5,121
0103121A	U.S. Space Command Activities (H)	1988, 1991, 1993–94	5,184	5,745
0103121F	U.S. Space Command (SPACECOM) Activities (H)	1986–95	106,894	122,148
0103121M	U.S. Space Command (SPACECOM) Activities (H)	1987–95	9,514	10,824
0103121N	U.S. Space Command (SPACECOM) Activities (H)	1986–95	28,916	33,073
0103122A	U.S. Element NORAD Activities	1987–88, 1992–95	7,584	8,657
0103122F	U.S. Element NORAD Activities	1986–95	54,267	61,539
0103122M	U.S. Element NORAD Activities	1986–95	1,256	1,437
0103122N	U.S. Element NORAD Activities	1986–95	10,385	12,035
0103198A	Management Headquarters (U.S. Element NORAD)	1986–95	9,080	10,829
0103198F	Management Headquarters (U.S. Element NORAD)	1986–95	64,912	74,004
0103198M	Management Headquarters (U.S. Element NORAD)	1986–89	234	298
0103198N	Management Headquarters (U.S. Element NORAD)	1986–95	3,022	3,584
0103298A	Management Headquarters (U.S. Space Command)	1987–95	40,666	47,238
0103298F	Management Headquarters (U.S. Space Command)	1986–95	100,611	113,583
0103298M	Management Headquarters (U.S. Space Command)	1986–95	7,514	8,555
0103298N	Management Headquarters (U.S. Space Command)	1986–95	35,443	40,695
	SUBTOTAL MFP 1—STRATEGIC FORCES		425,305,301	952,291,705
0201117A	Airborne Command Post (CINCEUR)	1962–95	13,806	28,150
0201117F	Airborne Command Post (CINCEUR)	1964–95	364,370	744,974
0201117M	Airborne Command Post (CINCEUR)	1988–91, 1995	587	690
0201117N	Airborne Command Post (CINCEUR)	1965–95	9,144	17,921
0201118A	Airborne Command Post (CINCPAC)	1962–86, 1988, 1990–91	7,213	16,534
0201118F	Airborne Command Post (CINCPAC) (H)	1965–93	331,425	704,607
0201118N	Airborne Command Post (CINCPAC)	1966–95	11,513	20,209
0201120A	Airborne Command Post (CINCLANT)	1973–86, 1988–92, 1994-95	7,015	11,299
0201120F	Airborne Command Post (CINCLANT) (H)	1973–93	195,903	299,795
0201120M	Airborne Command Post (CINCLANT)	1973–92	1,463	2,281
0201120N	Airborne Command Post (CINCLANT)	1974–93	35,327	45,872

TABLE B-1. Department of Defense Future Years Defense Program Database, 1962–95 (*continued*)

Thousands of dollars

Program element number	*Program element title*	*Years active*	*Total then-year cost*	*Total adjusted cost (1996 dollars)*
0201132N	CINCLANT ABNCP Communications Facilities (H)	1975–77	3,402	8,754
0202081A	Theater Air Defense Forces	1989–95	3,129,196	3,573,118
0202082A	Theater Missile Forces (H)	1989–91	398,503	469,608
0202085A	Theater Defense Forces	1989–95	3,091,787	3,452,982
0202086A	Special Mission Support (H)	1989–92	180,880	209,359
0202089A	Communications Support	1989–95	538,925	600,581
0202091A	Intelligence Support	1989–95	1,989,385	2,198,638
0202092A	Special Activities	1989–95	14,973,279	16,438,286
0202381A	Europe Air Defense Forces	1962–88	8,312,501	16,219,617
0202382A	Europe Missile Forces	1962–88	3,935,096	8,923,397
0202386A	Special Mission Support	1962–88	111,224	342,296
0202391A	Intelligence Support	1965–88	223,939	330,962
0202392A	Special Activities	1975–88	22,644	32,365
0202481A	Pacific Air Defense Forces	1962–88	495,002	2,132,654
0202482A	Pacific Missile Forces	1962–88	205,779	737,401
0202483A	Special Operations Forces	1962–87	221,060	979,622
0202484A	Support to Other Services (H)	1962–84	365,429	1,093,865
0202486A	Special Mission Support	1962–88	409,491	1,414,074
0202489A	Communications Support	1962–75	113,382	543,198
0202491A	Intelligence Support	1966–88	96,541	161,441
0202492A	Special Activities	1972–88	646,808	1,163,110
0202588A	Intelligence Support (H)	1975–84, 1987	31,249	58,395
0202681A	Theater Air Defense Forces	1962–86	629,615	2,107,440
0202682A	Theater Missile Forces	1962–75, 1980–88	802,084	3,929,541
0202692A	Special Activities	1962–88	753,690	1,368,841
0202891A	Intelligence Support	1962–88	625,949	1,010,804
0203711A	LITTLE JOHN (H)	1962–63	1,015	6,089
0203712A	HONEST JOHN (H)	1962–63	1,040	6,210
0203730A	CHAPARRAL (H)	1974–84	118,880	205,092

0203734A	PERSHING (H)	1962–74	278,559	1,467,659
0203736A	NIKE HERCULES (H)	1962–68	13,191	74,238
0203737A	SERGEANT (H)	1963–67	13,423	72,654
0203739A	Air Defense C3I Modifications	1981–83, 1988–92	49,562	59,318
0203801A	Missile/Air Defense Product Improvement Program	1985–95	534,907	621,480
0204111N	Attack Carriers (H)	1962–75	8,249,630	35,849,648
0204112N	Multi-Purpose Aircraft Carriers	1972–95	64,652,052	89,792,736
0204133N	A-4 Squadrons (H)	1962–76	814,285	4,222,407
0204134N	A-6 Squadrons	1962–95	12,327,182	24,219,043
0204135N	A-7 Squadrons	1964–91	6,931,647	19,045,906
0204136N	F/A-18 Squadrons	1976, 1978–95	24,919,047	30,701,851
0204143N	F-111 Squadrons (H)	1963–68	359,862	1,810,826
0204144N	F-14 Squadrons	1970–95	22,449,169	37,089,136
0204150N	Navy TACAIR/ASW Carrier Airwing Staff Flying	1988–95	278,745	315,104
0204152N	E-2 Squadrons	1962–95	10,471,128	19,084,047
0204153N	Reconnaissance Squadrons	1962–83	1,320,313	6,354,994
0204158N	F/A-18 Fleet Readiness Squadron (Attack) (H)	1992–95	120	130
0204211N	ASW Carriers (H)	1962–74	1,212,427	6,004,567
0204220N	Battleships	1981–95	3,197,873	4,336,618
0204221N	Cruisers	1962–95	47,329,851	74,079,250
0204222N	Destroyers, Missile	1962–95	46,107,389	82,093,992
0204223N	Destroyers, Nonmissile	1962–95	22,061,044	60,341,849
0204224N	Frigates, Missile	1962–95	17,061,068	30,225,256
0204225N	Frigates, Nonmissile	1962–95	14,138,868	32,084,306
0204227N	Support Forces	1962–95	8,781,239	17,212,361
0204228N	Surface Support	1974–95	14,412,317	20,335,121
0204229N	Tomahawk and Tomahawk Mission Planning Center (TMPC)	1973–95	31,669,283	44,048,134
0204231N	A-4 Squadrons (H)	1966–70	9,178	43,781
0204232N	S-2 Squadrons (H)	1962–76	566,839	2,863,381
0204233N	SH-3/SH-60F Squadrons	1962–95	4,375,588	7,402,982
0204234N	S-3 Squadrons	1971–95	6,163,733	12,277,152
0204251N	ASW Patrol Squadrons	1962–95	16,609,871	36,416,228
0204271N	Air-Launched Ordnance and Missiles	1962–95	6,448,902	11,344,532
0204281N	Submarines	1962–95	73,442,730	142,505,128
0204282N	Support Forces	1962–95	9,215,146	15,375,049
0204283N	Submarine Support	1972–95	8,327,969	11,148,424
0204284N	Submarines Ordnance and Missiles	1962–69, 1974–95	6,760,172	10,814,516

TABLE B-1. Department of Defense Future Years Defense Program Database, 1962–95 (*continued*)

Thousands of dollars

Program element number	*Program element title*	*Years active*	*Total then-year cost*	*Total adjusted cost (1996 dollars)*
0204311N	Integrated Surveillance System	1962–95	6,473,703	12,843,766
0204454N	Special Combat Support Forces	1962–95	1,025,533	3,721,640
0204561N	Deep Submergence Systems	1962–95	1,750,578	3,729,986
0204572N	Space Activities	1980–95	155,548	180,981
0204633N	Fleet Support Training	1962–95	2,578,203	6,187,082
0204641N	Ship Special Support Equipment	1990	7,825	9,185
0204660N	Navy Command and Control Systems (NCCS)	1976–95	1,593,606	2,013,764
0205620N	Surface ASW Combat System Integration	1978–95	305,898	389,290
0205621N	Air Anti-Submarine Warfare Fleet Support (H)	1966–69	6,717	32,027
0205622N	DASH Weapons System (H)	1962–67	11,163	62,363
0205628N	ASROC Weapons System (H)	1962–67	16,209	90,146
0205629N	Torpedo MK-46 (H)	1962–69	76,308	424,701
0205630N	Torpedo Support Equipment (H)	1976–78	1,555	3,721
0205634N	Submarine Silencing	1967–86	253,082	572,658
0205635N	Ship Support (ASWEPS) (H)	1962–72	17,971	93,811
0205660N	MK 48 Torpedo (H)	1963–77	339,363	1,519,460
0205661N	Submarine ASW Weapon Improvement (H)	1976–77	2,139	5,222
0207111F	B-57 Squadrons (H)	1962–72	242,430	1,203,477
0207112F	B-66 Squadrons (H)	1962	6,800	40,865
0207122F	F-84 Squadrons (H)	1962–65	133,441	785,618
0207123F	F-86 Squadrons (H)	1962–63, 1968–69	19,698	105,510
0207124F	F-100 Squadrons (H)	1962–73	1,801,332	9,288,870
0207129F	F-111 Squadrons	1962–95	20,609,036	55,507,086
0207221F	KB-50 Squadrons (H)	1962–65	105,421	618,277
0207223F	KC-135s	1993–95	539,883	566,239
0207311F	MACE (H)	1962–70	143,342	784,090
0207312F	MATADOR Squadrons (H)	1962	1,300	7,813
0207314F	Ground Launched Cruise Missile	1979–93	4,004,735	5,639,433
0207417F	Airborne Warning and Control System (AWACS)	1974–95	9,938,868	15,493,862

0207589F	Base Physical Security Systems	1986–95	154,458	183,864
0207593F	Nuclear, Biological, and Chemical Defense Program	1977–95	1,309,802	1,682,474
0208009N	TOMAHAWK Cruise Missile	1978–95	3,614,578	4,743,467
0208012A	Defense Special Projects Group (DSPG) (H)	1967–72	67,304	300,804
0208012D	Defense Special Projects Group (DSPG) (H)	1967–72	96,522	417,431
0208012F	Defense Special Projects Group (DSPG) (H)	1966–72	655,224	2,924,318
0208013A	Special Ammunition Control, Non-United States	1962–95	2,161,687	4,364,439
0208060C	Theater Missile Defenses	1992–94	438,046	463,440
0208060F	Theater Missile Defenses	1992, 1995	30,439	31,399
	SUBTOTAL MFP 2—GENERAL PURPOSE FORCES		595,649,597	1,099,130,379
0301333N	Fleet Intelligence Support	1972–95	113,057	181,628
0301357F	NUDET Detection System	1986–88, 1990–91, 1993	91,706	112,276
0302011F	National Military Command Center (NMCC)	1964–95	163,865	280,808
0302012A	Alternate National Military Command Center (ANMCC)	1962–92	350,782	1,023,780
0302015F	National Emergency Airborne Command Post and E-48 Class V Mods	1962–95	1,367,987	2,195,655
0302016F	National Military Command System-Wide Support	1962–82, 1984–92	56,839	219,231
0302016J	National Military Command System-Wide Support	1965–95	258,902	511,171
0302016K	National Military Command System-Wide Support	1962–95	553,790	1,537,773
0302016N	National Military Command System-Wide Support (H)	1964–72	4,827	24,130
0302017K	WWMCCS ADP–JTSA	1971–95	538,183	842,203
0302018K	WWMCCS ADP–NMCS	1974–95	1,122,378	1,612,662
0302019K	Joint/Defense Information Systems Engineering and Integration	1976–95	770,154	1,006,009
0302051N	National Emergency Command Post Afloat (NECPA), Communications (H)	1962–70	162,852	858,397
0302052F	National Emergency Airborne Command Post (NEACP), Communications	1963–95	237,279	364,791
0302053A	NMCS-Wide Support, Communications	1965–92	137,122	313,775
0302053F	NMCS-Wide Support, Communications	1962–95	247,566	480,016
0302053N	NMCS-Wide Support, Communications (H)	1967–68, 1970, 1972–73	7,192	32,071
0303109N	Satellite Communications	1964–95	6,172,705	9,038,267
0303110F	Defense Satellite Communications System (DSCS)	1966–95	2,722,154	4,916,223
0303111A	Strategic Army Communications (STARCOM)	1962–95	5,341,200	10,775,633
0303112F	Air Force Communications (AIRCOM)	1962–95	9,381,658	21,222,996
0303113N	Navy Communications (NAVCOM)	1962–95	7,099,589	16,726,110
0303127K	Support of the National Communications System	1981–95	766,873	942,433
0303127M	Support of the National Communications System	1994–95	128	132
0303129A	Defense Message System	1991	2,368	2,655

TABLE B-1. Department of Defense Future Years Defense Program Database, 1962–95 (*continued*)

Thousands of dollars

Program element number	*Program element title*	*Years active*	*Total then-year cost*	*Total adjusted cost (1996 dollars)*
0303129F	Defense Message System	1991–95	56,593	58,905
0303131A	Minimum Essential Emergency Communications Network (MEECN)	1973–76, 1978–91	23,663	49,474
0303131F	Minimum Essential Emergency Communications Network (MEECN)	1971–95	910,943	1,295,946
0303131K	Minimum Essential Emergency Communications Network (MEECN)	1971–95	163,533	262,054
0303131N	Minimum Essential Emergency Communications Network (MEECN)	1971, 1973–95	57,191	102,995
0303140A	Information Systems Security Program	1990–95	259,390	276,337
0303140F	Information Systems Security Program	1992–95	168,224	174,346
0303140G	Information Systems Security Program	1994–95	949,998	981,643
0303140K	Information Systems Security Program	1995	6,479	6,627
0303140N	Information Systems Security Program	1992–95	240,892	252,601
0303142A	SATCOM Ground Environment	1962–95	4,945,445	7,464,688
0303144F	Electromagnetic Compatibility Analysis Center (ECAC)	1962–95	299,453	552,239
0303145A	EUCOM C3 Systems	1976–95	721,009	964,957
0303150F	WWMCCS/Global Command and Control System	1994–95	36,641	37,499
0303150J	WWMCCS/Global Command and Control System	1995	20,400	20,865
0303150M	WWMCCS/Global Command and Control System	1994–95	563	581
0303151A	World-Wide Military Command and Control Systems (WWMCCS) ADP	1974–92	258,549	359,959
0303151F	World-Wide Military Command and Control Systems (WWMCCS) ADP	1974–95	617,763	851,879
0303151H	World-Wide Military Command and Control Systems (WWMCCS) ADP	1974–94	83,878	119,257
0303151N	World-Wide Military Command and Control Systems (WWMCCS) ADP	1976–95	280,341	391,348
0303152A	World-Wide Military Command and Control Systems, Information System	1984–95	678,174	804,072
0303152F	World-Wide Military Command and Control Systems, Information System	1982–95	349,915	412,232
0303152H	World-Wide Military Command and Control Systems, Information System	1984–88	3,760	4,970
0303152K	World-Wide Military Command and Control Systems, Information System	1982, 1984–89	40,914	53,834
0303152N	World-Wide Military Command and Control Systems, Information System	1982–95	141,953	177,411
0303154F	WWMCCS ADP Modernization (H)	1983–90	302,697	395,170
0303154J	WWMCCS ADP Modernization	1992–94	38,435	40,451
0303154K	WWMCCS ADP Modernization	1989–95	182,978	204,053
0303298A	Management Headquarters (WWMCCS ADP)	1973, 1976–92	138,388	229,312
0303298N	Management Headquarters (WWMCCS ADP)	1974–95	272,124	403,183

0303398A	Management Headquarters (WWMCCS Information System)	1982–95	31,961	35,638
0303401K	Communications Security (COMSEC) (H)	1964, 1967–70	1,018	5,550
0303601F	Milstar Satellite Communications System	1993–95	2,264,612	2,391,319
0303603F	MILSTAR Satellite Communications System	1992–94	873,358	960,586
0303603N	Milstar Satellite Communications System	1986–90	21,267	26,588
0303605F	Satellite Communications Terminals	1992–95	257,008	271,025
0303606F	UHF Satellite Communications	1995	34,450	35,236
0305106LC	Consolidated Imagery Activities	1993–95	139,609	144,780
0305108K	Command and Control Research	1984–95	23,956	28,757
0305111F	Weather Service	1962–95	6,141,840	13,271,369
0305111N	Weather Service	1962–95	1,726,465	3,236,644
0305112N	Oceanography	1962–95	1,930,601	2,847,937
0305115H	Nuclear Weapons Operations	1962–95	1,685,715	3,747,801
0305121F	Manned Orbiting Laboratory (H)	1964–70	1,451,237	6,786,591
0305130F	AFSCN Operations	1981–95	2,599,556	3,167,831
0305131A	Mapping, Charting, and Geodesy (H)	1962–73	836,753	4,052,775
0305131B	Mapping, Charting, and Geodesy	1973–95	9,569,100	13,940,228
0305131F	Mapping, Charting, and Geodesy (H)	1962–74	934,218	4,626,385
0305131N	Mapping, Charting, and Geodesy	1962–95	3,004,654	6,974,621
0305132B	Defense Mapping Agency Communications	1973–95	237,724	295,683
0305133V	Industrial Security Activities	1981–95	427,722	533,414
0305134N	Physical Security	1986, 1988–95	171,353	196,408
0305135BA	On-Site Inspection Agency Activities	1988–95	537,507	583,505
0305136BA	Nuclear Weapons Operations Communications	1989–95	17,252	18,730
0305145A	Arms Control Implementation	1991–95	102,043	108,205
0305145F	Arms Control Implementation	1991–95	229,896	244,273
0305145N	Arms Control Implementation	1991–95	154,259	164,274
0305152H	Nuclear Weapons Operations Communications	1962–95	41,958	59,166
0305155F	Theater Nuclear Weapon Storage & Security System	1984–91, 1993–95	172,997	213,935
0305159B	Defense Reconnaissance Support Activities	1982–95	374,933	489,419
0305159D	Defense Reconnaissance Support Activities	1986	2,988	4,011
0305159F	Defense Reconnaissance Support Activities (H)	1984–90, 1992	1,265,766	1,557,355
0305159I	Defense Reconnaissance Support Activities	1982–95	4,329,960	5,556,358
0305160F	Defense Meteorological Satellite Program (DMSP)	1963–95	2,930,213	4,681,239
0305160N	Defense Meteorological Satellite Program (DMSP)	1976–95	201,875	275,876
0305162F	Defense Meteorological Satellite Program Communications	1970–95	36,907	65,158
0305164A	NAVSTAR Global Positioning System (User Equipment)	1985–93	182,466	219,924
0305164F	NAVSTAR Global Positioning System (User Equipment)	1984–95	1,073,251	1,263,970

TABLE B-1. Department of Defense Future Years Defense Program Database, 1962–95 (*continued*)

Thousands of dollars

Program element number	*Program element title*	*Years active*	*Total then-year cost*	*Total adjusted cost (1996 dollars)*
0305164N	NAVSTAR Global Positioning System (User Equipment)	1983–95	293,937	334,464
0305165F	NAVSTAR Global Positioning System (Space and Control Segments)	1982–95	2,809,099	3,435,024
0305170F	Space Support Program (H)	1977–82	18,427	36,059
0305171F	Space Shuttle Operations	1979–95	4,165,093	5,584,807
0305175F	Space-Based Radar Operations	1992–95	2,054	2,161
0305181F	Western Space Launch Facility (WSLF)	1991–95	574,547	612,444
0305182F	Eastern Space Launch Facility (ESLF)	1991–95	1,273,765	1,353,471
0305598LC	Management Headquarters–Central Imagery Office	1993–95	13,569	14,143
0305810A	Service Support to OSIA	1989, 1991–95	49,931	53,408
0305810M	Service Support to OSIA	1988–95	4,593	4,939
0305810N	Service Support to OSIA	1988–95	15,438	16,715
0305816A	Service Support to OSIA (NFIP)	1993–95	793	820
0305816F	Service Support to OSIA (NFIP)	1992–95	919	971
0305821A	Service Support to CIO	1994–95	3,789	3,907
0305821M	Service Support to CIO	1995	208	213
0305821N	Service Support to CIO	1994–95	3,271	3,380
0305902F	Ballistic Missile Tactical Warning/Attack Assessment System	1993–95	18,819	19,685
0305904F	Space Defense Interface Network	1993–95	6,686	6,985
0305905F	Improved Space Based TW/AA	1993–94	342,129	362,833
0305906F	NCMC—TW/AA System	1992–95	836,269	875,441
0305907F	NCMC—Space Defense Systems	1993–95	47,286	49,240
0305908F	TW/AA Interface Network	1993–95	63,523	66,409
0305909F	Ballistic Missile Early Warning System (BMEWS)	1992–95	230,936	241,339
0305910F	SPACETRACK	1993–95	401,661	419,704
0305911F	Defense Support Program	1993–95	1,477,861	1,540,102
0305912F	Submarine-Launched Ballistic Missile (SLBM) Radar Warning System	1993–95	117,827	123,131
0305913F	NUDET Detection System	1993–95	147,897	153,980
	SUBTOTAL MFP 3—C3I		108,860,217	190,568,042

0501111F	F-86 Squadrons (H)	1962–65	79,263	462,722
0501112F	F-89 Squadrons (H)	1962–70	249,155	1,369,333
0501113F	F-100 Squadrons (H)	1962–65	52,716	306,280
0501114F	F-102 Squadrons (ANG) (H)	1962–76	1,045,040	4,635,618
0501115F	F-104 Squadrons (H)	1962–64	18,871	112,365
0501117F	F-101 Squadrons (ANG) (H)	1969–82	585,736	1,581,633
0501118F	Defense System Evaluation Squadron (H)	1970–72	4,902	19,158
0501120F	F-106 Squadrons (ANG) (H)	1972–88	1,302,138	2,411,983
0501123F	EB-57 Squadrons (ANG) (H)	1974–82	118,241	267,019
0501124F	F-4 Fighter Interceptor Squadrons (ANG)	1976–91	1,712,826	2,379,409
0501196F	Base Operations–(Offensive) (AFR) (H)	1962–93	35,139	66,073
0501198F	Management Headquarters (Strategic Forces)	1962–95	14,899	26,718
0501216F	F-16 Air Defense Squadrons (ANG)	1985–95	2,049,736	2,287,678
0501217F	F-15 Air Defense Squadrons (ANG)	1987–95	510,454	562,362
0501218F	Air Defense Competitive Aircraft (ANG) (H)	1987	550	716
0501296F	Base Operations–(Defensive) (AFR) (H)	1962–80, 1988–93	10,458	36,933
0501311F	Command Control and Warning (ANG)	1962–95	371,406	801,080
0501312F	Airborne Early Warning and Control Systems (AFR) (H)	1972–79	46,190	124,410
0501313F	Surveillance Radar Stations/Sites (AFR) (H)	1962–81	3,536	12,421
0501411F	KC-135 Squadrons (ANG)	1975–95	5,623,658	7,490,342
0501412F	KC-97 Squadrons (ANG) (H)	1976–78	224,202	560,402
0501611N	Support Ships (FBM)	1974–95	36,304	51,403
0501628F	B-1B Squadrons (ANG)	1994–95	139,318	142,916
0501631N	Operational Headquarters (Fleet Ballistics Missile)	1974–95	29,237	38,050
0501720F	B-52 Squadrons (AFR)	1994–95	70,105	72,080
0501801A	NIKE-HERCULES (ARNG) (H)	1962–75	777,780	3,535,063
0501802A	NIKE-AJAX (ARNG) (H)	1962–64	84,233	499,149
0501928A	Service Support to FEMA (AR)	1977–95	23,499	31,206
0502324N	Early Warning Aircraft Squadrons	1971–95	163,434	239,031
0502325N	Reconnaissance Squadrons	1971–92	53,430	96,860
0502330N	Carrier ASW Squadrons (H)	1962–74	164,670	810,414
0502341N	ASW Patrol Squadrons	1962–95	2,999,459	5,179,625
0502363N	Undersea Surveillance Systems (H)	1974–76	626	1,789
0502386N	Deep Submergence Systems	1974–94	8,415	11,725
0503127F	Defense Special Security System (AFR) (H)	1962–79	6,628	24,317
0505165F	Nuclear/Biological/Chemical Defense Program (ANG) (H)	1990–91	11,169	12,947
0505166F	Nuclear/Biological/Chemical Defense Program (AFR)	1990–95	20,415	22,925

TABLE B-1. Department of Defense Future Years Defense Program Database, 1962–95 (*continued*)

Thousands of dollars

Program element number	*Program element title*	*Years active*	*Total then-year cost*	*Total adjusted cost (1996 dollars)*
	SUBTOTAL MFP 5—GUARD AND RESERVE FORCES		18,647,838	36,284,154
0602102E	CLOUD GAP (H)	1964	831	4,687
0602107E	JOINT ARPA/DOE Third Generation Weapon Technology (H)	1984	6,840	9,777
0602113A	Hardened BMD Materials (H)	1970–72, 1974	12,167	43,641
0602117A	Nuclear Munitions and Radiacs (H)	1962–72, 1974	75,675	382,022
0602118A	Nuclear Weapons Effects Research and Test (H)	1971–75	28,284	93,389
0602119A	Nuclear Power Applications (H)	1971–72, 1974	3,712	12,834
0602304A	Exploratory Ballistic Missile Defense Development (H)	1972–74	104,490	348,987
0602306A	Hardened Ballistic Missile Defense Materials (H)	1973, 1975	7,660	23,104
0602314N	Undersea Surveillance Weapon Technology	1986–95	959,469	1,117,144
0602323N	Submarine Technology	1986–93	113,028	134,461
0602324N	Nuclear Propulsion Technology	1986–91, 1993	211,964	264,961
0602331N	Missile Propulsion Technology (H)	1962–85	212,561	726,538
0602332N	Surface/Aerospace Weaponry Technology (H)	1962–85	820,035	2,966,622
0602542N	Nuclear Propulsion Technology (H)	1962–85	684,230	1,926,347
0602543N	Ship and Submarine Technology (H)	1962–85	576,237	1,775,272
0602615A	Nuclear Munitions (H)	1973, 1975	2,614	7,768
0602633N	Undersea Warfare Weaponry Technology	1962–85, 1994–95	568,503	1,693,031
0602701E	Nuclear Monitoring Research (H)	1962–80	636,152	2,964,892
0602704H	Nuclear Weapons Effects Development (H)	1962–80	1,095,723	3,817,773
0602707E	Particle Beam Technology	1982–92	204,390	278,459
0602710H	Nuclear Weapons Effects Test (H)	1962–80	1,362,920	5,523,792
0602711N	Undersea Target Surveillance Technology (H)	1962–85	717,489	2,301,479
0602713H	Nuclear Weapons Survivability and Security (H)	1978–80	31,679	61,384
0602714E	Treaty Verification	1981–92	257,903	334,567
0602715H	Defense Nuclear Agency	1962–95	7,479,434	14,964,624
0602735N	High Energy Laser Technology (H)	1981–83	156,739	241,085
0602764N	Chemical, Biological and Radiological Defense Technology (H)	1962–85	23,196	62,956
0602768N	Directed Energy Technology (H)	1982–84	32,836	48,150

0603201N	Airborne ASW Detection System	1972–81	17,360	43,393
0603214C	Space Based Interceptors	1991–93	1,513,318	1,676,390
0603215C	Limited Defense System	1991–94	4,113,050	4,448,041
0603215N	Long-Range Airborne ASW System	1979	1,000	2,042
0603216C	Theater Missile Defense Advanced Development	1991–94	3,438,348	3,669,595
0603217C	Ballistic Missile Defense Advanced Development	1991–93	1,563,544	1,725,278
0603218C	Research and Support Activities	1991–94	2,382,585	2,592,493
0603220C	SDI-Surveillance, Acquisition, Tracking and Kill Assessment	1984–90	5,581,893	7,040,552
0603221C	SDI-Directed Energy Weapons	1984–90	4,526,548	5,743,277
0603222C	SDI-Kinetic Energy Weapons	1984–90	3,930,521	4,954,238
0603223C	SDI-Systems and Battle Management	1984–90	2,322,295	2,894,623
0603224C	SDI-Survivability, Lethality, and Key Support Technology	1984–90	1,874,273	2,357,142
0603227E	Relocatable Target Detection Technology Program	1988–92	83,391	95,732
0603228N	CV ASW Module	1972–87, 1989–91	66,159	119,624
0603229F	CONUS Air Defense Interceptor (H)	1970	50	210
0603252F	Bomber Penetration Evaluation (B-1) (H)	1980	69,900	127,811
0603254N	ASW Systems Development	1963–72, 1975–95	433,072	1,099,919
0603258F	Common Strategic Rotary Launcher (H)	1982–85, 1990	203,065	292,301
0603259N	Acoustic Search Sensors	1969–76, 1979–85	81,772	217,360
0603272A	Joint Tactical Missile Defense	1989–90	44,324	52,599
0603302A	Joint Tactical Missile Defense Program (H)	1983–88	159,886	215,455
0603304A	Army BMD Support to SDI	1967–95	1,809,098	4,608,484
0603304F	Air Force Support to SDIO, Reimbursable (H)	1987	380	495
0603305A	ZMAR Sprint Defense (H)	1962–63	116,306	686,195
0603305F	Advanced ICBM Technology (H)	1963–79	576,502	1,643,688
0603308A	Army Missile Defense Systems Integration (Dem/Val)	1971–86	2,149,087	4,292,008
0603309F	Reinforced Grain Solid Rocket (H)	1963–64	5,500	31,474
0603310F	High Energy Solid Propulsion Rocket Motor (H)	1963–64	2,500	14,124
0603311A	PERSHING II (H)	1975–76	21,000	55,029
0603311F	Ballistic Missile Technology	1963–95	3,302,109	9,761,732
0603312F	Advanced Concepts (H)	1983–88	7,223,428	9,487,119
0603314F	Strategic Laser Systems Technology (H)	1963–65, 1970–79, 1984	216,762	533,250
0603314N	TRIDENT System (H)	1968–71	60,215	243,865
0603317F	Theater Ballistic Missile (H)	1979–80	21,200	43,036
0603318F	Counter SUAWACS Technology Program (H)	1980–81	19,751	34,782
0603319F	Airborne Laser Technology	1983, 1994–95	48,221	61,391
0603361N	TOMAHAWK Cruise Missile (H)	1973–77	150,058	398,862
0603362N	Cruise Missile (H)	1972–73	6,999	24,805

TABLE B-1. Department of Defense Future Years Defense Program Database, 1962–95 (*continued*)

Thousands of dollars

Program element number	*Program element title*	*Years active*	*Total then-year cost*	*Total adjusted cost (1996 dollars)*
0603367F	Relocatable Target Capability Program (H)	1987–90	39,760	48,719
0603369F	Cruise Missile Engagement Systems Technology (H)	1987	487	634
0603371N	TRIDENT II Missile System	1978–84	2,214,928	3,245,705
0603392A	Anti-Satellite Weapon (ASAT)	1990–93	224,134	253,510
0603393A	TRACTOR TRAILER	1990–92	20,985	23,548
0603401A	Satellite Communications (H)	1962–68	205,213	1,174,764
0603401N	Navigation Satellite System	1967–81	95,299	255,921
0603402F	Space Test Program	1967–95	1,077,099	1,830,160
0603403A	NAVSTAR Global Positioning System (H)	1970–78	23,102	61,736
0603408F	Advanced Liquid Rocket Technology (H)	1965–72	54,082	250,850
0603411F	Space Shuttle (H)	1963–80	709,091	1,841,318
0603413F	Program 626 (H)	1962–64	27,700	163,031
0603414F	Space Test Electric Propulsion (H)	1962–65	7,658	44,676
0603415F	Space Power Unit (H)	1962–63, 1966	5,100	29,558
0603418F	DYNASOAR (H)	1962–64	294,099	1,726,746
0603419F	GEMINI (H)	1964–66	26,985	149,810
0603420F	Program 706 (H)	1962–64	56,500	335,198
0603421F	NAVSTAR Global Positioning System (H)	1969–79	281,179	691,913
0603424F	Cruise Missile Surveillance Technology (H)	1969–87	179,548	420,715
0603425F	Advanced Warning System (H)	1980, 1982–84, 1992	112,987	139,667
0603429F	Warning Information Correlation (H)	1973–81	16,417	38,225
0603435F	Integrated Operational NUDET Detection System (H)	1976–80	33,500	69,175
0603438F	Satellite Systems Survivability	1973–95	222,637	361,007
0603501N	Reactor Propulsion Plants	1962–83	160,736	606,239
0603507N	ASW Ship Integrated Combat Systems (H)	1965–72	36,275	175,752
0603528N	Nonacoustic Antisubmarine Warfare (ASW)	1979–89, 1991	163,551	229,167
0603529N	Advanced ASW Target	1979–91	101,129	129,324
0603531N	HY 130 Steel (New SSN Material)	1969–82	36,291	112,427
0603541N	Nuclear Electronic Power Plants (H)	1969–73	2,206	8,794
0603542N	Radiological Control	1985–95	31,862	36,834

0603553N	Surface ASW	1973–82, 1984–93	442,871	599,632
0603569E	Advanced Submarine Technology	1989–95	450,547	506,767
0603575N	Special Test Systems (H)	1980–81	46,835	83,516
0603578N	A4W/A1G Nuclear Propulsion Plant	1966–87	191,396	539,478
0603579N	D2W Nuclear Propulsion Reactor	1968–83	128,340	327,314
0603580N	Advanced Design Submarine Nuclear Propulsion	1969–81	141,138	437,812
0603588N	SSBN Survivability	1977–82, 1987–91	81,023	122,288
0603604A	Nuclear Munitions, Adv Dev	1966–94	83,221	153,484
0603634N	Electromagnetic Effects Protection Development	1977–94	82,657	105,222
0603638A	Nuclear Hardening Advanced Technology (H)	1984	466	666
0603702F	Over-the-Horizon Radar Technology (H)	1966–73	16,499	70,290
0603703F	CONUS Over-the-Horizon Radar (H)	1972–82	142,666	320,883
0603703N	Mobile Anti-Submarine Warfare Targets (H)	1965–69	13,901	67,847
0603704N	ASW Oceanography	1965–91	99,206	193,488
0603708N	ASW Signal Processing	1977–93	188,801	260,023
0603714N	Nuclear Vulnerability/Survivability (H)	1970–73, 1975–77	6,620	21,243
0603716F	Atmospheric Surveillance Technology (H)	1985–87	30,733	40,718
0603717F	Technical On-site Inspection Program (H)	1987–90	30,025	37,732
0603723N	ASW Force Command and Control System (H)	1972–75	18,210	55,743
0603735F	WWMCCS Architecture (H)	1969–72, 1974, 1976–87	105,782	197,543
0603735K	WWMCCS Architecture	1977–84	8,298	14,996
0603735N	WWMCCS Architecture Support	1975–85, 1989–90, 1992–93	27,894	45,064
0603741N	Satellite Laser Communications (H)	1985, 1987, 1989	23,359	30,429
0603743D	Theater Tactical Ballistic Missile Defense	1991	214,124	240,049
0603747N	Undersea Warfare Advanced Technology	1987–95	345,104	379,520
0603754N	High Energy Laser (H)	1969–80	224,535	584,448
0603788N	Moored Surveillance System	1975–85	122,481	237,001
0603793N	ASW Sensors (Prototype) (H)	1973–79	11,623	30,180
0603806A	NBC Defense System-Adv Dev	1985–95	262,938	308,216
0604202F	XB-70 (H)	1962–67	665,036	3,856,837
0604204F	YF-12A (H)	1962–67	204,520	1,159,672
0604212N	ASW and Other Helo Development	1987–95	1,107,537	1,778,438
0604213F	ASW-18/GAR-9 (H)	1962–63	39,200	232,596
0604214F	Tanker Aircraft Improvements (H)	1975	1,596	4,459
0604215F	B-1 (H)	1965–79	3,600,966	10,625,840
0604217N	S-3 Weapon System Improvement	1979–87, 1993–95	282,249	406,769
0604219N	Airborne ASW Developments	1967–87, 1990–91	287,468	592,302
0604221F	Special Improvements Projects (H)	1984–85	740,842	1,045,440

TABLE B-1. Department of Defense Future Years Defense Program Database, 1962–95 (*continued*)

Thousands of dollars

Program element number	*Program element title*	*Years active*	*Total then-year cost*	*Total adjusted cost (1996 dollars)*
0604221N	P-3 Modernization Program	1980–95	886,635	1,111,354
0604222F	Nuclear Weapons Support	1980–95	52,290	63,700
0604225C	Theater Missile Defense Acquisition EMD Programs	1994	42,097	43,915
0604226F	B-1B	1981–90, 1992–95	3,777,815	5,298,439
0604229N	Carrier Inner Zone ASW Helicopter	1985–87	37,460	50,662
0604234F	Common Strategic Rotary Launcher (H)	1986–88	61,788	82,104
0604240F	B-2 Advanced Technology Bomber	1989–95	9,602,110	10,859,533
0604244F	Short Range Attack Missile II (SRAM II)—Eng Dev (H)	1990–91	345,229	398,134
0604245F	Short Range Attack Missile–Tactical (SRAM-T) (H)	1990–91	77,461	89,693
0604301A	NIKE-X (H)	1964–68	1,794,967	9,166,719
0604302A	Air Defense Control and Coordination System (H)	1969–77	29,439	100,527
0604303A	Missile Effectiveness Evaluation (H)	1962–71	14,443	74,213
0604304A	NIKE-ZEUS Testing (H)	1962–65	541,411	3,186,132
0604305F	MMRBM (H)	1962–65	79,957	456,304
0604307A	PATRIOT Air Defense Missile System (H)	1965–86	2,100,971	5,529,484
0604307F	Hard Rock Silo Development (H)	1968–70	49,047	212,826
0604308F	Short-Range Air-to-Air Missile (H)	1969–71	16,846	69,554
0604309F	HOUND DOG II (H)	1971–73	6,026	21,492
0604311A	PERSHING II (H)	1977–78, 1980–84	644,934	1,091,757
0604312F	ICBM Modernization	1979–93	17,157,080	24,316,317
0604355N	Vertical Launch ASROC	1984–90	209,711	276,025
0604361F	Air Launched Cruise Missile (ALCM) (H)	1973–90	1,376,170	2,784,186
0604362F	Ground-Launched Cruise Missile (GLCM) (H)	1978–86, 1988	381,617	636,193
0604363N	TRIDENT II	1972–78, 1985–91, 1993	10,620,423	18,495,450
0604367N	TOMAHAWK—Theater Mission Planning Center	1977–91	1,397,058	2,407,897
0604370N	SSN-688 Class Vertical Launch System	1981–91	259,543	362,701
0604406F	Space Defense System (H)	1972–88, 1990–91	1,527,372	2,324,532
0604408F	National Launch System (H)	1990–93	164,165	186,830
0604411F	Space Shuttle (H)	1981–86	1,629,510	2,401,436
0604478F	NAVSTAR Space and Control Equipment (H)	1979	32,300	65,959

0604502N	Submarine Communications	1967–91	129,543	294,998
0604503N	SSN-688 and Trident Modernization	1963, 1965–95	826,656	1,384,987
0604523N	ASW Acoustic Warfare (H)	1971–72, 1974	12,550	45,922
0604524N	Submarine Combat System	1982–95	2,708,834	3,316,371
0604558N	New Design SSN	1994–95	465,297	480,729
0604559N	Deep Submergence Technology	1974–80	37,926	86,958
0604560N	Trident Submarine System (H)	1972–78	623,236	1,778,623
0604561N	SSN-21 Developments	1977–84, 1987–95	1,411,172	1,671,066
0604562N	Submarine Tactical Warfare System	1962–69, 1972–95	902,290	1,370,197
0604563N	Physical Security—Eng Dev	1984–88	24,932	32,596
0604570N	CSGN Development (H)	1977–78	63,193	146,023
0604577N	EHF SATCOM	1983–87, 1989–91	341,793	459,885
0604603A	Nuclear Munitions—Eng Dev	1962–93	362,509	849,317
0604706A	Radiological Defense Equipment (H)	1968–84	13,190	36,459
0604711F	Systems Survivability (Nuclear Effects)	1969–94	210,999	387,338
0604712N	Special Electromagnetic Interferences (H)	1975–79	10,292	25,380
0604713N	Surface ASW System Improvement	1978–84, 1986, 1990–91	328,883	462,420
0604721A	Nuclear Power Systems (H)	1962–66	21,003	120,661
0604723F	E-4 (H)	1969–71, 1973–76	171,184	500,341
0604747F	Electromagnetic Radiation Test Facilities	1973–93	148,681	293,461
0604778F	NAVSTAR Global Positioning System (H)	1979–85	695,119	1,099,500
0604778N	NAVSTAR Global Positioning System (User Equipment)	1979–81	37,933	68,586
0604806A	NBC Defense System-Eng Dev	1985–95	361,988	420,133
0605003A	R&D Facility-Redstone (H)	1962, 1964–65, 1968	10,470	60,335
0605101F	RAND Project Air Force	1962–95	529,726	1,303,613
0605301A	Army Kwajalein Atoll	1962, 1964–95	3,694,612	6,904,798
0605301F	Space and Missile Test Center (SAMTEC) (H)	1962, 1964–75	228,884	1,083,695
0605302A	White Sands Missile Range (H)	1962–75, 1992	1,119,494	5,070,623
0605302F	Eastern Test Range (H)	1962–72	1,949,600	9,993,428
0605351N	Pacific Missile Range	1962–95	1,193,889	5,651,146
0605605A	DOD High Energy Laser Test Facility	1989–95	189,288	209,637
0605703F	Joint Task Force 2 Instrumentation Support (H)	1967–68	5,493	26,639
0605704A	Deseret Test Center (H)	1969–74	74,689	289,468
0605708A	Theater Nuclear Force Survivability (H)	1976–79	6,333	14,424
0605806A	DOD High Energy Laser Systems Test Facility (H)	1982–84	112,986	167,139
0605856N	Strategic Technical Support	1963–65, 1967–95	141,428	399,737
0605870N	Strategic Systems Test Support	1981–83	39,901	60,658
0605898C	Management Headquarters (Strategic Defense Initiative)	1984–89	123,396	158,118

TABLE B-1. Department of Defense Future Years Defense Program Database, 1962–95 (*continued*)

Thousands of dollars

Program element number	*Program element title*	*Years active*	*Total then-year cost*	*Total adjusted cost (1996 dollars)*
	SUBTOTAL MFP 6—RESEARCH AND DEVELOPMENT		155,698,745	292,476,713
0702009A	Missile Facilities (IF) (H)	1962–89	6,749,944	17,179,520
0702009N	Missile Facilities (IF)	1962–84	649,140	1,655,317
0702010A	Revenues (Missile Facilities) (IF) (H)	1962–89	(6,109,665)	(15,550,546)
0702010N	Revenues (Missile Facilities) (IF) (H)	1968–84	(514,655)	(1,197,804)
0702207F	Depot Maintenance (Non-IF)/Aerospace Maintenance & Regeneration Center	1988, 1990, 1992–95	45,384	51,260
0702828N	Surveillance Systems Electronic Support	1976–89	1,321,160	2,013,389
0708022F	Eastern Test Range	1972–92	2,441,616	4,383,691
0708023F	Eastern Test Range Communication (H)	1971–80	27,852	76,127
0708032F	Western Test Range (H)	1978–92	1,267,060	1,794,870
0708034F	SAMTEC Communications (H)	1979–90	97,654	140,109
07080160F	Inactive Aircraft Storage and Disposal	1977–95	188,171	282,472
	SUBTOTAL MFP 7—CENTRAL SUPPLY AND MANAGEMENT		5,975,490	10,545,933
0901119M	WWMCCS ADP and WIS–Marine Corps	1974–93	21,133	27,974
	SUBTOTAL MFP 9—ADMINISTRATION AND ASSOCIATED ACTIVITIES		21,133	27,974
1001005A	NATO Infrastructure (H)	1965–79	917,727	3,117,111
1001005D	NATO Infrastructure	1979–95	4,354,816	5,820,302
1001012F	NATO AEW&C Program	1979–95	1,871,394	2,814,970
	SUBTOTAL MFP 10—SUPPORT OF OTHER NATIONS		7,143,937	11,752,384
	GRAND TOTAL		1,317,302,258	2,593,077,284

C

Nuclear Weapons Production and Naval Nuclear Propulsion Facilities

Note: Budget data for 1997 reflect actual expenditures in 1997 (expressed in constant 1999 dollars). Accounting data for stored quantities of plutonium and highly enriched uranium exclude (for uranium) materials in intact nuclear weapons, materials not in Department of Energy custody (such as deployed weapons) and materials in spent fuel and irradiated fuel targets. both categories exclude materials designated as radioactive waste (including 3,919 kilograms of plutonium). These figures are accurate as of September 30, 1994 (plutonium), and December 1996 (uranium).

Operational Facilities

Ames Laboratory (Ames, Iowa)
ESTABLISHED: 1947
SIZE: 10 acres (435,600 square feet)
BUDGET: $23.8 million (4.7 percent defense-related) (1997)
EMPLOYEES: 0 federal; 375 contractor (as of September 30, 1997)
FUNCTION: Conducts basic research on nuclear materials and nuclear waste remediation
RADIOACTIVE MATERIALS ON-SITE: 15.5 grams of plutonium and 31 grams of uranium-235
CONTRACTOR: Iowa State University (formerly Iowa State College)

Argonne National Laboratory (ANL); Argonne, Illinois (ANL-East), 22 miles southwest of downtown Chicago, and Idaho National Engineering and Environmental Laboratory, Idaho (ANL-West)
ESTABLISHED: July 1, 1946
SIZE: 1,704 acres (2.7 square miles) (ANL-E)
BUDGET: $286.3 million ANL-East (6.2 percent defense-related); $92.1 million ANL-West (16.3 percent defense-related) [not including DOE's Chicago Operations Office] (1997)
EMPLOYEES: 315 federal; 3,862 contractor (as of September 30, 1997)
FUNCTION: Conducts research on advanced nuclear reactor technologies
RADIOACTIVE MATERIALS ON-SITE: 1.15 kilograms of plutonium and less than 1 metric ton of uranium-235 (ANL-E); 4.0 metric tons of plutonium-239 and less than 10 metric tons of uranium-235 (ANL-W)
CONTRACTOR: University of Chicago and Argonne Universities Association

Bettis Atomic Power Laboratory (West Mifflin, Pennsylvania)
ESTABLISHED: 1948
BUDGET: $346.0 million (including DOE's Pittsburg Naval Reactors Office) (100 percent defense-related)
SIZE: 160 acres (0.25 square miles)
EMPLOYEES: 67 federal; 2,972 contractor (as of September 30, 1997)
FUNCTION: Designs, builds, and tests prototype naval nuclear reactors and trains U.S. Navy personnel in their operation and maintenance
RADIOACTIVE MATERIALS ON-SITE: 272 grams of plutonium and 5.5 kilograms of uranium-235
CONTRACTOR: Westinghouse Bettis Co. (formerly Westinghouse Electric Corp., Atomic Power Division)

Brookhaven National Laboratory (BNL) (Upton, Long Island, New York, 60 miles east of New York City)
ESTABLISHED: January 31, 1947
SIZE: 5,300 acres (8.3 square miles)
BUDGET: $357.9 million (4.5 percent defense-related) (1997)
EMPLOYEES: 33 federal; 3,101 contractor (as of September 30, 1997)
FUNCTION: Conducts research on nuclear weapons, nuclear waste, nuclear materials production, nuclear safeguards, and security and verification and control technologies
RADIOACTIVE MATERIALS ON-SITE: 0.3 metric tons of uranium-235 (all declared excess by President Bill Clinton on March 1, 1995)
CONTRACTOR: Brookhaven Science Associates (a partnership led by the Research Foundation of the State University of New York on behalf of the State University of New York at Stony Brook and Battelle Memorial Research Institute
FORMER CONTRACTOR: Associated Universities, Inc. (a consortium founded in 1946 by Columbia University, Cornell University, Harvard University, Johns Hopkins University, Massachusetts Institute

of Technology, University of Pennsylvania, Princeton University, University of Rochester, and Yale University), 1947–98

Holston Army Ammunition Plant (Kingsport, Tennessee, 85 miles northeast of Knoxville)
ESTABLISHED: 1942; began making high explosives for nuclear weapons in 1961
SIZE: 6,000 acres (9.4 square miles)
EMPLOYEES: 475 (as of November 30, 1997)
FUNCTION: Sole source (since 1961) of a high-explosive (HE) chemical powder used to fabricate high-explosive lenses for nuclear weapons
CONTRACTOR: Managed for the U.S. Army by the Holston Defense Corporation, a subsidiary of Eastman Chemical Company

Idaho National Engineering and Environmental Laboratory (INEEL) (42 miles Northwest of Idaho Falls, Idaho)[1]
ESTABLISHED: 1949
SIZE: 571,800 acres (893 square miles)
BUDGET: $726.7 million (including DOE's Idaho Operations Office) (87.9 percent defense-related) (1997)
EMPLOYEES: 393 federal; 5,868 contractor (as of September 30, 1997)
FUNCTION: Researches, develops, tests, and evaluates naval and breeder reactors, and manages high-level and transuranic nuclear waste. Fabricates depleted uranium armor for M1-A1/A2 tanks. From 1953 to 1992, the Idaho Chemical Processing Plant (ICPP)[2] reprocessed spent naval reactor fuel to recover uranium-235 (some of which was fabricated into HEU fuel for the Savannah River reactors beginning in 1968) and krypton-85. Facilities include fifty-two reactors (fourteen of which are still operating or operable, and two of which are run by the navy's Nuclear Reactors Office) and eleven stainless steel high-level waste underground storage tanks
RADIOACTIVE MATERIALS ON-SITE: 0.5 metric tons of plutonium-239 (0.4 metric tons declared excess by President Clinton on March 1, 1995), 26.2 metric tons of uranium-235 (23.4 metric tons declared excess by President Clinton on March 1, 1995), and 40 metric tons of uranium-233
CONTRACTORS: Lockheed Idaho Technologies Company (composed of Lockheed and Babcock & Wilcox Idaho, Coleman Research, Duke Engineering and Services, NUMATEC, Parsons Environmental Services, Rust International (Rust Federal Services) and the Thermo Electron Corporation (Thermo Technology Ventures), a subsidiary of Lockheed Martin Corp.; Lockheed Idaho Technologies Com-

1. Originally known as the National Reactor Testing Station. From August 1974 until January 28, 1997, the site was known as the Idaho National Engineering Laboratory.

2. Formerly the Idaho Fuels Processing Facility.

pany (ICPP); Westinghouse Electric Corp. (Naval Reactor Facility); Argonne National Laboratory-West (fast breeder reactor program); Lockheed Idaho Technologies Company (SMC) (Special Manufacturing Capability for depleted uranium M1-A1/A2 tank armor)

FORMER CONTRACTORS: Phillips Petroleum Co., Atomic Energy Division, 1950–66; American Cyanamid Co. (ICPP), 1953; Combustion Engineering Inc., Nuclear Division (Naval Reactor Facility), 1959–65; Aerojet General Corp. and Aerojet General Nucleonics, 1959–65; Aerojet General Corp., 1965–66; General Electric Company, 1965–68; Idaho Nuclear Corp. (a jointly owned subsidiary of Aerojet General Corp., Allied Chemical Corp. and (beginning in 1969) Phillips Petroleum Co.), 1966–71; Aerojet Nuclear Co. (a wholly owned subsidiary of Aerojet General Corp.), 1971–76; Allied Chemical Corp. (ICPP), 1971–80; Exxon Nuclear Idaho Company (ICPP), 1980–84; EG&G Idaho, Inc.,[3] 1984–94; Westinghouse Idaho Nuclear Co. (ICPP), 1984–94; Rockwell International Corp. (SMC) (Special Manufacturing Capability for M1-A1/A2 tank armor), December 1986–91; Babcock and Wilcox (SMC) (Special Manufacturing Capability for M1-A1/A2 tank armor), 1991–94

Kansas City Plant (12 miles south of Kansas City, Missouri)

ESTABLISHED: 1949

SIZE: 136 acres (0.2 square miles; 113 acres of process buildings covering 3.2 million square feet)

BUDGET: $296.3 million (100 percent defense-related) (1997)

EMPLOYEES: 61 federal; 3,679 contractor (as of September 30, 1997)

FUNCTION: Produces or procures electronic, electromechanical, rubber, plastic, and metal components for nuclear weapons, including arming, fuzing, and firing systems; radars and coded safety locks known as PALs (permissive action links)

RADIOACTIVE MATERIALS ON-SITE: 1.2 grams of plutonium

CONTRACTOR: Bendix Kansas City Division of Allied-Signal (formerly the Bendix Aviation Corporation)

Knolls Atomic Power Laboratory (KAPL) (Niskayuna and West Milton, New York; Windsor, Connecticut)

ESTABLISHED: 1947

SIZE: 170 acres (0.3 square miles) at Niskayuna; 3,900 acres (6.1 square miles) at West Milton; 10.8 acres at Windsor

BUDGET: $280.1 million (including DOE's Schenectady Naval Reactors Office) (100 percent defense-related) (1997)

3. EG&G stands for Edgerton, Germeshausen & Grier.

EMPLOYEES: 65 federal; 2,700 contractor (as of September 30, 1997)
FUNCTION: Designs, builds, and tests prototype naval nuclear reactors and trains U.S. Navy personnel in their operation and maintenance. Maintains three operational test reactors at Niskayuna, New York, and one nonoperational reactor at Windsor, Connecticut (shut down in March 1993)
RADIOACTIVE MATERIALS ON-SITE: 1.6 metric tons of uranium-235 and 171.7 grams of plutonium
CONTRACTOR: Lockheed Martin-KAPL Co., Inc. (a subsidiary of Lockheed Martin Corporation), formerly Martin Marietta KAPL Co., Inc.
FORMER CONTRACTOR: General Electric Company, 1947–93

Lawrence Livermore National Laboratory (LLNL) (Livermore, California)[4]
ESTABLISHED: July 1952; opened September 1952
SIZE: 7,321 acres (11.4 square miles)
BUDGET: $862.2 million (not including DOE's Oakland Operations Office) (93.4 percent defense-related) (1997)
EMPLOYEES: 110 federal; 6,403 contractor (as of September 30, 1997)
FUNCTION: Conducts research, development, and testing activities associated with all phases of the nuclear weapons life cycle, as well as research on nonproliferation, arms control, and treaty verification technology. Facilities include an explosives test site, a tritium facility, the NOVA laser, the Atomic Vapor Laser Isotope Separation (AVLIS) plant, Inertial Confinement Fusion (ICF) facilities, the High-Explosive Application Facility (HEAF), and the National Ignition Facility (NIF, under construction)
RADIOACTIVE MATERIALS ON-SITE: 0.3 metric ton of plutonium-239, 0.2 metric ton of uranium-235, and 3.1 metric tons of uranium-233
CONTRACTOR: University of California, Board of Regents

Los Alamos National Laboratory (LANL) (Los Alamos, New Mexico)[5]
ESTABLISHED: Site selected on November 25, 1942 (code name Site Y)
SIZE: 27,520 acres (43 square miles)
BUDGET: $1,042.8 million (not including DOE's Albuquerque Operations Office) (89.5 percent defense-related) (1997)

4. Founded as the Livermore Laboratory, originally a branch of and co-directed by the University of California Radiation Laboratory (UCRL) in Berkeley, California. In 1958 the laboratory was renamed the E. O. Lawrence Radiation Laboratory in honor of physicist Ernest O. Lawrence. In mid-1971 the Board of Regents of the University of California gave the laboratories in Berkeley and Livermore separate independent status and removed the word "radiation" from Livermore's name.

5. Originally it was known as the Los Alamos Project, then Los Alamos Scientific Laboratory, later renamed Los Alamos National Scientific Laboratory (LANSL). During the Manhattan Project, because the name "Los Alamos" was classified, the site was known by a number of euphemisms, including Site Y, Project Y, Zia Project, Santa Fe, Area L, Shangri-La, and Happy Valley. Residents of Los Alamos and Santa Fe called it "The Hill."

EMPLOYEES: 70 federal; 6,687 contractor (as of September 30, 1997)

FUNCTION: Conducts research, development, and testing activities associated with all phases of the nuclear weapons life cycle, as well as arms control and nuclear proliferation. Facilities include plutonium- and tritium-processing plants, an 8-megawatt research reactor, and various laser and high-explosives buildings. Also operates the only U.S. facility capable of fabricating and testing plutonium-238 heat sources for radioisotope thermoelectric generators (RTGs) used in interplanetary probes, surveillance satellites, and classified military programs. Until fiscal 1984, Los Alamos had the capability to fabricate and assemble nuclear weapons test devices.[6]

RADIOACTIVE MATERIALS ON-SITE: 2.7 metric tons of plutonium-239 (1.5 metric tons declared excess by President Clinton on March 1, 1995), 3.2 metric tons of uranium-235 (0.5 metric tons declared excess by President Clinton on March 1, 1995), and more than 1 metric ton of uranium-233

CONTRACTOR: University of California, Board of Regents

Nevada Test Site (NTS) (65 miles northwest of Las Vegas)[7]

ESTABLISHED: Selected in December 1950; first nuclear test on January 27, 1951; last on September 23, 1992; 928 total tests (100 atmospheric, 828 underground, including 24 joint U.S.-U.K. tests)

SIZE: 864,000 acres (1,350 square miles)

BUDGET: $396.4 million (including DOE's Nevada Operations Office) (91.7 percent defense-related) (1997)

EMPLOYEES: 17 federal; 2,345 contractor (as of September 30, 1997)

FUNCTION: Field tests nuclear weapons for development, safety, and weapons effects purposes. From 1959 through 1972 a portion of the site, designated the Nuclear Rocket Development Station (NRDS), was used to test 21 aboveground prototypes of space nuclear propulsion reactors.[8] In mid-1993, construction was completed on the $109 million Device Assembly Facility, a 100,000-square-foot building within a highly secured 22-acre section of the test site. The facility includes five high-explosives containment cells, called "Gravel Gerties," three weapon assembly bays, two radiographic areas, and storage bunkers

---

6. This function was terminated and transferred to the Nevada Test Site due to serious security lapses at the assembly and storage areas. Los Alamos is currently the only site in the complex capable of producing plutonium pits (in a facility known as TA-55) and has reportedly fabricated a small number in recent years. On February 28, 1996, Secretary of Energy Hazel O'Leary announced that any future plutonium pit production would occur at the laboratory. TA-55 is currently being modified and upgraded to allow for production of up to 20 pits a year by 2007. Production of an "early development unit" pit (a copy of the kind used in W88 warhead) was demonstrated in March 1998.

7. Originally known as the Nevada Proving Ground, the site was annexed from the existing Las Vegas Bombing and Gunnery Range.

8. Major contractors for this effort, a joint project between the Atomic Energy Commission and the National Aeronautics and Space Administration, were the Los Alamos Scientific Laboratory, Pan American World Airways, and Westinghouse Electric Corp.

RADIOACTIVE MATERIALS ON-SITE: 16 kilograms of plutonium-239 and 217 grams of uranium-235 (does not include significant residues resulting from testing activities)

CONTRACTORS: Bechtel Nevada Corporation; Lockheed Martin Nevada Technologies, Inc.; Johnson Controls Nevada, Inc.; Wackenhut Services, Inc.

FORMER CONTRACTORS: Test Division of the Santa Fe (later Albuquerque) Operations Office, 1951–62; Holmes & Narver, Inc., 1956–90; Fenix & Sisson of Nevada, Inc., 1963–90; EG&G Energy Measurements, Inc., 1951–95; Reynolds Electrical and Engineering Co. (REECo), 1953–95; Raytheon Services Nevada (RSN), 1990–95

Nuclear Fuel Services, Inc. (Erwin, Tennessee)

ESTABLISHED: Constructed in 1957; developed naval fuel fabrication process between 1964 and 1968; awarded contract for the USS *Nimitz* reactors in 1968.

SIZE: 66 acres (0.1 square miles)

EMPLOYEES: 380 (as October 1, 1997)

FUNCTION: Sole facility (since 1978) to convert uranium hexafluoride into the chemical and physical form used in naval reactor fuel elements.[9]

RADIOACTIVE MATERIALS ON-SITE: Unknown

CONTRACTOR: Nuclear Fuel Services, Inc.[10]

Oak Ridge Reservation (ORR) (Oak Ridge, Tennessee)[11]

ESTABLISHED: Site selected on September 19, 1942 (code name Site X)

SIZE: 35,252 acres (55.1 square miles) (2900 acres/4.5 square miles (ORNL); 1,500 acres/2.3 square miles (K-25 Plant); 811 acres/1.3 square miles (Y-12 Plant)

BUDGET: $1,143.8 million (not including DOE's Oak Ridge Operations Office) (64.6 percent defense-related) (1997)

EMPLOYEES: 593 federal; 14,046 contractor (as of September 30, 1997)

FUNCTION: Currently produces weapon components to support the activities of the design laboratories and the Nevada Test Site, fabri-

9. The uranium hexafluoride comes from the Portsmouth Gaseous Diffusion Plant.

10.The Nuclear Fuel Services facility has had a number of corporate owners throughout its history, including Davison Chemical Co. (a division of W. R. Grace and Company), 1957–69; Getty and Skelly Oil Co., 1969–84; and Texaco Inc., 1984–87. Since 1987 the plant has been owned by a private limited partnership.

11. Officially designated the Clinton Engineer Works in early 1943, after a nearby small town. In 1947 the entire reservation was designated the "City of Oak Ridge." Oak Ridge is also the site of Oak Ridge National Laboratory (ORNL), originally known as Clinton Laboratories, which conducted early, small-scale work on plutonium production and processing prior to full-scale operation of facilities at Hanford. The X-10 reactor (originally known as the Clinton Pile), the first true plutonium production reactor, began operating on November 4, 1943. The site was briefly known as the Holifield National Laboratory, after staff members on the Joint Committee on Atomic Energy acted unilaterally in late 1974 and changed the name to honor their retiring chairman, Representative Chet Holifield (Democrat of California). Congress, at the behest of the Tennessee congressional delegation and Oak Ridge community leaders, took action to restore the name Oak Ridge National Laboratory to the site in late 1975.

cates materials for the naval nuclear reactor program and stores (in the Y-12 plant) highly enriched uranium (HEU) returned from dismantled weapons. Formerly produced uranium-235 (483 metric tons) and lithium-6 deuteride (442.4 metric tons) for nuclear weapons. Site of Oak Ridge National Laboratory (ORNL)

RADIOACTIVE MATERIALS ON-SITE: 189 metric tons of uranium-235 and 3.0 metric tons of low-enriched uranium at the Y-12 Plant,[12] 1.5 metric tons of uranium-235 at the K-25 Plant,[13] and 1.4 metric tons of uranium- 235 and 424 metric tons of uranium-233 at Oak Ridge National Laboratory (84.9 metric tons of uranium-235 declared excess by President Clinton on March 1, 1995)

CONTRACTORS: Lockheed Martin Energy Research Corporation (a subsidiary of Lockheed Martin Corporation), formerly Martin Marietta Energy Systems, Inc.; Bechtel Jacobs Company LLC (a joint venture of Bechtel National, Inc., and Jacobs Engineering Group, Inc.); Westinghouse Environmental Management Co.; Martin Molten Metal Technology; M-K Ferguson Oak Ridge, Co.; Oak Ridge Associated Universities; Southeastern Universities Research Association

FORMER CONTRACTORS: Built by E. I. Du Pont de Nemours and Company; Tennessee Eastman Corporation, a subsidiary of Eastman Kodak (Y-12 Plant), 1943–47; Metallurgical Laboratory of the University of Chicago (X-10 Plant), 1943–45; Monsanto Chemical Corporation (X-10 Plant), 1945–47; Union Carbide Corp. Nuclear Division (formerly Carbide and Carbon Chemical Corp.) (K-25 Plant), 1943–84; Union Carbide Corp. Nuclear Division (formerly Carbide and Carbon Chemical Corp.) (Y-12 Plant), 1947–84; Union Carbide Corp. Nuclear Division (formerly Carbide and Carbon Chemical Corp.) (ORNL), 1948–84; Lockheed Martin Energy Systems, Inc. (a subsidiary of Lockheed Martin Corporation formerly Martin Marietta Energy Systems, Inc.), 1984–98

Pantex Plant (17 miles northeast of Amarillo, Texas)[14]

ESTABLISHED: 1942, to load TNT and other explosives into conventional shells. Site selected for nuclear weapons work in 1950; extensive renovations completed in 1952 and first assembly (of Mk-6 bombs) occurred in May 1952

SIZE: 16,000 acres (25 square miles)

BUDGET: $319.9 million (100 percent defense-related) (1997)

12. This does not include an estimated 600 kilograms of uranium-235 purchased from Kazakhstan and transported to Oak Ridge during October–November 1994, as part of a joint Department of Energy and Department of Defense operation code-named "Project Sapphire."

13. Does not include material that will eventually be recovered during decontamination of buildings and equipment or material in waste.

14. Known as the Pantex Ordnance Plant from 1951 until September 1963.

EMPLOYEES: 89 federal; 2,920 contractor (as of September 30, 1997)
FUNCTION: Currently evaluates, refurbishes, and modifies stockpiled weapons, fabricates high-explosive components[15] and disassembles retired nuclear weapons. Formerly assembled weapons. Last new nuclear weapon (W88 warhead) assembled on July 31, 1990
RADIOACTIVE MATERIALS ON-SITE: Classified. More than 10,500 plutonium pits (as of March 1998) and an indeterminate number of assembled weapons are presently stored in protective bunkers called igloos. There are 66.1 metric tons of plutonium-239 in currently deployed weapons, weapons destined for disassembly at Pantex, and currently stored at Pantex. Of that total, 21.3 metric tons was declared excess by President Clinton on March 1, 1995. An additional 16.7 metric tons of uranium-235 was also declared excess
CONTRACTOR: Mason and Hanger-Silas Mason Company, Inc.
FORMER CONTRACTOR: Procter & Gamble Defense Corporation, 1952–56

Sandia National Laboratories (SNL) (inside Kirtland Air Force Base, Albuquerque, New Mexico;[16] Livermore, California; Tonopah Test Range (northwest of the Nevada Test Site), Nevada)
ESTABLISHED: 1945 (in Albuquerque), 1956 (in Livermore)
SIZE: 7,600 acres (11.9 square miles) at Kirtland/Albuquerque; 413 acres (0.6 square miles) at Livermore; 409,600 acres (640 square miles) at Tonopah
BUDGET: $948.9 million (not including DOE's Albuquerque Operations Office (89.4 percent defense-related) (1997)
EMPLOYEES: 46 federal; 7,576 contractor (as of September 30, 1997)
FUNCTION: Responsible for research, development and testing of all nonnuclear components in nuclear weapons; develops transportation and storage systems for nuclear weapons; assesses nuclear weapons safety, security and control and helps train military personnel in the assembly and maintenance of completed weapons
RADIOACTIVE MATERIALS ON-SITE: 0.9 metric tons of uranium-235 (0.2 metric tons declared excess by President Clinton on March 1, 1995) and 8.1 kilograms of plutonium (Livermore)
CONTRACTOR: Sandia Corporation (a subsidiary of Lockheed Martin Corporation)

15. High-explosive lenses are fabricated from a chemical high-explosive powder produced by the U.S. Army's Holston Ammunition Plant in Kingsport, Tennessee (the sole producer of HE powder since 1961). Before 1961 this powder was apparently manufactured at a second facility, the Cornhusker Army Ammunition Plant in Grand Island, Nebraska. High-explosive lenses were also fabricated at the Salt Wells Pilot Plant near China Lake, California, using ingredients obtained from Holston and possibly Cornhusker. Previous production and assembly of high explosives took place at the Los Alamos Scientific Laboratory, Kirtland Air Force Base (assembly only), and the Iowa Army Ordnance Plant.

16. Originally known as Sandia Base and home to Z division, a makeshift branch of the Los Alamos Project, later referred to as Los Alamos Scientific Laboratory. Subsequently known as Sandia Laboratory.

FORMER CONTRACTORS: University of California, Board of Regents, 1945 to October 31, 1949; Sandia Corporation, a wholly owned subsidiary of Western Electric Company, Inc. (later AT&T Technologies, Inc.), a subsidiary of the American Telephone and Telegraph Company, November 1, 1949 to 1993

Savannah River Site (SRS) (12 miles south of Aiken, South Carolina)[17]
ESTABLISHED: Site selected on November 22, 1950; operations began on October 3, 1952, with basic plant construction completed in 1956
SIZE: 198,400 acres (310 square miles; production facilities occupy approximately 16 square miles)
BUDGET: $1,401.4 million (including DOE's Savannah River Operations Office) (98.7 percent defense-related) (1997)
EMPLOYEES: 556 federal; 13,231 contractor (as of September 30, 1997)
FUNCTION: Manages high-level nuclear wastes and refills tritium reservoirs. Processes plutonium-238 for use in radioisotope thermoelectric generators (RTGs). Earlier, produced weapon-grade plutonium (36.1 metric tons), tritium and deuterium for nuclear weapons. Facilities include five reactors, two chemical separation plants, two tritium facilities, fifty-one high-level waste underground storage tanks, a high-level waste plant (the Defense Waste Processing Facility), and a completed but unopened naval reactor fuel fabrication facility
RADIOACTIVE MATERIALS ON-SITE: 2.0 metric tons of plutonium-239 (1.3 metric tons declared excess by President Clinton on March 1, 1995) and 24.4 metric tons of uranium-235 (22 metric tons declared excess by President Clinton on March 1, 1995)
CONTRACTORS: Westinghouse Savannah River Company; Bechtel; Wackenhut Services, Inc.
FORMER CONTRACTOR: Built and operated by E. I. Du Pont de Nemours and Company, 1950–89

Waste Isolation Pilot Plant (WIPP) (26 miles east of Carlsbad, New Mexico)
ESTABLISHED: Conceptual work in mid-1970s; construction began on July 4, 1981
SIZE: 10,240 acres (16 square miles)
BUDGET: $193.2 million (not including DOE's Albuquerque Operations Office) (100 percent defense-related) (1997)
EMPLOYEES: 57 federal; 636 contractor (as of September 30, 1997)
FUNCTION: Completed but unopened site to assess the feasibility of safe underground storage of transuranic (TRU) waste from nuclear

17. Known as the Savannah River Plant (SRP) until April 1, 1989.

weapons–manufacturing processes. The Department of Energy currently plans to begin waste shipments to WIPP in June 1998

RADIOACTIVE MATERIALS ON-SITE: None

CONTRACTOR: Westinghouse WIPP Company (a subsidiary of Westinghouse Electric Corp.)

Yucca Mountain Project (65 miles NW of Las Vegas, adjacent to the Nevada Test Site)

ESTABLISHED: Surface-based studies began in May 1986. The Nuclear Waste Policy Act Amendment of 1987 designated Yucca Mountain as the sole site to be studied as a potential underground repository for high-level radioactive waste

BUDGET: $216.2 million (61.0 percent defense-related) (1997)

EMPLOYEES: 95 federal; 1,475 contractor (as of September 30, 1997

FUNCTION: Proposed site for underground storage of some vitrified high-level defense wastes and spent nuclear fuel from commercial power reactors

RADIOACTIVE MATERIALS ON-SITE: None

CONTRACTORS: TESS (TRW Environmental and Safety Systems); B&W Fuel Company; Duke Engineering and Services; Fluor Daniel; INTERA, Inc.; Morrison-Knudson Corporation; Woodward-Clyde Federal Services

Transitional/Closed Facilities[18]

Apollo Plant (Apollo, Pennsylvania), 1957–78

FUNCTION: Earlier, converted uranium hexafluoride to naval reactor fuel, manufactured plutonium fuel rod elements for the Fast Flux Test Facility (FFTF) reactor at the Hanford Reservation, and (as of November 30, 1961) fabricated plutonium-beryllium neutron sources

FORMER CONTRACTORS: Nuclear Materials and Equipment Corporation (NUMEC), 1957–67; Atlantic Richfield Co., 1967–71; Babcock and Wilcox, 1971–78

18. In addition to the larger and relatively well-known facilities listed here, several hundred smaller sites have contributed to the U.S. nuclear weapons effort since its inception. For example, the Atomic Energy Commission estimated that during the last six months of 1955, some 925 domestic uranium mines were in operation. That figure remained relatively steady until the early 1960s (as production per mine increased) and then declined until mining operations for the weapons program were curtailed in 1970. At peak production in 1961, twenty-six uranium ore processing plants were in operation. The Department of Energy currently oversees the remediation of twenty-four former uranium ore processing sites and approximately 5,000 vicinity properties through the Uranium Mill Tailings Remedial Action Project. As of February 1996, surface cleanup at sixteen of the twenty-four sites was completed, but groundwater cleanup had yet to commence. (The program's 1997 budget was $48.2 million.) An additional forty-six sites in fourteen states, once used for research on or processing of radioactive materials, are part of the Formerly Utilized Site Remedial Action Program. By December 1997, remediation had been completed at twenty-five of these sites, with the remainder scheduled to be finished by 2016. (This program's 1997 budget was $74 million) Effective October 1, 1997, management of the program passed from the Department of Energy to the U.S. Army Corps of Engineers.

Buffalo Works (Buffalo, New York), 1944–57[19]

FUNCTION: Former site for weapon production, research and development engineering, and testing (functions transferred to South Albuquerque Works)

SIZE: 191 acres (0.3 square miles)

FORMER CONTRACTOR: ACF Industries, Inc. (formerly American Car & Foundry, Inc.)

Burlington AEC (Atomic Energy Commission) Plant (Burlington, IA), 1947–75[20]

ESTABLISHED: Began producing high-explosive (HE) components in 1948; first assembly (of a Mk-4 bomb) occurred in 1949

FUNCTION: Former site for nuclear weapon fabrication and final assembly (functions transferred to Pantex)

FORMER CONTRACTORS: Ordnance Corps, U.S. Army, 1947–63; Mason & Hanger-Silas Mason Co., 1963–75

Clarksville Modification Center (Clarksville, Tennessee), 1960 to September 1965[21]

FUNCTION: Warhead component testing and modification (functions transferred to Pantex)

FORMER CONTRACTOR: Mason & Hanger-Silas Mason Co., Inc.

Dana Heavy Water Plant (Newport, Indiana), April 1952 to May 24, 1957 (on standby until July 29, 1959)

FUNCTION: Produced heavy water (deuterium) used for moderating and cooling production reactors and as a fusion source in early hydrogen bombs

FORMER CONTRACTOR: Designed and built by the Girdler Corporation (under the direction of E. I. Du Pont de Nemours and Company) and operated by E. I. Du Pont de Nemours and Company

Destrehan Street Plant (St. Louis, Missouri), 1943 to June 1958

FUNCTION: Supplied uranium "feed materials" to facilities producing fissionable materials. Currently undergoing decontamination and decommissioning (D&D)

FORMER CONTRACTOR: Mallinckrodt Chemical Works

19. The Lake Ontario Ordnance Works, 25 miles north of Buffalo in Lewiston, New York, was used to store waste generated from uranium ore during the Manhattan Project. This 191-acre site is now called the Niagara Falls Storage Site. It consists of four buildings and an engineered cell containing 250,000 cubic yards of radiologically contaminated soils and approximately 4,000 cubic yards of radium-bearing residues. Since 1944, NFSS has stored low-level radioactive material from Manhattan Engineer District/Atomic Energy Commission facilities. Current site activities involve the surveillance and maintenance of the containment structure. The adjacent Niagara Falls Storage Site Vicinity Property was not fully remediated until the early 1990s.

20. Known as the Iowa Army Ordnance Plant, then the Iowa Ordnance Plant, from 1947 until September 1963, when control was transferred from the army to the Atomic Energy Commission.

21. Formerly known as the Clarksville Facility.

Fernald Environmental Management Project (Fernald, Ohio, 17 miles northwest of Cincinnati), 1953 to the present[22]

ESTABLISHED: Construction began in 1951 and was completed in May 1954; production operations began in 1953 and ceased in 1989

SIZE: 1,050 acres (1.6 square miles); 136 acres of process buildings

BUDGET: $269.7 million (not including DOE's Ohio Field Office) (100 percent defense-related) (1997)

EMPLOYEES: 55 federal; 1,989 contractor (as of September 30, 1997)

FUNCTION: Earlier, converted various forms of uranium into uranium metal for use as target and fuel elements in SRS production reactors. Processed depleted uranium for use in artillery shells and tank armor. Currently undergoing decontamination and decommissioning (D&D)

RADIOACTIVE MATERIALS ON-SITE: 3,373 metric tons of depleted uranium and 2,170 metric tons of low-enriched uranium

CONTRACTOR: Fluor Daniel Fernald (known until September 1996 as Fluor Daniel Environmental Restoration Management Corp. (FERMCO), a subsidiary of Fluor Corp

FORMER CONTRACTORS: National Lead Company of Ohio (NLO, a subsidiary of NL Industries, Inc.), 1951–85;[23] Westinghouse Materials Co. of Ohio, 1986–92

---

22. Formerly known as the Feed Materials Production Center.

23. According to a 1986 DOE memorandum, NLO used eighty-three subcontractors and vendors to support its work at Fernald (a partial list from existing records follows). These subcontractors and vendors handled various forms and quantities of radioactive materials (dates in parentheses indicate approximate duration of work, as recalled by the manager of NLO in October 1976; sites in italics were involved in handling and producing large quantities of radioactive material for NLO): *Allegheny-Ludlum Steel Corp.,* Watervliet, New York (March 1952); American Machine and Foundry, Brooklyn, New York (October 1952, July 1953), Landis Machine Tool Co., Waynesboro, Pennsylvania (September 1952); *Bethlehem Steel Corp.,* Buffalo, New York (February 1952); Bliss & Laughlin Steel, Buffalo, New York (September–October 1952); Besley-Wells, South Beloit, Wisconsin (May 1953); Door Corp., Westpoint, Connecticut (January 1955); *Oregon Bureau of Mines (Albany Research Center),* Albany, Oregon (October 1954–June 1955); *Superior Steel Co.,* Carnegie, Pennsylvania (December 1955–January 1957); Atlas Steels, Ltd., Welland, Ontario (February 1957-November 1957); Armour Research Foundation, Chicago, Illinois (September 1957); *Alba Craft Laboratories,* Oxford, Ohio (1952–March 1957 [NLO manager only indicated March 1957]); Chambersburg Engineering Co., Chambersburg, Pennsylvania (March 1957); Knoxville Iron Co., Knoxville, Kentucky (October 1957–October 1958); Podbeilniac Corp., Chicago, Illinois (February 1957); *Associated Aircraft Tool & Manufacturing Co.,* Fairfield, Ohio (1956); Magnus Metals, Cincinnati, Ohio (December 1957, March 1958); *Simonds Saw & Steel Co.,* Lockport, New York (February 1952–July 1957); Watertown Arsenal, Watertown, Massachusetts (November 1957); *Vitro Rare Metals Co.,* Canonsburg, Pennsylvania (August 1954–August 1956); Ohio State University, Columbus, Ohio (December 1956, May 1969); Tube Reducing Corp., Wallington, New Jersey (January 1958); American Bearing Corp., Indianapolis, Indiana (July 1958); Ajax-Magnetherimc Corp., Youngstown, Ohio (October 1958, November 1961); Westinghouse Electric, Bloomfield, New Jersey (May 1958, June 1959); *Oregon Metallurgical Corp.,* Albany, Oregon (November 1958); U.S. Steel, National Tube Division, McKeesport, Pennsylvania, April 1959, February 1960); Sutton, Steele and Steele, Dallas, Texas (November 1959); North Carolina State College, Chapel Hill, North Carolina (1958); Hunter Douglas Plant of Bridgeport Brass, Riverside, California (August 1959); *Bridgeport Brass Co.,* Adrian, Michigan (February 1959); Petrolite Corp., St. Louis, Missouri (September 1959); Heald Machine Co., Worchester, Massachusetts (March 1960, May 1960); Dubois Chemical, Cincinnati, Ohio (May 1960); Pioneer Division, Bendix Aviation, Davenport, Iowa (June 1960, September 1960); American Machine and Metals, Inc., East Moline, Illinois (May 1960); Stauffer Metals, Inc., Richmond, California (April 1961); Ithaca Gun Co., Ithaca, New York (September 1960, August 1961, November 1961); R. W. LeBlond Machine Tool Co., Cincinnati, Ohio (November 1961); American Manufacturing of Texas, Fort Worth, Texas (July 1961, August 1961, August 1961, April 1963); Gleason Works, Rochester, New York (October 1961); Hood Machinery & Chemical Corp., Nitro, West Virginia (1962); Oliver Corp., Battle Creek, Michigan (April 1962); Battelle Memorial Institute,

Hanford Reservation (Richland, Washington), 1943 to the present[24]

ESTABLISHED: Site selected on February 8, 1943 (code name Site W); reactor operations began in September 1944. Production of plutonium-239 ceased in 1988

SIZE: 360,000 acres (562.5 square miles)

BUDGET: $1,626.3 million (including DOE's Richland Operations Office) (87.5 percent defense-related) (1997)

EMPLOYEES:170 federal; 11,137 contractor (as of September 30, 1997)

FUNCTION: Earlier, produced 54.5 metric tons plutonium-239 and 13 kilograms of tritium for nuclear weapons, as well as 12.9 metric tons of reactor-grade plutonium. Built and tested advanced reactor concepts. Currently focuses on high-level waste management and decontamination and decommissioning (D&D). Facilities include nine reactors, five reprocessing plants, 177 high-level waste underground storage tanks built between 1943 and 1976, and a disposal site for dismantled submarine reactor vessels

RADIOACTIVE MATERIALS ON-SITE: 11.0 metric tons of plutonium-239 (1.7 metric tons declared excess by President Clinton on March 1, 1995) and 0.6 metric tons of uranium-235 (0.5 metric tons declared excess by President Clinton on March 1, 1995)

CONTRACTORS: Fluor Daniel Hanford, Inc.; Lockheed Martin Hanford Corporation; Rust Federal Services of Hanford, Inc.; Duke Engineering & Services Hanford, Inc.; B & W Hanford Company; Numatec Hanford Corporation; BNFL, Inc.; Bechtel National Inc.; GTS Duratek; Science Applications International Corp. (SAIC); Lockheed Martin Advanced Environmental Systems; M4 Environmental L.P.; Nukem Nuclear Technologies; Los Alamos Technical Associates Inc; AEA Technology; OHM Remediation Services Corporation; Battelle Memorial Institute (Pacific Northwest National Laboratory).[25]

FORMER CONTRACTORS: Built and operated by E. I. Du Pont de Nemours and Company, 1943–46; Garrett Corporation, 1943–46; General Electric Company, 1946–64; General Electric Company (Hanford Laboratories, Hanford Atomic Products Operation), 1946–64; Isochem Inc. (a joint venture of the U.S. Rubber Corp. and Martin-Marietta Corp.), 1965–67; United Nuclear, Inc. (formerly Douglas

---

Columbus, Ohio (December 1962); National Lead Company, Nuclear Division, Albany, New York (July 1962); University of Florida, Gainesville, Florida (October 1963–November 1969); Cincinnati Milling Machine, Cincinnati, Ohio (October 1963); New England Lime Co., Canaan, Connecticut (June 1963); Charles Taylor & Sons, Cincinnati, Ohio (August 1964, January 1965); Southern Research Institute, Birmingham, Alabama (December 1964, September 1965); University of Denver Research Institute, Denver, Colorado (February 1965); New England Materials Lab., Inc. (Teledyne Materials Res.), Medford, Massachusetts (January 1965, April 1967); Tocco Heat Treating Co., Cleveland, Ohio (April 1967, February 1968); Fenwal, Inc., Ashland, Massachusetts (May 1967, November 1967); Robbins & Myers, Co., Springfield, Ohio (1975).

24. Originally called the Hanford Engineering Works and later shortened to Hanford Works.

25. Known as Hanford Laboratories, Hanford Atomic Products Operation, until the Battelle Memorial Institute assumed control in 1965.

United Nuclear, Inc., a joint venture of Douglas Aircraft and United Nuclear Corp.), 1964–77; Atlantic Richfield Hanford Co., 1967–76; Rockwell Hanford Operations, 1977–87; Westinghouse Hanford Co. 1987–96; ICF Kaiser Hanford Co., 1987–96; UNC Nuclear Industries, 1987–96; Bechtel Hanford Inc., 1987–96

Medina Modification Center (San Antonio, Texas), late 1958 to July 1966[26]

FUNCTION: Warhead component testing and modification, weapon repairs and retirements (functions transferred to Pantex)

FORMER CONTRACTOR: Mason and Hanger-Silas Mason Co., Inc.

Mound Laboratory (Miamisburg, Ohio), 1947–present[27]

ESTABLISHED: 1947

SIZE: 306 acres (0.5 square miles)

BUDGET: $119.9 million (not including DOE's Ohio Field Office) (93.7 percent defense-related) (1997)

EMPLOYEES: 34 federal; 740 contractor (as of September 30, 1997)

FUNCTION: Until October 1994, produced nonnuclear components of nuclear weapons (for example, detonators, timers, cable assemblies, pyrotechnic devices). Earlier, developed tritium reservoirs; currently analyzes, disassembles, and recovers tritium from weapon components. Earlier, produced plutonium-238 heat sources for radioisotope thermoelectric generators (RTGs) used in interplanetary probes, surveillance satellites, and classified military programs. Until November 30, 1961, Mound fabricated plutonium-beryllium neutron sources

RADIOACTIVE MATERIALS ON-SITE: 2.2 kilograms of uranium-235 and 25 kilograms of plutonium

CONTRACTOR: Babcock & Wilcox of Ohio, a division of BWX Technologies (a wholly owned subsidiary of McDermott International, Inc.)

FORMER CONTRACTORS: Monsanto Research Corporation, a wholly owned subsidiary of Monsanto Chemical Company (formerly the Monsanto Chemical Company), 1948–88; EG&G Mound Applied Technologies, a subsidiary of EG&G, Inc., 1988–97

Pacific Proving Ground (Enewetak, Pacific Ocean), 1947–58 (on standby to July 1960)[28]

26. Formerly known as the Medina Facility.

27. Originally called the Dayton Engineer Works. On September 8, 1993, the Department of Energy approved a plan to transfer all defense program activities at Mound to the Kansas City Plant and the Savannah River Site by October 1995, and to decontaminate and decommission facilities at Mound. Except for tritium extraction and purification work, all activities associated with maintaining the nuclear stockpile ceased in September 1994. Tritium extraction and purification work continued through 1997. On January 26, 1998, the DOE transferred ownership of the site to the Mound Community Improvement Corporation, which plans to convert it into a technology-based research park.

28. Known as the Enewetak Proving Ground until the spring

ESTABLISHED: Selected on October 11, 1947; first nuclear test[29] on April 14, 1948; last on August 8, 1958

FUNCTION: Used for above-ground and underwater testing of sixty-six nuclear weapons (activities gradually transferred to Nevada Proving Ground during the 1950s). Some sites, notably Bikini Atoll, are still undergoing monitoring and decontamination

FORMER CONTRACTORS: Test Division of the Santa Fe (later Albuquerque) Operations Office, 1947–49; Holmes & Narver, Inc., 1949–58

Paducah Gaseous Diffusion Plant (PGDP) (16 miles west of Paducah, Kentucky), 1951 to the present[30]

ESTABLISHED: Facilities built between 1951 and 1954; production operations for the weapons program began in 1953 and ceased in 1992

SIZE: 3,422 acres (5.3 square miles); site encompasses 750 acres (1.2 square miles), including 74 acres of process buildings

BUDGET: The U.S. Enrichment Corporation does not release budget data for this facility; $46.6 million (DOE-funded activities) (0 percent defense-related) (1997)

EMPLOYEES: 8 federal; 8 USEC; 2,101 contractor (as of December 5, 1997)

FUNCTION: Enriches uranium (formerly for nuclear weapons, currently for civilian power reactors)

RADIOACTIVE MATERIALS ON-SITE: 1,071 metric tons of low-enriched uranium

CONTRACTOR: Lockheed Martin Utility Services (a subsidiary of Lockheed Martin Corporation), formerly Martin Marietta Utility Services; Bechtel Jacobs Company LLC (a joint venture of Bechtel National, Inc., and Jacobs Engineering Group, Inc.)

FORMER CONTRACTORS: Union Carbide Corporation Nuclear Division (formerly Carbide and Carbon Chemical Corp.), 1952–84; Lockheed Martin Energy Systems, Inc. (a subsidiary of Lockheed Martin Corporation, formerly Martin Marietta Energy Systems, Inc.), 1984–98

---

of 1954, when Bikini Atoll was added. Enewetak Atoll, part of the Marshall Islands, consists of some forty-six islands (comprising 2.75 square miles of dry land) surrounding a 388-square-mile lagoon. It is located approximately 2,380 nautical miles southwest of Honolulu, Hawaii. Bikini Atoll is 189 nautical miles east of Enewetak. Control of the site was transferred from the Atomic Energy Commission to the U.S. Navy on July 1, 1960.

29. Before the establishment of the Enewetak Proving Ground, Bikini was the site of two atomic bomb tests, Able and Baker, as part of Operation Crossroads, at that time the largest peacetime military operation ever conducted, which involved 240 ships, 156 aircraft, and 42,000 personnel. The device used in shot Able was dropped from a B-29 bomber on June 30, 1946, while the device used in shot Baker was detonated underwater on July 24, 1946.

30. On July 1, 1993, control of Paducah passed from the Department of Energy to the United States Enrichment Corporation, a wholly owned government corporation. The USEC leases facilities at Paducah from the DOE (this lease expires in mid-1999). The USEC was created by Congress in the Energy Policy Act of 1992 in an attempt to transform the DOE's uranium enrichment enterprise into a profitable business.

Pinellas Plant (approximately six miles north of St. Petersburg, Florida), 1957 to September 1994[31]

ESTABLISHED: Construction began in 1956, production in 1957

SIZE: 90 acres (0.14 square miles)

BUDGET: $64.1 million (100 percent defense-related) (1997)

EMPLOYEES: 12 federal; 5 contractor (as of September 30, 1997)

FUNCTION: Manufactured neutron generators, thermal batteries, lithium ambient batteries, special capacitors, and switches and other electrical and electronic components for nuclear weapons. Also manufactured radioisotope thermoelectric generators (RTGs), using plutonium-238 capsules provided by the Mound Laboratory

RADIOACTIVE MATERIALS ON-SITE: None

FORMER CONTRACTOR: Built and operated by the General Electric Company, 1956–92; Lockheed Martin Specialty Components, Inc. (a subsidiary of Lockheed Martin Corporation), formerly Martin Marietta Specialty Components, Inc., 1992–94

Portsmouth Gaseous Diffusion Plant (PORTS) (Piketon, Ohio, 20 miles north of Portsmouth), 1952 to the present[32]

ESTABLISHED: Facilities built between November, 1952 and 1956; production operations for the weapons program began in 1956 and ceased in 1992

SIZE: 3,708 acres (5.8 square miles), including 93 acres of process buildings

BUDGET: The U.S. Enrichment Corporation does not release budget data for this facility; $61.2 million (DOE-funded activities) (3.7 percent defense-related) (1997)

EMPLOYEES: 14 federal; 6 USEC; 2,595 contractor (as of December 1, 1997)

FUNCTION: Enriches uranium (formerly for nuclear weapons and naval reactors: 511 metric tons from 1956 to 1992; currently for civilian power reactors)

RADIOACTIVE MATERIALS ON-SITE: 23 metric tons of uranium-235 (22.5 metric tons declared excess by President Clinton on March 1, 1995)

CONTRACTOR: Lockheed Martin Utility Services (a subsidiary of Lockheed Martin Corporation), formerly Martin Marietta Utility Ser-

31. Formerly known as the Pinellas Peninsula Plant. On September 8, 1993, the Department of Energy approved a plan to transfer all defense program activities at Pinellas to the Kansas City Plant, Los Alamos National Laboratory, and Sandia National Laboratories by October 1995, and to decontaminate and decommission facilities at Pinellas. All work associated with maintaining the nuclear stockpile ceased in September 1994. The Department of Energy sold the plant to the Pinellas County Industrial Council in 1995, completed remediation work, and formally returned the site to the community on September 12, 1997. It is now known as the Pinellas Science, Technology and Research Center.

32. On July 1, 1993, control of Portsmouth passed from the Department of Energy to the United States Enrichment Corporation. The USEC leases facilities at Portsmouth from the DOE (this lease expires in mid-1999).

vices; Bechtel Jacobs Company LLC (a joint venture of Bechtel National, Inc., and Jacobs Engineering Group, Inc.)

FORMER CONTRACTORS: Goodyear Atomic Corporation, 1956–86; Lockheed Martin Energy Systems, Inc. (a subsidiary of Lockheed Martin Corporation, formerly Martin Marietta Energy Systems, Inc.), 1986–98

RMI Titanium Company Extrusion Plant (Ashtabula, Ohio), 1952–90[33]

FUNCTION: Extruded uranium ingots into tubes and billets as a step in the fabrication of fuel and targets for the Savannah River production reactors. Production ceased on October 31, 1990. Currently undergoing decontamination and decommissioning (D&D)

SIZE: 8.2 acres (357,192 square feet)

RADIOACTIVE MATERIALS ON-SITE: 1 metric ton of depleted uranium

CONTRACTOR: Owned and operated by RMI Titanium Company (formerly Reactive Metals Inc.), which is jointly owned by the National Distillers and Chemical Corporation and the USX (formerly United States Steel) Corporation

FORMER CONTRACTOR: Bridgeport Brass Company, 1952–63

Rock Island Arsenal (Rock Island, Illinois), 1947–51; circa 1956–63 (Davy Crockett)

ESTABLISHED: 1862; Atomic Energy Commission support began in 1947

SIZE: 946 acres (1.5 square miles)

FUNCTION: Site apparently produced armored steel bomb casings for Mk-3 and Mk-4 atomic bombs between 1947 and 1951. Casings were shipped via train to Iowa, where the train was joined to one carrying high explosive lenses from the Iowa Army Ordnance Plant. The train then proceeded to Kirtland Air Force Base in New Mexico. From there, the casings were trucked to Sandia Base for storage and eventual assembly into weapons. From about 1956 until 1963, the arsenal also designed and built the nonnuclear components for the Davy Crockett infantry nuclear weapon

CONTRACTOR: U.S. Army

Rocky Flats Environmental Technology Site (21 miles northwest of Denver, Colorado), 1951 to the present[34]

ESTABLISHED: Construction began in 1951; production commenced in 1952 and ceased in 1990

SIZE: 6,550 acres (10.2 square miles)

BUDGET: $588.1 million (including DOE's Rocky Flats Field Office (92.3 percent defense-related) (1997)

33. Formerly known as the Ashtabula Extrusion Plant.

34. Known as the Rocky Flats Plant until July 11, 1994.

EMPLOYEES: 280 federal; 3,410 contractor (as of September 30, 1997)
FUNCTION: Currently undergoing decontamination and decommissioning (D&D). Fabricates and repairs Safe Secure Transporters (SSTs) used to transport assembled weapons, weapons components and special nuclear materials (SNM). Earlier, fabricated and assembled plutonium-239 "pits," uranium-235 and uranium-238 components, beryllium components, and tritium reservoirs
RADIOACTIVE MATERIALS ON-SITE: 12.7 metric tons of plutonium-239 (11.9 metric tons declared excess by President Clinton on March 1, 1995), 6.7 metric tons of uranium-235 (2.8 metric tons declared excess by President Clinton on March 1, 1995, and 262 metric tons of depleted uranium.[35]
CONTRACTOR: Kaiser-Hill Company, L.L.C. (a joint venture subsidiary of ICF Kaiser International Inc. and CH2M Hill Cos. Ltd., and composed of Westinghouse Electric Corp., Babcock & Wilcox Co., Rocky Mountain Remediation Services (a joint effort of Morrison-Knudson Corp., and British Nuclear Fuels Limited), Dyncorp, Inc., Wackenhut Services Inc., and Quanterra Environmental Services)
FORMER CONTRACTORS: Dow Chemical Co., 1952–75; Rockwell International Corp., North American Space Operations (formerly Atomics International Division), 1975–89; EG&G Rocky Flats, Inc., 1989–95

Sequoyah Fuels Corporation Plant (Gore, Oklahoma), 1970–92
ESTABLISHED: 1970
FUNCTION: Parts of the plant are closed and undergoing decontamination and decommissioning (D&D). Currently reprocesses depleted uranium hexafluoride (UF-6) to produce uranium tetrafluoride, commonly known as "green salt." Used to process natural uranium ("yellowcake") into UF-6 for use in the Paducah and Portsmouth Gaseous Diffusion Plants
CONTRACTOR: General Atomics
FORMER CONTRACTOR: Kerr-McGee Corp., 1970–88

South Albuquerque Works (Albuquerque, New Mexico, 2 miles west of Kirtland Air Force Base), 1952–67
FUNCTION: Former site for weapons research, development engineering, testing, production, and fabrication activities, as well as operations associated with reactors and space programs.[36]
FORMER CONTRACTOR: ACF Industries, Inc. (formerly American Car & Foundry, Inc.), Albuquerque Division

35. Does not include material that will eventually be recovered during decontamination of buildings and equipment or material in waste.

36. The U.S. Air Force took possession of the site in 1967, which was then operated by the General Electric Company to produce jet aircraft engines. General Electric purchased the site in 1984 and is the current owner.

United Nuclear Corporation Plant (Hermatite, Missouri), 1961–72
FUNCTION: Earlier, converted UF-6 to naval reactor fuel
FORMER CONTRACTOR: United Nuclear Corporation, Chemicals Division (formerly Mallinckrodt Chemical Works)

Weldon Spring Feed Materials Plant (Weldon Spring, Missouri, 27 miles west of St. Louis), 1958–67
ESTABLISHED: Built between 1955 and 1958; operations began in May, 1957
SIZE: 229 acres (0.4 square miles)
BUDGET: $63.7 million (100 percent defense-related) (1997)
FUNCTION: Supplied uranium and thorium "feed materials" to facilities producing fissionable materials (consolidated at Fernald)
FORMER CONTRACTOR: Mallinckrodt Chemical Works

Sources

Cochran, Thomas, and others. *Nuclear Weapons Databook.* Vol. 2, *U.S. Nuclear Warhead Production.* Cambridge, Massachusetts: Ballinger, 1987.

Cochran, Thomas B., and others. *Nuclear Weapons Databook.* Vol. 3. *U.S, Nuclear Warhead Facility Profiles.* Cambridge, Mass.: Ballinger, 1987.

Natural Resources Defense Council. Nuclear Weapons Databook Project.

U.S. Atomic Energy Commission. *Semiannual and Annual Reports to Congress,* 1947–71.

Department of Energy. Assistant Secretary for Human Resources and Administration. Office of Worker and Community Transition.

U.S. Enrichment Corporation.

Memorandum from Edward G. DeLaney, Director, Division of Facility and Site Decommissioning Projects, Office of Nuclear Energy, U.S. Department of Energy to Robert E. Lynch, Procurement and Contracts Division, Oak Ridge Operations Office, July 28, 1986.

Department of Energy. *Plutonium Working Group Report on Environmental Safety and Health Vulnerabiilties Associated with the Department's Plutonium Storage.* Vol. 1, DOE/EH-0415 Washington, D.C.: Department of Energy, November 1994.

Department of Energy. Office of Environmental Management. *Taking Stock: A Look at the Opportunities and Challenges Posed by Inventories from the Cold War Era.* Vol. 1, EM-0275. Washington, D.C.: Department of Energy, January 1996.

Department of Energy. *Plutonium: The First 50 Years: The United States Plutonium Production, Acquisition, and Utilization from 1944 to 1994* (Washington, D.C.: Department of Energy, February 1996.

Department of Energy, Office of Environmental Management. *The Baseline Environmental Management Report. DOE/EM-0290* (Washington, D.C.: Department of Energy, June 1996), vols. 2 and 3

Department of Energy. *Highly Enriched Uranium Working Group Report on Environmental, Safety and Health Vulnerabilities Associated with the Department's Storage of Highly Enriched Uranium.* Vol. 1, DOE/EH-0525. Washington, D.C.: Department of Energy, December 1996.

Department of Energy. "FY 1999 Congressional Budget Laboratory/Facility Table," March 6, 1998.

D

Assessing the Costs of Other Nuclear Weapon States

The preceding discussion raises the obvious question of whether an analysis similar to the one presented in this volume might be undertaken in other countries that have produced or deployed nuclear weapons. The answer is yes, but with varying degrees of difficulty.[1] Indeed, one purpose of the current study is to encourage similar efforts for the other nuclear powers. With the exception of Russia, the significantly smaller size of these arsenals should ease the sizable data collection requirements of the present effort. The clearest candidate for such an assessment is the former Soviet Union. Unfortunately it is also the one least likely to yield anything approaching the level of detail in this book. The central problem is that the political and heavily militarized economic system of the USSR provided "no way to accurately measure these costs," even though throughout Soviet history, the issue of defense spending was at the heart of civilian-military relations:

> Detailed discussions by Soviet leaders on the trade-offs between civilian and military spending or the burden imposed by the military on the economy as a whole were simply not possible. . . . Because of the fundamental belief that it was immoral and unpatriotic to question the absolute priority

1. Too little is known about the nuclear programs and arsenals of Israel, India, and Pakistan to include them here.

> of the motherland, the very idea of calculating the costs of defense was implicitly suspect. As a result, much of the data relating to defense industry were not even collected, and when they were, they were not shared with civilian planners and policymakers.[2]

Such conditions make it exceedingly difficult if not impossible to comprehend the total historical and current costs of the Soviet/Russian nuclear weapons program. Even the recent dramatic political changes in Russia apparently have not improved matters much: "What is notable is how little substantial new information has been obtained about the defense-industrial complex, even after the collapse of the Soviet government and the accession to power of the democrats in the Yeltsin government."[3] And even if this should change, the fact that the Soviet Union was not a market economy and therefore lacked market prices means that measuring the true costs of any economic activity is essentially impossible.

One may nevertheless infer from the scale of the effort that costs were quite high, perhaps even roughly comparable to those in the United States in certain areas (for example, the production of fissile materials).[4] At the same time, the near total lack of environmental concerns (as can be seen in the widespread practice of injecting high-level radioactive wastes directly into the ground or dumping fully fueled naval propulsion reactors at sea) would have reduced the cost of production but resulted in a potentially grave environmental legacy, which continues to have serious repercussions for the peoples of the former Soviet Union and, in the case of sea-based disposal, Norway (see chapters 6 and 7). The use of slave or conscripted labor to construct many facilities and to mine uranium in the 1940s and 1950s also lowered monetary costs, but with a correspondingly high cost in human health. There is no doubt that the intangible environmental and human costs of nuclear weapons production in the former Soviet Union dwarf those of the United States, whose record in this regard is far from unblemished.

What about China, the only other nonmarket (until recently) nuclear power? Here there is even less certainty and practically no data. The small size and relatively slow pace of China's nuclear weapons program (it has an estimated 450 warheads and has con-

2. Clifford G. Gaddy, *The Price of the Past: Russia's Struggle with the Legacy of a Militarized Economy* (Brookings, 1996), pp. 2–3.

3. Gaddy, *The Price of the Past,* p. 11.

4. However, because the Soviet economy was substantially smaller than that of the United States, the opportunity cost to Soviet citizens was much higher in terms of expenditures diverted to nuclear weapons, which in a market economy might have been allocated to other things. It is worth bearing in mind that whereas the Soviet Union presented the only serious military threat to the United States throughout the cold war, it had to contend not only with the United States and NATO but with the nuclear arsenals of Great Britain, France, and China. Furthermore, U.S. and Western military bases literally surrounded the Soviet Union, increasing the forward-based threat. With the sole exception of the 1962 Cuban Missile Crisis, the United States was never threatened in this manner.

ducted just 45 tests since 1964 versus 1,030 for the United States since 1945) would indicate a modest scale of effort, but it might also indicate production problems that would have the effect of increasing costs. Several hundred thousand people were reportedly involved in the production and testing of China's first atomic bomb (1955–64), a significantly larger work force than required for the Manhattan Project. To keep costs down, Chinese officials carefully studied everything that was known about the U.S., British, and Soviet programs and proceeded with great caution: "They approved each move only after careful comparison to the ones already taken by other nations, with special attention paid to the American program," a policy characterized by one Chinese leader as "great and deliberate redundancy." The total cost of the effort has been estimated at $28 billion, which was "about 37 percent of the entire state budget for . . . 1957, and . . . slightly more than 100 percent of the defense budget for the two years 1957–58."[5]

Two factors caused delays and thus increased costs on the project. The first was Mao Zedong's "Great Leap Forward," which encouraged innovation and improvisation in the name of technological progress. At the gaseous diffusion plant under construction at Lanzhou, workers tampered with equipment and modified designs over the objections of their director. This resulted "in over 290 accidents, of which more than 20 were ranked as major." The director later recalled that this set work back six months. A second and far more serious setback was the Soviet Union's withdrawal from its nuclear cooperation agreements with China in July and August 1960, following a period of increased tension between the two countries (in part because the Soviet Union refused in June 1959 to provide China with the technical details or a working model of an atomic bomb). Without blueprints to construct their plant (which were held back by the Soviet Union apparently because they duplicated an enrichment facility in the Urals), the Chinese were left in the dark about how it was supposed to be built, let alone operated. In addition, all the remaining equipment at the site was deliberately left in a state of disarray, further complicating attempts to assemble it. Nevertheless, they undertook the effort and at the expense of an additional 700 days succeeded in producing just enough highly enriched uranium to fuel the first atomic test in 1964. There are no other cost figures available for the Chinese nuclear weapons program.[6]

Little is known about the cost of the British program as well, although the unit cost of some weapons systems is available.[7] The con-

5. John Wilson Lewis and Xue Litai, *China Builds the Bomb* (Stanford University Press, 1988), pp. 52, 106–08.

6. Lewis and Litai, *China Builds the Bomb*, pp. 117–25. Additional information on China's nuclear weapons may be found in Robert S. Norris, Andrew S. Burrows, and Richard W. Fieldhouse, *Nuclear Weapons Databook*, vol. 5: *British, French, and Chinese Nuclear Weapons* (Boulder, Colo.: Westview Press, 1994).

7. See Norris and others, *British, French, and Chinese Nuclear Weapons*.

tinuing restrictions under the Official Secrets Act make it difficult to ascertain costs in a truly comprehensive way. As with China, the small size of Great Britain's arsenal (currently estimated at about 200 warheads) would appear to indicate that costs have been relatively low.

In early 1997 the secretary of state for defense provided the House of Commons with the operating cost of the four submarine Polaris fleet from 1981 through 1996 (this dropped to three in May 1992, and all the submarines were withdrawn from service by August 1996, to be eventually replaced by 2001 with an equal number of Vanguard class submarines carrying U.S.-built Trident II missiles).[8] These figures indicate a total operating cost of roughly $7.0 billion since 1981, with annual costs in the 1980s running between $600 million and $780 million before steadily dropping during the 1990s to just over $100 million in 1995–96. An additional $130 million is expected to be spent through 2007 to defuel and retire the submarines and scrap the Polaris missiles. The costs of reactor and reactor core disposal and the ultimate disposition of the nuclear warheads is not included in this total.[9]

The historical costs associated with the French nuclear arsenal are likewise murky, although some figures on weapons procurement and operating costs are available.[10] Because the nuclear testing program was carried out entirely overseas (Algeria and Mururoa), U.S. experience suggests that expenditures for this activity would have been considerable. Among the smaller nuclear powers, France was also the only one to deploy a triad of intermediate-range ballistic missiles, submarine-launched ballistic missiles, and nuclear bombers (although China is slowly moving toward acquiring this capability), in addition to tactical nuclear weapons. On July 31, 1996, France retired its fifteen remaining Mirage IVP nuclear bombers and on September 16, 1996, it shut down the eighteen-missile IRBM force in the Plateau d'Albion in southeastern France (which had been operational since 1971). The base will be completely dismantled and all the missiles and their 1-megaton warheads removed by 1998, at a cost of about $78 million. The future nuclear force will consist of forty-five Mirage 2000N nuclear strike fighters carrying the medium-range Air-Sol Moyenne Portée standoff missile and four ballistic-missile submarines. Available data indicate that France's nuclear weapons budget consumed 3 percent of the defense budget in 1960, 18 percent in 1970, 14 percent in 1980, and 17 percent in 1990 (the reported nuclear share of the budget peaked in 1967 at 26 percent). More recently, actual expenditures dropped from about $6.9 billion (F35.8 billion) in 1990 to about $2.7

8. Robert S. Norris and William M. Arkin, "Nuclear Notebook—British, French, and Chinese Nuclear Forces," *Bulletin of the Atomic Scientists*, vol. 52, no. 6 (1996), p. 64.

9. House of Commons, "Operating Costs of British Polaris Fleet," January 13, 1997 (courtesy of Nicola Butler of the British-American Security Information Council).

10. Norris, Burrows, and Fieldhouse, *British, French, and Chinese Nuclear Weapons.*

billion (F16.3 billion) in 1998 and now account for about 20 percent of weapon spending.[11]

Finally, there is the case of South Africa, which from the 1960s through 1989 built six nuclear weapons (out of a planned program of seven; the seventh was half-finished) fueled by highly enriched uranium before dismantling them by September 1991 as a prelude to rejoining the international community (and as a result of the increasing cost of the effort). The existence of the program was revealed by President F. W. de Klerk on March 24, 1993. This secret program employed about a thousand people, relied on minimal outside assistance (which increased both its cost and duration), and could produce just one or two weapons a year. Hence its costs were "only a fraction of south Africa's total defense budget." During its early production phase in 1987, operating costs were some $6 million to $7 million as year, up from about $3 million in the early 1980s. Total estimated costs were about $850 million, not including the considerable costs of a ballistic missile program.[12]

11. These figures are based on official data that are not adjusted for inflation and may not represent the total costs of producing and maintaining the French nuclear arsenal. Author's electronic mail communications with Camille Grand, Institut de Relations Internationales et Stratégiques (Paris), October 11–12, 1997; Marcel Duval and Yves Le Baut, *L'arme Nucléaire Française Pourquoi et Comment?* (Paris: S.P.M., 1991), pp. 247–48. For additional perspective on the French nuclear arsenal see Camille Grand, *A French Nuclear Exception?* Occasional Paper 38 (Washington, D.C.: Henry L. Stimson Center), January 1998; Giovanni de Briganti, "France Continues to Pare Down Nuclear Forces," *Defense News*, October 14–20, 1996, p. 40; and Reuters, "France Scraps Arsenal of Land-Based Nukes," *Washington Times*, September 17, 1997, p. A14.

12. Bill Keller, "South Africa Says It Built 6 Atom Bombs," *New York Times*, March 25, 1993, p. A1; R. Jeffrey Smith; "South Africa's 16-Year Secret: The Nuclear Bomb," *Washington Post*, May 12, 1993, p. A1; David Albright, "South Africa and the Affordable Bomb," *Bulletin of the Atomic Scientists*, vol. 50 (July/August 1994), pp. 37–47.

E

Steering Committee of the U.S. Nuclear Weapons Cost Study Project

DAVID ALBRIGHT is president of the Institute for Science and International Security (ISIS), a nongovernmental organization working to inform the public about science and policy issues affecting national and international security, including the spread of weapons of mass destruction, arms races and war, and the environmental, safety, and health hazards of nuclear weapons production. He is a contributing editor for the *Bulletin of the Atomic Scientists* and the coauthor of *World Inventory of Plutonium and Highly Enriched Uranium 1992* (Oxford University Press, 1993) and *Plutonium and Highly Enriched Uranium 1996: World Inventories, Capabilities and Policies* (Oxford University Press, 1997). He has published numerous articles on nuclear weapons proliferation and on civilian and military and fissile material inventories in *Arms Control Today*, the *Bulletin of the Atomic Scientists*, the *FAS Public Interest Report*, *Science*, *Scientific American*, *Science and Global Security*, the *New York Times*, and the *Washington Post*. In 1992 he received an Olive Branch Award for a series of articles he wrote with Mark Hibbs on the Iraqi nuclear weapons program for the *Bulletin of the Atomic Scientists* ("Iraq and the Bomb: Were They Even Close?" [March 1991], "Hyping the Iraqi Bomb" [March 1991], and "Iraq's Nuclear Hide-and-Seek" [September 1991]). Since 1992 Albright has cooperated with the International Atomic Energy Agency's Action Team. In June 1996 he was invited to be the first nongovernmental inspector of Iraq's nuclear program and questioned Iraqi officials about that country's uranium enrichment program. Also in 1996 Albright was appointed to the Department of Energy's Openness Advisory Panel, which is charged with reviewing the DOE's efforts to lift the veil of cold war secrecy surrounding many of its programs. Albright has also testified before Congress on a variety of nuclear weapons production issues. Before founding ISIS, Albright was senior staff scientist at the Federation of American Scientists. From 1984 to 1986 he was also on the research staff of Princeton University's Center for Energy and Environmental Studies. Albright holds an M.S. in physics from Indiana University, and an M.S. in mathematics from Wright State University.

BRUCE G. BLAIR is a senior fellow in the Foreign Policy Studies Program at the Brookings Institution, a private, nonprofit organization founded in 1916 and devoted to nonpartisan research, education, and publication in economics, government, foreign policy, and the social sciences generally. He is an expert on the security policies of the United States and the former Soviet Union, defense conversion, and nuclear forces command and control systems. Blair has frequently testified before Congress on this latter subject. He has also extensively studied the Russian military and military-industrial economy. While at Brookings, he has taught defense analysis as a visiting professor at Yale and Princeton universities. Before joining Brookings in 1987, Blair served in the Department of Defense and was a project director at the Congressional Office of Technology Assessment for a highly classified study on the vulnerability of the U.S. strategic command and control system. He received his B.S. in communications from the University of Illinois in 1970 and then served as a U.S. Air Force officer in the Strategic Air Command from 1970 to 1974, as a Minuteman ICBM launch control officer, and as a support officer for SAC's Airborne Command Post, while simultaneously pursuing graduate studies in business administration at the University of Montana. He earned an M.S. in management sciences at Yale University in 1977 and was awarded a Ph.D. in operations research by Yale in 1984. Blair is the author of numerous books, occasional papers, and articles on defense issues in such publications as *Scientific American.* His books include *Strategic Command Control* (Brookings, 1985), winner of the Edgar S. Furniss Award for its contribution to the study of national security, and *The Logic of Accidental Nuclear War* (Brookings, 1993). His most recent occasional paper is *Global Zero Alert for Nuclear Forces* (Brookings, 1995).

THOMAS S. BLANTON is the executive director of the National Security Archive, located at the George Washington University in Washington, D.C. Founded in 1985, the Archive has become the most prolific and successful nonprofit user of the Freedom of Information Act and has built what the *Christian Science Monitor* called "the largest collection of contemporary declassified national security information outside of the U.S. Government." Blanton served as the Archive's first director of planning and research beginning in 1986, became deputy director in 1989 and executive director in 1992. Previously he worked as a journalist, foundation staffer, and congressional aide. His most recent book is *White House E-Mail: The Top Secret Computer Messages the Reagan-Bush White House Tried to Destroy* (The New Press, 1995). Blanton also coauthored *The Chronology* (Warner Books, 1987) on the Iran-Contra affair and served as contributing editor to several other books, including *Litigation under the Federal Open Government Laws* (American Civil Liberties Union, 1995). His articles have appeared in the *International Herald Tribune, New York Times, Wall Street Journal, Washington Post, Atlanta Journal/Constitution, Los Angeles Times,* and other publications. Trained in history at Harvard University, he won Harvard's 1979 Newcomen Prize in Material History for his honors thesis, and the American Library Association's 1996 James Madison Award Citation for "preserving the public's right to know" for his efforts to defend the expansion of the Freedom of Information Act.

WILLIAM BURR is an analyst at the National Security Archive, where he directs the Archive's nuclear history documentation project. He has edited a microfiche collection, *U.S. Nuclear History: Nuclear Weapons and Politics in the Missile Age, 1955–1968* (Chadwyck-Healey, 1997), which includes more than 1,400 documents on U.S. government decisions and follow-up activity on weapons systems development; force levels and deployments; war plans; and command, control, and warning arrangements, among other issues. He is also responsible for a long-term documentation project, "The United States and Nuclear China." Burr edited and supervised the Archive's project, *The Berlin Crisis: 1958–1962* (Chadwyck-Healey, 1992), a comprehensively indexed collection of more than 3,000 documents. While working on this project, he participated in the Nuclear History Program's oral history project on the Berlin Crisis. He has written articles and reviews for *Bulletin of the Atomic Scientists, International History Review, Diplomatic History* (where he serves on the editorial board) and the *Cold War International History Project Bulletin.* Burr received his Ph.D. in history from Northern Illinois University and has taught courses on U.S. diplomatic and military history at Catholic University of America, American University, and George Mason University.

STEVEN M. KOSIAK is director of budget studies at the Center for Strategic and Budgetary Assessments (formerly the Defense Budget Project), a nonpartisan research organization committed to a coherent national security policy that reflects a realistic assessment of available fiscal resources and national security needs. He has previously served as a senior analyst at the Center for Defense Information, worked on Capitol Hill, and served in the Office of the Defense Advisor at the U.S. Mission to the North Atlantic Treaty Organization (NATO). Kosiak specializes in the analysis of defense spending trends, force structure, and weapon system costs and the budgetary consequences of arms reduction measures. He is the author of the center's annual defense budget analysis and contributes significantly to other center reports. His publications include *Air Force Plans for the 21st Century: A Budgetary Perspective* (Center for Strategic and Budgetary Assessments, 1996), *Nonproliferation and Counterproliferation: Investing for a Safer World?* (Defense Budget Project, 1995), and *The Lifecycle Costs of Nuclear Forces: A Preliminary Assessment* (Defense Budget Project, 1994). He is frequently cited in national news stories and has appeared on network television news and radio programs. He has also lectured on defense issues before professional, academic, and civic organizations. Kosiak holds an M.A. in public affairs from the Woodrow Wilson School of Public and International Affairs at Princeton University and a B.A. (summa cum laude) from the University of Minnesota.

ARJUN MAKHIJANI is president of the Institute for Energy and Environmental Research (IEER), an independent nonprofit organization located in Takoma Park, Maryland. The IEER produces technical studies on a wide range of environmental issues to provide advocacy groups and policymakers with sound scientific information and to promote the understanding and democratization of science. Makhijani is frequently cited in national news stories and has appeared on numerous network television news and radio programs. His articles have appeared in, among other publications, the *Bulletin of the Atomic Scientists, New York Times,* and *Washington Post.* He is the author and coauthor of numerous reports and books on topics such as radioactive waste storage and disposal, nuclear testing, disposition of fissile materials, energy efficiency, and ozone depletion, including *High-Level Dollars, Low-Level Sense* (Apex Press, 1992), *Fissile Materials in a Glass, Darkly* (IEER Press, 1995), *The Nuclear Safety Smokescreen: Warhead Safety and Reliability and the Science Based Stockpile Stewardship Program* (IEER, 1996), and *Containing the Cold War Mess: Restructuring the Environmental Management of the U.S. Nuclear Weapons Complex* (IEER, 1997). He is also the principal editor of *Nuclear Wastelands: A Global Guide to Nuclear Weapons Production and Its Health and Environmental Effects* (MIT Press, 1995). Makhijani has served as a consultant to numerous organizations, including the Congressional Office of Technology Assessment, Lawrence Berkeley Laboratory, and the Tennessee Valley Authority. He has testified before Congress and is a consultant to the Radiation Advisory Board Committee of the Environmental Protection Agency's Science Advisory Board. Makhijani studied engineering at the University of Bombay and

Washington State University and earned a Ph.D. in engineering at the University of California at Berkeley, specializing in nuclear fusion.

ROBERT S. NORRIS is senior staff analyst with the Natural Resources Defense Council and director of the Nuclear Weapons Databook Project. NRDC is a nonprofit membership organization dedicated to the protection of natural resources and the human environment. Norris's principal areas of expertise include nuclear weapons research and production, arms control and disarmament, and nuclear weapons testing. He is coeditor of NRDC's *Nuclear Weapons Databook* series and is a coauthor of *U.S. Nuclear Warhead Production*, vol. 2 (Ballinger, 1987); *U.S. Nuclear Warhead Facility Profiles*, vol. 3 (Ballinger, 1987); *Soviet Nuclear Weapons*, vol. 4 (Harper and Row, 1989); *British, French and Chinese Nuclear Weapons*, vol. 5 (Westview Press, 1994); and *Making the Russian Bomb: From Stalin to Yeltsin* (Westview Press, 1995). Norris coauthored the chapter on nuclear weapons production in the 1985–92 editions of the *SIPRI Yearbook* and is an author of six recent NRDC working papers. His writings have appeared in *Arms Control Today* and *Security Dialogue*, and, since May 1987, he has prepared the "Nuclear Notebook" column for the *Bulletin of the Atomic Scientists*. Norris also coauthored the article on nuclear weapons in the 1990 printing of *The New Encyclopedia Britannica* (15th edition, vol. 29, pp. 575–80). He was a senior research analyst for the Center for Defense Information before joining NRDC in 1984. Norris received his Ph.D. in political science from New York University and has taught at New York University; Miami University in Oxford, Ohio: Miami University, Luxembourg; and American University.

KEVIN O'NEILL is deputy director of the Institute for Science and International Security (ISIS). Since his arrival at ISIS in 1994, O'Neill has been deeply involved in all aspects of the institute's work. His research has focused principally on the proliferation risk posed by the collapse of the former Soviet Union, efforts to secure fissile material stockpiles in Russia and the former Soviet republics, and the threat of nuclear terrorism. He also works on issues related to nuclear testing and the control of fissile materials stockpiles in the United States and has contributed to ISIS's efforts to promote regional nuclear safeguards in the Middle East and to uncover the strategies that proliferant states have utilized in the pursuit of nuclear weapons. Before joining ISIS, he was a research intern at several arms control organizations, including the Congressional Arms Control and Foreign Policy Caucus, the Arms Control Association, and the Center for Defense Information. O'Neill has authored or coauthored several articles on nuclear proliferation and nuclear testing for the *Bulletin of the Atomic Scientists, Defense News*, and the *Washington Times*. He is also the author of the May 1996 *ISIS*

Report, "Securing Former Soviet Nuclear Assets." He holds a B.A. in political science from the University of Connecticut at Storrs and an M.A. in public administration from the American University.

JOHN E. PIKE directs the Space Policy Project at the Federation of American Scientists, a nongovernmental organization founded in 1945 as the Federation of Atomic Scientists (by scientists who had worked on the Manhattan Project) and currently comprising 4,000 natural and social scientists and engineers. Pike coordinates research, analysis, and advocacy on military and civilian space policy and other national security issues and has pioneered the use of the internet for public policy communication. A former political consultant and science writer, Pike is the author of more than 200 studies and articles on space and national security. He is a fellow of the Interplanetary Society and a member of the Council on Foreign Relations. In 1991 Pike received the Public Service Award of the Federation of American Scientists and in 1994 he was named one of the twenty-five "Rising Stars Who Will Lead Us into the Next Space Age" by the National Space Society's *Ad Astra* magazine. He is frequently called upon by print and broadcast media for commentary, and by congressional committees for testimony, on space and national security issues. Pike earned a B.A. in technology and public policy from Vanderbilt University.

STEPHEN I. SCHWARTZ is a guest scholar with the Foreign Policy Studies Program at the Brookings Institution and director of the U.S. Nuclear Weapons Cost Study Project. Before joining Brookings in May 1994, Schwartz was the Washington representative for the Military Production Network (now known as the Alliance for Nuclear Accountability), a national alliance of more than forty organizations addressing nuclear weapons production and environmental issues at the Department of Energy's (DOE) nuclear weapons complex. From 1988 until early 1992, he was legislative director for nuclear campaigns with Greenpeace, focusing on the DOE's nuclear weapons programs and naval nuclear weapons issues. Schwartz has also served as associate director of the Santa Monica, California-based Council on Nuclear Affairs (1987–88) and as senior research assistant for the Adlai E. Stevenson Program on Nuclear Policy at the University of California at Santa Cruz (1985–87). He has testified before Congress on various nuclear weapons production issues and given presentations to academic organizations, Department of Energy employees, and military personnel. His writings have appeared in the *Atlanta Journal/Constitution, Bulletin of the Atomic Scientists, Los Angeles Times, New York Times, San Jose Mercury News, Wall Street Journal, Washington Post, Washington Times,* and *Disarmament Diplomacy*. Schwartz's monographs include "Nuclear Weapons Primer: A Supplement to the UCSC Nuclear Information Handbook"

(Adlai E. Stevenson Program on Nuclear Policy, 1986), "The ABM Treaty: Problems in Compliance" (Adlai E. Stevenson Program on Nuclear Policy, 1987), and "Rhetoric vs. Reality: Admiral James D. Watkins at the Helm—The Department of Energy, 1989–1992 and Beyond" (Military Production Network, 1992). Schwartz earned a B.A. in Sociology (summa cum laude and college honors) from the University of California at Santa Cruz.

WILLIAM J. WEIDA is a professor of economics at Colorado College in Colorado Springs, Colorado, and a project director with the New York-based Global Resource Action Center for the Environment. Weida has taught at Colorado College since 1985, serving as cochair of the Economics and Business Department from August 1985 through May 1990, and as chair from June 1990 through June 1993. From March 1982 through July 1985, he worked at the Department of Defense in the Economic Policy and Analysis Division under the assistant secretary of defense for international security affairs, first as assistant director (1982–84) and then as director (1984–85). While at the Pentagon, Weida formulated DOD policy on international economic and energy issues, including security assistance, burdensharing, sanctions and economic warfare trade restrictions, energy, and defense trade. During 1983 he also served on the Blue Ribbon Commission on Security and Economic Assistance. Weida served as an officer and pilot in the U.S. Air Force from June 1965 through January 1971. He taught at the U.S. Air Force Academy from 1970 to 1972 and again from 1975 to 1982, when he also managed more than forty research projects. From June 1981 through March 1982 he served as professor and acting head of the academy's Department of Economics, responsible for curricula, pedagogy, budget, and administration of faculty. He also taught courses in macro- and microeconomics, statistics, and econometrics. His research and articles have appeared in the *International Journal of Social Economics* and *Journal of Technology Transfer,* and his books include *Paying for Weapons: The Politics and Economics of Offsets and Countertrade* (Frost and Sullivan, 1986); *The Political Economy of National Defense* (with Frank L. Gertcher, Westview Press, 1987); *Beyond Deterrence: The Political Economy of Nuclear Weapons* (with Frank L. Gertcher, Westview Press, 1990); and *Regaining Security: A Guide to the Costs of Disposing of Plutonium and Highly Enriched Uranium* (London: Avebury Press, 1997). Weida holds a B.S. in engineering from the U.S. Air Force Academy, an M.B.A. in management theory from the University of California at Los Angeles, and a D.B.A. in econometrics and operations research from the University of Colorado.

Selected Bibliography

Abrams, Herbert L. "Human Reliability and Safety in the Handling of Nuclear Weapons." *Science & Global Security,* vol. 2 (1991), pp. 1–26.

_______. "Sources of Human Instability in the Handling of Nuclear Weapons." In *The Medical Implications of Nuclear War,* pp. 490–528. Washington, D.C.: National Academy Press, 1986.

Adams, Colonel Gerald M. *A History of U.S. Strategic Air Bases in Morocco, 1951–1963.* Omaha, Nebr.: Moroccan Reunion Association, 1992.

Adler, Allan Robert. "Public Access to Nuclear Energy and Weapons." In *Controlling the Atom in the 21st Century,* edited by David P. O'Very, Christopher E. Paine, and Dan W. Reicher, pp. 73–106. Boulder, Colo.: Westview Press, 1994.

_______. "Unclassified Secrets." *Bulletin of the Atomic Scientists,* vol. 41 (March 1985), pp. 26–28.

_______, ed. *Litigation under Federal Open Government Laws.* 18th ed. Washington, D.C.: American Civil Liberties Union Foundation, 1993.

Aerospace Defense Command. *Statistical Data Book—Aircraft and Missiles.* Vol. 2. April 1973.

_______. *Statistical Data Book—Budget, Personnel and Air Bases.* Vol. 1. April 1973.

_______. *Statistical Data Book—Radar.* Vol. 2. April 1973.

_______. "The Air Defense of Atomic Energy Installations, March 1946—December 1952." ADCOM Special Historical Study, August 3, 1953.

Albright, David. "South Africa and the Affordable Bomb." *Bulletin of the Atomic Scientists,* vol. 50 (July/August 1994), pp. 37–47.

Albright, David, William Walker, and Frans Berkhout. *Plutonium and Highly Enriched Uranium 1996: World Inventories, Capabilities, and Policies.* New York: Oxford University Press, 1997.

Allison, Graham T. "U.S. Strategic Offensive Forces in the 1960's." In *The Report of the U.S. Commission on the Organization of the Government for the Conduct of Foreign Policy.* Appendix K, Vol. 4, pt. 2, "Adequacy of Current Organization: Defense and Arms Control," pp. 139–49. GPO, 1975.

Allison, Graham T., and others. *Avoiding Nuclear Anarchy: Containing the Threat of Loose Russian Nuclear Weapons and Fissile Material.* Cambridge, Mass.: MIT Press, 1996.

Alsop, Joseph, and Stewart Alsop. "We Accuse!" *Harper's* Magazine, October 1954, pp. 24–25.

Anders, Roger M., ed. *Forging the Atomic Shield: Excerpts from the Office Diary of Gordon E. Dean.* University of North Carolina Press, 1987.

ARADCOM. "The History of ARADCOM. Volume I: The Gun Era—1950–1955." Historical Project ARAD 5M-I. September 19, 1972.

Arkin, William M. "Bring on the Radiation." *Bulletin of the Atomic Scientists,* vol. 53 (January/February 1997), p. 72.

_______. "The Buildup That Wasn't." *Bulletin of the Atomic Scientists,* vol. 45 (January/February 1989), pp. 6–10.

_______. "Calculated Ambiguity: Nuclear Weapons and the Gulf War." *Washington Quarterly,* vol. 19, no. 4 (1996), pp. 3–18.

_______. "New, and Stupid." *Bulletin of the Atomic Scientists,* vol. 52 (January/February 1996), p. 64.

_______. "Nuclear Excuses." *Bulletin of the Atomic Scientists,* vol. 52 (May/June 1996), p. 64.

_______. "Preparing for World War IV." *Bulletin of the Atomic Scientists,* vol. 41 (May 1985), pp. 6–7.

_______. "Provocations at Sea." *Bulletin of the Atomic Scientists,* vol. 41 (November 1985), p. 67.

_______. "The Six-Hundred Million Dollar Mouse." *Bulletin of the Atomic Scientists,* vol. 52 (November/December 1996).

Arkin William M., and Richard W. Fieldhouse. "Focus on the Nuclear Infrastructure." *Bulletin of the Atomic Scientists,* vol. 41 (June/July 1985), pp. 11–15.

_______. *Nuclear Battlefields: Global Links in the Arms Race.* Cambridge, Mass.: Ballinger, 1985.

Arkin, William M., and Joshua Handler. *Naval Accidents 1945–1988.* Neptune Papers no. 3. Washington, D.C.: Greenpeace, June 1989.

Arkin, William M., and Robert S. Norris. *Nuclear Alert after the Cold War.* NWD 93-4. Natural Resources Defense Council, October 18, 1993.

Arkin, William M., Robert S. Norris, and Joshua Handler. *Taking Stock: Worldwide Nuclear Developments 1998.* National Resources Defense Council, March 1998.

Arkin, William M., and others. *Encyclopedia of the U.S. Military.* Philadelphia: Harper & Row, 1990.

Armacost, Michael H. *The Politics of Weapons Innovation: The Thor-Jupiter Controversy.* Columbia University Press, 1969.

Art, Robert J. *The TFX Decision: McNamara and the Military.* Boston: Little, Brown, 1968.

Bacevich, A. J. *The Pentomic Era: The U.S. Army between Korea and Vietnam.* National Defense University Press, 1986.

Ball, Desmond. "The Development of the SIOP, 1960–1983." In *Strategic Nuclear Targeting,* edited by Desmond Ball and Jeffrey Richelson, pp. 57–83. Cornell University Press, 1986.

_______. *Politics and Force Levels: The Strategic Missile Program of the Kennedy Administration.* University of California Press, 1980.

Ball, Desmond, and Jeffrey Richelson, eds. *Strategic Nuclear Targeting.* Cornell University Press, 1986.

Ball, Desmond, and Robert C. Toth. "Revising the SIOP: Taking War-Fighting to Dangerous Extremes." *International Security,* vol. 14, no. 4 (1990), pp. 65–92.

Bamford, James. *The Puzzle Palace.* New York: Penguin Books, 1984.

Barlow, Jeffrey G. *Revolt of the Admirals: The Fight for Naval Aviation, 1945–1950.* Washington, D.C.: Naval Historical Center, 1994.

Baylis, John. *Ambiguity and Deterrence: British Nuclear Strategy, 1945–1964.* Oxford University Press, 1995.

Beard, Edmund. *Developing the ICBM: A Study in Bureaucratic Politics.* Columbia University Press, 1976.

Benson, Lawrence R. *USAF Aircraft Basing in Europe, North Africa, and the Middle East, 1945–1980.* Ramstein Air Base, Germany: Office of History, Headquarters, United States Air Forces in Europe, April 23, 1981.

Benson, Robert Louis, and Michael Warne. *Venona: Soviet Espionage and the American Response, 1939–1957.* Washington, D.C.: National Security Agency and Central Intelligence Agency, 1996.

Berenson, Douglas. "DOD Concedes Strategic Missile Detargeting Deal Is Easily Reversed." *Inside the Pentagon,* May 29, 1997, p. 1.

Berkowitz, Bruce D., and Jeffrey T. Richelson. "The CIA Vindicated: The Soviet Collapse *Was* Predicted." *National Interest,* no. 41 (Fall 1995), pp. 36–47.

Bernstein, Barton J. "Eclipsed by Hiroshima and Nagasaki." *International Security,* vol. 15, no. 4 (1991), pp. 149–73.

_______. "The Oppenheimer Loyalty-Security Case Reconsidered." *Stanford Law Review,* vol. 342 (July 1990), pp. 1383–84.

_______. "Radiological Warfare: The Path Not Taken." *Bulletin of the Atomic Scientists* (August 1985), pp.44–49.

Beschloss, Michael R. *Mayday: Eisenhower, Khrushchev and the U-2 Affair.* New York: Harper & Row, 1986.

Betts, Richard. *Nuclear Blackmail and Nuclear Balance.* Brookings, 1987.

Blair, Bruce G. *Global Zero Alert for Nuclear Forces.* Brookings, 1995.

_______. *The Logic of Accidental Nuclear War.* Brookings, 1993.

_______. *Strategic Command and Control: Redefining the Nuclear Threat.* Brookings, 1985.

Blechman, Barry M., and Victor A. Utgoff. "The Macroeconomics of Strategic Defenses." *International Security,* vol. 11, no. 3 (1986–87), pp. 33–70.

Blue Ribbon Task Group. *Report to the President on Nuclear Weapons Program Management.* July 1985. Partly declassified and released to the U.S. Nuclear Weapons Cost Study Project. National Security Archive, Washington, D.C.

Borden, William L. Memorandum for Senator Brien McMahon, February 25, 1950. JCAE General Correspondence Files, Record Group 128, Box 17, AEC Budget (Folder 2). National Archives, Washington, D.C.

Boulding, Kenneth E. *The Structure of a Modern Economy: The United States 1929–1989.* New York University Press, 1993.

Bowen, Lee, Robert D. Little, and others. *A History of the Air Force Atomic Energy Program, 1943–1953.* Vol. 3, *Building an Atomic Air Force, 1949–1953.* Washington, D.C.: U.S. Air Force Historical Division, 1959.

Boyer, Paul. *By the Bomb's Early Light: American Thought and Culture at the Dawn of the Atomic Age.* New York: Pantheon Books, 1985.

Broscious, Chuck. *Citizens Guide to the Idaho National Engineering Laboratory.* Troy, Idaho: Environmental Defense Institute, February 1996.

_______. "Gaining Information on the Legacy of Nuclear Weapons Production." *Gonzaga Law Review,* vol. 31, no. 1 (1995/96), pp. 137–46.

Brown, Michael E. *Flying Blind: The Politics of the U.S. Strategic Bomber Program.* Cornell University Press, 1992.

Bruce-Briggs, B. *The Shield of Faith: A Chronicle of Strategic Defense from Zeppelins to Star Wars.* New York: Simon & Schuster, 1988.

Buderi, Robert. *The Invention That Changed the World: How a Small Group of Radar Pioneers Won the Second World War and Launched a Technological Revolution.* New York: Simon & Schuster, 1996.

Budiansky, Stephen. "Keeping Research under Wraps." *U.S. News & World Report,* March 22, 1993, pp. 48–50.

Bukharin, Oleg. "The Future of Russia's Plutonium Cities." *International Security,* vol. 21, no. 4 (1997), pp. 126–58.

Bunn, Matthew, and Kosta Tsipis. "The Uncertainties of Preemptive Nuclear Attack." *Scientific American,* vol. 249 (November 1983), pp. 38–46.

Burleson, Clyde W. *The Jennifer Project.* Englewood Cliffs, N.J.: Prentice-Hall, 1977.

Burrows, William E. *Deep Black: Space Espionage and National Security.* New York: Random House, 1986.

Bush, Vannevar. *Modern Arms and Free Men: A Discussion of the Role of Science in Preserving Democracy.* New York: Simon & Schuster, 1949.

Butler, George Lee. "Time to End the Age of Nukes." *Bulletin of the Atomic Scientists,* vol. 53 (March/April 1997), pp. 33–36.

Cabasso, Jacqueline, and John Burroughs. "End Run around the NPT." *Bulletin of the Atomic Scientists,* vol. 51 (April 1995), pp. 27–29.

Cahn, Anne Hessing, and John Prados. "Team B: The Trillion Dollar Experiment." *Bulletin of the Atomic Scientists,* vol. 49 (April 1993), pp. 22–31.

Capaccio, Tony. "The B-2's Stealthy Skins Need Tender, Lengthy Care." *Defense Week,* May 27, 1997, p. 1.

_______. "A New Look at Why B-1B Bombers Sat Out the Gulf War." *Defense Week,* September 12, 1994, p. 2.

_______. "Spy Agency's 1995 Surplus Tallied at Near $4 Billion." *Defense Week Special,* May 15, 1996, p. 1.

_______. "Top Pentagon Tester Gives B-2 Mixed Review." *Defense Week,* September 8, 1997, p. 1.

Carlisle, Rodney P., with Joan M. Zenzen. *Supplying the Nuclear Arsenal: American Production Reactors, 1942–1992.* Johns Hopkins University Press, 1996.

Caute, David. *The Great Fear: The Anti-Communist Purge under Truman and Eisenhower.* New York: Simon & Schuster, 1978.

Center for Defense Information. "More Bang, More Bucks: $450 Billion for Nuclear War." *Defense Monitor,* vol. 12, no. 7 (1983).

_______. "The Nuclear Nineties: Broken Promises, Misplaced Priorities." *Defense Monitor,* vol. 24, no. 8 (1995).

_______. "Nuclear Weapons after the Cold War: Too Many, Too Costly, Too Dangerous." *Defense Monitor,* vol. 22, no. 1 (1993).

_______. "Preparations for Nuclear War: Still More than $1 Billion a Week." *Defense Monitor,* vol. 19, no. 7 (1990).

_______. "Preparing for Nuclear War: President Reagan's Program." *Defense Monitor,* vol. 10, no. 8 (1982).

_______. "President Reagan's Civil Defense Program." *Defense Monitor,* vol. 11, no. 5 (1982).

_______. "U.S. Nuclear Weapons Accidents: Danger in Our Midst." *Defense Monitor,* vol. 10, no. 5 (1981).

Charles, Daniel. "Labs Struggle to Promote Spin-offs." *Science,* no. 240 (May 13, 1988), pp. 874–76.

Charlton, Michael. *From Deterrence to Defense: The Inside Story of Strategic Policy.* Harvard University Press, 1987.

Cirincione, Joseph. "Why the Right Lost the Missile Defense Debate." *Foreign Policy,* no. 106 (Spring 1997), pp. 39–55.

Clark, Ian. *Nuclear Diplomacy and the Special Relationship: Britain's Deterrent and America, 1957–1962.* Oxford: Clarendon Press, 1994.

Cleary, Mark C. *The 655th: Missile and Space Launches through 1970.* Forty-Fifth Space Wing, Office of History, 1991.

Cochran, Thomas B., William M. Arkin, and Milton M. Hoenig. *Nuclear Weapons Databook.* Vol. 1, *U.S. Nuclear Forces and Capabilities.* Cambridge, Mass.: Ballinger, 1984.

Cochran, Thomas B., Robert S. Norris, and Oleg A. Bukharin. *Making the Russian Bomb: From Stalin to Yeltsin.* Boulder, Colo.: Westview Press, 1995.

Cochran, Thomas B., and Christopher E. Paine. "The Amount of Plutonium and Highly-Enriched Uranium Needed for Pure Fission Nuclear Weapons." Natural Resources Defense Council, Washington, D.C., April 13, 1995.

Cochran, Thomas B., and others. *Nuclear Weapons Databook.* Vol. 2, *U.S. Nuclear Warhead Production.* Cambridge, Mass.: Ballinger, 1987.

_______. *Nuclear Weapons Databook.* Vol. 3, *U.S. Nuclear Warhead Facility Profiles.* Cambridge, Mass.: Ballinger, 1987.

Cockburn, Andrew. *The Threat: Inside the Soviet Military Machine.* New York: Vintage Books, 1984.

Cockburn, Andrew, and Alexander Cockburn. "The Myth of Missile Accuracy." *New York Review of Books,* November 20, 1980, pp. 40–44.

Cohen, Linda R., and Roger G. Noll. "Privatizing Public Research." *Scientific American,* September 1994, pp. 72–77.

Collina, Tom Zamora. "The National Ignition Facility: Buyer Beware." *Technology Review,* vol. 100 (February/March 1997), pp. 35–40.

Collins, A. S. "Current NATO Strategy: A Recipe for Disaster." In *The Nuclear Crisis Reader,* edited by Gwyn Prins, pp. 24–41. New York: Vintage Books, 1984.

Cotter, Donald R. "Peacetime Operations: Safety and Security." In *Managing Nuclear Operations,* edited by Ashton B. Carter, John D. Steinbruner, and Charles A. Zraket, pp. 17–74. Brookings, 1987.

Dahl, Robert. *Controlling Nuclear Weapons, Democracy versus Guardianship.* Syracuse University Press, 1985.

Danish Institute of International Affairs. *Grønland under den Kolde Krig* (Greenland during the Cold War). Vol. 2. Copenhagen: Dansk Udenrigspolitisk Institut, 1997.

D'Antonio, Michael. *Atomic Harvest: Hanford and the Lethal Toll of America's Nuclear Arsenal.* New York: Crown, 1993.

Davis, Merton, and William Harris. "RAND's Role in the Evolution of Balloon and Satellite Observation Systems and Related U.S. Space Technology." Santa Monica, Calif.: Rand, 1988.

De Selding, Peter B. "A Broken Arrow's Dark Legacy." *Nation,* June 25, 1988, pp. 888–91.

Dean, Gordon. *Report on the Atom: What You Should Know about Atomic Energy.* London: Eyre & Spottiswoode, 1954.

DePuy, William E., Jr., and others. *U.S. Military Aircraft Cost Handbook.* Falls Church, Va.: Management Consulting & Research, 1983.

DeVolpi, A., and others. *Born Secret, The H-Bomb, the Progressive Case, and National Security.* New York: Pergamon Press, 1981.

Directorate of Historical Services. "Nuclear Weapons in the Air Defense System." Air Defense Command, Special Historical Study 2, n.d.

"Document One: Memorandum Op-36C/jm, 18 March 1954." *International Security,* vol. 6, no. 3 (1981–82), pp. 18–28.

Donnelly, Charles H. *The United States Guided Missile Program.* Prepared for the Preparedness Investigating Subcommittee of the U.S. Senate Committee on Armed Services. 86 Cong. 1 sess. GPO, 1959.

Duffy, Gloria. *Compliance and the Future of Arms Control.* Palo Alto, Calif.: Stanford University, Center for International Security and Arms Control, 1988.

Dumas, Lloyd J. "Human Fallibility and Weapons." *Bulletin of the Atomic Scientists,* vol. 36 (November 1980), pp. 15–20.

_______, ed. *The Socio-economics of Conversion from War to Peace.* Armonk, N.Y.: M. E. Sharpe, 1995.

Dyke, Richard W., and Francis X. Gannon. *Chet Holifield: Master Legislator and Nuclear Statesman.* Lanham, Md.: University Press of America, 1996.

Edelstein, Michael. *What Price Cold War? The Accumulation of Physical Capital, and Economic Growth: The United States, 1890–1980.* Canberra: Australian National University, 1986.

Eden, Lynn. "Capitalist Conflict and the State: The Making of United States Military Policy in 1948." In *Statemaking and Social Movements: Essays in History and Theory,* edited by Charles Bright and Susan Harding, pp. 233–61. University of Michigan Press, 1984.

Eisenbud, Merill, and Thomas Gessel. *Environmental Radioactivity.* San Diego, Calif.: Academic Press, 1997.

Eisenhower, Dwight D. *Mandate for Change, 1953–1956: The White House Years.* Garden City, N.Y.: Doubleday, 1963.

_______. *The White House Years: Waging Peace, 1956–1961.* Garden City, N.Y.: Doubleday, 1965.

Elliot, David C. "Project Vista and Nuclear Weapons in Europe." *International Security,* vol. 11, no. 1 (1986), pp. 163–83.

Emerson, Steven. "America's Doomsday Project." *U.S. News & World Report,* August 7, 1989, pp. 26–31.

Enthoven, Alain C., and K. Wayne Smith. *How Much Is Enough? Shaping the Defense Program, 1961–1969.* New York: Harper & Row, 1971.

Etzold, Thomas H., and John Lewis Gaddis. *Containment: Documents on American Policy and Strategy, 1945–1950.* Columbia University Press, 1978.

Evangelista, Matthew A. "Stalin's Postwar Army Reappraised." *International Security,* vol. 7, no. 3 (1982/83), pp. 110–38.

Fallows, James. *National Defense.* New York: Vintage Books, 1981.

Feaver, Peter Douglas. *Guarding the Guardians: Civilian Control of Nuclear Weapons in the United States.* Cornell University Press, 1992.

"The Final Report of the Joint Chiefs of Staff Evaluation Board for Operation Crossroads." JCS 1691/10, June 30, 1947. In *America's Plans for War against the Soviet Union, 1945–1950,* edited by Steven T. Ross and David A. Rosenberg. Vol. 9, *Concepts and Capabilities,* pp. 101–39. New York: Garland, 1989.

Findlay, Trevor. *Nuclear Dynamite: The Peaceful Nuclear Explosions Fiasco.* Sydney: Brassey's Australia, 1990.

Fioravanti, Marc, and Arjun Makhijani. *Containing the Cold War Mess: Restructuring the Environmental Management of the U.S. Nuclear Weapons Complex.* Takoma Park, Md.: Institute for Energy and Environmental Research, October 1997.

Foerstel, Herbert N. *Secret Science: Federal Control of American Science and Technology.* Westport, Conn.: Praeger, 1993.

Foran, Virginia. "Strategic Non-Proliferation: Balancing Interests and Ideals." In *U.S. Nuclear Non-Proliferation Policy, 1945–1991,* edited by Virginia Foran. Alexandria, Va.: Chadwyck-Healey, 1992.

Ford, Daniel. *The Button: The Pentagon's Strategic Command and Control System.* New York: Simon & Schuster, 1985.

Forty-Fifth Space Wing History Office, *The 45th Space Wing: Its Heritage, History & Honors, 1950–1994.* GPO, 1995.

Foster, Nancy. "Citizens Jam Nuclear Radio Network." *Bulletin of the Atomic Scientists,* vol. 44 (November 1988), pp. 21–26.

Frank, W. J. *Summary Report of the Nth Country Experiment.* UCRL-50249. Lawrence Radiation Laboratory, March 1967.

Franke, Bernd, and K. R. Gurney. *Estimates of Lung Burdens for Workers at the Feed Materials Production Center, Fernald, Ohio.* Takoma Park, Md.: Institute for Energy and Environmental Research, July 1994.

Franklyn D. Holzman, "Politics and Guesswork: CIA and DIA Estimates of Soviet Military Spending." *International Security,* vol. 14, no. 2 (1989), pp. 101–31.

Freedman, Lawrence. *U.S. Intelligence and the Soviet Strategic Threat.* 2d ed. Princeton University Press, 1986.

Friedman, Herbert, Luther B. Lockhart, and Irving H. Blifford. "Detecting the Soviet Bomb: Joe-1 in a Rain Barrel." *Physics Today,* vol. 49 (November 1996), pp. 38–41.

Frye, Alton. *A Responsible Congress: The Politics of National Security.* New York: McGraw-Hill, 1975.

Fuhrman, R. A. "The Fleet Ballistic Missile System Polaris to Trident." American Institute of Aeronautics and Astronautics, February 1978.

Fulghum, David A. "Cobra Ball Revamped for Battlefield Missions"; "Endurance, Standoff Range Remain Crucial Attribute"; and "Multi-Sensor Cobra Ball Tackles Missile Defense." *Aviation Week & Space Technology,* August 4, 1997, pp. 48–57.

Gaddy, Clifford G. *The Price of the Past: Russia's Struggle with the Legacy of a Militarized Economy.* Brookings, 1996.

Galison, Peter, and Barton Bernstein. "In Any Light: Scientists and the Decision to Build the Superbomb, 1952–1954." *Historical Studies in the Physical Sciences,* vol. 19 (1989), pp. 267–347.

Gallagher, Carole. *American Ground Zero: The Secret Nuclear War.* Cambridge, Mass.: MIT Press, 1993.

Garthoff, Raymond L. *The Great Transition: American-Soviet Relations and the End of the Cold War.* Brookings, 1994.

_______. *Intelligence Assessment and Policymaking: A Decision Point in the Kennedy Administration.* Brookings, 1984.

Gates, Robert M. *From the Shadows: The Ultimate Insider's Story of Five Presidents and How They Won the Cold War.* New York: Simon & Schuster, 1996.

Gavin, James M. *War and Peace in the Space Age.* New York: Harper & Brothers, 1958.

Gayler, Noel. "A Commander-in-Chief's Perspective on Nuclear Weapons." In *The Nuclear Crisis Reader,* edited by Gwyn Prins. New York: Vintage Books, 1984.

Gleason, S. Everett, and Fredrick Aandahl, eds. *Foreign Relations of the United States 1950.* Vol. 1, *National Security Affairs; Foreign Economic Policy.* GPO, 1977.

Glennan, T. Keith. Memorandum to Chairman Gordon Dean and others, May 9, 1952. Records of the Atomic Energy Commission, Office of Secretary. General Correspondence, Record Group 324, Box 73, file "Organization and Management 8, Progress Reports by Division, Vol. 1." National Archives, Washington, D.C.

Gold, David. *The Impact of Defense Spending on Investment, Productivity, and Economic Growth.* Defense Budget Project, Washington, D.C., 1990.

Goldfischer, David. *The Best Defense: Policy Alternatives for U.S. Nuclear Security from the 1950s to the 1990s.* Cornell University Press, 1993.

Goncharov, German A. "Thermonuclear Milestones." *Physics Today,* vol. 49 (November 1996), pp. 44–61.

Grand, Camille. *A French Nuclear Exception?* Occasional Paper 38. Washington, D.C.: Henry L. Stimson Center, January 1998.

Green, Harold P. "Q-Clearance: The Development of a Personnel Security Program." *Bulletin of the Atomic Scientists,* vol. 20 (May 1964), pp. 9–15.

Green, Harold P., and Alan Rosenthal. *Government of the Atom: The Integration of Powers.* New York: Atherton Press, 1963.

Greenwood, Ted. *Making the MIRV: A Study of Defense Decision Making.* Cambridge, Mass.: Ballinger, 1975.

Grossman, Elaine M. "Russian Failure to Ratify Start II Would Cost U.S. $10 Billion After FY-00." *Inside the Pentagon,* April 25, 1996, p. 1.

_______. "To Save Funds, Pentagon May Let Some Start I Nuclear Forces Age Out." *Inside the Pentagon,* May 29, 1997, p. 1.

Groves, Leslie R. *Now It Can Be Told: The Story of the Manhattan Project.* New York: Harper & Brothers, 1962.

Gulley, Bill, with Mary Ellen Reese. *Breaking Cover.* New York: Simon & Schuster, 1980.

Gup, Ted. "The Doomsday Blueprints." *Time,* August 10, 1992, pp. 32–39.

_______. "Doomsday Hideaway." *Time,* December 9, 1991, pp. 26–29.

_______. "How FEMA Learned to Stop Worrying about Civilians and Love the Bomb." *Mother Jones,* January/February 1994, pp. 28–31, 75–76.

_______. "The Ultimate Congressional Hideaway." *Washington Post Magazine,* May 31, 1992, pp. 10–15, 24–27.

Gusterson, Hugh. "NIF-ty Exercise Machine." *Bulletin of the Atomic Scientists,* vol. 51 (September/October 1995), pp. 22–26.

_______. *Nuclear Rites: A Weapons Laboratory at the End of the Cold War.* University of California Press, 1996.

Hacker, Barton C. *Elements of Controversy: The Atomic Energy Commission and Radiation Safety in Nuclear Weapons Testing, 1947–1974.* University of California Press, 1994.

Haines, Gerald K. "CIA's Role in the Study of UFOs, 1947–90." *Studies in Intelligence,* vol. 1, no. 1 (1997), pp. 67–84.

Hales, Peter Bacon. *Atomic Spaces: Living on the Manhattan Project.* University of Illinois Press, 1997.

Hall, R. Cargill. "The Truth about Overflights." *MHQ: Quarterly Journal of Military History,* vol. 9, no. 3 (1997), pp. 24–39.

Halperin, Morton H. *National Security Policy-Making: Analyses, Cases, and Proposals.* Lexington, Mass.: D. C. Heath, 1975.

Hamilton, Walter. Memorandums to William L. Borden, February 22 and May 23 (with attachment), 1950. JCAE General Correspondence Files, Record Group 128, Box 17, AEC Budget (Folder 2). National Archives, Washington, D.C.

Handler, Joshua, and William M. Arkin. *Nuclear Warships and Naval Nuclear Weapons 1990: A Complete Inventory.* Neptune Papers no. 5. Washington, D.C.: Greenpeace, September 1990.

Hansen, Chuck. *The Swords of Armageddon.* Sunnyvale, Calif.: Chuckelea Publications, 1995.

_______. *U.S. Nuclear Weapons: The Secret History.* Arlington, Tex.: Aerofax, 1988.

Hargreaves, C. D. *Introduction to the Historical Report of the Corps of Engineers Ballistic Missile Construction Office and History of the Command Section, Pre-CEBMCO Thru December 1962.* Los Angeles, Calif.: CEBMCO, n.d. (circa 1963).

Hart, Gary, and Barry Goldwater. *Recent False Alerts from the Nation's Missile Attack Warning System.* Report to the U.S. Senate Committee on Armed Services. 96 Cong. 2 sess. GPO, 1980.

Herken, Gregg. "The Earthly Origins of Star Wars." *Bulletin of the Atomic Scientists,* vol. 43 (October 1987), pp. 20–28.

Hewlett, Richard G., and Oscar E. Anderson, Jr. *A History of the United States Atomic Energy Commission.* Vol. 1, *The New World: 1939/1946.* Oak Ridge, Tenn.: U.S. AEC Technical Information Center, 1972.

Hewlett, Richard G., and Francis Duncan. *A History of the United States Atomic Energy Commission.* Vol. 2, *Atomic Shield: 1947/1952.* Oak Ridge, Tenn.: U.S. AEC Technical Information Center, 1972.

_______. *Nuclear Navy: 1946–1962.* University of Chicago Press, 1974.

Hewlett, Richard G., and Jack M. Holl. *Atoms for Peace and War, 1953–1961: Eisenhower and the Atomic Energy Commission.* University of California Press, 1989.

"The Hidden Struggle for the H-Bomb." *Fortune,* May 1953, pp. 108–10, 210.

Hilgartner, Stephen, Richard C. Bell, and Rory O'Connor. *Nukespeak: The Selling of Nuclear Technology in America.* New York: Penguin Books, 1983.

History Associates Incorporated. *History of the Production Complex: The Methods of Site Selection.* Prepared for U.S. Department of Energy, Assistant Secretary for Defense Programs, Office of Nuclear Materials, September 1987.

Hitch, Charles J., and Roland N. McKean. *The Economics of Defense in the Nuclear Age.* Harvard University Press, 1960.

Hoddeson, Lillian, with contributions from Gordon Balm and others. *Critical Assembly: A Technical History of Los Alamos during the Oppenheimer Years, 1943–1945.* Cambridge University Press, 1993.

Holloway, David. *The Soviet Union and the Arms Race.* 2d ed. Yale University Press, 1984.

_______. *Stalin and the Bomb: The Soviet Union and Atomic Energy, 1939—1956.* Yale University Press, 1994.

Hopkins, J. C., and Sheldon A. Goldberg. *The Development of Strategic Air Command, 1946–1986 (The Fortieth Anniversary History).* Offutt Air Force Base, Nebr.: Office of the Historian, Strategic Air Command, September 1, 1986.

Hopkins, Robert S. III. "Cobra Ball and Cobra Eye: Alaskan Observers." *World Air Power Journal,* vol. 8 (Spring 1992), pp. 128–39.

Horgan, John. "'Peaceful' Nuclear Explosions." *Scientific American,* June 1996, pp. 14–15.

Huntington, Samuel R. *The Common Defense: Strategic Programs in National Politics.* Columbia University Press, 1961.

Independent Project Analysis, Inc. *The Department of Energy, Office of Environmental Restoration & Waste Management: Project Performance Study.* November 1993.

Institute for Energy and Environmental Research. *Plutonium: Deadly Gold of the Nuclear Age.* Cambridge, Mass.: International Physicians Press, 1992.

_______. *Radioactive Heaven and Earth: The Health and Environmental Effects of Nuclear Weapons Testing in, on, and above the Earth.* New York: Apex Press, 1991.

Institute of Medicine. *Mortality of Veteran Participants in the Crossroads Nuclear Test.* Washington, D.C.: National Academy Press, 1996.

Intelligence Community Experiment in Competitive Analysis: Soviet Strategic Objectives—An Alternative View. Report of Team "B," December 1976. Record Group 263, National Archives, Washington, D.C.

Isaacs, Terry. "Silos and Shelters in the Pecos Valley: The Atlas ICBM in Chaves County, New Mexico, 1960–1965." *New Mexico Historical Review,* vol. 68 (October 1993), pp. 347–70.

Jockel, Joseph Thomas. "The United States and Canadian Efforts at Continental Air Defense, 1945–1957." Ph.D. dissertation, Johns Hopkins University, 1978. University Microfilms 7906466.

Johnson, Charles E. "Memorandum of the President's Decisions at the Meeting on Nuclear Weapons Requirements on May 3, 1962." Draft, May 4, 1962. Formerly Top Secret/Restricted Data. National Security Archive, Washington, D.C.

Johnson, Kent, and others. "Stockpile Surveillance: Past and Future." Lawrence Livermore National Laboratory, Los Alamos National Laboratory, Sandia National Laboratories, September 1995.

Johnson, Leland, and Daniel Schaffer. *Oak Ridge National Laboratory: The First Fifty Years.* University of Tennessee Press, 1994.

Joint Committee on Atomic Energy. Minutes of an Executive Meeting, April 6, 1949. Records of Joint Committees of Congress, Record Group 46, Box 202, JCAE Document 1059. National Archives, Washington, D.C.

_______. Staff. "The Scale of Our Atomic Weapons Effort." Memorandum to the Joint Committee on Atomic Energy, May 23, 1950. JCAE General Correspondence Files, Record Group 128, Box 17, AEC Buget (Folder 2). National Archives, Washington, D.C.

Joint Security Commission. *Redefining Security: A Report to the Secretary of Defense and the Director of Central Intelligence.* Washington, D.C., February 28, 1994.

Jones, Vincent C. *Manhattan: The Army and the Atomic Bomb.* Washington, D.C.: Center for Military History, U.S. Army, 1985.

Kahan, Jerome H. *Security in the Nuclear Age: Developing U.S. Strategic Arms Policy.* Brookings, 1975.

Kaplan, Fred. "Some Second Thoughts about a First Strike." *Environment,* vol. 26, no. 3 (1984), pp. 6–13.

_______. *The Wizards of Armageddon.* New York: Simon & Schuster, 1983.

Karber, Philip A., and Michael D. Yaffe. *U.S. Strategic Nuclear Forces, 1946–1990.* Vols. 1–3. Washington, D.C., Nuclear History Program, August 13, 1992.

Kidder, R. E. *Maintaining the U.S. Stockpile of Nuclear Weapons during a Low-Threshold or Comprehensive Test Ban.* UCRL-53820. Livermore, Calif.: Lawrence Livermore National Laboratory, October 1987.

Kincade, William H. *Nuclear Proliferation: Diminishing Threat?* Boulder, Colo.: Institute for National Security Studies, U.S. Air Force Academy, 1995.

Klass, Philip J. *Secret Sentries in Space.* New York: Random House, 1971.

Knaack, Marcelle Size. *Encyclopedia of U.S. Air Force Aircraft and Missile Systems.* Vol. 2, *Post–World II Bombers, 1945–1973.* Washington, D.C.: Office of Air Force History, 1988.

Kohn, Richard H., and Joseph P. Harahan. "U.S. Strategic Air Power, 1948–1962." *International Security,* vol. 12, no. 4 (1988), pp. 78–95.

Kolodziej, Edward A. *The Uncommon Defense and Congress, 1945–1963.* Ohio State University Press, 1966.

Korff, Kal K. "What *Really* Happened at Roswell." *Skeptical Inquirer,* vol. 21 (July/August 1997), pp. 24–31.

Kosiak, Steven. *The Lifecycle Costs of Nuclear Forces: A Preliminary Assessment.* Defense Budget Project, Washington, D.C., October 1994.

Kotz, Nick. *Wild Blue Yonder: Money, Politics, and the B-1 Bomber.* New York: Pantheon Books, 1988.

Kristensen, Hans M. "Targets of Opportunity." *Bulletin of the Atomic Scientists,* vol. 53 (September/October 1997), pp. 22–28.

Kristensen, Hans M., William M. Arkin, and Joshua Handler. *Aircraft Carriers: The Limits of Power.* Neptune Papers no. 7. Washington, D.C.: Greenpeace, June 1994.

_______. *U.S. Naval Nuclear Weapons in Sweden.* Neptune Papers no. 6. Washington, D.C.: Greenpeace, September 1990.

Lanouette, William. *Tritium and the Times: How the Nuclear Weapons-Production Scandal Became a National Story.* Cambridge, Mass.: Harvard University, Joan Shorenstein Barone Center, May 1990.

Lapp, Ralph E. *Atoms and People.* New York: Harper & Brothers, 1956.

Lapp, Ralph E., and Stewart Alsop. "We Can Smash the Red A-Bombers." *Saturday Evening Post,* March 21, 1953, p. 19.

Lashmar, Paul. *Spy Flights of the Cold War.* Annapolis, Md.: Naval Institute Press, 1996.

Lebow, Richard Ned, and Janice Gross Stein. *We All Lost the Cold War.* Princeton University Press, 1994.

Lemert, Ann Arnold. *First You Take a Pick and Shovel: The Story of the Mason Companies.* Lexington, Ken.: John Bradford Press, 1979.

Lewis, John Wilson, and Xue Litai. *China Builds the Bomb.* Stanford University Press, 1988.

Lilienthal, David E. *The Journals of David E. Lilienthal.* Vol. 2, *The Atomic Energy Years, 1945–1950.* New York: Harper & Row, 1964.

Lipschutz, Ronnie D. *Radioactive Waste: Politics, Technology and Risk.* Cambridge, Mass.: Ballinger, 1980.

Lockwood, Dunbar. "The Nunn-Lugar Program: No Time to Pull the Plug." *Arms Control Today,* June 1995, pp. 8–13.

Lonnquest, John C., and David F. Winkler. *To Defend and Deter: The Legacy of the United States Cold War Missile Program.* USACERL Special Report 97/01. Rock Island Ill.: Defense Publishing Service, November 1996.

Loper, Herbert B. "Current U.S. Nuclear Energy Programs, 1956–1959." Address by Assistant to the Secretary of Defense (Atomic Energy) delivered before the Air War College, Montgomery, Ala., November 19, 1956. Formerly classified Secret. National Security Archive, Washington, D.C.

Lowenhaupt, Henry S. "The Description of a Picture." *Studies in Intelligence,* vol. 11 (Summer 1967), pp. 41–53.

Lyman, Edwin S. "Weapons Plutonium: Just Can It." *Bulletin of the Atomic Scientists,* vol. 52 (November/December 1996), pp. 48–52.

Mabon, David W., ed. *Foreign Relations of the United States, 1961–1963.* Vol. 8, *National Security Policy.* GPO, 1996.

Machta, Lester. "Finding the Site of the First Soviet Nuclear Test in 1949." *Bulletin of the American Meteorological Society,* vol. 73, no. 11 (1992), pp. 1797–1806.

Mackenzie, Donald. *Inventing Accuracy: A Historical Sociology of Nuclear Missile Guidance.* Cambridge, Mass.: MIT Press, 1990.

_______. "Moving Toward Disinvention." *Bulletin of the Atomic Scientists,* vol. 52 (September/October 1996), p. 4.

Mackenzie, Donald, with Graham Spinardi. "Tacit Knowledge and the Uninvention of Nuclear Weapons." In *Knowing Machines: Essays on Technical Change,* edited by Donald MacKenzie, pp. 215–60. Cambridge, Mass.: MIT Press, 1996.

Makhijani, Annie, and Arjun Makhijani. *Fissile Materials in a Glass, Darkly.* 2d ed. Takoma Park, Md.: IEER Press, 1995.

Makhijani, Arjun. "Calculating Doses from Disposal of High-Level Radioactive Waste: Review of a National Academy of Sciences Report." *Science for Democratic Action,* vol. 4. no. 4 (1995), p. 1.

_______. "Energy Enters Guilty Plea." *Bulletin of the Atomic Scientists,* vol. 50 (March/April 1994), pp. 18–28.

Makhijani, Arjun, and David Albright. *Irradiation of Personnel During Operation Crossroads: An Evaluation Based on Official Documents.* Washington, D.C.: International Radiation Research and Training Institute, 1983.

Makhijani, Arjun, Robert Alvarez, and Brent Blackwelder. *Deadly Crop in the Tank Farm.* Washington, D.C.: Environmental Policy Institute, 1986.

Makhijani, Arjun, and Bernd Franke. *Addendum to the Report: Release Estimates of Radioactive and Non-Radioactive Materials to the Environment by the Feed Materials Production Center 1951–85.* Takoma Park, Md.: Institute for Energy and Environmental Research, 1989.

Makhijani, Arjun, and Bernd Franke. "Worker Radiation Dose Records Deeply Flawed." *Science for Democratic Action,* vol. 6, no. 2 (1997), p. 1.

Makhijani, Arjun, Howard Hu, and Katherine Yih, eds. *Nuclear Wastelands: A Global Guide to Nuclear Weapons Production and Its Health and Environmental Effects.* Cambridge, Mass: MIT Press, 1995.

Makhijani, Arjun, and Scott Saleska. *High-Level Dollars and Low-Level Sense: A Critique of Present Policy for the Management of Long-Lived Radioactive Wastes and Discussion of an Alternative Approach.* New York: Institute for Energy and Environmental Research, 1992.

Makhijani, Arjun, and others. "The United States." In *Nuclear Wastelands: A Global Guide to Nuclear Weapons Production and Its Health and Environmental Effect,* edited by Arjun Makhijani, Howard Hu, and Katherine Yih, pp. 169–284. Cambridge, Mass.: MIT Press, 1995.

Maroni, Alice C. "Estimating Funding for Strategic Forces: A Review of the Problems." Congressional Research Service Report 84-652F. May 31, 1984.

Marsh, John O., Jr. *Congressional Oversight of National Security: A Mandate for Change.* Washington, D.C.: Center for Strategic and International Studies, October 1992.

Maust, R. L., G. W. Goodman, Jr., and C. E. McLain, *History of Strategic Defense.* Final Report SPC 742, Log No. 81-3735, DTIC ADB 066294. System Planning Corporation, September 1981.

McDougall, Walter A. *The Heavens and the Earth: A Political History of the Space Age.* New York: Basic Books, 1985.

McMullen, Richard F. *Interceptor Missiles in Air Defense, 1944–1964.* ADC Historical Study 30. February 1965.

McPhee, John. *The Curve of Binding Energy.* New York: Farrar, Straus & Giroux, 1974.

Mello, Greg. "New Bomb, No Mission." *Bulletin of the Atomic Scientists,* vol. 53 (May/June 1997), pp. 28–32.

Melman, Seymour. *The Pentagon and the National Debt: The Consequences of the Global Military Mission of the United States.* Northampton, Mass.: Aletheia Press, 1994.

Metzger, H. Peter. *The Atomic Establishment.* New York: Simon & Schuster, 1972.

Midgley, John J., Jr. *Deadly Illusions: Army Policy for the Nuclear Battlefield.* Boulder, Colo.: Westview Press, 1986.

Miller, Jay. *Lockheed U-2.* Austin, Texas: Aerofax, 1983.

Miller, Richard L. *Under the Cloud: The Decades of Nuclear Testing.* New York: Free Press, 1986.

Moody, Walton S. *Building a Strategic Air Force.* Washington, D.C.: Air Force History and Museums Program, 1996.

Morland, Howard. *The Secret That Exploded.* New York: Random House, 1981.

Morrison, David C. "And Not a Single Bang for Their Bucks." *National Journal,* August 13, 1994, pp. 1924–25.

———. "Bombs? What Bombs?" *National Journal,* April 25, 1987, p. 1036.

———. "Fuses Are Short over Tall Towers." *National Journal,* May 31, 1986, pp. 1324–26.

———. "Gold Plating." *National Journal,* April 26, 1986, p. 1026.

———. "Here's One Costly Relic." *National Journal,* January 29, 1994, pp. 247–49.

———. "Is the Navy Losing Its Edge in ASW?" *National Journal,* April 8, 1989, pp. 870–71.

———. "Japanese Principles, U.S. Policies." *Bulletin of the Atomic Scientists,* vol. 41 (June/July 1985), pp. 22–24.

———. "The Nuclear Buildup That Wasn't." *National Journal,* November 26, 1988, p. 2994.

———. "Nuking the Constitution." *National Journal,* vol. 23, no. 49 (1991), p. 2993.

———. "Radar Diplomacy." *National Journal,* January 3, 1987, pp. 17–21.

———. "Second Thoughts about Soviet Lasers." *National Journal,* August 5, 1989, p. 1993.

———. " 'Star Wars' Healing Spin-Offs." December 7, 1991, p. 1140.

Nash, Philip. *The Other Missiles of October: Eisenhower, Kennedy, and the Jupiters, 1957–1963.* University of North Carolina Press, 1997.

National Academy of Sciences. Panel on Reactor-Related Options for the Disposition of Excess Weapons Plutonium, Committee on International Security and Arms Control. *Management and Disposition of Excess Weapons Plutonium—Reactor-Related Options.* Washington, D.C.: National Academy Press, 1995.

National Cancer Institute. *Estimated Exposure and Thyroid Doses Received by the American People from Iodine-131 in Fallout Following Nevada Atmospheric Nuclear Bomb Tests.* NIH 97-4264. GPO, October 1997.

National Academy of Sciences. Committee on International Security and Arms Control. *The Future of U.S. Nuclear Weapons Policy.* Washington, D.C.: National Academy Press, 1997.

_______. Committee on International Security and Arms Control. *Nuclear Arms Control: Background and Issues.* Washington, D.C.: National Academy Press, 1985.

_______. Committee on International Security and Arms Control. *Management and Disposition of Excess Weapons Plutonium.* Washington, D.C.: National Academy Press, 1994.

National Research Council. Committee on the Biological Effects of Ionizing Radiation. *Health Effects of Exposure to Low Levels of Ionizing Radiation: BEIR V.* Washington, D.C.: National Academy Press, 1990.

_______. Committee on Declassification of Information for the Department of Energy Environmental Remediation and Related Programs. Board on Radioactive Waste Management. Commission on Geosciences, Environment, and Resources. *A Review of the Department of Energy Classification Policy and Practice.* Washington, D.C.: National Academy Press, 1995.

_______. Committee on the Technical Bases for Yucca Mountain Standards, Board on Radioactive Waste Management. *Technical Bases for Yucca Mountain Standards.* Washington, D.C.: National Academy Press, 1995.

_______. Waste Isolation Systems Panel, Board on Radioactive Waste Management. *A Study of the Isolation System for Geologic Disposal of Radioactive Wastes.* Washington, D.C.: National Academy Press, 1983.

Neufeld, Jacob. *The Development of Ballistic Missiles in the United States Air Force, 1945–1960.* Washington, D.C.: Office of Air Force History, 1990.

Neustadt, Richard E. *Alliance Politics.* Columbia University Press, 1970.

Nicholas, Ted, and Rita Rossi. *U.S. Historical Military Aircraft and Missile Data Book.* Fountain Valley, Calif.: Data Search Associates, 1991.

_______. *U.S. Missile Data Book, 1995.* 19th ed. Fountain Valley, Calif.: Data Search Associates, November 1994.

Nimroody, Rosy. "The Trillion Dollar Brain Drain." *Science Digest,* August 1986, pp. 51–57.

Nolan, Janne E. *Guardians of the Arsenal: The Politics of Nuclear Strategy.* New York: Basic Books, 1989.

Norris, Robert S., and William M. Arkin, "Beating Swords into Swords." *Bulletin of the Atomic Scientists,* vol. 46 (November 1990), pp. 14–16.

_______. "Nuclear Notebook—British, French, and Chinese Nuclear Forces." *Bulletin of the Atomic Scientists,* vol. 52 (November/December 1996), pp. 64–67.

_______. "NRDC Nuclear Notebook—Known Nuclear Tests Worldwide, 1945–1995." *Bulletin of the Atomic Scientists,* vol. 52 (May/June 1996), pp. 61–63.

_______. "NRDC Nuclear Notebook—U.S. Nuclear Stockpile, July 1997." *Bulletin of the Atomic Scientists,* vol. 53 (July/August 1997), pp. 62–63.

_______. "Nuclear Notebook (Pantex Lays Nukes to Rest)." *Bulletin of the Atomic Scientists,* vol. 48 (October 1992), pp. 48–49.

_______. "Nuclear Notebook—U.S. Strategic Nuclear Forces, End of 1996." *Bulletin of the Atomic Scientists,* vol. 53 (January/February 1997), pp. 70–71.

Norris, Robert S., Andrew S. Burrows, and Richard W. Fieldhouse. *Nuclear Weapons Databook.* Vol. 5, *British, French, and Chinese Nuclear Weapons.* Boulder, Colo.: Westview Press, 1994.

Norris, Robert S., and Thomas B. Cochran. *United States Nuclear Tests: July 1945 to 31 December 1992.* NWD-94-1. Natural Resources Defense Council, February 1, 1994.

_______. *US-USSR/Russian Strategic Offensive Nuclear Forces, 1945–1996.* NWD-97-1. Natural Resources Defense Council, January 1997.

Norris, Robert S., Thomas B. Cochran, and William M. Arkin. "History of the Nuclear Stockpile." *Bulletin of the Atomic Scientists,* vol. 41 (August 1985), pp. 106–09.

O'Keefe, Bernard J. *Nuclear Hostages.* Boston: Houghton Mifflin, 1983.

O'Neill, Dan. *The Firecracker Boys.* New York: St. Martin's Press, 1994.

O'Rourke, Ronald. *Nuclear-Powered and Nuclear-Weapon-Capable Ships in the U.S. Navy: An Aid to Identification.* Congressional Research Service Report 86-659F. Washington, D.C: Library of Congress, April 16, 1986.

Oden, Michael Dee. "Military Spending Erodes Real National Security." *Bulletin of the Atomic Scientists,* vol. 44 (June 1988), pp. 36–42.

Orlans, Harold. *Contracting for Atoms: A Study of Public Policy Issues Posed by the Atomic Energy Commission's Contracting for Research, Development, and Managerial Services.* Brookings, 1967.

Osgood, Robert Endicott. *NATO: The Entangling Alliance.* University of Chicago Press, 1962.

Paine, Christopher E., and Matthew G. McKinzie. *End Run: The U.S. Government's Plan for Designing Nuclear Weapons and Simulating Nuclear Explosions under the Comprehensive Test Ban Treaty.* Natural Resources Defense Council Nuclear Program, August 1997.

Parnas, David Lorge. "Software Aspects of Strategic Defense Systems." DCS-47-IR. University of Victoria (British Columbia), Department of Computer Science, July 1985.

Pasternak, Douglas, with Peter Cary. "A $200 Billion Scandal." *U.S. News & World Report,* December 14, 1992, pp. 34–47.

Peacock, Lindsay. *Strategic Air Command.* London: Arms & Armour Press, 1988.

Peebles, Curtis. *The Moby Dick Project.* Washington, D.C.: Smithsonian Institution Press, 1991.

Pike, John. "Buying Votes with B-2s." *Bulletin of the Atomic Scientists,* vol. 52 (May/June 1996), p. 4.

Pocock, Chris. *Dragon Lady: The History of the U-2 Spyplane.* Shrewsbury, Great Britain: Airlife, 1989.

Polmar, Norman. *Strategic Weapons: An Introduction.* New York: Crane, Russak, 1975.

Poole, Walter S. *The History of the Joint Chiefs of Staff.* Vol. 4, *1950–1952.* Wilmington, Del.: Michael Glazer, 1980.

Powell, Colin L., with Joseph E. Perisco. *My American Journey.* New York: Random House, 1995.

Powers, Thomas. *Heisenberg's War: The Secret History of the German Bomb.* New York: Alfred A. Knopf, 1993.

Prados, John. *The Soviet Estimate: U.S. Intelligence Analysis and Russian Military Strength.* New York: Dial Press, 1982.

President's Air Policy Commission. *Survival in the Air Age.* January 1, 1948.

Pringle, Peter, and William Arkin. *SIOP.* London: Sphere Books, 1983.

Pringle, Peter, and James Spigelman. *The Nuclear Barons.* New York: Holt, Rhinehart & Winston, 1981.

Quanbeck, Alton H., and Barry M. Blechman, *Strategic Forces: Issues for the Mid-Seventies.* Brookings, 1973.

Quist, Arvin S. *Security Classification of Information.* Vol. 1, *Introduction, History, and Adverse Impacts.* U.S. Department of Energy, Oak Ridge Gaseous Diffusion Plant, 1989.

Ray, Thomas W. "A History of Texas Towers in Air Defense, 1952–1964." Air Defense Command Historical Study 29, March 1965.

Reed, Thomas, and Arnold Kramish. "Trinity at Dubna." *Physics Today,* vol. 49 (November 1996), pp. 30–35.

Report of the President's Commission on Strategic Forces (Scowcroft Commission). April 6, 1983.

Reynolds, Gary K. "The Ground Wave Emergency Network (GWEN)." Congressional Research Service, Foreign Affairs and National Defense Division, March 27, 1989.

Rhodes, Richard. *Dark Sun: The Making of the Hydrogen Bomb.* New York: Simon & Schuster, 1995.

_______. *The Making of the Atomic Bomb.* New York: Simon & Schuster, 1986.

Rich, Ben R., and Leo Janos. *Skunk Works: A Personal Memoir of My Years at Lockheed.* New York: Little, Brown, 1994.

Richelson, Jeffrey T. *American Espionage and the Soviet Target.* New York: William Morrow, 1987.

_______. *America's Secret Eyes in Space: The U.S. Keyhole Spy Satellite Program.* New York: Harper & Row, 1990.

_______. *A Century of Spies: Intelligence in the Twentieth Century.* Oxford University Press, 1995.

_______. "Cold War Recon Planes Find New Missions." *Defense Week,* September 5, 1995, pp. 6–7.

_______. "Scientists in Black." *Scientific American,* February 1998, pp. 48–55.

_______. *The U.S. Intelligence Community.* 3d ed. Boulder, Colo.: Westview Press, 1995.

Roman, Peter. "Strategic Bombers over the Missile Horizon, 1957–1963." *Journal of Strategic Studies,* vol. 18, no. 1 (1995), pp. 198–236.

Rosenberg, David Alan. "American Atomic Strategy and the Hydrogen Bomb Decision." *Journal of American History,* vol. 66, no. 1 (1979), pp. 62–87.

_______. "The Origins of Overkill: Nuclear Weapons and American Strategy, 1945–1960." In *Strategy and Nuclear Deterrence,* edited by Steven E. Miller, pp. 113–81. Princeton University Press, 1984.

_______. "'A Smoking Radiating Ruin at the End of Two Hours': Documents on American Plans for Nuclear War with the Soviet Union, 1954–1955." *International Security,* vol. 6, no. 3 (1981/82), pp. 3–17.

_______. "U.S. Nuclear Stockpile, 1945 to 1950." *Bulletin of the Atomic Scientists,* vol. 38 (May 1982), pp. 25–30.

Rosenberg, Eric. "The Price of Navy Nuclear Missiles? Take Your Pick." *Defense Week,* August 8, 1994, p. 2.

Rowen, Henry S. "Reforming Intelligence: A Market Approach." *American Intelligence Journal,* vol. 14 (Autumn–Winter 1993–94), pp. 49–54.

Ruffner, Kevin C., ed. *CORONA: America's First Satellite Program.* Washington, D.C.: Center for the Study of Intelligence, Central Intelligence Agency, 1995.

Sachs, Noah. *Risky Relapse into Reprocessing: Environmental and Non-Proliferation Consequences of the Department of Energy's Spent Fuel Management Program.* Institute for Energy and Environmental Research, 1995.

Saffer, Thomas H., and Orville E. Kelly. *Countdown Zero.* New York: Penguin Books, 1982.

Sagan, Scott D. *The Limits of Safety.* Princeton University Press, 1993.

_______. "SIOP-62: The Nuclear Plan Briefing to President Kennedy." *International Security,* vol. 12, no. 1 (1987), pp. 22–40.

Saleska, Scott. *Nuclear Legacy: An Overview of the Places, Problems, and Politics of Radioactive Waste in the United States.* Washington, D.C.: Public Citizen Critical Mass Energy Project, September 1989.

Sapolsky, Harvey M. *Creating the Fleet Ballistic Missile System: The Interaction of Technology and Organization in the Development of a Major Weapon System.* Cambridge, Mass.: MIT Press, October 1969.

Sastry, M. Anjali, Joseph J. Romm, and Kosta Tsipis. "Can the U.S. Economy Survive a Few Nuclear Weapons?" *Technology Review,* vol. 92 (April 1989), pp. 23–29.

Schaffel, Kenneth. *The Emerging Shield: The Air Force and the Evolution of Continental Air Defense, 1945–1960.* Washington, D.C.: Office of Air Force History, 1991.

Scheer, Robert. *With Enough Shovels: Reagan, Bush and Nuclear War.* New York: Vintage Books, 1982.

Schwartz, David N. *NATO's Nuclear Dilemmas.* Brookings, 1983.

Schwarzkopf, H. Norman, with Peter Petre. *It Doesn't Take a Hero: General H. Norman Schwarzkopf, The Autobiography.* New York: Bantam Books, 1992.

Scott, William B. "USAF Nuclear Detectives Assume New Roles," "Sampling Missions Unveiled Nuclear Weapon Secrets," and "Debris Collection Reverts to Ground Sites." *Aviation Week & Space Technology,* November 3, 1997, pp. 50–59.

Seaborg, Glenn T. "Secrecy Runs Amok." *Science,* vol. 264 (June 3, 1994), pp. 1410–11.

Selden, Zachary. *Nunn-Lugar: New Solutions for Today's Nuclear Threats.* Washington, D.C.: Business Executive for National Security, September 1997.

Shircliffe, David W. *NORAD's Underground COC, Initial Requirement to Initial Operation: 1956–1966.* Historical Reference Paper 12. NORAD Public Affairs Office, January 1966.

Shuey, Robert D., Steven R. Bowman, and Zachary S. Davis. "Proliferation Control Regimes: Background and Issues." Congressional Research Service Report 97-343F, March 19, 1997.

Shulman, Seth. "Code Name: Corona." *Technology Review,* October 1996, pp. 22–31.

"SIOP-62 Briefing: JCS 2056/281 Enclosure, September 13, 1961." *International Security,* vol. 12, no. 1 (1987), pp. 41–51.

Sorenson, David S. *The Politics of Strategic Aircraft Modernization.* Westport, Conn.: Praeger, 1995.

Stares, Paul B. *The Militarization of Space: U.S. Policy, 1945–1984.* Cornell University Press, 1985.

Stein, Peter, and Peter Feaver. *Assuring Control of Nuclear Weapons: The Evolution of Permissive Action Links.* Lanham, Md.: University Press of America, 1987.

Steiner, James E., and Franklyn D. Holzman. "Correspondence: CIA Estimates of Soviet Military Spending." *International Security,* vol. 14, no. 4 (1990), pp. 185–98.

Stern, Philip M., with the collaboration of Harold P. Green. *The Oppenheimer Case: Security on Trial.* New York: Harper & Row, 1969.

Sterste-Perkins, Dagnija. "Long-Range Bomber Facts: Background Information." Congressional Research Service Report for Congress, March 10, 1995.

Strategic Air Command. *The Development of the Strategic Air Command, 1946–1986.* Offutt Air Force Base, Nebr.: Office of the Historian, September 1, 1986.

_______. *From Snark to Peacekeeper: A Pictorial History of Strategic Air Command Missiles.* Offutt Air Force Base, Nebr.: Office of the Historian, May 1, 1990.

_______. *SAC Missile Chronology, 1939–88.* 3d ed. Offutt Air Force Base, Nebr.: Office of the Historian, May 1, 1990.

Takahasi, T., and others. "An Investigation Into the Prevalence of Thyroid Disease on Kwajalein Atoll, Marshall Islands." *Health Physics,* vol. 73, no. 1 (1997), pp. 199–213.

Taylor, Maxwell D. *Precarious Security.* New York: W. W. Norton, 1976.

_______. *The Uncertain Trumpet.* New York: Harper, 1960.

Thirtieth Space Wing History Office. *The Heritage of the 30th Space Wing and Vandenberg Air Force Base.* GPO, 1995.

"The Truth about Our Air Defense." *Air Force Magazine,* May 1953, pp. 25–36.

Thomas, Dave. "The Roswell Incident and Project Mogul." *Skeptical Inquirer,* vol. 19 (July/August 1995), pp. 15–18.

Thomas W. Ray, "Nuclear Armament: Its Acquisition, Control and Application to Manned Interceptors, 1951–1963." Air Defense Command Historical Study 20 (n.d.).

Thorn, Robert N., and Donald R. Westervelt, "Hydronuclear Experiments." In *Nuclear Nonproliferation, 1945–1990,* edited by Virginia Foran. Alexandria, Va.: Chadwick-Healey, 1992.

Titus, A. Costandina. "Selling the Bomb: Public Relations Efforts by the Atomic Energy Commission During the 1950s and Early 1960s." *Government Publications Review,* vol. 16 (January/February 1989), pp. 15–29.

Torres, Louis. *A History of Huntsville Division, U.S. Army Corps of Engineers, 1982–1987 Update.* Huntsville, Ala.: U.S. Army Corps of Engineers, 1990.

Trauth, Kathleen M., Stephen C. Hora, and Robert V. Guzowski. *Expert Judgement on Markers to Deter Inadvertent Human Intrusion into the Waste Isolation Pilot Plant.* SAND92-1382. Albuquerque, N.M.: Sandia National Laboratories, 1993.

Turner, Stansfield. *Caging the Nuclear Genie: An American Challenge for Global Security.* Boulder, Colo.: Westview Press.

USAF Nuclear Safety. AFRP 122-1 Jan/Feb/Mar 1970, vol. 65, no. 1 (pt. 2). Special Edition, pp. 2-97.

U.S. Advisory Committee on Human Radiation Experiments. *Final Report.* GPO, 1995.

U.S. Air Force. *A History of Strategic Arms Competition 1945–1972.* Vol. 2, *A Handbook of Selected U.S. Weapon Systems.* June 1976.

_______. *The Roswell Report: Fact vs. Fiction in the New Mexico Desert.* GPO, 1995.

_______. *SAC Operations in the United Kingdom, 1948–1956.* Washington, D.C.: Historical Division, 7th Air Division, n.d.

_______. Air Research and Development Command. *Development of the SM-64 Navaho Missile, 1954–1958.* Historical Branch: Wright Air Development Division, January 1961.

U.S. Arms Control and Disarmament Agency. *START—Treaty between the United States of America and the Union of Soviet Socialist Republics on the Reduction and Limitation of Strategic Offensive Arms.* GPO, 1991.

U.S. Army Corps of Engineers (Omaha District). *The Federal Engineer—Damsites to Missile Sites: A History of the Omaha District, U.S. Army Corps of Engineers.* Omaha, Nebr., 1984.

U.S. Atomic Energy Commission. *Fifth Semiannual Report of the Atomic Energy Commission.* GPO, 1949.

_______. *History of Expansion of AEC Production Facilities.* AEC 1140. August 16, 1963.

_______. *In the Matter of J. Robert Oppenheimer: Text of Principal Documents and Letters of Personnel Security Board, General Manager, Commissioners.* GPO, 1954.

_______. "Summary of Relations between the AEC and the Photographic Industry Regarding Radioactive Contamination from Atomic Weapons Tests, from January through December 1951." Report by the Director of Military Application, January 17, 1952. Record Group 325, Secretariat Collection, Box 1258, Folder MH&S 3-3, Contamination & Decontamination, Department of Energy Archives. (Formerly confidential; declassified March 28, 1983.)

U.S. Central Intelligence Agency. "Possible Soviet Responses to the U.S. Strategic Defense Initiative." NIC M 83-10017. September 12, 1983, copy 458.

_______. History Staff. *Intentions and Capabilities: Estimates on Soviet Strategic Forces 1950–1983.* Washington, D.C., 1996.

U.S. Commission on the Roles and Capabilities of the United States Intelligence Community. *Preparing for the 21st Century: An Appraisal of U.S. Intelligence.* GPO, 1996.

U.S. Congress. House. *American Nuclear Guinea Pigs: Three Decades of Human Radiation Experiments on U.S. Citizens.* Report. 99 Cong. 2 sess. GPO, 1986.

_______. House. Committee on Armed Services. *The Ailing Defense Industrial Base: Unready for Crisis.* Report of the Defense Industrial Base Panel. GPO, 1980.

_______. House. Committee on Energy and Commerce. Subcommittee on Oversight and Investigations. *DOE and Contractor Litigation Costs.* Hearings. 103 Cong. 2 sess. GPO, 1994.

_______. House. Committee on Foreign Affairs. *U.S. Nuclear Policy,* Hearings. 103 Cong. 2 sess. GPO, 1994.

_______. House. Committee on Government Operations. *NORAD Computer Systems Are Dangerously Obsolete.* Report 97-449. 97 Cong. 2 sess. GPO, 1982.

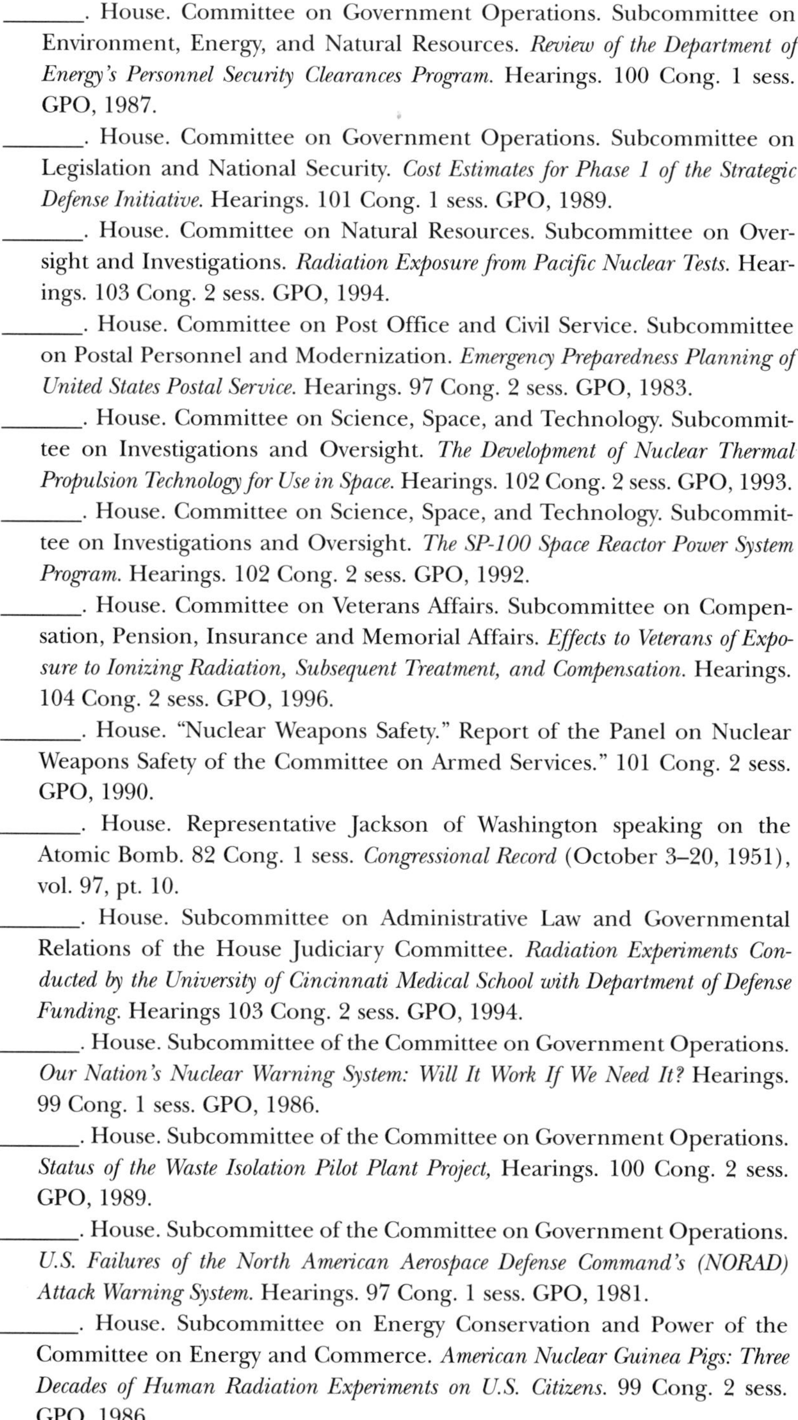

_______. House. Committee on Government Operations. Subcommittee on Environment, Energy, and Natural Resources. *Review of the Department of Energy's Personnel Security Clearances Program.* Hearings. 100 Cong. 1 sess. GPO, 1987.

_______. House. Committee on Government Operations. Subcommittee on Legislation and National Security. *Cost Estimates for Phase 1 of the Strategic Defense Initiative.* Hearings. 101 Cong. 1 sess. GPO, 1989.

_______. House. Committee on Natural Resources. Subcommittee on Oversight and Investigations. *Radiation Exposure from Pacific Nuclear Tests.* Hearings. 103 Cong. 2 sess. GPO, 1994.

_______. House. Committee on Post Office and Civil Service. Subcommittee on Postal Personnel and Modernization. *Emergency Preparedness Planning of United States Postal Service.* Hearings. 97 Cong. 2 sess. GPO, 1983.

_______. House. Committee on Science, Space, and Technology. Subcommittee on Investigations and Oversight. *The Development of Nuclear Thermal Propulsion Technology for Use in Space.* Hearings. 102 Cong. 2 sess. GPO, 1993.

_______. House. Committee on Science, Space, and Technology. Subcommittee on Investigations and Oversight. *The SP-100 Space Reactor Power System Program.* Hearings. 102 Cong. 2 sess. GPO, 1992.

_______. House. Committee on Veterans Affairs. Subcommittee on Compensation, Pension, Insurance and Memorial Affairs. *Effects to Veterans of Exposure to Ionizing Radiation, Subsequent Treatment, and Compensation.* Hearings. 104 Cong. 2 sess. GPO, 1996.

_______. House. "Nuclear Weapons Safety." Report of the Panel on Nuclear Weapons Safety of the Committee on Armed Services." 101 Cong. 2 sess. GPO, 1990.

_______. House. Representative Jackson of Washington speaking on the Atomic Bomb. 82 Cong. 1 sess. *Congressional Record* (October 3–20, 1951), vol. 97, pt. 10.

_______. House. Subcommittee on Administrative Law and Governmental Relations of the House Judiciary Committee. *Radiation Experiments Conducted by the University of Cincinnati Medical School with Department of Defense Funding.* Hearings 103 Cong. 2 sess. GPO, 1994.

_______. House. Subcommittee of the Committee on Government Operations. *Our Nation's Nuclear Warning System: Will It Work If We Need It?* Hearings. 99 Cong. 1 sess. GPO, 1986.

_______. House. Subcommittee of the Committee on Government Operations. *Status of the Waste Isolation Pilot Plant Project,* Hearings. 100 Cong. 2 sess. GPO, 1989.

_______. House. Subcommittee of the Committee on Government Operations. *U.S. Failures of the North American Aerospace Defense Command's (NORAD) Attack Warning System.* Hearings. 97 Cong. 1 sess. GPO, 1981.

_______. House. Subcommittee on Energy Conservation and Power of the Committee on Energy and Commerce. *American Nuclear Guinea Pigs: Three Decades of Human Radiation Experiments on U.S. Citizens.* 99 Cong. 2 sess. GPO, 1986.

U.S. Congress. Joint Committee on Armed Services and Committee on Aeronautical and Space Sciences. Subcommittee on Preparedness Investigating. *Missile and Space Activities.* Hearings. 86 Cong. 1 sess. GPO, 1959.

U.S. Congress. Joint Committee on Atomic Energy. *Atomic Energy Report to Congress.* Hearings. 81 Cong. 1 sess. GPO, 1949.

_______. Joint Committee on Atomic Energy. *Investigation into the United States Atomic Energy Project.* Hearings. 81 Cong. 1 sess. GPO, 1949.

_______. Joint Committee on Atomic Energy. Subcommittee on Military Applications. *Military Applications of Nuclear Technology.* Hearings. 93 Cong. 1 sess. GPO, 1973.

_______. Joint Committee on Atomic Energy. Subcommittee on Research and Development. *Aircraft Nuclear Propulsion Program.* Hearings. 86 Cong. 1st sess. GPO, 1959.

U.S. Congress. Joint Committee on Defense Production. *Economic and Social Consequences of Nuclear Attacks on the United States.* A Study. GPO, 1979.

U.S. Congress. Joint Committee on Government Operations and Governmental Affairs. *Nuclear Reactor Safety at the Department of Energy's Savannah River Plant.* Hearings. 100 Cong. 2 sess. GPO, 1988.

U.S. Congress. Office of Technology Assessment. *Complex Cleanup: The Environmental Legacy of Nuclear Weapons Production.* OTA-O-484. GPO, 1991.

_______. Office of Technology Assessment. *Defense Conversion: Redirecting R&D.* OTA-ITE-522. GPO, May 1993.

_______. *Dismantling the Bomb and Managing the Nuclear Materials.* OTA-O-572. GPO, September 1993.

_______. Office of Technology Assessment. *Long-Lived Legacy: Managing High-Level and Transuranic Waste as the DOE Nuclear Weapons Complex.* Background Paper OTA-BP-O-83. GPO, 1991.

_______. *MX Missile Basing.* OTA-IS-140. GPO, September 1981.

_______. Office of Technology Assessment. *Technologies Underlying Weapons of Mass Destruction.* Background Paper ISC-115. GPO, 1993.

U.S. Congress. Senate. *Atoms for Peace Manual: A Compilation of Official Materials on International Cooperation for Peaceful Uses of Atomic Energy, December 1953–July 1955.* 84 Cong. 1 sess. GPO, 1955.

_______. Senate. *Report of the Commission on Protecting and Reducing Government Secrecy.* Doc. 105-2. GPO, 1997.

_______. Senate. Committee on Appropriations. *Attack Submarine Requirements: Department of Defense Appropriations for Fiscal Year 1991.* 101 Cong. 2 sess. GPO, 1990.

_______. Senate. Committee on Armed Services. *Strategic Forces and Nuclear Deterrence.* Hearings. 102 Cong. 1 sess. GPO, 1991.

_______. Senate. Committee on Armed Services in Conjunction with the Committee on Aeronautical and Space Sciences. Subcommittee on Preparedness Investigating. *Missiles, Space, and Other Major Defense Matters.* Hearings. 86 Cong. 2 sess. GPO, 1960.

_______. Senate. Committee on Armed Services. Subcommittee on the Air Force. *Study of Airpower.* Hearings. Vols. 1 and 2. 84 Cong. 2 sess. GPO, 1956.

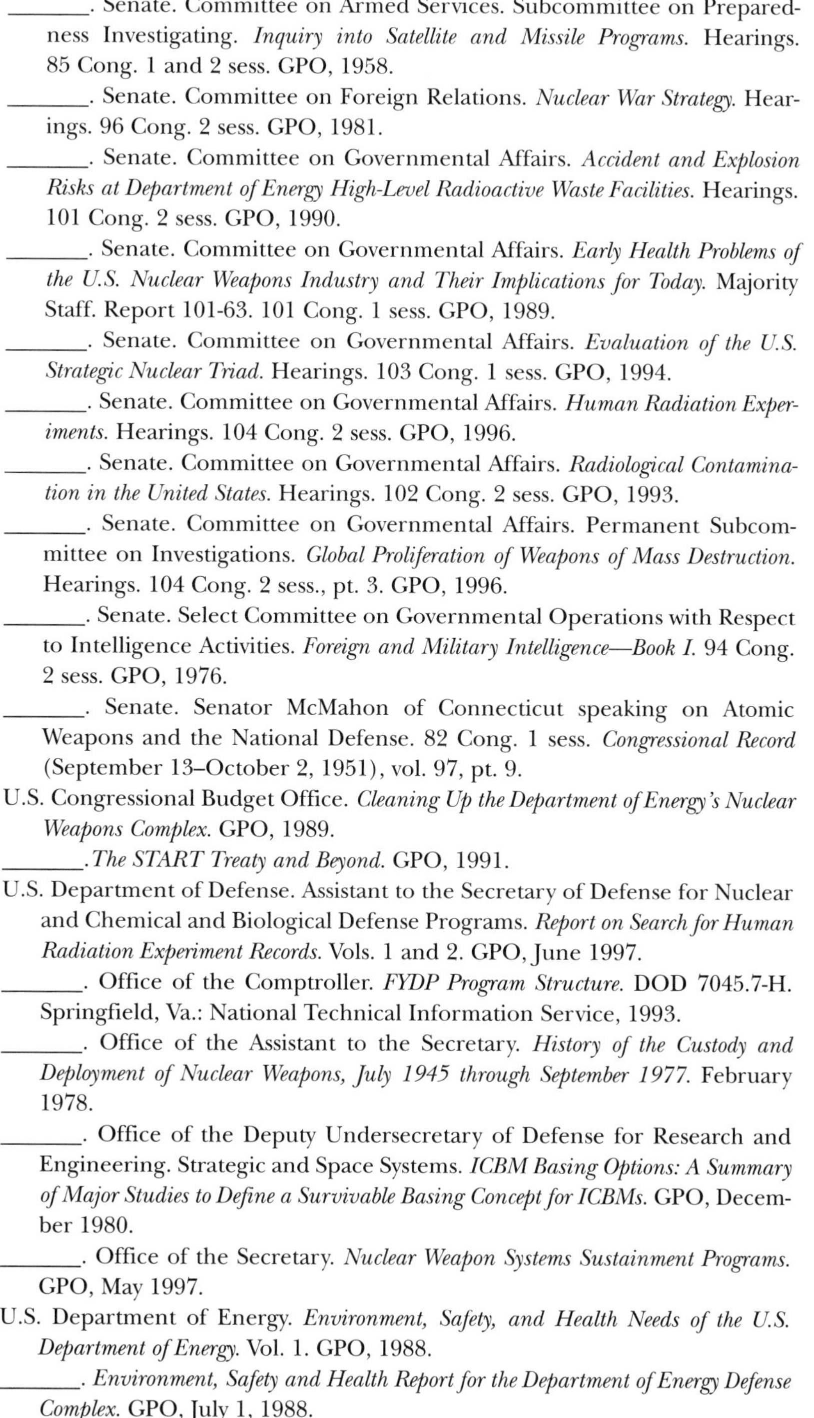

_______. Senate. Committee on Armed Services. Subcommittee on Preparedness Investigating. *Inquiry into Satellite and Missile Programs.* Hearings. 85 Cong. 1 and 2 sess. GPO, 1958.

_______. Senate. Committee on Foreign Relations. *Nuclear War Strategy.* Hearings. 96 Cong. 2 sess. GPO, 1981.

_______. Senate. Committee on Governmental Affairs. *Accident and Explosion Risks at Department of Energy High-Level Radioactive Waste Facilities.* Hearings. 101 Cong. 2 sess. GPO, 1990.

_______. Senate. Committee on Governmental Affairs. *Early Health Problems of the U.S. Nuclear Weapons Industry and Their Implications for Today.* Majority Staff. Report 101-63. 101 Cong. 1 sess. GPO, 1989.

_______. Senate. Committee on Governmental Affairs. *Evaluation of the U.S. Strategic Nuclear Triad.* Hearings. 103 Cong. 1 sess. GPO, 1994.

_______. Senate. Committee on Governmental Affairs. *Human Radiation Experiments.* Hearings. 104 Cong. 2 sess. GPO, 1996.

_______. Senate. Committee on Governmental Affairs. *Radiological Contamination in the United States.* Hearings. 102 Cong. 2 sess. GPO, 1993.

_______. Senate. Committee on Governmental Affairs. Permanent Subcommittee on Investigations. *Global Proliferation of Weapons of Mass Destruction.* Hearings. 104 Cong. 2 sess., pt. 3. GPO, 1996.

_______. Senate. Select Committee on Governmental Operations with Respect to Intelligence Activities. *Foreign and Military Intelligence—Book I.* 94 Cong. 2 sess. GPO, 1976.

_______. Senate. Senator McMahon of Connecticut speaking on Atomic Weapons and the National Defense. 82 Cong. 1 sess. *Congressional Record* (September 13–October 2, 1951), vol. 97, pt. 9.

U.S. Congressional Budget Office. *Cleaning Up the Department of Energy's Nuclear Weapons Complex.* GPO, 1989.

_______. *The START Treaty and Beyond.* GPO, 1991.

U.S. Department of Defense. Assistant to the Secretary of Defense for Nuclear and Chemical and Biological Defense Programs. *Report on Search for Human Radiation Experiment Records.* Vols. 1 and 2. GPO, June 1997.

_______. Office of the Comptroller. *FYDP Program Structure.* DOD 7045.7-H. Springfield, Va.: National Technical Information Service, 1993.

_______. Office of the Assistant to the Secretary. *History of the Custody and Deployment of Nuclear Weapons, July 1945 through September 1977.* February 1978.

_______. Office of the Deputy Undersecretary of Defense for Research and Engineering. Strategic and Space Systems. *ICBM Basing Options: A Summary of Major Studies to Define a Survivable Basing Concept for ICBMs.* GPO, December 1980.

_______. Office of the Secretary. *Nuclear Weapon Systems Sustainment Programs.* GPO, May 1997.

U.S. Department of Energy. *Environment, Safety, and Health Needs of the U.S. Department of Energy.* Vol. 1. GPO, 1988.

_______. *Environment, Safety and Health Report for the Department of Energy Defense Complex.* GPO, July 1, 1988.

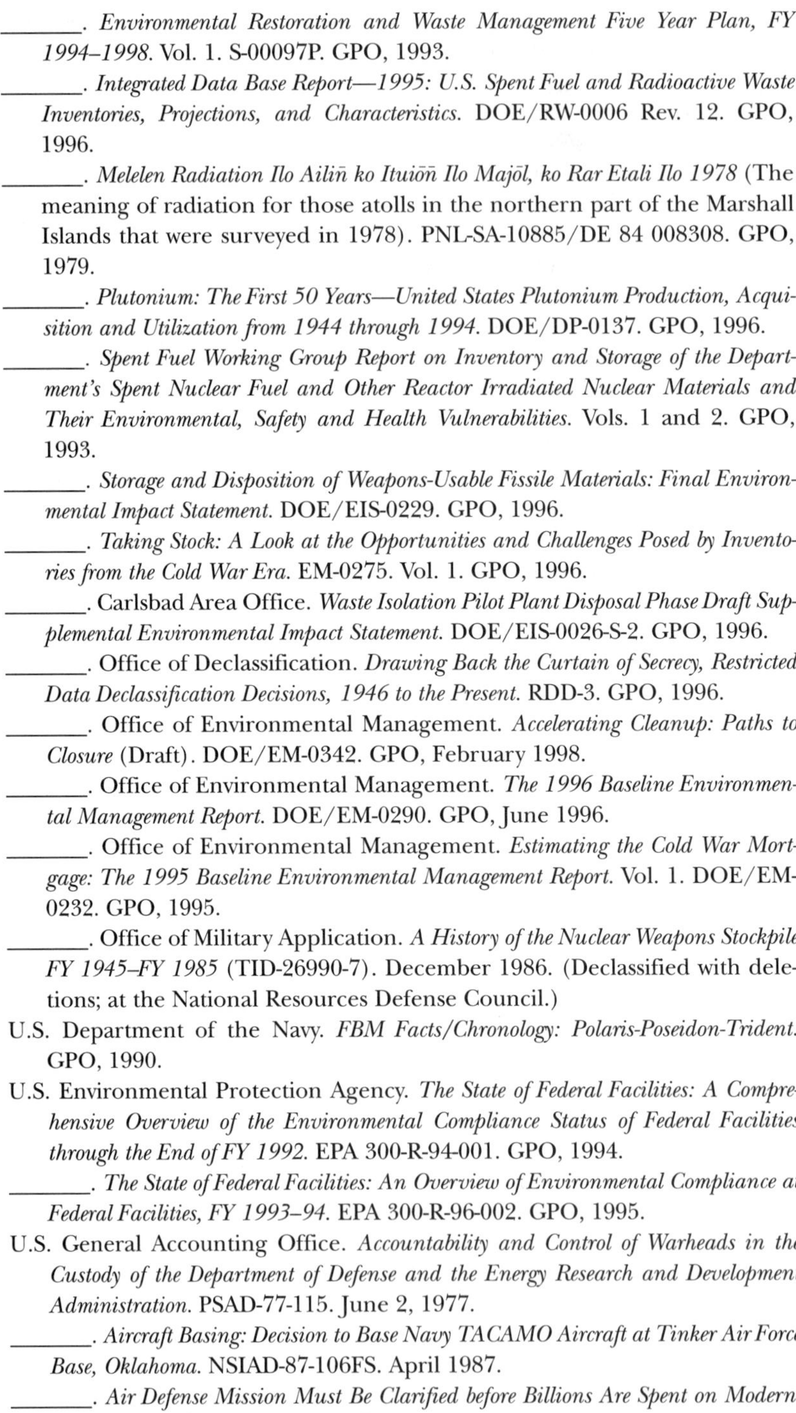

_______. *Environmental Restoration and Waste Management Five Year Plan, FY 1994–1998.* Vol. 1. S-00097P. GPO, 1993.

_______. *Integrated Data Base Report—1995: U.S. Spent Fuel and Radioactive Waste Inventories, Projections, and Characteristics.* DOE/RW-0006 Rev. 12. GPO, 1996.

_______. *Melelen Radiation Ilo Ailin̄ ko Ituiōn̄ Ilo Majōl, ko Rar Etali Ilo 1978* (The meaning of radiation for those atolls in the northern part of the Marshall Islands that were surveyed in 1978). PNL-SA-10885/DE 84 008308. GPO, 1979.

_______. *Plutonium: The First 50 Years—United States Plutonium Production, Acquisition and Utilization from 1944 through 1994.* DOE/DP-0137. GPO, 1996.

_______. *Spent Fuel Working Group Report on Inventory and Storage of the Department's Spent Nuclear Fuel and Other Reactor Irradiated Nuclear Materials and Their Environmental, Safety and Health Vulnerabilities.* Vols. 1 and 2. GPO, 1993.

_______. *Storage and Disposition of Weapons-Usable Fissile Materials: Final Environmental Impact Statement.* DOE/EIS-0229. GPO, 1996.

_______. *Taking Stock: A Look at the Opportunities and Challenges Posed by Inventories from the Cold War Era.* EM-0275. Vol. 1. GPO, 1996.

_______. Carlsbad Area Office. *Waste Isolation Pilot Plant Disposal Phase Draft Supplemental Environmental Impact Statement.* DOE/EIS-0026-S-2. GPO, 1996.

_______. Office of Declassification. *Drawing Back the Curtain of Secrecy, Restricted Data Declassification Decisions, 1946 to the Present.* RDD-3. GPO, 1996.

_______. Office of Environmental Management. *Accelerating Cleanup: Paths to Closure* (Draft). DOE/EM-0342. GPO, February 1998.

_______. Office of Environmental Management. *The 1996 Baseline Environmental Management Report.* DOE/EM-0290. GPO, June 1996.

_______. Office of Environmental Management. *Estimating the Cold War Mortgage: The 1995 Baseline Environmental Management Report.* Vol. 1. DOE/EM-0232. GPO, 1995.

_______. Office of Military Application. *A History of the Nuclear Weapons Stockpile FY 1945–FY 1985* (TID-26990-7). December 1986. (Declassified with deletions; at the National Resources Defense Council.)

U.S. Department of the Navy. *FBM Facts/Chronology: Polaris-Poseidon-Trident.* GPO, 1990.

U.S. Environmental Protection Agency. *The State of Federal Facilities: A Comprehensive Overview of the Environmental Compliance Status of Federal Facilities through the End of FY 1992.* EPA 300-R-94-001. GPO, 1994.

_______. *The State of Federal Facilities: An Overview of Environmental Compliance at Federal Facilities, FY 1993–94.* EPA 300-R-96-002. GPO, 1995.

U.S. General Accounting Office. *Accountability and Control of Warheads in the Custody of the Department of Defense and the Energy Research and Development Administration.* PSAD-77-115. June 2, 1977.

_______. *Aircraft Basing: Decision to Base Navy TACAMO Aircraft at Tinker Air Force Base, Oklahoma.* NSIAD-87-106FS. April 1987.

_______. *Air Defense Mission Must Be Clarified before Billions Are Spent on Modernization.* PSAD-78-86. May 10, 1978.

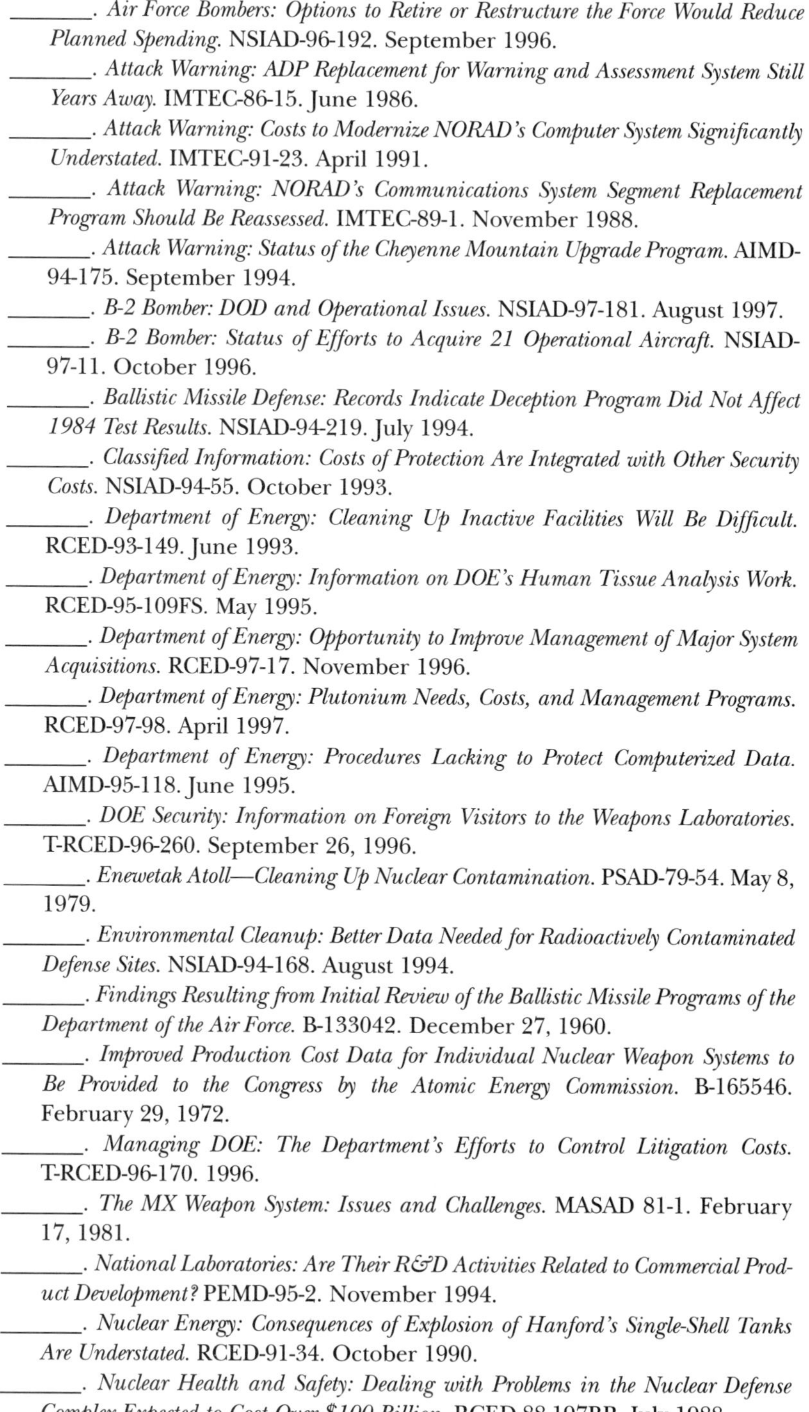

_______. *Air Force Bombers: Options to Retire or Restructure the Force Would Reduce Planned Spending.* NSIAD-96-192. September 1996.

_______. *Attack Warning: ADP Replacement for Warning and Assessment System Still Years Away.* IMTEC-86-15. June 1986.

_______. *Attack Warning: Costs to Modernize NORAD's Computer System Significantly Understated.* IMTEC-91-23. April 1991.

_______. *Attack Warning: NORAD's Communications System Segment Replacement Program Should Be Reassessed.* IMTEC-89-1. November 1988.

_______. *Attack Warning: Status of the Cheyenne Mountain Upgrade Program.* AIMD-94-175. September 1994.

_______. *B-2 Bomber: DOD and Operational Issues.* NSIAD-97-181. August 1997.

_______. *B-2 Bomber: Status of Efforts to Acquire 21 Operational Aircraft.* NSIAD-97-11. October 1996.

_______. *Ballistic Missile Defense: Records Indicate Deception Program Did Not Affect 1984 Test Results.* NSIAD-94-219. July 1994.

_______. *Classified Information: Costs of Protection Are Integrated with Other Security Costs.* NSIAD-94-55. October 1993.

_______. *Department of Energy: Cleaning Up Inactive Facilities Will Be Difficult.* RCED-93-149. June 1993.

_______. *Department of Energy: Information on DOE's Human Tissue Analysis Work.* RCED-95-109FS. May 1995.

_______. *Department of Energy: Opportunity to Improve Management of Major System Acquisitions.* RCED-97-17. November 1996.

_______. *Department of Energy: Plutonium Needs, Costs, and Management Programs.* RCED-97-98. April 1997.

_______. *Department of Energy: Procedures Lacking to Protect Computerized Data.* AIMD-95-118. June 1995.

_______. *DOE Security: Information on Foreign Visitors to the Weapons Laboratories.* T-RCED-96-260. September 26, 1996.

_______. *Enewetak Atoll—Cleaning Up Nuclear Contamination.* PSAD-79-54. May 8, 1979.

_______. *Environmental Cleanup: Better Data Needed for Radioactively Contaminated Defense Sites.* NSIAD-94-168. August 1994.

_______. *Findings Resulting from Initial Review of the Ballistic Missile Programs of the Department of the Air Force.* B-133042. December 27, 1960.

_______. *Improved Production Cost Data for Individual Nuclear Weapon Systems to Be Provided to the Congress by the Atomic Energy Commission.* B-165546. February 29, 1972.

_______. *Managing DOE: The Department's Efforts to Control Litigation Costs.* T-RCED-96-170. 1996.

_______. *The MX Weapon System: Issues and Challenges.* MASAD 81-1. February 17, 1981.

_______. *National Laboratories: Are Their R&D Activities Related to Commercial Product Development?* PEMD-95-2. November 1994.

_______. *Nuclear Energy: Consequences of Explosion of Hanford's Single-Shell Tanks Are Understated.* RCED-91-34. October 1990.

_______. *Nuclear Health and Safety: Dealing with Problems in the Nuclear Defense Complex Expected to Cost Over $100 Billion.* RCED-88-197BR. July 1988.

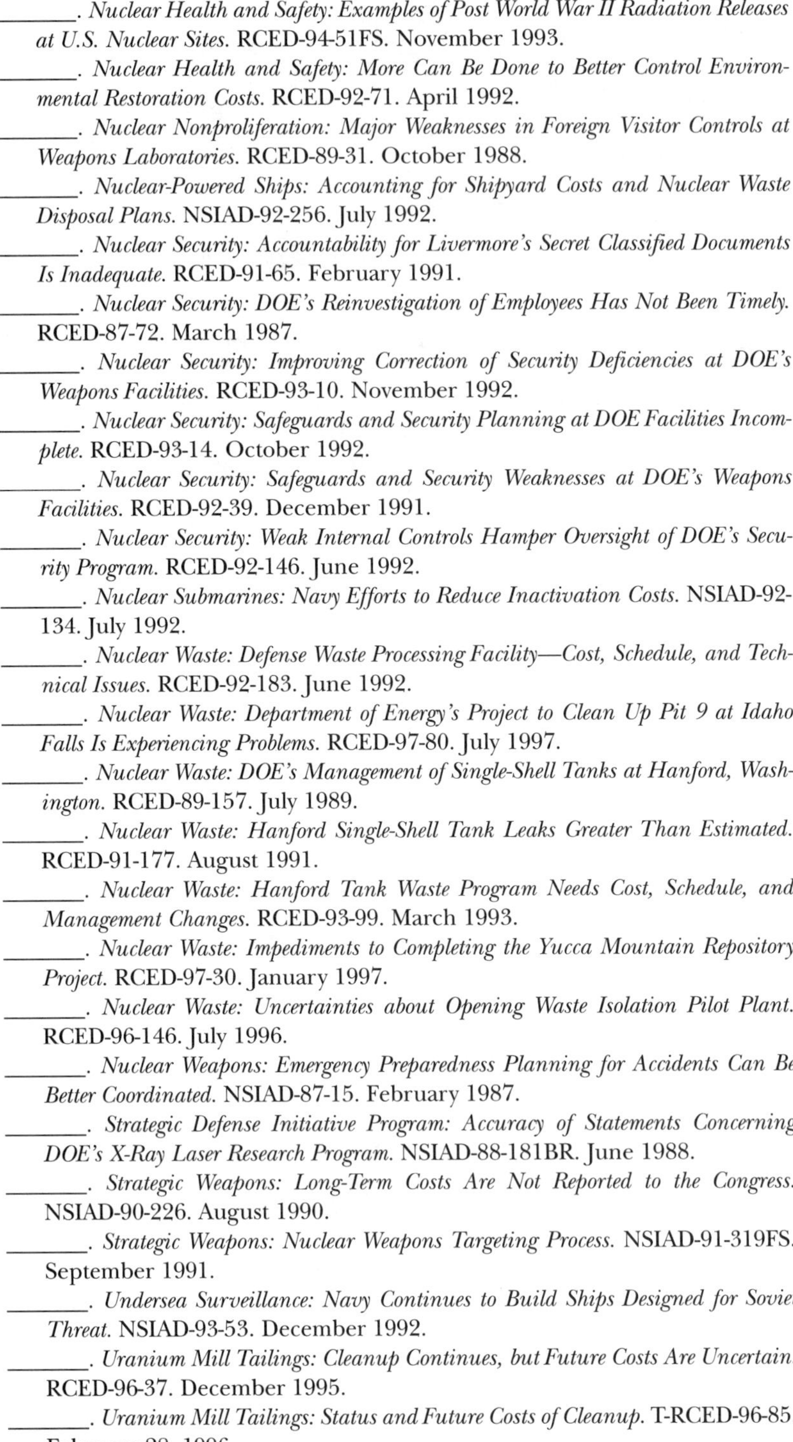

_______. *Nuclear Health and Safety: Examples of Post World War II Radiation Releases at U.S. Nuclear Sites.* RCED-94-51FS. November 1993.

_______. *Nuclear Health and Safety: More Can Be Done to Better Control Environmental Restoration Costs.* RCED-92-71. April 1992.

_______. *Nuclear Nonproliferation: Major Weaknesses in Foreign Visitor Controls at Weapons Laboratories.* RCED-89-31. October 1988.

_______. *Nuclear-Powered Ships: Accounting for Shipyard Costs and Nuclear Waste Disposal Plans.* NSIAD-92-256. July 1992.

_______. *Nuclear Security: Accountability for Livermore's Secret Classified Documents Is Inadequate.* RCED-91-65. February 1991.

_______. *Nuclear Security: DOE's Reinvestigation of Employees Has Not Been Timely.* RCED-87-72. March 1987.

_______. *Nuclear Security: Improving Correction of Security Deficiencies at DOE's Weapons Facilities.* RCED-93-10. November 1992.

_______. *Nuclear Security: Safeguards and Security Planning at DOE Facilities Incomplete.* RCED-93-14. October 1992.

_______. *Nuclear Security: Safeguards and Security Weaknesses at DOE's Weapons Facilities.* RCED-92-39. December 1991.

_______. *Nuclear Security: Weak Internal Controls Hamper Oversight of DOE's Security Program.* RCED-92-146. June 1992.

_______. *Nuclear Submarines: Navy Efforts to Reduce Inactivation Costs.* NSIAD-92-134. July 1992.

_______. *Nuclear Waste: Defense Waste Processing Facility—Cost, Schedule, and Technical Issues.* RCED-92-183. June 1992.

_______. *Nuclear Waste: Department of Energy's Project to Clean Up Pit 9 at Idaho Falls Is Experiencing Problems.* RCED-97-80. July 1997.

_______. *Nuclear Waste: DOE's Management of Single-Shell Tanks at Hanford, Washington.* RCED-89-157. July 1989.

_______. *Nuclear Waste: Hanford Single-Shell Tank Leaks Greater Than Estimated.* RCED-91-177. August 1991.

_______. *Nuclear Waste: Hanford Tank Waste Program Needs Cost, Schedule, and Management Changes.* RCED-93-99. March 1993.

_______. *Nuclear Waste: Impediments to Completing the Yucca Mountain Repository Project.* RCED-97-30. January 1997.

_______. *Nuclear Waste: Uncertainties about Opening Waste Isolation Pilot Plant.* RCED-96-146. July 1996.

_______. *Nuclear Weapons: Emergency Preparedness Planning for Accidents Can Be Better Coordinated.* NSIAD-87-15. February 1987.

_______. *Strategic Defense Initiative Program: Accuracy of Statements Concerning DOE's X-Ray Laser Research Program.* NSIAD-88-181BR. June 1988.

_______. *Strategic Weapons: Long-Term Costs Are Not Reported to the Congress.* NSIAD-90-226. August 1990.

_______. *Strategic Weapons: Nuclear Weapons Targeting Process.* NSIAD-91-319FS. September 1991.

_______. *Undersea Surveillance: Navy Continues to Build Ships Designed for Soviet Threat.* NSIAD-93-53. December 1992.

_______. *Uranium Mill Tailings: Cleanup Continues, but Future Costs Are Uncertain.* RCED-96-37. December 1995.

_______. *Uranium Mill Tailings: Status and Future Costs of Cleanup.* T-RCED-96-85. February 28, 1996.

U.S. Office of the Director of Defense Research and Engineering, *Report of the Defense Science Board Task Force on Secrecy.* July 1, 1970.

"U.S. Security Assistance to the Former Soviet Union." *Arms Control Today,* vol. 26, no. 7 (1996), pp. 25–26.

Udall, Stewart L. *The Myths of August: A Personal Exploration of Our Tragic Cold War Affair with the Atom.* New York: Pantheon Books, 1994.

Ullmann, Richard H. "The Covert French Connection." *Foreign Policy,* no. 75 (Summer 1989), pp. 3–33.

Vandercook, Wm. F. "Making the Very Best of the Very Worst." *International Security,* vol. 11, no. 1 (1986), pp. 184–95.

Varner, Roy, and Wayne Collier. *A Matter of Risk: The Incredible Inside Story of the CIA's Hughes Glomar Explorer Mission to Raise a Russian Submarine.* New York: Random House, 1978.

von Hippel, Frank N., and others. "Civilian Casualties from Counterforce Attacks." *Scientific American,* September 1988, pp. 36–42.

Wagner, Ray. *American Combat Planes.* 3d ed. Garden City, N.Y.: Doubleday, 1982.

Wainstein, Leonard, and others. *The Evolution of U.S. Strategic Command and Control and Warning, 1945–1972.* Institute for Defense Analyses Study S-467. June 1975.

Waite, J. L. *Tank Wastes Discharged Directly to the Soil at the Hanford Site.* WHC-MR-0227. Westinghouse Hanford Company, April 1991.

Waller, Douglas. "Fumbling the Football: Now It Can Be Told." *Newsweek,* October 7, 1991, p. 26.

_______. "Nuclear Ninjas." *Time,* January 8, 1996, pp. 38–40.

Warner, Michael, ed. *CIA Cold War Records: The CIA under Harry Truman.* Washington, D.C.: Central Intelligence Agency, 1994.

Watson, Bruce. "We Couldn't Run, So We Hoped We Could Hide." *Smithsonian,* April 1994, pp. 46–58.

Watson, Russell, with Daniel Glick and Mark Hosenball and others. "America's Nuclear Secrets." *Newsweek,* December 27, 1993, pp. 14–18.

Weart, Spencer R. *Nuclear Fear: A History of Images.* Harvard University Press, 1988.

Weida, William J., and Frank L. Gertcher. *The Political Economy of National Defense.* Boulder, Colo.: Westview Press, 1987.

Weisgall, Jonathan M. *Operation Crossroads: The Atomic Tests at Bikini Atoll.* Annapolis, Md.: Naval Institute Press, 1994.

Weisman, Jonathan. "Who's Minding the Store?" *Bulletin of the Atomic Scientists,* vol. 53 (July/August 1997), pp. 32–37.

Wells, Jim. *Protecting Department of Energy Workers Health and Safety.* Testimony before the House Subcommittee on Oversight and Investigations. T-RCED-94-143. GAO, March 17, 1994.

Werrell, Kenneth P. *The Evolution of the Cruise Missile.* Maxwell Air Force Base, Ala.: Air University Press, 1985.

West, George T. "United States Warhead Assembly Facilities (1945–1990)." Mason & Hanger—Silas Mason, Pantex Plant, March 1991.

Wetterhahn, Ralph F. "Death of the Beast: Saying Goodbye to a Trusty Old Cold Warrior." *Air & Space,* July 1995, pp. 24–31.

Whitfield, Stephen J. *The Culture of the Cold War.* Johns Hopkins University Press, 1991.

Williams, Robert C., and Philip L. Cantelon, eds. *The American Atom: A Documentary History of Nuclear Policies from the Discovery of Fission to the Present, 1939–1984.* University of Pennsylvania Press, 1984.

Wilson, Carroll L. "Nuclear Energy: What Went Wrong?" *Bulletin of Atomic Scientists,* vol. 35 (June 1979), pp. 13–17.

Winkler, Allan M. "A 40-Year History of Civil Defense." *Bulletin of the Atomic Scientists,* vol. 40 (June/July 1984), pp. 16–22.

Wohlstetter, A. J., and others. *Selection and Use of Strategic Air Bases.* Report R-266. Rand Corporation, April 1954.

York, Herbert. "The Origins of the Lawrence Livermore Laboratory." *Bulletin of the Atomic Scientists,* vol. 31 (September 1975), pp. 8–18.

_______. *Race to Oblivion: A Participant's View of the Arms Race.* New York: Simon & Schuster, 1970.

Zerriffi, Hisham, and Arjun Makhijani. *The Nuclear Safety Smokescreen: Warhead Safety and Reliability and the Science Based Stockpile Stewardship Program.* Takoma Park, Md.: Institute for Energy and Environmental Research, 1996.

Ziegler, Charles. "Intelligence Assessments of Soviet Atomic Capability, 1945–1949: Myths, Monopolies and *Maskirovka.*" *Intelligence and National Security,* vol. 12, no. 4 (1997), pp. 1–24.

_______. "Waiting for Joe-1: Decisions Leading to the Detection of Russia's First Atomic Bomb Test." *Social Studies of Science,* vol. 18, no. 2 (1988), pp. 197–229.

Ziegler, Charles A., and David Jacobson. *Spying without Spies: Origins of America's Secret Nuclear Surveillance System.* Westport, Conn.: Praeger, 1995.

Zimmerman, Peter. "The Thule, Fylingdales, and Krasnoyarsk Radars: Innocents Abroad?" *Arms Control Today,* vol. 17 (March 1987), pp. 9–11.

Zuckerman, Edward. *The Day after World War III.* New York: Viking Press, 1984.

Index